Tolley's
Inheritance Tax
2007–08

by
Jon Golding ATT TEP

LexisNexis®
Tolley

Members of the LexisNexis Group worldwide

United Kingdom	LexisNexis Butterworths, a Division of Reed Elsevier (UK) Ltd, Halsbury House, 35 Chancery Lane, LONDON, WC2A 1EL, and London House, 20–22 East London Street, EDINBURGH EH7 4BQ
Argentina	LexisNexis Argentina, BUENOS AIRES
Australia	LexisNexis Butterworths, CHATSWOOD, New South Wales
Austria	LexisNexis Verlag ARD Orac GmbH & Co KG, VIENNA
Benelux	LexisNexis Benelux, AMSTERDAM
Canada	LexisNexis Canada, MARKHAM, Ontario
Chile	LexisNexis Chile Ltda, SANTIAGO
China	LexisNexis China, Beijing and Shanghai
France	LexisNexis SA, Paris
Germany	LexisNexis Deutschland, Gmbh, MUNSTER
Hong Kong	LexisNexis Hong Kong, HONG KONG
India	LexisNexis, NEW DELHI
Italy	Giuffrè Editore, MILAN
Japan	LexisNexis Japan, TOKYO
Malaysia	Malayan Law Journal Sdn Bhd, KUALA LUMPUR
Mexico	LexisNexis Mexico, Mexico
New Zealand	LexisNexis NZ Ltd, WELLINGTON
Poland	Wydawnictwo Prawnicze LexisNexis Sp, WARSAW
Singapore	LexisNexis Singapore, SINGAPORE
South Africa	LexisNexis Butterworths, DURBAN
USA	LexisNexis, DAYTON, Ohio

© Reed Elsevier (UK) Ltd 2007

Published by LexisNexis Butterworths

A CIP Catalogue record for this book is available from the British Library.
ISBN 9 780754 532750

Typeset by Kerrypress Ltd, Luton, Bedfordshire

Printed in the United Kingdom by Polestar Wheatons Ltd

Visit LexisNexis Butterworths at www.lexisnexis.co.uk

About This Book

The text of this book states the law and practice as it stood up to and including 20 July 2007 and includes the current provisions relating to the Finance Act 2007 which received Royal Assent on 19 July 2007.

The Finance Act 2007 has again introduced a further graduated nil rate band for the year to 2011/12 rising to £350,000 in that year. Whilst the main changes to the inheritance tax legislation involved Alternatively Secured Pension (ASP) schemes, which are covered in detail in Chapter 37 Pension Schemes, there have been numerous pronouncements on various aspects such as pre-owned assets, case law and the 2006 trusts legislation changes. HMRC Inheritance Tax is also continuing to make changes to the IHT200 forms. The numerous examples have been updated and where tax cases and other non-tax cases have a bearing on the text and examples, these are included in the commentary and in Chapter 60 on Tax Cases for reference.

LexisNexis Butterworths are most obliged to Philip Laidlow LLM LLB of Laytons, for his agreement to the publication of a variety of forms, and readers are also referred to his book *Tolley's Tax Planning for Post-Death Variations*. We are also indebted to Robert Ham QC and Emily Campbell of Wilberforce Chambers for their permission to reproduce the precedent in Chapter 33 in respect of a Maintenance Fund Settlement. Forms IHT100 and IHT200 and supporting supplementary forms are reproduced by kind permission of HMRC Inheritance Tax. In addition, the continuing pronouncements by HMRC on inheritance tax in their IHT Newsletter and Tax Bulletin are reproduced in Chapter 61. Finally many thanks go to John Woolley LLB FCII FTII of Technical Connection who supplied three case studies on inheritance tax planning matters which can be found in Chapter 59 Working Case Study.

Comments on this book and suggestions for improvements are always welcome.

Contents

Abbreviations and References

ABBREVIATIONS

A-G	=	Attorney-General.
AIM	=	Alternative Investment Market.
CA	=	Court of Appeal.
CCA	=	Court of Criminal Appeal.
CCAB	=	Consultative Committee of Accountancy Bodies.
CGT	=	Capital Gains Tax.
Ch	=	Chapter.
Ch D	=	Chancery Division.
CIR	=	Commissioners of HMRC ('the Board').
Commr(s)	=	Commissioner(s) (General or Special).
CPA	=	Civil Partnership Act 2004.
CTO	=	HMRC Capital Taxes.
CTT	=	Capital Transfer Tax.
CTTA 1984	=	Capital Transfer Tax Act 1984.
DTR	=	Double Taxation Relief.
DV	=	District Valuer.
ESC	=	HMRC Extra-Statutory Concession.
FA	=	Finance Act.
Fam D	=	Family Division (formerly Probate, Divorce and Admiralty Division).
HC	=	House of Commons.
HL	=	House of Lords.
HMRC	=	Her Majesty's Revenue and Customs.
HMRCC	=	Her Majesty's Revenue and Customs Commissioners.
ICTA 1970	=	Income and Corporation Taxes Act 1970.
ICTA 1988	=	Income and Corporation Taxes Act 1988.
IHT	=	Inheritance Tax.
IHTA 1984	=	Inheritance Tax Act 1984.
IHTM	=	Inheritance Tax Manual
IPDI	=	Immediate Post-Death Interest
ITA	=	Income Tax Act 2007.
ITEPA 2003	=	Income Tax (Earnings and Pensions) Act 2003.
ITTOIA 2005	=	Income Tax (Trading and Other Income) Act 2005
NAO	=	National Audit Office.
NI	=	Northern Ireland.
PC	=	Privy Council.
PCm	=	Personal Contact (HMRC Manual).
PDA	=	Probate, Divorce and Admiralty Division (now Family Division).
Pt	=	Part.
QB	=	Queen's Bench Division.
R	=	Rex or Regina (i.e. The Crown).
RI	=	Republic of Ireland (Eire).
s	=	Section.
Sch	=	Schedule [4 Sch para 10 = 4th Schedule, paragraph 10].
SC	=	Supreme Court.
SCS	=	Scottish Court of Session.
SDLT	=	Stamp Duty Land Tax
SI	=	Statutory Instrument.
SP	=	HMRC Statement of Practice. (SP 7/87, 15 July 1987 = 7th Statement of Practice in 1987 issued on date shown).
SVD	=	Shares Valuation Division.
TCGA 1992	=	Taxation of Chargeable Gains Act 1992.

TSI	= Transitional Serial Interest
USM	= Unlisted Securities Market.
VOA	= Valuation Office Agency.

REFERENCES

(*denotes a series accredited for citation in court).

All ER	= *All England Law Reports, (Butterworths, Halsbury House, 35 Chancery Lane, London WC2A 1EL).
AC	= *Law Reports, Appeal Cases, (Incorporated Council of Law Reporting for England and Wales, 3 Stone Buildings, Lincoln's Inn, London WC2A 3XN).
ATC	= *Annotated Tax Cases (publication discontinued).
BTC	= British Tax Cases, CCH Editions Ltd, Telford Road, Bicester, Oxfordshire OX6 0XD.
Ch	= *Law Reports, Chancery Division.
EG	= Estates Gazette, (The Estates Gazette Ltd., 151 Wardour Street, London W1V 4BN).
ILT	= Irish Law Times.
IR	– *Irish Reports, (Law Reporting Council, Law Library, Four Courts, Dublin).
KB	= *Law Reports, King's Bench Division (1900–1952).
LT	= Decisions of the Lands Tribunal, (Lands Tribunal, 48–49 Chancery Lane, London WC2A 1JR).
[Year] QB	= *Law Reports, Queen's Bench Division (1891–1901 and 1952 onwards).
QBD	= Law Reports, Queen's Bench Division (1875–1890).
Sp C	= Special Commissioners' decisions, (The Court Service, 15/19 Bedford Avenue, London WC1B 3AS).
SLT	= Scots Law Times.
SCD	= *Simon's Special Commissioners' Decisions, (Butterworths, as above).
STC	= *Simon's Tax Cases, (Butterworths, as above).
STI	= Simon's Tax Intelligence, (Butterworths, as above).
TC	= *Official Reports of Tax Cases, (H.M. Stationery Office, as above).
TLR	= Times Law Reports.
TR	= *Taxation Reports (publication discontinued).
WLR	= *Weekly Law Reports, (Incorporated Council of Law Reporting, as above).

The first number in the citation refers to the volume, and the second to the page, so that [1979] 2 All ER 80 means that the report is to be found on page eighty of the second volume of the All England Law Reports for 1979. Where no volume number is given, only one volume was produced in that year. Some series have continuous volume numbers.

Where legal decisions are very recent and in the lower Courts, it must be remembered that they may be reversed on appeal. But references to the official Tax Cases ('*TC*'), and to the Appeal Cases ('*AC*') may be taken as final.

In English cases, Scottish and N. Irish decisions (unless there is a difference of law between the countries) are generally followed but are not binding, and Republic of Ireland decisions are considered (and vice versa).

Acts of Parliament, Command Papers, 'Hansard' Parliamentary Reports and Statutory Instruments are obtainable from The Stationery Office, (bookshops at 123 Kingsway, London WC2B 6PQ (Fax 0207 242 6394) and elsewhere; orders to P.O. Box 29, Norwich NR3 1GN). Fax orders should be made to 0870 600 5533. General enquiries should be made to 0870 600 5522. Telephone orders should be made to 0870 600 5522. **Hansard** (referred to as HC Official Report or HL Official Report) references are to daily issues and do not always correspond to the columns in the bound editions. **N.B.** Statements in Parliament, while useful as indicating the intention of enactments, have no legal authority if the Courts interpret the wording of the Act differently (except in the limited circumstances mentioned in 15.11 DETERMINATIONS AND APPEALS).

1   Introduction and Basic Principles

Simon's Direct Tax Service, parts I1.3, I1.4.

Other Sources. Foster, part A and E1.02.

1.1   **The aim of this chapter** is to provide a brief outline of the principal features and key concepts of inheritance tax. It is intended to illustrate only the basic mechanism of the tax as this is essential for an understanding of the detailed provisions covered in the following chapters. For complete details of any particular topic or area, reference should be made to the appropriate chapter.

1.2   **FUNCTION AND SCOPE OF TAX**

Inheritance tax is a tax on chargeable transfers made by an individual during his life and on the value of his estate on his death. Various exemptions and reliefs are available to lessen the impact of the tax.

The tax is charged on certain events relating to settled property and there is a separate charging structure for settlements without interests in possession. See SETTLEMENTS WITHOUT INTERESTS IN POSSESSION (44) for new trusts arising on or after 22 March 2006. In addition, certain transfers made by close companies may be attributed to the individual participators. See CLOSE COMPANIES (12).

Individuals domiciled in the UK are liable to inheritance tax on all chargeable transfers, whether or not the property transferred is situated in the UK. Individuals not domiciled in the UK are not liable to IHT on transfers of property situated outside the UK but are so liable, with certain exceptions, on chargeable transfers of property in the UK. In certain circumstances double tax relief may be available. See 17 DOMICILE for the extended IHT meaning of 'domicile', 20 EXCLUDED PROPERTY and 46 SITUS for full details of what property is outside the scope of the tax, and 18 DOUBLE TAXATION RELIEF for situations where DTR may be available.

1.3   **STARTING DATE AND MAIN CHANGES TO CTT**

The revised provisions relating to inheritance tax effectively replaced capital transfer tax for events occurring after 17 March 1986 although the name of the tax was not formally changed until 25 July 1986, the date of Royal Assent to the *Finance Act 1986*. The revised provisions do not affect the tax chargeable on a transfer of value occurring before 18 March 1986. [*FA 1986, Sch 19 para 40*]. However, chargeable transfers made before that date and within the lifetime cumulation period for IHT purposes may affect the tax payable on subsequent transfers.

The main amendments to the CTT provisions in the IHT legislation are

(*a*)   the removal of liability for tax on certain transfers of value where the transfer occurs at least seven years before the transferor's death;

(*b*)   the reduction in the period during which the values transferred by chargeable transfers are aggregated from ten to seven years;

(*c*)   the increase in the period before death within which tax on chargeable lifetime transfers is recomputed at the higher rates applicable on death from three to seven years (but subject to the introduction of taper relief where the transfer is more than three years before death); and

(*d*)   the re-introduction of legislation for GIFTS WITH RESERVATION (22) similar to the old estate duty provisions.

1.4   Introduction and Basic Principles

The *Capital Transfer Tax Act 1984* may be cited as the *Inheritance Tax Act 1984*. Any reference to CTT in the *1984 Act* or any other Act passed before or in the same session as the *FA 1986* or any document executed, made, served or issued on or before the passing of *FA 1986* has effect as a reference to inheritance tax unless relating to a liability to tax arising before 25 July 1986. [*FA 1986, s 100*].

1.4   **CHARGE TO TAX**

Inheritance tax is charged on the value transferred by a chargeable transfer. [*IHTA 1984, s 1*].

A chargeable transfer is any transfer of value made by an individual other than an EXEMPT TRANSFER (21). [*IHTA 1984, s 2(1)*].

A potentially exempt transfer (PET) is a transfer of value made by an individual after 17 March 1986 but before 22 March 2006 which would otherwise be a chargeable transfer and which is either a gift to another individual or a gift into an accumulation and maintenance trust or a trust for a disabled person. After 21 March 2006 a PET is a transfer of value made by an individual which would otherwise be a chargeable transfer and which is either a gift to another individual (see Example 1 below) or into a trust for a disabled person or into a trust for bereaved minors on the ending of an immediate post-death interest (IPDI). See 43.1 SETTLEMENTS WITH INTERESTS IN POSSESSION and 53.1 TRUSTS FOR BEREAVED MINORS. With respect to transfers of value made, and other events occurring, after 16 March 1987 but before 22 March 2006, certain gifts by individuals into and out of settlements with interests in possession are also included. From 22 March 2006, however, there are certain transitional rules that ensure that new interest in possession which are created out existing ones before 6 April 2008 ie TSIs ('transitional serial interests') still will qualify as PETs. See 38.1 POTENTIALLY EXEMPT TRANSFERS for full details. A potentially exempt transfer made seven years or more before the transferor's death is an exempt transfer and any other potentially exempt transfer is a chargeable transfer. A potentially exempt transfer is assumed to be an exempt transfer during the seven years following the transfer (or, if earlier, until immediately before the transferor's death). [*IHTA 1984, s 3A; FA 1986, Sch 19 para 1; F(No 2)A 1987, s 96; FA 2006, Sch 20 para 9*]. In summary therefore a PET will, from 22 March 2006, comprise:

- transfers by individuals to other individuals;

- transfers by individuals to certain trusts for the disabled (see 54 TRUSTS FOR DISABLED PERSONS);

- transfers on or after 22 March 2006 by an individual to a bereaved minor's trust on the coming to an end of an immediate post-death interest (see 53 TRUSTS FOR BEREAVED MINORS);

- transfers before 22 March 2006 by an individual to an accumulation and maintenance trust (see 3 ACCUMULATION AND MAINTENANCE TRUSTS);

- transfers by an individual into an interest in possession trust in which, for transfers on or after 22 March 2006, the beneficiary has a disabled person's interest (see 54.1 TRUSTS FOR DISABLED PERSONS); and

- certain transfers on the termination or disposal of an individual's beneficial interest in possession in settled property (these are in restricted circumstances following *FA 2006* at 30.1 LIFE ASSURANCE POLICIES AND ANNUITIES; 43.1 SETTLEMENTS WITH INTERESTS IN POSSESSION).

A transfer of value is any disposition made by a person as a result of which the value of his estate immediately after the disposition is less than it would be but for the disposition; and the amount by which it is less is the value transferred by the transfer. A person is treated as making a notional transfer of value of his whole estate immediately before his death. [*IHTA 1984, s 3(1), s 4(1)*]. A disposition is not a transfer of value if made in an arm's length (or similar) transaction. [*IHTA 1984, s 10*]. (See TRANSFER OF VALUE (49) for extended meanings of 'transfer of value' and 'disposition' and TRANSFERS ON DEATH (50) for provisions relating specifically to such transfers.)

Since the reduction in value in a person's estate includes the payment of the IHT itself where this is paid by the transferor, it is necessary in such cases to gross-up the 'net' value at the appropriate tax rate (see 1.6 below).

A person's estate is the aggregate of all the property to which *he* is beneficially entitled. However, a person's estate immediately before his death (on which inheritance tax is payable) does not include excluded property. A person beneficially entitled to an interest in possession in settled property is treated as beneficially entitled to that property excepting trust property held on statutory trusts applying at age 18 arising for minor children due to intestacy or trusts drawn in similar terms by reason of the parent's will or as a result of the Criminal Injuries Compensation Scheme. This treatment also applies where a person becomes beneficially entitled to an interest in possession after 21 March 2006 and the interest is not an immediate post-death interest or a disabled person's interest or a transitional serial interest. [*IHTA 1984, ss 5(1)(1A), s 49(1), 71A; FA 2006, Sch 20 para 10*]. See *Faulkner (Adams' Trustee) v CIR [2001] STC SCD 112 Sp C 278*. See 19 ESTATE for extensions and qualifications of this basic definition.

Example 1

A wishes to pay for his grandson AA's school fees in respect of attendance at independent school and contracts with the said school (see below) for a one-off payment to be made of £74,000 in advance which will ensure that the child's education is paid for from the age of 13 to 18 without any increases in school fees over the period. Mr A has only made previous transfers to his son in 2006/07 of £291,000 which equates to a cumulation of £285,000 after using available annual exemptions as at 6 April 2007. Mr A has also agreed with the school that there will not be a refund due to Mr A of the school fees on his death.

This agreement is made between the Governors of [**Select Independent School**] by their duly authorised officer [**A. Bursar**] (hereinafter called 'the school') of the first part; and [**Mr A**].

Whereas it is proposed that [**Mr A**] does make a payment of school fees to the school until [**Mr A's**] grandson [**Master AA**] completes full time education (or as the case may be). Such said fees shall be paid to the school by [**Mr A**] in advance in the sum of £74,000 and the receipt by the school shall be sufficient discharge.

1. In consideration of the payment by [**Mr A**] of the said school fees the school agrees to keep a place open for the child [**Master AA**] until he has completed full time education or cease such education at the agreement of the contracting parties.

Etc.

This is a transfer of value within *IHTA 1984, s 3(1)* since the value of A's estate is diminished by the disposition. However, Master AA does not receive any property from A so the gift is not within *IHTA 1984, s 3A(2)(a)*. But whilst benefiting Master AA is his estate increased? Is therefore the transfer a PET?

Under *IHTA 1984, s 3A(2)(b)*, where property does not becomes comprised in the estate of another person, a transfer may still be treated as a gift to an individual provided two conditions are satisfied. These conditions are that:

(*a*)   property does not become comprised in the estate of another person (not 'individual'), but (*b*)   the estate of another individual is increased.

The first condition is not satisfied because the cash given does not become directly comprised in the estate of Master AA. The second condition is not satisfied either even though the value of Master AA's estate is effectively increased by the gift. This is because the value transferred is attributable to property that has become comprised in the estate of another person. See also IHTM04058 and IHTM04060.

On the one hand tested against the definition of a PET, the gift is a transfer of value by Mr A which is chargeable but on the other hand it does not satisfy the condition that it is a transfer to an individual and cannot therefore be treated as a PET.

As IHT is based on the 'loss to the donor' principle the 'gift' of the payment to the school of the fees of the grandchild would potentially be immediately chargeable to IHT because the gift is not to an individual. Obviously if there is part (or all) of the Nil rate band available to cover the fees paid directly to the school then no actual tax would be payable. However, on death a chargeable transfer should be taken into account again when applying death rates. Whereas if the cash is given to the child or grandchild (bearing in mind the giving good receipt problem for grandchildren) then it will drop out of account after seven years. In this case though Mr A has already utilised a majority of his Nil rate band and the following calculation has to be made.

Transferor (Mr A) bears tax

		£	£
Value of gift			74,000
Deduct exempt transfers	note (A)		
Annual exemption 2007/08		3,000	
Annual exemption 2006/07		N/A	
			3,000
			71,000

Tax on £71,000 + £285,000 (per grossing-up table 41.1 2007.B2). See also 1.6 below.

0–300,000 = Nil + ¼ (356,000 – 300,000)	14,000
Mr A's chargeable transfer	**£85,000**
Tax payable by Mr A	**£14,000**

Notes to the example

(A)   As A has made previous transfers up to the Nil rate band threshold only part i.e. £15,000 (£300,000 – £285,000) to set against the transfer but also he will have only one year of annual exemption available to deduct from the transfer of value.

(B)   The transfer of value is £88,000. A's estate is reduced by the gift of £74,000 plus the tax of £14,000 and has proved to an expensive way of funding the fees. With better planning Mr A should have made the school fees contribution before the gift of £291,000 to his son and utilised part of the nil rate band to cover the gift. The gift to the son would be a PET and drop out of account after seven years or, if Mr A died within the seven years, be covered by part of the nil rate band and possibly attract tapering relief on the balance. See 51.1 TRANSFERS WITHIN SEVEN YEARS OF DEATH.

1.5   **AMOUNT OF TAX CHARGE**

Rates. After 14 March 1988 inheritance tax is charged at a single rate of 40%. After 17 March 1986 and before 15 March 1988 it was charged at progressively steeper rates. Only one table of rates is enacted which is applicable to transfers on death. Chargeable lifetime transfers are charged at one half of those rates throughout the range of rate bands. Transfers made within seven years of death are charged at the death rates but in the case of chargeable transfers made in that period and more than three years before death, the tax charge is tapered. See 41 RATES OF TAX for tables and 51.1 TRANSFERS WITHIN SEVEN YEARS BEFORE DEATH for taper relief.

Cumulation. Chargeable transfers are cumulated over a seven-year period and the rate of tax on any chargeable transfer will depend on the total value of any other chargeable transfers within the seven-year period ending with the date of the transfer (including, where applicable, chargeable transfers made before 18 March 1986 under the rules relating to CTT). After seven years transfers drop out of the cumulative total. After 5 April 2007 and before 6 April 2008 no tax is payable on the first £300,000 of chargeable transfers as the rate is nil per cent. For the following three years 2008–09, 2009–10 and 2010–11 the threshold will be increased to £312,000, £325,000 and £350,000 respectively. See 41 RATES OF TAX for tables. Lower limits applied previously. [*IHTA 1984, ss 7, 8, Sch 1; FA 1986, Sch 19 para 2; FA 1987, s 57; FA 1988, s 136; SI 1989/468; SI 1990/680; SI 1991/735; F(No 2)A 1992, s 72; FA 1993, s 196; FA 1994, s 246; SI 1994/3011; FA 1996, s 183; SI 1998/756; SI 1999/596; SI 2000/803; SI 2001/639; FA 2002, s 118; SI 2003/841; SI 2004/771; FA 2005, s 98; FA 2006, s 155; FA 2007, s 4*].

1.6   **Grossing-up.** Although inheritance tax is essentially a tax based on the loss to the person giving rather than on the benefit to the person receiving, the tax itself may be paid either by the transferor or the transferee. Where the tax is paid by the transferor, it is part of the diminution in value of his estate and is itself included in the transfer of value. A 'net' transfer has to be grossed-up to arrive at the amount of the chargeable transfer.

Example 2

A transfers £327,000 to a discretionary trust on 1 October 2007. He has made no previous transfers.

(i)   *Transferor (A) bears tax*

	£	£
Value of gift		327,000
Deduct exempt transfers note (A)		
Annual exemption 2007/08	3,000	
Annual exemption 2006/07	3,000	
		6,000
		321,000
Tax on £321,000 (per grossing-up table 41.1 2007.B2)		
0–321,000 = Nil + ¼ (321,000 – 300,000)		5,250
A's chargeable transfer		**£326,250**
Tax payable by A		**£5,250**

Notes to the example

(A)   As A has made no previous transfers he will have two years' annual exemptions available but in cases where *FA 1986, s 102(4)* creates a deemed PET the annual exemption is not available. See http://www.hmrc.gov.uk/manuals/ihtmanual/index.htm. 21.9 EXEMPT TRANSFERS; 22.1 GIFTS WITH RESERVATION.

(B)   The transfer of value is £332,250. A's estate is reduced by the gift of £327,000 plus the tax of £5,250.

(*ii*)   *Transferees (trustees) bear tax*

	£	£
Value of gift		327,000
Deduct exempt transfers (as in (i))		6,000
A's chargeable transfer		£321,000
Tax on £321,000 (per table 41.1 2007.B1)		
1–300,000 at 0%		
300,001–321,000 at 20%	4,200	
Tax payable by trustees		£4,200

Note. The transfer of value is £327,000. The value of the gift is the amount of the reduction in A's estate. See 8 CALCULATION OF TAX for more detailed examples.

1.7   **Reduction of tax rates.** There were frequent changes in the tax rates following the introduction of capital transfer tax. For IHT purposes (and previously for CTT purposes) the rate bands are indexed in line with the retail prices index and must be increased each year unless otherwise determined by Parliament. [*IHTA 1984, s 8*]. The increase for 2007–08 of the nil rate band to £300,000 was in excess of the increase in the retail prices index and the statutory indexing provisions to the RPI have been disallowed on this particular occasion and will resume from the year 2011–12 if Parliament decides. [*IHTA 1984, ss 7, 8, Sch ; FA 2005, s 98(6); FA 2006, s 155(5); FA 2007, s 4*]. Where there has been a rate change, the new rates are used to calculate the tax on any subsequent transfer. In certain cases, because of the cumulative nature of the tax, this may mean that earlier transfers need to be 'revised' before the calculation can be made. This revision does *not* affect the amount of earlier chargeable transfers or the actual tax paid on them.

Example 3

C made a gift to a discretionary trust of £244,000 on 1 February 2001. He had made no previous transfers. He makes a further gift of £150,000 to the discretionary trust on 1 October 2007. In each case he pays any tax due.

Gift on 1 February 2001

	£	£
Value of gift		244,000
Deduct exempt transfers		
Annual exemption 2000/01	3,000	
Annual exemption 1999/2000	3,000	
		6,000
		£238,000

Tax on net £238,000 per grossing-up table 41.1 2000.B2

0–238,000 = Nil + ¼ (234,000 – 238,000)	1,000
C's chargeable transfer	**£239,000**
Tax payable by C	**£1,000**

Gift on 1 October 2007

	£	Gross £	Tax £	Net £
Cumulative totals 1.2.2001		239,000	1,000	238,000
Revision for changes of rates (per table 41.1 2007.B1)		239,000	Nil	239,000
Value of gift	150,000			
Deduct annual exemption				
2007/08	(3,000)			
2006/07	(3,000)			
	£144,000	164,750	20,750*	144,000
		£403,750	£20,750	£383,000

*Tax on net £383,000 per grossing-up table 41.1 2007.B2

0–383,000 = Nil + ¼ (383,000 – 300,000)	20,750
Deduct tax on previous transfer at rates applicable at 1.10.2007	Nil
Tax payable by C	**£20,750**

Although the cumulative totals of tax and 'net' transfers are subject to change every time there is a change of rates, it is important to note that

(a) the figures change for the purpose of calculating the amount of any tax on subsequent transfers only: there is no question of any repayment of tax; and

(b) the chargeable transfer (sometimes called the gross transfer) never alters. See 8 CALCULATION OF TAX for more detailed examples.

1.8 **Death within seven years of transfer.** The tax on a chargeable lifetime transfer is initially calculated at one half of the death scale rates. Where the transferor then dies within seven years of the transfer, the tax is recomputed at the higher death scale but the tax rates are tapered where the death is more than three years after the gift. If there is a reduction in tax rates between the chargeable lifetime transfer and the date of death, the additional tax, if any, is calculated as if the new table applicable on death had applied to the transfer. The tax payable cannot be reduced below that originally chargeable at half death rates. [*IHTA 1984, s 7, Sch 2 para 2; FA 1986, Sch 19 para 2, para 37*].

Where potentially exempt transfers are made within seven years of death, no tax would have been payable at the time of the transfer. On death, tax is calculated at the full death rates applying at the time of death, subject to the tapering relief.

Where a death occurs after 17 March 1986, the above provisions do not affect the tax chargeable on a chargeable transfer occurring before 18 March 1986. The tax on such a chargeable transfer will only be recomputed at the higher death rates if the transferor dies within three years of the transfer. [*FA 1986, Sch 19 para 40*].

See 51 TRANSFERS WITHIN SEVEN YEARS BEFORE DEATH.

Example 4

C in Example 3 in 1.7 above dies on 1 April 2008. He leaves his entire estate to his wife so no tax is payable on his estate on death (see 21.8 EXEMPT TRANSFERS). No further tax is due on the gift made on 1 February 2001 as the gift was made more than seven years previously so no tax is payable. Further tax is due on the gift to the discretionary trust made on 1 October 2007.

	£
Gift on 1 October 2007	
Chargeable transfer	£164,750
Tax at death rates applicable on 1 April 2008	
(table 41.1 2007.A1)	
300,000 – 403,750 at 40%	41,500
Deduct tax paid by C	20,750
Further tax payable by the trustees of the discretionary trust	£20,750

1.9 INTERACTION WITH OTHER TAXES

Inheritance tax is levied separately from any other tax, so that it is possible, for example, for a transfer to suffer both inheritance tax and capital gains tax without any allowance in one for the other. See 9 CAPITAL GAINS TAX.

2   Accounts and Returns

Cross-reference. See also 4 ADMINISTRATION AND COLLECTION.

Simon's Direct Tax Service, part I11.2, I11.7.

Other Sources. Foster, part L; IHT 200 (Notes); IHTM10000.

2.1   ACCOUNTS AND RETURNS

An account is a document completed by a transferor or other taxable person providing details of a transaction in respect of which inheritance tax may apply.

A return is a document normally submitted by a person other than the transferor about transactions affecting others.

An account or return must be rendered in such form and containing such particulars as the Board may prescribe and an account must be supported by such books, papers and other documents, and verified (whether on oath or otherwise) in such manner as the Board may require. An account delivered to a probate registry i.e. the Probate Service (or the Probate and Matrimonial Office in Northern Ireland) is treated as delivered to the Board. [*IHTA 1984, s 257*]. See also 2.4 below. HMRC are satisfied that an accurate facsimile of an official account or other required document is within the scope of *IHTA 1984, s 257*. The most important criteria to be met are that the substitute document etc. must provide the same information as the official one; be readily recognisable as a substitute of the relevant official form; be in a form approved by HMRC and carry an agreed unique imprint; and bear the reference number of the issued official form it replaces or otherwise the taxpayer's reference. Application for approval should be made to the Customer Service Manager at the Nottingham or Edinburgh HMRC Inheritance Tax, (see below) as appropriate. (Inland Revenue Statement of Practice SP 2/93, 13 January 1993). The Board has power to make regulations by statutory instrument to dispense with the delivery of accounts and also to require information where accounts are not delivered. Secondary legislation provides for simplified IHT procedures in cases of minor nil-IHT paying estates and the *Finance Act 2004* extended this to bring in most non-taxpaying estates not already qualifying. This will also include estates which are substantially over the IHT threshold (currently £300,000) but are covered by the inter-spousal exemption or bequests to charitable organisations. Revised regulations that supplement *The Inheritance Tax (Delivery of Accounts) (Excepted Estates) Regulations 2002, SI 2002/1733* will be introduced to effect this change. See *Excepted estates* at 2.4 below. Under *IHTA 1984, s 256(1)(aa)* regulations will allow personal representatives to complete a short form of return which will meet the minimum requirements for both tax and probate purposes. Once such cases are dealt with under this simplified procedure they may be considered closed to further enquiry allowing the estate to be distributed and avoiding the necessity for a certificate of discharge. Further, *s 256(1A)* may require that the information and documents provided to the probate registry (England and Wales), the sheriff in Scotland and the Probate and Matrimonial Office in Northern Ireland can be passed on to HMRC and treated as if they had been passed originally to the Board of HMRC. The penalty position would be unaffected by this conduit process. See 36.1 PENALTIES. [*IHTA 1984, s 256 as amended by FA 2004, s 293*].

See 2.11 below for addresses to which accounts etc. should be delivered.

2.2   FORMS

The principal forms currently prescribed by the Board for IHT purposes are as follows. The forms should be used for deaths and other transfers after 17 March 1986 (chargeable events after 24 July 1986 for IHT 101).

2.2   Accounts and Returns

IHT 100

An account of a transfer of value (for use for lifetime transfers by individuals or the termination (during life or on death) of an interest in possession in settled property, but not where Form IHT 101 applies nor by personal representatives intending to obtain a grant of probate from a Probate Registry). Instruction booklet is IHT 110. This form was updated in December 2005 and includes a worksheet IHT100WS. For timber, trees or wood chargeable in connection with a death, Form C–5 (Timber) applies. Note that the old form IHT 100 and IHT 101 cannot be used after 31 October 2003. See http://www.hmrc.gov.uk/cto/forms/iht100_1.pdf.

IHT 101

An account of a chargeable event (which arises under the provisions relating to settlements without interests in possession in *IHTA 1984, Pt III, Ch III*). IHT 101 is now phased out with the introduction of the replacement IHT 100. The accompanying instruction booklet was IHT 111.

IHT 200

HMRC Account (See form IHT 200 below. A revised version was issued in December 2005 and may also be viewed below and at the HMRC website at http://www.hmrc.gov.uk/cto/forms/iht200_1.pdf) (for use in applying for a grant of representation where the deceased died domiciled in the UK, but not

(i)   for a grant of double probate, a grant *de bonis non administratis* or a grant following which an earlier grant will become cessate—Form Cap A5–C (Cap A5–N in NI) applies; or

(ii)   where IHT 202 was appropriate (this form is not now being issued); or

(iii)   where the deceased died domiciled in the UK and personal application for a grant is being made by the proposed legal personal representative *and* the net estate chargeable to tax does not exceed the threshold for the imposition of tax at the date of death (taking into account any reliefs claimed) *and* the property to be covered by the grant does not include any settled land. Form IHT 37 has been drawn up by the CTO in respect of land, which is being sent out with supplies of IHT 200. See below for the CTO telephone/fax orderline for stationery.

Instruction booklet is IHT 210. See http://www.hmrc.gov.uk/cto/forms/iht210_1.pdf.

A grant of representation granted by the High Court in England and Wales in respect of the estate of a person dying domiciled there and noting the domicile will be recognised throughout the UK. This can be achieved by the delivery of a single HMRC Account. If such a grant is obtained when the domicile is in Scotland or NI, the grant is limited to assets in England and Wales and a further grant (requiring a further HMRC Account) may be required. The appropriate form in Scotland is also now IHT 200 (a revised version came into effect in December 2005) as well as Inventory Form C1 where Confirmation is all that is required. See also 61 IHT NEWSLETTER AND TAX BULLETIN EXTRACTS and http://www.hmrc.gov.uk/cto/forms/c1_1.pdf. The IHT 200 must be used in all cases unless the gross value of the estate and the gifts within the previous seven years does not exceed £300,000. See 2.4 below. These forms replace the previous Forms A3, B3 and B4. Where an Eik (addition) to Confirmation is required for additional assets, a Corrective Inventory C4, available from the HMRC website and updated in April 2007, should also be used. See http://www.hmrc.gov.uk/cto/c4_2.pdf. However, where an Eik to Confirmation is required because the estate has not been fully administered or none of the original executors or substitutes remains in office, then the existing Form X-1, available from the Sheriff's Court, should be used. In NI it is IHT 200 which has replaced the 200N. [*SI 2003/1658; SI 2004/2543 as amended*].

IHT 200 (Form D2)	For use in applying for a grant of representation where the deceased died domiciled outside the UK even though the domicile is deemed to be in the UK under *IHTA 1984, s 267* (see 17.3 DOMICILE). See http://www.hmrc.gov.uk/cto/forms/d02_1.pdf. In NI the Form D2 replaces the original 201N. Instruction booklet is IHT 210. Updated at regular intervals.
IHT 22	**HMRC Account** (for use where a grant of representation is not required for small estates where money is deposited in a Savings Bank or is due from a Friendly or Industrial and Provident Society etc. and a certificate of exemption from tax is required to obtain payment of the money).
CAP D–3	**Corrective account** (for use where too much or too little tax has been paid on a previous account). D–1 in Scotland.

IHT 215 is the Practitioner's Guide which contains IHT 210 'How to fill in Form IHT 200', Notes D1–D21, IHT 213 'How to fill in Form IHT 200(WS)' and IHT 214 'Examples of inheritance tax calculations'. See IHT 200 notes which deals with information suggested to be provided with Accounts on Forms IHT 200 and may be obtained from HMRC Inheritance Tax. Booklet SP2 is the supplementary notes guide to enable completion of forms D1, D3, D4, D6, D7, D9, D10, D12, D17 and D18. See http://www.hmrc.gov.uk/cto/forms/iht215_1.pdf.

Forms relating to other matters are mentioned under the appropriate subject headings elsewhere in this book. Orders for forms should be sent by fax to HMRC Inheritance Tax Stationery Section on 0845 234 1010 for dispatch within five working days. Telephone enquiries should be made on 0845 30 20 900. See IHT NEWSLETTER AND TAX BULLETIN EXTRACTS (61), Tax Bulletin, December 2005.

2.3   **ACCOUNTS FOR LIFETIME TRANSFER**

(a)   Every transferor who is liable for tax on the value transferred by a chargeable transfer; and

(b)   every person liable for tax on the value transferred by a potentially exempt transfer (including, in relation to transfers and other events after 16 March 1987, such a transfer made under *IHTA 1984, s 52* as amended by *FA 2006, Sch 20 para 13* on the termination of an interest in possession) which proves to be a chargeable transfer; and

(c)   any person within (a) or (b) above who would be so liable if tax were chargeable on that value,

must deliver to the Board an account (see LIFETIME TRANSFERS (31) for Form IHT 100) specifying all property comprised in that transfer to which tax is or would be attributable and its value, unless some other person liable for the tax (other than a joint trustee) has already delivered such an account. [*IHTA 1984, s 216(1)(4)(5); FA 1986, Sch 19 para 29; F(No 2)A 1987, Sch 7 para 4; FA 2006, Sch 22 para 7*].

Potentially exempt transfers. There is no requirement to notify the Board on the making of such a transfer nor to deliver an account. In the case of a transfer on or after 17 March 1987 but before 22 March 2006 involving an interest in possession trust, that transfer may also become an exempt transfer if the transferor survives for seven years. In this connection, there is no immediate lifetime charge on a gift by an individual if the gift is into trust before 22 March 2006 under which another individual has a beneficial interest in possession in that gifted property, nor where the gift increases the value of trust property in which another individual has a beneficial interest in possession. After 21 March 2006 a PET is a transfer of value made by an individual which would otherwise be a chargeable transfer and which is either a gift to another individual or into a trust for a disabled person or into a trust for bereaved minors on the ending of an immediate post-death interest (IPDI). See 38.1 POTENTIALLY EXEMPT TRANSFERS. There was also no immediate lifetime charge on the termination or disposal of an individual's beneficial interest in possession in trust property before 22 March 2006 where another individual becomes beneficially entitled or that trust property becomes comprised of an accumulation and maintenance settlement or the value of another individual's estate is increased. An account must be submitted where there has been a potentially exempt transfer and the transferor has not survived for seven years. The donee of a potentially exempt transfer is liable to deliver an account if the transferor dies within seven years of the transfer.

Excepted transfers. No account need be delivered in respect of a chargeable transfer by an individual where

(i)   the value of the chargeable transfer, together with any other chargeable transfers by the same individual in the same tax year ending 5 April, does not exceed £10,000; and

(ii)   the value of the chargeable transfer, together with any other chargeable transfers by the same individual in the previous ten years (presumably to be amended to seven years) does not exceed £40,000; or

(iii)   an interest in possession comes to an end and the transferor gives the trustees a notice informing them of the availability of an annual or marriage or civil partnership exemption and the value transferred is wholly covered by that exemption.

The Board retain the right to call for an account by notice in writing to the individual. [*IHTA 1984, s 256(1)(a); SI 1981/1440; SI 2002/1731*]. See LIFETIME TRANSFERS (31) for IHT 100 and http://www.hmrc.gov.uk/cto/forms/iht110_2.pdf.

See 2.6 below for time limits and 2.7 for submission of accounts where transfer originally treated as 'excepted'.

Gifts with reservation. Property given but subject to a reservation where that reservation is retained until the death of the donor or where the reservation ceases within seven years of the death should be the subject of an IHT 100 account return. However, where a reservation ceases before the death of the donor then the donor is treated as having made a potentially exempt transfer of the property at the time the reservation ceases. In addition, the dismantling of pre-owned assets avoidance schemes by way of election on form IHT 500 in respect of any relevant year of assessment will ensure that the property is treated as being comprised in the original donor's estate for these purposes as a gift with reservation but will preclude the income tax charge on the annual taxable value of the pre-owned asset. See 22 GIFTS WITH RESERVATION; 59.40 WORKING CASE STUDY.

2.4   ACCOUNTS FOR TRANSFERS ON DEATH

The **personal representatives** of a deceased person must deliver to the Board an account of all property which formed part of the deceased's estate immediately before his death (other than property which only forms part of his estate by virtue of the provisions relating to GIFTS WITH RESERVATION (22)) and its value unless the estate is an 'excepted estate' (see below). For deaths on or after 9 March 1999 the information provided by the personal representatives must include details of any chargeable transfers made by the deceased within seven years of his death. The personal representatives may also provide a provisional estimate of the value of an asset included in their account where, despite making all reasonable enquiries to ascertain the value, they cannot establish the exact value. In such cases, the account must contain a statement to that effect and an undertaking to deliver a further account as soon as the value is ascertained. An executor in England and Wales of settled land need only give details of the trust property comprised in the transfer (see IHT 200 Form D5 below). See http://www.hmrc.gov.uk/cto/forms/d05_1.pdf. In the case of pension scheme administrators of alternatively secured pension (ASP) funds who become liable to the payment of IHT by reason of *IHTA 1984, s 151A–C* they are responsible for delivering an account to HMRC of the property expended on dependant's benefits. [*IHTA 1984, ss 216(1)(bca), 272; FA 2006, s 160, Sch 22 paras 7, 10*]. See also 2.6 below and 37.2 PENSION SCHEMES.

The account must be presented at a probate registry, and any tax payable on delivery paid, before a grant of representation can be obtained. In Scotland, such an account is called an inventory and it must be presented at a local Sheriff Court or the Commissary Office in Edinburgh. The Scottish equivalent of the grant of representation is the confirmation. See 2.11 below for addresses. The Board of HMRC may also give directions restricting assets to be included in accounts to be delivered by personal representatives. In *Robertson v CIR [2002] STC SCD 182 Sp C 309* the Executor R had instructed valuers to carry out valuations of the two properties; he had not received these valuations at the time of submitting the inventory. Later that month the contents of the Scottish house were valued at £24,845, and in December the house was sold for £82,000. In January 2000 the English cottage and its grounds were valued at £315,000. R submitted a corrective inventory to HMRC Inheritance Tax, and paid the additional IHT due. The CTO informed him that they considered that the executors had not made 'the fullest enquiries that are reasonably practicable', as required by *IHTA 1984, s 216(3A)*, and they proposed to charge a penalty of £9,000, under *IHTA 1984, s 247*. The Special Commissioner reviewed the evidence and held that R was not liable to any penalty, since he had made the fullest enquiries that were reasonably practicable in the circumstances. On the evidence, R had made a thorough examination of S's home shortly after her death, had appreciated that a valuation of the contents would be required, and had instructed a valuation promptly. In the meantime, he had, in accordance with accepted practice, inserted estimated valuations in the inventory and had disclosed that they were estimates. He had followed what was acceptable practice in the legal profession, and had fulfilled his duties as an executor and as a solicitor. HMRC was not justified in seeking to impose a penalty. [*IHTA 1984, s 216(1)(3)(3A)(3B)(4), s 261; FA 1986, Sch 19 para 29; FA 1999, s 105*].

Following the Senior District Judge's Direction of 27 October 2004 there are three alternative IHT certificates that may be used in varying circumstances to use in the oath to apply for a grant. These are detailed below. See also 61 IHT NEWSLETTER AND TAX BULLETIN EXTRACTS.

2.4   Accounts and Returns

In the case where the estate is not an excepted estate then the preferred oath is that applying at point 5 below:

IN THE HIGH COURT OF JUSTICE   Extracting Solicitor ....

Family Division   Address ....

The District Probate Registry at Leeds

IN the Estate of AB deceased

We CD of [address]

And EF of [address]

make Oath and say

1.   We believe the paper writing now produced to and marked by us to contain the true and original last will and testament of AB of [address in death certificate] formerly of [address in will] who died on the ..... day .... 200(7).. born on the ..... day .... 19./200 ..... aged .... years domiciled in England and Wales.

2.   To the best of my/our knowledge, information and belief there was no land vested in the said deceased which was settled previously to his death and not by his will and which remained settled land notwithstanding his death.

3.   We are the Executors named in the said will.

4.   We will

    (i)   collect, get in and administer according to the law the real and personal estate of the said deceased

    (ii)   when required to do so by the Court, exhibit on oath in the Court a full inventory of the said estate

And when so required render an account of the administration of the said estate to the Court; and when required to do so by the High Court, deliver up the grant of probate to that Court.

5.   To the best of my/our knowledge, information and belief the gross estate passing under the grant amounts to £ and the net estate amounts to £ .

SWORN by CD and EF the above named

Deponents   )
At   )
)
This day of 200(7)   )
)
Before me,   )

A Commissioner for Oaths/Solicitor.

Where there are no personal representatives because no grant of representation or confirmation has been obtained in the UK within twelve months of the end of the month in which death occurred,

(*a*)   every person in whom *any property* of the estate vests as beneficial owner or otherwise, or who is beneficially entitled to an interest in possession in such property, on or after the deceased's death, and

(*b*)   where property is comprised in a settlement with no person entitled to an interest in possession, every person for whose benefit any of that property, or income from it, is applied, on or after the deceased's death,

must deliver an account to the Board, specifying to the best of his knowledge and belief, the property in which he has an interest (or which is applicable for his benefit) and its value. Any property includes property which is expended on dependants' benefits arising from an alternatively secured pension (ASP) under *IHTA 1984, s 151A* or property paid to a charity within *IHTA 1984, ss 151B(4), 151C(3)(b)*. See 37.2 PENSION SCHEMES. Such an account is not required if the person concerned has satisfied the Board that an account will in due course be delivered by the personal representatives or has already been delivered by some other liable person. [*IHTA 1984, s 216(2)(4)(5)*]. See Form D11 below or http://www.hmrc.gov.uk/cto/forms/d11_1.pdf.

Gifts with reservation. Any person who is liable for tax on the value of property forming part of the deceased's estate by virtue only of the provisions relating to GIFTS WITH RESERVATION (22) (or would be so liable if tax were chargeable on that value) must deliver to the Board an account specifying all property to the value of which the tax is or would be attributable and its value unless some other person liable for the tax (other than a joint trustee) has already delivered such an account. [*IHTA 1984, s 216(1)(4)(5); FA 1986, Sch 19 para 29*].

Excepted estates. HMRC are presently considering revising and updating the excepted estates legislation and are asking for comments at http://www.hmrc.gov.uk/cto/etes.htm. At present no account need be delivered for the estate of any person who has died domiciled in the UK on or after 1 September 2006 where:

(i)   the estate comprises only property which has passed under the deceased's will or intestacy, or by nomination on death, or entitlement to a single interest in possession settlement, or beneficially by survivorship;

(ii)   the total gross value of the estate for tax purposes (inclusive of (iii)–(v) below, as may be the case) does not exceed £300,000 (£285,000 for deaths before 6 April 2007 and after 5 April 2006; £275,000 for deaths before 6 April 2006 but after 5 April 2005; £263,000 for deaths before 6 April 2005 but after 5 April 2004; £240,000 for deaths before 6 April 2004 but after 5 April 2002; £220,000 for deaths before 6 April 2003 but after 5 April 2002; £210,000 for deaths before 6 April 2002 but after 5 April 2000; £200,000 for deaths before 6 April 2000 but after 5 April 1998; £180,000 for deaths before 6 April 1998 but after 5 April 1996; £145,000 for deaths before 6 April 1996 but after 5 April 1995; £125,000 for deaths before 6 April 1995 but after 31 March 1991; £115,000 for deaths before 1 April 1991 but after 31 March 1990; £100,000 for deaths before 1 April 1990 but after 31 March 1989; and £70,000 for deaths before 1 April 1989) after ignoring transfers attracting APR or BPR within *IHTA 1984, ss 104, 116*;

(iii)   not more than £100,000 (£75,000 for deaths before 1 September 2006 but after 5 April 2002; £50,000 for deaths before 6 April 2002 but after 5 April 1998; £30,000 for deaths before 6 April 1998 but after 5 April 1996; £15,000 for deaths before 6 April 1996 but after 31 March 1989; £10,000 for deaths before 1 April 1989 but after 31 March 1987; and for deaths before 1 April 1987 the higher of 10% of the total gross value or £2,000) consists of property situated outside the UK and by reason of that person's death an ASP fund provision under *IHTA 1984, ss 151A–C* does not apply; and

(iv) the deceased died and had made no lifetime gifts chargeable to inheritance tax (including potentially exempt transfers becoming chargeable on death and gifts with reservation where the reservation subsists at death or where the property ceased to be subject to the reservation in the seven years before the donor's death) excepting lifetime transfers made within seven years of the deceased's death consisting of 'specified transfers' i.e. cash, listed shares or securities, an interest over land (and furnishings and chattels enjoyed with the land and transferred at the same time) that did not exceed £150,000 (£100,000 for deaths before 1 September but after 5 April 2000; £75,000 for deaths before 6 April 2000 but after 5 April 1998; £50,000 for deaths before 6 April 1998 but after 5 April 1996; before 6 April 1996 such transfers would have ruled out the excepted estates procedure) after ignoring transfers attracting APR or BPR within *IHTA 1984, ss 104, 116* and by reason of that person's death an ASP fund provision under *IHTA 1984, ss 151A-C* does not apply;

(v) not more than £150,000 represents value attributable to property which, immediately before the person's death, was settled property.

No account need be delivered for the estate of any person who died on or after 6 April 2004 who was domiciled in the UK or treated as domiciled in the UK [*FA 2004, s 293*] where:

(vi) the aggregate gross value of the deceased's estate (inclusive of (iii)–(v) above, as may be the case) is £1,000,000 or less after ignoring transfers attracting APR or BPR within *IHTA 1984, ss 104, 116* and after deducting any specified exemptions (e.g. spousal, charities, etc.) so that the net chargeable estate is less than £300,000. See Form IHT205 below (Form C5 in Scotland). See April 2005 IHT Newsletter at 61 IHT NEWSLETTER AND TAX BULLETIN EXTRACTS.

[*Inheritance Tax (Delivery of Accounts)(Excepted Estates)(Amendment) Regulations 2006, SI 2006/2141*].

For an excepted estate where the gross value does not exceed the IHT threshold (currently £300,000) the following certificate may be used in the oath to apply for a grant.

IN THE HIGH COURT OF JUSTICE   Extracting Solicitor ....

Family Division   Address ....

The District Probate Registry at Leeds

IN the Estate of AB deceased

We CD of [address]

And EF of [address]

make Oath and say

1. We believe the paper writing now produced to and marked by us to contain the true and original last will and testament of AB of [address in death certificate] formerly of [address in will] who died on the ..... day .... 200(7).. born on the ..... day .... 19./200 ..... aged .... years domiciled in England and Wales.

2. To the best of my/our knowledge, information and belief there was no land vested in the said deceased which was settled previously to his death and not by his will and which remained settled land notwithstanding his death.

3. We are the Executors named in the said will.

4. We will

(i)   collect, get in and administer according to the law the real and personal estate of the said deceased

(ii)   when required to do so by the Court, exhibit on oath in the Court a full inventory of the said estate

And when so required render an account of the administration of the said estate to the Court; and when required to do so by the High Court, deliver up the grant of probate to that Court.

5.   To the best of my/our knowledge, information and belief the gross estate passing under the grant does not exceed £300,000 and the net estate amounts to £   and this is not a case in which a HM Revenue and Customs Account is required to be delivered.

SWORN by CD and EF the above named

Deponents	)
At	)
	)
This day of 200(7)	)
	)
Before me,	)

A Commissioner for Oaths/Solicitor.

For an excepted estate where the gross value exceeds the IHT threshold (currently £300,000) but does not exceed £1m and the chargeable estate after deducting any spouse/civil partner or charitable exemptions does not exceed the current IHT threshold the following certificate may be used in the oath to apply for a grant.

IN THE HIGH COURT OF   Extracting Solicitor ....
JUSTICE

Family Division   Address ....

The District Probate Registry at Leeds

IN the Estate of AB deceased

We CD of [address]

And EF of [address]

make Oath and say

1.   We believe the paper writing now produced to and marked by us to contain the true and original last will and testament of AB of [address in death certificate] formerly of [address in will] who died on the ..... day .... 200(7).. born on the ..... day .... 19./200 ..... aged .... years domiciled in England and Wales.

2.   To the best of my/our knowledge, information and belief there was no land vested in the said deceased which was settled previously to his death and not by his will and which remained settled land notwithstanding his death.

3.   We are the Executors named in the said will.

---

4.   We will

    (i)   collect, get in and administer according to the law the real and personal estate of the said deceased

    (ii)   when required to do so by the Court, exhibit on oath in the Court a full inventory of the said estate

And when so required render an account of the administration of the said estate to the Court; and when required to do so by the High Court, deliver up the grant of probate to that Court.

5.   To the best of my/our knowledge, information and belief the gross estate passing under the grant amounts to £   and the net estate amounts to £   and this is not a case in which a HM Revenue and Customs Account is required to be delivered.

SWORN by CD and EF the above named

Deponents   )

At   )

)

This day of 200(7)   )

)

Before me,   )

A Commissioner for Oaths/Solicitor.

No account need be delivered for the estate of any person who died on or after 6 April 2002 who was never domiciled in the UK or treated as domiciled in the UK [*FA 1986, s 267*] where

(vii)   the value of such a person's estate that is situated in the UK which is attributable to cash or quoted shares or securities that pass by will, or by intestacy, or beneficially by survivorship and does not exceed £100,000. See Form IHT207 below (Form C5(OUK) in Scotland).

A grant of representation will still be required but applicants will only be required to swear as to the brackets into which the value of the estate falls. Under this procedure applicants in National Coal Board compensation claims can, instead of completing a full IHT account, send a D18 to HMRC Inheritance Tax together with a set declaration that the assets of the estate did not exceed the taxable limit or threshold at the date of death. It has been agreed by HMRC Inheritance Tax with the Court Service that, with immediate effect, the completion of a Form [P26A or] D18 will not be required. As a result, HMRC Inheritance Tax will no longer be part of the process. See IHT NEWSLETTER AND TAX BULLETIN EXTRACTS (61), May Special Edition 2003 and http://www.hmrc.gov.uk/cto/forms/d18_1.pdf.

Once it has been worked out that there is no tax to pay, put 'NIL' in box PS8 (or PS7 for the Form D18) and the form should then be signed. The form can then be sent directly to the probate registry. At the same time the HMRC Account, supporting papers and a copy of the will should be sent to HMRC Inheritance Tax. HMRC Inheritance Tax issued an extra module to the IHT 200 forms which can be completed by the taxpayer and delivered with the IHT 200. This Form D19 (shown below) will enable the taxpayer to apply to HMRC Inheritance Tax for confirmation that HMRC is satisfied with the information supplied to them and at the same time register a reference number. The D19 will not, however, have the standing of a statutory certificate of clearance. See IHT NEWSLETTER AND TAX BULLETIN EXTRACTS (61), March 1997, November 1999 and April 2000. See http://www.hmrc.gov.uk/cto/forms/d19_1.pdf.

The Board retain the right to call for an account by issuing a notice to the personal representatives within 35 days of the issue of the grant of probate. See Leaflet IHT 14, p 7. In Scotland, the Board may give notice to the personal representatives within 60 days of the issue of confirmation to the estate that the Registrar, HMRC Inheritance Tax at Edinburgh has required the Commissary Clerk or Sheriff Clerk to transmit to him an inventory of the excepted estate. If no notice is issued, the personal representatives will be automatically discharged from any further tax claims (unless there is fraud or non-disclosure of material facts) and any HMRC charge (see 35.8 PAYMENT OF TAX) is extinguished without formal application. See leaflet 'What to do after a death in Scotland'. See also IHT 14, p 7 and 8.

[*IHTA 1984, s 256; SI 1981/880, SI 1981/881, SI 1981/1441; SI 1983/1039, SI 1983/1040, SI 1983/1911; SI 1987/1127, SI 1987/1128, SI 1987/1129; SI 1989/1078, SI 1989/1079, SI 1989/1080; SI 1990/1110, SI 1990/1111, SI 1990/1112; SI 1991/1248, SI 1991/1249, SI 1991/1250; SI 1996/1470, SI 1996/1472,SI 1996/1473; SI 1998/1429, SI 1998/1430, SI 1998/1431; SI 2000/965, SI 2000/966, SI 2000/967; SI 2002/1733; SI 2003/1658; SI 2004/2543*].

Estates where the deceased had an interest in settled property are not excepted estates except insofar as that property from 6 April 2002 was wholly settled property the value of which immediately before the person's death amounted to not more than £100,000. Where the value of an estate is attributable in part to property passing by survivorship in a joint tenancy or, in Scotland by survivorship, it is the deceased's beneficial interest in that property which is taken into account for the purposes of the limit in (ii) above. (Inland Revenue Press Release, 2 July 1987). [*SI 2002/1733*].

See 2.6 below for time limits and 2.7 for submission of accounts where estate originally treated as 'excepted'.

A simpler reporting regime was announced by the Chancellor of the Exchequer in the Budget speech on 17 March 2004 and is now incorporated into *FA 2004, s 293* whereby an IHT account will be required only where there is tax to pay. In most other cases contact will only be with the Probate Service in England and the Sheriff's Court in Scotland. [*Supreme Court Act 1981, s 109(1); Probate and Legacy Duties Act 1808, s 42; Administration of Estates (Northern Ireland) Order 1979, SI 1979/1575 as amended by FA 2004, s 294(3); The Finance Act 2004, Section 294 (Appointed Day) Order 2004, SI 2004/2571*]. As a result, in a vast majority of cases applying from 1 November 2004, the information on deceased's estate will be provided once to the Probate Service (or the Sheriff's Court in Scotland) who in turn will provide HMRC with information from which HMRC will determine selected cases for enquiry. This change in administration procedure ensures that only the basic information will be provided in a vast majority of cases and not the full account as in past years. The changes are now incorporated in the *Inheritance Tax (Delivery of Accounts) (Excepted Estates) Regulations 2004, SI 2004/2543 as amended by The Tax and Civil Partnership (No 2) Regulations 2005, SI 2005/3230, Reg 15* ensuring that a new category of qualifying estate where the gross value does not exceed £1 million, subject to a number of provisos, is excluded. See above at (vi). [*IHTA 1984, s 256(3A) as inserted by FA 2004, s 293(6)*]. See 2.1 above and HMRC IHT Newsletter, April and August 2004 at IHT NEWSLETTER AND TAX BULLETIN EXTRACTS (61).

In order to ensure that compliance requirements are met the existing penalty rules (see 36 PENALTIES for failure to provide accounts, etc.) will apply to the delivery of incorrect information under these simplified reporting arrangements. As a result of this provision will be made to allow the information delivered to the Probate Service and then passed on to HMRC to be treated as having been delivered direct to HMRC as will be the case for the delivery of information via the Scottish Court Service. [*IHTA 1984, s 256(1A) as inserted by FA 2004, s 293(3)*]. Contact the Principal Probate Registry on 0207 947 7431/7414.

Many estates are exempt from IHT because most or all of the estate passes to a surviving spouse/civil partner, a UK charity or other exempt bodies. HMRC has identified certain circumstances where a reduced IHT 200 account may be delivered. These circumstances are as follows:

- the deceased was domiciled in the UK at the date of death, and

- most or all of the property passing by will or under intestacy passes to an 'exempt beneficiary' either:

    (i)   absolutely, or through an interest in possession trust, to the surviving spouse/civil partner, who must also be domiciled in the UK, or

    (ii)   so as to immediately become the property of a body listed in *IHTA 1984, Sch 3*, or

    (iii) so as to immediately become the property of a charity registered in the UK, or held on trusts established in the UK for charitable purposes only, and

- the gross value of the property passing by will or under intestacy to beneficiaries other than exempt beneficiaries together with the value of 'other property chargeable on death' and the chargeable value of any gifts made in the seven years prior to death do not, in total, exceed the IHT threshold.

Other property chargeable on death mentioned above includes:

(*a*)   joint property passing by survivorship to someone other than the deceased's surviving spouse/civil partner (assuming that he or she was domiciled in the UK);

(*b*)   settled property in which the deceased had a life interest, other than settled property which then devolves to the deceased's spouse/civil partner, to a body listed in *IHTA 1984, Sch 3*, or to a charity registered in the UK;

(*c*)   property that the deceased had given away but in which they reserved a benefit that either continued until death or ceased within seven years of death;

(*d*)   property situated outside the UK which does not devolve under the UK will or intestacy.

Where the circumstances above are met, the requirement to deliver an account containing all appropriate property and the value of that property is relaxed. The account must still be delivered on Form IHT 200 and the declaration on p 8 signed. See leaflet IHT 19 which details which sections of the IHT 200 that need to be completed.

2.5   **ACCOUNTS BY TRUSTEES OF SETTLEMENTS**

The **trustees** of a settlement liable for tax on the value transferred by a transfer of value or for tax under provisions relating to SETTLEMENTS WITHOUT INTERESTS IN POSSESSION (44) (or who would be so liable if tax were chargeable) must deliver an account specifying all property to which tax is or would be attributable and its value, unless some other person liable for the tax (other than as joint trustee) has already delivered such an account. [*IHTA 1984, s 216(1)(4)(5)*]. An account must be rendered to the best of a taxpayer's knowledge and belief. This does not mean that he can be compelled to act as an information gatherer if he does not have information himself. (*Re Clore (decd.) (No 3), CIR v Stype Trustees (Jersey) Ltd and Others Ch D, [1985] STC 394*). (The *Stype* case also held that foreign trustees liable to pay tax are also liable to produce accounts despite difficulties of enforcement.)

Excepted terminations. No account need be delivered on a termination of an interest in possession in settled property where

PAYMENT OF TAX (35.2) (Family Division Practice Note 30 November 1989). See IHT
NEWSLETTER AND TAX BULLETIN EXTRACTS (61).

Inheritance Tax Account

Fill in this account for the estate of a person who died on or after 18 March 1986.
You should read the related guidance note(s) before filling in this form.
The notes follow the same numbering as this form for ease of reference.

A Write in the name of the Probate Registry, Commissary Court or Sheriff Court District where you will apply for a grant

A1 [   ]   Date of Grant [   ]

B Provide the following information about the person who has died

Title B1 [   ]   Surname B2 [   ]

Other name(s) B3 [   ]

Date of birth B4 [dd / mm / yyyy]   Date of death B5 [dd / mm / yyyy]

Marital or civil partnership status   Write whichever is appropriate a, b, c or d in the box B6 [   ]

a married or in civil partnership   b single   c divorced or former civil partner   d widowed or surviving civil partner

Last known permanent address

B7 [   ]   Is B7 a care home? B13 Yes [ ] No [ ]

Postcode [   ]   Domicile B14 [   ]

Occupation B15 [   ]

Surviving relatives

Spouse or civil partner B8 [   ]   National insurance number B16 [   ]

Brother(s)/sister(s) B9 [   ]   Income tax district B17 [   ]

Parent(s) B10 [   ]   Income tax or self assessment reference B18 [   ]

Number of children B11 [   ]

Number of grandchildren B12 [   ]   Did the deceased grant a power of attorney? B19 Yes [ ] No [ ]

C If you want us to deal with a solicitor or other person provide the following information about them

Name and address of firm or person dealing with the estate

C1 [   ]   DX number and town

C2 DX [   ]

Contact name and reference

C3 [   ]

Telephone number

C4 [   ]

Postcode [   ]   Fax number

C5 [   ]

(Substitute)(LexisNexis Butterworths)

IHT 200   www.hmrc.gov.uk/cto   Helpline 0845 30 20 900   HMRC CT 08/06

D Supplementary pages

You must answer all of the questions in this section, by ticking the box that applies

If you answer "Yes" to a question you will need to fill in the supplementary page shown. If you do not have all the supplementary pages you need you can download them from the internet (www.hmrc.gov.uk/cto) or request them from the orderline: e-mail (hmrc.ihtorderline@gtnet.gov.uk) or telephone 0845 30 20 900.

		No	Yes	Page
• The Will	Did the deceased leave a Will?	☐	☐	D1
• Domicile outside the United Kingdom	Was the deceased domiciled outside the UK at the date of death?	☐	☐	D2
• Gifts and other transfers of value	Did the deceased make any gift or any other transfer of value on or after 18 March 1986 (including gifts with reservation and gifts involving previously owned assets)?	☐	☐	D3
• Joint assets	Did the deceased hold any asset(s) in joint names with another person?	☐	☐	D4
• Nominated assets	Did the deceased, at any time during their lifetime, give written instructions (usually called a "nomination") that any asset was to pass to a particular person on their death?	☐	☐	D4
• Assets held in trust	Did the deceased have any right to any benefit from any assets held in trust or in a settlement at the date of death?	☐	☐	D5
• Pensions	Did the deceased have a pension provision ofr retirement other than the State Pension?	☐	☐	D6
• Stocks and shares	Did the deceased own any stocks or shares?	☐	☐	D7
• Debts due to the estate	Did the deceased lend any money, either on mortgage or by personal loan, that had not been repaid by the date of death?	☐	☐	D8
• Life insurance and annuities	Did the deceased pay any premiums on any life insurance policies or annuities which are payable to either the estate or to someone else or which continue after death?	☐	☐	D9
• Household and personal goods	Complete form D10 in all cases. If the deceased did not own any household goods or personal possessions or they do note have any value, explain the circumstances on form D10.			D10
• Interest in another estate	Did the deceased have a right to a legacy or a share of an estate of someone who died before them, but which they had not received before they died?	☐	☐	D11
• Land, buildings and interests in land	Did the deceased own any land or buildings in the UK?	☐	☐	D12
• Agricultural relief	Are you deducting agricultural relief from the value of any farm or farmland owned by the deceased?	☐	☐	D13
• Business interests	Did the deceased own all or part of a business or were they a partner in a business?	☐	☐	D14
• Business relief	Are you deducting business relief?	☐	☐	D14
• Foreign assets	Did the deceased own any assets outside the UK?	☐	☐	D15
• Debts owed by the estate	Are you claiming a deduction against the estate for any money that the deceased had borrowed from relatives, close friends, or trustees, or other loans, overdrafts or guarantee debts?	☐	☐	D16

2.11 Accounts and Returns

E **Domicile in Scotland - entitlement to claim legal rights**

Scottish legal rights entitlement (jus relicti/æ and or legitim) is relevant to this estate? No ☐ Yes ☐

How many children are   under 18 ☐   18 and over ☐

F **Estate in the UK where tax may not be paid by instalments**

Open market value at the date of death

- Quoted stocks, shares and investments *(box SS1, form D7)* F1 £
- UK Government and municipal securities *(box SS2, form D7)* F2 £
- Unquoted stocks, shares and investments F3 £
- Traded unquoted stocks and shares F4 £
- Dividends or interest F5 £
- Premium Bonds *(including the value of any unclaimed or uncashed prizes)* F6 £
- National Savings investments *(show details on form D17, or inventory form C1 in Scotland)* F7 £
- Bank and building society accounts *(list each account or investment separately on form D17, or Inventory form C1 in Scotland)* F8 £
- Cash F9 £
- Debts due to the deceased and secured by mortgage *(box DD1, form D8)* F10 £
- Other debts due to the deceased *(box DD1, form D8)* F11 £
- Rent due to the deceased, but unpaid at the date of death *(Include the property itself on form D12)* F12 £
- Accrued income F13 £
- Apportioned income F14 £
- Other income due to the deceased *(box IP4, form D9, box PA1 form D6)* F15 £
- Life insurance polices *(box IP3, form D9)* F16 £
- Payments due to the deceased under private medical insurance to cover hospital or health charges incurred before death. F17 £
- Income tax or capital gains tax repayment F18 £
- Household and personal goods *(sold, box HG18, form D10)* F19 £
- Household and personal goods *(unsold, box HG17, form D10)* F20 £
- Interest in another estate unpaid at the date of death *(box UE1, form D11)* F21 £
- Interest in expectancy *(reversionary interest)* F22 £
- Other personal assets in the UK *(show details on form D17, or Inventory form C1 in Scotland)* F23 £

Total assets *(sum of boxes F1 to F23)* F24 £

Liabilities, funeral expenses, exemptions and reliefs

- Liabilities incurred by the deceased before the date of death

Name	Description of liability	

Total liabilities *(write in the total of the items listed above)* F25 £

- Funeral expenses

Total funeral expenses *(write in the total of the items listed above)* F26 £

Total liabilities and funeral expenses F27 £
(box F25 plus box F26. If box F27 is more than box F24 see explanatory notes)

Net total of assets less liabilities *(box F24 less box F27)* F28 £

- Exemptions and reliefs

Total exemptions and reliefs *(write in the total of the items listed above)* F29 £

Chargeable value of assets in the UK where tax may not be paid by instalments F30 £
(box F28 less box F29. Copy this figure to box WS1 on form IHT200WS)

2.11   Accounts and Returns

(G) **Estate in the UK where tax may be paid by instalments**

Do you wish to pay the tax on these assets by instalments? *(Tick appropriate box)* No ☐ Yes ☐

Interests in land owned by the deceased at the date of death

Open market value at the date of death

- Deceased's residence *(excluding farm houses)* **G1** £
- Other residential property **G2** £
- Farms, farmland, farm buildings and farmhouses. **G3** £
- Business property *(from which the deceased ran a business alone or in partnership)* **G4** £
- Timber and woodland which is not part of a farm. **G5** £
- Other land, buildings and rights over land **G6** £

	Interest in a business	Interest in a partnership		
• Farming business	**G7.1** £	**G7.2** £	**G7** £

	Interest in a business	Interest in a partnership		
• Other business interests	**G8.1** £	**G8.2** £	**G8** £

	Farm trade assets	Other business assets		
• Business assets	**G9.1** £	**G9.2** £	**G9** £

- Quoted shares and securities, control holding only **G10** £

	Control holding	Non-control holding		
• Unquoted shares	**G11.1** £	**G11.2** £	**G11** £

	Control holding	Non-control holding		
• Traded unquoted shares	**G12.1** £	**G12.2** £	**G12** £

Total assets *(sum of boxes G1 to G12)* **G13** £

Liabilities, exemptions and reliefs *(that relate to the assets described in this section)*

- Name and address of mortgagee

G14 £

- Other liabilities

Total of other liabilities **G15** £

Net total of assets less liabilities *(box G13 less boxes G14 and G15)* **G16** £

- Exemptions and reliefs

Total exemptions and reliefs **G17** £

Chargeable value of assets in the UK where tax may be paid by instalments
(box G16 less box G17) **G18** £

Summary of the chargeable estate

You should fill in form IHT200WS so that you can copy the figures to this section and to section J. If you are applying for a grant without the help of a solicitor or other agent and you do not wish to work out the tax yourself, leave this section and section J blank. Go on to section K. The corresponding box numbers from the IHT200WS are shown in *italics*.

Assets where tax may not be paid by instalments

- Estate in the UK *(box WS1)* — H1 £
- Joint property - passing by survivorship *(box WS2)* — H2 £
- Foreign property *(box WS3)* — H3 £
- Settled property on which the trustees would like to pay tax now *(box WS4)* — H4 £

  Total of assets where tax may not be paid by instalments *(box WS5)* — H5 £

Assets where tax may be paid by instalments

- Estate in the UK *(box WS6)* — H6 £
- Joint property - pasing by survivorship *(box WS7)* — H7 £
- Foreign property *(box WS8)* — H8 £
- Settled property on which the trustees would like to pay tax now *(box WS9)* — H9 £

  Total of assets where tax may be paid by instalments *(box WS10)* — H10 £

Other property taken into account to calculate the total tax

- Settled property *(box WS11)* — H11 £
- Alternatively secured pension *(box WS11A)* — H11A £
- Gift with reservation *(box WS12)* — H12 £

Chargeable estate *(box WS13)* — H13 £

Cumulative total of lifetime transfers *(box WS14)* — H14 £

Aggregate chargeable transfer *(box WS15)* — H15 £

2.11 Accounts and Returns

J **Calculating the tax liability**

Calculating the total tax that is payable

- Aggregate chargeable transfer *(box WS16)* — **J1** £
- Tax threshold *(box WS17)* — **J2** £
- Value chargeable to tax *(box WS18)* — **J3** £

Tax payable *(box WS19)* **J4** £

- Tax (if any) payable on lifetime transfers *(box WS20)* — **J5** £
- Relief for successive charges *(box WS21)* — **J6** £

Tax payable on total of assets liable to tax *(box WS22)* **J7** £

Calculating the tax payable on delivery of this account

- Tax which may not be paid by instalments *(box TX4)* — **J8** £
- Double taxation relief *(box TX5)* — **J9** £
- Interest to be added *(box TX7)* — **J10** £

Tax and interest being paid now which may not be paid by instalments *(box TX8)* **J11** £

- Tax which may be paid by instalments *(box TX12)* — **J12** £
- Double taxation relief *(box TX13)* — **J13** £
- Number of Instalments being paid now **J14** /10 *(box TX15)*
- Tax now payable *(box TX16)* — **J15** £
- Interest on instalments to be added *(box TX17)* — **J16** £
- Additional interest to be added *(box TX18)* — **J17** £

Tax and interest being paid now which may be paid by instalments *(box TX19)* **J18** £

Total tax and interest being paid now on this account *(box TX20)* **J19** £

K **Authority for repayment of inheritance tax**

In the event of any inheritance tax being overpaid the payable order for overpaid tax and interest in connection with this estate should be made out to

🅛 Declaration

Note: you may be liable to a penalty if you deliver this account late. See the declaration below for other circumstances in which a penalty may be imposed.

I/We wish to apply for a **L1**

To the best of my/our knowledge and belief, the information I/we have given and the statements I/we have made in this account and in supplementary pages **L2**

attached (together called "this account") are correct and complete (list the supplementary pages used).

I/We have made the fullest enquiries that are reasonably practicable in the circumstances to find out the open market value of all the items shown in this account. The value of items in box(es) (list the boxes)

L3   are provisional

estimates which are based an all the information available to me/us at this time. I/We will tell Capital Taxes the exact value(s) as soon as I/we know it and I/we will pay any additional tax and interest that may be due.

I/We understand that I/we may be liable to prosecution if I/we deliberately conceal any information that affects the liability to inheritance tax arising on the deceased's death, OR if I/we deliberately include information in this account which I/we know to be false.

I/We understand that I/we may have to pay financial penalties if this account is incorrect by reason of my/our fraud or negligence, OR if I/we fail to remedy anything in this account which is incorrect in any material respect within a reasonable time of it coming to my/our notice.

I/We understand that the issue of the grant does not mean that

● I/we have paid all the inheritance tax and interest that may be due on the estate, or

● the statements made and the values included in this account are accepted by Capital Taxes.

I/We understand that Capital Taxes

● will only look at this account in detail after the grant has been issued

● may need to ask further questions and discuss the value of items show in this account

● may make further calculations of tax and interest payable to help the persons liable for the tax make provision to meet the tax liability.

I/We understand that where we have elected to pay tax by instalments that I/we may have to pay interest on any unpaid tax according to the law.

Each person delivering this account, whether as executor, intending administrator or otherwise must sign below to indicate that they have read and agreed the statements above.

Full name and address	Full name and address
Signature Date	Signature Date
Full name and address	Full name and address
Signature Date	Signature Date

2.11 Accounts and Returns

HM Revenue & Customs

Assets held in trust (settled property)

Name

Date of death

/ /

You have said that the deceased had a right to benefit from a trust created by a deed or under someone else's Will or intestacy. Answer the following questions and give the further details we ask for. If necessary, use a separate form for each trust. You should read form D5(Notes) before filling this form.

1 Was the deceased's intersest in possession one of the following

- an interest in possession that commenced before 22 March 2006 and remained in existence between then and the date of death
  No Yes

- an immediate post death interest
  No Yes

- a disabled person's interest
  No Yes

- a transitional serial interest
  No Yes

*The types of interest listed above are defined in the guide **IHT210** - How to fill in the IHT200.*

If you have answered 'No' to all the above you do not need to fill in any more of this form and details of the settled property should not be included in form **IHT200**.

2 What is the name of the person who created the trust either during their lifetime or by their will or intestacy?

3 What are the names and addresses of the trustees?

4 On what date was the trust created?

/ /

5 **Settled property where tax may not be paid by instalments**

- Assets

Total of assets SP 1 £

D5 www.hmrc.gov.uk/cto Helpline 0845 30 20 900

HMRC 08/06

(Substitute)[LexisNexis Butterworths]

34

• Liabilities

| | Total of liabilities | SP2 | £ |

| | Net assets *(box SP1 less box Sp2)* | SP3 | £ |

• Exemptions and reliefs

| | Total exemptions and reliefs | SP4 | £ |

| Net total of settled property where tax may not be paid by installments *(box SP3 less box SP4)* | SP5 | £ |

6 Settled property where tax may be paid by installments

Do you wish to pay tax on these assets by installments?   **Yes**   **No**

• Assets

| | Total of assets | SP6 | |

• Liabilities

| | Total of liabilities | SP7 | £ |

| | Net assets *(box SP6 less box SP7)* | SP8 | £ |

• Exemptions and reliefs

| | Total exemptions and reliefs | SP9 | £ |

| Net total of settled property where tax may be paid by installments *(box SP8 less box SP9)* | SP10 | £ |

2.11 Accounts and Returns

<table>
<tr><td>
Inland Revenue
Capital Taxes Office
</td><td colspan="2">
Interest in another estate
</td></tr>
<tr><td>Name</td><td colspan="2">Date of death
/   /</td></tr>
</table>

Give details about the right the deceased had to a legacy or share in an estate of someone else who died before them, but which they had not received before they died. You should read form D11 (Notes) before filling in this form.

1 Full name of the person who died earlier (the 'predecessor')

2 On what date did the predecessor die?   /   /

3 State CTO reference of the earlier estate, if known

4 What was the deceased's entitlement from the other estate?

5 Had the deceased received any part of their entitlement before they died?   No   Yes

If the answer is "Yes", give details of the assets that the deceased had received before they died

6 Details of the entitlement the deceased had still to receive

Net value   UE1 £

Copy the total from box UE1 to box F21, page3, form IHT200.

D11   CTO Approval Ref No L3/00   R0G4111CTO11/99

(Substitute)(LexisNexis Butterworths)

HM Revenue & Customs

Return of estate information

Fill in this version of this form only when the person died on or after 1st September 2006.
Fill in this form where the person who has died ("the deceased") had their permanent home in the United Kingdom at the date of death and the **gross value of the estate for inheritance tax**
. is less than the excepted estate limit, **or**

"✓"

□

- is less than £1,000,000 **and** there is no inheritance tax to pay because of spouse, civil partner or charity exemption **only**.

□

About the person who has died

Title [1.1]   Surname [1.2]

Other name(s) [1.3]

Date of death [1.4] d d / m m / y y y y

Marital or civil partnership status   Write whichever is appropriate a,b,c or d in the box [1.5]

a. married or in civil partnership   *b. single*   *c. divorced or former civil partner*   *d. widowed or surviving civil partner*

Occupation [1.6]   National Insurance number [1.7]

Surviving relatives   "✓"   "✓"   "✓"

Husband/Wife or Civil Partner [1.8]   Brother(s)/Sister(s) [1.9]   Parent(s) [1.10]

Number of children [1.11]   Number of grandchildren [1.12]

The notes in booklet IHT206 will help you fill in this form. You must answer questions 2 - 10.

About the estate

2. Within seven years of death did the deceased

    No   Yes

    a. make any gifts or other transfers totalling more than £3,000 per year, other than normal birthday, festive, marriage or civil partnership gifts, **or**

    □   □

    b. give up the right to benefit from any assets held in trust that were treated as part of their estate for inheritance tax purposes (see booklet IHT206)?

    □   □

    If you answer 'Yes' to either part of question 2, include the chargeable value of the gifts in box 14.1. But if this value is more than £150,000 or the assets do not qualify as 'specified transfers' (see IHT206) stop filling in this form. You will need to fill in form IHT200 instead.

3. Did the deceased make

    a. a gift, on or after 18 March 1986, where they continued to benefit from, or had some right to benefit from, or use all or part of the asset? **Or**

    □   □

    b. a gift, on or after 18 March 1986, where the person receiving the gift did not take full possession of it? **Or**

    □   □

    c. an election that the income tax charge should not apply to

    □   □

    - assets they previously owned, in which they retained a benefit **or**

    - the deceased's contribution to the purchase price of assets acquired by another person, but in which the deceased retained a benefit?

    If you answer 'Yes' to any part of question 3, stop filling in this form. You will need to fill in form IHT200 instead.

4. Did the deceased have the right to receive the benefit from any assets held in a trust that were treated as part of their estate for inheritance tax purposes(see booklet IHT206)?

    □   □

    If you answer 'Yes' to question 4 and the deceased

    • *was entitled to benefit from a single trust, and*

    • *the value of the assets in that trust, treated as part of their estate, was less than £150,000.*

    include the value of the trust assets in box 14.2. But if the value is more than £150,000, or there is more than one trust, stop filling in this form. You will need to fill in form IHT200 instead.

5. Did the deceased own or benefit from any assets outside the UK?

    □   □

    If you answer 'Yes' to question 5 include the value of the overseas assets in box 14.5. But if the value of the overseas assets is more than £100,000, stop filling in this form. You will need to fill in form IHT200 instead.

IHT205 (2006)   *www.hmrc.gov.uk/cto*   *Helpline 0845 30 20 900*   HMRC 09/06

37

2.11 Accounts and Returns

6. Did the deceased pay premiums on any life insurance policies that were not for the deceased's own benefit or did not pay out to the estate?

   If you answer 'Yes' to question 6, you must also answer question 11.

7. Did the deceased benefit from an alternatively secured pension fund (see IHT206)

   *If you have answered 'Yes' to question 7 **stop filling in this form. You will need to fill in form IHT200 instead.***

8. Did the deceased benefit under a registered pension scheme, where

   • the benefit was unsecured **and**

   • they acquired the benefit as a relevant dependant of a person who died aged 75 or over?

   *If you have answered 'Yes' to question 8 **stop filling in this form. You will need to fill in form IHT200 instead.***

9. Was the deceased a member of a pension scheme or did they have a personal pension policy from which in either case, they had not taken their full retirement benefits before the date of death?

   If you answer 'Yes' to question 9, you must also answer question 12.

10. a. Was the deceased entitled to receive payments from a pension which continued to be paid after they had died (other than arrears of pension)?

    b. Was a lump sum payable under a pension scheme or pension policy as a result of the death?

    If you answer 'Yes' to question 10, see IHT206 to find out where to include the asset.

Do not answer questions 11 or 12 unless you answered 'Yes' to questions 6 or 9.

11. Within seven years of the death, did the deceased

    a. pay any premium on a life insurance policy under which the benefit is payable other than to the estate, or to the spouse or civil partner of the deceased, *and if so*

    b. did they buy an annuity at any time?

    *If you answer 'Yes' to question 11(a), see IHT206 to find out how to include the premiums paid on this form. If you answer 'Yes' to **both** question 11(a) & 11(b), **stop filling in this form. You will need to fill in form IHT200 instead.***

12. At a time when they were in poor health or terminally ill, did the deceased change their pension scheme or personal pension policy so as to

    a. dispose of any of the benefits payable, or

    b. make any change to the benefits to which they were entitled?

    *If you answer 'Yes' to question 12(a) or 12(b), **stop filling in this form. You will need to fill in form IHT200 instead.***

13. **Deceased's own assets (including jointly owned assets NOT passing by survivorship - see IHT206)**

    • *You must include the gross value for each item below, before deduction of any exemption or relief.*

    • *You must include all the assets that were part of the deceased's estate as at the date of death, ignoring any changes that may take place through an Instrument of Variation made after the death.*

    • *You must make full enquiries so that you can show that the figures that you give in this form are right. If you cannot find out the value for an item, you may include your best estimate.*

    Tick the box to show estimates "✓"

13.1	Cash, including money in banks, building societies and National Savings	13.1 £
13.2	Household and personal goods	13.2 £
13.3	Stocks and shares quoted on the Stock Exchange	13.3 £
13.4	Stocks and shares not quoted on the Stock Exchange	13.4 £
13.5	Insurance policies, including bonuses and mortgage protection policies	13.5 £
13.6	Money owed to the person who has died	13.6 £
13.7	Partnership and business interests	13.7 £
13.8	Freehold/leasehold residence of the person who has died	13.8 £

Address (including postcode)

www.hmrc.gov.uk/cto   *Helpline 0845 30 20 900*

Tick box to show estimates amounts "✓"

13.9   Other freehold/leasehold residential property   13.9 £ _____   ☐

Address (including postcode)
_____

13.10 Other land and buildings   13.10 £ _____   ☐

Address/location
_____

13.11 Any other assets not included above   13.11 £ _____   ☐

Total estate for which a grant is required (sum of boxes 13.1 to 13.11)   A £ _____

14.   **Other assets forming part of the estate**

14.1   Gifts and other lifetime transfers (after deduction of exemptions)   14.1 £ _____   ☐

Details of gifts
_____

14.2   Assets held in trust for the benefit of the deceased   14.2 £ _____   ☐

Details of assets held in trust
_____

14.3   Share of joint assets passing automatically to the surviving joint owner   14.3 £ _____   ☐

Details of joint assets
_____

14.4   Nominated assets   14.4 £ _____   ☐

14.5   Assets outside the United Kingdom (value in £ sterling)   14.5 £ _____   ☐

Total (sum of boxes 14.1 to 14.5)   B £ _____

Gross estate for inheritance tax (A + B)   C £ _____

15.   **Debts of the estate**

15.1   Funeral expenses   15.1 £ _____   ☐

15.2   Mortgage or share of a mortgage on a property in Section 13   15.2 £ _____   ☐

15.3   Other debts owed by the deceased in the UK   15.3 £ _____   ☐

Total debts owing in the UK (sum of boxes 15.1 to 15.3)   D £ _____

15.4   Debts payable out of trust assets   15.4 £ _____   ☐

15.5   Share of mortgage on a property owned as a joint asset   15.5 £ _____   ☐

15.6   Share of other debts payable out of joint assets   15.6 £ _____   ☐

15.7   Debts owing to persons outside the UK   15.7 £ _____   ☐

Total of other debts (sum of boxes 15.4 to 15.7)   E £ _____

Total debts (D + E)   F £ _____

Net estate for inheritance tax (C - F)   G £ _____

www.hmrc.gov.uk/cto   *Helpline 0845 30 20 900*

2.11   Accounts and Returns

16. | Use this space to provide any other information we have asked for or you would like taken into account. |

17.   **Exemptions (you should read IHT206 before filling in this section)**

In the box below, deduct any exemption for assets passing on death to
  * the spouse or civil partner of the deceased, or

  * a UK charity or for national purposes

Describe the extent of the exemption deducted. If for charities, etc give the name of the charity(s) or other organisation(s) benefiting. Where exemptions are deducted for particular assets, list those assets and show the amount deducted.

17.1

| **H** | £ |

Net qualifying value for excepted estates (G - H) | **J** | £ |

17.2   Tax district and/or income tax reference number | 17.2 | |

If the value in box J is more than the excepted estate limit, you must fill in form IHT200.

If you find something has been left out, or if any of the figures you have given in this form change later on, you only need to tell us if, taking all the omissions and changes into account,
  * the figure at box G is now higher than the inheritance tax threshold, **and**
  * there are no exemptions to deduct which keep the value at box J below the inheritance tax threshold.

If, at any time, the value at box J is more than the inheritance tax threshold, you must list any new items and the items that have changed in a Corrective Account (form C4) and send it to us with a copy of this form along with a cheque for the tax that has become payable.

The issue of the grant does not mean that there is no inheritance tax due on this estate.

To the best of my/our knowledge and belief, the information I/we have given in this form is correct and complete. I/We have read and understand the statements above.

I/We understand that I/we may have to pay financial penalties if the answers to the questions or figures that I/we give in this form are wrong because of my/our negligence or fraud, OR if the estate fails to qualify as an excepted estate and I/we do not deliver a corrective account within 6 months of the failure coming to my/our notice.

Full name and address	Full name and address
Signature Date	Signature Date
Full name and address	Full name and address
Signature Date	Signature Date

Summary

Gross estate in the United Kingdom passing under Will or by intestacy		**A**	£
Debts in the United Kingdom owed by the deceased alone		**D**	£
Net estate in the United Kingdom	**(A - D)**	**K**	£

HM Revenue & Customs

Return of estate information

*Fill in this form where the person who has died ("the deceased") had their permanent home abroad and their assets in the United Kingdom consisted of cash, or quoted stocks and shares **only**, the gross value of which was less than £100,000.*

About the person who has died

Title | 1.1 | Surname | 1.2

Other name(s) | 1.3

Date of death | 1.4 | d d / m m / y y y y

Maritial or civil partnership status Write whichever is appropriate a, b, c or d in the box | 1.5

a. married or in civil partnership b. single c. divorced or former civil partner d. widowed or surviving civil partner

Occupation | 1.6

Surviving relatives

Domicile | 1.7

Spouse or civil partner | 1.9

Last known usual address | 1.8

Brother(s)/sister(s) | 1.10

Parent(s) | 1.11

Number of children | 1.12

Postcode

Number of grandchildren | 1.13

You should read the notes about each question in booklet IHT208 as you fill in this form.

About residence in the United Kingdom (UK)

No   Yes

2. Was the deceased born in the UK?

3. Did the deceased live in the UK during their lifetime?

*If you answer 'Yes' to either question 2 or 3, **do not fill in any more of this form**. You will need to fill in form IHT200 instead.*

About the estate

4. Was the deceased receiving any benefit from any assets held by trustees who were resident in the UK?

5. Did the deceased make any gifts of UK assets within the 7 years before the date they died?

*If you answer 'Yes' to either question 4 or 5, **do not fill in any more of this form**. You will need to fill in form IHT200 instead.*

6. Did the deceased own any asset(s) in joint names with another person or people?

If you answer 'Yes' to question 6, describe the asset(s) and give their value(s) in box 7. Read IHT208 to find out how to include these assets in the rest of this form.

7. Use this space to provide any other information we have asked for or you would like taken into account

IHT 207
(Substitute)(LexisNexis Butterworths)

www.hmrc.gov.uk/cto   Helpline 0845 30 20 900   HMRC CT 12/05

2.11   Accounts and Returns

8.   Assets in the United Kingdom

- *You must include the gross value for each item below.*
- *You must make full enquiries so that you can show that the figures that you give in this form are right. If you cannot find out the value for an item, you may include your best estimate.*   Tick the box to show estimates *"✓"*

8.1 Cash, including money in banks and building societies	**8.1** £
8.2 Stocks and shares quoted on the Stock Exchange	**8.2** £
8.3 Assets held as tenants-in-common	**8.3** £
Total estate in the UK for which a grant is required	**A** £
8.4 Share of joint assets passing automatically to the surviving joint owner	**B** £
Gross estate for inheritance tax (A + B)	**C** £

9.   Debts payable in the United Kingdom

9.1 Debts owed in the UK by the deceased	**D** £
9.2 Share of debts in the UK payable out of joint UK assets	**E** £
Total debts (D + E)	**F** £
Net estate in the UK for inheritance tax (C - F)	**G** £

If you find something has been left out, or if any of the figures you have given in this form change later on so that the value in box G is more than £100,000, you must list any new items and the items that have changed in a Corrective Account (form C4) and send it to us with a copy of this form.

The issue of the grant does not mean that there is no inheritance tax due on this estate.

To the best of my/our knowledge and belief, the information I/we have given in this form is correct and complete. I/We have read and understand the statements above.

I/We understand that I/we may have to pay financial penalties if the answers to the questions or figures that I/we give in this form are wrong because of my/our fraud or negligence, OR if the estate fails to qualify as an excepted estate and I/we do not deliver an account within 6 months of the failure coming to my/our notice.

Full name and address	Full name and address
Signature *Date*	*Signature* *Date*
Full name and address	Full name and address
Signature *Date*	*Signature* *Date*

Summary

Gross estate in the United Kingdom passing under Will or by intestacy	**A** £
Debts in the United Kingdom owed by the deceased alone	**D** £
Net estate in the United Kingdom **(A - D)**	**H** £

www.hmrc.gov.uk/cto   *Helpline 0845 30 20 900*

Revenue
Inland
Capital Taxes

Probate summary

Fill in this form to give details of the estate that becomes the property of the personal representatives of the deceased. It is this property for which the grant of representation is to be made. You should read form D18(Notes) before filling in this form.

A Name and address

Probate registry

Date of grant
(for probate registry use)

B About the person who has died

Title

Surname

First name(s)

Date of death / /

Last known usual address

Domicile

Postcode

C Summary from IHT200
Add the value of any general power property on form D5 to boxes PS1-PS5

Gross assets, section F, box 24	PS1	£
Gross assets, section G, box 13	PS2	£
Gross value to be carried to Probate papers *(box PS1 plus box PS2)*	PS3	£
Liabilities, section F, box F27	PS4	£
Liabilities, section G, boxes G14 plus G15	PS5	£
Net value to be carried to Probate papers *(box PS3 less box PS4 less box PS5)*	PS6	£
Tax and interest paid on this account, section J, box J19	PS7	£

/ /

Signature of person or firm calculating the amount due   Contact name and /or reference   Date

(For IR CT use only)

IR CT reference

EDP

Cashier's reference

IR CT Cashiers

D18   Version 2.0.0.2

43

HM Revenue & Customs

Checklist

Have you remembered to include, if appropriate?

The numbers refer to the forms and guides where we ask you to provide the information requested.

1   Any professional valuation of **stock and shares** - *IHT210, "How to fill in form IHT200".*   Yes ☐ N/A ☐

2   Any professional valuation of **household or personal goods** - *D10(Notes).*   Yes ☐ N/A ☐

3   Any professional valuation of **land** - *IHT210, "How to fill in form IHT200".*   Yes ☐ N/A ☐

4   A copy of the **Will,** any codicils and any Instrument of Variation (if appropriate) - *D1(Notes).*   Yes ☐ N/A ☐

5   A copy of any **insurance policy** (and **annuity**, if appropriate) where the deceased was paying the premiums for the benefit of someone else - *D3(Notes)*   Yes ☐ N/A ☐

6   A copy of the **trust deed**, if the trustees are paying tax at the same time as you apply for the grant - *D5(Notes)*   Yes ☐ N/A ☐

7   Any evidence of **money owed** to the deceased, including loan agreements and related trusts or policies and any evidence of debts being released - *D8(Notes)*   Yes ☐ N/A ☐

8   A copy of any **joint life** insurance policy or policy on the life of another person - *D9(Notes)*   Yes ☐ N/A ☐

9   A copy of any structural survey and/or correspondence with the **loss adjuster** about stucturally damaged property - *D12(Notes)*   Yes ☐ N/A ☐

10 A plan of the property and a copy of the lease or agreement for letting (where appropriate) if you are claiming **agricultural relief** - *D13(Notes).*   Yes ☐ N/A ☐

11 A copy of the partnership agreement (where appropriate) and the last two years' accounts if you are claiming **business relief** - *D14(Notes).*   Yes ☐ N/A ☐

12 Any written evidence of **debts to close friends or family** - *D16(Notes).*   Yes ☐ N/A ☐

13 Your **payment** of tax where you are calculating your own tax - *IHT213, "How to fill in form IHT200(WS)".*   Yes ☐ N/A ☐

14 And please do not forget to sign page 8 of the **Inheritance Tax Account** IHT200.   Yes ☐

But do not send this checklist or form IHT200(WS) to Capital Taxes.

(Substitute)(LexisNexis Butterworths)

CHK 1   *www.hmrc.gov.uk/cto*   *Helpline 0845 30 20 900*   HMRC 08/06

3   Accumulation and Maintenance Trusts

Cross-reference. 44 SETTLEMENTS WITHOUT INTERESTS IN POSSESSION; 53 TRUSTS FOR BEREAVED MINORS.

Simon's Direct Tax Service, part I5.5.

Other Sources. Tolley's Tax Planning 2007–08; Foster, parts E5 and M8.04. CTO Leaflet IHT 16 'Settled property'; IHTM16000.

3.1   RESTRICTION OF LIABILITY TO TAX

Transfers into accumulation and maintenance trusts. After 17 March 1986 but before 22 March 2006, a gift by an individual into an accumulation and maintenance trust, by virtue of which property becomes comprised in the trust, is a potentially exempt transfer. After 21 March 2006, a gift by an individual into an accumulation and maintenance trust, is no longer treated as a PET. See 38 POTENTIALLY EXEMPT TRANSFERS for further details. Existing accumulation and maintenance settlements that are reviewed before 6 April 2008 and ensure that the beneficiaries will become absolutely entitled on or before the age of 18 will remain settlements to which *IHTA 1984, s 71* applies otherwise they will come within the charging provisions of 'age 18–25 trusts' (see 53.3 TRUSTS FOR BEREAVED MINORS) or within the relevant property taxing regime. [*IHTA 1984, ss 58, 71, 71E–F*].

In addition, with respect to transfers of value made, and other events occurring, after 16 March 1987 but before 22 March 2006, a potentially exempt transfer also occurs where an individual disposes of or terminates his beneficial interest in possession in settled property by gift and on that event the property is settled on accumulation and maintenance trusts. Provided the transferor survives seven years or more from the date of the gift, the gift is exempt for inheritance tax purposes. Where an individual has a beneficial interest in possession in settled property which was in existence at 22 March 2006 and it terminates before 6 April 2008 and on that event the property is settled on accumulation and maintenance trusts then the new interest will come within the old taxing regime. See 3.2 below and INTEREST IN POSSESSION (26).

See 38 POTENTIALLY EXEMPT TRANSFERS for further details. Also see 50.5 TRANSFERS ON DEATH for variation to create a trust. [*IHTA 1984, s 3A; FA 1986, Sch 19 para 1; F(No 2)A 1987, s 96; FA 2006, Sch 20 para 9*].

Transfers out of accumulation and maintenance trusts. Until property settled on accumulation and maintenance trusts vests, there will be no interest in possession so that, in the absence of special provisions, such settlements would be liable to tax under the provisions relating to SETTLEMENTS WITHOUT INTERESTS IN POSSESSION (44). Where, however, a settlement qualifies as an accumulation and maintenance trust, its liability to tax is limited to the circumstances mentioned in 3.3 and 3.4 below.

3.2   QUALIFICATION AS ACCUMULATION AND MAINTENANCE TRUST

Settlements created before 22 March 2006. To qualify as an accumulation and maintenance settlement prior to 22 March 2006, the following conditions must have been satisfied.

3.2 Accumulation and Maintenance Trusts

(a)   One or more 'persons' (beneficiaries) will on or before attaining a specified age, not exceeding 25, become beneficially entitled to, or to an interest in possession in, the settled property (see Example 4 below).

(b)   No interest in possession subsists in the settled property and the income from it is to be accumulated so far as not applied for the maintenance, education or benefit of a beneficiary.

(c)   Either

(i)   not more than 25 years have elapsed since the commencement of the settlement or, if it was later, since the time (or latest time) when the conditions stated in (a) and (b) above became satisfied with respect to the property; or

(ii)   all the persons who are or have been beneficiaries are or were either grandchildren of a common grandparent *or* 'children', widows or widowers or surviving civil partners of such grandchildren who were themselves beneficiaries but died before the time when, had they survived, they would have become entitled as mentioned in (a) above.

Accumulation and maintenance settlements created prior to 22 March 2006 will continue to be treated under the old regime but only until 6 April 2008. From that date onwards any existing accumulation and maintenance settlement must conform to the new rules so that the beneficiary or beneficiaries must obtain a right to *capital* on or before the age of eighteen and not as in (a) above at age 25 to continue to attract the taxing benefits of the old regime of *IHTA 1984, s 71*. This may be achieved by the existing terms of the settlement which already allow the beneficiary or beneficiaries to obtain a right to capital at eighteen or the terms of trust powers of appointment providing for such entitlement. See example in 3.3 below. All such existing accumulation and maintenance settlements will have ceased to exist by 22 March 2024. All other existing accumulation and maintenance settlements formed prior to 22 March 2006 will otherwise from 6 April 2008 become subject to the '18–25 trusts' taxing regime or they may in other circumstances become subject to the relevant property trust regime. See Example 1 below, SETTLEMENTS WITHOUT INTERESTS IN POSSESSION (44) and 53.3 TRUSTS FOR BEREAVED MINORS. [*IHTA 1984, ss 71, 71D; FA 2006, Sch 20 paras 1, 2, 3; Sch 26 Part 6*].

See [**Case Study 5**] at WORKING CASE STUDY (59). The mere existence of a power to appoint, as opposed to actual exercise, does not take a trust outside the common grandparent category. See HMRC Tax Bulletin, Issue 55.

'*Persons*' includes unborn persons; but the conditions in (a) and (b) above are not satisfied unless there is or has been a living beneficiary. A person's '*children*' include his illegitimate children, his adopted children and his stepchildren. [*IHTA 1984, s 71(1)(2)(7)(8)*].

There is no statutory definition of 'interest in possession' and the term has been the subject of judicial interpretation. See 26 INTEREST IN POSSESSION.

Settlements created after 21 March 2006. New trusts from 22 March 2006 will not qualify as an accumulation and maintenance settlement under the old *IHTA 1984, s 71* regime but alternative trusts designated 'bereaved minors' (see 53 TRUSTS FOR BEREAVED MINORS) may attract similar taxing benefits. In order to qualify as a trust for 'bereaved minors' one of the following conditions must be satisfied:

(a)   One or more 'persons' (beneficiaries) will, on or before attaining a specified age, not exceeding 18, become beneficially entitled to the settled property. See (b) below.

(b)   Settled property is held on statutory trust for the benefit of a 'bereaved minor' where the trust is established under either the will of a deceased parent or under intestacy under *Administration of Estates Act 1925, ss 46, 47(1)*. But see also (c) below. The bereaved minor must, prior to or upon the attainment of the age of 18 years, be absolutely entitled to the settled property, any income arising therefrom and any

46

income that has arisen but been accumulated in respect of the property held on trust. Whilst the beneficiary is under the age of 18 if any of the settled property is applied it must be applied for the benefit of the bereaved minor. If the trust property is not so applied then whilst the bereaved minor is under the age of 18 years the income arising, if any, must be a full entitlement or the income must not be applied for the benefit of any other person. In connection with the above, 'statutory trust' shall not be treated as failing the requirements of entitlement due to age, property, income or accumulations because of the requirements of the *Trustee Act 1925, s 32* or *Trustee Act (Northern Ireland) 1958, s 33*. See TRUSTS FOR BEREAVED MINORS (53).

(*c*)   Settled property is held on statutory trust for the benefit of a 'bereaved minor' as a result of payments from the Criminal Injuries Compensation schemes. Any such payments must be made for the benefit of the minor as a result of

   (i)   the scheme being established by arrangements under the *Criminal Injuries Compensation Act 1995*;

   (ii)   arrangements made by the Secretary of State for compensation for criminal injuries which were in operation before commencement of those Criminal Injuries Compensation schemes;

   (iii)   the scheme being established by arrangements under the *Criminal Injuries Compensation (Northern Ireland) Order 2002*.

[*IHTA 1984, ss 71, 71A, 71B, 71C; FA 2006, Sch 20 paras 1, 2, 3*].

'*Bereaved Minor*' means a person who has not yet attained the age of eighteen years and at least one of whose parents has died. For these purposes 'B' or 'bereaved minor' includes all beneficiaries within a relevant class provided they are alive and are under the specified age of 18. See CIOT/STEP clarification dated 29 June 2007. [*IHTA 1984, s 71C inserted by FA 2006, Sch 20 para 1*].

'*Parent*' for these purposes also means step-parent or person with 'parental responsibility' within the *Children Act 1989, s 3*. See TRUSTS FOR BEREAVED MINORS (53). [*IHTA 1984, s 71H inserted by FA 2006, Sch 20 para 1*].

Meaning of 'will' in 'will become entitled to'. The requirement in (*a*) above is regarded as being satisfied even if no age is specified in the trust instrument, provided that it is clear that a beneficiary will in fact become entitled to the settled property (or an interest in possession in it) by the age of 25 or, as the case may be, 18. See *Crawford Settlement Trustees v HMRC [2005] STC SCD 457*. (See F8 at 23 HMRC EXTRA-STATUTORY CONCESSIONS.) Where the trustees of a settlement exercise their powers of investment so that there is no certainty that anyone will be entitled to any income at any age (e.g. where all the investment by them is in non-income producing assets) this will not prevent a settlement from qualifying under (*a*) above provided the powers in the settlement deed are limited by a clause to the effect that none of the powers will ever be used so as to breach the provisions of *IHTA 1984, s 71* above (Tolley's Practical Tax 1990 p 159).

The existence of a power of revocation, which may be exercised for the benefit of other persons at ages exceeding 25 or, as the case may be, 18 is sufficient to prevent a settlement from qualifying under (*a*) above. The word 'will' implies a degree of certainty inconsistent with such a power (*Inglewood and Another v CIR CA 1982, [1983] STC 133*). However, the word 'will' does not require absolute certainty. Some qualification is required. See *Maitland's Trustees v Lord Advocate CS 1982, [1982] SLT 483* for the distinction drawn between a present contingency and a future or supervening contingency.

Powers of appointment and revocation limited to the class of beneficiaries. Where there is a trust for accumulation and maintenance of a class of persons who become entitled to the property (or to an interest in possession in it) at a specified age not exceeding 25 or, as the case may be, 18 it would not be disqualified under (*a*) above by the existence of a power to vary or determine the respective shares of members of the class (even to the extent of excluding some members altogether) provided the power is exercisable only in favour of a person under 25 or, as the case may be, 18 who is a member of the class. See HMRC Press Release 19 January 1976. (25.E1 HMRC STATEMENTS OF PRACTICE).

Settlements created before 15 April 1976. There are transitional provisions for settlements in existence on 15 April 1976 when the restrictions under (*c*) above became effective. Where such settlements (and the property comprised therein at that date) satisfied the conditions in (*a*) and (*b*) above on 15 April 1976,

(i) the 25 years referred to in (*c*)(i) above run from 15 April 1976 (i.e. to 14 April 2001) and not from the commencement of the settlement; and

(ii) the condition in (*c*)(ii) above is treated as satisfied if

(*a*) it is satisfied in respect of the period beginning with 15 April 1976, or

(*b*) it is satisfied in respect of the period beginning with 1 April 1977 and either there was no beneficiary living on 15 April 1976 or the beneficiaries on 1 April 1977 included a living beneficiary, or

(*c*) there is no power under the terms of the settlement whereby it could have become satisfied during the period beginning with 1 April 1977, and the settlement has not been varied after 15 April 1976.

[*IHTA 1984, s 71(6)*].

3.3 **TAXATION OF SETTLEMENTS FROM 22 MARCH 2006**

From 22 March 2006 new taxing rules apply with regard to accumulation and maintenance trusts in existence such that where one or more 'persons' (the beneficiaries) fail to, on or before attaining a specified age not exceeding 18, become beneficially entitled to the settled property that trust will come within the '18–25 trusts' or relevant property trust regime and be subject to an initial proportionate ten-yearly charge and charges on exit of funds from the trust. The *maximum* charge within the '18–25 trusts' will be 4.2% on, broadly, the value of the trusts fund over the period of the life of the trust if the beneficiary takes capital, income and accumulated income at the age of 25. If this event is deferred until the beneficiary is beyond that age before they take the capital then the maximum charge that will apply is 6%, the relevant property rules applying (see Table below and Example 2 below). Otherwise property leaving such trusts will be subject to a charge under *IHTA 1984, s 70*. [*IHTA 1984, ss 58, 71, 71D–71G; FA 2006, Sch 20 paras 1, 2, 3*].

0.15% for each	1	quarter	1 quarter	0.15%
0.15% for each of the next	4	quarters	1 year	0.6%
0.15% for each of the next	28	quarters	7 years	4.2%
0.15% for each of the next	40	quarters	10 years	6.0%

See also 44.3 SETTLEMENTS WITHOUT INTERESTS IN POSSESSION.

Example 1

On 6 April 1983 G settled £50,000 on trust equally for his grandchildren. The beneficiaries were to take absolute entitlements at age 25, income being accumulated for minor beneficiaries as detailed within the accumulation and maintenance trust deed below. By 2007 G had three grandchildren; Alex, who becomes 25 on 28 February 2008, and Stephanie, born 27 September 1994, and Roger, born 25 July 1996, who are 13 and 11 years old respectively.

On 28 February 2008 Alex became entitled to an interest in possession in one-third on reaching age 25. There is no charge on the distribution of capital entitlement under the old rules on Alex attaining the age of 25. The remaining two-thirds continues to be held equally for Stephanie and Roger but is not subject to an interest in possession. On 6 April 2008, 25 years will have elapsed since the date of the settlement but the settlement would not cease to qualify as an accumulation and maintenance trust as a result since all of the remaining beneficiaries have a common grandparent. The settlement does, however, cease to be an accumulation and maintenance settlement from that date because the remaining beneficiaries do not become entitled to settled property on or before attaining age 18 as required from that date by *IHTA 1984, s 71* as amended by *FA 2006, Sch 20 paras 2, 3*.

As this is an existing accumulation and maintenance settlement the existing pre-22 March 2006 rules for accumulation and maintenance trusts will continue until 5 April 2008 so that if the beneficiaries will become absolutely entitled no later than age 18, the settlement will remain within *IHTA 1984, s 71*. Otherwise the settlement will fall within the '18–25 trust' regime from 6 April 2008 within *IHTA 1984, s 71D(3)(4)* but in this case applying from each of their eighteenth birthdays. [*IHTA 1984, s 71F(1)(2)(a)*]. Consequently there would be no 'exit' tax charge on 6 April 2008 when the accumulation and maintenance settlement fails to qualify under the new rules under *IHTA 1984, s 71(1)(a)*. Also, there will be no entry charge when it fails and becomes a '18–25 trust' with effect from 6 April 2008 but a charge will commence from the date of each of their birthdays at 18. From that point onwards the exit charges will apply to distributions of capital entitlement on or before Stephanie and Roger becoming aged 25. The value of the remaining settlement is £600,000 and the IHT threshold is, say, £455,000 on 26 September 2019, Stephanie's birthday at 25 years, when the Trustees decide to distribute the respective capital entitlements to Stephanie of £325,000 and Roger of £275,000.

27 September 2019 distribution charge within *IHTA 1984, s 71F*

Assumed chargeable transfer (as above)	600,000
Assumed cumulative total	—
Deduct Nil rate band, say,	(455,000)
	£145,000
IHT at lifetime rates	£29,000

Effective rate

$$\frac{29,000}{600,000} = 4.83\%$$

Stephanie's exit charge: 27 September 2012 to 27 September 2019 = 7 years i.e. 28 complete quarters
Rate of Stephanie's exit charge:
$^{28}/_{40} \times 4.83\% = 3.381\%$
Exit charge: $^3/_{10} \times 3.381\% \times £325,000$ £3,296

Roger's exit charge: 25 July 2014 to 27 September 2019 = 5 years i.e. 20 complete quarters
Rate of Roger's exit charge:
$^{20}/_{40} \times 4.83\% = 2.415\%$
Exit charge: $^3/_{10} \times 2.415\% \times £275,000$ £1,992

Notes to the example

(A)   There was no charge to IHT on Alex becoming entitled to his one-third absolute interest on his 25th birthday in February 2008 but his brother and sister who are beneficiaries of the remainder of the trust will effectively suffer an exit charge when they take their benefit at the appropriate time but see (C) below.

(B)   As Stephanie and Roger are minors they may not be regarded as mature enough to receive distributions from the settlement at the age of 18. Therefore from 6 April 2008 the settlement can come within an '18–25 trust' within *IHTA 1984, s 71D(3)(4)* but the exit charge under *IHTA 1984, s 71F(5)* does not commence until each of them attain their 18th birthdays and ending on the day before the occasion of charge, eg their attaining age 25 or receiving capital entitlement or advance. One option may be to instead retain the trust assets on bare trusts for Stephanie and Roger and only inform them that they are objects when considering the appropriateness of any individual appointments to them. However, where individuals such as Stephanie and Roger have become aware of the existence of such a trust and that they are the objects of such power they may require that the trustees consider exercising the power from time to time. HMRC have confirmed that an absolute trust such as a bare trust is not a settlement for IHT purposes and therefore the trust property will form part of the beneficiary's estate and not be subject to the *FA 2006* rules. See CIOT Press Release, 23 March 2007.

(C)   In order to ensure that this existing pre-22 March 2006 accumulation and maintenance settlement continues to benefit from 6 April 2008 the assets in the trust must go to the beneficiaries absolutely on or before their attainment of the age of 18 years. Therefore Trustees may modify the terms of the settlement prior to 6 April 2008 to ensure that the power of appointment, where appropriately drafted in the original trust deed (see 3.1.1 of the Settlement Deed below), can be used to alter administrative provisions so that the beneficiaries will be fully entitled to the assets and accumulations on or before the age of 18. Notice that in the Settlement Deed extract below at 3.1.2 it states 'An appointment may create provisions and in particular …(b) dispositive or administrative powers exercisable by any other Person or Persons'. This enables the Trustees to alter administrative provisions in addition to beneficial provisions. Whilst a power of appointment may vary the terms of a settlement a power of resettlement may result in property being held by different trustees and with, if required, other proper law. Also, it will no longer be possible to pool the trust funds after 6 April 2008 so that separate trusts must exist for the beneficiaries who then become the sole beneficiary of that fund. Many existing trusts will not have been set up in this way and will have to be altered but in the example above this facility is in existence already. The costs of applying to the court to sanction such a change may prove prohibitive and the Trustees will have to consider other options or pay the tax. See 2 below.

(D)   The question trustees may ask is whether by using their administrative powers to ensure that the beneficiaries benefit absolutely in the assets and accumulated income at aged 18 years constitutes tax avoidance. This is unlikely to be a cause for concern here because *FA 2006, Sch 20* approves such alteration but the case of *Richards v Mackay* [1990] 1 OTPR regarding tax avoidance is interesting because Millett J contrasts situations to distinguish cases where the courts are satisfied proposed arrangements which include tax avoidance are not so inappropriate that no reasonable trustee would entertain them.

THIS ACCUMULATION AND MAINTENANCE SETTLEMENT made on 6 APRIL 1983

PARTIES

1.   "The Settlor" namely Alan George of …

2.   "The Original Trustees" namely Settlor and Alan Milburn of Melsons, Solicitors, 1 High Street, Netherington, Wilts SP3 1RP.

WHEREAS
The Settlor has [one] grandchild namely:

(1)   Alex George who was born on 28 February 1983

(2)   This settlement shall be known as the [Alan George Grandchildrens' Settlement 1983]

NOW THIS DEED WITNESSES AS FOLLOWS:

1.   DEFINITIONS

2.   TRUST INCOME

Subject to Overriding Powers conferred below:

2.1   The Trust Fund shall be divided into equal shares ("the Shares") so that there shall be a share for each of Principal Beneficiary.

2.2   While a Principal Beneficiary is living and under the age of 25

2.2.1   The Trustees may apply the income of his share for the maintenance and education of any Principal Beneficiaries who have not attained the age of 25.

2.2.2   Subject to that, the Trustees shall accumulate the income of the share during the Accumulation Period. That income shall be added to that Trust Fund.

2.2.3   Subject to that, section 31 of the Trustee Act 1925 shall apply to the Share but so that the proviso to section 31(1) be deleted.

2.3   The Trustees shall pay the income of the Share to the Principal Beneficiary during his life if he attains the age of 25.

2.4   Subject to that, if the Principal Beneficiary dies during the Trust Period, the Trustees shall pay the income of the Share to the Widow of the Principal Beneficiary during her life.

2.5   Subject to that, during the Trust Period, the Trustees shall pay or apply the income of the Share to or for the benefit of any one or more of the Beneficiaries, as they think fit.

3.   OVERRIDING POWERS

Subject to the following clause, during the Trust Period, the Trustees have the following powers termed "Overriding Powers"

3.1   Power of appointment

3.1.1   The Trustees may appoint that they shall hold the Trust Fund for the benefit of any Beneficiaries, on such terms as the Trustees think fit.

3.1.2   An appointment may create provisions and in particular (a) discretionary trusts (b) dispositive or administrative powers exercisable by any other Person or Persons.

3.1.3   An appointment shall be made by deed and may be revocable or irrevocable.

3.2   Transfer of Trust Property to new settlement.

3.2.1   The Trustees may by deed declare that they hold any Trust Property on trust to transfer it to trustees of a Qualifying Settlement, to hold on the terms of that Qualifying Settlement, freed and released from the terms of this settlement.

> 3.2.2 "A Qualifying Settlement" here means any settlement, wherever established, under which every person who may benefit is (or would be if living) a Beneficiary to this Settlement.
>
> 3.3 Power of Advancement
>
> 3.3.1 The Trustees may pay or apply any Trust Property for the advancement or benefit of any Beneficiary.

Example 2

On 31 December 2000 G, who had made no cumulative chargeable transfers within the previous 7 years, settled £150,000 on accumulation and maintenance settlement for his son GS born on that date. The trust is contingent on GS attaining the age of 25 years subject thereto to G's nephew N, aged 21 at 22 March 2006, attaining the age of 26, subject thereto for H absolutely with *Trustee Act 1925, s 31* being applicable. GS dies on 6 April 2009 at the age of 9 years.

The settlement is valued at £640,000 on 30 December 2010. The property in the settlement is valued at £700,000 at 21 March 2012, the day before N attains his 26th birthday when the funds are released to him.

As the settlement is an accumulation and maintenance settlement prior to 22 March 2006 it will continue to be so until 6 April 2008 when it will cease to be subject to *IHTA 1984, s 71* when there is no charge. *IHTA 1984, s 71D(3)(4)* '18–25 trust' subsequently applies by reason particularly of *s 71D(3)(a)*. Unfortunately, GS dies on 6 April 2009 and *s 71D* ceases to apply by reason of *s 71D(6)(c)* which, at that point, does not give rise to a charge. N, although entitled to income, does not yet have an interest in possession within *IHTA 1984, s 49(1A)* and therefore the relevant property trust regime will commence resulting in a 10-year anniversary charge on 31 December 2010 and an exit charge on 22 March 2012 when N reaches his birthday at 26 within the terms of the settlement.

	£
Ten-year anniversary charge 31 December 2010	
Value of relevant property on 31.12.2010	640,000
Less nil rate band, say, £325,000	325,000
IHT at lifetime rates on £315,000 @ 20%	£63,000

Effective rate
$$\frac{63,000}{640,000} = 9.84375\%$$

Rate of charge for period 6.4.2009 to 31.12.2010:
$3/10 \times 9.84375\% = 2.953125\% \times 6/40 \times £640,000$

Ten-year anniversary charge:	£1,019

Exit charge on N becoming absolutely entitled at 22 March 2012
Effective rate (as above) = 9.84375%
No. of complete successive quarters between 31.12.2010 to 22.3.2012 = 4
Proportionate charge:

$9.84375\% \times 3/10 \times 4/40 \times £700,000$	£2,067

Notes to the example

(A) The settlement qualifies as an accumulation and maintenance settlement until 6 April 2008 when it then fails to qualify as an accumulation and maintenance settlement under *IHTA 1984, s 71* but the settlement now qualifies within the '18–25 trust' provisions under *IHTA 1984, s 71D(3)(4)*. From 6 April 2009 the settlement will come within the relevant property charging regime as it no longer qualifies as an original accumulation and maintenance trust or an 'age 18–25 trust'.

(B)   No new accumulation and maintenance trusts can be set up on or after 22 March 2006 under *IHTA 1984, s 71*. Existing accumulation and maintenance trusts will not attract *section 71* treatment after 5 April 2008 unless the beneficiaries become absolutely entitled at age 18. Where existing accumulation and maintenance trusts do not comply with the entitlement at age 18 condition then the trust may come within the new regime for 18–25 trusts within *IHTA 1984, ss 71D–71H*. See also 53.3 TRUSTS FOR BEREAVED MINORS. If it does not come within the new regime for 18–25 trusts, as in this example, it becomes a relevant property trust and is subject to the discretionary trust regime. See 44 SETTLEMENTS WITHOUT INTERESTS IN POSSESSION.

In cases where an accumulation and maintenance settlement is replaced with a life interest in favour of a beneficiary prior to 22 March 2006 that beneficiary is treated as beneficially entitled to the property in which the interest subsists, i.e. he is treated as owning it absolutely. There is an IHT charge based on the value of the settled property in which his interest subsists when a beneficiary disposes of his interest or it otherwise comes to an end, i.e. either as a transfer on death or as a PET where the termination of the interest occurs during the lifetime of the tenant, for example where there is an exercise of a power of appointment. [*IHTA 1984, ss 49(1), 51(1), 51A, 52(1); FA 2006, Sch 20 paras 11–13*]. From 22 March 2006 newly created IIP settlements will be treated under the relevant property taxing regime unless the interest is an immediate post-death interest (IPDI) or a transitional serial interest (TSI) or a disabled person's interest. See 43 SETTLEMENTS WITH INTERESTS IN POSSESSION.

Example 3

On 6 June 1989 G settled shares on trust equally for his three grandchildren on an accumulation and maintenance settlement. He had made no cumulative chargeable transfers within the previous seven years. He settled shares in a property investment company that he had set up many years before on an accumulation and maintenance settlement for his grandchildren. The trust is contingent on the grandchildren attaining 25 years when they would receive life interests. The first born grandchild, Graham, attained the age of 25 years on 28 February 2007, while Stephanie, who was born 27 September 1994, and Roger, born 25 July 1996, are 13 and 11 years old respectively.

The settlement is comprised of 1,000 shares in the company which were valued at £100 per share but are valued at £6,000 per share on 6 June 2009. The property in the settlement is valued at £7,000 per share at 6 June 2019.

As the settlement is an accumulation and maintenance settlement prior to 22 March 2006 it will continue to be so until 6 April 2008 when it will cease to be subject to *IHTA 1984, s 71*, at which point there is no charge. Unfortunately, from 6 April 2008 it becomes a relevant property trust which, from that point, becomes subject to ten-yearly charges because the settlement is within *IHTA 1984, s 58*. The settlement will also suffer exit charges. The first charge arising after 6 April 2008 will be on 6 June 2009 and this is the first ten-yearly charge which will be appropriately apportioned. The next charge will be either a ten-yearly charge on 6 June 2019 or an exit charge prior to that date depending on the Trustees decisions.

3.3 Accumulation and Maintenance Trusts

	£
Ten-year anniversary charge 6 June 2009	
Value of relevant property on 6 June 2009 (see note A)	4,002,000
Value of other property (see note B)	33,333
Less nil rate band £325,000	325,000
IHT at lifetime rates on £3,710,333 @ 20%	£742,067

Effective rate

$$\frac{742,067}{4,002,000} = 18.5424\%$$

Rate of charge for period 6.4.2008 to 6.6.2009:
$^3/_{10} \times 18.5424\% = 5.56272\% \times 4/_{40} \times £4,002,000$

First ten-year anniversary charge	£22,262
Ten-year anniversary charge 6 June 2019	
Value of relevant property on 6 June 2019 (see note A)	4,669,000
Value of other property (see note B)	33,333
Less nil rate band, say, £425,000	425,000
IHT at lifetime rates on £4,277,333 @ 20%	£855,467

Effective rate

$$\frac{855,467}{4,669,000} = 18.32227\%$$

Rate of charge for period 7.6.2009 to 6.6.2019:
$^3/_{10} \times 18.32227\% = 5.496681\% \times 40/_{40} \times £4,669,000$

Second ten-year anniversary charge	£256,640

Notes to the example

(A) The value of the remaining 667 shares after deducting Graham's share under the old A&M rules is £6,000 per share. The ten-yearly charge then applies from 6 April 2008 when the new relevant property rules apply up to the date of the first ten-yearly anniversary date of the setting up of the settlement. This conveniently turns out to be only four quarters after the new rules come into force and the charge is a comparatively small £22,340. However, the Trustees will find it difficult to meet this liability if the company does not pay a dividend which is the case in many family grown businesses. Other options might be to sell back shares to the other existing shareholders/Directors, to borrow to settle the liability in the interim or sell to a third party individual; none of which are ideal. Action should be taken before 6 April 2008 to ensure that the beneficiaries either qualify within the '18–25 trust' provisions under *IHTA 1984, s 71D(3)(4)* or receive an absolute interest in their entitlement as soon as possible. This latter option may be inappropriate bearing in mind the value of the fund and age of the grandchildren. A bare trust may be set up or the funds may be transferred to a discretionary trust for the two younger grandchildren, but this depends on whether the terms of the settlement allow such conversions. See Notes B and C in Example 1 above.

(B) Graham's one-third portion must still be valued as other property under *IHTA 1984, s 66(4)(b)*, i.e. £100,000 × 33.3%.

3.4   **TAXATION ON CREATION OUT OF DISCRETIONARY TRUSTS**

Where property held on discretionary trusts is appointed on accumulation and maintenance trusts, there is a charge to tax under *IHTA 1984, s 65* (see 44.9 SETTLEMENTS
WITHOUT INTERESTS IN POSSESSION) as the property then ceases to be 'relevant
property'. See also the provisions under 44.15 and 44.16 SETTLEMENTS WITHOUT
INTERESTS IN POSSESSION which also apply to property settled on accumulation and
maintenance trusts.

3.5   **TREATMENT OF PAYMENTS, ETC. OUT OF ACCUMULATION AND
MAINTENANCE TRUSTS**

A charge to tax arises

(*a*)   where settled property ceases to be property which satisfies the necessary conditions
in 3.2 above (but see also 21.3, 21.5–21.7 EXEMPT TRANSFERS for certain situations
where there is no charge when property becomes held for charitable purposes only
without limit of time *or* that of a qualifying political party *or* a national body
mentioned in *IHTA 1984, Sch 3 or*, under certain conditions, a body not established
or conducted for profit), or

(*b*)   if the trustees make a 'disposition' which reduces the value of the settled property.
'*Disposition*' includes an omission to exercise a right, unless not deliberate, which is
treated as made at the latest time the right could have been exercised. [*IHTA 1984,
s 70(10), s 71(3)(5), s 76*].

No charge arises

(i)   on a beneficiary's becoming beneficially entitled to, or to an interest in possession in,
settled property on or before attaining the specified age, or

(ii)   on the death of a beneficiary before attaining the specified age, or

(iii)   if, under (*b*) above the trustees do not intend to confer a gratuitous benefit and either
the transaction is at arm's length between persons not connected with each other (see
13 CONNECTED PERSONS) or is such as might be expected in such a transaction (but
see 49.2 TRANSFER OF VALUE for unquoted securities in such a transaction), or

(iv)   if, under (*b*) above, the disposition is a grant of a tenancy of agricultural property in
the UK, Channel Islands or Isle of Man, for use for agricultural purposes and is made
for full consideration in money or money's worth, or

(v)   on the 'payment' of costs or expenses attributable to the property, or

(vi)   where any payment is, or will be, income for income tax purposes of any person (or, in
the case of a non-resident, would be if he were so resident), or

(vii)   in respect of a liability to make a payment under (v) or (vi) above.

'*Payment*' includes the transfer of assets other than money. [*IHTA 1984, s 63, s 70(3)(4),
s 71(4)(5)*].

Tax is charged on the amount by which the trust property is less immediately after the
event giving rise to the charge than it would have been but for the event (i.e. the loss to
donor principle), grossed-up where the settlement pays the tax.

The rate at which tax is charged is the aggregate of the following percentages for each
complete successive 'quarter' in the 'relevant period'.

3.6 Accumulation and Maintenance Trusts

	Cumulative Total
0.25% for each of the first 40 quarters	10%
0.20% for each of the next 40 quarters	8%
0.15% for each of the next 40 quarters	6%
0.10% for each of the next 40 quarters	4%
0.05% for each of the next 40 quarters	2%
Maximum rate chargeable after 50 years	30%

See also IHT 16, p 23 at http://www.hmrc.gov.uk/pdfs/iht16.pdf.

The rate charged may be reduced if any of the property is, or was, EXCLUDED PROPERTY (20). See 3.5 below.

'*Relevant period*' is the period beginning with the day on which the property became (or last became) held on accumulation and maintenance trusts, or 13 March 1975 if later, and ending on the day before the chargeable event.

'*Quarter*' is a period of three months. [*IHTA 1984, s 63, s 70(5)(6)(8), s 71(5)*].

Example 4

On 1 January 1982 G settled £50,000 on trust equally for his great nephews and nieces born before 1 January 2003. The beneficiaries were to take life interests at age 18, income being accumulated for minor beneficiaries. By 2003 G had three great nephews and nieces, A (his brother's grandson) born in 1979 and B and C (his sister's grandsons) born in 1993 and 1998 respectively. The settlement was valued at £150,000 on 1 January 2007.

On 1 January 2007 the settlement fails to qualify as an accumulation and maintenance settlement as more than 25 years have elapsed since the date of settlement and the beneficiaries do not have a common grandparent. A has an interest in possession in one-third as he is over 18, but the remaining two-thirds which is held equally for B and C is not yet subject to an interest in possession. There will be a charge to IHT on two-thirds of the value of the settlement on 1 January 2007.

The rate of tax is the aggregate of:

0.25% for each of the first	40	quarters	10%
0.20% for each of the next	40	quarters	8%
0.15% for each of the next	20	quarters	3%
	100		21%

The IHT charge is 21% × ⅔ × £150,000 = £21,000

Note to the example

(A)   There was no charge to IHT on A becoming entitled to an interest in possession in one-third on his eighteenth birthday in 1997 (see (i) above and IHT 16, p 23).

(B)   Where an accumulation and maintenance settlement was established before 15 April 1976 (see above) its qualification as an A & M settlement would have expired in 2001. However, the settlement may not have originally commenced as an A & M settlement as there may have been an intervening life interest or it may have commenced as a discretionary trust so that the expiration period could now be imminent. [*IHTA 1984, s 71(1)(2b)(5)*].

3.6   **Excluded property.** Where the whole or part of the amount on which tax is charged as in 3.4 above is attributable to property which was EXCLUDED PROPERTY (20) at any time during the relevant period, then, in determining the rate at which tax is charged in respect of that amount or part, no quarter throughout which the property was excluded property is to be counted. [*IHTA 1984, ss 70(7), 71(5)*].

4 Administration and Collection

Simon's Direct Tax Service, part I11.

Other Sources. CTO leaflet IHT 14 'The personal representatives' responsibilities'; Mellows, Chapter 5; Foster, part L; IHTM 30000, IHTM31000, IHTM38000, IHTM36000.

4.1 MANAGEMENT

Inheritance tax is 'under the care and management of the Board' (i.e. the Commissioners for Her Majesty's Revenue and Customs, 1 Parliament Street, London SW1A 2BQ). [*IHTA 1984, s 215*]. HMRC Inheritance Tax exist to deal with the levying of inheritance tax, and accounts and correspondence should be sent to them at the addresses given at 2.11 ACCOUNTS AND RETURNS.

HMRC's care and management powers take many forms: in this work special attention is given to 23 HMRC EXTRA-STATUTORY CONCESSIONS, 24 HMRC PRESS RELEASES, and 25 HMRC STATEMENTS OF PRACTICE, which are published by the Board. Reference is also made in context to other statements made by HMRC elsewhere, e.g. in HMRC's Tax Bulletin or memoranda issued by professional bodies.

Taxpayer's Charter and Codes of Practice. HMRC has also produced in the past, in accordance with Government initiatives generally, a Taxpayer's Charter which has set out the principles it tries to meet in its dealings with taxpayers, the standards it believes the taxpayer has a right to expect, and what people can do if they wish to appeal or complain. There is no current Taxpayer's Charter as the last one of any consequence was allowed to lapse and HMRC seem to rely on a mission statement. An Early Day Motion was tabled in the House of Commons for a new Taxpayer's Charter to set down the rights and obligations of the taxpayer and tax administration by the Finance Bill 2006 but did not garner enough parliamentary support. CIOT Press Release 16 March 2006 and Taxation, 25 May 2006 p 205.

A series of codes of practice, setting out the standards of service people can expect in relation to specific aspects of HMRC's work, are produced. The codes are not meant to represent any change of practice although some practices mentioned in them were not previously publicly available. Of the codes, Code of Practice 1 (COP 1), 'Putting things right when we make mistakes' issued by HMRC, is in principle applied to all HMRC functions (and thus including those relating to HMRC Inheritance Tax), although originally written mainly with tax and collection offices in mind (Inland Revenue Press Release 3 April 1996). See http://www.hmrc.gov.uk/leaflets/c11.htm. Under the most recently updated Code, the direct costs incurred by the taxpayer in dealing with HMRC will be reimbursed (this practice supersedes that contained in 25 HMRC STATEMENTS OF PRACTICE A31) and compensation paid where HMRC took an unreasonable view of the law. Other aspects of Code 1 are mentioned at 27.1 and 27.2 INTEREST ON TAX (both of which also mention reimbursement of the taxpayer's costs where there is unreasonable delay by HMRC) and 35.11 PAYMENT OF TAX.

The Adjudicator. A taxpayer who is not satisfied with the HMRC response to a complaint has the option of putting the case to the Adjudicator. The Adjudicator, who was appointed with effect from 1 July 1993, is able to deal with complaints about HMRC's handling of a taxpayer's affairs, e.g. excessive delay, errors, discourtesy or the exercise of HMRC discretion, where the events complained of occurred after 5 April 1993. Matters subject to existing rights of appeal are excluded.

Complaints normally go to the Adjudicator only after they have been considered by the Controller of the relevant HMRC office, and where the taxpayer is still not satisfied with the response received. The alternatives of pursuing the complaint to HMRC's Head office, to an MP, or (through an MP) to the Parliamentary and Health Service Ombudsman continue to be available. See http://www.ombudsman.org.uk/make_a_complaint/index.html.

The Adjudicator will review all the facts, consider whether the complaint is justified, and, if so, make recommendations as to what should be done. See http://www.hmrc.gov.uk/pdfs/ao1.pdf.

Contact can be made with the Adjudicator's Office, 3rd Floor, Haymarket House, 28 The Haymarket, London SW1Y 4SP. Tel: 020 7930 2292. Fax: 020 7930 2298. An explanatory leaflet A01 (in nine ethnic minority languages as well as English and Welsh) is available from the Adjudicator which describes the actions a taxpayer should take and how the Adjudicator will respond to complaints.

4.2   ACCOUNTS AND INFORMATION

Transferors and other taxable persons have a duty to provide the Board with accounts containing information about transfers within a certain time after the transfers. The Board also has power to require any person to furnish them with information for IHT purposes. [*IHTA 1984, ss 216–219, 256, 257, 261*]. See 2 ACCOUNTS AND RETURNS. The Board has powers of inspection for valuation purposes. [*IHTA 1984, s 220*]. See 55.1 VALUATION.

4.3   DETERMINATIONS AND APPEALS

When a transfer of value has been made, the Board issues a notice of determination (with a similar function to a notice of assessment for income tax, capital gains tax, etc.) showing the value of the transfer and the tax chargeable. A person who receives a notice of determination may appeal against it. The appeal will be heard by the Special Commissioners, or, in certain circumstances, by the Lands Tribunal or the High Court. [*IHTA 1984, ss 221–225*]. Special Commissioners' cases held publicly and reported may be obtained from the Special Commissioners' Office in London. See 15 DETERMINATIONS AND APPEALS.

4.4   PAYMENT OF TAX

Tax is generally due six months after the end of the month of the transfer, with an extension to the end of the following April where a chargeable lifetime transfer takes place after 5 April and before 1 October in any year. In the tax year 2005–06 the inheritance tax collected amounted to £3.2 billion and is expected to increase; no doubt this will continue to increase by degrees as the rise in property prices is reflected consequentially in subsequent values of estates on death. On the transfer of certain types of property, broadly land, shares and businesses, tax may be paid by instalments. Certain 'pre-eminent' types of property such as works of art, historic buildings etc. were accepted in lieu of tax up to an amount of £17 million (see also Capital Taxation and the National Heritage IR 67 and also IHT 200 'Practitioners' Guide'). See also [**Case Study 3**] in WORKING CASE STUDY (59).

Where tax is not paid an HMRC charge for the unpaid tax is imposed on the property transferred. However, a person who has paid tax on a transfer or who has confirmed with HMRC that no tax is due, may obtain a certificate of discharge which serves to free the property in question from any HMRC charge. [*IHTA 1984, ss 226–232, 237–239*]. See 35 PAYMENT OF TAX and IHT 14, pp 14 and 24. See http://www.hmrc.gov.uk/leaflets/iht14.htm.

4.5   INTEREST AND PENALTIES

Interest is charged on unpaid tax and paid on any repayment of tax overpaid (currently 3%). [*IHTA 1984, ss 233–236*]. See 27 INTEREST ON TAX. Penalties are charged for various failures to comply with the IHT legislation, for providing incorrect information and for failing to remedy errors. By reason of the *FA 2004* penalties have been increased substantially. [*IHTA 1984, ss 245–253; FA 2004, s 295*]. See 36 PENALTIES and IHT 14, pp 21–24.

4.6 **RECOVERY OF TAX**

The Board may issue a notice of determination (see 4.3 above) if it appears that a transfer of value has been made, even if no account or return (see 4.2 above) of the transfer has been made. If tax or interest on tax is unpaid, the Board may take legal proceedings to recover it. If it is discovered that too little tax has been paid, the underpayment is payable with interest. However, where tax is paid and accepted on the view of the law current at the time, the amount of tax due is not affected if it appears subsequently that that view was wrong. [*IHTA 1984, ss 240–244, 254, 255*]. See 35 PAYMENT OF TAX.

4.7 **SERVICE OF DOCUMENTS**

A notice or other document which is to be served on a person under *IHTA 1984* may be delivered to him or left at his usual or last known place of residence or served by post, addressed to him at that address or his place of business or employment. [*IHTA 1984, s 258*].

4.8 **PUBLICATIONS**

Booklets IHT 14–18 (replacing IHT 1) concerning inheritance tax generally, may be obtained from the HMRC Inheritance Tax (addresses at 2.11 ACCOUNTS AND RETURNS). The generally required leaflets are:

IHT 2*	Lifetime gifts (public)
IHT 3*	Introduction to IHT (public)
IHT 4*	Notes on informal calculation of inheritance tax
IHT 8*	Alterations to inheritance after death
IHT 11*	Payment of IHT from National Savings
IHT 11(S)*	IHT from National Savings (Scotland)
IHT 12*	When is an Excepted Estate Grant appropriate
IHT 12(S)*	When is an Excepted Estate Grant appropriate (Scotland)
IHT 13*	Penalties leaflet
IHT 14*	The personal representatives' responsibilities
IHT 15*	How to calculate the liability
IHT 16*	Settled property
IHT 17*	Businesses, farms and woodlands
IHT 18*	Inheritance tax – Foreign aspects
IHT 19*	Delivery of a reduced Inland Revenue Account
IHT 110*	Guide to completing IHT 100
IHT 113*	Guide to completing IHT 100(WS)
IHT 205*	Short form for Personal Applicants
IHT 206*	Notes to help you fill in Form IHT 205
IHT 210*	Guide to completing IHT 200
IR45*	What to do when someone dies (public)
IR156*	Our Heritage – your right to see tax exempt works of art
SV 1*	Shares Valuation Division (an introduction)
CIL*	Customer Information Leaflet
COP1*	Putting things right when we make mistakes
*	Denotes availability on website http://www.hmrc.gov.uk/leaflets/iht.htm

Those wishing to obtain booklets and pamphlets should fax their order to HMRC Inheritance Tax stationery order line 0845 234 1010 and those sending written application to Resources & Facilities Section, HMRC Inheritance Tax, Ferrers House, P O Box 38, Castle Meadow Road, Nottingham NG2 1BB. The Heritage leaflet IR156 (last updated December 1996) may be obtained by telephoning the Heritage Section of HMRC Inheritance Tax on 0115 9742490 or faxing orders to 0115 9742497. Reports regarding Special Commissioners' decisions on cases held publicly and reported may be obtained at cost of £6 per copy from the Administration Office at the Tax Tribunals, 15/19 Bedford Avenue, London WC1B 3AS quoting the case number. Cheques should be made payable to 'H M Paymaster General only'. See http://www.financeandtaxtribunals.gov.uk/decisions/ decisions.htm. The quarterly CTO Newsletter is available free from HMRC Inheritance Tax, Customer Services, Ferrers House, PO Box 38, Castle Meadow Road, Nottingham NG2 1BB. Tel: 0115 974 2424. Fax: 0115 974 3041. The DX is 701201 Nottingham 4. See http://www.hmrc.gov.uk/cto/newsletter.htm.

5   Agricultural Property

Cross-references. See 7 BUSINESS PROPERTY; 8.5 CALCULATION OF TAX for application of agricultural relief where transfer partly exempt; 22.7 GIFTS WITH RESERVATION where such a gift is of agricultural property or shares in an agricultural company; 33.3 NATIONAL HERITAGE; 35 PAYMENT OF TAX and 58 WOODLANDS; 59 WORKING CASE STUDY.

Simon's Direct Tax Service, parts I7.2, I7.3.

Other Sources. Foster, parts G2–3; Mellows, parts 5.36–5.50; IHTM24000, IHTM24036.

5.1   AGRICULTURAL PROPERTY RELIEF

Introduction. Where certain conditions are satisfied, relief from inheritance tax is available on the transfer of agricultural property in the UK, the Channel Islands and the Isle of Man. The relief is a percentage reduction in the value transferred by a transfer of value and is given automatically without claim. Relief is also available on occasions on which tax is chargeable under the provisions relating to SETTLEMENTS WITHOUT INTERESTS IN POSSESSION (44). *[IHTA 1984, ss 115(1)(5), 116(1)].*

Agricultural property means agricultural land or pasture and includes woodlands and any building used in connection with the intensive rearing of livestock or fish if the woodlands or building is occupied with agricultural land or pasture and the occupation is ancillary to that of the agricultural land or pasture. It also includes such cottages, farm buildings and farmhouses, together with the land occupied with them, as are of a character appropriate to the property. Agricultural land which is taken out of production can still qualify for APR (including GAEC land) because *IHTA 1984, s 117* does not require the land to be in production either continuously or at a specific time (though there must be an intention or expectation that the land will be back in production at some time in the future). So, for example, agricultural land set aside to rotational, or even permanent, fallow can still qualify as agricultural property within the definition of *IHTA 1984, s 115(2)* and as occupied for the purposes of agriculture within the meaning of *IHTA 1984, s 117.* See June 2005 Tax Bulletin Special Edition, IHT NEWSLETTER AND TAX BULLETIN EXTRACTS (61). The breeding and rearing of horses on a stud farm and the grazing of horses in connection with those activities is to be taken to be agriculture and any buildings used in connection with those activities to be farm buildings. See also *Wheatley and another (Executors of Wheatley Deceased) v CIR [1998] STC SCD 60 Sp C 149* e.g. grazing by draught horses. Livestock, deadstock and farm plant and machinery are not included but these may qualify for BUSINESS PROPERTY (7) relief, as may the value of land in excess of its agricultural value and milk quota where it is valued separately (HMRC Tax Bulletin February 1993 p 51). *[IHTA 1984, s 115(2)(4)].* From 6 April 1995 land used for short rotation coppice (a cultivation method of producing willow, poplar and elephant grass cuttings for renewable fuel for biomass-fed power stations) will count as agricultural property and qualify for either 100% or 50% relief depending on the circumstances as will buildings used in the cultivation which will be regarded as farm buildings. Similarly, farmland and buildings used for the management of the habitat land (see (*c*) below) counts as agricultural property for the purposes of relief at 100% or 50%. The new provisions apply from 26 November 1996 and apply to land dedicated under the Government's Habitat Schemes. *[SI 1994/1291, SI 1994/1292, SI 1994/1293, SI 1994/2710; SI 1995/134].* See 5.2 below and Inland Revenue Press Release 27 January 1995. *[IHTA 1984, ss 116, 124C; FA 1995, s 154(2)(3)(5); FA 1997, s 94].* According to the original CTO Advanced Instruction Manual, paras L246.2.2–2.4 (but now see IHTM24103) land used for agricultural purposes may occasionally be used for other purposes (e.g. an annual point to point horse race) without the relief being jeopardised. However, careful consideration is required where land is used for other purposes such as reeds for thatching (cultivation of a crop) and pheasants for sport (food for human consumption) which are not agricultural. In addition, where derelict land has been restored to previous levels of agricultural production due to the application of manures and calcified seaweed in order to make the grasses more palatable to cattle then even though the process is not considered an 'intensive agricultural purpose' it would constitute agricultural/pasture land and not moorland. See [**Case Study 1**] in 59.5 WORKING CASE STUDY.

The IHT 210 (Notes) at D13 (Notes) http://www.hmrc.gov.uk/cto/forms/ d13_notes_1.pdf states at point 4:

> 'Describe the agricultural activities that the deceased carried out. Do not use vague phrases like "general farming". Say whether it was
>
> • An arable, pastoral or mixed farm
>
> • The type of crops usually grown
>
> • The type of livestock that grazed the land
>
> If a variety of livestock grazed the land, give some idea about the number of animals and acreage used by each type.
>
> You should tell us here if the deceased left the property or stopped the agricultural activity. Say when this happened and why. Agricultural relief may still be due if the property was managed under an agro–environmental or habitat scheme arrangement.
>
> Our Helpline can tell you what the conditions are for the agro–environmental or habitat scheme arrangement.'

See 2.11 ACCOUNTS AND RETURNS for Helpline numbers and end of this chapter for Form D13.

In *Starke and another (Executors of Brown) v CIR CA, [1995] STC 689* the property in question comprised a site with an area of just over one hectare containing a farmhouse and an assortment of outbuildings, the site being used as part of a farm devoted to mixed farming, although the remainder of the farm, however, was substantially in the ownership of a farming company. The taxpayer, whilst successful in being granted leave to appeal direct to the High Court, a point of law being involved (see 15.4 DETERMINATIONS AND APPEALS), undertook in the application for leave not to contend that the land in question fell within the concluding part of *IHTA 1984, s 115(2)*, namely 'such cottages, farm buildings and farmhouses, together with the land occupied with them, as are of a character appropriate to the property'. The reason for such an undertaking being given was that the former Inland Revenue did not agree with the taxpayer that the appeal should be to the High Court and would have opposed the taxpayer's application for leave to appeal direct to the High Court if such contention had been made. In addition, because of the differing ownerships of the property in question and the remainder of the farm, such a contention may not have been possible. Consequently, because no contention was made concerning woodlands or buildings used for intensive rearing, the appeal turned on whether the land constituted 'agricultural land or pasture' within the first leg of that provision. The taxpayer contended that the *Interpretation Act 1978, Sch 1* definition of 'land' so as to include 'buildings and other structures' should apply in the expression 'agricultural land'. It was held that it did not apply because *Interpretation Act 1978, s 5* provides that definitions provided by that *Act* only apply 'unless the contrary intention appears' and by giving the expression 'agricultural land or pasture' the more limited and natural meaning for which the former Inland Revenue contended, namely that the primary meaning of 'agricultural property' was 'agricultural land or pasture' which meant 'bare land', i.e. fields or land used either for the cultivation of crops or for the grazing of animals, it was possible to give a sensible meaning to the remainder of the definition by extending the meaning of 'agricultural property' to include species of property which the expression 'agricultural land' did not cover. Because of the taxpayer's undertaking in the application for leave to appeal direct to the High Court, the decision in the case may have to be considered special to its circumstances. In a decision on 19 May 1995 the Court of Appeal dismissed the appeal by the executors.

In *Farmer v CIR [1999] STC SCD 321 Sp C 216* it was accepted that there was a single composite business comprising of farming and letting of various farm buildings. The Special Commissioners in this case came to the decision that on the application of the 'wholly or mainly' test and taking the business as a whole it consisted mainly of farming. In support of this were the facts that the property was a business property of landed estate with a majority of the land being used for farming. The lettings element was subsidiary to the farming enterprise and was of short duration. In viewing the capital that was employed in the business amounting to about £3.5 million, £1.25 million was attributable to the letting element and the balance to farming. Also, the employees and consultants spent a greater proportion of time on the farming activities and the farm turnover exceeded the letting turnover in six years out of eight but significantly the net profit of the lettings exceeded the net profit from the farming. This last point did not sway the view that the farm was a business rather than an investment because the 'wholly or mainly' test could not be determined solely on the basis of net profits but the character of the business should be looked at as a whole. In addition, it is necessary to consider the overall position over a period of time rather than for a particular period in isolation. (See also *Millington v Secretary of State for the Environment and Another CA, [1999] TLR 29 June 1999*). See also *Harrold and others (executors of Harrold deceased) v CIR [1996] STC SCD 195 Sp C 71* and *Dixon v CIR [2002] STC SCD 53 Sp C 297*. In the case of *Higginson's Executors v CIR [2002] STC SCD 483 Sp C 337* the farmhouse was originally a nineteenth century hunting lodge with 6 bedrooms, 63 acres of agricultural land, 3 acres of formal gardens and 68 acres of woodlands. The Special Commissioner dismissed the appeal, holding that 'for the purposes of *section 115(2)* the unit must be an agricultural unit: that is to say that within the unit, the land must predominate ... (and) any qualifying cottages, farm buildings or farmhouses must be ancillary to the land'. However, in view of the price paid for the property, it was clear that 'within this particular unit it is the house which predominates, and that what we have here is a house with farmland going with it (and not vice versa)'. Accordingly, the lodge was not a 'farmhouse' for the purposes of *s 115(2)*. In the case of *Lloyds TSB plc (Antrobus' Personal Representatives) v CIR [2002] STC SCD 468 Sp C 336* however the farmhouse, Cookhill Priory, comprised of 6 bedrooms and the farm was 126 acres of freehold land and 6.5 acres of tenanted land. It was accepted that the Priory and the land and surrounding buildings (including a chapel) were agricultural property. The Special Commissioner allowed the appeal, finding that the property 'was in a poor state of repair and maintenance'. The result was that, even if the dwelling-house had at one time been a family home of some distinction, it had, both in appearance and in use, become a farmhouse on a working farm. On the evidence, the house was 'a farmhouse with a farm and definitely not a house with land'. It was 'of a character appropriate to the property' for the purposes of *s 115(2)*. However, having lost the case at the Special Commissioners in October 2002 HMRC Inheritance Tax issued a notice of determination on the basis that the agricultural value of the farmhouse was less than the market value. Subsequently, the case went to the Lands Tribunal where the day-to-day operations were given more focus than the management of the farm when considering the actual business of farming. When considering the operational components of the farming business for the purposes of securing APR the Tribunal stated:

'There is, we think, no dispute about the definition when it is expressed in this way. The question is: who is the farmer of the land for the purposes of s 115(2)? In our view it is the person who lives in the farmhouse in order to farm the land on a day-to-day basis. It is likely, although it may not necessarily always be the case, that his principal occupation will consist of farming the land comprised in the farm. We do not think that a house occupied with a farm is a farmhouse simply because the person living there is in overall control of the agricultural business conducted on the land; and in particular we think that the lifestyle of the farmer, the person whose bid for the land is treated as establishing the agricultural value of the land, is not the farmer for the purposes of these provisions.'

It may be a matter of dispute whether the above *dictum* is persuasive enough to influence other cases where the farmhouse under scrutiny for APR incorporates this 'lifestyle buyers' application. The result did secure discount of 30% in the value for APR purposes. See *Lloyds TSB plc (Antrobus' Personal Representatives) v Twiddy [2004] DET/47/2004*, VALUATION (56) and IHTM24036 at http://www.hmrc.gov.uk/manuals/ihtmanual/ IHTM24036.htm.

In *Rosser v CIR [2003] STC SCD 311 Sp C 368* a former farmhouse was ostensibly treated as a 'retirement' home and did not qualify as agricultural property whereas a barn within the same curtilage was treated as such due to the fact that is was in general use for farming. The effect of *s 115(2)* was that 'broiler houses' on a farm could only qualify for relief if they had been 'a subsidiary part of the purpose of an overall agricultural activity carried out on the land'. Since they had been let to a separate company, this was not the case. Accordingly, the broiler houses were not 'ancillary' to the farm, within *s 115(2)*, and did not qualify for relief. See *Williams (Williams' Personal Representatives) v HMRCC [2005] STC SCD 782 Sp C 500*. In *Arnander, Lloyd & Villiers (McKenna's Executors)*, a small country estate comprising a large house with six acres of gardens and some domestic outbuildings, and 187 acres of land, most of which was farmland, the Special Commissioner reviewed the evidence in detail and held that three of the outbuildings qualified for relief but that the main house and eight of the outbuildings did not. The house which the couple lived in was not 'the main dwelling from which the agricultural operations over the land were conducted and managed'. See *Arnander, Lloyd & Villiers (McKenna's Executors) v HMRC, [2006] STC SCD 800 Sp C 565*. See 60 TAX CASES.

In connection with the above the CTO's previous Advanced Instruction Manual, para L231.4 (but now see IHTM24042), states that cases involving farming businesses of less than 20 acres or where the farmhouse is very valuable (say, over £250,000) and the acreage is comparatively small (say, less than 100 acres) then the case will be referred for review.

Whether a farmhouse is to be classed as agricultural property is mainly a question of the purpose of occupation rather than the actual use to which it is put by the owner/occupier. Peter Twiddy, formerly the HMRC Inheritance Tax Litigation Support Team stated in Taxation Magazine on 15 June 2000 in relation to farmhouses:

'The CTO asks the District Valuer to consider the appropriate test through the eyes of the rural equivalent of the reasonable man on the Clapham omnibus ...'

HMRC Inheritance Tax now appear to seek to apply the following tests in relation to farmhouses:

- *Primary character:* is the unit primarily a dwelling with some land or is it an agricultural unit incorporating such a dwelling as is appropriate?

- *Local practice:* is it normal for land of this quality, use and area to have with it a dwelling of this type and size?

- *Financial support:* is the size and character of the dwelling commensurate with the scale of agricultural operations appropriate for the land? We are not considering a strict economic viability test for the holding but adding information in context.

In applying these three criteria, a balanced view is taken 'in the round' and this stage has been referred to colloquially as 'the elephant test', i.e. 'difficult to describe, but you know one when you see one'. See now IHTM24036 at http://www.hmrc.gov.uk/manuals/ ihtmanual/IHTM24036.htm and also 59.4 WORKING CASE STUDY.

Where the prudent lotting of an agricultural estate rests on the basis of separate farm lots, the question of sporting rights should be considered as the value may be materially affected by the hypothesis of separate ownership of farms. (VOA IHT manual, section 9, para 9.3). If the whole of one or more of the lots is exempt then it is not necessary to value that lot and if it is only a part that is exempt the valuation should be done on a just and reasonable basis. (VOA IHT manual, section 9, para 9.4). See IR IHT Newsletter, April 2004 at IHT NEWSLETTER AND TAX BULLETIN EXTRACTS (61). See http://www.voa.gov.uk/instructions/Index.htm.

Farming companies. Relief extends to shares and securities if agricultural property forms part of the company's assets and part of the value of the shares or securities can be attributed to the agricultural value of the agricultural property. [*IHTA 1984, s 122*]. See 5.6 below.

In normal circumstances if the tenant of an agricultural holding is a company then there is less likelihood of the landlord eventually obtaining vacant possession than if the tenant is an individual because a company does not die. (VOA IHT manual, section 9, para 9.8).

Agricultural value applies to that part of the value of shares in or debentures of a company which is attributable to the agricultural value of qualifying agricultural property, provided that the particular conditions set out in *IHTA 1984, s 122* are satisfied. This will be determined by Shares Valuation Division (SVD). Also SVD will notify the DV of any agricultural property owned by a company which qualifies for relief (Form VAL 63 or 63A) when referring the case to the DV. (VOA IHT manual, section 16, para 16.21).

5.2 **NATURE OF RELIEF**

The relief is a percentage reduction of the value transferred by a transfer of value (including an occasion on which tax is chargeable under the rules on SETTLEMENTS WITHOUT INTERESTS IN POSSESSION (44)). The percentage reduction is made before deduction of the annual exemption and other EXEMPT TRANSFERS (21) and before grossing-up where the transferor pays the tax.

Subject to the conditions in 5.3 below, the percentage is

(*a*) **100%** in relation to transfers of value made, and other events occurring, after 9 March 1992 (previously 50%) of the agricultural value of the property transferred if either

    (i) the transferor immediately before the transfer enjoyed either the right to vacant possession or the right to obtain it within the next twelve months; or

    (ii) the transferor has been beneficially entitled to his interest since before 10 March 1981; and

        (1) if he had disposed of it by a transfer of value immediately before that date, he would have been entitled to claim the 50% relief available after 6 April 1976 and before 10 March 1981; and

        (2) that relief would not have been restricted by reference to the limits of £250,000 or 1,000 acres (whichever was the more favourable to the taxpayer) applying between those dates (see also Note (A) below); and

        (3) the interest did not in the period from 10 March 1981 to the date of transfer, give him the vacant possession rights in (*a*)(i) above and did not fail to give him those rights because of any act or deliberate omission by him during that period.

(*b*) **100%** in relation to transfers of value of farmland let for periods exceeding twelve months which is let on or after 1 September 1995 (the commencement date of the *Agricultural Tenancies Act 1995* and *Agricultural Holdings (Scotland) Act 1991, s 12* by right of succession in Scotland). [*IHTA 1984, s 116(2)(c) as inserted by FA 1995,* *s 155(1)*]. Previously the relief was 50% where let farmland which did not or still does not, under an existing pre-1 September 1995 agreement, entitle the transferor to vacant possession or the right to obtain vacant possession within the next twelve months. A tenancy starting on or after 1 September 1995 by reason of statutory succession to an existing tenancy is not excluded from the full relief but there is doubt regarding the adding of land to an existing tenancy (HMRC Tax Bulletin, August 1995 p 241). However, *FA 1996, s 185* enables a tenancy acquired by succession by way of death of the existing tenant to be treated as commencing on the date of death where this is on or after 1 September 1995. A statutory succession would normally take effect from the grant of succession to the new tenancy but this is overridden for the purposes of *IHTA 1984* and the commencement is taken as the date of death of the tenant being succeeded. In the case of a tenant's retirement in favour of a new tenant on or after 1 September 1995 but there is the landowner's death in between the notice of retirement and the succession by the new tenant, the date of the tenancy is deemed to have commenced for these purposes as just before the landowner's death. This has the effect of allowing 100% relief from the date of the death of the landowner whereas under normal rules the relief would only be available from the grant of the new tenancy. [*IHTA 1984, s 116(5A)–(5D)* as inserted by *FA 1996, s 185*].

The *Agricultural Holdings Act 1986* affords the opportunity to grant a new tenancy, on or after 1 September 1995, thereby permitting the landlord 100% agricultural property relief and allowing the tenant a tenancy under the *AHA 1986*. The common law principle of surrender and re-grant can sometimes apply where the terms of a tenancy are varied (*Friends' Provident Life Office v British Railways Board [1996] 1 All ER 336*. However, in the House of Lords (Report Stage, Col 895, 23 January 1995) Lord Howe said

'We accept in those circumstances it would be inequitable for the new tenancy to be excluded from the scope of the 1986 Act when the parties had not intended that to happen.'

Therefore a purported variation of the previous tenancy in the *AHA 1986* is meant to apply to the unintentional variations and not those deliberately effected to bring about surrender and re-grant. In view of this a deliberate variation may result in the landlord obtaining 100% agricultural property relief but not an *AHA 1986* tenancy for the tenant.

(*c*)　　100% in relation to chargeable transfers of value of farmland and related buildings that have been dedicated to wildlife habitats on or after 26 November 1996 which meet the usual ownership criteria. [*FA 1997, s 94* inserting new *IHTA 1984, s 124C*]. Land and any related buildings will be treated as agricultural land and associated farm buildings where the land and buildings are dedicated to the Government's Habitat Schemes under any of the following:

- *Habitat (Water Fringe) Regulations 1994, SI 1994/1291, Reg 3(1)* as amended by *SI 1996/1480* and *SI 1996/3106*.

- *Habitat (Former Set-Aside Land) Regulations 1994, SI 1994/1292* as amended by *SI 1996/1478* and *SI 1996/3107*.

- *Habitat (Salt-Marsh) Regulations 1994, SI 1994/1293* as amended by *SI 1995/2871 and SI 1995/2891; SI 1996/1479* and *SI 1996/3108*.

- *Habitats (Scotland) Regulations 1994, SI 1994/2710, Reg 3(2)(a)* as amended by *SI 1996/3035*.

- *Habitat Improvement Regulations (Northern Ireland) 1995, SR(NI) 1995/134, Reg 3(1)(a)*.

Previously these habitat schemes, which protect the environment and maintain the countryside by taking land out of agriculture for 20 years, could not satisfy the occupation test in 5.3(A) below. It was considered that this would put farmers at a disadvantage over those not engaging in such environmentally friendly schemes. The change in legislation was therefore introduced to rectify this. It does not affect in any way the situation where land is farmed in an ecologically benign i.e. organic way because this land, although dedicated in this way for ten years, attracts agricultural property relief in any case. Where land is let on or before 31 August 1995 and it qualifies as part of a Habitat Scheme as above the result will be that relief is available at the reduced rate of 50%. See example below.

Example

D has owned and farmed 700 acres of land since 1970. This land has been farmed for arable crops but under the set-aside scheme he has, since 1994 under the *Habitat (Former Set-Aside Land) Regulations 1994*, taken out 200 acres for a period of 20 years to be used for rare nesting owls in accordance with the Government's Habitat Scheme. Also two former grain storage warehouses, valued at £34,000, have been converted to a hide and an information centre. These have both been let to the Conservation Volunteer Development Society since 1994. The remaining 500 acres continue to be farmed as crops for human consumption. The value of the farmland is £1,500 per acre and the set-aside land is valued at £950 per acre. D dies on 30 September 2007 and leaves all the farmland including set-aside to his son E. The value of the farmhouse is £125,000.

	£
500 acres at £1,500 per acre	750,000
Farmhouse	125,000
200 acres of Habitat land at £950 per acre	190,000
Value of agricultural property	1,065,000
Less amount of agricultural relief @ 100%	(1,065,000)
Chargeable	Nil

	£
Former grain storage warehouse	34,000
Less amount of agricultural relief @ 50%	(17,000)
Total value of farm on which tax is chargeable	17,000

Notes to the example

(A)   As the former grain storage warehouses are associated farm buildings within the Habitat Scheme, the owner is entitled to agricultural property relief but because the buildings were rented out on or before 31 August 1995 only 50% relief is due.

(B)   The normal conditions for relief in 5.3 above apply to the land in the Habitat Scheme.

(d)   50% in relation to transfers of value made, and other events occurring, after 9 March 1992 (previously 30%) in cases not covered by (a), (b) or (c) above.

[*IHTA 1984, s 116(1)–(3) (5A)–(5E) (7); F(No 2)A 1992, s 73, Sch 14 paras 4, 8; FA 1995, ss 154(2), 155; FA 1996, s 185*]. See Tolley's Capital Transfer Tax 1986/87 and earlier editions for the agricultural property relief available for CTT purposes after 6 April 1976 and before 10 March 1981.

Example

A and B, who are brothers, farm 1,500 acres of arable land under a tenancy in common agreement with the landowner X. B dies on 26 July 2006 and leaves his share of the tenancy to A's son C. At the beginning of October 2006 A decides to retire and let his son C have his share of the tenancy as from 1 November 2006 and advises X by notice in writing. Landowner X dies on 16 November 2007. The tenancy agreement and the provisions of B's will are not resolved until 18 January and 28 August 2008 respectively.

In the case of C's succession to B's tenancy, this will be treated as having commenced on B's death notwithstanding X's death later on 16 November 2007. In the case of A's decision to retire in favour of his son C the tenancy will be treated as having commenced on 16 November 2007 for the purposes of the rate of any agricultural relief on the death of X. In this latter case of retirement the succession by C to the tenancy of the land let to A can take effect up to 30 months from November 2006. Therefore 100% agricultural property relief applies to the let land on gift or transfer subject to the other qualifying conditions.

Notes to the example

(A)   *IHTA 1984, s 116(5A)*, inserted by *FA 1996, s 185*, relates to successions to tenancies in Scotland whereas *section 116(5B)* relates to tenancies other than in Scotland. See also *Agricultural Holdings (Scotland) Act 2003, ss 20, 22* where a short limited duration tenancy or a limited duration tenancy may be bequeathed or transferred by reason of intestacy to a person entitled to succeed to the deceased's intestate estate and the executor shall be entitled so to transfer the interest without the consent of the landlord. This may well have been preceded by a Notice of Interest in Acquiring Land signed by a tenant under *The Agricultural Holdings (Forms)(Scotland) Regulations 2004* but still 100% APR should be available to the landlord in these cases.

(B)   *Section 116(5D)* relates to the situation above where X dies on or after 1 September 1995 following a notice of retirement but before the new tenancy has taken effect and takes place within 30 months of the notice being given (which also includes an assignment or assignation in Scotland).

(C)   The notice of retirement must be a notice or other written intimation given by the tenant (joint tenants or tenants in common) to the landowner indicating, under whatever terms, that the person or persons in the notice should become the tenant of the property. This may arise from, say, a three-generation tenancy renewable every five years.

The increases in the relief from 30% to 50%, and from 50% to 100%, mentioned above will be interpreted as applying not only to transfers of value made after 9 March 1992 but also to charges or further charges to IHT arising on a death after that date in respect of a transfer of value made before 10 March 1992 (Inland Revenue Press Release, 10 March 1992 and correspondence with the publisher).

Example

X has owned since 1983 1,000 acres of land. In June 1992 he began to farm the land, utilising 800 acres for that purpose. The remaining 200 acres are not used for any business purposes. On 1 July 2007 X transfers all the land to his son, Y, at a time when its agricultural value was £1,000 per acre and its open market value £1,500 per acre. He had not used his annual exemptions for 2006/07 and 2007/08. X dies on 6 September 2010. Y has continued to run the farm business since the date of the gift.

The value of the gift for inheritance tax purposes before relief is

5.2 Agricultural Property

	£	£
1,000 acres at £1,500 per acre		£1,500,000

The transfer subject to tax is

(i)	Agricultural value of land		
	800 acres × £1,000	800,000	
	Less agricultural property relief at 100%	(800,000)	—
(ii)	Non-agricultural value of land		
	800 acres × £500		400,000
(iii)	Value of land not used in business		
	200 acres at £1,500 per acre		300,000
			700,000
	Deduct annual exemptions (2006/07 and 2007/08)		6,000
	Value transferred by PET becoming chargeable on death		£694,000

Notes to the example

(A)   Business property relief may be available in respect of the £400,000 excess of the open market value over the agricultural value.

(B)   IHT will be charged at 80% of full rates as X died more than three but not more than four years after the gift.

(C)   The 100% relief applies in relation to transfers of value made, and other events occurring, after 9 March 1992, and replaced a 50% relief.

(e)   An Inland Revenue Press Release dated 13 February 1995 published an Extra-Statutory Concession F17 (see 23 HMRC EXTRA-STATUTORY CONCESSIONS and also IHT 17, p 10 on http://www.hmrc.gov.uk/leaflets/iht17.htm) which extends to 100% from 50% the agricultural property relief where the transferor's interest in the property either:

(aa)   carries the right to vacant possession within 24 months of the date of transfer; or

(bb)   is, notwithstanding the terms of the tenancy, valued at an amount broadly equivalent to the vacant possession value.

In the case of (aa) above the landlord may have a contractual right to serve notice to the tenant to vacate the property within twelve months of the date of transfer but because of the *Agricultural Holdings Act 1986* (and similar legislation in Scotland and Northern Ireland) vacant possession cannot be obtained for a further twelve months after the tenancy agreement is terminated. It also arises where there is a tenancy which lasts for more than one and less than two years (*Gladstone v Bower CA [1960] 3 All ER 353* type of arrangement).

In the case of (bb) above the transferor and the tenant are so closely connected that in practice the value of the property on the open market is broadly the same as with vacant possession e.g. land let to a company by the transferor who also controls that company. The above concession is to apply from the date of the press release but also in respect of earlier chargeable transfers where liability has not yet been agreed.

A summary of the above may be detailed as follows:

Summary of situations where 100% relief is due in respect of agricultural property

Circumstance	Qualifying requirements	Relevant legislation applicable
Vacant possession	Vacant possession of the agricultural property must be held by the transferor including land farmed subject to a licence. See (a) above.	*IHTA 1984, s 116(2)(a)*
Land let subject to a tenancy beginning on or after 1 September 1995.	Applies in respect of all land that is subject to a farm business tenancy. It applies to land let that is subject to a succession tenancy granted on or after 1 September 1995. An extension of the relief applies where either (i) a valid retirement notice for succession has been made after 1 September 1995, or (ii) the tenant has died after that date and the tenancy has become vested or obtained by another person. See (b) above.	*IHTA 1984, s 116(2)(c),(5A) –(5D)* as extended by *FA 1996, s 185(2); Agricultural Holdings Act 1986, s 25.*
Near vacant possession value or short-term loss of vacant possession.	Applies where the transferor's interest in the property does not carry vacant possession but is valued near vacant possession value e.g. land let to a company where the company is controlled by the transferor. See (e) above and 5.6 below. Alternatively, the transferor must have the right to obtain vacant possession within 24 months. See (e) above.	Extra-Statutory Concession F17. See 23 HMRC EXTRA-STATUTORY CONCESSIONS. *IHTA 1984, s 116(2)(a).*
Pre-1981 'full-time working farmer' provision.	Applies where land has been continuously let to a partnership or company since prior to 10 March 1981 which the transferor has previously farmed in some capacity. See (a) above.	*IHTA 1984, s 116(2)(b).*
Post 5 April 1995	Applies where land and buildings used in the cultivation of short-rotation coppice.	*FA 1995, s 154*
Post 25 November 1996 'dedicated wildlife habitats'.	Applies where land is being used or has been let on or after 26 November 1996 dedicated to wildlife habitats. See (c) above.	*IHTA 1984, s 124C.*

'Agricultural value' is the value of agricultural property on the assumption that it is subject to perpetual covenant prohibiting its use otherwise than as agricultural property.

Farm cottages occupied by persons employed solely for agricultural purposes in connection with the agricultural property are valued without taking any account of the fact that the cottages are suitable for the residential purposes of persons not so employed. *IHTA 1984, s 115(3)* does not require 'exclusive occupation' for agricultural purposes as evidenced in the case of, say, a country manor house which is purchased at a premium (because of the tax shelter relief obtained) where agricultural land adjoining the manor house is also acquired notwithstanding the fact that it is farmed under a contracting agreement. See Taxation Magazine, 3 April 2003 p 14. [*IHTA 1984, ss 115(3), 169*]. The Inland Revenue Press Release on 13 February 1995 published an ESC F16 (see also IHT 17, p 9) that gives relief to certain farm cottages that would not normally be relieved from IHT on a lifetime or death transfer. The condition that a farm cottage is occupied by persons employed solely for agricultural purposes is also satisfied in respect of chargeable transfers from 13 February 1995 where the cottage is occupied by a retired farm worker or his/her surviving spouse or civil partner if the occupation is either:

(*a*)   protected under the *Rent (Agriculture) Act 1976* or *Housing Act 1988* (or similar legislation in Scotland and Northern Ireland); or

(*b*)   under a lease granted as part of the worker's contract of employment in agriculture which has a similar effect to that of a protected tenancy or licence (e.g. lease granted as terms of employment).

Where the valuation of the land reflects the benefit of milk quota, agricultural relief is given on that value (HMRC Tax Bulletin February 1993 p 51 and http://www.hmrc.gov.uk/bulletins/tb6.htm).

The value of a farm cottage may be restricted, sometimes to its agricultural value, where the property is both agricultural and occupied as such. If the cottage is not occupied as such the value should reflect the use to which it may be legally put. (VOA IHT manual, section 9, para 9.18).

If at the date of transfer there are crops growing on the land these are legally part of the land until severed. However, the DV should exclude the value of growing crops from their report unless the CTO specifically requests otherwise and if the DV is aware that the value includes growing crops without a separate figure then the case should be returned to the CTO. (VOA IHT manual, section 9, paras 9.40 and 9.41). The value of permanent or temporary pasture and the value of cultivations or unexhausted manures should be included and where the value of growing crops have been included with the value of the land then the CTO will ask them to state their separate values. (VOA IHT manual, section 9, para 9.41).

Example

A has owned and occupied land for the purposes of agriculture for the last three years and transfers it to a discretionary trust in May 2007. He has not used his annual exemption for either the year 2006/07 or 2007/08. The value of the gift for inheritance tax purposes is £100,000 and the agricultural value is agreed at £70,000.

		£	£
Value transferred			100,000
Less relief of 100% on £70,000			70,000
			30,000
Less	Annual exemption 2007/08	3,000	
	Annual exemption 2006/07	3,000	6,000
Net value transferred (subject to grossing-up if tax paid by donor)			£24,000

5.3   CONDITIONS OF RELIEF

The agricultural property must have been either

(*a*)   **occupied** by the transferor for the purposes of agriculture throughout the period of two years ending with the date of transfer (see *Wheatley* 60 TAX CASES), or

(*b*)   **owned** by the transferor for the period of seven years ending with the date of transfer and have been occupied throughout that period (by him or another person) for the purposes of agriculture. [*IHTA 1984, s 117*]. See *Wheatley's Executors v CIR [1998] STC SCD 60 Sp C 149.*

See also IHT 17, p 14.

Interest in possession in settled agricultural property. A person with such an interest is regarded as the beneficial owner of the settled property. [*IHTA 1984, s 49(1)*].

Replacements. Where agricultural property *occupied* by the transferor on the date of transfer replaced other agricultural property, condition (*a*) above is satisfied if both properties together with any earlier agricultural property directly or indirectly replaced were occupied by that person for the purposes of agriculture for periods comprising at least two years within the five years ending with the date of the transfer. Where agricultural property *owned* by the transferor on the date of the transfer replaced other agricultural property, condition (*b*) is satisfied if the respective properties were both owned by the transferor and occupied (by him or another person) for the purposes of agriculture for at least seven years within the ten years ending with the date of the transfer.

In both cases relief is limited to what it would have been if any one or more of the replacements in the respective periods had not taken place. For this purpose, changes resulting from the formation, alteration or dissolution of a partnership are disregarded. [*IHTA 1984, s 118*].

Occupation by company or partnership. Occupation by a company controlled by the transferor is treated as occupation by the transferor. 'Control' is defined by *IHTA 1984, s 269*, see 35.4 PAYMENT OF TAX. Occupation by a Scottish partnership is treated as occupation by the partners. [*IHTA 1984, s 119*]. See also previous CTO Advanced Instruction Manual, para L266.6 (now IHTM24074).

Binding contract for sale. Relief will not be given if at the time of the transfer, the transferor has entered into a binding contract for sale of (i) agricultural property (unless the sale is to a company in return for an issue of shares which will give the transferor control of that company); or (ii) shares or securities in agricultural companies (see 5.6 below) except where the sale is made for the purpose of reconstruction or amalgamation. [*IHTA 1984, s 124*].

The IHT 210 (Notes) at D13 (Notes) http://www.hmrc.gov.uk/cto/forms/d13_notes_1.pdf states at point 8:

> 'If, before the deceased died, all or part of the property was subject to a binding contract for sale where contracts have been exchanged (or, in Scotland, when missives have been concluded), but the sale had not been concluded, agricultural relief will not be due. You should give details of the sale, and clearly identify the part of the property that was sold on the plan.'

Further conditions for lifetime transfers. Agricultural property relief is only available where any part of the value transferred by a POTENTIALLY EXEMPT TRANSFER (38) proves to be a chargeable transfer if, in addition to the conditions in 5.3 above, the conditions listed below are also satisfied. Similarly, where a chargeable lifetime transfer, other than a potentially exempt transfer, made within seven years of the transferor's death is reduced under the agricultural property relief provisions, the additional tax chargeable by reason of death must be calculated as if the relief had not been received unless the following additional conditions are satisfied.

5.3 Agricultural Property

Subject to the provisions below for replacement property, the additional conditions are

(*a*) that the original property was owned by the 'transferee' throughout the period beginning with the date of the chargeable transfer and ending with the transferor's death or, if earlier, the transferee's death (the 'relevant period') and is not at the time of death subject to a binding contract for sale; and

(*b*) except in a case falling within (*c*) below, the original property is agricultural property immediately before the death and has been occupied (by the transferee or another) for the purposes of agriculture throughout the relevant period; and

(*c*) where the original property consists of shares or securities of a company, that throughout the relevant period the agricultural property in question was owned by the company and occupied (by the company or another) for the purposes of agriculture.

'*Transferee*' means the person whose property the original property became on that chargeable transfer or, where on the transfer the original property became or remained settled property in which no qualifying interest in possession subsists, the trustees of the settlement.

Where any shares owned by the transferee immediately before the death would either be identified with the original property under the provisions of *TCGA 1992, ss 126–136* (reorganisations of share capital, conversion of securities and company reconstructions and amalgamations) *or* were issued to him in consideration of the transfer of agricultural property consisting of the original property (or part), his period of ownership of the original property is treated as including his period of ownership of the shares (in relation to transfers of value made, and other events occurring, before 17 March 1987 the shares were treated as if they were the original property (or part)).

Where part only of the original property satisfies the conditions in (*a*) to (*c*) above, proportionate agricultural property relief is given.

Example

A is the freehold owner of agricultural land which at current vacant possession value is estimated to be valued at £850,000. On 29 September 1989, he enters into an agricultural tenancy (with more than two years to run) with a farming partnership comprising his two sons and his grandson for a full market rental of £25,000 p.a. The tenanted value is estimated at £500,000.

In July 2007 his grandson is killed in a farming accident and a new letting agreement is made between the two sons and A for a full market rent of £35,000 p.a. on 15 September 2007.

A dies on 1 October 2007 when the tenanted value of the land has risen to £600,000.

	£
Transfer at death (tenanted valuation)	600,000
Deduct agricultural property relief	600,000
IHT payable	NIL

Notes to the example

(A) As the land is let under an agreement on or after 1 September 1995 relief of 100% is available. Only 50% relief would have been available if the existing tenancy had continued. [*IHTA 1984, s 116; FA 1995, s 155; FA 1996, s 185*].

(B)   The addition of land to an *AHA 1986* tenancy will have the effect of a surrender and re-grant on or after 1 September 1995 thereby ensuring the landlord receives 100% relief.

Replacement property. Where the transferee has disposed of all or part of the original property before the death of the transferor and applied the whole of the consideration received in acquiring a replacement property within the 'allowed period' after the disposal of the original property or part (or has entered into a binding contract to acquire replacement property within that time), then, provided the disposal and acquisition are both made in transactions at arm's length or on terms such as might be expected to be included in such a transaction, the conditions in (*a*) to (*c*) above are taken as satisfied if

(i)   the replacement property is owned by the transferee immediately before the transferor's death (or immediately before the transferee's death if earlier) and is not at that time subject to a binding contract; and

(ii)   throughout the period beginning with the date of the chargeable transfer and ending with the disposal, the original property was owned by the transferee and occupied (by him or another) for the purposes of agriculture; and

(iii) throughout the period beginning with the date when the transferee acquired the replacement property and ending with the death, the replacement property was owned by the transferee and occupied (by him or another) for the purposes of agriculture; and

(iv)   the replacement property is agricultural property immediately before the death.

If the transferor dies before the transferee and all or part of the original property has been disposed of before the transferor's death (or is subject to a binding contract for sale at that time) then if the replacement property is acquired (or a binding contract entered into) after the transferor's death but within the 'allowed period' after the disposal of the original property, or part, conditions (i) and (iii) above do not apply and any reference to a time immediately before the transferor's death is taken as a reference to the time when the replacement property is acquired.

Where any shares owned by the transferee immediately before the death would either be identified with the replacement property under the provisions of *TCGA 1992, ss 126–136* (as above) *or* were issued to him in consideration of the transfer of agricultural property consisting of the replacement property (or part), his period of ownership of the original property is treated as including his period of ownership of the shares (in relation to transfers of value made, and other events occurring, before 17 March 1987 the shares were treated as if they were the original property (or part)).

Where a binding contract for the disposal is entered into at any time before the disposal of the property, the disposal is regarded as taking place at that time.

'Allowed period' means the period of three years or such longer period as the Board may allow. In relation to transfers of value made, and other events occurring, before 30 November 1993, the legislation effectively provided for the allowed period to be twelve months. [*IHTA 1984, ss 124A, 124B; FA 1986, Sch 19 para 22; FA 1987, s 58, Sch 8 para 9; FA 1994, s 247(2)(3)*]. The three-year (or longer) allowed period will apply not only to transfers of value made after 29 November 1993 but also to charges or further charges to IHT arising on a death after that date in respect of a transfer of value made before 30 November 1993 (HMRC response in ICAEW Faculty of Taxation Memorandum TAX 9/94).

Where agricultural property which is a farming business is replaced shortly before the owner's death by non-agricultural business property the period of ownership of the original property will be relevant for applying the minimum ownership condition to the replacement property. If all the conditions for business property relief (see 7 BUSINESS PROPERTY) are satisfied relief will be available on the replacement business property. (HMRC Tax Bulletin December 1994 p 183).

5.4 Agricultural Property

In order to remove doubt that has arisen in the past in determining whether there is a PET or a chargeable transfer, the availability of APR is ignored for the purposes of the further conditions for lifetime transfers. This new subsection applies to any transfer of value on or after 28 November 1995. [*IHTA 1984, s 124A(7A); FA 1996, s 185(4)*].

5.4 SUCCESSIONS AND SUCCESSIVE TRANSFERS

Where property transferred had been inherited on a death, for the purposes of 5.3(*a*) and (*b*) above the transferor is deemed to have owned it (and, if he subsequently occupies it, to have occupied it) from the date of death. If the deceased was the transferor's spouse or civil partner the periods are extended to include any period of occupation or ownership of the spouse or civil partner. [*IHTA 1984, s 120(1); The Tax and Civil Partnership Regulations 2005, SI 2005/3229, Reg 22*]. See also 5.2 Note C above.

Agricultural property which does not satisfy the conditions in 5.3(*a*) or (*b*) above can qualify for relief if all the following conditions are satisfied.

(*a*) All or part of the value transferred by an earlier transfer was eligible for the relief in 5.2 above (or would have been if such relief had been capable of being given at the time of that transfer).

(*b*) All or part of that property became the property of the subsequent transferor or his spouse or civil partner because of the earlier transfer, and at the time of the subsequent transfer it was occupied for the purposes of agriculture by that person or the personal representative of the earlier transferor.

(*c*) That property, or any directly or indirectly replacing it, would otherwise have been eligible for relief were it not for 5.3(*a*) or (*b*) above. If the value transferred by the earlier transfer only partly relates to the property or any replacing it, only the same proportion of the value on the later transfer qualifies for relief.

(*d*) Either the earlier or the subsequent transfer is a transfer on the death of the transferor.

Where the property eligible for relief above replaced the property or part referred to in (*c*) above, relief is limited to what it would have been if any one or more of the replacements had not taken place. For this purpose, changes resulting from the formation, alteration or dissolution of a partnership are disregarded. [*IHTA 1984, s 121; The Tax and Civil Partnership Regulations 2005, SI 2005/3229, Reg 23*].

5.5 SHARES ETC. IN AGRICULTURAL COMPANIES

The transfer of shares or securities in a company may attract relief if

(*a*) agricultural property forms part of the company's assets and part of the value of the shares or securities can be attributable to the agricultural value of the property; and

(*b*) the shares or securities gave control of the company to the transferor immediately before the transfer. For 'control' see 35.4 PAYMENT OF TAX. If their value is reduced under the rules relating to sales of related property within three years after death (see 56.18 VALUATION) the shares or securities must be sufficient, without any other property, to give control; and

(*c*) either

(i) the agricultural property was occupied by the company for the purposes of agriculture throughout the period of two years ending with the date of the transfer and the shares or securities were owned by the transferor throughout that period; or

(ii) the agricultural property was owned by the company throughout the period of seven years ending with that date and was throughout that period occupied (by the company or another) for the purposes of agriculture *and* the shares or securities were owned by the transferor throughout that period.

Example

AC Ltd is an unquoted agricultural company of which A owns 60% of the shares.

	£
The company owns	
4,000 acres of land – agricultural value	4M
Other trading assets (net)	2M
Total value of company	£6M
A's shareholding is valued at	£4.5M

All necessary conditions for relief are satisfied.

If A were to die in, say, November 2007 the position as regards his shareholding would be as follows

	Total Value £	Land £	Other Assets £
Value of assets of company	£6M	£4M	£2M
Value of shares, split in same proportions	£4.5M	£3M	£1.5M
Agricultural property relief (100% of £3M)	(3.0M)		
Business property relief (100% of £1.5M)	(1.5M)		
Chargeable to IHT	Nil		

Note to the example

(A)   The legislation appears to require that both agricultural property relief and business property relief be given, each against its appropriate part of the value. [*IHTA 1984, s 114*]. When some of the land owned by the company is tenanted and attracts only 50% agricultural property relief, the total relief given will be less than would be the case if business property relief at 100% were given on the whole value.

Where the transferred shares etc. replaced other eligible property (i.e. either agricultural property, or shares etc. the value of which is wholly or partly attributable to agricultural property), the conditions regarding the transferor's period of ownership of the shares etc. are treated as satisfied if the transferor owned the shares etc. and the other eligible property which preceded it for at least two of the last five years in the case of (i) above and at least seven of the last ten years in the case of (ii) above.

The provisions relating to replacements of agricultural property at 5.3 above also apply to agricultural shares etc.

Notes

(A)   For the purposes of 5.2(A)(I) and 5.2(A)(II)(3) above the transferor's interest in agricultural property means the company's interest.

(B)   For the purposes of (*c*) above the company is treated as occupying land at any time when it was occupied by a person who subsequently controls the company.

[*IHTA 1984, ss 122, 123*].

5.6   **GRANTS OF AGRICULTURAL TENANCIES**

The grant of a tenancy of agricultural property in the United Kingdom, Channel Islands or Isle of Man for use for agricultural purposes is not a transfer of value if made for full consideration in money or money's worth. [*IHTA 1984, s 16*]. See also 56.2 VALUATION.

5.7   **SCOTTISH AGRICULTURAL LEASES**

Scottish agricultural leases: fixed terms. Where on a person's death any part of the value of his estate is attributable to the interest of a tenant in *an unexpired portion of a lease* for a fixed term of agricultural property in Scotland, any value associated with any prospect of renewal of the lease by tacit relocation is left out of account, provided either he had been tenant of that property for at least two years immediately preceding his death or he had become tenant of that property by succession. [*IHTA 1984, s 177(1)(3)*].

Scottish agricultural leases: tacit relocation. Where on a person's death any part of the value of his estate is attributable to the value of the interest of a tenant of agricultural property in Scotland *held by virtue of tacit relocation* (i.e. on a year to year basis), and the interest is acquired at his death by a new tenant, the value of that interest is left out of account, provided either he had been tenant of that property for at least two years immediately preceding his death or he had become tenant of that property by succession. The value to be left out of account does not include the value of any rights to compensation in respect of tenant's improvements. [*IHTA 1984, s 177(2)–(4)*]. See also 56.2 VALUATION.

5.8   **FOOT AND MOUTH**

The incidence of foot and mouth disease throughout the United Kingdom in the earlier part of 2001 and 2007 had an impact on the farming community resulting in the deferment of payment of tax and interest. See 27.4 INTEREST ON TAX. In a number of situations the deferral of tax as a result of the foot and mouth outbreak resulted in the late payment of inheritance tax and the consequent interest charge was not payable. [*FA 2001, s 107(1)*]. See also 33.3 NATIONAL HERITAGE.

5.9   **WILL PLANNING FOR AGRICULTURAL PROPERTY**

Where a farming business is to be left on death to beneficiaries there will be certain periods when the farm will be under the management of the executors or trustees. There are a number of factors that should be borne in mind with regard to such a situation, It must be remembered that the agricultural property (and business property) must be specifically gifted to the person concerned to qualify for the APR (and BPR where relevant). A legacy payable out of the property is not a specific gift and does not qualify. It should be incumbent on the will drafter to ensure that the executors or trustees have full power to run and manage the farm or have the powers to engage a manager to run the business. The Society of Trust and Estate Practitioners standard provisions do not include these powers. Therefore when drafting the will the executors or trustees, where a will trust is involved, should include powers to trade, delegate, manage etc. This might be on the following basis with regard to a will trust for a farming enterprise:

IN WITNESS etc

FIRST SCHEDULE

The Property

[Here identify the Property]

SECOND SCHEDULE

The Initial Settled Property

[Here specify the property that has been transferred to the Original Trustees.]

THIRD SCHEDULE

Additional administrative powers

The Trustees have the following additional powers:

---

1.   *Investment.* The Trustees may invest Trust Property in any manner as if they were beneficial owners. In particular the Trustees may invest in property in any part of the world and in unsecured loans. The Trustees are under no obligation to diversify the Trust Fund. The Trustees may invest in speculative or hazardous investments.

2.   *Joint Property.* The Trustees may acquire property jointly with any Person and may blend Trust Property with other property.

3.   *General Power of Management and Disposition:* The Trustees may effect any transaction relating to the management or disposition of Trust Property as if they were beneficial owners. The Trustees shall have power to employ serv-ants and independent contractors and to purchase plant and equipment in connection with any trade or business or the management of any property.

4.   *Delegation;* A Trustee may delegate in writing any of his functions to any Person. A Trustee shall not be responsible for the default of that Person (even if the delegation was not strictly necessary or expedient) provided that he took reasonable care in his selection and supervision.

5.   *Trade:* The Trustees may carry on a trade, in any part of the world, alone or in partnership.

6.   *Nominees:* The Trustees may vest Trust Property in any Person as nominee, and may place Trust Property in the possession or control of any Person. The Trustees may have the power to employ and remunerate a nominee or nomi-nees in any part of the world to hold any property subject to the trusts hereof.

The Schedule continues with other administrative powers.

A situation may arise where the farmer wishes to leave the farm and agricultural land to the wife to manage and then pass on to the children but by doing so would not benefit from the 100% APR as the gift/willed assets would in any case be exempt due to the inter spouse or civil partner exemption. If there are other non-agricultural/business assets that do not attract any relief an option may be to leave the farm and agricultural land to the children and the other assets to the wife as in the example below.

5.9 Agricultural Property

Example

Farmer A, who is married to W and has a daughter D, is the freehold owner of a farm and agricultural land which at current vacant possession value is estimated to be valued at £850,000. On 29 September 2007 A dies and leaves by his will the farm and agricultural property and his other assets including investments valued at £1.25 million into a two-year discretionary trust. There are specific powers in the will to appoint out before grant. Within the two-year period but not before the first three months have expired the Trustees appoint out of the trust £300,000 in cash and the farm to the daughter D. W is appointed £950,000 in cash and investments. After a period D sells the farm to W who pays for it out of part of the assets inherited from her late husband A as follows:

STEP 1

Daughter (D)	£
Transfer of farm by appointment from trust	850,000
Deduct agricultural property relief	850,000
IHT payable	NIL

Transfer of cash by appointment from trust	300,000
Deduct nil rate band	300,000
IHT payable	NIL

Wife (W)	£
Transfer of cash/investments by appointment from trust	950,000
Deduct inter-spouse/civil partner exemption	950,000
IHT payable	NIL

STEP 2	Assets
D	£
Cash for farm	850,000
Original nil rate band transfer	300,000
IHT payable	NIL

W	£
Farm	850,000
Balance of original inter-spouse/civil partner transfer	100,000
IHT payable	NIL

Notes to the example

(A) The Stamp Duty Land Tax implications have not been addressed here and this potential charge must be weighed up with the potential saving in IHT, i.e. £330,000 (£1,125,000 – 300,000 × 40%) if the cash and investments to the value of the farm and the Nil rate band had initially been left to D instead and the farm to the wife together with the balance of cash of £100,000. [*FA 2003, s 55(2)*].

(B) A transfer on death by W, assuming she will die first and has been farming the land for two years, to D of the farm and the assets of £100,000 of cash and investments will be covered by APR and part of the Nil rate band.

(C)   There may be a concern that the daughter may not wish to sell the farm to W but it must be in the daughter's own interests as any subsequent gift by W to D during lifetime or on death could incur IHT of up to £260,000 (£950,000 – 300,000 × 40%) if this does not happen.

(D)   In a case where, for example, a deceased's estate has a farm that would qualify for APR which is left to the wife and a share portfolio that would be taxable and is left to the daughter, a deed of variation may be entered into whereby there is an exchange of assets under *IHTA 1984, s 142(1)* i.e. '... the making, in respect of another of the dispositions, of a variation ...' so that the wife receives the share portfolio and the daughter receives the farm, each being exempt. In any other case a transfer, such as the one in the example above, by deed of variation might constitute transfers for any consideration, including consideration less than full consideration, which would be ineffective under *IHTA 1984, s 142(1)(3)*. See also 14.2 and 14.3 DEEDS OF VARIA-TION.

5.9   Agricultural Property

Revenue
Inland
Capital Taxes

Agricultural Relief

Name

Date of death

/   /

You have deducted agricultural relief on form IHT200. Answer the following questions and give the further details we ask for. If necessary, fill in a separate form for each item of property. You should read form D13(Notes) before filling in this form.

1   What is the address of the property concerned?

2a   Did the deceased occupy the property for the purposes of agriculture *throughout* the 2 years up to the date of death?

No   Yes

If the answer is "Yes" go to question 3 and ignore question 5. If "No", go to question 2b.

2b   Was the whole of the property owned by the deceased and occupied for agricultural purposes *throughout* the 7 years up to the date of death?

No   Yes

If the answer is "Yes", go to question 3 and ignore question 4. If "No", go to question 2c.

2c   As you have answered "No" to questions 2a and 2b, agricultural relief would not normally be available. If you feel the relief should be due, say why below.

3   When and how did the deceased acquire the property?

4   Describe the nature and extent of the agricultural operations carried out by the deceased.

5a   Who occupied the property during the 7 years up to the date of death?

5b   Describe the nature and extent of the agricultural operations carried out on the land

D13   www.hmrc.gov.uk/cto   Helpline 0845 30 20 900   **Please turn over**
R0K 4274 IRCT 12/02
(Substitute)(LexisNexis Butterworths)

5c Provide a copy of any lease, tenancy or other proprietary interest that applied to the property immediately before the deceased died. If there is nothing in writing, give details below. If the tenancy began after 31 August 1995, you need only give the date the tenancy started.

6 Did the deceased have the right to vacant possession immediately before the death, or the right to obtain it within 24 months?   No ☐ Yes ☐

If the answer is "Yes" say how the deceased would have been able to obtain vacant possession. If the answer is "No", but you feel relief is due at the higher rate, say why below.

7 Who occupied any farmhouse and buildings or cottage at the property and what was the nature of the occupation? Provide details for each building separately.

8 Was the property, or any part of it, subject to a binding contract for sale at the date of death?   No ☐ Yes ☐

If the answer is "'Yes", give details of the contract below

9 *Only answer question 9 if you are claiming agricultural relief in connection with a lifetime transfer.*

9a Was the property agricultural property immediately before the end of the relevant period?   No ☐ Yes ☐

9b Was the property owned by the person who received the gift throughout the relevant period?   No ☐ Yes ☐

9c Was the property occupied (by the person who received the gift or by someone else) for agricultural purposes *throughout* the relevant period?   No ☐ Yes ☐

9d Was the property subject to a binding contract for sale immediately before the end of the relevant period?   No ☐ Yes ☐

6 Anti-Avoidance

Cross-references. See 12.5 CLOSE COMPANIES; 21.16 EXEMPT TRANSFERS; 22 GIFTS WITH RESERVATION; 29.2 LIABILITY FOR TAX; 30.3 LIFE ASSURANCE POLICIES AND ANNUITIES; 39 PROTECTIVE TRUSTS; 43.5 SETTLEMENTS WITH INTERESTS IN POSSESSION; 44.10 and 44.16 SETTLEMENTS WITHOUT INTERESTS IN POSSESSION; 56.17 VALUATION.

Simon's Direct Tax Service, parts I2.2, I3.7.

Other Sources. Tolley's Income Tax 2007–08; IHTM09151 *et seq.*

6.1 APPROACH OF THE COURTS

For the general approach of the Courts to transactions entered into solely to avoid or reduce tax liability, leading cases are *Duke of Westminster v CIR HL 1935, 19 TC 490; W T Ramsay Ltd v CIR, Eilbeck v Rawling HL 1981, 54 TC 101; CIR v Burmah Oil Co. Ltd HL 1981, 54 TC 200; Furniss v Dawson (and related appeals) HL 1984, 55 TC 324.* See also *Coates v Arndale Properties Ltd HL 1984, 59 TC 516; Reed v Nova Securities Ltd HL 1985, 59 TC 516; Magnavox Electronics Co. Ltd (in liquidation) v Hall CA 1986, 59 TC 610; Commr of Inland Revenue v Challenge Corporation Ltd PC, [1986] STC 548; Craven v White; Baylis v Gregory HL 1988, 62 TC 1; Dunstan v Young Austen Young Ltd CA 1988, 61 TC 448; Shepherd v Lyntress Ltd; News International plc v Shepherd Ch D 1989, 62 TC 495; Hatton v CIR (and related appeals) Ch D, [1992] STC 140; Moodie v CIR and another (and related appeal) HL, [1993] STC 188; Countess Fitzwilliam and others v CIR (and related appeals) HL, [1993] STC 502; Ingram and another (Executors of the estate of Lady Ingram deceased) v CIR HL [1999] STC 37; MacNiven v Westmoreland Investments Ltd, HL [2001] STC 237; Mawson v Barclays Mercantile Business Finance Ltd (aka ABC Ltd v M), HL 2004, 76 TC 446; [2005] STC 1; [2004] UKHL 51; [2005] 1 All ER 97; CIR v Scottish Provident Institution, HL 2004, 76 TC 538; [2005] STC 15; [2004] UKHL 52; [2005] 1 All ER 325.*

The classical interpretation of the constraints upon the Courts in deciding cases involving tax avoidance schemes is summed up in Lord Tomlin's statement in the *Duke of Westminster* case that 'every man is entitled if he can to order his affairs so that the tax attaching … is less than it otherwise would be'. The judgment was concerned with the tax consequences of a single transaction, but in *Ramsay*, and subsequently in *Furniss v Dawson*, the House of Lords has set bounds on the ambit within which this principle can be applied in relation to modern sophisticated and increasingly artificial arrangements to avoid tax. *Ramsay* concerned a complex 'circular' avoidance scheme at the end of which the financial position of the parties was little changed but it was claimed that a large capital gains tax loss had been created. It was held that where a preconceived series of transactions is entered into to avoid tax and with the clear intention to proceed through all stages to completion, once set in motion, the *Duke of Westminster* principle does not compel a consideration of the individual transactions and of the fiscal consequences of such transactions in isolation. The opinions of the House of Lords in *Furniss v Dawson* are of outstanding importance, and establish, *inter alia*, that the *Ramsay* principle is not confined to 'circular' devices, and that if a series of transactions is 'preordained', a particular transaction within the series, accepted as genuine, may nevertheless be ignored if it was entered into solely for fiscal reasons and without any commercial purpose other than tax avoidance, even if the series of transactions as a whole has a legitimate commercial purpose. However, in *Craven v White* the House of Lords indicated that for the *Ramsay* principle to apply all the transactions in a series have to be preordained with such a degree of certainty that, at the time of the earlier transactions, there is no practical likelihood that the transactions would not take place. It is not sufficient that the ultimate transaction is simply of a kind that was envisaged at the time of the earlier transactions.

Countess Fitzwilliam and others v CIR is the first case in which the question of the application of the *Ramsay* principle to transactions entered into with a view to the avoidance of inheritance tax (or, more strictly, its predecessor, capital transfer tax) has arisen. The trustees of a will trust (who included the deceased's widow F and her daughter H) were empowered to appoint within 23 months of the death of the deceased (which occurred in September 1979) the residue of the estate amongst a class of beneficiaries which included F (then aged 81) and H. In order to avoid a heavy charge to tax on an appointment directly to H or, should an appointment be made to F, on her death when it was envisaged she would make H the beneficiary of her own will, a complex five-step scheme was entered into by F, H and the trustees ('the taxpayers'). It was claimed by the taxpayers that the five steps, the first of which took place on 20 December 1979 and the last on 7 February 1980, should be viewed separately with the result that by reason of a number of available reliefs (some of which still have application to inheritance tax) no liability to capital transfer tax arose. The former Inland Revenue issued notices of determination claiming that the five steps constituted a preordained single composite transaction effected to avoid tax and that *Ramsay* applied to permit a charge to tax on the deceased's estate on the basis of appointments directly to F and H.

The Special Commissioners (who, it was pointed out in the subsequent House of Lords' judgment, gave their determination prior to the House of Lords' decision in *Craven v White*) found for the Revenue, but this was rejected in both the Chancery Division and the Court of Appeal on the grounds that the only true and reasonable conclusion from the facts found by the Commissioners was contrary to their conclusion that the five steps formed a preordained series of transactions. In the House of Lords the Revenue accepted that step 1 did not form part of such a series but argued that the steps 2 to 5 did. The leading judgment in the House of Lords stated that the correct approach to a consideration of steps 2 to 5 was to ask whether realistically they constituted a single and indivisible whole in which one or more of the steps was simply an element without independent effect and whether it was intellectually possible so to treat them. It was held that both questions should be answered in the negative. The case put by the Revenue did not depend on disregarding for fiscal purposes any one or more of steps 2 to 5 as having been introduced for fiscal purposes only and as having no independent effect, nor on treating the whole of steps 2 to 5 as having no such effect. Each of the four steps had a fiscal effect of giving rise to an income tax charge on F or H for a period of time, and there was a potential capital transfer tax charge should either have died whilst in enjoyment of the income. Although steps 2 to 5 were 'preordained', in the sense that they formed part of a pre-planned tax avoidance scheme and that there was no reasonable possibility that they would not all be carried out, the fact of preordainment in that sense was not sufficient in itself to negative the application of an exemption from liability to tax which the series of transactions was intended to create, unless the series was capable of being construed in a manner inconsistent with the application of the exemption. In the particular circumstances of the case, the series of transactions could not be so construed. Two or more transactions in the series could not be run together, as in *Furniss v Dawson*, nor could any one or more of them be disregarded. There was no rational basis on which the four separate steps could be treated as effective for the purposes of one provision which created a charge to tax on a termination of an interest in possession but ineffective for the purposes of two other provisions which gave exemptions from that charge where the interest was disposed of for a consideration and where the interest reverted to the settlor. Accordingly, the case was one to which the *Ramsay* principle, as extended by *Furniss v Dawson*, did not apply.

In *Hatton*, a scheme to avoid tax, which bore some similarity to that in *Fitzwilliam*, was found by the Special Commissioners and Chancery Division to be preordained and one to which the *Ramsay* principle applied (although it should be noted that the Chancery Division judgment in the case was given prior to the judgments of the Court of Appeal and House of Lords in *Fitzwilliam*).

In the decision by the House of Lords in the *Ingram* case concerning a tax avoidance scheme Lord Hoffman stated 'The scope of the Ramsay principle does not arise and I

6.1 Anti-Avoidance

therefore prefer to say nothing about it.' Concerned at an outflow of funds from the Treasury, the former Inland Revenue sought to block this avoidance scheme by introducing legislation in *FA 1999, s 104* to combat any further loophole in the legislation. See Tolley's Inheritance Tax 1999 Post Budget Supplement for the full text of the decision in the *Ingram* case.

For an indication of the then Inland Revenue practice as to the application of the principles established in decided cases up to and including *Furniss v Dawson* to certain types of transfers, see ICAEW Guidance Note TR 588, 25 September 1985.

In the 2001 case of *MacNiven v Westmoreland Investments Ltd, HL [2001] STC 237* where the HL held that the '*Ramsay* principle' did not apply to a payment of interest, Lord Nicholls held that 'the very phrase "the *Ramsay* principle" is potentially misleading. In *Ramsay* the House did not enunciate any new legal principle. What the House did was to highlight that, confronted with new and sophisticated tax avoidance devices, the courts' duty is to determine the legal nature of the transactions in question and then relate them to the fiscal legislation'. Lord Hoffmann held that 'what Lord Wilberforce was doing in the *Ramsay* case was no more ... than to treat the statutory words "loss" and "disposal" as referring to commercial concepts to which a juristic analysis of the transaction, treating each step as autonomous and independent, might not be determinative'. Lord Hutton held that 'an essential element of a transaction to which the *Ramsay* principle is applicable is that it should be artificial'.

In another case *Melville v CIR [2000] STC 628; Ch D [2000] All ER(D) 832; CA [2001] STC 1271* the Court of Appeal held that powers over trusts are potential 'property' for inheritance tax purposes. This had the effect of creating an avoidance of IHT liability when used as part of an avoidance scheme because the holder of the power had effective dominion over the settled property, if he chose to exercise it. A power was different in character from a reversionary interest and in the *Melville* case clause 4(c) stated:

> 'The Settlor shall have power exercisable during his lifetime at any time or times after the Relevant Day and before the Vesting Day by deed or deeds to direct the Trustees to exercise any one or more of the powers conferred by sub-clause (a) above in such manner as shall be specified in such deed. And it is hereby declared that the Trustees shall forthwith exercise such power or powers accordingly (and for the avoidance of doubt the Settlor shall have power to direct the Trustees to transfer the whole of the trust fund to the Settlor absolutely freed and discharged from the trust powers and provisions of this settlement and join with the Settlor in making a claim to the [Inland Revenue] for hold-over relief from capital gains tax pursuant to section 260 of the Taxation of Chargeable Gains Act 1992 in respect of any assets thereby disposed of by the Trustees to the Settlor).'

The above clause was not exercisable in the first 90 days of the settlement but once that period was over the power became presently exercisable and was even less like a reversionary interest because there was nothing in *IHTA 1984* to suggest that a general power was a reversionary interest. The holder of a general power of appointment therefore had a valuable right, the value of which had to be taken into account in the holder's estate under *IHTA 1984, s 5(1)* unless excluded by some other provision. There was nothing in the settled property provisions which caused the power to be excluded property or prevented it from being a valuable right or interest to be included in the settlor's estate. Whilst in the case instant the decision had the effect of avoiding an IHT charge on the setting up of the discretionary settlement. However, this decision could have resulted in other cases in 'double counting' because the person entitled to an interest in possession in the settled property would have been treated as beneficially entitled and the general power of appointment would be property of the appointor's estate. This creation of unexpected liabilities where powers are created on the previously understood view that they were not 'property' for IHT purposes was one of the reasons that *IHTA 1984, s 47A inserted by FA 2002, s 119* defines a settlement power as any power over, or exercisable (whether directly or indirectly) in relation to, settled property or a settlement. However, for deaths on or before 16 April 2002 it disapplies charges on those earlier deaths which might have otherwise arisen from the stated side effects of the decision arising out of the *Melville* case. It appears therefore that the unintended effect of the decision which benefited the *Melville* case has given birth to anti-avoidance legislation that now benefits both taxpayers generally and the then Inland Revenue!

6.2   **LEGISLATION**

Anti-avoidance legislation is intended to counteract transactions designed to avoid taxation but *bona fide* transactions may sometimes be caught also. Because anti-avoidance legislation is often not formally designated as such it follows that it must be a matter of opinion whether any provision not so designated was enacted for anti-avoidance purposes. In the case, lost by the former Inland Revenue in the Court of Appeal, *CIR v Eversden and another (executors of Greenstock deceased) CA, [2003] STC 822*, a loophole within (*d*) below was declared as such by the IR and blocked with immediate effect from 20 June 2003 by legislation (*FA 1986, s 102(5A)–(5C) as amended by FA 2003, s 185*) because

> 'Ministers are aware of significant activity marketing schemes seeking to exploit this weakness and have introduced this new clause to curtail further loss to the Exchequer.'

Inland Revenue Press Release, 20 June 2003 'Corporation Tax & Inheritance Tax: Blocking Tax Avoidance'. See also a detailed exposition in Taxation Magazine 11 September 2003, pages 634–637.

In the *Eversden* case (see 60 TAX CASES) the strategy was effected by the husband making a gift into trust under which the wife took an initial interest in possession for life or six months, whichever was the shorter. Alternatively, the trustees of the settlement can be given wide powers to terminate the life interest and appoint on varied trusts. Husband and wife are capable of benefiting in a reversionary interest by being added as potential beneficiaries and without the gifts with reservation rules applying. Although the settlor will in these circumstances almost certainly have made a gift, the gifts with reservation rules in *FA 1986, s 102* did not apply as it was excluded by *FA 1986, s 102(5A)* with respect to the inter-spouse/civil partner exemption i.e. *IHTA 1984, s 18*. The settlor and wife were able therefore to reserve whatever benefits over the settled property as required. The exemption by *FA 1986, s 102(5A)* came into play only if the gift in settlement constituted a transfer of value and one which was exempt by virtue of the spousal exemption.

On occasions where a scheme of avoidance has been incorrectly drafted it may be set aside by applying *dicta* of Millett J in *Gibbon v Mitchell, Ch D [1990] 3 All ER 338*, 'wherever there is a voluntary transaction by which one party intends to confer a bounty on another, the deed will be set aside if the court is satisfied that the disponor did not intend the transaction to have the effect which it did'. In *Wolff & Wolff v Wolff and Others Ch D, [2004] STC 1633* a married couple owned a freehold property. They sought advice from a solicitor with a view to avoiding inheritance tax. On the solicitor's advice, in 1997 they entered into a reversionary lease of the property in favour of their daughters, to begin in 2017. Subsequently they became aware that the effect of the lease was that they would have no right to remain in the property after 2017. They applied to the Chancery Division to set aside the reversionary lease under the *Civil Procedure Rules 1998, SI 1998/3132, Part 8.* The Ch D granted their application. Mann J observed that the relevant deed was 'manifestly defective as a piece of drafting' and that the solicitor 'did not fully understand the implications of what he had brought about'. On the evidence, the couple 'did not know that the effect of the lease was to deprive them of their right to occupy the property in 2017'.

Accordingly, the following anti-avoidance provisions relating to inheritance tax include some which have not been formally so designated but have been selected from the legislation as being broadly of an anti-avoidance nature.

6.3   Anti-Avoidance

(*a*)   **Associated operations.** See 6.3 below.

(*b*)   **Close companies.** See 12.2 and 12.5 CLOSE COMPANIES.

(*c*)   **Exempt transfers.** See 21.8 for transfers between spouses/civil partners and 21.16 EXEMPT TRANSFERS for abatement of certain exemptions on death.

(*d*)   **Gifts with reservation.** See 22 GIFTS WITH RESERVATION.

(*e*)   **Liability for tax of transferor's spouse/civil partner.** See 29.2 LIABILITY FOR TAX.

(*f*)   **Annuity purchased in conjunction with life policy.** See 30.3 LIFE ASSURANCE POLICIES AND ANNUITIES.

(*g*)   **Protective trusts.** See 39 PROTECTIVE TRUSTS.

(*h*)   **Termination of an interest in possession.** See 43.3–43.5 SETTLEMENTS WITH INTERESTS IN POSSESSION.

(*i*)   **Initial interest of settlor or spouse/civil partner and property moving between settlements.** See 44.15 and 44.16 SETTLEMENTS WITHOUT INTERESTS IN POSSESSION.

(*j*)   **Related property.** See 56.17 VALUATION.

(*k*)   **Excluded property settlements.** See 20.2 and 20.10 EXCLUDED PROPERTY.

(*l*)   **Funds in alternatively secured pensions.** See 37.2 PENSION SCHEMES.

6.3   **ASSOCIATED OPERATIONS**

If inheritance tax applied only to each separate transaction, it would be possible to split some transfers of value into several parts, the sum of which was less than the total value actually transferred. To counter this, the separate transactions are treated as 'associated operations' which together comprise one transfer of value. But see *Rysaffe Trustee Co (CI) Ltd v CIR [2001] STC SCD 225 Sp C 290; [2002] STC 872; CA [2003] EWCA Civ 356.*

'*Associated operations*' are any two or more operations of any kind by the same person or different persons and whether simultaneous or not

(*a*)   which affect the same property, or one of which affects some property while the other or others affect property which represents, whether directly or indirectly, that property, or income arising from that property, or any property representing accumulations of any such income, or

(*b*)   where one operation is effected with reference to a second or with a view to enabling the other to be effected or facilitating its being effected, and any further operation having a like relation to any of those two, and so on.

'*Operation*' includes an omission.

Where a transfer of value is made by associated operations carried out at different times it shall be treated as made at the time of the last of them. The transfer of value is reduced by the value transferred by any earlier operations which were also transfers of value by the same transferor, except to the extent that the transfer made by earlier operations, but not the operations as a whole, was covered by the exemption for transfers between spouses/civil partners (see 21.8 EXEMPT TRANSFERS). [*IHTA 1984, s 268(1)(3)*].

Example 1

H owns a set of four Chippendale chairs valued, as a set, at £6,000. Individually they would be valued at only £1,000, although a pair would be worth £2,500 and three £4,000.

He gives one chair to his son each year over four years, during which time all values increase at 10% p.a. (simple). In the fifth year H dies.

	£	£
Year 1		
Value of four chairs	6,000	
Deduct value of three	4,000	
Value transferred		2,000
Year 2		
Basic computation ignoring the associated operations rule		
Current value of three chairs	4,400	
Deduct value of two	2,750	
Value transferred	£1,650	
Revised to take account of associated operations rule		
Current value of four chairs	6,600	
Deduct value of two	2,750	
	3,850	
Deduct value transferred in Year 1	2,000	
		1,850
Year 3		
Current value of four chairs	7,200	
Deduct value of one	1,200	
	6,000	
Deduct value transferred in Years 1 and 2	3,850	
		2,150
Year 4		
Current value of four chairs	7,800	
Deduct value transferred in Years 1, 2 and 3	6,000	
Value transferred		1,800
Total values transferred		£7,800

The following are *not* associated operations.

(i)   The granting of a lease for full consideration with any operation effected more than three years later.

(ii)   An operation effected on or after 27 March 1974 with any operation before that date. [*IHTA 1984, s 268(2)*].

See *CIR v Macpherson and Another, HL 1988 [1988] STC 362* where, by a majority decision, on the special facts of the case a commercial agreement (involving custody of paintings), which both facilitated an appointment made the following day and reduced the value of the property so appointed, was regarded as an operation associated with the appointment. See also *Reynaud & Others v CIR [1999] STC SCD 185 Sp C 196* where the transfer of shares in a company into a discretionary trust and the subsequent purchase by that company of its own shares was not a disposition affected by the associated operations rules.

6.3 Anti-Avoidance

In practice, HMRC will not use the associated operation provisions where a husband shares capital with his wife who 'chooses to make gifts out of the money she has received from her husband', unless it is a blatant case of a husband's gift to his wife made on condition that she should at once use the money to make gifts to others. (Official Report, Standing Committee A 13 February 1975 Col 1596). See also IHTM11091.

Example 2

If in the example above H had wished to give away the chairs over two years instead of four, he might first have given two chairs to his wife (exempt), so that each could give the son one chair each year.

	Year 1	£	£
(i)	Value transferred by husband to son		
	Value of two chairs (as half of a set of four linked by the related property rule)	3,000	
	Deduct value of one chair (as half of a pair)	1,250	
			1,750
(ii)	Value transferred by wife (similar calculation)		1,750

	Year 2		
	Value transferred by husband, applying the associated operations rule		
	Current value of four chairs	6,600	
	Deduct value transferred in Year 1 by H and W	3,500	
	Value transferred		3,100
	Total values transferred		£6,600

Notes to the example

(A) In this case, the total of the values transferred can exceed the value of the assets, although it must be doubtful whether the HMRC would seek to apply the full rigours of the section unless the transfer by the wife in Year 1 had fallen within her annual exemptions, or she had survived seven years so that the gift was exempt.

(B) See *IHTA 1984, s 161* for the related property rule, and see also 56.17 VALUATION.

(C) The result above could have been achieved in another way. The first transfer by the husband to his spouse is quantified at £3,000 – the second to the son is quantified at £1,750 as in the example. If through *section 268* one looks at the position as if the transfer of value was made on the last of the operations, the calculation would be:

Value in H's estate before any transfer
(i.e. value of 4 chairs at the date of last transfer   £6,600
Value in husband's estate after all transfers   Nil

Value transferred   £6,600
Deduct value of earlier operations:
Transfer to wife disregarded *s 268(3)*   Nil
Transfer to son   £1,750

Value transferred   £4,850

So the value transferred is £1,750 + £4,850 = £6,600. HMRC Inheritance Tax would not seek to raise a charge to tax on the actual transfers by the wife to the son.

The CTO may ask the DV for the value effectively transferred by one transfer being the last of a series of associated operations. If any of the earlier operations were themselves transfers of value, other than transfers between spouses/civil partners [*IHTA 1984, s 18*], then the adjustment will be dealt with by the CTO.

If the DV is aware from his office records that a transfer is an associated operation and the CTO has not referred to it then the papers should be returned to the CTO by the DV explaining the situation and to await further instructions. (VOA IHT manual, section 4, paras 4.40 and 4.41). See http://www.voa.gov.uk/instructions/chapters/inheritance_tax_ch_1b/sections/section_4/frame.htm.

6.4   **PRE-OWNED ASSETS**

Further anti-avoidance measures apply from 6 April 2005 which were introduced following a short consultation period (consultation document 'The Tax Treatment of Pre-Owned Assets') to counteract the free continuing use of assets that have been ostensibly gifted. HMRC's original consultative document concentrated mainly on a charge to income tax, under the former Schedule D Case VI [now see *ITTOIA 2005*], on former owners of assets on the benefit of using the asset(s) unless the asset has been sold to an unconnected party at arm's length. A subsequent consultative document issued on 18 August 2004 'Taxation of Pre-Owned Assets: Further Consultation' sought views of interested parties on matters to be covered by regulations. A Technical Guidance Note was subsequently issued on 17 March 2005 with further clarification in June 2005 and June 2006 at http://www.hmrc.gov.uk/poa/poa_news.htm. See also 59.42 WORKING CASE STUDY. It appears that this anti-avoidance has been instigated because of the large amount of tax that has been, and is likely to be, lost through for example the 'double trust' home loan schemes, successful *Eversden* structures (see above) and chattels that are gifted and then rented back under *FA 1986, Sch 20 para 6(1)(a)*. See also 59.40 WORKING CASE STUDY. The income tax charge is to be applied in respect of any benefit received in chargeable circumstances in the initial year of assessment or thereafter, but donor(s) will not be chargeable if the scheme is dismantled, or the donor(s) decides to pay a full market rent. This anti-avoidance legislation institutes latent retrospective taxation and applies to existing arrangements that have been in place for many years as well as future arrangements. The income tax charge can apply to assets in circumstances where the user of the asset does not own it but it was purchased with funds provided by him. Tangible assets e.g. a house or land or chattels, and intangible assets such as life assurance policies will come within the income tax charge. In the case of realty the 'appropriate rental value' is the annual rent equal to the annual value. See 59.40 WORKING CASE STUDY. For chattels the chargeable amount is the interest that would be payable for the taxable period at a prescribed rate on an amount equal to the value of the chattel at the valuation date. In the case of intangible assets the chargeable amount is the interest that would be payable for the taxable period at a prescribed rate on an amount equal to the value of the intangible asset at the valuation date. The prescribed rate is currently 5% and is related to the official rate of interest as defined in *ITEPA 2003, s 181*. In all three cases apportionment applies where the asset is not wholly within the charge due to retained ownership of part of the asset or in relation to part of the year of assessment by reference to the valuation date. [*FA 2004, Sch 15 paras 4, 7, 9; Charge to Income Tax by Reference to Enjoyment of Property Previously Owned Regulations 2005, SI 2005/724, Regs 2–4*]. See also 56.1 VALUATION. Regulations provide that land and chattels will be valued every five years. In the initial year *FA 2004, Sch 15; Charge to Income Tax by Reference to Enjoyment of Property Previously Owned Regulations 2005, SI 2005/724, Reg 4* applies a valuation will be made and this will apply to the following four succeeding years. In the fifth year *after* the first chargeable year a new valuation will be made on 6 April and this will then apply for that year and the four succeeding years and so on. The actual valuation date for these purposes will be 6 April in the year or if later the commencement of the 'taxable period' when the asset first becomes chargeable. Initially, therefore, the first valuation date may be any date in the tax year from 6 April but subsequent valuation dates after five years have expired will normally be on 6 April. However, no income tax charge will apply where the appropriate amounts for any given tax year is not more than £5,000. See Tolley's Income Tax 2007–08, chapter 4.21.

In order to provide an escape route from incurring the income tax charge detailed above, taxpayers who have existing schemes that come within the charge may elect for special transitional relief that allows them to avoid the charge to income tax by dismantling the original gift scheme. The timing of the election is not tied to a particular date as it is related to the point at which the individual first came within the charge but the latest date for existing schemes was to be 31 January 2007 for 2005/06. [*FA 2004, Sch 15 paras 21, 22 and 23*]. However, *FA 2007* inserted an amendment to the 2004 legislation so that HMRC may allow a later time limit in particular cases that are deemed appropriate. [*FA 2004, Sch 15 para 23(3); FA 2007, s 66*]. See http://www.hmrc.gov.uk/poa/late-election-guidance.htm. This election (see IHT500 below) will then ensure that the asset is treated as part of the individual's taxable estate for IHT purposes while he continues to enjoy the property in accordance with the gifts with reservation rules. Under the gifts with reservation rules the property would be potentially eligible for IHT reliefs and exemptions providing the necessary requirements for those reliefs and exemptions were met. However, it may still, in certain circumstances, be appropriate for the taxpayer to suffer the income tax charge under existing schemes and avoid the IHT charge. See 22.1 GIFTS WITH RESERVATION; 59.40 WORKING CASE STUDY.

In the Pre-Budget Report Statement on 5 December 2005 further anti-avoidance measures regarding the pre-owned assets regime were highlighted for reverter to settlor trusts; it suggests that there is a gap in the legislation so that an owner of an asset can transfer it into a trust but still enjoy the use of the asset. In order to prevent avoidance the pre-owned assets income tax charge will apply from 5 December 2005 to such situations so that where the former owner of an asset (or a person who contributed to its acquisition) enjoys the asset under the terms of the trust, and the trust property may in due course revert to the settlor (or to the spouse, civil partner or the widow, widower or surviving civil partner of the settlor) where an exemption is applicable under *IHTA 1984, ss 53(3)(4), 54(1)(2)* the income tax charge will apply subject to an election for the property to fall back into their estate for IHT purposes. It will apply to all trusts, whenever created, where the property will or could qualify for the reverter to settlor or settlor's spouse/civil partner exemption. See 59.41 WORKING CASE STUDIES. [*IHTA 1984, ss 53(3)(4), 54; FA 2004, Sch 15; FA 2006, s 80*].

The method of election recommended by HMRC is that prescribed in the form IHT500 as follows:

Inland
Revenue
Capital Taxes

Election for Inheritance Tax to apply to asset previously owned

Fill in this form if you are chargeable to income tax on the benefit you receive from property you previously owned but want to elect for the property to be treated as part of your estate for inheritance tax purposes.

You should read the notes in form IHT501 as you fill in this form. Please provide information for all sections, inserting "not applicable" where appropriate.

About the person making the election

Title

Surname

Other name(s)

Date of birth   /   /

Income Tax district and reference

Unique Taxpayer Reference (UTR)

National Insurance number

Address

About the property subject to the election

The property is: an interest in land ☑

a chattel ☐

intangible property ☐

Description of the property

IHT 500 **(Substitute)(LexisNexis Butterworths)**

IR CT Approval ref: L4/05

6.4   Anti-Avoidance

Who are the legal owners of the property?

What is the nature and extent of your interest in the property?

Name(s) of anyone else who receives a benefit from the property

Details of disposal(s) or contribution(s)

Is the property conditionally exempt from IHT or CGT on an earlier event?   Yes ☐   No ☐

If "yes", please provide details

The election

I elect that the property specified above is to form part of my estate for inheritance tax purposes under the provisions of paragraphs 21 to 23, Schedule 15 to the Finance Act 2004.

Signature of person making the election

Capacity

Date

This election applies from the year of Assessment beginning on 6 April

When you have completed this form send it to:

Pre-owned Assets Section
Inland Revenue Capital Taxes
PO Box 38
Castle Meadow Road
Nottingham
NG21BB

**Probate and inheritance tax
Helpline 0845 3020900**

Document Exchange: DX 701201 Nottingham 4.

7   Business Property

Cross-references. See 5 AGRICULTURAL PROPERTY; 6.1 ANTI–AVOIDANCE; 8.5 CALCULATION OF TAX for application of business relief where transfers partly exempt; and 22.7 GIFTS WITH RESERVATION where such a gift is of relevant business property; 59 WORKING CASE STUDY.

Simon's Direct Tax Service, part I7.1.

Other Sources. Tolley's Capital Gains Tax 2007–08; Foster, part G1; Mellows, parts 5.24–5.34; IHTM25000, IHTM18331.

Headings in this chapter are:

Business property relief:		**7.6**	Further conditions
7.1	Introduction	**Nature of business property relief:**	
Conditions for business property relief:		**7.7**	Conditions prior to 6 April 1996
		7.8	Valuation
7.2	Conditions	**7.9**	Settled property with interest in posses-
7.3	Qualifying business		sion
7.4	Relevant business property	**Business property — tax by instalments:**	
7.5	Minimum period of owner-	**7.10**	Conditions
	ship		

7.1   BUSINESS PROPERTY RELIEF

Introduction. Where certain conditions are satisfied, relief from inheritance tax is available on the transfer of 'relevant business property'. The relief is a percentage reduction in the value transferred by the transfer of value (see Table below) and applies to transfers in life and on death and to occasions on which tax is chargeable under the provisions relating to SETTLEMENTS WITHOUT INTERESTS IN POSSESSION (44). It should be noted that unlike agricultural property relief there is no territorial limitation on undertakings entitled to business property relief and therefore can include business situated worldwide. See also Foster on inheritance tax at section G1.11. For the purposes of the relief a company and all its subsidiaries are members of a group and 'holding company' and 'subsidiary' have the same meanings as in the *Companies Act 1985*. [*IHTA 1984, s 103(1)(2), s 104*]. Therefore shares in holding companies which own shares in trading subsidiaries benefit from the relief. However, there are categories of *excepted* assets that are left out of account when calculating whether there is an entitlement to business property relief and reference should be made to these circumstances below. [*IHTA 1984, s 112(2)*].

In relation to transfers of value made, and other events occurring, **after 5 April 1996** qualifying for business property relief (BPR) the relief given is as follows:

(a)	Unincorporated business (7.4(a) below)	**100%**
(b)	Unquoted securities which either by themselves or with other such securities or unquoted shares gave the transferor control (7.4(b) below)	**100%**
(c)	Any unquoted shares in a company not listed on a recognised stock exchange but including those traded in the USM or the AIM or OFFEX markets (7.4(b), (d) below)	**100%**
(d)	Shares or securities giving control of a 'quoted' company (7.4(b) below)	**50%**
(e)	Land, buildings, machinery or plant in a partnership or in a controlled company or in a settlement (but see (7.9) and (7.4(c) below)	**50%**

7.2 Business Property

CONDITIONS FOR BUSINESS PROPERTY RELIEF

The conditions to be satisfied are

(*a*) the business is a qualifying business, see 7.3 below; and

(*b*) the asset must be relevant business property, see 7.4 below; and

(*c*) the asset must have been owned for a minimum period, see 7.5 below.

There are further conditions to be satisfied by lifetime transfers, see 7.6 below.

7.3 **Qualifying business.** '*Business*' includes a business carried on in the exercise of a profession or vocation but does not include a business carried on otherwise than for gain which might include stud farms, painters, sculptors, musicians and many authors. [*IHTA 1984, s 103(3)*]. In contrast, a business would include an on-course bookmaker's 'pitch' because it is 'a serious undertaking earnestly pursued' from 8 October 1999 onwards, which is passed on by inheritance provided the statutory conditions are met. See *C & E Commissioners v Lord Fisher [1981] STC 238* for Ralph Gibson J's six tests on the factors to be considered in respect of a business carried on for gain. See HMRC Tax Bulletin October 1999, p 699.

Example

Bill 'the bet' Hill, an Authorised Bookmaker, is an on-course bookmaker with a 'pitch' at Sandown Park racecourse as well as his own independent bookmakers in Wallington, Surrey. He had originally obtained the bookmaking business by inheritance from his father many years previously. The 'pitch' is valued at £98,000 (see point (C) below) and the business in Wallington where he conducts his business other than on race days at Sandown Park is valued at £210,000. Bill also provides a deposit to the National Joint Pitch Council of £25,000, being the security required for a rails bookmaker. Bill dies on 25 December 2007 and leaves the business to his son Alan.

	£
Value of Wallington bookmakers	210,000
Pitch at Sandown Park	98,000
Deposit held by National Joint Pitch Council	25,000
Total	333,000
Deduct business property relief 100%	(333,000)
IHT payable	Nil

Notes to the example

(A) The business including pitch must meet the statutory requirements of *IHTA 1984, ss 103–114* in order to qualify for 100% BPR.

(B) Rule 17.1.3 of the National Pitch Rules (Fourth Edition) deals with the transfer of Seniority Positions and states that '... subject to no consideration in money or money's worth being paid, by transfer on retirement or Will, to a member of the Authorised Bookmaker's immediate family, being defined for the purposes of this Rule 17 as the Authorised Bookmaker's spouse, parents, children or sibling'. In this case a transfer of the 'pitch' to Bill's son is allowable under the Rules. See http://www.njpc-ltd.co.uk/index.htm.

(C) Under *TCGA 1992, s 274* where the market value of an asset has been 'ascertained' for IHT purposes then that value is also used for CGT purposes to be the market value. In the case of a bookmaker's pitch see HMRC Interpretation RI 210.

A business or interest in a business, or shares or securities of a company, do not qualify if the business (or the business of the company) consists wholly or mainly of dealing in securities, stock or shares, land or buildings or making or holding investments, unless the business is

(*a*)   wholly that of a 'market maker' (before the Stock Exchange reform, a jobber) or that of a discount house and, in either case, is carried on in the UK; or

(*b*)   that of a holding company of one or more companies whose business does qualify.

A land holding or dealing business, however, can qualify, provided it includes building construction or land development, and the housing stock of a building business can qualify if regarded as stock in trade.

> *Mr Lawson:* 'As with many, if not all building companies their stock of houses would be regarded as stock in trade—I know that in some cases the houses may rapidly be transferred to a holding company in the Group, but in the company which does the building they will be regarded as stock in trade—will the Chief Secretary assure us that that type of company is not comprised in the category of company that is described as that dealing in land or buildings.'

> *Mr Barnett:* 'I can give the hon and learned Gentleman that assurance.'

HC Official Report, 30 June 1976, cols 1268, 1269.

The meaning of '**consists wholly or mainly**' is on the face of it simple to deduce. That is, a business that satisfies the quantitative test of 50% or more will qualify for the BPR relief although there are no set guidelines in this regard. However, past cases have concluded that the 50% threshold for the relief is in respect of 'net' profits. See *Powell and Halfhide (executor of G E Pearce deceased) v CIR [1997] STC SCD 181 Sp C 120; Furness v CIR [1999] STC SCD 232 Sp C 202.* In the case of *Hall & Hall (Hall's Executors) v CIR [1997] STC SCD 126 Sp C 114;* the letting of caravans on 45-year leases which comprised 84% of the deceased's income in the form of rent and standing charges resulted in the determination that the business had consisted 'mainly of making or holding investments'. In contrast, the effect of net profitability lettings on a farm when compared with that of the less profitable farming business could not be held as a yardstick as to whether the business consisted 'mainly' of holding investments in *Farmer and another (Executors of Farmer deceased) v CIR [1999] STC SCD 321 Sp C 216.* As well as considering the net profitability element a distinction between industrial and residential letting makes no difference when determining what constitutes investment activity. See also *Weston (Weston's Executor) v CIR [2000] STC SCD 30 Sp C 222.* In this regard see *Burkinyoung (executor of Burkinyoung deceased) v CIR [1995] STC SCD 29 Sp C 3* for business of letting furnished flats on assured shorthold tenancies which was wholly one of making and holding investments and so is excluded from *s 105(3).* Also, in the similar case of *Martin and Horsfall (executors of Moore deceased) v CIR [1995] STC SCD 5 Sp C 2* the letting of properties as small industrial units was not a business as the units consisted wholly or mainly of the 'making or holding of investments'. In determining these cases, Stephen Oliver QC referred to an income tax decision and suggested that the provision of security services or heating/cleaning services, independent of the lease requirements, for specific charge would not be an activity of holding investments. As it was where services are provided under the lease then that may be deemed to be connected with and incidental to holding investments. [*IHTA 1984, s 105(3)*]. In a more recent case a woman owned a number of shares in a company which owned more than 100 different properties. Her executors claimed business property relief. HMRC rejected the claim on the basis that the shares were not 'relevant business property', because the company's business consisted mainly of 'making or holding investments', within *IHTA 1984, s 105(3)*. The executors appealed, contending that because the company carried out maintenance work on the properties, it should not be treated as falling within *s 105(3)*. The Special Commissioner rejected this contention and dismissed the executors' appeal, holding that 'the company's maintenance activity is not the separate provision of services; it is inherent in property ownership'. On the evidence, the company's business consisted 'mainly of holding investments'. See *Clark (executors of Clark deceased) v HMRC [2005] STC SCD 823 Sp C 502*. However, in a more recent case the activities of a money lender which encompassed lending to various family companies 'was in the business of making loans and not in the business of investing in loans … the loans were not investments for their own sake but the provision of a finance facility to the other companies'. Accordingly, the shares in the money lending company qualified for business property relief. *Phillips and Others (Phillips' Executors) v HMRC, [2006] STC SCD 639 Sp C 555*.

In contrast, the case of the Commissioners in *Stedman's Executors v CIR [2002] STC SCD 358 Sp C 323* determined that as '72% of the site fees goes in overheads (*sic*) … most of which relate to the provision of upkeep of the common parts' was 'the provision of services and not the business of holding investments'. This decision was reversed on appeal in *CIR v George and Another [2003] All ER (D) 376 (Feb)* in the Chancery Division with Laddie J stating that the business of receiving site fees from the owners of the mobile homes in return for the right to use the company's land, and the receipt of fees for the storage of caravans, constituted the exploitation of the proprietary rights in the land and amounted to the holding of an investment. However, the Court of Appeal then subsequently restored the original decision with Carnwath LJ stating that, on the evidence, the holding of property as an investment was only one component of the business, and did not prevent the company from qualifying for business property relief (*George & Loochin (Stedman's Executors) v CIR CA [2003] EWCA Civ 1763; [2004] STC 147*). As this was only the second time the Court of Appeal had considered BPR, the previous case being *Fetherston-augh and others v CIR [1984] STC 261*, it is interesting to note Carnwath LJ's comment in conclusion:

> 'I find it difficult to see any reason why an active family business of this kind should be excluded from business property relief, merely because a necessary component of its profit making activity is the use of land.'

In relation to the holding of '**investments**' HMRC Inheritance Tax may well seek to suggest that a company or business has become an investment company or business. In the Special Commissioner's case *Brown's Executors v CIR [1996] STC SCD 277 Sp C 83* it was held that the sale of a night club, an asset of the proprietor's unquoted UK company Gaslight, resulting in capital being held on deposit interest account pending the further investment in a future premises was not a change in the nature of the business carried on by the company. HMRC had contended that at the time of the proprietor's death the company's business consisted wholly or mainly in the making and holding of investments and therefore excluded the shares from being qualifying business property. However, the Commissioner found in favour of the taxpayer because the proprietor intended to purchase suitable alternative premises and the deposit account holding the proceeds was of necessity short term to conclude a purchase. In the case of *Beckman v CIR [2000] STC SCD 59 Sp C 226* monies in a business remaining a capital account on retirement of a partner was held on death to be 'simply those of a creditor of the business' and would therefore not qualify for BPR. The retention of large sums of money in the business after retirement should be avoided because there is no reason *per se* for such a retention which might be expected to be paid out as dividend or capital distribution. In order to counteract this an appropriation to trading stock might restore BPR.

A '**market maker**' is a person who holds himself out at all normal times in compliance with the rules of either The Stock Exchange or, after 22 March 1992, traders on the London Financial Futures and Options Exchange (LIFFE) who are recognised by LIFFE (Administration and Management) as willing to buy and sell securities etc. [*IHTA 1984, s 105(4)(7); FA 1986, s 106; SI 1992/3181*].

7.4   **Relevant business property**. Business property qualifying for relief is in the following classes. See IHT 17, p 3.

(a) **Unincorporated business:** property consisting of a qualifying business (see 7.3 above) or interest in such a business (e.g. sole trade, profession, share in partnership). [*IHTA 1984, s 105(1)(a)*]. The value of a business or of an interest in a business is the net value of the business or interest therein, i.e. the value of the assets used in the business including goodwill, less the business liabilities but not, according to IHT 17, p 5, money loaned to a business. In valuing an interest in a business, regard must only be had to assets and liabilities by reference to which the net value of the entire business would fall to be ascertained. In *Ninth Marquess of Hertford and others (Executors of eighth Marquess of Hertford deceased) v CIR, [2005] STC SCD 177 Sp C 444* part of a historic house was open to the public, while part was used as a private residence and not open to the public. The freeholder died in 1997. HMRC issued a notice of determination charging IHT on 22% of the value of the house, on the basis that only 78% of the house was open to the public and thus only 78% of the house qualified for business property relief. The freeholder's executors appealed, contending that the house was a single asset and that the effect of *IHTA 1984, s 110(b)* was that the whole of the house qualified for business property relief even though 22% of the house was not open to the public. The Special Commissioner accepted this contention and allowed the appeal, observing that *s 110* made no provision for apportionment. See also 33 NATIONAL HERITAGE. Also, IHT 210 (Notes) at D14 (Notes) 2 http://www.hmrc.gov.uk/cto/forms/d14_notes_1.pdf states at point 5a 'If the business owed any money to the deceased, often through a loan account, you must **not** add that value to the value of the capital and current accounts. A loan does not qualify for business relief.' [*IHTA 1984, s 110*]. See also *Hardcastle & Hardcastle (Vernede's Executors) v CIR, [2000] STC SCD 532 Sp C 259* and *Mallender & Others (Drury-Lowe's Executors) v CIR, Ch D [2001] STC 514* below.

In the case of **Lloyd's Underwriters** who converted to a NameCo, HMRC will by concession allow business property relief on the value of the underlying assets, subject to certain limitations, up to and including 31 December 2006. Previously, before Names converted to limited company status, it is understood that the CTO did restrict BPR treatment if assets so deposited were excessive compared with the underwriting undertaken. From 1 January 2007 regard must be had to the degree of likelihood that such assets that are put up as security will be drawn to meet the NameCo's losses. These may be met directly if they are third part Funds at Lloyd's (FAL) or indirectly if they are in the form of bank guarantee(s). The valuation of the assets needs to take into account the diminution in their value arising from the fact that the individual or his estate does not have unfettered use of the assets during the period the FAL requirements are in place or the guarantee(s) are available to be called upon. See Lloyd's Market Bulletin 86/411, 6 December 2003 and 31 May 2006. Also, the right to a share of the Lloyd's syndicate profit/loss is an asset/ liability of the business and HMRC regards that the loss should be a liability incurred for the purpose of the business and is not left out of account for BPR purposes. Restrictions on claiming BPR apply from 1 January 2007. See http:// www.lloyds.com/Lloyds_Market/Taxation/Taxation_bulletins/. In *Hardcastle v CIR [2000] STC SCD 532 Sp C 259* this underwriting case concerned trading profits and losses. However, HMRC also claims that land (or the interest in the reversion) which is 'not used' in the underwriting business but supported a guarantee should be left out of account for BPR purposes. See *Hardcastle & Hardcastle (Vernede's Executors) v CIR [2000] STC SCD 532 Sp C 259* and *CIR v Mallender and Others (Executors of Drury–Lowe deceased), Ch D [2001] STC 514.* (See Lloyd's Market Bulletin, 8 May 2001). The business of corporate Lloyd's members may qualify for relief. The address of the CTO dealing with Lloyd's Underwriters' inheritance tax is Shares Valuation Division, Fitz Roy House, PO Box 46, Castle Meadow Road, Nottingham NG2 1BD. Tel 0115 974 2222, fax 0115

7.4 Business Property

974 2197, DX 701203 Nottingham 4. See 7.9 below for the position regarding settled property used in the business of a person with an interest in possession in that property.

(b)   **Shares or securities** ('quoted' or 'unquoted' but note that, in relation to transfers of value made, and other events occurring before 6 April 1996, different rates of relief apply as in 7.7 below) of a company carrying on a qualifying business (see 7.3 above) which (either with or without other such shares or securities owned by the transferor) gave the transferor *control* of the company immediately before the transfer. [*IHTA 1984, s 105(1)(b)(cc); F(No 2)A 1992, s 73, Sch 14 paras 2(1)–(3), 8; FA 1996, s 184(2), Sch 41 Part VI*]. It is not necessary for either the transferor or the transferee to have control after the transfer. From 6 April 1996 100% relief is extended to all qualifying unquoted shareholdings whether or not the holding carries more than 25% voting control and therefore 'control' is not so important for the purposes of BPR. Also, unquoted securities such as loan stock which, either by themselves or with other securities or unquoted shares, give the transferor control of the company immediately before the transfer attract the 100% relief. IHT 210 (Notes) at D14 (Notes) http://www.hmrc.gov.uk/cto/forms/d14_notes_1.pdf states in connection with the definition of 'unquoted' the following: 'This means a company that is not listed on a recognised stock exchange. Some companies although they are listed in the Stock Exchange Daily List are still "unquoted" for business relief.' The note goes on to mention AIM and USM listed shares in this connection and would also include PLUS/OFEX and NASDAQ Europe listings. See IHTM18331. Whilst *FA 2007* inserted new definitions of 'recognised stock exchange' for the purposes of income tax and capital gains tax, the change did not include inheritance tax. HMRC have confirmed that AIM shares continue to be unlisted for the purposes of, for example, CGT taper relief (as they are not included on the UK official list, required by new *ITA 2007, s 1005(3)*. However, adopting the new definition for IHT will not in itself mean that the treatment of such shares will change for IHT purposes. See HMRC statement on 29 March 2007 at http://www.hmrc.gov.uk/budget2007/rec-stock-exch.htm. [*ITA 2007, s 1005; FA 2007, s 109, Sch 26*]. In the case of quoted shares or securities a person has 'control' of a company if that person has the control of powers relating to voting on all questions affecting the company as a whole. Control can therefore be deemed a subjective test which depends on the facts whether a person actually exercises control over a company. See the case of *Walding* below and at 59 TAX CASES. [*IHTA 1984, s 105(1)(b)(bb); FA 1996, s 184(2)*].

'*Quoted*' means quoted on a recognised stock exchange. The IHT 210 (Notes) in relation to 'Quoted company' at D14 (Notes) page 2 http://www.hmrc.gov.uk/cto/forms/d14_notes_1.pdf states: 'This means a company that is listed on a recognised stock exchange. This includes shares traded on the American NASDAQ and European EASDAQ for deaths after 9 March 1992.'

The word '*quoted*' on a recognised stock exchange is to be substituted by the word '*listed*'. Such interpretation has effect in relation to transfers of value or events occurring on or after 1 April 1996. [*FA 1996, Sch 38 para 2(1)(2)*].

For the purposes of inheritance tax the words 'recognised stock exchange' include those exchanges defined as such for the purposes of *ITA 2007, s 1005* previously *ICTA 1988, s 841* as amended by *Financial Services and Markets Act 2000, s 287*. See also EU Directive 22001/34/EC and http://www.hmrc.gov.uk/fid/rse.htm. In addition there are a number of other stock exchanges which have not yet have been designated by the Board for the purposes of *ITA 2007, s 1005* previously *ICTA 1988, s 841*. In practice, however, recognition for IHT purposes depends on whether the law of the country where it is situated recognises the exchange or market in question and whether it provides an adequate trading floor (this last requirement is now becoming obsolete). Also, both tiers of the NASDAQ stock market have recognised stock exchange status and securities traded thereon become quoted for IHT purposes (previously CTO Advanced Instruction Manual, para L 42 now see IHTM25192).

'*Control*' is defined by *IHTA 1984, s 269*. 'Control' is a subjective test and depends on whether the person can actually exercise control over the company, see *Walding and Others (Executors of Walding, deceased) v CIR [1996] STC 13* and 35.4 PAYMENT OF TAX. In determining whether the transferor has control, any shares or securities deemed to be related property must be added so that shares in the name of the deceased's grandson, aged 4 years, were *not* to be included with the main shareholder's (giving a controlling majority). The Judge held that *s 269(1)* allowed relief where the deceased controlled the powers of voting on all matters affecting the entire company. In this connection, the capabilities of persons in whose name the shares were registered was not an issue. The relief was denied. See 60 TAX CASES. See also IHT 17, p 4 for the CTO's meaning of 'control'. In IHT 210 (Notes) at D14 (Notes) http://www.hmrc.gov.uk/cto/forms/d14_notes_1.pdf it states in connection with the definition of 'control' the following: 'For inheritance a person controls a company if they can control the majority (more than 50%) of the voting powers on *all* questions affecting the company as a whole.' See also *Walker's Executors v CIR [2001] STC SCD 86 Sp C 275* where the casting vote gave control and entitlement to BPR.

There is no relief if the company is being wound up or otherwise in the process of liquidation at the time of the transfer unless the business of the company is to continue after a reconstruction or amalgamation which is either the purpose of the winding up etc. or takes place not later than one year after the transfer. [*IHTA 1984, s 105(5)*].

See below for binding contracts for sale and excepted assets.

Example 1

Alex, Bernard, Charlie and David own 25% each of the shares in ABCD Ltd. Alex has land in the company which is being used by the company for business purposes but he wants to transfer the land out of the company to his daughter. He does not have control for these purposes. However, the shares are divided into four separate classes in December 2006 which will carry control in January for Alex, February for Bernard, March for Charlie and April for David. In January 2008 Alex transfers his land out of the company as at that time he has 'control' and is therefore entitled to 50% BPR. The use of a *Bushell v Faith [1970] AC 1099* clause can be beneficial in these circumstances. See 60 TAX CASES.

Example 2

A has owned for many years 60,000 shares in X Ltd, a company now listed on the Alternative Investment Market (AIM), whose issued share capital is 100,000 shares of £1 each. All shares carry full voting rights. A gifts to his son 20,000 shares in June 2000, a further 20,000 in June 2002 and the remaining 20,000 in June 2004. The son agrees to pay any IHT on all gifts. A dies in May 2007, at which time his son still owns the shares.

The value of holdings at all three dates of transfer were as follows:

60% holding	£10 per share
40% holding	£4 per share
20% holding	£3 per share

7.4 Business Property

First gift	£
Value of holding before transfer	600,000
Value of holding after transfer	160,000
Reduction in value of estate	440,000
Deduct business property relief (100%) note (B)	440,000
Value transferred	Nil

Second gift	
Value of holding before transfer	160,000
Value of holding after transfer	60,000
Reduction in value of estate	100,000
Deduct business property relief (100%) note (B)	100,000
Value transferred	Nil

Third gift	
Value of shares transferred	60,000
Deduct business property relief (100%) note (B)	60,000
	Nil

Notes to the example

(A)   If A had made a single gift of his entire holding in June 1999, the computation would have been as follows:

	£
Value of gift	600,000
Deduct business property relief (100%)	(600,000)
Value transferred	Nil
IHT payable	Nil

(B)   There are advantages in transferring all the shares by gift at one time rather than piecemeal as in the example above. These advantages would include:

- the option to pay tax by instalments [*IHTA 1984, s 227(1)(b), s 228(1)(a)*]

- the use of *Bushell v Faith [1970] AC 1099* clauses commonly used to get around *Companies Act 1985, s 303* restrictions

- the transfer of, say, buildings or plant and machinery where the transferor controlled the company immediately before the transfer which attracts 100% relief under *IHTA 1984, s 104(1)(a), s 105(1)(b)*.

In this particular example A and his son are not connected and therefore 'control' for the purpose of *IHTA 1984, ss 269(2), 161* rests initially with A and then after the third gift with the son. Prior to 6 April 1996 business property relief on the first transfer is 100% as the gift was made from a controlling interest in an unquoted company. On the second transfer, 100% relief is due as the gift was from a holding yielding more than 25% of the voting rights. The third transfer satisfies neither of these criteria and relief would therefore have been at only 50%. However, from 6 April 1996 onwards all unquoted shares (not securities) in *qualifying* companies held for at least two years qualify for business relief at 100% regardless of the size of holding or voting entitlement.

Also, as mentioned previously, if the *FA 2007* new definitions of 'recognised stock exchange' for the purposes of income tax and capital gains tax are eventually duplicated to include inheritance tax then there might be the prospect of losing BPR. In such a case shares by gift at one time and not given in a piecemeal fashion (as above) would currently secure BPR with no limitations in the relief.

Example 3

A owns 85% of the share capital of H Ltd, an unquoted company which has two wholly-owned subsidiary companies S Ltd and P Ltd. H Ltd and S Ltd are trading companies and P Ltd is a property investment company. The issued share capital of H Ltd is 100,000 ordinary shares of £1 each valued at £8 per share. The values of the issued shares in S Ltd and P Ltd are £250,000 and £300,000 respectively.

A gave 10,000 shares in H Ltd to his son in August 2007. He had already made chargeable transfers using up his basic exemptions. His son agreed to pay any IHT. A dies in January 2010, at which time his son still owns the shares.

	£	£
Value of gift		80,000
Deduct business property relief 100% × £80,000	80,000	
Less 100% × 80,000 × $\frac{300,000}{800,000}$	30,000	
		50,000
PET becoming chargeable transfer on death		£30,000

Note to the example

(A)   The value of H Ltd shares at £8 each is for a holding of 75% or more therefore the transfer of 10% of his holding does not give rise to the 'Loss to donor' provisions. [*IHTA 1984, s 269*].

(*c*)   **Land, building, machinery or plant** which, immediately before the transfer, was used wholly or mainly for the purposes of a qualifying business (see 7.3 above) carried on by

    (i)   a company controlled by the transferor, or

    (ii)   a partnership of which he then was a partner, or

    (iii)   the transferor and was settled property in which he was then beneficially entitled to an interest in possession (but see 7.9 below). [*IHTA 1984, s 105(1)(d)(e)*].

Any assets under this heading *owned by the transferor* and used wholly or mainly for the purposes of a business under (i) to (iii) above, only qualify for relief if that business, or the transferor's interest in it, or the shares or securities in the company are also relevant business property. [*IHTA 1984, s 105(6)*].

7.4   Business Property

See below for binding contracts for sale and excepted assets. Also, IHT 210 (Notes) at D14 (Notes) http://www.hmrc.gov.uk/cto/forms/d14_notes_1.pdf states at point 5b '... you will need to obtain open market values for land and any other assets included at "book value" such as stock and goodwill.'

Example 4

M has for many years owned a factory used in the business of Q Ltd, of which he has control. In September 2007, M gives the factory to his son S when its value is £700,000. He has made no previous chargeable transfer, but made a gift of £3,000 in 2006/07. M dies in October 2008, when the factory is being used for business purposes by the partnership of which S is a member. S agreed to pay any IHT on the gift.

	£
Value of gift	700,000
Deduct business property relief (50%)	350,000
	350,000
Deduct annual exemption (2007/08)	(3,000)
PET becoming chargeable transfer on death	£347,000
IHT payable at full rates* (death within 3 years)	£14,000

* 6 April 2008 nil rate band of £312,000 (table 41.1 2008.A1)

Notes to the example

(A)   If M wishes also to dispose of shares in Q Ltd by sale or gift after which he would no longer have control, he should give the factory to his son *before* disposing of the shares, or else the business property relief would not be available on the gift of the factory.

(B)   If the factory had been used by Q Ltd at the date of M's death, no business property relief would be available on the gift since the factory would not be relevant business property in S's hands at the date of death.

(*d*)   **Minority holdings of 'unquoted' shares** in a company carrying on a qualifying business (see 7.3 above). Securities are eligible for relief as from 6 April 1996 onwards. [*IHTA 1984, s 105(1)(b)(c), (1A), (1B)* as repealed by *FA 1996, Sch 41 Part VI*]. See also IHT 17, pp 3–5.

General and transitional provisions. See (*b*) above for loss of relief if the company is in the process of winding up at the time of transfer. See below for binding contracts for sale and excepted assets.

See 7.6 below for certain transitional reliefs where shares have changed their status in relation to transfers of value made, and other events occurring after 16 March 1987, after 9 March 1992 and again after 5 April 1996.

Binding contracts for sale. If at the time of the transfer a binding contract for sale has been entered into, the property will not qualify as relevant business property unless

(i)   it is a business or an interest in a business and the sale is to a company which is to carry on the business and is in consideration wholly or mainly for shares or securities in the company, or

(ii)   it is shares or securities in a company and the sale is for the purpose of reconstruction or amalgamation. [*IHTA 1984, s 113*].

HMRC consider there is a binding contract for sale where partners or shareholder directors of companies enter into an agreement (known as a 'buy and sell' agreement) whereby, in the event of the death before retirement of one of them, the deceased's personal representatives are obliged to sell and the survivors are obliged to purchase the deceased's business interest or shares. Funds for the purchase are frequently provided by means of life assurance policies. (HMRC Statement of Practice SP 12/80, 13 October 1980). In order to circumvent the 'buy and sell' agreements constituting binding contracts, the use of an option to purchase that does not constitute a binding contract for sale should be considered as an alternative to protect the BPR. HMRC's attitude to several possible wordings of a partnership deed was subsequently discussed in correspondence between HMRC and the accountancy bodies. See ICAEW Memorandum TR 557, 19 September 1984 and Law Society Gazette, 4 September 1996.

Business property relief is accepted as being available in the circumstances detailed in the table below:

	Table	
Event	**IHT payable on**	**BPR available**
1. Partnership determines on death. Partnership assets realised and estate entitled to deceased's share of proceeds.	Value of partnership interest.	Yes
2. Partnership continues with estate entitled to represent the deceased.	Value of partnership interest.	Yes
3. Partnership continues with partnership share falling into the deceased's estate but with the option for other partners to acquire either on valuation or formula.	Value of partnership interest (valuation or formula).	Yes
4. Partnership continues with the share of the deceased partner accruing to the surviving partners with the estate entitled to payment on valuation or formula.	Value of partnership interest (valuation or formula).	Yes
5. A double option agreement is entered into under which the surviving partners have an option to buy and the PRs an option to sell, such options to be exercised within a stated period after the partner's death.	Value of partnership interest (valuation or formula).	Yes

Notes to the table

(A)   It is normal for the Testator to make provision in the partnership agreement rather than by testamentary disposition.

(B)   Concern has arisen in the past that the decision in *Spiro v Glencrown [1991] 1 All ER 680* provided authority for an option to be a contract for sale (see items 3 and 5 in Table above) thereby resulting in no BPR being available. Early in 1996 the CTO confirmed that there had been no change in their opinion regarding SP 12/80 (see above) and that the case would not be cited as an authority for an option constituting a binding contract for sale.

7.4 Business Property

Excepted assets. The value of any relevant business property which is attributable to 'excepted assets' does not qualify for relief.

Apart from business property relief qualifying under (c)(i) or (c)(ii) above only, '*excepted assets*' are those neither

(i)   used wholly or mainly for the purposes of the business concerned throughout the last two years before the transfer (or since acquisition if more recent); nor

(ii)   required at the time of the transfer for the future use of the business.

[*IHTA 1984, s 112(2)(a)*, (*b*)].

Where the business concerned is carried on by a group company, the use of an asset for the purposes of a business carried on by another company which at the time of use and immediately before the transfer was also a group member is treated as use for the purpose of the business concerned unless that other company's membership of the group is disregarded under *IHTA 1984, s 111*, see 7.8 below.

An asset is not relevant business property by virtue only of (c)(i) or (c)(ii) above unless

(A)   it was used for the purpose of the business carried on by the company or partnership throughout the two years immediately preceding the transfer; or

(B)   it replaced another asset so used and it and the other asset and any asset directly or indirectly replaced by that other asset were so used for periods comprising at least two years within the five years immediately before the transfer.

The qualifying period under (A) or (B) above is reduced in the case of successive transfers in a similar manner to the minimum period of ownership (see 7.5 below) provided the asset (or it and the assets replaced by it) was or were so used throughout the period between the earlier and subsequent transfer (or throughout the part of that period during which it or they were owned by the transferor or his spouse or civil partner). [*IHTA 1984, s 112(3); FA 2005 s 103; The Tax and Civil Partnership Regulations 2005, SI 2005/3229, Reg 21*].

'Land or building which is only partly used for the business must be separated into qualifying and non-qualifying parts for the purposes of relief. Qualifying parts would include a room or rooms in a doctor's house used as his waiting room and surgery, or the ground floor of a three-storey building used by its owner as a shop, provided they were exclusively used for business purposes.'

See previous CTO Advanced Instruction Manual, para L 114.2 now see IHTM25354.

For the above purposes, an asset is deemed not to have been used wholly or mainly for the purposes of the business concerned at any time when it was wholly or mainly for the personal benefit of the transferor or a person connected with him. [*IHTA 1984, s 112*]. See *Barclays Bank Trust Co Ltd v CIR [1998] STC SCD 125 Sp C 158* where the deceased held half the shares in an unquoted trading company which traded in bathroom and kitchen fittings. Rather than tie up money in working capital or premises it had substantial liquid funds on call at the bank amounting to £450,000 in comparison with a turnover of £600,000. The proprietor died and evidence was put forward that there had been consideration given to acquiring a new enterprise some eight months before her death. The target company was later liquidated with no further progress. Ultimately, seven years later the company spent £350,000 purchasing goods from China. The question arose whether the £300,000 cash on deposit at the time of death was required for the purposes of the business. The Special Commissioners held that the £300,000 was not required for the purpose of the business. This case illustrates that in considering *IHTA 1984, s 112(2)(b)*, i.e. (ii) above, surplus cash notwithstanding it is held in a limited company is an excepted asset. The monies should be earmarked or used for 'some palpable business purpose'.

One area of recent change in attitude by HMRC is that relating to hybrid companies where a company is entitled to BPR because of its trading activities but is also involved in investments. Previous guidance suggested that the Inspector of Taxes should consider whether investment interests are part of a 'hybrid' business activity and, if so, *s 112* could only apply to assets which are not used in either part of the business. More recent guidance suggests a relaxing of the rigid approach so that where companies appear to be conducting a normal business activity without using the company as a repository for non-business assets, there is a degree of flexibility. For instance, investigation should consider how directors (and shareholders) view matters in the company reports. The manual concludes: 'decisions in this area need to be commercially sensible and realistic'. Shares Valuation Manual, para 27710.

7.5 **Minimum period of ownership.** The property described in 7.4 above will not qualify for relief unless

(i)   it was owned by the transferor for a minimum period of two years immediately preceding the transfer, or

(ii)   it replaced other property which qualified (apart from the two year period) immediately before the replacement and both properties together (or all properties if other qualifying property had been previously replaced directly or indirectly) were owned by the transferor for at least two years out of the five years immediately preceding the transfer. [*IHTA 1984, ss 106, 107(1)*].

Minority shareholdings under 7.4(*d*) above and 7.7 below do not qualify as replacement property but where such shares owned by the transferor immediately before the transfer would be identified with other shares previously owned by him for capital gains tax purposes under *TCGA 1992, ss 126–136* (reorganisations of share capital, conversions, amalgamations and reconstructions), the combined period of ownership may be taken for the purposes of (i) above or the additional requirement for substantial minority shareholdings below. [*IHTA 1984, s 107(4); FA 1996, s 184(3), Sch 41 Part VI*]. A technical defect in the drafting of the Finance Bill clause meant that the replacement facility available to controlling shareholdings ((i) and (ii) above) would have been withdrawn. As this was not intended, amendments were made to allow both the existing replacement facilities for majority and minority holdings to be available to all unquoted holdings regardless of size. (See Inland Revenue Press Release 26 March 1996). [*IHTA 1984, s 107(4); FA 1996, s 184(3)*].

Relief cannot be more than what it would have been had the replacement (or any one or more of the replacements) not taken place (i.e. increases in value by replacement are ignored). For this purpose, changes resulting from formation, alteration or dissolution of a partnership, or from the acquisition of a business by a company controlled by the former owner of a business, are disregarded. [*IHTA 1984, s 107(2)(3)*].

Inherited property is treated as being owned from the date of death. If the spouse or civil partner inherits then ownership includes the period owned by the deceased spouse or civil partner. [*IHTA 1984, s 108; FA 2005 s 103; The Tax and Civil Partnership Regulations 2005, SI 2005/3229, Reg 19*].

Successive transfers. Relief is given on relevant business property not owned for the minimum period under (i) or (ii) above by the transferor if

(*a*)   he or his spouse or civil partner acquired property (or part) by an earlier transfer on which business property relief was, or would have been, due; and

(*b*)   that property, or any property directly or indirectly replacing it, would (apart from the two-year qualifying period) have been relevant business property in relation to the subsequent transfer; and

(*c*)   either the earlier transfer or the subsequent transfer took place on death.

Relief cannot be more than what it would have been had the replacement (or any one or more of the replacements) not taken place (i.e. increases in value by replacement are ignored). For this purpose, changes resulting from formation, alteration or dissolution of a partnership, or from the acquisition of a business by a company controlled by the former owner of a business, are disregarded. [*IHTA 1984, s 109*]. See IHT 17, p 7.

Example

In January 2007 A owns 85% of the share capital of Glum Ltd i.e. 85,000 shares, an unquoted company valued at £150,000. A transfers his business to Happy Ltd in exchange for shares. The replacement shares are comprised of one ordinary share in Happy and one share in its wholly-owned subsidiary company Sad Ltd for each share in Glum Ltd. Happy Ltd and Sad Ltd are trading companies. The issued share capital of Happy Ltd is 100,000 ordinary shares of £1 each valued at £1.50 per share. The value of the 100,000 issued shares in Sad Ltd is £30,000.

A gives half his new shares to his son in August 2007. He had already made chargeable transfers using up his basic exemptions. His son agreed to pay any IHT. A dies in January 2010, at which time his son still owns the shares.

	£	£
Value of gift to son		90,000
Deduct business property relief 100% × £90,000	90,000	
Less 100% × 90,000 × $\dfrac{30,000}{180,000}$	15,000	
		75,000
PET becoming chargeable transfer on death		£15,000

Note to the example

(A)   The value of Happy Ltd shares at A's death will attract business property relief on their value but under *IHTA 1984, s 107(2)* the business property relief is not to exceed what it would have been had the replacement shares or any one or *more* of the replacements not taken place. Therefore on the death of A HMRC will require evidence of the prior value of Glum Ltd and a similar computation will apply in respect of the value of the shares not attracting BPR as shown in the example above. Under *IHTA 1984, s 109* operates to extend BPR where *s 106* would deny relief (i.e. minimum period of ownership not met), however, *s 109(3)* similarly operates so as not to increase the amount of BPR available.

Additional requirement for substantial minority shareholdings prior to 6 April 1996. To qualify for relief in relation to transfers of value made, and other events occurring, after 16 March 1987 and before 6 April 1996 as a substantial minority share-holding under 7.7 below, the 25% control test must have been satisfied throughout the two years immediately before the transfer or, where the rules relating to inherited property or successive transfers above apply and the transferor owned the shares for a period of less than two years immediately before the transfer, throughout that lesser period. [*IHTA 1984, s 109A; FA 1987, s 58, Sch 8 para 7* now repealed by *FA 1996, Sch 41 Part VI*].

'Ownership' is not defined but would have its meaning in normal usage and includes both beneficial and legal ownership so that the two year rule must be satisfied by the life tenant in a settlement and by the trustees in a discretionary trust (Official Report Standing Committee E, 24 June 1976 cols 1275/1276).

7.6   Further conditions for lifetime transfers. Business property relief is only available where any part of the value transferred by a POTENTIALLY EXEMPT TRANSFER (38) proves to be a chargeable transfer if, in addition to the conditions in 7.3 to 7.5 above, the conditions listed below are also satisfied. Similarly, where a chargeable lifetime transfer, other than a potentially exempt transfer, made within seven years of the transferor's death is reduced under the business property relief provisions, the additional tax chargeable by reason of death must be calculated as if the relief had not been received unless the following conditions are satisfied.

Subject to the provisions below for replacement property, the additional conditions are

(*a*)   that the original property was owned by the 'transferee' throughout the period beginning with the date of the chargeable transfer and ending with the transferor's death or, if earlier, the transferee's death; and

(*b*)   in relation to a notional transfer of value made by the transferee immediately before the death in (*a*) above, the original property would, ignoring the minimum period of ownership requirement in *IHTA 1984, s 106* (see 7.5 above), be relevant business property unless, for transfers made, and other events occurring, after 16 March 1987, the original property consists of shares or securities

(i)   which were 'quoted' at the time of the chargeable transfer; or

(ii)   fell within 7.7 below in relation to the transfer and were 'unquoted' through-out the period referred to in (*a*) above.

'*Transferee*' means the person whose property the original property became on that chargeable transfer or, where on the transfer the original property became or remained settled property in which no qualifying interest in possession subsists, the trustees of the settlement.

'*Quoted*', and '*unquoted*', in relation to any shares or securities, have the same meanings as for defining relevant business property in 7.7 below.

Example

X transfers the share of his 25% interest in Amalgam Ltd (an AIM company) to his son Y and also transfers land and buildings in his partnership to his other son Z on 16 June 2004. X has already used up his annual exemptions for the current year and the previous one. The shares are valued at £640,000 and the land and buildings at £650,000. In February 2006 Amalgam Ltd is quoted on the London Stock Exchange and Y's share value increases to £1 million.

Z sells the land and property to one of the partners in May 2006 and invests the whole proceeds in an unquoted company receiving shares to the value of £800,000. X dies on 6 June 2007.

Theoretical computation on death if shares in Amalgam Ltd had remained unquoted.

	£	Gross	Tax
Value of shares to Y	640,000		
Deduct BPR 100%	640,000	Nil	Nil
Partnership assets to Z	650,000		
Deduct BPR 50%	325,000		
	325,000		
PET becoming chargeable transfer on death	£325,000	25,000	10,000

109

7.6 Business Property

The tax payable on failed BPR and PETs that have become chargeable because of X's death within 7 years:

Computation on death.

X's early death within 3 years of the gift of a non-controlling shareholding in Amalgam Ltd results in the loss of relief. Although Y did not own the shares for a minimum period of two years, i.e. June 2004 to February 2006 before they became quoted, this does not matter for the purposes of *IHTA 1984, s 113A* provided the shares were owned throughout the period by Y, which they were.

	£	£
Value of shares to Y	640,000	
Deduct annual exemption	Nil	
		640,000
Value of property to Z after BPR	325,000	
Deduct annual exemption	Nil	325,000
		965,000
Less nil rate band		(300,000)
		665,000 × 40% = £266,000

Apportionment of tax

Gift to Y

$$\frac{£640,000}{£965,000} \times £266,000 = £176,414$$

Gift to Z

$$\frac{£325,000}{£965,000} \times £266,000 = £89,586$$

Z has sold the business assets in the partnership and reinvested the proceeds in other relevant business property which attracts 100% BPR (i.e. unquoted shares) as opposed to 50% for the original assets (i.e. land and buildings) in the partnership. Z's replacement of the partnership assets with unquoted shares qualifies for replacement property relief *IHTA 1984, s 113B*. However, Z's position is affected by Y's loss of 100% BPR in respect of the transfer of shares to Y by X.

Notes to the example

(A)   In light of these circumstances Y and Z have tax liabilities on X's death that arise from a quotation on the London Stock Exchange of Amalgam Ltd shares. However, Y's interest (taken at book value) in Amalgam shares of £360,000 (£1 million – £640,000) is reduced immediately by the tax due of £176,414.

(B)   Z could have taken the view that his position was vulnerable to Y's decision to accept quoted shares (with no control) and X's death within seven years of the gifts. Insurance on a reducing basis could have been taken out by Z to protect his position and cover the liability of £79,586 (i.e. £89,586 – £10,000).

Where any shares owned by the transferee immediately before the death would either be identified with the original property under the provisions of *TCGA 1992, ss 126–136* (reorganisations of share capital, conversion of securities and company reconstructions and amalgamations) *or* were issued to him in consideration of the transfer of a business or

110

an interest in a business consisting of the original property (or part), the shares are treated as if they were the original property (or part).

Where part only of the original property satisfies the conditions in (a) and (b) above, proportionate relief is given.

Replacement property. Where the transferee has disposed of all or part of the original property before the death of the transferor and applied the whole of the consideration received in acquiring a replacement property within the 'allowed period' after the disposal of the original property or part (or has entered into a binding contract to acquire replacement property within that time), then, provided the disposal and acquisition are both made at arm's length or on terms such as might be expected to be included in such a transaction, the conditions in (a) and (b) above are taken as satisfied if

(i) the replacement property is owned by the transferee immediately before the transferor's death (or immediately before the transferee's death if earlier); and

(ii) throughout the period beginning with the date of the chargeable transfer and ending with the death (disregarding any period between the disposal and acquisition) either the original property or the replacement property was owned by the transferee; and

(iii) in relation to a notional transfer of value made by the transferee immediately before the death, the replacement property would, ignoring the minimum period of ownership requirement, be relevant business property.

If the transferor dies before the transferee and all or part of the original property has been disposed of before the transferor's death (or is excluded by the provisions relating to binding contracts for sale under 7.4 above from being relevant business property in relation to the notional transfer under (iii) above) then if the replacement property is acquired (or a binding contract entered into) after the transferor's death but within the 'allowed period' after the disposal of the original property, or part, condition (i) above does not apply and any reference to a time immediately before the death is taken as a reference to the time when the replacement property is acquired.

Where any shares owned by the transferee immediately before the death would either be identified with the replacement property under the provisions of *TCGA 1992, ss 126–136* (above) *or* were issued to him in consideration of the transfer of a business or an interest in a business consisting of the original property (or part), the shares are treated as if they were the replacement property (or part).

Where a binding contract for the disposal of any property is entered into at any time before the disposal of the property, the disposal is regarded as taking place at that time.

'*Allowed period*' means the period of three years or such longer period as the Board may allow. In relation to transfers of value made, and other events occurring, before 30 November 1993, the legislation effectively provided for the allowed period to be twelve months. [*IHTA 1984, ss 113A, 113B; FA 1986, Sch 19 para 21; FA 1987, s 58(1)(2), Sch 8 para 8; F(No 2)A 1992, s 73, Sch 14 paras 3, 8; FA 1994, s 247(1)(3)*]. The three-year (or longer) allowed period will apply not only to transfers of value made after 29 November 1993 but also to charges or further charges to IHT arising on a death after that date in respect of a transfer of value made before 30 November 1993 (HMRC response in ICAEW Faculty of Taxation Memorandum TAX 9/94).

Where business property which is relevant business property is replaced shortly before the owner's death by agricultural property, the period of ownership of the original property will be relevant for applying the minimum ownership condition to the replacement agricultural property. If all the conditions for agricultural property relief (see 5 AGRICULTURAL PROPERTY) are satisfied relief will be available on the replacement agricultural property. (HMRC Tax Bulletin December 1994 p 183).

Transitional provisions. The amendments made to *IHTA 1984* by *FA 1987, Sch 8* (broadly amendments to the status of Unlisted Securities Market shares and securities, business property, agricultural property and payments by instalments with effect in relation to transfers of value made, and other events occurring, after 16 March 1987) are disregarded in determining under (*a*) and (*b*) and (i)–(iii) above whether any property acquired by the transferee before 17 March 1987 would be relevant business property in relation to a notional transfer of value made after 16 March 1987. [*FA 1987, s 58(3)*]. In broad terms, this protects the position of shares and securities dealt in on the Unlisted Securities Market which were the subject of a transfer before 17 March 1987 in circumstances where the transferor died after 16 March 1987 and within seven years of the transfer.

Further provisions, which are to be read as one with the business property provisions of *IHTA 1984*, apply where by reason of a death occurring after 9 March 1992

(1)   a potentially exempt transfer made before 10 March 1992 proves to be a chargeable transfer, or

(2)   additional tax falls to be calculated in respect of a chargeable transfer (other than a potentially exempt transfer) made before 10 March 1992 and within seven years of the death.

In these circumstances, then, for the purposes of the replacement property provisions of *IHTA 1984, ss 113A, 113B* above, it is to be assumed that the amendments made by *F(No 2)A 1992, Sch 14* (broadly amendments to business property relief (including the status of Unlisted Securities Market shares and securities and increased relief in certain cases), agricultural property relief, payment by instalments and gifts with reservation with effect in relation to transfers of value made, and other events occurring, after 9 March 1992) came into effect at the time the transfer was made, and, in a case within (2) above, that so much of the value transferred as would have been reduced in accordance with the business property relief provisions as amended by *F(No 2)A 1992, Sch 14* was so reduced. Where disregarding the amendments made by *F(No 2)A 1992, Sch 14*, any shares or securities transferred fell within *IHTA 1984, s 105(1)(b)* (see 7.4(*b*) above) in relation to the transfer, those amendments are disregarded in determining whether (*b*) (i) and (ii) above apply to the shares or securities. [*F(No 2)A 1992, s 73, Sch 14 para 9*]. In broad terms, this protects the position of a transferee who receives Unlisted Securities Market shares and securities before 10 March 1992 out of a majority holding where the company acquires a recognised stock exchange listing, and the transferor dies, after 9 March 1992 and within seven years of the transfer.

In order to remove doubt that has arisen in the past a new *IHTA 1984, s 113A(7A)*, is inserted by *FA 1996, s 184(5)*, so that the availability of business relief is to be disregarded in determining whether a transfer falls within the rules in *section 113A*. The clawback rules will apply in respect of any potentially exempt or chargeable transfer to which *section 113A* applies and is effective after 27 November 1995. [*IHTA 1984, s 113A; FA 1986, Sch 19 para 21; FA 1996, s 184(5)*].

7.7   **NATURE OF BUSINESS PROPERTY RELIEF**

Conditions prior to 6 April 1996. The relief is a percentage reduction of the value transferred by the transfer of value (including occasions on which tax is chargeable on SETTLEMENTS WITHOUT INTERESTS IN POSSESSION (44)). The percentage reduction is made before deduction of the annual exemption and other EXEMPT TRANSFERS (21) and before grossing-up where the transferor pays the tax. The percentage rates appropriate to the different classes of relevant property detailed in 7.4 above are as follows. See IHT 17, pp 3 and 4.

In relation to transfers of value made, and other events occurring, **after 9 March 1992 and before 6 April 1996**:

(a)	Unincorporated business (7.4(a) above)	100%
(b)	Shares or securities giving control of an 'unquoted' company (7.4(b) above)	100%
(c)	Shares giving more than 25% voting control of an 'unquoted' company not within (b) above (see (i) below)	100%
(d)	Shares or securities giving control of a 'quoted' company (7.4(b) above)	50%
(e)	Shares in an 'unquoted' company not within (b) or (c) above (7.4(d)(ii))	50%
(f)	Land, buildings, machinery or plant in a partnership or in a controlled company or in a settlement (but see 7.9 below) (7.4(c) above)	50%

In relation to transfers of value made, and other events occurring, after 16 March 1987 and before 6 April 1996, minority holdings are classified as follows.

(i)   Substantial minority holdings, i.e. holdings not falling within (b) above which (either with or without other such shares or securities owned by the transferor) gave the transferor control of over 25% of the powers of voting on all questions affecting the company as a whole and for this purpose there was included any shares or securities which were related property, see 56.17 VALUATION. Where shares or securities were comprised in a settlement, any voting powers which they can give to the trustees were deemed to be given to the individual (if any) beneficially entitled in possession to those shares or securities. Where there were shares or securities of any class with voting powers only on the winding up of the company and/or on any question primarily affecting that class, the reference above to 'all questions affecting the company as a whole' was to be read as referring to all such questions except those to which the powers of the particular class applied. [IHTA 1984, s 105(1)(bb), (1A), (1B); FA 1987, s 58, Sch 8 para 5 as repealed by FA 1996, Sch 41 Part VI].

(ii)   Shares were excluded from the relief if they were insufficient by themselves, without other property, to satisfy the 25% test above immediately before the transfer and their value was reduced because of a qualifying sale within three years of death, see 56.18 VALUATION. [IHTA 1984, s 105(2A); FA 1987, s 58, Sch 8 para 5 as repealed by FA 1996, Sch 41 Part VI].

(iii)   Other minority holdings not falling within 7.4(b) or (i) above. [IHTA 1984, s 105(c); FA 1987, s 58, Sch 8 para 5 as repealed by FA 1996, Sch 41 Part VI].

In relation to transfers of value made, and other events occurring, after 9 March 1992 and before 31 March 1996, then, in relation to any shares or securities within 7.4(b) above or shares within this paragraph, 'unquoted' means not so quoted and for these purposes the Alternative Investment Market (AIM) is treated as unquoted. [IHTA 1984, s 105(1ZA); F(No 2)A 1992, s 73, Sch 14 paras 2(4), 8 (see HMRC Press Release, 20 February 1995)]. This definition only applies for the purposes of defining relevant business property above and payment by instalments (see 35.3 PAYMENT OF TAX). The HMRC'S Press Release dated 20 February 1995 stated 'securities on AIM will not fall to be treated as quoted or listed for tax purposes. They will therefore qualify for the various tax reliefs available for unquoted securities.' For inheritance tax purposes the press release specifically mentions those in IHTA 1984, Part V Chap 1 i.e. business property relief. Prior to 6 April 1996 shares or securities are excluded from relief if they are insufficient by themselves, without other property, to give control immediately before the transfer and their value is reduced because of a qualifying sale within three years of death, see 56.18 VALUATION. [IHTA 1984, s 105(2); F(No 2)A 1992, s 73, Sch 14 paras 2(5), 8]. (The shares by themselves may qualify for relief under as minority holdings of 'unquoted' shares.) From 6 April 1996 onwards quoted shareholdings and unquoted securities are only subject to the 'control' test and value reduction method. [IHTA 1984, s 105(2); FA 1996, Sch 14 Part VI].

7.7 Business Property

See 7.6 above for certain transitional reliefs where shares or securities have changed their status in relation to transfers of value made, and other events occurring after 9 March 1992 and before 6 April 1996.

In relation to transfers of value made, and other events occurring, **after 16 March 1987 and before 10 March 1992**:

(A)	Unincorporated business (7.4(A) above)	50%
(B)	Shares or securities giving control of a company (7.4(b) above)	50%
(C)	Shares giving more than 25% voting control of an 'unquoted' company not within (B) above	50%
(D)	Shares in an 'unquoted' company not within (B) or (C) above	30%
(E)	Land, buildings, machinery or plant in a partnership or in a controlled company or in a settlement (but see 7.9 below) (7.4(c) above)	30%

In relation to any shares or securities within the Table above '*quoted*' means quoted on a recognised stock exchange or dealt in on the Unlisted Securities Market and '*unquoted*' means neither so quoted nor so dealt in. [*IHTA 1984, s 272; FA 1987, s 58(2), 8 Sch 17*]. This definition applied for all IHT purposes, and *still* continues to do so, in relation to transfers of value made, and other events occurring, after 9 March 1992 for purposes *other* than defining relevant business property above and payment by instalments.

See 7.6 above for certain transitional reliefs where shares or securities have changed their status in relation to transfers of value made, and other events occurring after 16 March 1987 and before 10 March 1992.

In relation to transfers of value made, and other events occurring, **before 17 March 1987**:

(1)	Unincorporated business (7.4(a) above)	50%
(2)	Shares or securities giving control of a company (7.4(b) above)	50%
(3)	Shares in a company not within (2) above and not 'quoted' on a recognised stock exchange (7.4(d) above)	30%
(4)	Land, buildings, machinery or plant in a partnership or in a controlled company or in a settlement (but see 7.9 below) (7.4(c) above)	30%

In relation to transfers of value made, and other events occurring, before 17 March 1987, the classification of minority holdings was simply to shares in a company which were not within the Table at (2) above and which were not quoted on a recognised stock exchange. Shares in companies dealt in on the Unlisted Securities Market were *not* treated as quoted securities for this purpose and qualified for relief under this category. (HMRC Statement of Practice SP 18/80, 23 December 1980).

'*Quoted*' and '*unquoted*' have the same meanings as in 7.4(d) above subject to *FA 1996, Sch 38 para 2(1)(2)*. [*IHTA 1984, ss 104, 105; FA 1987, s 58, Sch 8 para 4; F(No 2)A 1992, s 73, Sch 14 paras 1, 2, 8*].

The increases in the relief from 30% to 50%, and from 50% to 100%, mentioned above will be interpreted as applying not only to transfers of value made after 9 March 1992 but also to charges or further charges to IHT arising on a death after that date in respect of a transfer of value made before 10 March 1992 (HMRC Press Release, 10 March 1992 and correspondence with the publisher).

Business property relief applies only to the part of a transfer represented by relevant business property (see 7.4 above). It is given without claim. It is not given on the agricultural value of land where AGRICULTURAL PROPERTY (5) relief is given. [*IHTA 1984, s 114(1)*].

Where woodlands are transferred and capital transfer tax or inheritance tax previously deferred (see 58 WOODLANDS) becomes chargeable, that tax is deducted from the later transfer before business property relief is applied. [*IHTA 1984, s 114(2)*]. See also IHT 17, p 25.

114

7.8 **Valuation.** For the valuation generally of property transferred see 56 VALUATION but for the purposes of business property relief the following particular provisions apply. See http://www.voa.gov.uk/ also for valuation information.

Unincorporated business, see 7.4(*a*) above. *Shares and securities* in a holding company will have their value reduced by the amount attributable to any group company not carrying on a qualifying business (see 7.3 above), but a group company with a business wholly or mainly in the holding of land or buildings occupied wholly or mainly by group companies, who themselves carry on qualifying businesses, is included in the value of the holding company's shares etc. [*IHTA 1984, s 111*]. The shares etc. will also have their value reduced by reference to any assets owned within the group which are not relevant business property (see 7.4 above under excepted assets). See Form D14 below http://www.hmrc.gov.uk/cto/forms/d14_1.pdf and also IHT 17, p 6.

7.9 **Settled property with interest in possession.** In *Fetherstonhaugh and Others v CIR* (formerly *Finch and Others v CIR) CA, [1984] STC 261* it was decided that relief at what was then 50% in 1977 (now 100%) was available in relation to land of which a sole trader was life tenant and on which he had carried on a farming business prior to his death. HMRC's understanding of this decision is that, where there is a transfer of value of a life tenant's business or interest in a business (including assets of which he was life tenant which were used in that business) the case falls within 7.4(*a*) above and 100% relief is available. Where, by contrast, the transfer of value is only of any land, building, machinery or plant, used wholly or mainly for the purposes of a business carried on by the life tenant and in which he has an interest in possession under a settlement, the relief is only available at 50% if the transfer takes place in circumstances in which the business itself is not being disposed of. (Law Society's Gazette, 14 May 1986). See also IHT 17, p 4.

7.10 **BUSINESS PROPERTY—PAYMENT OF TAX BY INSTALMENTS**

Where IHT payable is attributable to the value of either

(*a*) a business or interest in a business carried on for gain, or

(*b*) shares or securities in certain circumstances, or

(*c*) land of any description, wherever situated,

the person paying the tax may elect to pay it in ten equal yearly instalments if the transfer is made on death, *or* if it is one on which tax is charged on settled property under *IHTA 1984, Part III* and the property concerned remains in the settlement, *or* if the tax is borne by the person benefiting from the transfer. [*IHTA 1984, ss 227, 228*]. See 35.3 PAYMENT OF TAX for full details.

Interest on tax payable by instalments. With certain exceptions, interest on tax payable by instalments which is attributable to any shares or securities, business or interest in a business runs from the date of each instalment [*IHTA 1984, s 234*]. See 35.5 PAYMENT OF TAX.

7.10   Business Property

Revenue
Inland
Capital Taxes

Business relief,
business or partnership interests

Name	Date of death
	/ /

You have deducted business relief on form IHT200. Answer the following questions and give the further details we
ask for. If necessary, fill in a separate form for each business, holding of shares or business asset concerned.
You should read form D14 (Notes) before filling in this form.

1   Tick one of the boxes below to show the type of business interest concerned.

☐ a holding of unquoted shares *(see question 4)*   ☐ an interest in a business *(see question 5)*

☐ the whole business, *(see question 5)*   ☐ land or buildings, plant or machinery used
                                                             by a business or company *(see question 6)*

2   Did the deceased own the shares or business interest *throughout* the two years up
to the death?   No ☐   Yes ☐

If the answer is "No", business relief would not normally be due. If you feel that business relief should still be due,
say why below.

3   Was the business, interest in a business, shares, assets, or any part of them,
subject to a binding contract for sale at the date of death?   No ☐   Yes ☐

If the answer is " Yes ", give details of the contract below

4   **Unquoted shares and securities**

4a   What is the name of each company, the number, type and value of shares against
which you have deducted business relief?

4b   Had an order to wind up any company shown above been made, or was it otherwise
in liquidation at the date of death (or date of gift, if the shares had been transferred)?   No ☐   Yes ☐

If the answer is " Yes ", please give details in the box above.

D14   CTO Approval Ref No L3/03

Please turn over
R0H4263 IRCT 7/01

(Substitute)(LexisNexis Butterworths)

5   Business or interest in a business

5a What is the value of the deceased's business or interest in a business at the date of death?

BR1 £ _____

Include the total from box BRI in either box G7 or G8, page 5, IHT200.

5b What is the name and the main activity of the business? How has the value for the business or interest in a business been calculated?

5c Is the business an interest in a partnership?   No □ Yes □
If the answer is "Yes "give details below.

5d Is the business or interest in a business to be sold as a result of the death?   No □ Yes □

6   Asset(s) owned by the deceased and used by a business or company

6a Describe the assets owned by the deceased and used by a business or a company and give their value.

Include the value(s) in the appropriate boxes at G9, page 5, form IHT200.

6b What is the main activity of the business or company concerned and what was the extent of the deceased's interest in the business or company?

7   *Only answer question 7 if you are claiming business relief in connection with a lifetime transfer.*

7a Was the business, interest in a business, shares or asset concerned owned by the person who received the gift throughout the relevant period?   No □ Yes □

7b Would the business, interest in a business, shares or asset concerned have qualified for business relief if *the person who received the gift* had made a transfer of the property at the date of death?   No □ Yes □

7c Was the business, interest in a business, shares or asset concerned subject to a binding contract for sale immediately before the end of the relevant period?   No □ Yes □

D14

8 Calculation of Tax

Cross-references. See 1 INTRODUCTION AND BASIC PRINCIPLES; 5 AGRICULTURAL PROPERTY; 7 BUSINESS PROPERTY; 21 EXEMPT TRANSFERS; 22 GIFTS WITH RESERVATION; 38 POTENTIALLY EXEMPT TRANSFERS; 40 QUICK SUCCESSION RELIEF; 41 RATES OF TAX; 49 TRANSFERS OF VALUE; 50 TRANSFERS ON DEATH; 51 TRANSFERS WITHIN SEVEN YEARS BEFORE DEATH; 58 WOODLANDS and 59 WORKING CASE STUDY.

Simon's Direct Tax Service, parts I3.5, I4.1.

Other Sources. Tolley's Tax Computations 2007–08; IHTM26000.

8.1   Inheritance tax is levied on the value transferred by a CHARGEABLE TRANSFER (10) at the rate or rates applicable at the time of the transfer to the highest part of the aggregate of that value and the values transferred by any previous chargeable transfers made by the transferor in the period of seven years ending with the date of transfer. It is therefore the value transferred by a chargeable transfer made more than seven years previously which is omitted (i.e. the gift after exemptions e.g. the annual exemption and after grossing–up where applicable) and not the value of the gift itself. [*IHTA 1984, ss 1, 7*].

Only one table of rates is enacted which is applicable to transfers on death. Chargeable lifetime transfers are charged at one-half of those death rates throughout the range of rate bands. Transfers made within seven years of death are charged at the death rates but in the case of chargeable transfers made in that period and more than three years before death, the tax charge is tapered. [*IHTA 1984, s 7*]. See 41 RATES OF TAX and 51.1 TRANSFERS WITHIN SEVEN YEARS OF DEATH. There is no subsequent credit or repayment for tax paid on a transfer *before* a reduction in the scale rates even if less tax would have been payable if the transfer had been made after the reduction in rates. In certain cases, where tax is chargeable by reference to an event before a reduction of tax by the substitution of new rate tables, *IHTA 1984, Sch 2* provides that the new rates are to be used. See 33.5 and 33.15 NATIONAL HERITAGE, 44.14 SETTLEMENTS WITHOUT INTERESTS IN POSSESSION, 51.1 TRANSFERS WITHIN SEVEN YEARS BEFORE DEATH and 58.4 WOODLANDS.

The value transferred is the amount by which the value of the transferor's estate immediately after the disposition in question is less than it would be but for that disposition. [*IHTA 1984, s 3(1)*].

A chargeable transfer is any transfer of value made by an individual, other than an EXEMPT TRANSFER (21). [*IHTA 1984, s 2(1)*]. Certain lifetime transfers are designated potentially exempt transfers. A potentially exempt transfer is a transfer of value made by an individual after 17 March 1986 which would otherwise be a chargeable transfer and which is either a gift to another individual or a gift into an accumulation and maintenance trust or a trust for a disabled person. In relation to transfers of value made, and other events occurring, after 16 March 1987, certain gifts by individuals into and out of settlements with interests in possession are also included. See 38.1 POTENTIALLY EXEMPT TRANSFERS for full details. A potentially exempt transfer made seven years or more before the transferor's death is an exempt transfer and any other potentially exempt transfer is a chargeable transfer. A potentially exempt transfer is assumed to be an exempt transfer during the seven years following the transfer (or, if earlier, until immediately before the transferor's death). [*IHTA 1984, s 3A; FA 1986, Sch 19 para 1; F(No 2)A 1987, s 96*].

Where the transferor bears the tax on a lifetime transfer, the inheritance tax liability is taken into account in calculating the reduction in the value of his estate. [*IHTA 1984, ss 3(1), 162(3)*]. The 'net' transfer is grossed up at the appropriate rate(s) in order to arrive at the amount of the chargeable transfer. The chargeable transfer is always the gross, not the net, figure. See 41 RATES OF TAX for grossing-up tables. Where the transferee bears the tax on lifetime transfers, no grossing-up is required as the tax liability is not part of the reduction in value of the transferor's estate.

On death the tax is charged on the value of the deceased's estate immediately before his death and grossing-up is not required.

There are special rules for allocating the tax where the transfer is partly chargeable and partly exempt, see 8.5 below.

As the tax is charged on a cumulative basis, a careful record must be kept of all chargeable transfers made and the tax thereon.

8.2   **LIFETIME TRANSFERS—EXAMPLES**

(i)   **With transferor bearing the tax.**

A transfers £69,000 to a discretionary trust on 1 May 2007, £240,000 on 31 December 2007 and a further £43,000 on 1 February 2008. He bears the tax and he has made no other chargeable transfers. His inheritance tax position is as follows assuming for the purposes of this calculation that rates of tax remain unchanged after 5 April 2007.

	£	£
Gift on 1 May 2007		69,000
Deduct Annual exemption 2007/08	3,000	
Annual exemption 2006/07	3,000	6,000
		63,000

Covered by nil rate band of £300,000

		£
Gift on 31 December 2007		240,000
(*Note.* Annual exemption already used for 2007/08)		
Cumulative net transfers		£303,000

Tax thereon (see grossing-up table at 41.1 2007.B2)

0–300,000		—
300,001 – 303,000 (£3,000 × ¼)		750
Tax on gift		£750

Gift on 1 February 2007

	Gross	Tax	Net
Cumulative totals	303,750	750	303,000
Add Latest net transfer of £43,000	53,750	10,750*	43,000
	£357,500	£11,500	£346,000

*Tax on £346,000 per table 41.1 2007.B2

0–300,000		—
300,001–346,000 (£46,000 × ¼)		11,500
		11,500
Deduct Tax on previous transfers		750
Tax on latest gift		£10,750

8.3 Calculation of Tax

(ii) With transferee bearing the tax on the latest gift.

If, in example (i) above, the trustees agree to pay the tax on the latest gift, the tax will be calculated on that transfer (without grossing-up) using the table at 41.1 2007.B1 RATES OF TAX as follows.

	£
Previous chargeable transfers	303,750
Chargeable transfer on 1 February 2005	43,000
	£346,750

Tax on £43,000 is

303,750 – 346,750 (£43,000 × 20%)   £8,600

(iii) For transfers under the CTT provisions and more than 7 years before latest transfer, see previous editions.

8.3 TRANSFERS ON DEATH—EXAMPLE

A dies on 5 September 2007 leaving an estate valued at £313,000, of which he bequeaths £103,000 to his wife and the balance elsewhere. His lifetime chargeable transfers in the seven years before death totalled £97,265. Tax due from his estate (using the table at 41.1 2007.A1) is as follows.

	£	£
Previous chargeable transfers		97,265
Value of estate at death	313,000	
Deduct exempt bequest to wife	103,000	
Chargeable residue		210,000
Total cumulative chargeable transfers		£307,265
Tax due from estate on £210,000		
97,265–300,000 (£202,735 at nil%)		—
300,001–307,265 (£7,265 at 40%)		2,906
		£2,906

8.4 POTENTIALLY EXEMPT TRANSFERS AND ADDITIONAL TAX LIABILITY ON DEATH—EXAMPLE

A made the following lifetime transfers on which he paid any tax as appropriate

January 1979	Gift to individual C	£50,000
December 1985	Gift to individual D	£65,000
May 1992	Gift to individual C	£96,000
November 1992	Gift to discretionary trustees	£117,000

He died in November 1994 leaving his estate valued at £320,000 to his sons C and D.

120

Tax payable following lifetime transfers

			£	£
Gift to C in January 1979				50,000
Deduct	Annual exemption	1978/79	2,000	
		1977/78	2,000	
	Small gifts exemption		100	4,100
Cumulative net transfers				£45,900
Tax thereon				£2,128
Gross transfer				£48,028

		£	£
Gift to D in December 1985			65,000
Deduct annual exemption 1985/86		3,000	
1984/85		3,000	6,000
			£59,000

Tax on latest gift of £59,000 (*Note.* There has been a change in tax rates)

	Gross	Tax	Net
Gross transfers in previous ten years adjusted for change in rates applicable after 5 April 1985	48,028	—	48,028
Add latest net transfer of £59,000	66,824	7,824*	59,000
	£114,852	£7,824	£107,028

*Tax on £107,028 at grossing-up rates applicable after 5 April 1985

0–85,700	3,300
85,701–107,028 (£21,328 × ⁷⁄₃₃)	4,524
	7,824

Deduct tax on transfers in previous ten years at rates applicable after 5 April 1985 —

Tax on latest gift   £7,824

Gift to C in May 1992

The gift of £96,000 is a potentially exempt transfer to the extent it exceeds the available annual exemption (£3,000 for 1992/93 and £3,000 for 1991/92 brought forward), i.e. £90,000 (see 38.2 POTENTIALLY EXEMPT TRANSFERS), but incurs no immediate liability to tax

8.4   Calculation of Tax

Gift to discretionary trustees in November 1992

Tax on gift of £117,000

(*Note.* There has been a change in tax rates and the gift in January 1979 is more than seven years before the latest gift)

	Gross	Tax	Net
Gross transfers in previous seven years adjusted for change in rates applicable after 9 March 1992	66,824	—	66,824
Add latest net transfer of £117,000	125,456	8,456*	117,000
	£192,280	£8,456	£183,824

*Tax on £183,824 at grossing-up rates applicable after 9 March 1992 (see table at 41.1 1992.B2 RATES OF TAX)

0–150,000	—
150,000–183,824 (£33,824 × ¼)	8,456
	8,456

Deduct tax on transfers in previous seven years at rates applicable after 9 March 1992	—
Tax on latest gift	£8,456*

Tax payable following death in November 1994

Gift to C in January 1979

Gift to D in December 1985

These gifts are before 18 March 1986 and more than three years before death. No additional tax is payable (see 52.7 TRANSITIONAL PROVISIONS).

Gift to C in May 1992

The potentially exempt transfer of
£90,000 (see above) becomes a chargeable
transfer following A's death within seven
years. Since it is made not more than
three years before death, there is no
reduction in tax rate (see 51.1
TRANSFERS WITHIN SEVEN YEARS
BEFORE DEATH). The gift to D in
December 1985 is within seven years of
the gift and must be aggregated.

There has been a change in tax rates at
death.

	Gross	Tax	Net
Gross transfers in previous seven years adjusted for the change in rates applicable after 5 April 1992	66,824	—	66,824
Add latest gross transfer	90,000	2,730*	87,270
	£156,824	£2,730	£154,094

*Tax on £156,824 at rates applicable on death after 9 March 1992

0–150,000	—
150,001–156,824 (£6,824 × 40%)	2,730
Tax payable by C (but see 29.4 below)	£2,730

8.5   Calculation of Tax

Gift to discretionary trustees in November 1992

Additional tax is due following A's death within seven years. However, the gift is made not more than three years before death, so there is no reduction in tax rate. The gifts in December 1985 and May 1992 are within seven years of the gift of £117,000 and must be aggregated.

	Gross	Tax	Net
Gross transfers in previous seven years	156,824	2,730	154,094
Add latest gross transfer of £125,456	125,456	50,182*	75,274
	£282,280	£52,912	£229,368

*Tax on £282,280 at rates applicable on death after 9 March 1992

0–150,000	—
150,001–282,280 (£132,280 × 40%)	52,912
	52,912
Deduct tax on transfers in previous seven years at rates applicable after 9 March 1992	2,730
	50,182
Deduct tax already paid	8,456
Additional tax payable by trustees	£41,726

Transfer on death in November 1994

The gift to D in December 1985 is made more than seven years before death. The gifts made in May 1992 and November 1992 must be aggregated with the death estate as they are both made within seven years of death. These gifts entail gross transfers of £90,000 and £125,456 respectively resulting in cumulative chargeable transfers of £215,456 immediately prior to death.

Cumulative chargeable transfers in previous seven years	215,456
Value of estate	320,000
Total cumulative chargeable transfers	£535,456

Tax due from estate of £320,000
215,457–535,456 (£320,000 × 40%)   £128,000

8.5   **PARTLY EXEMPT TRANSFERS**

Where a transfer is partly exempt and partly chargeable, special provisions apply to allocate the tax chargeable and the benefit of the exemption. The circumstances will arise mainly with transfers on death but may also apply where, for example, an interest (other

124

than an interest in possession) in settled property comes to an end in lifetime and the property is distributed between exempt and non-exempt beneficiaries. On death, a common situation is where, after specific chargeable gifts, the residue of the estate is left to the widow and is therefore exempt. The provisions are contained in *IHTA 1984, ss 36–42*. *'Specific gift'* means any gift other than a gift of residue or any share in residue. [*IHTA 1984, s 42(1)*]. In Scotland legal rights claimed by a person entitled to claim such rights are treated as a specific gift which bears its own tax. In determining the value of such legal rights, any tax payable on the estate of the deceased is left out of account. [*IHTA 1984, s 42(4)*]. Any liability of the transferor which is not taken into account in arriving at the value of his estate (including liabilities non-deductible or abated under *FA 1986, s 103*, see 50.3 TRANSFERS ON DEATH) is treated as a specific gift. [*IHTA 1984, s 38(6); FA 1986, Sch 19 para 13*]. Any value transferred which is not a specific gift is made out of residue. [*IHTA 1984, s 39*].

See below for the application of business and agricultural property reliefs.

Attribution of value to specific gifts. If a specific gift is fully exempt (e.g. gift of specified property to spouse) then the value of that gift corresponds to such part of the total value transferred, and such gift will not bear any tax. By contrast an exempt residuary gift (e.g. gift of residue to spouse) may suffer the tax on a specific gift which does not bear its own tax (a tax-free gift). Where residue is part exempt and part chargeable (e.g. part to spouse and part to son) the exempt part will not bear any tax attributable to the chargeable part. [*IHTA 1984, ss 38(1), 41*]. See *Re Benham's Will Trusts; Lockhart v Harker, Read and the National Lifeboat Institution Ch D, [1995] STC 210* in which the testatrix listed A and B beneficiaries and those in List A were to benefit 3.2 times the size of the fund compared to List B beneficiaries. The Court's view of the testatrix's intention was that each beneficiary of the respective lists, whether charitable or not, should receive the same amount from the express terms of the will as the other beneficiaries within the same list. In view of this the beneficiaries who were not charities received grossed up shares so that they achieved equality with the charitable beneficiaries. (See also Taxation magazine 20 April 1995 p 53.) The case is now final and until the matter is re-examined in the courts those drafting wills should pay particular attention to the wording and executors are advised to review their interpretation of the terms of the will when *s 41* is to apply.

The effect of *Re Benham's Will Trusts* (see above) is that where there is exempt and non-exempt residue and the will is worded such that if the Testator/Testatrix has not ensured that the non-exempt residue bears its tax then the inheritance tax is likely to be borne out of the estate rather than by the non-exempt beneficiaries wholly out of their portion of the residue. Seemingly, following *Benham's* this will have the effect of increasing the size of the inheritance tax bill. This may not be a problem where the beneficiaries are husband/wife and sons/daughters who would wish to limit the inheritance tax liability in the first instance and amicably redefine the will to take advantage of the redefinition of gifts between themselves. However, as happened in the *Benham's* case, the beneficiaries were not family and the view of one of the exempt residuary beneficiaries that their charity should have the benefit of their exempt status and this therefore meant that the estate should pay as little inheritance tax as possible, did not hold sway. The Court's view that the intention of the Testatrix was that each beneficiary should receive the same amounts as the other beneficiaries (in each list) consequently the non-exempt residue had to be grossed up. It was clause 3 of the late Jane Mary Benham's will that centred around the problems and was drawn up as follows:

'As to the residue after such payment aforesaid to pay the same to those beneficiaries as are living at my death and who are listed in List A and List B hereunder written in such proportions as will bring about the result that the aforesaid beneficiaries named in List A shall receive 3.2 times as much as the beneficiaries in list B, and in each case for their own absolute and beneficial use and disposal.'

8.5 Calculation of Tax

To avoid this the will should state that the non-exempt residue is to bear its own tax or the result following *Benham's* will be a greater incidence of tax (see bullet point three below and Precedent). However, the CTO has stated:

> 'Generally speaking the Court is concerned in such cases to establish the intention of the testator or testatrix from the wording of the will and admissible extrinsic evidence. If the will is drafted in common form with a direction to ascertain residue after payment of funeral and testamentary expenses and debts followed by a bequest of that residue then it is focusing on the ascertainment and division of disposable residue rather than on what each residuary beneficiary is to receive. Accordingly wills so drafted would not appear to involve *Benham* style grossing up computations.'

See The Tax Journal, 5 September 1996, p 3. However, *Holmes & Another v McMullen & Others Ch D [1999] STC 262* in the Chancery Division did not follow *Benham*, and Blackburne J held that an equal division of disposable residue between relatives and charities meant that the IHT attributable to the relatives' shares had to be borne by those shares, since to subject the charities' share to any part of that burden was prohibited.

Will drafting post Benham

1. As to one share absolutely for my wife (husband) [*or give name already defined as such*] if she (he)survives me for 28 days

2. As to another share (or as to the whole if the preceding gift fails) for all of my children as are alive at my death [and reach the age of 18] and if more than one in equal shares PROVIDED that if any child of mine [is already dead or] dies before me [or before reaching that age] but leaves a child or children alive at the death of the survivor of my child and me who reach the age of [*18*] or marry under that age then such equal shares so much of the Trust Fund as that child of mine would have taken on attaining a vested interest

AND the shares given by (1) and (2) above shall be such shares as before [after] the deduction of any inheritance tax attributable to them respectively are of equal value [or are of equal values bearing to one another in the proportions (2:1) the larger share being given by (1)(2)].

Example

Assume that the net residue of £200,000 is to be divided equally between a charity and the surviving son. The estate rate is 40% (i.e. the nil rate band has been utilised).

The options:

*   Divide the residue equally so that the charity gets £100,000 and the son gets £100,000 and he then bears the tax of £40,000 out of the share he receives. This is the Charity's beneficial option: the *Holmes* option above which is now preferred by the courts following the decision in that case. See Tolley's Practical Tax Service Newsletter dated 10 March and 28 July 1999.

$£$

Charity	100,000
Son	60,000
HMRC	40,000
Total	$£200,000$

- Calculate the tax on the £100,000 (son's share) and the tax of £40,000 is then deducted from the £200,000 and the balance of £160,000 divided equally between the Charity and the son who each get £80,000. The son's beneficial option but precluded by *IHTA 1984, s 41(b)*.

$£$

Charity	80,000
Son	80,000
HMRC	40,000
Total	$£200,000$

- Gross up the son's share so that the charity and the son end up with the same net amount after the son's share has suffered tax i.e. the £200,000 divided in the proportions 60:60:40 as follows:

$£$

Charity	75,000
Son	75,000
HMRC	50,000
Total	$£200,000$

The above is HMRC's preferred option and that arrived at in the *Benham's* case.

Where two or more specific gifts are in excess of an exemption limit, relief for the exemption is given to gifts bearing their own tax before other gifts. Any excess relief is allocated to the other gifts in proportion to their values. [*IHTA 1984, s 38(2)*].

Where specific gifts which do not bear their own tax are the only chargeable part of a transfer the tax on them (found by grossing-up) is borne by the residuary estate. [*IHTA 1984, s 38(3)*].

Example 1

A dies in July 2007 leaving estate valued at £361,000. He leaves a tax-free legacy to his daughter of £306,000 and the residue to his widow. He has made no previous chargeable transfers.

8.5 Calculation of Tax

	£
Tax-free legacy	306,000
Tax thereon (see table at 41.1 2007.A2) is (6,000 × ⅔)	4,000
Grossed-up legacy	£310,000
Value of estate	361,000
Deduct chargeable estate	310,000
Exempt residue to widow	£51,000

Where tax-free specific gifts are not the only chargeable gifts very complex rules must be followed. An assumed rate of tax must be calculated on a hypothetical chargeable estate for the purpose of allocating values to the chargeable and exempt parts of an estate. [*IHTA 1984, s 38(4)(5)*].

Example 2

A dies in July 2007 leaving an estate valued at £510,000. He leaves a tax-free legacy to his daughter of £316,000, a property worth £10,000 bearing its own tax to a nephew, and the residue of his estate equally between his widow and his son. He has made no previous chargeable transfers.

	£	£
Hypothetical chargeable estate:		
Tax-free specific gift to daughter		316,000
Tax thereon (as if legacy was the only chargeable gift – £16,000 × ⅔)		10,666
Grossed-up specific gift to daughter		326,666
Specific gift bearing own tax to nephew		10,000
Total of specific gifts		336,666
Chargeable residue		
Gross estate	510,000	
Deduct total of specific gifts	336,666	
Residue	£173,334	
Half-share of residue to son		86,667
Hypothetical chargeable estate		£423,333

Calculation of assumed tax rate

Tax on £423,333 would be (see table at 41.1 2007.A1 RATES OF TAX)	£49,333

Assumed rate is

$$\frac{£49,333}{£423,333} \times 100 = \underline{11.65347\%}$$

Re-gross tax-free legacy to daughter using assumed rate

$$£316,000 \times \frac{100}{100 - 11.65347} \qquad £357,683$$

Calculate chargeable estate and tax thereon

Grossed-up value of tax-free legacy		357,683
Specific gift bearing own tax		10,000
Total of specific gifts		367,683
Chargeable residue:	510,000	
Deduct total of specific gifts	367,683	
Residue	£142,317	
Half-share of residue to son		71,158
Hypothetical chargeable estate		£438,841
Tax on chargeable estate of £438,841 (see table at 41.1 2007.A1 RATES OF TAX) is		£55,536

$$\text{Estate rate is} \frac{55,536}{438,841} \times 100 = 12.65515\%$$

Distribution of estate

Specific gifts payable:	to daughter		316,000
	to nephew		10,000
			326,000

Tax on gift to daughter

Gift grossed at assumed rate on £367,683 (see above)

Tax thereon at estate rate of 12.65515%	46,531

Note. The nephew pays the tax on his gift of £10,000 at the estate rate of 12.65515% which is £1,265

Total specific gifts plus tax	£372,531
Gross estate	510,000
Deduct total specific gifts plus tax	372,531
Residue	£137,469

8.5 Calculation of Tax

<table>
<tr><td></td><td>£</td><td>£</td></tr>
<tr><td>**Allocation of estate**</td><td></td><td></td></tr>
<tr><td>Widow (one half residue)</td><td></td><td>68,734</td></tr>
<tr><td>Son (one half residue)</td><td>68,735</td><td></td></tr>
<tr><td>Tax on son's share at estate rate</td><td></td><td></td></tr>
<tr><td>£68,735 at 12.65515%</td><td>8,699</td><td></td></tr>
<tr><td>Payable to son</td><td></td><td>60,036</td></tr>
<tr><td>Legacies to daughter and nephew</td><td></td><td>326,000</td></tr>
<tr><td>Tax borne by residue (£46,531 + £8,6992)</td><td></td><td>55,230</td></tr>
<tr><td></td><td></td><td>£510,000</td></tr>
</table>

Application of business and agricultural property relief where transfers partly exempt. With respect to transfers of value made after 17 March 1986, the rules for apportioning the value of an estate between specific gifts and residue (in order to determine the exempt and chargeable parts) are modified for transfers including property qualifying for business and agricultural property reliefs.

(*a*)   Specific gifts of business or agricultural property are to be taken at their value as reduced by the business or agricultural property relief attributable to such property.

(*b*)   Any other specific gifts not within (*a*) above are to be taken to be the fraction of their value given by the formula

$$\frac{V-S}{E-P}$$

where

V =   Total value transferred (i.e. as reduced by business and agricultural property reliefs)

S =   Specific gifts within (*a*) above as reduced by the attributable relief

E =   Total value transferred *before* deduction of business and agricultural property reliefs

P =   Specific gifts within (*a*) above *before* deduction of the attributable relief

For the purposes of the above provisions, the value of a specific gift of relevant business or agricultural property does not include the value of any other gift payable out of that property (e.g. a pecuniary legacy charged on the relevant property) and that other gift is not itself treated as a specific gift of relevant business or agricultural property.

IHTA 1984, ss 38 and *39* (see above) have effect subject to the above provisions. [*IHTA 1984, s 39A; FA 1986, s 105*].

Example 3

A dies in July 2007 leaving an estate valued at £405,000. The estate includes a sweet shop business valued at £30,000 (for which 100% business property relief is available) and a small tenanted farm valued at £10,000 (for which only 50% agricultural property relief is available as the tenancy commenced before 1 September 1995). He leaves a tax-free legacy to his daughter of £345,000, the tenanted farm bearing its own tax to his nephew and the residue of his estate equally between his widow and his son. He has made no previous chargeable transfers.

Application of business and agricultural property reliefs: Under (*a*) above, the value of the specific gift of the tenanted farm is taken as the value of it as reduced by the applicable agricultural property relief, i.e. £10,000 – £5,000 = £5,000.

Under (*b*) above

V = £405,000 – £30,000 – £5,000	=	£370,000
S = £10,000 – £5,000	=	£5,000
E	=	£405,000
P	=	£10,000

The value of the tax-free specific gift to the daughter is reduced to:

$$\frac{£370,000 - £5,000}{£405,000 - £10,000} \times £345,000 = £318,797$$

£26,203 (£345,000 – £318,797) of business property relief has therefore been allocated to the tax-free specific gift to the daughter, leaving £3,797 (£30,000 – £26,204) of business property relief to be allocated to residue.

	£	£
Hypothetical chargeable estate:		
Tax-free specific gift to daughter		318,797
Tax thereon (as if legacy was the only chargeable gift – £3,797 × ⅔)		2,531
Grossed-up specific gift to daughter		323,859
Specific gift bearing own tax to nephew		5,000
Total of specific gifts		328,859
Chargeable residue		
Gross estate	405,000	
Deduct total of agricultural and Business property reliefs	35,000	
Value transferred after reliefs	370,000	
Deduct total of specific gifts	328,859	
Residue	£41,141	
Half-share of residue to son		20,570
Hypothetical chargeable estate		£349,429

The calculation of the assumed tax rate, chargeable estate and tax thereon, distribution of the estate and allocation of the estate then proceed in the same manner (but with different amounts) as in *Example 2* above. Agricultural and business property reliefs will be apportioned as above in the distribution of the estate.

Note to the examples

The above example shows that business property relief will be apportioned to the exempt half-share of residue transferred to the widow and thereby effectively wasting some of the relief otherwise available. In this and similar situations the wastage can be avoided by ensuring that all agricultural and business property are subject of specific gifts to

8.6   Calculation of Tax

non-exempt beneficiaries if part of the estate is destined to go to an exempt beneficiary such as the widow/widower or a charity, as it is understood that HMRC Inheritance Tax insist on the strict application of *IHTA 1984, s 39A*. Also see Example at 5.9 AGRICULTURAL PROPERTY.

8.6   ABATEMENT

Abatement not attributable to tax. Where a gift would be abated because of an insufficiency of assets under the normal rules for the administration of estates, the abated value will be taken for the purposes of inheritance tax. [*IHTA 1984, s 37(1)*].

Abatement for tax: specific gifts. Where the grossed-up value attributable to specific gifts (see 8.5 above) exceeds the value transferred, they are treated as reduced to the extent necessary to reduce their value to that of the value transferred in the order in which, under the terms of the relevant disposition or any rule of law, the reduction would fall to be made on a distribution of assets. [*IHTA 1984, s 37(2)*].

8.7   GIFTS MADE SEPARATELY OUT OF DIFFERENT FUNDS

Where there are gifts taking effect on a death both out of the deceased's own estate and out of a settled fund, the provisions in 8.5 and 8.6 above are applied separately to each fund. [*IHTA 1984, s 40*]. Subject to the application of the *Ramsay* principle or the associated operations provisions, the Board consider that the rate of tax to be used for grossing up should be found by looking at each fund separately and in isolation. See 6.1 ANTI-AVOIDANCE. Previously they thought that the rate applicable to the total value of all property chargeable on the death should be used (letter from Capital and Valuation Division reproduced at 1990 STI 446).

Example

A dies in June 2007 with a nil cumulative total. Of his free estate of £1,000,000, the sum of £305,000 free of tax is left to his son and the residue is left to his widow. A was the life tenant of a settlement the funds of which were worth £500,000 at the date of his death. His interest under the settlement passed to his grandchildren. Under the Board's revised practice the chargeable estate and tax thereon would be calculated as follows.

	£
Hypothetical chargeable estate	
Tax-free specific gift to son	305,000
Tax thereon (see table at 41.1 2007.A2) is (£5,000 × ⅔)	3,333
Grossed-up specific gift to son	308,333
Life interest in settlement bearing own tax and passing to grandchildren	500,000
Hypothetical chargeable estate	£808,333

Calculation of assumed tax rate

Tax on £808,333 would be (see table at 41.1 2007.A1)   £203,333

Assumed rate is

$$\frac{203,333}{808,333} \times 100 = 25.1546\%$$

No further re-grossing is required and the assumed rate becomes the estate rate

Distribution of estate

Tax-free gift to son	305,000
Grossed-up gift to son is £305,333 and tax on this at the estate rate of 25.1546% is	76,805
Life interest bearing its own tax (so that trustees will be liable for tax on it at the estate rate, i.e. £125,773)	500,000
Widow's exempt residue	618,195
	£1,500,000

8.8   **TAX CHARGEABLE IN CERTAIN CASES OF FUTURE PAYMENTS**

Special provisions apply where a disposition made for a consideration in money or money's worth is a transfer of value and any payments made or assets transferred *by the transferor* in pursuance of the disposition are made more than one year after the disposition i.e. the provisions apply where the transferor acquires property at an overvalue.

Tax is charged as if any payment made etc. was made in pursuance of a separate disposition made, without consideration, at that time and the amount of the payment etc. was the 'chargeable portion' of the full payment.

The '*chargeable portion*' of any payment etc. is such proportion of its value at that time as is found by multiplying it by the fraction

$$\frac{A}{B}$$

where

A =   the value actually transferred by the disposition as a whole; and

B =   the value, at the time of that disposition, of the aggregate of the payments etc. made or to be made by the transferor.

[*IHTA 1984, s 262*].

Example

M acquires property from P on 1 January 2007 which is worth £30,000 but for which he agrees to pay £20,000 immediately and two further instalments of £10,000 each on 1 January 2008 and 1 January 2009. The discounted value of the two future instalments on 1 January 2007 at, say, 10% interest, is £17,355 (£9,091 + £8,264).

The value transferred by the disposition as at 1 January 2007 is

8.9 Calculation of Tax

	£
Immediate payment	20,000
Present value of future instalments	17,355
	37,355
Value of property received from P	30,000
Value transferred by disposition	£7,355

The chargeable portion of each of M's payments is

$$\frac{7,355}{37,355} = 19.69\%$$

i.e. the potentially exempt transfers are (ignoring annual exemptions)

On 1 January 2007 £20,000 × 19.69%	= 3,938
On 1 January 2008 £10,000 × 19.69%	= 1,969
On 1 January 2009 £10,000 × 19.69%	= 1,969
	£7,876

Note to the example

(A) 'The element of the bounty is ascertained by examining the entire position at the moment of the original disposition ...' see previous CTO Advanced Instruction Manual, para C58.

8.9 CHARGEABLE TRANSFERS AFFECTING MORE THAN ONE PROPERTY

Where more than one property is comprised in a chargeable transfer, the tax which is attributable to each separate property is in the proportions which the separate values bear to the whole (subject to any provisions reducing the amount of tax attributable to the value of any particular property). [*IHTA 1984, s 265*].

8.10 MORE THAN ONE CHARGEABLE TRANSFER ON ONE DAY

Where more than one lifetime chargeable transfer is made on the same day by the same person, the transfers are treated as made in the order which results in the lowest value chargeable and the rate of tax charged on each transfer is the effective rate (total tax divided by total transfers) which would apply if there has been one transfer of the total amount. The same rules regarding transfers on the same day apply to chargeable transfers from settlements without interests in possession if they are made out of property comprised in the same settlement. [*IHTA 1984, s 266*]. The previous CTO Advanced Instruction Manual stated that:

'It is important to bear in mind that a gift by cheque is not complete until the cheque itself is cashed ... and thus where transfers are made by way of several cheques IHTA 1984, s 266(1)/IHTA 1984, s 43(2) will operate only if the cheques are **cleared** on the same day. The date on which the cheque is **drawn** is immaterial.'

See also *Curnock (Curnock's Personal Representative) v CIR [2003] STC SCD 283 Sp C 365* where a cheque issued before the date but not cleared until after death still formed part of the deceased's estate on death. See TAX CASES (60).

8.11   **TRANSFERS REPORTED LATE**

Provisions are made to deal with the situation which arises where a transfer ('the earlier transfer') is not notified to the Board by an account or other information within the required period (see 2.6 ACCOUNTS AND RETURNS) and is not discovered until after the tax on a later transfer has been paid and accepted by the Board (or if no tax was payable, when the later transfer was notified in an account).

The provisions are as follows.

(*a*)   Where the transfer which is reported late ('the earlier transfer') is made within the [seven] years preceding the later transfer, the tax payable on the earlier transfer is the amount which would have been payable on that transfer if it had been reported at the correct time (i.e. using the table of rates applicable at that time) plus the additional tax that would have been charged on the later transfer if the earlier transfer had been taken into account. Where a later transfer (A) is itself an earlier transfer in relation to a subsequent later transfer (B), the additional tax chargeable on (A) by virtue of its being an earlier transfer in relation to (B) is left out of account in the calculation required when (A) itself is a later transfer.

(*b*)   Where two or more transfers in the [seven]-year period are reported late, the additional tax on a later transfer is apportioned between them on a pro rata basis; but if one of these unreported transfers is discovered after the liability on another has been settled, any further tax is payable on the latest transfer to be reported.

(*c*)   Where the earlier transfer is made more than seven years before the later transfer, the tax payable on the earlier transfer is still the amount which would have been payable on that transfer if it had been reported at the correct time. The tax payable on the later transfer is not affected because of the seven-year cumulation rule.

(*d*)   Where no account of a person's excepted estate is required by the Board, an account of that estate shall, be treated as having been delivered on the last day of the prescribed period in relation to that person. See 2.6 ACCOUNTS AND RETURNS.

[*IHTA 1984, s 264*].

Note. The legislation still refers to a ten-year period in (*a*) and (*b*) above but this should presumably be amended due to the reduction in the cumulation period from ten to seven years. The principle is, however, unaffected.

A transfer is discovered (i) if notified by an account etc. after the required period, on the date so notified or (ii) in any other case, on the date when the Board give notice of a determination (see 15.1 DETERMINATIONS AND APPEALS). [*IHTA 1984, s 264(9)*].

Interest on tax overdue will run from the due date of payment (see 35 PAYMENT OF TAX), but from that date to six months after the date of discovery the interest will be on the amount of tax which would have been payable if the transfer had been reported at the proper time. Thereafter, the interest will be on the actual tax payable. [*IHTA 1984, s 264(6)*].

Exemption limits. If the earlier transfer would have been wholly or partly exempt because it was within the limits of an exemption and the later transfer actually received the benefit of the same exemption, the later transfer is not disturbed and the exemption which would have applied to the earlier transfer is reduced accordingly. [*IHTA 1984, s 264(7)*].

Settled property. The provisions of *IHTA 1984, s 240(3)* apply to cases where any fraud, wilful default or neglect by the settlor of a SETTLEMENT WITHOUT INTERESTS IN POSSESSION (44) comes to the knowledge of the Board. See 35.11 PAYMENT OF TAX. In consequence, the provisions relating to transfers reported late do not apply to such settled property for IHT purposes.

8.11   Calculation of Tax

HM Revenue
& Customs
Capital Taxes

Inheritance
tax worksheet

Working out the value of the estate

Assets where tax may not be paid by instalments

- Estate in the UK *(box F30, form IHT200)*

  WS1 £
  Copy to box H1 on IHT200

- Joint property – **passing by survivorship**. Copy
  the figure from box JP5 on form D4. If you have
  filled in more than one form D4, there is space
  here to copy the figure off each form.

  Total £

  WS2 £
  Copy to box H2 on IHT200

- Foreign assets – copy the figure from box FP7 on
  form D15. If you have filled in more than one
  form D15, there is space here to copy the figure
  off each form.

  Total £

  WS3 £
  Copy to box H3 on IHT200

- Settled property – **on which the trustees would
  like to pay tax now**. Copy the figure from box
  SP5 on form D5. If you have filled in more than
  one form D5, there is space here to copy the
  figure off each form.

  Total £

  WS4 £
  Copy to box H4 on IHT200

  Total of assets where tax may not be paid by instalments
  (WS1 + WS2 + WS3 + WS4)

  WS5 £
  Copy to box H5 on IHT200

Assets where tax may be paid by instalments

- Estate in the UK *(box G18, form IHT200)*

  WS6 £
  Copy to box H6 on IHT200

- Joint property – **passing by survivorship**. Copy
  the figure from box JP10 on form D4. If you have
  filled in more than one form D4, there is space
  here to copy the figure off each form.

  Total £

  WS7 £
  Copy to box H7 on IHT200

- Foreign assets – copy the figure from box FP12
  on form D15. If you have filled in more than one
  form D15, there is space here to copy the figure
  off each form

  Total £

  WS8 £
  Copy to box H8 on IHT200

- Settled property – **on which the trustees would
  like to pay tax now**. Copy the figure from box
  SP10 on form D5. If you have filled in more than
  one form D5, there is space here to copy the
  figure off each form.

  Total £

  WS9 £
  Copy to box H9 on IHT200

  Total of assets where tax may be paid by instalments
  (WS6 + WS7 + WS8 + WS9)

  WS10 £
  Copy to box H10 on IHT200

IHT200 (WS)

(Substitute)(LexisNexis Butterworths)

136

Other property taken into account to calculate the total tax

- Settled property – copy the figure from boxes SP5 and SP10 on form D5. If you have filled in more than one form D5, there is space here to copy the figures off each form.

  Total £   WS11 £
  Copy to box H11 on IHT200

- Alternatively secured pensions included as part of the deceased's estate. Copy this figure from box PA6 form D6.

  Total £   WS11A £
  Copy to box H11A on IHT200

- Gift with reservation *(total of boxes LT2 and LT3, form D3)* WS12 £
  Copy to box H12 on IHT200

  Chargeable estate *(WS5 + WS10 + WS11 + WS11A + WS12)* WS13 £
  Copy to box H13 on IHT200

  Cumulative total of lifetime transfers *(box LT1, form D3)* WS14 £
  Copy to box H14 on IHT200

  Aggregate chargeable transfer *(WS13 + WS14)* WS15 £
  Copy to box H15 on IHT200

Working out the total tax that is payable

- Aggregate chargeable transfer *(WS15)* WS16 £
  Copy to box J1 on IHT200

- Tax threshold WS17 £
  Copy to box J2 on IHT200

- Value chargeable to tax *(WS16 – WS17)* WS18 £
  Copy to box J3 on IHT200

  Tax due (WS18 @ 40%) WS19 £
  Copy to box J4 on IHT200

- Tax (if any) on lifetime transfers *(box LT7)* WS20 £
  Copy to box J5 on IHT200

  Total of lifetime transfers LT3 £
  Copy from box WS14

  Tax threshold LT4 £
  Copy from box WS17

  Lifetime transfers chargeable to tax *(LT4 – LT5)* LT5 £

  Tax on lifetime transfers *(LT6 @40%)* LT6 £
  Copy to box WS20

- Relief for successive charges WS21 £
  Copy to box J6 on IHT200

  Tax payable on chargeable estate *(WS19 – WS20 – WS21)* WS22 £
  Copy to box J7 on IHT200

8.11 Calculation of Tax

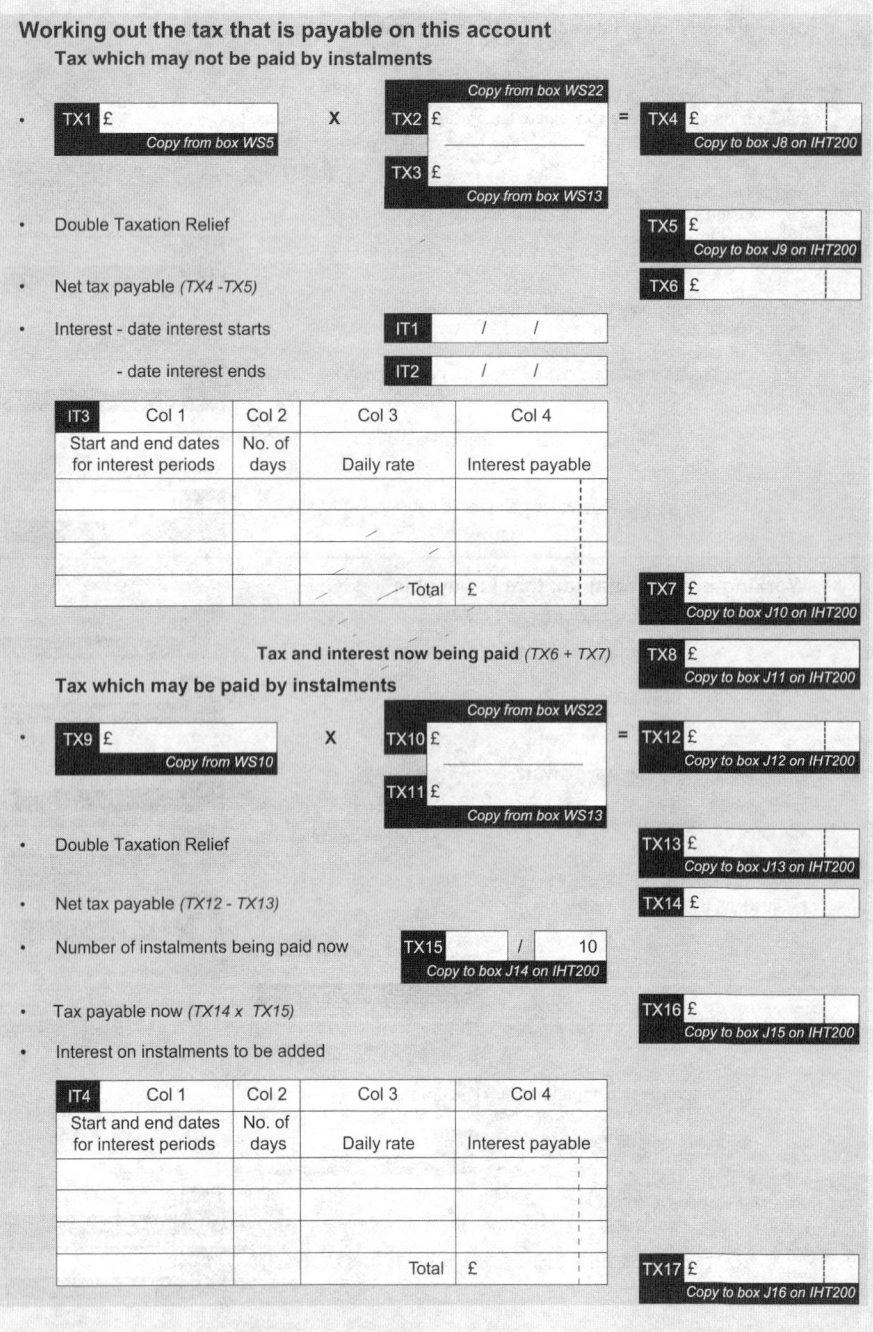

Working out the tax that is payable on this account

Tax which may not be paid by instalments

- TX1 £ _____ (Copy from box WS5) X TX2 £ _____ (Copy from box WS22) TX3 £ _____ (Copy from box WS13) = TX4 £ _____ (Copy to box J8 on IHT200)

- Double Taxation Relief — TX5 £ _____ (Copy to box J9 on IHT200)

- Net tax payable *(TX4 -TX5)* — TX6 £ _____

- Interest - date interest starts — IT1 / /

- - date interest ends — IT2 / /

IT3	Col 1	Col 2	Col 3	Col 4
	Start and end dates for interest periods	No. of days	Daily rate	Interest payable
			Total £	

TX7 £ _____ (Copy to box J10 on IHT200)

Tax and interest now being paid *(TX6 + TX7)* — TX8 £ _____ (Copy to box J11 on IHT200)

Tax which may be paid by instalments

- TX9 £ _____ (Copy from WS10) X TX10 £ _____ (Copy from box WS22) TX11 £ _____ (Copy from box WS13) = TX12 £ _____ (Copy to box J12 on IHT200)

- Double Taxation Relief — TX13 £ _____ (Copy to box J13 on IHT200)

- Net tax payable *(TX12 - TX13)* — TX14 £ _____

- Number of instalments being paid now — TX15 [/ 10] (Copy to box J14 on IHT200)

- Tax payable now *(TX14 x TX15)* — TX16 £ _____ (Copy to box J15 on IHT200)

- Interest on instalments to be added

IT4	Col 1	Col 2	Col 3	Col 4
	Start and end dates for interest periods	No. of days	Daily rate	Interest payable
			Total £	

TX17 £ _____ (Copy to box J16 on IHT200)

- Additional interest to be added

IT5	Col 1	Col 2	Col 3	Col 4
	Start and end dates for interest periods	No. of days	Daily rate	Interest payable
			Total £	

TX18 £

Copy to box J17 on IHT200

Tax and interest now being paid *(TX16 + TX17 + TX18)*   **TX19** £

Copy to box J18 on IHT200

Total tax and interest now being paid on this account *(TX8 + TX19)*   **TX20** £

Copy to box J19 on IHT200

Working out Successive Charges Relief
Estate of first person to die

Net value of estate for inheritance tax   **SC1** £

Legacies paid out from estate   **SC2** £

Inheritance Tax paid on estate   **SC3** £

Deceased's entitlement from estate   **SC4** £

Rate of relief   **SC5**   %

Formula for relief

$$\frac{\textbf{SC3}\ £}{\textbf{SC1}\ £} \times \textbf{SC4}\ £ \times \textbf{SC5}\ \% = \textbf{SC6}\ £$$

Working out Double Taxation Relief

Value of foreign property included in form IHT200 on which foreign tax has been paid (figure in sterling)   **DT1** £

Foreign tax paid (in sterling)   **DT2** £

Formula for relief

$$\frac{\textbf{WS22}\ £}{\textbf{WS13}\ £} \times \textbf{DT1}\ £ = \textbf{DT3}\ £$$

The relief is the **lower** of boxes DT2 and DT3.

9   Capital Gains Tax

Cross-reference. See 56.4 VALUATION for valuation at death for capital gains tax purposes.

Simon's Direct Tax Service, parts I3.611–I3.615, I5.915.

Other Sources. Tolley's Capital Gains Tax 2007–08.

9.1   **A lifetime disposition** may give rise to a chargeable gain subject to capital gains tax. There is no capital gains tax on property passing on death. For the purposes of inheritance tax no account is taken of any capital gains tax borne by the transferor in determining the reduction in value in his estate. [*IHTA 1984, s 5(4)*].

Example

A makes a gift of land to discretionary trustees valued at £10,000 on which there is capital gains tax of £4,000. The value for inheritance tax purposes (subject to grossing-up for the IHT payable) is £10,000 (i.e. the same as if A had sold the land and given the £10,000 proceeds to the trustees).

9.2   **Relief for CGT against IHT.** Capital gains tax paid is taken into account for IHT purposes in the following circumstances.

(*a*)   If the transferor fails to pay all or part of the capital gains tax within twelve months of the due date, an assessment may be made on the donee [*TCGA 1992, s 282 as amended by FA 2004, s 116*] and the amount of such tax borne by the donee is treated as reducing the value transferred. There is a similar effect when the transfer is from a settlement but this only applies if the capital gains tax is borne by a person who becomes absolutely entitled to the settled property concerned. [*IHTA 1984, s 165(1)(2)*].

Example

In the Example in 9.1 above, if A fails to pay the £4,000 capital gains tax and it is borne by the trustees, the value transferred by A is £6,000 for the purposes of inheritance tax.

(*b*)   Where a person sells, or is treated as having sold, national heritage property on the breach or termination of an undertaking (see 33.4 NATIONAL HERITAGE) any capital gains tax payable is deductible in determining the value of the asset for IHT purposes. [*TCGA 1992, s 258(8)*].

If IHT becomes payable in circumstances [other than the above], there is no relief for any of the CGT payable on the transfers. The Law Society revenue law committee memorandum recommended that where IHT becomes payable on transfers which have already suffered CGT then that CGT is given so that it reduces the subsequent IHT liability. On the 6 July 1994 at a meeting between the former Inland Revenue and the revenue law committee, the Inland Revenue thought that the problem was not a significant one but further representations by the Law Society were made to make it clear that the point is a priority for action (see Law Society's Gazette 7 December 1994).

9.3   **Relief for IHT against CGT.** In certain circumstances, where capital gains tax on a disposal not at arm's length has been held over under the provisions of *FA 1980, s 79* as extended by *FA 1981, s 78* and *FA 1982, s 82* (general relief for gifts etc. before 14 March 1989) or, where the disposal takes place after 13 March 1989, *TCGA 1992, s 165* (relief for gifts etc. of business assets), any inheritance tax payable (or which proves to be payable where a potentially exempt transfer becomes a chargeable transfer on the transferor's death within seven years) may be deducted from the chargeable gain arising on the transferee's subsequent disposal (but not so as to create an allowable loss). Where the inheritance tax is re-determined in consequence of the transferor's death within seven years of the chargeable transfer or is otherwise varied, all necessary adjustments are to be made whether by assessment, discharge or repayment. [*TCGA 1992, s 67(2)(3), s 165(10)(11); FA 2004, s 116*].

The same relief against the transferee's gain is available for chargeable transfers (not potentially exempt) after 13 March 1989 for which capital gains tax holdover relief is available under *TCGA 1992, s 260* (gifts on which inheritance tax is chargeable etc.). The foregoing relief is subject to the anti-avoidance provisions regarding private residence relief which is subject to a hold-over election under *TCGA 1992, s 260*. [*TCGA 1992, s 260(7)(8); FA 2004, s 116, Schs 21, 22*].

9.4   **For full details of capital gains tax,** see Tolley's Capital Gains Tax 2007–08.

9.5   **Claims for exemption.** Before the *Finance Act 1998* changes, there were no specified time limits for claiming the inheritance tax exemption. There is now a two-year time limit for making such claims. This does not affect the relief from CGT under *TCGA 1992, ss 258, 260* detailed above.

10   Chargeable Transfer

Simon's Direct Tax Service, parts I3–I4.

10.1   DEFINITION

A chargeable transfer is any TRANSFER OF VALUE (49) made by an individual other than an EXEMPT TRANSFER (21). [*IHTA 1984, s 2(1)*]. *Note*. A transfer of value can be made by a person but a chargeable transfer can be made only by an individual, although individual participators in a close company may be charged in respect of certain transfers made by the company (see 12 CLOSE COMPANIES). Inheritance tax is charged on the value transferred by a chargeable transfer. [*IHTA 1984, s 1*].

Certain lifetime transfers are designated potentially exempt transfers. See 59 WORKING CASE STUDY [**Case Study 6**]. A potentially exempt transfer is a transfer of value made by an individual after 17 March 1986 which would otherwise be a chargeable transfer and which is either a gift to another individual or a gift into an accumulation and maintenance trust or a trust for a disabled person. In relation to transfers of value made, and other events occurring, after 16 March 1987, certain gifts by individuals into and out of settlements with interests in possession are also included. See 38.1 POTENTIALLY EXEMPT TRANS-FERS for full details. A potentially exempt transfer made seven years or more before the transferor's death is an exempt transfer and any other potentially exempt transfer is a chargeable transfer. A potentially exempt transfer is assumed to be an exempt transfer during the seven years following the transfer (or, if earlier, until immediately before the transferor's death). [*IHTA 1984, s 3A; FA 1986, Sch 19 para 1; F(No 2)A 1987, s 96*].

The estate of a deceased person is treated as a transfer of value equal to the value of his estate made immediately before his death and is chargeable to inheritance tax. See 50 TRANSFERS ON DEATH for detailed provisions.

10.2   SEVEN-YEAR CUMULATION PERIOD

Chargeable transfers are cumulated over a seven-year period. After seven years transfers drop out of the cumulative total. The rate of tax on any chargeable transfer is determined from the tables at 41 RATES OF TAX by reference to the transferor's cumulative total of chargeable transfers within the previous seven years (including, where appropriate, poten-tially exempt transfers previously made becoming chargeable and chargeable transfers made before 18 March 1986 under the rules relating to CTT). [*IHTA 1984, s 7; FA 1986, Sch 19 para 2*].

10.3   NIL RATE TAX BAND

The first £300,000 of chargeable transfers in the seven-year cumulation period are taxable at nil per cent for the period 6 April 2007 to 5 April 2008. The nil rate band has also been set for 2008–09 at £312,000, for 2009–10 it has been set at £325,000 and for 2010–11 it has been set at £350,000. See 41 RATES OF TAX. The total of chargeable transfers is calculated after making any allowance for the annual exemptions but see 22.1 GIFTS WITH RESERVA-TION for circumstances where the annual exemption cannot be utilised although it may be available. No tax is payable but such transfers do have to be included in the transferor's cumulative total. [*IHTA 1984, ss 7, 8, Sch 1; FA 1986, Sch 19 para 36; FA 1987, s 57; FA 1988, s 136; SI 1989/468; SI 1990/680; SI 1991/735; F(No 2)A 1992, s 72; FA 1993, s 196; FA 1994, s 246; SI 1994/3011; SI 1995/3032; FA 1996, s 183, FA 1997, s 93; SI 1998/756; SI 1999/596; SI 2000/803; SI 2001/639; FA 2002, s 118; SI 2003/841; SI 2004/771; FA 2005, s 98; FA 2006, s 155; FA 2007, s 4*]. Various factors affect the application of the nil-rate band, including the effect of the annual exemption, previous chargeable transfers becoming 'out-of-time', potentially exempt transfers becoming chargeable and a reduction of tax rates where there are previous taxable chargeable transfers within the seven-year cumulation period. See examples at 1.7 and 1.8 INTRO-DUCTION AND BASIC PRINCIPLES, 8.4 CALCULATION OF TAX and also 41 RATES OF TAX. An account may still need to be submitted in respect of a chargeable transfer even if no tax is payable because it falls within the nil rate band. See 2.3–2.5 ACCOUNTS AND RETURNS.

10.4   **TIME OF GIFT**

As a basic rule no chargeable transfer can take place until there has been a disposition resulting in a shift of value from one estate to another. See 48 TIME OF DISPOSITION for details of when a disposition is considered to have occurred.

10.5   **POOLS SYNDICATES AND OTHER SIMILAR ARRANGEMENTS**

There is no chargeable transfer where football winnings, National Lottery (now Lotto) etc., are shared among the members of the syndicate in accordance with the terms of an agreement drawn up before the win. (25.E14 HMRC STATEMENTS OF PRACTICE and 59 WORKING CASE STUDY). The prior agreement can be verbal or written and it is recommended that a written record is made but it is not necessary to lodge this with HMRC Inheritance Tax. Providing an agreement is in existence any winnings by the syndicate leader which are passed on to the members of the syndicate are not chargeable to IHT. [**Case Study 9**].

11   Charities

Cross-references. See 21.2 and 21.3 EXEMPT TRANSFERS for gifts to charities; and 23.F2 HMRC EXTRA-STATUTORY CONCESSIONS for Roman Catholic religious communities; 59 WORKING CASE STUDY.

Simon's Direct Tax Service, parts I3.333, I4.215.

Other Sources. Tolley's Income Tax 2007–08; Tolley's Capital Gains Tax 2007–08; Foster, parts C3.33, D2.15; IHTM11101.

11.1   MEANING

'*Charity*' means any body of persons or trust established for charitable purposes only. [*ICTA 1988, ss 505, 506(1); IHTA 1984, s 272; ITTOIA 2005, s 878(1); FA 2006, ss 55, 56; ITA 2007, ss 519, 543(1)*].

'*Charitable purposes*' comprise the relief of poverty, the advancement of education and of religion and other purposes 'beneficial to the community' (Lord MacNaghten in *Special Commissioners v Pemsel HL 1891, 3 TC 53*). Under *Recreational Charities Act 1958, s 1*, the provision, in the interest of social welfare, of facilities for recreation or other leisure time occupation, is deemed to be charitable (subject to the principle that a trust or institution to be charitable must be for the public benefit). See in this connection *Guild v CIR HL*, [*1992*] *STC 162*, a CTT case where it was initially held in the SC that the phrase or for 'some similar purpose in connection with sport' in a bequest made to a sports centre might include non-charitable purposes and thus would not be 'for charitable purposes only' within *FA 1975, Sch 6 para 10* (now *IHTA 1984, s 23*). However, this was overturned in the HL, Lord Keith stating that, on a 'benignant construction', where the first part of the bequest (i.e. to the sports centre) was charitable, the phrase in the second part (i.e. 'or some similar purpose'), meaning the provision of facilities for the public at large, must also be charitable. For examples of purposes held to be charitable, see Tolley's Income Tax 2007–08. See Tolley's Capital Gains Tax 2007–08 for tax relief for gifts of qualifying investments and interests in land to a charity by an individual. Also gifts to Community Amateur Sports Clubs are exempt for inheritance tax purposes as well as capital gains tax. See for http://www.charity-commission.gov.uk/publications/cc22.asp a Model Agreement and http://www.hmrc.gov.uk/charities/casc.htm. [*ICTA 1988, s 587B inserted by FA 2002, s 43 and ICTA 1988, s 587C inserted by FA 2002, s 97; ITA 2007, ss 23, 24(1), 431(1), 445(1), Sch 1 paras 328, 536*]. See 59 WORKING CASE STUDY and [**Case Study 9**] for gifts to charities.

11.2   GIFTS

Gifts to charities are generally exempt from inheritance tax including the gifts of qualifying investments introduced by the *Finance Act 2000* for capital gains tax purposes (see above). See 59 WORKING CASE STUDY and [**Case Study 9**] for gifts to charities. There is no charge to tax when certain settled property becomes held for charitable purposes only without limit of time. See details at 21.2 and 21.3 EXEMPT TRANSFERS. See CTO Newsletter, July 1997 in 61 IHT NEWSLETTER AND TAX BULLETIN EXTRACTS.

11.3   TRUSTS

Where a charity takes the usual form of a trust in which there is no interest in possession i.e. a discretionary trust, special rules apply. Where the trusts on which property is held require part of the income to be applied for charitable purposes, a corresponding part of the settled property is regarded as held for charitable purposes, for the purposes of the rules in *IHTA 1984, Part III, Ch III* relating to SETTLEMENTS WITHOUT INTERESTS IN POSSESSION (44) (other than the provisions of *ss 78, 79* relating to conditionally exempt occasions and exemption from ten-yearly charge for National Heritage property). [*IHTA 1984, s 84*]. Provided the property is held for charitable purposes only, whether for a limited time or otherwise, it is not 'relevant property' and there is no ten-year anniversary charge under *IHTA 1984, s 64* (see 44.2 and 44.3 SETTLEMENTS WITHOUT INTERESTS IN POSSESSION). In addition, if the property becomes held for charitable purposes without any time limit, there is no charge to tax at other times (proportionate charge to tax) on distributions. See 11.4 below for property leaving temporary charitable trusts.

In the case of *St Dunstan's v Major [1997] STC SCD 212 Sp C 127* the gift to the Charity by way of Deed of Variation and the claiming of gift aid relief by the personal representative was precluded (see 60 TAX CASES). But where a bequest is part of a will or the assets are left to someone to make the gift to the charity then the charity exemption is in point under *IHTA 1984, s 23* and where the beneficiary makes a subsequent transfer to the charity gift aid relief will also be available; the charity being able to claim the basic rate relief in respect of the gift aid and the higher rate relief being claimed by donor who has been a beneficiary under the will and benefited the charity. Alternatively, providing the above procedures are adhered to the opportunity to claim gift aid relief and exemption under *section 23* will be available. A form of Trust document that utilises the Charities Aid Foundation documentation and flexible donation options is shown below but refer to CAF Trust Department regarding conditions applying before use. Tel. 01732 520026.

Trust document

1   *Definitions*

   (a)   The 'Donor' is the person whose name appears below under Donor Details.

   (b)   The 'Trustees' are the trustees for the time being of the Charities Aid Foundation.

   (c)   The 'Foundation' is the Charities Aid Foundation.

   (d)   The 'Trust Fund' is the amount of cash, or stocks and shares, given to the Charities Aid Foundation by the Donor and entered in the Schedule below together with any further sums or securities which may be given to the Foundation to be held upon the same terms and shall also be interpreted as the money, investments or property which may from time to time represent the original cash, stocks and shares or securities given to the Foundation.

   [(e)   The 'Conditions' are those conditions printed on the reverse of this Trust Document or any future amendment thereof.]

   (f)   The 'Successor' (or successors) is the person (or persons) duly appointed by way of a Successor Election Form who, following the death of the Donor, has the power to distribute the Trust Fund for charitable purposes.

2   *Donor Details*

Full Name ....

Title Mr/Mrs/Miss/Ms/Other ....

Address ....

....

Postcode .... Tel: ....

11.3 Charities

3 *Schedule*

Amount of cash £...............................

Or

Share details:-

Nominal	Holding
....	....
....	....

4 The Trust Fund, together with the income arising thereon, is to be held by the Trustees upon trust under the name of ....to the intent that it shall be distributed for charitable purposes as may from time to time be determined by the Donor during his/her lifetime and thereafter as may be determined by any Successors for their respective lives.

5 It is the wish of the Donor (without in any way seeking to fetter the investment powers of the Trustees) that initially the Trust Fund be invested as follows:-

	% (approx)
CAF UK Equity Growth Fund	....
CAF Bond Income Fund	....
CAF Equitrack Fund	....
CAF Socially Responsible Fund	....
Cash Deposit Fund	....
Other	....

6 The Donor shall, during his/her lifetime, have power to appoint a successor (or Successors) who upon the death of the Donor, will have all the rights and powers attributed to the donor including the power to appoint his/her own Successor (or Successors) subject to the Trustees having the discretion to limit the number of Successors to two in number at any one time.

7 The trust will terminate when the Trust Fund has been completely distributed or when the Trust Fund has been transferred to the Foundation Fund of the Charities Aid Foundation under condition (d) overleaf.

8 The management and operation of the Trust Fund shall be subject to the conditions and any future amendment thereof.

9 This document shall be governed by and construed in accordance with the Laws of England.

....

Donor's Signature

....

Date

....

Trust Manager (Countersigned on behalf of the Charities Aid Foundation).

....

Date

* Conditions apply to the Trust Document which are not reproduced here other than in (A) below.

Notes to the Trust Document

(A) In 7 above the reference to the condition is 'If and so far as the purposes of the Trust fund are, in the opinion of the Trustees, no longer possible or practical or should the trust upon which the Trust Fund is held fail for any reason then the Trust Fund together with any undistributed income arising therefrom shall be transferred to and held as part of the Foundation Fund of the Charities Aid Foundation'.

(B) For chargeable periods commencing after 21 March 2006, tax relief will be available for charities where only or part of a trade is carried on for a primary charitable purpose or where a trade is partly carried on by the beneficiaries of a charity. The trade must be split into two separate parts, a primary charitable purpose part, with tax relief under *ICTA 1988, s 505* given on the primary charitable purpose part or on the profits of the part carried on by the beneficiaries of the charity in respect of the non-primary purpose part. [*ICTA 1988, ss 505, 506 as amended by FA 2006, ss 55, 56; ITA 2007, ss 525(2)–(4), 539(2), 540(1)–(3), 541(2)–(6), 562(4)–(5), 563(2)–(6), Sch 1 paras 326, 327, Sch 2 para 107*]. See Tolley's Income Tax 2007–08 and Tolley's Capital Gains Tax 2007–08 for tax relief for gifts of qualifying investments and interests in land to a charity by an individual.

11.4 PROPERTY LEAVING TEMPORARY CHARITABLE TRUSTS

Property which is held on charitable trusts only until the end of a specific period (whether defined by date or in some other way) is subject to a charge when either

(*a*) it ceases to be held for charitable purposes otherwise than by being applied for charitable purposes (but see also 21.3 EXEMPT TRANSFERS for certain situations where there is no charge when property becomes that of a qualifying political party or a national body mentioned in *IHTA 1984, Sch 3* or, under certain conditions, a body not established or conducted for profit), or

(*b*) the trustees make a 'disposition' (otherwise than for charitable purposes) which reduces the value of the settled property. '*Disposition*' includes an omission to exercise a right, unless not deliberate, which is treated as made at the latest time that the right could be exercised. [*IHTA 1984, s 70(1)(2)(10), s 76*].

No charge arises

(i) if, under (*b*) above, the trustees do not intend to confer gratuitous benefit and either the transaction is at arm's length between persons not connected with each other (see 13 CONNECTED PERSONS) or is such as might be expected in such a transaction, or

(ii) if, under (*b*) above, the disposition is a grant of a tenancy of agricultural property in the UK, Channel Islands or Isle of Man, for use for agricultural purposes and made for full consideration in money or money's worth, or

(iii) on the payment of costs or expenses attributable to the property, or

(iv) where any payment is, or will be, income for income tax purposes of any person (or, in the case of a non-resident, would be if he were so resident), or

(v) in respect of a liability to make a payment under (iii) or (iv) above.

'*Payment*' includes a transfer of assets other than money.

[*IHTA 1984, s 63, s 70(3)(4)*].

Tax is charged on the amount by which the trust property is less immediately after the event giving rise to the charge than it would have been but for the event (i.e. the loss to the donor principle), grossed-up where the settlement pays the tax.

The rate at which tax is charged is the aggregate of the following percentages for each complete successive quarter in 'the relevant period'.

147

11.4　Charities

	Cumulative Total
0.25% for each of the first 40 quarters	10%
0.20% for each of the next 40 quarters	8%
0.15% for each of the next 40 quarters	6%
0.10% for each of the next 40 quarters	4%
0.05% for each of the next 40 quarters	2%
Maximum rate chargeable after 50 years	30%

The rate charged may be reduced if any of the property is, or was, EXCLUDED PROPERTY (20), see 11.5 below.

'*Relevant period*' is the period beginning with the day on which the property became (or last became) held on charitable trusts, or 13 March 1975 if later, and ending on the day before the chargeable event. Where property in respect of which tax is chargeable was relevant property (see 44.2 SETTLEMENTS WITHOUT INTERESTS IN POSSESSION) immediately before 10 December 1981 (e.g. in a discretionary trust) and became (or last became) comprised in a temporary charitable trust after 9 December 1981 and before 9 March 1982, the relevant period begins with the day on which the property became (or last became) relevant property before 10 December 1981 or 13 March 1975 if later. [*IHTA 1984, s 70(5)(6)(8)(9)*].

'*Quarter*' means a period of three months. [*IHTA 1984, s 63*].

See also 44.15 and 44.16 SETTLEMENTS WITHOUT INTERESTS IN POSSESSION which also apply to temporary charitable trusts.

Example 1

On 1 January 1972 A settled £100,000 on temporary charitable trusts. The income and capital were to be applied for charitable purposes only for a period of 25 years from the date of settlement, and thereafter could be applied for charitable purposes or to or for the settlor's grandchildren. On 1 January 2008 the trustees paid £50,000 to charity and the balance of the settlement, valued at £75,000, to the three grandchildren.

The relevant period is the period from settlement of the funds or, if later, 13 March 1975 to 1 January 2008, i.e. 131 complete quarters, and the amount on which tax is charged is £75,000 gross.

The rate of tax is

	%
0.25% for 40 quarters	10.00
0.20% for 40 quarters	8.00
0.15% for 40 quarters	6.00
0.10% for 11 quarters	1.10
	25.10%

IHT payable is 25.10% × £75,000 =　　　　　　£18,825

Example 2

Assume the same facts as in the above Example 1 except that the trustees apply £75,000 net for the settlor's three grandchildren, and the balance to charity.

The rate of tax is, as before, 25.10%

$$\text{IHT payable is} \frac{25.10}{100 - 25.10} \times £75,000 = £25,133$$

The gross payment to the beneficiaries is £75,000 + £25,133 = £100,133.

11.5   **Excluded property.** Where the whole or part of the amount on which tax is charged as in 11.4 above is attributable to property which was EXCLUDED PROPERTY (20) at any time during the relevant period, then, in determining the rate at which tax is charged in respect of that amount or part, no quarter throughout which the property was excluded property is to be counted. [*IHTA 1984, s 70(7)*].

12 Close Companies

Cross-references. See 5.6 AGRICULTURAL PROPERTY for agricultural companies; 7 BUSINESS PROPERTY; and 20.4 EXCLUDED PROPERTY for Government securities held by close companies.

Simon's Direct Tax Service, part I6.1.

Other Sources. Tolley's Corporation Tax 2007–08, chapter 13; Foster, part F1; IHTM14851.

12.1   MEANING

A company can make a TRANSFER OF VALUE (49) as a *person* but only an individual can make a CHARGEABLE TRANSFER (10). However, where a close company makes a transfer of value that value is apportioned among its participators and treated as if each had made a transfer of the apportioned part (except to the extent that the transfer is to that participator). [*IHTA 1984, s 94(1)*]. Also, where unquoted share or loan capital (or any rights attached thereto) is altered, the participators are treated as having made a disposition, see 12.5 below.

'*Close company*' is as defined by *ICTA 1988, s 414* for the purposes of corporation tax with the addition that companies resident outside the UK are treated as close companies if they would otherwise be within the definition. Broadly, a company is close if it is under the control of five or fewer participators or participators who are directors. [*IHTA 1984, s 102(1)*].

'*Participator*' in a company (whether resident in the UK or not) is as defined by *ICTA 1988, s 417* for the purposes of corporation tax but with the exclusion of a person who is a participator by reason only of being a loan creditor. [*IHTA 1984, s 102(1)*]. The definition includes any person

(i)   possessing, or entitled to acquire, share capital or voting rights, or

(ii)   possessing, or entitled to acquire, a right to receive, or to participate in, distributions, or

(iii)   entitled to ensure that present or future income or assets of the company will be applied, directly or indirectly, for his benefit.

See Tolley's Corporation Tax 2007–08 for full definitions of '*close company*' and '*participator*'.

12.2   APPORTIONMENT

The value transferred (see 12.3 below) by the company is apportioned among the participators according to their respective 'rights and interests' in the company *immediately before the transfer* and any amount so apportioned to a close company is further apportioned among its participators, and so on.

Exceptions. The following are not apportioned.

(*a*)   Any value attributable to any payment or transfer of assets to any person who brings it into account for the purposes of his income tax or corporation tax computations (including UK company dividends and other distributions not chargeable to income tax or corporation tax under *ICTA 1988, s 208*).

(*b*)   Any amount apportionable to an individual domiciled outside the UK which is attributable to any property outside the UK.

[*IHTA 1984, s 94(2)*].

'Rights and interests' in a company include those in the assets of the company available for distribution among the participators in a winding-up or in any other circumstances. They do not include

(i)   preference shares (as defined by *ICTA 1988, s 210(4)*) where any transfer of value by the company or any other close company has only a small effect on their value compared with the effect on the value of other parts of the company's share capital; or

(ii)   the rights and interests of 'minority participators' of a subsidiary company which disposes of an asset, as a transfer of value, to another 'group' company (within the terms of *TCGA 1992, ss 171(1), 171A(2)*) and that transfer has only a small effect on the value of the rights and interests of the minority participators compared with those of other participators.

A *'minority participator'* is a participator of the transferor company which is not, and is not a person connected with, a participator of the 'principal company' (before 14 March 1989, 'principal member') of the group or of any of the principal company's (before 14 March 1989, principal member's) participators.

'Principal company' and *'group'* are as defined in *TCGA 1992, s 170 as amended by FA 2000, Sch 29 para 14*. Before 14 March 1989, the *'principal member'* of a group is the member of which all the other members are '*75% subsidiaries*' (within *ICTA 1988, s 413(3)*).

[*IHTA 1984, ss 96, 97, 102(2); FA 1989, s 138(6); FA 2000, Sch 29 para 14; FA 2001, s 106; FA 2002, s 42(3)*].

12.3   VALUE TRANSFERRED

A transfer of value made by a close company is the amount by which the value of its assets immediately after a disposition is less than it would be but for the disposition, and this reduction (ignoring dispositions of EXCLUDED PROPERTY (20)) is the value transferred for apportionment among its participators. See 49 TRANSFER OF VALUE generally and 49.2 in particular for dispositions which are not transfers of value. The surrender by a close company of surplus advance corporation tax or losses within a group under *ICTA 1988, ss 240 (now repealed), 402* is not treated as a transfer of value. [*IHTA 1984, ss 3(1), 10, 94(3), 98(1)*]. A bonus issue of shares will not be a transfer of value nor will a genuine commercial transaction. In *Postlethwaite's Executors v HMRC* where a FURBS payment was not within *IHTA 1984, s 94* and that the payment was a disposition not intended to confer gratuitous benefit, within *IHTA 1984, s 10*. See 60 TAX CASES.

A dividend paid by a subsidiary to its parent is not a transfer of value nor is a transfer of assets between a wholly-owned subsidiary and its parent or between wholly-owned subsidiaries. (25.E15 HMRC STATEMENTS OF PRACTICE).

Example

The ordinary shares of companies A and B are held as follows (in January 2008)

		A	B
Individuals	X	80%	
	Y	20%	
	Z		10%
Company A			90%

Company B is non-resident and Z is domiciled in the UK. Company A sells a property valued at £220,000 to a mutual friend of X and Y for £20,000. The following month, company B sells a foreign property worth £100,000 to X for £90,000.

12.4 Close Companies

Company A

	£
The transfer of value is £220,000 – £20,000	200,000
Apportioned to X 80% × £200,000	160,000
Y 20% × £200,000	40,000
	£200,000

Company B

The transfer of value of £10,000 is apportioned

	£
To X 80% × 90% × £10,000	7,200
Deduct increase in X's estate	10,000
	—
To Y 20% × 90% × £10,000	1,800
To Z 10% × £10,000 note (C)	1,000
	£2,800

Notes to the example

(A)   If the sale by company A were to X (or Y), there would be no apportionment because the undervalue would be treated as a net distribution, thus attracting income tax.

(B)   On the sale by company B, X would not be liable to income tax.

(C)   If Z were not domiciled in the UK, his share of the transfer of value would not be apportioned to him. [*IHTA 1984, s 94(2)(b)*].

12.4   CHARGE ON PARTICIPATORS

Where a close company makes a transfer of value which is apportioned among its participators as above, inheritance tax becomes chargeable as if each such participator who is an individual had made a transfer of value after deduction of tax (if any) equal to the amount apportioned to him, less the amount (if any) by which his estate is more than it would be but for the company's transfer. For this purpose his estate is treated as not including any rights or interests (see 12.2 above) in the company. [*IHTA 1984, s 94(1)*].

Example

Assume the values transferred by X, Y and Z above in 12.3 and that X and Y have each made previous chargeable transfers in excess of £300,000 since January 2001 and have used up their annual exemptions for 2006/07.

Company A

	X	Y	Z
	£	£	£
Value transferred	160,000	40,000	
Annual exemptions 2007/08	(3,000)	(3,000)	
	157,000	37,000	
Tax (25% of net)	39,250	9,250	
Gross transfer	£196,250	£46,250	
IHT	£39,250	£9,250	

Company B

Value transferred	7,200	1,800	1,000
Deduct increase in X's estate	(10,000)	—	—
		1,800	1,000
Deduct annual exemption		—	1,000
		1,800	—
Tax (25% of net)		450	
Gross transfer		£2,250	
IHT		£450	

Note to the example

(A) Although it is understood that HMRC would follow this method of calculation in the above example, there is an alternative view which follows the exact wording of *IHTA 1984, s 94(1)*. This view is that the grossing-up should take place before the increase in X's estate is deducted. In the above example, it makes no difference as the gross transfer would still be less than the increase in X's estate. But suppose that X held 90% of the ordinary shares in Company A. His value transferred would then be £8,100 (90% × 90% × £10,000) and this alternative method would proceed as follows.

	£
Value transferred	8,100
Tax (25% of net)	2,025
	10,125
Deduct increase in X's estate	(10,000)
	£125
IHT thereon at 20%	£25

Where a close company makes a transfer of value to another company and an individual is a participator in both companies, any amount apportioned to him of the transferor company's transfer may be reduced by his apportioned part of the increase, due to the transfer, in the estate of the transferee company. [*IHTA 1984, s 95*].

Trustees. Where a person is a participator in his capacity as trustee of a settlement, any amount apportioned to him less the amount (if any) by which the value of the settled property is more than it would be apart from the company's transfer (leaving out of account the value of any rights or interests in the company) is treated as follows.

(*a*) If a qualifying interest in possession subsists in the settled property, a part of that interest corresponding to the amount apportioned (as reduced) is treated as having come to an end on the making of the transfer.

(*b*) If no qualifying interest in possession subsists in the settled property, the trustees are treated for the purposes of the rules relating to SETTLEMENTS WITHOUT INTERESTS IN POSSESSION (44) as having made, at the time of the transfer, a disposition as a result of which the value of the settled property is reduced by a corresponding amount.

[*IHTA 1984, s 99*].

Note. For transfers within (*b*) above the amount is grossed-up under *IHTA 1984, s 65(2)* (see 44.9 SETTLEMENTS WITHOUT INTERESTS IN POSSESSION) where the trustees pay the tax.

Where the amount apportioned to a person is not more than 5% of the value transferred, it is to be disregarded in determining the rate of tax on any later transfers made by him. [*IHTA 1984, s 94(4)*].

Exemptions. A participator can set his annual exemption against any amount apportioned to him but not the exemptions for small gifts, normal expenditure gifts, or gifts in consideration of marriage. The exemptions for gifts to charities and political parties and for national purposes or public benefit are available. [*IHTA 1984, ss 3(4), 19(5), 20(3), 21(5), 22(6), 94(5)*].

12.5 ALTERATION OF SHARE CAPITAL, ETC.

Where there is an alteration in the share or loan capital of a close company not consisting of quoted shares or securities (for transfers and other events occurring before 17 March 1987, shares or securities quoted on a recognised stock exchange) or in any rights attaching to its unquoted shares or debentures (for transfers and other events occurring before 17 March 1987, shares or debentures not quoted on a recognised stock exchange), the alteration is treated as having been made by a disposition by the participators whether or not it would otherwise fall to be so treated. Such a disposition is not a POTENTIALLY EXEMPT TRANSFER (38). Alterations are not to be taken to have affected the value of the unquoted shares etc. immediately before the alteration. '*Alteration*' includes extinguishment. [*IHTA 1984, s 98; FA 1986, Sch 19 para 20; FA 1987, s 58, Sch 8 para 2*]. Any decrease in value arising from an alteration brought about by a death is to be disregarded in arriving at the value of the estate on death. [*IHTA 1984, s 171(2)*].

Example

In January 2008 the share capital of company H, an investment company, is owned by P and Q as follows

P	600
Q	400
	1,000 ordinary £1 shares

The shares are valued at £10 per share for P's majority holding and £4 per share for Q's minority holding.

The company issues 2,000 shares at par to Q and the shares are then worth £3.50 per share for Q's majority holding and £1.50 per share for P's minority holding. P has previously made chargeable transfers in excess of £300,000 since January 2001 and has utilised his 2007/08 and 2006/07 annual exemptions.

The transfer of value for P is

	£
Value of holding previously	6,000
Value of holding now	900
Decrease in value	5,100
Tax (25% of net)	1,275
Gross transfer	£6,375
IHT thereon at 20%	£1,275

Notes to the example

(A)   P's transfer of value is *not* a potentially exempt transfer. [*IHTA 1984, s 98(3)*].

(B)   An alternative charge may arise under *IHTA 1984, s 3(3)* (omission to exercise a right) but the transfer would then be potentially exempt and only chargeable if P died within seven years.

For the above purposes, and in relation to transfers and other events after 16 March 1987, '*quoted*', in relation to any shares or securities, means quoted ('*listed*' from 1 April 1996) on a recognised stock exchange or dealt in on the Unlisted Securities Market, and '*unquoted*', in relation to any shares or securities, means neither so quoted nor so dealt in. [*IHTA 1984, s 272; FA 1987, s 58(2), Sch 8 para 17; FA 1996, Sch 38 para 2*]. In relation to transfers and other events after 9 March 1992, Unlisted Securities Market shares and securities are only treated as unquoted for the purposes of defining relevant business property (see 7.4 BUSINESS PROPERTY) and payment of tax by instalments (see 35.3 PAYMENT OF TAX). For all IHT purposes, and in relation to transfers and other events before 17 March 1987, Unlisted Securities Market shares and securities were not regarded as quoted on a recognised stock exchange (Inland Revenue Statement of Practice SP 18/80, 23 December 1980).

It is understood (see Law Society's Gazette 11 September 1991) that HMRC treat deferred shares issued after 5 August 1991 which subsequently come to rank equally, or become merged with, another class of shares as an alteration of rights within *IHTA 1984, s 98(1)(b)* (alteration in rights attaching to unquoted shares or debentures, etc.). Previously such an issue 'could' (the original statement by the former Inland Revenue said 'would' but it is understood they accepted 'could' as appropriate) have been treated as within *IHTA 1984, s 98(1)(a)* (alteration in unquoted share or loan capital).

HMRC have refused to confirm that either a purchase, redemption or repayment of a company's own shares or the alteration to any Articles of Association to enable it to make such a purchase etc. will not give rise to a transfer of value under *IHTA 1984, s 94*. (CCAB Memorandum, 22 June 1982). See 45.9 SHARES AND SECURITIES.

Trustees. Where a person is a participator in his capacity as trustee and the disposition would, if he were beneficially entitled to the settled property, be a transfer of value made by him, the following consequences arise.

(*a*)   *If an individual is beneficially entitled to an interest in possession* (e.g. a life interest) in the whole or part of so much of the settled property as consists of unquoted shares or securities of the close company (before 17 March 1987 shares or securities of the close company not listed on a recognised stock exchange), part of the individual's interest (equal to the amount of the decrease in value of the shares etc. in which the interest subsists) is treated as coming to an end. The amount of the decrease in value is the decrease caused by the alteration and is not grossed-up. [*IHTA 1984, s 100; FA 1987, s 58, Sch 8 para 3*].

(*b*) *If no individual is beneficially entitled to an interest in possession* in the whole of so much of the settled property as consists of the unquoted shares etc. then a charge to tax automatically arises under *IHTA 1984, s 65(1)(b)* (see 44.9 SETTLEMENTS WITH-OUT INTERESTS IN POSSESSION).

12.6 **LIABILITY FOR TAX**

(*a*) **On a transfer of value by the company apportioned to participators** (see 12.2 above). The company is primarily liable for the tax chargeable on amounts apportioned but, if it is unpaid by the time it ought to have been paid (see 35 PAYMENT OF TAX), the persons to whom any amounts have been apportioned and any individuals benefiting from the transfer become liable subject to the following limitations.

(i) A person to whom not more than 5% of the value transferred is apportioned is not liable for any of the tax.

(ii) Each of the other persons to whom any part of that value has been apportioned is liable only for the corresponding proportion of the tax.

(iii) A person benefiting from the transfer by an increase in value of his estate is liable only to the extent of that increase. [*IHTA 1984, s 202*].

Note. Whoever pays the tax, it is the participators (except those within (i) above) whose cumulative totals of transfers are increased. [*IHTA 1984, ss 3(4), 94(4)*].

A taxation warranty may be in order where transfers in shares in a close company are involved. In spite of the heading to *IHTA 1984, s 94* which states 'charge on participators' *section 202(1)(a)* makes it clear that tax is payable by the company. However, if the tax remains unpaid it can be collected from the participators by reason of *section 202(1)(b)*. In order to counteract the possibility of such a charge the following warranty may be inserted:

Taxation Warranty

1. General

All returns computations and payments which should or should have been made by the Company for any fiscal purpose have been prepared on a proper basis and submitted within the prescribed time limits and are up to date and correct and none of them is now the subject or likely to be the subject of any dispute with HMRC and will not give rise to any disallowance …

8. Inheritance Tax

The Company has made no transfer of value within the IHTA 1984, sections 94 or 99 in respect of close companies and charges on participators respectively.

No person has the power under IHTA 1984, section 212 to raise any capital transfer tax or inheritance tax by the sale of or charge over any of the Company's assets.

There is no unsatisfied liability to capital transfer tax or inheritance tax attached to or attributable to the assets of the Company or the shares of the Company and neither the assets nor the shares are subject to HMRC/Capital Taxes charge as is mentioned in IHTA 1984, section 237.

Note: *Further conditions apply to the Taxation Warranty that are not relevant to this work.*

(*b*) **On an alteration of share capital or rights** (see 12.5 above). The participators who own the shares or debentures are liable for the tax on the disposition made by them. [*IHTA 1984, s 98(1)*].

12.7 **INTEREST IN POSSESSION OWNED BY CLOSE COMPANY**

Where a close company is entitled to an interest in possession in settled property, the participators of that company are treated, for the purposes of inheritance tax (except for the provisions of *IHTA 1984, s 55* relating to the acquisition by a person of a reversionary interest expectant on an interest to which he is already entitled), as being entitled to that interest according to their respective rights and interests in the company.

If such participators include the trustees of a settlement and a person is beneficially entitled to an interest in possession in the whole or part of the settled property, that beneficiary is treated as entitled to the whole or a corresponding part of the interest to which the trustees would otherwise be treated as entitled. For consideration of this provision, see *Powell-Cotton v CIR Ch D, [1992] STC 625* where an interest in possession for the life of P in part of settled property was held by a close company shares in which were gifted to a charity by P who held a life interest in the remaining part of the settled property. It was held that there had been a termination of P's interest (which he was deemed to hold by virtue of *IHTA 1984, s 101*). [*IHTA 1984, s 101 as amended by FA 2006, Sch 20 para 26*].

From 22 March 2006 where a close company is entitled to an interest in possession in settled property, that interest in possession will also include an immediate post-death interest (IPDI) or a transitional serial interest (TSI). Where there is a disposal of rights and interests in the close company to 'a later participator' then for these purposes the later participator will be entitled to that interest in possession according to their respective rights and interests in the company. See 43 SETTLEMENTS WITH INTERESTS IN POSSESSION for full details. [*IHTA 1984, s 101 as amended by FA 2006, Sch 20 para 26*].

Note: In cases where property is held on SETTLEMENTS WITH INTEREST IN POSSESSION (43) which are settled on or after 22 March 2006, not being an IPDI or a TSI, whereby the close company acquired the interest for full consideration in money or money's worth from an individual who was beneficially entitled to it then it is not relevant property for the purposes of *IHTA 1984, s 58(1C)*. [*FA 2006, Sch 20 para 19(3)*].

13   Connected Persons

Simon's Direct Tax Service, part I3.142.

Other Sources. Foster, parts C1.42 and F2; IHTM04442.

> [*IHTA 1984, s 270; TCGA 1992, s 286; FA 2005, s 103; ITA 2007, ss 993, 994, Sch 1 para 411*]

13.1   **MEANING**

For many tax purposes, certain persons are treated as being so closely involved with each other that either they must be viewed as the same person or transactions between them must be treated differently from transactions 'at arm's length'. Any question of whether a person is connected with another is determined for the purposes of *IHTA 1984,* as it is for the purposes of capital gains tax, by *TCGA 1992, s 286 as amended by The Tax and Civil Partnership Regs 2005, SI 2005/3229, Reg 121* but with modification to the meaning of 'relative', 'settlement', 'settlor' and 'trustee'. [*ITA 2007, ss 993, 994*].

13.2   **Individuals. An individual** is connected with his spouse or civil partner, or with relatives (including their spouses) of his or of his spouse or civil partner. It appears that a widow or widower is no longer a spouse (*Vestey's Exors and Vestey v CIR HL 1949, 31 TC 1*). Spouses divorced by decree nisi remain connected persons until the decree is made absolute (*Aspden v Hildesley Ch D 1981, 55 TC 609*). See definition of relative in 13.8 below. [*ITA 2007, s 993(2)*].

13.3   **Settlements. A trustee of a settlement,** in his capacity as such, is connected with

(*a*)   the settlor (see 13.8 below) if an individual, and

(*b*)   any person connected with the settlor, and

(*c*)   a body corporate connected with the settlement (see 13.8 below).

HMRC has confirmed (*a*) above applies as regards the time when a settlement is created and property first transferred to it. On the death of the settlor, neither (*a*) nor (*b*) apply (former Inland Revenue Tax Bulletin February 1993 p 56). [*ITA 2007, s 993(3)*].

13.4   **Partner. A partner** is connected with any person with whom he is in partnership and with the spouse/civil partner or a relative of that person, except in relation to acquisitions and disposals of partnership assets pursuant to bona fide commercial arrangements. In the case of a civil partnership recognised under the *Civil Partnership Act 2004* from 5 December 2005 the individuals in such a union will be treated as 'connected persons' as they will be close relatives of each other. See 59.44 WORKING CASE STUDY.

13.5   **Company. A company is connected with another company** if

(*a*)   the same person controls both, or

(*b*)   one is controlled by a person [A] who has control of the other in conjunction with persons connected with him [A], or

(*c*)   a person [A] controls one company and persons connected with him [A] control the other, or

(*d*)   the same group of two or more persons control both, or

(*e*)   a group of two or more persons has control of each company and the groups can be regarded as the same by treating one or more members of either group as replaced by a person with whom he is connected.

[*ITA 2007, s 993(5)*].

13.6   A company is connected with another person if that person (either alone or with persons connected with him) has control of it.

[*ITA 2007, s 993(6)*].

13.7   Control. Persons acting together to secure or exercise control of a company are treated in relation to that company as connected with one another and with any person acting on the directions of any of them to secure or exercise such control. Control may be 'exercised' passively, see *Floor v Davis HL 1979, 52 TC 609*.

[*ITA 2007, s 993(7)*].

13.8   '*Relative*' means brother, sister, ancestor or lineal descendant, uncle, aunt, nephew and niece. In the circumstances regarding the taxation of 'pre-owned' assets within *FA 2004, s 84, Sch 15* 'relative' shall, as well as the definition of 'relative' in *ITA 2007, s 993(2), Sch 1 para 411* (formerly *ICTA 1988, s 839*), be extended to include uncle, aunt, nephew and niece. See 22.1 GIFTS WITH RESERVATION. [*ICTA 1988, s 839; TCGA 1992, s 286(8); IHTA 1984, s 270; FA 2004, Sch 15 para 2; The Tax and Civil Partnership Regs 2005, SI 2005/3229, Reg 121; ITA 2007, s 993(2), Sch 1 para 411*].

'*Company*' includes any body corporate or unincorporated association but does not include a partnership. [*TCGA 1992, s 288(1); ITA 2007, s 994(1)*].

'*Settlement*' and '*settlor*' are defined in *IHTA 1984, ss 43, 44* (see 42.6 SETTLEMENTS— GENERAL).

'*A body corporate connected with the settlement*' is a close company (or one which would be close if resident in the UK), the participators in which include the trustees of the settlement, or a company controlled by such a close company etc. 'Control' is as defined in *ITA 2007, s 995(1)–(3)* (formerly *ICTA 1988, s 840*), i.e. the power of a person by shareholding or voting power (whether directly or through another company), or under Articles of Association or other regulating documents, to secure that the company's affairs are conducted according to his wishes. See also *Walding and Others (Executors of Walding, deceased) v CIR [1996] STC 13* and 7.4 BUSINESS PROPERTY; TAX CASES (60). [*ICTA 1988, s 682A(2)*].

14   Deeds Varying Dispositions on Death

Cross-reference. See 50.5 TRANSFERS ON DEATH; 59 WORKING CASE STUDY; 61 IHT NEWSLET-TER AND TAX BULLETIN EXTRACTS.

Simon's Direct Tax Service, parts I4.411–I.423.

Other Sources. Foster, part D4; IR Leaflet IHT 8, 'Alterations to an inheritance following death', reissued 1 September 2002; HMRC IHT Newsletter, August 2002, April 2004, August 2004 and April 2006; IHTM35011.

14.1   DISCLAIMERS AND VARIATIONS

A disposition by a deceased person (by will, on an intestacy or otherwise) may be disclaimed or varied after the death. If the following conditions are met, the disclaimer or variation is treated for inheritance tax purposes as if made by the deceased, and any disclaimed benefit is treated as if never conferred, nor is the disclaimer or variation treated as a transfer of value. [*IHTA 1984, ss 17(a), 142(1)*].

Example

A dies in December 2007 leaving his estate of £329,000 to his wife absolutely. His wife, having an index-linked widow's pension and other assets of her own, agreed with her sons, B and C, that they could benefit from the estate to the extent of the nil rate band in the sum of £300,000 in equal shares, i.e. £150,000 each. As this is a variation after 31 July 2002 a separate election/statement is not required and instead it is sufficient for the instrument itself to state that a variation is to have effect for inheritance tax purposes only where additional tax is due. For variations before 1 August 2002 a deed of variation should be duly executed, and an election made under *IHTA 1984, s 142(2)*.

A had made no chargeable transfers before his death.

	£
Exempt transfer to widow	29,000
Transfer to B	150,000
Transfer to C	150,000
	£300,000
IHT payable	Nil

Note to the example

(A)   If A's widow died five years later when her estate was valued at, say, £354,000, IHT payable would be £1,600 (assuming the £350,000 nil rate band is in force). If no instrument including a variation had been made on A's death and his widow's estate was, as a result, £654,000 (i.e. £300,000 going to the sons now added to £354,000 in her estate in five years), the IHT payable on her death would have been £121,600. The instrument has thus saved IHT of £120,000 (ignoring any potential increase in value in the funds originally intended for the sons). [*FA 2006, s 155*].

14.2   DISCLAIMERS

(*a*)   The disclaimer must be made in writing within two years of the death.

(*b*)   The disclaimer must not be made for any consideration in money or money's worth, except the making, in respect of another of the deceased's dispositions, of another disclaimer or variation which is treated as made by the deceased. See IHTM35100.

[*IHTA 1984, s 142(1)(3)*].

THIS DEED OF DISCLAIMER is made by.............of............ ("Mr A")

WHEREAS

(A)   [..............] died on .... ("the Testator")

(B)   The Testator left a will dated .... ("the Will")

(C)   By clause 3(1) of the Will the Testator left Mr A a pecuniary legacy of ten thousand pounds (£10,000) ("the Legacy")

(D)   Mr A. wishes to disclaim the Legacy

NOW THIS DEED WITNESSES as follows:

1.   Mr A disclaims the Legacy

2.   Mr A confirms that he has accepted or received no benefit from the Legacy

EXECUTED AS A DEED on ....200(7).

SIGNED as a deed and delivered   )
by [Mr A] in the presence   )
of:)

Notes to the Precedent

(A)   The deed should be unilateral. The personal representative should not be a party.

(B)   There is no need (or reason) to recite details of the grant of probate if it has already been obtained, or to endorse a memorandum on the disclaimer subsequently if it has not.

(C)   Clause 2 is far from conclusive but is probably worth including.

(D)   The precedent assumes that Mr A is not a residuary beneficiary, as the disclaimed legacy will fall into residue.

(E)   No elections are required; *sections 62(6)* and *142(1)* have automatic effect.

(F)   No stamp is required.

14.3   VARIATIONS

(*a*)   The variation must be made in writing, by any of the persons who benefit or would benefit from the dispositions, within two years of the death.

(*b*)   For variations prior to 1 August 2002, an election must have been made in writing to the Board (i.e. the former Inland Revenue Capital Taxes for IHT and Inspector of Taxes for CGT) within six months (or such longer time as the Board allow) after the date of the instrument by

(i)   the person or persons making the instrument, and

(ii) where the variation results in additional tax being payable, the personal representatives. (See CTO Newsletter, March and December 1996 in IHT NEWSLETTER AND TAX BULLETIN EXTRACTS (61)).

(*c*) For instruments after 31 July 2002 it is no longer necessary for an election to be made and the instrument itself should contain a statement as to the variation. Where the variation results in additional tax being payable, any of the persons in (*b*)(i) or (ii) above shall, within six months after the day on which the instrument is made, deliver a copy of it to the Board of HM Revenue and Customs and notify them of the additional tax that is due. [*IHTA 1984, s 218A; FA 2002, s 120(2)*]. The penalty for not complying with *s 245A(1A)* is an amount not exceeding £100 and a further penalty of £60 for every day after the day on which the failure was declared by the court or Special Commissioners and up until the day before the day on which the requirements are complied with. In addition to the preceding penalty under *s 245A(1A)* a further penalty can arise where a disposition on death is varied by the beneficiaries and gives rise to an additional tax IHT liability. In these circumstances where there is a continuing failure to deliver an instrument varying a disposition and notification of additional tax payable within 18 months after the day on which the instrument is made, a penalty of up to £3,000 may be charged. No penalty arises under any of the above provisions where there is 'reasonable excuse' for the failure unless the failure is not remedied without unreasonable delay after the excuse has ceased. See 36.1 PENALTIES. [*IHTA 1984, s 245A(1A)(1B), (5); FA 2002, s 120(3); FA 2004, s 295(3)*].

(*d*) The variation must not be made for any consideration in money or money's worth, except the making, in respect of another of the deceased's dispositions, of another variation or disclaimer which is treated as made by the deceased. See, however, IHTM35100 which states: 'The bar against consideration relates only to extraneous consideration and will not prevent a rearrangement of assets within the will'. See also Note (D) in Example in 5.9 AGRICULTURAL PROPERTY.

[*IHTA 1984, s 142(1)–(3) as amended by FA 2002, s 120(1)*].

The two sample elections in use **prior** to 1 August 2002 (below) were for use outside the deed of variation.

Inland Revenue Capital Taxes
CTO ref:
date of death:
[solicitor's] ref:

AB deceased

We, being the parties making a deed of variation dated .... a certified copy of which is attached to this election, elect pursuant to section 142(2) of the Inheritance Tax Act 1984 that section 142(1) of that Act shall apply to such deed of variation.

Signed:

Dated:

Please sign and return the duplicate of this election as confirmation of receipt.

Notes to the election

(A) A certified copy is not in practice required. A photocopy is usually accepted.

(B)   The receipt notice will not amount to an acceptance of the election. It merely confirms receipt. This is useful in that receipt by HMRC Inheritance Tax within six months of the variation is vital. If an election is posted in time but lost in the post, HMRC Inheritance Tax will put the parties to strict proof. Failure to receive a receipt puts the practitioner on alert. Following *FA 2002, s 120* it is not necessarily relevant to include such a receipt for variations after 31 July 2002 as notification to the Board is only required if additional tax is due. Similarly, it is not relevant for a receipt for capital gains tax purposes (below) to be sent to the HMRC following *FA 2002, s 52*.

HMIT
HMIT ref:
solicitor's] ref:

AB deceased

We, being the parties making a deed of variation dated .... a certified copy of which is attached to this election, elect pursuant to section 62(7) of the Taxation of Chargeable Gains Act 1992 that section 62(6) of that Act shall apply to such deed of variation.

Signed:

Dated:

Please sign and return the duplicate of this election as confirmation of receipt.

14.4   GENERAL

Although *IHTA 1984, s 142* does not require the execution of a deed for the alteration of dispositions taking effect on death, but simply an instrument in writing, the use of a deed is considered prudent. (Law Society's Gazette 18 December 1991) (See also HMRC Inspector's Manual, para 3284b issue 12/94.)

It is understood that HMRC Inheritance Tax take the view that the desired IHT effect is not obtained unless the appropriate words of variation or disclaimer appear in the deed itself (and not merely in the recitals) (Law Society's Gazette 7 November 1984). In leaflet IHT8 the wording in the instrument should be as follows:

'The parties to this variation intend that the provisions of section 142(1) Inheritance Tax Act 1984 and section 62(6) Taxation of Chargeable Gains Act 1992 shall apply.'

It would appear that this does not take into account the *FA 2002* changes and the wording detailed should incorporate some reference to the *FA 2002* changes as shown below in the precedent. See IHT NEWSLETTER AND TAX BULLETIN EXTRACTS (61), August 2002, p 5.

Also, HMRC CGT manuals (CG31691) have not been updated for that particular piece of legislation and still refers to 'the deed contains clear and certain words of election'. However, the Tax Bulletin of August 2002 states in the section entitled 'Simpler rules for dealing with Instruments of Variation for IHT and CGT' the following:

'**When do I have to decide whether to include the statements or not?**
What these changes will mean in practice is that you can draft an IoV in the usual way, but to have retrospective effect for IHT and/or CGT purposes it must contain a statement of the parties' intent, rather than a formal election, although if an IoV follows old drafting precedents and refers to an election, this would be regarded as a statement of the parties' intent. As the statement must be part of the IoV, the parties

will need to consider both the IHT and CGT consequences at the time the IoV is being drafted and decide at that time whether or not they wish provisions of s.142 and/or s.62 to apply.

In practice most elections under the old rules were included in the IoV itself. So apart from minor changes from the standard wording which you may wish to adopt to reflect better the change from elections, the difference is that under the old rules it was possible, although an election had been made in the IoV, to prevent it having any retrospective effect for IHT and CGT by choosing not to send it to the Board within the six-month period. This option is no longer available.'

HMRC have also specified certain conditions which they consider must be satisfied before an instrument of variation can come within *IHTA 1984, s 142*.

(i)　The instrument must clearly indicate the dispositions that are the subject of it, and vary their destinations as laid down in the will, or the law of intestacy, or otherwise. It is not necessary that the instrument should purport to vary the will or intestacy provisions themselves: it is sufficient if the instrument identifies the disposition to be varied and varies its destination.

Deed of Variation in intestacy

THIS DEED OF VARIATION dated .... 200(7) .. is made between:

(1)　'the Administrators' ....[Names].........[Addresses]...................

(2)　'the Personal Representatives' [of, say, the widow/widower (*see note (A) below in Notes to the Deed*)]

(3)　'the substituted Beneficiary' ....[Name].........[Address]................

WHEREAS

1.1　XY ('the Deceased') died intestate on ....[Date]......... and Letters of Administration of his estate were granted to the Administrators by the Principal ..[Name].. District Probate Registry on ...[Date]....

1.2　AB (the widow/widower of the deceased) was entitled to the whole of the deceased's estate.

1.3　AB died on ....(2006).. and a grant of representation was made to the Personal Representatives by the Principal ....[Name].... District Probate Registry on ...[date].

(4)　The Personal Representatives and the substituted Beneficiary:

2.1　agree that the provisions of the Schedule shall be construed as if they constituted the deceased's will and his/her estate shall be administered accordingly;

2.2　direct the Administrators to distribute the estate of the deceased in accordance with the provisions of the Schedule.

(5)　The parties elect for [section 142 of the Inheritance Tax Act 1984] and [section 62 of the Taxation of Chargeable Gains Act 1992] as amended by Finance Act 2002, section 120 and/or section 52 to apply to this deed.

(6)　It is certified that this instrument falls within category M in the schedule to the Stamp Duty (Exempt Instruments) Regulations 1987.

SCHEDULE

Signed as a Deed by the Administrators in the presence of .... [Name] ....

.... [Address] ....

Signed as a Deed by the Personal Representatives in the presence of   [Name] ......

.... [Address] ....

Signed as a Deed by the substituted Beneficiary in the presence of ..... [Name] ....

.... [Address] ....

Notes to the Deed

(A) It will not necessarily be the case that the widow/widower will be entitled to the whole estate (see TRANSFERS ON DEATH (50.9)) and therefore references to widow/ widower of the deceased would be replaced by the 'original beneficiary' and the 'substituted beneficiary'.

(B) If a residuary beneficiary benefits under an intestacy but wishes to make a complete disclaimer then he/she needs clearly to disclaim both the residuary gift and the resulting entitlement under intestacy.

(ii) Where there is more than one variation in relation to the same will or intestacy, HMRC consider that an election validly made is irrevocable and that an instrument will not fall within *IHTA 1984, s 142* if it *further* redirects any item (or part of any item) that has already been redirected by an earlier instrument. (Law Society's Gazette 22 May 1985). This has been confirmed by the decision in the case of *Russell and Another v CIR Ch D, [1988] STC 195*. However, in *Lake v Lake and others Ch D, [1989] STC 865* an originating summons was sought for rectification of an original deed of variation where HMRC had claimed that a later deed entered into was inoperative following *Russell* above. The order for rectification was granted as it was shown that the original deed did not carry out the intentions of the parties concerned. See also in this connection *Matthews v Martin and others Ch D 1990, [1991] BTC 8048* where an order for rectification was granted as the original deed did not reflect the agreement reached between the parties because of errors in the preparation of the draft for execution.

HMRC Inheritance Tax have confirmed that they do not regard a deed as having been made for a consideration in money's worth where it is entered into solely to avoid or compromise a claim under the *Inheritance (Provision for Family and Dependants) Act 1975* (Tolley's Practical Tax 1984, p 112). See also Note (D) in Example in 5.9 AGRICULTURAL PROPERTY.

HMRC Inheritance Tax have also made it clear that under *section 142(1)(a)* the words 'or otherwise' can apply to the automatic inheritance of a deceased owner's interest in jointly held assets by the surviving joint owner(s) (Inland Revenue Tax Bulletin, October 1995, p 254). HMRC Inheritance Tax have stated that there has been confusion in this area suggesting that the surviving joint owner could not vary the inheritance in such circumstances and HMRC give the example below.

Example

A family home is owned by mother and son as beneficial joint tenants and, on the mother's death, her interest is passed by survivorship to the son who then becomes the sole owner of the property. The son could vary his inheritance of his mother's interest by redirecting it to his children and this would enable the half share of the property to skip one generation on transfer.

14.4 Deeds Varying Dispositions on Death

Where a variation to which the above provisions apply results in property being held in trust for a person for a period of not more than two years after the death, the disposition which takes place at the end of that period is treated as if it had taken place at the beginning of that period, but any distribution or application of property occurring in that period is unaffected (i.e. will be chargeable to inheritance tax under the provisions relating to settled property). In Scotland, property which is subject to a proper liferent is deemed to be held in trust for the liferenter. [*IHTA 1984, s 142(4)(7)*]. See also *Soutter's Executry v CIR [2002] STC SCD 385 Sp C 325* where a woman (S) died in November 1999 and the value of her estate was less than the IHT threshold. She owned a house, in which she lived with a friend (G). Under her will, she gave G the right to live in the house, rent free. G died in November 2000. In an attempt to reduce the IHT due on G's death, S's executors and G's executors purported to execute a deed of variation of S's estate, under *IHTA 1984, s 142*, removing the provision whereby G could live in the house rent free. The former Inland Revenue issued a notice of determination that the purported deed of variation was ineffective because the deed of variation was not a disposition of property and had no effect. S's executors appealed. The Special Commissioner dismissed the appeal, observing that 'the executors of a liferentrix have nothing they can vary'. G's executors 'had neither right, title or interest to any liferent'. They 'could not have continued to receive the liferent so they had nothing to give up or vary. The liferent was not and could not be assigned to them … a purported assignation of an expired liferent has no reality'. Some commentators suggest that the view that there was nothing to vary is incorrect and there is conceptually no difference between the position where a beneficiary has spent a gift or sold a gifted asset before the execution of a variation, which would be allowed, and the case in point. See Taxation Magazine, 22 May 2003, p 197. It remains to be seen whether the Executors appeal. See also HMRC IHT Newsletter, December 2001 in IHT NEWSLETTER AND TAX BULLETIN EXTRACTS (61).

The above provisions regarding disclaimers and variations apply whether or not the administration of the estate is complete or the property concerned has been distributed in accordance with the original dispositions. They apply to 'property comprised in a person's estate' immediately before his death which term includes EXCLUDED PROPERTY (20) but not any settled property in which the deceased had only an interest in possession nor property to which he was treated as entitled under the provisions relating to GIFTS WITH RESERVATION (22). [*IHTA 1984, s 142(5)(6); FA 1986, Sch 19 para 24*].

Example

Assume H dies worth £315,000, leaving it all to his wife W who herself is already worth £50,000. H has already made PETs a few years previously to his children amounting to £155,000. W then dies leaving her entire estate among the children. Though not strictly relevant assume also that the children would have been H's beneficiaries had W predeceased him. Assuming both deaths occurred in the current tax year then, for both to benefit from the nil rate band, between £65,000 and £145,000 needs to be read back through H's will to be taken by the children directly in that estate.

THIS DEED OF VARIATION is made ....200(7).

BETWEEN

1.	"the Wife's Executors"	Namely..............and.............. both.............solicitors of.............
2.	"the Husband's Executors"	Namely..............and.............. both.............solicitors of.............
3.	"the Children"	Namely:

166

(1)..............of..............
(2)..............of..............
(3)..............of..............

WHEREAS

(A)   H ("the Husband") late of .... died on ....

(B)   The Husband's Executors are the executors appointed under his will ("the Will") probate to which was granted by the Leeds District Probate Registry on ....

(C)   In his will the Husband left his entire estate to the Wife

(D)   W ("the Wife") late of .... died on ....

(E)   The Wife's Executors are the executors appointed under her will dated .... and who will be applying for Probate a memorandum of which will be endorsed on this deed

(F)   The Children are the residuary beneficiaries entitled between them to the entire estate of the Wife.

(G)   The parties wish to vary the dispositions of the Husband's estate as follows

(H)   Such variation will leave the estate of the Wife solvent and capable of answering all debts taxes liabilities and testamentary expenses

NOW THIS DEED WITNESSES

1.   The Will shall be deemed to read and always to have read as if in it the Husband had left (subject to tax) a pecuniary legacy of sixty thousand pounds (£60,000) to each of the Children

2.   It is certified that this instrument falls within category L in the schedule to the Stamp Duty (Exempt Instruments) Regulations 1987.

3.   The parties elect for [section 142 of the Inheritance Tax Act 1984] and [section 62 of the Taxation of Chargeable Gains Act 1992] as amended by section 120 and/or section 52 of the Finance Act 2002 to apply to this deed.

EXECUTED AS A DEED on the day and year first above written

SIGNED etc.

Notes to the example

(A)   The recital that the second estate will still be left solvent is considered extremely important.

(B)   Often the executors of H and W will be identical. They should be listed as two separate parties. There is no difficulty in the executors being parties twice to the deed in distinct capacities (see *Rowley, Holmes & Co v Barber [1977] 1 All ER 801*).

(C)   In the past a Stamp Duty certificate would have been included. It was not necessarily required as invariably there was no element of gift. The fact that category M originally mentioned deeds of variation did not mean that category M actually applied to all deeds of variation. The bulk of deeds of variation had an underlying element of gift and therefore were ordinarily stamped at category L. Prior to 1 December 2003 all instruments of variation were either liable to Stamp Duty, or certified as exempt from Stamp Duty under the categories L or M in *Stamp Duty (Exempt Instruments) Regulations 1987, SI 1987/597*. From 1 December 2003, any instrument involving a land transaction falls within the new Stamp Duty Land Tax

14.4 Deeds Varying Dispositions on Death

(SDLT) regime and does not need stamping. [*FA 2003, s 125*]. An instrument of variation that varies the devolution of land only, requires no certificate of exemption to be attached from 1 December 2003 onwards. Category M exemption certificate is only attached where an instrument of variation alters the destination of stocks and shares or marketable securities, e.g. where stocks and shares are left by the deceased in his will to the spouse and there is a variation of the will to take advantage of the nil rate band so as to benefit chargeable beneficiaries.

(D) The two tax elections will need to be made if the death occurred before 1 August 2002, see 14.3. However, it may not be applicable for both elections to be made as in the case of capital gains, for example, there may be assets with CGT losses to take into account or gains which may be covered by the annual CGT exemption, currently £9,200. And also from 1 August 2002 notification to the Board will be required only if additional tax is payable as a result of the variation.

(E) Where it is not practicable for all the beneficiaries of the second estate whose entitlements in practical terms are being varied, to join in the deed, perhaps because they are numerous and geographically diverse, it ought to suffice for the executors in the second estate to get clear authorities from each beneficiary to enter into the deed and then simply to recite that they are duly authorised and directed by all of those relevantly entitled to benefit under the will to enter into the variation.

No specific provision has been included to deal with the income position.

(F) Income tax has not been addressed in this precedent.

The case of *Marshall v Kerr HL, [1994] STC 638* concerned the effects on what is now *TCGA 1992, s 87* (overseas resident trusts) of what is now *TCGA 1992, s 60* (see Tolley's Capital Gains Tax 2007–08 under Death). Under this last provision, it is possible to vary or disclaim dispositions of the deceased so that, for capital gains tax purposes, a variation or disclaimer is ignored as a disposal and a variation is treated as made by the deceased and a disclaimed benefit is treated as never having been conferred. However, in many cases it will not be appropriate to elect to disclaim for CGT purposes such when it is wished to use up annual exemptions or where non-residents are involved or where the principal private residence is involved and (ESC D5) and has risen in value since the death. The wording of *IHTA 1984, s 142* is similar (but see below) in regard to the treatment of variations and disclaimers for inheritance tax purposes. In the case it was held that the execution of a written instrument of variation (whereunder a residuary bequest by will to the person executing the variation was settled on trusts administered by overseas resident trustees, the trusts having as one of its beneficiaries that person) at a time when the deceased estate was still being administered did not settle any specific assets comprised in the estate but settled a separate chose in action, the right to administration of the testator's estate. This would also seem pertinent for inheritance tax purposes. In addition it was held that in reality the person executing the variation was the settlor of the chose in action which comprised the property disposed of under the variation and there was nothing in the deeming provisions of *TCGA 1992, s 60* which required any assumption to the contrary. By virtue of the person making the variation being the settlor of the property varied, *TCGA 1992, s 87* was brought into operation. The decision that the person making the variation was the settlor of the property varied is of no application to inheritance tax since the deeming provisions of *IHTA 1984, s 142* are by reference to 'this Act' (i.e. *IHTA 1984*) whereas the relevant deeming provisions of *TCGA 1992, s 62* are by reference to 'this section'. On this view, confirmed by the former Inland Revenue Tax Bulletin February 1995, p 195, a variation or disclaimer would therefore for all inheritance tax purposes be deemed to be made by the deceased (e.g. for deciding whether settled property is EXCLUDED PROPERTY (20.2)).

Under Scots law there are certain circumstances in which a residuary legatee can make a partial disclaimer. Where this is possible HMRC accepts that *IHTA 1984, s 142* applies (see also E18 at 25 HMRC STATEMENTS OF PRACTICE). The same treatment may apply to partial disclaimers made under English law since they are thought to be valid where the part disclaimed is not onerous and either the legacy concerned is a pecuniary one or the will states expressly or by implication that partial disclaimers can be made (Tolley's Practical Tax 1994, pp 31 and 56).

See 50.5 TRANSFERS ON DEATH for other alterations of dispositions on death which are not transfers of value. For waiver of loans to be effected by deed, see 19.1 ESTATE.

14.5   PLANNING

Under *FA 2004, s 84, Sch 15 para 16* relating to 'Pre-owned assets' provides that under *IHTA 1984, s 17* where beneficiaries of a deceased's estate agree between themselves to vary the will or the intestacy provisions then any party to the variation is not to be taxed as a former owner by reason of having had an interest under the original will or intestacy provisions. There was some doubt expressed whether the wording of *FA 2004, s 84, Sch 15 para 16* protected a widow/widower from a charge where an interest in possession in a house is taken but subsequently that interest in possession is terminated and occupation still continues. HMRC have confirmed in an exchange of correspondence with the CIOT that such situations will be excluded from charge:

> '... all instruments of variation to which section 142(1) IHTA 1984 applies will come within the protection afforded by paragraph 16 of Schedule 15.'

As an election may be made within two years of the death under *IHTA 1984, s 17* this gives a period of grace with no charge arising in respect of rental value of the property or chattels in question where these are enjoyed by a 'relative' within *ITA 2007, ss 993, 994, Sch 1 para 411* (formerly *ICTA 1988, s 839*) including uncle, aunt, nephew, niece, settlement, settlor and trustee. This applies from 6 April 2005 and consequently the two-year period of grace mentioned above would only fully apply from deaths on or after that date. [*FA 2004, Sch 15 para 2*]. See 59.40 WORKING CASE STUDY.

The situation may arise where one spouse/civil partner may transfer shares to another spouse/civil partner on a nil gain/nil loss basis and the transferee spouse/civil partner dies sometime later leaving those same shares to the surviving spouse/civil partner with the attaching increased probate value unencumbered by the burden of an historic acquisition price, saving a substantial CGT charge and enjoying the benefit of the inter-spousal/civil partnership transfer exemption under *IHTA 1984, s 18*. However, if the transferee spouse/civil partner dies within days/weeks of the gift and the shares pass back by survivorship to the original donor then for transfer purposes the date of acquisition is the date of death and the surviving spouse's/civil partner's acquisition falls within the 30 days matching period for share disposals. [*TCGA 1992, s 106A(5)*]. This may give rise to a substantial CGT liability in the donor spouse's disposal computation. See example below.

Example

Wife W acquired 1,000 shares in Dido Ltd in June 1987 for £90,000 (the indexed cost in March 1998 being £143,640). W gives H 1,000 shares on 1 August 2007. H then dies on 30 August 2007 leaving his estate to W. The shares are valued at that time to be £342,000 and are left to his wife along with all his other assets. The inter spouse exemption rules out any charge under the excluded property provisions of *IHTA 1984, s 18* but under the matching CGT rules for shares the disposal on 1 August must be matched with the acquisition at the date of death on 30 August thereby negating any probate value uplift. Had H died one day later the shares would have been uplifted from an indexed cost of £143,640 to £342,000 with the opportunity for W to sell at that uplifted base value with little or no CGT.

In order to rectify this problem a deed of variation might be entered into by the parties; the deed of variation alters the late spouse's (H) will to create an interest in possession trust for the surviving spouse (W) enabling the trustees to pay capital to the surviving spouse. The deed of variation must be made before the shares are sold and within two years of the date of death. The result is that, even if the shares have been transferred to the surviving spouse, they will be treated as being acquired by the trustees at the value on death of the transferee spouse (H). [*TCGA 1992, s 62(1)*]. Subsequently the trustees make a capital appointment of the transfer of the shares to the surviving spouse (W) who acquires the shares at market value at the date of appointment and will not have reacquired them within 30 days of having given them to the late spouse thereby avoiding the matching rules. If the value of the shares has increased in the period between the date of death and appointment this may be covered by the annual CGT exemption or unused personal losses or there may be a loss to carry forward arising out of the appointment from the trust depending on the rise or fall in the market for those shares.

The beneficiaries of a will may decide amongst themselves to rearrange the distribution of the estate to effect different inheritance tax consequences by the use of a deed of variation or a disclaimer or by application to the Court either under the *Inheritance (Provision for Family and Dependants) Act 1975* or if they are *sui juris* under the *Variation of Trusts Act 1958*. See also Note (A) in the Example below. In this latter case the Court's consent which is embodied in a Court Order must be made within two years. In the case of *Goulding and Another v James and Another [1997] 2 All ER 239* the rearrangement of the beneficial interests to take advantage of tax planning schemes was successful despite the testatrix's previous intentions that the assets should devolve to the beneficiaries in another way. Such was the rearrangement that not only did it rearrange the division of the assets in contradiction of the testatrix's wishes but that there was also the subsidiary insertion of a tax planning scheme for the management of the funds.

In a Special Commissioners case a deed of variation redirecting a legacy to a charity was claimed as a gift by the original beneficiary eligible for gift aid relief for income tax purposes because the *FA 1990, s 25(2)(a)(e)* provisions for relief were met—this was disputed by the Inspector of Taxes. Also the transfer of value arising from the deed of variation was exempt from inheritance tax to the extent that the value transferred was attributable to property which is given to charities. [*IHTA 1984, s 23(1)*]. In this particular case the legacy of £20,000 to the charity, who had renounced probate and the deceased's son had applied for a Grant of Letters of Administration, was payable out of the property bequeathed to the son, W. The terms of the will were that the residue was to be held in trust for the son, W. By effecting the deed of variation and reducing the inheritance tax by £8,000 (i.e. £20,000 @ 40%) the residue of the estate was £8,000 more than it would have been had the gift to the charity been made without taking advantage of *IHTA 1984, s 142*. As sole residuary beneficiary W ultimately benefited from the inheritance tax saving notwithstanding that the residue available to W had been reduced by £12,000. The charity's position remained unaffected in that it claimed repayment of tax from HMRC of £6,666.67 being the tax withheld at basic rate on the gift although the charity's appeal against the former Inland Revenue's assessment to recover this amount was dismissed. W therefore was by the timeous election under *section 142* able to redirect a legacy to the charity claiming gift aid relief for income tax purposes and relief for charitable donations under *IHTA 1984, s 23*. It is thought that if it can be arranged for the inheritance tax to accrue to a third party, or to be added to the gift to the charity, the scheme should succeed. See *St Dunstans v Major [1997] STC SCD 212 Sp C 127* and 11.3 CHARITIES.

On another matter, the fact that a solicitor failed to advise a testatrix of the possibility of executing a deed of arrangement under *section 142* and, on the testatrix's death, advising her residuary beneficiaries of the contents of the will in time for them to effect an election under that section; it was held by the court not to be a breach of duty in not advising the testatrix about the tax avoidance schemes of another estate and also the executor owed no duty to inform a legatee that there was a prospective legacy. Accordingly in this case there was no obligation on the executor to advise of the possibility of tax mitigation by way of *IHTA 1984, s 142*. However, a duty of care to an intended beneficiary is clear from Lord Nolan's dictum in *White v Jones [1995] 1 All ER 691* and this might extend to advising a beneficiary of circumstances that might jeopardise a claim being submitted under *section 142* (see *Cancer Research Campaign v Ernest Brown & Co, Ch D [1997] STC 1425*.

Also, IHT 210 (Notes) at D1 (Notes) had previously stated:

> 'If an Instrument of Variation or Disclaimer, which varies either the terms of the Will or the distribution of an estate under intestacy, has been signed, please attach a copy of the deceased's Will (if appropriate) and a copy of the Instrument of Variation or Disclaimer to form D1, irrespective of the value of the estate.'

In drawing up an Instrument of Variation it should be distinguished whether the interest is an absolute one or a life interest only. In the case of an absolute interest passed on to the survivor who in turn dies the property passed on subsists in the donee's estate and it is possible for those inheriting on the second death to redirect the estate of the first person to die provided the second death is within two years of the first death. See IHT NEWSLETTER AND TAX BULLETIN EXTRACTS (61), April 2006, p 2. Contrast this with the position where the survivor is given a life interest in property on the first death; that interest expires on the death of the life tenant and there is no property capable of disposition. Therefore where there is a life tenancy comprising part of an estate and that person dies, then as the variation is made after the death of the life tenant, at that time there is no interest in existence and hence no opportunity to redirect. In such a case a variation to assign a life interest might be considered. See *Soutter's Executry v CIR [2002] STC SCD 385 Sp C 325* above and example below.

Example

H dies on 31 August 2006 leaving an estate comprising farmland to his widow for life and thereafter to his two adult sons if they survive her, with substitution provisions in favour of grandchildren (those in existence being minors). The estate is non-chargeable because of the inter-spousal exemption but there is a potential problem that if the widow dies in excess of two years after the death of the husband there can be no variation of the husband's estate. The widow can vary her life interest in favour of her sons to ensure that some or the entire nil rate band is utilised.

THIS DEED OF VARIATION is made..............200(7).

BETWEEN

1.   "the Mother"   Namely..............of..............
2.   "the Sons"   Namely..............of..............
                           Namely..............of..............
3.   "the Executors"   Namely:
                               (1)..............of..............
                               (2)..............of..............
                               (3)..............of..............

WHEREAS

(A)   ....of ....('the father') died on.............. [2006]

(B)   The Father's will dated .....('the Will') appointed Executors to be executors and trustees of his estate.

(C)   The Executors obtained probate of the Will from the [........] District Probate Registry on .... [2006]

(D)   Under the Will the Mother is by Clause 3 entitled to the net income of the residuary estate for the remainder of her life ('her Life Interest')

(E)   The property detailed in the schedule ('the Property') is comprised of the residuary estate of the Testator

---

(F)   The Mother wishes to vary the dispositions of the Will as follows:

NOW THIS DEED WITNESSES

1.   The Will shall be deemed to read and always to have read (so far as on account of the contingent remainders such is possible) as if the Property has been left (subject to tax) to the sons as tenants in common in equal shares absolutely

2.   In furtherance of clause 1 the Mother assigns to the Sons her Life Interest to the extent of the Property (and no more) to hold the same unto themselves as tenants in common in equal shares absolutely

3.   The parties elect for [section 142 of the Inheritance Tax Act 1984] and [section 62 of the Taxation of Chargeable Gains Act 1992] as amended by Finance Act 2002, section 120 and/or section 52 to apply to this deed.

EXECUTED AS A DEED on the day and year first above written

the Schedule

.... and .... being

end of the Schedule

SIGNED etc.

Notes to the example

(A)   On account of the substitutional provisions a full *Saunders v Vautier 4 Beav 115* variation to deem the land direct to the sons is not possible as the consents of the minors and unborns are unavailable. It should be remembered that where any potential beneficiaries are minors, or are otherwise *sui juris*, it will be necessary for any variation to be approved on their behalf by the courts. This could include unborn children if the wording of the will is wide-ranging. Even though HMRC will normally accept that a woman who is aged over 55 is past child bearing age this is not necessarily true in practice. [*Variation of Trusts Act 1958; Trusts (Scotland) Act 1961*].

(B)   Pending the mother's death title to the land would remain in the trustees unless some arrangement were reached between the trustees and the sons to transfer title on a protected basis.

See below for Form D1.

HM Revenue & Customs

The Will

Name

Date of death

/ /

Give details and provide a copy of the latest Will made by the deceased, together with any codicils. If a Deed of Variation has been signed before applying for a grant, fill in the form to show the effect of the Will and the Deed together. You should read form D1(Notes) before filling in this form.

1 Is the address for the deceased as shown in the Will the same as the address on page 1 of form IHT200?

No Yes

If the answer is "No", say below what happened to the property shown in the Will.

2 Are all items referred to in the Will, for example, legacies referring to personal possessions, stocks and shares, loans or gifts made by the deceased, included in form IHT200?

N/A No Yes

If the answer is "No", say below why these items are not included.

3 Does the whole estate pass to beneficiaries who are chargeable to inheritance tax?

No Yes

If the answer is "No", deduct the exemption on form IHT200.

(Substitute)(LexisNexis Butterworths)

| D1 | www.hmrc.gov.uk/cto | Helpline 0845 30 20 900 | HMRC CT 08/06 |

15 Determinations and Appeals

Cross-reference. See 4 ADMINISTRATION AND COLLECTION.

Simon's Direct Tax Service, part I11.3.

Other Sources. Foster, part L3; IHTM37000.

15.1 **NOTICE OF DETERMINATION**

Where it appears to the Board that a transfer of value has been made (or a claim received in respect of such a transfer) it may issue a notice in writing to any person who appears to be the transferor, the claimant or to be liable for any of the tax chargeable stating that they have determined the matters specified in the notice. The matters are all or any of

(*a*) the date of the transfer;

(*b*) the value transferred and the value of any property to which the value transferred is wholly or partly attributable;

(*c*) the transferor;

(*d*) the tax chargeable and the persons who are liable to pay it;

(*e*) the amount of any payment made in excess of the tax for which a person is liable and the date from which, and the rate at which, tax or any repayment of tax overpaid carries interest; and

(*f*) any other matter that appears to the Board to be relevant.

This also applies to occasions on which tax is chargeable under the rules in *IHTA 1984, Part III, Ch III* relating to SETTLEMENTS WITHOUT INTERESTS IN POSSESSION (44), to events or occasions on which tax is chargeable under *IHTA 1984, s 32* or *s 32A* on conditionally exempt NATIONAL HERITAGE (33) property and to disposals of growing timber (see 58 WOODLANDS) left out of account on a previous death which gives rise to a charge under *IHTA 1984, s 126.*

The notice of determination will be based on any account or return which the Board are satisfied is correct or, otherwise, will be made according to the Board's best judgment. The notice must state the time and manner in which an appeal may be made. See *Two Settlors v CIR [2004] STC SCD 45 Sp C 385; Thomson (Thomson's Executor) v CIR [2004] Sp C 429.*

[*IHTA 1984, s 221(1)–(4)(6); FA 1985, Sch 26 para 5*].

15.2 **Conclusive nature of determination.** Subject to any variation agreed in writing or on appeal or later adjustments for underpaid or overpaid tax, a notice of determination is conclusive against the person on whom it is served. If it is served on the transferor and specifies the value of the transfer, or earlier transfers, it is also conclusive in respect of later transfers of value (whether or not made by the transferor) against any other person. [*IHTA 1984, s 221(5)*].

For all matters relating to the administration and collection of IHT, a notice of determination which can no longer be varied or quashed on appeal is sufficient evidence of the matters so determined. [*IHTA 1984, s 254(1)*].

15.3 **APPEALS AGAINST DETERMINATIONS**

Appeal to Special Commissioners. An appeal may be made against a notice of determination within 30 days of its service. The appeal must be in writing to the Board and must state the grounds of the appeal. See *Jacques v HMRC [2006] STC SCD 40 Sp C 513.* The Special Commissioners will generally hear appeals (but see 15.4 and 15.5 below for exceptions) and their decision is final except on a point of law (but see *Edwards v Bairstow and Harrison HL 1955, 36 TC 207* as a leading case on jurisdiction of Court on questions of fact) and they may confirm, vary or quash the determination appealed against. [*IHTA 1984, ss 222(1)(2), 224(5)*].

On an appeal before the Special Commissioners (see 15.7 below), they may allow the appellant to put forward any ground of appeal not specified in the notice of appeal and may take it into consideration if satisfied that the omission was not wilful or unreasonable. [*IHTA 1984, s 224(4)*]. See IHT 14, p 21.

15.4   **Appeal direct to High Court.** An appeal may be made direct to the High Court (or Court of Session in Scotland and Court of Appeal in Northern Ireland) if the appellant and the Board agree. If the Board does not agree, the High Court may, on application by the appellant, give leave for appeal direct to that Court if it is satisfied the matters to be decided are likely to be substantially confined to questions of law. [*IHTA 1984, s 222(3)(5)*]. In these circumstances, the High Court has the same powers to confirm, vary or quash a determination of the Board as the Special Commissioners would have had if the appeal had gone first to them. (*Von Ernst & Cie SA and Others v CIR Ch D 1979, [1979] STC 478*).

In *Bennett and Others v CIR Ch D 1994, [1995] STC 54* it was stated that whilst a precondition of the grant of leave is that the appeal is substantially confined to questions of law there will be instances where the case's 'novelty or importance or otherwise' is such that it can and should proceed to the High Court in the interests of justice.

15.5   **Appeal to Lands Tribunal.** Land valuation appeals (re land in the UK only) are determined by the Lands Tribunal and not by the Special Commissioners or the High Court. Any dispute on the value of land in an appeal to the Special Commissioners or High Court which is made on or after 27 July 1993, or has not begun to be heard before then, is referred to the Lands Tribunal. See *Prosser (personal representatives of Jempson deceased) v CIR [2003] STC SCD 250 Sp C 362*. Guidance on property valuations for IHT purposes may be obtained from the Royal Institution of Chartered Surveyors (RICS) in the form of their leaflet GN21. The contents of GN21 have been approved by the Valuation Office Agency. See http://www.voa.gov.uk/instructions/. See also HMRC Tax Bulletin Issue 63 'Guidance on Property Valuations'. [*IHTA 1984, s 222(4)–(4B); FA 1993, s 200(1)(3)*]. The Tribunal may be required to state a case for the Court of Appeal or the Court of Session in Scotland. [*Lands Tribunal Rules SI 1963 No 483*].

Prior to 27 July 1993, the question as to the value of an interest in UK land, taking into account the liability to repay a discount allowed to a purchaser under the 'right to buy' provisions of *Housing Act 1980*, was a question as to the value of land within the exclusive jurisdiction of the Lands Tribunal (*Alexander v CIR CA, [1991] STC 112*).

The address of the Lands Tribunal is at 48–49 Chancery Lane, London WC2A 1JR.

15.6   **Late appeals. A late appeal** may be accepted by the Board or the Special Commissioners. The Board must consent to the appeal if satisfied there was reasonable excuse for the delay and that the application was made thereafter without unreasonable delay. Otherwise it must refer the application to the Commissioners for their decision. [*IHTA 1984, s 223*].

15.7   **Special Commissioners: jurisdiction and procedure.** For appeal proceedings where the notice of the hearing of the appeal is given after 31 August 1994, formal rules of procedure and jurisdiction for the Special Commissioners are introduced by statutory instrument under wide regulatory powers granted to the Lord Chancellor. These wide regulatory powers have been used to include appeals under the *Proceeds of Crime Act 2002, s 320(1)*. [*TMA 1970, ss 46A, 56B–56D; IHTA 1984, s 225A; F(No 2)A 1992, s 76, Sch 16 para 8; FA 1994, s 254; SI 1994/1811 as amended by Special Commissioners (Jurisdiction and Procedure) (Amendment) Regulations 2003, SI 2003/968*].

An outline of the rules is given below where references to regulations refer to those of *SI 1994/1811*.

15.7 Determinations and Appeals

In preparation for a hearing rules are set down as regards the following: the listing of proceedings for hearing on the application of any party by notice served on the Clerk to the Special Commissioners (15/19 Bedford Avenue, London WC1B 3AS) Tel: 020 7612 970. [*Reg 3*]; the power of the Special Commissioner to give directions to assist in the determination of any procedural issue [*Reg 4*]; the summoning of witnesses [*Reg 5*]; the agreement of documents [*Reg 6*]; the power of the Presiding Special Commissioner to order that appeal proceedings be heard together or in succession where a common issue is involved [*Reg 7*]; the power of the Special Commissioners to direct that another party should be joined as a party in the proceedings, a preliminary hearing should be held and any proceedings should be postponed or adjourned [*Regs 8, 9, 11*]; the power of the Special Commissioners on a preliminary hearing or substantive appeal hearing to direct the delivery of relevant particulars and documents from any party to the appeal and the powers of those Commissioners or inspecting party to inspect and copy the particulars and documents so delivered [*Reg 10*]; and the adduction of expert evidence or report prepared by an assessor nominated under the *Proceeds of Crime Act 2000, s 320(2)*. [*Reg 12*].

As regards the hearing and determination of proceedings, rules are provided to cover the following matters: the constitution and sittings of a Tribunal formed by any one, two or three of the Special Commissioners [*Reg 13*]; the representation of the respondent by a barrister, advocate, solicitor or any officer of the Board and any other party to the appeal by a legally qualified person, a member of an incorporated society of accountants or, unless the Tribunal directs otherwise, any other person [*Reg 14*]; the hearing of an appeal before the Tribunal to be in public unless a party to the appeal is able to satisfy the Tribunal that the hearing should be in private and the Special Commissioner so directs [*Reg 15*]; the power of the Tribunal to decide to hear and determine proceedings if a party fails to attend or to be represented at a hearing for which notice has been given unless there is good cause, or to postpone or adjourn the hearing in the light of representations made in writing or otherwise [*Reg 16*]; and the procedure and evidence at the hearing of the appeal as regards such matters as the assessment of the truth and weight of any evidence and the appearance of witnesses [*Reg 17*]. The respondent in an appeal under *Proceeds of Crime Act 2002, s 320(2)* will be the Director of the assets Recovery Agency. See *Rose v Director of Assets Recovery Agency [2006] STC SCD 472 Sp C 543.*

A decision of the Tribunal is given by a majority of votes where it comprises two or three Special Commissioners, the Special Commissioner presiding in a Tribunal of two being entitled to a second or casting vote. A final determination of the Tribunal, whether given orally at the end of the hearing or reserved, must be recorded in a dated and signed document which must contain a statement of facts found and the reasons for the determination. A copy of the document must then be sent to each party, the date of sending it being treated as the date on which the final determination is made in the case of a reserved final determination, and must be accompanied by a notification of the provisions of *TMA 1970, SI 1994/1811* and the rules of court relating to appeals from the Special Commissioners, and of the time within which, and the manner in which, such appeals have to be made. After reserving final determination, the Tribunal can give a written decision in principle on one or more issues arising and this must contain a statement of facts and the reasons for the decision and a copy of it must be sent to each party. The making of the final determination is then adjourned until the parties agree any further questions or, failing agreement, the Tribunal decides those questions. The final determination need then only state facts and reasons insofar as these have not been dealt with already in any decision in principle given already. [*Reg 18*]. The Tribunal may review and set aside or vary the decision in principle or final determination (or both) where any party or the Clerk or any of the staff of the Special Commissioners makes an administrative error, a party failed to appear or be represented at the hearing but had good cause for such failure, or accounts or other information had been sent to the Clerk or the HMRC prior to the hearing but had not been received by the Tribunal until after the hearing. A written application for such a review stating grounds in full must be made within 14 days of the date on which the document recording the decision in principle or, as the case may be, the final determination was sent. A Tribunal proposing to review of its own motion must send notice of such a proposal to the parties within the same 14-day period. The Tribunal can determine the review by upholding the decision in principle or final determination, by substituting a new decision or determination in the same manner as in *Reg 18* above, or by ordering a rehearing. [*Reg 19*].

There are further rules relating to: the publication of reports of decisions in principle and final determinations where appropriate, but so that any report relating to an appeal heard in private is published so far as possible in a form which does not identify any of the persons whose affairs are dealt with therein [*Reg 20*]; the ordering of costs incurred by the Tribunal and, if required, the other parties against a party (including a party who has withdrawn his appeal or application) to the proceedings who has acted wholly unreasonably [*Reg 21*]; the referring of questions of values relating to land to the Lands Tribunal (see 15.5 above) by the Tribunal or, if the hearing of the appeal has not begun, by an officer of the Board [*Reg 23*]; the award of penalties (see 36 PENALTIES) against any party or person for failure to comply with Tribunal directions [*Reg 24*]; the treatment of clerical mistakes in documents recording a Tribunal direction or decision and of irregularities resulting from any failure to comply with any provision of *SI 1994/1811* itself or with any direction given by a Tribunal before a decision is reached [*Reg 25*]; the requiring of a notice under *SI 1994/1811* to be given in writing unless the Tribunal authorises the giving of an oral notice [*Reg 26*]; and the service and substituted service of documents [*Regs 27, 28*].

Prior to the commencement of *SI 1994/1811 as amended by Special Commissioners (Jurisdiction and Procedure) (Amendment) Regulations 2003, SI 2003/968* above, similar rules to those contained in *Regs 5, 10,* and *14* above applied. [*IHTA 1984, s 224(1)–(3); SI 1994/1813, Sch 1 para 20, Sch 2 Part I*]. For reports obtainable regarding Special Commissioners' decisions see 4.8 ADMINISTRATION AND COLLECTION.

15.8   **Appeal from determination of Special Commissioners.** Any party to an appeal, if dissatisfied in point of law with the determination of that appeal by the Special Commissioners, may appeal against that determination to the High Court (in Scotland, the Court of Session, and in NI, the Court of Appeal). See *Thorogood v CIR Ch D [2005] All ER (D) 201; STI 920* and 60 TAX CASES. As mentioned in 15.7 above, the final determination will be accompanied by a notification of the rules of court relating to such appeals, time limits and the manner in which appeals must be made.

The High Court etc. hears and determines any question of law arising on the appeal and may reverse, affirm or amend the determination appealed against, or remit the matter to the Special Commissioners with the Court's opinion on it, or make such other order in relation to the matter as the Court thinks fit. [*IHTA 1984, s 225; SI 1994/1813, Sch 1 para 21*].

Where notice of the appeal hearing was given before 1 September 1994, similar provisions applied save that an appellant had to make a written request to the Special Commissioners within 30 days of their determination for a case to be stated and signed and pay a fee of £25. Within 30 days of the case being received, the appellant had to send it to the High Court and, no later than the time of sending it, a copy of it to every other party. [*IHTA 1984, s 225*].

Cases may be continued up to the Court of Appeal and House of Lords under normal procedures.

15.9   **'Leapfrog' procedures.** See 15.4 above for appeal direct to the High Court. It is also possible to bypass the Court of Appeal and to appeal direct from the High Court to the House of Lords in certain cases where the appeal concerns a point of law of general public importance. [*Administration of Justice Act 1969, Pt II*].

15.10   **Judicial review.** A taxpayer who is dissatisfied with the exercise of administrative powers may in certain circumstances (e.g. where HMRC have exceeded or abused their powers or acted contrary to the rules of natural justice or where the Special Commissioners have acted unfairly or improperly) seek a remedy in one of the prerogative orders of mandamus, prohibition or certiorari. This is now done by way of application for judicial review under *Supreme Court Act 1981, s 31* and *Order 53* of the *Rules of the Supreme Court*. See also *Arkwright and Another (Williams' Personal Representatives) v CIR Ch D [2004] STC 1323*. The issue on an application for leave to apply for judicial review is whether there is an arguable case (*R v CIR (ex p Howmet Corporation and another) QB, [1994] STC 413*). The procedure is generally used where no other, adequate, remedy, such as a right of appeal, is available. See *R v Special Commrs (ex p Stipplechoice Ltd) (No 1) CA 1985, [1985] STC 248* and *(No 3) QB 1988, [1989] STC 93, R v HMIT (ex p Kissane and Another) QB, [1986] STC 152* and *R v CIR (ex p Goldberg) QB 1988, 61 TC 403*. There is a very long line of cases in which the courts have consistently refused applications where a matter should have been pursued through the ordinary channels as described above. See, for example, *R v Special Commrs (ex p Morey) CA 1972, 49 TC 71; R v Special Commrs (ex p Emery) QB 1980, 53 TC 555; R v Walton General Commrs (ex p Wilson) CA, [1983] STC 464; R v Special Commrs (ex p Esslemont) CA, 1984 STI 312; R v Brentford Commrs (ex p Chan) QB 1985, 57 TC 651*. See also, however, *R v HMIT and Others (ex p Lansing Bagnall Ltd) CA 1986, 61 TC 112* for a successful application where the inspector issued a notice under a discretionary power on the footing that there was a mandatory obligation to do so, and *R v CIR (ex p J Rothschild Holdings plc) CA 1987, 61 TC 178* where the former Inland Revenue was required to produce internal documents of a general character relating to their practice in applying a statutory provision. See, however, *R v CIR (ex p Taylor) CA, [1988] STC 832* where an application for discovery of a document was held to be premature. In *R v Inspector of Taxes, Hull (ex p Brumfield and others) QB 1988, 61 TC 589* the court was held to have jurisdiction to entertain an application for judicial review of a failure by the former Inland Revenue to apply an established practice not embodied in a published extra-statutory concession but this should be compared with *R v CIR (ex p Fulford-Dobson) QB 1987, 60 TC 168* where it was held that there had been no unfair treatment by the former Inland Revenue when it failed to apply a published extra-statutory concession because it was clear from the facts of the case that it was one of tax avoidance and this was a clearly stated general circumstance (see HMRC Pamphlet IR 131 mentioned in 23 HMRC EXTRA-STATUTORY CONCESSIONS) in which concessions would not be applied. It was held that there had been no unfairness by the former Inland Revenue when it refused to assess on the basis of transactions that the applicants claimed they would have entered into had an Inland Revenue statement of practice been published earlier (*R v CIR (ex p Kaye) QB, [1992] STC 581*). A similar view was taken in *R v CIR (ex p S G Warburg & Co Ltd)* where the Revenue declined to apply a previously published practice because not only was it not clear that the taxpayer's circumstances fell within its terms but also the normal appeal procedures were available.

There was held to have been no unfairness in two cases where the former Inland Revenue resiled from assurances given by its officers as to its course of action to be taken in regard to intended transactions put to it in 'advance clearance' form by the taxpayer where the latter, having received the assurances, subsequently entered into actual transactions similar to those envisaged in the request for clearance. In order to bind HMRC to any such assurances, it would seem necessary not only to make complete, clear, correct and unqualified representations of the circumstances in a written request and subsequently enter into actual transactions on all fours with those envisaged in the request but to ensure that request is sent to the appropriate HMRC officer or office (*R v CIR (ex p MFK Underwriting Agencies Ltd & Others) QB 1989, 62 TC 607; Matrix-Securities Ltd v CIR HL, [1994] STC 272*). See further Revenue Tax Bulletin August 1994, p 137.

The first step is to obtain leave to apply for judicial review from the High Court. Application for leave is made ex parte to a single judge who will usually determine the application without a hearing. The Court will not grant leave unless the applicant has a sufficient interest in the matter to which the application relates. See *CIR v National Federation of Self-employed and Small Businesses Ltd HL 1981, 55 TC 133* for what is meant by 'sufficient interest' and for discussion of availability of judicial review generally.

Time limit. Applications must be made within three months of the date when the grounds for application arose. The Court has discretion to extend this time limit where there is good reason, subject to conditions, but is generally very reluctant to do so. Grant of leave to apply for review does not amount to a ruling that application was made in good time (*R v Tavistock Commrs (ex p Worth) QB 1985, 59 TC 116*).

15.11   **Parliamentary history of legislation.** Following the decision in *Pepper v Hart HL, [1992] STC 898*, the Courts are prepared to consider the parliamentary history of legislation, or the official report of debates in Hansard, where all of the following conditions are met.

   (i)   Legislation is ambiguous or obscure, or leads to an absurdity.

   (ii)   The material relied upon consists of one or more statements by a Minister or other promoter of the Bill together if necessary with such other parliamentary material as is necessary to understand such statements and their effect.

   (iii)   The statements relied upon are clear.

Unfortunately the consideration of the parliamentary legislation is dependent on the legislative programme at the time of discussion and was aptly alluded to by Lord Higgins in Hansard debates, 10 May 2001, Col 2232 as follows:

'As I pointed out on Second Reading, the debates in another place were very heavily programmed and the discussion on this issue was rather limited.

There is a particular disadvantage in this context, in view of the extent to which the courts can, as a result of *Pepper v Hart*, take into account the *travaux préparatoires* of any Bill.'

15.12   **Reform of the tax appeals system.** A consultation white paper issued in July 2004 (Cm 6243) 'Transforming Public Services: Complaints Redress and Tribunals' (CP 07/05) regarding the reform of the tax appeals system with its emphasis on proceedings to cancel a tax advantage can be best accommodated in a unified tax jurisdiction under a new tribunal system was published in July 2004. Under the new system it is proposed that the new tribunal system will consists of two tiers; one of which will hear virtually all first instance direct and indirect tax appeals. This will include IHT appeals and especially where there has been a perceived tax advantage. Appeals against these first tier decisions will go to an appellate tier where permission has been granted or on a point of law. See below. Responses to the consultation document were required to be submitted by 25 May 2005. [*FA 2004, s 703*].

In a statement by the Courts Service regarding the future of the Reform of the Tax Appeals System it was stated:

'The Government has been determining how best to take the recommendations in Sir Andrew's report forward and has undertaken a formal consultation exercise. The summary of responses to this consultation has recently been published and can be accessed at http://www.lcd.gov.uk/civil/tribunals.htm.

The Government has decided that the best way to deliver sustainable improvements for tribunal users is through the creation of the Tribunals Service within the Department for Constitutional Affairs. This new Service will be established from the ten largest non-devolved central Government tribunals and will include the Tax Appeal System. The creation of the new Service will help to ensure that all tribunals continue to provide effective and efficient services for users while meeting the Government's aim of providing a modern, high quality service to more tribunal users.'

See http://www.courtservice.gov.uk/tribunals/gcit/reform.htm.

15.12 Determinations and Appeals

It was expected that the new Tribunals Service incorporating the Special Commissioners, the General Commissioners and VAT and Duties Tribunals would operate from April 2006. See The Tax Journal, 16 May 2005.

Appeal matters came under the responsibility of the Department for Constitutional Affairs as the Tribunals Service from 1 April 2006 (http://www.financeandtaxtribunals.gov.uk/). At the point of transfer and immediately after there is no change to the way that appeals are processed or where they are heard and 'customers' will continue to deal with the same people in the same offices and hearing venues. Forms and time limits will remain the same and appeals will still be heard by tribunals made up of a lawyer sitting with a doctor, accountant or disability expert, depending on the nature of the appeal. It is unlikely that there will be any further changes to these aspects until Parliament has approved further legislation. The transitional year of the new Tribunals Service (which also includes most other government tribunals apart from the Tax Commissioners) ran from 4 April 2005 to 31 March 2006.

A Tribunals, Courts and Enforcement Bill was introduced into the House of Lords on 16 November 2006 but it is thought that there will be no cessation of the current roles of the General and Special Commissioners until at least 2009.

16 Diplomatic Immunity

Simon's Direct Tax Service, part I9.327.

16.1 EXEMPTION

Diplomatic agents (i.e. heads of mission or members of diplomatic staff) of foreign states are exempt from all duties and tax except, *inter alia*, taxes on

(*a*) private immovable property situated in the UK;

(*b*) capital taxes on investments made in commercial undertakings in the UK; and

(*c*) 'estate, succession or inheritance duties' on property in the UK except on movable property which is in the UK solely due to the presence of the deceased as a member of the mission or as a member of the family of a member of the mission. [*Diplomatic Privileges Act 1964, s 2*].

The head of a diplomatic mission will normally supply the Foreign and Commonwealth Office with a list of the staff of the mission etc. and, once such persons have been accepted as *persona grata*, exemption from liability will apply where appropriate. See The London Diplomatic List, December 2006 (ISBN 0115917845). Any question which arises as to whether a person is entitled to privilege or immunity is to be settled conclusively by a certificate issued by or under the authority of the Secretary of State. [*DPA 1964, s 4; ITA 2007, s 841*]. See also IHTM11270.

Relief is extended to members of the families of diplomatic agents (provided they are not UK nationals) and members of the administrative and technical staff of the mission, together with their families (provided they are not nationals or permanent residents in the UK).

In interpreting inheritance tax and estate treaties between the UK and any other country consideration should be given as to whether the treaty was based on the OECD 1966 Estate Tax Draft Model or the OECD 1982 Estate Tax Model. This is because when interpreting certain terms in a treaty, either based on the 1966 Model or the 1982 Model, the 1982 version had a close relationship in application terms to the 1977 OECD Income Tax Model. Commentaries on the articles will vary significantly depending on the original model that was used. In the case of diplomatic and consular officials the 1982 Model refers to them in *Article 13*, whereas the 1966 Model refers to them in *Article 14*. *Article 13* of the 1982 Model convention provides that the convention does not affect the fiscal privileges of diplomatic agents or consular officials under the general rules of international law or under *special agreements*.

Consular officers, their families and staff. Similar provisions apply as to diplomatic agents except that the *Consular Relations Act 1968, Arts 49, 51* expressly exclude from exemption 'duties on transfers' unless on movable property belonging to a deceased and in the UK solely because of his presence as a member of the consular post etc.

A *member of a consular post* means a consular officer, a consular employee or a member of the service staff. A *consular officer* means the person charged with the duty of acting as head of a consular post and any other person entrusted with the exercise of consular functions. A *consular employee* means any person employed in the administrative or technical service of a consular post; and a *member of the service staff* means any person employed in the domestic service of the consular post. [*CRA 1968, Sch 1 para 1*].

Officials of international organisations including representatives, members of committees or missions etc. may be specified by Order in Council as exempt from certain taxes. [*International Organisations Act 1968; Arms Control and Disarmament (Privileges and*

16.1   Diplomatic Immunity

Immunities) Act 1988, s 1(2)]. The position of **officials etc.** **of the European Communities** is covered by the *Protocol on the Privileges and Immunities of the European Communities 1965*. [*European Communities Act 1972*].

17 Domicile

Cross-reference. See 18 DOUBLE TAXATION RELIEF; 59 WORKING CASE STUDY.

Simon's Direct Tax Service, part I9.2.

Other Sources. Tolley's Tax Planning 2007–08; Foster, part J2; IR Leaflet IR20 and 17 April 2002 Treasury Budget Report; IHTM13000.

17.1 APPLICATION

Inheritance tax applies to all dispositions by an individual domiciled in the UK but only to assets situated in the UK if he is domiciled abroad. To determine a person's domicile the general law applies (see 17.2 below) except in the special circumstances described in 17.3 below. In the 2002 Budget on 17 April 2002 the Chancellor of the Exchequer announced a review of the rules relating to the residence and domicile and taxation of those persons resident or domiciled outside the UK. Formal consultation commenced after the 2003 Budget. Past domicile reviews (1987 Law Commission Report, 1988 Consultation Paper and numerous earlier Commissions and Committees set up to look at the subject) have always been met with an adverse response and the Government states that it is keen to acknowledge its commitment to international business and encourage people with the right qualifications from abroad who reside in the UK long term and it continues to examine responses. Following the Budget on 16 March 2005 the Government continues to review residence and domicile and is continuing to seek further contributions to the debate; eventually a consultation paper will be issued setting out the various proposals for reform. The Budget 2007 briefly mentioned at paragraph 5.120 the domicile issue as follows:

> 'The review of the residence and domicile rules as they affect the taxation of individuals is ongoing.'

17.2 GENERAL LAW

A person may have only one place of domicile at any given time denoting the country or state considered his permanent home. He acquires a *domicile of origin* at birth (normally that of his father). It may be changed to a *domicile of choice*, but this must be proved by subsequent conduct. See *Re Clore (deceased) (No 2), Official Solicitor v Clore and Others Ch D, [1984] STC 609* for a case where English domicile of origin was retained as a result of failure to establish a settled intention to reside permanently in Monaco. Actual settlement abroad is necessary as well as intention; see *Plummer v CIR Ch D, [1987] STC 698*. If a domicile of choice is established but later abandoned (by actual action, not by intention or declaration only, see *Faye v CIR Ch D 1961, 40 TC 103*) reversion to domicile of origin is automatic. A case of this was *Civil Engineer v CIR [2002] STC SCD 72* where the abandonment of a Hong Kong domicile of choice, thereby reviving a UK domicile, resulted in a chargeable transfer in respect of the setting up of a discretionary trust in the interim that relied on the taxpayer's perception that he was non–UK domiciled. See also *Anderson (Anderson's Executor) v CIR [1997] 1998 STC SCD 43 Sp C 147* in which a domicile of choice of England in place of Scotland (origin) suggested by HMRC failed due to the insufficient persuasive elements of the abandonment of Mr Anderson's roots in Scotland. See *Allen & Hateley (executors of Johnson) v HMRC, [2005] STC SCD 614 Sp C 481* where the Special Commissioners determined whether a person of UK origin had lost her domicile of choice in Spain by coming to reside in England in order to be cared for by a relative (domicile held not to have been lost).

Domicile is a highly technical matter and does not necessarily correspond with either residence or nationality. See *Earl of Iveagh v Revenue Commissioners SC (RI), [1930] IR 431; Fielden v CIR Ch D 1965, 42 TC 501* and *CIR v Cohen KB 1937, 21 TC 301*. This last case shows how difficult it is to displace a *domicile of origin* by a *domicile of choice* but contrast *In re Lawton Ch D 1958, 37 ATC 216*. See also *In re Wallach PDA 1949, 28 ATC 486, Buswell v CIR CA 1974, 49 TC 334, Steiner v CIR CA 1973, 49 TC 13, CIR v Bullock CA 1976, 51 TC 522* and *In re Furse decd., Furse v CIR Ch D, [1980] STC 597; A Beneficiary v CIR [1999] STC SCD 134 Sp C 190; Moore's Executors v CIR [2002] Sp C 335*.

Minors. The domicile of a minor normally follows that of the person on whom he is legally dependent. Under *Domicile and Matrimonial Proceedings Act 1973, s 3* (which does not extend to Scotland), a person first becomes capable of having an independent domicile when he attains 16 (in Scotland, 14 for boys and 12 for girls) or marries under that age. Under *section 4* thereof, where a child's father and mother are alive but living apart, his domicile is that of his mother if he has his home with her and has no home with his father.

Married women. Up to 31 December 1973, a woman automatically acquired the domicile of her husband on marriage. From 1 January 1974 onwards, the domicile of a married woman is to be ascertained 'by reference to the same factors as in the case of any other individual capable of having an independent domicile' except that a woman already married on that date will retain her husband's domicile until it is changed by acquisition or revival of another domicile. [*Domicile and Matrimonial Proceedings Act 1973, ss 1, 17(5)*]. A woman married before 1974 does not reacquire her domicile of origin and retains her husband's domicile unless she subsequently establishes her own domicile of choice. See *CIR v Duchess of Portland Ch D 1981, 54 TC 648* and Form D31 of IHT 100. In the recent House of Lords decision involving a matrimonial case *Mark v Mark HL, [2005] UKHL 42* it was decided that the legality of a wife's presence in the UK was irrelevant when considering her domicile of choice within *Domicile and Matrimonial Proceedings Act 1973, s 5(2)* and therefore it was held that it is possible for someone who is present in the UK illegally to have a domicile of choice in the UK.

17.3 SPECIAL CIRCUMSTANCES

For the purposes of IHT and CTT only, an individual may be treated as domiciled in the UK at a time (the 'relevant time') when he is domiciled abroad under general law. This applies where

(a) he was domiciled (under general law) in the UK at any time during the three years immediately preceding the relevant time; or

(b) he was resident (see below) in the UK in not less than 17 of the 20 years of assessment (i.e. years ending on 5 April) ending with the year of assessment in which the relevant time falls.

[*IHTA 1984, s 267(1)*].

In IHT 210 (Notes) and in particular form D2 (Notes) states '… if a person has lived in the UK for a long time, so that they were resident for income tax purposes for at least 17 out of the 20 years ending with the tax year in which they died …we can charge inheritance tax on the deceased's worldwide estate, even though they were not domiciled in the UK when they died.'

In the circumstances regarding the taxation of 'pre-owned' assets within *FA 2004, s 84, Sch 15* 'domicile' for the purposes of the scope of the charge, includes deemed domicile within *IHTA 1984, s 267*, so that such treatment will include UK and, in some circumstances, overseas property. [*FA 2004, Sch 15 para 12*].

Example

David leaves the UK on 1 January 2005 and becomes a Dutch citizen. David moves to Brussels in Belgium during the later part of 2006 in order to avoid Dutch wealth tax. He owns a property in the Dordogne, France and owned a property in Cornwall which was given to his aged Aunt. He occupies it rent free for three months in the summer when she goes to reside in his Dordogne residence rent free for the same period, i.e. a reserved right. Neither of them pays the household bills when staying in the respective properties. He dies in a car crash in Belgium on 24 December 2007 and leaves all his assets to his brother who is resident in Spain.

The Netherlands levies estate duty on assets that pass on the death of an individual who was a Dutch resident at the moment of death, *or* who died a Dutch citizen within ten years of leaving the Netherlands i.e. 'trailing tax'. Dutch forced succession rules (legitieme portie) must also be taken into account.

Belgium levies estate duty taxes on non-resident donors if they die owning real estate situated in that jurisdiction. Belgium is party to treaties with only France and Sweden which allow Belgium to subject real property to estate duty.

France levies estate duties on immovable assets of non-residents such as real estate that pass on death. There are also forced heirship implications relevant to immovable property owned in France by non-residents.

Spain levies estate duty on a resident recipient, i.e. the beneficiary of a will if the person is resident in Spain.

United Kingdom levies inheritance tax on worldwide assets of *deemed* domiciliaries.

Summary: Although David is non-resident in France at the time of his death, France will tax the real estate i.e. the realty situated there, on the market value at the date of death. Similarly, although David is non-resident in the Netherlands the effect of the Dutch 'trailing taxes' regime which applies for a ten-year period, as detailed above, is to subject both the French and UK properties to Netherlands estate duty tax. There are no double tax treaties providing for exemption from estate duties levied on real estate. Spain will tax on the basis that the recipient i.e. David's brother is resident in Spain and not take into account the fact that David was non-resident and non-domiciled. The UK will tax David's worldwide assets (see above) and this will include the French and UK properties because he was domiciled (under general law) in the UK at any time during the three years immediately preceding the relevant time, i.e. 1 January 2005 to 24 December 2007, but this is less than three years. There is no statutory definition of 'year' and therefore in the absence of such a definition 'year' will mean a period of twelve calendar months. See *CIR v Hobhouse [1956] 1 WLR 1393*. In addition, from 6 April 2006 David will have a liability to IHT on the Cornwall property occupied by his Aunt because it was a gift of property which he now uses. David will also have a potential income tax liability under *FA 2004, Sch 15* for his use of the property for the three months in the summer of 2007 prior to his death. The property in the UK will be treated as part of his estate under *IHTA 1984, s 102* and by reason of his deemed UK domicile.

The result of the combined estate duty taxes in the UK, Netherlands, France and Spain and the possible income tax liability under former Schedule D Case VI in the UK could be that very little of the estate passes to the brother. The estate duty taxes exigible will be subject to unilateral double taxation relief where this is relevant. See *Heirs of Van-Hilten Van der Heijden v Inspecteur van de Belastingdienst/Particulieren/Ondernemingen buitenland te Heerlen* [2006] WTLR 919 (C-513/03) and 18.3 DOUBLE TAXATION RELIEF.

See below for Form D2 and 59 WORKING CASE STUDY **[Case Study 7]**.

The above provisions do not apply

(i)   in determining whether exempt government securities which are in the beneficial ownership of a non-domiciled person (or are settled property to which such a person is entitled to a qualifying interest in possession) are excluded property, see 20.4 EXCLUDED PROPERTY;

(ii) in determining whether certain savings to which persons domiciled in the Channel Islands or Isle of Man are beneficially entitled are excluded property, see 20.6 EXCLUDED PROPERTY;

(iii) where the domicile of a person is determined under the terms of a double taxation agreement which related to estate duty (and CTT) and still applies for IHT purposes;

(iv) in determining whether settled property which became comprised in a settlement before 10 December 1974 is excluded property, see 20.2 EXCLUDED PROPERTY; and

(v) in determining the settlor's domicile for the purposes of *IHTA 1984, s 65(8)* in relation to property which became comprised in the settlement before 10 December 1974, see 44.10 SETTLEMENTS WITHOUT INTERESTS IN POSSESSION.

Residence in the UK for years of assessment before 1993/94 was determined as for income tax purposes, but without regard to any dwelling-house available in the UK for the person's use. After 1992/93, residence in the UK is determined simply as for income tax purposes, but in practice the position may be unchanged because of the amendments for 1993/94 and subsequent years made by *FA 1993, s 208(1)(4)* to *ICTA 1988, s 336* (now *ITA 2007, s 831*) for income tax purposes so as to provide that the residence status of temporary residents in the UK be decided without regard being had to the availability of the use of living accommodation in the UK. Registration and voting as an overseas elector are removed from determination of domicile for tax purposes under *IHTA 1984, s 267(1)(a)*. [*IHTA 1984, s 267; FA 1993, s 208(3)(5), Sch 23 Part V; FA 1996, s 200; ITEPA 2003, s 722, Sch 6 paras 1, 48*].

A new account on Form IHT 100 (old Forms IHT 100 and IHT 101 were replaced as from April 2003) is required and also when there is a transferor who is non-UK domiciled and has transferred property that is not excluded property (i.e. asset held outside the UK) then supplementary form D31 should be completed as part of the IHT 100. This form asks for details of chargeable events if the transferor is domiciled in a foreign country or if the transferor is treated as domiciled in the UK. The form does not require details of foreign assets or foreign currency bank accounts held with the main UK banks or ANZ Grindlays Bank Plc, Banque Nationale de Paris Plc, Italian International Bank Plc or Wesleyan savings Bank Plc. In addition, if the transferor was not ordinarily resident in the UK at the date of the chargeable event UK government securities that are authorised as being exempt from tax is also treated as excluded property for these purposes. Even though the Channel Islands and Isle of Man are treated as not being included in the UK, if a transferor was domiciled in one of those jurisdictions at the date of the chargeable event, War Savings Certificates, National Savings Certificates, Ulster Savings Certificates, Premium Bonds, Save As You Earn schemes and deposits with the National Savings & Investments are treated as excluded property.

Form P86 which is normally completed by individuals coming to the UK to take up employment has been revised to include a section on domicile. In less straightforward cases a new Form DOM 1 will have to be completed to determine the domicile position of the individual (Inland Revenue Press Release 8 September 1994. See also Taxline March 1995 Item 38). See Form D2 above where non-UK domicile is claimed.

United Kingdom comprises England, Scotland, Wales and Northern Ireland. The Channel Islands (Jersey, Guernsey, Alderney and Sark) and the Isle of Man are not included. Great Britain comprises England, Scotland and Wales only.

17.4 FOREIGN ASPECTS

The concept of *domicile* in relation to inheritance tax and estate duties is particular to the UK but other jurisdictions depend on residency, source and nationality or citizenship. For instance, the UK, Ireland and Malta tax only if the non-resident is domiciled in that jurisdiction. Particularly, the UK applies inheritance tax to all dispositions by an individual domiciled in the UK but only to assets situated in the UK if he is domiciled abroad. This may be at odds with other jurisdictions that tax solely on a residency basis. Some jurisdictions tax assets located in the jurisdiction, commonly known as 'source' taxation. Invariably this includes immovable property such as realty and will also include movable property such as share certificates in companies based in that jurisdiction. Where registration of an asset is required by notarial deed in the jurisdiction this fact may also require that the asset be included as a taxable source where the non-resident owner dies. However, even though registration is a practical means of enforcement by some jurisdictions moveables may be exempt where held by non-domiciles. See 59.22 WORKING CASE STUDY.

Nationality and/or citizenship is an important factor in a number of jurisdictions. In jurisdictions where this is a dominant requirement tax can be applied on the basis that the deceased is a national even though that individual was non-resident at the time of death.

The concept of domicile when considered with other countries with which the UK has agreements (see 18.2 DOUBLE TAXATION RELIEF) can give rise to some disparate domicile treatment.

(*a*)   **Ireland** (1978/1107), the definition of domicile includes the deemed domicile rules of *IHTA 1984, s 267* but introduction of the Irish capital acquisitions tax (CAT) should be referred to in terms of residence superseding domicile. [*Irish Finance Act 2000*].

(*b*)   **India** (1956/998), the UK deemed domicile rules of *IHTA 1984, s 267* cannot be applied to the worldwide assets of someone who dies with an Indian domicile under local law.

(*c*)   **Pakistan** (1957/1522), the UK deemed domicile rules of *IHTA 1984, s 267* cannot be applied to the worldwide assets of someone who dies with an Indian domicile under local law. However, the foregoing does not apply to Bangladesh.

(*d*)   **USA** (1979/1454), where an individual does not have a permanent home in the UK or USA he is deemed to be domiciled in the country in which he has his centre of vital interests rather than the country of habitual abode.

(*e*)   **France** (1963/1319), under *Article V(2)* where the deceased was domiciled in Great Britain the French succession duty is not applied to property situated outside of France. See 59.21 WORKING CASE STUDY.

17.4   Domicile

Domicile outside the United Kingdom

Name	Date of death
	/ /

You have said that the deceased was not domiciled in the United Kingdom. Answer the following questions and give the further details we ask for. You should read form D2(Notes) before filling in this form.

1   Write a brief history of the life of the deceased. If the deceased was female, and had married at any time on or before 1 January 1974, include a history of the life of the deceased's husband (or husbands) while she was married and up until 1 January 1974.

2   Was the deceased domiciled in the UK at any time during the 3 years up to the date of death?

No   Yes

3   Was the deceased resident in the UK for income tax purposes during the 4 years up to the date of death?

No   Yes

If the answer is "Yes" give details of any periods that the deceased was treated as resident in the UK during the last 20 years.

Please turn over

D2   www.hmrc.gov.uk/cto   *Helpline 0845 30 20 900*   HMRC CT 12/05

(Substitute)(LexisNexis Butterworths)

4 Who will benefit from the deceased's estate under the law that applies in the country of domicile?

5 Do you claim surviving spouse or civil partner exemption?   No   Yes

If you have answered "No" go on to question 6 below. If you have answered "Yes", provide the details we ask for below.

5a Give brief details of the property the surviving spouse or civil partner will receive following the death.

5b Was a community of property established in the foreign country?   No   Yes

If you have answered "No" go on to question 6. If you have answered "Yes" give full details of the rights each party to the marriage or civil partnership had over property.

5c Was any property under the community situated in the UK at the date of death?   No   Yes

If you have answered "Yes" give full details of the property.

5d Has the form IHT200 been completed on the basis of the community?   No   Yes

6 Did the deceased leave any assets of any description outside the UK?   No   Yes
   If so, give their approximate value. £

7 Do you expect the terms of a Double Taxation Convention or Agreement to apply to any of the assets owned by the deceased?   No   Yes

8 Is any foreign tax to be paid on assets in the UK as a result of the deceased's death?   No   Yes

18 Double Taxation Relief

Cross-references. See 17 DOMICILE; 46.2 SITUS; 59 WORKING CASE STUDY.

Simon's Direct Tax Service, parts I9.123, F7.1.

Other Sources. Tolley's Tax Planning 2007–08; Foster, part J5; IR Leaflet IHT 18; IHTM27000.

18.1 **GENERAL**

Where inheritance tax is chargeable in the UK, and tax of a similar character or which is chargeable on or by reference to death or gifts inter vivos is also charged by another country (an 'overseas territory') on the same property, relief may be available

(*a*)   under the specific terms of a double tax agreement between the UK and that other country [**Case Study 7**], or

(*b*)   under the unilateral double tax relief provisions contained in the UK legislation. [*IHTA 1984, ss 158(1), 159(1)*].

Leaflet IHT 10 (see also IHT 18) is available from HMRC Inheritance Tax and provides a summary of the information required from tax practitioners submitting an HMRC Account in respect of a deceased person who was UK domiciled but whose estate includes property situated outside the UK. A Green Paper was issued regarding the proposed EU Succession Directive entitled 'Wills and Succession in Europe' which required responses by September 2005. The European Parliament was still debating the 'Green Paper on Succession and Wills', COM (2005) 65 published in March 2005 and further clarifications were debated from the beginning of June 2006. See *Heirs of Van-Hilten Van der Heijden v Inspecteur van der Belastingdienst/Partculieren/Ondernemingen buitenland te Heerlen* [2006] WTLR 919 (Case: C-513/03) and example at 17.3 DOMICILE.

18.2 **DOUBLE TAX AGREEMENTS**

An agreement with another country is made by Order in Council after a draft has been approved by resolution by the House of Commons and may give retrospective relief. See IHT 18, pages 9 and 10.

The Board is authorised to exchange with the other government any information required provided the Board or its authorised officer is satisfied as regards confidentiality. This authority has been further enhanced by changes in the *FA 2003* which relax the obligations of secrecy and insert changes to the wording governing the exchange of information by changing the wording *in IHTA 1984, ss 158(1A), 220A* from 'necessary for the carrying out of' to 'foreseeably relevant to the administration or enforcement of'. [*IHTA 1984, ss 158(1A), 220A inserted by FA 2000, s 147(1) and as amended by FA 2003, ss 197, 198*].

Any provisions relating to estate duty in an existing agreement are extended to capital transfer tax and inheritance tax payable on a death (but not on lifetime transfers). Provisions in such agreements relating to the determination of domicile are not affected by *IHTA 1984, s 267* which treats certain persons as domiciled in the UK when they are domiciled abroad under the general law, see 17.3 DOMICILE. [*IHTA 1984, s 158*].

The existing estate duty agreements which now apply to inheritance tax on death are (country and statutory instrument year and number). See also **Case Study 7**.

France (1963/1319), **India** (1956/998), **Italy** (1968/304), **Pakistan** (1957/1522) and **Switzerland** (1957/426) (see also 1994/3214 below).

The existing capital transfer tax agreements which now apply to inheritance tax on chargeable lifetime transfers and death are (country and statutory instrument year and number).

Ireland (1978/1107), South Africa (1979/576), Sweden (1981/840 with amending protocol 1989/986) and USA (1979/1454).

Inheritance tax agreements entered into in respect of chargeable transfers on death are (country and statutory instrument year and number).

Switzerland (1994/3214), Netherlands (1980/706 with amending protocol 1996/730).

The specific provisions of the particular agreement concerned must be studied carefully. For instance, the agreement with France does not extend to Northern Ireland, the Pakistan convention remains in force despite the abolition of the death duties law in 1978 and the agreement with India remains in force despite the abolition of Indian estate duty law in 1985, see 17.4 DOMICILE. See HMRC Tax Bulletin, June 2001. See also UK and Netherlands Protocol which entered into force on 3 June 1996 amending the Convention signed in The Hague on 11 December 1979. (*Treaty Series No 73 (1996) Cmnd 3336*).

The IHT 210 (Notes) at D2 (Notes) http://www.hmrc.gov.uk/cto/forms/d02_notes_1.pdf point 7 states:

> 'As both countries may have the right to tax the assets, these agreements usually have rules that say which country may tax the different assets. We will not give up our right to tax any assets until we have evidence from the foreign authority that the assets have been included for tax in the foreign country and tax has been paid. If you feel that certain assets should not be taxed in the UK because an agreement says so, you should let us have evidence that foreign tax has been paid on the assets as soon as you can.'

18.3   **UNILATERAL RELIEF BY UK**

Where relief is not available under a double tax agreement, relief may be obtained by means of a credit for the overseas tax against the UK inheritance tax. This unilateral relief is also applied if greater relief is obtained than under an agreement. See IHT 18, pp 11 and 12. The relief is as follows.

(*a*)   Where the property is situated in the overseas territory and not in the UK, the credit is the whole amount of the overseas tax.

Example 1

Where property is situated in an overseas territory only

A, domiciled in the UK, owns a holiday home abroad valued at £396,000 which he gives to his son in July 2007. He is liable to local gifts tax of, say, £8,830. He has made no previous transfers and does not use the home again at any time before his death in February 2012. Assumes that nil rate band in force at that time is £350,000. See 41 RATES OF TAX.

	£	£
Market value of holiday home		396,000
Annual exemption 2007/08	(3,000)	
Annual exemption 2006/07	(3,000)	
		(6,000)
Chargeable transfer		£390,000
IHT payable at 60% of full rates by son (death between 4 and 5 years after gift) £40,000 × 40% × 60%		9,600
Unilateral relief for foreign tax		(8,830)
IHT borne		£770

18.3 Double Taxation Relief

Note to the example

(A)   If the overseas tax suffered exceeded the UK liability before relief, there would be no IHT payable but the excess would not be repayable.

Example 2

Where property is situated in both the UK and an overseas territory

M, domiciled in the UK, owns company shares which are regarded as situated both in the UK and country X under the rules of the respective countries. On M's death in June 2007 the shares pass to M's son S. The UK IHT amounts to £5,000 before unilateral relief. The equivalent tax liability arising in country X amounts to £2,000.

Apply the formula

$$\frac{A}{A+B} \times C$$

shown below

The unilateral relief available is

$$\frac{5,000}{5,000 + 2,000} \times £2,000 = £1,429$$

IHT payable = £5,000 – £1,429 = £3,571

(*b*)   Where the property is

   (i)   situated neither in the UK nor the overseas territory, or

   (ii)   situated both in the UK and the overseas territory,

the credit is in accordance with the following formula.

$$\frac{A}{A+B} \times C$$

where

A =   the amount of inheritance tax,

B =   the overseas tax, and

C =   whichever of A or B is the smaller.

(*c*)   Where tax is imposed in two or more overseas territories in respect of property which is

   (i)   situated neither in the UK nor in any of those territories, or

   (ii)   is situated in the UK and in each of those territories

the formula above applies but

A =   the amount of inheritance tax,

B =   the aggregate of the overseas tax imposed in each of those territories, and

C =   the aggregate of all, except the largest, of A and the overseas tax imposed in each of them.

Where credit is allowed under (*a*) above or under the terms of a double tax agreement in respect of overseas tax imposed in one overseas territory, any credit under (*b*) above in respect of overseas tax imposed in another is calculated as if the inheritance tax at A in the formula were reduced by that credit. Similarly, where in the case of an overseas territory within (*b*) or (*c*) above, credit is allowed against the overseas tax for tax charged in a territory in which the property is situated, the overseas tax at B in the formula is treated as reduced by the credit.

References to tax imposed in an overseas territory are references to tax chargeable under the laws of that territory and paid by the person liable to pay the tax. [*IHTA 1984, s 159*].

Example 3

Where tax is imposed in two or more overseas territories on property situated in the UK and each of those territories

Assume the facts in the example in 2 above except that a third country imposes a tax liability on the death as the shares are regarded as also situated in that country.

UK IHT before unilateral relief	£5,000
Tax in country X	£2,000
Tax in country Y	£400

Apply the formula

$$\frac{A}{A+B} \times C$$

shown above

The unilateral relief available is

$$\frac{5,000}{5,000+2,000+400} \times (2,000+400) = £\,1,622$$

IHT payable £5,000 − £1,622 = £3,378

19 Estate

Cross-references. See 28 LAND for estates of land; 42 SETTLEMENTS–GENERAL, 43 SETTLE-MENTS WITH INTERESTS IN POSSESSION, 53 TRUSTS FOR BEREAVED MINORS and 56 VALUATION.

Simon's Direct Tax Service, part I4.111.

19.1 MEANING OF ESTATE

'Estate' is one of the key concepts of IHT because of the loss to donor principle which underlies the tax. (See 1 INTRODUCTION AND BASIC PRINCIPLES for general exposition). During life, the value transferred by a transfer of value is the amount by which the transferor's estate is reduced by that transfer. On death, a person is treated as having made a transfer of value equal to the value of his estate immediately before his death. [*IHTA 1984, ss 3(1), 4(1)*].

Where a loan is made between individuals, HMRC Capital Taxes will not accept that the loan has been waived and the estate of the lender reduced unless the waiver was effected by deed. (Law Society's Gazette, 18 December 1991). See also *Moggs (Moggs' Executor) v CIR [2005] STC SCD 394 Sp C 464*.

THIS DEED is made by:

(1) "Father" namely [   ] of [   ]

In favour of

(2) "Son" namely [   ] of [   ]

RECITALS

A.   Son is indebted to Father for the loan brief details of which are set out in the schedule below ("the Loan")

B.   By this waiver Father intends to utilise the annual exemption available to him under section 19 of the Inheritance Tax Act 1984

WAIVER

1.   Father waives and releases in favour of Son Three Thousand pounds (£3,000.00) of the Loan

2.   The continuing balance of the indebtedness due under the Loan following this waiver is set out in part 2 of the schedule

The Schedule

Part 1 – [details of "the Loan"]

Part 2 – balance now [ ]

EXECUTED AS A DEED   )
and DELIVERED on   )
                                     200(7)   )
FATHER in the presence of   )

Note to the waiver

It is imperative that waivers of loan are made by Deed. Estoppels apart (which should not be relied on) waivers under hand, by letter etc. are simply ineffective due to a lack of consideration.

A person's estate, for IHT purposes, is the aggregate of all the 'property' to which he is *beneficially entitled*, except that the estate of a person immediately before his death does not include EXCLUDED PROPERTY (20) or property to which *IHTA 1984, ss 71A, 71D* (i.e. bereaved minor's trust and an 'aged 18–25 trust') apply and does not include, from 22 March 2006, certain interests in possession other than an IPDI, a TSI, a disabled person's trust. These trusts will be charged to IHT under the trusts taxing regimes applicable depending on whichever trust is in point. See *Anand v CIR [1997] STC SCD 58 Sp C 107* and *O'Neill and others v IRC [1998] STC SCD 110 Sp C 154*. 'Property' includes rights and interests of any description but does not include property to which he is entitled as a corporation sole (e.g. as Archbishop of Canterbury). His liabilities, including his liability for IHT (but not any other tax or duty) on the value transferred, are taken into account in determining the value of his estate. However, a liability not incurred for a consideration in money or money's worth is left out of account unless it is a liability imposed by law. [*IHTA 1984, ss 5(1)(3)–(5), 271, 272; FA 2006, Sch 20 para 10, 28*].

Estate on death. There are additional rules for the valuation of a person's estate immediately before his death. See 50.2 TRANSFERS ON DEATH.

19.2   GENERAL POWERS

A person who has a 'general power' (or would have if he were *sui juris*) to dispose of, or to charge money on, any property other than settled property is treated as beneficially entitled to the money or property. *'General power'* means a power or authority enabling a person by whom it is exercisable to appoint or dispose of property as he thinks fit. [*IHTA 1984, s 5(2)*]. See *Kempe and Roberts (personal representatives of Lyon, deceased) v CIR [2004] STC SCD 467 Sp C 424*. In the case of a Power of Attorney care should be exercised as applying *dicta* of Russell J in *Re Reckitt, CA [1928] 2 KB 244*, 'the primary object of a power of attorney is to enable the attorney to act in the management of his principal's affairs. An attorney cannot, in the absence of a clear power to do so, make presents to himself or to others of his principal's property.' See *McDowall & Others (McDowall's Executors) v CIR [2004] STC SCD 22 Sp C 382*. As settled property is specifically excluded, the existence of a general power of appointment in a trust deed does not result in the settled property being deemed to be included in the estate of the trustee. It has been held that a right reserved by the settlor to require his trustees to revest in him settled property was property forming part of his estate immediately after the settlement. This could have resulted in 'double counting' because the person entitled to an interest in possession in the settled property would have been treated as beneficially entitled and the general power of appointment would be property of the appointor's estate. *Melville v CIR, [2000] STC 628; CA [2001] STC 1271*. In this case the position has now been rectified by legislation in *FA 2002, s 119(4)*. The section reverses the effects of the *Melville* case from 17 April 2002 by providing expressly that powers over trusts are not to be treated as property. Powers which have been acquired for money or money's worth will not be disregarded for IHT purposes by reason of *FA 2002, s 119(3)* inserting new *IHTA 1984, s 55A*. Interestingly, in *Sillars and Another v CIR [2004] STC SCD 180 Sp C 401* the deceased transferred her building society account into the names of herself and her two daughters. In putting the account into their joint names the deceased had intended to make an immediate gift. The daughters did regard a one-third share of the balance in the account as being theirs. Withdrawals from the account were made either to or for the benefit of the mother until her death. On the mother's death the whole of the account formed part of her estate. Although the deceased's power over the account was not a *general power* in the ordinary sense it did fit the definition. The deceased was able to dispose of the balance as she thought fit and there was no accounting to see whether more than one-third was being extracted from the account. The daughters did not therefore have a general power over the account 'enabling the person by whom it is exercisable to dispose of or appoint property as he thinks fit'. See also 6.1 ANTI-AVOIDANCE.

19.3   SETTLED PROPERTY

A person beneficially entitled to an interest in possession in settled property is treated as beneficially entitled to the property in which the interest subsists, i.e. his estate for IHT purposes includes the value of any settled property in which he has such an interest (and not the actuarial value of the interest itself). [*IHTA 1984, s 49(1)*]. See 50.2 TRANSFERS ON DEATH for exceptions to the above where settled property reverts to the settlor, or in certain circumstances to the settlor's spouse, on the death of a person entitled to an interest in possession in that property. For the position from 22 March 2006 see SETTLEMENTS–GENERAL (42) and SETTLEMENTS WITH INTERESTS IN POSSESSION (43).

A reversionary interest in settled property is generally EXCLUDED PROPERTY (20), i.e. it continues to form part of a person's estate except immediately before his death (see 19.1 above), although it is not taken into account in determining the value transferred by any transfer of value. Where a person entitled to an interest (whether in possession or not) in any settled property acquires a reversionary interest expectant (whether immediately or not) on that interest, the reversionary interest is not part of his estate. See also ANTI-AVOIDANCE (6). [*IHTA 1984, ss 3(1)(2), 5(1), 48, 55(1); FA 2006, Sch 20 para 10*].

A trustee of settled property is the legal, not the beneficial, owner of the property so the property does not form part of his estate. See 19.2 above for the position where a trustee has general powers of appointment etc. Where a trustee is remunerated for his services by an interest in possession in settlement property (e.g. an annuity) the interest is not part of his estate except to the extent that it represents more than reasonable remuneration. [*IHTA 1984, s 90*].

HMRC Inheritance Tax normally expects to deal with the reversionary interest but the DV may be asked by HMRC Capital Taxes whether or not consideration paid by the lessee represented the full consideration for the grant of the lease for life. It is only these cases that the DV will be involved in the use of Life Tables in order to arrive at the required value. HMRC Inheritance Tax will inform the DV of the age and sex of the person by reference to whose death the lease will determine. (VOA IHT manual, section 8, para 8.22).

20   Excluded Property

Cross-references. See 46 SITUS; 49 TRANSFER OF VALUE; 59 WORKING CASE STUDY.

Simon's Direct Tax Service, part I9.3.

Other Sources. Foster, parts C2.17, C4.43, D1.21, E7.02, J3; IHTM04251.

20.1   APPLICATION

Excluded property is property excluded from the scope of inheritance tax. The value transferred by a transfer of value does not take account of the value of any excluded property ceasing to form part of a person's estate as a result of a disposition [*IHTA 1984, s 3(1)(2)*] and a person's estate immediately before his death (on which inheritance tax is payable) does not include excluded property. [*IHTA 1984, s 5(1)*]. Similarly, if the excluded property is settled property, the termination of an interest in possession in it is not taxable (see 43 SETTLEMENTS WITH INTERESTS IN POSSESSION) and nor is it relevant property for the purposes of the rules for SETTLEMENTS WITHOUT INTERESTS IN POSSESSION (44). [*IHTA 1984, ss 53(1), 58(1)*]. The types of excluded property are described below.

20.2   PROPERTY ABROAD

Property not comprised in a settlement (but including a reversionary interest in settled property, see 20.3 below) which is situated outside the UK is excluded property if the person beneficially entitled to it is an individual domiciled outside the UK. [*IHTA 1984, ss 6(1)(1A), 48(3), (3A) as inserted by FA 2003, s 186(2)(3)*]. [**Case Study 7**]. A double tax treaty may specify where property is situated. [*IHTA 1984, s 158(1)*]. See 17.3 DOMICILE for special provisions and 46 SITUS for situation of property generally.

Settled property (including a reversionary interest which is itself settled property) situated outside the UK is excluded property if the settlor was domiciled outside the UK when the settlement was made. See *A Beneficiary v CIR [1999] STC SCD 134 Sp C 190*. For property in a settlement before 10 December 1974, the special provisions relating to domicile in *IHTA 1984, s 267* (see 17.3 DOMICILE) do not apply. Anti-avoidance measures flagged in Pre-Budget Report Statement release PBR05 apply from 5 December 2005 to prevent UK domiciled individuals who become entitled directly or indirectly to interests in pre-existing foreign trusts originally settled by non-UK domiciliaries which are treated as excluded property within *IHTA 1984, s 48(3)* from being treated as excluded property if it is acquired for money or money's worth. It is immaterial whether the consideration is given by the person acquiring the interest in possession in the settlement or someone else or whether the entitlement arises by way of will or intestacy. Any IHT arising as a result of this avoidance provision applying from 5 December 2005 to the day before enactment of the *Finance Act 2006* on 19 July 2006 will be due 14 days after enactment. If the acquired interest is subsequently resettled by someone who is domiciled outside the UK relief may still be available under *IHTA 1984, s 48(3)* in respect of the new settlement. See 20.10 below and 44.10 SETTLEMENTS WITHOUT INTERESTS IN POSSESSION. [*IHTA 1984, ss 48(3), (3)(B)(C), 267(3); FA 2006, s 157(2)(4)–(6)*]. For this purpose, property is regarded as becoming comprised in a settlement when it (or other property which it represents) is introduced by the settlor (25.E9 HMRC STATEMENTS OF PRACTICE). However, see 44.15 SETTLEMENTS WITHOUT INTERESTS IN POSSESSION where either the settlor or his spouse/civil partner is entitled to an initial interest in possession in property settled after 26 March 1974, and see 44.16 where property moves from one settlement to another. The status of excluded property is determined immediately before vesting (*Von Ernst & Cie SA and Others v CIR CA 1979, [1980] STC 111*). See also 20.6

below regarding persons domiciled in the Channel Islands or Isle of Man and 22.6 GIFTS WITH RESERVATION for liability where excluded property which is settled property ceases to be subject to a reservation.

Situs. See 46 SITUS for the rules determining where property is situated.

See below for form D15.

20.3	**REVERSIONARY INTEREST**

A reversionary interest is excluded property unless

(*a*)   it has at any time been acquired (whether by the person entitled to it or by a person previously entitled) for a consideration in money or money's worth, or

(*b*)   it is the interest expectant on the determination of a lease which is treated as a settlement because the lease is for life or lives, or for a period ascertainable only by reference to death, or which is terminable on, or at a date ascertainable only by reference to, a death, and was not granted for full consideration in money or money's worth. Where a lease, not granted at a rack rent, is at any time to become a lease at an increased rent, it shall be treated as terminable at that time, or

(*c*)   for a settlement made after 15 April 1976, it is one to which either the settlor or his spouse or civil partner is (or, for a reversionary interest acquired after 9 March 1981, has been) beneficially entitled.

If a reversionary interest falls into one of the exceptions in (*a*) to (*c*) it may still be excluded property in certain circumstances if it is situated outside the UK. See 20.2 above. Additionally, a reversionary interest is to be treated as excluded property where the reversioner to that property is non-UK domiciled. This assists non-UK domiciled individuals who have a reversionary interest but die before that interest falls in and will no longer have the threat of an IHT charge in those particular circumstances for instance. [*IHTA 1984, s 48(3A)(b) as inserted by FA 2003, s 186(3)*].

Where more than one person is the settlor in relation to a settlement and the circumstances so require, the above provisions apply as if the settled property were comprised in separate settlements.

[*IHTA 1984, ss 43(3), 44(2), 48(1)(2)(3A)(b); FA 2003, s 186(3)*]. See also 42.6 SETTLEMENTS—GENERAL for meaning of reversionary interest.

20.4	**GOVERNMENT SECURITIES**

Government securities issued on terms giving exemption from taxation to persons of a description specified in the condition with beneficial ownership are excluded property if

(*a*)   they are beneficially owned by such a person and are not settled property, or

(*b*)   they are settled property and such a person is entitled to a qualifying interest in possession in them. If a close company is the person entitled, the participators in the company are treated as being entitled to the interest according to their respective rights and interests in the company, or

(*c*)   they are settled property in which there is no qualifying interest in possession and all known persons for whose benefit the settled property or income from it has been or might be applied or who are or might become beneficially entitled to an interest in possession in it are of a description specified in the condition in question. See *Montague Trust Co (Jersey) Ltd and Others v CIR Ch D [1989] STC 477.*

Where

(i)   after 19 April 1978 and before 10 December 1981 property ceased to be comprised in one settlement and, by the same disposition, became comprised in another settlement, or

(ii)   after 9 December 1981 property ceased to be comprised in one settlement and became comprised in another without any person in the meantime having become entitled to the property (and not merely to an interest in possession in it)

the property in the second settlement will only be excluded property if these requirements are satisfied by both settlements. However, this does not apply where a reversionary interest in the property expectant on the termination of a qualifying interest in possession subsisting under the first settlement was settled on the trusts of the second settlement before 10 December 1981.

A charity cannot be a 'known person for whose benefit the settled property … might be applied' (*Von Ernst & Cie SA and Others v CIR CA 1979, [1980] STC 111*).

For the above purposes 'description specified in the condition' will also mean free of tax to those who are ordinarily resident abroad and the special provisions relating to domicile in *IHTA 1984, s 267* (see 17.3 DOMICILE) do not apply. See 44.1 SETTLEMENTS WITHOUT INTERESTS IN POSSESSION for the meaning of '*qualifying interest in possession*'. The former CTO Advanced Instruction Manual, para G33 states that on or after 29 April 1996 securities which are issued by the Treasury are exempt from taxation irrespective of the domicile of the person by whom or on whose behalf they are held. Such securities are excluded property for IHT purposes if the beneficial owner of the security or, where the security is settled property, the beneficiary or beneficiaries concerned are ordinarily resident outside the UK. Now see IHTM13025 and IHTM27241.

[*IHTA 1984, ss 6(2), 48(4)–(7), 101(1), 267(2); FA 1996, s 154, Sch 28 paras 7, 8*].

Example

Where exempt gilts are used for planning for the emigrant

M, domiciled in the UK, emigrates to Australia on 6 April 2007 and intends to become an Australian citizen and domiciliary. Australia has no death duties legislation. M owns a property which he has put on the market to sell at £560,000. M is not married and on his death his estate would go to his nieces and nephews in equal shares. His total estate would be valued at £750,000 if the house sells for its current stated value. The potential maximum liability to IHT for three years under the deemed domicile provisions of *IHTA 1984, 267(2)* would be £180,000.

In order to circumvent this he could take out a loan up to £450,000 (i.e. £750,000 – £300,000) secured on the prospective sale of his property to invest in exempt gilts. He might consider the purchase of gilts issued by the Treasury on or after 29 April 1996 which are excluded property where the person beneficially entitled is ordinarily resident abroad. See also *Shepherd v IRC Ch D* [2006] STC 1821 and 17.3 DOMICILE. Alternatively, he could establish a temporary life interest trust for his benefit where the trustees also invest in exempt post 28 April 1996 gilts. Should he then die within the three-year period of deemed domicile having shed his ordinary residence the monies borrowed against the property would be allowed for IHT purposes and the released capital, comprising of exempt gilts constituting excluded property. [*IHTA 1984, ss 6(2), 162; FA 1996, s 154*].

All Government securities (issued before or after 6 April 1998) are excluded property after 5 April 1998 if satisfying the conditions in (*a*)–(*c*) above.

[*IHTA 1984, s 65; FA 1998, s 161(3)*].

20.4 Excluded Property

The securities below are those that were redeemed after 17 March 1986 and before 6 April 1998 which were specifically treated as excluded prior to the *FA 1998*. The IHT manual now states at IHTM27241:

> 'As a result of FA96/S154, the Treasury adapted its conditions so that securities could be issued with the condition that they are exempt from taxation providing the beneficial owner was not ordinarily resident in the UK. Thus, domicile was no longer a determining factor for taxation of securities issued under these new conditions.'

Treasury 8½% 1984/86

Funding 6½% 1985/87

Treasury 7¾% 1985/88

Exchequer 11% 1990

Treasury 8¼% 1987/90

Treasury 13% 1990

Treasury Convertible 8% 1990

Funding 5¾% 1987/91

Treasury Convertible 10% 1991

Treasury 8% 1992

Treasury 12¾% 1992

Treasury Convertible 10½% 1992

Treasury 10% 1993

Treasury 9% 1992/96

Index-linked Treasury 2% 1992

Treasury 12½% 1993

Funding 6% 1993

Treasury 13¾% 1993

Treasury 14½% 1994

Treasury 10% 1994

Treasury 9% 1994

Treasury 12¾% 1995

Treasury 15¼% 1996

Exchequer 13¼% 1996

Treasury 13¼% 1997

Treasury 8¾% 1997

Treasury Convertible 7% 1997

Terms of issue of Government securities are set by the Treasury, although promulgated in prospectuses etc. published by the Bank of England. Accordingly, further information relating to the above list, together with any changes made since publication to it, should be obtained from FICO, Fitz Roy House, PO Box 46, Nottingham, NG2 1BD. Tel: 0115 974 2400. Also, see IHTM27243 and IHTM27244.

20.5   **OVERSEAS PENSIONS**

Transfers on death only. Any pension receivable from a fund set up under the *Government of India Act 1935, s 273* (or a corresponding fund under *Overseas Pensions Act 1973, s 2*) is to be left out of account in determining the value of a person's estate immediately before his death. See IHT 18, p 8.

Transfers generally. Any pension, gratuity, sum payable on or in respect of death or a return of contributions (including interest thereon) paid from certain pension funds relating to service in overseas territories is to be treated as paid by the government of the territory concerned. It will thus constitute property situated outside the UK (see 46 SITUS) and will be excluded property if the pensioner is domiciled overseas (see 20.2 above). The pensions are those

(a)   paid out of any fund established in the UK by the government of any country which at the time the fund was established was, or formed part of, a colony, protectorate, protected state or 'UK trust territory' for the sole purpose of paying pensions etc. in respect of service under that government e.g. DFID Overseas Pensions Department;

(b)   paid out of the Central African Pension Fund established by *Federation of Rhodesia and Nyasaland (Dissolution) Order in Council 1963, s 24*;

(c)   paid under a scheme made under *Overseas Pensions Act 1973, s 2* which is constituted by the *Pensions (India, Pakistan and Burma) Act 1955* (or similar);

(d)   paid under the scheme constituted under *Overseas Pensions Act 1973, s 2* by *Overseas Service Act 1958, ss 2, 4(2)* (or similar); and

(e)   for which the UK has assumed responsibility within the meaning of *Overseas Pensions Act 1973, s 1* exclusive of any increase in the pension under *Pensions (Increase) Act 1971* or any enactment repealed by that Act.

'*UK trust territory*' means a territory administered by the UK government under the trusteeship system of the United Nations.

[*IHTA 1984, s 153*].

20.6   **PERSONS DOMICILED IN CHANNEL ISLANDS OR ISLE OF MAN**

Savings. The following savings to which persons domiciled in the above Islands are beneficially entitled are excluded property.

(a)   War savings certificates.

(b)   NS&I National savings certificates (including Ulster savings certificates).

(c)   NS&I Premium bonds.

(d)   NS&I Deposits with the National Savings Bank or with a trustee savings bank.

(e)   Any certified contractual savings scheme (e.g. SAYE schemes with qualification in the prospectus) within the meaning of *ICTA 1988, s 326(2)(6)* and *ITEPA 2003, Sch 3 para 48(1) as replaced by ITTOIA 2005, ss 702(1), 703(2)(3), 704(2), 705(1), 707(1)*.

For the above purposes, the special provisions relating to domicile in *IHTA 1984, s 267* (see 17.3 DOMICILE) does not apply.

[*IHTA 1984, ss 6(3), 267(2)*].

20.7   Excluded Property

20.7   VISITING FORCES

Emoluments paid by the Government of a country designated by Order in Council to a member of a visiting force of that country (including the member of a civilian component) are excluded property provided that member is not a British citizen, a British Dependent Territories citizen or a British Overseas citizen. Any tangible movable property in the UK solely because of the presence of that member is also excluded. [*Visiting Forces (Inheritance Tax) (Designation) Order 1998, Art 1; ITA 2007, s 833*].

A period during which any such member is in the UK by reason solely of his being such a member is not treated for inheritance tax purposes as a period of residence in the UK or as creating a change of residence or domicile. [*IHTA 1984, ss 6(4), 155*].

The *Visiting Forces (Inheritance Tax) (Designation) Order 1998, SI 1998/1516* comes into effect in respect of the following countries on the later of the date the country becomes party to the agreement or the day after the date on which the Order was made (i.e. 25 June 1998).

Designated countries:

Armenia

Austria

Azerbaijan

Belarus

Finland

Georgia

Kazakhstan

Kyrgyzstan

The Former Yugoslav Republic of Macedonia

Moldova

Russia

Switzerland

Turkmenistan

Ukraine

Uzbekistan

20.8   SPECIAL DISCRETIONARY TRUSTS

Where tax is charged when property leaves certain trusts, no account is taken of any quarter throughout which the property was excluded property when determining the appropriate rate of tax. [*IHTA 1984, ss 70(7), 71(5), 72(5), 73(3), 74(3)*]. See 3.5 ACCUMULATION AND MAINTENANCE TRUSTS; 11.5 CHARITIES; 39.3 PROTECTIVE TRUSTS; 54.3 TRUSTS FOR DISABLED PERSONS; and 55.8 TRUSTS FOR EMPLOYEES.

20.9   CHEVENING ESTATE AND APSLEY HOUSE

Inheritance tax does not apply to property held on trusts under the *Schedule* to the *Chevening Estate Act 1959* or rights conferred by the *Wellington Museum Act 1947*. [*IHTA 1984, s 156*].

20.10   **NON-UK DOMICILES (AUT AND OEIC INVESTMENTS)**

Inheritance tax does not apply to property held in investments in authorised unit trusts (AUTs) or open-ended investment companies (OEICs) by non-domiciled individuals or trusts of which they were the settlor when non-UK domiciled—these investments in these circumstances are to be disregarded for the purposes of IHT. This section has been added to *IHTA 1984* to boost the competitiveness of UK-authorised funds when competing for investment business overseas. These changes to excluded property apply to IHT occasions of charge on or after 16 October 2002. The IHT anti-avoidance measures flagged in Pre-Budget Report Statement release PBR05 mentioned in 20.2 above apply from 5 December 2005 to prevent UK domiciled individuals who purchase interests in pre-existing foreign trusts originally settled by non-UK domiciliaries which benefit from the exemption attaching to such property or under *IHTA 1984, s 48(3A)* relating to holdings in AUTs and OEICs from obtaining the benefit of excluded property. It is immaterial whether the consideration is given by the person with the interest in possession in the settlement or someone else arising by way of will or intestacy. Any IHT arising as a result of this avoidance provision applying from 5 December 2005 to the day before enactment of the *Finance Act 2006* on 19 July 2006 will be due 14 days of enactment. If the acquired interest is subsequently resettled by someone who is domiciled outside the UK relief may still be available under *IHTA 1984, s 48(3A)* in respect of the new settlement. See 20.2 above. [*IHTA 1984, ss 6(1A), 48(3A)(a) as inserted by FA 2003, s 186(3) and amended by FA 2006, s 157(3)–(6)*]. See IHT NEWSLETTER AND TAX BULLETIN EXTRACTS (61), May 2003.

20.10 Excluded Property

Inland Revenue Capital Taxes Office

Foreign assets

Name

Date of death

/ /

Give details about any assets situated outside the UK that the deceased owned. You should read form D15(Notes) before filling in this form.

1 **Assets outside the UK where tax may not be paid by instalments**

- Assets

Stocks, shares and securities

	Total	**FP1**

Other foreign assets

	Total	**FP2**

Total of assets *(box FP1 plus box FP2)* **FP3** £

- Liabilities

Total of liabilities **FP4** £

Net assets *(box FP3 less box FP4)* **FP5** £

- Exemptions and reliefs

Total exemptions and reliefs **FP6** £

Net total of foreign property where tax may not be paid by instalments *(box FP5 less box FP6)* **FP7** £

D15

CTO Approval Ref No ☐ L3/00

Please turn over
R0K4134CTO11/99

(Substitute)(LexisNexis Butterworths)

2 **Assets outside the UK where tax may be paid by instalments**

Do you wish to pay tax on these assets by instalments?   No ☐   Yes ☐

• Assets

Total assets   FP8 £

• Liabilities

Total   FP9 £

Net assets *(box FP8 less box FP9)*   FP10 £

• Exemption and reliefs

Total exemptions and reliefs   FP11 £

Net total of foreign property where tax may be paid by instalments
(box FP10 less box FP11)   FP12 £

D15

21 Exempt Transfers

Cross-references. See 5 AGRICULTURAL PROPERTY; 7 BUSINESS PROPERTY; 11 CHARITIES; 14 DEEDS VARYING DISPOSITIONS ON DEATH; 16 DIPLOMATIC IMMUNITY; 33 NATIONAL HERITAGE; 38 POTENTIALLY EXEMPT TRANSFERS; 55 TRUSTS FOR EMPLOYEES; 59 WORKING CASE STUDY.

Simon's Direct Tax Service, parts I3.3, I4.2.

Other Sources. Form P11(Notes); CTO Leaflet IHT 15 'How to calculate the liability' pages 4–8; Foster, parts C and D; IHT 110; IHT 210 (Notes), Form D3 (Notes); IHTM11000.

Headings in this chapter are:

General exemptions:	21.9 Annual gifts
21.1 Nil rate tax band	21.10 Gifts in consideration of marriage or
21.2 Gifts to charities	civil partnership
21.3 Settled property becoming	21.11 Dispositions for maintenance of family
held for charitable purposes	21.12 Normal expenditure out of income
21.4 Gifts to housing associations	21.13 Transfers allowable for income tax or
21.5 Gifts for national purposes	conferring retirement benefits
21.6 Gifts for political parties	**Transfers on death only:**
21.7 Gifts for public benefit	21.14 Death on active service,etc.
21.8 Transfers between spouse or	21.15 Non-residents' bank accounts
civil partner	21.16 Abatement of exemptions
Lifetime transfer only:	

21.1 NIL RATE TAX BAND

Currently, the first £300,000 of chargeable transfers in any seven-year period are taxable at nil%. See 10.3 CHARGEABLE TRANSFER and 41 RATES OF TAX.

21.2 GIFTS TO CHARITIES

Gifts to charities are exempt from inheritance tax. [*IHTA 1984, s 23(1)*]. [**Case Study 9**]. See also 21.3 below for transfer of property from certain trusts to charities. See IHTM11101.

Property is given to a charity if it becomes the property of the charity or is held on trust for charitable purposes only. [*IHTA 1984, s 23(6)*]. Where the value transferred (i.e. the loss to the transferor's estate as a result of the disposition) exceeds the value of the gift in the hands of the charity (or political party), the exemption extends to the whole value transferred. (See E13 at 25 HMRC STATEMENTS OF PRACTICE).

'*Charity*' has the meaning given by *ITA 2007, ss 519, 543(1)* (formerly *ICTA 1988, ss 506(1) as amended by FA 2006, s 55(2), 507* and *ITTOIA 2005, ss 108(4), 878(1)*) for income tax purposes, i.e. 'any body of persons or trust established for charitable purposes only' and excludes foreign charities. A community amateur sports club, if it is a registered club, will be treated as a charity for these purposes. Following *Finance Act 2002* the '*charity*' exemption is also extended to include a club that is registered as a community amateur sports club, and is required by its constitution to be, and is a club that (a) is open to the whole community; (b) is organised on an amateur basis; and (c) has as its main purpose the provision of facilities for, and the promotion of participation in, one or more eligible sports. [*FA 2002, Sch 18 paras 1–3, 9(2); ITA 2007, s 430(1)(d)*]. See *Dreyfus (Camille & Henry) Foundation Inc v CIR HL 1955, 36 TC 126.* [*IHTA 1984, s 272*]. See also 11 CHARITIES.

Exceptions. The exemption above does not apply under any of the following circumstances.

(*a*) If the testamentary or other disposition giving the property

(i)   takes effect on the termination of any interest or period after the transfer is made (e.g. a gift to a person for life and then to the charity), or

(ii)   depends on a condition which is not satisfied within twelve months after the transfer, or

(iii)   is defeasible. (For this purpose, any disposition which has not been defeated within twelve months of the transfer and is not defeasible after that time is treated as not being defeasible (whether or not it was capable of being defeated before that time).)

(*b*)   If the property is

(i)   an interest in other property and that interest is less than the donor's, or

(ii)   an interest in other property and that property is given for a limited period, or

(iii)   an interest in possession in settled property and the settlement does not come to an end in relation to that settled property on the making of the transfer (unless the transfer is a disposition whereby the use of money or other property is allowed by one person to another) (see *Powell-Cotton v CIR Ch D, [1992] STC 625*), or

(iv)   land or a building given subject to an interest reserved or created by the donor entitling him, his spouse or civil partner or a person connected with him to possess or occupy the whole or part of the property rent-free or at a rent less than obtainable in an arm's length transaction between unconnected persons, or

(v)   not land or a building and is given subject to an interest reserved or created by the donor other than an interest created by him for full consideration in money or money's worth or an interest which does not substantially affect the enjoyment of the property by the person or body to whom it is given, or

(vi)   property of which any part may become applicable for purposes other than charitable purposes or those of a body within 21.4 to 21.7 below, or

(vii)   given in consideration of the transfer of a reversionary interest which under *IHTA 1984, s 55(1)* (see 19.3 ESTATE) does not form part of the estate of the person acquiring that interest.

(*c*)   If immediately before the time when it becomes the property of the charity, the property is comprised in a settlement and, at or before that time but after 11 April 1978, an interest under the settlement is or has been acquired for a consideration in money or money's worth by that or another charity or body within 21.4 to 21.7 below (otherwise than *from* another charity or body within 21.4 to 21.6 below). For these purposes, a person is treated as acquiring an interest for a consideration in money or money's worth if he becomes entitled to it as a result of transactions which include a disposition for such consideration (whether to him or another) of that interest or other property. The exception does not apply if the transfer is a disposition whereby the use of money or other property is allowed by one person to another.

In (*b*)(i) above any question whether any interest is less than the donor's and in (*b*)(iv) and (v) above whether property is given subject to an interest, is decided at a time twelve months after the transfer.

See 49.3 TRANSFER OF VALUE for modification of the above where the transfer of value is an uncommercial loan. See also 21.16 below.

[*IHTA 1984, ss 23(2)–(5), 56(1)(3)–(6)(8); F(No 2)A 1987, Sch 7 para 2; FA 1998, s 143(2)(a); FA 2002, Sch 18 para 9(2)*].

21.3 SETTLED PROPERTY BECOMING HELD FOR CHARITABLE PURPOSES

No charge to tax arises when property ceases to be relevant property in a SETTLEMENT WITHOUT INTERESTS IN POSSESSION (44) or ceases to be comprised in a temporary charitable trust (see 11.4 CHARITIES), a maintenance fund for historic buildings (see 33.11 NATIONAL HERITAGE), an ACCUMULATION AND MAINTENANCE TRUST (3), a TRUST FOR EMPLOYEES (55), a PROTECTIVE TRUST (39), or a TRUST FOR DISABLED PERSONS (54) and becomes property held for charitable purposes only without limit of time (defined by date or otherwise). Also exempt is the settlement on discretionary trusts by a person's will of property which then becomes held, within two years of death, for charitable purposes only without limit of time. See 50.5 TRANSFERS ON DEATH. See also Tolley's Income Tax 2007–08 for information on gifts to charity from certain settlements. [*FA 2000, s 44*].

The exemption does not apply under the following circumstances.

(*a*)   The disposition is defeasible. (For this purpose any disposition which has not been defeated within twelve months of the transfer and is not defeasible after that time is treated as not being defeasible (whether or not it was capable of being defeated before that time).)

(*b*)   The property or any part of it can be applied otherwise than for charitable purposes or the purposes of a body within 21.5 to 21.7 below (but see *FA 1998, s 143(4)*).

(*c*)   At or before the time of the disposition, an interest in the settlement is, or has been, acquired for a consideration in money or money's worth (or as a result of transactions which include a disposition for such consideration, whether to that body or another person, of that interest or other property) by a charity or body within 21.5 to 21.7 below otherwise than *from* a charity or body within 21.5 or 21.6 below.

If the amount on which tax would otherwise be charged (before grossing-up if applicable and before BUSINESS PROPERTY (5) relief or AGRICULTURAL PROPERTY (7) relief) exceeds the value of the property immediately after it becomes the property of the recipient body (less any consideration for the transfer received by the trustees), the amount on which tax is charged is restricted to the excess. [*IHTA 1984, ss 76(1)(3)–(8), 144; FA 1998, s 143*].

These provisions also apply where the settled property mentioned above becomes that of the bodies within 21.5 to 21.7 below. See also 44.16 SETTLEMENTS WITHOUT INTERESTS IN POSSESSION.

21.4 GIFTS TO HOUSING ASSOCIATIONS

Transfers of value after 13 March 1989 to registered social landlords (within the meaning of *Housing Associations Act 1985* or *Housing (Northern Ireland) Order 1981, Part VII (SI 1981 No 156)* and *Housing Act 1996, Part I*) are exempt to the extent that the value transferred is attributable to land in the United Kingdom. [*IHTA 1984, s 24A(1)(2); FA 1989, s 171*]. See IHTM11211.

Exceptions are the same as those applying to gifts to charities, see 21.2 above [*IHTA 1984, ss 23(2)–(5), 24(3), 56(1)(3)–(6)(8); FA 1998, s 143 (3)*].

21.5 GIFTS FOR NATIONAL PURPOSES

Gifts to certain national bodies (see list under 33.16 NATIONAL HERITAGE) are exempt from inheritance tax. [*IHTA 1984, s 25(1), Sch 3*]. (See IR 67, Capital Taxation and the National Heritage). See IHTM11221.

Exceptions are the same as those applying to gifts to charities, see 21.2 above, but 21.2(B)(I) and (II) do not prevent the exemption from applying in relation to property consisting of the benefit of an agreement restricting the use of land. [*IHTA 1984, ss 23(2)–(5), 25(2), 56(1)(3)–(6)(8)*].

See also 21.3 above which applies equally to settled property becoming the property of a national body under *IHTA 1984, s 25(1)*. [*IHTA 1984, ss 76(1)(3)–(8), 144; FA 1998, s 143(4)*].

21.6   GIFTS TO POLITICAL PARTIES

All gifts made to qualifying political parties after 14 March 1988 are exempt from inheritance tax. For gifts made before 15 March 1988 exemption was limited to £100,000 if made on or within one year of death. Certain uncommercial loans which were transfers of value were not subject to the £100,000 limit. See 49.3 TRANSFER OF VALUE. A political party qualifies for exemption if, at the last general election (i.e. by-elections are ignored) preceding the transfer of value

(*a*)   two members of that party were elected to the House of Commons, or

(*b*)   one member of that party was elected to the House of Commons and not less than 150,000 votes were given to candidates who were members of that party.

[*IHTA 1984, s 24(1)(2); FA 1988, s 137*].

Qualifying parties have been listed in House of Commons written answers. [*Hansard, 1988 vol 132 col 329 (29 April 1988*) and *1988 vol 138 cols 106–107 (25 July 1988*)]. See also IHTM11199.

Exceptions are the same as those applying to gifts to charities, see 21.2 above. [*IHTA 1984, ss 23(2)–(5), 24(3), 56(1)(3)–(6)(8)*].

See also 21.3 above which applies equally to settled property becoming the property of a qualifying political party. [*IHTA 1984, ss 76(1)(3)–(8), 144; FA 1998, s 143 (4)*].

21.7   GIFTS FOR PUBLIC BENEFIT

Disposals before 17 March 1998. Gifts of eligible property to bodies not established or conducted for profit were, if the Board so directed (whether before or after the transfer), exempt from inheritance tax. [*IHTA 1984, s 26(1); FA 1985, s 95*].

Exceptions were the same as those applying to gifts to charities, see 21.2 above. [*IHTA 1984, ss 23(2)–(5), 26(7), 56(1)(3)–(6)(8)*].

Eligible property was

(*a*)   land which in the opinion of the Board was of outstanding scenic, historic or scientific interest;

(*b*)   a building for the preservation of which special steps should in the opinion of the Board be taken by reason of its outstanding historic, architectural or aesthetic interest and the cost of preserving it;

(*c*)   land used as the grounds of a building within (*b*) above;

(*d*)   an object which at the time of the transfer was ordinarily kept in, and was given with, a building within (*b*) above;

(*e*)   property given as a source of income for the upkeep of property within these sub-paragraphs;

(*f*)   a picture, print, book, manuscript, work of art or scientific collection which in the opinion of the Board was of national, scientific, historic or artistic interest. ('*National interest*' included interest within any part of the UK.)

[*IHTA 1984, s 26(2)(9); FA 1985, s 95*].

The Board did not give a direction (i) unless in their opinion, the body who received the property was an appropriate one to be responsible for its preservation or the preservation of the character of the land with (*a*); or (ii) in relation to property within (*e*) above, if or to the extent that the property would, in their opinion, produce more income than was needed (with a reasonable margin) for the upkeep of the other property in question.

Before giving a direction, the Board could require undertakings (which could be varied by agreement) concerning the use, disposal, and preservation of the property and reasonable access to it for the public. Any obligation imposed by an undertaking was enforceable by injunction (in Scotland by petition under *Court of Session Act 1988, s 45* (before 29 September 1988, *Court of Session Act 1868, s 91*)), and any purported disposition in contravention of an undertaking was void. [*IHTA 1984, s 26(3)–(6); FA 1985, s 95*].

See also 21.3 above which applied equally to settled property becoming the property of a body not established or conducted for profit. The restrictions on eligible property and Board requirements was as above. [*IHTA 1984, ss 76, 144; FA 1985, s 95*].

Disposals after 16 March 1998. The above provisions are repealed due in main to the unrestricted exemption on transfers to charitable bodies existing elsewhere in the legislation. [*FA 1998, s 143 (4)*].

21.8   TRANSFERS BETWEEN SPOUSES OR CIVIL PARTNERS

Transfers of value between spouses or civil partners are exempt from inheritance tax

(*a*)   where property becomes comprised in the transferee's estate, by the amount by which the transferor's estate is diminished, or

(*b*)   in any other case (e.g. payment by the transferor of his spouse's or civil partner's debt), by the amount by which the transferee's estate is increased.

For these purposes, property is given to a person if it becomes his property or is held in trust for him.

[*IHTA 1984, s 18(1)(4); The Tax and Civil Partnership Regulations 2005, SI 2005/3229, Reg 7*].

If, immediately before the transfer, the transferor, but not the transferor's spouse or civil partner, is domiciled in the UK the exemption is limited to a cumulative total of £55,000, without grossing-up for tax. [*IHTA 1984, s 18(2)*]. See IHT 15, page 4. [**Case Study 7**]. See also IHTM11011. In *Burden & Burden v United Kingdom* [2006] ECHR Case 13378/05 two elderly sisters lived together in a jointly-owned house on land which they had inherited from their parents. They lodged a complaint with the ECHR, contending that the provisions of *IHTA 1984, s 18* (as amended by the *Tax and Civil Partnership Regulations 2005*) were a breach of *Article 14* of the *European Convention on Human Rights*, because when one of them died, the survivor would be required to pay IHT on her sister's share of their home, whereas no IHT would have been charged if they had lived together as a registered lesbian civil partnership. The ECHR rejected their application holding that 'the inheritance tax exemption for married and civil partnership couples ... pursues a legitimate aim, namely to promote stable, committed heterosexual and homosexual relationships by providing the survivor with a measure of financial security after the death of the spouse or partner'. See 60 TAX CASES.

Exceptions. Unless the transfer of value is a loan of money or property (see 49.3 TRANSFER OF VALUE) the above exemption does not apply

(i)   if the testamentary or other disposition giving the property takes effect on the termination of any interest (e.g. a life interest in settled property) or period after the transfer is made, but this does not exclude a gift which is dependent on the spouse/civil partner surviving the donor spouse/civil partner by a specified period, or

(ii)   if it depends on a condition which is not satisfied within twelve months after the transfer is made, or

(iii)   if property is given in consideration of the transfer of a reversionary interest which under *IHTA 1984, s 55(1)* (see 19.3 ESTATE) does not form part of the estate of the person acquiring that interest. [*IHTA 1984, ss 18(3), 56(1)*].

Where a spouse purchased a reversionary interest in settled property after 15 April 1976 for a consideration in money or money's worth, the exemption does not apply on the falling in of the reversion by the termination of the interest on which the reversionary interest is expectant unless a loan of money or property is involved, see 49.3 TRANSFER OF VALUE. For these purposes, a person is treated as acquiring an interest for a consideration in money or money's worth if he becomes entitled to it as a result of transactions which include a disposition for such consideration (whether to him or another) of that interest or other property. [*IHTA 1984, s 56(2)(5)–(7); F(No 2)A 1987, Sch 7 para 2*].

See also 21.16 below.

21.9   ANNUAL GIFTS

(*a*)   **Annual exemption.** Transfers of value during the lifetime of a person up to a total of £3,000 per fiscal year are exempt from inheritance tax. See IHTM14141 and IHT 110, 210 and D3 (Notes) at http://www.hmrc.gov.uk/cto/forms/d03_notes_1.pdf. [*IHTA 1984, s 19(1)(4)*]. [**Case Study 9**].

Where the gifts (if any) fall short of the above limit, the shortfall is carried forward to the next following year and added to the allowance *for that year only*.

Where the gifts exceed the limit, the excess must,

(i)   if the gifts were made on different days, be attributed, so far as possible, to a later rather than an earlier transfer; and

(ii)   if the gifts were made on the same day, be attributed to them in proportion to the values transferred by them.

[*IHTA 1984, s 19(2)(3)*].

Where a transfer of value is a POTENTIALLY EXEMPT TRANSFER (38), in the first instance it is left out of account for the above purposes. However, if it proves to be a chargeable transfer, it is taken to have been made in the year in which it was made later than any transfer of value which is not a potentially exempt transfer. [*IHTA 1984, s 19(3A); FA 1986, Sch 19 para 5*]. The relevance of this provision is discussed at 38.2 POTENTIALLY EXEMPT TRANSFERS. See also 19.1 ESTATE for loan waiver using annual exemption.

For the purposes of the pre-owned assets anti-avoidance legislation within *FA 2004, Sch 15*, the disposal of any property which is an outright gift to an individual and is for the purposes of *IHTA 1984* a transfer of value that is *wholly* exempt by reason of *s 19* will be an excluded transaction. [*FA 2004, Sch 15 para 10(1)(e), (2)(e)*].

Example

S, who has made no other transfers of value, made gifts to his sister of £5,000 on 1 June 2006 and £4,000 on 1 May 2007. S dies on 1 September 2009 with an estate valued at £325,000. See 41 RATES OF TAX.

21.10   Exempt Transfers

Annual exemptions are available as follows

2006/07	£	£
1 June 2006 Gift		5,000
Deduct 2006/07 annual exemption	3,000	
2005/06 annual exemption (part)	2,000	
		5,000
		Nil

2007/08		£
1 May 2007 Gift		4,000
Deduct 2007/08 annual exemption		3,000
PET becoming chargeable on death		£1,000

The PET, having become a chargeable transfer as a result of death within seven years, is covered by the nil rate band but is aggregated with the death estate in computing the IHT payable on death and therefore £1,000 is chargeable at 40%.

(b)   **Small gifts to same person.** Transfers of value during the lifetime of a person up to a total of £250 per fiscal year *to any one person* are exempt from inheritance tax. The gifts must be outright (i.e. not settled) but include free use of property (see 49.3 TRANSFER OF VALUE). This exemption is in addition to the annual exemption under (a) above and applies to any number of gifts up to £250 to separate persons but it cannot be used to cover part of a larger gift i.e. the exemption will only apply where the value of all gifts in a year *to any individual* does not exceed £250. [**Case Study 9**]. Form P11(Notes) states that 'This exemption covers gifts at birthdays and Christmas' but is not actually solely restricted to such gifts. [*IHTA 1984, s 20*]. See IHTM14180.

Notes to (a) and (b) above.

(i)   The exemptions apply separately to husband, wife or civil partners.

(ii)   The value of gifts is calculated without tax (i.e. they are not grossed-up). [*IHTA 1984, ss 19(1), 20(1)*]. The exemptions apply only to transfers actually made (i.e. during lifetime) and not where deemed to have been made (such as on death or on a transfer by a settlement), but (a) does apply to transfers of value by a close company which are apportioned among its participators (see 12.4 CLOSE COMPANIES) and to the value chargeable on the termination of an interest in possession in settled property (see 43.3 SETTLEMENTS WITH INTERESTS IN POSSESSION). [*IHTA 1984, ss 3(4), 19(5), 20(3), 57, 94(5)*].

(iii)   For the purposes of the pre-owned assets anti-avoidance legislation within *FA 2004, Sch 15*, the disposal of any property which is an outright gift to an individual and is for the purposes of *IHTA 1984* a transfer of value that is *wholly* exempt by reason of *s 20* will be an excluded transaction. [*FA 2004, Sch 15 para 10(1)(e), (2)(e)*].

21.10   GIFTS IN CONSIDERATION OF MARRIAGE OR CIVIL PARTNERSHIP

Gifts in consideration of any one marriage or civil partnership by any one transferor (e.g. husband and wife are treated separately) are exempt from inheritance tax on the value transferred without tax (i.e. there is no grossing-up) up to the following limits

(a)   £5,000 by a parent of either party to the marriage or civil partnership.

(*b*)   £2,500 by one party to the marriage or civil partnership to the other or by a grandparent or remoter ancestor.

(*c*)   £1,000 in any other case.

Any excess of gifts over the above limits is attributed in proportion to the values transferred. Form P11(Notes) prior to the civil partnership legislation being introduced stated that the gift should be made 'on or shortly before the marriage' and 'to be fully effective on the marriage taking place'. The common usage form of '… on the occasion of the marriage …' is also acceptable. See IHTM14201.

Gifts must be outright to a party to the marriage or civil partnership, or settled gifts exclusively for the following persons who are or may become entitled to any benefit under the settlement (using Form 222).

(i)   The parties to the marriage or civil partnership, issue of the marriage or civil partnership, or a wife or husband or civil partner of any such issue.

(ii)   A subsequent spouse or civil partner of a party to the marriage or civil partnership, or any child of the family, or the spouse or civil partner of any such child, of a subsequent marriage or civil partnership of either party.

(iii) As respects a reasonable amount of remuneration, the trustees of the settlement.

'*Child of the family*' above includes in relation to parties to a marriage or civil partnership, a child of one or both of them. [*The Tax and Civil Partnership Regulations 2005, SI 2005/3229, Reg 8(6)*].

'*Issue*' includes any person legitimated by a marriage, or adopted by husband and wife jointly. [*IHTA 1984, s 22(1)–(5)*].

The exemptions apply only to actual lifetime gifts, not to transfers deemed to have been made (but include a loan of money or property, see 49.3 TRANSFER OF VALUE) and to the value chargeable on the termination of an interest in possession in settled property (see 43.3 SETTLEMENTS WITH INTERESTS IN POSSESSION). [*IHTA 1984, ss 3(4), 22(6), 57*]. See IHTM14201 for examples of non-qualification vis:

'Where before the marriage or civil partnership the donor has taken steps towards making the gift, for example, by instructing their solicitors or brokers, but the gift is not completed until after the marriage or civil partnership, it does not qualify.'

Note. The exemption will not be lost

(A)   if some other person can benefit from the settlement only in the event of any child to the marriage or civil partnership dying without attaining a specified age; or

(B)   on the operation of a protective trust to which a person within (i) or (ii) above is the principal beneficiary.

21.11   DISPOSITIONS FOR MAINTENANCE OF FAMILY

A disposition is not a transfer of value if it is made during lifetime

(*a*)   by one party to a marriage or civil partnership for the maintenance of the other party, or

(*b*)   by one party to a marriage or civil partnership for the maintenance, education or training of a child of either party for a period up to 5 April after attaining the age of eighteen or, if later, after ceasing full-time education or training. '*Child*' includes step–child and adopted child, or

(c)   by any person for the maintenance, education or training of a child not in the care of a parent of his for a period up to 5 April after attaining the age of eighteen or, if the child has been in the care of the disponer for substantial periods before that age, after ceasing full-time education or training, or

(d)   in favour of an illegitimate child of the person making the disposition and is for the maintenance, education or training of the child for a period up to 5 April after attaining the age of eighteen or, if later, after ceasing full-time education or training, or

(e)   as a reasonable provision for the care or maintenance of a dependent relative (i.e. a relative of self, spouse or civil partner who is incapacitated by old age or infirmity from maintaining himself or his mother or father or his spouse's or civil partner's mother or father). By concession, such a disposition is also exempt if made by a child in favour of his unmarried mother if she (although not so incapacitated) is genuinely financially dependent on that child. (See F12 at 23 HMRC EXTRA–STATUTORY CONCESSIONS).

'*Marriage*' or '*civil partnership*' includes a former marriage or civil partnership where a disposition has been made on its dissolution or varied later.

'*Step-child*' in relation to a civil partner is the meaning given within *Civil Partnership Act 2004, s 246.*

For the purposes of the pre-owned assets anti-avoidance legislation within *FA 2004, Sch 15*, the disposal of any property which is a disposition falling within the requirements of this paragraph will be an excluded transaction. [*FA 2004, Sch 15 para 10(1)(d), (2)(d)*].

If a disposition as above only partially satisfies the conditions, it will be separated into exempt and non-exempt parts. An exempt disposition which is a disposal of an interest in possession in settled property is not treated as terminating that interest so as to make it chargeable to tax under *IHTA 1984, s 51(1)* (see 43.3 SETTLEMENTS WITH INTERESTS IN POSSESSION). [*IHTA 1984, ss 11, 51(2); The Tax and Civil Partnership Regulations 2005, SI 2005/3229, Reg 4*]. The non-exempt part may qualify as a POTENTIALLY EXEMPT TRANSFER (38).

21.12   NORMAL EXPENDITURE OUT OF INCOME

A transfer of value during lifetime is exempt if, or to the extent that, it is shown

(a)   that it was made as part of the normal (i.e. typical or habitual) expenditure of the transferor, and

(b)   that (taking one year with another) it was made out of his income, and

(c)   that, after allowing for all transfers of value forming part of his normal expenditure, the transferor was left with sufficient income to maintain his usual standard of living.

[*IHTA 1984, s 21(1)*].

For these purposes 'normal' is not defined but in reply to questions raised by the Committee of the Association of Corporate Trustees the HMRC Capital Taxes have stated 'There is no rule of thumb. We basically judge each case on its merits. We do look very closely at the standard of living of the transferor. The test of normality requires patterns of giving to be established. That is why it is not always possible to say that, at the time it is made, a particular gift is or is not exempt as normal.' STEP Newsletter, May 1998, p 17. However, see note (C) to the example below. Note that from February 2004 Form D3 (see 51) has been revised to include a new Box 1e asking whether the deceased made any regular gifts out of income. A new Form D3a is added to the IHT 200 supplementary forms and requires details of the income and expenditure to support the claim under *IHTA 1984, s 21*. The form will be included in the next issue of this publication.

The exemption applies only to transfers actually made and not where deemed to have been made. [*IHTA 1984, ss 3(4), 21(5)*]. The first gift in a series can qualify as 'normal' provided there is clear evidence that further gifts are intended. 'Income' for the purposes of exemption, means net income after income tax and is determined in accordance with normal accountancy rules rather than income tax rules (HMRC Pamphlet IHT 1 paras 5.13 and 5.14 originally stated the above but this explanation is now absent from the replacement IHT 15, p 7). In the new IHT 110 (Notes) it additionally states 'A one-off payment, even if it was out of income, will not be exempt'.

In the case *Bennett and Others v CIR Ch D 1994, [1995] STC 54* Lightman J stated that a pattern of gifts is intended to remain in place for more than a nominal period and for a sufficient period (barring unforeseen circumstances). Also, the amount of the expenditure need not be fixed nor the individual recipient be the same but a pattern established by proof of the existence of a prior commitment or resolution or by reference only to a sequence of events. In this particular case the deceased had adopted a pattern of expenditure in respect of the surplus income which was part of her normal expenditure despite her death just over one year after executing a form of authority to distribute her surplus income (see also Taxline March 1995 Item 40). See also *Nadin v CIR [1997] STC SCD 107 Sp C 112* at 60 TAX CASES.

To the trustees of [   ] trust ('the Trust')

1   I request and direct you to pay fifty per cent of the net after tax income due to me from the Trust to my son [   ]

2   My son's receipt shall be a complete discharge to you for my strict entitlement under the terms of the Trust

3   This authority shall be revocable by me at will but

    3.1   I confirm that I have no current intention of revoking it

    3.2   May be acted on by you unless and until you have notice of such revocation]

4   I confirm that I have taken such legal or other professional advice as I see fit

5   For the avoidance of doubt this authority is given to you under seal

SIGNED AS A DEED and   )
DELIVERED on   )
                       200(7)   )
By   )
in the presence of:—   )

Note to deed

(A)   Clause 3 is thought to be consistent with *Bennett*.

Example

A wife pays annual life assurance premiums on a policy in favour of her son. The income of her husband and herself for 2007/08 is

	£
Husband's salary	25,000
Wife's salary	6,295
	£31,295

Income levels are not expected to fluctuate wildly from year to year.

The wife's disposable income is

	£
Salary	6,295
Tax thereon (personal allowance £5,225)	107
Personal income	£6,188

Notes to the example

(A)   Depending on her lifestyle, the wife is probably able to show that she has sufficient income to justify a 'normal expenditure' gift of, say, a £1,000 premium paid annually (and therefore habitual). In Form P11(Notes) HMRC state that 'Examples of usual expenditure are where the deceased was paying a regular premium on an insurance policy for the benefit of another person, or perhaps they were making a monthly or other regular payment'.

(B)   If the wife was also accustomed to pay personally for an annual holiday costing, say, £2,500, it might be difficult to show that the life assurance premium was paid out of income.

(C)   It has been suggested that HMRC Capital Taxes do not, as a general guide, review cases where the gift out of income is not greater than one third of net income i.e. £2,056 in the above case.

A premium on a life insurance policy. A premium on a life insurance policy on his own life paid directly or indirectly by the transferor is not part of his normal expenditure if at any time an annuity was purchased on his life, unless it is shown that the purchase of the annuity and the making or varying of the insurance (or any prior insurance for which the first-mentioned insurance was directly or indirectly substituted) were not associated operations (see 6.3 ANTI-AVOIDANCE) (i.e. were not 'back to back'). [*IHTA 1984, s 21(2)*]. The practice 'is to regard policies and annuities as not being affected by the associated operations rule if, first, the policy was issued on full medical evidence of the assured's health, and, secondly, it would have been issued on the same terms if the annuity had not been bought'. (Official Report, Standing Committee A, 5 February 1975 Col 872). See also 30.3 LIFE ASSURANCE POLICIES.

Income does not include the capital element of a life annuity purchased after 12 November 1974. [*IHTA 1984, s 21(3)(4)*].

Loans of property etc. Loans of property etc. will be exempt from inheritance tax if instead of (*a*) and (*b*) above there were substituted the condition that the transfer was a normal one by the transferor. See 49.3 TRANSFER OF VALUE. [*IHTA 1984, s 29(1)(4)*].

21.13   **TRANSFERS ALLOWABLE FOR INCOME TAX OR CONFERRING RETIREMENT BENEFITS**

A disposition is not a transfer of value if

(*a*)   it is allowable in computing profits or gains for income tax or corporation tax; or (*b*)   it is a contribution to an approved retirement benefit scheme (occupational pension scheme); or

(*c*)   it is to provide

(i)   benefits on or after retirement for a person not connected with the transferor who is or has been in his employ; or

(ii)   benefits on or after the death of such a person for his widow or dependants or surviving civil partner; or

(*d*)   it is a contribution after 22 July 1987 under approved personal pension arrangements entered into by an employee of the person making the disposition.

Where benefits under (*c*) are greater than could be provided under (*b*), the excess is a transfer of value. Dispositions under more than one of the kinds described in (*b*), (*c*) and (*d*) in respect of service by the same person, are exempt only to the extent that the benefits do not exceed what could be provided by a disposition of the kind described in any one of those subparagraphs. For the purposes of (*c*) above, the right to occupy a dwelling at a rent less than would be expected in a transaction at arm's length between persons not connected with each other is regarded as equivalent to a pension equal to the additional rent that might be so expected.

If a disposition as above only partially satisfies the conditions, it will be separated into exempt and non-exempt parts. From 6 April 2006 a person's contributions to an employees' registered pension scheme or scheme within *ICTA 1988, s 615(3)* will also not be a transfer of value as above. [*IHTA 1984, s 12; F(No 2)A 1987, s 98(2)(3); FA 2004, s 203(2); The Tax and Civil Partnership Regulations 2005, SI 2005/3229, Reg 5; FA 2006, Sch 22 para 2*].

The above exemptions apply to lifetime dispositions only. (Official Report Standing Committee E, 29 June 1976 Col 1435).

21.14   DEATH ON ACTIVE SERVICE, ETC.

No inheritance tax is payable on the death of a person from wound, accident or disease contracted whilst on active service against an enemy (or on service of a similar nature) during that time or from aggravation during that time of a previously contracted disease. See IHTM11281. This exemption only applies when the CTO receives a valid certificate issued by the Ministry of Defence. These types of certificate are detailed at IHTM11301 and IHTM11302 and may be obtained from: Wendy Gower
JCCC Deceased Estates
Room 115 Building 182 RAF Innsworth Gloucester GL3 1HW Tel 01454 715680

The following information should be provided:

•   the deceased's service number

•   a copy of the death certificate

•   any relevant supporting medical evidence such as a post-mortem report.

Exemption applies to a person certified by the Defence Council or the Secretary of State as dying from the above causes inflicted or incurred whilst in the armed forces, or if not a member of those forces, whilst subject to the law governing any of those forces by reason of association with or accompanying them. [*Armed Forces Act 1981; IHTA 1984, s 154*]. The wound does not have to be the only or direct cause of death, provided it is a cause (*Executors of 4th Duke of Westminster (otherwise Barty-King) v Ministry of Defence QB 1978, [1978] STC 218*). The exemption applies to the estates of those killed on active service in the Falklands conflict (HMRC Press Release 23 June 1982) and to estates of members of the former Royal Ulster Constabulary who die from injuries caused in NI by terrorist activity. (See F5 at 23 HMRC EXTRA-STATUTORY CONCESSIONS.)

21.15   Exempt Transfers

Where a common seaman, marine or soldier died before 12 March 1952 in the service of the Crown and his estate was wholly exempt from estate duty and under his will he left a limited life interest, no inheritance tax is charged on such exempted property which passes under the terms of the will on the termination of the limited interest. (See F13 at 23 HMRC EXTRA-STATUTORY CONCESSIONS.)

21.15   NON-RESIDENTS' BANK ACCOUNTS

See 50.2 TRANSFERS ON DEATH for the exemption of certain foreign currency bank or Post Office accounts held by persons not domiciled, resident or ordinarily resident in the UK at death. See IHT 18, p 8. A foreign currency account with any of the High Street banks will qualify as will a foreign currency account with:

- ANZ Grindlays Bank Plc

- Banque Nationale de Paris Plc

- Italian International Bank Plc

- Wesleyan Savings Bank Plc

'Bank' for this purpose takes the same meaning as *ITA 2007, s 991* (formerly *ICTA 1988, s 840A*) and includes the Bank of England and any institution authorised by the *Financial Services and Markets Act 2000, Part 4.*

21.16   ABATEMENT OF EXEMPTIONS

Where a transfer on a death after 26 July 1989 is wholly or partly exempt under any of 21.2 or 21.4–21.8 above or under 33.11, 33.12 NATIONAL HERITAGE or 55.4 TRUSTS FOR EMPLOYEES, and the recipient of the property (the trustees where applicable) disposes of property not derived from the transfer on death in settlement of all or part of a claim against the deceased's estate, the exemption for the transfer on death is abated. The (otherwise exempt) gift on death is treated instead as a chargeable specific gift not bearing its own tax, up to the lower of

(i)   the value of the property transferred in that gift

(ii)   the amount by which the estate of the recipient of the property immediately after the disposition settling the claim is less than it would be but for the disposition.

In determining the value of the recipient's estate for the purposes of (ii), no deduction is made for the claim, no account is taken of any liability of the recipient for any tax on the disposition, and the provisions giving relief for AGRICULTURAL PROPERTY (5.1) and BUSINESS PROPERTY (7.1) are disregarded.

The abatement does not apply to the extent that the claim against the deceased's estate is in respect of a liability to be taken into account in determining the value of that estate for inheritance tax purposes. See 50.3 TRANSFERS ON DEATH for liabilities to be taken into account.

[*IHTA 1984, s 29A; FA 1989, s 172*].

22 Gifts with Reservation

Cross-references. See 2.4 ACCOUNTS AND RETURNS; 6.3 ANTI-AVOIDANCE for associated operations; 29.3 LIABILITY FOR TAX; 37.2 PENSION SCHEMES.

Simon's Direct Tax Service, part I3.4.

Other Sources. Form P11(Notes); IHT 110; IR Leaflet IHT 15, pages 11–12; Foster, parts C4 and C5; IHTM24191.

22.1 APPLICATION

Subject to the exceptions in 22.2 below, where, after 17 March 1986, an individual disposes of any property (by way of gift or otherwise) and either

(*a*)   possession and enjoyment of the property is not *bona fide* assumed by the donee at or before the beginning of the 'relevant period'; or

(*b*)   *at any time* in the relevant period the property is not enjoyed to the entire exclusion, or 'virtually' to the entire exclusion, of the donor; or

(*c*)   *at any time* in the relevant period the property is not enjoyed to the entire exclusion, or virtually to the entire exclusion, of any benefit to the donor by contract or otherwise (and for this purpose a benefit which the donor obtained by virtue of any associated operations (see 6.3 ANTI-AVOIDANCE), of which the gift is one, is treated as a benefit to him by contract or otherwise);

then, if and so long as any of the conditions in (*a*) to (*c*) above apply, the property is referred to (in relation to the gift and the donor) as '*property subject to a reservation*'. See *HD Lyon's Personal Representatives v HMRC; Trustees of the Alloro Trust v HMRC* [2007] Sp C 616 where the manner in which a trust, set up by the settlor, had been operated meant that the 'possession and enjoyment of the property' within (*a*) above had not been 'bona fide assumed by the donee at the beginning of the relevant period', within *s 102(1)(a)*. HMRC have set out examples of 'virtually the entire exclusion' which come within the *de minimis* occupation criteria in Revenue Interpretation 55. See http://www.hmrc.gov.uk/leaflets/iht.htm.

'*Relevant period*' is the period ending on the date of the donor's death and beginning seven years before that date or, if later, on the date of the gift.

'*Virtually*' is not defined but it is intended to prevent the rules applying where the benefit enjoyed by the donor is small, e.g. a gift of a house or picture would not be a gift with reservation if the donor happened to 'enjoy' either the house or picture on short visits to the donee (HMRC Booklet IHT 15, page 11) http://www.hmrc.gov.uk/pdfs/iht15.pdf. Further examples of benefits enjoyed by a donor which are considered by the Revenue to be similarly *de minimis*, together with examples which are not so considered (e.g. a gift of a house in which the donor then stays most weekends, or for a month or more each year) are provided in Inland Revenue Tax Bulletin November 1993 p 98. See IHTM14333 for meaning of 'virtually' and IHTM14334 for examples of gifts with exclusion.

Any question where property falls within (*b*) or (*c*) above is, so far as that question depends on the identity of the property, determined by reference to the property which is at that time treated as comprised in the gift. See 22.3 to 22.6 below for special rules where the property changes after the gift or the donee predeceases the donor.

Life policies. Any property comprised in a gift made after 17 March 1986 falls within (*b*) above if the gift consists of or includes, or is made in connection with, a policy of insurance on the life of the donor or his spouse/civil partner or their joint lives *and* the benefits which will or may accrue to the donee as a result of the gift vary by reference to benefits accruing to the donor or his spouse/civil partner (or both) under that or another policy. Policies on joint lives include those on joint lives and the life of the survivor. Benefits accruing to the donor or his spouse/civil partner (or both of them) include benefits accruing by virtue of the exercise of rights conferred on either or both of them. For the HMRC's understanding of when an insurance is made, see 48.1 TIME OF DISPOSITION.

The effect of the above is that

(i)   if, immediately before the donor's death, there is any property which, in relation to him, is property subject to a reservation then, to the extent that the property would not otherwise form part of his estate immediately before death, it is treated as property to which he was beneficially entitled at that time; and

(ii)   if at any time before the end of the relevant period, any property ceases to be property subject to a reservation, the donor is treated as having at that time made a disposition of the property by a disposition which is a POTENTIALLY EXEMPT TRANSFER (38).

In the case of *Ingram and Another (Executors of the Estate of Lady Ingram deceased) v IRC, HL [1999] STC 37; [1999] 1 All ER 297* the case revolved around the transfer of property on 29 March 1987 by Lady Ingram to her Solicitor who then, as nominee, granted Lady Ingram 20-year leasehold interests and then transferred the land subject to the leases to Trustees to hold on trust for specified beneficiaries. The widow continued to live at the property until her death in 1989. HMRC treated the transfer as a gift with reservation and issued a notice of determination accordingly. The House of Lords allowed the executors' appeal. Lord Hoffmann held that:

'although (*s 102*) does not allow a donor to have his cake and eat it, there is nothing to stop him from carefully dividing up the cake, eating part and having the rest. If the benefits which the donor continues to enjoy are by virtue of property which was never comprised in the gift, he has not reserved any benefit out of the property of which he disposed.'

For these purposes, 'property' was 'not something which has physical existence like a house but a specific interest in that property, a legal construct, which can co-exist with other interests in the same physical object. *Section 102* does not therefore prevent people from deriving benefit from the object in which they have given away an interest. It applies only when they derive the benefit from that interest'. The policy of *section 102* was to require people to 'define precisely the interests which they are giving away and the interests, if any, which they are retaining'. The interest, which the widow retained, was 'a proprietary interest, defined with the necessary precision'. The gift was 'a gift of the capital value in the land after deduction of her leasehold interest in the same way as a gift of the capital value of the fund after deduction of an annuity'.

From 9 March 1999 counter avoidance measures were introduced whereby if a gifted interest is treated as being property where the donor or his spouse/civil partner enjoys a significant right or interest, or is a party to a significant arrangement, in relation to the land then the avoidance measures below apply. A right, interest or arrangement in relation to the land is significant only if it entitles the donor to occupy all or part of the land, or enjoy a right in relation to it, otherwise than for full consideration in money or money's worth but is not significant if

*   it does not and cannot prevent the enjoyment of the land to the entire exclusion (or virtually the entire exclusion) of the donor;

*   it does not entitle the donor to occupy all or part of the land immediately after the gift, but would do so were it not for the interest gifted; or

*   it was granted or acquired more than seven years before date of the gift.

The question had been raised as to planning opportunities afforded by the *Ingram* decision *prior* to the anti-avoidance provisions being introduced with effect from 9 March 1999. [*FA 1999, s 104*]. The solicitors for the appellant have expounded in 'Trusts and Estates' the following:

- A transfer of the freehold by the donor to the donee, contingent upon the donee granting a lease at a proper market rent, with reviews on a regular basis advised by an appropriately qualified valuer. This would fall within *paragraph 6* of *Schedule 20* to the *Finance Act 1986*. Both parties should take independent legal and valuation advice.

- A transfer of the freehold to a nominee, who grants a lease to the donor (the lease being carefully drawn to ensure that there is no reservation of benefit to the donor). The nominee would then transfer the freehold to the intended donees who would receive it subject to the lease.

- A deferred 999-year lease, to start in no more than, say, 20 years. This type of arrangement was discussed in the *Ingram* case and, in argument, counsel for HMRC thought that it would not fall within the gift with reservation of benefit provisions. Lord Hoffmann was of the same view.

- In an appropriate case, the grant of a lease by the sole freeholder to himself and his spouse/civil partner, followed by a gift of the freehold to the intended donees. If the house is jointly owned, then the lease could be granted by the joint owners to one of them (probably the one with the longest life expectancy), who could leave the lease to the other joint owner by will.

In addition, the gift of an undivided share in land on or after 9 March 1999 will be treated as a gift with reservation unless either

- the donor does not occupy the property;

- the donor occupies the land to the exclusion of the donee for full consideration in money or money's worth; or

- the donor and donee occupy the land and the donor receives no material benefit, other than a negligible one, by or at the donee's expense in connection with the gift.

[*FA 1986, s 102B(4)*].

Further, from 20 June 2003 additional anti-avoidance provisions were introduced following HMRC's failure in the Court of Appeal in the *CIR v Eversden and another (executors of Greenstock deceased) [2003] STC 822*. See TAX CASES (60). Thereafter an anti-avoidance provision applies from 20 June 2003 that ensures that *s 102(5)* is amended to disapply the exception from *s 102(5)* where a gift is made to a spouse/civil partner and

(*a*)   the property becomes settled property by virtue of the gift; and

(*b*)   the trusts of the settlement give an interest in possession to the donor's spouse/civil partner, so that the gift is exempt from IHT because the exemption for transfers between spouses/civil partners and the rule that treats an interest in possession as equivalent to outright ownership; and

(*c*)   between the date of the gift and the donor's death the interest in possession comes to an end; and

(*d*)   when that interest in possession comes to an end, the beneficiary does not become beneficially entitled either to the settled property, or another interest in possession in it.

The anti-avoidance provisions also apply to ensure that *FA 1986, s 102(5B)* is to apply as if the gift had been made immediately after the relevant beneficiary's interest in possession has ended so that it is only the circumstances after that date which determine whether the property is subject to reservation even in the case where the donor dies within seven years. In addition, *FA 1986, s 102(5C)* duplicates the rule in *FA 1986, s 51(b)* which treats an interest in possession as coming to an end when it is disposed of and reinforces the fact that a reference to property or an interest in property includes part of any property or interest. [*FA 1986, s 102(5)(A), (B), (C); FA 2003, s 185(3); The Tax and Civil Partnership Regulations 2005, SI 2005/3229, Reg 44*].

The above provisions do not make the gift of land a gift with reservation where

- the gift was itself an exempt transfer covered by the main exemptions from inheritance tax in *FA 1986, s 102(5)* (including transfers between spouses) until 19 June 2003. See *Essex and another (executors of Somerset deceased) v CIR [2002] STC SCD 39* and *Eversden*; or

- due to unforeseen circumstances, the donor occupies the land because he/she becomes unable to maintain himself/herself through old age, infirmity or otherwise, and, the interest in land represents reasonable care and maintenance provided by the donee, who is a relative.

Example 1

Alistair, aged 79 years, owns a property that is valued at £340,000. He gives the property to his daughter on 31 March 2007 at the time he enters a nursing home as an infirm resident. However, on 31 December 2007 the nursing home closes due to the imposition of onerous Local Authority regulations imposed on the nursing home. *Care Standards Act 2000, s 23.* In view of the fact that there is a shortage of nursing home beds available in the vicinity Alistair returns to the former family home to live with his daughter who gives up her job to care for him full time. Under *FA 1986, Sch 20 para 6(1)(b)* Alistair's occupation of the property, now owned by his daughter, will not be treated as a gift with reservation because

(*a*) the change resulting in the reoccupation of the property arose out of 'unforeseen' circumstances which were not brought about by the donor; and

(*b*) it occurs at a time when the donor is unable to maintain himself because of old age, infirmity or otherwise; and

(*c*) the gift represents reasonable care and maintenance provided by the donee which in this case can be equated with the loss of earnings by the daughter; and

(*d*) the daughter is a relative.

Alistair dies on 16 June 2012. Providing that within (*c*) above it can be determined that the care and maintenance was 'reasonable' and the other factors within (*a*), (*b*) and (*d*) are in point, the donor's occupation and enjoyment of the gifted land will be disregarded concerning the provisions on gifts with reservation. HMRC does not state what 'reasonable' equates to but states in a letter dated 19 February 1987 'What is *reasonable* will of course depend on the facts of the case'. However, in Tax Bulletin, Issue 9 November 1993 within *FA 1986, Sch 20 para 6(1)(b)* a definition is made by comparison with the shorter Oxford English Dictionary and the corollary of this when defining 'reasonable' would be that the care and maintenance is 'as much as is appropriate or fair; moderate'. In these circumstances the care and maintenance which is full time might be argued to be appropriate and fair for an infirm person commensurate with nursing home standards.

[*FA 1986, ss 102(1)–(5)(5A)–(5C), 102A–B, Sch 20 para 6(1)(c)(2), 7; FA 1999, s 104; FA 2003, s 185(2)(3); The Tax and Civil Partnership Regulations 2005, SI 2005/3229, Regs 44, 45*].

Notes

1. The disposition by which the property becomes subject to a reservation may itself be a chargeable transfer (e.g. a gift to a discretionary trust with the settlor among the

class of beneficiaries). Provided certain conditions are met, regulations provide for the avoidance of a double charge to tax in these circumstances. See 22.10 below.

2.   The amount of the benefit or enjoyment retained by the donor is not important. If a gift falls within the provisions the value of all the property subject to the reservation is taken into account.

3.   Any property which the donor's spouse/civil partner enjoys or benefits from does not automatically fall within the above provisions.

4.   See 38.2 POTENTIALLY EXEMPT TRANSFERS for HMRC treatment of the annual exemption in relation to the potentially exempt transfer deemed to be made as in (ii) above.

Example 2

On 19 June 1992 D gave his house and contents to his grandson G, but continued to live in it alone paying no rent. The agreement between D and G read as follows:

'I give to ....[Grandson G]....... my house known as ...[Postal address]..... that constitutes my principal private residence but subject to his bearing any inheritance tax attributable to its value. I also give to ....[Grandson G].... those of my personal chattels, specified in the schedule annexed hereto, in my house known as ......[Postal address].... which constitute furniture or articles of household use or ornament; jewellery or articles of personal use or adornment; books photographs and articles relating to any sport hobby or other pastime also subject to his bearing any inheritance tax attributable to their value.'

The house and contents were valued at £130,000. On 5 May 2003 D remarried, and went to live with his new wife F. G immediately moved into the house, which was then valued at £308,000.

On 3 January 2008 D died, leaving his estate of £200,000 equally to his granddaughter H and his wife F.

Gift 19 June 1992

As the gift was made more than seven years before death, it is a PET which has become exempt.

5 May 2003 release of reservation

The release of D's reservation is a PET which becomes chargeable by reason of D's death between 4 and 5 years later. IHT is charged, at 60% of full rates on the basis of the Table of rates in force at the time of death, on the value of the house at the date of release of reservation.

22.1 Gifts with Reservation

		£	£
Gift			308,000
Deduct annual exemptions	2003/04*	Nil	
	2002/2003*	Nil	
* see note (C) below			
			Nil
Chargeable transfer			£308,000

Tax thereon (assuming no change in rates)

0–300,000 at nil%	—
300,001–308,000 at 40%	3,200
	£3,200

IHT payable at 60% of full rates, 60% × £3,200 =	£1,920

Death 3 January 2008

IHT is charged at full rates on the chargeable estate of £100,000 (£100,000 passing to the wife is exempt) in the bracket £308,000 to £408,000.

Tax thereon

£308,001–408,000 at 40%	£40,000

Notes to the example

(A) The reference to principal private residence is designed to secure exemption under *TCGA 1992, s 222* but an election should exist where there are two or more properties (inclusive of those abroad).

(B) The agreement between the D and his grandson G above is not ideal as there are likely to be a number of factors that might be open to dispute, particularly the schedule if it does not have, say, an insurance valuation and photographs attaching.

(C) It would appear that under *FA 1986, s 102(4)* HMRC practice is not to reduce a PET by the available annual exemption. This is detailed in the Tax Bulletin, issue 9, November 1993 which stated '... but the value of the PET cannot be reduced by any available annual exemption under section 19 IHTA 1984. The statement in paragraph 3.4 IHT 1 booklet, which indicates that the annual exemption may apply if the reservation ceases to exist in the donor's lifetime and a PET is treated as made at that time, is incorrect'. The new version of IHT 110 definitively states 'The law states that the exemption for gifts out of income and the annual exemption do not apply to a gift with reservation'.

Further anti-avoidance measures apply from 6 April 2005 have been introduced following a short consultation period on the consultation document 'The Tax Treatment of Pre-Owned Assets' to counteract the free continuing use of assets that have been ostensibly gifted. Subsequently, a Technical Guidance note was issued on 17 March 2005. A further Technical Guidance Note was subsequently issued in June 2005 and June 2006 at http://www.hmrc.gov.uk/poa/poa_news.htm. See also 6.4 ANTI-AVOIDANCE. HMRC's consultative document concentrated mainly on a charge to income tax, under Schedule D Case VI [now see *ITTOIA 2005*], on former owners of assets on the benefit of using the asset(s) unless the asset has been sold to an unconnected party at arm's length. [*FA 2004, Sch 15 paras 4, 7, 9; Charge to Income Tax by Reference to Enjoyment of Property Previously Owned Regulations 2005, SI 2005/724, Regs 2–4*]. Taxpayers who have existing schemes that come within the charge may, by the relevant filing date i.e. 31 January in the year of assessment immediately following the initial year or such later date as HMRC may allow, elect for special transitional relief that allows them to avoid the charge to income tax by dismantling the original gift scheme. [*FA 2004, Sch 15 para 23(3)* as amended by *FA 2007, s 66*]. For IHT 500 election form see 59.42 WORKING CASE STUDY. This will then ensure that the asset is treated as part of the individual's taxable estate for IHT purposes in accordance with the gifts with reservation rules while the individual continues to enjoy the property. Under those rules the property would be potentially eligible for IHT reliefs and exemptions (e.g. APR and BPR) providing the necessary requirements for those reliefs and exemptions were met. However, it may still in certain circumstances be appropriate to suffer the income tax charge under existing schemes and avoid the IHT charge. In addition, the charging provisions do not apply to property within an 'exemption from charge' or to the extent that it comes within an 'excluded transaction' category. See 59.40 WORKING CASE STUDY.

Where a person is beneficially entitled to settled property and continues to be treated as owning the property after 21 March 2006 and that interest is an immediate post death interest (IPDI) or a transitional serial interest (TSI) or a disabled person's interest and that interest comes to an end during that person's lifetime then it is to be treated as if it was a gift for the purposes of the gifts with reservation rules above. See also 43 SETTLEMENTS WITH INTERESTS IN POSSESSION and 54 TRUSTS FOR DISABLED PERSONS. Therefore where the interest in the property has terminated by gift or otherwise and the individual with the former interest in possession still has use of that property then a charge under the gifts with reservation rules may apply subject to exclusions from charge noted below. In addition, where an individual has use of property that was derived, directly or indirectly, from the original property whether in the form of a loan or not then that property will be treated as subject to the gifts with reservation provisions. [*FA 1986, ss 102, 102ZA; FA 2006, Sch 20 para 33*].

22.2   **Exceptions.** The above provisions do not apply in the following circumstances.

(a)   To the extent that the disposal by way of gift is an exempt transfer by virtue of

(i)   *IHTA 1984, s 18 as amended by FA 2003, s 185(2)* (transfers between spouses/civil partners except where provided by *FA 1986, s 102(5A)(5B)*, see 21.8 EXEMPT TRANSFERS);

(ii)   *IHTA 1984, s 20* (small gifts, see point (*b*) at 21.9 EXEMPT TRANSFERS);

(iii)   *IHTA 1984, s 22* (gifts in consideration of marriage, see 21.10 EXEMPT TRANSFERS);

(iv)   *IHTA 1984, s 23* (gifts to charities, see 21.2 EXEMPT TRANSFERS);

(v)   *IHTA 1984, s 24* (gifts to political parties, see 21.6 EXEMPT TRANSFERS);

(vi)   *IHTA 1984, s 24A* (gifts to housing associations, see 21.4 EXEMPT TRANSFERS);

(vii)   *IHTA 1984, s 25* (gifts for national purposes, see 21.5 EXEMPT TRANSFERS);

(viii)   *IHTA 1984, s 27 as amended by FA 1998, s 144* (maintenance funds for historic buildings, see 33.11 NATIONAL HERITAGE); or

(ix)   *IHTA 1984, s 28* (employee trusts, see 55 TRUSTS FOR EMPLOYEES).

[*FA 1986, s 102(5); The Tax and Civil Partnership Regulations 2005, SI 2005/3229, Reg 44*]. *Note.* The annual exemption (see further 38.2 POTENTIALLY EXEMPT TRANSFERS) and the normal expenditure out of income exemption are not included.

22.2 Gifts with Reservation

(*b*)   If the disposal by way of gift is made under the terms of a policy issued in respect of an insurance made before 18 March 1986 *unless* the policy is varied on or after that date so as to increase the benefits secured or extend the term of the insurance. Any change in the terms of the policy made in pursuance of an option or other power conferred by the policy is deemed to be a variation of the policy except for the exercise of an indexation option with respect to benefits or premiums before 1 August 1986 if the option or power could only be exercised before that date. [*FA 1986, s 102(6)(7)*].

(*c*)   In the case of property which is an interest in land or a chattel (corporeal movable in Scotland), retention or assumption by the donor of actual occupation of, or actual enjoyment of an incorporeal right over, the land or actual possession of the chattel (corporeal movable in Scotland) is disregarded for the purposes of 22.1(B) and (C) above if it is for full consideration in money or money's worth. [*FA 1986, Sch 20 para 6(1)(a),(3)*]. HMRC considers that for this provision to apply full consideration should be provided throughout the relevant period (see 22.1 above), so that any rent passing should be reviewed at appropriate intervals to reflect market changes. Any consideration passing will be treated as full if it lies within a range of values reflecting normal valuation tolerances (Inland Revenue Tax Bulletin November 1993 p 98).

CHATTEL LEASE

PARTIES:

1.   'The Parents' namely, ...

2.   'The Children' namely ....

BACKGROUND

A.   The Children are the beneficial owners of the chattels set out in the Schedule below ('the Chattels')

B.   The Children wish to allow the Parents the use and enjoyment of the Chattels on the basis of full consideration payable by the Parents

AGREEMENT

1.   Bailment

The Children grant a lease of the Chattels to the Parents for the following term and generally on the terms and conditions following:

2.   The Term

The term of the lease shall be equal to the joint lives and life of the survivor of the Parents, terminable earlier:

2.1   Upon six months written notice given by either party

2.2   Immediately upon default of any obligations contained in clause 9

2.3   Immediately upon both the Parents or the survivor of them becoming mentally incapable within the meaning of section 94 (2) of the Mental Health Act 1983.

3.   Ownership

3.1   The Children retain the ownership of the Chattels

3.2   The Children reserve the right to fix any plating or other means of identification to the Chattels or any of them

3.3   The Parents covenant not (nor take steps) to sell, deal, charge or part with the Chattels in any other way contrary to the ownership of the Children

3.4   The Parents will immediately pay any sum required to remove any lien which may arise over the Chattels.

4.   Enjoyment and Housing

4.1   The Children covenant with the Parents (provided the Parents pay the rent and perform the Parents' covenants) that the parents shall peaceably hold and enjoy the Chattels during the term without any interruption by the Children or any person rightfully claiming under or in trust for any of them

4.2   The Chattels shall be housed at ....[Name of property]... or at other locations from time to time agreed between the Parents and the Children

5.   Rental

5.1   The initial annual rental for the Chattels shall be £....... per annum (which is agreed by the Children and the Parents to reflect .....% of the current open market value of the Chattels)

5.2   The rental shall be paid annually; the first year's rental is due on the signing of this agreement (and the Children acknowledge receipt of it); further annual rental payments shall be due on the anniversaries of this agreement. Such adjustment as is necessary on the termination of the agreement by the death of the survivor of the Parents shall be made as is required; otherwise there shall be no adjustment

5.3   The rental shall be reviewable by agreement at three yearly intervals from the date of this Agreement to ensure that the Parents give full consideration for the use and enjoyment of the Chattels. In default of agreement the reviewed rent shall be determined by a valuer appointed by the President for the time being of the Incorporated Society of Valuers and Auctioneers acting as expert and not an arbitrator; either party shall be at liberty to request the President to make such an appointment.

6.   Insurance

6.1   The Parents will insure the Chattels for their full replacement cost comprehensively against all risk with the interest of the Children noted on the Policy and will duly and punctually pay all premiums and on request will promptly produce the insurance policy and proof of payment of premiums to the Children. All claims under such insurance policy will be dealt with in accordance with the written direction of the Children. All claims and moneys received by the Parents under such insurance policy shall be held by the parents in trust for the Children

7.   Preservation and Repair

7.1   The Parents undertake to preserve the Chattels

7.2   The Parents undertake to keep the Chattels clean and in good and substantial repair and will bear the cost of any repairs not covered by insurance

7.3   The Parents will permit the Children and any person authorised by them at any reasonable hour to view or survey the state and condition of the Chattels

7.4   The Parents will forthwith after being required to do so by the Children make good any want of repair in the Chattels

PROVIDED that nothing in this clause shall require the Parents to maintain the Chattels in anything other than their current condition or require the Parents to improve or put the Chattels into first rate condition

8.   Security

8.1   The Parents undertake to put in place, maintain and bear the cost of such security arrangements as are from time to time agreed between the Parents and Children or as are reasonably stipulated by the Children to reflect the requirements of any relevant insurance company, advice from the Police or advice otherwise specifically received from a specialist security company engaged for the purpose

9.   Default

If the Parents default in the punctual payment of any of the instalments of rent provided for, or default in the payment of the insurance premiums as provided for, or default in the performance of any of the terms and conditions of this agreement, the Children may immediately retake possession of the Chattels, without notice to the Parents, with or without legal process, and the parents by this agreement authorise and empower the Children to enter the premises or other places where the Chattels may be found and to take and carry away the Chattels. All moneys due under this agreement shall become immediately due and payable plus all reasonable costs of repossession

EXECUTED on .... 200(7)

Signed by ....

Note to the Precedent

(A)   The initial rent should be arrived at preferably by written negotiation between two competent valuers aware of the terms of the lease, the value and condition of the chattels, cost of insurance and security, etc.

(B)   The agreement is said to be a chattel lease as that is the common understanding. Strictly it is a bailment agreement though nothing turns on that.

(*d*)   In the case of property which is an interest in land, any occupation by the donor of the whole or any part of the land is disregarded for the purposes of 22.1(*b*) and (*c*) above if

(i)   it results from a change in circumstances of the donor since the time of the gift, being a change which was unforeseen at that time and was not brought about by the donor to receive the benefit of this provision; *and*

(ii)   it occurs at a time when the donor has become unable to maintain himself through old age, infirmity or otherwise; *and*

(iii)   it represents a reasonable provision by the donee for the care and maintenance of the donor; *and*

(iv)   the donee is a relative of the donor or his spouse/civil partner. [*FA 1986, Sch 20 para 6(1)(b); The Tax and Civil Partnership Regulations 2005, SI 2005/3229, Reg 46*].

See also IHT 15, page 11 and http://www.hmrc.gov.uk/pdfs/iht15.pdf.

22.3   **SUBSTITUTIONS AND ACCRETIONS OF UNSETTLED PROPERTY**

Special rules are required to cover cases where the property changes hands after the gift or the donee predeceases the donor.

Basic rule. Where the donor makes a gift which is not a sum of money in sterling or any other currency then if at any time before the 'material date' the donee ceased to have the possession and enjoyment of any of the gifted property, the property, if any, received by him in substitution for that property is treated as if it had been comprised in the original gift instead of the property of which the donee ceased to have possession and enjoyment. This includes, in particular

(*a*)   in relation to any property disposed of by the donee, any benefit received by him by way of consideration for the sale, exchange or other disposition; and

(*b*)   in relation to a debt or security, any benefit received by the donee in or towards the satisfaction or redemption thereof; and

(*c*)   in relation to any right to acquire property, any property acquired in pursuance of that right. Any consideration given by the donee, in money or money's worth, is allowed as a deduction in valuing the original gift at any time after the consideration is given. This does not apply to any part (not being a sum of money) of that consideration which is property comprised in the same or another gift from the donor and is treated either as forming part of his estate immediately before death or as being attributable to the value transferred by a potentially exempt transfer made by him.

The '*material date*' is the date of the donor's death, or, if earlier the date on which the property ceases to be property subject to a reservation.

Gift by donee. Where, before the material date, the donee makes a gift of the property comprised in the gift to him or otherwise voluntarily divests himself of it (except under compulsory purchase) for less than the value of the property at that time, then, unless he does so in favour of the donor, he is treated as continuing to have possession and enjoyment of that property. For these purposes, the donee is treated as divesting himself, voluntarily and without consideration, of any interest in property which merges or is extinguished in another interest held or acquired by him in the same property. [*FA 1986, Sch 20 paras 1, 2(1)–(5), 3(1)*].

The effect of the above is as follows:

(i)   If the original gift subject to a reservation is of money in sterling or other currency it appears that the reservation ceases when the money is spent on acquiring any property.

(ii)   If the disposal by the donee is for full consideration, the property received in substitution is treated as the original gift. As drafted, one interpretation is that this provision only applies to the first substitution and that on a second substitution (e.g. the application of the proceeds of sale of the original property for full consideration) the reservation ceases. It is understood that HMRC Inheritance Tax do not agree with this interpretation, and their view is that the property received on second and subsequent substitutions is also treated as the original gift. This point is unlikely to be resolved until the matter is tested in the courts.

(iii)   If the disposal by the donee is for less than full consideration, the donee is treated as continuing to have possession and enjoyment of the original property.

22.4   **Shares and debentures.** Where any shares in or debentures of a body corporate are comprised in the original gift and the donee is issued with, or granted rights to acquire, further shares or debentures (in the same or any other body corporate) otherwise than by way of exchange, the further issue or rights granted are treated as having been comprised in the gift in addition to the original property. (Where the shares etc. are issued by way of exchange, the *basic rule* above applies.)

This applies where the issue or grant of rights is

(*a*)   made to the donee as holder or as having been the holder; or

(*b*)   made to him in pursuance of an offer or invitation made to him as being or having been the holder; or

(*c*)   an offer or invitation in connection with which any preference is given to him as being or having been the holder. [*FA 1986, Sch 20 para 2(6)(7)*].

Consideration by donee. Any consideration given by the donee, in money or money's worth, for the issue or grant of rights is allowed as a deduction in valuing the original gift at any time after the consideration is given. This does not apply to any part of that consideration

(i)   which, not being a sum of money, is property comprised in the same or another gift from the donor and is treated either as forming part of his estate immediately before death or as being attributable to the value transferred by a potentially exempt transfer made by him; or

(ii)   as consists in the capitalisation of reserves or in the retention of any property distributable by the body corporate; or

(iii)   is otherwise provided (directly or indirectly) out of the assets or at the expense of the body corporate or any associated body corporate. For this purpose, two bodies are deemed to be associated if one has control of the other or if another person has control of both. [*FA 1986, Sch 20 para 3*].

22.5   **Early death of donee.** Where there is a gift and the donee dies before the material date (see 22.3 above) the provisions of 22.3 and 22.4 above apply to any property comprised in the gift as if

(*a*)   the donee had not died and the acts of his personal representative were his acts; and

(*b*)   property taken by any person under his testamentary dispositions or his intestacy (or partial intestacy) were taken under a gift made by him at the time of his death. [*FA 1986, Sch 20 para 4*].

22.6   **SETTLED GIFTS**

Settlement by donor. Where there is a disposal by way of gift and the property becomes settled property by virtue of the gift, the provisions relating to gifts with reservation apply as if the property comprised in the gift consisted of the property in the settlement on the 'material date' except insofar as that property neither is, nor represents, nor is derived from, property in the original gift. For these purposes

(*a*)   any property comprised in the settlement on the material date which is derived, directly or indirectly, from a loan made by the donor to the trustees is treated as derived from property originally comprised in the gift; and

(*b*)   where, under any trust or power relating to settled property, income arising from that property after the material date is accumulated, the accumulations are not treated as derived from the property.

The '*material date*' is the date of the donor's death or, if earlier, the date at which the property ceased to be property subject to a reservation.

If the settlement comes to an end before the material date as respects all or any part of the property which, if the donor had died immediately before that time, would be treated as comprised in the gift, then

(i)   the property in question (other than property to which the donor then becomes absolutely and beneficially entitled in possession); and

(ii)   any consideration (not consisting of rights under the settlement) given by the donor for any of the property to which he so becomes entitled,

is treated as comprised in the original gift in addition to any other property so comprised. [*FA 1986, Sch 20 para 5(1)(2)(4)(5)*].

It is understood that HMRC Inheritance Tax accepts that the interaction of *FA 1986, s 102(3)* in 22.1(i) above and *IHTA 1984, s 48(3) as amended by FA 2006, s 157* (see 20.2 EXCLUDED PROPERTY) is such that if a non-UK domiciled settlor creates a discretionary settlement of assets situated outside the UK and is included as a possible beneficiary, the gifts with reservation rules do not apply because the excluded property provisions are paramount. The fact that the settlor becomes domiciled in the UK after creating the settlement would also not give rise to the operation of *FA 1986, s 102(3)* should he die while so domiciled but should the settlor become so domiciled and then cease to be a beneficiary, such cesser is deemed to be a potentially exempt transfer of the settled assets (notwithstanding that they are excluded property) by reason of *FA 1986, s 102(4)* in 22.1(ii) above and will be liable to tax in accordance with 51 TRANSFERS WITHIN SEVEN YEARS OF DEATH (Tolley's Practical Tax 1989 p 176).

Settlement by donee. Where the donor's gift is not settled property but the property is settled by the donee before the material date, the above provisions for settlements by the donor apply as if the settlement had been made by the original gift. For this purpose, property which becomes settled property under any testamentary disposition of the donee or his intestacy (or partial intestacy) is treated as settled by him. [*FA 1986, Sch 20 para 5(3)*].

22.7   AGRICULTURAL PROPERTY AND BUSINESS PROPERTY

Where there is a disposal by way of gift which, in relation to the donor, is at that time

(*a*)   relevant business property (see 7.4 BUSINESS PROPERTY); or

(*b*)   agricultural property to which *IHTA 1984, s 116* applies (see 5.2 AGRICULTURAL PROPERTY); or

(*c*)   shares or securities in agricultural companies to which *IHTA 1984, s 122(1)* applies (see 5.6 AGRICULTURAL PROPERTY),

and that property is subject to a reservation, then, subject to the exception below, any question as to the availability and appropriate percentage of agricultural or business property relief on the 'material transfer of value' is determined as if, so far as it is attributable to the gifted property, the transfer was made by the donee. For these purposes only, in determining whether the requirements as to minimum period of ownership and/or occupation are fulfilled (see 5.3 AGRICULTURAL PROPERTY and 7.5 BUSINESS PROPERTY) the donor's ownership prior to the gift is treated as the donee's and any occupation by the donor (before or after the gift) is treated as occupation by the donee.

The exception is that any question as to whether, on the material transfer of value, any shares or securities qualify for business property relief where control or 25% voting control is an issue is determined as if the shares or securities were owned by the donor and had been owned by him since the gift.

Where the gift falls within (*c*) above, agricultural property relief is not available (for transfers and other events occurring before 17 March 1987 the above provisions did not

231

apply) unless *IHTA 1984, s 116* (see 5.2 AGRICULTURAL PROPERTY) applied in relation to the value transferred by the disposal *and* throughout the period from the gift to the 'material date' the shares and securities are owned by the donee. For this purpose only, in determining whether the requirements of 5.6(C) AGRICULTURAL PROPERTY are fulfilled the requirements as to the ownership of the shares or securities there mentioned are assumed to be fulfilled.

The '*material transfer of value*' is, as the case requires, the transfer of value on the donor's death or on the property concerned ceasing to be subject to a reservation and '*material date*' is construed accordingly.

Early death of donee. If the donee dies before the material transfer of value, then, as respects any time after his death, references to the donee include references to his personal representatives or, if appropriate, the person by whom the property or shares etc. concerned were taken under a testamentary disposition made by the donee or under his intestacy (or partial intestacy). [*FA 1986, Sch 20 para 8; FA 1987, s 58, Sch 8 para 18; F(No 2)A 1992, s 73, Sch 14 para 7*].

22.8   ESTATE DUTY CASES

The estate duty legislation contained similar, but not identical, provisions relating to gifts with reservation. It is, therefore, currently uncertain to what extent the estate duty cases are relevant for IHT purposes. In *Pearson and Others v CIR HL, [1980] STC 318* it was held that the meaning of 'interest in possession' for estate duty purposes was not relevant for CTT purposes but this does not necessarily mean that similar decisions will be applied with respect to gifts with reservation.

The following decisions in estate duty cases must, therefore, be considered subject to this background.

(*a*)   *Exclusion of the donor from enjoyment under* 22.1(B) *above*. This condition is not fulfilled if at some later date after the gift the property or income therefrom is voluntarily applied by the donee to the donor, even if the latter is under an obligation to repay sums used by him (*New South Wales Commissioners of Stamp Duties v Permanent Trustee Co. of New South Wales Ltd PC, [1956] AC 512*). The deceased may remain as a guest in a house he has given without tax being attracted provided that there was no agreement to this effect and it was a *bona fide* gift (*A-G v Seccombe KB, [1911] 2 KB 688*—contrast *Revenue Commissioners v O'Donohoe SC (RI), [1936] IR 342*) but this proposition is open to question following *Chick v New South Wales Commissioners of Stamp Duties PC, [1958] AC 435*.

(*b*)   *Exclusion of the donor from any benefit under* 22.1(C) *above*. Arrangements between the donee and a third party to give the donor benefit is within this provision, but retention of rights under a contract made prior to the gift and quite separate from it, is not. The gift of land already subject to a lease to the donor is not a gift with reservation as the lease is not part of the gift (*Munro v New South Wales Commissioners of Stamp Duties PC 1933, [1934] AC 61*). But compare *Nicholas v CIR CA, [1975] STC 278* where the donor's lease was acquired at the same time as the gift. (*Note.* The question of whether the owner of property (in particular, land) can grant a lease to himself or a nominee for himself may need to be answered by reference to the legal jurisdiction concerned. In the Scottish stamp duty case of *Kildrummy (Jersey) Ltd v CIR CS, [1990] STC 657* the grant of a lease of land by the owners of the freehold interest to a nominee for themselves prior to the transfer of the freehold reversion to a third party was declared a nullity on the ground that a person cannot contract with himself. In the English law of property case of *Rye v Rye HL 1961, [1962] AC 496* it was held that *Law of Property Act 1925, s 72(3)* does not enable a person or persons who are the freeholders of land to grant a lease to himself or themselves but, although not at issue, the judgment of Radcliffe LJ suggests the use of a nominee in such circumstances would be valid. These cases may be pertinent when considering the *Munro* decision in the context of IHT and gifts with reservation.)

Examples of 'benefit' include a covenant by the donee to pay the donor's debts and funeral expenses (*Grey (Earl) v A-G HL, [1900] AC 124*); a power reserved to the donor to charge a capital sum on the subject matter of the gift (*Re Clark, (1906) 40 ILT 117*); a collateral annuity to the donor secured by personal covenant (*A-G v Worrall QB 1894, [1891–94] All ER 861*); remuneration paid to the settlor as trustee, but *not* money spent on maintenance and education of the donor's children (*Oakes v New South Wales Commissioners of Stamp Duties PC 1953, [1954] AC 57*).

(*c*)   *Settlements.* A reservation of benefit arises where a settlor is included as a potential beneficiary under a discretionary trust (see *A-G v Heywood QB, [1887] 19 QBD 326; A-G v Farrell CA, [1931] 1 KB 81*; and *Gartside v CIR HL, [1968] AC 553*) but not necessarily where a spouse is included. The inclusion of the spouse may have income tax disadvantages (unless the trust contains non-income producing assets) but the inclusion of a widow or widower will not do so (*Lord Vestey's Executors and Vestey v CIR HL 1949, 31 TC 1*). Trustees are treated as having possession on behalf of the beneficiaries (*Oakes v New South Wales Commissioners of Stamp Duties PC 1953, [1954] AC 57*). A settlement of shares in favour of an infant child with absolute gift provided he reached the age of 21 but with a resulting trust to the donor if the child failed to reach that age is not a gift with reservation as the property comprised in the gift is the equitable interest which the donor had created in the shares (*New South Wales Commissioners of Stamp Duties v Perpetual Trustee Co. Ltd PC, [1943] AC 425*).

22.9   **VARIATIONS AND DISCLAIMERS**

The provisions relating to variations and disclaimers in *IHTA 1984, s 142* (see 14.1 DEEDS VARYING DISPOSITIONS ON DEATH) do not apply to property to which the deceased was treated as entitled under the gifts with reservation rules. [*IHTA 1984, s 142(5); FA 1986, Sch 19 para 24*].

22.10   **DOUBLE CHARGES—GIFTS WITH RESERVATION AND DEATH**

Without specific relief, a double charge to tax could arise where there is a transfer by way of gift of property which is or subsequently becomes a chargeable transfer and the property is, by virtue of the rules relating to gifts with reservation, subject to a further transfer which is chargeable as a result of the transferor's death. The pre-owned assets regulations relating to income tax now include provisions to avoid a double charge to IHT where a chargeable person elects that the gift with reservation provisions apply to the relevant property. [*FA 1986, s 104(1); Charge to Income Tax by Reference to Enjoyment of Property Previously Owned Regulations 2005, SI 2005/724, Reg 6; Inheritance Tax (Double Charges Relief) Regulations 2005, SI 2005/3441, Reg 3*]. A double charge can arise where the chargeable person makes a gift of property or a debt that is a potentially exempt transfer for IHT purposes. If that same property is then liable to the income tax charge the person may decide to make an election on form IHT500 under *FA 2004, Sch 15 para 21* that the property is subject to the IHT reservation of benefits rules. See 59.42 WORKING CASE STUDY. If that person then dies within seven years of the original gift a double charge to IHT may arise, firstly, by reason of the original transfer and secondly when the property is added back into the death estate for the purposes of the gift with reservation rules. The new provision avoids the double charge by opting for the IHT on transfer that produces the highest overall amount of IHT and thereby reduces the other transfer to nil. See example 1 below.

Relief from double charge to tax is given where the following conditions are fulfilled.

(*a*)   An individual ('the deceased') makes a transfer of value by way of gift of property after 17 March 1986 which transfer is or proves to be a chargeable transfer.

(*b*)   The property in relation to the gift and the deceased is property subject to a reservation.

(*c*)   *Either*

    (i)   the property is treated as property to which the deceased was beneficially entitled immediately before his death (as the property is then subject to a reservation); *or*

    (ii)   the property ceases to be property subject to a reservation and is the subject of a potentially exempt transfer at that time.

(*d*)   *Either*

    (i)   the property is comprised in the estate of the deceased immediately before his death and value attributable to it is a chargeable part of this estate on death; *or*

    (ii)   the property is property transferred by the potentially exempt transfer in (*c*)(ii) above, value attributable to which is transferred by a chargeable transfer.

Where the above conditions are fulfilled, there must be separately calculated the total tax chargeable as a consequence of the death of the deceased

(A)   disregarding so much of the value transferred by the transfer of value under (*a*) above as is attributable to property to which (*d*) above refers; and

(B)   disregarding so much of the value of property to which (*d*) above refers as is attributable to property to which (*a*) above refers.

Whichever of the two calculations produces the higher amount of IHT as a result of the death remains chargeable and the value of the other transfer is reduced by reference to the value of the transfer which produced that amount.

Where the higher amount is calculated under (A) above

(I)   credit is available for tax already paid on the lifetime chargeable transfer which is attributable to the value disregarded under that calculation (but not exceeding the amount of tax due on death attributable to the value of the property in question); and

(II)   to avoid the value of the same property entering twice into the tax calculations, the reduction in value applies to all IHT purposes except a ten-year anniversary charge or proportionate charge to tax on a discretionary trust arising before the transferor's death if the transfer by way of gift was chargeable to tax when made.

Where the total tax chargeable under (A) and (B) above is identical, calculation (A) is treated as producing the higher amount. [*FA 1986, s 104(1)(c); SI 1987/1130, Regs 5, 8*].

Relief is given where a double charge to IHT arises in situations where arrangements are caught by the pre-owned assets income tax provisions in *FA 2004, Sch 15* which are subsequently dismantled by the individual but he/she dies within seven years. The conditions for double charge relief in these circumstances are as follows:

(*a*)   the disposal condition or the contribution condition (see 59.41 WORKING CASE STUDY) is met as respects the relevant property, and

(*b*)   the deceased makes a transfer the result of which a third party becomes entitled to the benefit of a debt owed to the deceased, and

(*c*)   before the deceased's death, any outstanding part of the debt is wholly written off, waived or released, and the write off, waiver or release is made otherwise than for full consideration in money or money's worth, and

(*d*)   the following conditions must be fulfilled:

    (i)   the deceased dies on or after 6 April 2005; and

    (ii)   on the deceased's death, the transfer of value treated as made immediately before the deceased's death included the relevant property, or any property representing that relevant property; and

    (iii) as a result of the deceased's death, the transfer of value referred to in (*b*) above has become a chargeable transfer.

See http://www.hmrc.gov.uk/poa/poa_guidance4.htm#9 for HMRC examples of how the double charge relief works in practice. [*Inheritance Tax (Double Charges Relief) Regulations 2005, SI 2005/3441*].

Example 3

A entered into a lifetime loan scheme, commonly known as a 'double trust' scheme, in June 2003. He then sold his house to a trust fund for £500,000 and he is a life tenant of that trust fund. The trustees do not pay the purchase price but give A an IOU instead. A then gifts the IOU to a second trust for the benefit of his children B and C. A remains in occupation of the property but the outstanding debt will reduce A's estate on death under *IHTA 1984, s 162* by the amount of the loan. Under *FA 2004, Sch 15* A makes an election under *ibid* paragraph 21 so that the value of the house becomes subject to the gifts with reservation rules. A dies in July 2007 and the house at that date is valued at £750,000 and A's estate is worth £500,000. See 51 TRANSFERS WITHIN SEVEN YEARS OF DEATH. However, the house is also chargeable within the estate because it constitutes a gift with reservation following the election under *FA 2004, Sch 15, para 21*.

As a double charge would now arise each calculation should be considered in isolation.

First calculation: charge to tax using the original gift in the death estate.

Transfer in June 2003	£	£
Taxable gift	500,000	
Less Nil rate band using the table at 41.1 2007.A1	(300,000)	
Taxable balance	200,000	
Tax payable @ 40%	80,000	
Less Taper relief @ 40% (i.e. between 4 and 5 years)	(32,000)	48,000
Taxable estate	500,000	
Tax payable @ 40%	200,000	200,000
Total IHT payable		248,000

Second calculation: charge to tax using the gifts with reservation rules in the death estate (ignoring PET in June 2003).

22.10 Gifts with Reservation

	£	£
Estate	500,000	
Add Gift with reservation	750,000	
Taxable balance	1,250,000	
Less Nil rate band using the table at 41.1 2007.A1	(300,000)	
	950,000	
Tax payable @ 40%	380,000	
Total IHT payable		380,000

Notes to the example

(A) The charge to tax using the gift with reservation will be used by HMRC Inheritance Tax and the charge using the original gift will be reduced to nil by using the double charge relief. [*Inheritance Tax (Double Charges Relief) Regulations 2005, SI 2005/3441, Reg 4(4)*].

(B) It should be noted that the double charge relief provisions will not always apply when a perceived double charge arises. This will happen where an election is made in respect of the property subject to an '*Eversden*' type scheme (see 6.2 ANTI-AVOIDANCE) with the result that one spouse/civil partner has made a potentially exempt transfer and the other spouse's/civil partner's estate includes property subject to a reservation so that both charges are unaffected by the double charge relief provisions. The provisions only apply where there is a double charge in respect of one individual.

Example 4

A made a potentially exempt transfer of £150,000 to B in January 1997. In March 2003, A made a gift of land worth £311,000 into a discretionary trust of which he is a potential beneficiary. The gift was a gift with reservation but also a chargeable lifetime transfer on which IHT of £12,200 would have been paid at rates current at the time assuming there were no other previous transfers; the trustees paid the tax; no annual exemptions were available.

A dies in February 2008 without having released his interest in the trust. His estate is valued at £440,000 including the land in the discretionary trust currently worth £360,000.

First calculation: charge the land subject to the gift with reservation in A's death estate and ignore the gift with reservation.

236

IHT
payable
£

January 1997
Potentially exempt transfer (now exempt)   —
March 2003
Gift with reservation (ignored)   —
February 2008
Death estate £440,000
Tax £56,000 less £12,200 already paid on the gift with reservation*   43,800

Total tax due as result of A's death   £43,800

* Credit for the tax already paid cannot exceed the amount of the death tax attributable to the value of the gift with reservation property i.e.

$$\frac{360,000}{440,000} \times £56,000 = £45,818.$$

Credit is therefore given for the full amount of tax paid £12,200.

Second calculation: charge the gift with reservation and ignore the land in the death estate

IHT
payable
£

January 1997
Potentially exempt transfer (now exempt)   —
March 2003
Gift with reservation £311,000
Tax £2,640 less £12,200 already paid (see note (A))   Nil
February 2008
Death estate £80,000 (ignoring gift with reservation land) as top slice of
£387,000   32,000

Total tax due as result of A's death   £32,000

Notes to the example

(A)   60% of the full rate for the date of death for a transfer more than 4 years but not more than 5 years before death i.e. 60% × 40% × (£311,000 – £300,000).

(B)   The first calculation gives the higher amount of tax. The value of the gift with reservation transfer is reduced to nil and tax on death is charged as in the first calculation with credit for the tax already paid. However, the credit provisions do *not* affect the choice of calculation, even if they operate to turn what was the higher amount of tax into the lower amount. So, in the first calculation if the tax paid previously had been greater than £24,000 (i.e. £360,000 – £300,000 × 40%) as opposed to £12,200 then the first calculation would still have been used. See IHTM14590.

23 HMRC Extra-Statutory Concessions

This chapter has been expanded to include the full text of HMRC extra-statutory concessions relevant to IHT.

The following is the full text of the concessions published (or to be published) in HMRC Pamphlet IR 1. Any concessions announced but not yet designated by a formal prefix are listed at the end of the chapter in date order. In the pamphlet it is stated: 'The concessions described within are of general application, but it must be borne in mind that in a particular case there may be special circumstances which will require to be taken into account in considering the application of the concession. A concession will not be granted in any case where an attempt is made to use it for tax avoidance'. See 15.10 DETERMINATIONS AND APPEALS.

F.	**INHERITANCE TAX**
F1	**Mourning.** A reasonable amount for mourning for the family and servants is allowed as a funeral expense.

See 50.3 TRANSFERS ON DEATH.

F2	**Property of Roman Catholic religious communities.** The property of Roman Catholic religious communities whose purposes are charitable is treated as trust property, held for a charitable purpose even where there is no enforceable trust, with a result that inheritance tax is not claimed on the death of one of the nominal owners of the property.
F5	**Deaths of members of the Royal Ulster Constabulary.** The relief from inheritance tax under *IHTA 1984, s 154 (FA 1975, 7 Sch 1)*, granted in certain circumstances to the estates of members of the armed forces, is applied to the estates of members of the Royal Ulster Constabulary who die from injuries caused in Northern Ireland by terrorist activity.

See 21.14 EXEMPT TRANSFERS.

F6	**Blocked foreign assets.** Where, because of restrictions imposed by the foreign government, executors who intend to transfer to this country sufficient of the deceased's foreign assets for the payment of the inheritance tax attributable to them cannot do so immediately, they are given the option of deferring payment until the transfer can be effected. If the amount in sterling that the executors finally succeed in bringing to this country is less than this tax, the balance is waived.

See 35.14 PAYMENT OF TAX.

F7	**Foreign owned works of art.** Where a work of art normally kept overseas becomes liable to inheritance tax on the owner's death solely because it is physically situated in the United Kingdom at the relevant date, the liability will—by concession—be waived if the work was brought into the United Kingdom solely for public exhibition, cleaning or restoration. The liability will similarly be waived if a work of art which would otherwise have left the United Kingdom to be kept overseas is retained in the United Kingdom solely for those purposes. If the work of art is held by a discretionary trust (or is otherwise comprised in settled property in which there is no interest in possession), the charge to tax arising under *IHTA 1984, s 64 (FA 1982, s 107)* will, similarly, be waived.

See 35.14 FOREIGN ASSETS.

F8	**Accumulation and maintenance settlements.** The requirement of *FA 1975, 5 Sch 15(1)(a)* or *IHTA 1984, s 71(1)(a)* (*FA 1982, s 114(1)(a)*) is regarded as being satisfied even if no age is specified in the trust instrument, provided that it is clear that a beneficiary will in fact become entitled to the settled property (or to an interest in possession in it) by the age of 25. See 3.2 ACCUMULATION AND MAINTENANCE TRUSTS.

F8   **Accumulation and maintenance settlements.** The requirement of *FA 1975, 5 Sch 15(1)(a)* or *IHTA 1984, s 71(1)(a)* (*FA 1982, s 114(1)(a)*) is regarded as being satisfied even if no age is specified in the trust instrument, provided that it is clear that a beneficiary will in fact become entitled to the settled property (or to an interest in possession in it) by the age of 25.
See 3.2 ACCUMULATION AND MAINTENANCE TRUSTS.

F10   **Partnership assurance policies.** A partnership assurance scheme under which each partner effects a policy on his own life in trust for the other partners is not regarded as a settlement for inheritance tax purposes if the following conditions are fulfilled.

(*a*)   The premiums paid on the policy fall within *IHTA 1984, s 10* (*FA 1975, s 20(4)*) (exemption for dispositions not intended to confer a gratuitous benefit on any person);

(*b*)   the policy was effected prior to 15 September 1976 and has not been varied on or after that date (but the exercise of a power of appointment under a 'discretionary' trust policy would not be regarded as a variation for this purpose); and

(*c*)   the trusts of the policy are governed by English law or by Scottish law, provided that in the latter case the policy does not directly or indirectly involve a partnership itself as a separate persona.

See 34.1 PARTNERSHIPS.

F11   **Property chargeable on the ceasing of an annuity.** Where an inheritance tax charge arises when an annuitant under a settlement either dies or disposes of his interest and

(i)   the annuity is charged wholly or in part on real or leasehold property, and

(ii)   the Board is satisfied that a capital valuation of the property at the relevant date restricted to its existing use, reflects an anticipated increase in rents obtainable for that use after that date

appropriate relief will be given in calculating the proportion of the property on which tax is chargeable.

See 43.2 SETTLEMENTS WITH INTERESTS IN POSSESSION.

F12   **Disposition for maintenance of dependent relative.** A disposition by a child in favour of his unmarried mother (so far as it represents a reasonable provision for her care or maintenance) qualifies for exemption under *IHTA 1984, s 11(3)* (*FA 1975, s 46(3)*) if the mother is incapacitated by old age or infirmity from maintaining herself. By concession such a disposition is also treated as exempt if the mother (although not so incapacitated) is genuinely financially dependent on the child making the disposition.

See 21.11 EXEMPT TRANSFERS.

F13   **Subsequent devolutions of property under the wills of persons dying before 12 March 1952 whose estates were wholly exempted from estate duty under *FA 1894, s 8(1)*.** Where a person died before 12 March 1952 and his estate was wholly exempted from estate duty as the property of a common seaman, marine or soldier who died in the service of the Crown and under his will he left a limited interest to someone who dies on or after 12 March 1975, inheritance tax is not charged on any property exempted on the original death which passes under the terms of the will on the termination of the limited interest.

See 21.14 EXEMPT TRANSFERS.

F15   **Woodlands.** *FA 1986, 19 Sch 46* denies potentially exempt transfer treatment for Inheritance tax purposes to all property comprised in a single transfer any part of which, however small, is woodlands subject to a deferred Estate Duty charge. By concession the scope of this paragraph will henceforth be restricted solely to that part of the value transferred which is attributable to the woodlands which are the subject of the deferred charge.

See 38.3 POTENTIALLY EXEMPT TRANSFERS and 58.5 WOODLANDS.

F16   **Agricultural property and farm cottages.** On a transfer of agricultural property which includes a cottage occupied by a retired farm employee or their widow(er), the condition in *IHTA 1984, s 117* and *IHTA 1984, s 169* concerning occupation for agricultural purposes is regarded as satisfied with respect to the cottage if either

- the occupier is a statutorily protected tenant, or
- the occupation is under a lease granted to the farm employee for his/her life and that of any surviving spouse as part of the employee's contract of employment by the landlord for agricultural purposes.

See 5.2 AGRICULTURAL PROPERTY.

F17   **Relief for agricultural property.** On a transfer of tenanted agricultural land, the condition in *IHTA 1984, s 116(2)(a)* is regarded as satisfied where the transferor's interest in the property either

- carries a right to vacant possession within 24 months of the date of the transfer, or
- is, notwithstanding the terms of the tenancy, valued at an amount broadly equivalent to the vacant possession value of the property.

See 5.2 AGRICULTURAL PROPERTY.

F18   **Treatment of income tax in Canada on capital gains deemed to arise on a person's death.**

1. Under *IHTA 1984, s 5(3)* a person's liabilities at the time of death are taken into account in arriving at the value of their estate for the purposes of IHT. The Board of Inland Revenue will by concession regard this provision as applying to income tax in Canada charged on a deemed disposal immediately before death, even though the liability may not in strictness have arisen until the person had died.

2. Where there is an IHT charge on a deceased person's world-wide estate, and income tax in Canada is charged on deemed gains which are attributable to assets forming part of the estate, the Canadian tax will rank as a deduction in arriving at the value of the estate for IHT purposes. The Canadian tax will normally be treated as reducing the value of assets outside the United Kingdom whether those assets are liable to IHT or not; but if the Canadian tax exceeds the value of those assets, the excess will be set off against the value of the United Kingdom assets.

F19   **Decorations awarded for valour or gallant conduct exempt from IHT.**

Decorations awarded for valour or gallant conduct that have never been sold will be treated as exempt from inheritance tax under a concession published today [21 August 2000].

The concession will have immediate effect, and apply to all cases yet to be settled. Its text is reproduced below.

The purpose of this concession is to allow these decorations to be handed on, without having to bear inheritance tax (IHT) charges.

Decorations which are awarded for valour or gallant conduct can, owing to their nature and history, command significant values and so increase the value of an estate or transfer for IHT purposes. Beneficiaries may therefore be faced with the dilemma of wishing to keep the decorations for personal or sentimental reasons, but not being able to afford to pay the tax on them.

As long as it can be shown that the decorations have *never* changed hands for consideration in money or money's worth, they will be excluded from claims for IHT. If they have ever changed hands for consideration in money or money's worth they will be liable to IHT like any other asset.

The concession regularises a broadly similar existing informal practice whereby honourable decorations that have been bestowed on a deceased individual or a member of his or her family were exempt from IHT. It will be effective from today and will apply to all cases yet to be settled. Any settled cases where the previous informal practice was not applied will be considered on their merits, if brought to the attention of the Capital Taxes Office [now HMRC Inheritance Tax].

All enquiries about this concession in particular cases should apply to — Heritage Section, Capital Taxes Office [now HMRC Inheritance Tax], Ferrers House, PO Box 38, Castle Meadow Road, Nottingham NG2 1BB; DX 701201 NOTTINGHAM 4.

Please provide the full name of the deceased or transferor and the date of death or transfer plus the CTO reference number if known. Please give full details of the decorations awarded (for valour or gallant conduct) and evidence of their value and the tax charged at the date of the chargeable occasion. [See IHT Newsletter, December 2005 issue in IHT NEWSLETTER AND TAX BULLETIN EXTRACTS (61)].

F20   **Late compensation for World War II claims.**
Schemes continue to be established in the UK and abroad which provide compensation for wrongs suffered during the Second World War era. When this is received by the original victim or their surviving spouse, this almost inevitably comes late in life when their plans for the disposal of their wealth have already been made. Ministers have agreed that the cash value of these claims may be excluded from inheritance tax in the following cases where compensation is paid in modest round-sum, or otherwise cash-limited, amounts:

- single ex-gratia lump sums of £10,000 payable to each surviving member of British groups interned or imprisoned by the Japanese during the Second World War or their surviving spouse as announced by the Government on 7 November 2000;

- financial compensation of fixed amounts payable from the German foundation 'Remembrance, Responsibility and Future' to claimants – or their surviving spouse – who were slave or forced labourers or other victims of the National Socialist regime during the Second World War;

- financial compensation of $1,000 payable from the Holocaust Victim Assets Litigation (Swiss Bank Settlement) to each of the slave or forced labourers qualifying under the aforementioned German foundation scheme;

- financial compensation by way of fixed amounts to the victim or their surviving spouse from the Swiss Refugee Programme;

- financial compensation by way of fixed amounts to the victim or their surviving spouse from Stichting Maror-Gelden Overheid (Dutch Maror); and

- financial compensation by way of a one-time payment to the victim or their surviving spouse from the following:
- monies allocated by the Federal German Government (the Hardship Fund);
- the Austrian National Fund for Victims of Nazi Persecution;
- the French Orphan Scheme.

Payments of this kind would normally increase the value of a deceased person's chargeable estate at death, either because a claim paid in their lifetime has increased their total assets, or because the right to a claim not yet paid is itself an asset of their estate.

By concession, where such a payment has been received at any time, either by the deceased or his or her personal representatives under the arrangements, the amount of the payment may be left out of account in determining the chargeable value of his or her estate for the purposes of inheritance tax on death. Similarly, where a person qualifies for more than one payment then each amount may be left out of account.

All enquiries about this extra-statutory concession in particular cases (quoting the full name and date of death of the deceased plus the Inland Revenue Capital Taxes reference number if known) should be directed to:

Inland Revenue Capital Taxes – IHT, Ferrers House, PO Box 38, Castle Meadow Road, Nottingham NG2 1BB.

For members of the DX system:

Inland Revenue Capital Taxes, DX 701201, Nottingham 4.

See 59.28 WORKING CASE STUDY.

B.   **Other tax concessions applied to inheritance tax**

B41   **Claims to repayment of tax.** Under *TMA 1970* unless a longer or shorter period is prescribed, no statutory claim for relief is allowed unless it is made within six years from the end of the tax year to which it relates.

However, repayments of tax will be made in respect of claims made outside the statutory time limit where an over-payment of tax has arisen because of an error by the Inland Revenue or another Government Department, and where there is no dispute or doubt as to the facts.

See 35.11 PAYMENT OF TAX.

24   HMRC Press Releases

The following is a summary in date order of Press Releases referred to in this book (other than those containing Extra-Statutory Concessions and Statements of Practice, as to which see 23 HMRC EXTRA-STATUTORY CONCESSIONS and 25 HMRC STATEMENTS OF PRACTICE). Certain pre-18 July 1978 Press Releases were reissued as Statements of Practice on 18 June 1979.

Copies of any individual Press Release may be viewed on HMRC website below. The Tax Bulletin could be purchased separately for an annual charge (£22). However, from 1 January 2007 the Tax Bulletin (former Inland Revenue publication) will be replaced by a unified online only free publication; HM Revenue & Customs Brief. This will be issued as and when the Department has news to give. HMRC are planning to move to an online only version of the IHT Newsletter by August 2007. See 61 IHT NEWSLETTER AND TAX BULLETIN EXTRACTS, April 2007.

It can be found in the library section of HMRC's website (http://www.hmrc.gov.uk/briefs/index.htm). For Press Releases see under 'Contacts' at http://www.hmrc.gov.uk/about/press.htm.

12.2.76	**Interests in possession: inheritance tax: settled property.** The Board do not consider that a mere power of revocation or appointment, in certain conditions, will prevent an interest being an 'interest in possession'. See 26.2 INTEREST IN POSSESSION.
17.1.79	**Life assurance premiums—measure of value for purposes of IHT.** See 30.2 LIFE ASSURANCE POLICIES AND ANNUITIES.
23.6.82	**Killed in war exemption—Falkland Islands.** The estates of those killed on active service in the Falklands conflict will be exempt from CTT and IHT. See 21.14 EXEMPT TRANSFERS.
18.3.86	**Gifts with reservation and insurance policies.** The Revenue's understanding of when an insurance is made is given. See 48.1 TIME OF DISPOSITION.
2.7.87	**Inheritance tax—reductions in requirements for delivery of accounts on death.** Advice is given. See 2.4 ACCOUNTS AND RETURNS.
10.3.92	**Increases in agricultural and business property relief.** The effective commencement of the increases is explained by the Revenue. See 5.2 AGRICULTURAL PROPERTY and 7.7 BUSINESS PROPERTY.
17.12.92	**Public access to conditionally exempt works of art.** See 33.3 NATIONAL HERITAGE.
17.2.93	**Revenue Adjudicator and Codes of Practice.** The appointment of an independent adjudicator and the publication of codes of practice are announced. See 4.1 ADMINISTRATION AND COLLECTION.
10.5.93	**Public access to conditionally exempt works of art.** See 33.3 NATIONAL HERITAGE.
2.8.93	**Inheritance tax—The Register of conditionally exempt works of art.** See 33.3 NATIONAL HERITAGE.
8.9.94	**Individuals coming to the United Kingdom to take up employment: Administrative measures.** See 17.3 DOMICILE.
6.3.95	**Double taxation agreement: Switzerland.** See 18.2 DOUBLE TAXATION RELIEF.
16.1.96	**The Register of conditionally exempt works of art.** See 33.3 NATIONAL HERITAGE.
16.1.96	**Law of domicile.** See 17.3 DOMICILE.
25.1.2000	**Inland Revenue account—reduced account for exempt estates.** See 2.4 ACCOUNTS AND RETURNS.

25   HMRC Statements of Practice

This chapter has been expanded to include the full text of HMRC Statements of Practice relevant to IHT.

The following is the full text of those Statements of Practice published in HMRC Pamphlet IR 131 (November 1996), or subsequently announced for inclusion therein, which are referred to in this book.

Statements are divided into those originally published before 18 July 1978 (which are given a reference letter (according to the subject matter) and consecutive number, e.g. E11) and later Statements (which are numbered consecutively in each year, e.g. SP 10/86).

Certain statements marked in IR 131 as obsolete will continue to be referred to in the text (having been relevant in the last six years), and the original source is quoted in such cases, as it is where the Statement awaits inclusion in IR 131.

ACCUMULATION AND MAINTENANCE SETTLEMENTS: IHTA 1984, s 71

E1   Powers of appointment

1. It is not necessary for the interests of individual beneficiaries to be defined. They can for instance be subject to powers of appointment. In any particular case the exemption will depend on the precise terms of the trust and power concerned, and on the facts to which they apply. In general, however, the official view is that the conditions do not restrict the application of *IHTA 1984, s 71* to settlements where the interests of individual beneficiaries are defined and indefeasible.

2. The requirement of *IHTA 1984, s 71(1)(a)* (formerly *FA 1982, s 114(1)(a)*) is that one or more persons will, on or before attaining a specified age not exceeding twenty five, become beneficially entitled to, or to an interest in possession in, the settled property or part of it. It is considered that settled property would meet this condition if at the relevant time it must vest for an interest in possession in some member of an existing class of potential beneficiaries on or before that member attains 25. The existence of a special power of appointment would not of itself exclude *section 71* if neither the exercise nor the release of the power could break the condition. To achieve this effect might, however, require careful drafting.

3. The inclusion of issue as possible objects of a special power of appointment would exclude a settlement from the benefit of *section 71* if the power would allow the trustees to prevent any interest in possession in the settled property from commencing before the beneficiary concerned attained the age specified. It would depend on the precise words of the settlement and the facts to which they had to be applied whether a particular settlement satisfied the conditions of *s 71(1)*. In many cases the rules against perpetuity and accumulations would operate to prevent an effective appointment outside those conditions. However the application of *s 71* is not a matter for a once-for-all decision. It is a question that needs to be kept in mind at all times when there is settled property in which no interest in possession subsists.

4. Also, a trust which otherwise satisfies the requirement of *s 71(1)(a)* would not be disqualified by the existence of a power to vary or determine the respective shares of members of the class (even to the extent of excluding some members altogether) provided the power is exercisable only in favour of a person under 25 who is a member of the class.

Examples

The examples set out below are based on a settlement for the children of X contingently on attaining 25, the trustees being required to accumulate the income so far as it is not applied for the maintenance of X's children.

Example A

The settlement was made on X's marriage and he has as yet no children.

IHTA 1984, s 71 will not apply until a child is born and that event will give rise to a charge for tax under *IHTA 1984, s 65* (formerly *FA 1982, s 108*).

Example B

The trustees have power to apply income for the benefit of X's unmarried sister.

IHTA 1984, s 71 does not apply because the conditions of *subsection (1)(b)* are not met.

Example C

X has power to appoint the capital not only among his children but also among his remoter issue.

IHTA 1984, s 71 does not apply (unless the power can be exercised only in favour of persons who would thereby acquire interests in possession on or before attaining age 25). A release of the disqualifying power would give rise to a charge for tax under *IHTA 1984, s 65* (formerly *FA 1982, s 108*). Its exercise would give rise to a charge under *IHTA 1984, s 65*.

Example D

The trustees have an overriding power of appointment in favour of other persons.

IHTA 1984, s 71 does not apply (unless the power can be exercised only in favour of persons who would thereby acquire interests in possession on or before attaining age 25). A release of the disqualifying power would give rise to a charge for tax under *IHTA 1984, s 65* (formerly *FA 1982, s 108*). Its exercise would give rise to a charge under *IHTA 1984, s 65*.

Example E

The settled property has been revocably appointed to one of the children contingently on his attaining 25 and the appointment is now irrevocable.

If the power to revoke prevents *IHTA 1984, s 71* from applying (as it would for example, if the property thereby became subject to a power of appointment as at C or D above), tax will be chargeable under *IHTA 1984, s 65* (formerly *FA 1982, s 108*) when the appointment is made irrevocable.

Example F

The trust to accumulate income is expressed to be during the life of the settlor.

As the settlor may live beyond the 25th birthday of any of his children the trust does not satisfy the condition in *subsection (1)(a)* and *IHTA 1984, s 71* does not apply.

See 3.2 ACCUMULATION AND MAINTENANCE TRUSTS.

SUPERANNUATION, LIFE INSURANCE AND ACCIDENT SCHEMES

E3   **Superannuation schemes**

1. This Statement clarifies the IHT liability of benefits payable under pension schemes.

2. No liability to IHT arises in respect of benefits payable on a person's death under a normal pension scheme except in the circumstances explained immediately below. Nor does a charge to IHT arise on payments made by the trustees of a superannuation scheme within *IHTA 1984, s 151* (formerly *FA 1975, 5 Sch 16*) in direct exercise of a discretion to pay a lump sum death benefit to any one or more of a member's dependants. It is not considered that pending the exercise of the discretion the benefit should normally be regarded as property comprised in a settlement so as to bring it within the scope of *IHTA 1984 Part III* (formerly *FA 1975, 5 Sch*). The protection of *IHTA 1984, s 151* would not of course extend further if the trustees themselves then settled the property so paid.

3. Benefits are liable to IHT if:

    (*a*) they form part of the freely disposable property passing under the will or intestacy of a deceased person. This applies only if the executors or administrators have a legally enforceable claim to the benefits; if they were payable to them only at the discretion of the trustees of the pension fund or some similar persons they are not liable to IHT; or

    (*b*) the deceased had the power, immediately before his death, to nominate or appoint the benefits to any person including his dependants.

4. In these cases the benefits should be included in the personal representatives' account (schedule of the deceased's assets) which has to be completed when applying for a grant of probate or letters of administration. The IHT (if any) which is assessed on the personal representatives' account has to be paid before the grant can be obtained.

5. On some events other than the death of a member information should be given to the appropriate Capital Taxes Office [now HMRC Inheritance Tax]. These are:

    (i) the payment of contributions to a scheme which has not been approved for income tax purposes;

    (ii) the making of an irrevocable nomination or the disposal of a benefit by a member in his or her lifetime (otherwise than in favour of a spouse) which reduces the value of his or her estate (e.g. the surrender of part of the pension or lump sum benefit in exchange for a pension for the life of another);

    (iii) the decision by a member to postpone the realisation of any of his or her retirement benefits.

6. If IHT proves to be payable the Capital Taxes Office [now HMRC Inheritance Tax] will communicate with the persons liable to pay the tax.

7. See also Statement of Practice 10/86. Tax Bulletin No 2 of February 1992; the article INHERITANCE TAX—Retirement Benefits, etc.

See 37.2 PENSION SCHEMES.

E4	**Associated operations.** Life assurance policies and annuities are regarded as not being affected by the associated operations rule if, first, the policy was issued on full medical evidence and, secondly, it would have been issued on the same terms if the annuity had not been bought.

See 30.3 LIFE ASSURANCE POLICIES AND ANNUITIES.

INTERESTS IN POSSESSION SETTLEMENTS

E5	**Close companies.** The Board consider that the general intention of *Section 101 IHTA 1984* is to treat the participators as beneficial owners for all the purposes of that Act. Consequently, the conditions of *IHTA 1984, s 52(2)*, and *53(2)*, are regarded as satisfied where it is the company that in fact becomes entitled to the property or disposes of the interest.

See 43.3 SETTLEMENTS WITH INTERESTS IN POSSESSION.

E6	**Power to augment income.** This statement sets out the effect for IHT of the exercise by trustees of a power to augment a beneficiary's income out of capital.

In the normal case, where the beneficiary concerned is life tenant of the settled property this will have no immediate consequences for IHT. The life tenant already has an interest in possession and under the provisions of *IHTA 1984, s 49(1)* (formerly *FA 1975, 5 Sch 3(1)*) is treated as beneficially entitled to the property. The enlargement of that interest to an absolute interest does not change this position (*IHTA 1984, s 53(2)*; formerly *FA 1975, 5 Sch 4(3)*) and it is not affected by the relationship of the beneficiary to the testator.

In the exceptional case, where the beneficiary is not the life tenant, or in which there is no subsisting interest in possession, the exercise of the power would give rise to a charge to tax under *IHTA 1984, s 52(1)*, although on or after 17 March 1987 this may be a potentially exempt transfer, or a charge under *IHTA 1984, s 65(1)(a)* (formerly *FA 1975, 5 Sch 4(2) or 6(1)*). But if the life tenant is the surviving spouse of a testator who died before 13 November 1974, exemption might be available under *IHTA 1984, 6 Sch 2* (formerly *FA 1975, 5 Sch 4(7)*). The exercise of the power would be regarded as distributing the settled property rather than as reducing its value, so that *IHTA 1984, s 52(3)* and *IHTA 1984, s 65(1)(b)* (formerly *FA 1975, 5 Sch 4(9)* and *6(3)*) would not be in point.

See 26.7 INTEREST IN POSSESSION.

E7	**Protective trusts.** In the Board's view, the reference to trusts 'to the like effect as those specified in *Section 33(1)* of the *Trustee Act 1925*'—contained in *IHTA 1984, ss 73* and *88* (both derived from *FA 1975, 5 Sch 18*)—is a reference to trusts which are not materially different in their tax consequences.

The Board would not wish to distinguish a trust by reason of a minor variation or additional administrative duties or powers. The extension of the list of potential beneficiaries to brothers and sisters is not regarded as a minor variation.

See 39.1 PROTECTIVE TRUSTS.

E8	**Age of majority.** Where Trustee Act 1925, s 31 applies to property appointed after the commencement date for the *Family Law Reform Act 1969* out of a settlement created before that date, the beneficiary's interest in possession is regarded as arising at age 18.

See 26.8 INTEREST IN POSSESSION. Following the decision by the High Court in *Begg-MacBrearty v Stilwell, [1996] STC 455* which upheld the Inland Revenue's view as set out above, this Statement of Practice has been withdrawn with effect from 30 September 1996.

SETTLED PROPERTY: MISCELLANEOUS

E9　　Excluded property. Property is regarded, for the purposes of *IHTA 1984, s 48(3)* (formerly *FA 1975, 5 Sch 2(1)*) as becoming comprised in a settlement when it, or other property which it represents, is introduced by the settlor.

See 20.2 EXCLUDED PROPERTY.

E11　　Employee trusts.

This statement clarifies the application of *IHTA 1984, s 13(1)* (formerly *FA 1976, s 90(1)*) where employees of a subsidiary company are included in the trust.

The Board regard *IHTA 1984, s 13(1)* (formerly *FA 1976, s 90(1)*) as requiring that where the trust is to benefit employees of a subsidiary of the company making the provision those eligible to benefit must include all or most of the employees and officers of the subsidiary and the employees and officers of the holding company taken as a single class. So it would be possible to exclude all of the officers and employees of the holding company without losing the exemption if they comprised only a minority of the combined class. But the exemption would not be available for a contribution to a fund for the sole benefit of the employees of a small subsidiary. This is because it would otherwise have been easy to create such a situation artificially in order to benefit a favoured group of a company's officeholders or employees. But even where the participators outnumber the other employees the exemption is not irretrievably lost. The requirement to exclude participators and those connected with them from benefit is modified by *IHTA 1984, s 13(3)* (formerly *FA 1976, s 90(4)*). This limits the meaning of 'a participator' for this purpose to those having a substantial stake in the assets being transferred and makes an exception in favour of income benefits. So even where most of the employees are also major participators or their relatives an exempt transfer could be made if the trust provided only for income benefits and the eventual disposal of the capital away from the participators and their families. This restriction does not affect the exemptions offered by *IHTA 1984, s 86* (formerly *FA 1975, 5 Sch 17*) from tax charges during the continuance of a trust for employees which meets the conditions of that paragraph.

See 55.5(A) TRUSTS FOR EMPLOYEES.

NON-SETTLED PROPERTY: MISCELLANEOUS

E13　　Charities.

1. *IHTA 1984, ss 23* and *24* (formerly *FA 1975, 6 Sch 10* and *11*) exempt from IHT certain gifts to charities and political parties to the extent that the value transferred is attributable to property given to a charity etc. *IHTA 1984, ss 25* and *26* (formerly *FA 1975, 6 Sch 12* and *13*) exempt certain gifts for national purposes and for the public benefit.

2. Where the value transferred (i.e. the loss to transferor's estate as a result of the disposition) exceeds the value of the gift in the hands of a charity, etc., the Board take the view that the exemption extends to the whole value transferred.

See 21.2 EXEMPT TRANSFERS.

E14　　Pools etc. syndicates. No liability to IHT arises on winnings by a football pool or similar syndicates provided that the winnings are paid out in accordance with the terms of an agreement drawn up before the win.

Where for example football pool winnings are paid out, in accordance with a pre-existing enforceable arrangement, among the members of a syndicate in proportion to the share of the stake money each has provided, each member of the syndicate receives what already belongs to him or her. There is therefore no 'gift' or 'chargeable transfer' by the person who, on behalf of the members, receives the winnings from the pools promoter.

Members of a pool syndicate may think it wise to record in a written, signed and dated statement, the existence and terms of the agreement between them. But the Inland Revenue cannot advise on the wording or legal effect of such a statement, nor do they wish copies of such statements to be sent to them for approval or registration. Where following a pools win the terms of the agreement are varied or part of the winnings are distributed to persons who are not members of the syndicate, an IHT liability may be incurred. The same principles apply to premium bonds syndicates and other similar arrangements.

See 10.5 CHARGEABLE TRANSFER.

E15   **Close companies: group transfers.** This statement clarifies the position concerning dividend payments and transfers of assets from a subsidiary company to a parent or sister company as appropriate. The statement refers to capital transfer tax (CTT), but applies equally to IHT.

Whether or not a disposition is a transfer of value for CTT purposes has to be determined by reference to *IHTA 1984, s 3(1)*, (2), and *section 10* which provides that a disposition is not a transfer of value if it was not intended to confer any gratuitous benefit on any person, subject to the other provisions of that subsection.

In the Board's view, the effect is that a dividend paid by a subsidiary company to its parent is not a transfer of value and so *IHTA 1984, s 94* does not start to operate in relation to such dividends. Nor do the Board feel that they can justifiably treat a transfer of assets between a wholly-owned subsidiary and its parent or between two wholly-owned subsidiaries as a transfer of value.

See 12.3 CLOSE COMPANIES.

SCOTS LAW

E18   **Partial disclaimers of residue.** Under Scots law there are certain circumstances in which a residuary legatee can make a partial disclaimer. Where this is possible the Inland Revenue accepts that the provisions of *IHTA 1984, s 142*, which deal with disclaimers, apply.

See 14.2, 14.4 DEEDS VARYING DISPOSITION ON DEATH.

STATEMENTS AFTER JULY 1978

SP 10/79   **Power for trustees to allow a beneficiary to occupy a dwelling house.** Many wills and settlements contain a clause empowering the trustees to permit a beneficiary to occupy a dwelling house which forms part of trust property as they think fit. The Board do not regard the existence of such a power as excluding any interest in possession in the property.

Where there is no interest in possession in the property in question the Board do not regard the exercise of power as creating one if the effect is merely to allow non-exclusive occupation or to create a contractual tenancy for full consideration. The Board also take the view that no interest in possession arises on the creation of a lease for a term or a periodic tenancy for less than full consideration, though this will normally give rise to a charge for tax under *IHTA 1984, s 65(1)(b)* (formerly *FA 1982, s 108(1)(b)*). On the other hand if the power is drawn in terms wide enough to cover the creation of an exclusive or joint right of residence, albeit revocable, for a definite or indefinite period, and is exercised with the intention of providing a particular beneficiary with a permanent home, the Revenue will normally regard the exercise of the power as creating an interest in possession. And if the trustees in exercise of their powers grant a lease for life for less than full consideration, this will also be regarded as creating an interest in possession in view of *IHTA 1984, ss 43(3)* and *50(6)* (formerly *FA 1975, 5 Sch 1(3)* and *3(6)*).

A similar view will be taken where the power is exercised over property in which another beneficiary had an interest in possession up to the time of exercise.

See 26.6 INTEREST IN POSSESSION.

SP 12/80   **Business relief: 'Buy and Sell' agreements.** The Board understand that it is sometimes the practice for partners or shareholder directors of companies to enter into an agreement (known as a 'Buy & Sell' agreement) whereby, in the event of the death before retirement of one of them, the deceased's personal representatives are obliged to sell and the survivors are obliged to purchase the deceased's business interest or shares, funds for the purchase being frequently provided by means of appropriate life assurance policies.

In the Board's view such an agreement, requiring as it does a sale and purchase and not merely conferring an option to sell or buy, is a binding contract for sale within *IHTA 1984, s 113*. As a result the Inheritance Tax business relief will not be due on the business interest or shares. (*IHTA 1984, s 113* provides that where any property would be relevant business property for the purpose of business relief in relation to a transfer of value but a binding contract for its sale has been entered into at the time of the transfer, it is not relevant business property in relation to that transfer.)

See 7.4 BUSINESS PROPERTY at *Binding contracts for sale.*

SP 18/80   **Securities dealt in on the Stock Exchange Unlisted Securities Market: status and valuation for tax purposes.** The Stock Exchange introduced an organised market in unlisted securities—the Unlisted Securities Market—on 10 November 1980.

In the view of the Inland Revenue securities dealt in on the Unlisted Securities Market will not fall to be treated as 'listed' or 'quoted' for the purposes of those sections of the Taxes Acts which use these terms in relation to securities. The securities will, however, satisfy the tests of being 'authorised to be dealt in' and 'dealt in (regularly or from time to time)' on a recognised stock exchange.

Where it is necessary for tax purposes to agree the open market value of such securities on a given date, initial evidence of their value will be suggested by the details of the bargains done at or near the relevant date. However other factors may also be relevant and the Shares Valuation Division of the Capital Taxes Office [now HMRC Inheritance Tax] will consider whether a value offered on the basis of those bargains can be accepted as an adequate reflection of the open market value.

See 56.20 VALUATION (but note that the statement is superseded for inheritance tax purposes by legislation after 16 March 1987).

SP 1/82   **The interaction of income tax and inheritance tax on assets put into settlements.**

1. For many years the tax code has contained legislation to prevent a person avoiding higher rate income tax by making a settlement, while still retaining some rights to enjoy the income or capital of the settlement. This legislation, which is embodied in *ICTA 1988, Part XV*, [now *ITTOIA 2005 Part 5 Chapter 5*] provides in general terms that the income of a settlement shall, for income tax purposes, be treated as that of the settlor in all circumstances where the settlor might benefit directly or indirectly from the settlement.

2. If the trustees have power to pay or do in fact pay inheritance tax due on assets which the settlor puts into the settlement the Inland Revenue have taken the view that the settlor has thereby an interest in the income or property of the settlement, and that the income of the settlement should be treated as his for income tax purposes under *ICTA 1988, Part XV*. [now *ITTOIA 2005 Part 5 Chapter 5*]

3. The inheritance tax legislation ([*IHTA 1984, s 199*]) however provides that both the settlor and the trustees are liable for any [inheritance tax] payable when a settlor puts assets into a settlement. The Board of Inland Revenue have therefore decided that they will no longer, in these circumstances, treat the income of the settlement as that of the settlor for income tax purposes solely because the trustees have power to pay or do in fact pay inheritance tax on assets put into settlements.

4. This change of practice applies to settlement income for 1981–82 *et seq.*

See 29.2 LIABILITY FOR TAX.

SP 8/86   **Treatment of income of discretionary trusts.** This statement sets out the Board's existing practice concerning the inheritance tax/capital transfer tax treatment of income of discretionary trusts.

The Board of Inland Revenue take the view that:

• Undistributed and unaccumulated income should not be treated as a taxable trust asset; and

• For the purposes of determining the rate of charge on accumulated income, the income should be treated as becoming a taxable asset of the trust on the date when the accumulation is made.

This practice applies from 10 November 1986 to all new cases and to existing cases where the tax liability has not been settled.

See 44.2 SETTLEMENTS WITHOUT INTERESTS IN POSSESSION.

SP 10/86   **Death benefits under superannuation arrangements.** The Board confirm that their previous practice of not charging capital transfer tax on death benefits that are payable from tax-approved occupational pension and retirement annuity schemes under discretionary trusts also applies to inheritance tax.

The practice extends to tax under the gifts with reservation rules as well as to tax under the ordinary inheritance tax rules. See 37.2 PENSION SCHEMES.

SP 6/87   **Acceptance of property in lieu of Inheritance Tax, Capital Gains Tax and Estate Duty**

1. The Revenue may, with the agreement of the Secretary of State for National Heritage (and, where appropriate, other departmental ministers), accept heritage property in whole or part satisfaction of an inheritance tax, capital transfer tax or estate duty debt. Property can be accepted in satisfaction of interest accrued on the tax as well as the tax itself.

2. No capital tax is payable on property that is accepted in lieu of tax. The amount of tax satisfied is determined by agreeing a special price at which the departmental ministers reimburse the Revenue. This price is found by establishing an agreed value for the item and deducting a proportion of the tax given up on the item itself, using an arrangement known as the 'douceur'. The terms on which property is accepted are a matter for negotiation.

3. *FA 1987, s 60* and *F(No 2)A 1987, s 97* provide that, where the special price is based on the value of the item at a date earlier than the date on which it is accepted, interest on the tax which is being satisfied may cease to accrue from that earlier date.

4. The persons liable for the tax which is to be satisfied by an acceptance in lieu can choose between having the special price calculated from the value of the item when they offer it or when the Revenue accept it. Since most offers are made initially on the basis of the current value of the item, the Revenue considers them on the basis of the value at the 'offer date', unless the offeror notifies them that he wishes to adopt the 'acceptance date' basis of valuation. The offeror's option will normally remain open until the item is formally accepted. But this will be subject to review if more than two years elapse from the date of the offer without the terms being settled. The Revenue may then give six months notice that they will no longer be prepared to accept the item on the 'offer date' basis.

5. Where the 'offer date' option remains open and is chosen, interest on the tax to be satisfied by the item will cease to accrue from that date.

See 35.6 PAYMENT OF TAX.

SP 7/87   **IHT—deduction of reasonable funeral expenses.** The Board take the view that the term 'funeral expenses' in *IHTA 1984, s 172* allows a deduction from the value of a deceased's estate for the cost of a tombstone or gravestone.

See 50.3 TRANSFERS ON DEATH.

SP 2/93   **Inheritance tax—the use of substitute forms**
Introduction

1. This Statement explains the Board of Inland Revenue's approach towards the acceptance of facsimiles of inheritance tax forms as substitutes for officially produced printed forms.

Legislative context

2. *IHTA 1984, s 257(1)* says that all accounts and other documents required for the purposes of the Act shall be in such form and shall contain such particulars as the Board may prescribe. The Board of Inland Revenue are satisfied that an accurate facsimile of an official Account or other required document will satisfy the requirements of the Section.

What will be considered an accurate facsimile?

3. For any substitute inheritance tax form to be acceptable, it must show clearly to the taxpayer the information which the Board have determined shall be before him or her when he or she signs the declaration that the form is correct and complete to the best of his or her knowledge. In other words, the facsimile must accurately reproduce the words and layout of the official form. It need not, however, be colour printed.

4. The facsimile must also be readily recognisable as an inheritance tax form when it is received in the Capital Taxes Offices [now HMRC Inheritance Tax], and the entries must be distinguishable from the background text. Where a facsimile is submitted instead of a previously supplied official form it is important that it bears the same reference as appeared on the official form. It is equally important that if no official form was supplied the taxpayer's reference should be inserted on the facsimile.

5. Advances in printing technology now mean that accurate facsimile forms can be produced. The Board will accept such forms if approval by the Capital Taxes Offices [now HMRC Inheritance Tax] of their wording and design has been obtained before they are used. Any substitute which is produced with approval will need to bear an agreed unique imprint so that its source can be readily identified at all times.

Applications for approval

6. Applications for approval should be made to in England, Wales and Northern Ireland

    The Customer Service Manager
    Inland Revenue
    Capital Taxes Office [now HMRC Inheritance Tax]
    Ferrers House
    PO Box 38
    Castle Meadow Road
    NOTTINGHAM NG2 1BB
    or
    DX 701201 Nottingham 4
    or in Scotland
    The Customer Service Manager
    Inland Revenue
    [Meldrum House
    15 Drumsheugh Gradens
    EDINBURGH EH3 7UG]
    or
    DX 542001 EDINBURGH 14
    All applications will be considered as quickly as possible.
    Further information available

7. A set of guidelines giving further details on the production of substitute forms is available on application to the appropriate office at the above address.

    See 2.1 ACCOUNTS AND RETURNS.

SP 6/95   **Legal entitlement and administrative practices.** Where an assessment has been made and this shows a repayment due to the taxpayer, repayment is invariably made of the full amount. But where the end of the year check applied to Schedule E taxpayers shows an overpayment of £10 or less, an assessment is not normally made and the repayment is not made automatically.

As regards payment of tax assessed, where a payment to the Collector exceeds the amount due and the discrepancy is not noted before the payment has been processed, the excess is not repaid automatically unless it is greater than £1.

For inheritance tax (and capital transfer tax), assessments that lead to repayments of sums overpaid are not initiated automatically by the Capital Taxes Offices [now HMRC Inheritance Tax] if the amount involved is £25 or less.

The aim of these tolerances is to minimise work which is highly cost-ineffective; they cannot operate to deny repayment to a taxpayer who claims it.

See 35.11 PAYMENT OF TAX.

A31   **Reimbursement of taxpayers' expenses.** The practice of the Board of Inland Revenue with regard to the reimbursement of taxpayers' expenses was set out in a letter of 16 June 1975 from Sir Norman Price KCB, the then Chairman of the Board, to the Clerk to the Select Committee on the Parliamentary Commissioner for Administration. The letter is reproduced in full below.

'In response to a number of questions from the Select Committee over the last year or so, I have undertaken to give further thought to the Board's policy in allowing compensation in various circumstances in which a taxpayer may suffer loss as the result of enquiries set in hand (justifiably or unjustifiably) by the Board, which do not in the event result in an additional charge to tax. Typically, the loss will be in respect of compliance costs—covering such things as agent's fees.

As you know, the Board does not as a general rule reimburse a taxpayer for his costs in establishing and subsequently meeting his tax obligations. This rule extends both to any preliminary discussions between the Board and the taxpayer to establish the facts relating to a particular transaction and the tax liability arising therefrom, and to any subsequent proceedings up to and including an appeal before the General or Special Commissioners. The same rule applies whether the point under enquiry is a question of fact (including a possible omission of income, leading to a back duty enquiry) or a question of law. By the same token, the Board naturally does not claim its costs against the taxpayer, if the proceedings before the Appeal Commissioners succeed in establishing a charge to tax. This rule no doubt owes much to practical considerations—the fact that the amount which a taxpayer may spend in circumstances of this kind may be very much at the taxpayer's own discretion. But as a general principle, it has long been thought desirable that, in what I may call the preliminary stages of an enquiry, each side should be free to explore the position and develop the argument in its exploratory stages, without fear of penalties if, in the event, it appears that the other side has the better case.

If I may broaden the argument for a moment, it is the case that over a very wide field of activity, it is thought reasonable that the citizen should bear the cost of compliance with laws passed by the community for the common good, and the same principle is naturally extended to the administrative cost to the citizen of reasonable enquiries, undertaken by the responsible Government Department, carrying out its duty to ensure that the law is being complied with.

My conclusion, after very careful review, is that the reasons which led to our present general policy over the payment of taxpayer's costs are still valid today. To abandon the general principle—to pay costs in cases generally where an enquiry undertaken by the Board or its officers does not in practice result in an additional charge to tax—would in my judgment significantly inhibit the Board in undertaking reasonable enquiries for the purpose of carrying out its duties and functions under the law.

At one point I was asked whether we could distinguish between cases where the result was 'not proven', rather than 'not guilty'. As a concept, I think that this is perhaps relevant only to potential back duty enquiries; and even there it is not altogether easy to relate to the standard of proof required for a civil case (as distinct from a criminal case) before the Appeal Commissioners. However that may be, it carries the implication that the Board, acting as judge in our own cause, should discriminate between taxpayer A and taxpayer B, in the matter of reimbursing costs, on the grounds that we suspected taxpayer B to be guilty of evasion, even though we had no adequate evidence to support that suspicion. With respect, I do not believe that the Board could possibly support such a posture.

Having said that, my review has led me to the conclusion that the balance of the argument shifts significantly, when the taxpayer's costs arise directly out of a serious error on the part of the Board itself. Inevitably, cases will arise from time to time when the Department does something—I am not thinking just of a mere error of judgment—but something which no responsible person, acting in good faith and with proper care, could reasonably have done. There will also be cases when the original action was based on a pardonable error, or even an innocent misunderstanding, but becomes more serious because it is persisted in. It is a prime responsibility of the Board to ensure that such cases arise very seldom. Nevertheless, as a direct consequence of such an error, a taxpayer will take reasonable action which involves him in unnecessary loss or unnecessary expenditure. The circumstances in which such cases may arise will vary widely, and each case will need to be considered on its individual facts. However, as a general principle, I believe now that it would be right for the Board to consider compensation—on the facts of each case—in cases of this kind, and this will be the Board's future practice.'

(Letter from Chairman of the Board to the Clerk of the Select Committee on the Parliamentary Commissioner for Administration 16 June 1975.) (This practice has been superseded by Code of Practice 1 from 17 February 1993.)

See 4.1 ADMINISTRATION AND COLLECTION.

26   Interest in Possession

Cross-references. See 42 SETTLEMENTS—GENERAL; 43 SETTLEMENTS WITH INTERESTS IN POSSESSION; 44 SETTLEMENTS WITHOUT INTERESTS IN POSSESSION.

Simon's Direct Tax Service, part I5.1.

Other Sources. CTO Leaflet IHT 16 'Settled property', pages 6 and 7; Foster, part E2; IHTM16000.

26.1   SIGNIFICANCE OF TERM 'INTEREST IN POSSESSION'.

A person with an interest in possession in all or part of settled property is treated as beneficially entitled to the property or part in which his interest subsists. Alternatively, if there is no 'qualifying interest in possession' (see 44.1 SETTLEMENTS WITHOUT INTERESTS IN POSSESSION) the special charging rules relating to such settlements apply. [*IHTA 1984, ss 49, 50, 58, 59*]. For IHT purposes it is therefore necessary to establish into which category a settlement falls.

26.2   MEANING OF 'INTEREST IN POSSESSION'

There is no statutory definition of 'interest in possession' in the IHT legislation (except see 26.3 below for Scotland). The explanation of the expression 'qualifying interest in possession' (see 44.1 SETTLEMENTS WITHOUT INTERESTS IN POSSESSION) merely clarifies what is meant by 'qualifying'. What is meant by an interest in possession is therefore a matter of general law as interpreted by the courts in the light of the specific IHT legislation.

The authoritative statement on the meaning of the term for CTT (and therefore IHT) purposes is to be found in the majority opinions in the House of Lords in *Pearson and Others v CIR HL, [1980] STC 318*. The salient facts to be derived from this case are as follows.

(*a*)   There must be a **present right to the present enjoyment** of something for there to be an interest in possession in settled property. So a person with an interest in possession will have an immediate right to trust income as it arises. See *Oakley & Hutson (Jossaume's Personal Representatives v CIR [2005] STC SCD 343 Sp C 460* at 60 TAX CASES.

(*b*)   If the trustees have **any power to withhold income** as it arises there is no interest in possession. There is a distinction between a power to terminate a present right to present enjoyment and a power which prevents a present right of present enjoyment arising. It follows that

(i)   *a power to accumulate income* is sufficient to prevent a beneficiary from having an interest in possession. (*Note.* per Inland Revenue Press Release 12 February 1976, if any accumulations must be held solely for the person having the interest or his personal representatives, this does not amount to a power to withhold income.) The position is the same if there is a trust to accumulate. Whether or not income is in fact accumulated is irrelevant.

(ii)   *an overriding power of appointment* which could be used to defeat the interest of a beneficiary does not prevent that interest from being in possession if it does not affect the right of the beneficiary to the income which has already arisen.

(iii)   *the possibility of future defeasance* of an interest does not prevent it from being in possession until the occurrence of the relevant event.

(iv)   *a power of revocation* does not prevent an interest from being in possession until it is exercised.

(*c*)   There is a distinction between trustees' **administrative powers**, such as those to pay duties, taxes etc. and their **dispositive powers** to dispose of the net income of the trust. The existence of the former does not prevent an interest from being in possession. Any interest in possession will be in the net income of the trust after deduction of administrative expenses.

(*d*)   An interest in settled property which is not in remainder or reversion or contingent is not necessarily an interest in possession.

The **HMRC view** is expressed in their Press Release of 12 February 1976 which they regard as not inconsistent with the majority HL opinions in *Pearson*.

26.3   **Scotland. In Scotland,** any reference to an interest in possession in settled property is a reference to an interest of any kind under a settlement by virtue of which the person in right of that interest is entitled to the enjoyment of that property, or would be so entitled if the property were capable of enjoyment, (including an interest of an assignee under an assignation of an interest of any kind in property subject to a proper liferent, other than a reversionary interest) and that person is deemed to be entitled to a corresponding interest in the whole or any part of the property comprised in the settlement. [*IHTA 1984, s 46*]. For further background on Scottish Trusts see IR Trust Manual, supplement to Appendix 2.

In a Scottish case, an individual (D) transferred certain securities and investments to trustees in 1962. The income arising from the trust was treated for tax purposes as income of the settlor under *FA 1958, s 22* (now *ITTOIA 2005, ss 624–628*). D died in 1981 and then his wife died in 2002. HMRC issued a notice of determination on the basis that she had enjoyed an interest in possession in the settled property. The trustees appealed. The Special Commissioner dismissed the appeal, finding that D's widow had effectively enjoyed 'a power of veto: the whole of the free annual income of the trust fund had to be paid or applied to her or for her benefit from year to year unless or until she should concur with a consideration by the trustees that it was proper and expedient for a lesser amount to be so paid or applied'. Accordingly the trust deed had conferred an interest in possession. See *Trustees of the Douglas Trust (for Mrs I Fairbairn) v HMRC* [2007] STC SCD 338 Sp C 593.

26.4   **Trustee Act 1925. Trustee Act 1925, s 31** can affect a beneficiary's right to trust income with a corresponding effect on whether or not he has an interest in possession. In *Swales and Others v CIR Ch D, [1984] STC 413*, an appointment of income contingent upon the occurrence of a vesting event was intended to carry the right to the intermediate income of the fund, and *Trustee Act 1925, s 31(1)(ii)* applied to that intermediate income with the effect that the beneficiary was entitled to an interest in possession in the trust fund. In *Re Delamere's Settlement Trusts, Kenny and Others v Cunningham-Reid and Others CA 1983, [1984] 1 All ER 584*, the point at issue was whether, on the facts, *Trustee Act 1925, s 31(2)* applied, as this determined whether or not the beneficiaries had interests in possession. It was held not to apply, with the result that the beneficiaries did have interests in possession.

26.5   **Sole object of discretionary trust.** The fact that income from trust funds is to be held upon 'protective trusts' to be paid to or applied for a class of beneficiaries at the trustees' absolute discretion has been held not to give the sole existing beneficiary a protected life interest. Nor does that beneficiary have an interest in possession by virtue of being the sole existing object of the discretionary trust. The possibility, however remote, that another discretionary object could come into existence is sufficient to prevent him from having the necessary immediate entitlement to trust income as it arises. (*Moore and Osborne v CIR Ch D, [1984] STC 236*).

26.6   **Occupation of dwelling-house by beneficiary.** Trustees under a will or settlement may have power to allow a beneficiary to occupy a dwelling-house comprised in the trust on

26.6   Interest in Possession

such terms as they think fit. Where there is no interest in possession in the dwelling house HMRC do not regard the exercise of the power as creating one if the effect is merely to allow non-exclusive occupation, or to create a contractual tenancy for full consideration. The creation of a lease for a term or a periodic tenancy for less than full consideration does not create an interest in possession, though it may give rise to a charge under *IHTA 1984, s 65*. (See 44.9 SETTLEMENTS WITHOUT INTERESTS IN POSSESSION.) On the other hand, if the power is drawn in terms wide enough to cover the creation of an exclusive or joint right of residence, albeit revocable, for a definite or indefinite period, and is exercised with the intention of providing a particular beneficiary with a permanent home, HMRC will normally regard the exercise of the power as creating an interest in possession. A lease for life for less than full consideration will also be regarded as an interest in possession. (In another context see *Harrison and Another v Gibson and Others Ch D [2005] TLR 24 January 2006* where the testator's intentions as to occupancy of his bungalow 'in trust to my wife' did not give an absolute interest to his wife under *Administration of Justice Act 1982, s 22.*) (See also 42.6(*E*) SETTLEMENTS—GENERAL.) A similar view will be taken where the power is exercised over property in which another beneficiary had an interest in possession up to the time of the exercise. In the recent case of *Judge and another (personal representatives of Walden deceased) v HMRC [2005] STC SCD 863 Sp C 506* a deceased husband's will gave his house to trustees, with a declaration that they should allow his widow (W) to occupy the house 'for such period or periods as they shall in their absolute discretion think fit'. W continued to occupy the house until her death in 2003. HMRC issued a notice of determination on the basis that her husband's will had given her an interest in possession in the house (see also Inland Revenue Statement of Practice SP 10/79, 15 August 1979). Her personal representatives appealed. The Special Commissioner allowed their appeal, holding that the effect of W's husband's will was that she 'had no right to occupy the property but the trustees were given a discretion (but not a duty) to allow her to occupy'. In the summary the Commissioner stated:

> 'With the exclusion of the words "with the consent in writing of my wife during her lifetime" this asset creates a trust for the sale of Perrymead Street and provides that the proceeds of sale are to be held as for the residuary (discretionary) fund. However, the words 'with the consent in writing of my wife during her lifetime' prevents the sale taking place during the life of Mrs Walden unless she consents in writing. In the absence of such consent, the sale cannot take place, but any net rents and profits until sale are to be held on the (discretionary) trusts of the residuary fund. In my view, this part of clause 3 manifests the intention of Mr Walden that Mrs Walden, during her lifetime, could unilaterally postpone the sale of Perrymead Street but that, if she did, then the rents and profits were to be held on the discretionary trusts of the residuary fund. This part of the clause makes it clear that Mrs Walden had no right to the income of Perrymead Street pending sale.'

Accordingly therefore, Mrs Walden did not have the right to occupy Perrymead Street and did not have an interest in possession in the property. Despite the case being found in favour of the taxpayer and the husband's will being held to create discretionary trusts with no tax being payable by the estate, it does raise the continuing spectre of creation of an interest in possession where the trustees exercise a discretion by permitting occupation of such property. In order to reduce such an inference, trustees should perhaps regularly reconsider their discretionary powers documenting such deliberations in writing for record and possibly even creating a formal licence to occupy. An incidental consequence arising from this case was that the husband's estate had obviously been taxed on the wrong basis! See also *CIR v Lloyds Private Banking Ltd [1998] STC 559 Sp C 133* at 42.6 SETTLEMENTS—GENERAL. (Inland Revenue Statement of Practice SP 10/79, 15 August 1979 at HMRC STATEMENTS OF PRACTICE (25)). See also Taxation Magazine, 20 May 2004 p 183.

Agreement between the Trustees and Beneficiary for the occupation of trust property [pursuant to *Trusts of Land and Appointment of Trustees Act 1996, section 13*]

THIS AGREEMENT is made the .... day of .... 200(7)... between

.... [Trustee]....... of ....[Address]....... and ....[Trustee]....... of ....[Address].......... hereinafter known as 'the Trustees' and ....[Beneficiary].......... of ....[Address]............ hereinafter known as 'the Beneficiary'.

WHEREAS

(1)   The Trustees are the present Trustees of:

    (a)   a conveyance ('the Conveyance') dated ....[date]..... and made between the parties and

    (b)   a settlement ('the Settlement') of even date with and made between the same parties in the same order as the Conveyance.

(2)   The freehold property (the 'Property') described in the schedule is vested in the Trustees and is held on trusts under which the Beneficiary is entitled to an interest in possession.

(3)   The Trustees have determined in accordance with the provisions of the Trusts of Land and Appointment of Trustees Act 1996, section 13 that the Beneficiary may occupy the Property on the following terms and conditions including the payment by the Beneficiary to ....[Name of second Beneficiary]....... of ....[Address]......... hereinafter known as ....[Name]..... (who is also entitled to an interest in possession under the trusts affecting the Property) of such annual sums as are stated in this agreement.

NOW IT IS AGREED as follows:

1   *Licence*

The Trustees permit the Beneficiary to reside in and occupy the Property until the agreement is determined in accordance with the provisions below.

2   *Tenant not to assign*

This licence is personal to the Beneficiary and he/she shall not assign it or allow any other person or persons to occupy the whole or any other part of the property.

3   *Payment*

The Beneficiary undertakes to pay to ....[Name]..... the annual sum of £....... by equal half yearly instalments payable in arrears throughout the currency of this licence so long as ...[Name].... is entitled to an interest in possession under the Trusts affecting the property, the first such instalment to be paid on ...[Date]... and the subsequent instalments to be paid on ...[Date].... and ...[Date]...... in each year and the last payment to be made on the termination of the licence or on such earlier date as ...[Name]... ceases to be entitled to an interest in possession under the trusts affecting the property (whether due to the death of ...[Name].... or for any other reason) and to be a proportionate payment.

26.7   Interest in Possession

Notes to the Agreement

(A)   Further provisions on powers, proper law, etc. and full administrative provisions are required to effect this agreement.

(B)   Note that in the above agreement the second Beneficiary is excluded from occupying land under the *Trusts of Land and Appointment of Trustees Act 1996, s 13(1)* but he/she still retains an interest in possession in that land. On the death of the occupying Beneficiary and upon the second Beneficiary becoming sole life tenant of the trust fund he/she can no longer be excluded from occupation under *s 13(1)* nor will he/she be required to pay compensation (see point 3 'Payment' in Agreement above) under *s 13(6)*.

26.7   **Power to augment income out of capital.** Where a trustee exercises a power to augment the income of a beneficiary out of capital, this will have no immediate IHT effect if the beneficiary is a life tenant who has an interest in possession, as by virtue of *IHTA 1984, s 49(1)* he is already treated as beneficially entitled to the property. In other circumstances the exercise of the power is likely to give rise to a tax charge. (25.E6 HMRC STATEMENTS OF PRACTICE).

26.8   **TIME OF CREATION OF INTEREST IN POSSESSION**

Age of majority. Under *Family Law Reform Act 1969, s 1*, the age of majority is reduced from 21 to 18 although for settlements created before 1 January 1970, the relevant age of majority remains 21. Where an interest is created by a special power of appointment made after 31 December 1969 under a settlement made before 1 January 1970, HMRC regard the beneficiary's interest in possession as arising at 18. (25.E8 HMRC STATEMENTS OF PRACTICE but now withdrawn—IR Press Release 30 September 1996).

Administration period. Where a person would have been entitled to any interest in possession in the whole or part of the residue of the estate of a deceased person had the administration of the estate been completed, he is regarded for inheritance tax purposes as becoming entitled to an interest in possession in the unadministered estate and in the property (if any) representing ascertained residue, or a corresponding part of it, on the date as from which the whole or part of the income of the residue would have been attributable to his interest had the residue been ascertained immediately after the date of death. [*IHTA 1984, s 91*].

Survivorship clauses. Where under the terms of a will or otherwise property is held for any person on condition that he survives another for a specified period not exceeding six months, the disposition taking effect at the end of the period (or on death if the person does not survive until then) is treated as having had effect from the beginning of the period. This has no effect on distributions etc. occurring before the disposition. [*IHTA 1984, s 92*].

27   Interest on Tax

Cross-references. See 8.11 CALCULATION OF TAX for transfers reported late and 35 PAYMENT OF TAX.

Simon's Direct Tax Service, part I11.405.

Other Sources. Foster, part L5.31–2; IHTM36000.

27.1   **Interest on tax overdue.** Interest is chargeable on unpaid inheritance tax from the due date (see 35.1 PAYMENT OF TAX) to the date of payment at the following rates. See http://www.hmrc.gov.uk/rates/interest.htm.

After 5 August 2007	5% p.a.
After 5 September 2006 and before 6 August 2007	4% p.a.
After 5 September 2005 and before 6 September 2006	3% p.a.
After 5 September 2004 and before 6 September 2005	4% p.a.
After 5 December 2003 and before 6 September 2004	3% p.a.
After 5 August 2003 and before 6 December 2003	2% p.a.
After 5 November 2001 and before 6 August 2003	3% p.a.
After 5 May 2001 and before 6 November 2001	4% p.a.
After 5 February 2000 and before 6 May 2001	5% p.a.
After 5 March 1999 and before 6 February 2000	4% p.a.
After 5 October 1994 and before 6 March 1999	5% p.a.
After 5 January 1994 and before 6 October 1994	4% p.a.
After 5 December 1992 and before 6 January 1994	5% p.a.
After 5 November 1992 and before 6 December 1992	6% p.a.
After 5 July 1991 and before 6 November 1992	8% p.a.
After 5 May 1991 and before 6 July 1991	9% p.a.
After 5 March 1991 and before 6 May 1991	10% p.a.
After 5 July 1989 and before 6 March 1991	11% p.a.
After 5 October 1988 and before 6 July 1989	9% p.a.
After 5 August 1988 and before 6 October 1988	8% p.a.
After 5 June 1987 and before 6 August 1988	6% p.a.
After 15 December 1986 and before 6 June 1987	8% p.a.
After 17 March 1986 and before 16 December 1986	
—transfers on death and potentially exempt transfers	9% p.a.
—all other transfers	11% p.a.

From 18 August 1989 the Treasury may, in an order in the form of a statutory instrument, prescribe formulae for computing interest rates so that if circumstances change so as to change the rate of interest prescribed, the Board must by order specify the new rate and the day from which it has effect. Prior to 18 August 1989 the Treasury had to prescribe each change of rate in an order in the form of a statutory instrument.

Any interest accruing on or after 6 April 1997 is calculated as if every year is a leap year (i.e. 366 days). This will give a small advantage to the taxpayer in three out of every four years. See IHT NEWSLETTER AND TAX BULLETIN EXTRACTS (61), March 1997.

Interest is payable gross and it is not deductible in computing income, profits or losses for tax purposes. It is refundable to the extent that the tax concerned is subsequently cancelled.

For the above purposes, where

(*a*)   additional tax becomes chargeable as a result of the transferor's death within seven years of a chargeable transfer (including tax payable under the provisions relating to SETTLEMENTS WITHOUT INTERESTS IN POSSESSION (44) because of the settlor's death within that period), and

27.1 Interest on Tax

(b)   a political party is liable for tax on the death of the transferor within one year after a gift in excess of £100,000 made before 15 March 1988

the chargeable transfer is deemed to have been made on death.

Acceptance of property in satisfaction of tax. Where after 16 March 1987, the Board agree to accept property (acceptance by the AIL Panel of Resource) in satisfaction of any IHT, CTT or estate duty (see 35.6 PAYMENT OF TAX) on terms that the value to be attributed to the property for the purposes of the acceptance is determined at a date earlier than that on which the property is actually accepted, the terms of the agreement may provide that the amount of tax which is satisfied by the acceptance of the property does not carry interest from that earlier date. [*IHTA 1984, ss 233, 236(1)(1A); FA 1986, Sch 19 paras 32, 33; FA 1987, s 60; F(No 2)A 1987, s 97; FA 1988, Sch 14; FA 1989, ss 178, 179; SI 1985/560; SI 1986/1944; SI 1987/887; SI 1988/1280; SI 1988/1623; SI 1989/1002; SI 1989/1297; SI 1989/1298*].

Example 1

B died on 10 February 2007. The executors made a payment on account of IHT of £70,000 on 30 June 2007 on delivery of the account. The final notice of determination was raised by HMRC Inheritance Tax on 19 June 2008 in the sum of £102,500. The rate of interest for these purposes is assumed to be 5%.

Date of chargeable event (death)	10 February 2007
Date on which interest starts to accrue	1 September 2007
	£
IHT payable	102,500
Payment made on account 30 June 2007	70,000
Balance due	£32,500

Assessment raised by HMRC Inheritance Tax 19 June 2008

Interest payable (1.9.2007 to 19.6.2008)

£32,500 at 5% for 292 days	£1,300

Example 2

F gave his holiday home in Cornwall to his granddaughter G on 7 August 2003. On 23 May 2007 F died. He had made no use of the property at any time after 7 August 2003. G made a payment of £15,000, on account of the IHT due, on 1 January 2008. The liability was agreed at £27,000, and the balance paid, on 17 February 2008. The rate of interest for these purposes is assumed to be 5%.

Date of PET	7 August 2003
Date on which PET becomes chargeable	23 May 2007
Date on which IHT is due	1 December 2007
	£
IHT payable	27,000
Payment made on account 1 January 2008	15,000
Balance due	£12,000

Interest payable
On £27,000 from 1.12.2007 to 1.1.2008

£27,000 at 5% for 31 days	115

On £12,000 from 1.1.2008 to 17.2.2008

£12,000 at 5% for 47 days	77
Total interest payable	£192

Where HMRC delay their reply to a letter or other enquiry for no good reason, and the delay in total exceeds by more than six months its 28-day target for replies, then no interest will be charged on tax that was unpaid during the period of the delay, and any reasonable costs incurred directly because of the delay will be reimbursed (HMRC Code of Practice 1).

27.2   **Interest on tax repaid.** Any repayment of tax or interest paid will carry interest from the date of payment until the order for repayment is issued at the above rates and such interest will be tax-free. [*IHTA 1984, s 235*]. Where inheritance tax is repaid as a result of an order that is made under the *Inheritance (Provision for Family and Dependants) Act 1975, ss 2, 19* as amended by the *Family Law Act 1996, s 66* special treatment applies, see 27.4 below.

Where HMRC delay their reply to a letter or other enquiry for no good reason, and the delay in total exceeds by more than six months its 28-day target for replies, then interest will be paid on repayments of tax due but not repaid during the period of the delay, and any reasonable costs incurred directly because of the delay will be reimbursed as well as consolatory payments in serious cases (revised HMRC Code of Practice 1 issued in April 1996). (*IHTA 1984, s 235* above would normally cover *by statute* all circumstances involving interest on repayments of tax including those of HMRC delay.) See http://www.hmrc.gov.uk/rates/interest-repayments.htm.

27.3   **Interest on payment by instalments.** See 35.5 PAYMENT OF TAX.

27.4   **Special cases.** Tax overpaid or underpaid in consequence of the *Inheritance (Provisions for Family and Dependants) Act 1975* (or NI equivalent) (see 50.6 TRANSFERS ON DEATH) does not carry interest before the date of the order. [*IHTA 1984, s 236(2)*].

In 2001 and 2007 HMRC introduced a cancellation of interest in respect of deferred tax resulting from financial difficulty brought about by the outbreak of foot and mouth disease. The circumstances where this may apply to inheritance tax is detailed in NATIONAL HERITAGE (33) and IR Tax Bulletin 'Special Edition on Foot and Mouth Disease', May 2001 http://www.hmrc.gov.uk/bulletins/tb-se(2001).htm.

Interest will normally become payable on the unpaid inheritance tax six months after the end of the month in which the chargeable event occurred (see 35.1 PAYMENT OF TAX). In the case of foot and mouth disease which affected farming businesses both these interest payments arising on the IHT and CGT tax liabilities payable but deferred will be cancelled. [*FA 2001, s 107(1)*]. The Government declared the United Kingdom free of the disease at midnight on 14 January 2002 but HMRC were aware that for some time after that the financial and economic effect would remain and they continued to help those affected. See IR Press Release 18 March 2002.

28 Land

Cross-reference. See 15.5 DETERMINATION AND APPEALS re land valuation.

Simon's Direct Tax Service, parts I4.311, I7.3, I8.361.

28.1 LAND

'Land' includes (unless the contrary intention appears) buildings and other structures, land covered with water, and any estate, interest, easement, servitude or right in or over land, but does not include any estate, interest or right by way of mortgage or other security. In *Chelsea Yacht and Boat Co Ltd v Pope, CA [2001] 2 All ER 409* where a houseboat moored to a pontoon and embankment wall by ropes constituted a chattel and not part of the land which consequently would affect the option to pay by instalments. In contrast in *Cinderella Rockerfellas Ltd v Rudd [2003] All ER 219* a floating nightclub permanently attached to the land by ropes and chains would constitute part of the land which consequently would affect the option to pay by instalments. See 35.3 PAYMENT OF TAX. In any Act passed before 1 January 1979, 'land' includes messuages, tenements and heraditaments, houses and buildings of any tenure. [*Interpretation Act 1978, s 5, Sch 1, Sch 2 para 5(b); IHTA 1984, s 272*]. See also IHTM23001. The Land Registry Office is the preferred source of information for HMRC. See http://www.landregistry.gov.uk/register_dev/.

28.2 Inheritance tax applies to chargeable transfers of land situated in the UK and to land situated abroad but in which an interest is held by a person domiciled in the UK. Certain special provisions apply as below.

28.3 AGRICULTURAL LAND AND BUSINESS LAND

Where property in the UK is transferred, and that property was used for agricultural purposes or was held as an asset of a business or used for the purposes of a business, a reduction in value for the purposes of inheritance tax may be claimed. See 5 AGRICULTURAL PROPERTY and 7 BUSINESS PROPERTY for details. In the case of agricultural or business property that may qualify for 100% relief HMRC Capital Taxes state that the open market value should still be used. Personal representatives may consider using their own estimate of the value of the property in the expectation that the business will in any case be covered by the 100% agricultural or business relief. A reason for using a nominal value may be the cost of a professional valuer's fees to the estate. However, nominal or ill considered values should be avoided because if relief is not due for some reason and there is an uplift in the nominal value put on the business by the personal representatives, then the consequent uplift to the correct value may incur a penalty. Also, for the purposes of *TCGA 1992, s 274* the value for CGT purposes should be 'ascertained' and not a nominal estimated value. See example in 7.3 BUSINESS PROPERTY and also IHT NEWSLETTER AND TAX BULLETIN EXTRACTS (61), April 2004.

See IHT 110 and 210 (Notes) and D12 (Notes) which at point 3 states:

'If any of the properties is suffering from any major damage, its value may be affected. Things like a poor state of internal and external decoration are not so important. But if the property is damaged in a way that is covered by buildings insurance, we have to value the property in a special way.'

28.4 FREE USE OF LAND

A charge to inheritance tax may arise where an owner allows the use of land to another person for a fixed or minimum period for inadequate consideration. See 49.3 TRANSFER OF VALUE for details.

28.5   **HOUSING ASSOCIATIONS**

Gifts of land in the UK to registered housing associations after 13 March 1989 are exempt. See 21.4 EXEMPT TRANSFERS.

28.6   **NATIONAL HERITAGE LAND**

Land and buildings which are of outstanding historic or other interest may be exempt from inheritance tax under certain conditions, see 33 NATIONAL HERITAGE.

28.7   **PAYMENT OF TAX BY INSTALMENTS**

Under certain conditions, where a liability to inheritance tax arises on the transfer of land and buildings of any description, wherever situated, an election to pay the tax by ten annual instalments may be made. See 35.3 PAYMENTS OF TAX for details and IHT 17, p 27.

28.8   **SALES WITHIN THREE (OR FOUR) YEARS AFTER DEATH**

Special provisions apply, see 56.6 VALUATION.

28.9   **TRANSFERS WITHIN SEVEN YEARS BEFORE DEATH**

See 51 TRANSFERS WITHIN SEVEN YEARS BEFORE DEATH for special provisions.

28.10   **WOODLANDS**

See 58 WOODLANDS for special provisions.

28.10 Land

HM Revenue & Customs

Land, buildings and interests in land

Give the details we ask for about the land included in the deceased's estate. You should read form D12(Notes) before filling in this form.

1

Name

Date of death
/ /

CT reference

Name and address of the person that the Valuation Office should contact

Reference

Telephone number

2

A Item No.	B Full address or description of property		C Tenure	D Lettings/leases	E Agricultural, timber or heritage element	F Open market value
		Post Code				

| | | | Total(s) carried forward | £ | | £ |

www.hmrc.gov.uk/cto   Helpline 0845 30 20 900

Please turn over
HMRC CT 12/05

D12

266

A Item No.	B Full address or description of property	Post Code	C Tenure	D Lettings/leases	E Agricultural, timber or heritage element	F Open market value
			Total(s) brought forward		£	£

Total (s) £   £   £

3 Were any of the properties subject to any damage that may affect their value? No ☐ Yes ☐

If the answer is "Yes", fill in the box below using the same item number(s) that you have used in column A above.

Item No.	Details of damage

4 Have any of the properties been sold, or do you intend to sell any of them within 12 months? No ☐ Yes ☐

If the answer is "Yes", fill in table below using the same item number(s) that you have used in column A above.

G Item No.	H Present position of sale	I Sale price	J Type of sale	K Price for fixtures, carpets and curtains	L Use sale price as value

29 Liability for Tax

Cross-references. See 12.6 CLOSE COMPANIES for liability of participators; 33.4 NATIONAL HERITAGE for persons liable on a chargeable event; 35 PAYMENT OF TAX; 37.2 PENSION SCHEMES; 50.7 TRANSFERS ON DEATH for liability where legitim is claimed in Scotland; 58.3 WOODLANDS for person liable on a disposal; 59 WORKING CASE STUDY.

Simon's Direct Tax Service, part I10.

Other Sources. CTO Leaflet IHT 15 'How to calculate the liability'; Foster, part K; IHTM28000.

29.1 MORE THAN ONE PERSON LIABLE

According to the nature of a chargeable transfer, one or more persons may be liable for the tax and if they do not pay then other persons may be liable up to certain limits and with a right of recovery. Except as provided otherwise, where two or more persons are liable for the same tax each of them is liable for the whole of it. [*IHTA 1984, s 205*].

29.2 LIFETIME TRANSFERS

Subject to the rules in 29.4 below for lifetime transfers within seven years of death, the primary person liable is the transferor. If the tax remains unpaid after it ought to have been paid, the following persons are also liable.

(*a*) Any person the value of whose estate is increased by the transfer.

(*b*) Any 'person in whom the property is vested' (whether beneficially or otherwise) or who is beneficially entitled to an interest in possession in it at any time after the transfer (e.g. a nominee, trustee, life tenant, but see 29.6 below) to the extent that the tax is attributable to the value of that property. See 29.3 below for the extension of the meaning of 'person in whom property is vested' which also applies to lifetime transfers.

(*c*) Where by the chargeable transfer any property becomes comprised in a settlement, any person for whose benefit any of the property or income from it is applied.

References to property include any property directly or indirectly representing it.

Limitation of liability. The liability of persons within (*a*) to (*c*) above is limited to the tax which would be payable on the value transferred as reduced by the tax remaining unpaid (i.e. the liability cannot be for a greater amount than tax on the property transferred without grossing-up). Liability is further limited as follows.

(i) In the case of a trustee, it is limited to the value of the property he has received, disposed of or has become liable to account for to the beneficiaries and any other property as is for the time being available in his hands for the payment of tax (or might have been so available but for his own neglect or default). *Note.* For income tax purposes, the income of a settlement is treated as that of the settlor where he might benefit directly or indirectly from the settlement. HMRC do not take the view that, solely because the trustees have power to pay, or do in fact pay, inheritance tax due on assets which the settlor puts into the settlement, the settlor has an interest in the income or property of the trust and any income should be treated as the settlor's. (former Inland Revenue Statement of Practice SP 1/82 6 April 1982 see 25 HMRC STATEMENTS OF PRACTICE).

(ii) A person within (*b*) above, other than a trustee, is only liable to the extent of the property concerned.

(iii) A person within (*c*) above is liable only to the extent of the property or income (as reduced by income tax borne by him in respect of that income) applied for his benefit by the trustees. [*IHTA 1984, ss 199(1)(4)–(5), 204(2)(3)(5)(6)*].

Example 1

A settled £78,000 on discretionary trusts in December 2007, having previously made chargeable transfers on 31 March 2007 totalling £303,000.

A's liability is as follows	£
Gift	78,000
Deduct 2007/08 annual exemption	3,000
	£75,000
Grossed at 20%	£93,750
IHT thereon at 20%	£18,750

Example 2

Transferee

In the example above A pays only £10,000 of IHT and defaults on the balance of £8,750, so that the trustees become liable as transferee.

The trustees' liability is not, however, £8,750 but is as follows

	£
Original gross	93,750
Deduct IHT unpaid	8,750
Revised gross	£85,000
IHT thereon at 20%	17,000
Deduct IHT paid by A	10,000
Now due from trustees	£7,000

Example 3

Person in whom property is vested

In January 2008 C transferred to trustees of a discretionary trust shares in an unquoted property company worth, as a minority holding, £50,000. However, the transfer deprives C of control of the company with the result that the value of his estate is reduced by £210,000. He has already used his nil rate band and annual exemptions.

29.3 Liability for Tax

C's liability is as follows

Net loss to him	£210,000
Grossed at 20%	£262,500
IHT thereon at 20%	£52,500

C fails to pay so that the trustees become liable, as follows

	£
Original gross	262,500
Deduct unpaid IHT	52,500
	£210,000
IHT thereon at 20%	£42,000

Notes to the example

(A)   The trustees' liability cannot exceed the value of the assets which they hold, namely the proceeds of sale of the shares, less any CGT and costs incurred since acquisition, plus any undistributed income in their hands.

(B)   Prior to 2004/05 when there was a differential between the marginal income tax rate (40%) and the rate applicable to trusts (34%) a further liability on the beneficiary could arise. If the trustees had already distributed net income of £2,000 to beneficiary D who is liable to pay additional higher rate income tax of £182 thereon (i.e. £3,030 x 6%), D could have been made to pay IHT of £1,818, being the net benefit received by him. From 6 April 2004 this will not arise as the rate applicable to trusts was increased to 40%. [*ICTA 1988, s 686(1A)* as amended by *FA 2004, s 29(2)* and *ITA 2007, s 9(1)(2)*].

Transferor's spouse or civil partner. Where a transferor is liable for tax on a chargeable transfer and has made another, separate transfer to his spouse or civil partner and both transfers took place while they were married to each other, the spouse or civil partner is also liable for the tax on the chargeable transfer. The liability of the spouse or civil partner is limited to the market value of the gift to the spouse or civil partner at the time of the spouse/civil partner transfer. In addition, where the transfer to the spouse or civil partner is *before* the chargeable transfer and the property transferred to the spouse or civil partner is not tangible movable property, the liability of the spouse or civil partner is limited to the market value of the gift received *at the time of the chargeable transfer* (or if the gift has been sold, its market value at the time of the sale) if this is lower than the market value at the time of the spouse/civil partner transfer. [*IHTA 1984, s 203; The Tax and Civil Partnership Regulations 2005, SI 2005/3229, Reg 36*]. This is an anti-avoidance provision to enable tax to be recovered from the spouse or civil partner where it cannot be recovered from the transferor or other person as above.

29.3   TRANSFERS ON DEATH

The persons liable are as follows.

(a)   The deceased's '*personal representatives*' in respect of property not comprised in a settlement immediately before death and settled land in the UK which devolves upon or vests in them. The liability is a personal rather than a representative liability of the personal representatives (see also Personal Contact manual, para 3.19 issue 12/94), and their non-UK residence does not prevent either liability or the UK courts' jurisdiction to deal with IHT claims (*CIR v Stype Investments (Jersey) Ltd; Re Clore (deceased) CA, [1982] STC 625* and *CIR v Stannard Ch D, [1984] STC 245*). However, the liability is limited to the unsettled assets received and the UK land settled immediately before the death and available at any time in their hands for the payment of tax (or such assets and land which might have been available but for their own neglect or default). In Scotland, an executor is not liable under this provision for tax on any heritable property vested in him under *Succession (Scotland) Act 1964, s 18*.

Under certain wills, the deceased may not have given any indication of how the burden of inheritance tax is to be allocated among the items of property in the estate. Where personal representatives are liable for tax on chargeable transfers on death, then, subject to any contrary intention in the will, any tax payable on the value of unsettled UK property which vests in them is to be treated as part of the general testamentary and administration expenses of the estate. Where any tax paid by the personal representatives does not fall to be treated in this way, the tax must, where necessary, be repaid to them by the person in whom the property is vested. References to tax include interest on tax.

(b)   *The trustees of a settlement* which immediately before death comprised property passing on the death. The liability is limited to the value of the property the trustees have received, disposed of or have become liable to account for to the beneficiaries and any other property for the time being as is in their hands for the payment of tax (or might have been so available but for their own neglect or default).

(c)   *Any person in whom property is vested* (whether beneficially or otherwise) *or who is beneficially entitled to an interest in possession in it* at any time after the death (but see 29.6 below) to the extent that tax is attributable to the value of the property. The liability is limited to the extent of the property.

(d)   *Any person for whose benefit any of the property or income comprised in a settlement immediately before death was applied after death*. The liability is limited to the property or income (as reduced by income tax borne by him on that income) applied for his benefit by the trustees.

(e)   *The administrator of any registered pension scheme in respect of funds which are chargeable under IHTA 1984, ss 151A or 151C*. The liability is intended to apply in the case where individuals use alternatively secured pension (ASP) to pass on tax-privileged retirement savings to their dependants rather than to provide a pension in retirement. See 37.2 PENSION SCHEMES.

References to property include any property directly or indirectly representing it.

[*IHTA 1984, ss 200(1), 204(1)–(3)(5), 209(1), 211; FA 2006, s 160, Sch 22 para 5*].

For the above purposes, entitlement to part only of the income of any property is deemed to be entitlement to an interest in the whole property. The whole tax attributable to the property can therefore be recovered from any beneficiary. [*IHTA 1984, s 200(3)*].

Example

Personal representatives of E, who died on 30 September 2007, received the following assets.

	£
Free personal property	143,265
Land bequeathed to F (which, under the terms of the will, bears its own IHT)	29,735
Private residence, bequeathed to spouse/civil partner	51,000

A trust in which E had a life interest was valued at £141,000. Under the will of E, legacies of £15,000, each free of IHT, were given to F and G and the residue was left to H. E had made no chargeable transfers during his lifetime.

29.4 Liability for Tax

	Persons liable	£	IHT £
IHT is borne as to			
Chargeable transfer			
Free personal property	PRs	143,265	2,555
Land bequeathed to F	F	29,735	530
Private residence to spouse/civil partner	—	Exempt	Nil
Trust fund	Trustees	141,000	2,515
		£314,000	£5,600

	£	£
The residue left to H is as follows		
Free personal property		143,265
Deduct IHT	2,555	
Legacies to F and G	30,000	32,555
		£110,710

Note to the example

(A) If the will had not directed that the IHT on the land bequeathed to F be borne by F, the IHT would be payable out of residue. [IHTA 1984, s 211].

'*Personal representative*' includes any person by whom or on whose behalf an application for a grant of administration or for the resealing of a grant made outside the UK is made; and also includes persons within (i) below. [*IHTA 1984, s 272*]. See IHT 14 'The personal representatives' responsibilities'.

'*Persons in whom the property is vested*' includes (i) any person who becomes liable as executor or trustee by taking possession of or intermeddling with property (or in Scotland, intromits with property or has become liable as a vitious intromitter) and (ii) any person to whom the management of property is entrusted on behalf of a person not of full legal capacity. [*IHTA 1984, ss 199(4), 200(4)*].

A person who transfers the sale proceeds of English property belonging to the estate of a deceased person out of English jurisdiction has been held to have intermeddled with the estate and to be liable for IHT as *executor de son tort* (*CIR v Stype Investments (Jersey) Ltd Re Clore (deceased) CA, [1982] STC 625*).

Gifts with reservation. Where property is treated as forming part of a deceased person's estate under the rules relating to GIFTS WITH RESERVATION (22), a personal representative is only liable for the tax on that property if it remains unpaid for twelve months after the end of the month in which death occurs and, subject to that, only to the extent mentioned in (*a*) above. [*IHTA 1984, s 204(9); FA 1986, Sch 19 para 28*].

29.4 **LIFETIME TRANSFERS WITH ADDITIONAL LIABILITY ARISING THROUGH DEATH**

For transfers of value before 15 March 1988, if death occurred within one year of a gift to a political party (see 21.6 EXEMPT TRANSFERS) in excess of £100,000, the tax due on death was the liability of the political party only. [*IHTA 1984, s 206; FA 1988, Sch 14*].

Death within seven years. Where a transferor dies within seven years of making a POTENTIALLY EXEMPT TRANSFER (38) or a chargeable lifetime transfer, the persons liable for the tax on the value transferred by the potentially exempt transfer or the additional tax on the chargeable transfer are as follows.

(*a*)   The personal representatives but only to the extent that

(i)   no other person within (*b*) below is liable for the tax because of their limitation of liability as detailed below; or

(ii)   tax remains unpaid twelve months after the end of the month in which death occurs.

Subject to the above, the personal representatives are only liable to the extent of the unsettled assets received and the UK land settled immediately before death and available at any time in their hands for the payment of tax (or such assets and land which might have been available but for their own neglect or default).

Without prejudice to the application of *IHTA 1984, s 199(2)*, HMRC will not usually pursue personal representatives who, having obtained a certificate of discharge (see 35.9 PAYMENT OF TAX) and distributed the estate before a chargeable lifetime transfer comes to light, have made the fullest enquiries that are reasonably practicable in the circumstances to discover lifetime transfers and done all in their power to make a full disclosure of them to HMRC (letter from Capital and Valuation Division reproduced at [1991] STI 238).

The previous CTO Advanced Investigation Manual stated at paragraph U.27:

'The liability of the transferor's personal representatives is a sensitive area of the legislation. Staff should alert the personal representatives at an early stage where recourse to them *might* occur. In cases where the transferee is not resident in this country we are of course likely to be aware of that fact from the replies on page 3 of the IRA, but nevertheless we should still warn the personal representatives of their potential liability, failing payment by the transferee and any other persons who may be liable under IHTA 1984, s 199(1).'

The manual continued:

'It is emphasised that the facility to have recourse to the transferor's personal representatives is not to be regarded as a soft option. We are to make all attempts at recovering from the persons liable under IHTA 1984, s 199(1) that we would presently contemplate in a similar situation against any liable person. But having warned the personal representatives that we may look to them to discharge the tax liability, we must ensure firstly that they are kept fully in the picture and secondly that a decision actually to collect from them is not delayed for years.'

However, at IHTM10811 it now states:

'The general rule is that the personal representatives (IHTM05012) are accountable. They have to complete and return an IHT 200 for the deceased's estate. The only exception to this rule is where the estate is an 'excepted estate' (IHTM06011).'

(*b*)   Any person within 29.2(*a*) to (*c*) above subject to the limitation of liability as in 29.2(i) to (iii) above (but *not* the preambles thereto).

[*IHTA 1984, ss 199(1)(2)(5), 204(1)–(3)(5)(7)(8); FA 1986, Sch 19 paras 26, 28*].

Example 1

On 31 December 2007, H, who had made no earlier chargeable transfers other than to utilise his annual exemptions for 2007/08 and earlier years, transferred £343,000 into a discretionary trust and, a month later, settled an asset worth £20,000 into the same trust. H paid the appropriate IHT. On 30 June 2010 H died.

29.5 Liability for Tax

The trustees become liable to further IHT as follows

	£	£
Original net gift	£343,000	£20,000
Grossed-up at half of full rates	£353,750	£25,000
IHT (paid by H) See 41.1 RATES 2007.B2	£10,750	£5,000
IHT at 80% of death rates applicable in June 2010 on original gross (death between 3 and 4 years after gifts)	1,200	8,000
Deduct IHT paid originally by H	10,750	5,000
Now due from trustees	Nil	£3,000

Note to the example

(A)   The additional IHT on death is calculated using the rates in force at the date of death assumed for these purposes to be that applying at 6 April 2010. See 41.1 RATES 2010.A1. If the IHT at the new death rates, as tapered, was less than the IHT paid on the original chargeable transfer, there would be no repayment as in this case.

Example 2

The second gift in the example above had fallen in value to £18,000 by the time of H's death.

The trustees may claim to reduce the IHT payable as follows

	£
Original gross gift	25,000
Deduct drop in value (£20,000 – £18,000)	2,000
Revised gross	£23,000
IHT thereon at 80% of death rate applicable in June 2011	7,360
Deduct IHT paid by H	5,000
	£2,360

Note to the example

(A)   If the asset had fallen in value to £10,625 or less, so that the revised gross became £15,625 or less and the IHT at 80% of death rates £5,000 or less, the trustees would have no liability because H had already paid IHT of £5,000.

29.5   SETTLED PROPERTY

Where a chargeable transfer is made, or is deemed to be made, out of settled property, the persons liable for the tax are

(*a*)   the trustees of the settlement (to the extent shown in 29.3(*b*) above), or, if they do not pay,

(*b*)   any person entitled (whether beneficially or not) to an interest in possession in the settled property (but liability of a person entitled to a beneficial interest is limited to the extent of the property); and

(c)   any person for whose benefit any of the settled property or income from it is applied at or after the time of transfer (but liability is limited to the extent of the property or income (as reduced by income tax borne by him in respect of that income) applied for his benefit by the trustees); and

(d)   the settlor, where the chargeable transfer is made during his lifetime and the trustees are not for the time being resident in the UK except that

        (i)   where the chargeable transfer is made within seven years of the death of the transferor but, after 16 March 1987, is not a potentially exempt transfer, the settlor is not liable for the extra tax due because of the death within seven years; and

        (ii)   there is no liability where the settlement was made before 11 December 1974 if the trustees were resident in the UK when the settlement was made but have not been resident in the UK at any time between that date and the time of the transfer; and

        (iii)   after 16 March 1987, there is no liability if a potentially exempt transfer proves to be a chargeable transfer where the settlement was made before 17 March 1987 if the trustees were resident in the UK when the settlement was made but have not been resident in the UK at any time between 16 March 1987 and the death of the transferor.

For these purposes, the trustees of a settlement are regarded as not resident in the UK unless the general administration of the settlement is ordinarily carried on in the UK and the trustees or a majority of them (including a majority of each class where there is more than one class of trustees) are for the time being resident in the UK. Where more than one person is a settlor in relation to a settlement, for these purposes the property is treated as comprised in separate settlements.

References to property include any property directly or indirectly representing it. [*IHTA 1984, ss 201, 204(2)(3)(5)(6); FA 1986, Sch 19 para 27; F(No 2)A 1987, Sch 7 para 3*].

Retiring UK trustees need to ensure that they have in place an indemnity which they can rely on, or they will have to retain sufficient cash to meet tax liabilities when they retire in favour of non-resident trustees. Whilst these tax liabilities will normally be in respect of capital gains there may be an IHT liability. Therefore the trustees' indemnity should be effected in similar terms to the following.

Recitals

The retiring Trustee(s) having made full enquiries of the Appointer and the continuing Trustee(s) and the new Trustees and in reliance on the answers to these enquiries is satisfied that (as the Appointer and the continuing Trustee(s) and the new Trustees hereby confirm) there is no proposal that the Trustees of the Settlement may become neither resident nor ordinarily resident in the United Kingdom.

In consideration of the retiring Trustee(s) retiring and being discharged from the trusts of the Settlement the continuing Trustees and the new Trustee(s) have agreed to give indemnity which appears below.

Operative Part

The continuing Trustee(s) and the new Trustee(s) hereby jointly and severally COVENANT with the retiring Trustee(s) at all times fully and effectually to indemnify [him/her/them] and [his/her/their] personal representatives and estates from and in respect of all United Kingdom tax liabilities (e.g. Inheritance

---

Tax, Income Tax, etc.), fiscal and other outgoings, claims, costs, expenses, and liabilities whatsoever to be incurred following the appointment of the new Trustee(s) as Trustee(s) in place of the retiring Trustee(s) including (but without limitation) any Capital Gains Tax which may at any future time or times become payable in the event of the Trustees of the Settlement becoming neither resident nor ordinarily resident in the United Kingdom at any time or times.

Note to the Recital

(A)   If a tax liability does subsequently arise then the retiring trustees may have recourse to the *Misrepresentation Act 1967*. Section 2(1) of the *Misrepresentation Act 1967* provides:

'Where a person has entered into a contract after a misrepresentation has been made to him by another party thereto and as a result thereof he has suffered loss, then, if the person making the misrepresentation would be liable to damages in respect thereof had the misrepresentation been made fraudulently, that person shall be so liable notwithstanding that the misrepresentation was not made fraudulently, unless he proves that he had reasonable ground to believe and did believe up to the time the contract was made that the facts represented were true'.

29.6   **A PURCHASER OF PROPERTY**

A 'purchaser' of 'property' and a person deriving title from or under such a purchaser, is not liable for any tax attributable to the property unless the property is subject to an HMRC charge (see 35.8 PAYMENT OF TAX). [*IHTA 1984, ss 199(3), 200(2)*].

'*Purchaser*' means a purchaser in good faith for consideration in money or money's worth other than a nominal consideration and includes a lessee, mortgagee or other person who for such a consideration acquires an interest in the property in question.

'*Property*' includes rights and interests of any description. [*IHTA 1984, s 272*].

29.7   **DEED OF INHERITANCE TAX INDEMNITY**

PARTIES

1.   "Father" namely

2.   "Son" namely

RECITAL

Immediately after the execution of this deed Father intends to give Son a cheque for £......... as a gift subject to inheritance tax ("the Gift")

IHT INDEMNITY

1.   The Liability

"The Liability" means any [additional] liability to inheritance tax probably chargeable in respect of the Gift arising or crystallising on or by reason of the death of Father

2.   Incidence

Son acknowledges that the burden of inheritance tax (if any) on the Gift shall be borne by Son

3.   Covenant and Indemnity

Son covenants with Father and his personal representatives to pay the Liability (whether by direct discharge to HMRC or by reimbursement to Father's estate or otherwise) immediately upon demand following an assessment on Father's estate and generally to keep Father and his personal representatives indemnified against the liability

4.   Effluxion

The indemnity given by this deed shall lapse and be extinguished on the seventh anniversary of the date of the Gift if Father is still then living

5.   Limitation

The indemnity given by this deed shall be limited to £..........

EXECUTED as a deed on 200(7)

SIGNED AS A DEED AND   )
DELIVERED by
FATHER in the presence of:—   )

Witness' signature

Address

Occupation

SIGNED AS A DEED AND   )
DELIVERED by
SON in the presence of:—   )

Witness' signature

Address

Occupation

Note to the deed

An indemnity of this nature will be sufficient to ensure there is no grossing up and to mark for family purposes who carries the burden in the event of premature death. If there is any serious prospect of it having to be relied on through enforcement then further provisions may be needed e.g. dealing with interest after the due date, reporting, costs, etc.

30 Life Assurance Policies and Annuities

Cross-reference. See 3.2 ACCUMULATION AND MAINTENANCE TRUSTS; 34.1 PARTNERSHIPS for partnership assurance policies; 59 WORKING CASE STUDY.

30.1 APPLICATION

Where a life assurance policy matures on the death of the person who took out the policy and remained the beneficial owner, the policy monies are included in his estate for the purposes of inheritance tax. [*IHTA 1984, s 171(1)*]. See IHTM20000 at http://www.hmrc.gov.uk/manuals/ihtmanual/index.htm.

Where the policy is expressed to be for the benefit of the spouse, civil partner or children under the *Married Women's Property Act 1882*, a trust is created in their favour so that the person whose life is assured never has an interest in the policy and the proceeds will not be included in his estate on his death. [*Married Women's Property Act 1882, s 11 as amended by Civil Partnership Act 2004, s 70*].

To [   ] Life Assurance Company

MWPA TRUST

This request is an integral part of the attached application and I declare that such application is made by me as settlor ("the Settlor") and request that the policy(ies) issued pursuant thereto shall be issued under the provisions of [Married Women's Property Act 1882] or [Married Women's Policies of Assurance (Scotland) Act 1880] or [Law Reform (Husband and Wife) Act (Northern Ireland) 1964] and subject to the powers and provisions in the Schedule below upon trust and for the benefit of:

I wish to appoint as trustees additional to myself the following persons whose concurrence is evidenced by execution hereto (and "the Trustees" shall be a reference to the trustees for the time being) of these trusts.

The receipt of the Trustees shall be a complete discharge to [...] for moneys payable under the policy.

Schedule of Further Trust Provisions

1. The Trustees shall have power to invest any moneys in their hands in or upon any investment of any nature and wherever situated and whether income producing or not and whether an investment strictly so called (including the effecting of policies of life assurance or annuities for the life of any beneficiary or other person and further including the purchase of freehold or leasehold land as an investment or the residence of a beneficiary) free from all duties of diversification as if the Trustees were the absolute beneficial owners

2. The Trustees shall have full power to surrender/convert/sell/auction or otherwise deal with any policy subject to these trusts notwithstanding that the sum assured may be increased or decreased

3. Section 31 of the Trustee Act 1925 shall apply as if:

    3.1 the words "may in all the circumstances be reasonable" had been omitted from paragraph (i) of subsection (1) and in substitution there

---

278

had been inserted the words "the Trustees may in their absolute discretion think fit" and as if the proviso at the end of subsection (1) had been omitted

3.2   in subsection (2) the words "as follows:—" and the paragraphs (i) and (ii) thereof had been omitted and replaced by "upon trust for that person absolutely"

4.   Section 32 of the Trustee Act 1925 shall apply as if the words "one half" were omitted from proviso (a) to subsection (1)

5.   The Trustees shall have power as they in their absolute discretion think fit to pay or apply any moneys for the time being subject to the trusts hereof (or borrowed hereunder) in or towards the discharge of any Inheritance Tax or other fiscal imposition the liability for which would otherwise fall either directly or indirectly on any beneficiary whether or not the interest or such beneficiary under the trusts hereof is absolute or contingent or vested in possession or in remainder or reversion PROVIDED that no such payment shall exceed the value of such beneficiary's interest at the time of such payment

6.   The power of appointing new or additional trustees shall be exercisable by the Settlor during his lifetime

7.   The receipt of a parent or guardian in respect of any benefit payable or transferable to a minor beneficiary shall be a sufficient discharge to the Trustees who shall be under no obligation to see to its application

8.   Neither the Settlor nor the Trustees shall be under any obligation whatsoever to keep up any policy subject to these trusts or to reinstate the same if it becomes void and the Settlor shall have no right by way of lien or otherwise to reimbursement of any premiums paid or subsequently paid in respect of any policy subject to these trusts

9.   These trusts shall be governed by and construed in accordance with the Law of England

Dated _____ 200(7) _____

(The Settlor)
Signed

(The further Trustees)
Signed

Dated _____ 200(7) _____

Where an annuity under an approved trust scheme or contract or, after 22 July 1987, under approved personal pension arrangements or, from 6 April 2006, a registered pension scheme (or *ICTA 1988, s 615(3)* scheme) is payable on a person's death to the widow, widower, surviving civil partner or dependant and the terms of the scheme etc. gave the deceased the option to have a sum of money i.e. cash payable to his personal representatives, he is not treated as having been beneficially entitled to that sum which is therefore not included in his estate. [*IHTA 1984, s 152; F(No 2)A 1987, s 98(5); FA 2004, s 203(5); The Tax and Civil Partnership Regulations 2005, SI 2005/3229, Reg 33*]. For the valuation of an annuity which is an interest in possession (IIP) chargeable on property, see 43.2 SETTLEMENTS WITH INTERESTS IN POSSESSION.

Compensation fund payments arising out the 11 September 2001 terrorist attacks that comprise part of the UK victims' estates are not subject to IHT. The Victim's Compensation Fund of 2001 was established by the US government as an alternative to any legal proceedings that the victims' estates could take under the law as it stood on 11 September. The legislation was actually passed after 11 September 2001 but claims under the compensation fund have no value at that date for IHT purposes. Payments made after that date are not chargeable to IHT in any case so that part of a victim's estate comprising of the compensation fund payment is not subject to IHT. See also April/May 2002 issue 61 IHT NEWSLETTER AND TAX BULLETIN EXTRACTS.

Transitional serial interest (TSI). Where a person (stipulated as being 'C' in the legislation) is beneficially entitled to a present interest in settled property with regard to a life insurance policy entered into before 22 March 2006, those rights under the contract or in property in the settlement directly or indirectly representing rights under the contract are, for the purposes of *IHTA 1984, Part III, Ch III*, a transitional serial interest only if a number of conditions are satisfied:

- The first condition is that the settlement must have commenced before 22 March 2006 and the property comprised in the settlement was property which consisted of or included rights under the insurance contract to which 'C', or some other person, was beneficially entitled an interest in possession which for these purposes is designated 'the earlier interest';

- The second condition is either:

  that 'the earlier interest' in the insurance contract came to an end on or after 6 April 2008 on the death of the person beneficially entitled to it and 'C' became beneficially entitled to the present interest at one of the following times:

  (i)   at the time of the ending of the earlier interest; or

  (ii) on the death of the person beneficially entitled to an interest in possession at the time of the ending of the earlier interest (i.e. (i) above); or

  (iii) on the ending of a second or last in a series of unbroken consecutive sequences of interests in possession to the first where a person becomes beneficially entitled at the time of the ending of the earlier interest (i.e. (i) above) each of which has ended on the death of the person with beneficial entitlement;

  or that 'C' became beneficially entitled to the present interest:

  (i)   on the coming to an end of an interest in possession that is a TSI under *s 49C* on the death of the person who is beneficially entitled to it. See 43.1 SETTLEMENTS WITH INTERESTS IN POSSESSION; or

  (ii) on the ending of a second or last in a series of unbroken consecutive sequences of interest in possession the first of which is a TSI under *s 49C* each of which has ended on the death of the person with beneficial entitlement.

- The third condition is that rights under the contract of insurance were comprised in the settlement from 22 March 2006 to the date when 'C' became beneficially entitled;

- The fourth condition is that neither *IHTA 1984, s 71A* (bereaved minor's trust) applies to the property in which the interest subsists nor is the interest a disabled person's interest.

This TSI category relating to life assurance policies is more limited than the other two categories at 43.1 SETTLEMENTS WITH INTERESTS IN POSSESSION in that it does not apply to any property settled before 22 March 2006, but only to property settled which comprises rights under a contract of life insurance entered into before 22 March 2006. The benefit of this TSI category is that it can apply to more than one of a chain of successive interests in possession, provided each one qualifies as a TSI. Similarly to the category 2 spouse/civil partner TSI at 43.1 SETTLEMENTS WITH INTERESTS IN POSSESSION it only applies to TSIs falling into possession on the death of a person previously entitled to an interest in possession.

The legislation in *IHTA 1984, s 49E* above provides for TSI treatment to apply to contracts of insurance after 5 April 2008 for contracts set up before 22 March 2006 and pre-22 March 2006 settlements. The main purpose being to allow TSI relief on premiums that continue to be paid after 22 March 2006 on a policy settled on IIP or accumulation and maintenance trusts before that date. However, if after 5 April 2008 a power of appointment is exercised to appoint any new beneficiary who is not absolutely entitled this will result in the trust coming within the new regime. See Example 1 below.

[IHTA 1984, s 49E; FA 2006, Sch 20 para 5].

Pre-22 March 2006 life insurance within an IIP trust. Where a life policy has been settled on an interest in possession (IIP) trust before 22 March 2006 but that premiums continue to be paid on that policy the whole of the value of the policy itself still qualifies for transitional protection as an asset of a trust in existence before 22 March 2006. This transitional treatment will continue to apply as long as the original terms of the policy continue. Also, where someone succeeds to the policy on the death of the policy holder then transitional protection will continue. *[IHTA 1984, s 46A; FA 2006, Sch 20 para 11]*. See Fosters Inheritance Tax, para E1.56 and also WORKING CASE STUDY (59).

Pre-22 March 2006 life insurance within an A & M trust. Similar to above where a life policy has been settled on accumulation and maintenance (A&M) trust before 22 March 2006 but that premiums continue to be paid on that policy the whole of the value of the policy itself still qualifies for transitional protection as an asset of a trust in existence before 22 March 2006. This transitional treatment will continue to apply as long as the original terms of the policy continue. Also, where someone succeeds to the policy on the death of the policy holder then transitional protection will continue. See Fosters Inheritance Tax, para E5.26 and also ACCUMULATION AND MAINTENANCE TRUSTS (3). *[IHTA 1984, s 46B; FA 2006, Sch 20 para 11]*.

Care needs to be taken regarding the payment of further premiums as detailed in IHTM20331:

> 'If a transferor puts a policy into an accumulation and maintenance trust or a disabled trust and then pays the renewal premiums direct to the insurance company, PET treatment will therefore not be available. This is because the premiums as such do not become settled property. However, if the transferor makes payments to the trustees and they use those payments to pay the renewal premiums PET treatment is available – even if payment by the transferor is by a cheque which the trustees endorse in favour of the insurance company. Neither the associated operations provisions nor the principle in Ramsey/Furniss should be invoked to deny PET treatment in these cases.'

Example 1

A is to pay premiums of £4,000 p.a. on a policy on his own life (policy 1) which commenced on 1 January 2006. He assigns the policy into trust in favour of a number of potential beneficiaries including his wife (see Deed of Assignment below). The market value of the policy at the date of gift is £3,000. A also pays annual premiums of £2,000 on a policy (policy 2) on his life which commenced on 2 January 2006 written in favour of his son S. The original policy terms permit a variation of beneficiaries and the policy is assigned on discretionary trust in favour of his grandson GS on 6 April 2008. The cumulative premiums paid to that date are £6,000 and the value of the policy is £4,000. In July 2014 A becomes gravely ill and the value of the policy at 2 January 2016 is £155,000. A has utilised

30.1 Life Assurance Policies and Annuities

his £275,000 of his nil rate band in the previous seven years to 2 January 2016. The nil rate band at that stage is assumed to be £350,000. See RATES OF TAX (41).

THIS DEED OF ASSIGNMENT AND DECLARATION OF TRUST is made the *first* day of *January* 2006

BETWEEN:

"the Settlor" namely [...............] .
and
"The Trustees" namely the Settlor and [.................] and [....................].
which expression shall include other trustees or trustee for the time being of these trusts

WHEREAS:

A.   The Settlor is the beneficial owner of the policy(ies) of life assurance detailed in the Second Schedule below ("the Policy")

B.   The Settlor wishes to settle the Policy upon the following trusts

NOW THIS DEED WITNESSES

1.   The Settlor ASSIGNS the Policy and all its benefits and all moneys payable under it and any other property representing the same from time to time to the Trustees UPON TRUST (and subject to the powers and provisions of the Schedule of Further Trust Provisions) for the benefit of such one or more exclusively of the other or others of:

    A.   Any spouse, widow or widower of the Settlor

    B.   Any children of the Settlor whenever born

    C.   Any grandchildren of the Settlor whenever born

    D.   Any spouse, widow or widower or anyone falling within B or C

    E.   Any one or more individual(s) benefiting from the estate of the Settlor under Will or under intestacy

    F.   Any other individual nominated by the Settlor during lifetime in writing to the Trustees other than the Settlor

    in such shares and upon such trusts (and subject to such powers and provisions) as the Trustees being at least two in number or a trust corporation shall appoint by Deed or Deeds revocable or irrevocable executed not later than two years following the death of the Settlor and in default of any such appointment

UPON TRUST for Scope and Red Cross in equal shares absolutely

EXECUTED as a deed on *first January 2006.*

Assignment of policy (policy 1)

The gift is valued either at

  (i)   market value (£3,000), or

  (ii) the accumulated gross premiums paid (£4,000) if greater i.e. £4,000.

Continued premiums paid into a policy effected in trust before the Budget (22 March 2006) will not cause the policy to be subject to the new IHT trust provisions that apply to post-21 March 2006 trusts. Provided that the original policy terms permit, the terms of a policy can be varied post-21 March 2006 without causing the policy to be subject to the new IHT provisions. This means that the benefits can be increased or the term of the policy extended without changing the inheritance tax treatment of the policy. If one of the policy named (see extract above) becomes entitled to an interest in possession via an appointment to him before 6 April 2008 (a TSI), this will not cause the policy to be subject to the new IHT rules. If one of the named in A to F in the policy document becomes entitled to an interest in possession following the death of the previous holder of the interest in possession, this will not cause the policy to be subject to the new IHT rules provided the previous holder of the interest:

- held that interest on Budget day (22 March 2006); or

- held that interest as a TSI (so that it had been made via an appointment to him before 6 April 2008).

Annual premiums (policy 2)

The payment of an annual premium is regarded as an annual gift, the amount of the transfer being the net premium after deduction of any tax relief at source or the gross premium where paid without deduction. In this case no tax relief is due so £2,000 is the figure that is taken for these purposes. Continuing payment of premiums paid into a policy effected in trust before the Budget (22 March 2006) will not result in the policy becoming subject to the new IHT trust provisions that apply to post-21 March 2006 trusts. Premiums paid after Budget day to these trusts will continue to be treated as PETs and will not be chargeable lifetime transfers. Also, providing the original policy terms permit, the terms of a policy can be varied post-21 March 2006 without resulting in the policy becoming subject to the new IHT provisions. The result is that, in those circumstances, the benefits can be increased or the term of the policy extended without changing the inheritance tax treatment of the policy. Whilst the gifts of the premiums after 21 March 2006 where there has been a subsequent appointment of a new beneficiary will no longer be treated as PETs within *s 46A(4)* transfers should still be exempt under the annual exemption or gifts out of normal expenditure. See 21 EXEMPT TRANSFERS.

Re-assignment of policy (policy 2)

Where there is the possibility of a change in the named/default beneficiaries after 5 April 2008 it should be avoided unless the appointment is absolute. In this particular case the power to appoint a new beneficiary within the terms of the policy has been exercised in favour of GS after 5 April 2008 but on discretionary trusts and therefore brings the policy into the new regime of charge (see below) and triggers a chargeable lifetime transfer by the son S. Providing S's transfer is less than £10,000 per annum or £40,000 cumulative over the past ten years it will not need to be reported on Forms IHT100 and IHT100a. This will depend on previous cumulative total of gifts to date and adding the accumulated premiums or the market value of the policy at that point.

30.2 Life Assurance Policies and Annuities

Ten-yearly charge

	£
Initial ten-yearly charge for period 6 April 2008 to 2 January 2016	
Value of relevant property on 2.1.2016	155,000
Value of property in related settlements	—
	155,000
Assumed cumulative total	275,000
	£430,000
IHT at lifetime rates after assumed nil rate band of £350,000	£16,000

Effective rate

$$\frac{16,000}{430,000} = 3.72093\%$$

Rate of ten-year anniversary charge:
$^3\!/_{10} \times 3.72093\% = 1.116279\%$

Ten-year anniversary charge: $30^*\!/_{40} \times 1.116279\% \times £155,000$	£1,298

* i.e. 30 complete quarters from 6 April 2008 to first ten-year anniversary.

Notes to the example

(A)   Pre-22 March 2006 life policy trusts will not be subject to the new IHT taxing rules provided the original terms of the policy continue and where someone succeeds to the policy on the death of the policy holder then transitional protection will continue. The payment of ongoing premiums for life policies owned by trusts will not constitute additions to the trust thereby bringing them into the new IHT charging provisions. On the premature death of the wife prior to A the life policy trust above would still qualify as subsequent beneficiaries would be entitled and therefore the terms of the trust would not have altered since it was set up pre-22 March 2006 within the stipulations of *IHTA 1984, s 46A inserted by FA 2006, Sch 20 para 11.*

(B)   In the case of the life policy trust assigned for the benefit of the grandson GS after 5 April 2008 as this is not an absolute appointment then the new taxing regime within *IHTA 1984, s 43(2)* will apply with the prospect of 20% life time charge (where gifts to the trust exceed the nil rate band) ten yearly charge on the value of the trust fund on the tenth anniversary of the policy and potential exit charge when the policy proceeds are paid out to the beneficiary. In this case the ill health of A prior to the first ten-yearly charge has resulted in a substantial revaluation of the policy.

(C)   Existing accumulation and maintenance settlements that hold life policies will need to be reviewed before 6 April 2008. See ACCUMULATION AND MAINTENANCE TRUSTS (3).

30.2   ASSIGNMENT OF POLICY

Where the benefits of a life policy (or contract for an annuity payable on a person's death) are assigned as a gift or for less than full value, there is a transfer of value and inheritance tax is chargeable (unless any reliefs may be claimed, see 21 EXEMPT TRANSFERS).

The value of a life policy or contract *transferred before death* is to be taken as not less than

(a)   the total premiums or other consideration paid at any time (under the policy or contract or any policy or contract for which it was substituted) before the transfer of value; *less* (*b*)   any sum received, at any time before the transfer of value, for a surrender of any right conferred by the policy or contract (or a policy or contract for which it was substituted).

This provision does not apply unless the policy or contract ceases to be part of the transferor's estate as the result of the transfer of value. [*IHTA 1984, s 167(1)(2); FA 1986, Sch 23 Part X*].

The special rules for valuing a policy above do not apply where the policy is one under which the sum assured becomes payable only if the person whose life is insured dies (i) before the expiry of a specified term, or (ii) both before the expiry of a specified term and during the life of a specified person. Where under the policy the term ends, or can be extended to end, more than three years after the making of the insurance, if neither the person whose life is insured nor the specified person dies before the expiry of the specified term, the rules do not apply if the policy satisfies the conditions that the premiums are payable during at least two–thirds of that term and at yearly or shorter intervals, *and* the premiums payable in any one period of twelve months are not more than twice the premiums payable in any other twelve months. [*IHTA 1984, s 167(3)*].

Unit linked policies. Where the benefit secured under a policy is expressed in units the value of which is published and subject to fluctuation and the payment of each premium secures the allocation to the policy of a specified number of such units, then the value to be taken as above will take into account any investment loss on those units. This is done by deducting from the total premiums etc. paid, the difference between the value of the units when they were first allocated and their value at the time of the transfer of value. [*IHTA 1984, s 167(4)*].

Settlements. References above to a transfer of value include an event on which there is a charge to tax under the provisions relating to SETTLEMENTS WITHOUT INTERESTS IN POSSESSION (44) in *IHTA 1984, Part III, Ch III* (except *section 79*, see 33.10 NATIONAL HERITAGE), other than an event on which tax is chargeable in respect of the policy or contract by reason only that its value is reduced otherwise than by these provisions. [*IHTA 1984, s 167(5)*].

Premiums continued by donor. Where a policy is transferred and the donor continues to pay the premiums, or provides the money for this purpose, then a transfer of value occurs on each occasion, based on the decrease in value of the donor's estate (i.e. the special rules above for valuing the policy on its assignment do not apply to later payments of premiums). These payments may be exempt, see 21 EXEMPT TRANSFERS. HMRC take the view that where the payment of a premium on a life assurance policy is a transfer of value, the amount of the transfer is the net amount of the premium after deduction under ICTA 1988, s 266(5) (tax relief at source) or the gross premium where paid without deduction. (HMRC Press Release 17 January 1979 and IHT 15, p 9.

Example 2

A has paid premiums of £2,000 p.a. for six years on a policy on his own life. He gives the policy to his son B. The market value of the policy at the date of gift is £11,000 but due to a demutualisation policy enhancement is uplifted to £12,500 (see HMRC Tax Bulletin, April 1998, p 520). A also pays annual premiums of £2,000 on a policy on his life written in favour of his son.

Assignment of policy

The gift is valued either at

(i)   market value (£12,500), or

(ii)   the accumulated gross premiums paid (£12,000) if greater (but they are not).

30.3   Life Assurance Policies and Annuities

Annual premiums

The payment of an annual premium is regarded as an annual gift, the amount of the transfer being the net premium after deduction of any tax relief at source or the gross premium where paid without deduction. [**Case Study 4**].

Notes to the example

(A)   The gifts are PETs. The assignment of the policy will only become chargeable if A dies within seven years, and only the annual premiums paid within seven years of A's death will be chargeable.

(B)   Exemptions available for reduction of the chargeable transfer on assignment include the annual exemption and the marriage exemption.

(C)   The normal expenditure exemption may be available to A for premiums paid and the annual exemption may also be claimed to exempt the gift in whole or in part.

(D)   Normal expenditure relief is not available when a policy and annuity have been effected on a back-to-back basis (with certain exceptions).

30.3   ANNUITY PURCHASED IN CONJUNCTION WITH LIFE POLICY

The use of annuities in conjunction with life policies is known as 'back to back' arrangements.

Example 3

The purchase of an immediate annuity for a lump sum would reduce the purchaser's estate and provide him with an income for life. If he arranged an insurance on his own life but for the benefit of another person whom he wished to benefit at his death, the proceeds would be free of tax because they are not part of his estate. There would be further advantages if he paid the premiums on the policy and could obtain exemption from inheritance tax on them, e.g. as normal expenditure out of income (see 21.12 EXEMPT TRANSFERS).

The following provisions reduce the effectiveness of 'back to back' arrangements.

Where a life insurance is made, varied or substituted and an annuity on the life of the insured is purchased at any time before or after that date and the benefit of the insurance policy is vested in a person other than the purchaser of the annuity, the purchaser of the annuity is treated as making a transfer of value at the time the benefit of the policy became vested in the other person. The value transferred is the lesser of

(*a*)   the aggregate of (i) the value of the consideration given for the annuity and (ii) any premium paid or other consideration given under the policy on or before the transfer; and

(*b*)   the value of the greatest benefit capable of being conferred at any time by the policy, calculated as if that time were the date of the transfer.

The above provisions also apply where an annuity payable on a person's death is substituted for 'life insurance policy'.

The above provisions do *not* apply if it can be shown that the purchaser of the annuity and the making, variation or substitution of the insurance were not associated operations (see 6.3 ANTI-AVOIDANCE). [*IHTA 1984, s 263*].

In practice, such policies and annuities are not regarded as being affected by the associated operations rule if the policy was issued on full medical evidence of the insured's health and it would have been issued on the same terms if the annuity had not been bought. (See at 25 HMRC STATEMENTS OF PRACTICE). See also *AC Smith v HMRC (and related appeals) [2007] Sp C 605 at 60* TAX CASES.

If the transferor pays, either directly or indirectly, a premium on a life insurance on his life and an annuity on his life is purchased at any time, the premium will not be treated as part of his normal expenditure out of income unless it can be shown that the associated operations rule (see above) does not apply. [*IHTA 1984, s 21(2)*].

See 21.12 EXEMPT TRANSFERS for normal expenditure out of income and that chapter generally for exemptions which might be applied to the transfers of value mentioned above.

31 Lifetime Transfers

Cross-references. See 1 INTRODUCTION AND BASIC PRINCIPLES; 2.3 ACCOUNTS AND RETURNS and 8 CALCULATION OF TAX; 59 WORKING CASE STUDY.

Simon's Direct Tax Service, part I3.

31.1 GENERAL

An individual is subject to inheritance tax on every CHARGEABLE TRANSFER (10) made by him after 17 March 1986. Chargeable transfers are any transfers of value made by an individual other than EXEMPT TRANSFERS (21). For inheritance tax purposes, certain lifetime transfers are designated POTENTIALLY EXEMPT TRANSFERS (38). Such a transfer made seven years or more before the death of the transferor is an exempt transfer and any other such transfer is a chargeable transfer. The tax is normally levied on the value of the reduction in the transferor's ESTATE (19) caused by the chargeable transfer which includes the inheritance tax on the value of the gift where the transferor pays that tax (i.e. the value of the gift, after taking account of any exempt transfers, is grossed-up). If the transferee bears the tax, the transferor's estate is reduced only by the value of the gift itself (after exemptions). See 31.2 below. Dispositions not intended to confer gratuitous benefit are not transfers of value. See point (*a*) at 49.2 TRANSFER OF VALUE. For definition of estate, see 19 ESTATE. The chargeable transfers are aggregated during a seven-year period to arrive at the scale rate of tax applicable (see 8 CALCULATION OF TAX). [*IHTA 1984, ss 2(1)(2), 3, 3A, 7, 10; FA 1986, Sch 19 para 1; F(No 2)A 1987, s 96; FA 2006, Sch 20 para 9*].

See also IHTM14000 at http://www.hmrc.gov.uk/manuals/ihtmanual/index.htm.

31.2 SHORT FORM MEMORANDUM EVIDENCING A GIFT OF SHARES SUBJECT TO TAX

MEMORANDUM OF GIFT OF

Father: Of
Son   Of

MEMORANDUM that on Father transferred by way of gift to Son (subject to the payment of any Inheritance Tax) the shares listed in the schedule below to the intent that they have become and are the absolute property of Son and IN CONSIDERA-TION of such transfer Son undertook to pay any Inheritance Tax in respect of such gift assessed upon Father or his personal representatives and indemnifies Father and his personal representatives accordingly.

SCHEDULE

Dated:
Signed by Father:
Signed by Son:

31.3 SHORT FORM MEMORANDUM EVIDENCING A GIFT OF CHATTEL(S)

The gift of a chattel(s) during lifetime should normally be evidenced so that when the gift is called into question there is proof on both sides, the donor and the donee, that such a gift was effected at the time stated. This may be useful not only for the purposes of determining future IHT liabilities but also in connection with bankruptcy, winding-up and divorce, for example. It is important that there is no reservation of benefit in the gift once it has been disposed for IHT purposes and a short form memorandum is detailed below:

MEMORANDUM OF GIFT OF CHATTEL(S)

THIS MEMORANDUM records that on the ...... day of .... 200(7) the undersigned [*Donor*] of [*Address*] ('the Donor') gave and by word of mouth expressed himself/herself to give to the undersigned [*Donee*]of [*Address*] ('the Donee) [all the furniture effects and moveable property] which [are] specified in the Schedule attached hereto ('the Chattel(s)) for the absolute sole use of the and benefit of the Donee and at the same time the Donor delivered the Chattel(s) to the Donee and placed the Donee in possession and unrestricted control of the Chattel(s) and at the same time the Donee accepted the gift.

Dated:

SCHEDULE

[Identification is made here of all chattels which have been given by the Donor]

Signed by [*Donor*]:

Signed by [*Donee*]:

See 59.11 WORKING CASE STUDY for additional precedent regarding the preservation of evidence by means of a third party statutory declaration which records the actual events of the gift as they occurred at the time in question.

31.4   **LIFETIME TRANSFERS AND IHT100**

An account on Form IHT 100 (old forms IHT 100 and IHT 101 have been replaced as from April 2003) is required when there is a chargeable event described below.

- Lifetime transfers made by an individual that are chargeable to inheritance tax at the time they are made (supplementary event form IHT 100a) subject to the exclusion mentioned in paragraph 31.5 below.

- A potentially exempt transfer where the transferor has died within seven years bearing in mind that there is no requirement to tell HMRC Inheritance Tax regarding the transfer while the transferor is still alive.

- A termination of an interest in possession in settled property (supplementary event form IHT 100b) e.g. the ending of a life interest, which occurs during the life of the life tenant and is chargeable to inheritance tax at the time of the event. If the interest in possession is not chargeable at the time it is made then there is no requirement to advise HMRC Inheritance Tax unless the life tenant dies within seven years of the event.

- A termination of an interest in possession in settled property within seven years of the death of the life tenant.

- A termination of an interest in possession in settled property *arising* as a result of the life tenant's death.

- Property is given subject to a reservation where the reservation is retained until the death of the transferor.

- Property ceases to be held on discretionary trusts and there is a proportionate charge or exit charge (supplementary event form IHT 100c).

31.5   Lifetime Transfers

• A ten-year anniversary charge on a discretionary trust (supplementary event form IHT 100d).

• Assets are no longer held on special trusts (supplementary event form IHT 100e) e.g. the flat rate charge.

• Recapture charges are exigible e.g. the ceasing of an entitlement to conditional exemption (supplementary event form IHT 100f).

• Assets ceasing to benefit from conditional exemption and being subject to a recapture charge (supplementary event form IHT 100f) e.g. sale of trees, timber or underwood.

Initially IHT 100 is completed together with supplementary Forms D31 to D40 which provide for information on the assets where required. In addition, there is the Form IHT 100WS which can be used to calculate the tax that will be due regarding the chargeable event.

31.5   EXCLUSION FROM IHT100 SUBMISSION

There are exceptions to the above cases where an IHT100 does not have to be submitted and these apply in the following circumstances:

(*a*)   where a gift or other transfer of value by an individual is wholly exempt;

(*b*)   where a gift or other transfer of value by an individual in circumstances where the amount of the gift and any other chargeable transfer made by the individual in the same tax year does not exceed £10,000 and the amount of the gift and any other chargeable transfer made by the individual in the ten years previously ending on the date of the gift does not exceed £40,000 (an increase in the threshold to £200,000 is being considered but has not yet been implemented);

(*c*)   where there is a termination of an interest in possession where the life tenant has given the trustees notice advising them of the availability of the annual exemption and/or marriage exemption and that/those exemptions cover the whole of the value transferred.

HMRC retain the right to call for an account by notice in writing to the individual. [*IHTA 1984, s 256(1)(a); SI 1981/1440; SI 2002/1731*]. See also 2.3 ACCOUNTS AND RETURNS and http://www.hmrc.gov.uk/cto/forms/iht110_2.pdf.

HM Revenue & Customs

Inheritance Tax Account

Fill in this account to tell us about any of the events listed below. You should read the related guidance notes before filling in any particular box on this or the accompanying forms. Complete all names and addresses in CAPITALS.

A About the Chargeable event

Tick one of the following boxes.

		Tick box	Event form
A1	Gifts and other transfers of value including failed potentially exempt transfers.		IHT100a
A2	Ending of an interest in possession in settled property.		IHT100b
A3	Assets in a discretionary trust ceasing to be relevant property (proportionate charge).		IHT100c
A4	Discretionary trust ten-year anniversary (principal charge).		IHT100d
A5	Assets ceasing to be held on special trusts (flat rate charge). See form IHT110 "How to fill in form IHT100".		IHT100e
A6	Cessation of conditional exemption and disposal of trees or underwood (recapture charge).		IHT100f
A7	Chargeable event in respect of an alternatively secured pension fund on death of scheme member, death of a dependant or relevant dependant, or relevant dependant ceasing to be a relevant dependant		IHT100g

This account must be accompanied by the event form shown against the box you have ticked.

B About the transferor/settlement

Title of transferor/settlor
B1

Surname of the transferor/settlor
B2

Forename(s) of the transferor/settlor
B3

Address, or last usual address of the transferor/settlor
B4

Post Code

Date of birth of the transferor/settlor
B5 / /

Date of death of the transferor/settlor (where appropriate)
B6 / /

IHT reference for the transferor/settlor (where appropriate)
B7

Tax District of the transferor/settlor
B8

Income tax or self assessment reference of the transferor/settlor
B9

National Insurance number of the transferor/settlor
B10

Domicile of the
• settlor when the settlement was made, or
• testator at the date of death, or
• transferor at the date of transfer
B11

Name of the settlement (where appropriate)
B12

IHT reference for the settlement (if known)
B13

Income tax reference for the settlement
B14

Write whichever is appropriate a, b, c or d in the box
a married or in civil partnership
b single
c divorced or former civil partner
d widowed or surviving civil partner
B15

IHT100   www.hmrc.gov.uk/cto   Helpline 0845 30 20 900   HMRC 08/06

(Substitute)(LexisNexis Butterworths)

31.5   Lifetime Transfers

Ⓒ Person we should contact

Name and address of the person to whom
communications should be sent

C1

Post code

Contact name | C2 |

DX number and exchange

| C3 |

Telephone number

| C4 |

Reference

| C5 |

Capacity | C6 |

Important. Read the following notes and the more detailed instructions in IHT110 "How to fill in form IHT100" before filling in the rest of this form. One of the event forms IHT100a, IHT100b, IHT100c, IHT100d, IHT100e, IHT100f or IHT100g must be filled in and returned with this form.

Fill in section **D**, **E** and **F** to tell us about *the assets included in the chargeable event you are telling us about as follows:*

If you have ticked box
- **A1** *tell us about the assets that were given or transferred.*
- **A2** *tell us about the assets in respect of which this interest in possession ceased.*
- **A3** *tell us about the assets that ceased to be relevant property. (Proportionate charge).*
- **A4** *tell us about the relevent property in the settlement. (Principal charge).*
- **A5** *tell us about the assets which ceased to be held on special trusts. (Flat rate charge).*
- **A6** *tell us about the assets on which a charge to inheritance tax arises. (Recapture charge).*
- **A7** *tell us about the assets in the alternatively secured or unsecured pension fund.*

Ⓓ Supplementary pages - Do not complete section D if you are telling us about the assets in an alternatively secured or unsecured pension fund - go to section E.

You must answer all the questions in this section. You should read the notes starting at page 12 of form IHT 100 before answering the questions. If you answer **yes** to a question you will need to fill in the supplementary pages shown. If you do not have all of the supplementary pages you should telephone our Orderline on 0845 234 1000.

			Yes	No	
•	**Domicile outside the United Kingdom**	Was the transferor domiciled outside the UK at the date of the transfer or the date of the settlement?	☐	☐	D31
•	**Stocks and shares**	Do the assets about which you are telling us include stocks and shares?	☐	☐	D32
•	**Debts due to the settlement**	Was there any money on loan from the settlement either on mortgage or by personal loan, that had not been repaid at the date of the chargeable event?	☐	☐	⟩⟩⟩ D33
•	**Insurance**	Were any insurance policies included in the transfer?	☐	☐	⟩⟩⟩ D34
•	**Household and personal goods**	Do the assets being reported include household and personal goods?	☐	☐	⟩⟩⟩ D35
•	**Land and buildings: Interests in land: Trees or underwood**	Do the assets being reported include any land, buildings, trees or underwood in the UK?	☐	☐	D36
•	**Agricultural relief**	Are you deducting agricultural relief?	☐	☐	⟩⟩⟩ D37
•	**Business relief**	Are you claiming business relief?	☐	☐	⟩⟩⟩ D38
•	**Foreign assets**	Do the assets being reported include any assets outside the UK?	☐	☐	D39
•	**Other information**	Use this form to provide any additional information.	☐	☐	⟩⟩⟩ D40

2

292

E *Assets in the UK where tax may not be paid by instalments*

- Quoted stocks, shares and investments *(box SS1 form D32)* — **E1** £
- UK Government and municipal securities *(box SS2 form D32)* — **E2** £
- Unquoted stocks and shares *(details from form D32)* — **E3** £
- Traded unquoted stocks and shares *(details from form D32)* — **E4** £
- Dividends or interest *(details from form D32)* — **E5** £
- National Savings Investments *(show details on form D40)* — **E6** £
- Bank and building society accounts *(show details on form D40)* — **E7** £
- Cash — **E8** £
- Debts due to the settlement, trust or fund and secured on mortgage *(box DD1 form D33)* — **E9** £
- Other debts due to the settlement or fund *(box DD1 form D33)* — **E10** £
- Life assurance policies *(box IP1 form D34)* — **E11** £
- Capital gains tax repayment — **E12** £
- Household and personal goods *(box HG1 form D35)* — **E13** £
- Other assets *(show details on form D40)* — **E14** £

Total assets *(sum of boxes E1 to E14)* — **E15** £

- **Liabilities**

Name of creditor	Description of liability	Amount £

Total liabilities — **E16** £

Net total of assets less liabilities *(box E15 less box E16)* — **E17** £

- **Exemption and reliefs** *(Do not include any annual exemption)*

Total Exemptions and reliefs — **E18** £

Chargeable value of assets in the UK where tax may **not** be paid by instalments *(box E17 less box E18)* — **E19** £

3

31.5 Lifetime Transfers

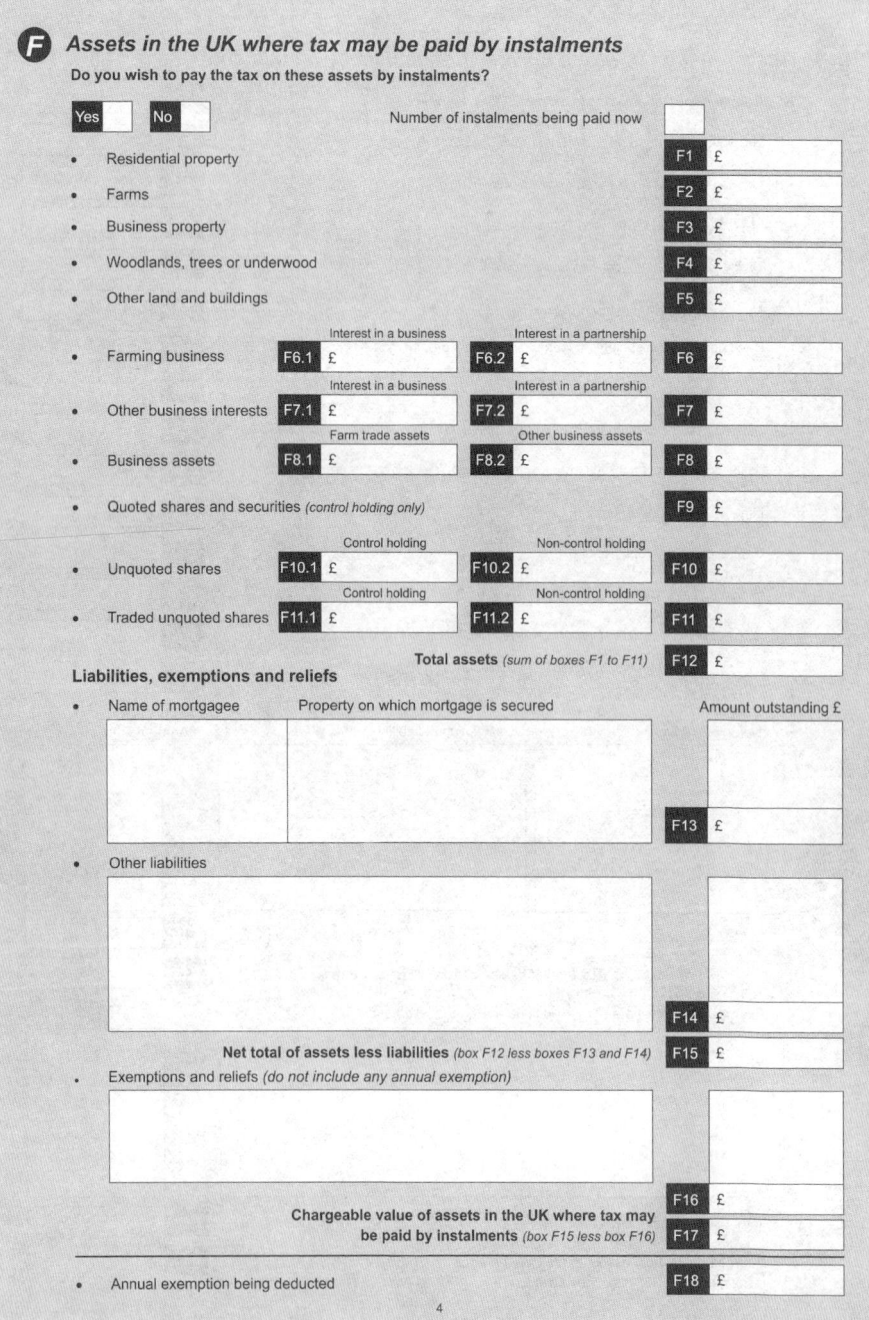

F *Assets in the UK where tax may be paid by instalments*

Do you wish to pay the tax on these assets by instalments?

| Yes | | No | | | Number of instalments being paid now | |

- Residential property — **F1** £
- Farms — **F2** £
- Business property — **F3** £
- Woodlands, trees or underwood — **F4** £
- Other land and buildings — **F5** £

	Interest in a business	Interest in a partnership	
Farming business	**F6.1** £	**F6.2** £	**F6** £

	Interest in a business	Interest in a partnership	
Other business interests	**F7.1** £	**F7.2** £	**F7** £

	Farm trade assets	Other business assets	
Business assets	**F8.1** £	**F8.2** £	**F8** £

- Quoted shares and securities *(control holding only)* — **F9** £

	Control holding	Non-control holding	
Unquoted shares	**F10.1** £	**F10.2** £	**F10** £

	Control holding	Non-control holding	
Traded unquoted shares	**F11.1** £	**F11.2** £	**F11** £

Total assets *(sum of boxes F1 to F11)* **F12** £

Liabilities, exemptions and reliefs

• Name of mortgagee	Property on which mortgage is secured	Amount outstanding £
		F13 £

- Other liabilities

F14 £

Net total of assets less liabilities *(box F12 less boxes F13 and F14)* **F15** £

- Exemptions and reliefs *(do not include any annual exemption)*

F16 £

Chargeable value of assets in the UK where tax may be paid by instalments *(box F15 less box F16)* **F17** £

- Annual exemption being deducted **F18** £

4

Ⓖ Summary of the chargeable event

If you wish to work out the tax yourself you should fill in form IHT100WS so that you can copy the figures to this section and to section H. *You do not have to work out the tax. If you do not wish to do so, leave this section and section H blank and go straight to section J.*
Guidance on how to fill in parts G and H are given on page 25 of the guide - "How to fill in form IHT100". The box number WSA1 etc, refer to the boxes in the worksheet from which the figures come.

Lifetime transfers (event forms IHT100a and IHT100b)

Previous transfers made by the transferor which need to be taken into account *(box WSA1)*	**G1** £
Threshold at date of transfer *(box TX2)*	**G2** £
Balance of threshold available *(box TX3)*	**G3** £

Assets where the tax may not be paid by instalments

• Assets in the UK *(box WSA2)*	**G4** £
• Foreign assets *(box WSA3)*	**G5** £
Value of assets where tax may not be paid by instalments *(box WSA4)*	**G6** £

Assets where the tax may be paid by instalments

• Assets in the UK *(box WSA5)*	**G7** £
• Foreign assets *(box WSA6)*	**G8** £
Total assets where tax may be paid by instalments *(box WSA7)*	**G9** £
Total value of transfer *(box WSA8)*	**G10** £
Annual exemption *(box WSA9)*	**G11** £
Chargeable transfer *(box WSA10)*	**G12** £

Go to box H1 on page 6 to work out the tax.

Non-interest in possession settlements (event forms IHT100c and IHT100d)

Assets where the tax may not be paid by instalments

• Assets in the UK *(box WSB1)*	**G13** £
• Foreign assets *(box WSB2)*	**G14** £
Value of assets where tax may not be paid by instalments *(box WSB3)*	**G15** £

Assets where the tax may be paid by instalments

• Assets in the UK *(box WSB4)*	**G16** £
• Foreign assets *(box WSB5)*	**G17** £
• Value of assets where tax may be paid by instalments *(box WSB6)*	**G18** £
• **Total value on which tax is chargeable** *(box WSB7)*	**G19** £

Go to box H7 on page 6 to work out the tax

5

31.5 Lifetime Transfers

Flat rate charge and Recapture charge (event forms IHT100e and IHT100f)

- Value of assets where tax may not be paid by instalments
  (flat rate charge box WSC3: recapture charge box WSD3) G20 £

- Value of assets where tax may be paid by instalments
  (flat rate charge box WSC6: recapture charge box WSD4) G21 £

- Total value of assets on which tax arises
  (flat rate charge box WSC7: recapture charge box WSD5) G22 £

Ⓗ Working out the tax

Lifetime transfers (event forms IHT100a and IHT100b)

- Value chargeable to tax *(box WSA10)* H1 £
- **Tax** *(box TX9)* H2 £
- Relief on successive charges *(box TX10)* H3 £
- Double taxation relief *(box TX11)* H4 £
- Tax previously paid on this transfer, if any *(box TX12)* H5 £
- **Tax due on this transfer** *(box TX13)* **Go to box H13** H6 £

Principal and proportionate charges (event forms IHT100c and IHT100d)

Value on which tax is chargeable *(box WSB7)* H7 £

Rate *(box R24)* H8 £

Tax *(principal charge box TX39 plus box TX46: proportionate charge box TX59 plus box TX67)* H9 £

Reduction against tax *(principal charge only box TX40 plus box TX47)* H10 £

Double taxation relief *(principal charge box TX42 plus box TX49: proportionate charge box TX60 plus box TX68)* H11 £

Tax payable on this transfer
(principal charge box TX43 plus box TX50: proportionate charge box TX61 plus box TX69) H12 £

Working out the tax that is payable on this account

• Lifetime transfers	• Principal charge	• Proportionate charge

- Tax which may not be paid by instalments
  (lifetime: box TX18, principal: box TX41, proportionate: box TX59) H13 £

- Successive charges relief *(lifetime: box TX19)* H14 £

- Double taxation relief
  (lifetime: box TX20, principal: box TX42, proportionate: box TX60) H15 £

- Tax previously paid, if any *(box TX21)* H16 £

- Interest *(lifetime: box TX23, principal: box TX44, proportionate: box TX62)* H17 £

Tax and interest which may not be paid by instalments
(lifetime: box TX24, principal: box TX45, proportionate: box TX63) H18 £

6

- Tax which may be paid by instalments
  (lifetime box TX29: principal box TX48: proportionate box TX67)

  H19 £ _____

- Successive charges relief *(lifetime box TX30)*

  H20 £ _____

- Double taxation relief
  (lifetime box TX31: principal box TX49: proportionate box TX68)

  H21 £ _____

- Tax previously paid *(lifetime box TX32)*

  H22 £ _____

- Number of instalments being paid now
  (lifetime box TX34: principal box TX51: proportionate box TX70)

  H23 _____ / 10

- Tax now payable
  (lifetime box TX35: principal box TX52: proportionate box TX71)

  H24 £ _____

- Interest on instalments to be added
  (lifetime box TX36: principal box TX53: proportionate box TX72)

  H25 £ _____

- **Tax and interest being paid now which may be paid by instalments**
  (lifetime box TX37: principal box TX54: proportionate box TX73)

  H26 £ _____

- **Total tax and interest payable on this account**
  (lifetime box TX38: principal box TX55: proportionate box TX74)

  H27 £ _____

Working out the tax   Flat rate charge (event form IHT100e)
Recapture charge (event form IHT100f)

- Tax which may not be paid by instalments
  (flat rate charge box TX75: recapture charge box TX104 or box TX117)

  H28 £ _____

- Double taxation relief on the tax which may not be paid by
  instalments *(flat rate charge box TX76)*

  H29 £ _____

- Tax not payable by instalments *(flat rate charge box TX77)*

  H30 £ _____

- Interest *(flat rate charge box TX78: recapture charge box TX105 or box TX118)*

  H31 £ _____

- **Tax which may not be paid by instalments and interest now
  payable** *(flat rate charge box TX79: recapture charge box TX106 or box TX119)*

  H32 £ _____

- Tax which may be paid by instalments
  (flat rate charge box TX80: recapture charge box TX110 or box TX120)

  H33 £ _____

- Double taxation relief on the tax which may be paid by instalments
  (flat rate charge box TX81)

  H34 £ _____

- Tax which may be paid by instalments
  (flat rate charge box TX82)

  H35 £ _____

- Number of instalments due *(flat rate charge box TX83: recapture charge
  box TX111 or box TX121)*

  H36 _____ / 10

- Tax now payable *(flat rate charge box TX84: recapture charge box TX112 or
  box TX122)*

  H37 £ _____

- Interest *(flat rate charge box TX85: recapture charge box TX113 or box TX123)*

  H38 £ _____

- **Tax which may be paid by instalments and interest now payable**
  (flat rate charge box TX86: recapture charge box TX114 or box TX124)

  H39 £ _____

- **Tax and interest now payable on this account**
  (flat rate charge box TX87: recapture charge box TX115 or box TX125)

  H40 £ _____

7

31.5 Lifetime Transfers

J **Authority for repayment of inheritance tax**

In the event of any inheritance tax being overpaid the payable order for the overpaid tax and interest in connection with this chargeable event estate should be made out to:

K **Declaration**

To the best of my/our knowledge and belief, the information I/we have given and the statements I/we have made in this account and in the event form

K1

and the supplementary pages

K2

attached (together called "this account") are correct and complete.

I/We understand that I/we may be liable to prosecution if I/we deliberately conceal any information that affects the liability to inheritance tax arising on the chargeable event OR if I/we deliberately include information in this account which I/we know to be false.

I/We understand that I/we may have to pay financial penalties if this account is incorrect by reason of my/our negligence or fraud OR if I/we fail to remedy anything in this account which is incorrect in any material respect within a reasonable time of it coming to my/our notice.

I/We understand that where we have elected to pay tax by instalments that I/we may have to pay interest on any unpaid tax according to the law.

Each person delivering this account whether as transferor, transferee or trustee, must sign below to indicate that they have read and agreed the statements above.

Full name and address	*Full name and address*
Signature *Date*	*Signature* *Date*
Capacity: Transferee, transferor, trustee, other(specify)	*Capacity: Transferee, transferor, trustee, other(specify)*
Delete the ones that do not apply	*Delete the ones that do not apply*
Full name and address	*Full name and address*
Signature *Date*	*Signature* *Date*
Capacity: Transferee, transferor, trustee, other(specify)	*Capacity: Transferee, transferor, trustee, other(specify)*
Delete the ones that do not apply	*Delete the ones that do not apply*

See notes. *Remember to fill in and return the correct event form.*

8

298

HM Revenue & Customs

Inheritance tax worksheet

Working out the taxable transfer and inheritance tax.

Section A: Use this section to work out the tax on lifetime transfers and the ending of interests in possession.

Section B: Use this section to work out the tax on principal and proportionate charges.

Section C: Use this section to work out the tax on a flat rate charge.

Section D: Use this section to work out the tax on a recapture charge.

A   Lifetime transfers (event forms IHT100a or IHT100b).

Other transfers of value to be taken into account to calculate the total tax.

Total value of lifetime transfers made during the 7 years ending on the date of this transfer to be taken into account.
(Take this figure from the following: IHT100a box 2.4 or IHT100b box 2.4).

WSA1 £
Copy to box G1 on IHT100

Assets where the tax may not be paid by instalments.

* Assets in the UK *(box E19 on form IHT100).*

WSA2 £
Copy to box G4 on IHT100

* Foreign assets *(box FP7 form D39).*

WSA3 £
Copy to box G5 on IHT100

* Total value of assets where the tax may not be paid by instalments *(box WSA2 plus box WSA3).*

WSA4 £
Copy to box G6 on IHT100

Assets where the tax may be paid by instalments.

* Assets in the UK *(box F17 form IHT100).*

WSA5 £
Copy to box G7 on IHT100

* Foreign assets *(box FP12 form D39).*

WSA6 £
Copy to box G8 on IHT100

* Total assets where the tax may be paid by instalments *(box WSA5 plus box WSA6).*

WSA7 £
Copy to box G9 on IHT100

* Total value of transfer *(box WSA4 plus box WSA7).*

WSA8 £
Copy to box G10 on IHT100

* Annual exemption *(box F18 IHT100).*

WSA9 £
Copy to box G11 on IHT100

* **Chargeable transfer** *(box WSA8 minus box WSA9).*

WSA10 £
Copy to box G12 on IHT100

IHT100 WS (Substitute)(LexisNexis Butterworths)

1

HMRC CT 12/05

31.5   Lifetime Transfers

- Annual exemption applicable to the property on which the tax may **not** be paid by instalments.

| £ | X | *(box WSA4)* | £ | = | WSA11 | £ |
| *(box WSA9)* | | *(box WSA8)* | £ | | | |

- Annual exemption applicable to the property on which the tax may be paid by instalments.

| £ | X | *(box WSA7)* | £ | = | WSA12 | £ |
| *(box WSA9)* | | *(box WSA8)* | £ | | | |

Working out the total tax that is payable.

- Other transfers of value to be taken into account *(box WSA1)*.

  TX1 £

- Threshold at the date of transfer *(box IHT100a 2.6 or IHT100b 2.6)*.

  TX2 £
  Copy to box G2 on IHT100

- Balance of tax threshold available *(box TX2 minus box TX1)*.
  If the result is a negative amount enter nil at box TX3.

  TX3 £
  Copy to box G3 on IHT100

- Amount chargeable to tax *(box WSA10)*.

  TX4 £

- Amount on which tax is payable *(box TX4 minus box TX3)*.

  TX5 £

Is the transferee paying the tax or does the transfer consist of the
ending of an interest in possession in settled property?

| Yes | *Copy the amount in box TX5 to box TX6.* | No | *Use the calculation below to work out the amount to write in box TX6.* |

Grossing-up *(For boxes TX6 and TX7 the rate of tax is 40% if the charge arose because of the transferor's death otherwise it is 20%).*

| (TX5) £ | X | 100 | or | 100 | | **TX6** £ |
| | | 100-40 | | 100-20 | | |

| Tax on TX6 | £ | @ 40% or 20% | **TX7** £ |

Taper relief. Taper relief is allowable on a transfer of value made more than
three years and not more than seven years before the date of the transferor's
death. *(If you wish to claim taper relief work out the relief using the table on page 16
copy the amount from TR2).*

  TX8 £

- Tax *(box TX7 minus box TX8)*.

  TX9 £
  Copy to box H2 on IHT100

- Relief on successive charges. *(Work out the relief using the calculation
  on page 17 and copy the result from box SC8).*

  TX10 £
  Copy to box H3 on IHT100

- Double taxation relief. *(Work out the relief using the calculation on page 17.
  Copy the lower of boxes DT2 and DT5 to this box).*

  TX11 £
  Copy to box H4 on IHT100

- Tax previously paid on this transfer (if any). *(From box 7.3 on form IHT100a
  or box 7.3 on form IHT100b).*

  TX12 £
  Copy to box H5 on IHT100

- **Tax due on this transfer** *(box TX9 minus box TX10, box TX11 and
  box TX12).*

  TX13 £
  Copy to box H6 on IHT100

2

Tax which may not be paid by instalments.

- Chargeable value of the assets on which tax may **not** be paid by instalments *(box WSA4 minus box WSA11).*

TX14 £

(Copy from box TX9) *(Copy from box TX14)*

Tax TX15 £ X TX16 £ = TX18 £
Copy to box H13 on IHT100

(Copy from box WSA10) TX17 £

- Successive charges relief attributable to the assets on which tax may **not** be paid by instalments. *(Work out the relief using the calculation on page 17. Copy the results from SC6 to this box).*

TX19 £
Copy to box H14 on IHT100

- Double taxation relief attributable to the property on which tax may not be paid by instalments. *(Work out the relief using the calculation on page 17 and the value of the foreign assets on which the tax may not be paid by instalments. Copy the lower of DT2 and DT5 to this box).*

TX20 £
Copy to box H15 on IHT100

- Tax previously paid on this transfer which may not be paid by instalments. *(From box 7.1 form IHT100a or box 7.1 form IHT100b).*

TX21 £
Copy to box H16 on IHT100

- **Tax which may not be paid by instalments** *(box TX18 minus box TX19, box TX20 and box TX21).*

TX22 £

- Interest - You may use the tables on page 15 to work out any interest due *(Copy the figure from box IT4).*

TX23 £
Copy to box H17 on IHT100

Tax which may not be paid by instalments and interest now being paid *(box TX22 plus box TX23).*

TX24 £
Copy to box H18 on IHT100

Tax which may be paid by instalments.

- Chargeable value of the property on which tax may be paid by instalments *(box WSA7 minus box WSA12).*

TX25 £

(Copy from box TX9) *(Copy from box TX25)*

Tax TX26 £ X TX27 £ = TX29 £
Copy to box H19 on IHT100

(Copy from box WSA10) TX28 £

- Successive charges relief attributable to the assets on which tax may be paid by instalments. *(Work out the relief using the calculation on page 17. Use the amounts that relate to assets on which the tax may not be paid by instalments. Copy the results from SC7 to this box).*

TX30 £
Copy to box H20 on IHT100

- Double taxation relief attributable to property on which tax may be paid by instalments. *(Work out the relief using the calculation on page 17 and the value of the foreign assets on which the tax may be paid by instalments. Copy the lower of DT2 and DT5 to this box).*

TX31 £
Copy to box H21 on IHT100

3

31.5   Lifetime Transfers

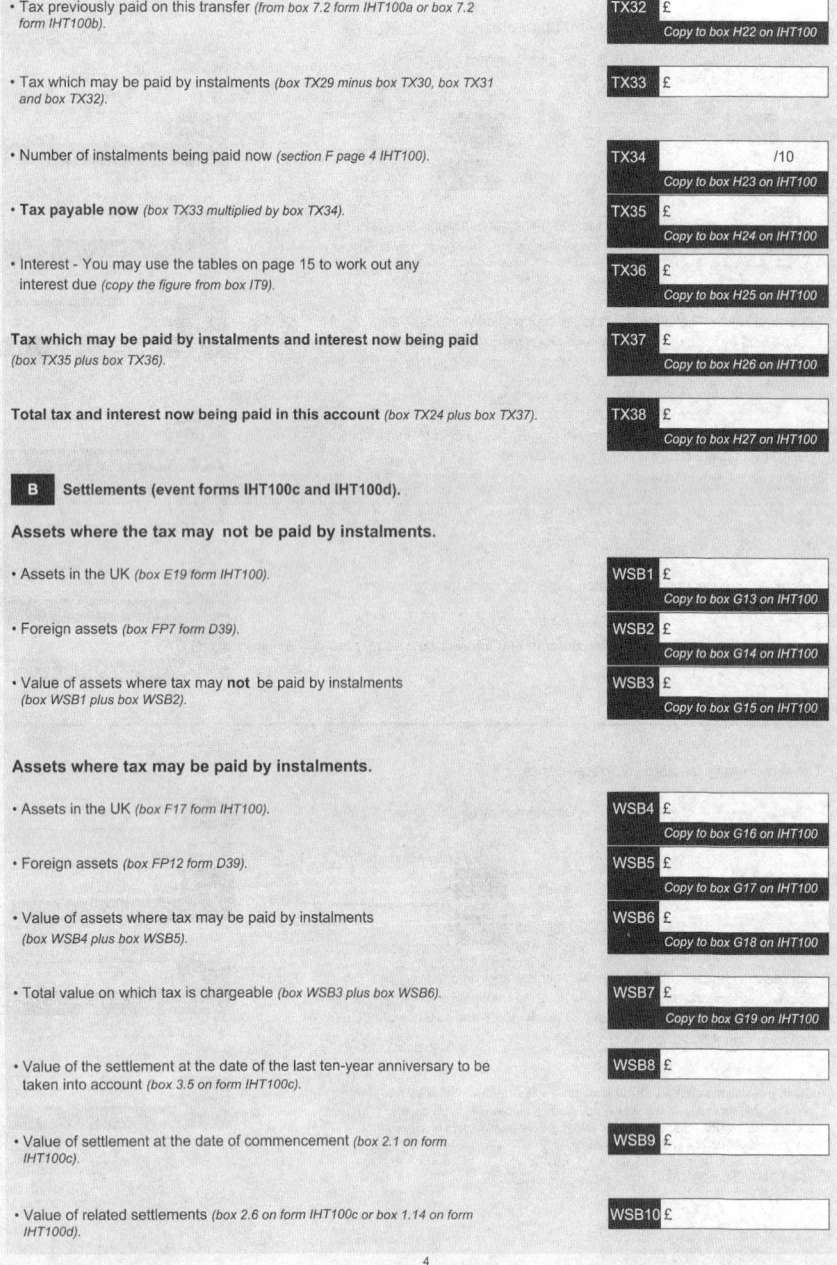

- Tax previously paid on this transfer *(from box 7.2 form IHT100a or box 7.2 form IHT100b).*

TX32 £
Copy to box H22 on IHT100

- Tax which may be paid by instalments *(box TX29 minus box TX30, box TX31 and box TX32).*

TX33 £

- Number of instalments being paid now *(section F page 4 IHT100).*

TX34 /10
Copy to box H23 on IHT100

- **Tax payable now** *(box TX33 multiplied by box TX34).*

TX35 £
Copy to box H24 on IHT100

- Interest - You may use the tables on page 15 to work out any interest due *(copy the figure from box IT9).*

TX36 £
Copy to box H25 on IHT100

Tax which may be paid by instalments and interest now being paid *(box TX35 plus box TX36).*

TX37 £
Copy to box H26 on IHT100

Total tax and interest now being paid in this account *(box TX24 plus box TX37).*

TX38 £
Copy to box H27 on IHT100

B   Settlements (event forms IHT100c and IHT100d).

Assets where the tax may not be paid by instalments.

- Assets in the UK *(box E19 form IHT100).*

WSB1 £
Copy to box G13 on IHT100

- Foreign assets *(box FP7 form D39).*

WSB2 £
Copy to box G14 on IHT100

- Value of assets where tax may **not** be paid by instalments *(box WSB1 plus box WSB2).*

WSB3 £
Copy to box G15 on IHT100

Assets where tax may be paid by instalments.

- Assets in the UK *(box F17 form IHT100).*

WSB4 £
Copy to box G16 on IHT100

- Foreign assets *(box FP12 form D39).*

WSB5 £
Copy to box G17 on IHT100

- Value of assets where tax may be paid by instalments *(box WSB4 plus box WSB5).*

WSB6 £
Copy to box G18 on IHT100

- Total value on which tax is chargeable *(box WSB3 plus box WSB6).*

WSB7 £
Copy to box G19 on IHT100

- Value of the settlement at the date of the last ten-year anniversary to be taken into account *(box 3.5 on form IHT100c).*

WSB8 £

- Value of settlement at the date of commencement *(box 2.1 on form IHT100c).*

WSB9 £

- Value of related settlements *(box 2.6 on form IHT100c or box 1.14 on form IHT100d).*

WSB10 £

4

- Value of non-relevant property *(box 1.12 on form IHT100d).*   WSB11 £

- Additions to the settlement *(box 2.3 or 3.7 form IHT100c).*   WSB12 £

- Value of assets which became relevant property since the last ten-year   WSB13 £
  anniversary *(box 3.9 column E on form IHT100c).*

- Aggregable previous chargeable transfers *(box 2.8 or 3.4 on form IHT100c or*   WSB14 £
  box 1.10 on form IHT100d).

- Value on which proportionate charges have arisen *(box 3.3 on form IHT100c*   WSB15 £
  or box 1.5 on form IHT100d).

Working out the rate.

Value of assumed chargeable transfer.   *Box R1, complete in respect of principal charge only.*

Value of relevant property *(box WSB7).*	R1	£
Value of the transfer at the last ten-year anniversary *(box WSB8).*	R2	£
Value of settlement at date of commencement *(box WSB9).*	R3	£
Value of related settlements *(box WSB10).*	R4	£
Value of non-relevant property *(box WSB11).*	R5	£
Value of additions *(box WSB12).*	R6	£
Value of the assets which became relevant property since the last ten-year anniversary *(box WSB13).*	R7	£
Total value of assumed chargeable transfer *(Sum of boxes R1 to R7).*	R8	£

Aggregate value of assumed previous chargeable transfers.

Previous cumulative total *(box WSB14).*	R9	£
Value on which proportionate charges have arisen *(box WSB15).*	R10	£

Total   *(box R9 plus box R10)*   R11 £

Aggregable chargeable transfers *(box R8 plus box R11)*   R12 £

Tax on the aggregable chargeable transfers *(box R12) =*

Tax on the first   R13 £   R14 £   0.00
(Write the inheritance tax threshold at the date of the chargeable event in box R13).

Tax on the balance   R15 £   @ 20%   R16 £
(box R12 minus box R13. If the result is a negative amount write '0' in box R15).

Total *(box R14 plus box R16).*   R17 £

Tax on the aggregate value of assumed previous transfers *(R11).*

Tax on the first   R18 £   R19 £   0.00
Write the inheritance tax threshold at date of the chargeable event in box R18).

Tax on the balance   R20 £   @ 20%   R21 £
(box R11 minus box R18. If the result is a negative amount write '0' in box R20).

5

31.5 Lifetime Transfers

Total tax on assumed previous transfers *(box R19 plus box R21).* R22 £

Total tax *(R17 minus R22).* R23 £

Effective rate = $\dfrac{(R23)}{(R8)}$ x 30 = R24 %

Copy to box H8 on IHT100

Calculating the tax.

To calculate the inheritance tax on a principal charge continue below from box TX39.
To calculate the inheritance tax on a proportionate charge go to page 8 and continue from box TX56.

Principal Charge (Ten-Year Anniversary).

Tax which may not be paid by instalments.

      (box WSB3)   *(box R24)*

• Tax on £   x   %   =   TX39 £

Reduction against tax which may **not** be paid by instalments.

If the relevant property included in box WSB3 was not relevant property during the whole of the ten years ending on this anniversary the tax at TX39 may be reduced for each successive complete quarter during which it was not relevant property. Use the table to calculate the reduction where applicable (see guidance notes IHT113 "How to fill in IHT100WS").

Value of relevant property at the ten-year anniversary. *(From question 1.3 form IHT100d).*		Rate % *(box R24).*		Complete quarters between the last ten-year anniversary and the date on which the asset last became relevant property.		40		Reduction in tax.
A		B		C		D		E
						40		
	x		x		÷	40	=	
						40		
						40		
						40		

Total reduction TX40 £

• Tax *(box TX39 minus box TX40).* TX41 £

Copy to box H13 on IHT100

Double taxation relief attributable to property on which tax may **not** be paid by instalments. *(Work out the relief using the calculation on page 17 and the value of the foreign assets on which the tax may be paid by instalments. Copy the lower of DT2 and DT5 to this box).* TX42 £

Copy to box H15 on IHT100

Tax which may not be paid by instalments *(box TX41minus box TX42).* TX43 £

• Interest - *You may use the tables on page 15 to calculate any interest due. (Copy the figure from box IT4).* TX44 £

Copy to box H17 on IHT100

6

304

Tax which may not be paid by instalments and interest now being paid
(box TX43 plus box TX44).

TX45 £

Copy to box H18 on IHT100

Tax which may be paid by instalments.

(box WSB6)   *(box R24)*

• Tax on £ _____ x _____ % = TX46 £

Reduction against the tax which may be paid by instalments.

If the relevant property included in box WSB6 which may be paid by instalments was not relevant property during the whole of the ten years ending on this anniversary the tax at TX46 may be reduced for each successive complete quarter during which it was not relevant property. Use the table to calculate the reduction where applicable (see guidance notes IHT113 "How to fill in IHT100WS").

Value of relevant property at the ten-year anniversary. (From question 1.3 form IHT100d).		Rate % (box R24).		Complete successive quarters between the last ten-year anniversary and the date on which the asset last became relevant property.		40		Reduction in tax.
A	x	B	x	C	÷	D	=	E
						40		
	x		x		÷	40	=	
						40		
						40		
						40		

Total reduction   TX47 £

• Tax *(box TX46 minus box TX47).*   TX48 £

Copy to box H19 on IHT100

• Double taxation relief attributable to assets on which the tax may be paid
by instalments. *(Work out the relief using the calculation on page 17 and the value of
the foreign assets on which the tax may be paid by instalments. Copy the lower of DT2
and DT5 to this box).*   TX49 £

Copy to box H21 on IHT100

• Tax which may be paid by instalments *(box TX48 minus box TX49).*   TX50 £

• Number of instalments being paid now *(section F page 4 form IHT100).*   TX51 /10

Copy to box H23 on IHT100

• Tax which may be paid by instalments payable now *(box TX50 x box TX51).*   TX52 £

Copy to box H24 on IHT100

• Interest - *You may use the tables on page 15 to calculate any
interest due. (Copy the figure from box IT9).*   TX53 £

Copy to box H25 on IHT100

Tax which may be paid by instalments and interest now being paid
(box TX52 plus box TX53).   TX54 £

Copy to box H26 on IHT100

Total tax and interest now being paid on this account
(box TX45 plus box TX54).   TX55 £

Copy to box H27 on IHT100

7

31.5   Lifetime Transfers

Calculating the tax.

Proportionate Charge.

Tax which may not be paid by instalments.

Value on which tax may not be paid by instalments *(box WSB3).* | TX56 | £ |

*The amount of tax depends on when the assets which are subject to this chargeable event became comprised in this settlement.
Use the table below to calculate the tax which may **not** be paid by instalments. (See notes on "How to fill in IHT100WS").*

Complete the following table for assets on which tax may **not** be paid by instalments.

*Line1. Enter the value of the assets comprised in this chargeable event that were relevant property at the date on which the
settlement commenced or the date of the last ten-year anniversary if later.*

Remaining lines. Write in the figures from box 2.11 or box 3.11 on form IHT100c.

Date on which the asset last became relevant property or the date of the last ten-year anniversary if later.	Value of the assets at the date of this chargeable event. £	X	Rate % *(box R24).*	X	Number of quarters between the date in column **A** and the date of this chargeable event.	÷	40	=	Tax. £
A	**B**		**C**		**D**		**E**		**F**
1							40		£
2							40		£
3							40		£
4		X		X		÷	40	=	£
5							40		£
6							40		£

Total * | £ | Total tax | TX57 | £ |

*This amount should be equal to the amount in box TX56.

Grossing. *If the tax is **not** being paid out of relevant property in this settlement copy the amount in box TX56 to box TX58
and the amount in box TX57 to box TX59.
If the tax is being paid out of relevant property in this settlement the value of the assets which cease to be relevant property
must be grossed-up to find the true value of the transfer. Go to the grossing calculation on pages 15 to 16 to work out the
revised value of the transfer and bring the figures back to boxes TX58 and TX59.*

Revised value on which tax may not be paid by instalments
(from box GC4 page 16). | TX58 | £ |

Revised tax which may not be paid by instalments *(from box GC6 page 16).* | TX59 | £ |
                                                    Copy to box H13 on IHT100

- Double taxation relief applicable to assets on which the tax may **not** be
  paid by instalments. *(Work out the relief using the calculation on page 17 and the
  value of the foreign assets on which the tax may not be paid by instalments. Copy the
  lower of DT2 and DT5 to this box).* | TX60 | £ |
                                        Copy to box H15 on IHT100

- **Tax which may not be paid by instalments** *(box TX59 minus box TX60).* | TX61 | £ |

- Interest - *You may use the tables on page 15 to calculate any
  interest due. (Copy the figure from box IT4).* | TX62 | £ |
                                                    Copy to box H17 on IHT100

8

306

Tax which may not be paid by instalments and interest now being paid
(box TX61plus box TX62).

TX63	£
	Copy to box H18 on IHT100

Tax which may be paid by instalments.

Value on which tax may be paid by instalments is chargeable *(box WSB6).*

TX64	£

Complete the following table for assets on which the tax may be paid by instalments.

Line 1. Enter the value of the assets that were relevant property at the date on which the settlement commenced or the date of the last ten-year anniversary if later.

Remaining lines. Write in the figures from box 2.11 or box 3.11 on form IHT100c.

Date on which the asset last became relevant property or the date of the last ten-year anniversary if later.	Value of the assets at the date of this chargeable event. £		Rate % (box R24).		Number of quarters between the date in column A and the date of this chargeable event.		40		Tax. £
A	B	X	C	X	D	÷	E	=	F
1							40		£
2							40		£
3							40		£
4			X		X		÷	40	=	£
5							40		£
6							40		£

Total *   £ _____   Total tax | TX65 | £ |

*This amount should be equal to the amount in box TX64.

Grossing. *If the tax is not being paid out of the relevant property in this settlement, copy the amount in box TX64 to box TX66 and the amount in box TX65 to box TX67.*
If the tax is being paid out of relevant property in this settlement the value of the assets which ceased to be relevant property must be grossed up to find the true value of the transfer. Go to the grossing calculation on pages 15 to 16 to work out the revised value of the transfer and the tax and bring the figures back to boxes TX66 and TX67.

Revised value on which tax may be paid by instalments *(from box GC5).*

TX66	£

Revised tax which may be paid by instalments *(from box GC7).*

TX67	£
	Copy to box H19 on IHT100

- Double taxation relief applicable to assets on which the tax may be paid by instalments. *(Work out the relief using the calculation on page 17 and the amounts relating to assets on which the tax may be paid by instalments. Copy the lower of DT2 and DT5 to this box).*

TX68	£
	Copy to box H21 on IHT100

- **Tax which may be paid by instalments**
  (box TX67 minus box TX68).

TX69	£

- Number of instalments being paid now *(section F page 4 IHT100).*

TX70	/10
	Copy to box H23 on IHT100

- Tax which may be paid by instalments payable now *(box TX69 x box TX70).*

TX71	£
	Copy to box H24 on IHT100

9

31.5   Lifetime Transfers

- Interest - *You may use the tables on page 15 to calculate any interest due. (Copy the figure from box IT9).*

TX72 | *Copy to box H25 on IHT100*

Tax which may be paid by instalments and interest now being paid *(box TX71 plus box TX72).*

TX73 | *Copy to box H26 on IHT100*

Total tax and interest now being paid on this account *(box TX63 plus box TX73).*

TX74 | *Copy to box H27 on IHT100*

C   Flat Rate Charge.

Assets on which tax may not be paid by instalments.

- Assets in the UK *(box E19 IHT100).*

WSC1

- Foreign assets *(box FP7 form D39).*

WSC2

- Value on which tax may not be paid by instalments *(box WSC1 plus box WSC2).*

WSC3 | *Copy to box G20 on IHT100*

Assets on which the tax may be paid by instalments.

- Assets in the UK *(box F17 form IHT100).*

WSC4

- Foreign assets *(box FP12 form D39).*

WSC5

- Value on which tax may be paid by instalments *(box WSC4 plus box WSC5).*

WSC6 | *Copy to box G21 on IHT100*

- Assets on which the charge arises *(WSC3 plus WSC6).*

WSC7 | *Copy to box G22 on IHT100*

Calculating the tax.

Tax which may not be paid by instalments.
(Copy the information from box 1.6 on from IHT100e).

Use the table below to work out the tax which may not be paid by instalments.
To work out the tax to put in column D use the table R25 on page 12 below.

No.	Date asset last became subject to special trusts.	Value of assets at the date of this chargeable event. £	Number of complete quarters between the date in column **A** and the chargeable event.	Tax *(see table R25).* £
	A	B	C	D
1				
2				
3				
4				
5				
6				

Total value* £   Total tax   TX75 £ | *Copy to box H28 on IHT100*

* This amount should equal the amount in box WSC3.

- Double taxation relief attributable to the assets on which tax may not be paid by instalments. *(Work out the relief using the calculation on page 17 and the amounts relating to assets on which the tax may not be paid by instalments. Copy the lower of DT2 and DT5 to this box).*

  TX76 £

  Copy to box H29 on IHT100

- Tax which may not be paid by instalments *(box TX75 minus box TX76).*

  TX77 £

  Copy to box H30 on IHT100

Interest - You may use the tables on page 15 to calculate any interest due *(copy the figure from box IT4).*

TX78 £

Copy to box H31 on IHT100

Tax which may not be paid by instalments and interest now payable *(box TX77 plus box TX78).*

TX79 £

Copy to box H32 on IHT100

Tax which may be paid by instalments.
(Copy the information from box 1.6 on form IHT100e).

Use the table below to work out the tax which may be paid by instalments.
To work out the tax to put in column D use the table R25 on page 12 below.

No.	Date asset last became subject to special trusts.	Value of assets at the date of this chargeable event. £	Number of complete quarters between the date in column **A** and the chargeable event.	Tax *(see table R25).* £
	A	B	C	D
1				
2				
3				
4				
5				
6				

Total value* £   Total tax   TX80 £

Copy to box H33 on IHT100

* *This amount shound equal the amount in box WSC6.*

- Double taxation relief attributable to assets on which the tax may be paid by instalments. *(Work out the relief using the calculation on page 17 and the amounts relating to assets on which the tax may be paid by instalments. Copy the lower of DT2 and DT5 to this box).*

  TX81 £

  Copy to box H34 on IHT100

- Tax which may be paid by instalments *(box TX80 minus box TX81).*

  TX82 £

  Copy to box H35 on IHT100

- Number of instalments being paid now *(section F page 4 IHT100).*

  TX83   /10

  Copy to box H36 on IHT100

- Tax which may be paid by instalments payable now *(box TX82 x box TX83).*

  TX84 £

  Copy to box H37 on IHT100

- Interest - *You may use the tables on page 15 to calculate any interest due. (Copy the figure from box IT9).*

  TX85 £

  Copy to box H38 on IHT100

- **Tax which may be paid by instalments and interest now payable** *(box TX84 plus box TX85).*

  TX86 £

  Copy to box H39 on IHT100

Total tax and interest now being paid on this account *(box TX79 plus box TX86).*

TX87 £

Copy to box H40 on IHT100

11

31.5   Lifetime Transfers

Copy the result back to column "D" on the table at TX75 or TX80 on page 10 or 11 above.

Tax payable   Table R25

Use this table to work out the tax on each asset or group of assets that last became held on special trusts on the same date. If more than one asset or more than one group of assets is listed on the tables at TX75 or TX80 separate calculations will be needed for each asset or group of assets.

No.	Capital value (from col B). £	X	Number of quarters (from col C).	X	Rate.	=	Tax. £
	A		B		C		D
1			1- 40		0.25%		
2			41- 80		0.20%		
3			81-120		0.15%		
4			121-160		0.10%		
5			161-200		0.05%		

Total   **R25** £

Copy the result back to column "D" on the table at TX75 or TX80 on page 10 or 11 above.

D   Recapture Charges.

Calculating the tax.

Previous cumulative total to be taken into account *(box 5.3 form IHT100f).*

WSD1 £

Value of the transferors/settlors estate at the date of death for inheritance tax purposes *(box 5.1 form IHT100f).*

WSD2 £

Assets on which the tax may **not** be paid by instalments *(box E19 form IHT100).*

WSD3 £

Copy to box G20 on IHT100

Assets on which the tax may be paid by instalments *(box F17 form IHT100).*

WSD4 £

Copy to box G21 on IHT100

Value on which tax is now chargeable *(box WSD3 plus box WSD4).*

WSD5 £

Copy to box G22 on IHT100

Tax threshold *(box 5.4 form IHT100f).*

WSD6 £

Calculation of tax 1.

Use this calculation unless the asset was relevant property in a discretionary trust between the date on which it became conditionally exempt and the date of this chargeable event.

Previous lifetime transfers *(box WSD1).*

TX88 £

Value of the transferors/settlors estate at the date of death for inheritance tax purposes *(box WSD2).*

TX89 £

Total *(box TX88 plus box TX89).*

TX90 £

Threshold at the date of the chargeable event *(box WSD6).*

TX91 £

Balance of the threshold available *(box TX91 minus box TX90. If box TX91 minus box TX90 is a negative amount write "0" in this box).*

TX92 £

Amount on which tax is now chargeable *(box WSD5).*

TX93 £

Value on which tax is payable *(box TX93 minus box TX92).*

TX94 £

Rate of tax *(20% or 40%. Use the flowchart R26 on page 18 to find out the rate to use).*

TX95 [ ] %

Tax *(box TX94 X box TX95).*

TX96 £ [ ]

Proportion of tax charged *(30%, 40%, 100%. Use the flowchart R26 on page18 to find out the proportion to use).*

TX97 [ ] %

Tax = *(box TX96 X box TX97).*

TX98 £ [ ]

Tax previously paid *(disposals of timber or underwood from box 4.1 form IHT100f).*

TX99 £ [ ]

Tax on this chargeable event *(box TX98 minus box TX99).*

TX100 £ [ ]

Tax which may not be paid by instalments.

(Copy from box TX100)   *(Copy from box WSD3)*

TX101 £ [ ]   X   TX102 £ [ ]   =   TX104 £ [ ]
                                         Copy to box H28 on IHT100

TX103 £ [ ]

(Copy from box WSD5)

Interest - *You may use the tables on page 15 to calculate any interest due. (Copy the figure from IT4).*

TX105 £ [ ]
Copy to box H31 on IHT100

Tax which may not be paid by instalments and interest now payable *(box TX104 plus box TX105).*

TX106 £ [ ]
Copy to box H32 on IHT100

Tax which may be paid by instalments

(Copy from box TX100)   *(Copy from box WSD4)*

TX107 £ [ ]   X   TX108 £ [ ]   =   TX110 £ [ ]
                                         Copy to box H33 on IHT100

TX109 £ [ ]

(Copy from box WSD5)

Number of instalments being paid now *(section F page 4 IHT100).*

TX111 [ ] /10
Copy to box H36 on IHT100

Tax which may be paid by instalments payable now *(box TX110 box TX111).*

TX112 £ [ ]
Copy to box H37 on IHT100

Interest - *You may use the tables on page 15 to calculate any interest due. (Copy the figure from IT9).*

TX113 £ [ ]
Copy to box H38 on IHT100

Tax which may be paid by instalments and interest now payable *(box TX112 plus box TX113).*

TX114 £ [ ]
Copy to box H39 on IHT100

Tax and interest now payable *(box TX106 plus box TX114).*

TX115 £ [ ]
Copy to box H40 on IHT100

Calculation 2. Use this calculation if the asset became conditionally exempt when held in a discretionary trust and at that time it was and since then continued to be relevant property.

Value of assets on which the tax may not be paid by instalments *(box WSD3).*

TX116 £ [ ]

13

31.5 Lifetime Transfers

Use the table below to work out the tax which may not be paid by instalments.
To work out the tax to put in column D use the table R25 on page 12 above.
Take the information from box 5.5 form IHT100f.

No.	Date on which settlement commenced or of last ten-year anniversary before asset became settled property if later.	Value of asset at the date of the chargeable event. £	Number of complete quarters between the date in column A and the chargeable event.	Tax (See table R25). £
	A	B	C	D
1				
2				
3				
4				
5				
6				

Total value £   Total tax   **TX117** £
Copy to box H28 on IHT100

Interest - *You may use the tables on page 15 to work out any interest due. (Copy the figure from box IT4).*   **TX118** £
Copy to box H31 on IHT100

Tax which may not be paid by instalments and interest now due *(box TX117 plus box TX118).*   **TX119** £
Copy to box H32 on IHT100

Use the table below to work out the tax which may be paid by instalments.
To work out the tax to put in column D use the table R25 on page 12 above.
Take the information from box 5.5 form IHT100f.

No.	Date on which settlement commenced or of last ten-year anniversary before asset became settled property if later.	Value of asset at the date of the chargeable event. £	Number of complete quarters between the date in column A and the chargeable event.	Tax (See table R25). £
	A	B	C	D
1				
2				
3				
4				
5				
6				

Total value £   Total tax   **TX120** £
Copy to box H33 on IHT100

Number of instalments being paid.   **TX121**   /10
Copy to box H36 on IHT100

Tax now payable *(box TX120 x box TX121).*   **TX122** £
Copy to box H37on IHT100

Interest - *You may use the tables on page 15 to work out any interest due. (Copy the figure from box IT9).*   **TX123** £
Copy to box H38 on IHT100

Tax and interest that may be paid by instalments payable now *(box TX122 plus box TX123).*   **TX124** £
Copy to box H39 on IHT100

Total tax and interest payable now *(box TX119 plus box TX124).*   **TX125** £
Copy to box H40 on IHT100

Working out the interest.

Assets on which the tax may not be paid by instalments.

Date interest starts. **IT1** /   /

Date interest ends. **IT2** /   /

IT3	Start and end dates for interest.	No of days.	Daily rate.*	Interest payable.

*(Page 33 IHT113,
"How to fill in IHT100WS").*

Total **IT4** £

Assets where the tax may be paid by instalments.

IT5	Start and end dates for interest.	No of days.	Daily rate.*	Interest payable.

Total **IT6** £

Additional interest.

IT7	Start and end dates for interest.	No of days.	Daily rate.*	Interest payable.

Total **IT8** £

• **Total interest** *(IT6 plus IT8).* **IT9** £

Grossing.

If the tax is being paid out of the relevant property in this settlement, the amounts shown in column F of the tables at TX57 and TX65 must be grossed up to take account of the tax being paid.

Because the rate of tax is different for each of the assets or groups of assets shown in the tables, separate calculations must be done for each.

Use the formula below to gross the value transferred and work out the revised tax.

Box TX57/65 (column F)
─────────────────────   X 100 =   **GC1** £
Box TX57/65 (column B)

Box TX57/65 (column B)
─────────────────────   X 100 =   **GC2** £
100 - Box GC1

Revised tax payable *(box GC2)* £   X *(box GC1)*   % = **GC3** £

15

31.5   Lifetime Transfers

• Repeat the calculation for each entry in rows 1-6 in the tables at boxes TX57 and TX65.

• Add up the grossed-up values (taken from box GC2) on which tax may not be paid by instalments. (You may use the table below) and copy the total back to box TX58.

• Add up the grossed-up values (taken from box GC2) on which tax may be paid by instalments and copy the total back to box TX66.

• Add up the tax which may not be paid by instalments taking the results from box GC3 and copy the total back to box TX59.

• Add up the tax which may be paid by instalments taking the results from box GC3 and copy the total back to box TX67.

Calculation   Total

Revised value on which tax may not be paid by instalments.	1	2	3	4	5	6	GC4 £ _Copy to box TX58_

Revised value on which tax may be paid by instalments.	1	2	3	4	5	6	GC5 £ _Copy to box TX66_

Revised tax which may not be paid by instalments.	1	2	3	4	5	6	GC6 £ _Copy to box TX59_

Revised tax which may be paid by instalments.	1	2	3	4	5	6	GC7 £ _Copy to box TX67_

Taper relief

Use the table below to work out the taper relief.

Tax.	Time of transfer before the date of death.	Rate of relief.	Amount.
TR1			TR2
	Not more than three years	Nil	
	More than 3 but not more than 4 years	20%	
	More than 4 but not more than 5 years	40%	
	More than 5 but not more than 6 years	60%	
	More than 6 but not more than 7 years	80%	
	More than 7 years	Nil	

Take the figure for TR1 from box TX7.

16

314

Working out successive charges relief.

First transfer.

Net Value of first transfer for inheritance tax *(box 5.2 form IHT100a or 5.2 form IHT100b).*

SC1 £ [   ]

Inheritance tax paid on the first transfer *(box 5.3 form IHT100a or box 5.3 form IHT100b).*

SC2 £ [   ]

Assets in the first transfer included in this transfer

Assets on which tax may not be paid by instalments *(box 5.4 form IHT100a or box 5.4 form IHT100b).*

SC3 £ [   ]

Assets on which tax may be paid by instalments *(box 5.5 form IHT100a or box 5.5 form IHT100b).*

SC4 £ [   ]

Rate of relief *(box 5.6 form IHT100a or box 5.6 form IHT100b).*

SC5 [   ] %

Relief on assets on which tax may not be paid by instalments

$$\frac{\text{SC2 } £ \rule{2cm}{0.4pt}}{\text{SC1 } £}\quad X\quad \text{SC3 } £ \quad \text{SC5 } \% \quad = \quad \text{SC6 } £$$

Relief on assets on which tax may be paid by instalments

$$\frac{\text{SC2 } £ \rule{2cm}{0.4pt}}{\text{SC1 } £}\quad X\quad \text{SC4 } £ \quad \text{SC5 } \% \quad = \quad \text{SC7 } £$$

Total relief *(SC6 plus SC7).*   **SC8** £ [   ]

Working out double taxation relief.

Value of the foreign property included in form D39 on which foreign tax has been paid (in sterling).

DT1 £ [   ]

Foreign tax paid on the assets included in DT1 (in sterling).

DT2 £ [   ]

Formula for relief.

Tax on this transfer   *Value of foreign property*

$$\frac{\text{DT3 } £ \rule{2cm}{0.4pt}}{\text{DT4 } £}\quad X\quad \text{DT1 } £ \quad = \quad \text{DT5 } £$$

Value of this transfer

The relief is the **lower** of boxes DT2 and DT5.

17

31.5   Lifetime Transfers

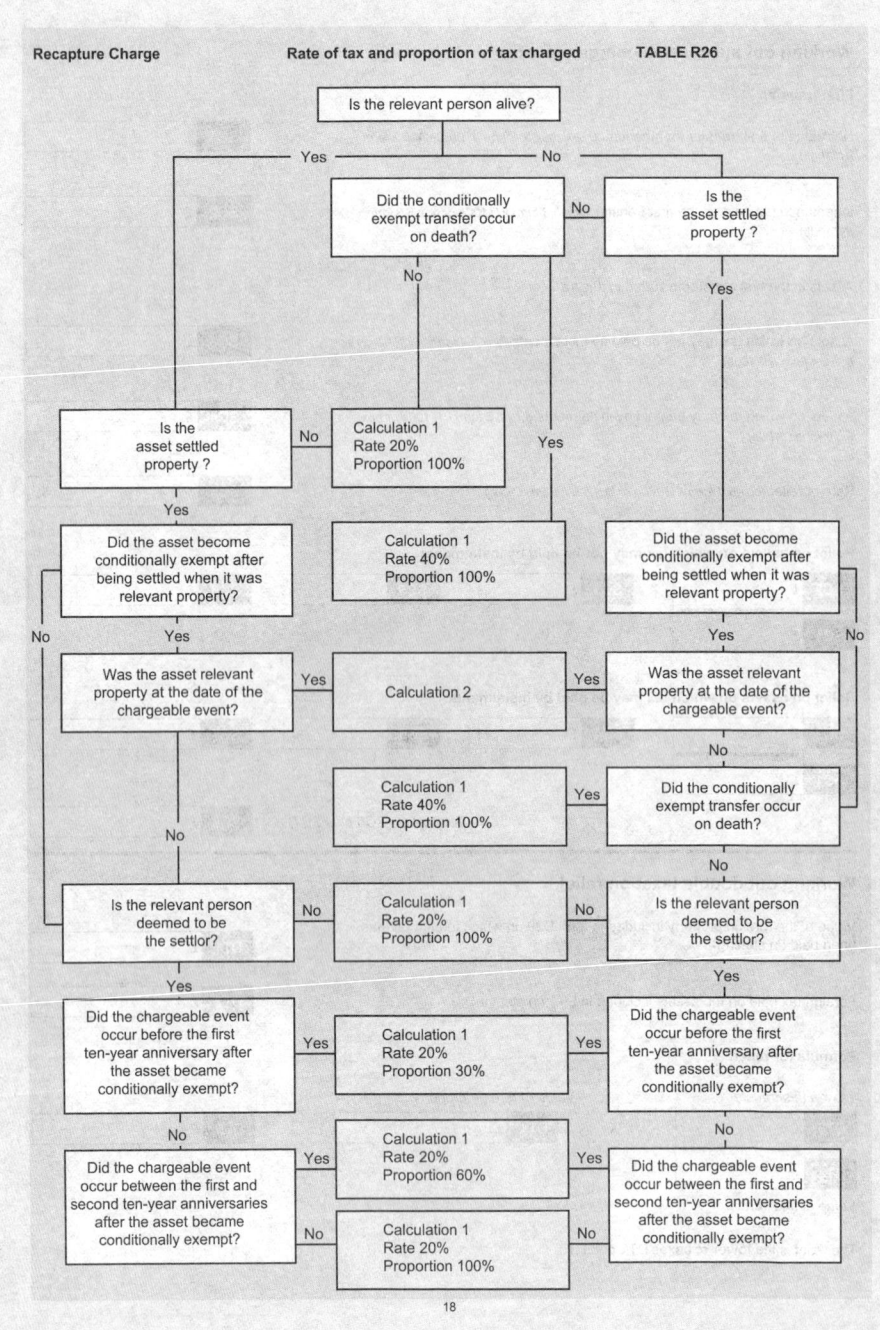

Recapture Charge   Rate of tax and proportion of tax charged   TABLE R26

Is the relevant person alive?

— Yes ——————— No ——

Did the conditionally exempt transfer occur on death? — No — Is the asset settled property?

No

Yes

Is the asset settled property? — No — Calculation 1 Rate 20% Proportion 100% — Yes

Yes

Did the asset become conditionally exempt after being settled when it was relevant property? | Calculation 1 Rate 40% Proportion 100% | Did the asset become conditionally exempt after being settled when it was relevant property?

No   No

Yes   Yes

Was the asset relevant property at the date of the chargeable event? — Yes — Calculation 2 — Yes — Was the asset relevant property at the date of the chargeable event?

No

Calculation 1 Rate 40% Proportion 100% — Yes — Did the conditionally exempt transfer occur on death?

No   No

Is the relevant person deemed to be the settlor? — No — Calculation 1 Rate 20% Proportion 100% — No — Is the relevant person deemed to be the settlor?

Yes   Yes

Did the chargeable event occur before the first ten-year anniversary after the asset became conditionally exempt? — Yes — Calculation 1 Rate 20% Proportion 30% — Yes — Did the chargeable event occur before the first ten-year anniversary after the asset became conditionally exempt?

No   Calculation 1 Rate 20% Proportion 60%   No

Did the chargeable event occur between the first and second ten-year anniversaries after the asset became conditionally exempt? — Yes — | Calculation 1 Rate 20% Proportion 100% | — Yes — Did the chargeable event occur between the first and second ten-year anniversaries after the asset became conditionally exempt?

No   No

18

316

32   Mutual Transfers

Simon's Direct Tax Service, part I3.502.

Other Sources. Foster, part C5.13.

32.1   **RELIEF**

Without specific relief, a double charge to tax could arise where a donor makes a gift to a donee who subsequently makes a gift back to the donor. Relief from double charge is provided for in three specified cases.

(*a*)   Where property given by a potentially exempt transfer is subsequently returned (otherwise than for full consideration) by the donee to the transferor and, as a result of the transferor's death, both that property and the potentially exempt transfer become chargeable to tax. See 32.2 below.

(*b*)   Where property given by a transfer of value which is chargeable when made is returned (otherwise than for full consideration) by the donee to the transferor and that property is also chargeable as part of the transferor's estate on his death. See 32.3 below.

(*c*)   Where a transfer of value is or subsequently becomes a chargeable transfer and, at the transferor's death, his estate owes to the transferee a debt which under the rules relating to such liabilities falls to be abated or disallowed in determining the value of the estate chargeable on the death. See 50.3 TRANSFERS ON DEATH.

32.2   **POTENTIALLY EXEMPT TRANSFERS AND DEATH**

Relief from double charge to tax is given where, after 17 March 1986, an individual ('the deceased') makes a transfer of value to a person ('the transferee') which is a potentially exempt transfer that proves to be a chargeable transfer and where immediately before his death the deceased was beneficially entitled to property

(*a*)   which he acquired from the transferee otherwise than for full consideration in money or money's worth after making the potentially exempt transfer; *and*

(*b*)   which was transferred to the transferee by the potentially exempt transfer or which is property directly or indirectly representing that property; *and*

(*c*)   value attributable to which is a chargeable part of his estate on death.

Where the above conditions are fulfilled, there must be separately calculated the total tax chargeable as a consequence of the death of the deceased

(i)   disregarding so much of the value transferred by the potentially exempt transfer as is attributable to the value of property within (*c*) above which is included in the chargeable transfer on death; and

(ii)   disregarding so much of the value of the property within (*c*) above which is included in the chargeable transfer on death as is attributable to property value of which is transferred by the potentially exempt transfer.

If charging the relevant property as part of the death estate under (i) above produces a higher amount of tax than would be payable if the charge on the potentially exempt transfer under (ii) was taken instead, the value transferred by the potentially exempt transfer is reduced by reference to the amount of the value of that property which is included in the chargeable transfer on death. Conversely, the potentially exempt transfer is charged if it produces the higher amount of tax with a corresponding reduction in the value of that property which is included in the chargeable estate on death. Where the

32.2 Mutual Transfers

amount calculated under (i) above is higher, to avoid the value of the same property entering twice into the tax calculations, this reduction applies for all IHT purposes.

Where the total tax chargeable under (i) and (ii) above is identical, calculation (i) is treated as producing a higher amount. [*FA 1986, s 104(1)(a); SI 1987/1130, Regs 4, 8*].

Example

A makes a potentially exempt transfer of £60,000 (annual exemptions having been used) to B in July 2001. In March 2003 A makes a gift of £261,000 (after annual exemptions) into a discretionary trust and the trustees pay IHT of £2,200. He makes a further gift of £55,000 (before annual exemption for the year) to the same trust in August 2003, the trustees paying IHT of £10,400.

B dies in January 2004 and the 2001 potentially exempt transfer returns to A. A dies in May 2007. His death estate of £310,000 includes the 2001 potentially exempt transfer, returned to him in 2003, which at the time of A's death is worth £216,000. It is assumed for the purposes of this computation that tax rates and bands remain as those pertaining from 6 April 2007.

First calculation: charge the returned potentially exempt transfer in A's death estate and ignore the potentially exempt transfer made in 2001

IHT payable

£

July 2001

Potentially exempt transfer £60,000 ignored — —

March 2003

Gift £261,000

Tax £NIL less £2,200 already paid (see note) —

August 2003

Gift £52,000 as top slice of £313,000

Tax £5,200 less £10,400 already paid —

May 2007

Death estate £310,000 as top slice of £626,000   124,000

Total tax due as a result of A's death   £124,000

Second calculation: charge the potentially exempt transfer made in 2001 and ignore the value of the returned potentially exempt transfer in A's death estate

318

IHT payable
£

July 2001
Potentially exempt transfer £60,000
Tax £NIL   —

March 2003
Gift £261,000 as top slice of £321,000
Tax £8,400 less £2,200 already paid   6,200

August 2003
Gift £52,000 as top slice of £373,000
Tax £20,800 less £10,400 already paid   10,400

May 2007
Death estate £94,000 as top slice of £467,000   37,600

Total tax due as a result of A's death   £54,200

The first calculation gives the higher amount of tax. The potentially exempt transfer made in 2001 will be ignored, and tax on other transfers will be as in the first calculation.

Note. In the first calculation, the tax of £124,000 on death does not allow for any QUICK SUCCESSION RELIEF (40) that might be due by reference to any tax charged in connection with B's death. Such relief could reduce the tax given by the first calculation. Credit for the tax already paid on the March 2003 and August 2003 gifts is restricted to the lower of the tax already paid and the tax payable as a result of death i.e. Nil. There is no repayment of the excess.

32.3   **CHARGEABLE TRANSFERS AND DEATH**

Relief from double charge to tax is given where, after 17 March 1986 and within seven years before his death, an individual ('the deceased') makes a transfer of value to a person ('the transferee') which is a chargeable transfer and where immediately before his death the deceased was beneficially entitled to property

(*a*)   which he acquired from the transferee otherwise than for full consideration in money or money's worth after making the chargeable transfer; *and*

(*b*)   which was transferred to the transferee by the chargeable transfer or which is property directly or indirectly representing that property; *and*

(*c*)   value attributable to which is a chargeable part of his estate on death.

Where the above conditions are fulfilled, there must be separately calculated the total tax chargeable as a consequence of the death of the deceased

(i)   disregarding so much of the value transferred by the lifetime chargeable transfer as is attributable to the value of property within (*c*) above which is included in the chargeable transfer on death; *and*

(ii)   disregarding so much of the value of the property within (*c*) above which is included in the chargeable transfer on death as is attributable to property, value of which is transferred by the lifetime chargeable transfer.

If charging the relevant property as part of the death estate under (i) above produces a higher amount of tax than would be payable if the charge on the lifetime chargeable transfer under (ii) was taken instead, the value transferred by the lifetime chargeable transfer is reduced by reference to the amount of the value of that property which is included in the chargeable transfer on death. Conversely, the lifetime chargeable transfer is charged if it produces the higher amount of tax with a corresponding reduction in the value of that property which is included in the chargeable estate on death.

Where the higher amount is calculated under (i) above

(A)   credit is available for tax already paid on the lifetime chargeable transfer which is attributable to the value disregarded under that calculation (but not exceeding the amount of tax due on death attributable to the value of the property in question); and

(B)   to avoid the value of the same property entering twice into the tax calculations, the reduction applies for all IHT purposes other than a ten-year anniversary charge or a proportionate charge to tax on a discretionary settlement arising before the death of the deceased.

Where the total tax chargeable under (i) and (ii) above is identical, calculation (i) is treated as producing the higher amount. [*FA 1986, s 104(1)(d); SI 1987/1130, Regs 7, 8*].

The pre-owned assets regulations relating to income tax now include provisions to avoid a double charge to IHT where a chargeable person elects that the gift with reservation provisions apply to the relevant property. [*FA 1986, s 104(1); Charge to Income Tax by Reference to Enjoyment of Property Previously Owned Regulations 2005, SI 2005/724, Reg 6; Inheritance Tax (Double Charges Relief) Regulations 2005, SI 2005/3441, Reg 3*]. A double charge can arise where the chargeable person makes a gift of property or a debt that is a potentially exempt transfer for IHT purposes. If that same property is then liable to the income tax charge the person may decide to make an election on Form IHT500 that the property is subject to the IHT reservation of benefits rules. See 59.42 WORKING CASE STUDY. If that person then dies within seven years of the original gift a double charge to IHT may arise, firstly, by reason of the original transfer and secondly when the property is added back into the death estate for the purposes of the gift with reservation rules. The new provision avoids the double charge by opting for the IHT on transfer that produces the highest overall amount of IHT and thereby reduces the other transfer to nil.

Relief is given where a double charge to IHT arises in situations where arrangements are caught by the pre-owned assets income tax provisions in *FA 2004, Sch 15* which are subsequently dismantled by the individual but he/she dies within seven years. The conditions for double charge relief in these circumstances are as follows:

(*a*)   the disposal condition or the contribution condition (see 59.41 WORKING CASE STUDY) is met as respects the relevant property; and

(*b*)   the deceased makes a transfer the result of which a third party becomes entitled to the benefit of a debt owed to the deceased; and

(*c*)   before the deceased's death, any outstanding part of the debt is wholly written off, waived or released, and the write off, waiver or release is made otherwise than for full consideration in money or money's worth;

(*d*)   further conditions apply so that

(i)   the deceased dies on or after 6 April 2005; and

(ii)   on the deceased's death, the transfer of value treated as made immediately before the deceased's death included the relevant property, or any property representing that relevant property; and

(iii)   as a result of the deceased's death, the transfer of value referred to in (*b*) above has become a chargeable transfer.

See http://www.hmrc.gov.uk/poa/poa_guidance4.htm#9 for HMRC examples of how the double charge relief works in practice. [*Inheritance Tax (Double Charges Relief) Regulations 2005, SI 2005/3441*].

33   National Heritage

Cross-references. See 2.6 ACCOUNTS AND RETURNS for rendering an account on ending of conditional exemption; 21.5 EXEMPT TRANSFERS for gifts for national purposes; 21.7 EXEMPT TRANSFERS for gifts for public benefit; 59 WORKING CASE STUDY.

Simon's Direct Tax Service, part I7.5.

Other Sources. VOA IHT manual, section 1; CTO Leaflet IHT 16; Foster, part G; IR Leaflet IR 88; IR67 (this is now out of print but the contents can be obtained in Word file format from the Heritage section of HMRC Capital Taxes).

33.1   GENERAL

On certain conditions, transfers of national heritage property can be exempted from inheritance tax. The Acceptance in Lieu Report 2005/06 details the works of art and heritage items offered to the Acceptance in Lieu Scheme in the year ending 31 March 2006. For that year, 38 items valued at approximately £25 million were accepted under the scheme and are now available for public benefit under the schemes rules. In March 2005, following the Goodison Report, the Museum, Libraries and Archive's Acceptance in Lieu Panel which advises on items that are acceptable in lieu of tax was given more power under the Contracting Out Order 2005 to act on behalf of the Secretary of State of the Department for Culture, Media and Sport (or the appropriate Minister outside England) to approve offers under *IHTA 1984, s 230* and allocation under the *National Heritage Act 1980, s 9*. See also http://www.mla.gov.uk/resources/assets//A/ail_report2006_10062.pdf.

National heritage property may also be given or sold by private treaty without tax liability to specified national bodies or may be transferred to individuals or settlements with conditional exemption. The detailed provisions are stated below.

33.2   NATIONAL HERITAGE PROPERTY

The following types of property are within the term 'national heritage property' provided they are so designated by the Board.

(*a*)   Any

(i)   picture, print, book, manuscript, work of art or scientific object, or any other thing not yielding income, which appears to the Board to be pre-eminent for its national, scientific, historic or artistic interest (introduced by *FA 1965*);

(ii)   any collections or groups of objects within (i) above which, taken as a whole, appears to the Board to be so pre-eminent (introduced by *FA 1973, s 46*); and

(iii)   any objects where they are associated with a particular building and where the Secretary of State believes it is desirable for that object to remain associated with a particular building or where objects have a significant association with a particular place.

'National interest' includes interest within any part of the UK.

'Pre-eminence'-in determining whether an object or collection is pre-eminent, any significant association with a particular place is to be taken into account ie the 'Waverley criteria'. The object or collection should be central, rather than of merely marginal significance, in the context of display in a public collection or important historic building and should satisfy one or more of the following tests which follow those laid down by the AIL Panel:

- Does the object have an especially close association with our history and national life? This category includes foreign as well as British works, e.g. gifts from foreign sovereigns or governments and objects that have been acquired abroad in circumstances associated with our history. It also includes objects closely associated with some part of the United Kingdom, or with the development of its institutions and industries. Some objects that fall under this category will be of such national importance that they deserve to enter a national museum or gallery. Others may well be of a lesser degree of national importance although they will be significant in a local context. This category will also include works which derive their significance from a local connection and which may therefore qualify as 'pre-eminent' to a local authority or independent museum or gallery.

- Is the object of especial artistic or art-historical interest? This category includes objects deserving of entering a national museum or gallery as well as other objects that may not be pre-eminent in a national museum or gallery but will be pre-eminent in local authority, university or independent museums or galleries which do not already possess items of a similar genre or quality. For example, outstanding items of decorative or applied art would come within this category for consideration.

- Is the object of especial importance for the study of some particular form of art, learning or history? This category includes a wide variety of objects, not restricted to works of art such as engineering plans or models, which are of especial importance for the study of, say, a particular scientific development. The category also includes objects forming part of an historical unity series or collection either in one place or in the country as a whole. Without a particular object or group of objects, both a unity and a series may be impaired.

- Does the object have an especially close association with a particular historic setting? This category will include primary works of art, manuscripts, furniture or other items that have an especially close association with an important historic building. The category may include paintings, furniture especially commissioned for a particular house or a group of paintings having an association with a particular location including those being returned to their original setting.

(See also IR 67, para 11.12 and Inland Revenue Press Release 17/99, 11 February 1999.)

Now HMRC Inheritance Tax refers offers of 'pre-eminent' or 'associated' objects (see (iii) above) to the Acceptance in Lieu (AIL) panel, which is comprised of 11 people and is currently under the chairmanship of Mark Wood. This panel, the council for museums, archives and libraries, takes into account the views of independent experts and advises the Secretary of State whether the property offered is suitable for acceptance in lieu by the Commissioners of HMRC in terms of the objects' pre-eminence. The AIL Panel also advises the Secretary of State on questions of allocation of objects (either temporary or permanent). Where land and buildings are offered the CTO refers to the Department of Culture Media and Sports (DCMS) who in turn consult advisers such as the Countryside Commission, the Forestry Authority and English Heritage. The Historic Manuscripts Commission advises the Secretary of State on the permanent allocation of records, archives and manuscripts.

For claims made before 31 July 1998, objects or collections within (i) and (ii) above could be designated if they appeared to the Board to be of national, scientific, historic or artistic interest. There was no requirement to satisfy the standard of 'pre-eminent' but only a lower standard of 'museum quality'.

(b)   Land which in the opinion of the Board is of outstanding scenic or historic or scientific interest.

(c)   A building for the preservation of which special steps should in the opinion of the Board be taken by reason of its outstanding historic or architectural interest.

(d)   Land which in the opinion of the Board is essential for the protection of the character and amenities of such a building as is mentioned in (c) above.

(e)   An object which in the opinion of the Board is historically associated with such a building mentioned in (c) above.

[IHTA 1984, s 31(1)(5); FA 1985, Sch 26 para 2(2); FA 1998, Sch 25 para 4].

The introduction of the pre-eminence test under (a) above may have the effect, in certain circumstances, of rendering previously exempted objects chargeable to a latent estate duty previously deferred but now exigible. Also, in the Finance Bill Committee Stage Debates the Financial Secretary's answer to questions on the definition of 'pre-eminent' exacted the following reply:

'An object must be pre-eminent or associated with a historical building; it does not have to be both. If the collection is pre-eminent in its own right, it should qualify. If it is not, its connection with a building may allow it to qualify as pre-eminent.'

(Hansard, 16 June 1998, Col 896).

33.3   **CONDITIONALLY EXEMPT TRANSFERS**

The Board may, on a claim (see below), designate property as eligible under 33.2 above and a transfer of such property is exempt from inheritance tax if certain conditions are met and undertakings given. Such a transfer is called a 'conditionally exempt transfer'. The failure to observe an undertaking is a 'chargeable event' and tax will become chargeable (see 33.4 and 33.5 below). It is understood that HMRC review all conditionally exempt transfers of land under 33.2(b) at five-yearly intervals to ensure that undertakings are observed (HC Written answer, Hansard 18 June 1992, Vol 209, Cols 629, 630). A gift cannot be conditionally exempt if it is entirely exempt as a gift to a spouse/civil partner or to a charity. See 21.2 and 21.8 EXEMPT TRANSFERS. [IHTA 1984, ss 30(1)(2)(4), 31, 32(1)(2); FA 1985, s 95, Sch 26 para 1; FA 1998, Sch 25 para 7].

Conditions. Exemptions may be given for transfers on death and lifetime gifts but the latter are eligible only if

(a)   the transferor or his spouse or civil partner has been beneficially entitled to the property throughout the six years ending with the transfer; or

(b)   the transferor acquired the property on a death and the acquisition was itself a conditionally exempt transfer.

[IHTA 1984, s 30(3); The Tax and Civil Partnership Regulations 2005, SI 2005/3229, Reg 11].

Interaction with potentially exempt transfers. The above provisions are disregarded in determining whether a transfer is a POTENTIALLY EXEMPT TRANSFER (38). Where the transfer in question is a potentially exempt transfer, no claim under the above provisions can be made until the transferor has died. [IHTA 1984, s 30(3A)(3B); FA 1986, Sch 19 para 7]. If the transferor survives for seven years after the transfer, the potentially exempt transfer becomes an exempt transfer and there is no need to make a claim for conditional exemption. If the transferor dies within the seven-year period, a claim for conditional exemption may be made and the question whether any property is appropriate for designation is determined by reference to circumstances existing after the transferor's death. [IHTA 1984, s 31(1A); FA 1986, Sch 19 para 8]. There is no conditional exemption if the property has been disposed of by sale before the transferor's death [IHTA 1984, *s 30(3C); FA 1986, Sch 19 para 7*] but a potentially exempt transfer which would have proved to be a chargeable transfer is an exempt transfer to the extent that the property has or could be designated under 33.2 above and, after the transfer in question and before the transferor's death, has been disposed of by way of sale by private treaty or otherwise to one of the bodies listed in 33.16 below or has been accepted by the Board in satisfaction of tax (see 35.6 PAYMENT OF TAX). [*IHTA 1984, s 26A; FA 1986, Sch 19 para 6*].

Where only part of a property is granted conditional exemption it is the actual transfer of value which is exempted rather than the property itself. Accordingly, the District Valuer should value the entire property and then apportion this figure on a just and reasonable approach between the value attributable to the heritage property and that attributable to the taxable non-heritage property. (VOA IHT manual, section 20, para 20.13).

Undertakings. An undertaking must be given (see notes to Form 700A), by such a person as the Board think appropriate in the circumstances of the case, that, until the person beneficially entitled to the property dies or the property is disposed of

(i)   in the case of property under 33.2(*a*) above, the property will be kept permanently in the UK and will not leave it temporarily except for a purpose and a period approved by the Board (see Form 700A over); and such steps as are agreed with the Board will be taken for the preservation of the property and for securing reasonable access to the public (but confidential documents may be excluded altogether or to a limited extent from the public access requirement), and

(ii)   in the case of land under 33.2(*b*), such steps as are agreed with the Board will be taken for its maintenance and the preservation of its character, and for securing reasonable access to the public, and

(iii) in the case of buildings, amenity land or objects within 33.2(*c*)–(*e*), such steps as are agreed with the Board will be taken for its maintenance, repair and preservation and for securing reasonable access to the public and, if it is an object within 33.2(*e*) above, for keeping it associated with the building concerned.

[*IHTA 1984, ss 30(1), 31(2)–(4); FA 1985, s 95, Sch 26 paras 1, 2(3)*].

Where the transfer in question is a POTENTIALLY EXEMPT TRANSFER (38) which has proved to be a chargeable lifetime transfer and at the time of the transferor's death an undertaking has been given by the appropriate person under *IHTA 1984, Sch 4 para 3(3)* (maintenance funds for historic buildings, see 33.11 below) or *TCGA 1992, s 258* with respect to any of the property to which the value transferred by the transfer is attributable, that undertaking is treated as having been given under the above provisions. [*IHTA 1984, s 31(4G); FA 1986, Sch 19 para 8*].

Reasonable access to the public. For undertakings given on or after 31 July 1998, public access cannot be confined to access by prior appointment only. [*IHTA 1984, s 31(4FA); FA 1998, Sch 25 para 5*]. As a result, in the case of objects within 33.2(*a*) above, the 'V & A list' procedure described below ceases to apply. Where an undertaking whether original or a replacement undertaking is given on or after 31 July 1998 then:

• public access to the tax-exempt assets cannot be restricted to 'appointment' access through the owner or his/her agent (see former Inland Revenue letter sent to owners of conditionally exempt chattels on 31 March 1999 below);

• the owner may be required to publicise the terms of the undertaking and any other information relating to exempt assets which will otherwise be considered confidential.

[*FA 1998, Sch 25 paras 5, 6*].

'Public access', above, means that all owners of exempt assets will have to provide a measure of 'open' access to those assets, but this will only be in accordance with the terms agreed with HMRC set out in the undertaking. The law requires 'public access' to be reasonable and this will depend upon the nature and type of the asset as well as the preservation and maintenance needs of that asset. See *Re Applications to Vary the Undertakings of 'A' and 'B' [2005] STC SCD 103 Sp C 439* below. For example, the measure of access for a large building may not be reasonable in the case of a smaller building or, say, a delicate object. In this latter case it may be appropriate to mix 'open' access with 'appointment' access if the preservation of the object requires it. In certain circumstances it may be appropriate to suspend or exclude public access. This occurred during 2001 when the foot and mouth outbreak resulted in the restriction of access to land and buildings which was exempted from IHT on condition that the appointed land and buildings were open to access by the general public. Provided the risk assessment at the time warranted the suspension of access to the land or building then it was not be necessary to make up the lost days of access later in that year. The CTO stated that a typical case for suspension of access by the public would be where a historic building is bounded by farm land that was subject to foot and mouth restrictions. See IR Tax Bulletin Special Edition — Foot and Mouth Disease, May 2001, IR Press Release 18 March 2002.

For chattels exempt in their own right 'open' access may be provided by displaying the objects at:

- the residence of the individual or at the place the object(s) is kept (restricted to the area in which the object is displayed, unless the building itself is tax exempt in which case this facility will not apply);

- a museum or gallery to which the public have access (see Revised DCMS model loan agreement for AIL in-situ offer revised at 30 December 2002 at http://www.culture.gov.uk/what_we_do/Cultural_property/QuickLinks/Forms/);

- any other building open to the public, e.g. a local Record office;

- the appropriate European Heritage Open Days event free of charge (i.e. Heritage Open Days (England), Doors Open Days (Scotland), London Open House, European Open Days in Wales and Northern Ireland); and

- local, regional or touring exhibitions.

Objects may be loaned for display in the public collection of a national institution, local authority, university or independent museum and this period will count as 'open'. Historically associated objects will normally be displayed in the building concerned.

If a chattel is located in a building which is itself tax exempt the period of access will be the same as that for the building, i.e. 25 to 156 days each year. In other situations the minimum period will be 5 to 100 days a year and the Museums, Archives and Libraries Council will advise HMRC where this applies. HMRC may be prepared to consider a two-year accounting period rather than a one-year period in certain circumstances.

In the case of exempt buildings and their amenity land the minimum period of 'open' access will be 25 to 156 days each year. In the case of land the access will, in general, be during daylight hours and on defined routes but with agreed closure periods for sporting activities, land management, nature conservation, etc. In most circumstances it will be open to the individual to charge a fee to view the exempt building but this must be reasonable from the point of view of the public at large.

Publicising access and undertakings is a requirement of conditional exemption for heritage assets. The *Finance Act 1998* tightened up on the rules and individuals will now be required to disclose more information. HMRC will expect the individual to make such an undertaking available to any member of the public who asks to view it. The undertaking in relation to the building or exempt chattel may be displayed at the premises and HMRC may also enter the details on their internet website. HMRC issued a letter on 31 March 1999 to all owners of conditionally exempt chattels stating that they should reply in writing detailing the 25 days the property would be open to the public without prior appointment.

Subsequently, HMRC indicated a degree of flexibility on the time limit for replies. HMRC issued a form titled 'Proposal' with the letter for signature by owners in connection with publicising their undertakings as follows:

'I/We shall give appropriate publicity to the public access arrangements, namely by agreeing that the Inland Revenue may:

- publicise the availability of this access via the internet or other appropriate means, and

- provide anyone who requests it with a copy of the undertaking.

I/We further agree to make public my/our undertakings in relation to conditionally exempt property and to disclose and/or copy them as appropriate to any third party who asks.'

The information required for the website will be a description of each object, full address of the building and opening times, and name, address and telephone number of the contact person (i.e. owner, agent, etc.). In the case of land HMRC may also require a copy of the undertaking together with any related management plan to be given free of charge to any local authority in which the land is situated. The authority and HMRC's advisers (e.g. Countryside Commission) will be free to make this information available to members of the public. The owner of amenity land must show the location of the land including the National Grid references for all points of entry onto that land. HMRC also require the name, address and telephone number of the person who can give further details of the amenity land on request. In the case of scenic land the owner may be required to advertise the details in the local tourist office and/or town hall, display map boards at each point of entry to the land and waymark the permitted paths, bridleways, etc. See http://www.countryside.gov.uk/livingLandscapes/finest_countryside/heritage_landscapes/benefits.asp.

A further letter was issued from the Capital Taxes Office [now HMRC Inheritance Tax] accepting that no obligation exists for owners to make proposals regarding the variation of existing undertakings. Also, HMRC have conceded that it is dependent on them to review existing undertakings and then make proposals for variations as well as leaving some existing arrangements in place under the old 'V & A List Arrangements'. See below. In addition the personal circumstances of those dictated by existing undertakings are relevant in deciding whether it is 'just and reasonable, in all the circumstances' for the terms of the current undertakings to be altered. [*IHTA 1984, s 35A(2)(c) as inserted by FA 1998, Sch 25 para 10(1)*]. See IHT NEWSLETTER AND TAX BULLETIN EXTRACTS (61), April 2001 and [**Case Study 3**].

Owners of buildings open to the public may be required to publicise the public access arrangements by:

1. advertising details in the local paper, tourist office and/or town hall;

2. advertising details in one of the annual national guides to historic houses, i.e. *Hudson's Historic Houses and Gardens* and *Johansens Historic Houses Castles & Gardens*;

3. placing a sign at the main entrance of the property with details of opening times; or

4. informing appropriate local council and education authorities.

For undertakings given before 31 July 1998, the HMRC issued guidelines on what was considered to be reasonable public access as regards works of art etc. within 33.2(*a*) above. See http://www.hmrc.gov.uk/manuals/ihtmanual/annex.htm. One option for securing access is for the owner to allow viewing by appointment and, subject to conditions, to lend it for special exhibitions on request to directors or curators of public collections for up to six months in any two-year period. A register ('the V & A list') of objects granted conditional exemption, computerised with database search, is available for public consultation at the Victoria and Albert Museum (London), National Library of Scotland (Edinburgh), National Museum of Wales (Cardiff) and Ulster Museum (Belfast). Access may be obtained through the internet on http://www.hmrc.gov.uk/heritage/rights.htm Publicity is given to the register in a number of ways and it is updated quarterly to ensure that the individual (who, for security reasons, does not have to be the owner concerned) shown as a contact point can be consulted. If a prospective viewer is unable to make viewing arrangements HMRC Inheritance Tax should be contacted. See also IR 156 'Our heritage: your right to see tax exempt works of art'. Previously a selective audit of the register ensured that undertakings on public access and preservation of objects in the UK were being observed. However, as from 1 April 2000 the Heritage Section took over the responsibility and now deals with owners and their agents directly. The reports are expected to be completed and returned to the Heritage Section within two months of request. (Inland Revenue Press Releases 17 December 1992, 10 May 1993, 2 August 1993 and subsequent Press Releases issued quarterly). See also former Inland Revenue Tax Bulletin August 1993 p 89. See CTO Newsletter December 1996 in Chapter 60 and IHT Newsletter October 2001. See IHT NEWSLETTER AND TAX BULLETIN EXTRACTS (61).

Publicity requirements regarding public access to land within 33.2(*b*) above were given in HC Written Answer 9 February 1987, Hansard Vol 110, Col 35. Undertakings regarding such land were reviewed every five years to ensure they are being observed (HC Written Answer 18 June 1992, Hansard Vol 209, Cols 629, 630). See also former Inland Revenue Tax Bulletin August 1993 p 89. [**Case Study 3**].

Additional undertaking for amenity land. An *additional* undertaking is required for amenity land within 33.2(*d*)above, called the '*relevant land*', which is over and above the requirement for an undertaking at (iii) above. The person seeking conditional exemption for the relevant land must provide (or secure, if necessary, from another person) undertaking(s) that until the death of the person beneficially entitled to the building for which the relevant land is an amenity or any other amenity land of that building which is either between it and the relevant land or physically closely connected with one of them, or until that property is disposed of, such steps as are agreed with the Board will be taken for the maintenance, repair, preservation and securing of reasonable public access to the building or other amenity land. Where different persons are entitled (either beneficially or otherwise) to the building and the other amenity land, separate undertakings are required in respect of each by whomever the Board think appropriate. These undertakings are required notwithstanding the fact that another undertaking is already effective for that building or other amenity land. Such undertakings will have been given with respect to the building etc., whereas the additional undertaking, although relating to the maintenance etc. of the building etc., is given with respect to the relevant amenity land. [*IHTA 1984, s 31(4A)–(4F); FA 1985, ss 94, 95, Sch 26 para 2(4)*].

Variations of undertakings. Undertakings may be varied by agreement between the Board and the person bound by the undertaking. Failing such agreement, a Special Commissioner may approve a proposed variation by the Board

• for any undertaking given on or after 31 July 1998; or

• for any undertaking given before 31 July 1998 (unless there has been a chargeable event after the giving of the undertaking and before that date) but only so as to impose wider requirements for

   (i)   public access where existing undertakings are confined to access by prior appointment only; and/or

   (ii) publication of details of the exemption.

For replacement undertakings sought on or after 31 July 1998 to preserve an existing exemption (IHT or CTT) the person will need to comply with the rules on undertakings in force on the date the undertaking is given. [*FA 1998, Sch 25 para 7*]. This does not affect any replacement undertakings given under the rules relating to estate duty. If the conditionally exempt item is sold there will normally be a charge to tax but a replacement undertaking may be given for another item. However, the Heritage Section of HMRC Inheritance Tax should be advised promptly of the change in such circumstances or they will be in breach of the undertaking. Form IHT100 (event form IHT 100f) should be completed where there is an ending of a conditional exemption and this should be delivered within six months from the end of month in which the event giving rise to the tax charge occurs. Form Cap100 is appropriate for the ending of a CTT conditional exemption. There is no prescribed form of account for the ending of an Estate Duty conditional exemption. In order to avoid interest and penalties an early submission of Form IHT 100 is recommended. See IHT NEWSLETTER AND TAX BULLETIN EXTRACTS (61), May 2003.

HMRC had stated that about 1,000 cases needed review arising from the undertakings given before 31 July 1998 but this would take some time. Originally, suggestions for access on terms not limited to access by prior appointment were sought by the end of June 1999 but this was extended to the end of the following month July. HMRC will accept advance proposals with regard to public access without prior appointment and if they consider that changes should be made to the undertaking and these cannot be mutually agreed then a right of appeal to the Special Commissioners exists. Up to the end of a six-month period the matter can be referred to the Special Commissioners who may either confirm the HMRC's proposals or reject them according to whether they consider the proposals just and reasonable. The Special Commissioners will only consider the reasonableness of HMRC proposals, not those of the person bound. There is no statutory right of appeal against the Special Commissioners' ruling but either side may be able to appeal to the Court for a review on a point of law. In *Re Applications to Vary the Undertakings of 'A' and 'B' [2005] STC SCD 103 Sp C 439* HMRC had agreed that the owners of certain valuable works of art should have the benefit of 'conditional exemption' from IHT. Subsequently, HMRC made applications, under *IHTA 1984, s 35A*, to vary the undertakings so as to give wider publicity to the existence of the items, and wider access to them. The Special Commissioner dismissed HMRC's applications, holding that 'the accumulated burdens placed on the particular owner' would 'so outweigh the benefit to the public as to make it neither just nor reasonable for me to direct that the proposals take effect'. There would be 'a serious intrusion into the family lives of the owners', and 'the increased risks of theft and damage to the owners' possessions' would go 'beyond what Parliament had in mind when empowering the inclusion of extended access requirements and publication requirements'. [*IHTA 1984, s 35A (2)(c)*]. This has now been acknowledged by HMRC Inheritance Tax [see **Case Study 3**] in their letter to owners and advisers and it is thought that HMRC Capital Taxes will now make their requests for greater access less burdensome following the above case.

HMRC will consider changes to their proposals by the person bound but the law:

• requires the undertaking to be appropriate to the asset concerned, so when they consider the changes they have regard to any change in the personal circumstances of the person bound; and

• does not provide for any appeal if the proposals put forward cannot be accepted.

[*IHTA 1984, s 35A; FA 1998, Sch 25 para 8*].

Claims. A claim should be made on Form 700A IHT (now revised). Copies are available from HMRC Inheritance Tax, Nottingham at the address shown in 2.11 ACCOUNTS AND RETURNS. In relation to transfers of property after 16 March 1998, the claim must be made no more than two years after the transfer of value or, in the case of potentially exempt transfers, the date of death. In either case the Board may allow a longer period. [*IHTA 1984, s 30(3BA); FA 1998, Sch 25 para 2*]. The Board will consider each application to extend the two-year period on its own merits but have stated that any oversight or mistake on the applicant's part or their adviser's, or the making of a post-death variation, will not normally by itself be an acceptable reason to allow a late claim. A primary claim for agricultural or business property relief may delay matters beyond the two-year claim period in which case a protective claim may be made to the CTO. See IHT NEWSLETTER AND TAX BULLETIN EXTRACTS (61), April 2001. Normally a claim may not be made in advance except in the cases of:

• any claim for exemption from the IHT ten-yearly charge on discretionary trusts must be made, and assets designated, before the date of the charge; and

• approval of a proposed heritage maintenance fund.

[IHTA 1984, s 79(3), Sch 4 para 1(2)].

HMRC expect applicants to make their claims without undue delay.

33.4   **CHARGEABLE EVENT**

Where there has been a conditionally exempt transfer of any property, tax is charged on the first occurrence after the transfer (or, if the transfer was a POTENTIALLY EXEMPT TRANSFER (38) after the transferor's death) of a chargeable event. Where properties are '*associated properties*' (i.e. a building within 33.2(*c*)above and any amenity land or objects within 33.2(*d*) or (*e*) related to that building), tax is chargeable on the first event after a conditionally exempt transfer (or, if the transfer was a potentially exempt transfer, after the transferor's death) of *any* of the associated properties (or part) on the *whole* of each of the associated properties (or part) for which the event is a chargeable event. Subject to exceptions below, there is a '*chargeable event*' on a material failure to observe an undertaking within 33.3 above, on the death of any person beneficially entitled to any property and on any disposal of any property. [*IHTA 1984, ss 32(1)–(3), 32A(1)–(4); FA 1985, Sch 26 para 4; FA 1986, Sch 19 paras 9, 10; FA 1998, Sch 25 para 7*].

Exceptions. There is no chargeable event in the following situations.

(*a*)   If a failure to observe an undertaking or a disposal relates to one only of the associated properties or part of it, and the associated properties as a whole have not been materially affected, the Board may, if so satisfied, direct that the chargeable event be limited to the property or part actually affected by the failure of undertaking, etc. [*IHTA 1984, s 32A(10); FA 1985, s 95, Sch 25 para 4*].

(*b*)   There is no chargeable event on death if within three years the personal representatives (or trustees or person next entitled if settled property, see 33.7 *et seq*. below) make a disposal of property by way of sale by private treaty or gift to one of the national bodies listed in *IHTA 1984, Sch 3*, or where the property is accepted in lieu of tax. A disposal is likewise not a chargeable event where it is one of this nature. Where there is then a subsequent death or disposal there is no chargeable event with respect to the property (or part) concerned unless there has been another, intervening, conditionally exempt transfer. The disposal of one or part of a group of 'associated properties' to a national body or in lieu of tax does not mean that the remaining associated properties are not chargeable. Conditional exemption only continues for the property retained if the necessary undertaking is given by such person or persons as the Board thinks appropriate. [*IHTA 1984, ss 32(4), 32A(5)–(7); FA 1985, Sch 26 para 4; FA 1998, Sch 25 para 7*].

(*c*)   Death, or disposal otherwise than by sale, is not a chargeable event if the transfer of value thereby made is itself a conditionally exempt transfer or if the necessary undertaking is given by such person or persons as the Board think appropriate. [*IHTA 1984, ss 32(5)(5AA), 32A(8)(8A); FA 1985, Sch 26 para 4; FA 1998, Sch 25 para 7*].

(*d*)   A disposal by sale of one or part of a group of associated properties gives rise to a chargeable event limited to that part of the associated properties actually disposed of (if it is not otherwise exempt) if the necessary undertaking is given by such person or persons as the Board think appropriate. [*IHTA 1984, s 32A(9); FA 1985, Sch 26 para 4; FA 1998, Sch 25 para 7*].

The person liable to pay the tax chargeable is

(i) in the case of breach of undertaking or death, the person who, if the property were sold at that time, would be entitled to receive (whether for his benefit or not) the proceeds of sale or any income arising from them; or

(ii) in the case of disposal, the person by whom or for whose benefit the property is disposed of.

[*IHTA 1984, s 207(1)–(2B); FA 1985, Sch 26 para 10*].

Conditional exemption on death before 7 April 1976. Similar rules apply in respect of conditional exemption granted under previous legislation on deaths before 7 April 1976. [*FA 1975, ss 32, 34(3)–(6); IHTA 1984, ss 35(2), 207(4)(5), Sch 5 paras 1, 3(1)–(4), Sch 6 para 4(2); FA 1985, Sch 26 paras 7, 13; FA 1986, Sch 19 para 12*].

33.5   CHARGE TO TAX

Different provisions apply according to the date of the conditionally exempt transfer or occasion (see 33.7 below) on which the chargeable event arises. In each case the tax is due six months after the end of the month in which the chargeable event occurs. [*IHTA 1984, s 226(4); FA 1985, Sch 26 para 11*]. See 33.4 above for person liable to pay the tax.

A conditionally exempt transfer can arise during lifetime or on death. The tax on a subsequent chargeable event is on the value of the property at the time of the event (i.e. there is no 'grossing-up') and where the event is a disposal on a sale not intended to confer any gratuitous benefit on any person and at arm's length between unconnected persons (or on similar terms), the value is equal to the sale proceeds (with proportionate reduction where the conditional exemption applied only to part of the property) [*IHTA 1984, s 33(1)(a)(3)(4)*] less any capital gains tax chargeable. [*TCGA 1992, s 258(8)*].

The rate at which tax on a subsequent chargeable event is charged is determined by reference to the relevant person. [*IHTA 1984, s 33(1)(b)*].

The 'relevant person' is

(i) if there has been only one conditionally exempt transfer or one conditionally exempt occasion (see 33.7 below) before the event, the person who made that transfer or the person who is the settlor in relation to the settlement in respect of which the occasion occurred;

(ii) if there have been two or more such transfers or occasions, and the last was before, or only one of them was within, the period of thirty years ending with the event, the person who made the last transfer or the person who is the settlor in relation to the settlement in respect of which the last occasion occurred;

(iii) if there have been two or more such transfers or occasions within that period, whichever person or settlor the Board may select. [*IHTA 1984, ss 33(5), 78(3)*].

The rate of tax will be, subject to the exceptions below,

(a) if the relevant person is alive, the rate applicable to the property if it were added to the cumulative total of his chargeable transfers at the date of the chargeable event and tax calculated using rates applicable to lifetime transfer. The amount is only notionally added for this purpose and does not affect the rate of tax on later transfers made by the relevant person unless he is also the person who made the last conditionally exempt transfer (see 33.6 below). The rates are not affected by the death of the relevant person after the chargeable event. [*IHTA 1984, ss 33(1)(b)(i)(2A), 34(1); FA 1986, Sch 19 para 11*].

(*b*)   if the relevant person is dead, the rate applicable to the property if it were added to the value of his estate on death and formed the highest part of that value. If the relevant person made the conditionally exempt transfer on death (but the property was not treated as forming part of his estate under the rules relating to GIFTS WITH RESERVATION (22)) the death rates are used. In any other case, tax is calculated using the rates applicable to lifetime transfers. If the relevant person is the settlor and the settlement was created on his death, the death rates are used, if not tax is calculated using the rates applicable to lifetime transfers. See also 59.11 WORKING CASE STUDY. If the chargeable event occurs after tax is reduced by the substitution of a new table of rates, the new rates are used. Where the relevant person died before 18 March 1986, nevertheless, the amount of tax payable is calculated as if the amendments to *IHTA 1984, s 7* in *FA 1986, 19 Sch 2* (rates of tax for transfers within seven years of death and tapering relief) had applied at the time of death. [*IHTA 1984, ss 9, 33(1)(b)(ii)(2), 78(4), Sch 2 para 5; FA 1985, Sch 26 para 5; FA 1986, Sch 19 paras 11, 19, 41*].

Exceptions. If the relevant person is determined as in (i) to (iii) above by reference to a conditionally exempt occasion (see 33.7 below)

(A)   the rates under (*a*) and (*b*) above will be reduced to **30%** of the full charge if the occasion occurred before the first ten-year anniversary (see 44.3 SETTLEMENTS WITHOUT INTERESTS IN POSSESSION) to fall after the property became comprised in the settlement concerned and **60%** of the full charge if the event occurred after the first and before the second ten-year anniversary.

(B)   the rate under (*b*) above is, where the relevant person died before 13 March 1975, and subject to (A) above, the rate applicable to the property as if the relevant person died when the chargeable event occurred and the chargeable amount were added to, and formed the highest part of, the value on which estate duty was chargeable when he in fact died. [*IHTA 1984, s 78(4)(5)*].

Conditionally exempt transfers or occasions in (i) to (iii) above do not include those made before any previous chargeable event on the same property or before any event mentioned in 33.4(*b*) above. [*IHTA 1984, s 33(6); FA 1985, Sch 26 para 6*].

On or before 6 April 1976, a conditionally exempt transfer could arise only on death. Where the chargeable event is more than three years after the death, the tax chargeable is on the value of the exempt property at the time of the chargeable event. This value is added to the chargeable estate at death and inheritance tax recalculated. The average rate of tax is then applied to the property to give the tax chargeable on the property ceasing to be exempt. The tax chargeable on the estate at death is not altered.

Where objects within 33.2(*a*) above formed a set at the time of the death and tax becomes chargeable on two or more of those objects by reason of chargeable events occurring at different times, the charge to tax is treated as if all the chargeable events occurred at the time of the earliest one (unless the chargeable events are disposals to different persons who are neither in concert nor connected with each other). [*IHTA 1984, Sch 5 paras 2, 4*].

Tax credit. Subject to below, where there is a chargeable transfer after a conditionally exempt transfer of the same property (wholly or in part), any tax charged is allowed as a credit

(*aa*)   if the chargeable transfer is also a chargeable event (see 33.4 above), against the tax chargeable on that chargeable event;

(*bb*)   if the chargeable transfer is not also a chargeable event, against the tax chargeable on the next chargeable event on the property.

Where after a conditionally exempt transfer of any property there is a potentially exempt transfer of all or part of that property, and *either* the potentially exempt transfer is a chargeable event with respect to the property *or* after the potentially exempt transfer but before the transferor's death a chargeable event occurs with respect to the property, the tax charged under the above provisions on the chargeable event is allowed as a credit against any tax which may become chargeable by reason of the potentially exempt transfer proving to be a chargeable transfer. No relief is due under (*aa*) or (*bb*) above. [*IHTA 1984, s 33(7)(8); FA 1986, Sch 19 para 11*].

Example 1

Chargeable event during lifetime of relevant person

C, who has made previous chargeable transfers during August 2001 of £230,000, makes a conditionally exempt gift of property in February 2002. In October 2007, the property is sold for £500,000 and capital gains tax of £100,000 is payable.

		£
Cumulative total of previous chargeable transfers of relevant person		230,000
Net sale proceeds of conditionally exempt property	500,000	
Deduct capital gains tax payable	(100,000)	
Chargeable transfer		400,000
Revised cumulative total for relevant person		£630,000

Inheritance tax payable (by reference to lifetime rates in October 2007)
£330,000 at 20% = £66,000

Example 2

Chargeable event after relevant person is dead

D died in April 1994 leaving a taxable estate of £350,000 together with conditionally exempt property valued at £600,000 at the breach in October 2007.

	£
Value of relevant person's estate at death	350,000
Value of conditionally exempt property at date of breach	600,000
	£950,000

Inheritance tax payable (by reference to full rates applicable in October 2007)
£600,000 at 40% = £240,000

Example 3

Property inherited in 1984 from A's estate by B, who gave the necessary undertakings so that the property is conditionally exempt, is given in December 2007 by B to C. C agrees to pay any inheritance tax arising from the transfer but does not wish to give the necessary undertakings, so a chargeable event arises. B dies in March 2008.

	£
A's estate at date of death in 1984	180,000
B's cumulative chargeable transfers at date of chargeable event in December 2007 (all in 2006/07)	73,000
Value of property at date of chargeable event	250,000

Inheritance tax on chargeable event (subject to tax credit)

	£
Value of A's estate at date of death	180,000
Value of property at date of chargeable event	250,000
	£430,000

Inheritance tax payable	
£130,000 (£430,000 – 300,000) at 40% =	£52,000

Inheritance tax on B's gift

Cumulative total of previous transfers		73,000
Value of property gifted	250,000	
Deduct annual exemption 2007/08	3,000	247,000
		£320,000

Inheritance tax arising on gift of £247,000	£8,000

Tax credit

IHT on B's gift		8,000
IHT on chargeable event	52,000	
Deduct tax credit	(8,000)	
		44,000

Total inheritance tax borne	£52,000

33.6   EFFECT OF CHARGEABLE EVENT ON SUBSEQUENT TRANSFERS

The person who made the last conditionally exempt transfer before the chargeable event (not necessarily the relevant person) will have his cumulative total of chargeable transfers increased by the amount of the property on which tax is paid on the chargeable event and, consequently, the rate of tax applicable to all his subsequent chargeable transfers is increased. Where that person is dead, but he is the relevant person in relation to a later chargeable event, the value of his estate at death will be increased by the amount on which tax is paid on the first chargeable event to determine the rates applicable to the later chargeable event. [*IHTA 1984, s 34(1)(2); FA 1985, Sch 26 para 5*].

Settlor. If the 'relevant person' is not the person who made the last conditionally exempt transfer of the property and at the time of the chargeable event, or at any time within the preceding five years, the property is or has been comprised in a settlement made within 30 years before that event and a person who is a settlor of that settlement has made a conditionally exempt transfer of the property within those 30 years (excluding any made before any previous chargeable event on the same property or before any event mentioned in 33.4(*b*) above), then the amount of the property chargeable at the time of the chargeable event is added to the cumulative total of the settlor (and not to that of the person who made the last conditionally exempt transfer). [*IHTA 1984, s 34(3)(4); FA 1985, Sch 26 para 6*].

Where the last conditionally exempt transaction before a chargeable event was a conditionally exempt occasion (see 33.7 below) as opposed to a conditionally exempt transfer, the above does not apply. [*IHTA 1984, s 78(6)*].

Example

Multiple conditionally exempt transfers

D died in December 1983 leaving a conditionally exempt property to his son E. D's taxable estate at death was £230,000. In 1992 E gave the property to his daughter F. F gave the necessary undertakings so this transfer was also conditionally exempt. In December 2007 F sold the property for its market value of £500,000 and paid capital gains tax of £80,000. During 1992 E had made chargeable transfers of £20,000 and he has made no other transfers.

	£	£
Value of relevant person's estate at death		230,000
Net sale proceeds of conditionally exempt property	500,000	
Deduct capital gains tax	80,000	
Chargeable transfer		420,000
		£650,000

Inheritance tax payable by F

£350,000 at 40% =	£140,000
Previous cumulative total of E	20,000
Add chargeable transfer	420,000
E's revised cumulative total	£440,000

Notes to the example

(A)   There have been two conditionally exempt transfers within the period of 30 years ending with the chargeable event in December 2007. HMRC may select either D or E as the 'relevant person' for the purpose of calculating the tax due. The IHT liability will be higher if D is selected. [*IHTA 1984, ss 33(5), 78(3)*].

(B)   As F receives the proceeds of sale, she is the person liable to pay the IHT. [*IHTA 1984, s 207(1)*].

(C)   Although the IHT is calculated by reference to D's cumulative total, it is E whose cumulative total is adjusted as he made the last conditionally exempt transfer of the property. [*IHTA 1984, s 34(1)*].

(D)   As the chargeable event occurs after a reduction in the rates of tax, the new rates are used to calculate the tax payable. [*IHTA 1984, Sch 2 para 5*].

33.7   **SETTLEMENTS**

Conditionally exempt occasions. A national heritage property (see 33.2 above) comprised in a SETTLEMENT WITHOUT INTERESTS IN POSSESSION (44) may be transferred with exemption from inheritance tax provided

(a)   the property has been comprised in the settlement throughout the six years ending with the transfer, and

(b)   on a claim being made, the property is designated by the Board as being within 33.2 above, and

(c)   the requisite undertaking (or undertakings) in 33.3 above are given by such person as the Board thinks appropriate.

Any event, other than a transfer, which would otherwise give rise to a charge under the provisions relating to SETTLEMENTS WITHOUT INTERESTS IN POSSESSION (44), is also exempt if the above conditions are satisfied. An exempt transfer or event as above, is a '*conditionally exempt occasion*'. [*IHTA 1984, s 78(1)(2); FA 1985, s 95, Sch 26 para 8*].

In relation to transfers of property or other events occurring after 16 March 1998, the claim under (b) above must be made no more than two years after the date of the transfer or other event in question, although the Board may allow a longer period. [*IHTA 1984, s 78(1A); FA 1998, Sch 25 para 3*].

33.8   **Chargeable events.** Chargeable events giving rise to a tax liability are as in 33.4 above with appropriate modification so that references to a conditionally exempt transfer include references to a conditionally exempt occasion; references to a disposal otherwise than by sale include references to any occasion on which tax is chargeable under the provisions relating to settlements without qualifying interests in possession (other than the ten-year anniversary charge for which see 33.10 below); and references to an undertaking in 33.3 above include the undertaking in 33.7 above. [*IHTA 1984, s 78(3); FA 1985, Sch 26 para 8*].

Example

A, who is still alive, settled property and investments on discretionary trusts in September 1988, conditional exemption being granted in respect of designated property. In April 2002, the designated property was appointed absolutely to beneficiary C who gave the necessary undertakings for exemption to continue. However, in February 2008, C sold the property for £135,000 net of costs, suffering a capital gains tax liability of £20,000. At the time of C's sale, A had cumulative chargeable transfers of £40,000.

	£
Cumulative total of previous chargeable transfers of relevant person	40,000
Net sale proceeds of conditionally exempt property	115,000
	£155,000

Inheritance tax payable by C

£110,000	At Nil	—	
£5,000	At 20%	1,000	
£115,000		£1,000	£1,000

Notes to the example

(A)   A is the relevant person in relation to the chargeable event as he is the person to effect the only conditionally exempt transfer *and* the person who is settlor in relation to the settlement in respect of which the only conditionally exempt occasion arose. [*IHTA 1984, ss 33(5), 78(3)*].

(B)   HMRC have discretion to select either the conditionally exempt transfer (by A to the trustees) in 1988 or the conditionally exempt occasion (from the trustees to C) in 2002 as the 'last transaction' for the purposes of determining who is the relevant person. A is the relevant person regardless of which is selected but the HMRC are more likely to choose the earlier transfer as this will result in a greater amount of tax being collected. [*IHTA 1984, ss 33(5), 78(3)(4)*].

(C)   The chargeable amount of £115,000 does not increase either A's cumulative total or that of the trustees for the purpose of calculating the IHT liability on any subsequent transfers. As the last conditionally exempt transaction before the chargeable event was a conditionally exempt occasion rather than a conditionally exempt transfer, the provisions of *IHTA 1984, s 34* (which allow for an increase in the cumulative total) do not apply. [*IHTA 1984, s 78(6)*].

33.9   **Charge to tax.** The tax on a chargeable event is on the value of the property at the time of the event (i.e. there is no grossing-up) and where the event is a disposal on a sale not intended to confer any gratuitous benefit on any person and at arm's length between unconnected persons (or on similar terms), the value is equal to the sale proceeds (with proportionate reduction where the conditional exemption applied only to part of the property) [*IHTA 1984, ss 33(1)(a)(3)(4), 78(3)*] less any capital gains tax chargeable. [*TCGA 1992, s 258(8)*].

The rate of tax will be as in 33.5 above.

Tax is due six months after the end of the month in which the chargeable event occurs. [*IHTA 1984, s 226(4); FA 1985, Sch 26 para 11*].

Tax credit. The same credit applies as in 33.5 above with the substitution of 'conditionally exempt occasion' for 'conditionally exempt transfer'.

33.10   **Exemption from the ten-year anniversary charge.** Where, on or before the occasion on which property became comprised in the settlement, there has been

(a)   a conditionally exempt transfer of the property, or

(b)   a disposal to which *TCGA 1992, s 258(4)* applies (capital gains tax relief for works of art etc.)

there is no liability to the ten-year anniversary charge (see 44.3 SETTLEMENTS WITHOUT INTERESTS IN POSSESSION) on any such anniversary that falls before such a time as where (a) applies a chargeable event occurs, or where (b) applies, property is treated as sold under *TCGA 1992, s 258(5)*.

Where (a) or (b) above do not apply but the Board have, on a claim, designated under 33.2 above relevant settled property (see 44.2 SETTLEMENTS WITHOUT INTERESTS IN POSSESSION) and the requisite undertaking or undertakings have been given, the ten-year charge will not apply but a charge will arise on the first occurrence of any event that would be a chargeable event under 33.4 above. No charge will arise, however, if after the property becomes settled property and before the occurrence of a chargeable event, there has been a conditionally exempt occasion (see 33.7 above) in respect of the property.

Tax is charged on the value of the property at the time of the event. The rate at which tax is charged is the aggregate of the following percentages for each complete successive quarter in 'the relevant period'.

	Cumulative Total
0.25% for each of the first 40 quarters	10%
0.20% for each of the next 40 quarters	8%
0.15% for each of the next 40 quarters	6%
0.10% for each of the next 40 quarters	4%
0.05% for each of the next 40 quarters	2%
Maximum rate chargeable after 50 years	30%

33.10　National Heritage

'*Relevant period*' is the period beginning with the latest of

(i)　the day on which the settlement commenced; and

(ii)　the date of the last ten-year anniversary of the settlement to fall before the day on which the property became comprised in the settlement; and

(iii)　13 March 1975

and ending with the day before the event giving rise to the charge.

'*Quarter*' means a period of three months.

Where National Heritage property became comprised in the settlement in the previous ten years and exemption from the ten-year anniversary charge on qualifying property has been obtained as above, the value of the consideration given for that property is nevertheless taken into account when calculating the rate at which tax is charged on the other (non-national heritage) property in the settlement. The amount is included under *IHTA 1984, 66(5)(b)* as a previous chargeable transfer by the notional transferor (see 44.5 and 44.7 SETTLEMENTS WITHOUT INTERESTS IN POSSESSION).

[*IHTA 1984, ss 61(1), 63, 79(1)–(9); FA 1985, s 95, Sch 26 para 9*].

An account must be delivered within six months from the end of the month in which the chargeable event occurs and any tax payable is due at the expiration of that period. Interest on overdue tax runs from the due date (see 27 INTEREST ON TAX). [*IHTA 1984, ss 216(7), 226(4), 233(1)(c); FA 1985, Sch 26 para 11; FA 1989, s 179(1)*].

The persons liable for the tax are the trustees of the settlement and any person for whose benefit any of the property or income from it is applied at or after the time of the event occasioning the charge. [*IHTA 1984, s 207(3)*].

Example

Trustees own National Heritage property for which the necessary undertakings have been given and the property has been designated by the Treasury. The property was settled in July 1974 and is the sole asset of the trust. No appointments or advances of capital have been made. On 30 October 2007, there is a breach of the undertakings. At this date the property is valued at £150,000.

Ten-year anniversary charge
There is no liability in 1984, 1994 or 2004.

Breach in October 2007
Value of property at time of event　　　　　　　　　　　　　　　£150,000

The relevant period is the period from the date of settlement or, if later, 13 March 1975 to 29 October 2007, i.e. 130 complete quarters.

The rate of tax is

	%
0.25% for 40 quarters	10.00
0.20% for 40 quarters	8.00
0.15% for 40 quarters	6.00
0.10% for 10 quarters	1.00
	25.00%

IHT payable is 25% × £150,000 =　　　　　　　　　　　　　　£37,500

33.11   **MAINTENANCE FUNDS FOR HISTORIC BUILDINGS**

The capital transfer tax provisions detailing the conditions to be met to exempt transfers into maintenance funds for historic buildings were introduced, with effect from 2 May 1976, by *FA 1976, s 84* and amended in 1980 and 1981. These provisions were replaced in 1982 by legislation subsequently consolidated as *IHTA 1984, ss 27, 57(5), Sch 4 paras 1–7* in relation to events after 8 March 1982 although much of the previous legislation was reproduced. Previously existing exempt funds are treated as approved under the revised provisions relating to CTT and the provisions relating to IHT, and designations, under- takings and acceptances are likewise treated as having been made under *CTTA 1984, Sch 4 para 3(3)* or *IHTA 1984, Sch 4 para 3(3). [IHTA 1984, Sch 4 paras 1(3), 3(5)].*

Provided the necessary conditions are met, there is no charge to inheritance tax either when the property is settled (but see 21.16 EXEMPT TRANSFERS for abatement of this exemption) or applied for approved purposes. See IHT 16, page 26.

33.12   **Qualifying conditions.** A transfer of value is an exempt transfer to the extent that the value transferred by it is attributable to property which by virtue of a transfer becomes, or immediately after the transfer remains, comprised in a settlement and in respect of which a Board direction has effect at or after the time of the transfer. The Board may give a direction in respect of property proposed to be comprised in the settlement. *[IHTA 1984, ss 27(1), 57(5), Sch 4 para 1(2)].* Exemption will not apply to a transfer which falls within certain situations in *IHTA 1984, ss 23, 56.* See 21.2(*a*), (*b*)(i)(ii)(iii)(vii) and point (*c*) at 21.2 EXEMPT TRANSFERS. *[IHTA 1984, ss 27(2), 56(1)(3)(4)].*

The Board *must* so direct (on a claim being made, see below) if they are satisfied

(*a*)   that its property during the six years from the date on which it became comprised in the settlement can only be applied

(i)   for the maintenance, repair or preservation of, or making provision for public access to, property which is for the time being qualifying property as defined in 33.2(*b*) above in relation to which the requisite undertaking has been given under 33.3 above and no tax has become chargeable since the last undertaking given, or for defraying the expenses of the trustees or for reasonable improve- ment of property so held; or

(ii)   as respects income not so applied or accumulated, for the benefit of a body mentioned in 33.16 below or a charity which exists wholly or mainly for maintaining, repairing or preserving for the public benefit, buildings of historic or architectural interest, land of scenic, historic or scientific interest or objects of national, scientific, historic or artistic interest; and

(*b*)   that any property ceasing at any time in that period (or before the death of the settlor if earlier) to be comprised in the settlement can only devolve on a body or charity as mentioned in (ii) above; and

(*c*)   that income arising from property in the settlement can at any time after the end of that period only be applied as mentioned in (i) and (ii) above; and

(*d*)   that the property is of a character and amount appropriate for the purposes of the settlement.

The provisions as to variations of undertakings in 33.3 above also apply to undertakings under (*a*)(*i*) above. *[IHTA 1984, Sch 4 para (3A); FA 1998, Sch 25 para 8].*

Note: In (*a*)(i) above structural 'repair' to the heritage property will normally qualify but alterations will not unless they are 'necessary to preserve the existing property' such as a new roof but not the conversion of a new wing of a house. Running repairs and maintenance costs will normally qualify e.g. preservation of stonework and fabric, internal redecorations and general maintenance. Heating costs will qualify where they are necessary either to maintain or preserve the building or its qualifying contents or as a consequence of public access. Where land is concerned, clearance, provision of fences and firebreaks, upkeep of ditches and fences and provision of sluices are allowable. In the gardens, seeds, plants, materials, implements, greenhouse heating costs and gardeners' wages are allowed. (VOA IHT manual, section 20, para 20.24).

FA 1998, s 144 introduces *IHTA 1984, s 27(1A)* which imposes the need to make a claim no more than two years after the date of the transfer or such longer period as the Board may allow for transfers of value made on or after 17 March 1998. The requirement of *IHTA 1984, s 27(1A)* does not apply where property enters a maintenance fund from an interest in possession trust already in existence following the death of a person entitled to that interest — see 33.14 below.

Where the transfer into the maintenance fund was an exempt transfer made by a person entitled to a beneficial interest in possession in the property (the 'beneficiary') or the transfer fell within 33.14 below, for directions given after 16 March 1987 for the reference to the settlor in (*b*) above there is substituted a reference to either the settlor or the beneficiary.

If a trust has been, or is to be, set up for the maintenance etc. of a property within 33.2(*b*)–(*e*) above but the property has not been subject to a conditionally exempt transfer, the Board can, on a claim, designate the property and accept the necessary undertakings and it will then be treated as qualifying property.

[*IHTA 1984, Sch 4 para 1(1), 2(1)(a), 3; FA 1985, s 95, Sch 26 para 12; FA 1987, s 59, Sch 9 paras 2, 5*].

Where property is transferred from one settlement to another and a tax charge is excluded under *IHTA 1984, Sch 4 para 9* (see 33.15(iii) below) or would have been excluded but for *IHTA 1984, Sch 4 para 9(4)* (see 33.15(iii)(*b*) below) then (*a*) and (*b*) above do not apply and (*c*) applies with the omission of 'at any time after the end of that period'. The full restrictions do, however, continue to apply until the qualifying conditions have been satisfied for a period of six years from the date on which the property became comprised in the earlier maintenance settlement. [*IHTA 1984, Sch 4 para 4*].

Where more than one person is the settlor in relation to a settlement and the circumstances so require *IHTA 1984, Sch 4 paras 1–7* apply as if the settled property was comprised in separate settlements. [*IHTA 1984, s 44(2)*].

The Board may, by notice in writing, withdraw the direction from a specified date if the facts cease to warrant its continuance. [*IHTA 1984, Sch 4 para 5; FA 1985, s 95*].

The trustees must

(i) be approved by the Board;

(ii) include either a trust corporation (i.e. a person so constituted for the purposes of the *Law of Property Act 1925* or the *Administration of Estates (Northern Ireland) Order 1979, Article 9*), or a solicitor, or a member of an incorporated society of accountants or a member of such other professional body as the Board allow; and

(iii) at the time the direction is given, be resident in the UK. For this purpose, trustees are regarded as resident in the UK if the general administration is ordinarily carried on there and the trustees or a majority of them (including a majority of each class where there is more than one class of trustees) are resident there. Where a trust corporation is a trustee, residence is determined as for corporation tax.

The trustees must furnish the Board with such accounts and other information as it reasonably requires. The trusts on which the property is held are enforceable at the suit of the Board which has the rights and powers of a beneficiary regarding the appointment, removal and retirement of trustees.

[IHTA 1984, Sch 4 paras 2(1)(b)(2)(3), 6, 7; FA 1985, s 95].

The precedent below sets out these and other points in respect of the creation of a Maintenance Fund Settlement and has been kindly provided by Robert Ham QC and Emily Campbell of Wilberforce Chambers, 8 New Square, Lincoln's Inn, London WC2A 3QP.

THIS SETTLEMENT is made the   200(7)

BETWEEN:-

1. [   ] of [   ] ("the Settlor") of the one part

2. THE SETTLOR

[   ] of [   ]

[   ] of [   ] and

[   ] of [   ] ("the Original Trustees") of the other part

WHEREAS:-

(A) The Settlor wishes to establish a fund for the maintenance repair or preservation of the property known as [   ] as more particularly specified in the First Schedule hereto ("the Property") which is qualifying property for the purposes of paragraph 3(1) of Schedule 4 ("Schedule 4") to the Inheritance Tax Act 1984 ("the 1984 Act").

(B) With a view to this Settlement the Settlor has transferred the property specified in the Second Schedule hereto ("the Initial Settled Property") into the names of the Original Trustees.

(C) The Original Trustees have agreed to act as the first trustees of this Settlement and have been approved by the Board of HMRC ("the Board") under paragraph 2(1)(b) of Schedule 4.

(D) [The Board has given a direction under paragraph 1(2) of Schedule 4].

NOW THIS DEED WITNESSES as follows:-

Name of Settlement

1.   This Settlement created shall (unless the Trustees otherwise determine) be known as "the _____ Maintenance Fund Settlement".

Definitions

2.   In this Settlement where the context so admits:-

"the Accumulation Period" means the period of 21 years from the date of this Settlement

"the Beneficiaries" means:-

the Settlor

the children and remoter issue of the Settlor

the spouse and former spouses of the Settlor and [his] [her] children and remoter issue

any charity or charities

---

all Heritage Bodies (as defined below)

such other person or persons (including bodies classes and descriptions of persons) as the Trustees may by deed or deed executed during the Trust Period (with the consent in writing of the Settlor during [his] [her] lifetime but thereafter in their absolute discretion) appoint

"charity" has the same meaning as in the 1984 Act and "charities" has a corresponding meaning

"Heritage Bodies" means:-

the bodies mentioned in Schedule 3 to the 1984 Act and

any qualifying charity for the purposes of Schedule 4 as specified in paragraph 3(4) of that Schedule

"the Heritage Property" means such of the following for the time being designated by the Board under section 31(1) or paragraph 3(3) of Schedule 4 to the 1984 Act:-

the Property

land or buildings associated with the Property within the meaning of Section 32A(1) of the 1984 Act

any object historically associated with the Property or such land or buildings

"the Qualifying Purposes" means:-

the maintenance, repair or preservation of, or making provision for public access to, all or any part of the Heritage Property

the maintenance, repair or preservation of property forming part of the Trust Fund or such improvement of such property as is reasonable having regard to the purposes of the trusts of this Settlement

defraying the expenses of the Trustees in relation to all or any part of the Trust Fund

"the Specified Period" means:-

in relation to such part of the Trust Fund as from time to time represents the Initial Settled Property the period of 6 years beginning with the date of this Settlement [or such shorter period as ends on the death of the Settlor]

in relation to such part of the Trust Fund as from time to time represents any property added by way of further settlement after the date of this Settlement the period of 6 years beginning with the date of such addition [or such shorter period as ends on the person making such addition]

"the Trustees" means the Original Trustees or other trustees or trustee for the time being hereof

"the Trust Fund" means the Initial Settled Property all further property added to it by way of further settlement capital accretion accumulation of income or otherwise and the investments and property from time to time representing the same respectively

"the Trust Period" means the period of 80 years from the date of this Settlement which shall be the perpetuity period applicable hereto under the rule against perpetuities

expressions descriptive of relationship shall include adopted and legitimated persons and those tracing their descent through them but not (except as objects of powers) illegitimate persons and those tracing their descent through them

3.   **Trusts of income and capital in default of appointment**

(1)   The Trustees may from time to time during the Trust Period pay or apply all or any part of the income or capital of the Trust Fund for all or any one or more of the Qualifying Purposes And so that the Trustees may in exercise of this power reimburse the Settlor [or any other person] for any expenditure incurred by [him] [her] during the Trust Period which they themselves would have been authorised to incur under this power

(2)   Subject thereto the Trustees shall pay the income of the Trust Fund during the Trust Period for such one or more Heritage Bodies as the Trustees shall from time to time think fit

(3)   Notwithstanding the foregoing the Trustees may accumulate all or any part of the income of the Trust Fund during the Accumulation Period by investing it and the resulting income as authorised below and (subject to any payment or application thereof under sub-clause (1) above) shall pay or apply all such accumulations to or for such one or more of Heritage Bodies as the Trustees shall during the trust period think fit

(4)   From and after the expiration of the Trust Period the Trustees shall hold the Trust Fund (so far as not previously disposed of under sub-clause (1) above) and the future income thereof upon trust for such one or more of the Beneficiaries as the Trustees may by deed or deeds executed during the Trust Period appoint and subject thereto upon trust for such of the children and remoter issue or the Settlor as may be living at the expiration of the Trust Period and if more than one in equal shares absolutely according to their stocks with the Settlor's children as heads of stock

Overriding power of revocation and appointment

4. The Trustees shall have power by deed or deeds revocable or irrevocable executed from time to time during the Trust Period to revoke all or any of the trusts powers and provisions of this Settlement and to appoint such further or other trusts powers and provisions (whether beneficial or administrative in nature and whether or not involving any delegation by the Trustees and in particular including discretionary trusts and powers exercisable by any person or persons) in favour or for the benefit of any one or more of the Beneficiaries and if more than one in such shares and proportions and in such manner generally as the Trustees may with due regard to the law as to remoteness of vesting in their absolute discretion think fit And so that any such deed may direct the transfer of all or part of the Trust Fund to the trustees of any other settlement or trust in any part of the world to hold upon and with and subject to the trusts powers and provisions of such other settlement or trust

PROVIDED ALWAYS that:-

(1)   no such deed may provide that:-

(a)   any part of the capital of the Trust Fund is applicable other than for the Qualifying Purposes during the Specified Period or

(b)   any part of the income (so far as not accumulated) of any part of the Trust Fund is applicable other than for the Qualifying Purposes or for the benefit of one or more Heritage Bodies during the Specified Period or

(c)   any part of the income accumulated under the power contained in Clause 3(3) above is applicable other than for the Qualifying Purposes or for one or more Heritage Bodies

(d)   any part of the capital of the Trust Fund is to devolve other than on one or more Heritage Bodies if it ceases to be held on trusts set out in Clause 3 above during the Specified Period

(2)   no such deed shall prejudice or affect the validity of any payment of capital or income or other act or thing done prior thereto

Maintenance and advancement

5. The Statutory provisions for maintenance and advancement shall apply hereto provided that:-

the power of maintenance shall be exercisable at the absolute discretion of the Trustees and in particular free from the obligation to apply a proportionate part only of income for maintenance where other income is available for that purpose

the power of advancement shall extend to the whole and not merely one half of the share or interest of the person advanced

Ultimate trust

6. From and after the expiration of the Trust period it and so far as not otherwise disposed of hereby (for whatever reasons) the Trust Fund shall be held upon trust as to capital and income for [such charity or charities as the Trustees shall think fit]

Additional administrative powers

7. In addition to all powers of management and administration conferred on them by the law the Trustees shall have the powers set out in the Third Schedule hereto

General provisions with regard to trustee powers

8. The following provisions shall apply with regard to the powers and discretions hereby or by law conferred upon the Trustees:-

Every such power or discretion shall be exercisable only during the Trust Period or such longer period (if any) as the law may allow in the case of any particular power or discretion

Every such power or discretion shall be exercisable from time to time during the Trust Period or such longer period as aforesaid and at the absolute discretion of the Trustees

The Trustees shall have power by deed to release or restrict the future exercise of any such power or discretion either wholly and so to bind their successors or to any lesser extent as they think fit

Relaxation of equitable restrictions on trustees

9. Notwithstanding any rule of equity to the contrary:-

None of the Trustees shall be accountable for any remuneration or other benefit gained as an officer employee agent or adviser of any company or body or firm in any way connected with the Trust Fund

The Trustees may enter into any transaction (including a sale purchase lease or loan) notwithstanding that one or more of their number may have other interest therein whether in a personal or fiduciary capacity PROVIDED that (a) a person whom the Trustees reasonably believe to be a duly qualified independent valuer or other adviser has advised that the transaction is a fair and reasonable one for the Trustees to enter into and (b) a purchaser shall not be concerned to see that the foregoing provisions of this proviso have been complied with

Any of the Trustees who is engaged in any profession or business may charge and be paid all professional and other proper charges for work done services rendered advice given or time spent or his firm in connection with this Settlement whether or not within the scope of his profession or business and though not of a nature requiring the employment of a professional or business person

Appointment of trustees

10. The statutory power of appointment of new and additional trustees shall apply hereto subject to the following provisions:-

Those powers shall be exercisable by the Settlor for life

A person in any part of the world may be appointed as a trustee

A trustee shall be discharged from the trusts of this Declaration of Trust on the appointment of a new trustee or the retirement of a trustee without the appointment of a new trustee notwithstanding that there will be neither a trust corporation nor two individuals to act as trustees to perform the trusts

A corporation may be appointed as trustee hereof on such terms as to remuneration and otherwise as the person or persons making the appointment may approve or prescribe

Trustee indemnity

11. None of the Trustees who is not entitled to charge and be paid by virtue of Clause 9(3) or Clause 10(4) above shall be liable for any act or omission other than fraud, knowing misconduct or gross negligence

Inheritance tax

12.

(1) The Trustees shall from time to time furnish the Board with such accounts and other information as may reasonably be required under paragraph 6 of Schedule 4

(2) No power or other provision hereby or by law conferred shall be capable of being exercised in such a way as to prevent the conditions set out in paragraph 2 of Schedule 4 from being satisfied at a time when they would be satisfied but for such power or discretion being exercisable in that way

Stamp duty certificate

13. It is hereby certified that the transaction hereby effected falls within Category L of the Stamp Duty (Exempt Instruments) Regulations 1987

IN WITNESS etc

FIRST SCHEDULE

The Property

[Here identify the Property to be maintained.]

SECOND SCHEDULE

The Initial Settled Property

[Here specify the property that has been transferred to the Original Trustees.]

THIRD SCHEDULE

Additional administrative powers

33.12   National Heritage

1.   Power with the consent of the Board to accept additions to the Trust Fund and (if they think fit) to administer them as one fund therewith for all purposes

2.   Power to retain all or any part of the Trust Fund (including uninvested money) in its existing state of investment for any period and to vary or transpose investments within the range authorised below in either case without being under any obligation to diversify the investment thereof

3.   Power to apply trust moneys in the acquisition by purchase or otherwise of such shares stocks funds securities or other investments or property (movable or immovable) in any part of the world whether or not income producing or involving liability or by lending the same whether or not at interest and with or without security TO THE INTENT that the Trustees shall have all the powers of investment and applying trust moneys available to an absolute beneficial owner

4.   In relation to any property (movable or immovable) which (or the future proceeds of sale of which) is subject to the trusts hereof all the powers of leasing and alienation generally and of management exploitation insurance protection maintenance repair cultivation and improvement available to an absolute beneficial owner PROVIDED ALWAYS as mentioned in Clause 2 above

5.   Power to carry on whether alone or in partnership or any other form of joint venture with others any trade or business to assist or finance to any extent the carrying on of any trade or business by others

6.   Power to employ servants and independent contractors and to purchase plant and equipment in connection with any trade or business or the management of any property

7.   Power to promote and participate whether alone or with others in the formation and financing of any company or corporation for the purpose of acquiring or exploiting any property or carrying on any business

8.   Power to promote or join in promoting or otherwise concur or participate in any such scheme or arrangement and (either for the purpose of any such scheme or arrangement or otherwise) to enter into any agreement or grant any option for the disposition of any shares or other securities of any company or corporation subject to trusts hereof

9.   Power to obtain or join in obtaining any stock exchange quotation for or permission to deal in any securities and to sell or join with others in selling or disposing of securities with a view to creating a market in such securities whether or not such a sale or disposition would otherwise be desirable or prudent

10.   Power to borrow money for any purpose (including investment and payment of any tax or duty for which the Trustees are liable) and to mortgage or charge any property which (or the future proceeds of sale of which) is subject to the trusts hereof to secure repayment of any such borrowing

11.   Power to employ and remunerate a nominee or nominees in any part of the world to hold any property subject to the trusts hereof

12.   Power to employ and remunerate an agent (whether a solicitor banker broker or other person) to transact any business or do any act required to be done in the execution of the trusts hereof (including the receipt and payment of money and the management of property) without being responsible for the default of any such agent

13.	Without limiting or being limited by the foregoing power to employ remunerate and remove investment managers on such terms as the Trustees think fit and to delegate to them all or any of the Trustees' discretions in connection with the investment of the Trust Fund

14.	Power (without prejudice to or being limited by any of the other provisions of this Clause) to effect any such transaction as could be authorised under section 57 of the Trustee Act 1925 without the necessity of obtaining an order of the Court

15.	Power exercisable expressly or by implication to allot appropriate partition or apportion any property which (or the future proceeds of sale of which) is subject to the trusts hereof in or towards satisfaction of any share or interest in the capital or income of the Trust Fund in such a manner as the Trustees (without the necessity of obtaining any consent) consider just according to respective rights of the persons interested

16.	Power to permit any property (movable or immovable) which (or the future proceeds of sale of which) is subject to the trusts hereof to be used and enjoyed by any person for the time being entitled (or capable by the exercise of any power or discretion of becoming entitled) to the income thereof. And so that the Trustees shall not be liable for any loss or damage to such property but shall have power to take any steps they think fit for its insurance repair renewal or custody

17.	Power to lend trust money whether or not at interest and with or without security to any person for the time being entitled (or capable by the exercise of any power or discretion of becoming entitled) to the income thereof whether or not it would otherwise be proper for the Trustees to do so

18.	Power to mortgage or charge any property which (or the future proceeds of sale of which) is subject to the trusts hereof to secure repayment of any borrowing by any such person notwithstanding that such a loan mortgage or charge and whether or not it would otherwise be proper for the Trustees to do so

19.	Power with regard to any capital or income of the Trust Fund to be paid or applied or which the Trustees resolve to pay or apply to or for the benefit of any beneficiary who does not have capacity to give a valid receipt therefor to pay or transfer the same to and to accept the receipt of his or her parent or guardian without being liable to see the application thereof by such parent or guardian

20.	Power with regard to any capital or income of the Trust Fund to be paid or applied or which the Trustees resolve to pay or apply to or for the benefit of any Heritage Body or any charity to pay or apply to or for the benefit of any Heritage Body or any charity to pay or transfer the same to and to accept the receipt of the treasurer or appropriate officer of such Heritage Body or charity and so that such receipt shall be a complete discharge to the Trustees

21.	Powers to treat income as accruing at the date of its actual receipt instead of apportioning it pursuant to statute.

Notes to the Precedent

(A)	HMRC have the same powers in relation to the appointment, removal and retirement of trustees as any beneficiary under the settlement. See *IHTA 1984, Sch 4 para 7.*

(B)   The Trustee Indemnity is a narrower exoneration provision than that commonly found in practice, which extends even to professional Trustees who are paid for their services and protects against liability for anything except fraud or wilful wrong doing. In practice, the Trustees should submit an annual audited statement of accounts together with an annual report of the activities of the fund. It is particularly important in light of the charge in *ICTA 1988, s 694* for the Trustees to keep adequate records of accumulations of income. [*FA 2004, s 29, Sch 4 para 2*].

(C)   There is a specific exemption from *TCGA 1992, s 226A* where an election has been made under *ITA 2007, s 508* (formerly *ICTA 1988, s 691(2)*), i.e. income of the settlement to be applied for the maintenance of a historic building within point 3 of the Precedent above, whereby the trustees of the maintenance fund settlement acquired the heritage property by way of a holdover election for CGT purposes under *TCGA 1992, s 260*. In such a case the main residence relief is preserved on a later disposal of the property. [*TCGA 1992, s 226B inserted by FA 2004, Sch 22 para 6*].

33.13   **Transfers from discretionary settlements etc.** A charge to tax under *IHTA 1984, s 65* does not arise where property comprised in a SETTLEMENT WITHOUT INTERESTS IN POSSESSION (44) (the original settlement) ceases to be relevant property and either

(*a*)   becomes comprised in a settlement in respect of which a direction under 33.12 above then has effect (the maintenance fund), or

(*b*)   is transferred to an individual who in turn makes an exempt transfer to such a fund within the permitted period and the value of the exempt transfer is attributable to that property. The '*permitted period*' is 30 days from the date the property ceases to be relevant property or two years if that occasion was on the death of any person.

The exemption will not apply if

(i)   the amount on which tax would otherwise be charged (before grossing-up if applicable and before BUSINESS PROPERTY (7) relief or AGRICULTURAL PROPERTY (5) relief) exceeds the value of the property immediately after it becomes, in (*a*) above, property in respect of which the direction has effect or, in (*b*) above, comprised in the maintenance settlement (less any consideration received by the original trustees under (*a*) or the individual under (*b*)). In these cases, the amount on which tax is charged is restricted to the excess without grossing-up and ignoring business property relief and agricultural property relief, or

(ii)   the trustees of the maintenance fund under (*a*) above acquired an interest under the original settlement, at or before the time when the property in question is transferred, for a consideration in money or money's worth or as a result of transactions which include a disposition for such consideration (whether to them or another) of that interest or of other property, or

(iii)   the individual under (*b*) above has acquired the property for a consideration in money or money's worth or as the result of transactions which include a disposition for such consideration (whether to him or another) of that or other property.

[*IHTA 1984, Sch 4 paras 16–18*].

See also the provisions of 44.15 and 44.16 SETTLEMENTS WITHOUT INTERESTS IN POSSESSION which also apply to property settled or appointed on maintenance funds.

33.14   **Transfers from interest in possession settlements following the death of the beneficiary.** Where a person dies after 16 March 1987 but before 22 March 2006 and immediately before his death he was entitled to an interest in possession in settled property, then, subject to the exceptions below, if, within two years after his death, the property becomes held on qualifying trusts within 33.12 above (whether in the same or a different settlement) the disposition is treated as having been made by the deceased.

Accordingly, no disposition or other event occurring after his death and before the property becomes subject to those trusts is, so far as it relates to the property, a transfer of value or an occasion for a charge to tax.

Where a person dies on or after 22 March 2006 and immediately before his death he was entitled to an interest in possession in settled property, then, subject to the exceptions below, if, within two years after his death, the property becomes held on qualifying trusts within 33.12 above (whether in the same or a different settlement) the disposition is treated as having been made by the deceased but only if the interest in the settlement was:

(1)　an immediate post-death interest (see SETTLEMENTS WITH INTERESTS IN POSSESSION (43)),

(2)　a disabled person's interest (see TRUSTS FOR DISABLED PERSONS (54)), or

(3)　a transitional serial interest (see SETTLEMENTS WITH INTERESTS IN POSSESSION (43)).

Where the property becomes held on the qualifying trusts as a result of court proceedings (and could only have done so) the two year period is extended to three years.

The provisions do not apply if

(a)　the disposition by which the property becomes held on qualifying trusts depends on a condition or is defeasible;

(b)　the property which becomes held on those trusts is itself an interest in settled property;

(c)　the trustees who hold the property on those trusts have, for a consideration in money or money's worth, acquired an interest under a settlement in which the property was comprised immediately before the death of the beneficiary or at any time thereafter; or

(d)　the property which became held on those trusts does so for a consideration in money or money's worth, or is acquired by the trustees for such a consideration, or has at any time since the death of the beneficiary been acquired by any other person for such consideration.

If the value of the property when it becomes held on the qualifying trusts is lower than that part of the value transferred on the death which is attributable to the property, the provisions apply to the property only to the extent of the lower value.

For the purposes of (c) and (d) above a person is treated as acquiring property for a consideration in money or money's worth if he becomes entitled to it as a result of transactions which include a disposition for such consideration (whether to him or another) of that or other property. [*IHTA 1984, s 57A; FA 1987, s 59, Sch 9 paras 1, 4; FA 2006, Sch 20 para 17*].

33.15　**Property leaving a maintenance fund.** A charge to tax arises on property in an approved maintenance fund

(a)　which is applied otherwise than for the purposes in 33.12(a)(i) or (ii); or

(b)　which devolves otherwise than on a body or charity as mentioned under 33.12(a)(ii); or

(c)　which devolves on a qualifying body or charity under 33.12(a)(ii) above but, at or before the time of devolution, an interest under the settlement in which the property was comprised immediately before the devolution is or has been acquired for a consideration in money or money's worth (or as the result of transactions which include a disposition for such consideration, whether to that body, etc. or to another person) by that or another such body, etc. For this purpose, any acquisition from another such body, etc. is disregarded; or (*d*) where, if (*a*) or (*b*) above do not apply, the trustees make a disposition which reduces the value of the settled property. '*Disposition*' includes an omission to exercise a right, unless not deliberate, which is treated as made at the latest time the right could be exercised.

[*IHTA 1984, Sch 4 para 8(1)–(3)(5)(6)*].

No charge arises under the following circumstances

(i) If, under (*d*) above, the trustees do not intend to confer a gratuitous benefit and either the transaction is at arm's length between persons not connected with each other (see 13 CONNECTED PERSONS) or is such as might be expected in such a transaction.

(ii) If, under (*d*) above, the disposition is a grant of tenancy of agricultural property in the UK, Channel Islands or Isle of Man, for use for agricultural purposes made for full consideration in money or money's worth.

(iii) If the property becomes comprised in another approved maintenance fund as a result of an exempt transfer under 33.12 above within the permitted period i.e. 30 days from the date on which tax would otherwise be chargeable *or* two years if that occasion was the death of the settlor. Where the transfer into the maintenance fund was an exempt transfer made by a person entitled to a beneficial interest in possession in the property (the 'beneficiary') or the transfer fell within 33.14 above, for occasions of charge or potential charge after 16 March 1987 for the reference to the death of the settlor there is substituted a reference to either the death of the settlor or the beneficiary.

This exemption is not available.

(*a*) if the person making the exempt transfer acquired the property for money or money's worth or as a result of transactions which include a disposition for such consideration (whether to him or another) of that or other property, or

(*b*) if the amount on which tax would otherwise be charged (before grossing-up, if applicable, and before BUSINESS PROPERTY (7) relief or AGRICULTURAL PROPERTY (5) relief) exceeds the value of the property immediately after it becomes comprised in the settlement (less any consideration for the transfer received by the person who makes the transfer). The amount on which tax is charged is, however, limited to the excess, without grossing-up or taking into account business property relief or agricultural property relief.

(iv) If the settlor or his spouse or civil partner become beneficially entitled to the property, or, if the settlor has died in the preceding two years, the settlor's widow or widower or surviving civil partner become beneficially entitled to it. This exemption is not available:

(*a*) if, at or before the time when the settlor, etc. becomes beneficially entitled to the property, he acquires or has acquired an interest under the approved maintenance fund for a consideration in money or money's worth or as the result of transactions which include a disposition for such consideration (whether to him or another) of that or of other property, or

(*b*) if the amount on which tax would otherwise be charged (before grossing-up, if applicable, and before BUSINESS PROPERTY (7) relief or AGRICULTURAL PROPERTY (5) relief) exceeds the value of the property immediately after it becomes the property of the settlor, etc. (less any consideration for its transfer received by the trustees). The amount on which tax is charged is, however, limited to the excess, without grossing-up or taking into account business property relief or agricultural property relief, or

(*c*) if the property was relevant property before it became, or last became held in the approved maintenance fund and, by virtue of 33.13(*a*) or (*b*) above, no proportionate charge to tax arose (or no such charge would have arisen apart from 33.13(*i*)) on its ceasing to be relevant property. See 44.2 and 44.9 SETTLEMENTS WITHOUT INTERESTS IN POSSESSION for '*relevant property*' and '*proportionate charge to tax*' respectively, or

(*d*)   if, before the property last became comprised in an approved maintenance fund (the second fund) it was comprised in another such fund (the first fund) and it ceased to be comprised in the first fund and last became comprised in the second fund in circumstances such that by virtue of (iii) above no charge to tax arose (or no charge would have arisen but for (iii)(*b*) above), or

(*e*)   unless the person who becomes beneficially entitled to the property is domiciled in the UK at the time when he becomes so entitled.

Where the transfer into the maintenance fund was an exempt transfer made by a person entitled to a beneficial interest in possession in the property (the 'beneficiary') or the transfer fell within 33.14 above, for occasions of charge or potential charge after 16 March 1987 the above provisions do not apply if the beneficiary had died at or before the time when the property became property subject to the charge to tax. Otherwise, the above provisions apply with the substitution of 'beneficiary' for 'settlor' wherever occurring. Where, however, the property becomes property to which the beneficiary's spouse, civil partner, widow or widower or surviving civil partner is beneficially entitled, the charge to tax is only avoided where the spouse etc. would have become beneficially entitled to the property on the termination of the interest in possession if the property had not then become held on maintenance trusts.

(v)   Where the property becomes held for charitable purposes only without limit of time or the property of a political party qualifying for exemption under *IHTA 1984, s 24*, a national body mentioned in *IHTA 1984, Sch 3*, or, under certain conditions, a body not established or conducted for profit (see 21.3, 21.5–21.7 EXEMPT TRANSFERS).

[*IHTA 1984, s 76, Sch 4 paras 8(3), 9, 10, 15A; FA 1987, s 59, Sch 9 paras 3, 6; The Tax and Civil Partnership Regulations 2005, SI 2005/3229, Reg 39*].

Tax is charged on the amount by which the trust property is less immediately after the event giving rise to the charge than it would have been but for the event (i.e. the loss to the donor principle), grossed-up where the settlement pays the tax. [*IHTA 1984, Sch 4 para 8(3)*].

Note that for the purposes of the capital gains tax counter avoidance legislation within *FA 2004, s 117, Sch 22* where trustees acquire property with the benefit of *TCGA 1992, s 260* holdover relief and are denied the relief on disposal of the property, if it is property within the meaning of *IHTA 1984 Sch 4* the main residence relief is preserved on a subsequent disposal by them. [*TCGA 1992, s 226B as inserted by FA 2004, Sch 22 para 6*]. See Note C to the Precedent in 33.12 above.

Rates of tax. The rate at which tax is charged depends upon whether or not the chargeable property has previously been relevant property comprised in a SETTLEMENT WITHOUT INTERESTS IN POSSESSION (44).

(A)   Where the property chargeable was relevant property before it became (or last became) held in the approved maintenance fund and, by virtue of 33.13(*a*) or (*b*) above, no proportionate charge to tax arose (or no such charge would have arisen apart from 33.13(*i*)) on its ceasing to be relevant property, the rate at which tax is charged is the aggregate of the following percentages for each complete successive quarter in 'the relevant period'

	Cumulative Total
0.25% for each of the first 40 quarters	10%
0.20% for each of the next 40 quarters	8%
0.15% for each of the next 40 quarters	6%
0.10% for each of the next 40 quarters	4%
0.05% for each of the next 40 quarters	2%
Maximum rate chargeable after 50 years	30%

'*Relevant period*' is the period *beginning* with the latest of the date of the last ten-year anniversary of the settlement in which the property was comprised before it ceased (or last ceased) to be relevant property *or* the day on which the property became (or last became) relevant property before it ceased (or last ceased) to be such property *or* 13 March 1975 and *ending* on the day before the chargeable event. Where property in respect of which tax is chargeable has at any time ceased to be and again become property in an approved maintenance fund such that by virtue of (iii) above no charge to tax arose (or no charge would have arisen but for (iii)(*b*) above) it is treated for these purposes as having been the property of an approved maintenance fund throughout the permitted period in (iii) above.

'*Quarter*' means a period of three months.

[*IHTA 1984, Sch 4 paras 8(4), 11*].

(B)   In all other cases, the rate at which tax is charged is the higher of

(*aa*)   the aggregate of the percentages for each successive quarter in the relevant period as in the table in (A) above (but see below for the meaning of relevant period in this context), and

(*bb*)   if the settlor is alive, the effective rate applicable to the property if it were added to the cumulative total of his chargeable transfers at the date of the chargeable event and tax calculated using the rates applicable to lifetime transfers. The rate or rates determined in respect of any occasion are not affected by the death of the settlor after that occasion, and

(*cc*)   if the settlor has died since 12 March 1975, the effective rate applicable to the property if it were added to the value of his estate on death and formed the highest part of that value. If the settlement was made on death, the death rates are used, if not, the rates applicable to lifetime transfers are used, and

(*dd*)   if the settlor died before 13 March 1975, the effective rate that would be applicable to the property if the settlor dies when the chargeable event occurred and the chargeable amount were added to and formed the highest part of the value on which estate duty was chargeable when in fact he died. If the settlement was made on death, the death rates are used, if not, the rates applicable to lifetime transfers are used.

Where the transfer into the maintenance fund was an exempt transfer made by a person entitled to a beneficial interest in possession in the property (the 'beneficiary') or the transfer fell within 33.14 above, for occasions of charge or potential charge after 16 March 1987 for the reference in (*aa*) to (*dd*) above to the settlor there are substituted references to the beneficiary. Under (*cc*) and (*dd*) if the beneficiary had died at or before the time when the property became property subject to the charge, the death rates are used, if not the rates applicable to lifetime transfers are used.

Where (*dd*) above applies or where under (*cc*) above the settlor died before 18 March 1986, nevertheless, the amount of tax payable is calculated as if the amendments to *IHTA 1984, s 7* in *FA 1986, Sch 19 para 2* (rates of tax for transfers within seven years of death and tapering relief) had applied at the time of death.

'*Relevant period*' under (*aa*) above means the period beginning with the day on which the chargeable property became (or *first* became) comprised in an approved maintenance fund and ending with the day before the event giving rise to the charge. For this purpose, any occasion on which the property became comprised in an approved maintenance fund and which occurred before an occasion of charge to tax under (*a*) to (*d*) above (other than the event currently giving rise to the charge or an occasion which would not be an occasion of charge but for (iii)(*b*) above) is disregarded.

'*Effective rate*' in (*bb*) to (*dd*) is the rate found by expressing the tax chargeable as a percentage of the amount on which it is charged.

For the purposes of (*bb*) to (*dd*) above, where tax is chargeable on property which has previously been comprised in another settlement and ceased to be comprised in that first settlement in circumstances such that, by virtue of (iii) above no charge to tax arose (or no charge would have arisen but for (iii)(*b*) above), '*settlor*' is construed as a reference to the person who was settlor of the first settlement, or, if the Board so determine, the current settlement. Where property has previously been comprised in more than one settlement and ceased to be comprised in each of them and became comprised in another or the current settlement in similar circumstances, '*settlor*' is construed as a reference to the person who was settlor of the first of the previous settlements, or, if the Board so determine, any other of the previous settlements or the current settlement. Similarly, for occasions of charge after 16 March 1987 where the transfer into the maintenance fund was an exempt transfer made by a person entitled to a beneficial interest in possession in the property (the 'beneficiary') or the transfer fell within 33.14 above, '*beneficiary*' may be, if the Board so determine, construed as a reference to the person who was settlor of the current settlement or, where the property has previously been comprised in more than one settlement, any of the previous settlements or the current settlement.

Where, in the period of seven years preceding the current charge, there has been a previous charge where the tax was calculated at the rate under (*bb*) to (*dd*) above and the person who is the settlor for the purposes of the current charge was the settlor for the purposes of the previous charge, the amount on which tax was charged on the previous charge (or if there have been more than one, the aggregate of the amounts on which tax was charged on each) is taken for the purposes of calculating the rate of the current charge

(i)   under (*bb*) above, to be the value transferred by a chargeable transfer made by the settlor immediately before the occasion of the current charge; and

(ii)   under (*cc*) or (*dd*) above, to increase the value there mentioned by an amount equal to the amount or aggregate on which tax was previously charged.

This applies whether or not the settlements are the same and, if the settlor is dead, whether or not he has died since the other charge. Where the transfer into the maintenance fund was an exempt transfer made by a person entitled to a beneficial interest in possession in the property (the 'beneficiary') or the transfer fell within 33.14 above, for occasions of charge or potential charge after 16 March 1987 for the references to the settlor there are substituted references to the beneficiary.

[*IHTA 1984, Sch 4 paras 12–14, 15A; FA 1986, Sch 19 paras 38, 42; FA 1987, s 59, Sch 9 paras 3, 6*].

In (*cc*) and (*dd*) above, where tax is reduced by the substitution of a new Table of rates between the date of death and the chargeable event, the new rates are used. [*IHTA 1984, Sch 2 para 6*].

Property in pre-*FA 1982* maintenance funds which are treated as approved under the current provisions by *IHTA 1984, Sch 4 para 1(3)* (see 33.11 above) is for the purposes of calculation of the rates of charge treated as having become property in an approved maintenance fund at the time of the original transfer of value. [*IHTA 1984, Sch 4 para 15*].

Example

On 1 January 1989 P settled £500,000 in an approved maintenance fund for his historic mansion during the lives of himself and his wife, W. P died in February 1994, his taxable estate and lifetime transfers chargeable on death amounting to £175,000. On 1 January 2008, the date of death of W, the fund, which has been depleted by extensive repairs to the mansion, is valued at £300,000. £80,000 is transferred to the National Trust, which also accepts the gift of the mansion, and the balance is paid to P's grandson G.

No IHT is payable on the £80,000 paid to the National Trust, but the balance passing to G is liable to IHT at the higher of a tapered scale rate (the 'first rate') and an effective rate calculated by reference to P's estate (the 'second rate'). [*IHTA 1984, Sch 4 paras 12–14*].

First rate

The property was comprised in the maintenance fund for 19 years, i.e. 76 quarters.

The scale rate is

	%
0.25% for each of the first 40 quarters	10.0
0.20% for each of the next 36 quarters	7.2
	17.2%

Second rate

The effective rate is calculated, using half Table rates applying on 1 January 2008 (taken as those rates applying on 6 April 2007), as if the chargeable amount transferred (£220,000) had been added to the value transferred by P on his death (£175,000) and had formed the highest part of the total. Half Table rates at 41.1 **2007.A1** RATES OF TAX are used because the fund was set up in P's lifetime.

	£
£125,000 at nil	—
£95,000 at 20%	19,000
£220,000	£19,000

The effective rate is $\dfrac{19,000}{220,000} \times 100\% =$ 8.63%

As the second rate (8.63%) is lower than the first rate (17.2%) the first rate is used.

IHT payable is £220,000 at 17.2% = £37,840

33.16 GIFTS, ETC. TO NATIONAL BODIES

Gifts to the following bodies whether or not national heritage property are exempt from inheritance tax. For exceptions, see 21 EXEMPT TRANSFERS.

The National Gallery.

The British Museum.

The National Museums of Scotland.

The National Museum of Wales.

The Ulster Museum.

Any other similar national institution which exists wholly or mainly for the purpose of preserving for the public benefit a collection of scientific, historic or artistic interest and which is approved for this purpose by the Treasury.

Any museum or art gallery in the UK which exists wholly or mainly for that purpose and is maintained by a local authority or university in the UK.

Any library the main function of which is to serve the needs of teaching and research at a university in the UK.

The Historic Buildings and Monuments Commission for England.

The National Trust for Places of Historic Interest or Natural Beauty.

The National Trust for Scotland for Places of Historic Interest or Natural Beauty.

The National Art Collections Fund.

The National Endowment for Science, Technology and the Arts.

The Trustees of the National Heritage Memorial Fund.

The Friends of the National Libraries.

English Nature.

The Historic Churches Preservation Trust.

Scottish National Heritage.

Countryside Council for Wales.

Any local authority within *ITA 2007, s 838*.

Any Government department (including the National Debt Commissioners).

Any university or university college in the UK.

A health service body within *ICTA 1988, s 519A* and *FA 2004, s 148* .

Since the 1984 Act similar national institutions are, with Treasury approval or the Board of HMRC, also included in the list of bodies within *IHTA 1984, Sch 3*.

[*National Heritage Act 1980; IHTA 1984, s 25(1), Sch 3; FA 1985, s 95; National Heritage (Scotland) Act 1985, Sch 2 para 4; National Health Service and Community Care Act 1990, s 61(5); Environmental Protection Act 1990, Sch 6 para 25; National Heritage (Scotland) Act 1991, Sch 2 para 9*].

See also 21.3 EXEMPT TRANSFERS which equally applies to settled property becoming the property of bodies listed above. [*IHTA 1984, s 76*].

Sales by private treaty to national bodies. To encourage *sales* to approved bodies as above, the conditional exemption from IHT will not be lost on such a transaction (but see 33.4(b) above for exception where there are associated properties). [*IHTA 1984, ss 32(4),*

32A(5); FA 1985, Sch 26 para 4]. Even if the work of art has not been formally exempted from IHT, a sale of this character by concession will not normally attract CGT. The price paid by the museum etc. in a private treaty sale is based on an agreed valuation of the picture or object in the open market or at auction. The amount the buyer offers to pay takes into account the tax exemption and divides the benefit of the exemption between both parties. The government has advised museums etc. that, in general, the seller should receive 25% (10% in the case of real property) of the benefit of tax exemption, subject to negotiations above or below this figure where flexibility is appropriate. It has been suggested that this amount of 25% should be increased to 50% by Resource's *Acceptance in Lieu: A Review* in January 2001, para 3.21. The final sum received will therefore be more than the net sum on an open market sale (i.e. gross value less tax) because the seller shares in the amount of tax saved. The addition is sometimes known as 'the douceur' (see also HMRC Capital Gains Tax Manual, para 73370) and the arrangement is an administrative not a statutory one (see IR 67 paragraph 10.1).

A claim for exemption from inheritance tax on the transfer of a heritage object, whether in life or on death, is normally made on or shortly after the transfer. Where an estate includes an object in respect of which a claim might be made, and the executors or administrators wish to sell the object by private treaty while the estate is in the course of administration and before a claim has been made, nothing in the legislation prevents designation of the object as exempt before or on such sale. The price is a matter for free negotiation between the parties but there is no capital gains tax exemption where no undertaking has been given regarding maintenance, preservation and access unless allowed concessionally. (Hansard Vol 9 No 153 Col 697, Written Answer for 31 July 1981).

No CGT is charged if property is accepted in lieu of IHT although it is usually necessary for CTO to calculate a notional charge in arriving at the approximate tax credit. (See also VOA IHT manual, section 20, para 20.60).

Acceptance in satisfaction of tax. If IHT has to be paid on any assets, it may be possible to offer a work of art, chattel, etc. in satisfaction of the liability. This is known as acceptance in lieu and the work of art accepted is exempt from IHT, whether or not it has been formally exempted. If the Secretary of State agrees with advice received from the AIL panel then a particular item(s) may be accepted in lieu of tax. Each Secretary of State (England, Wales, Scotland and Northern Ireland) will be ultimately responsible for the decision. The standard of objects which can be so accepted is very much higher than that applicable for conditional exemption. They have to satisfy a test of 'pre-eminence' either in the context of a national, local authority, or university collection, or through association with a particular building. A further administration requirement has been introduced to ensure that due diligence procedure with respect to the provenance and title to the chattel offered in lieu of tax. This is a result of the claims for restitution of chattels by descendants of Holocaust victims.

The benefit of the tax exemption is taken into account by adding 25% (the douceur) of the value of that exemption to the estimated value of the object after payment of notional tax. The amount thus calculated is offset against the tax liability of the estate on other property. However, see Taxation, 10 November 1994 page 123 regarding the Capital Taxes Office [now HMRC Inheritance Tax] refusal in some cases to accept assets of national importance in lieu of tax chargeable on the estate where those assets are inheritance tax exempt for any other reason e.g. business property relief.

Example

Trustees of deceased Lord Charles offer to the AIL Panel a chattel estimated to be worth £1 million at auction and seven acres of land with an arboretum designed by Capability Brown valued at £500,000. The IHT liability at 40% would be £400,000 on the chattel and £200,000 on the land. The douceur in the case of the chattel is 25% of the IHT due and in the case of the land is 10%. Therefore, the amount accepted in lieu of tax with douceur in these two circumstances would be as follows:

Chattel (auction value)	£1,000,000
Less: IHT @ 40%	£(400,000)
	£600,000
Add: Douceur at 25% × £400,000	£100,000
Sub-total	£700,000
Land (Valuation by the RICS)	£500,000
Less: IHT @ 40%	£(200,000)
	£300,000
Add: Douceur at 10% × £200,000	£20,000
	£320,000
Total acceptance in lieu (AIL) for chattel and land	**£1,020,000**

Persons wishing to offer a work of art in lieu of tax should send details to the CTO, London at the address in 2.11 ACCOUNTS AND RETURNS. See also 35.6 PAYMENT OF TAX. When HMRC receives an offer in lieu of tax it normally seeks the following details relating to the taxable occasion for which the offer in lieu of tax relates.

1.   A full description of the items being offered, giving, where appropriate, the artist, the medium (oil on canvas, watercolour, porcelain, bronze, etc.) and dimensions. Any exhibition history, literature and provenance should also be supplied. For archival offers, a full calendar, if available, should be supplied. Where a calendar is not on hand, a detailed description should be provided with the number of pieces in each section of the archive.

2.   Three good quality photographs, preferably in colour, of each item being offered. This is not required for archival offers.

3.   The valuation at which each item is being offered and a justification of the value by reference to previous sales of that artist or the dale of similar works. Unless HMRC has agreed to the alternative, the valuation should be that for the date the offer is made to them.

4.   A statement explaining why the items are being proposed as pre-eminent or, where appropriate, the association with an historic property.

5.   A statement of any allocation wishes or conditions that are part of the offer.

Such evidence might best also be provided to the AIL panel at the same time as when sent to HMRC.

Property may also be accepted in satisfaction of interest accrued on CTT, IHT or ED as well as in lieu of the tax itself. When an offer is made in lieu of tax interest stops accruing on the tax that the item is being offered to settle under AIL. In the case where tax has been paid in advance to obtain Grant of Probate a successful completion of the offer will result in a repayment of tax and any interest. Where the AIL panel require an item on offer for AIL to be replaced by another item the 'interest holiday' will still apply from the original offer and not the requested revised offer. Where property is accepted neither CGT, Stamp Duty nor VAT is charged. (VOA IHT manual, section 20, para 20.30). [*IHTA 1984, s 230*].

33.17   **ESTATE DUTY**

On the occurrence of a chargeable event, estate duty may still be payable on heritage objects granted conditional exemption under the estate duty provisions. Where the object was conditionally exempt on an inter vivos gift the 'taper' relief of *FA 1960, s 64* is only given for clawback assessments made before 3 May 1984. (HMRC Press Release 3 May 1984). See also 52 TRANSITIONAL PROVISIONS. [**Case Study 3**].

34 Partnerships

Cross-references. See 5 AGRICULTURAL PROPERTY and 7 BUSINESS PROPERTY for relief applicable to disposal of partnership assets; 13 CONNECTED PERSONS; 35.3 PAYMENT OF TAX for payment by instalments.

Simon's Direct Tax Service, part I6.2.

Other Sources. VOA IHT manual, sections 7, 19; Foster, part F2.

34.1 ENGLISH PARTNERSHIPS

An English partnership is not a legal entity in the same way as a company, but a *collection of separate individuals*. This being so, the provisions of inheritance tax apply to each partner as an individual and to his interest in the firm's assets. (See also VOA IHT manual, section 19, para 19.8.)

The Law Commission's proposals regarding the reform of the *Partnership Act 1890* and the *Limited Partnerships Act 1907* were likely, when introduced, to have an impact on direct taxes including IHT. Department of Trade and Industry Press Release, DTI/04/163, 4 May 2004. The aims of the reforms were to

- preserve partnership as a flexible, informal and private business vehicle;

- encourage continuity of business by facilitating continuity of partnership; and

- preserve mutual trust and good faith as a critical components of the relationship between partners.

In reply to responses to the consultation the report dated November 2003 stated that:

'We regard it as important that our proposed reforms should not materially alter the treatment of partnerships for tax purposes although they may provide an opportunity for addressing some of the anomalies of the present law.'

See CM6015 and at http://www.lawcom.gov.uk/docs/lc283–2.pdf.

Part of the reforms proposed will focus on conferring 'legal personality' on the partnership within Part V of the Joint Consultation Report and this may have an impact with regard to IHT in that treatment as a legal entity will possibly necessitate taxation warranties where transfers in shares in a partnership are involved. In spite of *IHTA 1984, ss 10, 270* which concerns 'no gratuitous intent' and *bona fide* commercial arrangements there may be a transfer of value under new proposals. However, if the tax remains unpaid it might be collected from the partners in a similar way to *IHTA 1984, s 202(1)(b)* in relation to close companies. In order to counteract the possibility of such a tax charge a tax warranty similar to that used for close companies may be required. See 12.6 CLOSE COMPANIES. One area of potential benefit might be the ability to transfer 'shares' in the new legal entity partnership to, say, children without the current problems so that the potentially exempt transfer provisions might apply to the transfer(s). Partners are connected persons with each other and with the spouse or civil partner or relative (brother, sister, ancestor or lineal descendant, uncle, aunt, nephew and niece, etc.) of each other, except in relation to acquisitions and disposals of partnership assets pursuant to *bona fide* commercial arrangements. [*TCGA 1992, s 286; IHTA 1984, s 270; The Tax and Civil Partnership Regulations 2005, SI 2005/3229, Reg 121*]. Where there are transactions between partners there is no transfer of value where no gratuitous benefit is intended and the transaction is such as might be expected to be made in a transaction at arm's length between persons not connected with each other. These normal reliefs will equally be available to partners in new Limited Liability Partnership (LLP) as an old partnership. [*IHTA 1984, s 10*].

34.1 Partnerships

'Buy and sell' agreements. See 7.4 BUSINESS PROPERTY for the effect of a partnership 'buy and sell' agreement on the availability of business property relief on the transfer of a partner's interest in the partnership.

Goodwill. Where goodwill is ignored for incoming and outgoing partners then *IHTA 1984, s 10* would probably apply so that there is no transfer of value. It would also apply where consideration passes which is equal to the market value or the value which would pass between persons at arm's length. See also *A-G v Boden and Another KB 1911, [1912] 1 KB 539; A-G v Ralli 1936, 15 ATC 523* and *Re White (deceased) White v Minnis and Another, Ch D [1999] 2 All ER 663*.

Other partnership transactions. Many transactions between partners will be on the basis of arm's length values with consideration passing in some form or other. Otherwise the normal rules apply for inheritance tax purposes.

In the case of partnership property the starting point is the valuation of the whole, but it is recognised that because of the fragmented ownership, a purchaser would expect to pay a lower price than if the whole of the property had been available as a single entity. Note the discount should not exceed 10%. (VOA IHT manual, section 19, para 19.8 but also see 56.5 VALUATION).

Partnership assurance policies taken out before 15 September 1976 (and not varied since that date) on normal business terms on trusts under English law (or Scots law provided the policy does not directly or indirectly involve a partnership itself as a separate persona) will not be regarded as settlements for inheritance tax purposes if the premiums paid fall within *IHTA 1984, s 10* (see above). The exercise of a power of appointment under a 'discretionary' trust policy would not be regarded as a variation. (See F10 at 23 HMRC EXTRA-STATUTORY CONCESSIONS).

Scottish partnerships are legal entities, so that provisions relating to individuals might not strictly apply, but in practice it is thought that the provisions would be applied as for the rest of the UK. In this connection, a Scottish Limited Liability Partnership which forms the basis of a Lloyd's member's underwriting vehicle might form the claim for a 'fast track' application to distribute and in this connection apply for leave to distribute the estate on the basis that no further provision need be made for Lloyd's creditors. The claim form is supported by an affidavit (or witness statement) in the form of a Chancery Master's Practice Form adapted as necessary (see 59.25 WORKING CASE STUDY). It should also be accompanied by draft minutes (see Chancery Master's Practice Forms) and a statement of costs (see Costs Practice Direction). (VOA IHT manual, section 19, para 19.11).

The CTO will decide when a property in the occupation of a partnership is to be regarded as a partnership asset and advise the DV accordingly as well as all the partner's beneficial interests in the assets, or if not known, state the number of partners and the way in which the profits are divisible between them. (VOA IHT manual, section 7, para 7.34).

Under English law, unlike Scottish law, a partnership cannot of itself hold an interest in land and the grant of a tenancy is to one or more of the individual partners. (VOA IHT manual, section 9, para 9.9).

Limited Liability Partnership (LLP) members are treated as if they are partners in a partnership. This ensures that inheritance tax will be charged in respect of members' interests in a LLP as it relates to partners' interests in a partnership and that business property relief will be available on the same basis. See 7.4 BUSINESS PROPERTY. These provisions have still to come into effect from a date yet to be appointed. [*IHTA 1984, s 267A as inserted by Limited Liability Partnerships Act 2000, s 11*].

Civil partnerships. With the introduction of the *Civil Partnership Act 2004* (CPA 2004), which received Royal Assent on 18 November 2004, it is possible for same sex couples to have their relationship legally recognised following a registration process which will then entitle them to acquire legal rights similar to heterosexual married couples. See 59.48

WORKING CASE STUDY for the formal procedure required. There are certain restrictions and the individuals who must be of the same sex must be unmarried and not party to another civil partnership whilst also not being related to each other. [*CPA 2004, s 3, Sch 1*]. Once they have their registration certificate they will be treated similarly to married couples with regard to both legal and taxation matters including IHT. [*FA 2005, s 103; The Tax and Civil Partnership Regulations 2005, SI 2005/3229*]. See also 59.47 WORKING CASE STUDY.

35   Payment of Tax

Cross-references. See 4 ADMINISTRATION AND COLLECTION; 27 INTEREST ON TAX; 29 LIABILITY FOR TAX; 59 WORKING CASE STUDY.

Simon's Direct Tax Service, part I11.4, I11.5.

Other Sources. Foster, part K; IHTM30000.

35.1   DUE DATE OF TAX

Lifetime transfers. Inheritance tax is due six months after the end of the month in which the chargeable transfer is made unless made after 5 April and before 1 October in any year when tax is due on 30 April in the following year.

Exceptions. Tax chargeable on the ending of conditional exemption for works of art, historic buildings etc. on woodlands and on maintenance funds for historic buildings is always payable six months after the end of the month in which the chargeable event occurs.

It should be noted that tax will often become payable before accounts (see 2 ACCOUNTS AND RETURNS) are due to be rendered.

Transfers on death. Inheritance tax is due six months after the end of the month in which death occurs but personal representatives must pay the tax for which they are liable *on delivery of their account* (even if before the due date) and may also at the same time pay any other tax on the death at the request of the persons liable. The *FA 2007* changes make provision for situations where there is a left-over pension pot at the death of an ASP scheme member who was over the age of 75 on death and was traced after their death by the scheme administrator. In such cases the left-over ASP funds are brought within the charge to IHT by *IHTA 1984, s 151A(6)* but the scheme administrator has six months from the end of the month in which they discovered the scheme member's death to pay any IHT due. [*IHTA 1984, s 226(4) inserted by FA 2007, Sch 19 para 25*].

Lifetime transfers with additional liability on death. Where tax or additional tax is due at death because

(*a*)   a POTENTIALLY EXEMPT TRANSFER (38) proves to be a chargeable transfer; or

(*b*)   the transferor dies within seven years of making a chargeable lifetime transfer; or

(*c*)   gifts have been made before 15 March 1988 and within one year of death to a political party in excess of £100,000; or

(*d*)   the settlor dies within seven years of the transfer and a further liability arises under the rules relating to SETTLEMENTS WITHOUT INTERESTS IN POSSESSION (44),

the additional tax is due six months after the end of the month in which death occurs.

[*IHTA 1984, s 226(1)–(4); FA 1986, Sch 19 para 30; FA 1988, Sch 14*].

Without prejudice to the recovery of the remainder of any tax due, the Board may, in the first instance, accept or demand payment by reference to the value stated in an account delivered to them. [*IHTA 1984, s 226(5)*].

35.2   ADDRESSES FOR PAYMENT OF TAX

England and Wales   Section K, HMRC Inheritance Tax, Ferrers House, PO Box 38, Castle Meadow Road, Nottingham NG2 1BB
Tel. 0845 3020900
Fax. 0115 974 2432
DX 701205 Nottingham 4

	Note: Electronic transfer payments are made to Bank of England, Sort code 10-00-00, Account 23430303 when using BACS or CHAPS. When using Bank Giro Credit use the Sort code 10-53-92 but the same Account number.
Scotland	HMRC, Meldrum House, 15 Drumsheugh Gardens, Edinburgh EH3 7UG.

Tel. 0131–777 4050
Fax. 0131–777 4220
DX 542001 Edinburgh 14
Note: Electronic transfer payments regarding the Edinburgh office are now made to Bank of England, Sort code 10-00-00, Account 23430303 when using BACS or CHAPS. When using Bank Giro Credit use the Sort code 10-53-92 but the same Account number.
Note: Any payments sent by post should be marked for the attention of the Cashier.

Northern Ireland　HMRC, HMRC Inheritance Tax, Dorchester House, 52–58 Great Victoria Street, Belfast BT2 7QL.
Tel. 028 9050 5353
Fax. 028 9050 5305
DX 2001 NR Belfast 2
Note: Electronic transfer payments regarding the Belfast office are now made to Bank of England, Sort code 10-00-00, Account 23430303 when using BACS or CHAPS. When using Bank Giro Credit use the Sort code 10-53-92 but the same Account number.

Where personal representatives apply personally for a grant of representation (see 2.11 ACCOUNTS AND RETURNS for addresses) they will be told how much tax should be paid before the grant can be obtained and the address at which the tax should be paid. In a change to the system and following discussions between the British Bankers' Association and the Building Societies' Association HMRC have agreed that personal representatives can draw on funds held in the deceased's bank or building society account (National Savings are not within the scheme yet) solely for the purpose of paying inheritance tax prior to the grant. The Paymaster General, Dawn Primarolo stated on 21 January 2003:

'In proceedings in Finance Bill Standing Committee on 25 June we announced that work was in hand to allow inheritance tax to be paid out of an estate before probate is granted. We have now reached agreement in principle with the British Bankers' Association and the Building Societies' Association on a direct payment scheme for Inheritance Tax. Broadly, where the deceased person has sufficient funds to their credit, participating institutions will be ready to transfer funds direct to the Inland Revenue to pay the inheritance tax due. We are now working with the Associations to finalise the detail of the processes concerned, and help their members prepare for the launch. The Government hope to see the maximum possible take up of this welcome scheme which will start later this year.'

In this connection Forms D20 has been added to the existing IHT 200 for this use.

There is one problem with electronic lodgement payment that impacts on the speed of obtaining probate; the result of electronic lodgement is that it takes at least three working days for the paperwork to reach HMRC Inheritance Tax from the Bank of England and therefore if speed is essential sending a cheque is the recommended alternative. Also, a HMRC Inheritance Tax reference number should only be applied for prior to using the direct payment scheme where tax is due on the estate. To obtain a HMRC Inheritance Tax reference for use with this scheme, the HMRC Inheritance Tax recommend telephoning their Helpline on 0845 30 20 900. See IHT NEWSLETTER AND TAX BULLETIN EXTRACTS (61), December 1995, July 1997, August 2003, April 2006, December 2006 and April 2007.

35.3 PAYMENT BY INSTALMENTS

An election in writing to the Board may be made to pay the tax due by ten equal yearly instalments in respect of property listed below. The first instalment is payable on the due date on which the whole tax would otherwise be due if it were not payable by instalments, see 35.1 above. Where the transfer is on death, the first instalment is due six months after the end of the month in which death occurs even if the personal representatives must otherwise pay tax before that date. See IHT 14, p 16 to 18.

The tax outstanding (with interest to the time of payment) may be paid at any time. If the whole or any part of the property concerned is sold or ceases to be comprised in a settlement, then the related tax still outstanding (with accrued interest) becomes payable forthwith unless (i) the sale precedes the date that the first instalment is due in which case the tax does not become due until that date; or (ii) the sale is by the transferee following a POTENTIALLY EXEMPT TRANSFER (38) and the transferee dies before the transferor. For these purposes, the sale of an interest in a business is treated as a sale of part of the business and payment of a sum in satisfaction of the whole or part of an interest in a business otherwise than on sale is treated as a sale of the interest or part at the time of payment. Where there is a delay between the dates of contract and completion, the sale for the purposes of *IHTA 1984, s 227(4)* is deemed to take place at the completion date (Tolley's Practical Tax 1991 p 200). *Note.* Where *IHTA 1984, s 107* (see 7.5 BUSINESS PROPERTY) allows for the extension of business relief to property which replaces relevant business property in a situation where a business is acquired by a company controlled by the former owner of the business, the right to pay by instalments is in practice not lost because of the 'sale' of the business to the company (Tolley's Practical Tax 1989 p 191).

Transfers on death. The eligible property is

(*a*)   land and buildings of any description, wherever situated;

(*b*)   listed or unquoted shares or securities which gave control of the company (see 35.4 below) to the deceased;

(*c*)   unquoted shares or securities (in relation to transfers made, and other events occurring, before 17 March 1987, shares or securities not listed on a recognised stock exchange) not within (*b*) above

   (i)   which attract (together with tax on any other transfer under (*a*) to (*e*) on which the same person is liable) not less than 20% of the tax liable by that person in the same capacity, or

   (ii)   if the Board are satisfied that the tax attributable to the shares or securities cannot be paid in one sum without undue hardship;

(*d*)   unquoted shares (not securities) (in relation to transfers made, and other events occurring, before 17 March 1987, shares not quoted on a recognised stock exchange) not within (*b*) with a value exceeding £20,000 where either

   (i)   their nominal value is not less than 10% of the total nominal value of all the shares of the company at the time of death, or

   (ii)   they are ordinary shares (see 35.4 below) with nominal value not less than 10% of all ordinary shares of the company at the time of the death;

(*e*)   the net value of a business (see 35.4 below) or an interest in a business carried on for gain, including a profession or vocation.

Lifetime transfers. The right to elect to pay tax on lifetime transfers by instalments in respect of the property listed below is restricted to cases

(i)   where the tax is borne by the person benefiting from the transfer (understood to be taken by HMRC Inheritance Tax to mean the transferee) (but see (F) below), or

(ii)   where the transfer is made under the settled property provisions in *IHTA 1984, Part III* in respect of settled property which remains in the settlement.

In relation to transfers of value made, and other events occurring, after 16 March 1987, tax cannot be payable by instalments where a POTENTIALLY EXEMPT TRANSFER (38) proves to be a chargeable transfer or additional tax becomes payable due to the death of the transferor within seven years of the transfer unless *either* the property was owned by the 'transferee' throughout the period from the date of the transfer to the transferor's death (or, if earlier, his own death) *or*, for the purposes of determining the tax (or additional tax) due, the value of the property is reduced by agricultural or business property relief by virtue of the replacement property provisions. See 5.3 AGRICULTURAL PROPERTY and 7.6 BUSINESS PROPERTY. If the property consists of unquoted shares or securities, there is an additional condition that the shares or securities remained unquoted throughout the period from the date of the transfer to the transferor's death (or, if earlier, the transferee's death).

In relation to transfers of value made, and other events occurring, before 17 March 1987, where a POTENTIALLY EXEMPT TRANSFER (38) proved to be a chargeable transfer, the tax payable could not be paid by instalments unless the property transferred was owned by the 'transferee' immediately before the transferor's death (or, if earlier, his own death).

'Transferee' means the person whose property the qualifying property became on the transfer or, where on the transfer the property became comprised in a settlement in which no qualifying interest in possession subsists, the trustees of the settlement.

The eligible property is

(A)   land and buildings of any description, wherever situated;

(B)   listed or unquoted shares or securities which gave control (see 35.4 below) of the company to the transferor or to the trustees of the settlement;

(C)   unquoted shares or securities (before 17 March 1987 and after 9 March 1992, shares or securities not listed on a recognised stock exchange) not within (B) where the Board are satisfied (on the assumption that the shares etc. are retained by the person liable to pay the tax) that the tax attributable to the shares or securities cannot be paid in one sum without undue hardship;

(D)   unquoted shares etc.—as for transfers on death under (*d*) above;

(E)   the net value of a business (see 35.4 below) or an interest in a business carried on for gain, including a profession or vocation;

(F)   trees or underwood left out of account on death (see 58 WOODLANDS) and later disposed of in a lifetime transfer. In this case the right to pay by instalments is available to both the transferor and transferee and does not cease if the timber is later sold.

[*IHTA 1984, ss 227–229; FA 1986, Sch 19 para 31; FA 1987, s 58, Sch 8 paras 15–17; F(No 2)A 1992, s 73, Sch 14 paras 5, 6, 8; FA 1996, Sch 38 para 5*].

Example 1

F died on 17 December 2007 leaving a free estate of £382,000, including £75,000 (after business property relief at 50%) in respect of plant and machinery in a partnership. An election is made to pay inheritance tax on the plant and machinery by 10 equal yearly instalments.

35.3 Payment of Tax

Inheritance tax on free estate		£
On first	£300,000	Nil
On next	£82,000 at 40%	32,800
	£382,000	£32,800

IHT applicable to business property

$$\frac{75,000}{382,000} \times £32,800 \qquad\qquad £6,440$$

1st instalment due 1.7.2008	£644
2nd instalment due 1.7.2009 And so on	£644

Example 2

On 1 December 2007 G gave his land in a partnership of which G was a partner to his son S who agreed to pay any IHT on the transfer. The land was valued at £600,000. G had made prior chargeable transfers of £140,000, had already used his 2006/07 and 2007/08 annual exemptions, and he died on 31 December 2011.

Selected to pay the IHT by ten yearly instalments and paid the first on 1 August 2012, and the second on 1 September 2013. On 1 December 2013 he sold the land, and paid the balance of the IHT outstanding on 1 February 2014. It is assumed that the rate of interest on unpaid inheritance tax is 3% p.a. throughout.

Inheritance tax on gift

	£
Value of land	600,000
Deduct business property relief at 50%	300,000
PET becoming chargeable on death	£300,000

IHT payable in the band £140,001–£440,000

	£
£140,001–300,000	Nil
£300,001–440,000 at 40%	56,000
	£56,000

Total IHT payable at 60% of full rates (death between 4 and 5 years after gift)	£33,600

1st instalment due 1.7.2012   3,360
Interest at 3% from 1.7.2012 to 1.8.2012
$^{31}/_{366}$ × £3,360 × 3%   8
                                                           ‾‾‾‾‾
                                                                      3,368
2nd instalment due 1.7.2013   3,360
Interest at 3% from 1.7.2013 to 1.9.2013
$^{62}/_{366}$ × £3,360 × 3%   17
                                                           ‾‾‾‾‾
                                                                      3,377
Balance due on sale on 1.12.2013   26,880
Interest at 3% from 1.12.2013 to 1.2.2014
$^{62}/_{366}$ × £26,880 × 3%   137
                                                           ‾‾‾‾‾
                                                                     27,017
Total IHT and interest   £33,762
                                                                   ‾‾‾‾‾‾‾

Note to the example

(A)   Interest on unpaid tax after 5 April 1997 is calculated using 366 days as the denominator rather than 365 days. See CTO Newsletter Extract, March 1997. See 27.1 INTEREST ON TAX and IHT NEWSLETTER AND TAX BULLETIN EXTRACTS (61).

35.4   **Definitions. Definitions** relating to 35.3 above are as follows.

'*Control of company*' by a person is when he can exercise control of a majority of votes on all questions affecting the company as a whole, and for this purpose there will be included any shares or securities which are related property (see 56.17 VALUATION) and where shares or securities are comprised in a settlement, any voting powers which they give to the trustees of the settlement are deemed to be given to the individual beneficially entitled in possession to those shares or securities (or to the trustees if there is no such individual). In IHT210 (Notes) and form D14 (Notes) it states; 'For inheritance tax a person controls a company if they can control the majority (more than 50%) of the voting powers on *all* questions affecting the company as a whole.' See *Walker's Executors v CIR [2001] STC SCD 86 Sp C 275*. Where there are shares or securities of any class with voting powers only on the winding-up of the company and/or on any question primarily affecting that class, then the reference above to 'all questions affecting the company as a whole' are to be read as referring to all such questions except those to which the powers of the particular class apply. In the case of *Walding and Others (Executors of Walding deceased) v IRC Ch D [1996] STC 13* where the point at issue was whether the deceased had 'the control of powers of voting on all questions affecting the company as a whole'. *[IHTA 1984, s 269(1)]*. The deceased's holding of 45 shares out of 100 gave control, in the view of the Executors, because 24 shares held by a four year old grandson of the deceased could not realistically be exercised in the voting rights of the company due to the minor's mental or physical incapacity. The judge held that *s 269(1)* allowed relief where the deceased controlled the powers of voting on all matters affecting the company. However, even though the grandson was too young to exercise his voting rights, *s 269(1)* required his shareholding to be taken into account in determining overall control of the company at the date of death. The court dismissed the Executors' appeal and no BPR relief was due; *IHTA 1984, s 269(1)* deals with the ambit of the powers of voting, not the capabilities of the shareholders in whose names the shares were registered. *[IHTA 1984, s 269; ITA 2007, s 995]*.

'*Ordinary shares*' are shares which carry either (i) a right to dividends not restricted to dividends at a fixed rate or (ii) a right to conversion into shares carrying such a right as in (i). *[IHTA 1984, s 228(4); ITA 2007, s 989]*.

In relation to transfers of value made, and other events occurring, after 9 March 1992, then, in relation to any shares or securities, '*quoted*' means quoted on a recognised stock exchange, and '*unquoted*' means not so quoted. [*IHTA 1984, ss 227(1AA), 228(5); F(No 2)A 1992, s 73, Sch 14 paras 5, 6, 8*]. This definition applies additionally for defining relevant business property (see 7.4 BUSINESS PROPERTY) but otherwise, for transfers of value made, and other events occurring, after 9 March 1992 does not apply generally for IHT purposes. In relation to transfers of value made, and other events occurring, after 16 March 1987 but before 10 March 1992, '*quoted*', in relation to any shares or securities, means quoted on a recognised stock exchange or dealt in on the Unlisted Securities Market, and '*unquoted*', in relation to any shares or securities, means neither so quoted nor so dealt in. [*IHTA 1984, s 272; FA 1987, s 58(2), Sch 8 para 17*]. This applied for all IHT purposes and *still*, in relation to transfers of value made, and other events occurring, after 9 March 1992, does so for purposes other than defining relevant business property and the above provisions. It should also be noted that as from 1 April 1996 the word '*quoted*' on a recognised stock exchange is substituted by the word '*listed*'. [*FA 1996, Sch 38 paras 2, 5*]. In relation to transfers of value made, and other events occurring, before 17 March 1987, shares and securities in companies dealt in on the Unlisted Securities Market were not treated as quoted on a recognised stock exchange for all IHT purposes (Inland Revenue Statement of Practice SP 18/80, 23 December 1980). See IR Press Release, 25 April 2001 for the proposed revised listing arrangements and its effect on the term 'recognised stock exchange'. The Alternative Investment Market (AIM) opened for business on 19 June 1995 with transitional arrangements until 29 September 1995 (see also IRPR 20 February 1995). This market will ostensibly replace the USM which was wound up at the end of 1996. (See also Company Secretary's Review, Vol 18 No 12, 19 October 1994).

Whilst *FA 2007* inserted new definitions of 'recognised stock exchange' for the purposes of income tax and capital gains tax, the change did not include inheritance tax. HMRC have confirmed that AIM shares continue to be unlisted for the purposes of, for example, CGT taper relief (as they are not included on the UK official list, required by new *ITA 2007, s 1005(3)*. However, adopting the new definition for IHT will not in itself mean that the treatment of such shares will change for IHT purposes. See HMRC statement on 29 March 2007 at http://www.hmrc.gov.uk/budget2007/rec-stock-exch.htm. [*ITA 2007, s 1005; FA 2007, s 109, Sch 26*].

'*Net value of a business*' is the value of the assets used in the business (including goodwill) reduced by the total amount of any liabilities incurred for the purposes of the business; and in ascertaining the net value of an interest in a business, (e.g. a partnership share), regard is to be had only to those assets and liabilities which would have been used in calculating the net value of the entire business. [*IHTA 1984, s 227(7)*].

35.5   **Interest. Interest on the unpaid portion of tax payable by instalments** is added to each instalment where applicable and paid accordingly. See 27.1 INTEREST ON TAX above for rates of interest and IHT 14, p 19. [*IHTA 1984, ss 233, 234(1); FA 1989, s 179(1)*]. They apply as follows.

On the balance outstanding at each instalment date commencing with the due date of the first instalment in respect of

(i)   land under 35.3(*a*) and 35.3(A) above (unless it is a business asset under 35.3(*e*) or 35.3(E) above or agricultural property reduced by AGRICULTURAL PROPERTY (5) relief); and

(ii)   shares and securities under 35.3(*b*)(*c*) and (*d*) and 35.3(*b*)(*c*) and (*d*) in companies whose business is wholly or mainly dealing in securities, stocks or shares or making or holding investments *unless* the business consists of being a holding company for subsidiaries whose business does not fall within those categories or the business is wholly that of a 'market maker' (before the Stock Exchange reform, a jobber) or a discount house and, in either case, is carried on in the UK.

A '*market maker*' is a person who holds himself out at all normal times in compliance with the rules of either The Stock Exchange or, after 23 March 1992, LIFFE (Administration and Management) as willing to buy and sell securities etc. and is recognised as doing so by the investment exchange concerned. [*IHTA 1984, s 234(2)–(4); FA 1986, s 107; SI 1992/3181*].

No interest (except for late payment of an instalment) is payable apart from those cases in (i) and (ii) above.

35.6   **ACCEPTANCE OF PROPERTY IN SATISFACTION OF TAX**

The Board may, if they think fit and the Ministers agree, on application of any person liable to pay tax, accept property within the following categories in whole or part payment of tax and interest (see VOA IHT manual, section 20, para 20.31 and also http://www.culture.gov.uk/cultural_property/acceptance_lieu.htm.)

(*a*)   Land. (In practice only land with a particular amenity value will normally be accepted. Agricultural land as such will not normally be accepted unless it is associated with an historic building. Buildings will normally only be accepted if they are of architectural or historic interest and can be put to amenity use such as display as part of the national heritage. See WORKING CASE STUDY (59) at **Case Study 3**.)

(*b*)   Any objects which are or have been kept in any building (i) accepted in satisfaction of IHT, CTT or estate duty or (ii) belonging to the Crown or Duchies of Lancaster or Cornwall or (iii) belonging to, or used for the purposes of, a government department or (iv) protected under the *Ancient Monuments and Archaeological Areas Act 1979* or the *Historic Monuments Act* (*Northern Ireland*) *1971* or (v) belonging to certain museums and other bodies specified in *IHTA 1984, Sch 3* (see list under 33.16 NATIONAL HERITAGE). It must appear desirable to 'the Ministers' for the objects to remain associated with the building.

(*c*)   Any picture, print, book, manuscript, work of art, scientific object or other thing which the Ministers are satisfied is pre-eminent for its national, scientific, historic or artistic interest. This includes a collection or group of such objects. (The test of 'pre-eminence' is 'would the object be a pre-eminent addition to a public collection, whether national, local authority or university?'. The object must be something which stands out for its particular qualities and will attract special attention when displayed, and is not merely a normal addition to a public collection.) However, see Taxation, 10 November 1994, p 123 regarding restrictions on the acceptance of assets of national importance in lieu of tax where those assets are exempt for other reasons e.g. BPR.

[*National Heritage Act 1980, ss 12, 13; IHTA 1984, s 230;* Capital Taxation and the National Heritage (IR67)].

HMRC have confirmed that if a claim is made under *IHTA 1984, s 230* for acceptance in lieu of tax but the offeror has already paid the IHT they will not accept a subsequent offer to transfer assets in lieu. However, HMRC will entertain an offer where:

•   all the tax has been paid in advance in order to obtain the grant or confirmation, provided that at or around the time of payment HMRC are notified of the possibility that an offer in lieu of the tax will be made; or

•   HMRC are holding money on account of a liability to pay interest and tax where the money is held to the taxpayer's order but remains unpaid.

See IHT NEWSLETTER AND TAX BULLETIN EXTRACTS (61), May Special Edition 2003 p 2.

The Department for Culture, Media and Sport drew up a model *in situ* loan agreement for use when drawing up a loan agreement covering Chattel(s) accepted in whole or part

35.6 Payment of Tax

satisfaction of capital taxes and any other liabilities under the provisions of *IHTA 1984*, *s 230* but which are to be displayed to the public *in situ* at the Borrower's premises.

THIS AGREEMENT is made the .... day of .... 200(7)

BETWEEN

(1) **A BORROWER** ('the Borrower')

(2) **[A MUSEUM]** ('the Museum')

WHEREAS

(A) .... died on .... and was [the owner of] [tenant for life of] property including the Chattels *[alternatively use 'Painting'/ 'Sculpture', etc. for Agreements in respect of individual items or categories of items]*.

(B) The Commissioners of HMRC have recognised the Chattels as being pre-eminent for their scientific historic or artistic interest within the meaning of section 230 of the Inheritance Tax Act 1984 and have accepted the Chattels in partial satisfaction of Inheritance Tax payable on the death of .... and other liabilities.

(C) The Chattels have been transferred to the Museum pursuant to a Direction by the Secretary of State of Culture, Media and Sport on the .... day of .... 200(7) under section 9 of the National Heritage Act 1980 (the 'Direction').

(D) The Museum has agreed, in pursuance of the Direction, to lend the Chattels to the Borrower on the terms of this Agreement.

NOW THIS DEED WITNESSES as follows:

1.1 In this Agreement unless the context otherwise requires the following words and expressions shall have the following meanings:

'the Arbitrator'-such person as is nominated in accordance under the provisions of clause 16 hereof

'the Chattels'-the Chattels specified in Schedule 1 of this Agreement and the expression 'the Chattels' shall include all or any of them

'the Compensation Value'-a sum equivalent to the Tax Settlement Price increased on April 1 in each year by the percentage measures in the Retail Prices (All Items) for the 12 months immediately preceding

'Current Market Value'-the current value of the Chattels on the open market as agreed in respect of each year beginning on .... by the parties

'the Director'-the Director for the time being of the Museum or such other official of the Museum who shall from time to time have day-to-day management of the Museum

'the Loan'-the free loan of the Chattels from the Museum to the Borrower, subject to the terms of this agreement

'the Premises'-..

'relative'-brother sister ancestor lineal descendant or spouse/civil partner of any such person or a spouse/civil partner of the Borrower

'the Secretary of State'-the Secretary of State for Culture, Media and Sport or such other person or body as shall for the time being exercise the functions of the Secretary of State in relation to section 9 of the National Heritage Act 1980

'the Tax Settlement Price'-the special price agreed as the value of the Chattel(s) on [their] [its] acceptance in lieu of Inheritance Tax as specified [for each Chattel] in Schedule 1 to this Agreement

1.2 The interpretation and construction of this Agreement shall be subject to the following provisions:

(a)   headings and marginal notes are for convenience only and shall not affect the interpretation of this Agreement;

(b)   where the context so admits:

(i)   words importing the singular include the plural and vice-versa;

(ii)   words denoting the masculine gender include the feminine;

(c)   reference to a clause is to a Clause of this Agreement unless otherwise specified; and

(d)   reference to any enactment shall be construed as a reference to the enactment as amended or re-enacted by subsequent enactment, order, regulation or instrument.

THE LOAN

2.1 In pursuance of the Direction the Museum agrees to lend the Chattels to the Borrower and the Borrower agrees to accept the Chattels on loan subject to the terms of this Agreement.

2.2 The Museum and the Borrower agree that the Chattels shall remain at the Premises for the duration of the Loan.

2.3 The Borrower agrees that the Museum is the owner of the Chattels and that the Borrower has no proprietary or other right or interest in the Chattels and will not by virtue of this Agreement acquire any such right or interest.

TEMPORARY REMOVAL

3 The Museum may remove the Chattels from the Premises at its expense and upon reasonable notice in writing to the Borrower without the consent of the Borrower for the purpose of conservation works.

4 Upon the Museum giving reasonable notice to the Borrower and the Borrower giving his consent (which consent shall not be unreasonably withheld) the Museum may at its own expense remove the Chattels from the Premises for the purpose of temporary exhibition.

PROVIDED ALWAYS that the period of removal under the Clauses 3 and 4 above shall be limited to the time reasonably necessary to effect the conservation works or stage the temporary exhibition (including such time as is needed for the transportation and installation of the Chattels).

BORROWER'S OBLIGATIONS

5 The Borrower agrees that he will:

(a)   keep the Chattels at the Premises in their positions on the date of this Agreement or such other positions as shall be agreed in writing and will not affix the Chattels in any way without the prior written agreement of the Director;

(b)   permit the Chattels to be moved only by the Director or someone authorised by the Director except in an emergency;

35.6   Payment of Tax

(c)   allow public access to the Chattels on at least [100] days in each year (or such other number of days as may be sufficient to comply with the Secretary of State's requirement from time to time concerning reasonable public access to the Premises) for a period of not less than three hours on each day and by prior appointment at other reasonable times;

(d)   keep the Chattels in as good repair as the same are now (as recorded in the Note of Condition contained in Schedule 1 which is accepted as an accurate record of the condition of the Chattels), fair wear and tear and ageing excepted, and will take proper precautions to prevent damage to the Chattels and to control the environment within which the Chattels are housed within reasonable limits as to dust smoke temperature humidity lighting and vibration levels and allow the Museum to install at its own expense such thermo-hydrographs or other appropriate measuring devices as the Museum shall from time to time request in order to monitor the environmental precautions and to maintain proper precautions for the security of the Chattels within the Premises as specified by the Museum or the Museum Security Adviser of the Museums & Galleries Commission. For the avoidance of doubt IT IS HEREBY AGREED that the precautions in force at the date of this Agreement provided always that the Museum shall be entitled to provide at its own expense such more effective security or damage prevention measures developed during the currency of this covenant as it may choose;

(e)   allow the Museum to display adjacent to or in front of the Chattels such notices with such dimensions as may be agreed in writing from time to time by the Borrower and the Director to publicise the ownership of the Chattels;

(f)   allow the Director or other officials of the Museum or the Museums Security Adviser or persons authorised by them free access to the Premises at all reasonable times by prior arrangement to inspect the Chattels or the environmental conditions or the security arrangements and to carry out such photography conservation and other works at all reasonable times as may be necessary after reasonable notice;

(g)   allow the Director or any person authorised by him access at any time without notice when the Director has reason to believe the Chattels to be at risk;

(h)   maintain the existing decor and furnishings of the room or rooms at the Premises in which the Chattels are situate in a style which provides a suitable historic physical and aesthetic setting for the Chattels and not make any changes thereto otherwise than as may be agreed in writing by the Director or in default of agreement decided by Arbitrator;

(i)   not allow reproduction of or publicity relating to the Chattels except upon terms and conditions approved in writing by the Director; and

(j)   comply with the terms of Clause 7 below.

CONSERVATION AND INSURANCE

6 The Museum agrees that it will:

(a)   conserve the Chattels at its own expense and take such suitable advice and carry out such necessary work as seems fit to the Director after consultation with the Borrower; and

(b)   where appropriate insure the Chattels by obtaining an undertaking from the Secretary of State under section 16 of the National Heritage Act 1980 to indemnify the Museum in respect of any repairable damage to the Chattels up to 99 per cent of the tax Settlement Price.

7 The Borrower agrees that it will indemnify the Museum against costs and expenses incurred by the Museum in making good repairable damage to the Chattels up to 1 per cent of the Compensation Value of the Chattels.

TERMINATION OF THE LOAN AGREEMENT

DEATH OF THE BORROWER

8.1 In the event of the death of the Borrower, subject always to the provisions of clauses 8.2 hereof, the Loan shall be determined and the Museum may remove the Chattels from the Premises.

8.2 If:

(a)   the body or person in whom the Premises shall become vested following the death of the Borrower shall be a relative of his or her family company or other vehicle controlled by a relative of the Borrower, a trust established for the primary benefit of any such person;

(b)   such body or person shall notify the Museum in writing of an intention to enter into a new Agreement within six months of the death of the Borrower; and

(c)   the condition of eligibility for renewal is established in accordance with clause 10 below

the Museum, subject to Clause 10.6 below, shall execute an Agreement in favour of such body or person in substantially the same terms as this Agreement, such new Agreement to include (*inter alia*) a provision containing a similar right to a new Agreement to take effect on the death of the successor to the Borrower as owner or occupier of the Premises.

TRANSFER OF THE PREMISES

9.1 In the event of the transfer, lease or other disposition of the Premises by the Borrower, subject always to the provisions of clause 9.2 and clause 9.3 hereof, the Loan shall determine and the Museum may remove the Chattels from the Premises.

9.2 If:

(a)   the body or person in whom the Premises shall become vested following a transfer lease or other disposition by the Borrower shall be a relative of his or a family company or other vehicle controlled by a relative of the Borrower a trust established for the primary benefit of any such person;

(b)   such person or body notifies the Museum in writing of an intention to enter into a new Agreement before the transfer, lease or other disposition; and

(c)   the condition of eligibility for renewal is established in accordance with Clause 10 below

the Museum, subject to clause 10.4 below, shall execute an Agreement in favour of such person or body in substantially the same terms as this Agreement, such new Agreement to include (*inter alia*) a provision containing a similar right to a new Agreement to take effect at the end of the Loan if the Premises transfers to the primary beneficiary or another company or trust undertaking the same function.

9.3 The Borrower shall give three months' written notice to the Museum of any intention to transfer, lease or otherwise dispose of the Premises or of his beneficial interest therein.

RENEWING THE LOAN

10.1 The condition of eligibility for renewal specified in the Clause 8.2(c) and Clause 9.2(c) above is that it has been agreed in writing between the Museum and the person in whom the Premises have or will become vested (or in default of agreement in writing determined by an Arbitrator appointed in accordance with clause 16) that it is appropriate for the Chattels to continue to be kept at the Premises.

10.2 Matters which shall be taken into account by the Arbitrator in making a determination under Clause 10.1 above include (*inter alia*):

(a)   the Chattels' historic and aesthetic association with the Premises and the use of the Premises;

(b)   the record of the Museum and the deceased or transferring Borrower's compliance with the terms and conditions of the loan Agreement;

(c)   the arrangements for the future display and conservation of the Chattels; and

(d)   the continuing benefit to the public of the Chattels being kept at the Premises;

and the Arbitrator may rely (*inter alia*) on:

(i)   such expert advice as appears to him to be appropriate; and

(ii) policy or guidelines (if any) from time to time adopted or issued by the Secretary of State in determining whether it is appropriate for Chattels accepted in satisfaction of tax to be kept at the premises with which they are associated.

10.3 A determination made by the Arbitrator under Clause 10.1 above may be made on such conditions as the Arbitrator may consider appropriate (including conditions as to the duration and terms of the new Agreement) and the conditions of eligibility for a new Agreement under Clauses 8 and 9 above shall extend to compliance with any conditions so imposed.

10.4 It shall be a term of any agreement made in pursuance of a condition of eligibility for renewal with a family, a trust or any vehicle other than a company (whether or not a charity) that after 21 years have elapsed from the date of the agreement the Museum or the Borrower may at any time seek a determination from an Arbitrator appointed in accordance with Clause 16 as to whether it is appropriate for the Chattels to continue to be kept at the Premises. The Museum and Borrower may not seek such a determination within 21 years of a previous one.

10.5 Should the Arbitrator, taking into account the circumstances of the case, including the matters specified in clause 10.2 above, determine that it is no longer appropriate for the Chattels to continue to be kept at the Premises the Museum may by not less than six months notice in writing terminate the Loan and/or remove the Chattels from the Premises.

10.6 Should the Arbitrator determine that it is appropriate for the Chattels to continue to be kept at the Premises but on different terms and conditions the Agreement (or the new Agreement as the case may be) shall take effect as varied by the Arbitrator, provided that the Borrower may then by not less than two months notice in writing (or such shorter period as the Arbitrator may allow) terminate the Loan and the Museum may remove the Chattels from the Premises.

TERMINATION OF THE LOAN – MISCELLANEOUS

11.1 If:

(a)   there is any material breach by the Borrower of any of the covenants contained in this Agreement or circumstances shall have arisen which are materially prejudicial to the condition, repair, well-being, or security of the Chattels or public access to them and substantial steps to remedy the breach or alleviate the risk to the condition, repair, well-being or security of the Chattels have not been taken within any reasonable period after the service of the written notice on the Borrower by the Museum requiring him to remedy that breach; or

(b)   the Borrower shall give the Museum not less than two months' written notice that it is desirous of determining the Loan

the Loan shall determine and the Museum shall recover the Chattels.

11.2 In default of agreement between the Borrower and the Museum as to whether:

(a)   any situation act or omission constitutes a breach of the covenants or obligations herein contained; or

(b)   circumstances have arisen which materially prejudice the condition, repair, well being or security of the Chattels or public access thereto; or

(c)   a particular period of time is reasonable in the circumstances in which to remedy a breach of covenant or other obligation;

(d)   it would be reasonable for the Borrower to withhold any consents required under this Agreement;

the provisions of Clause 16 will apply.

REMOVAL OF CHATTELS

12 In the event of the Loan determining and the Museum becoming entitled to recover the Chattels from the Premises under Clause 8.1, 9.1 or 11.1 above the Museum shall give the Borrower or his successor not less than two month's written notice of the removal of the Chattels and shall not remove the Chattels pending the determination in accordance with Clause 10 above of the entitlement of such successors to a new Agreement but this shall be without prejudice to the provisions of Clause 13 below.

13 If the Director is of the opinion that the Chattels are at any time at immediate risk of damage, loss or destruction for whatever reason, the Museum may remove the Chattels from the Premises without giving notice to be held by the Museum in a place of safety. Except where the Chattels were at risk by reason of the Borrower's breach of the covenants and obligations herein contained and the Museum has, in consequence of this breach, determined the Loan the Chattels shall be returned to the Premises when in the opinion of the Director they are no longer at risk.

14 Wherever the Loan is determined under the terms of this Agreement or the Chattels are removed from the premises by the Borrower it shall be responsible for the reasonable removal expenses of the Chattels and shall be responsible for all physical damage reasonably caused to the Premises by or in the course of such removal.

MISCELLANEOUS

15 Termination of this Agreement by either party under the terms of this Agreement shall be without prejudice to and shall not affect the liability of either party in respect of events occurring prior to the termination.

16 Any dispute or difference between the parties (other than a decision by the Museum to remove the Chattels to safe keeping in accordance with Clause 13 when the Directors decision shall be final and conclusive) shall be referred to and determined by a sole Arbitrator to be appointed by agreement between the parties or in default of agreement by the President for the time being of the Law Society. Such arbitration shall take place in London and the cost of arbitration shall be within the Arbitrator's discretion.

IN WITNESS whereof the Borrower and the duly authorised officers of the Museum have executed this instrument as a Deed on the date first before written.

35.6   Payment of Tax

Schedule 1 – the Chattels

Chattel　　　　　　*Condition*　　　　　*Tax Settlement Price*

Schedule 2 – Security and Damage Prevention Devices

Security: [The Chattels must be supervised during the whole of the time the public are admitted. A Security Officer is resident and on duty 24 hours per day (other items should be added depending on the specific circumstances)]

Fire: [Detection system – either smoke or heat detectors are installed throughout the building]

SIGNED as a DEED by ....

in the presence of ....

Witness Signature:

Witness Name:

Address:

Occupation:

SIGNED as a DEED on behalf of

[A MUSEUM] by ....

in the presence of:

Witness Signature:

Witness Name:

Address:

Occupation:

Notes to the Loan Agreement

(A)   The model Loan Agreement reflects policy on *in situ* loan arrangements and should be used by interested parties when drawing up loan agreements for the Secretary of State's approval. The Secretary of State will need to be persuaded that a departure from the above model is justified and in the public's interest if other arrangements are entered into. (See the revised DCMS model loan agreement for AIL in-situ offer revised at 30 December 2002 at http://www.culture.gov.uk/what_we_do/ Cultural_property/QuickLinks/Forms/).

For acceptances after 16 March 1987, the special price at which the item is accepted is calculated from the value of the item on the date the property is offered unless the person liable for the tax which is to be satisfied by an acceptance in lieu notifies HMRC that he wishes them to adopt the value of the property on the date of acceptance. See Inland Revenue Statement of Practice SP 6/87, April 1987. Before 17 March 1987, only the 'acceptance date' arrangements were available. Where the 'offer date' arrangements are chosen, interest on the tax satisfied by the item ceases to accrue on that date, see 27.1 INTEREST ON TAX.

A person having power to sell property in order to raise money for payment of tax may agree with the Board for the property to be accepted under the above conditions and such agreement shall be treated as a sale made under the said power. [*IHTA 1984, ss 231, 233(1A); FA 1987, s 60; F(No 2)A 1987, s 97*]. Before 1 April 1998 an amount equal to the Estate Duty, CTT or IHT had to be paid over by the Department of Culture, Media and

Sport (DCMS) to the Board under the *National Heritage Act 1980, s 8*. From 1 April 1998 this reimbursement system is abolished. In order to facilitate the above the *Exchequer Audit Department Act 1866, s 10* will be required to contain information about property accepted in lieu of tax on or after 1 April 1998. [*FA 1998, s 145*]. The appointed day for the purposes of this section is 4 November 1998. [*Finance Act 1998, Section 145, (Appointed Day) Order 1998, SI 1998/2703*].

'*The Ministers*' means the Secretary of State and the Lord President of the Council. [*National Heritage Act 1980, s 12(1); IHTA 1984, s 230(5); SI 1986/600*].

APPLICATION FOR ACCEPTANCE OF LAND IN SATISFACTION OF TAX

I/We* .... of .... apply for acceptance by the Board of HMRC of the property herein detailed in the accompanying Schedule in satisfaction of tax and accrued interest by way of sections 230 and 233 of the Inheritance Tax Act 1984. In support of this application I/we* the offeror(s) supply the following:

(a)   Four copies of a valuation of the land at the date of 'offer' for acceptance in satisfaction of tax;

(b)   Full colour photographs of the land;

(c)   Valuation and full description of the land;

(d)   Application for inspection of the land may be addressed to:

Name: ....

Address: ....

....

Telephone: ....

(e)   Certain wishes/conditions apply to the said land and these are attached to the enclosed documents.

I/We* look forward to receiving your reply concerning the above application under sections 230 and 233, IHTA 1984.

Signed ....

Capacity: ....

Dated: ....

* Delete as appropriate

Note to the claim

(A)   In preparing the 'full description' attaching to the claim in (c) above the following particulars, which are considered by the VOA when they present a report to the CTO, are likely to be of importance where relevant:

(1)   the situation of the property;

(2)   its general amenities;

(3)   any known matters of historical interest;

35.7 Payment of Tax

    (4)   any accepted features of architectural merit;

    (5)   elevations (e.g. Georgian), constructions, accommodation and condition of all buildings;

    (6)   public services available;

    (7)   any sporting rights with the property;

    (8)   total areas of the land;

    (9)   the tenure of the property;

    (10)   particulars of growing timber;

    (11)   any restrictions, rights or covenants affecting the property;

    (12)   whether any of the property is situated in a Special Site of Scientific Interest under the *Wildlife and Countryside Act 1981*;

    (13)   mention should be made of any easements and reservations necessitated by a division of the land previously;

    (14)   the nature and condition of any private roads and access drives;

    (15)   the nature and condition of any boundary fences shown on the map and which of these are provided or maintained with the property;

    (16)   tenancies attaching to the property with a note of any portions of the property where vacant possession can be offered;

    (17)   rents and outgoings;

    (18)   any valuable fixtures (e.g. chandeliers, panelling, tapestries, etc.) and whether these are to pass with the property;

    (19)   the existing use of the property and any proposals, applications and decisions under the *Town and Country Planning Acts and Regulations* which may affect it;

    (20)   whether any part of the property is scheduled as an ancient monument or a building of special architectural or historical interest;

    (21)   if the property is situated in a National Park;

    (22)   any prospective acquisition by a public body;

    (23)   any published material on the property e.g. brochures, press articles, etc. should be attached.

(See VOA IHT manual, section 20, para 20.33 and Appendix 29 and see also SP 6/87 at 25 HMRC STATEMENTS OF PRACTICE.)

35.7   CERTIFICATES OF TAX DEPOSIT

Certificates of tax deposit Series 7, which enable money to be set aside for payment of future tax liability, may be used in payment of inheritance tax. Interest from 11 May 2007 (maximum rates are currently between 2.25% – 4.75% for deposits of £100,000 or more) is received on these certificates from the date of purchase until the date on which the tax in respect of which they are surrendered falls due. Certificates may also be encashed but a lower rate of interest is then paid (currently 1% (for less than 1 month) – 2% for deposits of £100,000 or more). Deposits of less than £100,000 attract interest rates of 2% (if applied against tax) and the interest is 1% if withdrawn for cash. Application may be made for certificates of tax deposit from HMRC Finance, Accounting Services, Cash Management, CTD Team, Room B2 South Block, Barrington Road, Worthing, West Sussex BN12 4XH. Tel. 01903 509064/6. Fax: 01903 508707. DX 90951 WORTHING 3. See also IHTM10253.

35.8   **HMRC CHARGE**

Where any tax or interest is unpaid, an HMRC charge is imposed for that amount on

(a)   any property to which the tax is attributable by its transfer;

(b)   any property comprised in a settlement where the chargeable transfer arises on the creation of the settlement or is made under *IHTA 1984, Part III* in respect of settled property; and

(c)   any property relating to heritage assets charged under the existing provisions of *IHTA 1984, ss 32, 32A, 79, Sch 4 para 8* or *Sch 5 para 1* or *3*. Where the event giving rise to the charge is a disposal to a purchaser of the property or object in question, no charge may be imposed on that property or object or any property for the time being representing it.

The charge may be imposed on any property directly or indirectly representing the above.

[*IHTA 1984, s 237(1)(2)(3B)(3C); FA 1999, s 107*].

No charge may be imposed on

(i)   personal or movable property in the UK (excluding leaseholds in relation to deaths after 8 March 1999) treated as transferred on the death of the beneficial owner (other than settled property in which the deceased was beneficially entitled to an interest in possession) and which vests in his personal representatives;

(ii)   heritable property situated in Scotland (but where this is disposed of, any property representing it is subject to the charge).

[*IHTA 1984, s 237(3)(4); Trusts of Land and Appointment of Trustees Act 1996, Sch 14; FA 1999, s 107*].

Priority of charge. An HMRC charge on any property is effective after any incumbrance thereon which is allowable as a deduction in valuing that property for the purposes of IHT e.g. a mortgage. [*IHTA 1984, s 237(5)*].

Validity of charge on disposition. A disposition of property subject to an HMRC charge takes effect subject to that charge. However, property disposed of to a purchaser will not be subject to any HMRC charge if at the 'time of disposition'

(A)   in the case of land in England and Wales, the charge was not registered as a land charge or, in the case of registered land, was not protected by notice on the register; or

(B)   in the case of land in Northern Ireland the title to which is registered under the *Land Registration Act (Northern Ireland) 1970*, the charge was not entered as a burden on the appropriate register maintained under that *Act* or was not protected by a caution or inhibition or, in the case of other land in NI, the purchaser of the property had no notice of the facts giving rise to the charge; or

(C)   in the case of personal property situated in the UK other than in (A) and (B) above, and of any property situated outside the UK, the purchaser had no notice of the facts giving rise to the charge; or

(D)   in the case of any property, a certificate of discharge (now 'closure letter', see 35.9 below) had been given by the Board and the purchaser had no notice of any fact invalidating the certificate.

In the above circumstances, the charge ceases to apply to the property but then applies to the property representing it. (Note that the above does not apply to a donee who would receive property subject to any charge whether or not it was registered or he had notice of it.) [*IHTA 1984, ss 237(6), 238(1)*].

'*Time of disposition*' means (i) in relation to registered land, the time of registration of the disposition; and (ii) in relation to other property, the time of completion. [*IHTA 1984, s 238(3)*].

Where a POTENTIALLY EXEMPT TRANSFER (38) proves to be a chargeable transfer, property concerned which has been disposed of to a purchaser before the transferor's death is not subject to an HMRC charge but property concerned which has been otherwise disposed of before the death and property which at the death represents any property disposed of to a purchaser is subject to the charge. [*IHTA 1984, s 237(3A); FA 1986, Sch 19 para 34*].

Where property is disposed of to a purchaser subject to an HMRC charge, such charge ceases to apply after six years from the later of the date on which the tax became due and the date on which a full and proper account of the property was first delivered to the Board in connection with the chargeable transfer concerned. [*IHTA 1984, s 238(2)*].

A closure letter (previously a certificate of discharge, see 35.9 below) cancels any HMRC charge applying to the property specified. [*IHTA 1984, s 239(3)*]. Applications for the cancellation of an HMRC charge entered on property under the *Land Registration Acts 1925–1971* should be made on Form Cap 37. See 2.4 ACCOUNTS AND RETURNS for automatic discharge of 'excepted estates' and 2.5 for 'excepted terminations' of settled property.

35.9   **CLOSURE LETTERS**

On the application of the person liable for tax on the transfer of specified property, the Board may give (must give if the property is transferred on death or the transferor has died), if satisfied that the tax has been or will be paid, a closure letter to that effect. An application with respect to the tax which is or may become chargeable by a POTENTIALLY EXEMPT TRANSFER (38) may not be made earlier than two years after the transferor's death (except as allowed by the Board at any earlier time after death). Such a closure letter will discharge the property from HMRC charge (see 35.8 above) on its acquisition by a purchaser. [*IHTA 1984, s 239(1)(2A)(3)(5); FA 1986, Sch 19 para 35*].

On the application of the person who is, or might be liable for the whole or part of the tax on a transfer of value, the Board may determine the amount of the tax or determine that no tax is chargeable and, subject to the payment of any tax, may give (must give if the transfer of value is made on death or the transferor has died) a closure letter of their determination. The application must be after two years from the transfer (or earlier if the Board allow) and delivery made of a full account (see 2 ACCOUNTS AND RETURNS). An application with respect to the tax which is or may become chargeable by a POTENTIALLY EXEMPT TRANSFER (38) may not be made earlier than two years after the transferor's death (except as allowed by the Board at an earlier time after the death). Such a closure letter discharges all persons from any further tax on the transfer and extinguishes any HMRC charge for that tax. [*IHTA 1984, s 239(2)(2A)(3)(5); FA 1986, Sch 19 para 35*]. 'Closure letters' replaced the previous certificate of discharge and apply from 30 April 2007. The closure letter will confirm either that no tax is due or that all the tax due has been paid or, in the case of deferred/instalment property e.g. timber/land that the tax has, but for those items, been paid. Application for clearance should not be made until the applicants are reasonably certain that all aspects of the estate have been settled. This means that executors should have checked with the trustees that the value of all settled property has been notified and agreed with HMRC Inheritance Tax. Trustees should have made similar enquiries of executors before lodging their application (CTO Practice Note published in Taxation Practitioner August 1994, p 6). As a majority of non-tax estates remain that way indefinitely an extra module has been added to IHT 200 which, where appropriate, may be completed by the taxpayer and delivered with IHT 200. This form D19 informs the executors of HMRC Inheritance Tax reference number and although it does not have the standing of a statutory closure letter of clearance it confirms there is no IHT to pay. Forms D19 and D42 will be withdrawn in due course, see IHT NEWSLETTER AND TAX BULLETIN EXTRACTS (61), April 2007.

Effect of fraud or failure to disclose material facts etc. The above closure letters are invalid in a case of fraud or failure to disclose material facts and do not affect any further tax on further property afterwards shown to be included in a deceased's estate immediately before his death or arising from an alteration of dispositions under a deed of family arrangement or similar document. They are valid in favour of a purchaser of property who had no notice of any invalidation. [*IHTA 1984, s 239(4)*]. See also IHT NEWSLETTER AND TAX BULLETIN EXTRACTS (61), April 2006.

For HMRC's practice regarding the liability of personal representatives previously issued with a closure letter who discover a further chargeable lifetime transfer, see 29.4 LIABILITY FOR TAX.

Excepted estates. Subject to the same rules regarding fraud etc. (see above), where an estate is an excepted estate (see 2.4 ACCOUNTS AND RETURNS), if the Board do not issue a notice calling for an account, the personal representatives will automatically be discharged from any further claim for tax or charge on property at the end of the prescribed period. In these cases, there is no need to apply for a closure letter. If the Board issue a notice calling for details of the estate, automatic discharge does not apply and the normal course must be followed. [*SI 1981/880, SI 1981/881; SI 1981/1441* and *SI 2002/1733*; Inland Revenue Press Release 2 July 1987].

Excepted terminations. Where the termination of an interest in possession is an 'excepted termination' (see 2.5 ACCOUNTS AND RETURNS), unless within the period of six months from the termination the Board issue a notice requiring an account, the trustees will be discharged from any claim for tax on the value of that property. This provision does not discharge any person in a case of fraud or failure to disclose material facts. [*SI 1981/1440; SI 2002/1731*].

35.10   **RECOVERY OF TAX**

No legal proceedings to recover tax or interest can be taken by the Board unless the amount has been agreed in writing or specified in an undisputed notice of determination (see 15 DETERMINATIONS AND APPEALS). Tax and interest may, without prejudice to any other remedy, be sued for and recovered in a Scottish sheriff court if the amount sought does not exceed the sum for the time being specified in the *Sheriff Courts (Scotland) Act 1971, s 35(1)(a)*.

Where proceedings to recover tax or interest are taken in a county court or sheriff court, the court may be addressed by any authorised officer of the Board, and a certificate by an officer of the Board that the tax or interest is due or that, to the best of his knowledge and belief, it is unpaid is sufficient evidence of that fact in any proceedings for its recovery.

If an appeal to the Special Commissioners, or direct to the High Court, is pending, only agreed undisputed tax is recoverable. Where an appeal is taken a stage further, the disputed tax is payable (and adjusted after that appeal has been determined). [*IHTA 1984, ss 242–244, 254(2); FA 1993, s 200(2)(3)*].

35.11   **ADJUSTMENT OF TAX**

Underpayments. Where too little tax has been paid, the deficiency is payable with interest whether or not the original payment was stated in a notice of determination; but where the payment was made and accepted in full satisfaction of tax in accordance with an account duly delivered to the Board no proceedings for any additional tax may be brought after six years from the later of

(*a*)   the date on which the payment (or last instalment) was made and accepted; and

(*b*)   the date on which the tax (or last instalment) became due.

At the end of that period any liability for additional tax and any HMRC charge for that tax is extinguished. See also 35.9 above.

If there is fraud, wilful default or neglect by a person liable for tax, the six years begin when the Board first has knowledge of these circumstances. This also applies to fraud by the settlor of a settlement in the case of tax chargeable under the rules relating to SETTLE-MENTS WITHOUT INTERESTS IN POSSESSION (44). [*IHTA 1984, s 240*].

Where the fraud etc. is by a settlor, HMRC have confirmed that they would not seek to recover the full amount of the additional tax due from the trustees of the settlement personally where the trustees had acted in good faith and had insufficient trust funds left with which to pay the tax. (Law Society's Gazette 12 December 1984).

It is understood from HMRC's Press Office that the concession A19 (revised on 11 March 1996) in the HMRC Pamphlet IR1 (Arrears of tax arising through official error) is unavailable where an inheritance tax liability is in point. HMRC's statement that the principles of Code of Practice 1 (wherein the concession is mentioned) are applied 'to all parts of the Inland Revenue' (Inland Revenue Press Release 17 February 1993) should be read in the light of this.

Overpayments. Where an overpayment of tax or interest is proved to the satisfaction of the Board, repayment will be made provided the claim is made within six years from the payment (or last payment). Where the sum overpaid is £25 or less, the assessment leading to repayment is not automatically initiated by HMRC Inheritance Tax and must be requested by the taxpayer. [*IHTA 1984, s 241* and see SP 6/95 at 25 HMRC STATEMENTS OF PRACTICE].

If too much tax was paid because of a mistake by HMRC or any other Government department, repayment can be claimed within twenty years of the original overpayment (see B41 at 23 HMRC EXTRA-STATUTORY CONCESSIONS and Code of Practice 1). See CTO Newsletter, March 1996 in IHT NEWSLETTER AND TAX BULLETIN EXTRACTS (61).

For Scotland only, the time limits above of six years do not apply to adjustments of tax arising due to a person claiming or renouncing his right to legitim. [*IHTA 1984, s 147(8)(9)*].

35.12 PAYMENT BY COURT

Where IHT is attributable to any property in the possession or control of a court pending proceedings for its administration, the court must provide any unpaid tax, or interest, out of such property. [*IHTA 1984, s 232*].

35.13 PAYMENT ON PREVIOUS VIEW OF LAW

Any payment made and accepted in satisfaction of any liability for tax and on a view of the law then generally adopted, will only be disturbed on the same view of the law, notwithstanding that it appears from a subsequent legal decision or otherwise that the view was or may have been wrong. [*IHTA 1984, s 255*].

35.14 FOREIGN ASSETS

Payment out of foreign assets. Where, because of restrictions imposed by the foreign government, executors cannot immediately transfer to this country sufficient of the deceased's foreign assets for payment of the inheritance tax liability attributable to them, they are given the option of deferring payment until the transfer can be effected. If the amount in sterling that the executors finally succeed in bringing to this country is less than this tax, the balance is waived. (See F6 at 23 HMRC EXTRA-STATUTORY CONCESSIONS).

Foreign-owned works of art. Where a work of art normally kept overseas becomes liable to inheritance tax on the owner's death solely because it is physically situated in the UK at the relevant date, the liability will be waived if the work was brought into the UK solely for public exhibition, cleaning or restoration. Despite the flexibility of concession F7 it is perhaps wise to ensure that IR Capital Taxes are approached in these circumstances to ensure that no IHT liability will be attached if the foreign domiciliary dies with an artwork in the United Kingdom and a chargeable event arises. If the work of art is held by a discretionary trust (or is otherwise comprised in settled property in which there is no interest in possession) the charge to tax under *IHTA 1984, s 64* (ten-year anniversary charge) will similarly be waived. (See written ministerial statement by Dawn Primarolo MP, Hansard Col 11 WS, 25 February 2003 and F7 which has been now amended to include this provision at 23 HMRC EXTRA-STATUTORY CONCESSIONS).

35.15   POWERS TO RAISE TAX ETC.

Any transferee or devisee who is liable to tax (including interest) on the value of any property may raise the money by sale or mortgage of, or a terminable charge on, that property whether or not the property is vested in him. A person with limited interest in the property who pays the tax is entitled to a similar charge on the property as if raised by a mortgage to him. [*IHTA 1984, s 212*].

35.16   REFUND BY INSTALMENTS

Where a person has paid tax which is or might at his option have been payable by instalments and he is entitled to recover part or the whole of it from another person, that other person (unless otherwise agreed between them) is entitled to refund the tax by the same instalments (and with the same interest thereon) as might have been paid to the Board. [*IHTA 1984, s 213*].

A clause regarding *IHTA 1984, s 213* such as that detailed below might be appropriate where, for instance, a company is a close company where it paid IHT by a lump sum where it could have paid by instalments. These circumstances are likely to arise where there may have been gifts or settlement of the company's shares or gifts to the company prior to the sale to the purchaser. Where the close company paid the IHT by a lump sum in circumstances where it could have paid by instalments, 'the Covenantors' must reimburse 'the Purchaser' by lump sum and may not pay by instalments unless it is agreed otherwise as seen below.

Taxation Indemnity

THIS TAX DEED is made the .... day of .... BETWEEN

(1)   The persons whose names and addresses are set out in Part I of the Schedule ('the Covenantors');

(2)   The companies whose names and registered offices are set out in Part II of the Schedule ('the Companies');

(3)   ....[Name of Company]......... registration number ....[reg. number]......... whose registered office is at ....[address]......... ('the Purchaser' which expression shall where the context so admits include its successors and assigns).

35.17   Payment of Tax

> WHEREAS pursuant to an agreement ('the Agreement') dated ......[date]....... the Purchaser has today completed the purchase from the Covenantors of the whole of the issued share capital of ....[Name of company]...... in reliance *inter alia* upon the indemnities contained in this deed.
>
> NOW IT IS AGREED as follows:
>
> **1 General** ... *etc.*
>
> **2 The indemnities**
>
> The Covenantors jointly and severally covenant with the Company and the Purchaser to indemnify them and hold them harmless against any liability:
>
> 2.1   The Inheritance Tax Act 1984, section 213 shall not apply in relation to any payments to be made by the Covenantors under this deed.
>
> 2.2   *etc.*
>
> *Note*: Further conditions apply to the Tax Indemnity that are not relevant to this book

35.17   CERTIFICATES OF TAX PAID

A person who has paid tax not ultimately due from him may apply to the Board for a certificate specifying the tax paid and the debts and incumbrances allowed in valuing the property and any certificate is conclusive evidence of payment as between the payer and the person by whom the tax specified falls to be borne. [*IHTA 1984, s 214*].

 **HM Revenue & Customs**   *Application to transfer funds to pay inheritance tax*

Fill in this form if you want to pay the inheritance tax that is due on delivery of form IHT200 by transferring money from the deceased's bank or building society account(s). To request a Capital Taxes (CT) reference, telephone our helpline on 0845 30 20 900 or alternatively fill in the deceased's name and date of death and send this form to us with your return address completed overleaf. You should read form D20(Notes) before filling in this form.

Name of deceased
Surname

CT reference

Date of death / /

I/We, the person(s) entitled to apply for a grant of representation/Confirmation to the estate of the above named deceased request

Name of deceased's bank **TR1**

Branch address **TR2**

to transfer the sum of (in words) (in figures)

TR3 **TR4** £

to

TR5 *"✓"*

	Bank of England	10-00-00	23430303
	Royal Bank of Scotland	83-06-08	00132961
	Bank of Ireland	90-21-27	23350265

in payment of the inheritance tax now due.

The money should be transferred from the following account

Sort code	**Account number**	**Amount**
TR6		£

The deceased's surname and CT reference number must be quoted on the transfer.

I/We certify that the amount shown above is required to pay all or part of the tax now due under s.226(2) IHTA 1984. If, before a grant has been issued, it proves necessary to refund the tax transferred hereunder I/we authorise Capital Taxes to return the money to the account shown in box TR6 above.

Full name and address	Full name and address
Signature Date	Signature Date
Full name and address	Full name and address
Signature Date	Signature Date

D20   www.hmrc.gov.uk/cto   Helpline 0845 30 20 900   HMRC CT 12/05

(Substitute)(LexisNexis Butterworths)

35.17   Payment of Tax

If you would like us to send you the CT reference by post, please complete the boxes below.

Name and address to return form to

Solicitors/agents reference

Application for Capital Taxes reference

Inland Revenue
Capital Taxes

Fill in this form if you need a Capital Taxes reference number so you can pay inheritance tax by transferring money from the deceased's bank or building society account(s). You should apply for a reference number at least two weeks before you intend to send form IHT200 to us.

Full name of deceased

Any other names that the deceased was known by

Date of death ___/___/___   Date of birth ___/___/___

Domicile of deceased (tick one)   England and Wales ☐   Scotland ☐   Northern Ireland ☐   Other ☐

When you have filled in this form, you should send it to the Capital Taxes office where you intend to send form IHT200. Our addresses are on page 2 of the guide IHT210 *"How to fill in form IHT200"*. You should send the form to

• our Nottingham office, if you intend to apply for a grant of representation in England & Wales *other than at the Newcastle District Probate Registry*

• our Edinburgh office, if you intend to apply for Confirmation in Scotland, or for a grant of representation at the Newcastle District Probate Registry

• our Belfast office, if you intend to apply for a grant of representation in Northern Ireland.

Remember to fill in the boxes below with the name of the deceased and your return address.

- -

Name and address to return this form to

Your Reference

Name of deceased

IR CT reference

D21
(Substitute)(LexisNexis Butterworths)

L3/00

36 Penalties

Simon's Direct Tax Service, part I11.7.

Other Sources. HMRC Inheritance Tax Leaflet IHT 13; Foster, part L7; Adjudicator's Leaflet AO 1; IHTM36000.

36.1 APPLICATION

Failure to deliver an IHT account under *IHTA 1984, s 216* or a corrective supplementary account under *IHTA 1984, s 217*. See 2.3 to 2.7 ACCOUNTS AND RETURNS.

Penalty of £100 (£50 for accounts to be delivered before 27 July 1999) unless the tax payable is less than £100 or there is a reasonable excuse (see below). For accounts due to be delivered on or after 27 July 1999, a further penalty of £100 where proceedings in which the failure could be declared are not commenced within the period of six months from the date that the account was due to be delivered and where the account has not been delivered at the end of that six-month period. The total of these penalties cannot exceed the amount of tax payable.

A daily penalty of up to £60 (£10 for accounts due to be delivered before 27 July 1999) from the date the failure is declared by a court or the Special Commissioners until the account is delivered.

These provisions come into effect where the period within which the person is required to deliver the account expires after six months from the date of Royal Assent to the *FA 2004* i.e. from 22 January 2005 onwards. [*FA 2004, s 295(5)*].

Failure to make a return under *IHTA 1984, s 218* (non-resident trustees) and failure to comply with a notice under *IHTA 1984, s 219 as amended by FA 2000, s 147(2)* (power to require information). See 2.8 AND 2.9 ACCOUNTS AND RETURNS.

Penalty up to £300 (£50 for returns/notices required to be delivered before 27 July 1999) plus a daily penalty of up to £60 (£10 for returns/notices required to be delivered before 27 July 1999) from the date the failure is declared by a court or the Special Commissioners until the return is made.

Failure to comply with a notice under *IHTA 1984, s 219A* (power to call for documents, etc.). See 2.9 ACCOUNTS AND RETURNS.

Penalty up to £50 plus daily penalty of up to £30 from the date the failure is declared by a court or the Special Commissioners until the notice is complied with.

Continued failure to deliver an IHT account under *IHTA 1984, s 216(6), (7)*. See 2.6 ACCOUNTS AND RETURNS.

A penalty charge of up to £3,000 applies if the failure to deliver an account continues after the anniversary of the filing dates within *IHTA 1984, s 216(6), (7)* unless there is a reasonable excuse for the late delivery. These penalty provisions apply from the end of the period of twelve months beginning with the date on which the *FA 2004* received Royal Assent i.e. 22 July 2004 where the failure to deliver an account under this section is on or before that date. Where failure to deliver an account under this section is on or before that date then the anniversary for delivery is twelve months from the expiry date given within *IHTA 1984, s 216(6), (7)*.

Failure to comply with requirements of *IHTA 1984, s 218(A)*. See 14.3 DEEDS VARYING DISPOSITIONS ON DEATH.

A penalty can arise where a disposition on death is varied by the beneficiaries and gives rise to an additional tax liability. In these circumstances where there is a failure to deliver instrument varying a disposition and notification of additional tax payable within eighteen months after the day on which the instrument of variation is made, a penalty of up to £3,000 may be charged. Where the due date for notification expired before Royal Assent i.e. 22 July 2004 the penalty charge does not apply until 12 months after that date. No penalty arises where there is 'reasonable excuse' for the failure and that failure continues after the anniversary of the six-month period.

'Reasonable excuse'. No penalty arises under any of the above provisions where there is reasonable excuse for the failure unless the failure is not remedied without unreasonable delay after the excuse has ceased. From 1 April 2003 HMRC Inheritance Tax changed the process by which they deal with potential penalties on tax paying accounts sent to them outside the normal 12-month period allowed under *IHTA 1984, s 216*. A standard letter will now automatically be issued by them, as part of their initial processing of the new account, which explains that the account is late and a penalty arises. At the bottom of the letter is a payment slip to accompany the payment of any penalty.

Attached to the letter is a form that allows the personal representatives or their agent to provide an explanation if they believe a reasonable excuse exists (IHT 13, pp 3 and 4 detail what HMRC Inheritance Tax constitute 'reasonable excuse') so that the penalty does not have to be paid. An extract from leaflet IHT 13 will also be provided in every case. It contains examples of what they consider to be a reasonable excuse. See IHT NEWSLETTER AND TAX BULLETIN EXTRACTS (61), May Special Edition 2003, August 2004 HMRC Inheritance Tax.

[*IHTA 1984, ss 245, 245A as amended by FA 1999, s 108; FA 2004, s 295(2), (3) and (5)–(8)*].

36.2   **Special Commissioners. Failure to comply with direction of Special Commissioners** under *SI 1994/1811* (see 15.7 DETERMINATIONS AND APPEALS) including *Reg 10* thereof (**power of Special Commissioners to obtain information**; see 2.9 ACCOUNTS AND RETURNS), or **failure to attend in obedience to witness summons of Special Commissioners**; refusal to be sworn, answer questions or provide documents under *Reg 5* thereof (subject to certain exceptions including those relating to legal privilege and documents of tax advisers), where the appeal hearing is notified after 31 August 1994. Penalty up to £10,000. [*SI 1994/1811, Reg 24*].

Failure to answer summons of Special Commissioners or refusal to be sworn or to answer questions where the appeal hearing was notified before 1 September 1994. Penalty up to £50. [*IHTA 1984, s 246; SI 1994/1813, Sch 1 para 20, Sch 2 Part I*].

36.3   **Fraud and neglect. Fraudulent or negligent supply of information** or documents to the Board under the provisions of *FA 2004*. Following *FA 2004* the distinction between 'fraud' and 'negligence' is redundant and there is no *per se* actual fixed monetary amount of penalty. The penalty is now limited to the difference between the true tax payable, the additional tax, and the tax based on the incorrect information supplied. The result of this is that if there is no additional tax due there is no penalty notwithstanding the incorrect information being supplied. [*IHTA 1984, s 247(1) as amended by FA 2004, s 295(4)*]. Under *IHTA 1984, s 247(3)* the distinction between 'fraud' and 'negligence' is also redundant as the new amending provisions in *FA 2004* charge a penalty for providing incorrect information, whatever the reason, at a maximum of £3,000 in all cases. This could mean, oddly, that someone not liable for the tax but furnishes incorrect information or documents could suffer a penalty of up to £3,000 where there is no increase in the amount of the tax payable, whereas the person liable for the tax would not! It remains to be seen how this disparity will work in practice. The effective date of these changes is in respect of incorrect information supplied following the date of Royal Assent to *FA 2004* i.e. 23 July 2004. See IHT NEWSLETTER AND TAX BULLETIN EXTRACTS (61), August 2004. [*IHTA 1984, s 247(3) as amended by FA 2004, s 295(9)*].

Fraudulent or negligent supply of information or documents to the Board up to and including Royal Assent to *FA 2004* i.e. 22 July 2004:

(*a*)   by any person liable for the tax:

36.4 Penalties

(i) **if fraud**—penalty up to £3,000 plus an amount equal to the difference between the true tax and the tax based on the fraudulent information etc. (before 27 July 1999, £50 plus twice that amount).

(ii) **if negligence**—penalty up to £1,500 (before 27 July 1999, £50) plus the difference between the true tax and the tax based on the negligent information etc.

(b) by any person not liable for the tax:

(i) **if fraud**—penalty up to £3,000 (before 27 July 1999, £500).

(ii) **if negligence**—penalty up to £1,500 (before 27 July 1999, £250).

[*IHTA 1984, s 247(1)–(3); FA 1999, s 108*].

36.4 **Assistance. Assisting in, or inducing, the supply of any information or document known to be incorrect.** Penalty up to £3,000. [*IHTA 1984, s 247(4); FA 1999, s 108*].

36.5 **Discovery. Errors discovered** of a material respect in any information or document supplied by a person without fraud or negligence shall be treated as negligence under 36.3 parts (a)(ii) or (b)(ii) above unless remedied without unreasonable delay. If any other person notices an error in a return etc. not submitted by him whereby tax for which that other person is liable has been or might be underpaid, he must inform the Board without unreasonable delay, otherwise he will be subject to the penalty for negligence under 36.3(b)(ii) above. [*IHTA 1984, s 248*].

36.6 **Procedure.** Penalty proceedings are by the Board (in Scotland, by the Board or the Lord Advocate) and may be commenced before the Special Commissioners or in the High Court (or the Court of Session as the Court of Exchequer in Scotland) as civil proceedings by the Crown. An appeal may be lodged by either party against decisions by the Special Commissioners on a question of law and by the defendant (or, in Scotland, the defender) against the amount of penalty awarded which may be confirmed, reduced or increased by the Court. Any penalty awarded by the Special Commissioners is recoverable by the Board as a debt due to the Crown. [*IHTA 1984, ss 249, 252*]. *Summary penalties* may be awarded by the Special Commissioners in respect of 36.1(d) and 36.2 above with appeal available to the High Court (or Court of Session in Scotland). [*IHTA 1984, s 251; SI 1994/1813, Sch 1 para 22*]. The Board may mitigate penalties before or after judgment. [*IHTA 1984, s 253*].

36.7 **Time limits.** No proceedings for penalties may be brought more than three years after notification by the Board of the tax properly payable in respect of the chargeable transfer concerned. Proceedings may be continued or commenced against the personal representatives of a deceased person and any penalties awarded are payable out of his estate. [*IHTA 1984, s 250*].

36.8 **False statements. 'False statements to prejudice of Crown and public revenue'** are indictable as a criminal offence (*R v Hudson CCA 1956, 36 TC 561*). In the case of *R v Fogon [2003] STC 461* a question arose as to whether the appellant fell within *Criminal Justice Act 1988, s 71(4)* 'a person benefits from an offence' or *s 71(5)* 'a person derives a pecuniary advantage'. The Judge held that the prosecution's approach was correct and that the case was covered by *s 71(4)* as

'He diverted the money to a concealed account for his own purposes and failed to declare it to the Inland Revenue.'

Therefore it was concluded that 'money transferred to the account [Company] was property obtained in connection with the commission of the offence' and came within *s 71(4)*.

36.9 **Mitigation.** The Finance Act 2007 introduced a new framework of penalty impositions relating to direct tax matters including 'careless', 'deliberate' and 'concealed' actions which result in loss of tax; however, inheritance tax is excluded and has its own framework for penalty sanctions. [*IHTA 1984, s 253*]. In practice, HMRC Inheritance Tax will exercise their statutory power to charge a lower penalty in a negotiated settlement. Starting with the maximum figure of penalty HMRC Inheritance Tax will reduce it depending on how much is disclosed to them, how co-operative the parties are and how grave the offence. The rule of thumb that HMRC Inheritance Tax use in their negotiations will be as follows:

Disclosure – a reduction in the penalty of up to 20% (or even up to 30% with full and voluntary disclosure). However, if there is denial that anything is wrong until the last possible moment then there will be little or no reduction. Full and voluntary disclosure without prompting from HMRC Inheritance Tax will attract the maximum reduction or thereabouts. HMRC Inheritance Tax indicated that in between these two extremes a wide variety of circumstances are possible and consideration will be given to the amount of information given, how soon it was given and how that information contributed to the settling of the enquiries by HMRC Inheritance Tax.

Co-operation – a reduction in the penalty of up to 40%. If information is supplied to HMRC Inheritance Tax promptly after discovery and questions are answered honestly and accurately then the maximum reduction will apply. In addition, the maximum reduction is dependent on the relevant facts being supplied and the tax, once it is calculated, being paid promptly. Delays, untrue or evasive answers, or nothing was done until HMRC Inheritance Tax took formal action will not attract a reduction at all.

Gravity – a reduction of 40%. HMRC Inheritance Tax takes into account the reasons for failing to deliver an account and the amount of money involved. The less serious the matter the bigger the reduction in the penalty.

37 Pension Schemes

Cross-references. See 20.5 EXCLUDED PROPERTY for overseas pensions; 21.13 EXEMPT TRANS-FERS for dispositions conferring retirement benefits; 30 LIFE ASSURANCE POLICIES AND ANNUITIES; 59 WORKING CASE STUDY.

Simon's Direct Tax Service, parts I4.125, I5.636, I5.637.

Other Sources. Foster, parts C1.55, D1.25, E6.36–37, K1.25.

37.1   **Treatment of pension rights etc.** Property held as part of a superannuation scheme or fund (including retirement annuity contracts) approved by HMRC for income tax purposes or, after 22 July 1987, held under approved personal pension arrangements and, from 6 April 2006, registered pension schemes (or *ICTA 1988, s 615(3)* schemes) is not subject to inheritance tax under the provisions relating to SETTLEMENTS WITHOUT INTERESTS IN POSSESSION (44). However, where a benefit has become payable under such a scheme etc. and subsequently becomes comprised in a settlement made by a person other than the person entitled to the benefit, the person entitled to the benefit is treated as the settlor and the usual provisions relating to such settlements apply. In addition, the Treasury may make provision for or in connection with the application of IHT in relation to the Pension Protection Fund, Fraud Compensation Fund and the Board of the Pension Protection Fund so that regulations may include provision for and in connection with the taxation of compensation payments made under the *Pensions Act 2004, s 162.* The regulations may apply from any time after 5 April 2005. Unregistered pension schemes with no contributions on or after 6 April 2006 will be that relief in place at 5 April 2006 and those pension schemes with post 5 April 2006 contributions which are protected will attract limited relief from IHT inclusive of an indexation factor. In order to ensure that lump sum rights cannot fall below the value of the fund as at 6 April 2006 for IHT purposes minor amendments have been made to ensure that the formula in *FA 2004, Sch 36 para 57* for calculating the value is not compromised, [*IHTA 1984, ss 58, 151(1)(1A)(5); F(No 2)A 1987, s 98(4); FA 2004, s 203(3), (4), Sch 36 paras 56–58; FA 2005, s 102, Sch 10 para 58*]. See 44.2 SETTLEMENTS WITHOUT INTERESTS IN POSSESSION and Fosters Inheritance Tax, para E6.33 and E6.34.

37.2   **Application.** Where a person is entitled to an interest in or under a scheme etc. which ends on his death, the interest will not be included in his estate if it

     (*a*)   is, or is a right to, a pension or annuity, and

     (*b*)   is not an interest resulting from the application of any benefit provided under the fund or scheme otherwise than by way of a pension or annuity.

Other rights (e.g. rights to repayment of contributions on death before retirement age) are chargeable to IHT.

A person entitled to a pension or annuity satisfying the conditions of (*a*) and (*b*) above is not treated as being beneficially entitled to the property in which the interest subsists. The fund is not, therefore, liable to IHT on his death. In the case of Guaranteed Annuities if the deceased was receiving payments under an annuity and died before the end of the annuity period, the right to receive the remainder of the payments is an asset of the estate and the value should be included on Form D6 at question 1. HMRC Inheritance Tax has prepared an annuity calculator on its website which calculates the open market value of remaining period.

Where a person has a general power to dispose of his benefits as he thinks fit, he is treated as beneficially entitled to the interest. If a benefit passes only at the discretion of the trustees of the scheme and is not a legally enforceable claim by the personal representatives (PRs), there is no liability to inheritance tax. See [**Case Studies 2** and **6**] and *Kempe and Roberts (personal representatives of Lyon, deceased) v CIR [2004] STC SCD 467 Sp C 424.*

Where there is a tax liability, it is due from the pensioner or his personal representatives but not from the trustees of the scheme etc.

Changes arising from *FA 2004, s 203* ensure that IHT relief is applicable to contributions to registered pension schemes and for pension schemes for non-residents within *ICTA 1988, s 615(3)* such that transfers of value are not treated as chargeable transfers for IHT purposes.

An anti-avoidance measure is introduced to charge IHT on the death of a registered scheme member on or after the age of 75 where funds are held in an alternatively secured pension (ASP) within *FA 2004, s 165*. The charge is intended to apply in the case where individuals use ASPs to pass on tax-privileged retirement savings to their dependants within six months of death by reason of Rules 5 and 6 of *FA 2004, s 167* rather than to provide a pension in retirement. Broadly, an IHT charge will be made on the left-over ASP funds on death of the scheme member passed on to a 'relevant dependant' including:

- a dependant's scheme pension;

- a dependant's annuity;

- a dependant's unsecured pension; or

- a dependant's ASP

but funds paid to charity within a specified period will be exempt. A 'relevant dependant' for these purposes is includes spouse, civil partner or person financially dependant on the scheme member before their death. [*FA 2004, Schs 28, 29; FA 2007, s 69, Sch 19 paras 19–23*]. The charge will be based on the value of the taxable property at the time the charge arises and will be calculated by reference to the tax-free threshold and rate of tax in place at that time by way of *IHTA 1984, Sch 1*. See 41.1 RATES OF TAX. In the case of the 'relevant dependant's' benefits the charge will be deferred until entitlement to such benefits ceases. See also 62 FINANCE ACT 2007 — SUMMARY OF IHT PROVISIONS.

Example 1

Fredrick, a widower – who is a member of the Allied plc Pension Scheme which is registered – is aged 75 on 18 July 2006 and sets up an alternatively secured pension (ASP) within Rule 6 of *FA 2004, s 165*. Fred dies on 31 December 2006. The fund in the undrawn ASP is valued at £160,000 which is subjected to IHT under *IHTA 1984, s 151A*, as shown in the computation below. Alternatively, in the second part of the example, if the ASP is passed along with his estate valued £610,000 to his sister, Alexandra, who has been financially dependent upon him for many years, within six months of his death and she receives a dependant's unsecured pension then a calculation will be made on her death. See Letter of Wishes below. Alexandra dies three years later on 26 November 2009 when remaining funds in the ASP are valued at £100,000. Fred has previous chargeable transfers of £97,265.

37.2 Pension Schemes

IHTA 1984, s 151A calculation when Frederick dies

	£	£
Previous chargeable transfers		97,265
Value of estate at death excluding ASP	450,000	
Add Value of ASP at 31 December 2006	160,000	
Chargeable residue		610,000
Total cumulative chargeable transfers		£707,265
Tax due from estate on £707,265		
97,265–285,000 (£187,735 at nil%)		—
285,001–707,265 (£422,265 at 40%)		168,906
		£168,906

IHT due on ASP = £160,000/£707,265 × 168,906 = £38,210

IHTA 1984, s 151B calculation when Alexandra dies

	£	£
Previous chargeable transfers		97,265
Value of estate at death excluding ASP	450,000	
Add Value of ASP at 26 November 2009	100,000	
Chargeable residue		550,000
Total cumulative chargeable transfers		£647,265
Tax due from estate on £647,265		
97,265–325,000 (£227,735 at nil%)		—
325,001–647,265 (£322,265 at 40%)		128,906
		£128,906

IHT payable by the ASP fund administrator:
Revised IHT due on ASP = £100,000 × 40% = £40,000.

Notes to the example

(A) Frederick will have had the option to draw alternatively secured income (ASI) which can be between the lower limit of nil up to 70% of the notional annuity that could be purchased under annuity assumptions set by the Government Actuary's Department (GAD) using the member's available drawdown fund. This reduced upper limit and the required annual revaluation of the drawdown fund should result in the fund not being depleted to nil over the period. When the ASP member dies where the scheme rules allow the dependants of the deceased member may benefit from the residual (see letter of wishes below). However, no lump sum may be paid but pension income can continue to be paid to the chosen dependant(s). Alternatively, where there are no dependants the residual lump sum may be paid to a charity or it may be paid back to the original sponsoring company i.e. Allied plc Pension Scheme in this case or used to augment the fund for existing scheme members.

(B) The IHT payable by the ASP fund administrator under *IHTA 1984, s 151A(3)(4)* in the first computation applies if the ASP is not applied to provide dependant's benefits within six months of death whereas if Frederick passes the fund in the undrawn ASP to Alexandra within the six-month period *s 151B* will apply as in the second computation. The calculations are mutually exclusive and the ASP administrator would have a IHT liability of £38,210 on Frederick's demise or £40,000 if the undrawn ASP is passed on to Alexandra and she dies later so that the liability is

394

recalculated. This latter liability is because *IHTA 1984, s 151B(5)* inserted by *FA 2006, s 160(2), Sch 22 paras 1, 4* to ensure that tax is charged at the rate, or rates, at which it would have been charged on the death of the scheme member if the aggregate amounts (reduced by any charitable payment) had been included in the value transferred and the amount on which the tax is charged had formed the *highest* part of that value. Note that the position for IHT purposes changed from 6 April 2007. See examples below. [*IHTA 1984, ss 151A, 151B, Sch 2 para 6A inserted by FA 2006, Sch 22 paras 4–6, 9, 10*].

(C) In the case where a scheme member who died before the age of 75 years and, for example, a dependant of theirs takes the pension benefits in a dependant's unsecured scheme only later, on reaching 75 years themselves, for it to become an ASP the dependant's chargeable estate will then include the value of the ASP on their death. Any payments made to charity within six months beginning with the end of the month in which the death occurs will be deducted before the charge to IHT. [*IHTA 1984, s 151C inserted by FA 2006, Sch 22 para 4*].

For the guidance of the Management Committee, I nominate the person(s) named above to be the beneficiary/beneficiaries in the event of my death. I request the Management Committee to consider paying a pension to the above person under Rules 5 and 6 of *FA 2004, s 167*. I understand that my wishes cannot be binding on the Management Committee but that they will be considered when benefits become payable.............

Please read these notes carefully before completing the form.

On your death, certain benefits will be paid from the .... Pension Scheme.

So that these benefits can be paid free of inheritance tax, the Rules of the .... Pension Scheme give the Management Committee absolute discretion regarding the people to whom pensions and cash are paid.

In reaching its decision, however, the Management Committee will take account of your wishes and you can complete this nomination form with details of the person(s) you would like to receive a benefit on your death.

The above provisions are to take effect on the death of a scheme member after 5 April 2006. The pension scheme administrator is the person who is liable for tax chargeable under *IHTA 1984, s 151B*. [*IHTA 1984, ss 151(2)–(4), 151A–C, 210; FA 2004, s 203(4); FA 2006, s 161, Sch 22 paras 3, 4, 6; Inheritance Tax (Delivery of Accounts)(Excepted Estates)(Amendment) Regulations 2006, SI 2006/2141*].

The *Finance Act 2007, Sch 19 paras 19–23* changes the inheritance tax rules to take into account an income tax charge arising because of an unauthorised payment under *FA 2004, Part 4* when calculating the IHT liability arising after such an income tax charge has been imposed. In addition, any liabilities on an alternatively secured pension (ASP) scheme arising under *IHTA 1984, s 151A* are 'top-sliced' for deaths arising from 6 April 2007 to ensure that the nil rate band, if available, is used against the non–ASP part of the estate in priority to the ASP. See Example 2 below for the post-5 April 2007 position. If there is part of the nil rate band remaining after setting it against the non–ASP estate of the scheme member then this may be available to set against ASP funds, and any IHT liability arising thereon is settled by the ASP scheme administrator. Where a scheme member dies with funds in a pension scheme that would have been an ASP had the scheme administrator been able to trace the member before he/she reached the age of 75 years then the date that the scheme administrator becomes aware of the scheme member's death will be the date for the purposes of *s 151A(a)(b)* in calculating the 'relevant amount' to be subject to tax.

37.2 Pension Schemes

Any liabilities on an alternatively secured pension (ASP) scheme arising under *IHTA 1984, s 151B* are 'top-sliced' from 6 April 2007 to ensure that the nil rate band, if available, is used against the non-ASP part of the estate of the original scheme member in priority to the ASP. See Examples 3–6 below that show the treatment where there is an IHT charge before an unauthorised payment charge and where there is an IHT charge after an unauthorised payment charge where part of the nil rate band is available. Where a relevant dependant entitled to a pension fund inherited from a scheme member dies with funds in a pension scheme that would have been an ASP had the scheme administrator been able to trace the scheme member before their reaching the age of 75 years, the date that the scheme administrator becomes aware of the scheme member's death will be the date for the purposes of *s 151B(a)(b)* in calculating the amount to be subject to tax. New taxing rules in such circumstances follow those within *s 151A* allowing, on the cessation of the relevant dependant's pension, for unused nil rate band of the original scheme member to be grossed up under *s 151A(4C)* and set against the balance of the ASP funds remaining on the cessation of the dependant's pension. The nil rate band to be taken into account for these purposes is that applying at the time of the cessation of the relevant dependant's pension. If there has been a reduction in the tax rates since the scheme member's death then for these purposes the tax rate to be applied will be the latest as if it had been in force at the time of the scheme member's death.

Where a relevant dependant dies with another pension fund within *s 151C*, any ASP arising under *IHTA 1984, s 151C* is 'top-sliced' from 6 April 2007 to ensure that the nil rate band, if available, is used against the non-ASP part of the estate of the original scheme member in priority to the ASP. Any income tax charge arising because of an unauthorised payment under *FA 2004, Part 4* is taken into account in calculating the IHT tax liability. The income tax relieved within *s 151C(3)(a)* in this way is that which arose before IHT was charged in relation to any unauthorised member payments and reduces the subsequent IHT charge.

Where there is an ASP and any unused nil rate band of the original scheme member has not been fully utilised against the non-ASP funds the balance may be grossed up under *s 151C(3C)* and set against the balance of the ASP funds not previously assessed under *s 151A*. This 'previously untaxed dependant's alternatively secured pension fund amount' is that part of an individual's ASP that has not given rise to an unauthorised payment charge before IHT arose on the ASP. In addition, under *s 151C(3D)* where an amount of ASP charged under *s 151C* has previously been charged under *s 151A* then this amount shall be excluded from the IHT charge on the later event. *[IHTA 1984, ss 151A–C as amended by FA 2007, Sch 19 paras 19–23]*. See ACCOUNTS AND RETURNS (2), PAYMENT OF TAX (35), IHT AND TAX BULLETIN EXTRACTS (61), April 2007 and 62 FINANCE ACT 2007 — SUMMARY OF IHT PROVISIONS.

Example 2

Frederick, a widower (as in Example 1 above but reflecting the IHT situation after 5 April 2007) – who is a member of the Allied plc Pension Scheme which is registered – is aged 75 on 18 July 2007 and sets up an alternatively secured pension (ASP) within Rule 6 of *FA 2004, s 165*. Frederick dies on 31 December 2007. The fund in the undrawn ASP is valued at £160,000 which is subjected to IHT under *IHTA 1984, s 151A(2) as amended by FA 2007, Sch 19 para 20(2)*, as shown in the computation below. Frederick has previous chargeable transfers of £97,265.

IHTA 1984, s 151A calculation when Frederick dies	£	£
Previous chargeable transfers		97,265
Value of estate at death including ASP	610,000	
Deduct value of ASP at 31 December 2007	160,000	
Chargeable residue		450,000
Total cumulative chargeable transfers		£547,265
Tax due from estate on £547,265		
97,265 – 300,000 (£202,735 at nil%)		—
300,001– 547,265 (£247,265 at 40%)		98,906
IHT due on estate excluding ASP settled by PRs.		£98,906
IHT due on ASP = £160,000 × 40% = £64,000 i.e. top slice.		£64,000

IHT liability of £64,000 is settled by the ASP scheme administrator.

Notes to the example

(A) If Frederick died in 2007/08 then under the *FA 2007*, Sch 19 changes the ASP fund in his estate would be treated as the top slice in contrast to 2006/07 when the rules ensured that IHT payable by the ASP fund administrator under *IHTA 1984, s 151A(3)(4)* in Example 1 above attracted a proportion of the nil rate band. This only applies if the ASP is not applied to provide dependant's benefits within six months of death. The ASP administrator would have an IHT liability of £64,000, a substantial increase on the 2006/07 amount even taking into account the increase of £15,000 in the nil rate band. [*IHTA 1984, ss 151A(2) as inserted by FA 2007, Sch 19 paras 20(2)*].

(B) As the value of the estate excluding ASP funds is in excess of the nil rate band, any top-slicing relief that might have been available, *s 151A*, is not available and the ASP administrator suffers an IHT charge of 40% without any 'top-slicing'. Whereas if Frederick passes the fund in the undrawn ASP to Alexandra within the six-month period *section 151B* will apply and there would be no IHT charge at that time.

Example 3

Fred, a widower – who is a member of the Allied plc Pension Scheme which is registered – is aged 75 on 18 July 2007 and sets up an alternatively secured pension (ASP) within Rule 6 of *FA 2004, s 165*. Fred dies on 31 December 2007. The fund in the undrawn ASP is valued at £200,000 and there is an IHT charge *before* an unauthorised payment charge. The ASP is valued at £200,000. Fred has no previous chargeable transfers prior to his death.

Calculation when Fred dies	£	£
Previous chargeable transfers		Nil
Value of estate at death excluding ASP	200,000	
Deduct Proportion of nil rate band used at 31 December 2007	200,000	
Chargeable residue		Nil
Tax due from estate		£Nil

Calculation *IHTA 1984, s 151A*

Balance of nil rate band available £100,000 (£300,000 – £200,000)

Value of ASP funds becoming chargeable = £200,000		200,000
Unused nil rate band available grossed up £100,000 × (100/100 – 70)% =		333,333
IHT due on ASP funds		£Nil

Notes to the example

(A) Fred dies with an ASP that has not previously been subject to an unauthorised payment charge and he leaves an estate (excluding the ASP value) that does not exceed his available nil rate band. [*IHTA 1984, s 151A(4B)*]. In these circumstances the balance of the nil rate band is set against the ASP value and under *s 151A(4C)* the balance of the nil rate band i.e. £100,000 in this example is grossed up and set against the ASP value of £200,000.

(B) The *FA 2007, Sch 19 para 20* insertion of *s 151A(4C)* where the previously untaxed ASP is grossed up as follows in accordance with the following formula:

$$\frac{UNRB \times 100}{100 - MUPR}$$

where

UNRB = unused nil rate band in excess the chargeable transfers less any previously untaxed ASP fund; and

MUPR = the maximum unauthorised payment rate i.e. the maximum aggregate rate chargeable by FA 2004, Part 4 i.e. 70% in this example by reason of *FA 2004, ss 208, 209(6), 240*.

Example continued

Fred, as above, dies on 31 December 2007. The fund in the undrawn ASP is valued at £200,000 and there is an IHT charge unauthorised payment charge *before* the IHT is due when the ASP is valued at £200,000. Fred has no previous chargeable transfers prior to his death.

Calculation when Fred dies	£	£
Previous chargeable transfers		Nil
Value of estate at death excluding ASP	200,000	
Deduct Proportion of £300,000 nil rate band used at 31 December 2007	200,000	
Chargeable residue		Nil
Tax due from estate		£Nil

Calculation *IHTA 1984, s 151A*

Unauthorised payment charge = £200,000 × 70% = 140,000		
ASP funds chargeable to IHT will therefore be £200,000 – £140,000 unauthorised payment charge =	60,000	
Balance of nil rate band available (£300,000 – £200,000 above) =	£100,000	
IHT due on ASP funds		£Nil

Note to the example

(A)   The amount of the ASP funds charged to IHT differs depending on whether or not the unauthorised payment charges have arisen before or after the IHT due date. Where the unauthorised payment charges have been deducted before IHT is due then IHT is calculated by reference to the net value of the ASP funds as in this example. And conversely, as in the previous example, where IHT is due before the unauthorised payment charges are made then IHT is calculated by reference to the gross value of the ASP funds with an adjustment to the unused nil-rate band to set against the ASP funds.

Example 4

Bert, a widower – who is a member of the Allied plc Pension Scheme which is registered – is aged 77 and has an alternatively secured pension (ASP) within Rule 6 of *FA 2004, s 165*. The fund in the undrawn ASP is valued at £200,000 which is subjected to IHT as shown in the computation below. The ASP is passed along with Bert's estate valued at £280,000 to his sister, Adriana, who has been financially dependent upon him for many years, within six months of his death and she receives a dependant's unsecured pension; a calculation then will be made on her death. Adriana dies three years later on 26 November 2010 when remaining funds in the ASP are valued at £200,000. Bert has no previous chargeable transfers prior to his death.

Calculation when Bert dies	£	£
Previous chargeable transfers		Nil
Value of estate at death excluding ASP	280,000	
Deduct Proportion of nil rate band of £300,000	280,000	
Chargeable residue		Nil
Tax due from estate		£Nil

IHTA 1984, s 151B calculation when Adriana dies

	£
Balance of nil rate band available in 2010/11 is £350,000 – £280,000 = £70,000	
Unused nil rate band available grossed up £70,000 × (100/100 – 70)% =	233,333
Balance of ASP funds remaining on Adriana's death i.e. cessation of dependant's pension =	200,000
IHT on ASP funds	£Nil

Notes to the example

(A)   Bert dies with an ASP that has not previously been subject to an income tax charge under *FA 2004, Part 4* before IHT was charged. In these circumstances the balance of the nil rate band in 2010/11, i.e. £70,000 in this example, is grossed up and set against the ASP fund. [*IHTA 1984, s 151BA*].

(B)   The unused nil rate band is grossed up by application of the formula in *IHTA 1984, s 151A(4C)*. Had the ASP fund been subject to income tax, the relief provision as inserted by *FA 2007, Sch 19 para 20* would have applied where the income tax resulting from unauthorised pension payment charges would have been applied and would reduce the amount chargeable to IHT 'by the amount previously charged to income tax', i.e. 70% in the example above.

37.2 Pension Schemes

Example 5

Alan, a widower – who is a member of the Allied plc Pension Scheme which is registered – is aged 78 and has an alternatively secured pension (ASP) within Rule 6 of *FA 2004, s 165*. Alan dies on 31 December 2007. The fund in the undrawn ASP is valued at £200,000. The ASP is passed along with Alan's estate valued at £320,000 to his sister, Amanda, who has been financially dependent upon him for many years, within six months of his death and she receives a dependant's unsecured pension; a calculation then will be made on her death. Amanda dies three years later on 26 November 2010 when remaining funds in the ASP are then valued at £100,000. Alan had no previous chargeable transfers prior to his death.

Calculation when Alan dies	£	£
Previous chargeable transfers		Nil
Value of estate at death excluding ASP	320,000	
Deduct nil rate band of £300,000	300,000	
Chargeable residue		Nil
Tax due from estate £20,000 × 40%		£8,000

IHTA 1984, s 151B calculation when Amanda dies

Balance of nil rate band available in 2009/10 = £30,000 (£350,000 – £320,000)	
Unused nil rate band then grossed up by reference to *IHTA 1984, s 151A(4C)* i.e. £30,000 × (100/100 – 70)% =	100,000
Balance of ASP fund on cessation of Amanda's entitlement	100,000
IHT on ASP funds	£Nil

Note to the example

(A) Alan dies with an ASP that has not previously been subject to a tax charge and he leaves an estate (excluding the ASP value) that exceeds his available nil rate band in 2007/08. In these circumstances the nil rate band which has increased on Amanda's death in 2010/11 is deducted from the chargeable estate in 2007/08 and grossed up under *s 151A(4C)* and set against the ASP value at that time.

Example 6

Alan, as in Example 5 above, a widower – who is a member of the Allied plc Pension Scheme which is registered – is aged 78 and has an alternatively secured pension (ASP) within Rule 6 of *FA 2004, s 165*. Alan dies on 31 December 2007. The fund in the undrawn ASP is valued at £200,000. The ASP is passed along with Alan's estate valued £320,000 to his sister, Amanda, who has been financially dependent upon him for many years, within six months of his death and she receives a dependant's unsecured pension; a calculation then will be made on her death. Amanda dies some years later on 26 November 2012 when remaining funds in the ASP are then valued at £100,000 but there is an unauthorised payment charge *before* any IHT is due. Alan had previous chargeable transfers prior to his death of £97,265.

Calculation when Alan dies	£	£
Previous chargeable transfers		97,265
Value of estate at death including ASP	422,735	
Deduct Value of ASP at 31 December 2007	200,000	
Chargeable residue		222,735
Total cumulative chargeable transfers		£320,000
Tax due from estate on £320,000		
97,265 – 300,000 (£202,735 at nil%)		—
300,001– 320,000 (£20,000 at 40%)		8,000
IHT due on estate excluding ASP		£8,000

No IHT due on ASP at this stage as it is used to provide pension benefits for a relevant dependant.

IHTA 1984, s 151B calculation when Amanda dies

Balance of nil rate band available in 2012/13 (£350,000 – £320,000) =	30,000	
Balance of ASP fund chargeable to IHT on cessation of Amanda's entitlement = £100,000 – £70,000 unauthorised payment charge =	30,000	
IHT on ASP funds		£Nil

Notes to the example

(A)   When Alan dies with an ASP that has not previously been subject to an unauthorised payment charge and he leaves an estate (excluding the ASP value) that exceeds his available nil rate band then a charge to IHT will arise on his estate at that time. In these circumstances the whole of the nil rate band in 2007/08 is utilised against the non-ASP estate. However, when Amanda dies in 2012/13 (assuming there has been no change in the nil rate band of £350,000) the ASP value at that time forms the highest part of the estate i.e. ASP of £100,000 is added to £320,000. The nil rate band at that stage is £350,000 and under *s 151A(4B)(4C)* the remaining unused balance of the nil rate band i.e. £30,000 (see Note B below) in this example is set against the ASP value after the unauthorised payment charge on Amanda's death. [*IHTA 1984, s 151A(4B) as inserted by FA 2007, Sch 19 para 20(4)*].

(B)   Note in the above calculation that the balance of available nil rate band in 2012/13 of £30,000 is calculated by reference to the original non-ASP estate of £320,000 as this is 'the value actually transferred by that chargeable transfer (or nil if there is no such chargeable transfer)…' less the current nil rate band of £350,000 in 2012/13. [*IHTA 1984, s 151A(4B)(a) as inserted by FA 2007, Sch 19 para 20(4)*].

IHT concessionary practice dating from 1992 in relation to pension choices by scheme members who die under the age of 75 is to be put on a statutory footing. Under the concession, IHT is not charged under *IHTA 1984, s 3(3)* if a scheme member does not exercise their right to take pension benefits, for example, when an enhanced death benefit is paid to a beneficiary who is a spouse, civil partner or a financial dependant of the scheme member, at the time of their death, as a result of the member not taking their pension when their life expectancy was seriously impaired. If the scheme member makes a disposition of their pension benefit within two years of their death and even though the scheme member was in good health at that time but their life expectancy was seriously impaired then a *section 3(3)* charge will apply in respect of the deferral of the pension. However, any charge to IHT under *s 3(3)* arising from a failure to exercise pension rights which on death of the scheme member are paid to a relevant dependant or a charity will not be treated as a transfer of value for these purposes. See also HMRC Statement of Practice SP E3 regarding CTT, and HMRC Statement of Practice SP 10/86, 9 July 1986, see 25 HMRC STATEMENTS OF PRACTICE, confirming that their existing CTT practice is extended to IHT (including the gifts with reservation rules). [*IHTA 1984, ss 3(3), 12(2A)–(2G) inserted by FA 2006, s 160, Sch 22 para 2*].

37.3   **Cash options.** When a person dies and his widow or other dependant becomes entitled to an annuity under the terms of a superannuation scheme or fund (including annuity contracts) or, after 22 July 1987, the terms of approved personal pension arrangements or, after 5 April 2006, registered pension schemes (or *ICTA 1988, s 615(3)* schemes) the fact that the deceased could have chosen instead that a cash sum be paid to his personal representatives is not to be regarded as giving him the type of 'general power' within *IHTA 1984, s 5(2)* (see 19.2 ESTATE) which would result in that sum being included in his estate on death. [*IHTA 1984, s 152; F(No 2)A 1987, s 98(5); FA 2004, s 203(5)*].

37.4   **Death benefits.** Where a trust of the death benefit payable under a pension policy is created, a charge under *IHTA 1984, s 3(3)* may arise. HMRC Inheritance Tax has stated, in a letter to the Association of British Insurers, that a charge in this connection will be raised in very limited circumstances only. For example, where a policyholder is aware that he is terminally ill and at or after that time either takes out a new policy and assigns the death benefit, or assigns on trust the death benefit of an existing policy, or pays further contributions to a single premium policy or enhanced contributions to a regular premium policy, the death benefit of which has previously been assigned on trust, a charge under *section 3(3)* may be contemplated as the arrangements were not intended to make provision for the policyholder's own retirement, given the prospect of an early death. However, HMRC Inheritance Tax have indicated that they would not pursue a claim in these circumstances where the death benefit was paid to the policyholder's spouse and/or dependants (See ICAEW TR 854, 1991 STI 1118, HMRC Tax Bulletin, February 1992, p 11, The Tax Journal, 19 June 2000 and CTO guidance note 'The Inheritance Tax Treatment of Deferral of Annuity Purchase and Income Withdrawal under Personal Pensions'.) See [**Case Study 2**]. A Discussion Paper on Inheritance Tax (IHT) and Simplification issued on 21 July 2005 asked for proposals regarding the *FA 2006* tightening of the above relaxed rules currently in force concerning chargeability under *IHTA 1984, s 3(3)* with regard to omissions/deferrals of pension rights. Legislation has now been introduced so that lump sum payments in respect of registered pension schemes and *ICTA 1988, s 615(3)* schemes with effect from 6 April 2006 will not attract charges under the relevant property regime if they are paid within the stipulated time frame by the pension scheme trustees or persons having control of the scheme. The time allowed for the payment of lump sum by the scheme will run from the date on which the pension scheme is notified of the scheme member's death or, if earlier, when the scheme trustees or persons having control of the scheme could reasonably have been aware of that member's death. Prior to 6 April 2006 and the A-day pension rules being implemented, HMRC did consider relevant property rules applied in the cases of death benefits held on trusts for distribution amongst relatives or dependants. This HMRC concessionary practice only applies now to distributions within two years of the scheme member's death. [*IHTA 1984, s 58(2A)(a)(b); FA 2007, Sch 20 paras 20, 24(9)*].

In IHT 210 (Notes) at D6 (Notes) point 3 states: 'The value of the benefits given away or the impact of the changes made will depend to a large extent on the deceased's health at the date of the nomination, appointment or change. So that we can establish the value, please provide some evidence of the deceased's state of health and life expectancy at that time. A letter from the deceased's doctor is the best sort of evidence.' Note that from February 2004 Form D6 was revised to include a new Box 4 asking whether the deceased or his employer made any contributions to a pension scheme within two years of the death.

HM Revenue & Customs

Pensions

Name

Date of death

/   /

Answer the following questions and give the further details we ask for about the provision for pension(s) made by, or for, the deceased. You should read form D6(Notes) before filling in this form.

1 Did any payments made under a pension scheme or a personal pension policy continue after the deceased's death?

No   Yes

If the answer is "Yes" give details below

Include the figure from box PA1 in box F15, page 3, IHT 200.   **Total**   PA1 £

2 Was a lump sum payable under a pension scheme or a personal pension policy as a result of the deceased's death?

No   Yes

If the answer is "Yes" give details below

If the lump sum was payable as described in the notes, include the total from box PA2 in box F23, page 3, IHT 200.   **Total**   PA2 £

3 Did the deceased, **within 2 years of the death**
• dispose of any of the benefits payable, or
• make any changes to the benefits to which they were entitled
under a pension scheme or a personal pension policy?

No   Yes

If the answer is "Yes" give details below

4 Did the deceased (or his/her employer) make any contributions to a pension scheme for the deceased, within 2 years of the death?

No   Yes

If the answer is "Yes" give details below

D6   www.hmrc.gov.uk/cto   Helpline 0845 30 20 900   HMRC 08/06

(Substitute)|LexisNexis Butterworths)

37.4 Pension Schemes

5   Did the deceased benefit from an alternatively secured pension fund (ASP) at the time of their death?

     Yes   answer question 6

     No   go to question 7

6   How did the benefit arise? Please tick the appropriate box

     a.   The deceased was the original scheme member in their own right.   ☐   answer questions 8d - 8j

     b.   The deceased died (aged 75 or over) with an ASP that they became entitled to as a **'relevant dependant'** of someone who died aged 75 or more with an ASP.   ☐   answer questions 8a – 8g and questions 8i - 8j

     c.   The deceased died (aged 75 or over) with an ASP that they became entitled to as a **'dependant'** of someone who has died.   ☐   answer questions 8a - 8g and 8i - 8j

     d.   The deceased died (aged 75 or over) with an ASP that they became entitled to as a **'relevant dependant'** of someone who died before they reached the age of 75.   ☐   answer questions 8a - 8g and 8i - 8j

7   Did the deceased benefit under a registered pension scheme, where

     •   the benefit was unsecured **and**

     •   they became entitled to the benefit as a **'relevant dependant'** of a person who died aged 75 or over?

     Yes   Answer questions 8a - 8f

     No   you do not need to answer any further questions on form D6

8   a.   What was the original scheme member's name?

     b.   What was the original scheme member's date of death?

     c.   What was the original scheme members Capital Taxes reference number? (If known)

     d.   What is the name of the scheme provider?

     e.   What is the address of the scheme provider?

     f.   What is the scheme reference number?

     g.   What was the value of the fund at the date of the deceased's death?   **PA3**

     h.   What is the value of the fund that is now being applied for the benefit of the deceased's 'relevant dependant(s)'?   **PA4**

     i.   What is the value of the fund being applied for the benefit of charity?   **PA5**

     j.   What is the net value chargeable to tax ?
         (box PA3 less boxes PA4 and PA5)   **PA6**

38   Potentially Exempt Transfers

Cross-references. See 2.3 and 2.5 ACCOUNTS AND RETURNS; 5.3 AGRICULTURAL PROPERTY; 7.6 BUSINESS PROPERTY; 8 CALCULATION OF TAX; 27.1 INTEREST ON TAX; 29.4 LIABILITY FOR TAX; 33.3 NATIONAL HERITAGE; 35.1 PAYMENT OF TAX for due date of payment; 35.3 for payment by instalments; 35.8 for HMRC charges; 35.9 for certificates of discharge; 49.4 TRANSFER OF VALUE for the repayment of certain debts during lifetime being treated as potentially exempt transfers; 59 WORKING CASE STUDY.

Simon's Direct Tax Service, parts I3.311–I3.319.

Other Sources. CTO Leaflet IHT 15, p 5; Foster, parts C3, C4 and C5.

38.1   DEFINITION

Except as provided to the contrary under 38.3 below, a potentially exempt transfer is a transfer of value made by an individual which would otherwise be a chargeable transfer and which falls into one of the following categories.

(*a*)   A gift to another individual of property which

   (i)   becomes comprised in his estate; or

   (ii)   if not falling within (i) above, increases the value of his estate.

   Included is a gift made by an individual into a settlement or which increases the value of settled property, and, in either case, another individual has a beneficial interest in possession in that settlement.

(*b*)   A gift into an accumulation and maintenance trust before 22 March 2006 which gift, by virtue of the transfer, becomes *property* to which *IHTA 1984, s 71* applies, see 3.2 ACCUMULATION AND MAINTENANCE TRUSTS.

(*c*)   A gift to a disabled trust which gift, by virtue of the transfer, becomes *property* to which *IHTA 1984, s 89* applies, see 54.1 TRUSTS FOR THE DISABLED.

(*d*)   The disposal or termination by an individual of his beneficial interest in possession in settled property by gift before 22 March 2006 on which event

   (i)   another individual becomes beneficially entitled to the property in which the interest subsisted or an interest in possession in that property; or

   (ii)   that property is settled on accumulation and maintenance trusts or trusts for the disabled; or

   (iii)   the value of another individual's estate is increased.

(*e*)   A gift to a trust for a bereaved minor on or after 22 March 2006 which gift, on the ending of an immediate post-death interest (IPDI) which, by virtue of the transfer, becomes property to which *IHTA 1984, s 71A* applies but whereby the beneficial entitlement is passed on to the trust and was effected during the beneficiary's lifetime. [*IHTA 1984, s 3B inserted by FA 2006, Sch 20 para 9(5)*].

Note. For the purposes of (*b*) and (*c*) above some identifiable property must become subject to the trusts, otherwise the gift remains a chargeable transfer. For example, the payment by the settlor of an insurance premium on a policy written for the beneficiaries of an accumulation and maintenance trust would be a chargeable transfer. If, however, the settlor provides the trust with the funds from which to pay the premiums, the gift would be a potentially exempt transfer. For the purposes of (*d*), however, there are certain transitional rules that ensure that new interests in possession which are created out existing ones before 6 April 2008 ('transitional serial interests') still will qualify as PETs. See 43 SETTLEMENTS WITH INTERESTS IN POSSESSION.

In summary therefore a PET will, from 22 March 2006, comprise:

* transfers by individuals to other individuals;

* transfers by individuals to certain trusts for the disabled (see 54 TRUSTS FOR DISABLED PERSONS);

* transfers on or after 22 March 2006 by an individual to a bereaved minor's trust on the coming to an end of an immediate post-death interest (see 53 TRUSTS FOR BEREAVED MINORS);

* transfers before 22 March 2006 by an individual to an accumulation and maintenance trust (see 3 ACCUMULATION AND MAINTENANCE TRUSTS);

* transfers by an individual into an interest in possession trust in which, for transfers on or after 22 March 2006, the beneficiary has a disabled person's interest (see 54.1 TRUSTS FOR DISABLED PERSONS); and

* certain transfers on the termination or disposal of an individual's beneficial interest in possession in settled property (these are in restricted circumstances following *FA 2006* at 30.1 LIFE ASSURANCE POLICIES AND ANNUITIES; 43.1 SETTLEMENTS WITH INTERESTS IN POSSESSION).

Transfers before 17 March 1987

Transfers before 17 March 1987 were potentially exempt transfers only if they fell within (*b*) or (*c*) above, or within (*a*) above but excluding property becoming comprised in the individual's estate as settled property or increasing the value of settled property in his estate.

[*IHTA 1984, s 3A(1)–(3)(6)(7), 3B; FA 1986, Sch 19 para 1; F(No 2)A 1987, s 96(1)–(3); FA 2006, Sch 20 para 9, Sch 26 Part 6*].

38.2   **CONSEQUENCES OF TREATMENT AS POTENTIALLY EXEMPT TRANSFER**

A potentially exempt transfer made seven years or more before the death of the transferor is an exempt transfer and any other potentially exempt transfer is a chargeable transfer. [*IHTA 1984, s 3A(4); FA 1986, Sch 19 para 1*]. A potentially exempt transfer is assumed to be an exempt transfer during the seven years following the transfer or, if earlier, until immediately before the transferor's death. [*IHTA 1984, s 3(A)(5); FA 1986, Sch 19 para 1*].

As potentially exempt transfers are assumed to be exempt at the time of the transfer, no IHT is payable at that time. If the transferor makes a subsequent chargeable lifetime transfer (e.g. a gift to a discretionary trust) the earlier potentially exempt transfer does not enter into the transferor's cumulative total at that time. Where, however, the transferor dies within seven years of the potentially exempt transfer, it becomes a chargeable transfer at the actual date of the gift. Tax is calculated at the full death rates applying at the time of death, subject to taper relief, see 51.1 TRANSFERS WITHIN SEVEN YEARS BEFORE DEATH. Tax on subsequent chargeable lifetime transfers may, therefore, not only need to be revised under the rules for TRANSFERS WITHIN SEVEN YEARS BEFORE DEATH (51) but will also be affected by the revision of the transferor's cumulative total.

Example

X makes a potentially exempt transfer to Y of £313,000 on 1 January 2001 and then on 1 August 2006 makes a chargeable transfer of £150,000 to Z Discretionary Trust. X dies on 31 December 2007 with an estate valued at £500,000.

On the initial gift of the £313,000 to Y this will be a PET and no charge arises and no cumulation either. The subsequent gift to Z Trust is chargeable but at the time of the gift the nil rate band is greater than the gift into the Trust and therefore there is no charge to lifetime rates. However, with the death of X the PET now becomes chargeable because the gift was within seven years of X's death and this will be a charge to tax at death rates after the reallocation of the nil rate band to the gift. This has a knock-on effect in that the chargeable gift into the Trust which was made later and was not subject to tax because of the nil rate band now becomes chargeable to inheritance tax at death rates.

		£		
Y's liability becomes:		313,000		
Less 2000/01, 1999/2000		6,000		
		307,000		
Less nil rate band		300,000		
		£7,000	@ 40% =	£2,800
Less taper relief (80% for surviving six years)				2,240
Tax payable by Y				£560
Z Trust liability becomes:		150,000		
Less 2006/07, 2005/06		6,000		
		144,000	@ 40% =	£57,600
X's death estate liability becomes:		£500,000	@ 40% =	£200,000

As the gift into the Trust was within three years of the death there is no taper relief. The liability arising on Y and the Z Trustees and X's personal representatives will probably not be planned for and therefore either or both may be unable to pay the additional liability thereby shifting the burden of tax onto X's personal representatives. Situations such as this should ideally be planned for by both Y and Z Trustees and X's personal representatives taking out insurance cover for the period of seven years after the gifts. As personal representatives do not have an implied power to take out such insurance cover it makes sense for the original will to be drawn up with the empowering clause. Also, X should have planned his gifts in a better way by transferring the gift to the Trust firstly and the gift to Y second. This would have had the effect of providing the nil rate band for the Trust which would have had an impact in reducing future rates of charge on the discretionary trust.

Treatment of annual exemption in relation to a potentially exempt transfer. Where a transfer of value is a potentially exempt transfer, in the first instance it is left out of account for the purposes of allocating the £3,000 annual exemption. However, if the transfer subsequently proves to be a chargeable transfer, it is taken to have been made in the tax year in which it was actually made but later than any transfer of value in the same year which is not a potentially exempt transfer. [*IHTA 1984, s 19(3A); FA 1986, Sch 19 para 5*].

Prior to the publication of the January 1991 edition of their booklet IHT 1, HMRC had indicated that the effect of *IHTA 1984, s 19(3A)* was that where the annual exemption had been used in determining the amount of a chargeable lifetime transfer in the same tax year, it was not necessary to revise that amount by reallocating the annual exemption to an earlier potentially exempt transfer made in the same year which proved to be chargeable. However, on this analysis, where an unused annual exemption was carried forward to the following year and set against a chargeable transfer in that year, a potentially exempt transfer in the earlier year which became chargeable received the benefit of that exemption, rather than the chargeable transfer in the later year.

The HMRC view, whilst giving sense to *IHTA 1984, s 19(3A)*, appeared to conflict with the words of *IHTA 1984, s 3A(1)(b)*, namely 'Any reference in this Act to a potentially exempt transfer is a reference to a transfer of value ... which, apart from this section, would be a chargeable transfer (or to the extent to which, apart from this section, it would be such a transfer)' (see 38.1 above and 38.3(*a*) below). In this context it should be noted that *IHTA 1984, s 2(1)* defines chargeable transfer as a transfer of value which is made by an individual but which is not an exempt transfer. In the January 1991 edition of IHT 1, HMRC stated (at paragraph 5.16) that 'If a gift to an individual [or, presumably, one of the other qualifying categories in 38.1 above] is entitled to the annual exemption it is an exempt transfer and not a potentially exempt transfer'. At paragraph 5.17 it provided the following example:

'A makes a gift of £10,000 in May 1987. In October 1987 she makes a gift into a discretionary trust (so it is a gift chargeable when made). The annual exemption for 1987/88 is set against the first £3,000 of the May gift, leaving a potentially exempt transfer of £7,000. The whole of the October gift into discretionary trust is immediately chargeable. Any relief carried forward from 1986/87 is also set against the May gift. So if A has made no transfers in 1986/87 there will be a total of £6,000 to be set against the May gift, leaving a potentially exempt transfer of £4,000.'

Unfortunately the IHT 15 replacing the IHT 1 does not duplicate the example but under this previous treatment it would appear HMRC currently ignore *IHTA 1984, s 19(3A)*. Its treatment would also mean that it is to the taxpayer's benefit to arrange transfers that have to be made in the same year so that a chargeable transfer (against which the annual exemption is set) precedes a potentially exempt transfer which may never become chargeable (in which case, any set-off of annual exemption would have been wasted).

On similar arguments to the above, HMRC have stated that where a potentially exempt transfer is treated as made under *FA 1986, s 102(4)* as a result of a reservation of benefit ceasing to exist in the donor's lifetime (see example at 22.1 GIFTS WITH RESERVATION), no deduction of annual exemption can be made if the potentially exempt transfer proves to be a chargeable transfer (HMRC Tax Bulletin November 1993 p 98).

38.3   **EXCEPTIONS**

The following transfers are not to be regarded as potentially exempt transfers.

(*a*)   A transfer to the extent to which it would in any case be an EXEMPT TRANSFER (21). [*IHTA 1984, ss 2, 3A(1)(b); FA 1986, Sch 19 para 1; FA 2006, Sch 20 para 9*].

(*b*)   A transfer on which tax is in any circumstances to be charged *as if* a transfer of value has been made other than, after 16 March 1987, a transfer made under *IHTA 1984, s 52* (charge on the termination of an interest in possession). [*IHTA 1984, s 3A(6); FA 1986, Sch 19 para 1; F(No 2)A 1987, s 96(1)(2)*]. This excludes from treatment as a potentially exempt transfer the charge on

(i)   participators where a close company makes a transfer of value, see 12.1 CLOSE COMPANIES; and

(ii)   the termination of an interest in possession in settled property before 17 March 1987, see 43.3 SETTLEMENTS WITH INTERESTS IN POSSESSION.

(*c*)   Before 17 March 1987 a transfer of value resulting from the giving of consideration in money or money's worth where a person became entitled to an interest in possession in settled property as a result of the disposition. [*IHTA 1984, s 49(3); FA 1986, Sch 19 para 14; F(No 2)A 1987, s 96(4)*].

(*d*)   Before 17 March 1987 a disposition by which a reversionary interest (whether immediate or not) is acquired by a person entitled to an interest (whether in possession or not) in the settled property. [*IHTA 1984, s 55(2); FA 1986, Sch 19 para 15; F(No 2)A 1987, s 96(5)*].

(*e*)   A disposition treated as having been made by the participators of a close company where there is an alteration in the share or loan capital of a close company not consisting of quoted shares or securities (in relation to transfers of value made, and other events occurring, before 17 March 1987, shares or securities quoted on a recognised stock exchange) or in any rights attaching to its unquoted shares or debentures (in relation to transfers of value made, and other events occurring, before 17 March 1987, shares or debentures not quoted on a recognised stock exchange). [*IHTA 1984, s 98(3); FA 1986, Sch 19 para 20; FA 1987, s 58, Sch 8 para 2*]. See 12.5 CLOSE COMPANIES.

(*f*)   If made after 1 July 1986, the first transfer of value including woodlands on which estate duty was deferred on a death before 13 March 1975. [*FA 1986, Sch 19 para 46*]. Although this provision denies treatment as a potentially exempt transfer to all property comprised in a single transfer of value any part of which, however small, is woodlands subject to a deferred estate duty charge, by concession after 4 December 1990 it will be restricted in its scope to that part of a transfer of value which is attributable to such woodlands (see F15 at 23 HMRC EXTRA-STATUTORY CONCESSIONS).

39 Protective Trusts

Cross-reference. See also 44 SETTLEMENTS WITHOUT INTERESTS IN POSSESSION.

Simon's Direct Tax Service, part I5.6.

Other Sources. CTO Leaflet IHT 16, p 25; Foster, part E6.

39.1 **GENERAL**

'Protective trust' is defined by the *Trustee Act 1925, s 33* and, broadly, is a trust under which a person ('the principal beneficiary') is entitled to an interest in possession in the settled property for the trust period unless he forfeits his interest e.g. by attempting to assign his interest or by becoming bankrupt. Usually, if the interest of the principal beneficiary is forfeited, the trust property is held on discretionary trusts for a class of beneficiaries. The class includes the principal beneficiary and his spouse and his children or more remoter issue or, in the absence of spouse and issue, the principal beneficiary and the persons who would be entitled to the trust fund or the income thereof on his death. Where property is held on trusts to the like effect as those specified in *Trustee Act 1925, s 33(1)*, special provisions apply. Trusts of 'like effect' to those defined in the *Trustee Act* are those that are not materially different in their tax consequences i.e. where there are only minor variations or additional administrative powers or duties. A 'minor variation' does not include the extension *ab initio* of the class of beneficiaries to brothers and sisters (although it is appreciated that so long as the principal beneficiary has no spouse or issue the statutory trusts extend to the next of kin for the time being who might well be brothers and sisters) (see E7 at 25 HMRC STATEMENTS OF PRACTICE with additions derived from the original source which was a former Inland Revenue letter published in the Law Society's Gazette of 3 March 1976 and reprinted in British Tax Review 1976, p 421). A protective trust of income for the benefit of the settlor is a trust of 'like effect' (*Thomas & Thomas v CIR Ch D 1981, [1981] STC 382*).

39.2 **FORFEITURE BEFORE 12 APRIL 1978**

The following provisions apply where the principal beneficiary's interest in possession came to an end before 12 April 1978.

There is a charge to tax.

(*a*) where the settled property ceases to be held on discretionary trusts similar to those specified in *Trustee Act 1925, s 33(1)(ii)* (see 39.1 above) otherwise than by being applied for the principal beneficiary (but see also 21.3 EXEMPT TRANSFERS for certain situations where there is no charge when property becomes held for charitable purposes only without limit of time or that of a qualifying political party *or* a national body mentioned in *IHTA 1984, Sch 3* or, under certain conditions, a body not established or conducted for profit), or

(*b*) if the trustees make a 'disposition' otherwise than by way of payment for the benefit of the principal beneficiary which reduces the value of the settled property. '*Disposition*' includes an omission to exercise a right, unless not deliberate, which is treated as made at the latest time that the right could have been exercised.

[*IHTA 1984, ss 70(10), 73(1)(2), 76*].

No charge arises.

(i) if, under (*b*) above, the trustees do not intend to confer a gratuitous benefit and either the transaction is at arm's length between persons not connected with each other (see 13 CONNECTED PERSONS) or is such as might be expected in such a transaction, or

(ii)   if, under (*b*) above, the disposition is a grant of a tenancy of agricultural property in the UK, Channel Islands or Isle of Man, for use for agricultural purposes and is made for full consideration in money or money's worth, or

(iii)   on the 'payment' of costs or expenses attributable to the property, or

(iv)   where any payment is, or will be, income for income tax purposes of any person (or, in the case of a non-resident, would be if he were so resident), or

(v)   in respect of a liability to make a payment under (iii) or (iv) above.

'*Payment*' includes the transfer of assets other than money. [*IHTA 1984, ss 63, 70(3)(4), 73(3)*].

Tax is charged on the amount by which the trust property is less immediately after the event giving rise to the charge that it would have been but for the event (i.e. the loss to the donor principle), grossed-up where the settlement pays the tax.

The rate at which tax is charged is the aggregate of the following percentages for each complete successive 'quarter' in 'the relevant period':

	Cumulative Total
0.25% for each of the first 40 quarters	10%
0.20% for each of the next 40 quarters	8%
0.15% for each of the next 40 quarters	6%
0.10% for each of the next 40 quarters	4%
0.05% for each of the next 40 quarters	2%
Maximum rate chargeable after 50 years	30%

'*Relevant period*' is the period beginning with the day on which the property became (or last became) held on the discretionary trusts, or 13 March 1975 if later, and ending on the day before the chargeable event.

'*Quarter*' means any period of three months. [*IHTA 1984, ss 63, 70(5)(6)(8), 73(3)*].

39.3   **Excluded property.** Where the whole or part of the amount on which tax is charged as in 39.2 above is attributable to property which was EXCLUDED PROPERTY (20) at any time during the relevant period, then, in determining the rate at which tax is charged in respect of that amount or part, no quarter throughout which the property was excluded property is to be counted. [*IHTA 1984, ss 70(7), 73(3)*].

See also the provisions under 44.15 and 44.16 SETTLEMENTS WITHOUT INTERESTS IN POSSESSION which also apply to property settled or appointed on protective trusts.

Example

In 1951 X left his estate on protective trusts for his son Z. On 1 January 1978 Z attempted to assign his interest and the protective trusts were accordingly determined. On 1 May 1983 the trustees advanced £25,000 to Z to enable him to purchase a flat. At the same time, they also advanced £10,000 (net) to his granddaughter D. On 1 May 2007 Z died and the trust fund, valued at £200,000, passed equally to his grandchildren absolutely.

1 May 1983

There is no charge to IHT on the payment to Z, but a charge arises on the payment to D.

The relevant period is the period from the determination of the protective trusts (1 January 1978) to 1 May 1983, i.e. 21 complete quarters.

The rate of tax is 0.25% for each of 21 quarters 5.25%

39.4   Protective Trusts

IHT payable is

$$\frac{5.25}{100-5.25} \times £\,10,000 = £554$$

The gross payment is £10,554

1 May 2007

There is a charge to IHT when the trust vests on the death of Z. 117 complete quarters have elapsed since the protective trusts determined.

The rate of tax is:

	%
0.25% for each of the first 40 quarters	10.00
0.20% for each of the next 40 quarters	8.00
0.15% for the next 37 quarters	5.55
	23.55%

IHT payable is 23.55% × £200,000 = £47,100

39.4   FORFEITURE AFTER 11 APRIL 1978

Where the principal beneficiary's interest in possession comes to an end after 11 April 1978, the 'failure or determination' of such trusts before the end of the trust period will be disregarded for the purposes of inheritance tax and the principal beneficiary will continue to be treated as beneficially entitled to an interest in possession while discretionary trusts similar to those in *Trustee Act 1925, s 33(1)(ii)* (see 39.1 above) continue to apply under the *Trustee Act*. The effect is that any distribution to the principal beneficiary is not chargeable (because he is treated as having an interest in possession) but distributions to any other beneficiary will be chargeable. Also, the value of the principal beneficiary's deemed interest will form part of his estate on his death. [*IHTA 1984, s 88*]. For a consideration of the meaning of '*failure or determination*' see *Cholmondeley and Another v CIR Ch D, [1986] STC 384*.

39.5   FORFEITURE ON OR AFTER 22 MARCH 2006

Where protective trusts are created by the forfeiting of a beneficiary's interest, e.g. when he tries to sell the interest on or after 22 March 2006, then *IHTA 1984, s 88(3)* treats forfeiture out of a protective trust interest in possession created on or before that date as if it had happened on or before that date. The effect is that the deemed interest in possession arising on forfeiture is treated as created before 22 March 2006 and therefore the *FA 2006* rules do not apply and 39.4 above applies. In circumstances where a protective trust is created under *Trustee Act 1925 s 33(1)(i)* after 21 March 2006 the beneficiary has an interest in possession to which the new rules apply then the interest of the principal beneficiary is forfeited and the trust property is held on discretionary trusts for a class of beneficiaries. The class includes the principal beneficiary and his spouse and his children or more remoter issue or, in the absence of spouse and issue, the principal beneficiary and the persons who would be entitled to the trust fund or the income thereof on his death. However, the transitional rules apply to attract continuing favourable treatment in circumstances where the underlying interest of the principal beneficiary is either an 'immediate post-death interest' (IPDI), a disabled person's interest within *IHTA 1984, s 89B(1)(c)(d)* or a 'transitional serial interest' (TSI). See SETTLEMENTS WITH INTERESTS IN POSSESSION (43) and TRUSTS FOR THE DISABLED (54). [*IHTA 1984, s 88(3)–(6) as inserted by FA 2006, Sch 20 para 24*].

40 Quick Succession Relief

Cross-reference. See also 50 TRANSFERS ON DEATH.

Simon's Direct Tax Service, part I5.283.

Other Sources. CTO Leaflet IHT 15; Foster, part D1.65, D1.65, E2.83; IHTM22000.

40.1 **APPLICATION**

Where there is a later transfer of any property within five years of an earlier transfer ('the first transfer') which increased the transferor's estate and the later transfer

(a) arises on death; or

(b) is of settled property and (i) the transferor was entitled to an interest in possession in the property, (ii) the first transfer was of the same property, and (iii) the first transfer either was or included the making of the settlement or was made after the making of the settlement,

the tax payable on the later transfer is reduced by

$$\text{Percentage} \times \frac{(G-T)}{G} \times T$$

where

G = gross (chargeable first transfer);

T = tax on first transfer.

The percentages are as follows:

Period between transfers	Percentage
One year or less	100%
More than 1 year but not more than 2 years	80%
More than 2 years but not more than 3 years	60%
More than 3 years but not more than 4 years	40%
More than 4 years but not more than 5 years	20%

Where in relation to the first transfer there is more than one later transfer, if full relief cannot be given because the tax charge on the earliest of them is insufficient, credit may be given on later transfers in chronological order until credits representing the whole of (G – T) × T/G have been given. Credit of (for example) £1,200 on a later transfer after 2½ years represents £1,200/60% = £2,000, and the maximum relief on any later transfer would be limited to the appropriate percentage (60%, 40% or 20%) of ((G – T) × T/G – £2,000).

In calculating whether or to what extent the first transfer increased the value of the transferor's estate (i.e. (G – T)/G), any excluded property consisting of a reversionary interest to which he became entitled either on the occasion of, or before, that transfer is left out of account. [*IHTA 1984, s 141*].

Where the earlier occasion was a lifetime transfer and the transferee dies before the transferor, relief may still be available even though it cannot be determined whether any tax is in fact payable on the potentially exempt transfer (or further tax in respect of a lifetime transfer chargeable when made) until seven years have elapsed from the date of the gift or the transferor dies before the expiry of that period. Provided the transferee dies within five years of the gift, quick succession relief will be given in the transferee's estate in the normal way once the amount of the tax on the gift is quantified.

413

40.1   Quick Succession Relief

Example

On 1 January 2008 A died with a net estate valued at £375,000. In December 2003 he had received a gift from B of £20,000. B died in November 2005 and A paid the IHT (amounting to £8,000) due as a result of B's potentially exempt transfer becoming chargeable.

A was also entitled to an interest in possession in the whole of his father's estate. His father had died in February 2005 with a net estate of £269,000 on which the IHT paid was £2,400. On A's death, the property passed to A's sister and was valued at £145,000. A had made no previous transfers and left his estate to his brother.

	£
Free estate	375,000
Settled property	145,000
Taxable estate	£520,000

IHT on an estate of £520,000 = £88,000

Quick succession relief

The gift from B was made more than four but not more than five years before A's death so quick succession relief at 20% is available.

$$\text{QSR} = 20\% \times £\,8,000 \times \frac{12,000}{20,000} \qquad\qquad £960$$

	£
Interest in possession in father's will trust	
Net estate before tax	269,000
Tax	2,400
Net estate after tax	£266,600

A's death was more than two but not more than three years after his father's so relief is given at 60%.

$$\text{QSR} = 60\% \times £\,2,400 \times \frac{266,600}{269,000} \qquad\qquad £1,427$$

Tax payable on death of A	£	£
IHT on an estate of £520,000		88,000
Deduct QSR		
On gift from B	960	
On father's estate	1,427	
		2,387
IHT payable		£85,614

On free estate $\dfrac{375,000}{520,000} \times £\,85,614$ $£61,741$

On settled property $\dfrac{145,000}{520,000} \times £\,85,614$ $£23,873$

Note to the example

(A)   The relief is given only by reference to the tax charged on the part of the value received by the donee. Therefore, the tax paid must be apportioned by applying the fraction 'net transfer received divided by gross transfer made'.

41 Rates of Tax

Cross-references. See 8 CALCULATION OF TAX and 51 TRANSFERS WITHIN SEVEN YEARS BEFORE DEATH; 59 WORKING CASE STUDY.

Simon's Direct Tax Service, parts I3.5, I4.1.

41.1 RATES

Inheritance tax is levied on the value transferred by a CHARGEABLE TRANSFER (10) at the rate or rates applicable to the highest part of the aggregate of that value and the values transferred by any chargeable transfers made by the transferor in the period of seven years ending with the date of the transfer. [*IHTA 1984, ss 1, 7(1)*].

Only one table of rates is enacted which is applicable to transfers on death. Chargeable lifetime transfers are charged at one half of those death rates throughout the range of rate bands. Transfers made within seven years of death are charged at the death rates but in the case of chargeable transfers made in that period but more than three years before death (including potentially exempt transfers which become chargeable transfers), the tax charged is tapered, see 51.1 TRANSFERS WITHIN SEVEN YEARS BEFORE DEATH. [*IHTA 1984, s 7(2)–(4), Sch 1; FA 1986, Sch 19 paras 2, 36*].

The rate bands are indexed annually unless Parliament determines otherwise. If the Retail Prices Index as published by the Office of National Statistics for September in any year is higher than that for the previous September, then from the following 6 April the lower and upper limits of the rate bands in the tables applying in the previous year are increased by the same percentage as the percentage increase in the index. [*Transfer of Functions (Registration and Statistics) Order 1996, SI 1996/273*]. The figures are rounded up, if necessary, to the nearest £1,000. The Treasury specifies the new rate bands by statutory instrument before the start of the tax year in question. There is no provision for a reduction in the bands on a fall in the Index. For years before 1994/95 the calculation was made by reference to the change in the Index during the year to the previous December. The indexing provisions are not applied for 1987/88, 1988/89, 1992/93, 1993/94, 1994/95, 1996/97 and 2002/03 but were relevant for 1995/96, 1997/98, 1998/99, 1999/2000, 2000/01, 2001/02, 2003/04, 2004/05, 2005/06 and the rates of the nil rate band for 2006/07 and 2007/08 have been fixed (see Tables below). [*IHTA 1984, s 8; FA 1986, Sch 19 para 3; FA 1987, s 57; FA 1988, s 136; SI 1989/468; SI 1990/680; SI 1991/735; F(No 2)A 1992, s 72; FA 1993, ss 196, 197; FA 1994, s 246; SI 1994/3011; FA 1996, s 183; SI 1998/756; SI 1999/596; SI 2000/803; SI 2001/639; FA 2002, s 118; SI 2003/841; SI 2004/771; FA 2005, s 98; FA 2006, s 155; FA 2007, s 4*].

Although only one table of rates is enacted, a table for chargeable lifetime transfers is also given below. Grossing-up tables are included to simplify calculations which involve net transfers.

TRANSFERS ON DEATH AFTER 5 APRIL 2010 AND BEFORE 6 APRIL 2011
2010.A1 Tax on transfers

	Gross taxable transfers £	Gross cumulative totals £	Rate
First	350,000	0–350,000	Nil
Above	350,000		40% for each £ over 350,000

2010.A2 Grossing-up of specific transfers on death which do not bear their own tax

	Net transfers	Tax payable thereon
	£	£
0–	350,000	Nil
Above	350,000	Nil + ⅔ (66.666%) for each £ over 350,000

CHARGEABLE LIFETIME TRANSFERS AFTER 5 APRIL 2010 AND BEFORE 6 APRIL 2011

2010.B1 Tax on gross transfers

	Gross taxable transfers	Gross cumulative totals	Rate
	£	£	
First	350,000	0–350,000	Nil
Above	350,000		20% for each £ over 350,000

2010.B2 Grossing-up of net lifetime transfers

	Net transfers	Tax payable thereon
	£	£
0–	350,000	Nil
Above	350,000	Nil + ¼ (25%) for each £ over 350,000

TRANSFERS ON DEATH AFTER 5 APRIL 2009 AND BEFORE 6 APRIL 2010

2009.A1 Tax on transfers

	Gross taxable transfers	Gross cumulative totals	Rate
	£	£	
First	325,000	0–325,000	Nil
Above	325,000		40% for each £ over 325,000

2009.A2 Grossing-up of specific transfers on death which do not bear their own tax

	Net transfers	Tax payable thereon
	£	£
0–	325,000	Nil
Above	325,000	Nil + ⅔ (66.666%) for each £ over 325,000

CHARGEABLE LIFETIME TRANSFERS AFTER 5 APRIL 2009 AND BEFORE 6 APRIL 2010

2009.B1 Tax on gross transfers

	Gross taxable transfers	Gross cumulative totals	Rate
	£	£	
First	325,000	0–325,000	Nil
Above	325,000		20% for each £ over 325,000

41.1 Rates of Tax

2009.B2 Grossing-up of net lifetime transfers

Net transfers £	Tax payable thereon £
0– 325,000	Nil
Above 325,000	Nil + ¼ (25%) for each £ over 325,000

TRANSFERS ON DEATH AFTER 5 APRIL 2008 AND BEFORE 6 APRIL 2009
2008.A1 Tax on transfers

	Gross taxable transfers £	Gross cumulative totals £	Rate
First	312,000	0–312,000	Nil
Above	312,000		40% for each £ over 312,000

2008.A2 Grossing-up of specific transfers on death which do not bear their own tax

Net transfers £	Tax payable thereon £
0– 312,000	Nil
Above 312,000	Nil + ⅔ (66.666%) for each £ over 312,000

CHARGEABLE LIFETIME TRANSFERS AFTER 5 APRIL 2008 AND BEFORE 6 APRIL 2009
2008.B1 Tax on gross transfers

	Gross taxable transfers £	Gross cumulative totals £	Rate
First	312,000	0–312,000	Nil
Above	312,000		20% for each £ over 312,000

2008.B2 Grossing-up of net lifetime transfers

Net transfers £	Tax payable thereon £
0– 312,000	Nil
Above 312,000	Nil + ¼ (25%) for each £ over 312,000

TRANSFERS ON DEATH AFTER 5 APRIL 2007 AND BEFORE 6 APRIL 2008
2007.A1 Tax on transfers

	Gross taxable transfers £	Gross cumulative totals £	Rate
First	300,000	0–300,000	Nil
Above	300,000		40% for each £ over 300,000

2007.A2 Grossing-up of specific transfers on death which do not bear their own tax

	Net transfers	Tax payable thereon
	£	£
0–	300,000	Nil
Above	300,000	Nil + ⅔ (66.666%) for each £ over 300,000

CHARGEABLE LIFETIME TRANSFERS AFTER 5 APRIL 2007 AND BEFORE 6 APRIL 2008

2007.B1 Tax on gross transfers

	Gross taxable transfers	Gross cumulative totals	Rate
	£	£	
First	300,000	0–300,000	Nil
Above	300,000		20% for each £ over 300,000

2007.B2 Grossing-up of net lifetime transfers

	Net transfers	Tax payable thereon
	£	£
0–	300,000	Nil
Above	300,000	Nil + ¼ (25%) for each £ over 300,000

TRANSFERS ON DEATH AFTER 5 APRIL 2006 AND BEFORE 6 APRIL 2007

2006.A1 Tax on transfers

	Gross taxable transfers	Gross cumulative totals	Rate
	£	£	
First	285,000	0–285,000	Nil
Above	285,000		40% for each £ over 285,000

2006.A2 Grossing-up of specific transfers on death which do not bear their own tax

	Net transfers	Tax payable thereon
	£	£
0–	285,000	Nil
Above	285,000	Nil + ⅔ (66.666%) for each £ over 285,000

CHARGEABLE LIFETIME TRANSFERS AFTER 5 APRIL 2006 AND BEFORE 6 APRIL 2007

2006.B1 Tax on gross transfers

	Gross taxable transfers	Gross cumulative totals	Rate
	£	£	
First	285,000	0–285,000	Nil
Above	285,000		20% for each £ over 285,000

2006.B2 Grossing-up of net lifetime transfers

Net transfers	Tax payable thereon
£	£
0– 285,000	Nil
Above 285,000	Nil + ¼ (25%) for each £ over 285,000

TRANSFERS ON DEATH AFTER 5 APRIL 2005 AND BEFORE 6 APRIL 2006
2005.A1 Tax on transfers

	Gross taxable transfers	Gross cumulative totals	Rate
	£	£	
First	275,000	0–275,000	Nil
Above	275,000		40% for each £ over 275,000

2005.A2 Grossing-up of specific transfers on death which do not bear their own tax

Net transfers	Tax payable thereon
£	£
0– 275,000	Nil
Above 275,000	Nil + ⅔ (66.666%) for each £ over 275,000

CHARGEABLE LIFETIME TRANSFERS AFTER 5 APRIL 2005 AND BEFORE 6 APRIL 2006
2005.B1 Tax on gross transfers

	Gross taxable transfers	Gross cumulative totals	Rate
	£	£	
First	275,000	0–275,000	Nil
Above	275,000		20% for each £ over 275,000

2005.B2 Grossing-up of net lifetime transfers

Net transfers	Tax payable thereon
£	£
0– 275,000	Nil
Above 275,000	Nil + ¼ (25%) for each £ over 275,000

TRANSFERS ON DEATH AFTER 5 APRIL 2004 AND BEFORE 6 APRIL 2005
2004.A1 Tax on transfers

	Gross taxable transfers	Gross cumulative totals	Rate
	£	£	
First	263,000	0–263,000	Nil
Above	263,000		40% for each £ over 263,000

2004.A2 Grossing-up of specific transfers on death which do not bear their own tax

Net transfers £	Tax payable thereon £
0– 263,000	Nil
Above 263,000	Nil + ⅔ (66.666%) for each £ over 263,000

CHARGEABLE LIFETIME TRANSFERS AFTER 5 APRIL 2004 AND BEFORE 6 APRIL 2005

2004.B1 Tax on gross transfers

	Gross taxable transfers £	Gross cumulative totals £	Rate
First	263,000	0–263,000	Nil
Above	263,000		20% for each £ over 263,000

2004.B2 Grossing-up of net lifetime transfers

Net transfers £	Tax payable thereon £
0– 263,000	Nil
Above 263,000	Nil + ¼ (25%) for each £ over 263,000

TRANSFERS ON DEATH AFTER 5 APRIL 2003 AND BEFORE 6 APRIL 2004

2003.A1 Tax on transfers

	Gross taxable transfers £	Gross cumulative totals £	Rate
First	255,000	0–255,000	Nil
Above	255,000		40% for each £ over 255,000

2003.A2 Grossing-up of specific transfers on death which do not bear their own tax

Net transfers £	Tax payable thereon £
0– 255,000	Nil
Above 255,000	Nil + ⅔ (66.666%) for each £ over 255,000

CHARGEABLE LIFETIME TRANSFERS AFTER 5 APRIL 2003 AND BEFORE 6 APRIL 2004

2003.B1 Tax on gross transfers

	Gross taxable transfers £	Gross cumulative totals £	Rate
First	255,000	0–255,000	Nil
Above	255,000		20% for each £ over 255,000

41.1 Rates of Tax

2003.B2 Grossing-up of net lifetime transfers

	Net transfers £	Tax payable thereon £
0–	255,000	Nil
Above	255,000	Nil + ¼ (25%) for each £ over 255,000

TRANSFERS ON DEATH AFTER 5 APRIL 2002 AND BEFORE 6 APRIL 2003
2002.A1 Tax on transfers

	Gross taxable transfers £	Gross cumulative totals £	Rate
First	250,000	0–250,000	Nil
Above	250,000		40% for each £ over 250,000

2002.A2 Grossing-up of specific transfers on death which do not bear their own tax

	Net transfers £	Tax payable thereon £
0–	250,000	Nil
Above	250,000	Nil + ⅔ (66.666%) for each £ over 250,000

CHARGEABLE LIFETIME TRANSFERS AFTER 5 APRIL 2002 AND BEFORE 6 APRIL 2003
2002.B1 Tax on gross transfers

	Gross taxable transfers £	Gross cumulative totals £	Rate
First	250,000	0–250,000	Nil
Above	250,000		20% for each £ over 250,000

2002.B2 Grossing-up of net lifetime transfers

	Net transfers £	Tax payable thereon £
0–	250,000	Nil
Above	250,000	Nil + ¼ (25%) for each £ over 250,000

TRANSFERS ON DEATH AFTER 5 APRIL 2001 AND BEFORE 6 APRIL 2002
2001.A1 Tax on transfers

	Gross taxable transfers £	Gross cumulative totals £	Rate
First	242,000	0–242,000	Nil
Above	242,000		40% for each £ over 242,000

2001.A2 Grossing-up of specific transfers on death which do not bear their own tax

	Net transfers £	Tax payable thereon £
0–	242,000	Nil
Above	242,000	Nil + ⅔ (66.666%) for each £ over 242,000

CHARGEABLE LIFETIME TRANSFERS AFTER 5 APRIL 2001 AND BEFORE 6 APRIL 2002

2001.B1 Tax on gross transfers

	Gross taxable transfers	Gross cumulative totals	Rate
	£	£	
First	242,000	0–242,000	Nil
Above	242,000		20% for each £ over 242,000

2001.B2 Grossing-up of net lifetime transfers

	Net transfers	Tax payable thereon
	£	£
0–	242,000	Nil
Above	242,000	Nil + ¼ (25%) for each £ over 242,000

TRANSFERS ON DEATH AFTER 5 APRIL 2000 AND BEFORE 6 APRIL 2001

2000.A1 Tax on transfers

	Gross taxable transfers	Gross cumulative totals	Rate
	£	£	
First	234,000	0–234,000	Nil
Above	234,000		40% for each £ over 234,000

2000.A2 Grossing-up of specific transfers on death which do not bear their own tax

	Net transfers	Tax payable thereon
	£	£
0–	234,000	Nil
Above	234,000	Nil + ⅔ (66.666%) for each £ over 234,000

CHARGEABLE LIFETIME TRANSFERS AFTER 5 APRIL 2000 AND BEFORE 6 APRIL 2001

2000.B1 Tax on gross transfers

	Gross taxable transfers	Gross cumulative totals	Rate
	£	£	
First	234,000	0–234,000	Nil
Above	234,000		20% for each £ over 234,000

2000.B2 Grossing-up of net lifetime transfers

	Net transfers	Tax payable thereon
	£	£
0–	234,000	Nil
Above	234,000	Nil + ¼ (25%) for each £ over 234,000

41.1 Rates of Tax

TRANSFERS ON DEATH AFTER 5 APRIL 1999 AND BEFORE 6 APRIL 2000
1999.A1 Tax on transfers

	Gross taxable transfers £	Gross cumulative totals £	Rate
First	231,000	0–231,000	Nil
Above	231,000		40% for each £ over 231,000

1999.A2 Grossing-up of specific transfers on death which do not bear their own tax

	Net transfers £	Tax payable thereon £
0–	231,000	Nil
Above	231,000	Nil + ⅔ (66.666%) for each £ over 231,000

CHARGEABLE LIFETIME TRANSFERS AFTER 5 APRIL 1999 AND BEFORE 6 APRIL 2000
1999.B1 Tax on gross transfers

	Gross taxable transfers £	Gross cumulative totals £	Rate
First	231,000	0–231,000	Nil
Above	231,000		20% for each £ over 231,000

1999.B2 Grossing-up of net lifetime transfers

	Net transfers £	Tax payable thereon £
0–	231,000	Nil
Above	231,000	Nil + ¼ (25%) for each £ over 231,000

TRANSFERS ON DEATH AFTER 5 APRIL 1998 AND BEFORE 6 APRIL 1999
1998.A1 Tax on transfers

	Gross taxable transfers £	Gross cumulative totals £	Rate
First	223,000	0–223,000	Nil
Above	223,000		40% for each £ over 223,000

1998.A2 Grossing-up of specific transfers on death which do not bear their own tax

	Net transfers £	Tax payable thereon £
0–	223,000	Nil
Above	223,000	Nil + ⅔ (66.666%) for each £ over 223,000

CHARGEABLE LIFETIME TRANSFERS AFTER 5 APRIL 1998 AND BEFORE 6 APRIL 1999
1998.B1 Tax on gross transfers

	Gross taxable transfers £	Gross cumulative totals £	Rate
First	223,000	0–223,000	Nil
Above	223,000		20% for each £ over 223,000

1998.B2 Grossing-up of net lifetime transfers

	Net transfers	Tax payable thereon
	£	£
0–	223,000	Nil
Above	223,000	Nil + ¼ (25%) for each £ over 223,000

TRANSFERS ON DEATH AFTER 5 APRIL 1997 AND BEFORE 6 APRIL 1998

1997.A1 Tax on transfer.

	Gross taxable transfers	Gross cumulative totals	Rate
	£	£	
First	215,000	0–215,000	Nil
Above	215,000		40% for each £ over 215,000

1997.A2 Grossing-up of specific transfers on death which do not bear their own tax

	Net transfers	Tax payable thereon
	£	£
0–	215,000	Nil
Above	215,000	Nil + ⅔ (66.666%) for each £ over 215,000

CHARGEABLE LIFETIME TRANSFERS AFTER 5 APRIL 1997 AND BEFORE 6 APRIL 1998

1997.B1 Tax on gross transfers

	Gross taxable transfers	Gross cumulative totals	Rate
	£	£	
First	215,000	0–215,000	Nil
Above	215,000		20% for each £ over 215,000

1997.B2 Grossing-up of net lifetime transfers

	Net transfers	Tax payable thereon
	£	£
0–	215,000	Nil
Above	215,000	Nil + ¼ (25%) for each £ over 215,000

TRANSFERS ON DEATH AFTER 5 APRIL 1996 AND BEFORE 6 APRIL 1997

1996.A1 Tax on transfers

	Gross taxable transfers	Gross cumulative totals	Rate
	£	£	
First	200,000	0–200,000	Nil
Above	200,000		40% for each £ over 200,000

1996.A2 Grossing-up of specific transfers on death which do not bear their own tax

	Net transfers	Tax payable thereon
	£	£
0–	200,000	Nil
Above	200,000	Nil + ⅔ (66.666%) for each £ over 200,000

41.1   Rates of Tax

CHARGEABLE LIFETIME TRANSFERS AFTER 5 APRIL 1996 AND BEFORE 6 APRIL 1997

1996.B1 Tax on transfers

	Gross taxable transfers £	Gross cumulative totals £	Rate
First	200,000	0–200,000	Nil
Above	200,000		20% for each £ over 200,000

1996.B2 Grossing-up of net lifetime transfers

	Net transfers £	Tax payable thereon £
0–	200,000		Nil
Above	200,000	Nil + ¼ (25%) for each £ over 200,000

TRANSFERS ON DEATH AFTER 5 APRIL 1995 AND BEFORE 6 APRIL 1996

1995.A1 Tax on transfers

	Gross taxable transfers £	Gross cumulative totals £	Rate
First	154,000	0–154,000	Nil
Above	154,000		40% for each £ over 154,000

1995.A2 Grossing-up of specific transfers on death which do not bear their own tax

	Net transfers £	Tax payable thereon £
0–	154,000		Nil
Above	154,000	Nil + ⅔ (66.666%) for each £ over 154,000

CHARGEABLE LIFETIME TRANSFERS AFTER 5 APRIL 1995 AND BEFORE 6 APRIL 1996

1995.B1 Tax on gross transfers

	Gross taxable transfers £	Gross cumulative totals £	Rate
First	154,000	0–154,000	Nil
Above	154,000		20% for each £ over 154,000

1995.B2 Grossing-up of net lifetime transfers

	Net transfers £	Tax payable thereon £
0–	154,000		Nil
Above	154,000	Nil + ¼ (25%) for each £ over 154,000

TRANSFERS ON DEATH AFTER 9 MARCH 1992 AND BEFORE 6 APRIL 1995

1992.A1 Tax on transfers

	Gross taxable transfers £	Gross cumulative totals £	Rate
First	150,000	0–150,000	Nil
Above	150,000		40% for each £ over 150,000

1992.A2 Grossing-up of specific transfers on death which do not bear their own tax

	Net transfers £	Tax payable thereon £
0–	150,000	Nil
Above	150,000	Nil + ⅔ (66.666%) for each £ over 150,000

CHARGEABLE LIFETIME TRANSFERS AFTER 9 MARCH 1992 AND BEFORE 6 APRIL 1995

1992.B1 Tax on gross transfers

	Gross taxable transfers £	Gross cumulative totals £	Rate
First	150,000	0–150,000	Nil
Above	150,000		20% for each £ over 150,000

1992.B2 Grossing-up of net lifetime transfers

	Net transfers £	Tax payable thereon £
0–	150,000	Nil
Above	150,000	Nil + ¼ (25%) for each £ over 150,000

TRANSFERS ON DEATH AFTER 5 APRIL 1991 AND BEFORE 10 MARCH 1992

1991.A1 Tax on transfers

	Gross taxable transfers £	Gross cumulative totals £	Rate
First	140,000	0–140,000	Nil
Above	140,000		40% for each £ over 140,000

1991.A2 Grossing-up of specific transfers on death which do not bear their own tax

	Net transfers £	Tax payable thereon £
0–	140,000	Nil
Above	140,000	Nil + ⅔ (66.666%) for each £ over 140,000

CHARGEABLE LIFETIME TRANSFERS AFTER 5 APRIL 1991 AND BEFORE 10 MARCH 1992

1991.B1 Tax on gross transfers

	Gross taxable transfers £	Gross cumulative totals £	Rate
First	140,000	0–140,000	Nil
Above	140,000		20% for each £ over 140,000

1991.B2 Grossing-up of net lifetime transfers

	Net transfers £	Tax payable thereon £
0–	140,000	Nil
Above	140,000	Nil + ¼ (25%) for each £ over 140,000

41.1   Rates of Tax

TRANSFERS ON DEATH AFTER 5 APRIL 1990 AND BEFORE 6 APRIL 1991
1990.A1 Tax on transfers

	Gross taxable transfers £	Gross cumulative totals £	Rate
First	128,000	0–128,000	Nil
Above	128,000		40% for each £ over 128,000

1990.A2 Grossing-up of specific transfers on death which do not bear their own tax

	Net transfers £	Tax payable thereon £
0–	128,000		Nil
Above	128,000	Nil + ⅔ (66.666%) for each £ over 128,000

CHARGEABLE LIFETIME TRANSFERS AFTER 5 APRIL 1990 AND BEFORE 6 APRIL 1991
1990.B1 Tax on gross transfers

	Gross taxable transfers £	Gross cumulative totals £	Rate
First	128,000	0–128,000	Nil
Above	128,000		20% for each £ over 128,000

1990.B2 Grossing-up of net lifetime transfers

	Net transfers £	Tax payable thereon £
0–	128,000	Nil
Above	128,000	Nil + ¼ (25%) for each £ over 128,000

TRANSFERS ON DEATH AFTER 5 APRIL 1989 AND BEFORE 6 APRIL 1990
1989.A1 Tax on transfers

	Gross taxable transfers £	Gross cumulative totals £	Rate
First	118,000	0–118,000	Nil
Above	118,000		40% for each £ over 118,000

1989.A2 Grossing-up of specific transfers on death which do not bear their own tax

	Net transfers £	Tax payable thereon £
0–	118,000	Nil
Above	118,000	Nil + ⅔ (66.666%) for each £ over 118,000

CHARGEABLE LIFETIME TRANSFERS AFTER 5 APRIL 1989 AND BEFORE 6 APRIL 1990
1989.B1 Tax on gross transfers

	Gross taxable transfers £	Gross cumulative totals £	Rate
First	118,000	0–118,000	Nil
Above	118,000		20% for each £ over 118,000

1989.B2 Grossing-up of net lifetime transfers

	Net transfers	Tax payable thereon
	£	£
0–	118,000	Nil
Above	118,000	Nil + ¼ (25%) for each £ over 118,000

TRANSFERS ON DEATH AFTER 14 MARCH 1988 AND BEFORE 6 APRIL 1989

1988.A1 Tax on transfers

	Gross taxable transfers	Gross cumulative totals	Rate
	£	£	
First	110,000	0–110,000	Nil
Above	110,000		40% for each £ over 110,000

1988.A2 Grossing-up of specific transfers on death which do not bear their own tax

	Net transfers	Tax payable thereon
	£	£
0–	110,000	Nil
Above	110,000	Nil + ⅔ (66.666%) for each £ over 110,000

CHARGEABLE LIFETIME TRANSFERS AFTER 14 MARCH 1988 AND BEFORE 6 APRIL 1989

1988.B1 Tax on gross transfers

	Gross taxable transfers	Gross cumulative totals	Rate
	£	£	
First	110,000	0–110,000	Nil
Above	110,000		20% for each £ over 110,000

1988.B2 Grossing-up of net lifetime transfers

	Net transfers	Tax payable thereon
	£	£
0–	110,000	Nil
Above	110,000	Nil + ¼ (25%) for each £ over 110,000

TRANSFERS ON DEATH AFTER 16 MARCH 1987 AND BEFORE 15 MARCH 1988

1987.A1 Tax on transfers

	Gross taxable transfers	Gross cumulative totals	Rate	Equal to tax of	Cumulative totals	
					Taxable transfers	Tax thereon
	£	£		£	£	£
First	90,000	0–90,000	Nil	Nil	90,000	Nil
Next	50,000	90,001–140,000	30%	15,000	140,000	15,000
Next	80,000	140,001–220,000	40%	32,000	220,000	47,000
Next	110,000	220,001–330,000	50%	55,000	330,000	102,000
Above	330,000		60%			

41.1   Rates of Tax

1987.A2 Grossing-up of specific transfers on death which do not bear their own tax

Net transfers £	Tax payable thereon £			Cumulative totals Net Transfers £	Gross equivalent £
0– 90,000	Nil		Nil	90,000	90,000
90,001– 125,000	Nil + 3/7	(42.857%) for each £ over 90,000	125,000	140,000
125,001– 173,000	15,000+2/3	(66.666%) " " " "	125,000	173,000	220,000
173,001– 228,000	47,000+1	(100%) " " " "	173,000	228,000	330,000
Above 228,000	102,000+3/2	(150%) " " " "	228,000		

CHARGEABLE LIFETIME TRANSFERS AFTER 16 MARCH 1987 AND BEFORE 15 MARCH 1988
1987.B1 Tax on gross transfers

Gross taxable transfers £	Gross cumulative totals £	Rate	Equal to tax of £	Cumulative totals Taxable transfers £	Tax thereon £
First 90,000	0–90,000	Nil	Nil	90,000	Nil
Next 50,000	90,001–140,000	15%	7,500	140,000	7,500
Next 80,000	140,001–220,000	20%	16,000	220,000	23,500
Next 110,000	220,001–330,000	25%	27,500	330,000	51,000
Above 330,000		30%			

1987.B2 Grossing-up of net lifetime transfers

Net transfers £	Tax payable thereon £			Cumulative totals Net transfers £	Gross equivalent £
0– 90,000	Nil			90,000	90,000
90,001– 132,500	Nil + 3/17	(17.647%) for each £ over 90,000	132,500	140,000
132,501– 196,500	7,500 + 1/4	(25%) " " " "	132,500	196,500	220,000
196,501– 279,000	23,500 + 1/3	(33.333%) " " " "	196,500	279,000	330,000
Above 279,000	51,000+ 3/7	(42.857%) " " " "	279,000		

TRANSFERS ON DEATH AFTER 17 MARCH 1986 AND BEFORE 17 MARCH 1987
1986.A1 Tax on transfers

Gross taxable transfers £	Gross cumulative totals £	Rate	Equal to tax of £	Cumulative totals Taxable transfers £	Tax thereon £
First 71,000	0–71,000	Nil	Nil	71,000	Nil
Next 24,000	71,001–95,000	30%	7,200	95,000	7,200
Next 34,000	95,001–129,000	35%	11,900	129,000	19,100
Next 35,000	129,001–164,000	40%	14,000	164,000	33,100
Next 42,000	164,001–206,000	45%	18,900	206,000	52,000
Next 51,000	206,001–257,000	50%	25,500	257,000	77,500
Next 60,000	257,001–317,000	55%	33,000	317,000	110,500
Above 317,000		60%			

430

1986.A2 Grossing-up of specific transfers on death which do not bear their own tax

Net transfers £	Tax payable thereon £		Cumulative totals Net transfers £	Gross equiva- lent £
0– 71,000	Nil		71,000	71,000
71,001– 87,800	Nil + 3/7	(42.857%) for each £ over 71,000	87,800	95,000
87,801– 109,900	7,200 + 7/13	(53.846%) " " " "	87,800	109,900	129,000
109,901– 130,900	19,100 + 2/3	(66.666%) " " " "	109,900	130,900	164,000
130,901– 154,000	33,100 + 9/11	(81.818%) " " " "	130,900	154,000	206,000
154,001– 179,500	52,100 + 1	(100%) " " " "	154,000	179,500	257,000
179,501– 206,500	77,500 + 11/9	(122.222%) " " " "	179,500	206,500	317,000
Above 206,500	110,500 + 3/2	(159%) " " " "	206,500		

CHARGEABLE LIFETIME TRANSFERS AFTER 17 MARCH 1986 AND BEFORE 17 MARCH 1987
1986.B1 Tax on gross transfers

Gross taxable transfers £	Gross cumulative totals £	Rate	Equal to tax of £	Cumulative totals Taxable transfers £	Tax thereon £
First 71,000	0–71,000	Nil	Nil	71,000	Nil
Next 24,000	71,001–95,000	15%	3,600	95,000	3,600
Next 34,000	95,001–129,000	17½%	5,950	129,000	9,550
Next 35,000	129,001–164,000	20%	7,000	164,000	16,550
Next 42,000	164,001–206,000	22½%	9,450	206,000	26,000
Next 51,000	206,001–257,000	25%	12,750	257,000	38,750
Next 60,000	257,001–317,000	27½%	16,500	317,000	55,250
Above 317,000		30%			

1986.B2 Grossing-up of net lifetime transfers

Net transfers £	Tax payable thereon £		Cumulative totals Net transfers £	Gross equiva- lent £
0– 71,000	Nil + 3/7		71,000	71,000
71,001– 91,400	Nil + 3/17	(17.647%) for each £ over 71,000	91,400	95,000
91,401– 119,450	3,600 + 7/33	(21.212%) " " " "	91,400	119,450	129,000
119,451– 147,450	9,550 + ¼	(25%) " " " "	119,450	147,450	164,000
147,451– 180,000	16,550 + 9/31	(29.032%) " " " "	147,450	180,000	206,000
180,001– 218,250	26,000 + ⅓	(33.333%) " " " "	180,000	218,250	257,000
218,251– 261,750	38,750 + 11/29	(37.931%) " " " "	218,250	261,750	317,000
Above 261,750	55,250 + 3/7	(42.857%) " " " "	261,750		

42   Settlements—General

Cross-references. See also 26 INTEREST IN POSSESSION; 43 SETTLEMENTS WITH INTERESTS IN POSSESSION; 44 SETTLEMENTS WITHOUT INTERESTS IN POSSESSION; 59 WORKING CASE STUDY.

Simon's Direct Tax Service, part I5.

Other Sources. CTO Leaflet IHT 16 'Settled property'; Foster, parts E and M8; IHTM16000.

42.1   Inheritance tax applies to certain transactions and events relating to settlements. For this purpose settlements are divided into two main categories.

(*a*)   Settlements with qualifying interests in possession.

(*b*)   Settlements without qualifying interests in possession.

The charging provisions for the two types of settlement are completely different and are detailed at 43 SETTLEMENTS WITH INTERESTS IN POSSESSION; 44 SETTLEMENTS WITHOUT INTERESTS IN POSSESSION. See 26 INTEREST IN POSSESSION for meaning of '*interest in possession*'. A '*qualifying*' interest in possession is an interest in possession to which an individual (or a company in the business of acquiring such interests on commercial terms) is beneficially entitled. From 22 March 2006 a '*qualifying*' interest in possession will also include an immediate post-death interest (IPDI), a disabled person's interest, a transitional serial interest (TSI) or an interest in possession to which a company is beneficially entitled. [*IHTA 1984, s 59 as amended by FA 2006, Sch 20 para 20*].

42.2   TAX ON SETTLEMENTS WITH INTERESTS IN POSSESSION

The normal charging provisions for ordinary transfers of value (see 1 INTRODUCTION AND BASIC PRINCIPLES) apply with some modification to settlements with interests in possession. A person beneficially entitled to an interest in possession in settled property is treated as beneficially entitled to that property, and on the termination or disposal of that interest tax is charged as if he had made a transfer of value of the property in which his interest subsisted. In relation to transfers of value made, and other events occurring, after 16 March 1987, certain gifts of beneficial interests in possession in settled property are potentially exempt transfers. From 22 March 2006 a person beneficially entitled to an interest in possession in settled property which is terminated is charged to tax as if he had made a transfer of value of the property in which his interest subsisted only if his interest is an IPDI or a TSI or in circumstances where an interest continues to be an interest in possession but ceases to satisfy the rules for an IPDI. See 38.1 POTENTIALLY EXEMPT TRANSFERS. See 43 SETTLEMENTS WITH INTERESTS IN POSSESSION for full details regarding IPDIs and TSIs. [*IHTA 1984, ss 49, 51, 51A, 52; FA 2006, Sch 20 paras 11–13*].

42.3   TAX ON SETTLEMENTS WITHOUT INTERESTS IN POSSESSION

There is a separate charging regime for settlements without interests in possession. There are also special rules for certain types of settlements without interests in possession. See 3 ACCUMULATION AND MAINTENANCE TRUSTS; 11 CHARITIES; 33 NATIONAL HERITAGE; 37 PENSION SCHEMES; 39 PROTECTIVE TRUSTS; 53 TRUSTS FOR BEREAVED MINORS; 54 TRUSTS FOR DISABLED PERSONS; 55 TRUSTS FOR EMPLOYEES.

42.4   PROPERTY ENTERING SETTLEMENT

Tax is charged on the settlor in the normal way when he transfers property into a settlement. A transfer made by an individual after 17 March 1986 and before 22 March 2006 is a potentially exempt transfer (PET) to the extent that it constitutes a gift into an accumulation and maintenance trust or a trust for the disabled. In relation to transfers of value made, and other events occurring, after 16 March 1987 and before 6 April 2008, certain gifts by individuals into settlements with interests in possession are also included.

In this latter case certain transitional rules apply to ensure that new interests in possession which are created out of existing ones before 6 April 2008 ('transitional serial interests') still will qualify as PETs. See 38.1 POTENTIALLY EXEMPT TRANSFERS for full details. Such transfers made seven years or more before the transferor's death are exempt transfers. Any other potentially exempt transfer is a chargeable transfer. See 43 SETTLEMENTS WITH INTERESTS IN POSSESSION; 44.16 SETTLEMENTS WITHOUT INTERESTS IN POSSESSION for property moving between such settlements.

42.5   **SETTLEMENTS NOT LIABLE TO IHT**

Broadly, settled property situated outside the UK escapes IHT if the settlor did not have a UK DOMICILE (17) at the time the settlement was made but see *Civil Engineer v CIR [2002] STC SCD 72*. A reversionary interest in settled property is also normally outside the scope of IHT. From 5 December 2005 anti-avoidance measures apply to prevent UK domiciled individuals who become entitled directly or indirectly to interests in pre-existing foreign trusts which were originally settled by non-UK domiciliaries and would be treated as excluded property within *IHTA 1984, s 48(3)* from benefiting from such treatment if that interest is acquired for money or money's worth. This also applies to the excluded property provisions regarding such property under *IHTA 1984, s 48(3A)* relating to holdings in AUTs and OEICs, [*IHTA 1984, s 48(3), (3A), (3B), (3C); FA 2006, s 157*]. See 20 EXCLUDED PROPERTY, 46 SITUS and former IR Tax Bulletin, February 1997, pp 398 and 399.

42.6   **DEFINITIONS**

'**Settlement**' means any disposition or dispositions of property, whether effected by instrument, by parol (i.e. verbal or oral) or by operation of law, or partly in one way and partly in another whereby the property is for the time being

(*a*)   held in trust for persons in succession or for any person subject to a contingency, or

(*b*)   held by trustees on trust to accumulate the whole or any part of any income of the property or with power to make payments out of that income at the discretion of the trustees or some other person, with or without power to accumulate surplus income, or

(*c*)   charged or burdened (otherwise than for full consideration in money or money's worth paid for his own use or benefit to the person making the disposition), with the payment of any annuity or other periodical payment payable for a life or any other limited or terminable period. [*IHTA 1984, s 43(1)(2)*].

In the case of *CIR v Lloyds Private Banking Ltd [1998] STC 559 Sp C 133* the following clause in the will created a settlement pursuant to *IHTA 1984, s 43(2)* viz.

'(1) While my Husband … remains alive and desires to reside in the property and keeps the same in good repair and insured comprehensively to its full value with Insurers approved by my Trustee and pays and indemnifies my Trustee against all rates taxes and other outgoings in respect of the property my Trustee shall not make any objection to such residence and shall not disturb or restrict it in any way and shall not take any steps to enforce the trust for sale on which the property is held or to realise my share therein or to obtain any rent or profit from the property.

On the death of my said Husband … I devise and bequeath the said property … to my Daughter … absolutely'.

The Commissioner accepted the Trustee's contention that the words 'on the death of' might simply be read as 'subject to the foregoing'. The facts of this appeal showed an instance where the rule stated by Wood V C in *Maddison v Chapman (1859) 4 K & J 709* might be approved and it was held that there was an absolute gift of the separate share to the daughter, subject only to a direction to the Trustee to postpone sale. See also *Rysaffe*

Trustee Co (CI) Ltd v CIR [2003] STC 536 where in the Court of Appeal the Judges upheld Park J in the original case: A settlor had executed five settlements within a period of 35 days, and transferred shares of equal value to each settlement. HMRC had issued a notice of determination that the five holdings should be treated as a single settlement for the purposes of the charge to tax under *IHTA 1984, s 64*. The company which acted as the trustee of the settlements appealed. The Ch D allowed the appeal, holding that there were five separate settlements for the purposes of *s 64*. Park J held that 'it is up to the settlor who places property in trust to determine whether he wishes to create one trust or several trusts, or for that matter merely to add more property to a settlement which had already been created in the past'. Each settlement was created by a 'disposition' within *IHTA 1984, s 43*. The 'associated operations' provisions of *IHTA 1984, s 268* did not apply, since their 'practical operation' was 'comparatively limited'. *IHTA 1984, s 268* was 'not an operative provision which of itself imposes inheritance tax liabilities. It is a definition of an expression (associated operations) which is used elsewhere. The definition only comes into effect in so far as the expression "associated operations" is used elsewhere, and then only if the expression in another provision is relevant to the way in which that other provision applies to the facts of the particular case.'

The following are also treated as settlements.

(d)   *A foreign settlement.* Any disposition which would fall within (*a*) to (*c*) above if it were regulated by the law of any part of the UK, or if under foreign law the administration of the property is governed by provisions equivalent in effect. [*IHTA 1984, s 43(2)*]. See also 20.2 EXCLUDED PROPERTY.

(e)   A lease of property for life or lives, or for a period ascertainable only by reference to a death, or which is terminable on, or at a date ascertainable only by reference to, a death, *unless* the lease was granted for full consideration in money or money's worth.

For this purpose a lease not granted at a rack rent which is at any time to become a lease at an increased rent is to be treated as terminable at that time.

In Northern Ireland, this does not apply to a lease in perpetuity within the meaning of the *Renewable Leasehold Conversion Act 1849, s 1* or a lease to which *section 37* of that *Act* applies. [*IHTA 1984, s 43(3)(5)*].

(f)   *In Scotland*, (i) an entail; (ii) any deed by virtue of which an annuity is charged on, or on rents of, any property (the property being treated as the property comprised in the settlement); and (iii) any 'deed' creating or reserving a proper liferent of any property whether inheritable or movable (the property from time to time subject to the proper liferent being treated as the property comprised in the settlement). '*Deed*' includes any disposition, arrangement, contract, resolution, instrument or writing. [*IHTA 1984, s 43(4)*].

(g)   *In Northern Ireland*, references to property held in trust for persons include references to property standing limited to persons. [*IHTA 1984, s 43(5)*].

'Settlor' includes any person by whom the settlement was made directly or indirectly and any person who has provided funds directly or indirectly for the purpose of or in connection with the settlement or has made with any other person a reciprocal arrangement for that other person to make the settlement. Where more than one person is a settlor in relation to a settlement, and the circumstances so require, the settled property is treated as if comprised in separate settlements for the purposes of the provisions relating to inheritance tax on settled property other than *IHTA 1984, s 48(4)–(6)* (exempt gilts, see 20.4 EXCLUDED PROPERTY). [*IHTA 1984, s 44*].

The words 'for the purpose or in connection with' contained in *IHTA 1984, s 44* imply there must at least be a conscious association of the provider of funds with the settlement in question. It is insufficient that the settled funds should historically have been derived from the provider of them. If it were otherwise, anyone who gave funds unconditionally to another person which that other person later settled would fall to be treated as the settlor or as a settlor of the funds (*Countess Fitzwilliam and others v CIR (and related appeals) HL, [1993] STC 502*).

For those Trustees wishing to make an appointment of part of an unappropriated residue a possible alternative open to the Trustees would be to appoint an amount of cash to be raised from the disposal of part of the estate. This might be worded as follows:

Appointment by supplemental deed under the Trustee Act 1925

THIS DEED OF APPOINTMENT is made the .... day of ....200(7) BETWEEN ....[Trustee]..... of ....[Address]...... and .....[Trustee]....... of ....[Address]........ hereinafter known as the APPOINTERS and ....[Name]....... of ....[Address]...... hereinafter known as the BENEFICIARY.

WHEREAS

(1) The Appointers hereby irrevocably appoint and direct that the sum of £.............. shall forthwith be raised by the Trustees of the said settlement .... [Name of settlement]........ out of the trust funds and property comprised therein and shall be paid by them to ....[Name].

Notes to the Appointment

(A) Further provisions of powers and proper law etc. are required to give effect to this appointment.

(B) It may be necessary for the Trustees to have assented to the relevant property before the appointment can be made. In the case of land a written assent is needed before the legal estate vests in the Trustees *Re King's Will Trusts 1964 Ch 542*.

'**Trustee**' means, if there would otherwise be no trustees apart from this definition, any person in whom the settled property or its management is for the time being vested. [*IHTA 1984, s 45*].

'**Interest in possession**' is explained in 26 INTEREST IN POSSESSION.

'**Reversionary interest**' means a future interest under a settlement, whether vested or contingent (including an interest expectant on the termination of an interest in possession which, by virtue of *IHTA 1984, s 50* (see 43.1 SETTLEMENTS WITH INTERESTS IN POSSESSION) is treated as subsisting in part of any property); and in relation to Scotland includes an interest in the fee of property subject to a proper liferent. [*IHTA 1984, s 47*].

'**Modernising the Tax System for Trusts**' consultation paper was issued on 11 December 2003. One of the consultation paper's many proposals with regard to income tax and capital gains tax was the standardisation of the definitions of 'settlement', 'settlor' and 'settlor interested trusts' from April 2005. It is proposed that settlors will be more closely identified with settlor interested trusts with regard to income tax and capital gains, and this will impact on the inheritance tax position to a degree as well (see 43.1 SETTLEMENTS WITH INTERESTS IN POSSESSION). In reported responses to the consultation paper on 4 May 2004 it was suggested that most respondents favour the existing *IHTA 1984, s 43(2)* definition of 'settlement' as a starting point for an all encompassing definition. Consultation in this area continues following both the 2005 and 2006 Budget statements – a basic rate band applying to the first £1,000 applicable from 6 April 2006 will apply to trusts that pay tax at the rate applicable to trusts. Also a number of definitions and tests used in taxing trusts to income tax and capital gains tax are to be altered and aligned between the two taxes. See Tolley's Income Tax 2007–08 and Tolley's Capital Gains Tax 2007–08. [*FA 2005, ss 23–45; FA 2006, ss 88, 89, Schs 12, 13*].

42.7   LIFE INTEREST SETTLEMENT

THIS SETTLEMENT is made on   200(7)

PARTIES

1. "The Settlor" namely

2. "The Original Trustees" namely

RECITALS
(Usual recitals)

NOW THIS DEED IRREVOCABLY WITNESSES

1.   DEFINITIONS

The following terms (where the context permits) shall have the following meanings:—

1.1   "the Appointed Class" means the following persons now living or born during the Trust Period

    1.1.1   the Primary Beneficiary

    1.1.2   the children and remoter issue of the Primary Beneficiary

    1.1.3   the spouses former spouses widows and widowers of the persons within 1.1.1 and 1.1.2

    1.1.4   any other person or persons added by Clause 2

    1.1.5   the [widow] [widower] of the Settlor

1.2   "Excluded Person" means

    1.2.1   the Settlor

    1.2.2   any spouse of the Settlor

    1.2.3   any person declared to be an Excluded Person by Clause 2.

1.3   "the Primary Beneficiary" means [   ] born on [   ]

1.4   "the Trust Fund" means

    1.4.1   the sum specified in the First Schedule

    1.4.2   any further money or property accepted by the Trustees as additions to the Trust Fund

    1.4.3   the assets from time to time representing such sum and additions

1.5   "the Trust Period" means the period beginning on the date of this Settlement and ending

    1.5.1   80 years from the date (which period shall be the applicable perpetuity period) or

    1.5.2   on such earlier date as the Trustees shall by deed prospectively specify

1.6   "the Trustees" means the Original Trustees or other trustees or trustee for the time being of this Settlement

2.   POWER TO ADD OR EXCLUDE BENEFICIARIES

THE trustees shall have the power in their absolute discretion (with the prior written consent of the Settlor during the lifetime of the Settlor) exercisable by deed executed within the Trust Period to add any person or persons (not being an Excluded Person) to the Appointed Class or to declare any person or persons to be an Excluded Person with effect from the date of such deed

3.   BASIC TRUSTS OR CAPITAL AND INCOME

THE Trustees shall hold the capital and income of the Trust Fund upon trust

3.1   to pay the income to the Primary Beneficiary for life with power in their absolute discretion to transfer or raise and pay to or for the advancement or benefit of the Primary Beneficiary the whole or any part of the capital of the Trust Fund and subject to that

3.2   to pay the income to the surviving spouse of the Primary Beneficiary for life with the same power for the benefit of such surviving spouse as the Trustees have under this clause 3.1 for the Primary Beneficiary and subject to that

3.3   for such of the children of the Primary Beneficiary who attain the age of 25 years or are living and under that age at the end of the Trust Period and if more than one in such shares as the Primary Beneficiary shall by deed or will appoint and in default of such appointment in equal shares absolutely

4.   OVERRIDING POWER OF APPOINTMENT

4.1   NOTWITHSTANDING the trusts above the Trustees shall have power by deed or deeds executed during the Trust Period to declare such trusts in respect of all or any part or parts of the capital or income of the Trust Fund for the benefit of the members of the Appointed Class or any one or more of them exclusive of the other or others in such shares and subject to such terms and limitations and with and subject to such provisions for maintenance education or advancement or for accumulation of income or for forfeiture in the event of bankruptcy or otherwise and with such discretionary trusts and powers exercisable by such persons as the Trustees may think fit

4.2   to the extent that such trusts powers and provisions shall not be exhaustive of the entire beneficial interest in the Trust Fund it shall continue to be held upon the preceding trusts

4.3   no exercise of this power shall invalidate any prior payment or application of all or any part or parts of the capital or income of the Trust Fund made under any other power or powers conferred by this Settlement

5.   ULTIMATE TRUSTS

SUBJECT to the above trusts the capital and income of the Trust Fund shall be held upon trust for such charitable purposes as the Trustees shall in their absolute discretion select

42.7 Settlements—General

Note to the Precedent

Further provisions on powers, proper law, etc. plus full administrative provisions required. Following the enactment of the enactment of the *Civil Partnership Act 2004* references to 'spouse' and 'widow/widower' above would be amended to include 'civil partner' and 'surviving civil partner' where appropriate.

43   Settlements with Interests in Possession

Cross-references. See also 26 INTEREST IN POSSESSION; 30 LIFE ASSURANCE POLICIES AND ANNUITIES; 42 SETTLEMENTS—GENERAL; 44 SETTLEMENTS WITHOUT INTERESTS IN POSSESSION.

Simon's Direct Tax Service, parts I3.524–I3.527, I5.141–I5.155.

Other Sources. HMRC Inheritance Tax Leaflet IHT 16 'Settled property'; Foster, parts E1–4; IHTM16000.

43.1   EFFECT OF INTEREST IN POSSESSION (IIP)

A person beneficially entitled to an interest in possession in settled property in existence prior to 22 March 2006 is treated as beneficially entitled to the property in which the interest subsists, i.e. he is treated as owning it absolutely. There is an IHT charge based on the value of the settled property in which his interest subsists when a beneficiary disposes of his interest or it otherwise comes to an end i.e. either as a transfer on death or as a PET where the termination of the interest occurs during the lifetime of the tenant for example where there is an exercise of a power of appointment. [*IHTA 1984, ss 49(1), 51(1), 51A, 52(1); FA 2006, Sch 20 paras 11–13*]. See 38.1 POTENTIALLY EXEMPT TRANSFERS. See 26 INTEREST IN POSSESSION for meaning of 'interest in possession'. *Note* that the actual actuarial value of the interest is irrelevant except in the limited cases where an interest is acquired for money or money's worth. See 43.4 below.

From 22 March 2006 newly created IIP settlements will be treated under the relevant property taxing regime unless the interest is an immediate post-death interest (IPDI) or a transitional serial interest (TSI) or a disabled person's interest. See below and 30 LIFE ASSURANCE POLICIES AND ANNUITIES; 44 SETTLEMENTS WITHOUT INTERESTS IN POSSESSION. [*IHTA 1984, ss 49(1A), 51(1A); FA 2006, Sch 20 paras 4, 11*]. Any new trusts created from 22 March 2006 which are not IPDI or TSI trusts will be subject to certain requirements before they qualify for exclusion from the relevant property regime. See SETTLEMENTS WITHOUT INTEREST IN POSSESSION (44) and TRUSTS FOR DISABLED PERSONS (54).

Immediate post-death interest (IPDI). An IPDI arises for IHT purposes where a person (stipulated as being 'L' in the legislation) is beneficially entitled on or after 22 March 2006 to an interest in possession in settled property and a number of conditions are satisfied. For such trusts set up by will or intestacy the following conditions must apply:

- the first condition is the requirement that the interest in settled property arises immediately on the death of the settlor by reason of will or intestacy;

- the second condition is that 'L' becomes beneficially entitled to an interest in possession on the death of the testator or intestate;

- the third condition is that rules regarding bereaved minor's trusts under *IHTA 1984, s 71A* do not apply in these circumstances to property in which the interest subsists and the interest is not a disabled person's interest—see TRUSTS FOR BEREAVED MINORS (53);

- the fourth condition is that at all times since 'L' became beneficially entitled to the interest in possession that neither *IHTA 1984, s 71A* (bereaved minor's trust) applies to the property in which the interest subsists nor is the interest a disabled person's interest.

[*IHTA 1984, ss 49(1), 49A, 51A, 52(2A), 53(2A); FA 2006, Sch 20 paras 5, 11–13*].

43.1 Settlements with Interests in Possession

Example 1

X, who is married to L (his second wife), dies on 12 January 2008 having already made gifts on 21 May 2006 of £291,000 utilising his available annual exemptions and nil rate band. By his will he leaves his assets to his second wife L in trust for life and then on her death on trusts to his son S now aged 30. See extract below. His estate is valued at £760,000 including the value of the house in which they live of £340,000. X had made no gifts in the year to 5 April 2006 but had used his annual exemptions prior to 2005/06.

L dies on 8 January 2010 when the trust assets are valued at £800,000. The terms of the trust are that the assets are to be held on trusts with overriding powers to apply capital and accumulated income to the beneficiary son S.

TRUST INCOME

Subject to the Overriding Powers below I leave my residuary estate on trust:

(1)   My Trustees shall pay the income of the Trust Fund to my widow during her life and my Trustees shall have power to pay or apply capital for her benefit;

(2)   Subject thereto, my Trustees shall have power to accumulate the whole or any part of the Residuary Fund and that income shall be added to the Trust Fund;

(3)   Subject to that, the Trust Fund shall be held on trust for ....[Name]................ absolutely.

Calculation on death of X

	£	£
Value transferred on 21 May 2006		291,000
Deduct annual exemption 2006/07	3,000	
annual exemption 2005/06	3,000	6,000
		£285,000

IHT on chargeable gift of £285,000 is charged in the nil rate band up to £300,000. Balance of estate held on trust for wife L is exempt under *IHTA 1984, s 18.*

	£
£0–285,000 at Nil%	Nil
Estate chargeable	Nil

Calculation on death of L

	£
Value of L's estate at 8 January 2010 by reason of *IHTA 1984, s 49(1)(1A)*. See above.	£800,000

See table at 41.1 2009.A1 RATES OF TAX.

	£
£0–325,000	Nil
£325,001–£800,000 at 40%	£190,000
IHT payable	£190,000

See Note (B).

Notes to the example

(A)   Most married couples and those in civil partnerships would want to defer the IHT burden until the last death especially where there is a property of substantial value in

440

the estate which may have to be sold. In this particular case it is a second marriage and X wishes to benefit his spouse with a life interest but that his son S ultimately benefits on the death of his step-mother. Under *IHTA 1984, s 49A* L has an IPDI which arises under the will of X and L is treated as beneficially entitled to an interest in possession in settled property in which the interest subsists, i.e. see (1) in extract above where L is treated as owning it absolutely and certain disposals of interests in possession by individuals may be potentially exempt transfers. However, as L did not survive seven years but dies within three years of her husband's death, and as part of her estate is an IIP, that interest is chargeable potentially at 40% after the deduction of her nil rate band. Note that an IPDI does not necessarily have to be in favour of a surviving spouse/civil partner and could be an alternative source of providing funds for the next generation or younger individuals.

(B) The settlement of the trust assets in favour of the son would have been treated as an IIP settlement but following *FA 2006, Sch 20 para 4* it will not now be treated as such. See SETTLEMENTS WITHOUT INTERESTS IN POSSESSION (44). Therefore, as this IIP in favour of the son is created out of an existing IIP after 6 April 2008 it cannot be either a transitional serial interest (TSI see below) or an IPDI. An immediate charge of 40% has been levied as above and there will be further charges incurred under the relevant property taxing rules for discretionary trusts to the extent that the assets are held on continuing trusts. See SETTLEMENTS WITHOUT INTEREST IN POSSESSION (44) for a continuation of this example.

Transitional serial interest (TSI).

1. On or after 22 March 2006 and before 6 April 2008 (Category 1)

Where a person (stipulated as being 'B' in the legislation) is beneficially entitled on or after 22 March 2006 but before 6 April 2008 to an interest in possession in settled property then for the purposes of *IHTA 1984, Part III, Ch II* that interest is a transitional serial interest only if a number of conditions are satisfied:

- the settlement must have commenced before 22 March 2006 and the property comprised in the settlement was property to which 'B' (the beneficiary of the current interest), or some other person, was beneficially entitled an interest in possession which for these purposes is designated 'the prior interest';

- the prior interest came to an end on or after 22 March 2006 but before 6 April 2008;

- 'B' becomes beneficially entitled to the current interest on or after 22 March 2006 and before 6 April 2008;

- neither *IHTA 1984, s 71A* (bereaved minor's trust) applies to the property in which the interest subsists nor is the interest a disabled person's interest.

2. On death of spouse or civil partner on or after 6 April 2008 (Category 2)

Alternatively, a TSI arises where a person (stipulated as being 'E' in the legislation) is beneficially entitled to an interest in possession in settled property then for the purposes of *IHTA 1984, Part III, Ch II* that interest is a transitional serial interest only if a number of conditions are satisfied:

- the settlement must have commenced before 22 March 2006 and the property comprised in the settlement was property to which a person other than 'E' was beneficially entitled an interest in possession which for these purposes is designated 'the previous interest';

- the previous interest came to an end on or after 6 April 2008 on the death of the other person who for these purposes is designated as 'F';

- immediately before 'F' died, F was the spouse or civil partner of 'E';

- E became beneficially entitled to the successor interest on F's death;

- neither *IHTA 1984, s 71A* (bereaved minor's trust) nor a disabled person's interest applies to the property in which the successor interest subsists.

[*IHTA 1984, ss 49B–D, 51(1A), 52(2A), 54A(1A); FA 2006, Sch 20 paras 5, 12, 13, 16*].

In circumstances where there is a settled life insurance contract under *IHTA 1984, s 49E* that is to be treated as a TSI see 30.1 LIFE ASSURANCE POLICIES AND ANNUITIES.

Example 2

A transferred £260,000 on 1 October 2002 into an interest in possession trust of which his brother C is the life tenant. On 31 August 2006, C released his life interest i.e. 'the prior interest' in the first condition above, then valued at £320,000, to an IIP settlement in favour of his child 'B'. A's cumulative chargeable transfers in the last seven years amounted to £230,000. A was still alive on 31 August 2006, at which date C's cumulative chargeable transfers in the last seven years amounted to £130,000 and he (C) had not used his annual exemptions for 2006/07 and 2005/06. See table at 41.1 2008.A1 RATES OF TAX.

The transfer by A on 1 October 2002 is a potentially exempt transfer which will not become chargeable unless A dies before 1 October 2009. See also Example 4 below.

The transfer by C meets the four conditions above and B's interest is therefore a TSI. The transfer is therefore a potentially exempt transfer and is not charged at lifetime rates, i.e. one-half of death rates 20%, after taking into account cumulative transfers of £130,000.

If, however, C released his life interest i.e. 'the prior interest' on 5 May 2008 when valued at £350,000 then the second condition above would not be met and the IHT relevant property regime would apply going forward with the following results.

Normal calculation

	£	£
Value transferred by C on 5 May 2008		350,000
Deduct annual exemption 2008/09	3,000	
Annual exemption 2007/08	3,000	6,000
		£344,000

IHT on £344,000 is charged in the band £130,001 to £474,000.
See table at 41.1 2008.A1 RATES OF TAX.

	£
£130,001–312,000	Nil
£312,001–474,000 at 20%	32,400
IHT payable	£32,400

Notes to the example

(A) C's cumulative chargeable transfers following the gift on 5 May 2008 will incur an immediate 20% IHT charge due to his having made other chargeable transfers prior to that date but within seven years of the gift. In addition, if C dies within seven years of the gift then his estate will be subject to a further 20% charge. A report of the transfer on 5 May 2008 should be made to HMRC Inheritance Tax on Form IHT 100 and 100a with C paying the tax due. See ACCOUNTS AND RETURNS (2).

(B) The funds of £350,000 in the trust for B will be held under the discretionary trust taxing regime so that a charge on the trust fund assets will occur every 10th anniversary of up to 6%. See SETTLEMENTS WITHOUT INTEREST IN POSSESSION (44) for a continuation of this example including exit charges. [*IHTA 1984, ss 51, 51A; FA 2006, Sch 20 para 12*].

(C)   Had C died after 6 April 2008 and chosen to leave his interest in possession to his wife so that she succeeded his interest and the five Category 2 conditions mentioned above are met then a succeeding interest will arise to the wife. This is potentially very useful in the context of a trust that is an IIP for one spouse with a succeeding IIP for the survivor which under normal rules applying under *IHTA 1984, s 49C* would not have applied after 5 April 2008.

Where a *close company* is entitled to an interest in possession, this is treated for IHT purposes as being owned by the participators. From 22 March 2006 where a close company is entitled to an interest in possession in settled property, that interest in possession will also include an immediate post-death interest (IPDI) and a transitional serial interest (TSI). See below and 12.7 CLOSE COMPANIES.

43.2   VALUE OF PROPERTY IN WHICH INTEREST SUBSISTS

Entitlement to all income or property. If the interest is in all the income arising from the settled property, the beneficiary is treated as owning the whole property. The position is the same where there is no income but the beneficiary is entitled to the use or enjoyment of the property.

Entitlement to part only of the income (if any) of the property is treated as giving an interest in possession in the same proportion of the property as his income entitlement bears to the whole income. Where a person is entitled to a specified amount of income i.e. an annuity (or the whole income less a specified amount) in any period, his interest in the settled property is such part (or the whole less such part) of the property as produces that amount in that period. Where there is a chargeable transfer of such an interest, the Treasury prescribe higher and lower income yields (to prevent manipulation of the value transferred by altering the income). Where it is the property supporting an annuity which is to be charged, the minimum value is the 'actual' dividend yield compiled for the FT Actuaries Share Indices in place of the previous method which took the 'gross' yield. Where the remainder of the settled property is to be charged, the maximum value of the property supporting the annuity is the annuity grossed up at the gross dividend yield for British Government Stocks ('Irredeemables') at the date the property has to be valued (the balance of the settled property being the value of the property to be charged). The Treasury has power to alter the higher and lower values by statutory instrument and the most recent change was on 28 January 2000. [*IHTA 1984, s 50(1)–(4); SI 1980, No 1000; SI 2000, No 174*].

Cessation of annuity. Where an annuitant dies or disposes of his interest in possession, and the annuity is charged wholly or in part on real or leasehold property and the Board is satisfied that a capital valuation of the property at the relevant date restricted to its existing use reflects an anticipated increase in rents obtainable for that use after that date, appropriate relief will be given in calculating the 'slice', i.e. proportion of the property on which tax is payable (see F11 at 23 HMRC EXTRA-STATUTORY CONCESSIONS).

Entitlement to shared use of property. Where a person entitled to an interest in possession is not entitled to any income of the property but is entitled, jointly or in common with one or more other persons, to its use and enjoyment, his interest is taken to subsist in such part of the property as the proportion which the annual value of his interest bears to the aggregate annual value of his and the other interest(s). See *Woodhall (Woodhall's Personal Representatives) v CIR [2000] STC SCD 558* regarding the right to occupy a house jointly. [*IHTA 1984, s 50(5)*].

Leases. Where a lease is treated as a settlement (see point (*e*) at 42.6 SETTLEMENTS— GENERAL), the lessee's interest in the property is in the whole of the property less the value of the lessor's interest, see 55.14 VALUATION. [*IHTA 1984, s 50(6)*].

43.3 TERMINATION OF AN INTEREST IN POSSESSION

Inheritance tax is chargeable (but see exceptions below) when a beneficial interest in possession in settled property comes to an end because of (i) the death of the person entitled to the interest or (ii) the actual or deemed termination of that person's interest during his life (including disposal to a third party). That person is treated as if he had made a transfer of value and the value chargeable is the value of the property in which his interest subsisted, as if he were the transferor of that property, so that tax is charged at his personal cumulative rate of tax (but see also 43.5 below). References to property or to an interest in property include references to part of any property or interest. [*IHTA 1984, ss 51(1)(3), 52(1)*]. In *Mrs Patch's Executors v HMRC [2007] Sp C 600 a* deed of partition had resulted in a transfer of value under *IHTA 1984, s 52(1)*. See *Miller and Others v CIR CS 1986, [1987] STC 108* where, on the death of the life tenant, it was held that the trustees' powers regarding disposition of the trust fund were administrative and not dispositive and CTT on the whole fund was chargeable. From 22 March 2006 where the interest disposed of is IPDI or a TSI (see 43.1 above) and is not an interest to which *IHTA 1984, s 71A* (bereaved minor's trust) applies then that person is treated as if he had made a transfer of value and the value chargeable is the value of the property in which his interest subsisted, as if he were the transferor of that property. In such circumstances tax is charged at his personal cumulative rate of tax. References to property or to an interest in property include references to part of any property or interest. [*IHTA 1984, ss 51(1), 52(1) as amended by FA 2006, Sch 20 paras 12, 13*].

From 22 March 2006 where a close company is entitled to an interest in possession in settled property, that interest in possession will also include an immediate post-death interest (IPDI) and a transitional serial interest (TSI) as an interest in possession to which a company is beneficially entitled. Where there is a disposal of rights and interests in the close company to 'a later participator' then for these purposes the later participator will be entitled to that interest in possession according to their respective rights and interests in the company. See 12 CLOSE COMPANIES for full details. [*IHTA 1984, s 101 as amended by FA 2006, Sch 20 para 26*].

Subject to the application of the *Ramsay* principle or the associated operations provisions, the Board consider that, where an interest in possession comes to an end during the lifetime of the person entitled to it, the settled property in which the interest subsisted should be valued in isolation without reference to any similar property. Previously they thought that the value should be determined as a rateable proportion of the aggregate value of that settled property and other property of a similar kind in the person's estate (letter from Capital and Valuation Division reproduced at 1990 STI 446). The value of settled property continues to be determined by the Board in this latter manner where the interest in possession is terminated through the death of the person entitled to it. The construction of the legislation supports this view. See also (*c*) below where the settled property is excluded property. See also 43.2 above for the value of property in which the interest subsists.

Although termination of an interest in possession during a person's life is generally treated as if he were the transferor, the exemption for small gifts and for normal expenditure out of income (see 21 EXEMPT TRANSFERS) do not apply. The annual exemption and the exemption for gifts in consideration of marriage apply subject to the transferor giving notice in such form as the Board may prescribe (currently Form 222) to the trustees, within six months of the transfer, informing them of the availability and extent of the exemption. For the purposes of gifts in consideration of marriage (see 21.10 EXEMPT TRANSFERS) references to outright gifts and settled gifts include cases where property respectively ceases or remains settled property after the termination of the interest in possession.

SETTLED PROPERTY—ANNUAL AND MARRIAGE GIFTS EXEMP-
TION

Notice under Inheritance Tax Act 1984, sections 57(2) and/or (3) to
......................[Trustees full names].................................... the Trustees of the
...........................[Name and title of settlement]..............................

I ....[Full name]............................... in the knowledge that my beneficial
interest in possession in property in the sum of £............................. comprised in
the above Trust was terminated on ......[Date]........................... hereby give notice
that the amounts of

(a)   £.............................. of the annual exemption*

(b)   £.............................. of the exemption for gifts in consideration of marriage*

was/were then available to me and is/are to be applied against the transfer value
deemed to be made by the termination.

Signed..
Dated...

* Delete as appropriate

Notes to the Claim

(A)   The Trustees should retain the completed form in case it is subsequently required for
presentation to HMRC Inheritance Tax.

(B)   If the person signing the form later becomes aware that any correction is required
he/she should inform the Trustees immediately.

(C)   Notice has to be given within six months of the release.

It is also possible to incorporate the notice into the deed of release so that the releasor signs
the notice at one and the same time. This may be worded as below:

DEED OF RELEASE

The Releasor ....[Name]................. gives notice to the Trustees of
.........[Name]............... Settlement that pursuant to Inheritance Tax Act 1984,
sections 57(2) and/or (3)* that the £3,000 annual exemption and/or the [£1,000/
£2,500/£5,000*] gift in consideration of marriage exemption for 2007/08 are
available to him/her and are to be applied against the transfer of value deemed to be
made by this deed. The Releasor undertakes to notify the Trustees if he/she
becomes aware that a correction is necessary to the notice contained in this clause.

Signed... Dated..

Releasor [Name]

Notes to the Release

(A)   The annual exemption for the previous year may also be used by the Releasor if it is
available.

(B)   *Asterisks denote where deletion of non-applicable exemptions should be made by the Releasor.

If the interest is disposed of for a consideration in money or money's worth, the amount of the value transferred is reduced by that consideration (but excluding from the consideration the value of any reversionary interest in the property or any interest in other property in the same settlement). Where the property consists of an interest in a pre-owned asset which is disposed of by an individual in an arm's length transaction to a person not connected with him then that property will be treated as excluded for the purposes of *FA 2004, Sch 15. [IHTA 1984, s 52(2); FA 2004, Sch 15 para 10(1)]*. A reduction also applies where a close company disposes of the interest (25.E5 HMRC STATEMENTS OF PRAC-TICE). See 43.4 part (*b*) below for position of person acquiring the interest.

Tax is not chargeable in the following circumstances.

(*a*)   Where, after 16 March 1987, the disposal of a beneficial interest in possession by a beneficiary is a POTENTIALLY EXEMPT TRANSFER (38) which is made seven years or more before death (and is consequently an exempt transfer). [*IHTA 1984, s 3A(2)(4); FA 1986, s 101(3), Sch 19 para 1; F(No 2)A 1987, s 96(1)(2), Sch 9 Part III*].

(*b*)   On a *disposal* of an interest in possession for maintenance of family, see 21.11 EXEMPT TRANSFERS. [*IHTA 1984, s 51(2)*].

(*c*)   Where the settled property is EXCLUDED PROPERTY (20). [*IHTA 1984, s 53(1)*]. For consideration of the position where settled property is excluded property in relation to a person who holds similar property in his free estate (e.g. shares in a company) in the light of the Board's statement mentioned above regarding principles of valuation, see Taxation, 9 July 1992, p 371.

(*d*)   Where the person whose interest comes to an end becomes on the same occasion beneficially entitled to the property or to another interest in possession in the property (but if the value of the new interest is less than the old, tax is chargeable on the difference). [*IHTA 1984, ss 52(4)(b), 53(2)*]. This also applies where a close company becomes entitled to an absolute interest, etc. (25.E5 HMRC STATEMENTS OF PRACTICE).

(*e*)   Where the interest comes to an end and reverts to the settlor in his lifetime, unless the settlor (or his spouse after 11 April 1978) had purchased the reversion for money or money's worth. This relief does not apply where its application depends on a reversionary interest having been transferred into a settlement after 9 March 1981. [*IHTA 1984, ss 53(3)(5)(7), 54(1)(3)*. (See Notes (i) and (ii) below, 6.3 ANTI-AVOIDANCE and also 50.2 TRANSFERS ON DEATH.)

(*f*)   Where the interest comes to an end and the settlor's spouse or civil partner becomes beneficially entitled to the settled property, provided the settlor's spouse or civil partner is then domiciled in the UK and neither the settlor nor the spouse or civil partner had acquired a reversionary interest in the property for money or money's worth. This exemption also applies where the property reverts to the settlor's widow or widower or surviving civil partner if the settlor died less than two years before the interest comes to an end. This relief does not apply where its application depends on a reversionary interest having been transferred into a settlement after 9 March 1981. [*IHTA 1984, ss 53(4)(5), 54(2)(3)*]. (See Notes (i) and (ii) below, 6.3 ANTI-AVOIDANCE and also 50.2 TRANSFERS ON DEATH.)

(*g*)   On the coming to an end of an interest held by a surviving spouse (or surviving former spouse) of a person who died before 13 November 1974 where estate duty was paid on that death on the property in which the interest subsists (or would have been paid but for any exemption). [*IHTA 1984, Sch 6 para 2*]. (See also 50.2 TRANSFERS ON DEATH.)

(*h*)   Where the principal beneficiary's interest in a protective trust is determined, see 39 PROTECTIVE TRUSTS.

(*i*)   Where a trustee is remunerated for his services as a trustee by an interest in possession in settlement property (e.g. an annuity) except to the extent that it represents more than reasonable remuneration. [*IHTA 1984, s 90*].

(*j*)   Where a person disclaims an interest in settled property to which he has become entitled. This does not apply if the disclaimer is made for a consideration in money or money's worth. [*IHTA 1984, s 93*].

(*k*)   Where property comprised in a settlement (but not a reversionary interest in settled property, see 44.10) is a holding in an authorised unit trust or a share in an open-ended investment company unless the settlor was domiciled in the UK at the time the settlement was made. [*IHTA 1984, s 48(3A)(a) as inserted by FA 2003, s 186*].

(*l*)   Where a person's beneficial interest entitlement before 22 March 2006 comes to an end on or after that date but the interest was one to which *IHTA 1984, s 71A* (bereaved minor's trust) applies. See 53.1 TRUSTS FOR BEREAVED MINORS. [*IHTA 1984, s 53(1A) inserted by FA 2006, Sch 20 para 14*].

(*m*)   Where the person whose interest comes to an end becomes on the same occasion beneficially entitled to the property but that interest is not a disabled person's interest. See 54.1 TRUSTS FOR DISABLED PERSONS. [*IHTA 1984, s 53(2A) inserted by FA 2006, Sch 20 para 14*].

Notes

(i)   For the purposes of (*e*) and (*f*) above, a person is treated as acquiring an interest for a consideration in money or money's worth if he becomes entitled to it as a result of transactions which include a disposition for such consideration (whether to him or another) of that interest or of other property. [*IHTA 1984, s 53(6)(8)*].

(ii)   For the purposes of (*e*) and (*f*) above as they apply on the termination by death of an interest in possession, where it cannot be known which of two or more persons died first, they are assumed to have died at the same instant. [*IHTA 1984, s 54(4)*]. See also 50.4 TRANSFERS ON DEATH.

(iii)   For relief for successive charges on an interest in possession, see 40.1 QUICK SUCCESSION RELIEF.

Example 3

A had an interest in possession in a settlement valued at £240,000 with remainder to his son S. On 1 July 2007, A released his life interest to S in consideration of S's marriage on 2 July 2007. A had made no gifts since 5 April 2007 but had used his annual exemptions prior to that date. His cumulative total of chargeable transfers at 5 April 2007 was £88,000, and these had all been made since 1 July 2000. A died on 30 June 2008.

The release of A's life interest is a potentially exempt transfer which becomes chargeable by reason of A's death within seven years. The charge is at full rates with no tapering relief as the transfer took place within three years before death. See table at 41.1 2008.A2 RATES OF TAX.

43.3 Settlements with Interests in Possession

	£	£
Value of property		240,000
Exemptions		
Annual 2007–08	3,000	
In consideration of marriage	5,000	
		8,000
Chargeable transfer		£232,000

	Gross £	Tax £	Net £
Cumulative total b/f	88,000	—	88,000
Chargeable transfer	237,333	5,333.00	232,000
See table at 41.1 2008.A2	£325,333	£5,333.00	£320,000
Tax payable by trustees as a consequence of A's death			£5,333

Notes to the example

(A)   The annual gifts exemption and the exemption of gifts in consideration of marriage apply if notice is given to the trustees by the donor within six months of the gift—see Deed of Release form earlier. This requirement seems to apply even though the gift is potentially exempt when made.

(B)   The tax payable is computed by reference to the transferor's cumulative total of chargeable transfers within the previous seven years, and the chargeable transfer forms part of his cumulative total carried forward.

(C)   The release of A's life interest to S in consideration of S's marriage is a PET because S's interest becomes a transitional serial interest (TSI) because a new settlement is created on or after 22 March 2006 but out of an old IIP which commenced before 22 March 2006 and the original interest came to an end prior to 6 April 2008 i.e. 1 July 2007 when S (stipulated as being 'B' in the legislation) became beneficially entitled to the interest in possession on 1 July 2007. S will benefit from the transitional rules as detailed in Example 4 below.

Example 4

A typical case to which both category 1 and category 2 TSIs will apply is where property is settled before 22 March 2006 upon trust for S for life, with remainder to S's spouse (or civil partner) for life. Say S dies before 6 April 2008 leaving a widow, her successor life interest will be a category 1 TSI within 43.1 above. But if S dies on or after 6 April 2008, that life interest will be a spouse/civil partner category 2 TSI within 43.1 above. It should be noted that were S to surrender his life interest before 6 April 2008 so that his wife's life interest then fell into possession, her life interest would be a category 1 TSI, whereas if S surrendered his life interest on or after 6 April 2008, his wife's successor life interest would not be a TSI since an interest in possession will only be a category 1 TSI when it falls into possession before 6 April 2008, and will only be a spouse/civil partner category 2 TSI when it falls into possession on the death of the holder of the previous interest.

Notes to the example

(A)   It does not seem to be a requirement of a category 2 spouse/civil partner TSI at 43.1 above (or indeed a category 1TSI) that the trust of the successor (or current) interest is declared or appointed before 22 March 2006. Therefore, where property is settled before 22 March 2006 upon trust for S for life remainder to S's children, and on or after 22 March 2006 but during S's lifetime and in exercise of a special power of appointment in the settlement deed, a life interest is appointed to S's widow, S's widow's life interest should be a category 1 or 2 TSI if and when it falls into possession following S's death.

(B)   One important consequence of a surviving spouse's or civil partner's interest in possession being a TSI is that the spouse/civil partner exemption from inheritance tax should apply on the death of the first spouse/civil partner to die to the extent of the settled property in which both interests in possession subsist.

43.4   ANTI-AVOIDANCE

Anti-avoidance provisions apply as follows.

(*a*)   Where there is a transaction between the trustees of a settlement and a person who is, or is connected with:

    (i)   the person beneficially entitled to an interest in the property, or

    (ii)   a person beneficially entitled to any other interest in that property or to any interest in any other property comprised in the settlement, or

    (iii)   a person for whose benefit any of the settled property may be applied,

and, as a result of the transaction, the value of the first-mentioned property is reduced, a corresponding part of the interest is deemed to come to an end (with consequent tax liability). An exception to this provision is where there would be no TRANSFER OF VALUE (49) if the trustees themselves were beneficially entitled to the property (e.g. an arm's length transaction with no gratuitous benefit intended). [*IHTA 1984, s 52(3)*].

(*b*)   Where the person acquires an interest in possession in settled property as a result of a disposition for a consideration in money or money's worth, the actuarial value of the interest acquired and not the value of the underlying assets supporting the interest, must be looked at to determine whether the consideration given equals the market value of the interest. [*IHTA 1984, s 49(2)*]. The difference between the consideration given and the actuarial value of the interest acquired is a transfer of value. In relation to transfers of value made, and other events occurring, before 17 March 1987, no transfer of value resulting from the giving of consideration so mentioned could be a POTENTIALLY EXEMPT TRANSFER (38). [*IHTA 1984, s 49(3); FA 1986, Sch 19 para 14; F(No 2)A 1987, s 96(4)*].

43.5   Chargeable transfer on termination of interest in possession where funds settled by a potentially exempt transfer.

Where the circumstances below apply, special anti-avoidance provisions apply to a chargeable transfer of a '*relevant interest*' i.e. a chargeable transfer made on the coming to an end of an interest in possession in settled property during the lifetime of a person beneficially entitled to it or on the death of a person beneficially entitled to an interest in possession in settled property. From 22 March 2006, in this latter case where special anti-avoidance provisions apply to a chargeable transfer of a '*relevant interest*' on the death of a person beneficially entitled to an interest in possession in settled property that interest is either a disabled person's interest or a transitional serial interest. See above and TRUSTS FOR DISABLED PERSONS (54). The circumstances are as follows.

(*a*)   The whole or part of the value transferred by the chargeable transfer is attributable to property in which the relevant interest subsisted and which became settled property in which there subsisted an interest in possession (whether the relevant interest or an earlier one) on the making by the settlor of a potentially exempt transfer after 16 March 1987 and within seven years of the chargeable transfer.

(*b*)   The settlor is alive at the time when the relevant interest comes to an end.

(c)   On the coming to an end of the relevant interest, any of the property in which the interest subsisted becomes settled property in which no 'qualifying interest in possession' subsists other than property to which *IHTA 1984, s 71* applies (accumulation and maintenance trusts). From 22 March 2006 references to *IHTA 1984, s 71* (accumulation and maintenance settlements) are omitted. For '*qualifying interests in possession*' see 44.1 SETTLEMENTS WITHOUT INTERESTS IN POSSESSION.

(d)   Within six months of the coming to the end of the relevant interest, any of the property in which that interest subsisted has neither become settled property in which a qualifying interest in possession subsists nor the subject of an accumulation and maintenance trust, but only in this latter case up until 21 March 2006, nor become property to which an individual is beneficially entitled.

The IHT chargeable in such circumstances is the greater of the tax calculated under the special rate of charge below and the tax calculated under the normal rules (i.e. as if the person entitled to the interest in possession has made a transfer of the trust property).

The special rate of charge is the aggregate of

(i)   IHT at lifetime rates on an *assumed chargeable transfer* equal to the value transferred by the relevant transfer (or where only part of the value is attributable to 'special rate property' that part of the value) and which is made at the time of the relevant transfer by an *assumed transferor* who has made aggregate chargeable transfers in the preceding seven years equal to the aggregate of the values of chargeable transfers made by the settlor in the seven years ending with the date of the settlor's potentially exempt transfer; and

(ii)   IHT, if any, that would otherwise have been chargeable on the value transferred by the relevant transfer and which is attributable to the value of the property other than the special rate property.

The tax under (i) above is treated as tax attributable to the value of the settled property in which the relevant interest subsisted.

'*Special rate property*' means the property in which the relevant interest subsisted or, where any part of that property does not fall within (a) above or does not become settled property of the kind mentioned in (c) above, so much of that property as appears to the Board (or, on appeal, the Special Commissioners) to be just and reasonable.

The death of the settlor after the chargeable transfer cannot increase the tax chargeable unless, at the time of the transfer, the tax under the special rule is greater than the tax under the normal rules.

The death of the person beneficially entitled to the relevant interest in possession after the chargeable transfer cannot increase the tax chargeable unless, at the time of the transfer, the tax under the normal rules is greater than the tax under the special rules.

Where two or more previous chargeable transfers within these provisions have been made during the period of seven years ending on the date of the current transfer and the settlor is the same in each case, on calculating the tax on the current transfer, the value relating to the previous transfer or transfers attributable to the value of property which was special rate property in relation to those transfers is deemed to be the value of a chargeable transfer of equivalent value made by the settlor immediately before the potentially exempt transfer. This applies whether or not the transfers relate to the same settlement. [*IHTA 1984, ss 54A, 54B; F(No 2)A 1987, s 96, Sch 7 para 1; FA 2006, Sch 20 para 16; Sch 26 Part 6*].

Example 5

B transferred £100,000 on 1 October 2003 into an interest in possession trust of which his brother C is the life tenant. On 31 August 2007, C released his life interest, then valued at £157,000, to a discretionary settlement in favour of his children. B's cumulative chargeable transfers in the last seven years amounted to £230,000. B was still alive on 31 August 2007, at which date C's cumulative chargeable transfers in the last seven years amounted to £155,000 and he (C) had not used his annual exemptions for 2007/08 and 2006/07. See table at 41.1 2007.A1 RATES OF TAX.

The transfer by B on 1 October 2003 is a potentially exempt transfer which will not become chargeable unless B dies before 1 October 2010.

The transfer by C is a chargeable lifetime transfer, which is charged at lifetime rates, i.e. one half of death rates, taking into account cumulative transfers of £155,000. If, however, a higher tax liability would be produced by substituting B's cumulative transfers at the time of his PET for those of C at the time of his transfer, this takes precedence over the normal calculation.

Normal calculation

	£	£
Value transferred by C on 31 August 2007		157,000
Deduct annual exemption 2007/08	3,000	
annual exemption 2006/07	3,000	6,000
		£151,000

IHT on £151,000 is charged in the band £155,001 to £306,000.

	£
£155,001–300,000	Nil
£300,001–306,000 at 20%	1,200
	£1,200

Calculation under Section 54A

Value transferred by C on 31 August 2007, after exemptions as above	£151,000

IHT on £151,000 is charged in the band £230,001 to £381,000.

£230,001–300,000	Nil
£300,001–381,000 at 20%	£16,200

IHT payable is therefore £16,200.

Notes to the example

(A)   C's cumulative chargeable transfers following the gift in August 2007 will be £306,000 (*not* £381,000).

(B)   If B dies after 31 August 2007 and before 1 October 2010, the IHT liability of £16,200 may increase. For example, B's cumulative chargeable transfers at 1 October 2003 may increase due to his having made other PETs prior to that date but within seven years of death. If the IHT liability had been determined under normal rules because this produced a liability greater than that produced by a calculation under *IHTA 1984, s 54A*, such liability could not be affected by the death of B. [*IHTA 1984, s 54B(1)*].

44 Settlements without Interests in Possession

Cross-references. See 3 ACCUMULATION AND MAINTENANCE TRUSTS; 11 CHARITIES; 26 INTEREST IN POSSESSION for meaning of interest in possession; 33.6 NATIONAL HERITAGE for settlements of such property and 33.11 for maintenance funds for historic buildings; 39 PROTECTIVE TRUSTS; 42 SETTLEMENTS—GENERAL for definitions of settlement and settlor; 53 TRUSTS FOR BEREAVED MINORS; 54 TRUSTS FOR DISABLED PERSONS; 55 TRUSTS FOR EMPLOYEES; 59 WORKING CASE STUDY.

Simon's Direct Tax Service, parts I5.3, I5.4.

Other Sources. HMRC CTO Leaflet IHT 16 'Settled property'; Foster, part E3–4.

44.1 GENERAL

Separate charging provisions apply to settlements without interests in possession. For CTT purposes, the original provisions were substantially incorporated in *FA 1975, Sch 5 paras 6–14* but this legislation was superseded, in relation to events after 8 March 1982, by revised provisions in *IHTA 1984, ss 58–69, 80–85*.

For transfers and events occurring after 17 March 1986, amendments are made to the rules governing the calculation of tax to incorporate the reduction in the cumulation period for the settlor's chargeable transfers before the commencement of the settlement to seven from ten years.

From 22 March 2006 any new trusts that are set up *inter vivos* or on death which are trust other than:

- trusts created by will or intestacy whereby the life interest created on death is for the benefit of a life tenant whose interest cannot be replaced i.e. IPDI or a TSI (see 43.1 SETTLEMENTS WITH INTERESTS IN POSSESSION);

- accumulation and maintenance trusts set up for bereaved minor whose full entitlement vests at the age of 25 years and certain existing A & M trusts up until 6 April 2008 (see 3.2 ACCUMULATION AND MAINTENANCE TRUSTS); or

- trusts set up for disabled persons (see 54 TRUSTS FOR DISABLED PERSONS)

are to be subject to an IHT charge of up to 6% on the value of the assets in the trust every tenth anniversary. In addition, there will also be an exit charge of up to 6% on the value of capital distributions to beneficiaries in line with 44.3 and 44.9–44.12 below.

There is a charge to IHT (under the ordinary rules, see INTRODUCTION AND BASIC PRINCIPLES (1)) when property enters a settlement without an interest in possession with the exception of certain lifetime transfers into accumulation and maintenance trusts and trusts for the disabled which are POTENTIALLY EXEMPT TRANSFERS (38). There is also a ten-yearly charge on property remaining in the settlement and a proportionate charge to tax, based on the time that has elapsed since the date of settlement or the last full ten-year charge, on property leaving the settlement. For this treatment of existing trusts without interest in possession existing before 22 March 2006 and those created after that date see below.

The legislation refers to a 'principal charge to tax at the ten-year anniversary' and a 'principal charge to tax at other times'. In this chapter, the terms 'ten-year anniversary charge' and 'proportionate charge' have been adopted.

Certain special trusts are singled out for favourable treatment, principally accumulation and maintenance trusts, charitable trusts, maintenance funds for historic buildings, employee trusts, protective trusts, trusts for bereaved minors and trusts for the disabled. This is achieved by excluding property held on such trusts from the definition of 'relevant property'. (See 44.2 below.) These trusts are dealt with in other chapters. See the cross-references at the beginning of this chapter.

Qualifying interest in possession. The special charging rules apply to relevant property which is settled property in which there is no qualifying interest in possession. 'Interest in possession' is not defined in the IHT legislation and its interpretation is a matter of general law as applicable in the context of IHT. See 26 INTEREST IN POSSESSION. A '*qualifying interest in possession*', for the purposes of the special charging rules, means an interest in possession to which

(*a*)   an *individual* is beneficially entitled, or

(*b*)   a *company* is beneficially entitled provided

    (i)   that the business of the company consists wholly or mainly in the acquisition of interests in settled property, and

    (ii)   that the company has acquired the interest for full consideration in money or money's worth from an individual who was beneficially entitled to the interest.

'*Individual*' includes participators of a close company which is entitled to an interest in possession. See 12.7 CLOSE COMPANIES for full details.

Where the acquisition under (*b*)(ii) was before 14 March 1975, the condition in (*b*)(i) above is satisfied if the business of the company was as described at the time of the acquisition or the company has permission to carry on contracts of long term insurance under the *Financial Services and Markets Act 2000, Part 4*. 'Contracts of long term' means contracts which fall within *Financial Services and Markets Act 2000 (Regulated Activities) Order 2001, SI 2001/544, Sch 1, Part II*. Also, if it carries on, through a branch or agency in the United Kingdom, the whole or any part of any long term business which it is authorised to carry on by an authorisation granted outside the UK for the purposes of the first long term insurance Directive. [*IHTA 1984, s 59; FA 1995, s 52(4)(5)*].

44.2   KEY CONCEPTS

Relevant property. The provisions impose a charge to tax on relevant property i.e. settled property in which there is no qualifying interest in possession, other than

(*a*)   property held for charitable purposes only, whether for a limited time or otherwise (see 11 CHARITIES),

(*b*)   property held in ACCUMULATION AND MAINTENANCE TRUSTS (3), including from 22 March 2006, TRUSTS FOR BEREAVED MINORS (53) and 'age 18–25 trusts',

(*c*)   property held on discretionary trusts arising on the forfeiture of a protective life interest before 12 April 1978 (see 39 PROTECTIVE TRUSTS),

(*d*)   property held on TRUSTS FOR DISABLED PERSONS (54) settled before 10 March 1981,

(*e*)   property held in TRUSTS FOR EMPLOYEES (55), including property held on SETTLEMENTS WITH INTERESTS IN POSSESSION (43) which are settled on or after 22 March 2006 which are not an IPDI, a TSI or a disabled person's interest,

(*f*)   property held in approved maintenance funds for historic buildings (see 33.11 NATIONAL HERITAGE),

(*g*)   property held in PENSION SCHEMES (37) (but not benefits which, having become payable under a fund or scheme, become comprised in a settlement), (*h*) property comprised in a trade or professional compensation fund i.e. any fund, maintained or administered by a representative association of persons carrying on a trade or profession, the only or main objects of which are compensation for, or relief of, losses or hardship that, through the default (or alleged default) of persons carrying on the trade or profession or their agents or servants, are incurred or likely to be incurred by others,

(*j*) EXCLUDED PROPERTY (20),

(*k*) a sum received in respect of and assets representing (but not income or gains arising from them) a payment made in lieu of pool betting duty for football ground improvements or to support games etc. and,

(*l*) property forming part of a premiums trust fund or ancillary trust fund of a corporate member of Lloyd's,

(*m*) property held on SETTLEMENTS WITH INTERESTS IN POSSESSION (43) which are settled on or after 22 March 2006 which are an IPDI or a TSI,

(*n*) property held on SETTLEMENTS WITH INTERESTS IN POSSESSION (43) which are settled on or after 22 March 2006 whereby CLOSE COMPANIES (12) acquired the interest for full consideration in money or money's worth from and individual who was beneficially entitled to it and that acquired entitlement was not an IPDI or a TSI,

(*p*) property applied to pay a lump sum death benefit within *FA 2004, s 168(1)* (registered pension scheme lump sum death benefits) from the date of death of the scheme member to the date when the payment is made by the pension scheme,

(*q*) property held in an *ICTA 1988, s 615(3)* scheme where the lump sum benefit is paid out within two years beginning with the earlier of the:

  (a) date of notification to the scheme trustees, or persons having control of the scheme, of the scheme member's death, or

  (b) day on which the trustees, or persons having control of the scheme, could reasonably be expected to know of the scheme member's death.

[*IHTA 1984, s 58(1)(1A)(1B)(1C),(2),(2A); FA 1990, s 126(1)(5); FA 1991, s 121(1)(4); FA 1994, s 248; FA 2006, Sch 20 para 19; FA 2007, Sch 20 paras 20, 24(9)*].

See the appropriate chapters for events giving rise to a charge to tax.

Treatment of income. In respect of all new cases after 10 November 1986 and any existing cases where the tax liability has not been settled by that date, HMRC takes the view that

(*a*) *undistributed* and *unaccumulated* income should not be treated as a taxable trust asset; and

(*b*) for the purposes of determining the rate of charge on *accumulated income*, the income should be treated as becoming a taxable asset of the trust on the date when the accumulation is made.

Previously, the view had been taken that *undistributed* and *unaccumulated* income was a taxable trust asset in the hands of the trustees. For the purposes of determining the rate of charge, income (whether or not accumulated) was regarded as having been comprised in the trust for as long as the original trust property from which the income or accumulation was derived. (See SP 8/86 at 25 HMRC STATEMENTS OF PRACTICE).

Related settlements. These are brought into account when considering the rate at which tax is charged. Two settlements are related only if they have the same settlor and they commenced on the same day. If, however, the property in either settlement is held for charitable purposes only without limit of time (defined by date or otherwise) the settlements will not be related. [*IHTA 1984, s 62*]. The concept of related settlements is only relevant to settlements commencing after 26 March 1974.

Commencement of a settlement is the time when property first becomes comprised in the settlement. [*IHTA 1984, s 60*].

Property becoming comprised in a settlement in pursuance of a will or intestacy is treated for the purposes of the rules on settlements without interests in possession, *IHTA 1984, Part III, Ch III*, as having become so comprised on the death of the testator or intestate. [*IHTA 1984, s 83*].

44.3   **TEN-YEAR ANNIVERSARY CHARGE**

A charge to tax arises if, immediately before the ten-year anniversary of a settlement, all or any part of the settled property is relevant property (see 44.2 above). Tax is calculated on the value of the relevant property at that time. See *Henderson & Henderson (Black's Trustees) v CIR, Sp C November 2000, Sp C 263; Rysaffe Trustee Co (CI) Ltd v CIR [2001] STC SCD 225 Sp C 290; CA [2003] EWCA Civ 356*. [*IHTA 1984, s 64*]. See 44.2 above for the treatment of income. All Trustees must sign Form IHT 101 'Account of a Chargeable Event' relating to the ten-year anniversary charge: note 10 of IHT 111.

'Ten-year anniversary' is the tenth anniversary of the commencement of the settlement (see 44.2 above) and subsequent anniversaries at ten-yearly intervals but where a settlor or his spouse or civil partner, widow or widower or surviving civil partner is beneficially entitled to an interest in possession in property immediately after it becomes comprised in a settlement, and as a result of *IHTA 1984, s 80* (see 44.15 below) the property or part is treated as becoming comprised in a separate settlement at the time when neither of those persons are so entitled, the ten-year anniversaries are the dates that are (or would be apart from that *section*) the anniversaries of the original settlement. No date falling before 1 April 1983 could be a ten-year anniversary. Where the first ten-year anniversary would otherwise have fallen in the year ending 31 March 1984 it was postponed to 1 April 1984 where the circumstances were as in *IHTA 1984, s 61(3)* (chargeable event in year ending 31 March 1984 resulting from court proceedings) (but without affecting the dates of later anniversaries). [*IHTA 1984, s 61*]. See also IHT 16 'Settled property', p 12.

44.4   **Rate of ten-year anniversary charge.** The rate at which the charge is levied depends upon whether a settlement commenced before, or on or after, 27 March 1974.

Where a settlement commenced before 27 March 1974, the rate is determined by reference to the settlement's cumulative transfers in the ten years preceding the anniversary.

Where a settlement commenced on or after 27 March 1974, the rate is determined by reference to the settlor's cumulative transfers in the seven years preceding the date on which the settlement commenced, as well as the settlement's cumulative transfers in the ten years preceding the anniversary.

Tax is calculated using lifetime Tables at the following rates

(*a*)   where the whole of the relevant property has been comprised in the settlement throughout the ten-year period ending immediately before the ten-year anniversary, at 30% of the effective rate (see 44.5 and 44.7 below),

(*b*)   and where the whole or part of the relevant property was not relevant property or was not comprised in the settlement throughout the ten years ending immediately before the ten-year anniversary, at 30% of the effective rate reduced by one-fortieth for each successive 'quarter' in the ten-year period which expired before the property became, or last became, relevant property.

The '*effective rate*' is the rate found by expressing the tax chargeable as a percentage of the amount on which tax is charged on an assumed chargeable transfer by an assumed transferor. See 44.5 below. [*IHTA 1984, s 66(1)(2)*]. See IHT 16, p 13.

44.5 Settlements without Interests in Possession

'*Quarter*' means a period of three months. [*IHTA 1984, s 63*].

44.5 **Post-26 March 1974 settlements. The effective rate for post-26 March 1974 settlements** is defined as the rate at which tax would be charged on

(*a*)   an *assumed chargeable transfer* equal to the aggregate of

    (i)   the value of the relevant property immediately before the ten-year anniversary (see 44.2 above for the treatment of income), and

    (ii)   the value immediately after it became comprised in the settlement of any property which was not then relevant property and has not subsequently become relevant property while remaining in the settlement, and

    (iii)   the value immediately after a related settlement (see 44.2 above) commenced of any property comprised in it,

(*b*)   made immediately before the ten-year anniversary by an *assumed transferor* who, subject to the adjustment for added property etc. in 44.8 below, has made chargeable transfers in the preceding seven years equal to the aggregate of

    (i)   the values of chargeable transfers made by the settlor in the seven years ending with the day on which the settlement commenced (but disregarding transfers made on that day or before 27 March 1974), and

    (ii)   the amounts on which any proportionate charges (see 44.9 below) have been imposed in the ten years before the anniversary concerned, and

    (iii)   in relation to the first ten-year anniversary of a settlement which commenced after 26 March 1974 and before 9 March 1982, the amounts of any distribution payments made in that period (or in some circumstances later) and within ten years before that anniversary.

[*IHTA 1984, s 66(3)–(6); FA 1986, Sch 19 para 16*].

44.6   *Post-26 March 1974 settlements—Examples.*

Example 1

This example is a continuation of *Example 1* from 43.1 SETTLEMENTS WITH INTERESTS IN POSSESSION. X, who is married to L (his second wife), dies on 12 January 2008 having already made gifts on 21 May 2005 of £281,000 utilising his available annual exemptions and nil rate band. By his will he left his assets to his second wife L in trust for life and then on her death to his son S now aged 30.

L dies on 8 January 2011 when the trust assets originally passed on to her in trust are passed to her step-son S. The terms of the trust are that the assets, now valued at £610,000, are to be held on relevant property trusts with overriding powers to apply capital and accumulated income to the beneficiary S. In consequence therefore on 12 January 2018, being the first ten yearly anniversary charge date, the value of the settlement is £640,000 and the IHT threshold is, say, £455,000.

The trustees made the following advances (gross) to beneficiary S on 8 January 2026 of £180,000.

	£
Assumed chargeable transfer	
Value of relevant property on 12.1.2018	640,000
Value of property in related settlements	—
	640,000
Assumed cumulative total in 7 years to 12 January 2008	275,000
	£915,000
IHT at lifetime rates	£92,000

Effective rate

$$\frac{92,000}{640,000} = 14.375\%$$

Rate of ten-year anniversary charge:
$^3/_{10} \times 14.375\% = 4.3125\%$

Ten-year anniversary charge: $^{28}/_{40} \times 4.3125\% \times £640,000$	£19,320

(*a*) *Appointment on 8 January 2026*
Effective rate

$$\frac{92,000}{640,000} = 14.375\%$$

No. of complete successive quarters between 12.1.2018
and 8.1.2026 = 31
Proportionate charge:
$14.375\% \times \, ^3/_{10} = 4.3125\%$

$4.3125\% \times \, ^{31}/_{40} \times £180,000$	£6,016

Notes to the example

(A)   The first ten-year anniversary arises on the tenth anniversary when the settlement commenced, this being the date on which property first became comprised in the settlement. [*IHTA 1984, s 60*]. When property is left on will trust the date of death is the commencement of the settlement i.e. 12 January 2008. Even though the property is held on IIP settlement for the wife the actual date of the commencement is still taken as 12 January 2008 when calculating any subsequent ten-yearly charges appropriately apportioned for the number of complete quarters that have elapsed since L's death on 8 January 2011 to the ten-year anniversary on 12 January 2018. After calculating the deemed chargeable transfer and the deemed cumulative total after deducting the nil rate band the effective lifetime rate of 20% is used to calculate the tax due.

(B)   The exit charge between the ten-year anniversaries takes the rate charged on the last ten-year charge and then scales the percentage rate down by reference to the number of complete quarters which have elapsed since the last charge on 12 January 2018 and the date of the exit charge event on 8 January 2026 i.e. 31 quarters.

Example 2

On 22 May 1997, M, who had already used all available exemptions, settled property worth £56,000 on each of two settlements. One settlement is discretionary and the other is subject to a life interest. By 22 May 2007, the discretionary settlement is valued at £252,000, ignoring assets representing undistributed income.

Assuming no prior proportionate charge to tax or distribution payment, the first ten-year anniversary charge will be

	£
Assumed chargeable transfer	
Value of relevant property on 22.5.2007	252,000
Value of property in related settlement on 22.5.97	56,000
	308,000
Assumed cumulative total	—
	£308,000
IHT at lifetime rates	£1,600

Effective rate

$$\frac{1,600}{308,000} = 0.51948\%$$

Rate of ten-year anniversary charge:
$^3/_{10} \times 0.51948\% = 0.155844\%$

Ten-year anniversary charge: $0.155844\% \times £252,000$ £393

Example 3

Assume the same facts as in example 2 above except that the settlement subject to a life interest was made on 21 May 1997.

	£
Assumed chargeable transfer	
Value of relevant property on 22.5.2007	252,000
Assumed cumulative total	—
Value of chargeable transfers made by settlor in seven years to 22.5.97	56,000
	£308,000
IHT at lifetime rates	£1,600

Effective rate $\dfrac{1,600}{252,000} = 0.63492\%$

Rate of ten-year anniversary charge: $^3/_{10} \times 0.63492\% = 0.190476\%$
Ten-year anniversary charge: $0.190476\% \times £252,000$ £480

Example 4

Assume the facts in example 2 above except that the settlement subject to a life interest was made on 23 May 1996.

	£
Assumed chargeable transfer (as (2) above)	252,000
Assumed cumulative total	—
	252,000
IHT at lifetime rates	Nil
Ten-year anniversary charge	Nil

Example 5

On 22 May 1997, M's brother N, who had already used all available exemptions, settled £67,000. One half of the settlement was discretionary and the other half was subject to a life interest. On 22 May 2001, the life tenant dies and all the property of the trust becomes held on discretionary trusts. By 22 May 2007, the settlement is valued as follows.

Original discretionary fund, ignoring net assets representing undistributed income	£97,000
Funds previously subject to a life interest, ignoring net assets representing subsequent undistributed income	£198,000

The first ten-year anniversary charge will be:

Assumed chargeable transfer	
Value of relevant property on 22.5.2007	310,000
Assumed cumulative total	—
	£310,000
IHT at lifetime rates	£2,000
Effective rate	

$$\frac{2,000}{310,000} = 0.64516\%$$

Rate of ten-year anniversary charge: $^3/_{10} \times 0.64516\% = 0.193548\%$

Ten-year anniversary charge:

$0.193548\% \times £97,000$	188
$^{24}/_{40} \times 0.193548\% \times £198,000$	230
	£418

44.7   **Pre-27 March 1974 settlements. The effective rate for pre-27 March 1974 settlements** is defined as the rate at which tax would be charged

(*a*)   on an *assumed chargeable transfer* equal to the value of the relevant property immediately before the ten-year anniversary

(*b*)   made immediately before that anniversary by an *assumed transferor* who, subject to the adjustments for added property etc. in 44.8 below, has made chargeable transfers in the preceding seven years equal to the aggregate of

(i)   the amounts on which any proportionate charges (see 44.9 below) have been imposed in the ten years before the anniversary concerned, and

(ii)   in relation to the first ten-year anniversary, the amount of any distribution payment made out of the settled property before 9 March 1982 (or in some circumstances later) and within ten years before that anniversary.

44.7 Settlements without Interests in Possession

[*IHTA 1984, s 66(3)–(6); FA 1986, Sch 19 para 16*].

See 44.2 above for the treatment of undistributed or unaccumulated income.

Example

On 1 June 1971 T settled property on discretionary trusts. The trustees made the following advances (gross) to beneficiaries:

1.1.74	H	£10,000
1.1.77	B	£20,000
1.1.82	C	£60,000
1.1.88	D	£40,000
1.1.94	E	£80,000

On 1 June 1991 the settled property was valued at £175,000 and on 1 June 2001 £180,000.

1 June 1991 Ten-year anniversary charge

		£	£
Assumed chargeable transfer			
Value of relevant property			£175,000
Assumed transferor's cumulative total			
(i) Aggregate of distribution payments made between 1 June 1981 and 8 March 1982		60,000	
(ii) Aggregate of amounts on which proportionate charge arises between 9 March 1982 and 1 June 1991		40,000	£100,000

	Gross	Tax
	£	£
Assumed cumulative total	100,000	—
Assumed chargeable transfer	175,000	27,000
	£275,000	£27,000

Effective rate of tax =

$$\frac{27,000}{175,000} \times 100 = 15.429\%$$

Ten-year anniversary charge

The IHT payable is at 30% of the effective rate on the relevant property.

IHT payable = 30% × 15.429% × £175,000 = £8,100

1 June 2001 Ten-year anniversary charge

Assumed chargeable transfer		£180,000
Value of relevant property		
Assumed transferor's cumulative total		£80,000

Aggregate of amount on which proportionate charge arises between 1 June 1991 and 1 June 2001

	Gross £	Tax £
Assumed cumulative total	80,000	—
Assumed chargeable transfer	180,000	3,600
	£260,000	£3,600

Effective rate of tax =

$$\frac{3,600}{180,000} \times 100 \ = \ 2\%$$

Ten-year anniversary charge

The IHT payable is at 30% of the effective rate on the relevant property.

IHT payable = 30% × 2% × £180,000 = £1,080

44.8   **Adjustments for added property, etc.** The previous chargeable transfers of the assumed transferor in 44.5(*b*) and 44.7(*b*) above are adjusted in the following circumstances.

(*a*)   Where after the settlement commenced and after 8 March 1982, but before the ten-year anniversary concerned, the settlor makes a chargeable transfer which increases the *value* of the property in the settlement, the aggregate of the values of chargeable transfers made by the settlor in the seven years before the chargeable transfer in question is

(i)   if the settlement commenced after 26 March 1974, substituted for 44.5(*b*)(i) above if greater than that figure, and

(ii)   if the settlement commenced before 27 March 1974, added to the aggregate at 44.7(*b*) above.

For the purposes of both (i) and (ii) above, transfers made on the same day as the chargeable transfer in question are disregarded and any values attributable to property brought into account under 44.5(*a*) or 44.7(*a*) above, and any amounts on which proportionate charges have been imposed and which are already taken into account in 44.5(*b*)(ii) or 44.7(*b*)(i) above are excluded. Where the settlor makes two or more such chargeable transfers in the period, the transfer which gives rise to the highest aggregate is used.

It is immaterial whether the *amount* as well as the *value* of the property in the settlement is increased as a result of the chargeable transfer. Where, however, the *amount* of the property is not increased, these provisions will not apply if the transfer was not primarily intended to increase the value of the settled property and it did not increase that value immediately after the transfer by more than 5% of its value immediately before the transfer.

[IHTA 1984, s 67(1)–(5); FA 1986, Sch 19 para 17].

(*b*) Where property subject to the ten-year anniversary charge has previously, on ceasing to be relevant property within the preceding ten years, been subject to a proportionate charge (see 44.9 below), the aggregate of items at 44.5(*b*) and 44.7(*b*) above is reduced by the lesser of the amount subject to the proportionate charge *and* the value of the relevant property at the ten-year anniversary. Where only a part of the settled property was previously subject to the proportionate charge, the reduction is based on so much of the amounts mentioned above as is attributable to the part in question. If there were two or more occasions in the preceding ten years when the property was subject to a proportionate charge, the reduction above applies to each occasion. *[IHTA 1984, s 67(6)(7)]*.

44.9 CHARGE AT OTHER TIMES (THE PROPORTIONATE CHARGE)

A charge to tax arises

(*a*) where property comprised in a settlement, or any part, ceases to be relevant property (see 44.2 above) whether because it ceases to be comprised in the settlement or otherwise, and

(*b*) where (*a*) does not apply, where the trustees of the settlement make a disposition which reduces the value of the relevant property. '*Disposition*' includes an omission to exercise a right (unless not deliberate) which is treated as made at the latest time that the right could be exercised.

See 12.4 CLOSE COMPANIES for details of when a charge arises on a close company's transfer of value being apportioned to trustees.

Tax is charged on the amount by which the value of the relevant property is reduced as a result of the chargeable event (i.e. the loss to donor principle) grossed-up where the settlement pays the tax.

[IHTA 1984, s 65(1)(2)(9)].

44.10 Exceptions from charge. No charge arises

(i) if, under 44.9(*b*) above, the trustees do not intend to confer gratuitous benefit and either the transaction is at arm's length between persons not connected with each other (see 13 CONNECTED PERSONS) or is such as might be expected in such a transaction (see 49.2(*a*) TRANSFER OF VALUE), or

(ii) if, under 44.9(*b*) above, the disposition is a grant of tenancy of agricultural property in the UK, Channel Islands or Isle of Man for use for agricultural purposes made for full consideration in money or money's worth, or

(iii) on the payment of costs or expenses so far as they are fairly attributable to relevant property, or

(iv) where any payment is, or will be, income for income tax purposes of any person (or, in the case of a person not resident in the UK, would be if he were so resident), or

(v) in respect of a liability to make a payment under (iii) or (iv) above, or

(vi) if the chargeable event occurs in the three month period beginning with either the day on which the settlement commenced or a ten-year anniversary (see 44.3 above), or

(vii) if the settlor was domiciled outside the UK at the time the settlement was made, and by virtue of *IHTA 1984, s 48(3)(a)* relevant property comprised in the settlement becomes excluded property by ceasing to be situated in the UK; but see 44.15 below where the settlor or his spouse or civil partner retains an interest in the settlement and 44.16 below where property moves between settlements, or

(viii) if the settlor was domiciled outside the UK at the time the settlement was made and property comprised in the settlement is invested in exempt Government securities and becomes excluded property by virtue of *IHTA 1984, s 48(4)(b)* because all known beneficiaries are of a description specified in the condition in question. The 'condition in question' is usually that referred to in *FA (No 2) 1931, s 22* and modified by *FA 1940, s 60* relating to questions of domicile and ordinary residence but can now be references to residence abroad. [*IHTA 1984, s 48(4); FA 1996, s 154, Sch 28 para 8*]. See 20.4 EXCLUDED PROPERTY. The special provisions relating to domicile in *IHTA 1984, s 267* (see 17.3 DOMICILE) are disregarded. But see 44.15 below where the settlor or his spouse or civil partner retain an interest in the settlement and 44.16 below where property moves between settlements, or

(ix) if the property becomes held for charitable purposes only without limit of time *or* the property of a qualifying political party *or* national body mentioned in *IHTA 1984, Sch 3; or* the subject of a gift for public benefit (see 21.3, 21.5–21.7 EXEMPT TRANSFERS).

(x) if a reversionary interest, that is a future entitlement to trust assets currently subject to another interest e.g. a life interest in favour of someone else, where the property comprising in the trust is a holding in an authorised unit trust (AUT) and/or a share in an open-ended investment company (OEIC) where the reversioner to that property is non-UK domiciled. This assists, for instance, non-UK domiciled individuals who have a reversionary interest but die before that interest falls in and will no longer have the threat of an IHT charge in those particular circumstances. [*IHTA 1984, s 48(3A)(b) as inserted by FA 2003, s 186*].

See IHT 16 'Settled property', p 15 for exceptions above.

[*IHTA 1984, ss 65(4)–(8), 76*].

44.11 **Pre-ten-year anniversary charge. Rate of proportionate charge before** the first ten-year anniversary. On an occasion of charge before the first ten-year anniversary (see 44.3 above) the rate depends upon whether the settlement commenced before, or on or after, 27 March 1974.

Where a settlement commenced before 27 March 1974, the rate is calculated by reference to the settlement's own cumulative transfers in the preceding ten years.

Where a settlement commenced after 26 March 1974, the rate is determined by reference to the settlor's chargeable transfers in the seven years preceding the commencement of the settlement. [*IHTA 1984, ss 65(3), 68*].

44.12 **Post-26 March 1974 settlements tax calculation. The rate of tax for post-26 March 1974 settlements** is the 'appropriate fraction' of the 'effective rate' at which tax would be charged using lifetime rates,

(a) on an *assumed chargeable transfer* equal to the aggregate of

(i) the value of property comprised in the settlement immediately after it commenced (see 44.2 above), and

(ii) the value of any property comprised in a related settlement (see 44.2 above) immediately after its commencement and

(iii) the value, immediately after it became comprised in a settlement, of any property which became so comprised after the settlement commenced and before the occasion of charge (whether or not it has remained so comprised)

44.12 Settlements without Interests in Possession

(b) made at the time the proportionate charge arises by an *assumed transferor* who in the seven years ending with the day of the occasion to charge had aggregate chargeable transfers equal to those made by the settlor in the seven years ending with the day on which the settlement commenced (but excluding any transfers made on that day).

The '*effective rate*' is the rate found by expressing the tax chargeable as a percentage of the amount on which it is charged.

The '*appropriate fraction*' is three-tenths multiplied by so many fortieths as there are complete successive quarters in the period beginning with the day on which the settlement commenced and ending with the day before the occasion of charge. However, where the whole or part of the amount on which tax is charged was not relevant property or was not comprised in the settlement throughout that period, no quarter which expires before the day on which the property became, or last became, relevant property comprised in the settlement is counted except that if that day fell in the same quarter as that in which the period ends, that quarter is counted whether complete or not.

'*Quarter*' is a period of three months. [*IHTA 1984, ss 63, 68*].

See 44.2 above for the treatment of undistributed or unaccumulated income.

Example

On 19 May 1998, R settled £169,000 on discretionary trusts. He had previously made cumulative chargeable transfers of £142,000 in the previous seven years and had already used all available exemptions. On 18 July 2007, the trustees appoint £180,000 to beneficiaries absolutely (with the beneficiaries paying the IHT), and on 31 December 2007 appoint the remaining funds, then valued at £60,000 (ignoring assets representing undistributed income), to beneficiary C absolutely (who again pays the tax). The proportionate charges will be:

(a) 18 July 2007

	£
Assumed chargeable transfer	
Value of property in settlement at 19.5.98	169,000
Assumed cumulative total	
Aggregate chargeable transfers by settlor in seven years to 19.5.98	142,000
	£311,000
IHT at lifetime rates on £311,000	2,200
Deduct IHT at lifetime rates on £142,000	—
IHT on assumed chargeable transfer	£2,200

Effective rate

$$\frac{2,200}{169,000} = 1.30177\%$$

No. of complete successive quarters between 19.5.98 and 17.7.07 = 36

Proportionate charge:

1.30177% × ³/₁₀ × ³⁶/₄₀ × £180,000	£633

(*b*) *31 December 2007*
Effective rate (as above) = 1.30177%
No. of complete successive quarters between 19.5.98
and 30.12.07 = 38
Proportionate charge:
1.30177% × ³⁄₁₀ × ³⁸⁄₄₀ × £60,000   £223

44.13   **The rate of tax for pre-27 March 1974 settlements** is 30% of the 'effective rate' at which tax would be charged, using lifetime rates,

(*a*)   on an *assumed chargeable transfer* equal to the amount on which the proportionate charge is calculated (see 44.9 above)

(*b*)   which is made at the time of the proportionate charge by an *assumed transferor* who in the seven years ending with the day of the occasion of charge has made aggregate chargeable transfers equal to the aggregate of

(i)   any amounts on which any proportionate charges have previously been imposed in the period of ten years ending with that day, and

(ii)   any distribution payments made out of the settled property after 26 March 1974 and before 9 March 1982 (or in some circumstances later), and within that ten-year period.

The '*effective rate*' is the rate found by expressing the tax chargeable as a percentage of the amount on which it is charged.

[*IHTA 1984, s 68; FA 1986, Sch 19 para 18*].

See 44.2 above for the treatment of undistributed or unaccumulated income.

44.14   **Rate of the proportionate charge between ten-year anniversaries.** Where an occasion of charge arises following one or more ten-year anniversaries, tax is calculated as follows.

(*a*)   The rate of tax is, subject to (*b*) below, the 'appropriate fraction' of the rate charged at the most recent ten-year anniversary ignoring any reduction made under 44.4(*b*) above.

(*b*)   If, at any time before the occasion of charge and on or after the most recent ten-year anniversary

(i)   property becomes comprised in the settlement; or

(ii)   property which was comprised in the settlement immediately before that anniversary, but was not then relevant property (see 44.2 above) has become relevant property

then, whether or not the property has remained comprised in the settlement or has remained relevant property, the rate of tax is the appropriate fraction of the rate at which tax would have been charged at the most recent ten-year anniversary (see 44.4–44.8 above) if the property under (i) or (ii) above had then been relevant property comprised in the settlement. For these purposes, any property under (i) above which was relevant property immediately after it became comprised in the settlement or was not then, and has not subsequently become, relevant property while remaining comprised in the settlement, is included at its value immediately after becoming comprised in the settlement. All other property is included at its value when it became, or last became, relevant property.

44.15 Settlements without Interests in Possession

The '*appropriate fraction*' is so many fortieths as there are complete successive quarters in the period beginning with the most recent ten-year anniversary and ending with the day before the occasion to charge. Where the whole or part of the property on which tax is charged was not relevant property, or was not comprised in the settlement, throughout that period, no quarter which expired before the day on which the property became or last became relevant property comprised in the settlement is counted except that if that day fell in the same quarter as that in which the period ends, that quarter is counted whether or not complete.

[*IHTA 1984, ss 68(3), 69*].

Where the most recent ten-year anniversary fell before 18 March 1986 the rate at which tax was charged must be recalculated for the purposes of the proportionate charge as if the amendments made by *FA 1986, Sch 19* had then been in force i.e. as if the provision outlined in 44.4 to 44.8 above applied at that time. [*FA 1986, Sch 19 para 43*].

See 44.2 above for the treatment of undistributed or unaccumulated income.

Reduction of rates. For the purposes of (*a*) and (*b*) above, where there have been one or more substitutions of new Tables of rates between the most recent ten-year anniversary and the occasion of charge, the latest Table of rates is to be used in calculating the rate at which tax would have been charged at that most recent ten-year anniversary (and not the Table in force at the ten-year anniversary). [*IHTA 1984, Sch 2 para 3; FA 1986, Sch 19 para 37*].

44.15   INITIAL INTEREST OF SETTLOR OR SPOUSE OR CIVIL PARTNER

General. Where a settlor, or his spouse or civil partner (including widow or widower or surviving civil partner), is beneficially entitled to an interest in possession in property immediately after it becomes comprised in a settlement (the 'first' settlement), then, if that event occurs after 27 March 1974, the property is treated as not having become comprised in the settlement on that occasion for the purposes of the rules on settlements without interests in possession in *IHTA 1984, Part III, Ch III*. Instead, when the property or any part of it becomes held on trusts under which neither the settlor nor spouse (or civil partner) is beneficially entitled to an interest in possession, such property is treated as becoming comprised at that time in a separate settlement (the 'second' settlement) made by whichever of them last ceased to be so entitled. But the dates of the ten-year anniversaries of the deemed second settlement are those of the actual first settlement (see 44.3(*c*) above). From 22 March 2006 where a settlor, or his spouse or civil partner was beneficially entitled to an interest in possession in property immediately after it becomes comprised in a settlement (the 'first' settlement) and then it is passed on to a widow or widower or surviving civil partner, if that event occurs after 21 March 2006, the property is treated as not having become comprised in the settlement on that occasion for the purposes of the rules on settlements without interests in possession in *IHTA 1984, Part III, Ch III* unless it is an IPDI or disabled person's interest. [*IHTA 1984, ss 61(2), 80; FA 2006, Sch 20 para 23*].

Excluded property. Property will only qualify as excluded property in the above circumstances for the purposes of the rules on settlements without interests in possession in *IHTA 1984, Part III, Ch III* (but see application below) if it is situated outside the UK and the settlors of both the 'first' and 'second' settlements were domiciled outside the UK when their respective transfers were made. [*IHTA 1984, ss 48(3), 82(1)(3)*].

Where the property in the 'second' settlement is relevant property which becomes excluded property on being invested in Government securities within *IHTA 1984, s 48(4)(b)* (see 20.4(*c*) EXCLUDED PROPERTY and 44.10(viii) above) it will only be exempt from the proportionate charge on that occasion if both the settlor of the first settlement and the deemed settlor of the second settlement were domiciled outside the UK at their respective dates of settlement. For this purpose, where property became comprised in the settlement before 10 December 1974, the special provisions relating to domicile in *IHTA 1984, s 267* (see 17.3 DOMICILE) are disregarded. [*IHTA 1984, ss 65(8), 82(2)(3), 267(3)*].

Application. The above applies to provisions on settlements without interests in possession in *IHTA 1984, Part III, Ch III* except that the provisions on excluded property above do not apply to the rules relating to NATIONAL HERITAGE (33) property in *IHTA 1984, ss 78, 79, Chapter III* includes both the general rules for settlements without interests in possession and also the provisions for various special trusts. See ACCUMULATION AND MAINTENANCE TRUSTS (3), CHARITIES (11), NATIONAL HERITAGE (33) for settlements for heritage property and maintenance funds for historic buildings, PROTECTIVE TRUSTS (39), TRUSTS FOR DISABLED PERSONS (54) and TRUSTS FOR EMPLOYEES (55).

44.16   PROPERTY MOVING BETWEEN SETTLEMENTS

General. For the purposes of the rules on settlements without interests in possession in *IHTA 1984, Part III, Ch III* where **after 9 December 1981** property ceases to be comprised in one settlement (the 'first settlement') and becomes comprised in another (the 'second settlement'), then, unless in the meantime any person becomes beneficially entitled to the property (and not merely to an interest in possession in it), it is treated as remaining comprised in the first settlement. For events *after 14 March 1983*, this does not apply where a reversionary interest in the property expectant on the termination of a qualifying interest in possession under the first settlement was settled in the second settlement before 10 December 1981. Where **after 26 March 1974 and before 10 December 1981** property ceased to be comprised in one settlement (the 'first settlement') and became comprised in another (the 'second settlement') by the same disposition, it is treated as remaining in the first settlement. [*IHTA 1984, s 81*].

Excluded property. Where property in the second settlement is treated as remaining in the first settlement, it will only qualify as excluded property for the purposes of the rules on settlements without interests in possession in *IHTA 1984, Part III, Ch III* (but see application below) if it is situated outside the UK and the settlors of both the first and second settlements were domiciled outside the UK when their respective settlements were made but also see 44.10(X) above. [*IHTA 1984, ss 48(3), 82(1)(3)*]. See also IR Tax Bulletin, February 1997, pages 398 and 399.

Where the property in the second settlement is relevant property which becomes excluded property on being invested in Government securities or and AUT or OEIC within *IHTA 1984, s 48(3A), (4)(b)* (see 20.4(C) EXCLUDED PROPERTY and 44.10(VIII) above) it will only be exempt from the proportionate charge on that occasion if both settlors were domiciled outside the UK at the respective dates of settlement. For this purpose, where the property became comprised in the settlement before 10 December 1974, the special provisions relating to domicile in *IHTA 1984, s 267* (see 17.3 DOMICILE) are disregarded. [*IHTA 1984, ss 65(8), 82(2)(3), 267(3)*].

Application. The above applies to the provisions on settlements without interests in possession in *IHTA 1984, Part III, Ch III* except that the provisions on excluded property above do not apply to the rules relating to NATIONAL HERITAGE (33) property in *IHTA 1984, ss 78, 79. Chapter III* includes both the general rules for settlements without interests in possession and also the provisions for various special trusts. See ACCUMULATION AND MAINTENANCE TRUSTS (3), CHARITIES (11), NATIONAL HERITAGE (33) for settlements of heritage property and maintenance funds for historic buildings, PROTECTIVE TRUSTS (39), TRUSTS FOR DISABLED PERSONS (54) and TRUSTS FOR EMPLOYEES (55).

44.17   CREDIT FOR TAX PAID UNDER THE FA 1975 PROVISIONS

Any tax charged on a foreign settlement under *FA 1975, Sch 5 para 12(2)* (annual charge of 3% under the periodic charge provisions was allowable as a credit against subsequent capital distributions made (but not later annual charges). Any excess could be carried forward against capital transfer tax chargeable on the settlement under the 1982 provisions. Any further excess is allowed as a credit against the tax chargeable under *IHTA 1984, Part III, Ch III* (other than tax on NATIONAL HERITAGE (33) property under *IHTA 1984, s 79*) in respect of the settled property or part. [*IHTA 1984, s 85*].

44.18   **DISCRETIONARY SETTLEMENT EXCLUDING SETTLOR AND SPOUSE OR CIVIL PARTNER**

THIS DISCRETIONARY SETTLEMENT made on 200(7)

PARTIES

1.   "The Settlor" namely

2.   "The Original Trustees" namely

RECITALS
(Usual recitals)

NOW THIS DEED IRREVOCABLY WITNESSES:

1.   DEFINITIONS

The following terms (where the context permits) shall have the following meanings:—

1.1   "the Accumulation Period" means the period of 21 years from the date of this Settlement of the Trust Period if shorter

1.2   "the Beneficiaries" means

    1.2.1   [the [grand]children and remoter issue of the Settlor]

    1.2.2   the spouse's or civil partner's widows and widowers or surviving civil partners of persons within 1.2.1

1.3   "Excluded Person" means

    1.3.1   the Settlor

    1.3.2   any spouse or civil partner of the Settlor

1.4   "the Trust Fund" means

    1.4.1   the sum specified in the First Schedule

    1.4.2   any further money or property accepted by the Trustees as additions to the Trust Fund

    1.4.3   all accumulated income

    1.4.4   the assets from time to time representing such sum additions and accumulations

1.5   "the Trust Period" means the period beginning on the date of this Settlement and ending

    1.5.1   80 years from that date (which period shall be the applicable perpetuity period) or

    1.5.2   on such earlier date as the Trustees shall by deed prospectively specify

1.6   "the Trustees" means the Original Trustees or the other trustees or trustee for the time being of this Settlement

---

2.   INCOME

THE Trustees shall

2.1   Have the power during the Accumulation Period to accumulate all or any part of the income of the Trust Fund as an accretion to it and to apply the whole or any part or parts of the accumulated income as if it were income arising in the then current year

2.2   otherwise during the Trust Period pay or apply the income of the Trust Fund to or for the benefit of such of the Beneficiaries who are living in such shares as the Trustees in their absolute discretion think fit

3.   POWER OF APPOINTMENT

3.1   NOTWITHSTANDING the above trusts the Trustees shall hold the capital and income of the Trust Fund upon such trusts in favour or for the benefit of all or any one or more of the Beneficiaries exclusive of the other or others of them in such shares and with and subject to such powers and provisions for their respective maintenance education or other benefit or for the accumulation of income (including administrative powers and provisions and discretionary trusts and powers to be executed and exercised by any persons or person whether or not being or including the Trustees of any of them) as the Trustees in their absolute discretion think fit

3.2   The exercise of this power of appointment may be delegated to any extent and in such manner generally as the Trustees (subject to the application (if any) of the rule against perpetuities) by any deed or deeds revocable during the Trust Period or irrevocable and executed during the Trust Period shall with the written consent of the Settlor during his life but otherwise in their absolute discretion appoint

3.3   No exercise of this power shall invalidate any prior payment or application of all or any part or parts of the capital or income of the Trust Fund made under any other power or powers conferred by this Settlement or by law

4.   ULTIMATE TRUSTS

SUBJECT to and in default of the above trusts powers and provisions the Trustees shall hold the capital and income of the Trust Fund upon trust for such charitable purposes as the Trustees in their absolute discretion select

Notes to the Precedent

(A)   The provisions of *ss 31, 32*, powers, proper law, etc. plus full administrative provisions required to be added.

(B)   The settlor and spouse or civil partner are excluded from this discretionary settlement extract.

45   Shares and Securities

Cross-reference. See 12 CLOSE COMPANIES; 59 WORKING CASE STUDY.

Simon's Direct Tax Service, parts I4.301, I7.102, I8.241.

Other Sources. HMRC CTO leaflets IHT 15 'How to calculate the liability'; SVD 1 'Shares Valuation Division'; Foster, part H3; IHTM18000.

45.1   DEFINITIONS

In relation to transfers of value made, and other events occurring, after 16 March 1987, '*quoted*' in relation to any shares or securities, means quoted on a recognised stock exchange or dealt in on the Unlisted Securities Market (Alternative Investment Market (AIM) from 19 June 1995), and '*unquoted*', in relation to any shares or securities, means neither so quoted nor so dealt in. [*IHTA 1984, s 272; FA 1987, s 58(2), Sch 8 para 17*]. As from 1 April 1996 the word '*quoted*' on a recognised stock exchange is substituted by the word '*listed*'. [*FA 1996, Sch 38 para 2*]. In IHT 110 the definition of '*quoted*' and '*unquoted*' respectively are as follows:

> 'This means a company that is listed on a recognised stock exchange. This includes shares traded on the American NASDAQ and European EASDAQ for chargeable events after 9 March 1992.'

and

> 'This means a company that is not listed on a recognised stock exchange. Some companies although they are listed in the Stock Exchange Daily Official List are still "unquoted" for business relief.
>
> This includes shares
>
> • shares listed on the Alternative Investment Market (AIM)
>
> • shares listed on the Unlisted Securities Market (USM), there are some complicated rules that apply to chargeable events before 10 March 1992. You should telephone our Helpline if the transferor owned shares listed on the USM and the date of the chargeable event, is before 10 March 1992.'

The above definition applies for all IHT purposes except that, in relation to transfers of value made, and other events occurring, after 9 March 1992, an alternative definition, whereby Unlisted Securities Market shares and securities are treated as unquoted, applies for the purposes of defining relevant business property (see 7.4 BUSINESS PROPERTY) and payment by instalments (see 35.3 PAYMENT OF TAX).

In relation to transfers of value made, and other events occurring, before 17 March 1987, shares and securities in companies dealt in on the Unlisted Securities Market were not treated as 'quoted on a recognised stock exchange' for all IHT purposes (Inland Revenue Statement of Practice SP 18/80, 23 December 1980). For amendment to the term 'recognised stock exchange' see 7.4 BUSINESS PROPERTY. Whilst *FA 2007* inserted new definitions of 'recognised stock exchange' for the purposes of income tax and capital gains tax the change did not include inheritance tax. However, it may be that in the future the inheritance tax definition will fall into line with the *FA 2007* changes. [*ITA 2007, s 1005; FA 2007, s 109, Sch 26 paras 1, 3, 4*].

See also 56.20 VALUATION.

45.2   AGRICULTURAL AND BUSINESS PROPERTY RELIEFS

Controlling shares in agricultural companies may attract AGRICULTURAL PROPERTY (5) relief.

Shares and securities in companies carrying on a business may attract BUSINESS PROPERTY (7) relief.

45.3   PAYMENT OF TAX BY INSTALMENTS

Under certain conditions, inheritance tax on shares and securities transferred may be paid by annual instalments over ten years, see 35.3–35.5 PAYMENT OF TAX for details.

45.4   RELATED PROPERTY

See 56.17 VALUATION.

45.5   SALES WITHIN ONE YEAR AFTER DEATH

Special provisions apply, see 56.21 VALUATION.

45.6   TRANSFERS WITHIN SEVEN YEARS BEFORE DEATH

See 51 TRANSFERS WITHIN SEVEN YEARS BEFORE DEATH for special provisions.

45.7   TRADING COMPANIES

Controlling shares or securities or a minority holding of unquoted shares may attract BUSINESS PROPERTY (7) relief.

45.8   VALUATION

See 56.20 VALUATION for valuation of quoted and unquoted shares and securities. See also http://www.voa.gov.uk.

45.9   PURCHASE BY COMPANY OF OWN SHARES

A payment by an *unquoted trading* company (or *holding company* of a trading group) on the purchase, redemption or repayment of its own shares is not treated as a distribution if the price received from the company is used to meet the recipient's inheritance tax liability on a death. Substantially the whole of the payment (apart from any sum applied in paying capital gains tax on the purchase etc.) must be used for this purpose within two years of the death. The IHT liability must be one which could not be met without undue hardship otherwise than by means of such purchase etc. [*ICTA 1988, s 219*].

An *unquoted company* is one which has none of its shares listed in the official list of a stock exchange and which is not a 51% subsidiary of a company so listed.

A *trading company* is one whose business consists wholly or mainly of the carrying on of a trade or trades, excluding dealing in shares, securities, land or futures.

A *holding company* is one whose business, disregarding any trade carried on by it, consists wholly or mainly in the holding of shares or securities of one or more companies which are its 75% subsidiaries. [*ICTA 1988, s 229*].

Certain changes in company law have enabled listed companies to acquire their own shares as well as hold or dispose of them. *FA 2003, s 195* treats own shares held without cancellation as if they were cancelled for tax purposes. Up until the change in the treatment of listed companies in the *FA 2003* concerning the purchase by a company of its own shares the relieving provisions of *ICTA 1988, s 219* did not apply to listed companies. However, the change now secures equal treatment so that a payment by a *listed* company on the purchase, redemption or repayment of its own shares is not treated as a distribution if the price received from the company is used to meet the recipient's inheritance tax liability on a death. [*ICTA 1988, s 219; FA 2003, s 195*].

HMRC have refused to confirm that either a purchase etc. of a company's own shares or the alteration to any Articles of Association to enable it to make such a purchase etc. will

45.9 Shares and Securities

not give rise to a transfer of value under *IHTA 1984, s 94* (tax charge on close company participators—see 12.5 CLOSE COMPANIES). (CCAB Memorandum, 22 June 1982).

46 Situs

Cross-reference. See 20 EXCLUDED PROPERTY; 59 WORKING CASE STUDY.

Simon's Direct Tax Service, part I9.4.

46.1 GENERAL LAW

As the inheritance tax legislation contains no specific rules for determining whether property is or is not situated in the UK, the general law situs rules apply. It is important to note that the *Finance (No 2) Act 2005* included new rules for the determination of situs relevant for CGT purposes and whilst the new provisions do not affect the position for IHT it may be a precursor for future changes regarding non-domiciliaries and the situs of their assets. [*F(No 2)A 2005, s 34, Sch 4*].

Registered shares and securities are situated where they are registered unless transferable in more than one country when they are situated in the one in which they would be likely to be dealt with in the ordinary course of affairs. (*Standard Chartered Bank Ltd v CIR Ch D, [1978] STC 272; Treasurer for Ontario v Aberdein PC 1946, [1947] AC 24; R v Williams and Another PC, [1942] 22 All ER 95*).

Renounceable letters of allotment of shares in UK private companies have been held to be situated in the UK. (*Young and Another v Phillips Ch D 1984, 58 TC 232*).

Bearer shares and securities are situated in the country in which the certificate of title is kept. (*Winans and Another v A-G (No 2) HL 1909, [1910] AC 27*).

Interests in land and chattels. Situs depends upon actual physical situation. See [**Case Study 7**]. However, *ships* are situated where registered unless within UK territorial or national waters when this is displaced by the actual situs. (*The Trustees Executors and Agency Co Ltd v CIR Ch D 1972, [1973] 1 All ER 563*). For IHT purposes the application of extra-statutory concession F7 'Foreign owned works of art' ensures that even though a work of art is in the UK temporarily for cleaning or restoration or for a loan to a public exhibition by a non-UK domicile and a chargeable event arises then no charge to tax arises. This concession on the usual situs rules is perhaps designed to ensure that those owners of art works that are domiciled abroad do not remove valuable works of art from this country in fear of a tax charge arising out of the temporary situs in the UK of the work of art at a time of a chargeable event. See HMRC EXTRA-STATUTORY CONCESSIONS (23).

Debts. Generally, a simple contract debt is situated where the debtor resides (*Kwok Chi Leung Karl v Commissioner of Estate Duty PC, [1988] STC 728*). However, if there is more than one country of residence the terms of the contract may serve to localise the debt. (*New York Life Insurance Co Ltd v Public Trustee CA, [1924] 2 Ch 101*). A specialty debt is situated where the bond or specialty is kept. (*Royal Trust Co v A-G for Alberta PC 1929, [1930] AC 144*). A debt owed by a bank (e.g. bank account) is situated at the branch where it is primarily recoverable. (*R v Lovitt, [1912] AC 212*). A judgment debt is situated where the judgment is recorded.

Other assets. See also 20.5 EXCLUDED PROPERTY for foreign pensions and 35.14 PAYMENT OF TAX for foreign-owned works of art temporarily in the UK.

46.2 DOUBLE TAXATION AGREEMENTS

A double taxation agreement may determine where property is to be treated as situated for IHT purposes. [*IHTA 1984, s 158(1)*]. See [**Case Study 7**].

46.3 INTER-AMERICAN DEVELOPMENT BANK

Securities issued by this Bank are treated as situated outside the UK. [*FA 1976, s 131*].

46.4   **INTERNATIONAL ORGANISATIONS**

Securities issued by certain international organisations may be designated by the Treasury as being situated outside the UK for IHT purposes. The Asian Development Bank, the African Development Bank, the three European Communities and the European Investment Bank have been so designated. [*ICTA 1988, s 324 now repealed and replaced by ITTOIA 2005, s 774; FA 1985, s 96; SI 1984/1215; SI 1984/1634; SI 1985/1172*].

47   Time Limits

In some cases the periods can be extended at the discretion of HMRC. See IHTM30151–30159.

Simon's Direct Tax Service, parts I11.2, I11.3.

47.1   TIME LIMITS OF ONE YEAR OR LESS

(*a*)   **30 days**

(i)   Appeal against a notice of determination. See 15.3 DETERMINATIONS AND APPEALS.

(ii)   Stated case from Special Commissioners, request. See 15.8 DETERMINATIONS AND APPEALS.

(iii)   Information must be furnished if requested by the Board. See 2.9 ACCOUNTS AND RETURNS.

(iv)   Appeal against an information notice issued by HMRC. See 2.9 ACCOUNTS AND RETURNS.

(*b*)   **Three months**

(i)   Return to be made, in certain circumstances, by professional advisers acting for settlors. See 2.8 ACCOUNTS AND RETURNS.

(*c*)   **Six months**

(i)   Accounts to be delivered after ending of conditional exemption for works of art, historic buildings etc. and disposal of woodlands. See 2.6 ACCOUNTS AND RETURNS.

(ii)   Board may call for an account following an 'excepted termination'. See 2.5 ACCOUNTS AND RETURNS.

(iii)   Corrective and supplementary accounts to be delivered after discovery of defect. See 2.7 ACCOUNTS AND RETURNS. This limit applies also in cases of innocent reporting errors where the CTO do not seek a penalty. See IHT 13, p 10.

(iv)   Payment of tax. Normal due date after end of month in which chargeable transfer occurs. See 35.1 PAYMENT OF TAX.

(v)   A scheme administrator of an Alternatively Secured Pension (ASP) has six months from the end of the month in which he becomes aware or discovers the scheme member's death to pay IHT due. See 37.2 PENSION SCHEMES.

(*d*)   **Twelve months**

(i)   Delivery of accounts after lifetime transfers, transfers on death and transfers by trustees of settlements. See 2.6 ACCOUNTS AND RETURNS.

(ii)   Valuation reduced for certain quoted shares if sold for less within twelve months after death. See 56.21 VALUATION.

(iii)   Waiver of dividends within previous twelve months before any right accrues is not a transfer of value. See 49.1 TRANSFER OF VALUE.

(iv)   Unused portion of annual exemption can be utilised against transfers during following twelve months. See 21.9 EXEMPT TRANSFERS.

(v)　In relation to transfers of value made, and other events occurring, before 30 November 1993, property which is the subject of a lifetime transfer for which agricultural or business property relief is claimed but which is subsequently disposed of by the transferee, must be replaced by similar property within twelve months of the disposal. See 5.3 AGRICULTURAL PROPERTY and 7.6 BUSINESS PROPERTY.

(vi)　A scheme administrator of an ASP has twelve months from the end of the month in which he becomes aware or discovers the scheme member's death to file a return. See 37.2 PENSION SCHEMES.

47.2　TWO-YEAR TIME LIMITS

(a)　Variations and disclaimers of dispositions on death are valid if made within two years after death. See 14 DEEDS VARYING DISPOSITIONS ON DEATH.

(b)　Woodlands. Election after a death to defer tax on trees and underwood. See 58.1 WOODLANDS.

(c)　Scottish executors may elect to pay tax, ignoring legitim. See 50.7 TRANSFERS ON DEATH.

(d)　Heritage property. A claim for conditional exemption on or after 17 March 1998 relating to death or other transfers and heritage property held in a discretionary trust. See 33.3 NATIONAL HERITAGE .

(e)　Heritage property. A claim for exemption for transfers into maintenance funds for historic buildings, etc. See 33.3 NATIONAL HERITAGE and 9.5 CAPITAL GAINS TAX.

47.3　THREE-YEAR TIME LIMITS

(a)　Penalties. No proceedings by Board after notification of tax payable. See 36.7 PENALTIES.

(b)　Valuation reduced for land or 'related property' sold for less within three years (four years in certain cases) after death. See 56.6 and 56.18 VALUATION.

(c)　Woodlands. Expenses of replanting trees and underwood within three years after disposal are deductible. See 58.4 WOODLANDS.

(d)　In relation to transfers of value made, and other events occurring, after 29 November 1993, property which is the subject of a lifetime transfer for which agricultural or business property relief is claimed but which is subsequently disposed of by the transferee, must be replaced by similar property within three years of the disposal. See 5.3 AGRICULTURAL PROPERTY and 7.6 BUSINESS PROPERTY.

47.4　FIVE-YEAR TIME LIMIT

(a)　Quick succession relief is available. See 40.1 QUICK SUCCESSION RELIEF.

47.5　SIX-YEAR TIME LIMIT

(a)　Repayment of tax overpaid claimable. See 35.11 PAYMENT OF TAX.

(b)　Claims. Normal limit where not otherwise specified.

47.6　TWENTY-FIVE YEAR TIME LIMIT

(a)　Interests in certain accumulation and maintenance trusts must vest within twenty-five years of creation of settlement. See 3.2(C) ACCUMULATION AND MAINTENANCE TRUSTS.

47.7 **SUNSET TIME LIMITS**

(a) Election by the former owner of a pre-owned asset(s) for the asset(s) to be treated for IHT purposes as if it were a gift with reservation under existing rules is on or before 'the relevant filing date'. The relevant filing date means 31 January in the year of assessment that immediately follows the initial year but following *FA 2007, s 66* the filing date may be later if in a particular case the officer of Revenue and Customs allows. In most cases this will be 31 January 2007, but HMRC do give examples of circumstances where the late election option may be appropriate at http://www.hmrc.gov.uk/poa/late-election-guidance.htm. [*FA 2004, Sch 15 para 23*]. See 22.1 GIFTS WITH RESERVATION; 59.40 WORKING CASE STUDY.

(b) Non-disclosure in connection with undeclared funds in estate returns incurring no additional IHT penalties was 30 September 2003. See also 36.9 PENALTIES.

48   Time of Disposition

Simon's Direct Tax Service, part I3.131.

48.1   BASIC RULE

As a basic rule no CHARGEABLE TRANSFER (10) can take place until there has been a disposition resulting in a shift of value from one estate to another. The legal requirements that must be fulfilled to ensure such a shift vary depending on the subject matter of the gift. Usually all the requirements relating to the species of gift must be satisfied by the donor before the gift becomes effective. One common exception is where the donor has done all in his power to transfer the property e.g. signed a stock transfer form and delivered the scrip. See 31.2 LIFETIME TRANSFERS.

Freehold or leasehold land is gifted on the conveyance or assignment under seal or declaration of trust evidenced in writing.

Choses in possession (e.g. motor cars, furniture) are gifted when the appropriate formalities are completed. This could be the execution of a deed, declaration of trust or actual or constructive delivery. In the case of chattels that are capable of being physically handed over by a donor then constructive delivery may be the preferred option in a formal presentation in, say, domestic surroundings. Where an item is large and not portable then it may still be the subject of a constructive delivery if the donor expresses to the donee that he is making the gift of the item to the donee and places his hands on the item in question (see *Rawlinson v Mort (1905) 21 TLR 774*). Alternatively, the donor may hand over the physical means of making the item the ownership of the donee by surrendering the keys to, say, a locked bureau (See *Dublin City Distillery Limited v Doherty [1914] AC 823, 843*). In the case of leases relating to chattels the anti-avoidance provisions introduced by *FA 1999, s 104* only apply to land and not chattels. Therefore leases of chattels are possible but the law of bailment should be taken into account as there is a suggestion that this counters such a lease arrangement. See also 22.1 GIFTS WITH RESERVATION and Memorandum of Gift in 59.11 WORKING CASE STUDY.

Choses in action (e.g. shares, insurance policies) are normally gifted on the completion of the appropriate transfer or assignment although negotiable instruments are transferable by delivery. A transfer of shares is not complete until all the requirements of the company's articles have been complied with or the individual has complied with them to the best of his powers (*Re Rose, Rose and Others v CIR CA, [1952] 1 All ER 1217*).

Interests under trusts are gifted when the necessary formalities have been completed. A disposition of an equitable interest must be in writing (*Grey and Another v CIR HL, [1959] 3 All ER 603* and *Oughtred v CIR HL, [1959] 3 All ER 623*). See *Stenhouse's Trustees v Lord Advocate CS 1983, [1984] STC 195* for position when trustees make an appointment which is in part in breach of trust until a later date.

Cheques are gifted on payment (not when the cheque is received) i.e. the gift remains incomplete until the cheque is cleared by the paying bank (*Re Owen, Owen v CIR Ch D, [1949] 1 All ER 901*). There has now been a decided case since the old estate duty case and the IR Capital Taxes view is that a cheque constitutes a revocable instrument. See *Curnock (Curnock's Personal Representative) v CIR [2003] STC SCD 283 Sp C 365* where monies represented by a cheque issued before the date but not cleared until after death still formed part of the deceased's estate on death. See TAX CASES (60).

Insurance policies (e.g. where written to benefit a person other than the person insured or paying the premiums) are treated by HMRC as made when one party has unconditionally accepted an offer (or counter-offer) from the other party and has notified the other party accordingly (see Inland Revenue Press Release 18 March 1986).

48.2   **Omission to exercise a right. An omission to exercise a right** (unless not deliberate) is treated as a disposition if it decreases the value of one person's estate and increases the estate of another person or the value of a settlement without an interest in possession. The disposition is treated as made at the time, or latest time, the right could have been exercised. [*IHTA 1984, s 3(3)*]. See *Macauley & Another v Premium Life Assurance Co Ltd, Ch D 29 April 1999 unreported* where a scheme failed to take account of *s 3(3)* so that the whole of the free estate became liable to IHT on death. A claim that the six-year time limit laid down by the *Limitation Act 1980* precluded liability was rejected by the court.

49   Transfer of Value

Cross-references. See 10 CHARGEABLE TRANSFER; 19 ESTATE; 21 EXEMPT TRANSFERS; 59 WORKING CASE STUDY.

Simon's Direct Tax Service, part I3.1.

Other Sources. HMRC CTO leaflet IHT 15, page 9; Foster, part C1; IHTM04000.

49.1   **DEFINITION**

A **transfer of value** is any disposition (see 49.2 below) made by a *person* ('the transferor') as a result of which the value of his estate immediately after the disposition is less than it would be but for the disposition; and the amount by which it is less is the value transferred by the transfer. No account is taken of the value of EXCLUDED PROPERTY (20), which ceases to form part of a person's estate as a result of a disposition. References in *IHTA 1984* to a transfer of value made include references to events on the happening of which tax is chargeable *as if* a transfer of value had been made. [*IHTA 1984, s 3(1)(2)(4)*].

The reduction in the transferor's estate will include any inheritance tax (but no other tax or duty or expenses of sale) borne by him on the value transferred. [*IHTA 1984, s 5(4)*]. For individuals, the 'net' value transferred, i.e. after taking account of any EXEMPT TRANS-FERS (21), is grossed-up at the appropriate tax rate (see 8 CALCULATION OF TAX and 41 RATES OF TAX) when the transferor bears the tax (but not when the transferee pays it) in order to obtain the CHARGEABLE TRANSFER (10). If the transferee bears any related capital gains tax or incidental expenses (e.g. professional fees, stamp duties etc.) relating to the transfer, the value transferred is reduced by those charges. The reduction for capital gains tax applies to settled property only if the tax on the gain accruing to the trustees is borne by a person who becomes absolutely entitled to the settled property concerned. [*IHTA 1984, ss 164, 165*].

There is no transfer of value in the following circumstances

(*a*)   **Grant of agricultural tenancies.** See 5.7 AGRICULTURAL PROPERTY. See also 5.8 for the transfer of Scottish agricultural leases.

(*b*)   **Waiver of remuneration** (including the repayment of remuneration already received) if such remuneration would otherwise have been subject to income tax as employment income [formerly Schedule E] and is not allowable as a deduction to the employer for purposes of income tax and corporation tax. [*IHTA 1984, s 14; ITEPA 2003, s 7*]. The employment income assessment must not have become final, the remuneration must be formally waived (usually by deed) and the employer's profits or allowable losses must be adjusted accordingly. (Inland Revenue Press Release 11 November 1975).

(*c*)   **Waiver of dividends** by any person provided the waiver is within twelve months *before* any right to the dividend has accrued does not by itself make a transfer of value. [*IHTA 1984, s 15*]. See IHTM04052 regarding the use of the word 'person'.

49.2   **DISPOSITION**

Disposition is not defined in absolute terms. It includes the following.

(i)   A disposition effected by associated operations. See 6.3 ANTI-AVOIDANCE. [*IHTA 1984, s 272*].

(ii)   An omission to exercise a right (unless shown not to be deliberate) by a person which diminishes his estate and increases the estate of another person or the value of a discretionary trust. The time of the disposition is the time or latest time when the right could be exercised. [*IHTA 1984, s 3(3)*].

(iii)   Certain arrangements involving life insurance in conjunction with an annuity (a 'back to back' arrangement). [*IHTA 1984, s 263*]. See 30 LIFE ASSURANCE POLICIES AND ANNUITIES.

(iv)   Certain loans of money or property for a fixed or minimum period granted for inadequate consideration. See 49.3 below.

(v)   A disposition effected on the death of a registered scheme member on or after the age of 75 where funds are held in an alternatively secured pension (ASP) within *FA 2004, s 165*. The disposition on which a tax charge is imposed is the relevant amount of the ASP within *IHTA 1984, s 151A(2)(3)*. See 37.2 PENSION SCHEMES.

A disposition is not a transfer of value in the following circumstances.

(*a*)   It is shown that it was not intended, and was not made in a transaction (or series of transactions or by associated transactions) intended, to confer any gratuitous benefit on any person and either

    (i)   it was made in a transaction at arm's length between persons not connected with each other, [**Case Study 6**] or

    (ii)   it was such as might be expected to be made in a transaction at arm's length between persons not connected with each other.

The above exception does not apply to a disposition whereby a person entitled to an interest (whether in possession or not) in any settled property acquires a reversionary interest expectant (whether immediately or not) on the interest. It also does not apply to a sale of unquoted shares or debentures (in relation to transfers of value made, and other events occurring, before 17 March 1987, shares or debentures not quoted on a recognised stock exchange) unless it is shown that it was at a price freely negotiated at the time of the sale or at a price such as might be expected to have been freely negotiated at that time. [*IHTA 1984, ss 10, 55; FA 1986, Sch 19 para 15; FA 1987, s 58, Sch 8 para 1*]. It is not sufficient, for example, that the shares were sold at a price which had been fixed under a provision of the company's articles of association (Originally in former Inland Revenue Booklet IHT 1 (1991) para 8.10 but not now duplicated in IHT 15, p 15).

The question of whether a disposition is excepted from being a transfer of value in the circumstances of (ii) above is one of fact although the burden of proof is on the taxpayer (*CIR v Spencer-Nairn CS 1990, [1991] STC 60*). (The facts were special in that a seller of land did not realise, at the time of sale, he was connected with the purchaser, and it was later found the advice he had received in connection with the sale, to the effect that he was liable under statute to incur expenditure to improve the land, was erroneous, with the effect that the sale was carried out at an apparent undervalue.)

The relevance of associated operations was considered in *CIR v Macpherson and Another HL, [1988] STC 362*. See 6.3 ANTI-AVOIDANCE.

(*b*)   It is a disposition for family maintenance etc. see 21.11 EXEMPT TRANSFERS.

(*c*)   It is allowable for income tax or corporation tax. [*IHTA 1984, s 12(1)*].

(*d*)   It is a contribution to an approved retirement benefit scheme (occupational pension scheme) or is to provide retirement benefit for employees and their dependants or is a contribution under approved pension arrangements or, from 6 April 2006, a registered pension scheme (or *ICTA 1988, s 615(3)* scheme) entered into by an employee of the person making the disposition. [*IHTA 1984, s 12(2)–(5); F(No 2)A 1987, s 98(2)(3); FA 2004, s 203(2); FA 2006, Sch 22 para 2*]. See 21.13 EXEMPT TRANSFERS and 37.2 PENSIONS SCHEMES.

(*e*) It is by a close company to trustees for benefit of employees. [*IHTA 1984, s 13 as amended by FA 2000, s 138(1)*]. See 55 TRUSTS FOR EMPLOYEES. See [**Case Study 2**].

(*f*) It is a capital gains tax liability of a close relative paid by an individual which has previously been postponed under *FA 1984, Sch 14*. [*IHTA 1984, s 163(5)*]. See 56.15 VALUATION.

(*g*) The disposition falls within the provisions relating to GIFTS WITH RESERVATION (22).

49.3 **LOANS, ETC.**

A loan for a fixed or minimum period granted for inadequate consideration may be a transfer of value under the rules in *IHTA 1984, ss 3, 10*, see 49.1 and 49.2(*a*) above. The value transferred is the difference between the amount or value of the property lent and the value of

(*a*) the right to receive repayment or the return of the property when the loan has expired, plus

(*b*) the right to receive any interest or other consideration agreed between the parties.

See IHTM19010.

In the case of a lease, it is the difference between the value of the lessor's interest before the lease was granted and the value of his interest subject to the lease. The values are those at the time the loan is made. See 19.1 ESTATE for a deed of loan waiver.

Modification of exemptions for loans. The exemptions that apply to outright gifts (see 21 EXEMPT TRANSFERS) apply, with appropriate modifications, to loans as follows.

(i) In the case of loans etc. to political parties (see 21.6) the exemption limit in respect of transfer of value made within a year of death (which applied for transfers before 15 March 1988) does not apply.

(ii) For the purposes of loans etc. to charities (21.2), registered housing associations (to which only loans of land made after 13 March 1989 can be exempt) (21.4), political parties (21.6) or used for national purposes (see 21.5) or public benefit (see 21.7) the funds or property lent must be used solely for charitable purposes or the purposes of the appropriate political party or body. The value transferred is then treated as attributable to the property the borrower is allowed to use and the property is treated as having been given to, or having become the property of, the borrower. In addition, the exceptions to the exemptions in each of those paragraphs do not apply.

(iii) For the purposes of loans etc. between spouses or civil partners (see 21.8) the borrower's estate is treated as increased by the amount of the value transferred but see *Phizackerley* below.

(iv) For the purposes of the small gifts exemption (see 21.9(*b*)) and gifts in consideration of marriage (see 21.10) the transfer of value is treated as made by outright gift.

(v) The normal expenditure out of income exemption (see 21.12) applies if the transfer is a normal one on the part of the transferor and, after allowing for all transfers of value forming part of his normal expenditure, he is left with sufficient income to maintain his usual standard of living.

[*IHTA 1984, ss 29, 56(6); FA 1988, Sch 14*].

49.4 **Repayment of certain debts during lifetime.** Under *FA 1986, s 103* certain debts may not be deducted from the value of a deceased's estate if owed to a person who has received property from the deceased, see 50.3 TRANSFERS ON DEATH. Where a debt incurred after 17 March 1986 which would have been disallowed under those provisions is repaid by the donor in whole or in part during lifetime, he is treated as having made a transfer of value at the time of the payment equal to the money or money's worth paid or applied by him and such transfer is treated as a POTENTIALLY EXEMPT TRANSFER (38). [*FA 1986, s 103(5)(6)*]. The effect of this is that the repayment (or part repayment) of a gift loaned back to the donor, although reducing the amount disallowed on death, is treated as a potentially exempt transfer and may be subject to tax if the donor dies within seven years of the repayment. In a recent case a married woman died in 2000 and by her will she left an amount equal to the IHT nil rate band to a discretionary trust for her husband (P) and their children, and the residue to P. P agreed to pay £150,000 plus indexation to the discretionary trust in return for his wife's half-share in the matrimonial home. P died in 2002, and HMRC issued a notice of determination charging IHT on his estate. His personal representative appealed, contending that the £153,222 which P owed to the discretionary trust should be deducted from the value of his estate. The Special Commissioner rejected this contention and dismissed his appeal, holding that the effect of *FA 1986, s 103* was that the debt was not deductible. The Commissioner also held that *IHTA 1984, s 11* (providing that a 'disposition for maintenance' is not a 'transfer of value') did not apply to a situation 'when a husband puts a house in joint names of himself and his wife during their marriage'. The effect of this decision is that where there is a nil rate band discretionary trust with residue passing to a surviving spouse, and that proportion owned by the deceased is different from the financial contribution proportion, then it is likely that HMRC will review the case. In the absence of any definitive comment from HMRC a review of wills should be undertaken to ensure that residue passing on spouse/civil partner exempt interest is to IPDI so that the debt is incurred by the Trustees (preferably not inclusive of the spouse/civil partner) of the IPDI. See 43.1 SETTLEMENTS WITH INTERESTS IN POSSESSION. See also Tax Adviser, June 2007 and *Phizackerley (Personal Representative of Dr PJR Phizackerley) v HMRC [2007] STC SCD 328 Sp C 591* at TAX CASES (60).

Example 1

On 19 March 1999 Bernard gives his brother Charlie a plot of land worth £250,000. On 25 April 1999 Bernard borrows £250,000 from Charlie. Then on 7 April 2007 Bernard dies, at which time Charlie still retains the land which produces no income.

The potentially exempt transfer of the land has dropped out of cumulation so that no claim can arise and *IHTA 1984, s 103(1)(a)* is ineffective because the consideration for the debt was not derived from the deceased. In order to counter this *s 103(1)(b)* has been drafted and it precludes the deduction of liabilities to the extent that the consideration given consists of consideration given by any person who is at any time entitled to any property from the deceased or whose resources at *any* time include property derived from the deceased.

Example 2

Bernard gives his son Andrew shares worth £200,000. Andrew, who is wealthy, lends his father £250,000 at a time when the shares have dropped in value to £170,000. Bernard dies and a deduction is claimed of the £250,000 owing by the Executors to Andrew.

In such a situation it is open to the parties to claim that the whole of the loan is to be allowed on the grounds that the gift was not made to facilitate the loan. If the parties cannot establish this to the satisfaction of the Inspector then the 'realisable value' at the time the debt was created will be in point and not £250,000. That is to say £80,000 (i.e. £250,000 −£170,000 shares). *IHTA 1984, s 103(2)* permits the deduction to the extent that the value of the consideration for the debt is shown by the parties to have exceeded the amount available by the application of all the property derived by the creditor from the deceased.

49.5   **ESTATE**

A person's estate is the aggregate of all the property to which he is beneficially entitled, except that the estate of a person immediately before his death does not include

49.5   Transfer of Value

EXCLUDED PROPERTY (20). It includes the value of any settled property in which the person has a beneficial INTEREST IN POSSESSION (26) except that it does not include property to which *IHTA 1984, ss 71A, 71D* (i.e. bereaved minor's trust and an 18 to 25 trust) apply nor does it include from 22 March 2006 an IPDI, a TSI, a disabled person's trust. These trusts will be charged to IHT under the trusts taxing regimes applicable depending on whichever trust is in point. [*IHTA 1984, ss 5(1), 49(1); FA 2006, Sch 20 paras 4, 10*]. See 19 ESTATE for full details of meaning of estate.

50   Transfers on Death

Cross-references. See 2.4 ACCOUNTS AND RETURNS; 8 CALCULATION OF TAX; 14 DEEDS VARYING DISPOSITIONS ON DEATH; 19 ESTATE; 21.16 EXEMPT TRANSFERS; 35 PAYMENT OF TAX; 40 QUICK SUCCESSION RELIEF; 51 TRANSFERS WITHIN SEVEN YEARS BEFORE DEATH; 52 TRANSITIONAL PROVISIONS; 56 VALUATION; 59 WORKING CASE STUDY.

Simon's Direct Tax Service, part I4.

Other Sources. Mellows, chapter 5; Foster, part D; IHTM05000.

50.1   APPLICATION

On the death of any person after 17 March 1986, inheritance tax is chargeable as if he had made a transfer of value of his 'estate' immediately before his death. [*IHTA 1984, s 4(1)*].

'*Estate*' of a deceased person is the aggregate of all the property to which he was beneficially entitled immediately before death, but not including EXCLUDED PROPERTY (20). [*IHTA 1984, s 5(1) as amended by FA 2006, Sch 20 para 10*]. See 19 ESTATE for details, and in particular for the extended IHT meaning of 'beneficially entitled'.

The rules applying on intestacy are set out periodically in the weekly magazine Taxation but see 50.9 below.

50.2   VALUATION OF ESTATE ON DEATH

The value transferred on death is the total value of all the property in the deceased's estate (see above) at a price which the property might reasonably be expected to fetch if sold in the open market at that time, less liabilities (see 50.3 below). [*IHTA 1984, ss 5(3), 160*]. See 56 VALUATION.

Where an investor in a mutual building society dies after the issue of the relevant Transfer Document or Prospectus and before vesting day, there may be IHT consequences in respect of their entitlement to receive either free shares or a cash bonus on de-mutualisation. Following the death others may become entitled to any free shares or cash bonus due in respect of the account held by the deceased. The precise consequences depend on a number of factors, including the rules of the particular society, the terms of the Transfer Document covering the de-mutualisation and whether the deceased was the sole or first-named holder of the account.

Since 6 April 1996, a person's death has not been an occasion of charge under the accrued income scheme (AIS) and valuations of holdings of AIS stocks have included gross interest and IHT has been charged on that gross interest. However, this has led to a double charge to tax: that is, IHT is charged on the gross interest to the date of death and when the next interest payment is made a further charge arises on the personal representatives on the whole payment of interest including that accruing up to the date of death. The personal representatives have had no recourse to a deduction of the deceased's element of the accrued interest. HMRC Inheritance Tax have now confirmed that interest on AIS securities quoted 'cum-dividend' should be included net of tax at basic rate in the valuation. Similarly, where the securities are 'ex-dividend' at the date of death the allowance for interest accruing after death should be net of tax to the personal representatives. See IHT NEWSLETTER AND TAX BULLETIN EXTRACTS (61), May Special Edition 2003.

The only exception to the general valuation rule applies in certain cases involving the valuation of development sites or where building work is incomplete. The CTO will normally ask the DV to value the property at the relevant date as if the work had been completed. The CTO will then deduct the cost of completion as a charge against the deceased's estate. (VOA IHT manual, section 7, para 7.13 a).

Changes in the value of the estate by reason of the death (e.g. life assurance monies receivable or loss of goodwill) are included as if occurring before death except

(a)   the termination on the death of any interest, or

(b)   the passing of any interest by survivorship, or

(c)   a decrease in value resulting from an alteration of a close company's unquoted share or loan capital or any rights attached thereto, see 12.5 CLOSE COMPANIES.

See IHTM04046 for further examples of changes in value deemed to occur before death. [*IHTA 1984, s 171*].

Claims for reduction in value may be made where

(A)   quoted shares are sold at a loss within one year of death (Form IHT 35), see 56.21 VALUATION;

(B)   land is sold at a loss within three years (four years in certain cases) of death (Form IHT 38), see 56.6 VALUATION; or

(C)   'related property' is sold at less value within three years of death, see 56.18 VALUATION.

[*IHTA 1984, ss 176, 179, 191*].

Settled property. Where the deceased was entitled to an interest in possession which terminated on his death, the value of the settled property would normally be included in his estate. See 19 ESTATE and Form D5 below. However, where such settled property

(I)   reverts to the settlor who is still living and neither the settlor (nor his spouse after 11 April 1978) had acquired the reversionary interest for money or money's worth, or

(II)   reverts to the settlor's spouse or civil partner who is domiciled in the UK at the time of death and neither the settlor nor his spouse (or civil partner as the case may be) had acquired a reversionary interest for money or money's worth,

the value of the settled property is left out of account in determining the deceased's estate. The exemption also applies as under (II) where the reversion is to the widow or widower or surviving civil partner of the settlor where the settlor died less than two years before the deceased. Relief under these provisions does not apply to a reversionary interest transferred into a settlement after 9 March 1981. Where more than one person is the settlor in relation to such a settlement and the circumstances so require these provisions apply as if the settled property were comprised in separate settlements. From 22 March 2006 where a person becomes beneficially entitled to an interest in possession then it is included as part of his estate unless it is a disabled person's trust or a TSI. The exemption also applies as under (II) where the reversion is an IPDI to the widow or widower or surviving civil partner of the beneficiary where the settlor has died less than two years before the deceased beneficiary the value of the settled property is left out of account in determining the deceased's estate. See SETTLEMENTS WITH INTERESTS IN POSSESSION (43). [*IHTA 1984, ss 44(2), 54; FA 2006, Sch 20 para 15*].

The IHT 210 (Notes) at D5 (Notes) are somewhat limited in the advice given and state; 'Sometimes, a trust will give trustees a choice about who can benefit under the trust. These trusts are called "discretionary trusts". As no one has a *right* to benefit from a discretionary trust, you should not fill in Form D5 for such a trust, even if the deceased has been receiving some benefit.'

Surviving spouse exemption. Where a surviving spouse has received a life interest in property under the will of the deceased spouse who died before 13 November 1974, no inheritance tax will arise on that interest when the surviving spouse dies (because estate duty was or would have been payable on the first death). [*IHTA 1984, Sch 6 para 2*]. See 52.3 TRANSITIONAL PROVISIONS.

Survivorship clauses. Where under the terms of a will, or otherwise, property is held for a person if he survives another for a specified period of six months or less, the subsequent dispositions at the end of that period (or on the person's earlier death) are treated as having had effect from the beginning of the period. This does not affect any distributions or applications of property occurring before those dispositions take effect. [*IHTA 1984, s 92*]. The *Law Reform (Succession) Act 1995, s 1* inserting a new *subsection 2A to section 46* in the *Administration of Estates Act 1925* applying to all deaths after 1 January 1996 states that a survivorship provision of at least 28 days where a husband or wife dies intestate; this will prevent problems where the intestate's assets are inherited by the spouse or civil partner where in most circumstances either, or both, would not wish this to occur on such deaths in quick succession.

Example

Mr and Mrs A both die in a boating accident on 12 July 2007 whilst on holiday but neither has made a will. They do not have any children but both have parents still living. The estates are valued at £300,000 and £310,000 for Mr and Mrs A respectively. As there is no will or survivorship provision made by either there is the possibility that the parents of either Mr A or Mrs A may wish to prove their son/daughter survived the spouse and thereby share in both estates.

The *Administration of Estates Act 1925, s 46(2A)* has the effect of ensuring that where such deaths occur the survivorship of the one spouse over the other must be at least 28 days. In comparison *IHTA 1984, s 92* provides that the 'dispositions taking effect' under a survivorship clause will be treated as having 'had effect from the beginning of the period'. Therefore, if the survival of either Mr A or Mrs A did not exceed 6 months *IHTA 1984, s 92(1)* then *AEA 1925, s 46(2A)* has the effect in Mr A's and Mrs A's case of their assets passing to their issue (not applicable in this case) which enables them in this case utility of the £300,000 nil rate band. However, a surviving spouse or civil partner to whom *subsection (2A)* applies and whose estate is less than £300,000 will lose the use of a proportion of the nil rate band up to that limit as the predeceased's assets will pass directly to their issue, in this case the parents under the intestacy rules. See also 59.49 WORKING CASE STUDIES.

Notes to the example

(1)   It may be appropriate for interests on intestacy to be reallocated by the use of a deed of variation so that the unutilised nil rate band of up to £300,000 might be utilised. See *Daffodil (Daffodil's Administrator) v CIR [2002] STC SCD 224 Sp C 311* and also the Precedent in 14 DEEDS VARYING DISPOSITIONS ON DEATH.

(2)   The *Law of Property Act 1925, s 184* provides for the younger to have survived the elder in cases of disaster and where it is not known which of them died first. Section 184 may be overridden where a clause is inserted in the will which states 'provided that […] survives me for a period of twenty-eight days' so that the normal distribution is in accordance with testator's wishes. The twenty-eight day clause insertion in a will under the *Law Reform (Succession) Act 1995, s 1* results in each estate passing as though the other had predeceased and for IHT purposes this will mean that, for instance, couples in partnerships may in such circumstances wish their estate to go to their own family members so utilising their relevant nil rate bands.

(3)   In the case of spouses or civil partners who die in *commorientes* circumstances (see paragraph 50.4 below) then the situation is complicated further by the inter-spouse/civil partner exemption under *IHTA 1984, s 18*; as there is an exempt transfer on the death under section 18(1) then the transfer to the younger spouse or civil partner is not a chargeable transfer. However, the younger of the spouses/civil partners is deemed to have inherited the elder spouse's/civil partner's estate under the *Law of Property Act 1925, s 184*, but for the purposes of IHT under *IHTA 1984, s 4(2)* eliminates mutual gifts between individuals in such circumstances and there is no

transfer of value to the younger spouse/civil partner on which inheritance tax can be charged. There is a view therefore that the elder's estate escapes inheritance tax completely and therefore a survivorship condition, which is normally desirable, is deliberately excluded in the event of the spouses/civil partners dying simultaneously. In the case of civil partnerships this may not be desirable for the reasons as noted above, but in a case where a married couple's children benefit from their parents' estates then, depending on the size of the elder parent's estate, there could be a substantial saving in IHT. This view is not universally accepted but see the HMRC's IHT manual at IHTM12197 for text and a useful example, which supports the view above that the elder spouse's estate is not subject to IHT at all.

Non-residents' bank accounts. On the death of a person not domiciled, resident or ordinarily resident in the UK immediately before his death, the balance on any 'qualifying foreign currency account' is not included in the value of his estate immediately before his death. This also applies to such an account held by trustees of settled property in which the deceased held a beneficial interest in possession unless the settlor was domiciled in the UK at the time he made the settlement or the trustees are domiciled, resident and ordinarily resident there at the time of the beneficiary's death. Residence and ordinary residence are determined as for income tax purposes. The trustees of a settlement, however, are for these purposes regarded as not resident or ordinarily resident in the UK unless the general administration is ordinarily carried on there and the trustees or a majority of them (and where there is more than one class of trustees, a majority of each class) are resident and ordinarily resident in the UK. '*Qualifying foreign currency account*' means any foreign currency account with a bank or the Post Office. [*IHTA 1984, s 157; FA 1996, Sch 37 para 12(1), Sch 41 Part VIII*].

For these purposes 'bank' has the same meaning as that given by *ITA 2007, s 991* (formerly *ICTA 1988, s 840A*). [*FA 1996, Sch 37 para 12(2)*].

NHS Continuing Care Scheme payments. Payments under the NHS Continuing Care Scheme whereby a right exists to make a reimbursement claim is to be treated as an asset of the deceased's estate. Where a claim is underway at the date of death and an offer has been made by the Strategic Health Authority/ Primary Care Trust then that offer should be included as an asset on Form IHT200. If the claim has not been quantified or is not known about at the time of death a corrective account should be submitted to HMRC Inheritance Tax as soon as possible. A discounted valuation should be applied to the expected/actual payment and this discount is dependent on the date of death as detailed below and in the December 2005 issue of the IHT Newsletter at IHT NEWSLETTER AND TAX BULLETIN EXTRACTS (61). [*IHTA 1984, s 160*]. The discount reflects the potential uncertainty of success in a claim for reimbursement and arises from the Coughlan case and subsequent reports by the Health Service Ombudsman. See also *R v North East Devon Health Authority, ex p Coughlan (Secretary of State for Health and another intervening [2000] 3 All ER 850.*

Date of death	Discount
Prior to 17/7/99	100%
17/7/99–13/2/03	75%
14/2/03–16/12/04	40%
On or after 17/12/04	10%

50.3   **LIABILITIES DEDUCTIBLE**

In determining the value of a person's estate his liabilities at that time must be taken into account except as otherwise provided by *IHTA 1984*. Except in the case of a liability imposed by the law, a liability incurred by the transferor may be taken into account only to the extent that it was incurred for a consideration in money or money's worth. [*IHTA 1984, s 5(3)(5)*]. By concession, income tax in Canada charged on deemed gains immediately before death will be allowed as a deductible liability. A deceased's worldwide estate of which the Canadian tax on deemed gains comprises a liability may be set-off against the value of UK assets where it exceeds assets (liable or not to IHT) held outside the UK. (ESC F18, to be included in the next update of IR 1). *IHTA 1984, s 5(3)* provides that 'in determining the value of a person's estate at any time his liabilities at that time shall be taken into account, except as otherwise provided by this Act ...' and in *Robertson v HMRC [2005] STC SCD 723 Sp C 494* lump sum maintenance payments made to an ex-wife, which were not sanctioned under the maintenance agreement or by the court, were not to be treated as a liability to be returned to him and should be treated as part of the deceased ex-wife's estate for IHT purposes on her death.

Liabilities deductible (apart from normal debts) include the following.

(i)   Reasonable funeral expenses (including a reasonable amount for mourning for the family and servants, see F1 at 23 HMRC EXTRA-STATUTORY CONCESSIONS and the cost of a tombstone or gravestone, see Inland Revenue Statement of Practice SP7/87, 15 July 1987). The word 'reasonable' depends upon the standard of living of the deceased so that in a case similar to the funeral of the Duke of Athol in 1996, where the expense of his private army acting as an honour guard would have been allowed, any expenses that are reasonable for the attendance of family and servants will be allowed as a funeral expense. For deaths abroad embalming and transport costs will be allowed as an expense (see also Foster Inheritance Tax, para D1.42).

(ii) Inheritance tax or capital transfer tax liabilities outstanding from a previous transfer, but if the tax is not eventually paid out of the estate, an adjustment must be made.

(iii) Expenses in administering or realising property situated outside the UK, up to five per cent of the property's value where the expenses are shown to be attributable to the situation of the property. (The allowance is intended to cover the costs (in excess of the normal costs) of resealing a grant of probate etc. and obtaining the relevant tax clearance and not substantive expenses e.g. tax liabilities.) A separate note of charges should be kept to justify the claim. (Tolley's Practical Tax 1981, p 151).

(iv) Liabilities for future payments or transfer of assets taxable under *IHTA 1984, s 262*, see 8.7 CALCULATION OF TAX. Such liabilities are to be valued by reducing the amount of the further payments or assets by the chargeable portion.

(v)   Income tax liabilities arising on deemed disposals on death in respect of offshore income gains under the provisions in *ICTA 1988, ss 757–764, 27, Sch 28* as amended by *FA 2004, Sch 26* and deep discount securities under the provisions in the former *ICTA 1988, s 57* as amended by *FA 1996, Sch 15*.

[*IHTA 1984, ss 172–175; FA 1996, Sch 13 para 4, Sch 14 para 2*].

Treatment of certain debts and encumbrances. Certain liabilities may not be deducted if owed to a person who has received property from the deceased. Specifically, subject to below, where a debt incurred or encumbrance created by the deceased after 17 March 1986 would otherwise be taken into account in valuing his estate immediately before death, that liability is subject to abatement proportionate to the value of any consideration given for the debt etc. which consisted of

(*a*)   'property derived from the deceased'; or

(*b*)   consideration (not within (*a*) above) given by any person who was at any time entitled to, or amongst whose resources there was at any time included, any property derived from the deceased.

The abatement under (*b*) above does not apply to the extent it can be shown that the donee's loan etc. to the deceased was greater than the gifts received from the donor or was not made out of property derived from the deceased or that the deceased's gift was not made to facilitate the loan.

'*Property derived from the deceased*' means any property which was the subject matter of a disposition by the deceased (alone or with any other person) or which represented any of the subject matter of such a disposition (directly or indirectly) by one or more intermediate dispositions. If, however, the disposition by the deceased was neither

(A)   a transfer of value; nor

(B)   part of associated operations which included a disposition *by the deceased* (with or without another person) otherwise than for full consideration in money or money's worth to the deceased for his own use or benefit or a disposition *by any other person* which reduced the value of the deceased's property

it is left out of account. [*FA 1986, s 103(1)–(4)(6)*].

Double charges—liabilities subject to abatement and death. Relief from double charge to tax is given where, after 17 March 1986, a transfer of value which is or proves to be a chargeable transfer ('the transfer') is made by an individual ('the deceased') by virtue of which the estate of the transferee is increased or by virtue of which property becomes comprised in a settlement of which the transferee is a trustee *and* at any time before his death the deceased incurs a liability to the transferee ('the liability') which is subject to abatement under the provisions above.

Two separate calculations of tax payable as a result of death are made. In the first, the amount of the transfer of value is reduced by the amount of the debt which is disallowed or abated and, in the second, the amount of the transfer of value and of the debt are both taken into account. The higher amount of total tax is payable and, subject to below, relief is given, as the case may be, by either reducing the value of the transfer of value or by allowing the debt and charging the transfer of value in full.

Where the first calculation gives the higher amount,

1.   credit is available for any tax which became payable before the death of the deceased as is attributable to the amount of the reduction in that calculation (but not exceeding the difference between the amount of tax under the first calculation and the amount of tax which would have been paid under the second calculation if the liability had been taken into account); and

2.   the reduction applies for all IHT purposes other than a ten-year anniversary charge or a proportionate charge to tax on a discretionary settlement arising before the death of the deceased if the transfer of value was a chargeable transfer when it was made.

Where the total tax chargeable under the first and second calculations is the same, the first calculation is treated as producing the higher amount of tax.

Where there are a number of transfers by the deceased before his death which are relevant to the abated liability on death, the above provisions are applied to those transfers in reverse order i.e. latest first. [*FA 1986, s 104(1)(c); SI 1987/1130, Regs 6, 8*]. See also 22.10 GIFTS WITH RESERVATION regarding double charges relief in connection with pre-owned assets.

Example

A makes a potentially exempt transfer to B of £203,000 on 1 May 2003 and a further such transfer to him of £40,000 on 1 January 2004. On 1 July 2004 A makes a gift into a discretionary trust of £160,000 on which the trustees pay tax of £Nil. He makes a further potentially exempt transfer to B of £30,000 on 1 January 2005 but on 1 July 2005 B makes a loan to A of £100,000. No annual exemptions are available.

A dies on 1 December 2007 with a death estate of £200,000 against which a deduction is claimed for the debt of £100,000 due to B.

First calculation: disallow the debt and ignore corresponding amounts of potentially exempt transfers from A to B, starting with the latest

	IHT payable £
1 May 2003	
Potentially exempt transfer now reduced to £173,000*	—
1 January 2004	
Potentially exempt transfer now reduced to nil	—
1 July 2004	
Gift into trust £160,000 as top slice of £333,000	
Tax £13,200 less Nil already paid	13,200
1 January 2005	
Potentially exempt transfer now reduced to nil	—
1 December 2007	
Death estate £200,000 as top slice of £533,000	80,000
Total tax due as result of A's death	£93,200

* See note (C) below.

Second calculation: allow the debt and charge the potentially exempt transfers in full

	IHT payable £
1 May 2003	
Potentially exempt transfer £203,000	—
1 January 2004	
Potentially exempt transfer £40,000 as top slice of £243,000	—
1 July 2004	
Gift into trust £160,000 as top slice of £403,000	
Tax £41,200 less Nil already paid	41,200
1 January 2005	
Potentially exempt transfer £30,000 as top slice of £433,000	12,000
1 December 2007	
Death estate £100,000 as top slice of £533,000	40,000
Total tax due as a result of A's death	£93,200

Notes to the example

(A)   If the two calculations above result in the same tax chargeable, as in this case, the first of the calculations is taken by reason of *Inheritance Tax (Double Charges Relief) Regulations 1987, SI 1987/1130, Reg 8* but no such provision applies in respect of *Inheritance Tax (Double Charges Relief) Regulations 2005, SI 2005/3441*.

(B)   For examples where the calculation gives a marginal difference see 1996/97 edition and earlier.

(C)   In the first calculation the debt of £100,000 is disallowed from B to A less the corresponding amounts of potentially exempt transfers from A to B which are ignored, starting with the latest i.e. (£30,000 + £40,000 + £203,000) = £173,000 balance.

Life insurance policies. In determining the value of a person's estate immediately before death, no account is to be taken of any liability arising under or in connection with life insurance made after 30 June 1986 unless the whole of the sums assured under the policy form part of that person's estate immediately before his death. [*FA 1986, s 103(7)*]. See also April/May 2002, p 2 IHT Newsletter. 61 IHT NEWSLETTER AND TAX BULLETIN EXTRACTS.

50.4   **COMMORIENTES**

For the purposes of establishing if there has been a transfer on death, where it cannot be known which of two or more persons died first they are assumed to have died at the same instant (i.e. the rule in the *Law of Property Act 1925, s 184* that the elder is deemed to have died first does not apply for these purposes). [*IHTA 1984, s 4(2)*].

Example

If father and son die in the same accident, any property bequeathed by the father to the son passes to the son's estate (since the father is deemed under the rule quoted above to have died first) and then to the beneficiaries under the son's will, but inheritance tax is chargeable only on the transfer of the property to the son's estate and not again on the transfer of it to the beneficiaries of the son's estate.

In the case of spouses or civil partners who die in *commorientes* circumstances then the situation is complicated further by the inter-spouse/civil partner exemption under *IHTA 1984, s 18 as amended by The Tax and Civil Partnership Regulations 2005, SI 2005/3229, Reg 7*; as there is an exempt transfer on the death under *section 18(1)* then the transfer to the younger spouse or civil partner is not a chargeable transfer. However, the younger of the spouses/civil partners is deemed to have inherited the elder spouse's/civil partner's estate under the *Law of Property Act 1925, s 184* but for the purposes of Inheritance Tax under *IHTA 1984, s 4(2)* eliminates mutual gifts between individuals in such circumstances and there is no transfer of value to the younger spouse/civil partner on which inheritance tax can be charged. There is a view therefore that the elder's estate escapes inheritance tax completely and therefore a survivorship condition, which is normally desirable, is deliberately excluded in the event of the spouses/civil partners dying simultaneously (see Taxation magazine 24 September 1992 p 649 and 6 July 1995 p 362). This view is not universally accepted (see British Tax Review 1995 p 390). See also 50.2 above. See IHTM12197 for text and a useful example, which supports the view above that the elder spouse's estate is not subject to IHT at all.

See [**Case Study 6**], also 50.2 above regarding survivorship clauses and 40 QUICK SUCCESSION RELIEF.

50.5   **ALTERATIONS OF DISPOSITIONS ON DEATH**

Dispositions under a will or on an intestacy may be varied or disclaimed by an instrument in writing made by the persons who benefit or would benefit under the dispositions. Such variation or disclaimer may not be a transfer of value and may be treated as if effected by the deceased. For full details see 14 DEEDS VARYING DISPOSITIONS ON DEATH.

Where property was settled by a person's will and, within two years after his death and before any interest in possession has subsisted in the property, an event occurs on which tax would otherwise be chargeable under the provisions for SETTLEMENTS WITHOUT INTERESTS IN POSSESSION (44) (except in relation to a ten-year anniversary charge), no tax is chargeable and the event is treated as if the will had provided for it. Where the event within two years of death is one on which tax would be chargeable but for *IHTA 1984, ss 75, 76, Sch 4 para 16(1)* (property becoming subject to employee trusts or held for charitable purposes, national purposes, public benefit or a qualifying political party or comprised in a maintenance fund for historic buildings) then the will is deemed to have provided that the property should be held on the testator's death as it is after the event (i.e. the subsequent distribution to the employee trust etc.). Where a testator dies after 21 March 2006 an interest in possession in settled property mentioned above will also include an immediate post-death interest (IPDI) and an interest in a disabled person's trust. Also, where a testator dies after 21 March 2006 and his estate is held on trusts for up to two years from the date of death and would have qualified as IPDI or under *IHTA 1984, ss 71A, 71D* (i.e. bereaved minor's trusts and 18–25 trusts) then providing no person has an interest in possession in the property at that time, no tax is chargeable and the event is treated as if the will had provided for it. A late amendment to the Finance Bill was made to ensure that trusts for a bereaved minor, an 18–25 trusts and an IPDI created under *section 144* write back into the will of a deceased within two years of death will be treated as if established by the will regardless of whether before or after 22 March 2006. [*IHTA 1984, s 144; FA 2006, Sch 20 para 27*].

Because a proportionate charge (as in 44.9 SETTLEMENTS WITHOUT INTERESTS IN POSSESSION) would not arise on a distribution from a discretionary settlement where made within three months of the settlement's creation, it is important not to make a distribution within three months of the death (see *Frankland v CIR CA [1997] STC 1450*). See also *Harding and Leigh v CIR* where a testator expressed a wish that property bequeathed by his will should be transferred by the legatee to other persons and the legatee transfers any of the property in accordance with that wish within two years after the testator's death, then the transfer is not a transfer of value (i.e. not liable to inheritance tax) and it is treated as if the property had been bequeathed by the will to the transferee. [*IHTA 1984, ss 17(b), 143*]. However, in the case of *Harding and Leigh v CIR [1997] STC SCD 321 Sp C 140* the Trustees could not be treated as legatees because the Trustees in this case exercised fiduciary powers and were not beneficially entitled. The Capital Taxes Sub-Committee asked HMRC's views on the interaction between *s 142* and *s 144* in relation to intestacy; HMRC replied that in their view an event under *s 144(1)* could follow a variation satisfying *s 142(1)*. Accordingly, it would be inconsistent to distinguish between testate and intestate estates when, all other things being equal, the ability to vary the disposition is the same. This is subject to the caveat that the tax position will depend on the facts as they are at the relevant time. See Taxation Practitioner, June 1999 p 9.

Where a surviving spouse/civil partner elects under the *Administration of Estates Act 1925, s 47A* that his life interest in residuary estate be redeemed by the personal representatives by payment of its capital value, the redemption is not a transfer of value and the surviving spouse/civil partner is treated as having been entitled to that capital value instead of the life interest. [*IHTA 1984, ss 17(c), 145 as amended by The Tax and Civil Partnership Regulations 2005, SI 2005/3229, Regs 6, 31*].

Where a person disclaims his entitlement to an interest in settled property, then providing the disclaimer is not made for a consideration in money or money's worth, he is treated as not having become entitled to the interest. [*IHTA 1984, s 93*].

See 50.6 below for orders made under *Inheritance (Provision for Family and Dependants) Act 1975* and 50.7 below for legitim. See also 33.14 NATIONAL HERITAGE where, for deaths after 16 March 1987, settled property is exempt from IHT on the death of a person who has an interest in possession in the property if the terms on which the property is held are altered after his death so that it goes into a heritage maintenance fund within two years particularly with regard to the position after 21 March 2006. [*IHTA 1984, s 57A; FA 1987, s 59, Sch 9 paras 1, 4; FA 2006, Sch 20 para 17*].

50.6 **INHERITANCE (PROVISION FOR FAMILY AND DEPENDANTS) ACT 1975**

Under the above *Act*, as amended by the *Law Reform* (*Successors*) *Act 1995* and *Civil Partnership Act 2004, Sch 4 paras 15–27*, a court may order financial provision for family, civil partners and dependants of a deceased person out of his net estate. If the deceased died on or after 1 January 1996 a new category of applicant is defined as a person who 'during the whole of the period of two years ending immediately before the date when the deceased died' was living (a) in the same household as the deceased, and (b) as the husband or wife of the deceased. However, in (a) above 'living in the same household as the deceased' could also mean a period of temporary separation due to prevailing circumstances at the time. See *Gully v Dix; In re Dix deceased CA [2004] TLR 28 January 2004.* See TAX CASES (60).

ORIGINATING SUMMONS BY A WIDOW FOR LEAVE TO APPLY OUT OF TIME AND FOR REASONABLE PROVISION

IN THE HIGH COURT OF JUSTICE

200(7)... B. No ... [Chancery or Family] Division

In the Matter of the Estate of B.B. deceased

Between

	A.B.	...	Claimant
	And		
(1)	C.D.		
(2)	D.D.		
(3)	J.K.		
(4)	L.M. (a minor)	...	Defendants

LET C.D. of (*address*), D.D. of (*address*), J.K. of (*address*) and L.M. of (*address*) attend before [*in the Chancery Division:* Master .... at Chancery Chambers, Room No .., Thomas More Building, Royal Courts of Justice, Strand, London WC2A 2LL, *or in the Family Division:* District Judge .... in chambers at Somerset House, Strand, London WC2R 1LP, *or in a district registry:* the District Judge in chambers at the district registry of the High Court of Justice at (*address*)] on [[Mon]day the .... day of ..... 200(7) at .. o'clock in the [fore]noon *or* a day to be fixed] on the hearing of an application by the Claimant A.B. of (*address*):

(1)   For an order that she be granted permission to make an application under the Inheritance (Provision for Family and Dependants) Act 1975 notwithstanding that a period of 6 months from the date on which representation in regard to the estate of the above-mentioned B.B, was first taken out has ended;

(2)   For an order that such reasonable financial provision as this Honourable Court thinks fit to be made for the Claimant out of the net estate of the above mentioned B.B.;

(3)   For such further or other relief as shall be just;

(4)   For an order that the costs of this application be paid out of the said estate.

This application is made under the Inheritance (Provision for Family and Dependants) Act 1975.

AND let the defendant within [14] days after service of this summons on him counting the day of service, return the accompanying Acknowledgement of Service to the appropriate Court Office.

DATED the .... day of .... 200(7).

This provision is subject to the Court taking into account the co-habitee's age, the length of the relationship with the deceased and the contribution made by the co-habitee to the welfare of the deceased's family. [*Inheritance (Provision for Family and Dependants) Act 1975, s 1(1A)* as inserted by *Law Reform (Succession) Act 1995, s 2*]. Where such an order is made under *section 2* of the *Act* in relation to any property in the estate, the property is treated for purposes of inheritance tax as having devolved on his death subject to the provisions of the order. [*IHTA 1984, s 146(1)*].

Between   A.B.   ...   Claimant
                 And
                 C.D.   ...   Defendant

UPON THE APPLICATION of the Claimant by originating summons AND UPON HEARING Counsel for the Claimant and for the Defendant AND UPON READING the documents recorded in the court file as having been read.

[AND the Claimant and the Defendant by their Counsel consenting to this Order]

IT IS ORDERED pursuant to the provisions of Section 2 (1) of the Inheritance (Provision for Family and Dependants) Act 1975 that a sum of £ ..... be paid to the Claimant out of the capital of the Testator's estate on ..... 200(7) together with interest at the rate of ... per cent per annum as from the date of the death of the Testator namely .... 200(7).

AND IT IS ORDERED that there be taxed

(1)   on the indemnity basis the costs of and incidental to the said application of the Defendant as Executrix of the said will

(2)   on the [standard] basis the costs of the Claimant of the said application and

(3)   on the [standard] basis the costs to which the Legal Aid Act 1988 applies incurred on behalf of the Claimant

AND IT IS ORDERED that the costs first and secondly herein before directed to be taxed be paid when taxed out of the residuary estate of the testator

Etc.

In the case of *Goodchild and another v Goodchild [1997] 3 All ER 63* mutual wills were drawn up by Mr Goodchild and his wife as follows:

'1. I REVOKE all former Wills and Codicils made by me. 2. IF my wife [..] survives me for the space of twenty-eight days then I DEVISE AND BEQUEATH all my real and personal estate to her absolutely and appoint her to be the sole Executrix of this my Will. 3. IF my said wife does not survive me for the period aforesaid then I APPOINT my son [..] and my daughter [..] to be the Executors and Trustees of this my Will and I DECLARE that the following clauses shall take effect ...

CLAUSE 5. UPON TRUST for my said son [..] if he survives me for the space of twenty-eight days and if he does not so survive me then UPON TRUST for …'

The Goodchilds' wills did not contain the legal words 'mutually agreed' and the subsequent alteration of his will after Mrs Goodchild's death in favour of his new wife was a moral obligation that overcame the lack of the legal obligation. In consequence the sum awarded to the son under *section 2* for reasonable financial provision was not overturned. A further interesting point to arise out of the was the opportunity given to the parties by Carnwath J in an earlier judgment for the parties 'to arrive at a sensible financial arrangement, which meets as far as possible their respective requirements and is tax effective'. No agreement could be reached and in February 1996 it was too late; the only way of achieving a similar result would be for an order to be made under *Inheritance (Provision for Family and Dependants) Act 1975, s 2* as amended by *IHTA 1984, s 146* of which the relevant part at subsection (b) states '… an order for the payment to the applicant out of that estate of a lump sum of such amount as may be so specified …'. *Section 2 (4) of the Inheritance (Provision for Family and Dependants) Act 1975* follows on to say that the court may order consequential and supplemental provisions to '… vary the disposition of the deceased's estate effected by the will … in such a manner as the court thinks fair and reasonable having regard to the provisions of the order and all the circumstances of the case …'. However, Morritt LJ stated that where the effect of the order is to confer substantial advantage on the parties at the expense of HMRC the court should be satisfied that the order is not only within its jurisdiction but is also one which may properly be made. He went on to say '… I think that it is important for the future that if an order such as this is to be made the grounds on which it is thought to be authorised by subsection (4) should be clearly demonstrated, for the consent and wishes of the parties is not enough'.

Where during his lifetime the deceased made a disposition of property, without full consideration, with the object of defeating an application under the *Act*, the court may order (under *section 10* of the *Act*) the donee to refund any money or property required for the deceased's family or dependants. In addition, if a subsequent windfall arises to the estate and a hearing decides that provision, whether or not a moral obligation, is required then the windfall may be deemed to make any previous provision unreasonable. *Snapes v Aram and others [1998] TLR, 8 May 1998.* If the disposition was a chargeable transfer, the *personal representatives* may claim the inheritance tax or capital transfer tax paid on that transfer be repaid to them (whether or not they paid the tax in the first instance) with interest from the date of claim. A reduction in the total of lifetime chargeable transfers by the deceased is made equal to the value of the transfer refunded. (*Note.* This reduction will affect the tax rate applicable to the deceased's estate but not the rate on the other chargeable lifetime transfers). [*IHTA 1984, ss 146(2)(3), 236(3); FA 1989, s 179(1)*].

The court may make orders for financial provision out of the net estate which is deemed to include property held by persons as a result of (i) *donatio mortis causa*; (ii) any sums nominated by the deceased under any statute; and (iii) the deceased's severable share of property held in joint tenancy. Any such property on which inheritance tax is payable is treated as part of the net estate after deduction of the tax and for this purpose the amount of tax deducted is not affected by any court order. Any repayment of that tax is made to the personal representatives and not to the person holding the property. [*IHTA 1984, s 146(4)*].

Any tax refund (including any interest thereon) to the personal representatives or property recovered is treated as part of the deceased's estate for the purposes of transfer of value made by him on his death. [*IHTA 1984, s 146(2)(5)(7)*].

The court may also order financial provision out of settled property, or for property to be settled on variation of a settlement. In this case there is no charge to tax under *IHTA 1984, s 52(1)* (deemed transfer of value on termination of a life interest in settled property). Anything done in compliance with such a court order is not an occasion for charge under the provisions relating to SETTLEMENTS WITHOUT INTERESTS IN POSSESSION (44). [*IHTA 1984, s 146(6)*].

Northern Ireland. Corresponding provisions are applied by *SI 1979/924* and *927*.

50.7 **LEGITIM**

Under Scottish law children (or remoter issue) have the right to share in the movable estate of a deceased parent. This is called legitim. Where a testator dies after 12 November 1974 bequeathing property to the surviving spouse/civil partner and leaving insufficient property in the estate to satisfy entitlement to legitim of a minor, inheritance tax is charged as if legitim had been satisfied (i.e. the spouse/civil partner exemption will not apply to that much of the property) but this may be varied as follows.

(*a*)   The executors or judicial factor of the testator may elect in writing (within two years of the death or longer if the Board permit) that tax be charged as if the gift to the surviving spouse/civil partner took effect in full (so obtaining benefit of the spouse/civil partner exemption). If the minor subsequently claims his legal rights or has not renounced his rights by his twentieth birthday (or longer if the Board permit), the spouse/civil partner exemption is lost to that extent and tax becomes payable (by the child) on the scale applicable at the date of death with interest from the original due date (i.e. six months after the end of the month in which death occurred). If the child claiming legitim does not pay the tax, see points (*b*)–(*d*) at 29.3 LIABILITY FOR TAX for persons with secondary liability.

(*b*)   The child may renounce his claim to legitim by his twentieth birthday (or longer if the Board permit) and tax will be repayable (because of the spouse/civil partner exemption) with interest (which shall not constitute income for any tax purposes) from the date on which the tax was originally paid. Such a renunciation is not a transfer of value.

(*c*)   Where a child dies before renouncing his claim under (*b*) above, his executors may renounce his claim within two years of his death, and his legal rights to legitim will not form part of his estate on his death.

[*IHTA 1984, ss 17(d), 147, 209(2)(3), 236(4); FA 1989, s 179(1)(3); The Tax and Civil Partnership Regulations 2005, SI 2005/3229, Regs 6, 32*].

50.8   **SCOTTISH AGRICULTURAL LEASES**

See 5.8 AGRICULTURAL PROPERTY for special rules regarding such leases passing on death.

50.9   **INTESTACY**

The Distribution of Intestate Estates

For deaths on or after 1 January 1996 under the *Administration of Estates Act 1925, s 49(1)(a)*; not applicable in Scotland.

Spouse and issue survive. Note. For these purposes spouse should also mean '*civil partner*'.

Spouse receives	*Issue receive*
All personal chattels; £125,000 absolutely (or the entire estate where this is less); life interest in one half of residue (if any).	One half of residue (if any) on statutory trusts *plus* the other half of residue on statutory trusts upon the death of the spouse.

Spouse survives without issue

Spouse receives	*Remainder distributable to*
All personal chattels; £200,000 absolutely (or the entire estate where this is less); one half share of residue (if any) absolutely.	(a) The deceased's parents. If no parent survives: (b) on trust for the deceased's brother and sisters of the whole blood and the issue of any such deceased brother or sister.

Spouse survives but no issue, parents, brothers or sisters or their issue

Whole estate to surviving spouse.

No spouse survives

Estate held for the following in the order given with no class of beneficiaries participating unless all those in a prior class have predeceased. Statutory trusts may apply except under (b) and (e).

(a)   Issue of the deceased.

(b)   Parents.

(c)   Brothers and sisters and the issue of a deceased brother or sister.

(d)   Half-brothers and half-sisters and the issue of any deceased half-brother or half-sister.

(e)   Grandparents.

(f)   Uncles and aunts and the issue of any deceased uncle or aunt.

(g)   Half-brothers and half-sisters of the deceased's parents and the issue of any deceased half-uncle or half-aunt.

(h)   The Crown, the Duchy of Lancaster or the Duchy or Cornwall.

Notes

(A)   See IHTM12177, IHTM35161 and IHTM35165 for disclaimer of absolute benefits under intestacy, election by spouse/civil partner of intestate and the treatment of settled property with regard to competency to dispose.

(B)   See Taxation Practitioner (now Tax Adviser), June 1999 Page 9 for the supposition that it would be inconsistent to distinguish between testate and intestate estates when the ability to vary the dispositions on death is the same.

(C)   In this context 'Spouse' means a person to whom the deceased was married at the date of death even where there is a separation or estrangement applicable. 'Spouse' does not mean cohabiter, who has no rights of benefit under the rules of intestacy or a divorced ex-spouse.

(D)   'Child' means an adopted child and an illegitimate child but excludes a stepchild or the child of a co-habitee.

(E)   Note that the *Civil Partnership Act 2004, Sch 4 paras 7–12* amends the *Administration of Estates Act 1925* to ensure that the remaining surviving partner in a civil partnership will effectively acquire the same rights as a spouse in a case of intestacy.

HM Revenue & Customs

Assets held in trust (settled property)

Name

Date of death

/   /

You have said that the deceased had a right to benefit from a trust created by a deed or under someone else's Will or intestacy. Answer the following questions and give the further details we ask for. If necessary, use a separate form for each trust. You should read form D5(Notes) before filling this form.

1 Was the deceased's intersest in possession one of the following

- an interest in possession that commenced before 22 March 2006 and remained in existence between then and the date of death

  No   Yes

- an immediate post death interest

  No   Yes

- a disabled person's interest

  No   Yes

- a transitional serial interest

  No   Yes

The types of interest listed above are defined in the guide IHT210 - How to fill in the IHT200.

If you have answered 'No' to all the above you do not need to fill in any more of this form and details of the settled property should not be included in form **IHT200**.

2 What is the name of the person who created the trust either during their lifetime or by their will or intestacy?

3 What are the names and addresses of the trustees?

4 On what date was the trust created?

/   /

5 **Settled property where tax may not be paid by instalments**

- Assets

Total of assets SP 1 £

D5

www.hmrc.gov.uk/cto

Helpline 0845 30 20 900

HMRC 08/06

(Substitute)(LexisNexis Butterworths)

50.9 Transfers on Death

- Liabilities

Total of liabilities	SP2 £
Net assets *(box SP1 less box Sp2)*	SP3 £

- Exemptions and reliefs

Total exemptions and reliefs	SP4 £
Net total of settled property where tax may not be paid by installments *(box SP3 less box SP4)*	SP5 £

6 **Settled property where tax may be paid by installments**

Do you wish to pay tax on these assets by installments?　　　　Yes　　No

- Assets

Total of assets	SP6

- Liabilities

Total of liabilities	SP7 £
Net assets *(box SP6 less box SP7)*	SP8 £

- Exemptions and reliefs

Total exemptions and reliefs	SP9 £
Net total of settled property where tax may be paid by installments *(box SP8 less box SP9)*	SP10 £

51   Transfers Within Seven Years Before Death

Cross-references. See 8 CALCULATION OF TAX; 41 RATES OF TAX; 50 TRANSFERS ON DEATH; 59 WORKING CASE STUDY.

Simon's Direct Tax Service, part I3.511.

51.1   GENERAL

The report by the Comptroller and Auditor General on 3 March 1999 indicated that in 1997–98 the NAO had identified £20 million lifetime transfers which had not been included in the initial accounts of estates. This is one of the reasons that Form D3 requires details of lifetime gifts. See below for the form but note that from February 2004 the Form D3 was revised to include a new Box 1e asking whether the deceased has made any regular gifts out of income. A new Form D3a requires details of the income and expenditure to support the claim under *IHTA 1984, s 21*. IHT 210 (Notes) at D3 (Notes) states

> 'It is not just outright gifts, such as giving a cheque for £10,000 to someone on a special occasion, that are relevant for inheritance tax. The law says that there will be a gift whenever there is "a loss to the donor" (the "donor" is the person the gift). This can happen in different ways. For example, a parent may sell a house to a son or a daughter for less than they could sell the property on the open market. This will be a loss to the donor. A person may hold some shares that gives them control of a company. They may sell only a few shares to a relative but losing control of the company reduces the value of their other shares. This too will be a loss to the donor. If you are not sure whether you should include details of a particular gift, please telephone our Helpline.'

Where a chargeable lifetime transfer is made, tax on the value transferred is initially charged at one half of the death rates. Where a transferor then dies within seven years of the transfer, the tax is recomputed at the death rates but the tax rates (but not the value of the lifetime chargeable transfer) are subject to below, tapered as follows.

Years between transfer and death	Percentage of full tax rate
Not more than 3	100%
More than 3 but not more than 4	80%
More than 4 but not more than 5	60%
More than 5 but not more than 6	40%
More than 6 but not more than 7	20%

Where, between the chargeable transfer and the date of death, tax rates are reduced by the substitution of a new table of rates, the additional tax is charged as if the new table applicable on death had applied to the transfer.

The tapering provisions above do not apply where the tapered tax as calculated would be less than the tax which would have been chargeable using half death rates if the transferor had not died within seven years of the transfer i.e. the tax payable cannot be reduced below that originally chargeable at half death rates. [*IHTA 1984, s 7(2)(4)(5), Sch 2 para 2; FA 1986, Sch 19 paras 2, 37*]. See IHT 15, pp 23–24.

Where POTENTIALLY EXEMPT TRANSFERS (38) are made within seven years of death, no tax would have been payable at the time of the transfer. On death, tax is calculated at the full death rates applying at the time of death, subject to the tapering of tax rates (but not of values) above. (There is no lower limit on the tax, as no tax was chargeable when the transfer was made.) [*IHTA 1984, s 7(4)(5), Sch 2 para 1A; FA 1986, Sch 19 paras 2, 37*].

If no tax is actually due on a death in relation to a lifetime chargeable transfer or potentially exempt transfer which proves to be a chargeable transfer (e.g. because the value concerned falls within the nil rate band), the above relief can have no effect.

51.2   Transfers Within Seven Years Before Death

See 29.4 LIABILITY FOR TAX for the persons liable for the additional tax.

Transitional provisions. Where a death occurs on or after 18 March 1986, the above provisions do not affect the tax chargeable on a transfer of value occurring before that date. [*FA 1986, Sch 19 para 40*]. The tax on such a chargeable transfer will continue only to be recomputed at the higher death rates if the transferor dies within three years of the transfer.

51.2   RELIEF

Where tax or additional tax becomes payable because of the transferor's death within seven years of a transfer, relief is available where all or part of the value transferred is attributable to the value of property which

(*a*)   at the date of death is the property of the transferee or his spouse or civil partner; or

(*b*)   before that date has been sold by the transferee or his spouse or civil partner by a 'qualifying sale'

unless the property is tangible movable property that is a wasting asset (i.e. if, immediately before the transfer, it had a predictable useful life not exceeding 50 years, having regard to the purposes for which it was held by the transferor; and always treating plant and machinery as wasting).

A *'qualifying sale'* is a sale at arm's length for a price freely negotiated at the time of sale where no person concerned as vendor (or any person having an interest in the proceeds) is connected with the purchaser (or any person having an interest in the purchase). No provision must be made in connection with the sale for the vendor etc. to have any right to acquire any part of the property sold or any interest in or created out of it.

Where the above conditions are satisfied, then on a claim by a person liable to pay the whole or part of the tax or additional tax payable as a result of the transferor's death within seven years of the transfer, the tax is calculated on the market value of the property at the 'relevant date' if lower than at the time of the chargeable transfer. [*IHTA 1984, ss 131, 132; FA 1986, Sch 19 para 23; The Tax and Civil Partnership Regulations 2005, SI 2005/3229, Reg 25*].

The *'relevant date'* is the date of death under (*a*) above or qualifying sale under (*b*) above.

Example

A makes transfers on 21 September 2003 to B of properties valued at that date at £490,000 and to C of cash of £240,116 on the same day. A died on 28 April 2007 when the properties gifted to B were valued at £390,000.

		Gross £	Tax £
Value of properties to B	£490,000		
Less annual exemption (apportioned) Note B	£4,027	485,973	113,854
Cash to C	£240,116		
Less annual exemption (apportioned) Note B	£1,973	238,143	55,792
		724,116	
Less nil rate band		300,000	
		£424,116	£169,646

Recalculate the tax on the gifts to take into account the 20% taper relief as gifts were made between three and four years before death and in the case of B there has also been a fall in value of £100,000 in the properties since the gift of them by A to B and the executors have completed form IHT 38. With regard to the completion of form IHT 38 by the executors or personal representatives see 56.5 VALUATION.

Tax payable on PETs that have become chargeable because of A's death within seven years.

Value of properties	£490,000
Less annual exemption	4,027
	485,973
Less fall in value	100,000
	385,973
Value of cash	238,143
	624,116
Less nil rate band	300,000
	£324,116 @ 40% = £129,646

Apportionment of tax:

Gift to B

$$£129,646 \times \frac{385,973}{624,116} \times 80\% = £64,142$$

Gift to C

$$£169,646 \times \frac{238,143}{724,116} \times 80\% = £44,634$$

Notes to the example

(A)   *Section 131* relief only reduces the value of a transfer for the purpose of calculating the tax on that transfer (i.e. B's gift) and it does *not* affect its value for cumulation purposes (i.e. C's gift). See IHT 15 pp 21–26.

(B)   A's gifts to B and C were made on the same day so the annual exemption for 2003/04 and the unutilised annual exemption for 2002/03 are apportioned between B and C's gifts respectively.

(C)   Tapering relief applies as the gifts were made between three and four years before death of A therefore 80% applies.

(D)   The claim should be signed by one or more of the persons liable and should

- identify the transfer and transferred property

- confirm the property is retained (or sold by a qualifying sale in which case provide details)

- confirm that the property is the same at the date of death (or sale) as it was at the date of transfer (or give details of any changes).

(See IHTM14627).

Market value. For these purposes, market value is the price which the property might reasonably be expected to fetch if sold in the open market but that price must not be assumed to be reduced on the ground that the whole property is on the market at one and the same time. In determining the price of unquoted shares (in relation to transfers of value made, and other events occurring, before 17 March 1987, shares not quoted on a recognised stock exchange), it is assumed that there is available to any prospective purchaser all the information which such a person might reasonably require if he were proposing to purchase them from a willing vendor by private treaty and at arm's length.

Where the property transferred is subject to AGRICULTURAL PROPERTY (5) or BUSINESS PROPERTY (7) relief, the market value at any time is calculated as reduced by the appropriate percentage under those provisions. [*IHTA 1984, ss 131(2A), 140(2); FA 1986, Sch 19 para 23*].

Special provisions apply to ascertaining the market value of specified property at the relevant date as follows:

(a) *Shares—capital receipts.* Any capital payment (i.e. any money or money's worth which is not income for the purposes of income tax), including the sale of a provisional allotment of shares, received by the transferee or his spouse or civil partner before the relevant date in respect of shares transferred is added to the market value of the shares unless already reflecting the right to the payment. See note 7 of form IHT 35.

(b) *Payments of calls* made by the transferee or his spouse or civil partner before the relevant date on the shares transferred reduce the market value unless already reflecting the liability.

(c) *Reorganisation of share capital etc.* A new holding received for the original shares transferred is treated as the same property, but where the transferee or his spouse or civil partner gives any consideration for the new holding before the relevant date, the market value is reduced accordingly unless already reflecting the liability.

Consideration for the new holding does not include any surrender, cancellation or other alteration of any of the original shares or rights attached thereto *or* any consideration consisting of the application, in paying up the new holding or any part of it, of assets of the company concerned or any dividend or other distribution declared out of those assets but not made.

(d) *Transactions of close companies.* Where the transferred property consists of shares in a close company and at any time after the chargeable transfer and before the relevant date, there is a 'relevant transaction' in relation to the shares the market value of the property transferred on the relevant date is increased by the difference between

 (i) the market value of the transferred property at the time of the chargeable transfer; and

 (ii) what that value would have been if the relevant transaction had occurred before rather than after that time.

Where the relevant transaction increases the estate of the transferor or his UK-domiciled spouse or civil partner, the increase to the market value of the property on the relevant date is reduced by that amount.

'*Relevant transactions*' is a transfer of value by the company or an alteration in the company's share or loan capital not consisting of quoted shares (in relation to transfers of value made, and other events occurring, before 17 March 1987, shares quoted on a recognised stock exchange) or in any rights attaching to unquoted shares or debentures in the company (in relation to transfers of value made, and other events occurring, before 17 March 1987, shares or debentures in the company not quoted on a recognised stock exchange).See Note below.

(e) *Interests in land.* Where there has been a change in the 'interest in land' or its state between the date of transfer and the relevant date, the difference between the market value at the date of transfer and what would have been the market value if the change had prevailed at that date is added to the market value at the relevant date. Any statutory compensation received is also added. '*Interest in land*' does not include any estate, interest or right by way of mortgage or other security.

See Note below.

(*f*)   *Leases.* Where the transferred property is a lease with less than fifty years to run at the time of the chargeable transfer, the market value on the relevant date is increased by the fraction

$$\frac{P(1)\text{-}P(2)}{[P(1)]}$$

where

P(1) = the appropriate percentage from the table for depreciation of leases contained in *TCGA 1992, Sch 8 para 1* for the duration of the lease at the time of the chargeable transfer; and

P(2) = the appropriate percentage for the duration of the lease on the relevant date.

(*g*)   *Other property.* Where the property at the relevant date is not the same in all respects as the property transferred, the difference between the value transferred and what that value would have been if the change in the property had prevailed at the time of the transfer, is added to the market value at the relevant date. Where, between the time of the chargeable transfer and the relevant date, any benefits in money or money's worth are derived from the property which exceed a reasonable return on its market value at the time of transfer, the excess is added to the market value at the relevant date. See Note below.

Note. In (*d*), (*e*) and (*g*) above, if the market value at the date of transfer is less than it would have been if a change had prevailed at that date, the market value at the relevant date is reduced to what it would have been if the change had not occurred. [*IHTA 1984, ss 133–140; FA 1987, s 58; Sch 8 paras 10, 11; The Tax and Civil Partnership Regulations 2005, SI 2005/3229, Regs 26–30*].

See 45.1 SHARES AND SECURITIES for the definition of 'quoted' or 'listed' and 'unquoted' in relation to shares and securities.

HM Revenue & Customs

Gifts and other transfers of value

Name

Date of death

/   /

You have said that the deceased had transferred assets during their lifetime. Answer the following questions and give the further details we ask for. You should read form D3(Notes) before filling in this form.

1   Did the deceased within seven years of their death

1a   make any gift or transfer to, or for the benefit of, another person?   No ☐   Yes ☐

1b   create any trust or settlement or transfer additional assets into an existing trust or settlement?   No ☐   Yes ☐

1c   pay any premium on a life insurance policy for the benefit of someone else other than the deceased's spouse or civil partner?   No ☐   Yes ☐

1d   cease to have any right to benefit from any assets held in trust or in a settlement?   No ☐   Yes ☐

1e   make any gifts which are claimed to be exempt because they were regular gifts made from income?   No ☐   Yes ☐

If the answer to any part of question 1 is "Yes", fill in the details we ask for below.
If the answer to question 1e is "Yes" fill in form D3(a) in addition to this form.

Date of gift	Name and relationship of recipient and description of assets	Value at date of gift	Amount and type of exemption claimed	Net value after exemptions

Total   LT1   £

Please turn over

| D3 | www.hmrc.gov.uk/cto | Helpline 0845 30 20 900 | HMRC 08/06 |

506

2   Pre-owned assets

2a   Did the deceased make an election that the income tax charge should
not apply to
• assets they previously owned and they retained a benefit in **or**
• the deceased contribution to the purchase price of assets acquired by another person, but in which the
deceased retained a benefit.

| N/A | No | Yes |

If you have answered 'yes' to question 2a, include details at question 2b.

2b

Date of gift	Date of election	Description of assets and POA reference number	Value at date of death	Amount and type of exemption	Net value after exemptions

Total **LT2** £

3   Gifts with reservation

3a   Did the deceased transfer, on or after 18 March 1986, any assets during their lifetime
but the person receiving the gift did not take full possession of it, or

| No | Yes |

3b   if the gift was of or involved land, did the deceased or their spouse or their civil partner
continue to enjoy a significant right or interest in that land enabling them to occupy
or enjoy some other benefit from it, or were they party to a significant arrangement in
relation to the land such as a lease or trust that allowed them to do so?

| No | Yes |

3c   if the gift was of any other asset, did the deceased continue to have some
right to benefit from all or part of the asset?

| No | Yes |

If the answer to any part of question 3 is "Yes", fill the details we ask for below.

Date of gift	Name and relationship of recipient and description of assets	Value at date of death	Amount and type of exemption claimed	Net value after exemptions

Total **LT3** £

4   Earlier transfers

Did the deceased make any *chargeable* transfers during the 7 years **before**
the earliest date of the gifts shown at boxes LT1, LT2 and LT3 above?

| No | Yes |

*If the answer to question 4 is "Yes", fill in the details below, **but do not include the value in any of the tax calculations.***

Date of gift	Name and relationship of recipient and description of assets	Value at date of gift	Amount and type of exemption claimed	Net value after exemptions

51.2 Transfers Within Seven Years Before Death

Inland Revenue Capital Taxes

Gifts made as part of normal expenditure out of income

Name		Date of death	IR CT reference
		/ /	

You should read form D3 (Notes) before filling in this form

Give details of the deceased's income and expenditure

	Income	Tax Year in which gifts made (6 April to 5 April) eg 2001/2002						
1		/	/	/	/	/	/	/
	Salary							
	Investments							
	Other							
	Gross Income							
	Less Tax Paid							
	Net Income							
2	**Expenditure**							
	Gifts							
	Bills							
	Expenses							
	Nursing Home Fees							
	Other							
	Total Expenditure							
	Surplus income for the year							

D3a

52 Transitional Provisions

Cross-references. See 59 WORKING CASE STUDY.

Simon's Direct Tax Service, part I1.207, I1.401.

52.1 **ESTATE DUTY**

Nature and abolition of estate duty. Estate duty was introduced by the *Finance Act 1894*. It levied a duty on all property passing on deaths after 1 August 1894, with certain exceptions and reliefs. The chargeable property was aggregated and the duty applied on successive slices at increasing rates. Gifts during the life of the donor were not subject to the duty unless they were made within seven years of the death (four years in Northern Ireland) and reduced rates applied if the death was during the fifth, sixth or seventh year (third and fourth in Northern Ireland).

Estate duty was abolished for property passing on deaths after 12 March 1975. [*FA 1975, s 49(1)*].

52.2 Any reference (in whatever terms) to estate duty or death duties in any document (whenever executed) is to have effect as if it included a reference to CTT and IHT. [*IHTA 1984, Sch 6 para 1; FA 1986, s 100(1)(b)*].

52.3 **Surviving spouse exemption.** Where a person's spouse (or former spouse) died before 13 November 1974 and left an interest in possession in property to the surviving spouse, estate duty would have been chargeable on that death. To avoid a double charge to tax, there is no charge to CTT or IHT on either the subsequent death of the surviving spouse, or on the lifetime termination of the interest provided that there would have been no charge on death. [*FA 1894, s 5(2); IHTA 1984, Sch 6 para 2; FA 1986, s 100(1)(b)*].

52.4 **Sales and mortgages of reversionary interests.** The CTT or IHT payable by a purchaser or mortgagee when a reversionary interest purchased or mortgaged for full consideration before 27 March 1974 falls into possession is not to exceed the estate duty which would have been charged before the introduction of CTT. This limitation does not apply if the interest was sold or mortgaged to a close company of which the seller or mortgagor was a participator except to the extent that other persons had rights or interests in the company. [*IHTA 1984, Sch 6 para 3; FA 1986, s 100(1)(b)*].

52.5 **National heritage objects.** Where there is a chargeable event in relation to objects of national etc. interest which were conditionally exempt for estate duty purposes, there may be a charge to estate duty rather than CTT or IHT in certain circumstances. [*IHTA 1984, Sch 6 para 4; FA 1986, s 100(1)(b)*]. See [**Case Study 3**].

52.6 **CAPITAL TRANSFER TAX**

Capital transfer tax was introduced by the *Finance Act 1975* and charged on lifetime transfers made after 26 March 1974 and on transfers on deaths occurring after 12 March 1975 when it replaced estate duty. Following the *Finance Act 1975* there were substantial alterations to the legislation including the reduction of the open-ended cumulation period to one of ten years and the introduction of a new regime for the taxation of discretionary trusts. The legislation was consolidated in *Capital Transfer Tax Act 1984* which came into force on 1 January 1985.

CTT was effectively replaced by the revised provisions relating to inheritance tax for events occurring after 17 March 1986.

The *Capital Transfer Act 1984* may be cited as the *Inheritance Tax Act 1984*. Any reference to CTT in the *1984 Act* or any other *Act* passed before or executed, made, served or issued

52.7   Transitional Provisions

on or before 25 July 1986 has effect as a reference to inheritance tax unless relating to a liability arising before that date. [*FA 1986, s 100*].

52.7   **Transfers before 18 March 1986.** Although the provisions relating to IHT apply to events occurring on or after 18 March 1986, where a death or other event occurs on or after that date, the amendments to the CTT legislation in *FA 1986, Sch 19, Part I* do not affect the tax chargeable on a transfer of value occurring before that date. [*FA 1986, Sch 19 para 40(1)*]. The effect of this provision is that any additional tax payable on a chargeable lifetime transfer made before 18 March 1986 as a result of the transferor's death after 17 March 1986 is calculated under the CTT rules. The tax is, however, calculated using the rates in force at the time of death. [*FA 1986, Sch 19 para 44*]. It should be noted that the rate of tax on a chargeable transfer (whether a lifetime chargeable transfer, a deemed transfer on death or a potentially exempt transfer proving to be a chargeable transfer) made after 17 March 1986 (i.e. when IHT rules apply) will depend on the cumulative value of previous chargeable transfers made within the seven-year period ending with the date of the transfer (including, where applicable, chargeable transfers made before 18 March 1986 when CTT rules applied). See 1.5 INTRODUCTION AND BASIC PRINCIPLES.

The above provision does not authorise the making of a claim under the rules relating to MUTUAL TRANSFERS (32) where the donee's transfer occurs after 17 March 1986. [*FA 1986, Sch 19 para 40(2)*].

53   Trusts for Bereaved Minors

Cross-reference. 3 ACCUMULATION AND MAINTENANCE TRUSTS; 44 SETTLEMENTS WITHOUT INTERESTS IN POSSESSION.

Other Sources. Taxation magazine, 27 July 2006, p 464; Tolley's UK Taxation of Trusts; Foster, part E1.02.

53.1   **Transfers into trusts for bereaved minors.** A trust created under the terms of someone's will or intestacy will not come within the relevant property trust regime if it is a trust for a bereaved minor. A 'trust for a bereaved minor' is a testamentary trust for the benefit of a person under the age of 18, at least one of whose parents, or as the case may be step-parent or person having parental responsibility e.g. legal guardian, has died and the trust arises in any one of the following circumstances:

(a)   Statutory trusts arising on an intestacy under *Administration of Estates Act 1925, ss 46, 47(1)* where such terms of statutory trust are invariable so that any trust adhering to that act will qualify; or

(b)   Settled property is held on statutory trusts for the benefit of a 'bereaved minor' where the trust is established under the will of a deceased parent or, as the case may be, step-parent; or

(c)   Settled property is held on statutory trust for the benefit of a 'bereaved minor' as a result of payments from the Criminal Injuries Compensation Scheme such that payments have been made for the benefit of the minor as a result of

(i)   the scheme being established by arrangements under the *Criminal Injuries Compensation Act 1995*;

(ii)   arrangements made by the Secretary of State for compensation for criminal injuries which were in operation before commencement of those Criminal Injuries Compensation schemes;

(iii)   the scheme being established by arrangements under the *Criminal Injuries Compensation (Northern Ireland) Order 2002*.

[*IHTA 1984, s 71, 71A, 71B , 71C, 71H; FA 2006, Sch 20 paras 1, 2, 3*].

In relation to (b) and (c) the bereaved minor must, prior to or upon the attainment of the age of 18 years, be absolutely entitled to the settled property and also absolutely entitled to any income arising therefrom and any income that has been accumulated. Whilst the beneficiary is under the age of 18 if any of the capital of the settled property is applied it must be applied for the benefit of the bereaved minor only. If the trust property is not so applied then whilst the bereaved minor is under the age of 18 years the income arising therefrom, if any, must be a full entitlement or the income must not be applied for the benefit of any other person.

In connection with the above paragraph, 'bereaved minor's trusts' are not treated as failing the requirements of entitlement due to age, property, income or accumulations because of the requirements of the *Trustee Act 1925, s 32* or *Trustee Act (Northern Ireland) 1958, s 33* or where trustees have similar powers. [*IHTA 1984, s 71A(4); FA 2006, Sch 20 para 1*].

For these purposes 'parent' includes step-parent or 'guardian' who has parental responsibility for the minor as defined within the *Children Act 1989, s 3* or where applicable the *Children Act (Scotland) Act 1995, s 1(3)* or the *Children (Northern Ireland) Order 1995*. [*IHTA 1984, s 71H; FA 2006, Sch 20 para 1*].

53.1 Trusts for Bereaved Minors

Example 1

Mr and Mrs A both die in a boating accident on 12 July 2007 whilst on holiday and it is not known who survived the other and neither has made a will but Mr A is the elder of the two. They have two children who are aged four years and are twins and both the deceased have parents still living. Their estates are valued at £300,000 and £310,000 for Mr and Mrs A respectively. As there is no will or survivorship provision made by either there is the possibility that the parents of either Mr A or Mrs A may wish to prove their son/daughter survived the spouse and thereby share in both estates, however, under the *Law Reform (Succession) Act 1995, s 1* in the case of intestate spouses each estate passes as though the other had predeceased i.e. the estates pass as though each died as widow and widower. Note that there is a different treatment for IHT purposes where there is intestacy and deaths have occurred in *commorientes* circumstances. See Example 2 below.

The *Administration of Estates Act 1925, s 46(2A)* has the effect in Mr A's and Mrs A's case of their assets passing to their issue (applicable in this case to be held on statutory trusts as they are minors) so that no class of beneficiaries can participate unless all those in a prior class have predeceased. The parents of Mr and Mrs A will not therefore benefit from their children's intestate estates. The parents of Mrs A have agreed to act as guardians to the two children as the parents of Mr A are living abroad. Statutory trusts for the children due to their minority therefore arise on an intestacy and come within (*a*) above. However, see Example 2 below regarding the situation where settled property on bereaved minors trusts ceases to be property which satisfies the necessary conditions of *IHTA 1984, s 71B(2)(3) as inserted by FA 2006, Sch 20 para 1*.

The Distribution of Intestate Estates

For deaths on or after 1 January 1996 under the *Administration of Estates Act 1925, s 49(1)(a)*; not applicable in Scotland.

No spouse survives

Estate held for the following in the order given with no class of beneficiaries participating unless all those in a prior class have predeceased. Statutory trusts may apply except under (b) and (e).

(a)   Issue of the deceased.

(b)   Parents.

(c)   Brothers and sisters and the issue of a deceased brother or sister.

(d)   Half-brothers and half-sisters and the issue of any deceased half-brother or half-sister.

(e)   Grandparents.

(f)   Uncles and aunts and the issue of any deceased uncle or aunt.

(g)   Half-brothers and half-sisters of the deceased's parents and the issue of any deceased half-uncle or half-aunt.

(h)   The Crown, the Duchy of Lancaster or the Duchy or Cornwall.

Notes to the example

(A)   There will probably need to be a clause in the statutory trust that enables funds to be paid to the legal guardians of the two children so that income can be applied for their benefit. Trustees may pay funds to a guardian that belong to the child and the trust deed can be worded to incorporate this as seen below. A minor cannot give good receipt for trust income unless he/she is married and that is not the case in this situation. [*Law of Property Act 1925, s 21*].

'Where the Trustees may apply the income for the benefit of a minor, they may do so by paying the income to the minor's guardian on behalf of the minor, or to minor if he has attained the age of 16. The Trustees are under no duty to enquire into the use of the income unless they have knowledge of circumstances which call for enquiry.'

(B)   In many cases where the bereaved minor's trust has been set up the funds pertaining to that trust will have been subject to death rates of IHT where the estate is in excess of the appropriate nil rate band.

(C)   Provided the grandparents secure parental responsibility for the minors within the meaning of the *Children Act 1989, s 3* then provided the requirements within (*a*)–(*c*) are met above on the death of one of the grandparents any trust set up in favour of the children under 18 will also become a trust for a bereaved minor thereby enabling capital to skip a generation. [*IHTA 1984, 71H; FA 2006, Sch 20 para 1*].

'*Bereaved Minor*' means a person who has not yet attained the age of 18 years and at least one of whose parents, or, as the case may be, step-parent has died. For these purposes '*bereaved minor*' includes all beneficiaries within a relevant class provided they are alive and are under the specified age of 18. See CIOT/STEP clarification dated 29 June 2007. [*IHTA 1984, s 71C inserted by FA 2006, Sch 20 para 1*].

'*Parent*' for these purposes also means step-parent or person with 'parental responsibility' within the *Children Act 1989, s 3*. [*IHTA 1984, s 71H inserted by FA 2006, Sch 20 para 1*].

Note that unlike accumulation and maintenance settlements where no interest in possession subsists in the settled property and the income from that settled property is to be accumulated so far as not applied for the maintenance, education or benefit of a beneficiary the new 'bereaved minor' can be given an interest in possession at the outset. Therefore there are varying possibilities in the drafting of the trust deed for the 'bereaved minor' which will need to address the fact whether a discretionary or interest in possession subsists. As it could be said that the discretionary trust and interest in possession trust regimes attract the same tax burdens now it might be preferable to ensure that an interest in possession trust is formed. See SETTLEMENTS WITH INTERESTS IN POSSESSION (43).

53.2   **Treatment of payments, etc. out of trusts for bereaved minors** A charge to tax arises

(*a*)   where settled property on bereaved minors trusts ceases to be property which satisfies the necessary conditions of *IHTA 1984, s 71A* as detailed in 53.1 at (*a*)–(*c*) above, or

(*b*)   if the trustees make a 'disposition' which reduces the value of the settled property. '*Disposition*' includes an omission to exercise a right, unless not deliberate, which is treated as made at the latest time the right could have been exercised. [*IHTA 1984, ss 70(10), 71B(1)(3)*].

The rate is determined by reference to the settlor's cumulative transfers in the seven years preceding the date on which the settlement commenced, as well as the settlement's cumulative transfers in the ten years preceding the anniversary.

Tax is calculated using lifetime Tables (see 41 RATES OF TAX) at the following rates

(1)   where the whole of the relevant property has been comprised in the settlement throughout the ten-year period ending immediately before the ten-year anniversary, at 30% of the effective rate,

(2) and where the whole or part of the relevant property was not relevant property or was not comprised in the settlement throughout the ten years ending immediately before the ten-year anniversary, at 30% of the effective rate reduced by one-fortieth for each successive 'quarter' in the ten-year period which expired before the property became, or last became, relevant property.

The '*effective rate*' is the rate found by expressing the tax chargeable as a percentage of the amount on which tax is charged on an assumed chargeable transfer by an assumed transferor. [*IHTA 1984, s 66(1)(2)*]. See IHT 16, p 13.

No charge arises

(i) on a beneficiary's becoming absolutely entitled to the settled property (not necessarily in fixed shares) on or before attaining the specified age of 18 years, or

(ii) on the death of a beneficiary before attaining the specified age of 18 years (but see temporary charitable exit rules below), or

(iii) on being paid or applied for the advancement or benefit of the bereaved minor(s), or

(iv) on the 'payment' of costs or expenses attributable to the property, or

(v) where any payment is, or will be, income for income tax purposes of any person (or, in the case of a non-resident, would be if he were so resident).

[*IHTA 1984, ss 70(3)(8)(10), 71B(2)(3); FA 2006, Sch 20 para 1*].

'*Payment*' includes the transfer of assets other than money. [*IHTA 1984, s 63, s 70(3)(4), s 71(4)(5)*].

Tax is charged on the amount by which the trust property is less immediately after the event giving rise to the charge than it would have been but for the event (i.e. the loss to donor principle), grossed-up where the settlement pays the tax. [*IHTA 1984, s 71B(3); FA 2006, Sch 20 para 1*].

The rate at which tax is charged is the aggregate of the following percentages for each complete successive 'quarter' in the 'relevant period'. [*IHTA 1984, ss 70(7); 71B(3); FA 2006, Sch 20 para 1*].

'*Quarter*' is a period of three months. [*IHTA 1984, s 63, s 70(5)(6)(8), s 71(5)*].

'*Relevant period*' is the period beginning with the day on which the property became (or last became) held on bereaved minors trusts, or which immediately before it became property held on bereaved minors trusts was property held on accumulation and maintenance trusts but which had ceased to be so held on or after 22 March 2006, and ending on the day before the chargeable event. [*IHTA 1984, ss 70(3)–(8)(10), 71B(3); FA 2006, Sch 20 paras 1, 2*].

Where *s 71A* ceases to apply as in (*a*) above then the rate of charge will be that given at *IHTA 1984, s 70(6)* i.e., the temporary charitable exit rules. Potential circumstances are a trust for a bereaved minor is established but the minor dies, for instance, before the age 18 and the trust continues after the death of the minor. See also Example 2 below. In such circumstances the temporary charitable trust rules would apply with a maximum rate of 30% after 50 years have elapsed. See table below. A charge does not arise where settled property held on trusts for bereaved minors ceases to be so because the bereaved minor becomes absolutely entitled on or before the age of 18 or dies under the age of 18 or the property is applied or advanced to the bereaved minor before the age of 18. [*IHTA 1984, ss 70(6); 71B(2)(3); FA 2006, Sch 20 paras 1, 2*].

	Cumulative Total
0.25% for each of the first 40 quarters	10%
0.20% for each of the next 40 quarters	8%
0.15% for each of the next 40 quarters	6%
0.10% for each of the next 40 quarters	4%
0.05% for each of the next 40 quarters	2%
Maximum rate chargeable after 50 years	30%

The rate charged may be reduced if any of the property is, or was, EXCLUDED PROPERTY (20).

Example 2

Following on from the example above the deceased's wills are located on 31 July 2018 as a result of which each of the deceased's assets are found to have been left in entirety to each other then to Mr and Mrs A's parents separately. The beneficiaries were, on or before attaining a specified age, not exceeding 18, to become beneficially entitled to the settled property under statutory trusts and therefore had qualified as bereaved minors for these purposes.

On 31 July 2018 as a result of the located wills the settlement fails to qualify as a bereaved minors trust and the clawback provisions apply. The settlement was valued at £594,000 on 12 July 2007 (see Note A) and at £750,000 on 31 July 2018. There will be a charge to IHT on the whole of the value of the settlement on 31 July 2018. The period from 12 July 2007 to 31 July 2018 is 44 complete quarters charged at the *IHTA 1984, s 70(6)* rate:

0.25% for each of the first	40	quarters	10%
0.20% for each of the next	4	quarters	0.8%
	44		10.8%

The IHT charge is 10.8% × £750,000 = £81,000

Notes to the example

(A)   There would also have been a charge to IHT originally in respect of each of the original intestate estates. See IHTM12197. In this case there are wills and by virtue of *IHTA 1984, s 4(2)* if it is not known which of the two survived the other then in assessing their respective estates neither is deemed to have survived the other. However, Mr A's estate devolves to Mrs A as he is the elder but his estate enjoys the benefit of the spouse exemption and in assessing Mrs A's estate no account is to be taken of Mr A's estate being passed on under the inter-spousal exemption. Therefore Mr A's estate is not taxable at all and Mrs A's estate is taxable on £4,000 (i.e. £310,000 – £300,000 × 40%). See 50.4 TRANSFER ON DEATH.

(B)   In the circumstances above or if trust for a bereaved minor continues after the death of that minor before his or her attaining the age of 18 years then the temporary charitable trust exit rules apply with a potential maximum rate of 30%. [*IHTA 1984, ss 70(6), 71B(3); FA 2006, Sch 20 paras 1, 2*].

53.3   **Age 18–25 trusts.** Existing accumulation and maintenance settlements that satisfy the requirements detailed below by 6 April 2008 and newly created trusts under the terms of someone's will or established under the Criminal Injuries Compensation Scheme for a bereaved minor will not come within the relevant property trust regime if it continues beyond bereaved minor's eighteenth birthday. [*IHTA 1984, s 71D(1)–(4) as inserted by FA 2006, Sch 20 para 1*]. Any such 'trust for a bereaved minor' detailed at 53.1 above or an

53.4   Trusts for Bereaved Minors

existing accumulation and maintenance trust to which *s 71* ceased to have effect in the period 22 March 2006 to 6 April 2008 may then be treated as an 'age 18–25 trust' subject to the IHT charges detailed below. In order for the trusts to qualify as an 'age 18–25 trust' the following requirements and conditions will necessarily apply:

(*a*)   The person for whom the trusts are held must, prior to or upon the attainment of the age of 25 years, be absolutely entitled to the settled property, and also absolutely entitled to any income arising therefrom together with any income that has arisen from the property but that has been accumulated; and

(*b*)   That whilst the beneficiary 'B' is living and under the age of 25 any settled property is applied solely for 'B's benefit. For these purposes 'B' or '*bereaved minor*' includes all beneficiaries within a relevant class provided they are alive and are under the specified age of 18. See CIOT/STEP clarification dated 29 June 2007; and

(*c*)   That whilst the beneficiary 'B' is living and under the age of 25 any income arising from the settled property is applied solely for 'B's benefit or, if not applied, it is not applied for anyone else's benefit.

The settled property is held on trust established by the will of a deceased parent for the benefit of a beneficiary or beneficiaries not having yet attained the age of 25 or as a result payments from the Criminal Injuries Compensation schemes within 53.1(*c*) above. [*IHTA 1984, s 71D(1)–(2)*].

Alternatively, it must be settled property to which *IHTA 1984, s 71* ceases to have effect in the period 22 March 2006 to 6 April 2008 but that settled property may then be treated as an 'age 18–25 trust' if it continues to be held on trusts for a person who has not yet attained the age of 25 years and the trusts satisfy the conditions in (*a*)–(*c*) above. [*IHTA 1984, s 71D(3)–(4)*]. See Example 2 at 3.3 ACCUMULATION AND MAINTENANCE SETTLEMENTS.

In relation to (*a*) to (*c*) above, whilst the beneficiary is living and under the age of 25 if any of the capital of the settled property is applied it must be applied for the benefit of the beneficiary only. If the trust property is not so applied then whilst the beneficiary is under the age of 25 years the income arising therefrom, if any, must be a full entitlement or the income must not be applied for the benefit of any other person. [*IHTA 1984, s 71D(6)*].

In connection with the above paragraph, an 'age 18–25 trust' shall not be treated as failing the requirements of entitlement due to age, property, income or accumulations because of the requirements of the *Trustee Act 1925, s 32* or *Trustee Act (Northern Ireland) 1958, s 33* or where trustees have similar powers. [*IHTA 1984, s 71D(7)*].

[*IHTA 1984, s 71D as inserted by FA 2006, Sch 20 para 1*].

53.4   **Treatment of payments, etc. out of age 18–25 trusts** A charge to tax arises

(*a*)   where 'B' becomes absolutely entitled the settled property, any income arising from it and any income that has arisen and been accumulated; on the death of 'B'; when the property settled is paid or applied for the advancement or benefit of 'B'; or

(*b*)   if the trustees make a 'disposition' which reduces the value of the settled property. '*Disposition*' includes an omission to exercise a right, unless not deliberate, which is treated as made at the latest time the right could have been exercised.

[*IHTA 1984, s 71E(1)(5), 71F(2) as inserted by FA 2006, Sch 20 para 1*].

No charge to tax arises

(i)   on a beneficiary at or under the age of 18 becoming absolutely entitled to, or to an interest in possession in, settled property on or before attaining the specified age of 25 years, or

(ii)   on the death of a beneficiary before attaining the specified age of 18 years (but see temporary charitable exit rules below), or

(iii)   on settled property becoming whilst the beneficiary is living and under the age of 18 property held under trust for a bereaved minor, or

(iv)   on settled property being paid or applied for the advancement or benefit of the beneficiary before attaining the age of 18 but whilst still living or on attaining the age of 18, or

(v)   on the 'payment' of costs or expenses attributable to the property, or

(vi)   where any payment is, or will be, income for income tax purposes of any person (or, in the case of a non-resident, would be if he were so resident).

[*IHTA 1984, s 71E(2)(3); FA 2006, Sch 20 para 1*].

'*Payment*' includes the transfer of assets other than money. [*IHTA 1984, s 63, s 70(3)(4), s 71(4)(5)*].

Calculation of tax charge. Where tax is charged in accordance with an event arising under (*a*) or (*b*) above and it occurs after the beneficiary has attained the age of 18 years then the amount of the tax is calculated as follows:

Chargeable amount × *Relevant fraction* × *Settlement rate* = *Tax due*

- *Chargeable amount* is the amount by which the value of the property in the settlement has been decreased by following the event that gave rise to the charge or where the amount by which the value of the property in the settlement is reduced as a result of the chargeable event (i.e. the loss to donor principle) grossed-up where the settlement pays the tax;

- *Relevant fraction* is three-tenths multiplied by so many fortieths in the period beginning with the day on which the beneficiary attained 18 years or, if later, on the day when the property became subject to an '18–25 trust' and ending on the day prior to the occasion of the charge. For these purposes one fortieth is a complete three-month period;

- *Settlement rate* is the effective rate at which tax would be charged on the value transferred by a chargeable transfer where

    - the value transferred is equal to the aggregate of the value of the settlement immediately after commencement, and

    - any related settlement on creation, and

    - any other property which became comprised in the settlement but before the charge arising under (*a*) or (*b*) above.

[*IHTA 1984, s 71F; FA 2006, Sch 20 para 1*].

Example 3

X, a widower, dies on 29 August 2008 and by his will leaves all his assets in trust for his daughter Emily, aged 20 on 20 September 2008. The capital in the bereaved minor's trust amounts to £640,000 after IHT deductions. Emily will become absolutely entitled to capital and income by the age of 25 and whilst she is living before that date the trustees will only apply the settled property for her benefit within the terms of the trust. On her birthday on 20 September 2013 at age 25 the trustees appoint the capital and any accumulated income to her. The capital and remainder of accumulated income amounts to £640,000 on that date. X had made no previous transfers in the seven years prior to his death.

53.4 Trusts for Bereaved Minors

Assumed chargeable transfer 20 September 2013:

	£
Value of relevant property on 20.9.2013	640,000
Less nil rate band, say, £350,000	350,000
	£290,000
IHT at lifetime rates on £290,000 @ 20%	£58,000

Effective rate

$$\frac{58,000}{640,000} = 9.0625\%$$

Rate of charge for period 29.8.2008 to 20.9.2013 (i.e. 20 complete quarters):

$^3\!/_{10} \times 9.0625\% = 2.71875\% \times {}^{20}\!/_{40} \times £640,000$

Exit charge on Emily becoming 25 payable by Emily:	£8,700

Notes to the example

(A) If between the ages of 18 and 25, the beneficiary becomes absolutely entitled or property is paid or applied out of the trust fund by the trustees for the beneficiary, or, the beneficiary dies, there will be a rateable apportionment of the non–IIP rate. See SETTLEMENTS WITHOUT INTERESTS IN POSSESSION (44).

(B) A clawback charge, a rare situation in the circumstances, similar to that shown in Example 2 above will apply where assets leave an 18–25 trust where *s 71D* above ceases to apply. In those unusual circumstances above then the rate of charge will be that given at *IHTA 1984, s 70(6)* i.e., the temporary charitable exit rules. [*IHTA 1984, ss 70(6)–(8), 71G; FA 2006, Sch 20 para 1*].

54   Trusts for Disabled Persons

Cross-reference. 44 SETTLEMENTS WITHOUT INTERESTS IN POSSESSION.

Simon's Direct Tax Service, part I5.626–628.

Other Sources. HMRC CTO leaflet IHT 16, p 26; Foster, part E6.26–6.28; IHTM04102.

54.1   **PROPERTY SETTLED AFTER 9 MARCH 1981**

Where property is transferred into settlement under which, during the life of a 'disabled person', no interest in possession subsists, and which secures that not less than half of the settled property which is applied during his life is applied for his benefit, then the disabled person is treated as beneficially entitled to an interest in possession in the property. From 22 March 2006 the restrictions imposed on IIP trusts have required a redrafting and amendment of existing legislation to ensure that a disabled person's trust still continues to benefit from special treatment. See below and 26 INTEREST IN POSSESSION and 43 SETTLEMENTS WITH INTERESTS IN POSSESSION.

A '*disabled person*' is one who, when property was transferred into settlement, was

(i)   incapable by reason of mental disorder within the meaning of the *Mental Health Act 1983* (but amended by the *Mental Health Act 2007* from 19 July 2007 and reference is made to any disorder or disability of the mind) of administering his property or managing his affairs, or

(ii)   in receipt of an attendance allowance under *Social Security Contributions and Benefits Act 1992, s 64* or *Social Security Contributions and Benefits (Northern Ireland) Act 1992, s 64*, or

(iii)   in receipt of a disability living allowance under *Social Security Contributions and Benefits Act 1992, s 71* or *Social Security Contributions and Benefits (Northern Ireland) Act 1992, s 71* by virtue of entitlement to the care component at the highest or middle rate. See also Taxation Magazine, 27 July 2006, p 468.

Note also that the *Mental Capacity Act 2005* has been brought into law from April 2007 to protect those who lack mental capacity and introduces Lasting Powers of Attorney which replace the current Enduring Powers of Attorney and will cover financial decisions. Under *Mental Capacity Act 2005, s 18* there is a list of the actions that the appointed 'deputy' can take with regard to the subject of the Lasting Power of Attorney's financial affairs which include drawing up a will, carrying on a trade, discharging debts, contractual matters, etc. There are certain stipulations regarding the suitability of the person (referred to as the 'donee') acting on the individual's behalf such that the individual (or Trust Corporation) must be 18 years or over, not a bankrupt and cannot appoint a successor. The new rules will be implemented from 1 October 2007. A settlement will not fall outside these provisions by reason only of the trustees' power of advancement contained in *Trustee Act 1925, s 32* or *Trustee Act (Northern Ireland) 1958, s 33*. The reference to disabled persons in *s 89(1)* from 22 March 2006 ignores the disallowance provisions relating to (ii) and (iii) above where the disabled person is in paid-for accommodation e.g. hospitalisation due to renal failure, or where the person is living outside the UK and would fail (ii) and (iii) above. [*IHTA 1984, s 89 as amended by FA 2006, Sch 20 para 6(2)*].

Example 1

On 31 July 2007 X who is British and is physically disabled but currently resides in Ireland settles £360,000 from liability insurance payments into a disabled trust for his benefit in the future. X who intends to return to the UK would have qualified for receipt of a disability living allowance under *Social Security Contributions and Benefits Act 1992, s 71* by virtue of entitlement to the care component at the highest rate (see Note D below) due to severe disability. Despite not qualifying for disability benefit because of not being resident for the relevant period X is still able to set up a trust and benefit from both the CGT and IHT advantages attaching to such settlements of property so that after seven years the £360,000 will effectively drop out of account for cumulation purposes. See (C) below.

Notes to the example

(A)   Prior to 22 March 2006 the transfer into trust would not have qualified as a trust for disabled persons within *IHTA 1984, s 89* but following the amendments in *FA 2006, Sch 20 para 6(2)* the residence conditions of *Social Security Contributions and Benefits Act 1992, s 71(6)* are treated as if they were fulfilled.

(B)   Similarly, if a disabled person's entitlement to attendance allowance is restricted because of *Social Security Contributions and Benefits Act 1992, s 64(1)* requirements of residence but the person would have qualified for attendance allowance then from 22 March 2006 the settlement may notwithstanding this be allowed as a trust for disabled person.

(C)   The IHT advantages are that the gift into the disabled trust is treated as a PET but the disabled beneficiary is deemed to have an interest in possession. The *FA 2006, Sch 20* amendments merely ensure that the beneficial treatment of IIP designation continues. See below for the position after 21 March 2006. [*IHTA 1984, ss 3A, 3B; FA 2006, Sch 20 paras 6, 9*].

(D)   The highest rate applies where the individual is so physically or mentally disabled that he/she requires:

    (1)   frequent attention throughout the day in connection with bodily functions, or continual supervision throughout the day to avoid substantial danger to them or others; and

    (2)   prolonged or repeated attention at night in connection with bodily functions, or in order to avoid substantial danger to themselves or others he/she requires another person to be awake at night for a prolonged period or at frequent intervals to watch them; or

    (3)   he/she is terminally ill.

In respect of the counter measures within *TCGA 1992 s 226A* to prevent exploitation of the interaction between private residence relief and gifts relief for CGT these measures do not apply in the case of beneficiaries of trusts for disabled persons as *IHTA 1984, s 89* provides that a beneficiary of such a settlement has an interest in possession in the settled property. As a consequence of this, any transfer to such a trust is a potentially exempt transfer for IHT purposes and does not fall within *TCGA 1992, s 260* gifts holdover relief. [*TCGA 1992, s 226A inserted by FA 2004, Sch 22 para 6*].

Transfers into trusts for disabled persons. In relation to transfers of value made, and other events occurring, after 17 March 1986, a gift by an individual into a trust for a disabled person, by virtue of which property becomes comprised in the trust, is a potentially exempt transfer subject to the transfer not being primarily exempt under *IHTA 1984, s 11* i.e. dispositions for family maintenance. In addition, in relation to transfers of value made, and other events occurring, after 16 March 1987, a potentially exempt transfer occurs where an individual disposes of or terminates his beneficial interest in settled property by gift and on that event the property is settled on disabled trusts. Provided the transferor survives seven years or more from the date of the original gift, the gift is exempt for inheritance tax purposes. See 38 POTENTIALLY EXEMPT TRANSFERS for further details. [*IHTA 1984, ss 3A, 3B; FA 1986, Sch 19 para 1; F(No 2)A 1987, s 96; FA 2006, Sch 20 para 9*].

Property settled after 21 March 2006. From 22 March 2006 where a person (designated 'A' in the legislation) transfers property into a settlement and that person was beneficially entitled to the property immediately before transferring it and satisfies the Commissioners of HMRC that he had a condition at the time which it was reasonable to expect that it would lead to him becoming

(i) incapable by reason of mental disorder within the meaning of the *Mental Health Act 1983* (but amended by the *Mental Health Act 2007* from 19 July 2007 and reference is made to any disorder or disability of the mind) of administering his property or managing his affairs, or

(ii) in receipt of an attendance allowance under *Social Security Contributions and Benefits Act 1992, s 64* or *Social Security Contributions and Benefits (Northern Ireland) Act 1992, s 64*, or

(iii) in receipt of a disability living allowance under *Social Security Contributions and Benefits Act 1992, s 71* or *Social Security Contributions and Benefits (Northern Ireland) Act 1992, s 71* by virtue of entitlement to the care component at the highest or middle rate (see Example 2 below)

and the property is held on trusts that do not give 'A' during his lifetime an interest in possession then 'A' is treated as beneficially entitled to an interest in possession. In addition, two conditions must apply:

• the requirement that if any of the settled property is applied during A's lifetime for the benefit of a beneficiary, it is applied for the benefit of A; and

• any power to terminate the trusts during the lifetime of A or another person is such that A or another person will have an absolute entitlement to, or a *disabled person's interest* subsisting in, the settled property. See also Fosters Inheritance Tax, para E6.29.

Disabled person's interest means

(1) an interest in possession to which a person is beneficially entitled under *IHTA 1984, s 89(2)*; or

(2) an interest in possession to which a person is beneficially entitled under *IHTA 1984, s 89A(4)*; or

(3) an interest in possession to which the disabled person is beneficially entitled where the property of the settlement was transferred into settlement on or after 22 March 2006; or

(4) an interest in possession in settled property, other than in (1) and (2) above, to which 'A' is beneficially entitled where A is the settlor and was entitled to the property immediately before its settlement on or after 22 March 2006 and satisfies the Commissioners of HMRC that he had a condition at the time which it was reasonable to expect that it would lead to him becoming within (i) to (iii) above where any application of the settled property is applied for his/her benefit solely.

[*IHTA 1984, ss 89, 89A, 89B; FA 2006, Sch 20 para 6*].

Example 2

On 31 July 2007 X, who is in the early stages of dementia and currently resides in a care home, settles £300,000 into discretionary trust for his benefit in the future. X has been assessed by the care home at which he is registered to attend as Elderly Mentally Incapable (EMI). The trust qualifies as a settlement under *s 89A* because X's present condition advancing from dementia to Alzheimer's satisfies the criteria of the definition of a disabled person within *IHTA 1984, s 89(4)* that is required. The trust has been set up by X in conjunction with MENCAP. See *Mental Health Act 2007*, and also Note (A) below. See also *Masterman–Lister v Brutton & Co*, CA [2003] WTLR 259; CA [2003] All ER (D) 59 (Jan). See 60 TAX CASES.

X is treated as beneficially entitled to an interest in possession in the settled property. The transfer into settlement of the property would be a potentially exempt transfer which may become chargeable in the event of the donor's death within seven years of the transfer, but as it is X himself making the transfer it is not chargeable for IHT purposes. See (A) below and 43.3 SETTLEMENTS WITH INTERESTS IN POSSESSION for an example of a notice under *IHTA 1984, s 57(3)* and the deed of release.

Notes to the example

(A)   In certain cases such as the example above it is often difficult to ensure that relatives or acquaintances have sufficient knowledge or time to act as trustees to the disabled trust. In these cases it is often possible to obtain independent trusteeship from a commercial organisation and one such as the Mencap Trust Company Ltd may be chosen. See http://www.mencap.org.uk/html/legacies/MTC_information.pdf. There is some dispute as to whether a transfer into a trust for a disabled person is a PET, a non-chargeable transfer or an exempt transfer. See Taxation magazine, 30 September 2004 and also Fosters Inheritance Tax, para E6.29. HMRC have confirmed in a letter that:

'Lifetime transfers into settlements for the disabled, that satisfy the conditions laid down in section 89, Inheritance Tax Act 1984, are indeed covered by the provisions of section 11, Inheritance Tax Act 1984. Accordingly such dispositions are not transfers of value if these conditions – depending on which apply – are satisfied. It follows that such dispositions do not require to be reported, at any time, to any office of Capital Taxes.'

HMRC reiterate that the provision must be 'reasonable provision for his care or maintenance' within *IHTA 1984, s 11(3)* and of course this is a subjective matter.

(B)   Under *TCGA 1992, Sch 1 para 1* (see quotation below) the settlement will qualify for a CGT annual exemption of half the annual amount ie £4,600 but settlements for disabled beneficiaries take the full allowance of £9,200.

For any year of assessment during the whole or part of which settled property is held on trusts which secure that, during the lifetime or a person in receipt of attendance allowance or of disability living allowance by virtue of entitlement to the care of the highest or middle rate

(a)   not less than half of the property which is applied is applied for the benefit of the person: and

(b)   that person is entitled to not less than half of the income arising from the property, or no such income may be applied for the benefit of any other person.

'Modernising the Tax System for Trusts' consultation paper was issued on 11 December 2003. One of the consultation paper's many proposals with regard to income tax and capital gains tax was the standardisation of the definitions of 'settlement', 'settlor' and 'settlor interested trusts' from April 2005. The consultation paper at paragraph 45 states with particular regard to trusts for the disabled:

'The exact definition of trusts to which this option [settlor-interested trusts] would be restricted needs to be decided but the existing CGT and IHT definitions of disabled trusts seem a good place to start.'

It was proposed that trusts for the disabled could elect to be treated as settlor-interested trusts which would enable income and gains/losses to be treated as the settlor's allowing set-off against personal allowances and exemptions (see also 43.1 SETTLEMENTS WITH INTERESTS IN POSSESSION). In the Budget press release (REV 10) issued on 16 March 2005 a standard rate band of £500 for all 'vulnerable' trusts paying tax at the rate applicable to trusts i.e. 40% would apply from 6 April 2005 and subsequently a basic rate band was introduced in *Finance Act 2005* applying to the first £500 from 6 April 2005 relevant to trusts that pay tax at the rate applicable to trusts. Consultation in this area continued following the 2005 and 2006 Budget statements and the basic rate band applying to the first £1,000 applicable from 6 April 2006 will apply to trusts that pay tax at the rate applicable to trusts. Also a number of definitions and tests used in taxing trusts to income tax and capital gains tax are to be altered and aligned between the two taxes. See Tolley's Income Tax 2007–08 and Tolley's Capital Gains Tax 2007–08. [*FA 2005, ss 23–45; FA 2006, ss 88, 89, Schs 12, 13*].

54.2   **PROPERTY SETTLED BEFORE 10 MARCH 1981**

Where property is held on trusts under which there is no interest in possession but the property is to be applied only or mainly for the benefit of a disabled person within 54.1(i)–(iii) above during his life, then there is a charge to tax

(*a*)   where it ceases to be settled property otherwise than by being applied for the benefit of the disabled person (but see also 21.3, 21.5–21.7 EXEMPT TRANSFERS for certain situations where there is no charge when property becomes held for charitable purposes only without limit of time or the property of a qualifying political party or a national body mentioned in *IHTA 1984, Sch 3* or, under certain conditions, a body not established or conducted for profit), or

(*b*)   if the trustees make a 'disposition' otherwise than for the benefit of the disabled person which reduces the value of the settled property. *Disposition* includes an omission to exercise a right (unless not deliberate), which is treated as made at the latest time that the right could be exercised.

[*IHTA 1984, ss 70(10), 74(1)(2)(4), 76*].

Example 3

In 1968 Q settled £50,000 in trust mainly for his disabled son P, but with power to apply property to his daughter S. On 1 January 2008 the trustees advanced £5,000 gross to S on her marriage.

There will be a charge to IHT on the payment to S

The relevant period is the period from settlement of the funds or, if later, 13 March 1975, to 1 January 2008, i.e. 131 complete quarters.

The rate of IHT is the aggregate of

0.25% for each of the first	40	quarters	10.00%
0.20% for each of the next	40	quarters	8.00%
0.15% for each of the next	40	quarters	6.00%
0.10% for each of the next	11	quarters	1.10%
	131		25.10%

IHT payable is £5,000 × 25.10% = £1,255

54.2   Trusts for Disabled Persons

Example 4

On 1 July 1982 Q settled £50,000 in trust mainly for his disabled son P, but with power to apply property to his daughter S as follows

'1.1   I give to my Trustees on the trusts set out hereinafter the sum of £50,000.

      1.1.1   'the Trust Fund' means the assets at a particular time held by my Trustees on the trusts set out in ....

      1.1.2   'my other Beneficiaries' means: my children other than .....P's name]......

1.2   My Trustees shall hold the Trust Fund on the following trusts:

      1.2.1   During the lifetime of ....[P's name]........

           (a)   to apply the capital of the Trust Fund for the benefit of ...[P's name].... and my other Beneficiaries as my Trustees think fit so long as not less than half of any capital applied is for the benefit of ....[P's name]....;

           (b)   to have the power to accumulate the whole of any part of the income arising from the Trust Fund and to apply any income not accumulated solely for the benefit of .....[P's name]......

      1.2.2   After the death of ....[P's name]......:

           (a)   to apply the capital of the Trust Fund for the benefit of such of my other Beneficiaries as my Trustees think fit;

           (b)   to apply the income of the Trust Fund for the benefit of such of my other Beneficiaries as my Trustees think fit or to accumulate the whole or any part of it;

           (c)   within ..[Year(s)]... of ....[P's name].... death to end these trusts by distributing the Trust Fund among such Beneficiaries as my Trustees think fit.

1.3   My Trustees shall have the following powers: ...' *Details of Trustees' powers continue*

On 1 January 2008 the trustees advanced £5,000 gross to S on her marriage.

If the trust secures that not less than half the settled property which is applied during P's life is applied for his benefit, then P is treated as beneficially entitled to an interest in possession in the settled property. The transfer to S is a potentially exempt transfer which may become chargeable in the event of P's death within seven years of the transfer. The gift in consideration of marriage exemption applies (£1,000 on a gift from brother to sister) subject to the required notice. See 43.3 SETTLEMENTS WITH INTERESTS IN POSSESSION for an example of a notice under *IHTA 1984, s 57(3)* and the deed of release.

Otherwise, the trust is discretionary and the IHT liability, if any, would be calculated under the rules applying to settlements without interests in possession.

No charge arises

    (i)   if, under (*b*) above, the trustees do not intend to confer gratuitous benefit and either the transaction is at arm's length between persons not connected with each other (see 13 CONNECTED PERSONS) or is such as might be expected in such a transaction, or

    (ii)   if, under (*b*) above, the disposition is a grant of tenancy of agricultural property in the UK, Channel Islands or Isle of Man, for use for agricultural purposes and is made for full consideration in money or money's worth, or

(iii)   on the payment of costs or expenses attributable to the property, or

(iv)   where any payment is, or will be, income for income tax purposes of any person (or, in the case of a person not resident in the UK, would be if he were so resident), or

(v)   in respect of a liability to make a payment under (iii) or (iv) above.

'*Payment*' includes the transfer of assets other than money.

[*IHTA 1984, ss 63, 70(3)(4), 74(3)*].

Tax is charged on the amount by which the trust property is less immediately after the event giving rise to the charge than it would have been but for the event (i.e. the loss to the donor principle), grossed-up where the settlement pays the tax.

The rate at which tax is charged is the aggregate of the following percentages for each complete successive quarter in 'the relevant period':

	Cumulative Total
0.25% for each of the first 40 quarters	10%
0.20% for each of the next 40 quarters	8%
0.15% for each of the next 40 quarters	6%
0.10% for each of the next 40 quarters	4%
0.05% for each of the next 40 quarters	2%
Maximum rate chargeable after 50 years	30%

The rate charged may be reduced if any of the property is, or was, EXCLUDED PROPERTY (20), see 54.3 below.

'*Relevant period*' is the period beginning with the day on which the property became (or last became) held on trusts for disabled persons or 13 March 1975 if later, and ending on the day before the chargeable event.

'*Quarter*' means any period of three months.

[*IHTA 1984, ss 63, 70(5)(6)(8), 74(3)*].

54.3   **Excluded property.** Where the whole or part of the amount on which tax is charged as in 54.2 above is attributable to property which was EXCLUDED PROPERTY (20) at any time during the relevant period, then, in determining the rate at which tax is charged in respect of that amount or part, no quarter throughout which the property was excluded property is to be counted. [*IHTA 1984, ss 70(7), 74(3)*].

54.4   See also the provisions under 44.15 and 44.16 SETTLEMENTS WITHOUT INTERESTS IN POSSESSION which also apply to property settled or appointed on pre-10 March 1981 trusts for the disabled.

55 Trusts for Employees

Cross-reference. See also 44 SETTLEMENTS WITHOUT INTERESTS IN POSSESSION; 59 WORKING CASE STUDY.

Simon's Direct Tax Service, part I5.631.

Other Sources. HMRC CTO leaflet IHT 16, pages 23–24; Foster, part E6.31; IHTM04100.

55.1 **GENERAL**

Subject to conditions, trusts for the benefit of employees of a company are exempt from inheritance tax liability on the ten-year anniversary charge (see 44 SETTLEMENTS WITHOUT INTERESTS IN POSSESSION). Also, transfers to such trusts may be made by individuals, close companies and settlements without interests in possession without liability to inheritance tax. See IHT 16, pp 23 and 24.

55.2 **CONDITIONS FOR THE TRUST**

The conditions are that the settled property is held on trusts which, either indefinitely or until the end of a period (whether defined by a date or in some other way) do not permit that property to be applied otherwise than for the benefit of

(*a*) persons employed in a particular trade or profession, or

(*b*) employees, or office holders, of a body carrying on a trade, profession or undertaking, or

(*c*) spouses, civil partners, relatives or dependants or partners of (*a*) or (*b*) above. See IHT NEWSLETTER AND TAX BULLETIN EXTRACTS (61), April 2006.

For the settled property to qualify under (*b*), either all or most of the employees or office holders must be included as beneficiaries or the trust must be an approved profit sharing scheme under formerly *ICTA 1988, Sch 9* (now repealed by *ITEPA 2003, s 722, Sch 6* but see *ITEPA 2003, s 723, Sch 7*) or an employee share ownership plan approved under *FA 2000, Sch 8*. Where there are beneficiaries falling within (*a*), (*b*) or (*c*) above, the trusts are not disqualified by reason only that they also permit settled property to be applied for charitable purposes. [*IHTA 1984, s 86(1)–(3) as amended by FA 2000, s 138(4); Sch 8; The Tax and Civil Partnership Regulations 2005, SI 2005/3229, Reg 18*]. See 55.9 below regarding newspaper trusts.

The settled property

(i) is treated as comprised in one settlement;

(ii) may contain an interest in possession (e.g. a right by a beneficiary to an annuity) of less than 5% of the whole. Such interests are disregarded for IHT purposes, with the exception of those in *IHTA 1984, s 55* relating to the acquisition by a person of a reversionary interest expectant on an interest to which he is already entitled; and

(iii) may cease to be comprised in one settlement and, if within one month it becomes wholly comprised in another settlement satisfying the above conditions, it is treated as if it had remained comprised in the first settlement.

[*IHTA 1984, s 86(4)(5)*].

55.3 **CREATION OF THE TRUST**

Separate provisions apply to the creation of employee trusts by individuals (see 55.4 below) and close companies (see 55.5 below) and to property transferred from discretionary trusts (see 55.6 below).

55.4 **Individual transferor.** A transfer to a trust as described in 55.2 above, by an individual who is beneficially entitled to shares in a company, is an exempt transfer if the value transferred is attributable to shares in or securities of the company, provided

(*a*) the beneficiaries of the trust include all or most of the persons employed by or holding office with the company;

(*b*) within one year of the transfer

(i) the trustees hold more than one half of the ordinary shares of the company, and have majority voting powers on all questions affecting the company as a whole (but ignoring powers of any class of shares or securities limited to questions of winding up the company or primarily affecting that class); *and*

(ii) there are no provisions or agreements which can affect (i) above without the trustees' consent;

(*c*) the trust does not permit *any* of the settled property (i.e. not only the shares or securities) *at any time* to be applied (except payments which are income of the recipient for income tax purposes, or would be if he were resident in the UK) for the benefit of

(i) a participator in the company, or

(ii) any other person who is a participator in any close company that has made a disposition under *IHTA 1984, s 13* whereby property became comprised in the same settlement, see 55.5 below, or

(iii) any other person who has been a participator as mentioned in (i) or (ii) above at any time after, or during the ten years before, the transfer now being made, or

(iv) any person connected with the persons in (i) to (iii) above.

For these purposes, a participator mentioned above does not include any participator in a company who is not beneficially entitled to, or to rights entitling him to acquire, 5% or more of, or of any class of shares comprised in, its issued share capital and would not, on a winding up of the company, be entitled to 5% or more of its assets. Also participator includes, in the case of a company which is not a close company, a person who would be a participator in the company if it were a close company.

[*IHTA 1984, ss 13(5), 28*].

See 21.16 EXEMPT TRANSFERS for abatement of the exemption.

55.5 **Close company transferor.** A close company may transfer property to a trust as described in 55.2 above without it being a transfer of value, provided

(*a*) the beneficiaries of the trust include all or most of either

(i) the persons employed by or holding office with the same company, or

(ii) the persons employed by or holding office with the company or any of its subsidiaries (but persons with a holding company may be excluded if they are in the minority, 25.E11 HMRC STATEMENTS OF PRACTICE); and

(*b*) the trust does not permit *any* property at *any time* to be applied to any of the persons mentioned in 55.4(*c*) above except as payments which are income of the recipient for the purposes of income tax (or would be if he were resident in the UK), or as an appropriation of shares from a profit sharing scheme under formerly *ICTA 1988, Sch 9* (now repealed by *ITEPA 2003, s 722, Sch 6* but see *ITEPA 2003, s 723, Sch 7*); or

(*c*) the trust is an employee ownership share plan approved under *FA 2000, Sch 8*.

55.6   Trusts for Employees

[*IHTA 1984, s 13 as amended by FA 2000, s 138 (2) and Sch 8*].

55.6   **Property transferred from a discretionary trust etc.** SETTLEMENTS WITHOUT INTERESTS IN POSSESSION (44) may transfer shares or securities in a company to trusts as described in 55.2 above without a proportionate charge to tax, provided

(*a*)   the beneficiaries of the trust include all or most of the persons employed by or holding office with the company, and

(*b*)   without taking account of shares etc. held on other trusts, both conditions in 55.4(*b*) above are satisfied at the date when the shares etc. cease to be comprised in the original settlement or within one year of that time, and

(*c*)   the trust does not permit *any* property at *any time* to be applied

(i)   to any of the persons mentioned in 55.4(*c*) above except as payments which are regarded as the income of the recipient for the purposes of income tax (or would be if he were resident in the UK); or

(ii)   for the benefit of the settlor; or

(iii)   for the benefit of any person connected with the settlor. [*IHTA 1984, s 75*].

See also the provisions of 44.15 and 44.16 SETTLEMENTS WITHOUT INTERESTS IN POSSESSION which also apply to property settled or appointed on trust for employees.

55.7   **POSITION OF THE TRUST**

Settled property held on the conditions in 55.2 above is not subject to the principal charge to tax at the ten-year anniversary or the proportionate charge to tax under *IHTA 1984, ss 64, 65* but where the property is held in a SETTLEMENT WITHOUT INTERESTS IN POSSESSION (44), the trust is subject to a charge when

(*a*)   the property ceases to be held on qualifying employee trusts otherwise than by virtue of a payment out of the settled property (but see also 21.3, 21.5–21.7 EXEMPT TRANSFERS for certain situations where there is no charge when property becomes held for charitable purposes only without limit of time or the property of a qualifying political party *or* a national body mentioned in *IHTA 1984, Sch 3* or, under certain conditions, a body not established or conducted for profit); or

(*b*)   a payment is made for the benefit of a person who is, or is connected with,

(i)   a person who has directly or indirectly provided any of the settled property by amounts over £1,000 in any tax year; or

(ii)   where the employment in question is by a close company, a participator of that company who *either* is beneficially entitled to, or to rights entitling him to acquire, 5% or more of, or of any class of shares comprised in, its issued share capital, *or* would, on a winding up of the company be entitled to 5% or more of its assets (but this does not apply to any appropriation of shares under a profit sharing scheme approved under formerly *ICTA 1988, Sch 9* now repealed by *ITEPA 2003, s 722, Sch 6* but see *ITEPA 2003, s 723, Sch 7*); or

(iii)   a person who has acquired an interest in the employee trust for money or money's worth or as a result of transactions which include a disposition for such consideration (whether to him or another) of that interest or of other property, or

(*c*)   the trustees make a 'disposition' (otherwise than by virtue of a payment out of the settled property) which reduces the value of the settled property.

'*Disposition*' includes an omission to exercise a right, unless not deliberate, which is treated as made at the latest time that the right could be exercised.

[*IHTA 1984, ss 70(10), 72, 76*].

No charge arises

(i)   if, under (*c*) above, the trustees do not intend to confer gratuitous benefit and either the transaction is at arm's length between persons not connected with each other (see 13 CONNECTED PERSONS) or is such as might be expected in such a transaction, or

(ii)   if, under (*c*) above, the disposition is a grant of tenancy of agricultural property in the UK, Channel Islands or Isle of Man for use for agricultural purposes and is made for full consideration in money or money's worth, or

(iii)   on the payment of costs or expenses attributable to the property, or

(iv)   where any payment is, or will be, income for income tax purposes of any person (or, in the case of a person not resident in the UK, would be if he was so resident), or

(v)   in respect of a liability to make a payment under (iii) and (iv) above, or

(vi)   if the trusts are those of an employee share ownership plan approved under *FA 2000, s 138(3b) and Sch 8*.

'*Payment*' includes the transfer of assets other than money.

[*IHTA 1984, ss 63, 70(3)(4), 72(5); FA 2000, s 138(3b), Sch 8*].

Tax is charged on the amount by which the trust property is less immediately after the event giving rise to the charge than it would have been but for the event (i.e. the loss to the donor principle), grossed-up where the settlement pays the tax.

The rate at which tax is charged is the aggregate of the following percentages for each complete successive quarter in 'the relevant period'.

	Cumulative Total
0.25% for each of the first 40 quarters	10%
0.20% for each of the next 40 quarters	8%
0.15% for each of the next 40 quarters	6%
0.10% for each of the next 40 quarters	4%
0.05% for each of the next 40 quarters	2%
Maximum rate chargeable after 50 years	30%

The rate charged may be reduced if any of the property is, or was, EXCLUDED PROPERTY (20), see 55.8 below.

'*Relevant period*' is the period beginning with the day on which the property became (or last became) held on employee trusts, or 13 March 1975 if later, and ending on the day before the chargeable event. Where property in respect of which tax is chargeable was relevant property (see 44.2 SETTLEMENTS WITHOUT INTERESTS IN POSSESSION) immediately before 10 December 1981 (e.g. in a discretionary trust) and became (or last became) comprised in an employee trust after 9 December 1981 and before 9 March 1982, the relevant period begins with the day on which the property became (or last became) relevant property before 10 December 1981, or 13 March 1975 if later.

'*Quarter*' means a period of three months.

[*IHTA 1984, ss 63, 70(5)(6)(8)(9), 72(5)*].

Example

A qualifying trust for employees of a close company was created on 1 July 1983. On 4 May 1993, £15,000 is paid to a beneficiary who is a participator in the close company and holds

15% of the issued ordinary shares. On 4 August 2007, the whole of the remaining fund of £200,000 ceases to be held on qualifying trusts.

4 May 1993

There is a charge to IHT. The relevant period is the period from 1 July 1983 to 4 May 1993, i.e. 39 complete quarters.

The rate of tax is

0.25% for 39 quarters = 9.75%

IHT payable is

$$\frac{9.75}{100 - 9.75} \times £\,15,000 = £\,1,620$$

1 July 1993 and 1 July 2003

There is no liability at the ten-year anniversaries.

4 August 2007

The relevant period is the period from 1 July 1983 to 4 August 2007, i.e. 96 complete quarters.

The rate of tax is:

0.25% for 40 quarters =	10.00
0.20% for 40 quarters =	8.00
0.15% for 16 quarters =	2.40
	20.40%

IHT payable is £200,000 × 20.40% = £40,800

55.8   **Excluded property.** Where the whole or part of the amount on which tax is charged as in 55.7 above is attributable to property which was EXCLUDED PROPERTY (20) at any time during the relevant period, then, in determining the rate at which tax is charged in respect of that amount or part, no quarter throughout which the property was excluded property is to be counted. [*IHTA 1984, s 70(7)*].

55.9   **NEWSPAPER TRUSTS**

Newspaper publishing companies (i.e. companies whose businesses consist wholly or mainly in the publication of newspapers in the UK) are included among the persons within 55.2(*a*) to (*c*) above as permissible beneficiaries. The only or principal property comprised in a newspaper trust must be shares in a newspaper publishing company or a newspaper holding company (i.e. a company which has as its only or principal asset shares in a newspaper publishing company and has majority voting powers on all or most questions affecting the publishing company as a whole). Shares are treated as the principal property in a settlement or the principal asset of a company if the remaining property in the settlement or assets of the company are such as may be reasonably required to enable the trustees or the company to secure the operation of the newspaper publishing company concerned. [*IHTA 1984, s 87*]. See IHT 16, p 25.

56   Valuation

Cross-references. See 6.3 ANTI-AVOIDANCE; 7.8 BUSINESS PROPERTY; 33.5 NATIONAL HERIT-
AGE; 43.2 AND 43.3 SETTLEMENTS WITH INTERESTS IN POSSESSION; 51 TRANSFERS WITHIN
SEVEN YEARS BEFORE DEATH; 59 WORKING CASE STUDY.

Simon's Direct Tax Service, part I8.

Other Sources. VOA IHT manual; HMRC CTO leaflets IHT 14–18 and SAV 1; Foster, part H;
IHTM09000.

56.1   GENERALLY

The general valuation rule is that the value at any time of any property for the purposes of
inheritance tax is the price which the property might reasonably be expected to fetch if sold
in the open market at that time; but that price shall not be assumed to be reduced on the
ground that the whole property is to be placed on the market at one and the same time.
[*IHTA 1984, s 160*]. The valuation of particular property or in particular circumstances is
dealt with below and under appropriate headings elsewhere in this book. See also the
Valuation Office Agency website on http://www.voa.gov.uk/. IHT 210 (Notes) at D10
(Notes) states,

> 'If you have a professional or specialist valuation, please attach a copy. If you have
> not had the items valued, you should group the items together according to the list
> above [household and personal goods] and include a value for each group. Add up all
> the figures and write the total in box HG2. If the deceased owned a motor car,
> including classic or vintage cars, you should include details of the make, exact
> model, year of registration and registration number. If the registration number has a
> value, please include it separately. You should include similar details as necessary if
> the deceased owned a caravan, boat or aeroplane etc.'

See Form D10 below.

'Open market value' has to be interpreted in the light of cases concerning other taxes,
chiefly estate duty and capital gains tax, which have or had a similar valuation rule. IHT
210 (Notes) at D10 (Notes) states:

> 'A valuation for a "forced sale" is not acceptable. A "valuation for insurance",
> although a good place to start, may be the cost to replace the items and not
> necessarily a realistic price for which the item might be sold. As a rough guide, it
> might be worth having any individual items specifically mentioned in the Will and
> any other items that individually are thought to be worth more than £500 valued.'

In particular see *CIR v Clay CA 1914, [1914–15] All ER 882* for position where special
circumstances would affect the market price, and *Duke of Buccleuch and Another v CIR HL
1966, [1967] 1 AC 506* for the need to assume property would be sold in 'natural units'.
The decision in this last case was applied in *Gray (Executor of Lady Fox) v CIR CA,
[1994] STC 360*, where the deceased was a freeholder of farm land and one of three
partners in a partnership which farmed the land under an agricultural tenancy. It was held
that a unit of property for the purposes of *IHTA 1984, s 160* above could comprise two or
more component parts where at least one of those parts was 'land' and at least one of those
parts was not 'land', and in this respect, although the question did not arise, the interest in
the partnership included 'land'. See IR Tax Bulletin, August 1996, p 337. The freehold
reversionary interest in the land and the 92.5% interest in the partnership held by the
deceased at the time of death did, on the facts, form a unit of property to which the
Buccleuch principle, as a matter of law, applied. The decision in the Lands Tribunal case of
Walton (Executor of Walton deceased) v CIR, [1996] STC 68 diverged from the Capital
Taxes Office [now HMRC Inheritance Tax] approach to a farm tenancy valuation. In this

case the actual circumstances and intentions of co-owners of a tenancy were properly brought into account in assessing the value of the share in the tenancy of the outgoing interest. This case shows that the facts as to whether the landlord was in the market to buy in a tenant and, if the landlord was not, the only value is likely to be the capitalisation of the difference between the rent actually charged and the full market rental. See Taxation Vol 134, No 3492 pp 486–487 and Taxation Practitioner February 1995 pp 7–10).

For the valuation of an interest in land taking into account the liability to repay a discount allowed to a purchaser under the 'right to buy' provisions of *Housing Act 1980*, see *Alexander v CIR CA, [1991] STC 112*. The appeal concerned the valuation of a flat for Capital Transfer Tax purposes which had recently been acquired from the Local Authority under the right to buy. The difficulty was that the lease, and the *Housing Act 1980*, required the discount to be repaid on a sliding scale if it was resold within five years.

The death of the deceased did not trigger this clause but if the flat was sold at the date of death, as this was within one year of the original purchase, the full amount of the discount would have been repayable.

The Lands Tribunal had determined the value, without deduction for this obligation at £63,000. The parties successfully argued at an earlier hearing before the Special Commissioners that this value should be reduced by the discount of £24,600. HMRC contended for the DV's valuation of £50,000, being what someone would pay on the footing that if they then resold within the relevant period the discount (or part of it) would be payable, but not otherwise, and no further deduction.

Ralph Gibson LJ said:

'The essential question may be described thus: is the value of the lease to be taken as the value which the lease would have, if transferred, on the basis that the transferee must pay the relevant percentage of repayable premium, or is the lease to be valued as in the hands of the deceased immediately before her death when nothing had happened to cause any proportion of premium to be repayable?'

Gibson LJ concluded that the principles stated in *Inland Revenue Commissioners v Crossman and Others HL, [1936] 1 All ER 762* are applicable.

The DV is reminded that the use of 'hindsight' is to be avoided whenever possible when considering evidence and the valuation should be based upon such knowledge as would be available on the particular date of the valuation. (VOA IHT manual, section 7, para 7.15).

The DV should have regard to the following when considering the effect on value of a restriction:

(a) the amount of the potential liability;

(b) the effective duration of the restriction;

(c) how onerous it is to comply with any restriction;

(d) the type of property;

(e) the state of the property market at the valuation date.

(VOA IHT manual, section 17, para 17.23).

The Royal Institute of Chartered Surveyors (RICS) published a new Guidance Note, GN 21, effective from 1 August 2003, which gives advice to members of RICS on the meaning of 'market value' for CGT and Inheritance Tax purposes. Further guidance on property valuations for CGT, IHT and other taxes, together with a full explanation of the 'market value' basis of valuation can be found in the VOA's CGT and IHT Manuals which can be viewed on their website http://www.voa.gov.uk/ under 'Publications'.

For the purposes of the pre-owned assets anti-avoidance legislation the valuation of any property is the price which the property might reasonably be expected to fetch if sold in the open market at that time, but with the price not being reduced because the whole of the property is being placed on the market at one and the same time. See 56.20 below. [*FA 2004, Sch 15 para 15*].

Where there is a disagreement with a land valuation by the Valuation Office the matter may be negotiated with HMRC Inheritance Tax or, if that is not possible, then it can be referred to the Lands Tribunal. Any complaint regarding delay, mistake or poor handling by the Valuation Office must initially be made to the individual at the VO, their manager or Group Customer Service Manager. If still dissatisfied then contact should be made with:

The Chief Executive's Office
Valuation Office Agency
New Court
Carey Street
London WC2A 2JE

A customer service leaflet 'Putting Things Right' is available on the VO's website http://www.voa.gov.uk/. Tel: 020 7506 1801. Fax: 020 7506 1996. See 61 IHT NEWSLETTER AND TAX BULLETIN EXTRACTS, April 2004.

Inspection of property. If the Board authorise any person to inspect any property to ascertain its value for IHT purposes, the person having custody or possession of that property must permit him to inspect it at such reasonable time as the Board considers necessary. Any person who wilfully delays or obstructs a person acting under these powers is liable on summary conviction to a fine not exceeding level 1 on the standard scale within the meaning of *Criminal Justice Act 1982, s 75*. [*IHTA 1984, s 220*].

Land registry and e-conveyancing. With the advent of e-conveyancing many estates which are not registered are going to encounter problems and time delays with regard to valuations. This will particularly impact upon the period for which interest on overdue tax is due on an estate on a chargeable transfer where there are timing delays trying to ascertain boundaries, etc. It is estimated that at least 60% of the country is not registered with the Land Registry Office and in order to assist in complying with registration for e-conveyancing the Land Registry is recommending voluntary registration. See http://www.landregistry.gov.uk/register_dev/.

For large estates in excess of £1 million the fee for a 'Registered Title' will be £525 and the estate is then on the registry with all formalities completed. This will enable Executors or Trustees to obtain valuations quickly which in turn will reduce the prospect of interest on overdue IHT.

56.2   **AGRICULTURAL PROPERTY**

See 5.2, 5.7 and 5.8 AGRICULTURAL PROPERTY for agricultural value, etc. See *Willett and Another v CIR Lands Tribunal, [1982] 264 EG 257* and *Gray (Executor of Lady Fox) v CIR* (see 56.1 above) for valuation of a freehold interest in tenanted agricultural property. See *Baird's Exors v CIR Lands Tribunal for Scotland 1990, [1991] 09 EG, 10 EG 153* for valuation of the tenant's interest in an agricultural lease containing a standard prohibition on assignation. Where there is an agricultural tie to a property it has been assumed that there should be a discount in the market value of that property, Traditionally this has been taken to be a one-third reduction, however, *IHTA 1984, s 115(3)* does not require the exclusive occupation of the property and this is a factor that should be borne in mind when assuming such discounts. Currently, many farming properties are being marketed with agricultural ties on the basis that they provide a tax shelter even with an agricultural tie. A discount in these circumstances would be inappropriate. In addition, in some cases there has been a breach of the agricultural tie for more than ten years and the legal protection for the tenant has expired so negating any perceived depression in the market value because of the agricultural tie. HMRC have had discussions with the Central Association of Agricultural Valuers on this matter. See Taxation Magazine, 3 April 2003, p 14. See Form D13 below.

56.3   Valuation

The Lands Tribunal in *Lloyds TSB plc (Antrobus' Personal Representative) v Twiddy* [2004] DET/47/2004 reviewed and rejected the contention that the market value of a farmhouse represented the agricultural value, holding that the open market value of the farmhouse should be discounted by 30% to arrive at its 'agricultural value'. HMRC Inheritance Tax IHT manual sets down eight considerations as to 'character appropriateness' of a farmhouse which should be reviewed when considering a claim for relief under *IHTA 1984, s 115(2)*. See http://www.hmrc.gov.uk/manuals/ihtmanual/IHTM24036.htm.

See 60 TAX CASES for Lands Tribunal decision.

56.3   CREDITORS' RIGHTS

In determining the value of a right to receive a sum it must be assumed that amounts receivable under any obligation will be received in full unless recovery of the sum is impossible or not reasonably practicable and has not become so by any act or omission of the person to whom the sum is due. [*IHTA 1984, s 166*].

IHT 210 (Notes) at D8 (Notes) states:

> 'The law says that if the deceased was owed some money when they died, you must assume that the debt will be repaid in full. On this basis, you must include the full value of the capital and interest outstanding. If, however, it is impossible or not reasonably possible for the money to be repaid, you may include a reduced figure. You must explain why you have included the reduced figure and show the figure has been worked out.'

See Form D8 below.

56.4   DEATH

See 50.2 TRANSFERS ON DEATH for the valuation of a deceased person's estate generally and also below for certain sales after death.

Capital gains tax. Where, on the death of any person, inheritance tax (or, when extant, capital transfer tax or estate duty) is chargeable on the value of his estate immediately before his death and the value of an asset forming part of his estate has been ascertained for those purposes, that value is to be taken as the market value at the date of death for capital gains tax purposes. [*TCGA 1992, s 274, Sch 11 para 9*]. Because of the existence for inheritance tax of such factors as the spouse/civil partner exemption and 100% business and agricultural property relief, it is unclear whether in an appropriate case inheritance tax is 'chargeable' and a value has been 'ascertained'. In such cases, and where no IHT is payable on the deceased's estate, the value of an asset is not ascertained for IHT purposes and therefore no IHT value is available, then the normal rules of *TCGA 1992, s 272* are applied to determine the capital gains tax acquisition of the beneficiary (see HMRC Tax Bulletin, April 1995 p 209).

A danger lies in cases where agricultural property comprises part of an estate and is expected to attract the 100% relief under *IHTA 1984, s 116* and a nominal or ill-considered valuation is made rather than a professional valuation. Subsequently, if relief is not due for any reason then the value of the asset will not have been 'ascertained' for the purposes of *TCGA 1992, s 274*. In such a case where there is an uplift in the value to the open market value then a penalty may be applicable. See 36.5 PENALTIES and 61 IHT NEWSLETTER AND TAX BULLETIN EXTRACTS, April 2004.

See 56.20 below in the case of quoted shares and securities.

56.5   JOINT PROPERTY

The value of a half share of land owned by tenants in common is half vacant possession value less a discount to reflect the restricted demand for this type of interest. An appropriate discount has been held to be 15%. (*Wight and Moss v CIR Lands Tribunal, [1982] 264 EG 935; Barrett (Barrett's Personal Representatives) v HMRC Lands Tribunal, 23 November 2005 unreported*). It should be borne in mind that the interests of tenants in common may well be 'related property'; see 56.17 below and 59 TAX CASES.

Where at the valuation date a co-owner remains in occupation the normal approach is for the DV to take half the freehold vacant possession value and deduct 15%. In cases where the co-owner has rights to occupy but does not and the purpose behind the trust for sale still exists then the discount would normally be 15% and 10% in other cases. A half share without rights of occupation will obtain a 10% deduction from the value. See paras 18.5 and 18.6 of section 18 in VOA IHT manual at http://www.voa.gov.uk/instructions/chapters/inheritance_tax_ch_1b/sections/section_18/frame.htm. The example in the VOA manual shows circumstances where the 10% and 15% discounts are appropriate as follows:

Example

Mr and Mrs A bought a house for their joint occupation. When Mr A died he left his one-half share to his son Mr B who lives elsewhere. Mrs A has now died and it is therefore necessary to value her one half-share.

When Mrs A dies the other co-owner is Mr B. Mr B is not in occupation and the house was not purchased for his occupation. When valuing Mrs A's one-half share a 10% discount should be applied.

If Mr B had died before Mrs A then, at the date of Mr B's death, the other co-owner, Mrs A, would still have been in occupation and the purpose behind the trust would still have existed. When valuing Mr B's one-half share a 15% discount should be applied.

Notes to the example

(A) The example in the VOA IHT manual shows in the first two paragraphs that a 10% discount would be due because the original purpose behind the trust for sale (be it a 'financial' trust for sale or an 'occupation' trust for sale) still exists on the death of the wife in occupation or the son not in occupation. However, in the third paragraph where Mr B dies first his estate would be entitled to the higher 15% discount because Mrs A is still in occupation of the property.

(B) Where an 'interest in land' in a deceased person's estate is sold within three years after the death by the '*appropriate person*', a claim (on Form IHT 38) may be made by that person for the 'sale value' to be substituted for the value on death of *every* interest in land owned by the deceased and sold within three years of death by the same 'appropriate person' for which such a claim would be available. See 56.6 below. However, in cases where a discount of 10% has been claimed and then the interest is sold and a claim is made under *IHTA 1984, s 191* the 10% discount for joint ownership is not allowed as a further deduction from the sale proceeds. This may have the effect of HMRC assessing a higher than expected figure than was the case intended by the appropriate person.

(C) This (point B above) of course places the estate in a disadvantageous position and, as in many cases of HMRC elections which, once made, cannot be withdrawn, HMRC are instructed to ensure that they consider any disadvantageous elections under Form IHT 38, see IHT manual extract at IHTM33182 where the claim is reviewed to 'help prevent the taxpayer making a disadvantageous claim'. See also Fosters at D3.12. However, HMRC confirm that such an instruction will not be binding where the IHT 38 has been made on a commercially supplied copy of the form and submitted unsolicited to HMRC under *IHTA 1984, s 191*.

See also *St Clair-Ford (Youlden's Executor) v Ryder, [2006] Lands Tribunal 22 June 2006 unreported*. When dealing with minority shares in property which is vacant, or commercially let, it is necessary to consider the purpose behind the trust for sale and if it exists and can be fulfilled then the discount may be increased. (VOA IHT manual, section 18, paras 18.3–18.7). In *HSBC Trusts Co (UK) Ltd (Farmbrough's Executor) v Twiddy, [2006] Lands Tribunal 24 August 2006 unreported*, a woman had held a 16.25% interest in two large buildings comprising 28 flats and 9 shops. The Lands Tribunal held that since this was a minority interest, it should be valued on an income basis, declining to follow the earlier decision in *Charkham v CIR, Lands Tribunal 1996, [2000] RVR 7*.

For varying treatment of accounts held in joint names see *Anand v CIR [1997] STC SCD 58 Sp C 107* and *O'Neill and others v CIR [1998] STC SCD 110 Sp C 154*. See also *Sillars and another v CIR [2004] STC SCD 180 Sp C 401*.

IHT 210 (Notes) at D4 (Notes) states:

'The amount of discount will vary depending on the circumstances of each property. To give us a standing point, you may reduce the arithmetical share of the value of the whole property by 10%. This will give us an indication of the value of the share of the property. This figure of 10% is only to give us a starting point. The amount of the discount, as well as the value estimated for the whole of the property may need to be changed after the grant has been issued.'

See Form D4 below.

Under Scots Law the 'survivorship destination' does not by itself pass the ownership of the funds in a joint account to the survivor. An account with a bank or building society is not a document of title as it is not a Deed of Trust in terms of the *Bank Bonds and Trusts Act 1696*. Instead, it is a contract between the bank and the customer which regulates the conditions on which the account is to be operated and is for administrative convenience only. See *Cairns v Davidson [1913] SC 1054*. If under the terms of the Will/Intestacy the funds in the account do not pass wholly to the surviving spouse then inheritance tax will be payable as appropriate. If under the terms of the Will/Intestacy the funds in the joint account pass to the spouse, then the spouse exemption should be claimed on page 4 of the IHT 200 under the head 'Exemptions and Reliefs'. Do not complete boxes JP3, 4 and 5 on the D4. This applies to all bank/building society accounts governed by Scots Law so this is a point which practitioners should bear in mind when administering an estate subject to Scots Law.

56.6 LAND SOLD WITHIN THREE YEARS (FOUR YEARS IN SOME CASES) OF DEATH

Claim. Where an 'interest in land' in a deceased person's estate is sold within three years after the death by the '*appropriate person*', a claim (on Form IHT 38) may be made by that person for the 'sale value' to be substituted for the value on death of *every* interest in land owned by the deceased and sold within three years of death by the same 'appropriate person' for which such a claim would be available. In the case of a death after 15 March 1990, a sale in the fourth year after death is treated as having occurred within three years of death unless *either* 56.10 below applies *or* the 'sale value' would exceed the value on death.

'*Interest in land*' does not include any estate, interest or right by way of mortgage or other security.

'*Appropriate person*' is the person liable for the tax or, if there is more than one such person and one of them is paying the tax, that person. For instance, if personal representatives pay the tax on the estate and then assent shares or land to a beneficiary who sells them at a loss, within the respective time limits, then no relief will be due as the beneficiary is not an 'appropriate person' under *IHTA 1984, ss 179(1), 191(1)*. In cases where 100% business or agricultural property relief is available then a substitution claim under *IHTA 1984, s 191* would not apply because there would not be an '*appropriate person*' who could make a claim. This may have a knock-on effect with regard to the capital gains tax position. See *Stoner and Another (Executors of Dickinson deceased) v CIR [2001] STC SCD 199 Sp C 288* which underlines the fact that a claim can only be made where an IHT issue (not a CGT saving issue) is at stake. This would also exclude cases where the value was covered by business property relief, the spouse/civil partner exemption and the nil-rate. See 60 TAX CASES.

'*Sale value*' is the 'sale price' as adjusted by the provisions in 56.8 to 56.13 below. Note that an abortive contract is not a sale and the sale price cannot be the said to be the price stated in the contract. (*Jones and Another (Balls' Administrators) v CIR, Ch D [1997] STC 359*).

'*Sale price*' is the price for which the land is sold or, if greater, the best consideration that could reasonably have been obtained at the time of sale, ignoring incidental expenses of commission, stamp duty or otherwise. [*IHTA 1984, ss 190, 191(1), 197A(1)(2); FA 1993, s 199*].

No claim is available if in respect of the interest in land giving rise to the claim

(*a*)   the sale value differs from the value on death by less than the lower of £1,000 and 5% of the value on death (see note 7 on IHT 38); or

(*b*)   the sale is by a personal representative or trustee to

    (i)   a person who, at any time between death and the sale, has been beneficially entitled to, or to an interest in possession in, property comprising the interest sold, or

    (ii)   the spouse, civil partner, child or remoter descendant of a person within (i) above, or

    (iii)   a trustee of a settlement under which a person within (i) or (ii) above has an interest in possession in property comprising the interest sold, or

(*c*)   the vendor or any person within (*b*) above obtains a right in connection with the sale to acquire the interest sold or any other interest in the same land.

For the above purposes, a person shall be treated as having the same rights in the property in an unadministered estate as he would have if the administration of the estate had been completed. In the case of (*b*)(ii) and (iii) above the restriction will not apply to a parent or sibling of the beneficiary or to the trustees of a discretionary settlement in which he is a potential object.

[*IHTA 1984, s 191(2)(3)*].

Because of the possibility of further purchases (see 56.12 below), the above loss on sale relief cannot be formally granted until four months have elapsed from the date of the last sale of an interest in land (see note 4 on IHT 38). In many estates there is one interest in land and it has to be sold to give effect to the terms of the deceased's will so that there is no prospect of further purchases. In such circumstances, the HMRC Inheritance Tax will accept a loss on sale relief claim in advance of the statutory time limit and make a provisional repayment of tax accordingly. However, formal clearance by way of certificate of discharge (see 35.9 PAYMENT OF TAX) must await the personal representatives' confirmation (subsequent to the expiry of the four-month statutory time limit) that no changes have taken place since the claim was made (CTO Practice Note published in Taxation Practitioner August 1994 p 6).

56.7   **Date applicable. Date of sale or purchase of land** by the 'appropriate person' is the date of the contract. If the transaction results from the exercise (by him or any other person) of an option granted not more than six months earlier, then the date of the transaction is the date on which the option is granted.

56.8 Valuation

Where an interest in land is acquired in pursuance of a notice to treat served by an authority possessing powers of compulsory purchase, the date of sale is whichever is the earlier of

(*a*)   the date when the compensation is agreed or otherwise determined (any variation on appeal being disregarded), and

(*b*)   the date when the authority enters on the land in pursuance of their powers.

If an interest in land is acquired from the 'appropriate person' by a general vesting declaration under the *Compulsory Purchase (Vesting Declarations) Act 1981* or, in Scotland, the *Town and Country Planning (Scotland) Act 1972, Sch 24* or, in NI, by a vesting order, the date of sale is the last day of the period specified in the declaration (in NI, the date on which the vesting order becomes operative). [*IHTA 1984, s 198*].

56.8   **Adjustments. Sales to beneficiaries etc. and exchanges** require adjustment where the person making the claim, acting in the same capacity as that in which he makes the claim,

(*a*)   sells land (or an interest in land) within three years after the death (a sale within four years after death which is treated as within three years under 56.6 above being ignored for this purpose) to any person within 56.6(*b*) or (*c*) above; or

(*b*)   within three years after the death exchanges (with or without payment) any interest in land which was comprised in the deceased's estate

and the sale price (or market value in the case of an exchange) exceeds its value on death. In such a case an addition is made to the sale price of any interest to which the claim relates. If the claim relates to one interest only, the addition is the amount of the excess. If there is more than one interest, the addition is that part of the excess given by the fraction

$$\frac{A}{B}$$

where

A =   the difference between the value on death of that interest and its sale price (as adjusted under 56.9 to 56.11 below); and

B =   the aggregate of that difference and the corresponding differences for all other interests to which the claim relates, calculated without regard to which is the greater, in the case of any particular interest, of its value on death and its sale price. [*IHTA 1984, ss 196, 197A(4); FA 1993, s 199*].

Example

A (a bachelor) died on 1 May 2004 owning four areas of land, as follows.

(*a*)   10 acres valued at death £20,000

(*b*)   15 acres valued at death £30,000

(*c*)   20 acres valued at death £30,000

(*d*)   30 acres valued at death £40,000

He also owned a freehold house valued at death at £50,000.

In the four years following A's death, his executors made the following sales.

(i)   Freehold house sold 15.11.04, proceeds £53,000, expenses £2,000

(ii)   Land area (*c*) sold 1.6.06, proceeds £29,500, expenses £1,500

(iii) Land area (*b*) sold 8.8.07, proceeds £27,000, expenses £1,000

538

(iv)   Land area (*d*) sold 19.9.07, proceeds £42,000, expenses £3,000

The following revisions must be calculated on a claim under IHTA 1984, Pt VI, Chapter IV

	£	
Gross sale proceeds of house	53,000	
Deduct probate value	50,000	£3,000
Gross sale proceeds of land area (*b*)	27,000	
Deduct probate value	30,000	£(3,000)
Gross sale proceeds of land area (*c*)	29,500	
Deduct probate value	30,000	£(500)

Notes to the example

(A)   The sale of area (*c*) is disregarded as the loss on sale (before allowing for expenses) is less than 5% of £30,000 (£1,500) and is also lower than £1,000. [*IHTA 1984, s 191*]. Note 7 on IHT 38.

(B)   The overall allowable reduction on all sales is therefore nil even though there is a loss after expenses.

(C)   For deaths after 15 March 1990, a sale *for less than the value at death* which is made in the fourth year after death is treated as having been made in the three years after death. [*IHTA 1984, s 197A; FA 1993, s 199*].

(D)   Note that if the gross sale proceeds of the house of £53,000 had been incorrectly discounted by 10% to take account of a joint ownership at the date of death then the calculation would be recomputed to preclude the discount and a revised figure of £52,500 taken into account. This would result in a further *increase* in the value of the taxable estate thereby imposing a further IHT charge on the personal representatives which may also incur interest. See implications regarding an erroneous submission of IHT 38 in the example in 56.5 above.

56.9   **Changes between death and sale.** Where there has been a change between the date of death and the date of sale so that the interest is not the same in all respects and with the same incidents and the land in which the interest subsists is not in the same state and with the same incidents, the sale price is adjusted by the difference between the value on death and what that value would have been if the changed circumstances had prevailed at the time of death. The difference is added to the sale price if the original value on death was more than the new valuation and deducted if less.

If compensation under any *Act* has been received by the 'appropriate person' (or any other person liable to tax on the interest in the land) between the death and the sale because of a restriction on the use or development of the land or because its value has been reduced for any other reason, such restriction or reduction is ignored for the adjustment of the sale price mentioned above but the sale price is increased by the amount of the compensation. [*IHTA 1984, s 193*]. See question 7 on form IHT 38.

56.10   **Compulsory acquisition more than three years after death.** Where an authority possessing powers of compulsory acquisition has served notice to treat before the death or within the following three years and has acquired the land *after* those three years from the 'appropriate person', the acquisition is treated in the same way as a sale during the three years. This provision is ignored if the sale value exceeds the value on death. [*IHTA 1984, s 197(1)(2)*].

56.11   **Other interests in same or other land.** If in determining the value at death of any interest to which the claim relates, any other interests, whether in the same or other land, were taken into account, an addition must be made to the sale price of the interest equal to the difference between the value on death of the interest and the value which would have been the value on death if no other interests had been taken into account. [*IHTA 1984, s 195*].

56.12   **Subsequent purchases. Further purchases** of any interests in land by the person making the claim as above in the same capacity during the period beginning with the death and ending four months after the date of the last sale may reduce the relief claimable on the sales. For this purpose any sale in the fourth year after death and taken into account under 56.6 above and any compulsory acquisition more than three years after death and taken into account under 56.10 above are ignored, and if the claim relates only to such sales, the following provisions are ignored.

The relief is lost if the aggregate of the purchase prices of all the interests purchased equals or exceeds the aggregate of the sale prices (as adjusted by 56.9 and 56.11 above and 56.13 below). Otherwise an addition is made to the sale price of every interest to which the claim relates given by the formula

$$(V-S) \times \frac{A}{B}$$

where

V =   value on death of the interest;

S =   sales price (as adjusted by 56.8, 56.9 and 56.11 above and 56.13 below as appropriate);

A =   aggregate of the purchase prices; and

B =   aggregate of the sales prices.

Where the value on death of an interest is less than its sale price as adjusted above, the sale price is reduced by the amount calculated from the above formula. [*IHTA 1984, ss 192, 197(3), 197A(3); FA 1993, s 199*].

Example

B died on 30 June 2007 owning a house and a seaside flat.

At death the valuations were

	£
House	50,000
Flat	30,000
	£80,000

Sales by the executors realised (gross)

House proceeds 1.7.2008	42,000
Flat proceeds 1.12.2008	33,000
	£75,000

On 1 May 2008, the executors bought a town house for the deceased's daughter for £40,000 (excluding costs).

Initially relief is due of £(80,000 – 75,000) = £5,000

Recomputation of relief

$$\text{Appropriate fraction}=\frac{\text{Purchase price}}{\text{Selling price}}=\frac{40,000}{75,000}=\frac{8}{15}$$

	House		Seaside Flat	
	£	£	£	£
Value on death		50,000		30,000
Sale price	42,000			
Add (£50,000 – £42,000) × ⁸/₁₅	4,267			
Revised value for IHT		46,267		
Sale price			33,000	
Deduct (£33,000 – £30,000) × ⁸/₁₅			1,600	
Revised value for IHT				31,400
Revised relief		£3,733		£(1,400)
Total		£2,333		

Note to the example

(A)   The purchase is taken into account because it is made within the period 30 June 2007 (date of death) and 1 April 2009 (four months after the last of the sales affected by the claim). [*IHTA 1984, s 192(1)*]. If a sale made in the fourth year after death was affected by the claim (under *IHTA 1984, s 197A*), it would *not* be taken into account in determining the above-mentioned period. [*IHTA 1984, s 197A(3); FA 1993, s 199*].

56.13   **Leases.** Where a claim relates to an interest in a lease of under fifty years duration at the date of death, the sale price is increased by the proportion of the amount of the value on death given by the fraction

$$\frac{P(1)-P(2)}{P(2)}$$

where

P(1) = the appropriate percentage from the table for depreciation of leases contained in *TCGA 1992, Sch 8 para 1* (see 9 CAPITAL GAINS TAX) for the duration of the lease at the date of death; and

P(2) = the appropriate percentage for the duration of the lease at the date of sale.

Note that on form IHT 38 the unexpired term of the lease at the date of death must be entered on the form under the heading 'Tenure'.

[*IHTA 1984, s 194*].

56.14   **LEASED PROPERTY**

If full consideration originally passed for the lease then the market value of the lease is taken when it is later transferred. Where a lessee's interest is for life or otherwise determinable by reference to a death, it may be treated as a settlement (see 42.6 SETTLEMENTS— GENERAL) and the value is calculated as the full value of the property less the value of the lessor's interest. The value of the lessor's interest is the proportion of the value of the property given by the fraction

$$\frac{A}{B}$$

where

A =   the value of the consideration given by the lessee at the time the lease was granted; and B

B =   the value of a full consideration in money or money's worth of the lease at that time.
[*IHTA 1984, ss 50(6), 170*].

56.15   LIABILITIES

In determining the value of a person's estate at any time his liabilities at that time must be taken into account, except as otherwise provided by *IHTA 1984*. Except in the case of a liability imposed by the law, a liability incurred by the transferor may be taken into account only to the extent that it was incurred for a consideration in money or money's worth. [*IHTA 1984, s 5(3)(5)*].

The following rules apply for determining the amount or value of the liability.

(*a*)   A liability in respect of which there is a right to reimbursement is taken into account only to the extent that reimbursement cannot reasonably be expected to be obtained.

(*b*)   Subject to (*c*) below, where a liability falls to be discharged after the time at which it is to be taken into account, it must be valued at the time of being taken into account (i.e. at its discounted value).

(*c*)   In determining the value of the transferor's estate immediately after the transfer, his liability for inheritance tax is computed

   (i)   without making any allowance for the fact that the tax will not be due immediately; and

   (ii)   as if any tax recovered otherwise than from the transferor (or, under certain circumstances, the transferor's spouse or civil partner, see 29.2 LIABILITY FOR TAX) were paid in discharge of a liability in respect of which the transferor had a right to reimbursement.

(*d*)   A liability which is an encumbrance on any property must, as far as possible, be taken to reduce the value of that property.

(*e*)   A liability due to a person resident outside the UK which neither falls to be discharged in the UK nor is an encumbrance on property in the UK must, as far as possible, be taken to reduce the value of property outside the UK. [*IHTA 1984, s 162*]. See *Whittaker v CIR, [2001] STC SCD 61 Sp C 272.*

Where an individual receives a capital payment from a non-UK resident trust and, under the provisions in *FA 1984, Sch 14* that payment crystallises a previously deferred capital gains tax liability of a close relative of his (see Tolley's Capital Gains Tax 1984/85 for full details), the payment by the individual of the capital gains tax is treated for inheritance tax purposes as made in satisfaction of a liability of his. [*IHTA 1984, s 165(3)*].

See also 50 TRANSFERS ON DEATH.

The value transferred is also reduced by

   (i)   any capital gains tax (or income tax on a development gain) borne by the donee. In the case of settled property the reduction applies only if the tax on the gain accruing to the trustees is borne by a person who becomes absolutely entitled to the settled property concerned;

(ii)   any incidental expenses incurred by the transferor in making the transfer but borne by the transferee. If borne by the transferor they are left out of account i.e. they do not have to be added to the amount of the gift.

[*IHTA 1984, ss 164, 165*].

See form D16 below and 56.3 VALUATION.

56.16   **LIFE ASSURANCE POLICIES AND ANNUITIES**

See 30 LIFE ASSURANCE POLICIES AND ANNUITIES for the valuation of policies and contracts and 43.2 SETTLEMENTS WITH INTERESTS IN POSSESSION for annuities which are interests in possession.

IHT 210 (Notes) at D9 (Notes) states:

'Life insurance policies taken out on one person's life may be held in trust for the benefit of others. Parents and grandparents may often take out a life insurance policy but put it in trust for their children or grandchildren. Business partners or the directors of a company also take out insurance on their lives but for the benefit of their partners and co–directors. So, if the deceased died whilst still working, or they died before their parent(s), there is a possibility that they may have a right to benefit under a policy held in trust. If the deceased had a right to benefit under a life insurance policy held in trust, that right may be settled property.'

See Form D9 below. Note that from February 2004 Form D9 has been revised to include a new Box 5b asking whether an annuity was purchased at any time and if so a copy should be provided. Also, at new Box 5a reference is made to Form D3.

56.17   **RELATED PROPERTY**

The value of any property in a person's estate is found by taking related property into account if by so doing a higher value for all or part of the property in his estate would be obtained. Property is related to the property in a person's estate if

(*a*)   it is in the estate of his spouse/civil partner, or

(*b*)   it is, or was during the preceding five years, the property of a charity, charitable trust, qualifying political party (see 21.6 EXEMPT TRANSFERS), specified national body (see 33.16 NATIONAL HERITAGE), non-profit making body (see 21.7 EXEMPT TRANSFERS) or registered housing association (see 21.4 EXEMPT TRANSFERS), and became so as the result of a transfer of value made by him or his spouse or civil partner after 15 April 1976 and was exempt to the extent that the value transferred was attributable to the property.

See IHT 15, p 14.

The value of the estate property and the related property taken together is then apportioned to the estate property in the proportion that its value on its own bears to the sum of the separate values. See *Arkwright and Another (Williams' Personal Representatives) v CIR ChD [2004] STC 1323, Sp C 392. [IHTA 1984, s 161(1)–(3); FA 1989, s 171(4)].*

Example 1

Husband owns a property worth £150,000 and his wife owns adjoining land worth £250,000. The combined value is £800,000.

The proportioned value of the husband's land is

$$\frac{150,000}{150,000 + 250,000} \times £\,800,000 = £\,300,000$$

56.18   Valuation

In the above example if the properties were each owned in equal shares and, say, the house was encumbered by mortgage of £60,000 in the husband's name sole then the value of the house is divisible in equal shares after the deduction of the mortgage even though this is in the husband's sole name in the sum of £45,000 (i.e. £150,000 − £60,000 ÷ 2).

In the case of shares etc. of the same class or similar units of property, the proportion is that which the number of shares in the estate bears to the total number of those and the related shares. Shares are of the same class if they are, or would be, so treated by the practice of a recognised stock exchange. [*IHTA 1984, s 161(4)(5)*].

The DV should value both interests together and make no reduction in the aggregate value because the related property is owned by the spouse/civil partner and not by the transferor. If vacant possession would become available on the merging of the interests the property should be valued with vacant possession. The aggregate value should reflect the full enhancement attributable to the merging of the transferor's property with the related property and no deduction should be made because more than one ownership is involved. (VOA IHT manual, section 15, para 15.5).

Example 2

On the death of a husband on 31 October 2007, the share capital of a private company was held as follows

	Shares	
Issued capital	10,000	
Husband	4,000	40%
Wife	4,000	40%
Others (employees)	2,000	20%
	10,000	100%

The value of an 80% holding is £80,000, while the value of a 40% holding is £24,000. In his will, the husband left his 4,000 shares to his daughter.

The related property rules apply to aggregate the shares of:

Husband	4,000	
Wife	4,000	
Related property	8,000	shares

Chargeable transfer on legacy to daughter

IHT value of 8,000 shares (80%)	£80,000

IHT value attributed to legacy of husband's shares (4,000)	£40,000

(Subject to 100% business property relief if conditions satisfied.)

56.18   **Sale within three years after death.** If property was valued on a death by reference to related property as in 56.17 above and is sold within the following three years at less than that valuation (allowing for any difference in circumstances between the times of death and sale), a claim may be made to revert to the value of that property at death without reference to the related property. The sale must qualify under the following conditions, namely that

(a)   the vendors are the persons in whom the property vested immediately after death or are the deceased's personal representatives; and

544

(b)   the sale is at arm's length for a price freely negotiated at the time of the sale and is not made in conjunction with a sale of any of the related property; and

(c)   no vendor (or any person having an interest in the sale proceeds) is, or is connected with, any purchaser (or any person having an interest in the purchase); and

(d)   neither the vendors nor any other person having an interest in the sale proceeds obtain in connection with the sale a right to acquire the property sold or any interest in or created out of it.

Where the property is shares or securities of a close company, the above relief does not apply if between the death and sale the value is reduced by more than 5% as a result of an alteration in the company's share or loan capital or rights attaching thereto.

The above rules also apply where the property was valued at death in conjunction with other property which did not devolve on the vendors e.g. property in a trust of which the deceased was life tenant. [*IHTA 1984, s 176*].

56.19   RESTRICTION ON FREEDOM TO DISPOSE

If the right to dispose of any property has been excluded or restricted by a contract made at any time, then, on the next chargeable transfer of the property, the exclusion or restriction will be taken into account only to the extent that consideration in money or money's worth was given for it. If the contract was before 27 March 1974, this provision applies only if the next chargeable transfer is a transfer made on death.

If the contract was itself a chargeable transfer (including part of an associated operation), an allowance is made for so much of the value transferred thereby (ignoring tax) as is attributable to the exclusion or restriction. [*IHTA 1984, s 163*]. See IHT 15, p 14.

56.20   SHARES AND SECURITIES

Unquoted shares and securities are valued at what they might reasonably be expected to fetch if sold in the open market on the assumption that there is available to any prospective purchaser all the information which a prudent prospective purchaser might reasonably require if he were proposing to purchase them from a willing vendor by private treaty and at arm's length. [*IHTA 1984, s 168; FA 1987, s 58, Sch 8 para 12*]. See also *CIR v Crossman and Others HL, [1936] 1 All ER 762; In re Lynall (decd.) HL 1971, 47 TC 375; Battle and Another v CIR Ch D 1979, [1980] STC 86.*

In a capital transfer tax case, both earlier arm's length transactions in the shares in question and previous agreements with HMRC were held to be admissible evidence for valuation purposes (*CIR v Stenhouse's Trustees CS 1991, [1992] STC 103*).

In order to ensure uniformity of approach, the DV should, unless otherwise instructed by Shares and Assets Valuation (SAV), value the underlying company property or assets on the basis of the statutory definition in *IHTA 1984, s 160* of 'open market value' disregarding any 'flooding of the market' effect and apply any relevant legal principles which have evolved over the years when the courts have ruled on the meaning of the similar definition for ED purposes contained in *FA 1894, s 7(5)* (VOA IHT manual, section 16, para 16.8). For these purposes the costs of sale are ignored.

The address of Shares and Assets Valuation is HMRC, Shares and Assets Valuation, Fitz Roy House, PO Box 46, Castle Meadow Road, Nottingham NG2 1BD. Tel: 0115–974 2222. Fax: 0115–974 2197. DX 701203 Nottingham 4. The address in Scotland is HMRC Inheritance Tax, Meldrum House, 15 Drumsheugh Gardens, Edinburgh EH3 7UH. Tel: 0131 777 4180. Fax. 0131 777 4220. DX 542002, Edinburgh 14.

Where it is evident that any possible variation in the value of shares in an unquoted company shown in the HMRC Account will still leave the total value of an estate below the IHT threshold, it is not necessary to ascertain the value of those shares. Where the total value of an estate is close to the IHT threshold, values may be considered but not necessarily 'ascertained'. For example, where SAV regard the value of such shares to be too high it is unlikely to negotiate an ascertained value for IHT when no tax is at stake. However, if the value of the shares seems too low, SAV may negotiate an ascertained value if the likely amount of IHT at stake warrants this (HMRC Tax Bulletin April 1995, pp 209, 210).

Quoted shares and securities are in practice (see IHT 15, p 15), unless there are special circumstances, valued (as for capital gains tax), at the lower of

(a)   the lower of the two prices quoted in the Stock Exchange Daily Official List for the relevant date, plus a quarter of the difference between those prices (*'the quarter-up rule'*), and

(b)   the average of the highest and lowest prices for normal bargains recorded on that date, if any.

If there was no trading on the relevant date, the prices are to be taken by reference to the latest previous date or to the earliest subsequent date, whichever produces the lower figure.

IHT 210 (Notes) at D7 (Notes) states, 'Another way to find out about share prices is to use the London Stock Exchange Historic Price service. The Stock Exchange can tell you what the end of day quotation (price) was for all stocks and shares on the Stock Exchange Daily Official List. If the shares are marked "xd" the Stock Exchange can also tell you the dividend per share that was to be paid to the deceased. There is a charge for this service.' [£8 for the first five quotations and £2 for each additional quotation]. and 'The Stock Exchange will reply by letter (or by fax if you ask them to) and will give you the end of day quotation. If the shares are marked "xd", they will also give you dividend per share. The address to write to is Historic Price Service, 4th Floor Tower, London Stock Exchange, Old Broad Street, London EC2N 1HP. See form D7 below.

Shares in unit trusts, subject as above, are valued at the lower of the two prices published by the managers on the relevant date or, if no price is published at that time, on the latest date before the relevant date. [*TCGA 1992, s 272(3)(4)*].

Note that in the case of sales of shares there is no *de minimis* amount applicable as applies to land and there is no restriction with regard to whom the sale is made.

Definitions. In relation to transfers of value made, and other events occurring, after 16 March 1987, *'quoted'*, in relation to any shares or securities, means quoted on a recognised stock exchange or dealt in on the Unlisted Securities Market (see Alternative Investment Market under 35.4), and *'unquoted'*, in relation to any shares or securities, means neither so quoted nor so dealt in. [*IHTA 1984, s 272; FA 1987, s 58(2), Sch 8 para 17*]. This applies for all IHT purposes except that, in relation to transfers of value made, and other events occurring, after 9 March 1992, an alternative definition whereby Unlisted Securities Market (and AIM) shares and securities are treated as unquoted, applies for the purposes of defining relevant business property (see 7.4 BUSINESS PROPERTY) and payment by instalments (see 35.3 PAYMENT OF TAX). As from 1 April 1996 the word *'quoted'* is substituted by the word *'listed'*. [*FA 1996, Sch 38 para 2*]. In relation to transfers of value made, and other events occurring, before 17 March 1987, shares and securities in companies dealt in on the Unlisted Securities Market were not treated as 'quoted' or 'listed' on a recognised stock exchange for all IHT purposes where those terms were used in tax provisions. The shares or securities did, however, satisfy the tests of being 'authorised to be dealt in' and 'dealt in (regularly or from time to time)' on a recognised stock exchange (HMRC Statement of Practice SP 18/80, 23 December 1980). See IHT 17, p 3.

56.21   **Quoted shares sold within twelve months after death.** Where 'qualifying invest-ments' comprised in a deceased person's estate are sold within twelve months for less than their value on death the 'appropriate person' may claim (specifying the capacity in which he makes the claim and using form IHT 35) a reduction in the estate values equal to the amount by which the aggregate of the value of *all* the qualifying investments included in the estate which are sold in the twelve-month period exceeds the aggregate of the 'sale values' of those investments (i.e. the loss on sale). See *Lee & Lee (Lee's Executors) v CIR [2002] Sp C 349* for strict adherence to the twelve-month time limit. For this purpose, if death occurred after 15 March 1992,

(*a*)   qualifying investments which are 'cancelled' (this term is not defined but may cover the final act of a company liquidation; if so, any 'capital payments' received during the liquidation will presumably be dealt with as below) within the twelve-month period without being replaced by other shares etc. are treated as having been sold immediately before cancellation for a nominal sum of £1, and

(*b*)   qualifying investments of which the listing is suspended at the end of the twelve-month period are treated as having been sold immediately before the end of that period at their value at that time (if this is lower than their value at death).

[*IHTA 1984, ss 178(1), 179, 186A(1), 186B(1)(2); FA 1993, s 198; FA 1996, Sch 38 para 4(1)(2)*].

'*Qualifying investments*' are shares or securities which at the date of the death in question are quoted (in relation to transfers of value made, and other events occurring, before 17 March 1987, quoted on a recognised stock exchange), holdings in an authorised unit trust and shares in any common investment fund established under the *Administration of Justice Act 1965, s 1* (i.e. certain funds managed by the Public Trustee and held in court on behalf of the persons entitled). Where a listing on a recognised stock exchange or, in relation to transfers of value made, and other events occurring, after 16 March 1987, dealing on the Unlisted Securities Market (see Alternative Investment Market under 35.4 PAYMENT OF TAX above) is suspended at the date of death, the investments are qualifying investments if they are again so listed or dealt in at the time of sale or exchange under 56.24 below. [*IHTA 1984, s 178(1)(2); FA 1987, s 58, Sch 8 para 13; FA 1996, Sch 38 para 4(1)(3)*].

The '*appropriate person*' is the person liable for the tax attributable to the value of the investment concerned or, if there is more than one such person and one of them is paying the tax, that person. Note 2 of Form IHT 35 states that the 'capacity' of the claimant (i.e. executor, administrator, trustee or donor) must be indicated but this must not include an agent. See 56.6 above.

'*Sale value*' of qualifying investments means the price for which they were sold or (except in the case of (*a*) or (*b*) above), if greater, the best consideration which could reasonably have been obtained for them at the time of the sale (ignoring incidental expenses of commission, stamp duty or otherwise). Any 'capital payment' (whether during or after the twelve months following the death) as is attributable to the investments comprised in the estate and sold by the appropriate person is added to the sale value. '*Capital payment*' includes consideration received for the disposal of a provisional allotment of shares or debentures and any money or money's worth which does not constitute income for income tax purposes. It does not include the price paid on the sale of the investment. [*IHTA 1984, ss 178(1)(5), 179(1), 181, 186A(2), 186B(3); FA 1993, s 198*].

Date of sale or purchase of investments by the 'appropriate person' is the date of the contract. If the transaction results from the exercise (by him or any other person) of an option, then the date of the transaction is the date on which the option was granted. [*IHTA 1984, s 189*].

Value at death of qualifying investments includes any calls on them paid by the 'appropriate person' during or after the twelve months following the death. [*IHTA 1984, s 182*]. Where part only of a holding of qualifying investments is comprised in a person's estate (e.g. if he is a joint tenant of settled property) and a claim is made as above, the whole of the holding is included in the calculation and the loss on sale is reduced by the proportion which the value of that part of the investments included in the estate bears to the entire value of those investments. [*IHTA 1984, s 186*].

56.22   **Further qualifying investments. Further purchases** of qualifying investments by the 'appropriate person', in the same capacity in which he made the claim above, during the period beginning with the death and ending two months after the date of the last sale will reduce the 'loss on sale' by the proportion which the total of the purchase prices (ignoring incidental expenses) bears to the total of the sales values in the claim. If the aggregate purchase prices equals or exceeds the sales values, the loss is extinguished. [*IHTA 1984, s 180(1)*]. See Form IHT 35, p 3.

If a person makes a claim other than as personal representative or trustee, any purchase as above is ignored unless it is of qualifying investments of *the same description* (i.e. they are not separately listed on a recognised stock exchange nor, in relation to transfers of value made, and other events occurring, after 16 March 1987, separately dealt in on the Unlisted Securities Market (or AIM) nor in a different unit trust or common investment fund) as included in the claim and the purchase is made otherwise than in the capacity of personal representative or trustee. [*IHTA 1984, s 180(2)(3); FA 1987, s 58, Sch 8 para 14; FA 1996, Sch 38 para 3*].

56.23   **Changes in holdings.** On any change within the period of twelve months following death due to a reorganisation, conversion, exchange, amalgamation or reconstruction to which *TCGA 1992, s 127* applies (or such a change in unit trust holding to which *TCGA 1992, s 127* is applied by virtue of *TCGA 1992, s 99*), the new holding is treated as the same as the original holding.

If within the twelve-month period the appropriate person sells any investment comprised in the new holding, the value on death of those investments are determined by the formula

$$\frac{Vs}{Vs+Vr} \times (H-S)$$

where

Vs =   sales value of the investment;

Vr =   market value at the time of sale of any investment remaining in the new holding after the sale;

H =   value on death of the new holding; and

S =   value on death of any investments which were originally comprised in the new holding but have been sold on a previous occasion or occasions.

The value on death of the new holding is the same as the value on death of the original holding increased by any consideration which the appropriate person gives, or becomes liable to give, as part of or in connection with the transaction by which he acquires the new holding. For this purpose, 'consideration' excludes any surrender, cancellation or other alteration of the investments comprised in the original holding or rights attached thereto. It also excludes any application, in paying up the new holding or part of it, of assets of the company concerned or any dividend or other distribution declared out of those assets but not made. [*IHTA 1984, s 183*].

56.24   **Exchange of qualifying investments.** If, apart from 56.23 above, an 'appropriate person' exchanges qualifying investments within twelve months of the death for other property of any kind (with or without any payment by way of equality of exchange) and the market value of the investments at the date of exchange is *greater* than their value at the date of death, they are treated as having been sold at their market value at the date of exchange. [*IHTA 1984, s 184*].

56.25   **Identification.** Where an 'appropriate person' has, in the same capacity, (i) investments comprised in the deceased's estate at death and (ii) investments of the same description subsequently acquired in some other way (but not under 56.23 above), any part of such investments sold within the twelve months after death is apportioned between (i) and (ii) in the same proportions as they bore to each other immediately before the sale. [*IHTA 1984, s 185*].

56.26   **Attribution of specific values.** It is necessary (for the purposes of both inheritance tax and capital gains tax) to attribute values to specific investments included in a claim as under 56.21 above. Generally, the value of a specific investment is its sale value. Where the loss on sale is reduced by further purchases (see 56.22 above), that reduction is apportioned over all the investments sold in proportion to the differences between their sale values and their values at death.

Where a call has been paid, the sale value of that investment is reduced by the amount of the call.

Where under a reorganisation etc. under 56.23 above, consideration has been paid for the new holding, the sale value of any specific investment comprised in the new holding is reduced by an amount which bears to that consideration the like proportion as the value on death of the specific investment sold bears to the value on death of the whole of the new holding.

In no case can the value of an investment be reduced to a minus quantity. [*IHTA 1984, ss 187, 188*].

Example

An individual died on 30 June 2007 and included in his estate was a portfolio of quoted investments. The executors sold certain investments within twelve months of death. The realisations were as follows.

	Probate Value £	Gross Sales £
Share A	7,700	7,200
Share B	400	600
Share C	2,800	2,900
Share D	13,600	11,600
Share E	2,300	2,300
Share F	5,700	5,100
Share G	19,400	17,450
Share H	8,500	8,600
	£60,400	55,750
Incidental costs of sale		2,750
Net proceeds of sale		£53,000

On 1 September 2007, share J, having a probate value of £200 and still held by the executors was cancelled.

On 1 December 2007, share K, having a probate value of £1,000 has its stock exchange quotation suspended. On 30 June 2008, the investment is still held by the executors, its estimated value is £49 and the quotation remains suspended.

On 30 April 2008, the executors purchased a new holding for £1,750.

The executors would initially be able to claim a reduction of

56.27 Valuation

$$(\pounds 60{,}400 - \pounds 55{,}750) + (\pounds 200 - \pounds 1) + (\pounds 1{,}000 - \pounds 49) = \pounds 5{,}800$$

After the purchase, the reduction is restricted as follows

$$\text{Relevant proportion} = \frac{\text{Reinvestment}}{\text{Total sales}} = \frac{1{,}750}{\pounds 55{,}750 + \pounds 1 + \pounds 49} = \frac{1{,}750}{55{,}800}$$

Original relief restricted by

$$\frac{1{,}750}{55{,}800} \times \pounds 5{,}800 = \pounds 182$$

Total relief £5,800 less £182 = £5,618

Notes to the example

(A) No costs of selling investments may be deducted from the sale proceeds. Note 5 on IHT 35.

(B) The cancelled shares are treated as sold for £1 immediately before cancellation. The suspended shares are treated as sold on the first anniversary of death at their value at that time (provided that value is less than their value on death). [*IHTA 1984, ss 186A, 186B; FA 1993, s 198*].

(C) The purchase is taken into account as it is made during the period beginning on date of death and ending two months after the end of the last sale taken into account (including deemed sales as in (B) above).

(D) The probate value of each of the investments sold will be adjusted, both for CGT and IHT purposes, to the gross sale proceeds plus the relevant proportion of the fall in value. Thus the probate value of share A will be revised from £7,700 to

$$\pounds 7{,}200 + \left(\frac{1{,}750}{55{,}800} \times (7{,}700 - 7{,}200) \right) = \pounds 7{,}216$$

and in the case of share B where the sales price exceeds the probate value (i.e. profit on sale) the revised value will be

$$\pounds 600 - \left(\frac{1{,}750}{55{,}800} \times \pounds 200 \right) = \pounds 594$$

(i.e. £600 – £6) = £594

(E) Although excluded from computation of the loss on sale for inheritance tax purposes, incidental costs of sale and deductible from proceeds in calculating CGT. For deaths after 5 April 2004 see Inland Revenue Statement of Practice SP2/04.

56.27 UNINCORPORATED BUSINESS

See 7.8 BUSINESS PROPERTY.

56.28 DEMUTUALISATIONS

Valuing the estate. The valuation of the deceased's share, or other interest, in a building society or mutual insurance company is not directly concerned with the actual amount of cash received or the value of free shares received by their successors on or after vesting day. Rather, it is a matter of determining the value by reference only to the information that was available at the date of death. This is generally the information provided for the qualifying members in the Transfer Document or Prospectus.

Each Transfer Document or Prospectus provides:

- an anticipated price per share of the free share, or

- details of the proposed cash bonuses

calculated by reference to the amounts involved.

These anticipated prices, or proposed amounts, are the starting point for determining the gross value of the qualifying member's share or other interest at the relevant time. A discount is then applied to reflect any uncertainty or delay. For example, if a qualifying member died after the issue of the Transfer Document but before the extraordinary general meeting at which the de-mutualisation was formally approved by the voting members, the discount would be greater than if the member died after the extraordinary general meeting but before vesting day.

In the interests of consistency, a Valuation Table is provided to help calculate the open market value of the deceased member's share, or other interest, in a mutual society where he or she died before vesting day. As explained below, this value is also relevant for capital gains tax purposes and local Tax Offices and Tax Enquiry Centres have also been provided with a similar Table.

Most societies making special provisions in their Transfer Documents to preserve the entitlement of those qualifying members who die before vesting day. Under those special provisions, the qualifying member's personal representatives, as the qualifying successors, generally receive the free shares or cash bonus in that capacity for the benefit of the estate. See *Ward and Others (Executors of Cook deceased) v IRC [1999] STC SCD 1 Sp C 175.*

For inheritance tax purposes, a person's estate is the aggregate of all the property to which that person is beneficially entitled. [*IHTA 1984, s 5(1)*]. The value of that property is the price which it might reasonably be expected to fetch if sold on the open market at that time. [*IHTA 1984, s 160*].

Society	*Vesting day*	*Date of death between*	*Percentage discount*	*Anticipated share price/Cash bonus*
Cheltenham & Gloucester	1.8.1995	10.8.1994–31.3.1995 1.4.1995–31.7.1995	32%–25% 10%–0%	Cash bonus £500 +13.3%
National & Provincial	6.8.1996	28.2.1996–11.4.1996 12.4.1996–5.8.1996	27.5%–25% 10%–0%	£500 in Abbey National shares
Alliance & Leicester	22.4.1997	28.10.1996–10.12.1996 11.12.1996–21.4.1997	27.5%–25% 10%–0%	£3.97 per share
Halifax	3.6.1997	11.1.1996–24.12.1996 25.12.1996–2.6.1997	30%–25% 7.5%–0%	11.1.1997–28.4.1997 £4.05 per share 29.4.1997–2.6.1997 £5.30 per share
Woolwich	8.7.1997	6.1.1997–11.2.1997 12.2.1997–7.7.1997	27.5%–25% 12.5%–0%	£1.81 per share
Northern Rock	2.10.1997	17.2.1997–15.4.1997 16.4.1997–1.10.1997	27.5%–25% 12.5%–0%	£2.68 per share
Bristol & West	26.8.1997	27.2.1997–15.4.1997 16.4.1997–25.8.1997	30%–25% 10%–0%	Cash bonus 6.5% or £250 in Bank of Ireland shares
Greenwich	30.7.1997	13.5.1997–17.6.1997 18.6.1997–29.7.1997	27.5%–25% 5%–0%	Cash bonus 5%
Norwich Union	16.6.1997	18.4.1997–15.6.1997	5%–0%	£2.31 per share

56.28 Valuation

Scottish Amicable	30.9.1997	27.5.1997–26.6.1997	27.5%–25%	Cash payment
		27.6.1997–29.9.1997	7.5%–0%	£550; immediate bonus £430; bonus on maturity £450
Colonial Mutual	23.5.1997	24.9.1996–10.11.1996	28%–25%	£1.30 per share
		11.11.1996–22.5.1997	17.5%–0%	

IR Tax Bulletin 1998, p 523.

Notes to the Valuation Table

(A)   The discount rates offered are not intended to be prescriptive but are a guide to an acceptable valuation for the qualifying member's share, or interest, in the society at the date of death. The amount of any discount will be lower the closer that the date of death is to vesting day.

Example

An individual who is a UK policy holder of AMP, the Australian insurer which undertook demutualisation, died on 1 May 1998 a few days before the prospectus was published on 6 May 1998. The estimated share price was between A$12.50–16.00 per share when trading commenced on the Australian and New Zealand stock exchange on 15 June 1998.

As the individual died before the issue of the transfer document/prospectus, the value of the individual's qualifying member's share has increased but a discount is given of approximately 25–30%. However, if the individual had died after the prospectus issue then the discount may have been between 0–10%. The personal representative's valuation of the right to the shares owned by the deceased at the date of death can be valued as:

Value of shares at vesting day, say,	£3,700
Less: 25%, discount prior to vesting	(925)
Executor's value for estate	£2,775

If the shares are disposed of within twelve months of the death for, say, £4,200 then where this comprises part of the aggregate sale values under *IHTA 1984, s 179(1)* the increase of £1,425 (i.e. £4,200 − £2,775) will serve to reduce any overall loss on sale.

Note to the example

(A)   In view of the effective loss of 'discount' where shares are sold within 12 months of the death and comprise part of a claim under *IHTA 1984, s 179* it is perhaps better to defer the disposal until a later date.

HM Revenue & Customs

Household and personal goods

Name

Date of death

/ /

Give details about the household goods or other personal property owned by the deceased. You should read form D10(Notes) before filling in this form. You should forward any professional valuations obtained.

HG1 Did the deceased own any of the following

Yes No

Motor vehicles including vintage and classic vehicles ☐ ☐

Motor cycles ☐ ☐

Caravans ☐ ☐

Aeroplanes ☐ ☐

Boats ☐ ☐

Other ☐ ☐

If you have answered yes to any of the above, go to question HG2 otherwise go to question HG5

HG2 Provided the following information in respect of respect of each item that has not been sold.

Manufacturer	Model	Year of manufacture or first registration	Registration number (where appropriate)	Condition	Value

Vehicles etc. that have not been sold Total HG2

HG3 Provided the following information in respect of respect of each item that has been sold.

Manufacturer	Model	Year of manufacture or first registration	Registration number (where appropriate)	Condition	Date of sale	Sale price or value at date of death

Vehicles etc. that have not been sold Total HG3

HG4 What was the relationship between the purchaser and the deceased?

Item	Relationship

D10 www.hmrc.gov.uk/cto Helpline 0845 30 20 900 HMRC CT 08/06

56.28 Valuation

		Yes	No
HG5	Did the deceased own any jewellery?	☐	☐

If you have answered yes to this question, go to question HG6 otherwise go to question HG9.

HG6 Provided the following information about the jewellery that has not been sold.

Item	Description	Value

Jewellery that has not been sold Total HG6 [ ]

HG7 Provided the following information about the jewellery that has been sold.

Item	Description	Date of sale	Sale price or value at date of death

Jewellery that has been sold Total HG7 [ ]

HG8 What was the relationship between the purchaser and the deceased?

Item	Relationship

		Yes	No
HG9	Did the deceased own any	☐	☐

- antiques or works of art including paintings, drawings, sculpture porcelain, glass, silver etc.? or
- collections of any kind such as books, stamps, coins, medals or wines and spirits

If you have answered yes to this question go to question HG10 otherwise go to question HG13.

HG10 Provided the following information about the jewellery that has not been sold.

Item	Description	Value

Antiques etc. that have not been sold Total HG10 [ ]

HG11 Give full details of the items that have been sold.

Item	Description	Date of sale	Sale price or value at date of death

	Antiques etc. that have been sold Total HG11	

HG12 What was the relationship between the purchaser and the deceased?

Item	Relationship

HG13 Give details all other household and personal goods that have not been sold. Include all televisions, audio video equipment, cameras and other specialist equipment, electrical equipment, furniture, household and domestic items, clothes, garden equipment, tools etc.

Item	Description	Value

Other household and personal goods that have not been sold Total HG13	

HG14 Give details of all other household and personal goods that have been sold. Include all televisions, audio video equipment, cameras and other specialist equipment, electrical equipment, furniture, household and domestic items, clothes, garden equipment, tools etc.

Item	Description	Date of sale	Sale price or value at date of death

Other household and personal goods that have been sold Total HG14	

56.28 Valuation

HG15 What was the relationship between the purchaser and the deceased?

Item	Relationship

HG16 If you have not obtained professional valuations please say how you valued the household and personal effects. If the household and personal effects are considered to be valueless please explain why. If the deceased did not own any household goods or personal possessions explain the circumstances here.

HG17 Bring the totals of the items that have not been sold forward and add them up.

Total HG2	
Total HG6	
Total HG10	
Total HG13	
Overall total for the unsold personal goods. Copy to box F20 on form IHT200	

HG18 Bring the totals of the items that have been sold forward and add them up.

Total HG3	
Total HG7	
Total HG11	
Total HG14	
Overall value of the personal goods that have been sold. Copy to box F19 on form IHT200	

The values to be included are those before exemptions. Exemptions should be shown on the IHT200.

Revenue
Capital Taxes

Agricultural Relief

Name

Date of death

/   /

You have deducted agricultural relief on form IHT200. Answer the following questions and give the further details we ask for. If necessary, fill in a separate form for each item of property. You should read form D13(Notes) before filling in this form.

1 What is the address of the property concerned?

2a Did the deceased occupy the property for the purposes of agriculture *throughout* the 2 years up to the date of death?

No ☐   Yes ☐

If the answer is "Yes" go to question 3 and ignore question 5. If "No", go to question 2b.

2b Was the whole of the property owned by the deceased and occupied for agricultural purposes *throughout* the 7 years up to the date of death?

No ☐   Yes ☐

If the answer is "Yes", go to question 3 and ignore question 4. If "No", go to question 2c.

2c As you have answered "No" to questions 2a and 2b, agricultural relief would not normally be available. If you feel the relief should be due, say why below.

3 When and how did the deceased acquire the property?

4 Describe the nature and extent of the agricultural operations carried out by the deceased.

5a Who occupied the property during the 7 years up to the date of death?

5b Describe the nature and extent of the agricultural operations carried out on the land

D13
(Substitute)(LexisNexis Butterworths)

www.hmrc.gov.uk/cto

Helpline 0845 30 20 900

Please turn over
ROK 4274 IRCT 12/02

56.28   Valuation

5c Provide a copy of any lease, tenancy or other proprietary interest that applied to the property immediately before the deceased died. If there is nothing in writing, give details below. If the tenancy began after 31 August 1995, you need only give the date the tenancy started.

6 Did the deceased have the right to vacant possession immediately before the death, or the right to obtain it within 24 months?

No ☐   Yes ☐

If the answer is "Yes" say how the deceased would have been able to obtain vacant possession. If the answer is "No", but you feel relief is due at the higher rate, say why below.

7 Who occupied any farmhouse and buildings or cottage at the property and what was the nature of the occupation? Provide details for each building separately.

8 Was the property, or any part of it, subject to a binding contract for sale at the date of death?

No ☐   Yes ☐

If the answer is "Yes", give details of the contract below

9 *Only answer question 9 if you are claiming agricultural relief in connection with a lifetime transfer.*

9a Was the property agricultural property immediately before the end of the relevant period?

No ☐   Yes ☐

9b Was the property owned by the person who received the gift throughout the relevant period?

No ☐   Yes ☐

9c Was the property occupied (by the person who received the gift or by someone else) for agricultural purposes *throughout* the relevant period?

No ☐   Yes ☐

9d Was the property subject to a binding contract for sale immediately before the end of the relevant period?

No ☐   Yes ☐

Inland
Revenue
Capital Taxes Office

Debts due to the estate

Name	Date of death
	/ /

Give details about any debts owed to the deceased. Use a separate form for each loan or mortgage. You should read form D8(Notes) before filling in this form.

1 On what date was the original loan made?   /   /

2 What was the original value of the loan on that date?   £

3 What was the value of the loan, including any
interest due, still outstanding at the date of death?   DD1 £

Copy the total from box DD1 to box F10 or F11, page 3, form IHT200.

4 If you do not think that the value in box DD1 should be included as part of the deceased's estate, say why in the box below. If you wish to include a reduced value in box F10 or F11, page 3, form IHT200, show how that value is calculated.

5 Give the name(s) of the borrower(s) and say whether they were related to the deceased.

6 Is there evidence to prove the existence of the loan?   No   Yes
If the answer is "Yes" give details below

7 Was interest charged on the loan?   No   Yes
If the answer is "Yes" give details below

8 Was any capital repaid to the deceased during their lifetime?   No   Yes
If the answer is "Yes" give details below

D8   CTO Approval Ref No L3/00   R0G4112CTO11/99
(Substitute)(LexisNexis Butterworths)

56.28   Valuation

2   **Land, buildings, business assets, control shareholdings and unquoted shares**

Do you wish to pay tax on these assets by instalments?   No ☐   Yes ☐

If the value of the deceased's share is **not** the **whole** value, say

- who the other joint owner(s) is or are
- when the joint ownership began
- how much each joint owner provided to obtain the item
- who received the income, if there was any
- whether the item passes to other joint owner(s) by survivorship or under the deceased's Will or intestacy.

	Whole value	Deceased's share
	Total of assets JP6 £	
• Liabilities		
	Total of liabilities JP7 £	
• Exemptions and reliefs	**Net assets** *(box JP6 less box JP7)* JP8 £	
	Total exemptions and reliefs JP9 £	
	Net total of joint assets *passing by survivorship* **where tax may be paid by instalments** *(box JP8 less box JP9)* JP10 £	

3   **Nominated property**

If the deceased nominated any assets to any person, describe the assets below and show their value.

Include the assets in the appropriate box in section F of form IHT200.

D4

560

Inland Revenue Capital Taxes Office

Debts owed by the estate

Name	Date of death
	/ /

You have deducted certain types of debts against the estate. Give the details of the debts we ask for below. You should read form D16(Notes) before filling in this form.

1 Debts due to close friends or relatives

2 Loans and overdrafts

3 Guarantee debts

4 Debts created on or after 18 March 1986

D16

CTO Approval Ref No L3/00

R0G4110CTO11/99

(Substitute)(LexisNexis Butterworths)

Life insurance and annuities

Name

Date of death

/   /

Give details about the life insurance policies and annuities that the deceased paid premiums for. You should read form D9(Notes) before filling in this form.

1 Were any sums payable by insurance companies to the estate as a result of the deceased's death?

No   Yes

If the answer is "Yes" give details below

Total   IP1   £

2

2a Was the deceased a life assured under a joint life insurance policy which continues after death?

No   Yes

If the answer is "Yes" give details of the policy and it's value on form D4.

2b Was the deceased entitled to benefit from a life insurance policy on the life of another person where the policy continues after death?

No   Yes

If the answer is "Yes" give details below

Total   IP2   £

Total value for life insurance policies *(box IP1 plus box IP2)*   IP3   £
Copy the total from box IP3 to box F16, page 3, form IHT200.

Please turn over

D9   *www.hmrc.gov.uk/cto*   *Helpline 0845 30 20 900*   **HMRC CT 12/05**

(Substitute)(LexisNexis Butterworths)

3 Did any payments made under a purchased life annuity continue after the deceased's death?

No ☐ Yes ☐

If the answer is "Yes" give details below

Total IP4 £ _____

Include the total from box IP4 in box F15, page 3, form IHT 200.

4 Was a lump sum payable under a purchased life annuity as a result of the deceased's death?

No ☐ Yes ☐

If the answer is "Yes" give details below

Total IP5 £ _____

Include the total from box IP5 in box F23, page 3, form IHT 200.

5a Did the deceased, within 7 years of their death, pay any premium on a life insurance policy for the benefit of someone else, other than the deceased's spouse or civil partner? If so, provide details on from D3.

No ☐ Yes ☐

5b Was an annuity purchased at any time? If so please provide a copy of the policy schedule and provisions.

No ☐ Yes ☐

6 Did the deceased have some right to benefit from a life insurance policy taken out on another person's life and held in trust for the benefit of the deceased (and others)?

No ☐ Yes ☐

If the answer to either question 5 or 6 is "Yes" you should read form D9(Notes) to find out what you should do.

Revenue
Capital Taxes

Stocks and
shares

Name

Date of death

Give details about the stocks and shares owned by the deceased. You should read form D7(Notes)
before filling in this form.

1   **Quoted stocks, shares and investments** *(see box 2 for government securities)*

Name of company and type of shares or stock, or **full** name of unit trust and type of units	Number of shares or units or amount of stock held	Market price at date of death	Total value at date of death	Dividend or interest due to date of death	For IR CT use only

Total(s)	SS1			

Copy the total from box SS1 to box F1, page 3, form IHT200.
Include the total of all dividends and interest in box F5, page 3.

D7   Version 2.0.0.3

Please turn over

2 UK Government and municipal securities

Description of stock	Amount of stock £	Market price at date of death	Total value at date of death	Interest due to date of death	For IR CT use only

Total(s) SS2

Copy the total from box SS2 to box F2, page 3, form IHT200.
Include the total of all dividends and interest in box F5, page 3.

3 Unquoted stocks, shares and investments

Name of company and type of share or stock	Number of shares	Price per share	Total value of shares	Dividend due to date of death	For IR CT use only

Include the value of the shares in box F3, page 3 or box G11, page 5, form IHT200.
Include the total of all dividends in box F5, page 3.

4 Traded unquoted stocks and shares

Name of company and type of share or stock	Number of shares	Price per share	Total value of shares	Dividend due to date of death	For IR CT use only

Include the value of the shares in box F4, page 3 or box G12, page 5, form IHT200.
Include the total of all dividends in box F5, page 3.

57   Voidable Transfers

Simon's Direct Tax Service, part I3.562.

57.1   APPLICATION

Where it can be shown that the whole or part of a chargeable transfer has been set aside by virtue of any enactment or rule of law as voidable or otherwise defeasible, a claim may be made for the transfer to be treated as void *ab initio* and for any tax paid to be repaid (with interest free of tax from the date of the claim). The tax rate applied to later chargeable transfers must be recalculated.

A similar claim may also be made for the repayment of inheritance tax in respect of any other chargeable transfer made before the claim that would not have been payable if the transfer that has been set aside had been void *ab initio*. Again, the liability is extinguished if the tax has not been paid. [*IHTA 1984, ss 150, 236(3); FA 1989, s 179(1)*].

58 Woodlands

Cross-references. See also 5 AGRICULTURAL PROPERTY; 7 BUSINESS PROPERTY; 59 WORKING CASE STUDY.

Simon's Direct Tax Service, parts I7.3, I7.4.

Other Sources. Foster, parts G3 and 4; HMRC CTO Leaflet IHT 17, pages 24–26; IHTM24000.

58.1 RELIEF

On a person's death an election may be made within two years (or such longer time as the Board allow *IHTA 1984, s 125(3)*) for the value of any trees or underwood on any land in the UK not being AGRICULTURAL PROPERTY (5) for the purposes of agricultural property relief to be left out of account in determining the value transferred on death. See [**Case Study** 2]. The value of the land cannot be excluded. The claim must be made by a person liable for the whole or part of the tax. The tax is deferred and becomes chargeable on a later disposal. [*IHTA 1984, s 125*].

The DV will advise the CTO if woodlands should be excluded from the relief because these are agricultural property as defined in *IHTA 1984, s 115(2)*. Land dedicated under the *Forestry Act 1967* is unlikely to be agricultural property. In woodlands relief cases the DV should value the underlying land leaving out the trees or underwood growing on it. (VOA IHT manual, section 10, paras 10.7 and 10.9). Note, however, this woodlands relief is uncommon due to the existence of 100% business relief (see Inspector's manual, para 3260 issue 12/94 'woodlands' does not include orchards or nurseries). For the treatment of orchards see *Dixon v CIR [2002] STC SCD 53 Sp C 297*.

HMRC Inheritance Tax
IHT reference
Date of death:..........................

A B deceased

1. Attached to this election are:

    1.1   Schedule 1 being details of the land on which the trees and underwood are growing and to which the election is to apply.

    1.2   Ordnance survey map of the area of trees and underwood to which the election is to apply with relevant areas boundaried in red. [*Note 1:10,000 or in Scotland 1:50,000 will normally suffice*].

    1.3   Copy of the deceased's will pertaining to the land to which this election is to apply.

2. The deceased AB was:

    2.1   beneficially entitled to the land on which the trees and underwood grow [for the five years immediately preceding AB's death]* [by entitlement otherwise than for money or money's worth].*

* Delete as appropriate

3. We, being the parties making the election, elect pursuant to section 125, Inheritance Tax Act 1984 shall apply to such woods and underwood referred to at 1 above.

Signed:............................... Capacity...............................

58.2 Woodlands

```
Address:.................................................................................

Date:.....................

Signed:............................... Capacity...............................

Address:.................................................................................

Date:.....................

Schedule 1

[Full description including the precise location of the land to be included at Schedule 1].
```

Notes to the election

(A) Normally it will be appropriate to pay the tax at the date of death where the trees are very young and in such a case the election would not be appropriate.

(B) This relief is also available where the deceased had an interest in possession in woodlands under a trust *IHTA 1984, ss 5(1), 49(1), 125(1).*

58.2   CONDITION

A condition for the election is that the deceased either was beneficially entitled to the land for the five years immediately preceding his death or became beneficially entitled to it otherwise than for money or money's worth. [*IHTA 1984, s 125(1)*]. A life tenant in possession under a settlement is treated as beneficially entitled but not a shareholder in a company owning woodlands.

IHT 210 (Notes) at page 39 states, 'This relief may apply if any part of the deceased's estate includes land on which trees are growing, but which does not qualify for agricultural relief. The trees may qualify for woodlands relief if all the conditions are met

- the land must be in the UK

- it must not qualify for agricultural relief

- the deceased must have owned the land throughout the five years up to death or

- have acquired the land other than by buying it **and**

- you must formally claim the relief within two years after the death.

58.3   TAX CHARGE

Tax becomes chargeable on any disposal (other than between spouses or civil partners) of the trees or underwood (whether with or apart from the land on which they grow) before another death (which would be either another chargeable occasion itself or another occasion for an election). See IHT 17, p 25. The liability for the tax is on the person who is entitled to the proceeds of sale or would be so entitled if the disposal were a sale. Where tax has been charged on a disposal under these provisions, it cannot be charged in relation to the same death on a further disposal of the same trees or underwood. [*IHTA 1984, ss 126, 208; The Tax and Civil Partnership Regulations 2005, SI 2005/3229, Reg 24*]. An account (Form C–5 (Timber)) must be delivered by the person liable within six months of the end of the month in which the disposal occurs. [*IHTA 1984, s 216(7)*]. Where the disposal is a chargeable transfer (e.g. by gift into a discretionary trust), tax will become chargeable both in respect of the previous death and on the later transfer, in which case the later value transferred is that value less the tax charged by reference to the previous death under 58.4 below. [*IHTA 1984, s 129*]. The deferred tax is payable in one sum but the tax on the lifetime transfer may be paid by instalments over ten years at the option of either the transferor or the transferee (see 35.3 PAYMENT OF TAX) and payment by instalments does not cease if the timber is later sold. [*IHTA 1984, s 229*]. See also IHT 17, p 28. A new account on Form IHT 100 (old forms IHT 100 and IHT 101 have been replaced as from April 2003) is required when there is a chargeable event described below:

- Assets ceasing to benefit from conditional exemption and being subject to a recapture charge (supplementary event form IHT 100f) e.g. sale of trees, timber or underwood.

Form D36, part of IHT 100, should be filled in to give details of land, buildings, timber and underwood included in the chargeable event. In box F4 of IHT 100 the value of any timber and woodland included in the chargeable event valued at the date of the chargeable event should be inserted which is not part of a farm. Most farms have coppices, small woods and belts of trees that shelter the land and these are to be valued separately and included in a separate box (F2) on the IHT 100. See LIFETIME TRANSFERS (31).

58.4   **TAX RATE**

The tax rate is what would have applied to the value of the deceased's (i.e. the last person to die) estate if the trees or underwood had been included at the highest part and is charged

(*a*)   if the disposal is a sale for full consideration in money or money's worth, on the 'net proceeds' of the sale; and

(*b*)   in any other case, on the 'net value', at the time of disposal, of the trees or underwood.

'*Net proceeds*' or '*net value*' mean the proceeds of sale or value after any deduction of any of the following expenses so far as not allowed for income tax.

(*a*)   if the disposal is a sale for full consideration in money or money's worth, on the 'net proceeds' of the sale; and

(*b*)   in any other case, on the 'net value', at the time of disposal, of the trees or underwood.

'*Net proceeds*' or '*net value*' mean the proceeds of sale or value after any deduction of any of the following expenses so far as not allowed for income tax.

(i)   The expenses incurred in disposing of the trees or underwood.

(ii)   The expenses incurred in replanting, within three years of a disposal (or such longer time as the Board may allow), to replace the trees or underwood disposed of.

(iii)   The expenses incurred in replanting to replace trees or underwood previously disposed of, so far as not allowed on the previous disposal.

Where, if the value of the trees or underwood had *not* been left out of account in determining the value of the deceased person's estate, BUSINESS PROPERTY (7) relief would have been available (assuming, if necessary, that the relevant provisions were in force at the date of death) the amount on which tax is charged is reduced by 50%.

Deferred tax which becomes chargeable after tax has been reduced by the substitution of a new table of rates will be calculated on the new scale, even though the death occurred when the old scale applied. [*IHTA 1984, ss 9, 127, 128, 130, Sch 2 para 4; FA 1986, Sch 19 para 45*]. See also 58.6(*b*) below.

In arriving at the 'net value' the DV's valuation should ignore any allowable expenses as well as any obligations to replant. The value will be the higher of (i) the value of the trees for sale for felling including any underwood, or (ii) the value of the standing trees or underwood as part of the transferor's estate. The DV's valuation will always exclude the value of the underlying land. The valuation on basis (ii) will probably only apply when immature woodland or growing timber of high amenity value is involved. (VOA IHT manual, section 10, para 10.16).

58.4 Woodlands

Example 1

A died owning woodlands valued at £275,000 being land valued at £200,000 and trees growing on the land valued at £75,000. The woodlands passed to his son D. The marginal IHT rate applicable was 50% but the executors elected to exclude the value of the trees from the taxable estate on A's death. D died six years later leaving the woodlands to trustees for his grandchildren. They were then valued at £400,000 being land at £250,000 and trees at £150,000. The rate of tax which would have applied to the value of trees on D's death was 40%, but once again the executors elected to exclude the value of the trees from his estate.

The trustees sold the woodlands for £500,000, including trees valued at £180,000, four years later.

The IHT on the trees is payable when the trees are sold. The trustees of the settlement pay IHT at what would have been the marginal rate on D's death had the tax scale at the time of the sale applied on D's death, e.g. 40% on £180,000 (the proceeds of sale) = £72,000.

Note to the example

(A)   If D had gifted the land (with the trees) just before his death, the IHT would have become payable on the trees at what would have been the marginal rate on A's death had the scale at the time of the gift applied on A's death, on the value of the trees at the date of the gift. IHT would also have been payable on D's lifetime transfer (this being a PET but becoming chargeable by virtue of D's death shortly afterwards) but the value transferred by this transfer would have been reduced by the deferred IHT charge. See Example 2 below.

Example 2

B died in 1984 leaving woodlands, including growing timber valued at £100,000, to his daughter C. The executors elected to exclude the value of the timber from the taxable estate on B's death. B had made prior transfers of £50,000 and his taxable estate (excluding the growing timber) was valued at £210,000.

On 1 February 2001 C gave the woodlands to her nephew N, when the land was valued at £330,000 and the growing timber at £125,000. N agreed to pay any IHT on the gift. C died in January 2008, and had made no prior transfers other than to use her annual exemptions each year. It is assumed that IHT rates remain at their current level.

IHT on B's death

No IHT is payable on the growing timber until C's disposal when tax is charged on the net value at that time. The rates are those which would have applied (using the death scale applying on 1 February 2001) if that value had formed the highest part of B's estate on death. The tax was payable on 1 September 2001.

Deferred IHT payable £125,000 at 40% =   £50,000

IHT on C's lifetime transfer

IHT is payable on C's gift to N as C died within seven years of the gift. The deferred IHT is deducted from the value transferred.

	£
Value of land and timber	455,000
Deduct deferred IHT	50,000
Chargeable transfer	£405,000
IHT at death rates	
On first £300,000	Nil
On next £105,000 at 40%	42,000
£405,000	£42,000
IHT payable at 40% of full rates (death between 5 and 6 years after gift)	£16,800
Total IHT payable	
Deferred IHT	50,000
Lifetime transfer	16,800
	£66,800

Note to the example

(A)   In the above calculations it has been assumed that the woodlands were not run as a business either at the time of B's death or at the time of C's gift. If B had been running the woodlands as a business, such that business property relief would have been available on his death, the amount chargeable on C's disposal would have been reduced by 50%, i.e. to £62,500, on which IHT payable would have been £25,000. [*IHTA 1984, s 127(2)*]. If C ran the woodlands as a business (whether or not B had done so), business property relief would be available on her gift to N provided N also ran the woodlands as a business, but would be given after the credit for the deferred IHT. (With business property relief now usually at 100%, the order of set-off is not so relevant.)

	£
Value of land and timber	455,000
Deduct deferred IHT say	25,000
	430,000
Deduct business property relief at, say, 100%	430,000
Chargeable transfer	Nil

58.5   ESTATE DUTY

F(1909–10)A 1910, s 61(5) is an estate duty provision and still applicable for deaths before 13 March 1975. It provides for the value of timber etc. to be left out of account on the deceased's death but with estate duty charged at the estate rate on subsequent net moneys (less outgoings since death) received from time to time in respect of cut or felled timber etc. sales in the period from the death until the underlying land, on the death of some other person, again became or would, but for the provision itself, have become liable to estate duty. However, if at any time the timber etc. is sold, with or without the underlying land, the amount of estate duty on its principal value which, apart from the provision itself, would have been payable on the death of the deceased, after deducting any amount of estate duty already paid as above on previous timber sales since death, becomes payable. For the purposes of inheritance tax it is provided that where estate duty is payable under *F(1909–10)A 1910, s 61(5)* on the net moneys received from the sale of timber etc. when felled or cut during the period referred to in that provision, that period ends immediately after the first transfer of value made in which the value transferred is, or is determined by reference to, the value of the land concerned, other than an exempt transfer between spouses or civil partners. [*FA 1975, s 49(4)*]. Where the first transfer of value including such woodlands is after 30 June 1986, that transfer cannot be a POTENTIALLY EXEMPT TRANSFER (38) (even if it would otherwise qualify). [*FA 1986, Sch 19 para 46*]. Although *FA 1986, Sch 19 para 46* denies treatment as a potentially exempt transfer to all property comprised in a single transfer of value any part of which, however small, is woodlands subject to a deferred estate duty charge, by concession after 4 December 1990 it will be restricted in its scope to that part of a transfer of value which is attributable to such woodlands (see former Inland Revenue Pamphlet IR1 (1996) F15).

58.6 OTHER RELIEFS

(*a*) AGRICULTURAL PROPERTY (5) relief applies instead of the above if the woodlands are occupied and the occupation is ancillary to that of agricultural land or pasture. [*IHTA 1984, ss 115(2), 125(1)*].

(*b*) NATIONAL HERITAGE (33) property. Conditional exemption on a transfer may apply in certain circumstances.

59 Working Case Study

Cross-references. See 2.6 ACCOUNTS AND RETURNS; 3 ACCUMULATION AND MAINTENANCE TRUSTS; 5 AGRICULTURAL PROPERTY; 7 BUSINESS PROPERTY; 8 CALCULATION OF TAX; 11 CHARITIES; 14 DEEDS VARYING DISPOSITIONS ON DEATH; 17 DOMICILE; 18 DOUBLE TAXATION RELIEF; 20 EXCLUDED PROPERTY; 21 EXEMPT TRANSFERS; 29 LIABILITY FOR TAX; 30 LIFE ASSURANCE POLICIES AND ANNUITIES; 31 LIFETIME TRANSFERS; 33 NATIONAL HERITAGE; 35 PAYMENT OF TAX; 37 PENSION SCHEMES; 38 POTENTIALLY EXEMPT TRANSFERS; 41 RATES OF TAX; 42 SETTLEMENTS-GENERAL; 44 SETTLEMENTS WITHOUT INTERESTS IN POSSESSION; 45 SHARES AND SECURITIES; 46 SITUS; 50 TRANSFERS ON DEATH; 51 TRANSFERS WITHIN SEVEN YEARS BEFORE DEATH; 55 TRUSTS FOR EMPLOYEES; 56 VALUATION; 58 WOODLANDS.

Other Sources. CTO Form IHT 215 Practitioners Guide; Butterworths Practical Inheritance Tax Planning; Butterworths Encyclopædia of Forms and Precedents.

59.1 INTRODUCTION

Netherington village in Wiltshire has a typical population with personal circumstances that impact on their inheritance tax position for the year 2007–08. The village has its own Lord of the Manor at Netherington Hall and there is both a farm and business that employ a number of the local villagers. Two villagers have recently died and others in the village wish to mitigate their perceived inheritance tax liabilities following an enlightening talk in the church hall by an insurance salesman. The individuals with each of their particular IHT problems are detailed below.

John Giles [**Case Study 1**] farms 610 acres of arable land at Sleepy Hollow Farm, which also has, in addition, 90 acres of woodlands. His wife assists him in the farming and they have a son who is at agricultural college and hopes to take over the farm in the future. The farm is not tenanted and a recent 'contract to purchase' offer of £250,000 has been received from Tresco Stores for 20 acres of the land to build a distribution warehouse. Roger Coleman [**Case Study 2**] owns a company called Coleman's Pies Ltd manufacturing meat pies and sausages on the outskirts of the village. He is the majority shareholder with 75% of the shares, his ex-wife holds 15% and the remaining 10% of the shares are held in trust for his infant son (aged seven). The current value of the company is £1.5 million and Roger owns a holiday home in Jersey valued at £500,000 as well as his cottage in the village, which is valued at £145,000. Roger dies in a boating accident on 18 July 2007 whilst on holiday in Jersey. Lord Charles of Netherington Hall [**Case Study 3**] inherited the Hall and its contents on the death of his father in a hunting accident on Boxing Day in 2000. The Hall has many antique works of art and is regularly open to the public. In order to avoid IHT on his death Lord Charles wishes to pass on some of his valuable personal chattels to his younger brother, Alexander, who lives in London. Lord Charles is married but he has no children. His brother in London is married and has two children. Alan and Mary Smith [**Case Study 4**] live comfortably in the village but within the last two month's Alan's widowed mother has died leaving him her property in Shaftesbury valued at £150,000 and a controlling interest in an unquoted company with the shares valued at £200,000. Alan and Mary have a son and two grandchildren. Angela Such [**Case Study 5**] wants to ensure that her granddaughter has sufficient funds to see her through university but she is loath to pass the money amounting to £50,000 to her son or his wife because of their profligacy which resulted in a gift of £311,000 in 2005 being spent on round the world trips and a new Mercedes Benz car. She wishes to set up a trust or donate the money direct to Oxford University, an educational charity, on the proviso that her granddaughter secures a place after taking her 'A' levels. Jill and Martin Oakley [**Case Study 6**] own their home without encumbrance valued at £400,000 but have only £150,000 capital and a small pension. They require further income to fund their grandchild's school fees and are concerned about the potential inheritance tax liability on the death of the survivor. They have a married son and unmarried daughter who will be the sole beneficiaries on the death of the second of them. Carlo Grimaldi [**Case Study** 7] retired to this country sixteen years ago but he is domiciled in France where he has property in Nice valued at £350,000 and €2.05 million worth of shares in French Telecom valued at £200,000. He is married to Elizabeth, who will benefit on his death, and she is UK domiciled. He also has a widowed mother living in Paris. He is concerned about paying two amounts of death duties should he die in the United Kingdom. Colonel Smithers [**Case Study** 8], a Lloyd's underwriter, died of a heart attack at his home in the village on 25 July 2006. He was unmarried and had no children but has a widowed mother of sufficient means still living at the nursing home in the village. His Estate (excluding Lloyd's assets) is valued at £300,000 and his Lloyd's assets are valued at £250,000. He has left a legacy to his mother, who disclaims/varies it, and the remainder of his estate as to two thirds to his niece and one third to the charity Scope. Betty Nairn [**Case Study** 9] a widow (twice!) lives in the village and with her friend Doreen in Lancashire she has won £4.5 million on the National Lottery (now Lotto). She has no family but wants to benefit the deserving of the village where she has always been very happy. She does not intend to move from her cottage or change her lifestyle in any way. Betty's late husband Jack, who died two years ago, was an Artillery Gunner during the Second World War and was captured and imprisoned by the Japanese. John and Jennifer Brown [**Case Study** 10] are 58 years old and are seeking long term inheritance tax planning. Their only daughter is wealthy in her own right. They are looking for long term planning with the scope for income later and added flexibility of whatever inheritance tax planning they undertake. Stanley and Sonia White [**Case Study** 11] who are 68 years old have three children and four grandchildren. Sonia has had heart trouble recently and could predecease her husband. They are looking for medium term inheritance tax planning with immediate income. Don and Sandra Black [**Case Study** 12] have effected a pre-owned assets scheme in respect of their property and a chattel which turns out to be worth far more than the initial value for charging a market rent. William and Mary Pink [**Case Study** 13] are both 73 years old and are both retired. They have two children and three grandchildren. Their private residence is worth £400,000 and owned in joint names and between them they have substantial investments. They are aware of the high potential inheritance tax liability on their joint estates but they are not prepared to make outright gifts because they need income from their investment capital. However, they are unlikely to need capital and require tax mitigation and planning. Carol and Amelie [**Case Study** 14] are in a same sex relationship and have been for many years. They plan to cement their relationship by obtaining a registration certificate under the *Civil Partnership Act 2004*. Amelie is a citizen of France and lives with Carol but rents out her own property in Salisbury. Both work at Coleman's Pies Ltd. They are concerned about the effect the new Act and their registration will have on their current personal situation and the potential financial implications.

59.2   CASE STUDIES

The following case studies look at the inheritance tax position of the various individuals. Where there is an income, capital gains tax, etc. impact this will be briefly mentioned. Each case study is cross-referenced to chapters in the earlier part of the book and some further examples pertinent to the case study are to be located in the relevant chapters. In addition, where applicable, useful internet websites of HMRC and others will be shown for additional access to source information. Each case study is then summarised with tax planning suggestions which should be read in conjunction with the relevant chapters in the earlier part of this work.

59.3   CASE STUDY 1 — JOHN GILES

John Giles is the owner of a 700 acre farm including woodlands of 90 acres. He and his wife also run a bed and breakfast business from the substantial five-bedroom farmhouse, which is valued at £525,000. The bed and breakfast business is valued at between £50,000 and £60,000 on the basis of return on capital invested calculations. John Giles expects to pass on his farm to his son who is undertaking an agricultural course at Cirencester College.

The farmland is valued at £1,500 per acre and the woodlands at £900 per acre. Mrs Giles operates the bed and breakfast business from the farmhouse in partnership with her husband. As a family they are concerned with the inheritance tax (IHT) implications of passing the farm on to their son together with the plant and machinery valued at £250,000 held personally by John Giles but used in the farming partnership. A contract to sell the 20 acres to Tresco Stores for development is being considered by John Giles.

59.4   **Compliance undertakings.** In order to obtain agricultural property relief under *IHTA 1984, s 115* the property must be comprised of agricultural property and have been occupied or owned for a minimum qualifying period. [*IHTA 1984, s 117*]. Agricultural property means land, pasture and woodlands. Also, it includes any building used in connection with the intensive rearing of livestock or fish as well as cottages, farm buildings and farmhouses. The relief of 100% is available if the property has been occupied by the transferor, John Giles, for agricultural purposes throughout the period of two years ending with the date of transfer. Alternatively, relief is available if it has been owned by the transferor throughout the period of seven years prior to the date of transfer and has been occupied throughout that period by him or a tenant for agricultural purposes. The former case applies to John Giles and therefore, on the face of it, he appears to be entitled to 100% APR. With effect from 1 September 1995 new leases entered into from that date ensure that tenanted farmland will attract 100% relief. This places tenanted farmland on a par with land to which the owner has vacant possession or the right to obtain vacant possession within 12 months (but by concession 24 months). The change was introduced to encourage farmers to let more of their land to young people trying to enter into farming but does not apply here unless John Giles was to let the farmland to his son as a tenant. John Giles intends to pass it on to his son. If this is on his death then the IHT 200 form D13 will be completed. See http://www.hmrc.gov.uk/ under 'HMRC Inheritance Tax' or 'Inheritance Tax'.

The farmhouse must be 'of a character appropriate to the property' and it is expected that even though the farmhouse is substantial, i.e. 15 rooms, it will attract APR in full. [*IHTA 1984, s 115 (2)*]. In connection with *s 115(2)* the previous CTO Advanced Instruction Manual, para L. 231.4 but now see IHTM24035), stated that cases will be referred for review which involve farming businesses of less than 20 acres or where the farmhouse is very valuable (say, over £250,000) and the acreage is comparatively small (say, less than 100 acres). See also *Lloyds TSB plc (Antrobus' Personal Representatives) v Twiddy [2004] DET/47/2004*, and VALUATION (55) where the farmhouse under scrutiny for APR incorporates this 'lifestyle buyers' application. The 'appropriate character' test is a somewhat difficult phrase to interpret but some guidance was given by Peter Twiddy of the Inland Revenue Capital Taxes Litigation Support Team who stated:

> 'We have regard to the basic principle enunciated by Mr Justice Blackburne in *Starke v CIR [1994] STC 298* "… cottages, farm buildings and farmhouses … will constitute agricultural property if used in connection with agricultural land or pasture provided that they are of a character appropriate to such agricultural land or pasture (that is, are proportionate in size and nature to the requirements of the farming activities conducted on the agricultural land in question) …" The Capital Taxes Office asks the District Valuer to consider the appropriate test through the eyes of the rural equivalent of the reasonable man on the Clapham Omnibus, and the following criteria may help: *Primary character* — Is the unit primarily a dwelling with some land, or is it an agricultural unit incorporating such a dwelling as is appropriate? This criterion might be considered an instinctive test, it seeks to gain a comprehensive impression of the nature of the property. *Local practice* — Is it normal for land of this quality, use and area to have with it a dwelling of this type and size? The comparison should be with local functioning agricultural holdings rather than primarily residential holdings. The underlying purpose is to establish a pattern of the type, size and quality of holdings that function primarily as agricultural properties in this area. *Financial support* — Is the size and character of the dwelling

commensurate with the scale of agricultural operations appropriate for the land? We are not considering a strict economic viability test of the holding, but adding information in context.

Having applied those criteria and such other information as is available, e.g. a large reduction in the area farmed from the house, we should then stand back and take a balanced view in the round, and that may be described as the elephant test – difficult to describe, but you know one when you see one.'

In Dymond's Capital Taxes it is perhaps more succinctly put as the farmhouse that is

'essentially a contrast between property recognisable as a working farmhouse and a house which is primarily a desirable residence with farmland enhancing the views and keeping the neighbours at a safe distance.'

There are two areas of the business that might jeopardise the claim for APR when one views the functions of the farmhouse and the lettings part of the business. If John Giles is to retire sometime in the future and pass on the farm to his son but decides to stay on in the farmhouse then, particularly if the son does not live in the farmhouse, there is a distinct possibility that the farmhouse may not qualify for any future APR; in *Rosser v CIR [2003] STC SCD 311 Sp C 368* a former farmhouse was ostensibly treated as a 'retirement' home of the former farmer and did not qualify as agricultural property. There is also the point that the bed and breakfast business may impact on the claim for relief for the whole enterprise including the bed and breakfast undertaking; however, in *Farmer v CIR [1999] STC SCD 321 Sp C 216* it was accepted that there was a single composite business comprising of farming and letting of various farm buildings. The Special Commissioners in this case came to the decision that on the application of the 'wholly or mainly' test and taking the business as a whole it consisted mainly of farming. In support of this were the facts that the property was a business property of landed estate with a majority of the land being used for farming.

The contract to purchase 20 acres by Tresco Stores unfortunately ensures that there is a potential binding offer for sale, which would affect the APR position. Relief would not be given if at the time of the transfer, the transferor has entered into a binding contract for sale of (i) agricultural property (unless the sale is to a company in return for an issue of shares which will give the transferor control of that company); or (ii) shares or securities in agricultural companies (see 5.6 AGRICULTURAL PROPERTY) except where the sale is made for the purpose of reconstruction or amalgamation. [*IHTA 1984, s 124*]. On IHT 200 Form D13 question 8 asks 'Was the property, or any part of it, subject to a binding offer for sale at the date of death?'. Clearly, therefore, entering into a binding offer for sale can limit the relief available from APR (and BPR). See below for tax planning and mitigation suggestions.

The IHT calculation that would result from the passing of the farm to John Giles' son, assuming a binding offer for sale is not applicable at the date of transfer, would be as follows:

	£
Farmland	
610 acres at £1,500 per acre	915,000
Farmhouse	525,000
90 acres of woodlands at £900 per acre*	81,000
Value of agricultural property	1,521,000
Less amount of agricultural relief @ 100%	(1,521,000)
Chargeable	Nil

	£
Bed and Breakfast business valued at	55,000
Less amount of business property relief @ 50% #	(27,500)
Chargeable	£27,500

	£
Plant and Machinery valued at	250,000
Less amount of business property relief @ 50%	(125,000)
Chargeable	125,000

* Growing timber left out of account under *IHTA 1984, ss 125–130*.
\# The mid–range figure of £55,000 has been taken as the value of the bed and breakfast business after a professional valuation. It is not certain that BPR will be given in full but in this case negotiation with the CTO secures 50% relief.

59.5   **Tax planning and mitigation.** John Giles may wish to pass on his farming business to his son, wholly or by partnership, as soon as is reasonably practical (i.e. when the son finishes at Agricultural College) to ensure that any future restriction in APR or BPR is circumvented. Primarily it would seem that it is important to ensure that agricultural land and pasture is actually used for agricultural purposes. In commenting on module D13 of IHT 200 HMRC Inheritance Tax state:

'We are still receiving vague descriptions of the agricultural activities carried out on farms. The answers 'general farming' or 'grazing' will ensure that the case is picked for enquiry, so please could you answer the character appropriate question on page 2 for each residential property on the farm individually.'

See April/May 2002 IHT Newsletter at 61 IHT NEWSLETTER AND TAX BULLETIN EXTRACTS. Therefore land that has been left to return to its natural state and referred to as grazing land e.g. moorland with potentially unrestricted access may come within HMRC's enquiry parameters. The importance of ensuring that the land has not returned to its natural habitat with boundary walls and fences that have fallen into disrepair is of major importance. In addition the application of manures, fertilisers and other additives such as calcified seaweed would indicate land used for a normal level of productivity. See *Alford v DEFRA QB [2005] TLR 30 May 2005*. See 60 TAX CASES.

Further, it would seem that the *Agricultural Holdings Act 1986, s 25* may afford the opportunity to grant a new tenancy, on or after 1 September 1995, thereby permitting the landlord, John Giles, 100% agricultural property relief and allowing the tenant a tenancy under the *AHA 1986*. The common law principle of surrender and regrant can sometimes apply where the terms of a tenancy are varied (*Friends Provident Life Office v British Railways Board [1995] EGCS 140*). Any farmer reaching retirement similar to John Giles may not wish to leave the farmhouse even though he wishes to pass on the farmhouse, land and the running of the farm to the next generation. This will not be conducive to attracting APR on the farmhouse at a later date when it is passed on to the next generation. The reservation of benefit rules will necessarily come into play thereby jeopardising the whole gift of land and farmhouse. Also if the farmhouse is severed from the land and John Giles continues to live in it he will be no longer occupying it for the purposes of agriculture and hence no APR will be due, as mentioned above in the previous paragraph. If such a gift is to be made John Giles may wish to retain a tenancy over the land through, say, a partnership with his son or alternatively retain enough land to meet the 'character appropriate' test. This latter option may mean that too much land remains in the possession of John Giles which hampers the commercial viability of the whole farm business or alternatively the inactivity of the retained portion may lead to the conclusion that he is not occupying the farmhouse for the purposes of agriculture.

Often successions are used as an opportunity to update tenancies but care should be taken in ensuring that the resulting tenancy still remains a 1986 Act tenancy and not a new Farm

Business Tenancy. The safest method to ensure this is to incorporate in the documentation deed of variation of the tenancy terms by including the new terms into the old tenancy and including an express recital that *AHA 1986, s 4(1)(f)* applies and the tenancy will remain under the provisions of the 1986 Act. Since 1 September 1995 any succession arrangements for 1986 Act tenancies should be concluded as always having regard to the provisions for the *Agricultural Tenancies Act 1995*. *ATA 1995, s 4* provides for the agricultural Land Tribunal to give succession directions under *AHA 1986, s 39* in the case of death or *s 53* in the case of retirement. Therefore, a purported variation of the previous tenancy in the *AHA 1986, s 4(1)(f)* is meant to apply to the unintentional variations and not those deliberately effected to bring about surrender and regrant. In view of this a deliberate variation may result in the landlord obtaining 100% agricultural property relief but not an *AHA 1986* tenancy for the tenant.

APR (or BPR) is not available if, at the date of transfer, there is a binding contract for sale of the relevant property. HMRC Inheritance Tax refuse APR on land that has been farmed by the transferor prior to his death if it is subject to a 'binding contract for sale' for the purposes of *IHTA 1984, s 124*. It has been inferred in a case where the land was subject to a 'binding contract for sale' at that time and the option had not been exercised at the date of transfer, that the CTO might argue the option is a 'binding offer for sale' even before its exercise. (*Thomson v Salah Ch D [1971] 47 TC 559*). The matter is currently of some conjecture but the CTO argue that the grant of an option over land must be taken to have subjected that land to a contract for sale such that, once the option is in place, there is a 'binding offer for sale'. Statement of Practice SP12/80 (25) HMRC STATEMENTS OF PRACTICE mentions the distinction between 'buy and sell' agreements and 'mere options to buy and sell' so distinguishing the fact that the option that might not eventually be exercised might not be treated as a binding offer for sale, thereby excluding APR. Clearly the agreement with Tresco Stores for the option to buy the 20 acres should be appropriately worded.

The plant and machinery should be brought into the business so that it attracts 100% relief thereby releasing the current £300,000 nil rate band to offset against the potential liability on the sale of the 20 acres to Tresco Stores.

The CTO have confirmed that valuations cannot be exact and that where there is a *reasonable* range and professional valuers have been given instructions by the taxpayer to give the open market value then the CTO would not seek to apply any penalty notice. For the practice of returning for probate purposes at the lower end of the valuer's range see *Re: Hayes [1971] 1 WLR 758*. When considering the word *reasonable* the CTO have stated that in assessing the 'open market' value there must not be a special range so that the value is widened and, as the case may often be, the value reduced. It is important that the professional valuer inspects the property. See *BNP Mortgages Ltd v Goadsby & Harding Ltd [1994] 2 EGLR 169* and *Scotlife Homeloans (No 2) Ltd v Kenneth Jones & Co [1995] EGCS 70*. In opting for a mid-range value for the bed and breakfast business of £55,000 the taxpayer should be within the CTO guidelines. Following the *Robertson v CIR* case the question of valuations, especially when these are estimated, elicited the following response from the former Inland Revenue in their IHT Newsletter dated May 2002:

> 'The Revenue is keen to provide assistance to personal representatives to enable them to fulfil their obligations without incurring penalties. In most circumstances we would expect the exact value of property to be given when form IHT200 is submitted and not merely an estimate. However we accept that if there is a proven need to obtain a grant urgently personal representatives may find themselves in a position where they think they need to submit an estimated account of the value of a particular item of property. In such circumstances they should ensure that they have made the fullest enquiries that are reasonably practicable before doing so, and the estimate should be as accurate as possible. The Personal Representatives should, for example, contact the professional who is going to value the property formally and ensure that the estimate is a reasonable one.'

'Reasonable' in terms of chattels is more difficult to gauge. This is because the chattels market is subject to a wider range of estimated valuations than, say, land because the art market is small and volatile. Due to the fact that there may be a single large buyer operating in the market or fashion influencing the market having an undue influence on prices the question as to what is a 'reasonable' value is even harder to gauge. It is therefore important that these factors and one-off 'new money' purchases may affect an estimate so that it is too low, or even in cases of 'new-money' purchases, be too high! Personal Representatives must take care in appointing a valuer that in establishing a range of values for the chattels full regard has been made to the market and the characteristics of the chattel have been fully explored. In *GREA Real Property Investments v Williams [1979] 1 EGLR 121* at page 122 Forbes J states:

> 'It is a fundamental aspect of valuation that it proceeds by analogy. The valuer isolates those characteristics of the object to be valued which in his view affects the value and then seeks another of known or ascertainable value presenting some or all of these characteristics with which he may compare the object he is valuing. Where no directly comparable object exists, the valuer must make allowance of one kind or another interpolating or extrapolating from his given data. The less closely analogous the object chosen for a comparison the greater the allowances which have to be made and the greater the opportunity for error.'

The Royal Institute of Chartered Surveyors (RICS) published a new Guidance Note, GN 21, effective from 1 August 2002, which gives advice to members of RICS on the meaning of 'market value' for CGT and Inheritance Tax purposes. The Guidance Notes form part of the RICS 'Appraisal and Valuation Manual' which is commonly referred to as 'The Red Book'. The contents of GN 21 have also been approved by the Valuation Office Agency (VOA). In the case where there is an agricultural tie the former Inland Revenue have had discussions with the Central Association of Agricultural Valuers on this matter. See Taxation Magazine, p 14, 3 April 2003.

Further, HMRC formerly Inland Revenue in their IHT Newsletter dated April 2004 stated:

> 'Nominal or ill-considered values should not be used in any circumstances, not least because if it transpires that relief [APR] isn't due, a substantial uplift in the market value may give rise to a penalty.'

See 61 IHT NEWSLETTER AND TAX BULLETIN EXTRACTS.

59.6   CASE STUDY 2 — ROGER COLEMAN

Roger Coleman built up and runs Coleman's Pies Ltd which is an unquoted company. Roger dies prematurely at the age of 52 in a boating accident in Jersey whilst he is on holiday. He owned 75% of the shares, his ex-wife owns 15% and a trust set up for the benefit of his seven year old son, owns the balance of 10%. In his will he provides for 35% of the shares he owns to go into an employee trust for the benefit of the workers of Coleman's Pies Ltd and the balance (40%) to his ex-wife. His son is to inherit the Jersey home, which will be kept for him until he comes of age. The personal chattels and the house in Netherington will be held for his ex-wife for life and on her death for the benefit of their son. A company pension scheme that he has set up for the company also exists and the trustees have been made aware through a letter of wishes that Roger would, on his death, wish his ex-wife and son to benefit, subject to the Trustees having the ultimate say in where the benefits should be directed. Roger has been taking a drawdown facility from his personal pension scheme since he reached the age of 50 years.

59.7   Compliance undertakings. From 6 April 1996 100% business property relief is extended to *all* qualifying unquoted shareholdings whether or not the holding carries more than 25% voting control. Roger Coleman has owned more than 25% of the shares in any case for a minimum period of two years immediately preceding the transfer and therefore the shares are relevant business property. IHT 200 form D14 'Business relief, business interests or partnerships' is to be completed on the fact that the notes state in relation to Box 4:

> 'Write in the name of the company, the number and type of shares. For example, 1000 £1 ordinary shares, A Company Ltd, and give their value. You can help us by writing down the company's registration number if you know it. You do not need to provide a copy of the accounts now, although we may ask you for these and other information later.'

and at Box 5a:

> 'The last set of accounts prepared before the deceased died is the best starting point for valuing a business. The value of the business or the deceased's interest in the business will be the sum of the deceased's capital and current accounts. Please attach a copy of the last two years' accounts.'

There is no reason to suppose that 100% BPR will not be due.

Had the transfer of the shares in Coleman's Pies Ltd into the employee trust not been covered by 100% BPR it is also an exempt transfer if the value transferred is attributable to shares or securities in the company provided:

- the beneficiaries of the trust include all or most of the person's employed by holding office with the company;

- within one year the trustees hold more than half of the ordinary shares of the company having majority voting powers (there being no provision or agreement affecting this without the trustees consent);

- the trust does not permit any of the settled property to be applied for the benefit of a participator in the company or a participator in another close company that has benefited the same trust or any person connected with the previously mentioned.

[*IHTA 1984, s 28*].

Property held in TRUSTS FOR EMPLOYEES (55) is not relevant property including property held on SETTLEMENTS WITH INTERESTS IN POSSESSION (43) which is settled on or after 22 March 2006 which is not an IPDI, a TSI or a disabled person's interest.

The settled property is held on trusts for the benefit of the persons employed in the company and spouses or civil partners or relatives of the employees using a settlement along these lines:

THIS SETTLEMENT is made the ... day of ... BETWEEN (1) [Settlor] of [address] ('the Settlor') and (2) [trustees] of [addresses] ('the Original Trustees')

WHEREAS

The Settlor wishes to make provision for the employees of *Coleman's Pies Ltd* and companies in the same group (if applicable) and has transferred into the names of the Original Trustees the investments specified in the first schedule ('the Investments') to be held by the Original Trustees and their successors as trustees for the time being of this settlement on and with and subject to the following trust powers and provisions

NOW THIS DEED WITNESSES as follows:

1. Definitions and interpretation

1.1   In this settlement unless the context otherwise requires the following expressions shall have the following meanings

---

1.1.1 'the Trustees' means the Original Trustees ... *continues*

1.1.2 'the Trust Fund' means the Investments ... *continues*

1.1.3 'the Beneficiaries' means such of the following persons (not being an Excepted Person) as shall for the time being during such period of 80 years be in existence namely:

1.1.3.1 persons for the time being and from time to time employed by or holding office with a Group Company and any wife husband widow widower or child or other issue or dependant of any such employee or officer or of any deceased employee or officer

1.1.3.2 any person who at any time has been or shall have been employed by or has held or shall have held office with a Group Company and any wife husband widow widower or child or other issue or dependant of any such past employee or officer

and 'Beneficiary' means any one of the 'Beneficiaries

The Precedent continues

It has been possible for a number of years for a member of a pension scheme to take a drawdown of funds between the ages of 50 and 75 thereby deferring the purchase of an annuity. Where an individual has been taking a drawdown on his/her pension and dies there are some consequences which arise. The personal pension scheme units that have been subjected to drawdown are normally segmented and therefore a 35% tax charge arises on those units before the trustees make the balance remaining available for distribution. [*ICTA 1988, s 648B*]. The surviving spouse/civil partner (not the case here as there is only an ex-spouse) and dependants may take a lump sum or purchase an annuity from a life office or receive an income drawdown. HMRC Inheritance Tax will consider applying an inheritance tax charge under *IHTA 1984, s 3(3)* where the aim has been to benefit others on death rather than to make provision for the member's retirement. If having elected to take income withdrawal it can be shown that the member was in normal health and the option for income drawdown was made for commercial and retirement planning reasons then a *IHTA 1984, s 3(3)* claim by HMRC Inheritance Tax would not arise. However, if Roger had been in ill health and died having reduced any payments received under the drawdown this would have given rise to a potential inheritance tax charge as the decision would have been driven by the fact that illness was the main factor. In this case Roger was not suffering through ill health when he died and therefore the balance of units subjected to the 35% charge and the other remaining units not used for drawdown will be available for distribution to the ex-wife and into trust for the son. See 37.2 PENSION SCHEMES.

59.8 **Tax planning and mitigation.** There are a number of important uses of an employee trust; the trust offers a non-quoted company the opportunity of creating a market for the sale and purchase of shares. These trusts can also be used to build up large shareholdings in sympathetic control so that the company will be protected against unwanted take-overs and outside interference, which may have been one of Roger Coleman's main concerns for a company he built up from scratch. The employee trust will also build up good relations between staff and the employer. The trust provides for protection of workers and ex-workers in times of hardship or ill health. [*IHTA 1984, s 13*]. The employee benefit trust will also attract corporation tax liability benefits in the accounting year in which the payments to the trust are made. However, it should be borne in mind that the anti-avoidance provisions of *FA 1989, s 43(11)* might come into play if the funds of the trust might be applied otherwise than in the definition of 'potential emoluments'. Therefore special care should be taken in the wording of the deed so that the funds are 'for the sole purpose' or 'with the dominant intention of' their being potential emoluments. Following the House of Lords decision in *Dextra* which confirmed the Court of Appeal decision, HMRC will be reviewing its guidance on employee benefit trusts so that transfers of capital by the company will be transfers of value for IHT purposes. See 12.4 CLOSE COMPANIES for apportionment amongst participators chargeable at 20% lifetime rates or 40% where death of the participator is within three years of the transfer. See *Dextra Accessories Ltd and Others v MacDonald CA [2004] STC 339; HL [2005] UKHL 47*.

In order to qualify for favoured treatment an employee trust must satisfy the conditions set out in *IHTA 1984, s 86* and the necessity that all or most of the employees must be within a class of potential beneficiaries (see above). If the trust falls outside *IHTA 1984, s 28* (or *ss 13, 86*) then contributions to the trust may be a transfer of value. If *IHTA 1984, s 86* does not apply then the trust will be subject to a ten-year anniversary charge and an exit charge when capital is distributed. An exit charge will in certain circumstances arise under *IHTA 1984, s 72*.

Sometimes the employee trust does not hold more than 50% of the shares in the employing company and therefore the exemption will not apply. [*IHTA 1984, s 28(2)*]. However, there are a number of options in that within the year the trustees may be able to purchase the sufficient quantity of shares from, in this case, the ex-wife. Whether the ex-wife, or other party to the transaction, is going to agree to this is probably dependent on a number of factors but if she does not agree then the inheritance tax liability in respect of her former husband's estate is going to increase thereby impacting on the distribution that is available to her. A sale of shares in sufficient quantity owned by her already to the trust (i.e. 15%) will not give the trust control but she may also alternatively redirect the will so that a 16% of the 40%, attracting 100% BPR, is transferred to the trust under a deed of variation so that the trust has 16% to add to the existing 35%. The deed must be made within the 12-month period.

59.9   **CASE STUDY 3 — LORD CHARLES**

Lord Alan died in 1952 leaving Netherington Hall in Wiltshire together with all its contents to his son Bertie. In the past public access by members of the general public has been allowed to the Hall. The contents of the Hall include a painting by Whistler of Netherington Hall and also a rare painting of Mary Queen of Scots alongside Lord Bothwell her second husband. The pictures and other items in the Hall were all exempted from estate duty which, at the time Lord Alan died, was applied at a marginal rate of 80%.

Unfortunately, the son Lord Bertie dies in a hunting accident on Boxing Day 2000 and the Hall together with contents passed to his son, now Lord Charles. The Board considered the painting by Whistler of the Hall to be pre-eminent as it has a special close association with its historical setting, i.e. Netherington Hall. The painting was accepted as pre-eminent and is re-exempted on the death of Lord Bertie, subject to a contingent liability to IHT on any breach of undertaking or subsequent disposal by sale when the rate of IHT would be 40%.

The Board did *not* consider the painting of Mary Queen of Scots, now valued at £5 million, to be pre-eminent in this context.

Lord Charles has also inherited a great many valuable personal chattels from his late father Lord Bertie and wishes to pass on a lot of these to his brother who lives in London. Clearly, one of the main objects of this, other than benefiting his brother of family heirlooms, is to avoid IHT in the future, if at all possible, as the valuable chattels will not form part of the estate subject to heritage property exemptions.

59.10   **Compliance undertakings.** As the Mary Queen of Scots painting fails the pre-eminence test, IHT of £2 million (£5 million x 40%) is due and paid by the estate. Lord Charles decides to sell the painting for £8 million (net of expenses and CGT) six months later in January 2008 thereby breaking the estate duty undertaking. *'Pre-eminence'*

– in determining whether an object or collection is pre-eminent, any significant association with a particular place is to be taken into account, i.e. the 'Waverley criteria'. The object or collection should be central, rather than of merely marginal significance, in the context of display in a public collection or important historic building and should satisfy one or more of the pre-eminence tests which follow those laid down by the AIL Panel. Does the object have an especially close association with a particular historic setting, i.e. Netherington Hall? This category will include primary works of art, manuscripts, furniture or other items that have an especially close association with an important historic building but in this case there is no close association.

In view of the Board's decision (but see below) there will be a tax charge in respect of the Mary Queen of Scots painting calculated as follows:

	£
Estate duty at 80% on £8 million	6,400,000
Less credit for IHT paid on Lord Bertie's death	2,000,000
Estate duty payable on sale	£4,400,000

The Board's rejection of the painting of Mary Queen of Scots for continuing exemption could be appealed on the grounds that it is closely associated with Scottish history.

Historical calculation

There is no IHT payable on Bertie's death because of the exemption of the chattels but these chattels remain subject to a charge to IHT at 40% on a breach of undertaking or sale by Charles.

If Charles were to breach the undertaking by taking the chattels out of the country there would be a charge to IHT (at 40%) on the chattels rather than incur the 80% estate duty conditional exemption being claimed on Bertie's death under *IHTA 1984, Sch 6 para 4(2)(a)*.

Reference to 'estate duty exemption' (see above) means estate duty exemption obtained on a death on or after August 1930 (*Finance Act 1930, s 40*). The conferring of an exemption on death deferred the liability to estate duty, but with the possibility of triggering the charge later whether this was by way of sale (*FA 1930, s 40(2)*), breach of undertaking (*FA 1950, s 48(1)(3)* or otherwise *FA 1965, s 31(7)*).

It is important that the Whistler painting, which is now treated as pre-eminent and which has been the subject of exemption from estate duty previously, continues to meet the test of pre-eminence because a failure to do so, or, the omission of a new exemption claim, will result in a similar treatment to that of the Mary Queen of Scots painting. HMRC state 'to qualify for exemption the object must have a close association with a particular building and make a significant contribution, whether individually or as part of a collection or scheme of decoration, to the appreciation of that building or history'. See guidance note 3.12 to the Inland Revenue Press Release 17/99, 11 February 1999.

59.11   **Tax planning and mitigation.** National heritage property may also be given or sold by private treaty without tax liability to specified national bodies or may be transferred to individuals or settlements with conditional exemption.

If IHT has to be paid on any assets, it may be possible to offer a work of art in satisfaction of the liability. This is known as 'acceptance in lieu' and the work of art accepted is exempt from IHT, whether or not it has been formally exempted. The standard of objects which can be so accepted is very much higher than that applicable for 'conditional' exemption. The work of art has to satisfy a test of 'pre-eminence' either in the context of a national, local authority, or university collection, or through association with a particular building.

59.11 Working Case Study

APPLICATION FOR ACCEPTANCE OBJECTS IN SATISFACTION OF TAX

I/We* .... of ....apply for acceptance by the Board of HM Revenue and Customs of the objects herein detailed in the accompanying Schedule in satisfaction of tax and accrued interest by way of sections 230 and 233 of the Inheritance Tax Act 1984. In support of this application I/we* the offeror(s) supply the following:

(a) Four copies of a valuation of the object(s) at the date of 'offer' for acceptance in satisfaction of tax;

(b) Full colour photographs of the object(s);

(c) Valuation and full description of the object(s);

(d) Application for inspection of the object(s) may be addressed to:

Name: ....

Address: ....

....

Telephone: ....

(e) Certain wishes/conditions apply to the said object(s) and these are attached to the enclosed documents.

I/We* look forward to receiving your reply concerning the above application under sections 230 and 233, IHTA 1984.

Signed ....

Capacity: ....

Dated: ....

* Delete as appropriate

It should be noted that if a wish or condition applies to the object by, say, offering it to a university or museum and this fails because the university or museum is unable to accept the offer then the process of applying to HMRC Inheritance Tax under *IHTA 1984, s 230* must recommence.

Even if an object has been exempted from tax on the grounds of its 'pre-eminence' the Secretary of State may decline to accept the object in satisfaction of tax. An item that qualifies for exemption because it is historically associated with an eligible building may not have satisfied the 'pre-eminent' test.

In preparing the 'full description' attaching to the claim in (c) above the following particulars, which form part of the framework of reference on the interpretation of 'pre-eminence' by the expert advisers (chosen from directors of relevant national museums and galleries), are likely to be of importance where relevant:

- Does the object have an especially close association with our history and national life?

- Is the object of especial artistic or art-historical interest?

- Is the object of especial importance for the study of some particular form of art, learning or history?

Does the object have an especially close association with a particular historical setting?

See Hansard 7 August 1980 'Objects in lieu of tax (Guidelines on the interpretation of 'pre-eminent')' and former Inland Revenue Press Release 17/99 and accompanying notes dated 11 February 1999.

The benefit of the tax exemption is taken into account by adding 25% of the value of that exemption to the estimated value of the object after payment of notional tax. The amount thus calculated is offset against the tax liability of the estate on other property. However, see Taxation, 10 November 1994 p 123 regarding HMRC Inheritance Tax refusal in some cases to accept assets of national importance in lieu of tax chargeable on the estate where those assets are inheritance tax exempt for any other reason, e.g. business property relief.

NATIONAL HERITAGE UNDERTAKING

I/We .... of ....
apply for exemption from IHT/CGT* in respect of the objects shown on the attached schedule in connection with

Either
the death of .... who died on ....

Or
the lifetime transfer or disposal made on .... by ....
who was born on ....

I/We undertake, as regards those objects designated by the Board of HM Revenue and Customs to be of national, scientific, historic or artistic interest:

(a)   that they will be kept permanently in the United Kingdom and will not leave it temporarily except as approved by the Board of HM Revenue and Customs;

(b)   that reasonable steps will be taken to preserve the objects;

(c)   that reasonable steps will be taken to provide reasonable public access on terms to be agreed with the Board of HM Revenue and Customs.

(Note: If the objects are disposed of by sale, by gift or otherwise, or if the beneficiary dies, HMRC Inheritance Tax should be told as soon as possible).

Signed...Dated ....

Please say in what capacity you have signed ....

1. For objects which are or will be on display in a privately-owned house or room open to the public.

(a)   At what address can the objects be seen by the public?

....

(b)   How often will public access be given?

....

(c)   How will the opening of the house be publicised?

....

2.   For objects which are not/will not be on display in a privately-owned house or room open to the public.

Either
I   Long term loan to a public collection

(a)   Give the name and address of the collection

(b)   State the terms (including the period) of the loan

....

Or

II   View by appointment and availability for temporary loans

(a)   Give the name and address of the person to whom requests to view the objects should be made

....

(b)   Confirm that the objects will be available for loan to appropriate public collections for special exhibitions

....

Heritage land and buildings can be exempted from IHT on condition that the public is allowed access to them, either at any time or by visiting on special days. Lord Charles had agreed with HMRC that on certain requisite days of the year he opens Netherington Hall to the general public but following *Re Applications to Vary the Undertakings of 'A' and 'B' [2005] STC SCD 103 Sp C 439* the matter may now be revisited. See 60 TAX CASES. Lord Charles confirmed his commitment to public access with an exchange of letters with HMRC in the following manner:

Ferrers House
PO Box 38
Castle Meadow Road
Nottingham
NG2 1BB
DX 701 201 Nottingham 4
Direct line: 0115 974 2484
Fax: 0115 974 2497

2 November 2003

Dear Lord Charles

(Review of Articles Exempt from Tax as of 'National etc' Interest)

Our records show that certain articles were allowed exemption from tax (until sale or disposal) in connection with Netherington Hall on 25 April 1995. In return for this exemption, certain undertakings were entered into by The Honourable Lord Bertie and these conditions are shown on the enclosed copy of the form which was signed at the time.

We check periodically that these undertakings are being met and I should be grateful if you would provide me with the following information for that purpose (by answering 'YES' or 'NO' and provide details if the answer is 'NO').

We have already been in touch with you about the possibility of revised access arrangements as part of the review of all chattels currently seen by appointment only. This letter is concerned solely with observance of the undertakings already given.

1. Have the conditions set out in the   YES/~~NO~~
enclosed form been adhered to?

---

2. Can you confirm that none of the   YES/~~NO~~
exempted articles has been sold, or given
away, or disposed of in any other way?
3i Our records show that public access to
exempted articles shown on the attached
list* was to be given by entry on the
Register of Conditionally Exempted
Works of Art.
Also enclosed is a print from our records   YES/~~NO~~
which shows what the public would see
to arrange viewing. Are the details of the
public's point of contact both correct and
current, please? (We or our agents may,
from time to time, seek an appointment
on a test basis.)
3ii Please say a) how many visitors have   114
arranged appointments to view the
conditionally exempted items, and
b) how many loans to public exhibitions   None
have taken place since our last review
letter of 25 April 1994.
In addition, were there any approaches to   One failed approach from the
you for visits or loans which fell through,   University of Carolina, USA due to
for whatever reasons?   insufficient Insurance cover for
If so, please give details.   transport.
4 Is the descriptive material on the   YES/~~NO~~
attached list full and accurate?
If not, please give details of the
appropriate addition(s) or amendment(s)
you consider helpful for identification
purposes.

Your signature.....................................
Date

* The list comprises the articles I understand to be exempt from tax and to which
these enquiries relate, but any errors or omissions will not be binding on the Board
of HM Revenue and Customs and will not preclude the Board from raising fiscal
claims or taking any other action that the circumstances might justify.

Under *IHTA 1984, s 31(1)(e)* any objects, where they are associated with a particular
building and where the Secretary of State believes it is desirable for that object to remain
associated with a particular building or where objects have a significant association with a
particular place, will attract conditional exemption. If Lord Charles is able to secure
approval for the chattels he inherited from Lord Bertie on his death gifts the chattels to his
brother but rents back the chattels at a gross annual rent of between 1% and 2% of market
value before deducting insurance, etc. the payment should be acceptable providing the
necessary formalities and documentation are adhered to when the agreement is drawn up.
As no real market exists for rental of domestic chattels or valuable pieces of art, the rental
value he must pay his brother should be calculated by way of a negotiated arm's length
bargain by parties who are independently advised and follow the normal commercial
criteria in force at the time the contract is negotiated. [*FA 1986, Sch 20 para 6*]. See
memorandum below and item 12 at http://www.hmrc.gov.uk/trusts/pubsummary.pdf.
Should Lord Charles be unable or unwilling to pay the rents due on the lease of the gifted
chattels he will have reserved a benefit in respect of those chattels on his death. However,
the potential IHT charge arising on his death under the gift with reservation rules will be

at lifetime rates and not at death rates by reason of *IHTA 1984, ss 7(2), 33(1)(b)(ii), (2)(b)*. This will therefore reduce the potential IHT liability on the chattels by 50% on Lord Charles' death. See Taxation Magazine, 27 April 2006 p 104, 33.5 NATIONAL HERITAGE and 59.41 below.

With regard to the transfer of *personal* chattels by Lord Charles to his brother who lives in London the gift might best be made by way of a short form memorandum of gift and a statutory declaration of evidence by a third party. It is not normally sufficient for the gift, being a tangible portable *chose in possession*, to be passed on by a verbal affirmation of change in ownership. Especially where there is a prospect that the chattel may at some stage become the subject of an enquiry by HMRC Inheritance Tax as to ownership at some later stage. For the purposes of English law there must be effected a 'giving' and a 'taking' of the object. See *Cochrane v Moore [1890] 25 QBD 57 (CA)*. Following the *FA 1999, s 104* legislation to prevent shearing arrangements in response to the *Ingram v CIR HL [1999] STC 37* case, which related to realty, there was the question raised by HMRC Inheritance Tax whether shearing arrangements could relate to chattels having regard to the law of bailment. See Taxation Magazine, 31 July 2003, p 481. In August 2003 the then Inland Revenue accepted that shearing arrangements relating to chattels were successful. Further, *FA 2004, Sch 15 para 6* includes equivalent provisions for chattels to be treated as pre-owned assets unless the disposal is an excluded transaction. In application to this case *FA 2004, Sch 15 para 6(1)* states 'This paragraph applies where (a) an individual ("the chargeable person") is in possession of, or has the use of, a chattel whether alone or together with other persons …'. Under the election rules the phrase '… is in possession of, or has the use of,…' is also used. [*FA 2004, Sch 15 para 21(4)*]. Therefore, Lord Charles should consider a statutory declaration in the presence of an independent third party of the gift of the chattels currently situated at Netherington Hall to his brother on the following lines:

THIS MEMORANDUM records that on the ...... day of .... 200(7) the undersigned [*Donor*] of [*Address*] ('the Donor') gave and by word of mouth expressed himself/herself to give to the undersigned [*Donee*]of [*Address*] ('the Donee) [all the furniture effects and moveable property] which [are] specified in the Schedule attached hereto ('the Chattel(s)) for the absolute sole use of the/and benefit of the Donee and at the same time the Donor delivered the Chattel(s) to the Donee and placed the Donee in possession and unrestricted control of the Chattel(s) and at the same time the Donee accepted the gift.

Dated:

SCHEDULE

[*Identification is made here of all chattels which have been given by the Donor*]

Signed by [*Donor*]: *Lord Charles*

Signed by [*Donee*]: *Alexander Wishbourne*

---

and then the statutory declaration of evidence of the third party's involvement in the gifted assets/chattels:

STATUTORY DECLARATION

I/We [*Alan Milburn*](Declarant)....... of [*Melsons Solicitors, Netherington Village*]............. do solemnly and sincerely DECLARE as follows;

---

1. I am [a Solicitor of the Supreme Court]/[over the age of 18 years] and competent to make this declaration.

2. On the ... day of ....2007 at 2.30 p.m. in the afternoon I was present at ..[*Netherington Hall*]... where:

(i) I saw [*Lord Charles*]... standing in the [hall of Netherington Hall] and adjacent to a George III mahogany Serpentine sideboard on which he placed his hand at the same time [*Lord Charles*].. stated to [*his brother Alexander Wishbourne*]... "I give you this George III Mahogany sideboard and you may remove it to your home in London". Immediately thereafter I saw [*Lord Charles*]... lock the sideboard by its key and hand the key to [*Alexander Wishbourne*].. who then took it from him.

(ii) I saw [*Lord Charles*]... standing in the picture gallery on the first floor of Netherington Hall. Placed on a chaise-longue in the gallery were all the oil paintings watercolours and prints which are listed in the schedule to the Memorandum which is now annexed to this declaration and marked SCHEDULE 1. I heard *Lord Charles* say to [*Alexander Wishbourne*]... "I am giving you all the pictures which are on this list to hold at your London address..". I then saw [*Lord Charles*]... hold forward in turn each of the pictures passing it to [*Alexander Wishbourne*].. who then took it from him and as he did so I saw him [*Lord Charles*]..initial on SCHEDULE 1 in the margin opposite each picture he had held up for inspection. Immediately after the handing over of the poictures I saw first [*Lord Charles*].. and then [*Alexander Wishbourne*].. sign FIRST SCHEDULE of which a true copy is annexed hereto and marked FIRST SCHEDULE.

(iii) I saw [*Lord Charles*]... standing in the reception room on the ground floor of Netherington Hall. I saw that [*Lord Charles*]..had in his hand a paper bearing upon it a list of items and I heard [*Lord Charles*].. say to [*Alexander Wishbourne*].. "I am now giving you all the furniture which is mentioned in this inventory including [all the chairs and table in this reception hall to take to your residence in London]". After [*Lord Charles*].. had said these words, he laid the paper on the reception hall table and then lifted up one of the [six] Chippendale chairs which were lined up against the wall and passed it to [*Alexander Wishbourne*].., who took it from him and inspected it. I then saw [*Lord Charles*].. lean over the table and on producing a pen from his jacket sign the paper bearing the list of items. [*Lord Charles*].. then passed the pen to [*Alexander Wishbourne*].. who also signed the list of items. the signed paper in question is that which I now annex to this statutory declaration and which is marked

SECOND SCHEDULE.

Declaration of gifted items continues ...

AND I make this solemn declaration conscientiously believing the same to be true and by virtue of the *Statutory Declarations Act 1835*

DECLARED at ....

this .... day of ....

(signature of declarant) *Alan Milburn* ....

200...

Before me

(signature of person before whom declaration is made)

[A solicitor or A Commissioner for Oaths or as appropriate].

59.12   Working Case Study

FIRST SCHEDULE

SECOND SCHEDULE

Lord Charles' brother has children and for the purposes of 'skipping' a generation for IHT mitigation it may be possible to ensure that the chattels become the property of the children. Clearly matters as to whether the children are old enough to give good receipt is important here. Also, under *FA 2004, Sch 15 para 2* connected persons includes nephews and nieces and therefore no advantage could be obtained by reason of 'excluded transactions' detailed in *paragraph 10(1)(a)*. However, should the nephews and nieces be of an age to give a good receipt or the chattels were placed in settlement for their benefit *without* Lord Charles receiving any use or enjoyment from the chattel's physical situation the provisions of *FA 2004, Sch 15* would not apply.

59.12   CASE STUDY 4 — ALAN AND MARY SMITH

Alan Smith's widowed mother has recently died leaving an estate which is comprised of a property in Shaftesbury valued at £150,000 and a controlling interest (51%) in a small company, Dot-United Ltd, solely to her son. The shares in the company are valued at £200,000. Alan and Mary Smith live comfortably and are keen to 'skip a generation' and pass the mother's assets on to their son or grandchildren depending on what is the most tax efficient way. Alan Smith has taken out a personal pension scheme policy in 2007, which he understands can be written in trust for his wife and beneficiaries.

59.13   **Compliance undertakings.** The property in Shaftesbury and the unquoted shares will be reported on IHT 200 Forms D12 and D14.

Alan's mother dies with an estate valued at £350,000, leaving it all to Alan, her son. He can redirect it to his son and the grandchildren thereby skipping generations. The Dot-United Ltd shares are redirected to his son and are covered by the 100% BPR. In order for Alan's son to benefit from his grandmother's nil rate band of £300,000 the remaining £150,000 needs to be redirected through Alan's mother's will to be taken by Alan's grandchildren directly in that estate.

THIS DEED OF VARIATION is made..............200(7).

BETWEEN

1. "the Son"   namely...................
2. "the Executors"   namely..............both.............solicitors
                                 of.............
3. "the Grandson"   namely:
4. "the Great Grandchildren"   (1).............of.............
                                 (2).............of.............

WHEREAS

(A)   ......("the Testatrix") late of.............died on..............

(B)   The Testatrix left a last will dated ...... (the 'Will')

(C)   The Executors are the executors and trustees of the Testatrix appointed under the Will and proved the Will in the Salisbury District Probate Registry on ......

(D)   The 'Son' is the sole beneficiary entitled to the estate of the Testatrix under the Will

(E) The Son wishes to vary the disposition of the Estate of the Testatrix in favour of his family as follows

NOW THIS DEED WITNESSES

1. The Will shall be read and deemed always to have read as if it contained the following legacies:

A. I give subject to inheritance tax to my Trustees the sum of one hundred and fifty thousand pounds (£150,000) upon trust at my Trustees absolute discretion to pay transfer or apply any part or parts of the capital or income for the benefit of my Great Grandchildren.

B. I give subject to inheritance tax my shares in Dot-United Ltd absolutely to my Grandson.

2. It is certified that this instrument falls within category L in the schedule to the Stamp Duty (Exempt Instruments) Regulations 1987.

3. The parties elect for section 142 of the Inheritance Tax Act 1984 and section 62 of the Taxation of Chargeable Gains Act 1992 as amended by Finance Act 2002, section 120 to apply to this deed.

EXECUTED AS A DEED on the day and year first above written

SIGNED etc.

The controlling interest in the unquoted shares attract 100% BPR but had there been a liability then the beneficiaries would have been entitled to claim instalment relief under *IHTA 1984, 227(1)*. The form of election, shown below:

I/We, ... the Executor(s) of the Estate of .... deceased, hereby give notice to the Board in terms of *Section 227(1)* of the *Inheritance Tax Act 1984* that tax in respect of the property(ies) detailed below is to be paid by 10 equal yearly instalments.

PROPERTY
[See Note A in **Notes to the election**]

Signature of Executor(s) ....

....

Dated ....

The property that is to be the subject of an election should be described in detail as well, i.e. the unquoted shares. Unpaid tax becomes payable if the property is sold, the relevant business or an interest in it is sold, or a payment is made under a partnership deed in satisfaction of an interest in a business (not the case here).

59.14 **Tax planning and mitigation.** An alternative to the Deed of Variation would have been for Alan Smith to have accepted the assets from his late mother and created a discretionary trust deed himself (see below) although that may be unnecessarily cumbersome in view of the opportunity afforded by the Deed of Variation procedure.

THIS DISCRETIONARY SETTLEMENT made
on   200(7)

PARTIES

1.   "The Settlor" namely Alan Smith

2.   "The Original Trustees" namely Settlor and Alan Milburn of Melsons, Solicitors, 1 High Street, Netherington, Wilts SP3 1RP.

RECITALS
(Usual recitals)

NOW THIS DEED IRREVOCABLY WITNESSES:

1.   DEFINITIONS

The following terms (where the context permits) shall have the following meanings:—

1.1   "the Accumulation Period" means the period of 21 years from the date of this Settlement of the Trust Period if shorter

1.2   "the Beneficiaries" means

1.2.1   [the [grand]children and remoter issue of the Settlor]

1.2.2   the spouses widows and widowers of persons within 1.2.1

1.3   "Excluded Person" means

1.3.1   the Settlor

1.3.2   any spouse of the Settlor

1.4   "the Trust Fund" means

1.4.1   the sum specified in the First Schedule

1.4.2   any further money or property accepted by the Trustees as additions to the Trust Fund

1.4.3   all accumulated income

1.4.4   the assets from time to time representing such sum additions and accumulations

1.5   "the Trust Period" means the period beginning on the date of this Settlement and ending

1.5.1   80 years from that date (which period shall be the applicable perpetuity period) or

1.5.2   on such earlier date as the Trustees shall by deed prospectively specify

1.6   "the Trustees" means the Original Trustees or the other trustees or trustee for the time being of this Settlement

2.   INCOME

THE Trustees shall

2.1   Have the power during the Accumulation Period to accumulate all or any part of the income of the Trust Fund as an accretion to it and to apply the whole or any part or parts of the accumulated income as if it were income arising in the then current year

2.2   otherwise during the Trust Period pay or apply the income of the
Trust Fund to or for the benefit of such of the Beneficiaries who are
living in such shares as the Trustees in their absolute discretion think
fit

3.   POWER OF APPOINTMENT

3.1   NOTWITHSTANDING the above trusts the Trustees shall hold the
capital and income of the Trust Fund upon such trusts in favour or for
the benefit of all or any one or more of the Beneficiaries exclusive of
the other or others of them in such shares and with and subject to such
powers and provisions for their respective maintenance education or
other benefit or for the accumulation of income (including administrative powers and provisions and discretionary trusts and powers to be
executed and exercised by any persons or person whether or not being
or including the Trustees of any of them) as the Trustees in their
absolute discretion think fit

3.2   The exercise of this power of appointment may be delegated to any
extent and in such manner generally as the Trustees (subject to the
application (if any) of the rule against perpetuities) by any deed or
deeds revocable during the Trust Period or irrevocable and executed
during the Trust Period shall with the written consent of the Settlor
during his life but otherwise in their absolute discretion appoint

3.3   No exercise of this power shall invalidate any prior payment or
application of all or any part or parts of the capital or income of the
Trust Fund made under any other power or powers conferred by this
Settlement or by law

4.   ULTIMATE TRUSTS

SUBJECT to and in default of the above trusts powers and provisions the
Trustees shall hold the capital and income of the Trust Fund upon trust for
such charitable purposes as the Trustees in their absolute discretion select

Where a life assurance policy matures on the death of the person who took out the policy
and remained the beneficial owner, the policy monies are included in his estate for the
purposes of inheritance tax. [*IHTA 1984, s 171(1)*]. Also, care should be taken regarding
the wording where the policy proceeds on death can be designated to/for the benefit of
relatives or others especially in the case of foreign policies which do not adhere to the usual
UK type of Nomination Form wording. See 37.2 PENSION SCHEMES. Some foreign
policies are in fact worded as a Beneficiary Designation Form naming individuals or
entities who will receive the benefits on death. This fact will ensure that the proceeds
payable on death are treated as part of the deceased's estate for IHT purposes whereas a
simple UK type Nomination Form wording would have prevented such treatment under
IHTA 1984, s 5(2). See *Kempe and Roberts (personal representatives of Lyon, deceased) v
CIR [2004] STC SCD 467 Sp C 424* for the full transcript of the case but the information
circulated to the participators in the *Kempe* case (shown first) is compared below with the
typical UK Nomination Form wording (shown second):

You can name anyone as your beneficiary, or name several beneficiaries. You may
also name non profit charitable or educational institutions. (If you name more than
one beneficiary without specifying how they will share in the proceeds they will
share equally.) You may also name contingent beneficiaries. It is important that you

carefully read the instructions on the Beneficiary Designation Form and promptly mail it to the address on the Form since your designation(s) will not be valid unless a signed Beneficiary Designation Form is on file .... If there is no beneficiary on record, death benefits will be paid to your estate.

You (or your assignee, if applicable) can change beneficiary designations at any time by completing a new Beneficiary Designation Form .... a change in beneficiary designation becomes effective the date your signed Form is received.

You may assign your ....Group Life Insurance .... coverage .... as a gift to someone else but not as collateral for a loan. When you assign your coverage it means that you irrevocably transfer all rights, title and interest you have under the [policy] (including the right to name and change your beneficiary) to an assignee. To assign coverage you must submit an application ....

For the guidance of the Management Committee, I nominate the person(s) named above to be the beneficiary/beneficiaries in the event of my death. I request the Management Committee to consider paying a pension and/or cash sum to the above person(s). I understand that my wishes cannot be binding on the Management Committee but that they will be considered when benefits become payable.............

Please read these notes carefully before completing the form.

On your death, certain benefits will be paid from the .... Pension Scheme.

So that these benefits can be paid free of inheritance tax, the Rules of the .... Pension Scheme give the Management Committee absolute discretion regarding the people to whom pensions and cash are paid.

In reaching its decision, however, the Management Committee will take account of your wishes and you can complete this nomination form with details of the person(s) you would like to receive a benefit on your death.

Where a policy is transferred and the donor continues to pay the premiums, or provides the money for this purpose, then a transfer of value occurs on each occasion, based on the decrease in value of the donor's estate. These payments may be exempt, see 21 EXEMPT TRANSFERS. HMRC take the view that where the payment of a premium on a life assurance policy is a transfer of value, the amount of the transfer is the net amount of the premium after deduction under *ICTA 1988, s 266(5)* (tax relief at source) or the gross premium where paid without deduction. (Inland Revenue Press Release 17 January 1979 and IHT 15, p 9).

The gifts of the premiums are PETs. The assignment of the policy will only become chargeable if Alan dies within seven years, and only the annual premiums paid within seven years of Alan's death will be chargeable. Exemptions available for reduction of the chargeable transfer on assignment include the annual exemption and the marriage exemption. The normal expenditure exemption may be available to Alan for premiums paid and the annual exemption may also be claimed to exempt the gift in whole or in part. Normal expenditure relief is not available when a policy and annuity have been effected on a back-to-back basis (with certain exceptions).

Where the policy is expressed to be for the benefit of the spouse or children under the *Married Women's Property Act 1882*, a trust is created in their favour so that the person whose life is assured never has an interest in the policy and the proceeds will not be included in his estate on his death.

With regard to his latest personal pension policy; the Trustees of the Assurance Company will be able to apply the proceeds of the policy outside his estate on Alan's death following his wishes.

Pre-22 March 2006 life policies written in trust will not be subject to the new IHT taxing rules provided the original terms of the policy continue and where someone succeeds to the policy on the death of the policy holder then transitional protection will continue. The payment of ongoing premiums for life policies owned by trusts will not constitute additions to the trust thereby bringing them into the new IHT charging provisions. On the premature death of his wife prior to Alan Smith the life policy trust above would still qualify as subsequent beneficiaries would be entitled and therefore the terms of the trust would not have altered since it was set up pre 22 March 2006 within the stipulations of *IHTA 1984, s 46A as inserted by FA 2006, Sch 20 para 11*.

Deed of assignment and declaration of flexible trust—life policies. THIS DEED OF ASSIGNMENT AND DECLARATION OF TRUST is made the *first* day of *January* 2007

BETWEEN:

"the Settlor" namely Alan Smith of 12 High Street, Netherington, Wiltshire SP3 4RP.
and
"The Trustees" namely the Settlor and Alan Milburn of Melsons, Solicitors, 1 High Street, Netherington, Wilts SP3 1RP and William Mart, Solicitor, MWP Assurance, Head Office, Wilmslow, Cheshire.
which expression shall include other trustees or trustee for the time being of these trusts

WHEREAS:

A.   The Settlor is the beneficial owner of the policy(ies) of life assurance detailed in the Second Schedule below ("the Policy")

B.   The Settlor wishes to settle the Policy upon the following trusts

NOW THIS DEED WITNESSES

1.   The Settlor ASSIGNS the Policy and all its benefits and all moneys payable under it and any other property representing the same from time to time to the Trustees UPON TRUST (and subject to the powers and provisions of the Schedule of Further Trust Provisions) for the benefit of such one or more exclusively of the other or others of:

A.   Any spouse widow or widower of the Settlor

B.   Any children of the Settlor whenever born

C.   Any grandchildren of the Settlor whenever born

D.   Any spouse widow or widower or anyone falling within B or C

E.   Any one or more individual(s) benefiting from the estate of the Settlor under Will or under intestacy

F.   Any other individual nominated by the Settlor during lifetime in writing to the Trustees other than the Settlor

in such shares and upon such trusts (and subject to such powers and provisions) as the Trustees being at least two in number or a trust corporation shall appoint by Deed or Deeds revocable or irrevocable executed not later than two years following the death of the Settlor and in default of any such appointment

UPON TRUST for Scope and Red Cross in equal shares absolutely

EXECUTED as a deed on *first January 2007*.

The First Schedule

The Schedule of Further Trust Provisions

[being administrative etc. provisions]

The Second Schedule

"The Policy"

Life Office :	MWC Assurance Co Ltd
Life/Lives Assured :	Alan Smith
Assured/Grantee :	See 1 in Deed of Assignment
Type of Policy :	Whole of Life with profits
Sum Assured :	£260,000
Policy Number :	U6758902

SIGNED as a deed and delivered by etc.

59.15   **CASE STUDY 5 — ANGELA SUCH**

Angela Such wishes to provide for her granddaughter's university education and is thinking of donating £50,000 to Oxford university in the hope, but only a hope, that the university will give her a place when required. The gift would also be charitable so benefiting the university. Angela Such has already given £311,000 in 2005 to her profligate son and wants to know her potential IHT liability if she were to die soon, say, 31 December 2007. Also, bearing in mind that the charitable gift allocated to the university would not meet the charity requirements under *IHTA 1984, s 23* because 'it or any part of it may become applicable for purposes other than charitable purposes'. Instead, the local solicitor or adviser may advise a discretionary trust although this would impact on the PET to the son in 2005 if Angela were to die on, say, 31 December 2007. In addition, whilst Angela is mindful of her son's profligacy she is keen for him to enjoy her chattels notwithstanding that her granddaughter is to benefit in the main with regard to her overall estate on her death by way of testamentary discretionary trust.

59.16   **Compliance undertakings.** Angela Such made a potentially exempt transfer to her son of £311,000 on 24 December 2005 and then on 1 August 2006 makes a chargeable transfer of £50,000 to the discretionary trust primarily for the benefit of her granddaughter. What if Angela were to die on 31 December 2007 with an estate valued at £500,000?

The initial gift of the £311,000 to the son is a PET and no charge arises and no cumulation either. The subsequent gift to the discretionary trust is chargeable but at the time of the gift the nil rate band is greater than the gift into the trust and therefore there is no charge to lifetime rates. However, on Angela's death on 31 December 2007 the PET would become chargeable because the gift was within seven years of Angela's death and this will be a charge to tax at death rates after the reallocation of the nil rate band to the gift. This has a knock-on effect in that the subsequent chargeable gift into the Trust, which was not subject to tax because of the nil rate band now becomes chargeable to inheritance tax at death rates.

	£		
Son's liability becomes:	311,000		
Less 2005/06, 2004/05 annual exemptions	6,000		
	305,000		
Less nil rate band	300,000		
	£5,000	@ 40% =	£2,000
Less taper relief			Nil
Tax payable by son			£2,000
Trust liability becomes:	50,000		
Less 2006/07 annual exemption	3,000		
	47,000	@ 40% =	£18,800
Angela Such's death estate liability becomes:	£500,000	@ 40% =	£200,000

As the PET and the gift into the Trust were both within three years of the death there is no taper relief. The liability arising on the son and the Trustees and Angela's personal representatives will probably not be planned for and therefore either or both may be unable to pay the additional liability thereby shifting the burden of tax onto Angela's personal representatives. Situations such as this should ideally be planned for by both the son and the Trustees and Angela's personal representatives taking out insurance cover for the period of seven years after the gifts. As personal representatives do not have an implied power to take out such insurance cover it makes sense for the original will to be drawn up with the empowering clause. Also, Angela should have planned her gifts in a better way by transferring the gift to the Trust first and the gift to her son second.

Specimen extract of a discretionary trust THIS DISCRETIONARY SET-TLEMENT is made on 1 August 2006

BETWEEN

1. "The Settlor" namely Angela Such

2. "The Original Trustees" namely Alan Milburn [Solicitor], Angela Such, Christopher Bank.

RECITALS
(Usual recitals)

NOW THIS DEED IRREVOCABLY WITNESSES

1. DEFINITIONS

   THE following terms (where the context permits) shall have the following meanings:–

   1.1 "the Accumulation Period" means the period of 21 years from the date of this Settlement or the Trust Period if shorter

   1.2 "the Beneficiaries" means

       1.2.1 the existing grandchild of the Settlor namely:–
             [Sarah Jane Such] who was born on [16 June 1997] etc

       1.2.2 the spouses widows and widowers of the persons within 1.2.1

   1.3 "Excluded person" means

1.3.1   the Settlor

1.3.2   any spouse of the Settlor

1.4   "the Trust Fund" means

1.4.1   the sum specified in the First Schedule

1.4.2   any further money or property accepted by the Trustees as additions to the Trust Fund

1.4.3   all accumulated income

1.4.4   the assets from time to time representing such sum additions and accumulations

1.5   "the Trust Period" means the period ending

1.5.1   80 years from the date of this Settlement (which period shall be the applicable perpetuity period) or

1.5.2   on such date as the Trustees shall by deed prospectively specify

1.6   "the Trustees" means the Original Trustees or other the trustees or trustee for the time being of this Settlement

2.   INCOME

The Trustees shall

2.1   Have the power during the accumulation Period to accumulate all or any part of the income of the Trust Fund as an accretion to it and to apply the whole or any part or parts of the accumulated income arising in the then current year *etc.*

2.2   Otherwise during the Trust Period pay or apply *etc.*

3.   POWER OF APPOINTMENT

3.1   Notwithstanding the trusts above the Trustees shall have power by deed or deeds executed during the Trust Period to declare such trusts in respect of all or parts of the capital or income of the Trust Fund for the benefit of the members of the Appointed Class or any one or more of them exclusive of the other or others in such shares and subject to such terms and limitations and with and subject to such provisions for maintenance education or advancement or for accumulation of income or for forfeiture in the event *etc.*

3.2   Continues etc.

4.   ULTIMATE TRUSTS

SUBJECT to the trusts above the capital and income of the Trust Fund shall be held upon trust for such charitable purposes as the Trustees in their absolute discretion select

Other provisions plus a set of administrative provisions will be required.

In 3.1 of the precedent above the Trustees can in their discretion exercise their power to provide funds to pay for the school fees (or university) of the beneficiary Sarah under the trust. However, see *Fuller v Evans and Others* 60 TAX CASES on the divorce between the settlor and his wife, where a consent order was made which included provision for the settlor to make periodical payments to the mother of his children for general maintenance and for school fees inclusive of reasonable extras.

With regard to the position on the chattels there are three probable ways of distributing personal chattels in this fashion:

1.   The Testatrix leaves the distribution of the personal chattels to the discretion of her Executors;

2.   During her lifetime the Testatrix decides the division by way of informal memorandum of wishes;

3.   The Testatrix leaves the division of the personal chattels to the chosen legatees.

In this particular case, Angela Such perceives that the second option is the most appropriate and less likely to cause disharmony at a later stage. With this in mind she requests her solicitor to draw up a clause to effect this option. See 59.17 below.

59.17   **Tax planning and mitigation.** Angela Such might have instead set up an Accumulation and Maintenance Trust for her grandchild which would have been a PET. After 17 March 1986 but before 22 March 2006, a gift by an individual into an accumulation and maintenance trust, by virtue of which property becomes comprised in the trust, was a potentially exempt transfer. After 21 March 2006, a gift by an individual into an accumulation and maintenance trust, is no longer treated as a PET unless it is a transfer of value made by an individual which would otherwise be a chargeable transfer and which is either a gift into trust on the death of a parent (or step-parent for their step-child) for his or her child where the child takes the trust assets at aged eighteen or into a trust for a disabled person. See 53.1 TRUSTS FOR BEREAVED MINORS. See 38 POTENTIALLY EXEMPT TRANSFERS for further details. Also see 50.5 TRANSFERS ON DEATH for variation to create a trust. [*IHTA 1984, s 3A; FA 1986, Sch 19 para 1; F(No 2)A 1987, s 96*]. Until property settled on an existing accumulation and maintenance trusts vests at the age of 18, there will be no interest in possession so that, in the absence of special provisions, such settlements would be liable to tax under the provisions relating to SETTLEMENTS WITHOUT INTERESTS IN POSSESSION (44).

The following clause is drawn up by her solicitor regarding the chattels that she means to bequeath to her son with the inheritance tax to be paid out of the estate so that they receive the chattels free of a tax charge:

1.1   I give all my personal chattels as defined in section 55(1)(x) of the Administration of Estates Act 1925 not otherwise specifically gifted by my Will or any codicil, free of inheritance tax, to my executors as beneficial legatees.

1.2   I request my Executors, within two years of my death but without imposing any binding trust or legal obligation and without conferring any interest on any other person.

1.2.1   to dispose of the same in accordance with any memorandum of wishes of mine which may come to my Executor's attention within [....] months of my death; and

1.2.2   to the extent that there are personal chattels not disposed of by any such note or memorandum, to distribute the same in such manner as they in their discretion think fit between the persons interested in my Estate.

Other provisions plus a set of administrative provisions will be required.

59.18   Working Case Study

The letter of wishes might read as follows:

Letter of Wishes

1.   To such of [my children i.e. son] as shall be living at my death as he shall select within two years of my death all my personal chattels as defined in section 55(1)(x) of the Administration of Estates Act 1925 not hereinbefore or otherwise specifically disposed of but so that any such chattels not so selected shall fall into and form part of my residuary estate.

Should Angela Such decide she might wish her son to share in her personal chattels with her best friend Maureen then her letter of wishes might read as follows:

Letter of Wishes

1.   To such of [my son and best friend] namely ..... and ..... as shall be living at my death as they shall select within two years of my death in the manner specified in clause (2) hereof all my personal chattels as defined in section 55(1)(x) of the Administration of Estates Act 1925 not hereinbefore or otherwise specifically disposed of but so that any such chattels not so selected shall fall into and form part of my residuary estate.

2.   Such personal chattels to be divided according to value amongst them as specified in clause (1) in such manner as they shall agree or if they are unable to agree as my Trustees in their absolute discretion think fit and which shall be final and binding.

A letter of wishes must be clear but a conflicting undated memorandum of wishes will result in disaffected legatees trying to enforce their perceived rights to the chattels.

59.18   **CASE STUDY 6 — JILL AND MARTIN OAKLEY**

Jill and Martin Oakley own their own home without mortgage and they have been looking at equity release schemes or shared appreciation mortgages (SAMs) to free some of their equity in their property to fund the grandchild's school fees. They are concerned about their IHT exposure on the death of the survivor. Their capital is limited to £150,000 invested in a building society and Martin Oakley has a small pension, which will cease on his death or that of his wife whomever shall outlive the other. The property they own is valued at £400,000. They receive a quote from a commercial bank which will take a lien on the property for the advance of £87,500 of which £50,000 will be used immediately for school fees. They do not at the moment have any wills drawn up and ask their Solicitor what would be the position if they were to die together.

59.19   **Compliance undertakings.** An immediate priority should be the drawing up of their wills because to die intestate would create problems. See 50.9 TRANSFERS ON DEATH.

In determining the value of a person's estate his liabilities at that time must be taken into account except as otherwise provided by *IHTA 1984.* Except in the case of a liability imposed by the law, a liability incurred by the transferor may be taken into account only to the extent that it was incurred for a consideration in money or money's worth. [*IHTA 1984, s 5(3)(5)*].

Assume Jill and Martin Oakley take out the shared appreciation mortgage (SAM) and then die between five and six years after making the gift of £50,000 to their son for school fees.

The Estate is then valued at £774,000. The gift itself is a PET exempt transfer but as the transferor has died within seven years of the transfer the tax is recomputed at the death tax rates with tapering relief for the period between five and six years since the transfer. With an indexed Nil rate band of, say, £354,000 the calculation in the future may be as follows:

	£
Estate value	774,000
Less SAM (IHTA 1984, s 162)	(87,500)
	686,500
Less Nil rate band balance (say, £354,000–44,000)	(310,000)
	376,500
IHT thereon	£150,600

Calculate tax payable on the PETs that has become chargeable because of the death within seven years:

Son's liability:

Cash for school fees (IHTA 1984, ss 131, 139)	50,000
Less available annual exemptions	(6,000)
	44,000
Less Nil rate band	(44,000)

If no transfer had been made by use of the SAM, then the IHT due on death would have been £168,000 (i.e. £774,000 – 354,000 × 40%).

The difference in tax of £17,400 (£168,000 – £150,600) must be compared with the fact that the son would inherit £606,000 (i.e. £774,000 – 168,000) on the second death whereas with the SAM he would inherit £535,900 (i.e. £774,000 – (87,500 (SAM) + 150,600 (IHT))); a difference of £70,100. However, the son has actually had the sum of £50,000 for school fees five to six years earlier and the typical interest on such borrowings from a bank at, say, 10% for six years would have amounted to around £30,000. Therefore if he had taken a loan from the bank for school fees and repaid this out of his inheritance he would have had to repay the £50,000 borrowed for school fees and the interest amounting to £80,000 in total. This payment from his inherited property to take into account the loan means he would have been left with £526,000 (i.e. £606,000 – 80,000). Therefore by Jill and Martin giving the gift of £50,000 for school fees at the earlier date, the effect has been to reduce the IHT payable by £17,400 and the son's estate has benefited from a further £9,900 (i.e. £535,900 – £526,000).

It is important for each spouse/civil partner to draw up a will. For the purposes of establishing if there has been a transfer on death, where it cannot be known which of two or more persons died first they are assumed to have died at the same instant (i.e. the rule in the *Law of Property Act 1925, s 184* that the elder is deemed to have died first does not apply for these purposes). [*IHTA 1984, s 4(2)*].

In the case of spouses/civil partners who die in *commorientes* circumstances then the situation is complicated further by the inter-spouse/civil partner exemption under *IHTA 1984, s 18*; as there is an exempt transfer on the death under *section 18(1)* then the transfer to the younger spouse/civil partner is not a chargeable transfer. However, the younger of the spouses/civil partners is deemed to have inherited the elder spouse's/civil partner's estate under the *Law of Property Act 1925, s 184* but for the purposes of IHT under *IHTA 1984, s 4(2)* eliminates mutual gifts between individuals in such circumstances and there is no transfer of value to the younger spouse/civil partner on which inheritance tax can be charged. There is a view therefore that the elder's estate escapes inheritance tax completely and therefore a survivorship condition, which is normally desirable, is deliberately excluded in the event of the spouses/civil partners dying simultaneously (see *Taxation* magazine 24 September 1992 p 649 and 6 July 1995 p 362). This view is not universally accepted (see British Tax Review 1995 p 390). See 50.4 TRANSFERS ON DEATH and IHTM12197 for text and a useful example, which supports the view above.

59.20   **Tax planning and mitigation.** From 20 June 2003 additional anti-avoidance provisions were introduced following the former Inland Revenue's failure in the Court of Appeal in *CIR v Eversden and another (executors of Greenstock deceased), CA [2003] STC 822*. See TAX CASES (60). Thereafter, an anti-avoidance provision applies to ensure that the exception from the gifts with reservation rules in *FA 1986, s 102(5A), (5B), (5C)* for transfers between spouses does not prevent the rules from applying if (or to the extent that):

(*a*)   the property becomes settled property by virtue of the gift; and

(*b*)   the trustees of the settlement give an interest in possession to the donor's spouse, so that the gift is exempt from IHT because of the exemption for transfers between spouses and the rule that treats an interest in possession as equivalent to outright ownership; and

(*c*)   between the date of the gift and the donor's death the interest in possession comes to an end; and

(*d*)   when that interest in possession comes to an end, the donor's spouse does not become beneficially entitled either to the settled property, or another interest in possession in it.

In view of the above where a settlor creates a settlement conferring an interest in possession in favour of his/her spouse and that interest terminates during lifetime a reservation of benefit potentially arises. If there is an exercise of a power of appointment creating a discretionary settlement under which the donor spouse is capable of benefiting then that is also a reservation of benefit. *FA 2004, Sch 15* may impose a charge to income tax under Schedule D Case VI [now *ITTOIA 2005*] as a benefit arising from a pre-owned asset. It may be possible to create a loan trust in each of Jill and Martin's wills so that they leave everything to each other (attracting the inter-spouse exemption) in return for a promise of repayment for an amount equal to the nil rate band at the time the first dies. At the first death the promissory loan is created and held in trust for the benefit of the survivor and the children. The surviving spouse receives all the assets from his spouse or her spouse and is able to use them, dispose of the capital or live off the income. On the second death the promissory note is deducted from the value of the estate. This scheme thereby utilises the full Nil rate band on the first death but allows the partner to continue to use the assets accordingly. It is understood that HMRC Inheritance Tax has no objections to this scheme but in this particular case it will not be of benefit to Jill and Martin because it does not provide capital to supplement the shortfall in capital that they are experiencing.

Another option for Jill and Martin Oakley depends on which ever of them the property is vested in. If it is vested in the name of the older spouse and it is likely the older spouse will predecease the younger then there is the possibility of planning arrangement such as follows. For instance, say Martin is older than Jill and is the sole owner of their matrimonial home he may, by his will, leave part of the home as a legacy to the children. The balance of his estate can be left on a flexible life interest trust to Jill with remainder to the children. The trustees of the life interest trust appoint a 95% share in the home on discretionary trust for the benefit of the children and Jill. The remaining 5% interest in the home remains on a life interest trust for the benefit of Jill. Jill has therefore made a chargeable transfer which should ideally be covered by her nil rate band. If Jill survives for another seven years and dies thereafter a further nil rate band will be available which would no doubt cover the potential liability of her remaining life interest in the settlement. This would enable Jill to continue to live in the family home free of rent. In this scenario the *trustees* have made the decision to appoint the share on discretionary trust to the children and Jill has **not** been involved in the decision by the trustees other than being advised by the trustees. Clearly Jill must have no involvement in the decision and therefore it is appropriate for Jill not to be a trustee. The terms of the settlement might advisably exclude the usual provision that ensures that the trustees have regard to Jill's interests above all others; otherwise the exercise of the power in creating the discretionary trust by the trustees might result in her tacit approval of the action by them if she did not, as a consequence, seek to set aside the decision by the trustees and thereby be deemed to have made a gift herself. Jill would have a statutory right of occupation of the property under *Trusts of Land and Appointment of Trustees Act 1996, s 12*. This would enable her to occupy the property rent free whereas if she had no right to reside in the property and *TLATA 1996, s 12* did not apply, a rent-free occupation would be hard to sustain. Contrastingly, as a beneficiary under a discretionary settlement, as opposed to an interest in possession settlement, Jill could be allowed to occupy the property under the terms of SP10/79 (see Taxation Magazine, 20 May 2004, p 183) but unhelpfully an interest in possession arises unless a full market rent is paid by her. The income tax charge on pre-owned assets in *FA 2004, Sch 15* would not appear to be in point here as Jill is not the owner of the whole of the home other than a 5% share which when valued for market rental purposes would be below the *de minimis* limit of £5,000 per annum. The circumstances of this scenario rely on Jill surviving more than seven years after Martin's death and this may not be guaranteed.

Where under the terms of a will, or otherwise, property is held for a person if he survives another for a specified period of six months or less, the subsequent dispositions at the end of that period (or on the person's earlier death) are treated as having had effect from the beginning of the period. This does not affect any distributions or applications of property occurring before those dispositions take effect. [*IHTA 1984, s 92*]. The *Administration of Estates Act 1925, s 46 (2A)* applies to all deaths after 1 January 1996 and states that where an intestate's husband (or wife) survives the intestate for less than 28 days, then the normal intestacy rules in *section 46* have effect as if the husband (or wife) had not survived the intestate. This will prevent problems where the intestate's assets are inherited by the spouse where in most circumstances either, or both, would not wish this to occur on such deaths in quick succession. In comparison *IHTA 1984, s 92* provides that the 'dispositions taking effect' under a survivorship clause will be treated as having 'had effect from the beginning of the period'. Therefore, if the survival of either Mr Oakley or Mrs Oakley did not exceed six months *IHTA 1984, s 92(1)* then *AEA 1925, s 46(2A)* has the effect in Mr Oakley's and Mrs Oakley's case of their assets passing to their issue which enables them in this case to utilise the current £300,000 nil rate band. However, a surviving spouse to whom *subsection (2A)* applies and whose estate is less than £300,000 will lose the use of a proportion of the nil rate band up to that limit as the predeceased's assets will pass directly to their issue, in this case the parents under the intestacy rules.

Another alternative might be for the survivor (Jill or Martin) Oakley to borrow further funds from the bank so those funds are then available to place in a nil rate band discretionary trust for the grand children. Immediately, or at some stage in the future the trustees purchase a property for the use by one or more of the grand children, say, when they attend university. The loan from the bank on security of the property will under *IHTA 1984, s 162(4)* be a 'liability which is an encumbrance on any property shall, so far as possible, be taken to reduce the value of that property'. This would provide a charge against the estate of the survivor so reducing the IHT liability. The nil rate band settlement of up to £310,000 would at some stage be used to purchase the property for the grand child(ren) as their main residence whilst at university and possibly thereafter. The trustees could exercise their power in favour of a beneficiary (the grandchild) who would take up residence and on a subsequent disposal the gain would be exempt from CGT under *TCGA 1992, s 225*. See *Sansom and another v Peay 52 TC 1*. Alternatively, at some future date the trustees might appoint the property out to a beneficiary rolling over the gain and, providing the beneficiary used the property as their main residence, the property would qualify for CGT exemption on disposal under *TCGA 1992, s 222*. The original gift into the discretionary settlement of cash has advantages in that there is no possibility of application of the gifts with reservation rule that might be a factor with assets and the fact that after seven years the gift will drop out of the donor's cumulative total thereby reinstating the nil rate band of the donor. In this particular case, on the face of it, Jill and Martin Oakley will have a mortgage charge deductible from their estate under *IHTA 1984, s 162(4)* and the nil rate band availability may prove academic. However, the expectation of legacies or other inheritances benefiting the Oakleys in the future may result in the requirement for use of the nil rate band after the discretionary trust capital has been gifted. The amendments to the CGT rules affecting private residence relief in *FA 2004, s 117, Sch 22* have restricted the potential for tax planning using the discretionary trust, as above, where the property is transferred into trust holding over any gain arising and then 'washing' it out with the principal private residence exemption utilised by the beneficiaries. With effect from 10 December 2003 where trustees acquire a property with the benefit of *TCGA 1992, s 260* holdover relief any main residence exemption is denied on a subsequent transfer/disposal. [*TCGA 1992, s 226A inserted by FA 2004, Sch 22 para 6*]. However, as there has been no gain on a property being held over i.e. the property was purchased by the trustees with cash supplied by the survivor (Jill or Martin) the trustees can in the future still transfer the property to the beneficiary without the beneficiary losing the opportunity to claim principal private residence relief. Had Jill or Martin had an existing property e.g. a holiday home that they transferred into the discretionary trust with a gain that was held over then the effect of new *TCGA 1992, s 226A* will be to deny relief in respect of any future claim by the beneficiaries.

It may be appropriate to use the nil rate band discretionary trust by the use of a deed of variation so that currently the nil rate band of up to £300,000 might be utilised by the survivor. In this case both the Oakleys benefit from the pension whomever dies first but if the pension ceased on Martin Oakley's death then it would probably not be appropriate for the survivor, Jill Oakley, to deplete her income further by having to forego the benefit of up to £300,000 redirected from her husband's estate into a discretionary trust. In the reverse situation, Martin Oakley surviving, the position will not be the same as his pension would still continue and there would be no loss of annual income arising out of his wife's death. See Precedent in 14 DEEDS VARYING DISPOSITIONS ON DEATH.

59.21   CASE STUDY 7 — CARLO GRIMALDI

Carlo Grimaldi recently married Elizabeth who is UK domiciled and has moved to Netherington village with the intention of spending the rest of his married life there. He has a property in Nice valued at £350,000 and a 40% unquoted share in a French telecom valued at £200,000. He is living with his wife at her residence in Netherington and wishes to make a gift to her of £70,000 as his share of half her house valued at £140,000. Under his French will is a holograph (i.e. document wholly written by the signer) will leaving all his assets to his new wife Elizabeth. He intends to make out an English will presently in which he will benefit his wife of all his worldly assets to the exclusion of all others. Some concern has been expressed over the possible double taxation of his assets on his death and the application of the forced heirship rules pertaining to French realty and immovable property.

59.22   **Compliance undertakings.** On the event of Carlo's death his domicile position will come to a head. Form D2 (IHT 200) will need to be completed by his executors and whilst he may have considered himself to be domiciled in France, if a person has lived in the United Kingdom for a long time, so that they were resident for income tax purposes for at least 17 out of the last 20 years of assessment ending with the year in which they died or made a lifetime transfer they can be treated as domiciled in the UK for IHT. France for these purposes looks at the residence position so that the two different taxing jurisdictions are applying inheritance tax by reference to 'domicile' in the UK and 'residence' in France.

This means that HMRC Inheritance Tax can charge Inheritance Tax on Carlo's assets in France. As there is a Double Taxation Convention with France the terms of the convention will say which domicile/residence position is to be used in taxing rights. For example, Article 3 of the Convention states at paragraph 2:

> 'Where by reason of the provisions of paragraph (1) an individual is a resident of both Contracting States, then this case shall be determined in accordance with the following rules:
>
> (a)   he shall be deemed to be resident in the Contracting State in which he has a permanent home available to him. If he has a permanent home available to him in both Contracting States, he shall be deemed to be resident of the Contracting State with which his personal and economic relations are the closest (centre of vital interests).
>
> (b)   If the Contracting State in which he has his centre of vital interests cannot be determined, or if he has not a permanent home available to him in either Contracting State, he shall be deemed to be a resident of the Contracting State in which he has an habitual abode.
>
> (c)   If he has an habitual abode in both Contracting States or in neither of them, he shall be deemed to be resident of the Contracting State of which he is a national.
>
> (d)   If he is a national of both Contracting States or neither of them, the competent authorities of the Contracting State shall settle the question by mutual agreement.'

Individuals resident in France are also subject to a 'wealth tax' (quite separate from inheritance tax) once their worldwide assets exceed the tax threshold provided by law i.e. currently €720,000. Those who are non-resident are only subject to wealth tax on their French situated assets at varying rates up to 1.80%. [*Code Generale des Impots, Article 777*]. Subject to international treaty as above, all their assets are taxable on the inheritors whether situated in France or overseas, e.g. in United Kingdom. Individuals resident outside of France are only taxed on their assets in France but their financial investments in unquoted shares of 34% or more (or 20% or more of quoted shares) held in France are exempt.

In this case it is likely in the early years that Carlo would, on his death, be considered to have died domiciled in France and the whole estate will be governed by French law. If, on the other hand, Carlo becomes resident in the United Kingdom for many years with no intention of returning to France then he may be determined to be UK domiciled with immediate effect. However, domicile is extraordinarily difficult to alter and France tends to look more at the residence of an individual with regard to tax rights. This may result in French immovables being governed by French law and French movables being governed by English law. Where French law is to apply e.g. on his early death, then the French Law of Succession has to be considered; in this particular case where the deceased has left no issue but is survived by a parent and the surviving spouse is appointed as a sole beneficiary, the reserved share taken by the mother, is limited to a life interest in one-quarter of the estate. [*Code Civile, Article 1094*]. The French heirship rules are complicated and need to be reviewed with regard to the necessary planning for non-French domiciled individuals or non-resident individuals with immovables in France. A surviving spouse's French rights were limited to one quarter of the deceased's estate and whilst this could be varied by several means in some instances the forced heirship regime favoured the children and family of the deceased and the surviving spouse attracted only a minimum legal right which sometimes meant that they were entirely disinherited. From 4 December 2001 the surviving spouse is now in the same position as the children with a minimum right limited to one-quarter share of the estate. Carlo's mother is still alive and lives in Paris. Therefore she will take one-quarter share in the estate under the new rules unless she has a claim to financial support in which case the division could be different. Where the French property is owned by the couple, or solely by the deceased, the surviving spouse has the right to claim to live in the property for one year with the estate paying the charges. This prevents the children being able to eject the surviving spouse from the property as was the potential scenario previously. However, as Elizabeth does not live in the French property in Nice, the right to a claim to live in the property is probably baseless.

The gift by Carlo to Elizabeth of £70,000 for his share of the property is not a transfer of value because he is receiving a half share in Elizabeth's property. The price paid is such that no gratuitous benefit has been conferred on either party and the transaction was such as might be expected to be made at arm's length between persons not connected with each other. [*IHTA 1984, s 10 (1b)*]. However, if the payment had not been a true reflection of the half share of the property then there may have been problems arising out of *IHTA 1984, s 18(2)*. If Elizabeth had given Carlo half the house valued at £70,000 then the gift would have breached the £55,000 limit in respect of gifts allowed to non-domiciled spouses. The balance of £15,000 and any more gifts from Elizabeth other than the usual annual, small gifts, etc. would be treated as potentially exempt transfers and only fall out of account after seven years. Full consideration has been given by Carlo for his half share of the house and therefore this problem does not arise.

59.23   **Tax planning and mitigation.** Wills are of limited importance in inheritance tax planning in France because of the effect of the heirship rules (although certain rights can be annulled under a notarial deed), the testator's marriage contract and the use of gifts '*mortis causa*'. However, the testator will often simply just appoint the wife, Elizabeth in this case, as the sole beneficiary under the will without reference to the children, not the case here, in order to preserve the surviving spouses right to elect under *Code Civile, Article 1094*. This enables Elizabeth, on Carlo's death, as the surviving spouse and sole beneficiary to ensure that the reserved share taken by ascendants is limited to (a) a life interest in one-quarter of the estate if only maternal/paternal; or (b) a life interest in one-half of the estate if maternal and paternal. There are no exemptions on transfers between spouses and each beneficiary is separately taxed so that no French inheritance tax liability will be relevant until the value of the estate exceeds the cumulative total of two nil bands (one for Elizabeth i.e. €76,000, one for Carlo's mother €46,000). [*Code Generale des Impots, Article 777*]. The estate duty agreement will ensure that the country of domicile will give the credit for relief for estate duty tax paid in the country in which the property is situated as determined by the agreements. Therefore if Carlo's domicile is determined to be the UK then the French estate tax paid will be given as a credit against the UK inheritance tax liability. A French Avocat should be approached to provide specialised local advice. See also The Tax Journal, 31 January 2005.

59.24   **CASE STUDY 8 — COLONEL SMITHERS**

Colonel Smithers, who is a Lloyd's underwriter has died of a heart attack and has left the following will:

This is the last will and testament of me **Colonel Barry Smithers** of The Warren, High Street, Netherington, Wiltshire

1.   **I revoke** all wills and testamentary dispositions heretofore made by me

2.   **I appoint** the Partners at the date of my death in the firm Melsons of 1 High Street, Netherington Wiltshire and Margaret Smithers of the Haven Rest Home, Mile End Road, Netherington, Wiltshire to be the Executors and Trustees of my will

3.   **I give** the following legacies free of Inheritance Tax to Margaret Smithers of Haven Rest Home, Mile End Road, Netherington, Wiltshire the sum of £250,000

---

4.   **I give** all my real and the remainder of my personal property whatsoever and wheresoever (including any property over which I may have a general power of appointment or disposition by will) to my Trustees upon trust to sell call in and convert the same into money with power to postpone such sale calling in and conversion for so long as they shall in their absolute and uncontrolled discretion think fit without being liable for loss

5.   Subject to the payment thereout of my just debts funeral and testamentary expenses my Trustees shall hold the net proceeds of the said sale calling in and conversion and my ready money and all parts of my estate for the time being unsold Upon Trust to divide the same into two equal parts and to hold such equal parts upon the following trusts respectively

    (a)   to hold two equal third parts absolutely for my niece Mary Denise Dingwall of 24 Sparrow Way, Canterbury, Kent as shall survive me

    (b)   to hold the remaining such equal third upon trust absolutely for the following charitable institution for their respective general purposes namely:

Scope, 6 Market Road, London N7 9PW.

His estate comprises of personal assets of £300,000 but in addition include his Lloyd's assets such as investments held as part of his funds, syndicate underwriting profits for open accounts and undistributed syndicate profits or unpaid losses which have been closed prior to death. Under *IHTA 1982, ss 104, 105* the late Colonel Smither's underwriting assets would normally qualify for 100% Business Property Relief. The 100% relief remains available even if Colonel Smither's had resigned from Lloyd's but not if he had ceased to be a member. The value on which relief is given is the lower of the values at the date of death or resignation. However, Colonel Smithers was one of the underwriters who took part in the finality settlement in 1996 by reinsuring the open syndicates into Equitas (the company) and this consequently means that his personal representatives may have a problem in distributing the estate. Following the case *Re Yorke, Stone v Chataway [1997] 4 All E R 907* a practice direction was issued on 21 November 1997 by Master Dyson (amended 25 May 2001) to create a 'fast track' procedure to allow personal representatives to apply for leave to distribute the estate notwithstanding all the open years syndicates are reinsured into Equitas. Because the late Colonel Smithers underwrote for the years 1992 and earlier his PRs can apply for the 'fast track' application to distribute and in this connection apply by a Part 8 Claim Form (For N208) issued by direction of the Vice Chancellor for leave to distribute the estate on the basis that no further provision need be made for Lloyd's creditors. See notes to Precedent below. The claim form is supported by an affidavit (or witness statement) in the form of a Chancery Master's Practice Form adapted as necessary (see 59.25 below). It should also be accompanied by draft minutes (see Chancery Masters' Practice Forms) and a statement of costs (see Costs Practice Direction). See http://www.hmcourts-service.gov.uk/cms/852.htm.

Margaret Smithers, his widowed mother aged ninety four, disclaims her legacy (as opposed to entering into a deed of variation) in view of the fact that she considers she will not live much longer and is amply provided for already. See 59.25 below the necessary disclaimer form and 59.26 for tax planning and mitigation.

59.25   **Compliance undertakings.** The completed Chancery Master's Practice form is submitted to the Master (London) or District Judge (elsewhere) as follows:

In the Matter of the Estate of Colonel Barry Smithers deceased (a Lloyd's Estate) and in the Matter of the Practice Direction dated 31 January 2007.

59.25 Working Case Study

We, [   ] of [   ] and [   ] of, [occupations] state as follows:

1. We are the personal representatives of *Colonel Barry Smithers* ('the Deceased) who died on *25 July 2006* having obtained a [grant of probate/~~letters of administration~~] from the *Salisbury* Registry on *18 December 2006*. And a copy of the grant [and the Deceased's will dated [16 January 1998]] is now produced and shown to us marked '1'. We make this witness statement in support of our application for permission to distribute the Deceased's estate [and to administer the will trusts of which we will be the Trustees following administration.]. This witness statement contains facts and matters which, unless otherwise stated, are within our knowledge obtained in acting in the administration of the estate. We believe them to be true.

2. The Deceased was before his death an underwriting member of Lloyd's of London whose underwriting activities are treated by Lloyd's as having ceased on *25 July 2006*. The estate was sworn for probate purposes at £[   ]. We are now in a position to complete the administration of the estate and to distribute it to the beneficiaries but we do not wish to do so [or to constitute the will trusts] without the authority of the Court because of the existence of contingent claims against the estate arising out of the Deceased's underwriting liabilities for which we might be liable.

3. The position concerning the Deceased's liabilities is as follows:

3.1 The Deceased's liabilities in respect of the years of account 1992 and earlier were reinsured into Equitas as part of the Lloyd's settlement. There is now produced and shown to us marked '2' a copy of the certificate or statement of reinsurance into Equitas.

3.2 [The syndicates in which the Deceased participated in the years of account 1993 and later have [closed by reinsurance in the usual way] [are the subject of an Estate Protection Plan issued to the Deceased by Centrewrite Limited] [are protected by an EXEAT policy obtained by the Claimants from Centrewrite Limited].

4. There is now produced and shown to us marked '3' a copy of a later dated [   ] from the estate's Lloyd's agents confirming that [all] the syndicates have been reinsured to close [with the exception of [   ] which syndicate is protected by [the Estate Protection Plan] [the EXEAT policy]] and confirming that in the case of failure of a reinsuring syndicate to honour its obligations, the primary liability to a creditor will fall on Lloyd's Central Fund. [A copy of the [Estate Protection Plan and Annual Certificate] [EXEAT policy] is now produced and shown to us marked '4'.]

5. The claimants believe that the interests of any Lloyd's claimant are reasonably secured by virtue of the fact that all the Lloyd's syndicates in which the Deceased participated have either been closed ultimately by reinsurance to close (in respect of any open years prior to 1992 into the Equitas group) or, in respect of subsequent years [have all closed by reinsurance] [are protected by the Estate Protection Plan] [are protected by the EXEAT policy.] Equitas remains licensed to conduct insurance business and there is presently no reason to doubt its solvency. A copy of the latest report and accounts of Equitas Holdings Limited is now produced and shown to us marked '5'. [The [Estate Protection Plan] [EXEAT policy] is provided by Centrewrite Limited which is a wholly-owned subsidiary of Lloyd's and the beneficiary of an undertaking by Lloyd's to maintain its solvency. We have no reason to doubt the solvency of Centrewrite. A copy of the latest report and accounts of Centrewrite Limited is now produced and shown to us marked '6'.]

6. As appears from the schedule now produced and shown to us marked '7' in which we summarise the assets and liabilities of the estate, we have paid all the debts of the Deceased known to us (apart from the costs and expenses associated with the final

administration of the estate) and we have also advertised for and dealt with claimants in accordance with s 27 of the Trustee Act 1925 [*or if not explain why*].

7. We know of no special reason or circumstances which might give rise to doubt whether the provision described above can reasonably be regarded as adequate provision for potential claims against the estate and we ask for permission to distribute accordingly.

SCHEDULE 2

[heading as in claim form]

UPON THE APPLICATION of the Claimants by Part 8 Claim Form dated [   ].

AND UPON READING the documents recorded on the Court files having been read.

IT IS ORDERED THAT:

1. The Claimants as [the personal representatives of the estate ('the Estate') of the above-named deceased ('the Deceased')] [and] [the trustees of the trusts of the Deceased's will dated [16 January 1998] ('the Will')] have permission to distribute the Estate [and] [administer the trusts of the Will and distribute capital and income in accordance with such trusts] without making any retention or further provision in respect of any contract of insurance or reinsurance underwritten by the Deceased in the course of his business as an underwriting member of Lloyd's of London.

2. The costs of the Claimants of this application [*either* in the agreed sum of [£   ]] [*or* summarily assessed in the sum £[ ] with permission to [the residuary beneficiaries] [*name beneficiaries*] to apply within 14 days of this order on them for the variation or discharge of this summary assessment] [*or* subject to a detailed assessment on the indemnity basis if not agreed by or on behalf of [the residuary beneficiaries] [*name beneficiaries*] be raised and paid or retained out of the Estate in due course of administration.

By direction of the Vice Chancellor

Note to the Precedent

(A)   The PRs may apply to the court but the following points must be satisfied before an application is made:

(i)   all liabilities of the Lloyd's syndicates of which the Name is a member have reinsured into Equitas for 1992 and earlier years; and

(ii)   other liabilities of Lloyd's syndicates of which the Name was a member for the year 1993 and later have been closed by reinsurance in the usual way, or are covered by the Estate Protection Plan issued by Centrewrite Ltd, or are protected by the terms of EXEAT insurance cover provided by Centrewrite Ltd; and

(iii)   the substantial reason for the delay in distribution of the assets in the estate is the possibility of a claim against the estate by Lloyd's creditors.

PF33CH

Order for Distribution of a Lloyd's Estate

IN THE HIGH COURT OF JUSTICE

CHANCERY DIVISION

Claim No

In the Matter of the Estate of deceased (a Lloyd's Estate)

And in the Matter of the Practice Statement dated 25 May 2001

Before   Master

Upon the Application of the Claimants by Part 8 Claim Form dated [   ]

And upon Reading

IT IS ORDERED THAT

(1)   the Claimants as personal representatives of the estate ('the Estate') of the above named deceased ('the Deceased') [and] [the trustees of the trusts of the Deceased's will dated [ ] ('the Will') have permission to distribute the Estate [and] [administer the trusts of the will and distribute capital and income in accordance with such trusts] without making any retention or further provision in respect of any contract of insurance or reinsurance underwritten by the Deceased in the course of his business as an underwriting member of Lloyd's of London,

(2)   the costs of the Claimants of this application [*either* in the agreed sum of [£][*or* summarily assessed in the sum of £[ ] (with permission to [the residuary beneficiaries][*name beneficiaries*] to apply within 14 days after service of this order on them for the variation or discharge of this summary assessment) [*or* subject to a detailed assessment on the indemnity basis if not agreed by or on behalf of [the residuary beneficiaries] [*name beneficiaries*] be raised and paid or retained out of the Estate in due course of administration.

Note to the Direction Form

(A)   The application will be considered in the first instance by the Master (or outside London, the District Judge) who, if satisfied that the order should be made, may make it without requiring the attendance of the Claimants and the Court will send it to them. If not so satisfied, the Master or District Judge may give directions for the further disposal of the application. The Form PF 33CH Order for Distribution of a Lloyd's Estate will then be issued as above.

THIS DEED OF DISCLAIMER is made by Margaret Smithers of Haven Rest Home, Mile End Road, Netherington, Wiltshire.

WHEREAS

(A)   [Colonel Barry Smithers] died on 25 July 2006. ("the Testator")

(B)   The Testator left a will dated *16 January 1998*. ("the Will")

(C)   By clause 3 of the Will the Testator left *Margaret Smithers* a pecuniary legacy of *two Hundred and fifty thousand pounds* (£250,000) ("the Legacy")

(D)   *Margaret Smithers* wishes to disclaim the Legacy

NOW THIS DEED WITNESSES as follows:

1.   *Margaret Smithers* disclaims the Legacy

2.   *Margaret Smithers* confirms that she has accepted or received no benefit from the Legacy

EXECUTED AS A DEED on 2 August 2006.
SIGNED as a deed and delivered   )
by [Margaret Smithers] in the presence)
of: Alan Milburn, Solicitor.   )

This will be followed by a deed of variation entered into by the PRs so as to redirect the Lloyd's assets to the niece thereby reducing the inheritance tax liability imposed upon the niece.

HMRC Inheritance Tax
CTO reference
date of death:
[solicitor's ref]

Colonel B Smithers deceased

1.   Attached to this election are:

    1.1   Certified copy of a deed of variation made on [12 October 2006]

    1.2   Certified copy of death certificate of Colonel B Smithers

    1.3   Office copy grant of probate to the estate of Colonel B Smithers

Continues...

4.   We, being the parties making the deed of variation (in the case of *Margaret Smithers* and *Alan Milburn* being the personal representatives of one of the parties elect pursuant to section 142(2) of the Inheritance Tax Act 1984 and section 142(1) of that Act shall apply to such deed of variation.

Signed: ....

Dated: ....

Please sign and return the duplicate of this election as confirmation of receipt.

For deaths after 31 July 2002 it is not necessary for an election to be made within six months of the instrument of variation but that the instrument itself should contain a statement as to the variation. [*F A 2002, s 120*].

59.26   **Tax planning and mitigation.** Where an individual member of Lloyd's dies, his or her Lloyd's interest may be chargeable to inheritance tax. The Lloyd's interest comprises assets held in Funds at Lloyd's and the Special Reserve Fund, underwriting profits or losses for open years of account and undistributed syndicate profits or unpaid losses for closed accounts. Individual members are entitled to 100% business property relief on the value of the assets that are used wholly or mainly for the purpose of their Lloyd's business provided certain conditions are met. Two past cases (*Mallender & Others v CIR Ch D [2000] All ER (D) 197* and *Hardcastle & Hardcastle v CIR [2000] STC SCD 532 Sp C 259*) have come to the courts which have raised questions as to the interpretation of 'Lloyd's Interests' for the purposes of business property relief. In the *Mallender* case the taxpayers contended that business property relief should be given on the total value of the assets backing a guarantee rather than being limited to the amount of the guarantee. The Court rejected this argument, finding that the asset that underlay the guarantee did not itself qualify for relief. HMRC have confirmed that they will continue to allow the bank guarantees used as part of a member's funds at Lloyd's for the purposes of 100% business property relief but not the total value of the asset backing the guarantee. In the case of Names who converted to a NameCo, HMRC will by concession allow business property relief on the value of the underlying assets, subject to certain limitations, up to and including 31 December 2006. See http://www.lloyds.com/Lloyds_Market/Taxation/Taxation_bulletins/ and TAX CASES (60).

In the *Hardcastle* case there were open year losses and the taxpayers argued that, although they entered into the valuation of the whole estate, these losses should not be deducted from the other net assets of the Lloyd's business in calculating the amount of business property relief due. HMRC normally includes profits or losses in the value of Lloyd's business for business property relief. The Special Commissioners decided in the taxpayer's favour in this case. HMRC considers this decision to have been decided on its own particular facts and not to be of general application. It therefore will continue its existing practice of deducting open year losses from the other Lloyd's assets in determining the amount of business property relief that is available. It will also continue to give business property relief on any open year profits. See TAX CASES (60).

Those members of Lloyd's who are part of Scottish Limited Partnerships will also be affected by the rulings in the above cases. See Lloyd's Market Bulletin, No Y2543, 8 May 2001.

In connection with the Lloyd's assets if the Master is satisfied that the papers are in order he may, without requiring the attendance of the PRs, make the order to distribute the estate on the basis that no further provision need be made for Lloyd's creditors. See 59.25 above.

Disclaimers originally were beneficial as opposed to deeds of variation when the latter were subject to ad valorem stamp duty. However as neither are subject to stamp duty now this advantage of a disclaimer no longer applies. Deeds of variation offer advantages as to the certainty of destination of the assets whereas disclaimers do not. Yet under *IHTA 1984, s 93* it states:

> 'Where a person becomes entitled to an interest in settled property but disclaims that interest, then, if the disclaimer is not made for a consideration in money or money's worth, this Act shall apply as if he had **not** become entitled to that interest'.

The main purpose of the planning here is the fact that by disclaiming the legacy Margaret Smithers renders the disclaimed interest void for income tax purposes and therefore there is no taxation of the income of the disclaimed interest on her. This is appropriate because of Mrs Smithers' age and current secure financial position. The disclaimed interest does not make Mrs Smithers a settlor. The disclaimer must be made within two years of Colonel Smithers' death. The disclaimed benefit simply falls into residue so that the niece and Scope will benefit in the proportions stipulated in the will. In *Townson v Tickell [1819] 3 Barnewall & Alderson Reports 31* if a legatee disclaims his/her benefit the estate is administered as at the date of death as if there were an increase in residue. Where a specific legacy or a pecuniary legacy is dislaimed then the residue will benefit, in this case the niece and Scope. The asset, i.e. £250,000 falls into the residue. It should be noted that disclaimers of residue could give rise to intestacy rules treatment unless such disclaimers are authorised in the will, as in the STEP Standard Administration provisions.

The PRs can enter into a deed of variation and redirect the Lloyd's assets (100% BPR) to the niece. This would have the effect of creating an exempt amount of £250,000 ensuring that the balance of the two thirds of the estate due to the niece is covered by the nil rate band. The one third balance of assets goes to the Scope charity and is exempt under *IHTA 1984, s 23*.

59.27   CASE STUDY 9 — BETTY NAIRN

Betty Nairn, a widow, who has won £4.5 million on the National Lottery (now termed Lotto) has a syndicate agreement in operation with her friend Doreen Bagley to share the winnings equally (see 59.28 below). In view of this the transfer of £2.25 million to Doreen

Bagley will not be treated as a potentially exempt transfer. Betty has no wish to improve her current lifestyle and intends to make charitable gifts from her of a majority of the lottery winnings to good causes in the village.

In consequence of the fact that Betty Nairn wishes to benefit the village to a great extent and has discussions with the leader of the Parish Council and they agree the following:

- to provide £250,000 in a Trust Fund for the education and benefit of local children;

- to build a church annex for Sunday school worship costing £75,000;

- to provide £500,000 for a centre for the training and welfare of the community;

- a gift of £250 to every individual in the village.

Betty has been contacted by the War Pensions Agency (WPA) through the local British Legion Office with regard to the ex-gratia payment of £10,000 in respect of her late husband's suffering. The WPA have sent her a claim form for completion and with the help of her local solicitor she completes and submits the form. She locates her late husband's 'Soldier's Release Book Class A' (Army Book X801) stamped by the Military Dispersal Unit No 2, York which states he was a Far East Repatriated Prisoner of War in 1946. See HMRC EXTRA-STATUTORY CONCESSIONS (23).

59.28   **Compliance undertakings.** The lottery syndicate below was drawn up and registered before the win by Betty and Doreen therefore there cannot be any suggestion that there has been a gift or otherwise between the two parties. Therefore if Betty were to die the transfer would not be considered a disposition from her estate. However, in the event of a big win such as this HMRC Inheritance Tax may wish to see such agreement between the parties.

Agreement between the members of the Nairn and Bagley Lottery* Syndicate

We, the parties hereunder, contributing [equal] amounts on a weekly/~~monthly/ yearly~~* basis to the syndicate hereby confirm that the winnings from such game of chance will be distributed in equal/~~proportionate~~* shares to the stake contributed by each individual member as shown below/~~in the accompanying schedule~~*. Such stakes/contributions applied in the purchase of such tickets or the winnings arising therefrom and distributed by the appointed manager in accordance with the agreed shares shall not be a gift within *IHTA 1984, sections 2, 3A* but shall be treated as having no liability to inheritance tax in accordance with Inland Revenue Statement of Practice E14. The above shall apply to the members of this syndicate including the appointed manager being the first named member below.

Syndicate member.	Stake/contribution.	% share of prize	Date
1) Betty Nairn.	£3 per week/~~month/year~~	50%	23 April 98
Signed Mill Cottage, Netherington, Wilts Address			
2) Doreen Bagley	£3 per week/~~month/year~~	50%	26 April 98
etc.			

* deleted as appropriate.

An accompanying schedule was used by Betty Nairn to indicate her duties as the appointed manager and how the numbers were to be selected, what happens if either member failed to pay their contribution and whether the syndicate wished publicity, etc. Camelot Group plc stated that the agreement should be witnessed by a solicitor, doctor or someone of similar standing and Betty had her solicitor witness the form as did Doreen. Although HMRC Inheritance Tax state that this is not necessary for their purposes syndicate members may wish to have such an agreement witnessed for their own peace of mind.

Betty also makes a gift of £250 to every person in the village. This totals £393,750 (i.e. £250 × 1,575 persons).

Betty completes the WPA '*Claim for an ex-gratia payment for a SURVIVING SPOUSE of an Ex-Far East Prisoner of War, a Merchant Seaman imprisoned by the Japanese or a Civilian Internee*' Form WPA0009W in respect of the claim for her late husband's war service and submits it for the claim of the ex-gratia payment of £10,000.

Claim for an Ex-Gratia Payment for a SURVIVING SPOUSE of an Ex-Far East Prisoner of War, a Merchant Seaman imprisoned by the Japanese or a Civilian Internee

Thank you for enquiring about a claim for an ex-gratia payment.

You may be eligible for the ex-gratia award if you are the surviving widow or widower of one of the following and you were still married to them at the time of their death.

- A former member of HM Armed Forces who was held as a prisoner of war in the Far East during the Second World War.

- A former service personnel who received payments under Article 16 of the 1951 Treaty of Peace under the auspices of the British Government. These were certain members of the then colonial forces, Indian Army and Burmese Armed Forces.

- A former member of the Merchant Navy who was imprisoned by the Japanese in the Far East during the Second World War. For the purposes of this scheme, a member of the Merchant Navy is a person who has been employed, or engaged as, or for service as, a mariner in a British ship, or

- A British civilian who was interned by the Japanese in the Far East during the Second World War.

- **What we want you to do**

Please print a copy of this form, answer the questions in the reply part then sign and date the Declaration part on page 9. If you are unable to answer any of the questions please give as much information as you can. For the questions you have been unable to answer we may have to get in touch with you again or make other enquiries to enable us to process your claim. Return this form as soon as possible:

War Pensions Agency, Norcross, Blackpool, FY5 3WP, England.

Please turn over

The Claim Form continues ...

59.29   **Tax planning and mitigation.** In order to ensure that Betty Nairn falls within the requirements of *IHTA 1984, s 23* so that her gifts are for charitable purposes only she must not take any benefit. This is likely to be the case as even though she is resident in the village she will not be likely to benefit from the subject of her gifts e.g. the educational trust, Sunday school and the training/welfare centre. Whilst this is not a matter that is going to cause a problem for IHT purposes with regard to *section 23(4)* it might have done for income tax purposes under *FA 1990, s 25(2)*.

THIS DECLARATION OF TRUST is made on *30 September 2006* by THE TRUSTEES of the BETTY NAIRN EDUCATIONAL FOUNDATION

The object of the Charity shall be to further the education (including social and physical training) of children attending [...............] in the County of *Wiltshire* ...

The Trustees shall apply the net income of the Trust Fund in one or more of the following ways:

in awarding scholarships, exhibitions, bursaries or maintenance allowances tenable at any school, university or other educational establishment approved by the Trustees to persons under 25 years of age who, or whose parents or guardians, are resident in *Netherington* or who are attending or have attended an educational establishment in that area for not less than 7 years and who are in need of financial assistance;

in providing financial assistance, outfits, clothing, tools, instruments or books to such persons on leaving school, university or other educational establishment to prepare them for or assist their entry into a trade, profession or service;

in awarding to such persons grants or maintenance allowances to enable them to travel whether in the United Kingdom or abroad in furtherance of their education;

in otherwise furthering the education of such persons.

The Trust Deed continues with Powers of Investment, etc.

In the case of the training/welfare charities and Sunday school the following objects clauses might be appropriate:

To educate, relieve and rehabilitate persons resident in *Netherington* who by reason of their social and economic circumstances are unable to gain employment or to further their formal education by providing for such persons for a period not exceeding... years for any one individual, workshops and such other training facilities as will enable them to obtain work experience and acquire and develop vocational skills.

---

and

To advance religious education in accordance with the doctrines and principles of the [*Name*] faith by means of Sunday schools and otherwise.

Betty Nairn still has a substantial amount of money on investment thereby bringing her within the charge to IHT at 40%. As her will has been redrawn to benefit various charities on her death these bequests will be will free of inheritance tax. Note that in the case of the training/welfare charitable donation above it may be too widely drawn so as to preclude relief. A trust for the relief of unemployment is not charitable whereas the relief of poverty is charitable as is the furtherance of education. Again, care needs to be taken when setting up the necessary trust deed. However, with the introduction of gifts to Community Amateur Sports Clubs (CASCs) being exempt for inheritance tax purposes as well as capital gains tax she might consider this option as an answer to bullet point three above at 59.27. CASCs must be open to the whole community and provide facilities for, and promote participation in, one or more eligible sports. These clubs must be registered with HMRC. In addition, the Charities Commission has a narrower 'healthy recreation' condition which bars certain sports from charitable status and this might include boxing, polo etc. See http://www.charity-commission.gov.uk/. HMRC's registration procedure is by way of forms CASC3 and CASC4 which should be sent together with the club's governing document, latest accounts and rule book, etc to HMRC Sports Clubs Unit. See for http://www.charity-commission.gov.uk/publications/cc22.asp a Model Agreement and http://www.hmrc.gov.uk/charities/casc.htm. [*ITA 2007, ss 431, 442* formerly *ICTA 1988, s 587B inserted by FA 2002, s 43 and ICTA 1988, s 587C inserted by FA 2002, s 97*].

The gift to the villagers totalling £393,750 is totally exempt. See 21.9 EXEMPT TRANS-FERS. If Betty's generosity had been more focused, say, she decided to give the poorest 500 villagers £750 each (total £375,000) then the gifts would have been treated as PETs. Her death within seven years would have effectively increased the IHT liability by £150,000 (i.e. £375,000 × 40%).

In respect of the claim to the WPA her claim is successful and an ex-gratia payment is made to her of £10,000. This payment will under Extra-Statutory Concession F20 be left out of account in determining the chargeable value of her estate for the purposes of inheritance tax on death. See HMRC EXTRA-STATUTORY CONCESSIONS (23). It is also possible, although rare, that if Betty was entitled to an ex-gratia payment in her own right or, say, that both her late husbands were Japanese prisoners of war then the amount left out of account for IHT purposes on her death would become £20,000 or more. It is important that the Executors of the estate are aware of such ex-gratia payments as, in many cases, it will be many years before the claimant dies thereby generating the claim for relief. In Betty's case such a claim for relief may not be that critical as it appears that she might be minded to leave a generous portion of her estate to charity. However, a will setting out her wishes in this respect is something she and her solicitor should resolve very soon.

59.30   **CASE STUDY 10 — JOHN AND JENNIFER BROWN**

John and Jennifer are both 58 years old. John is a partner in a firm of solicitors from which he enjoys a good income. He is due to retire in about seven years' time. He then expects to receive a reasonable income from his retirement annuity and personal pension policies. However, should John predecease Jennifer after his retirement, the pension available to her as his widow would be substantially reduced. They have one daughter, Sally, and two grandchildren. Sally is wealthy in her own right by virtue of her career as a fashion designer. Her husband, Mervyn, is a partner in a firm of stockbrokers.

John and Jennifer's assets amount to about £700,000. Their private residence and contents represent a large part of this (£450,000). The remainder is held as to £100,000 in stocks and shares and as to £200,000 on deposit in bank and building society accounts (£125,000 for John and £75,000 for Jennifer). Both have left their assets to the surviving spouse on the first death and so no inheritance tax will arise then but, on the second death, both estates will effectively be aggregated.

John and Jennifer, who have not made any previous gifts, would like to embark on some inheritance tax planning. However, absolute gifts of investments are out of the question due to the fact that John will require an income from his investments in retirement to supplement his pension. Indeed, should John retire and then predecease Jennifer there will be even more of a requirement for income to Jennifer from any investments.

John and Jennifer recognise the fact that by passing assets to their daughter this will add to her already substantial inheritance tax problem.

Therefore, John and Jennifer are seeking long-term inheritance tax planning that:

- can provide an income to them in retirement (and perhaps access to a part of the capital);

- is tax efficient; and

- will give some flexibility over which beneficiary(ies) will eventually receive the benefits of the gift.

59.31   **Solution.** John effects a Retained Interest Trust by investing £100,000 of his cash into a life assurance investment bond made subject to trust. Under the terms of the trust, after due consideration, John reserves 50% of the trust fund for his own absolute benefit (i.e. £50,000 at outset). This is called the Donor's Fund.

---

*THE DONOR'S FUND-the initial   50% of the Trust Fund
percentage*

THE GIFTED FUND-THE BENEFICIARIES

Box A *DISCRETIONARY* *BENEFICIARIES*		
	1.	*Any child or grandchild of the Donor.*
	2.	*Any child or grandchild of any person at 6 below.*
	3.	*Any charity or person other than the Donor nominated as a Possible Beneficiary in a written nomination signed by the Donor and addressed to the Trustees of the Trust Fund.*
	4.	*Any beneficiary (including any object of a discretionary power whether or not that power is exercised) under the will (in respect of which Probate is granted) or intestacy of the Donor or of any person at 6 below but excluding the Donor.*
	5.	*Any person shown in Box B below.*
	6.	*Any past present or future spouse of the Donor.*
	7.	*Any other named/class of beneficiary*

Box B *IMMEDIATE BENEFICIARIES*	*Full Names*	*Share*
		100%

The balance of the trust fund is held on discretionary trusts from which John is excluded from benefit. This is known as the Gifted Fund. This should not be a gift with reservation under *FA 1986, s 102* because the Donor's Fund is carved out for John's absolute benefit and he is excluded from benefit under the Gifted Fund. *FA 1986, Sch 20, para 7* should not apply because there is no variation of rights between donor and donee under the policy — any variation occurs under the terms of the trust.

Under the discretionary part of the trust John names his two granddaughters as default beneficiaries who will benefit in the unlikely event of the trustees not appointing benefits for 80 years. His daughter and granddaughters are discretionary beneficiaries under the trust. In other words, the trustees can appoint benefits to them in the future should they so wish.

As this is a discretionary trust, none of the beneficiaries will be treated for IHT purposes as owning any part of the Gifted Fund and this will not therefore directly affect their own inheritance tax position. *[IHTA 1984, s 52]*.

John's wife, Jennifer, is also a discretionary beneficiary under the trust under 6. and so the trustees can appoint benefits to her at a later date if they so desire. However, this is not recommended whilst John is alive as he would then be likely to enjoy a benefit from any sums appointed and the gift with reservation rules *[FA 1986, s 102]* could apply. Therefore an appointment of capital to her should only be made after John's death. No gift with reservation can occur at that time.

Under the trust, John is a trustee. He also appoints his wife Jennifer and his solicitor, Albert, as trustees.

59.32   Tax effects. When John makes the £100,000 investment bond subject to trust:

- Initially £50,000 is treated as remaining in his estate as his capital entitlement to the Donor's Fund.

- £50,000 passes to the Gifted Fund and is treated as a chargeable lifetime transfer *[IHTA 1984, s 2(1)]*. As this does not cause John to exceed his nil rate band on a seven-year cumulative basis, no immediate IHT is payable. The transfer will also drop out of account on John's survival for seven years.

John's taxable estate will possibly reduce in three ways:

1. The growth on the Gifted Fund will be outside his taxable estate;

2. The gift of £50,000 will drop out of account after seven years; and

3. Should John draw back any of his capital from the Donor's Fund and spend it, this will reduce his taxable estate.

HMRC has confirmed in its guidance notes that for an interest under a trust to be caught by the pre-owned asset tax (POAT) rules, there must be a settlement and the settlor must enjoy a benefit under that settlement. In the case of the Retained Interest Trust there are two 'trust funds', John's interest is held on bare trust for him so is not a settlement. The Donor's Fund is a settlement but John is excluded from benefit. Therefore the POAT rules do not apply to the arrangement.

Ongoing IHT implications for the trust itself

As this is a discretionary trust, this means that special IHT charging rules apply. Under these rules there may be IHT charges:

- on every ten-year anniversary of the trust—'the Periodic Charge'; or

- whenever property leaves the trust (e.g. when capital is advanced to a beneficiary)— 'the Exit Charge'.

The periodic charge. Periodic charges at ten-yearly intervals may be applied to the value of the assets in the trust. The rate of inheritance tax charged will be determined based on an assumed transfer by an assumed transferor. This will mean that (provided no other settlements are created on the same day – these are known as related settlements) it will, broadly, be necessary to take account of

- the value of the property in the trust on the ten-year anniversary (the assumed transfer);

- the settlor's cumulative total of transfers in the seven-year period immediately before he made the trust (the cumulative total of the assumed transferor) plus any sums on which exit charges were imposed in the ten years immediately preceding the date of the periodic charge.

The maximum liability will be 6% of the value of the trust property but frequently it will be much less or nil.

In cases where the settlor has not made any chargeable transfers in the seven years before he creates the trust (as is the case with John), no payments have been made out of the trust in the previous ten years and there has been no added property, there will be no liability provided the value of the trust does not exceed the nil-rate band applicable at the ten-year anniversary. Any excess over the then nil-rate band will suffer IHT at 6%.

For the purposes of calculating the value of the trust fund for the periodic charge, the value of the Donor's Fund should be deducted from the value of the trust fund (i.e. the investment bond) at the ten-year anniversary. This means that an amount in respect of the then value of the settlor's rights would need to be deducted from the value of the investment bond.

In light of the above, it is most unlikely that a ten-year periodic charge will arise on the trust fund.

If all the trust fund is distributed before the tenth anniversary, no tax charge will arise (see next section). If assets remain in the trust after a distribution (or in the unlikely event of further assets being added to the trust), the trustees will need to seek specialist tax advice.

The exit charge. Exit charges will be based on the value of property leaving the trust.

No exit charge will arise on payments made to the settlor in respect of the Donor's Fund because this property is already held absolutely on bare trust for him.

Exit charges within the first ten years will be nil if the value of the initial chargeable transfer going into the trust (i.e. the £50,000 passing to the Gifted Fund) plus the cumulative total of the settlor's chargeable transfers in the seven years prior to creating the trust plus the value of any added property is below the nil-rate band when the trust is created (this assumes no 'related settlements' were made). If an exit charge does arise, it will increase according to the number of quarters that have expired since the trust was created.

The amount of any exit charge occurring after the first ten years will depend on the rate of tax charged at the previous ten-year anniversary (if any) and the length of time (in quarters) that the property has been in the trust since the last periodic charge. If there is no periodic charge at the immediately preceding ten-year anniversary then there will be no exit charge in the next ten years.

No IHT charge will arise on property paid out of the trust if there was no IHT charge at the last ten-year anniversary.

It is most unlikely that any exit charge will arise in respect of John's Retained Interest Trust.

Certain transactions, such as the value of the trust property on ten-year anniversaries and capital payments to the beneficiaries, may also have to be reported to HM Revenue &

Customs on Forms IHT100c and 100d even if no actual tax liability arises. Form D34 is also required if a life assurance policy is involved.

59.33   **Further planning.** John and Jennifer can live comfortably on John's earned income at the moment. He decides he needs no capital payments from the trust for the time being. Therefore, although growth in the value of 50% of the investment bond will be taking place outside his taxable estate, his taxable estate will be increasing by the growth on the 50% attributed to the Donor's Fund.

On retirement in seven years, John decides he requires some capital payments to supplement his pension income. At that time the bond is worth £160,578 (assuming 7% growth per annum net of charges) and his Donor's Fund 50% share £80,289. He requests the trustees to pay him £5,000 per annum. These payments are treated as capital payments to him and so these are free of income tax in his hands. These payments reduce the value of his Donor's Fund under the trust.

The trustees finance the capital payments by making a 5% withdrawal (£5,000) from the investment bond. This does not give rise to a chargeable event. [*ITTOIA 2005, s 507*].

It should be noted that as no withdrawals have been made in the seven years since the investment bond was effected, more than 5% could be withdrawn if necessary without a chargeable event occurring because the twenty year 5% annual allowance is cumulative. Indeed, John could slowly increase his 'income' from the trust e.g. 6% after a further two years, 7% for the next two years and so on provided his outstanding capital entitlement was not exceeded.

As capital payments are made to John and spent by him, his taxable estate will reduce (i.e. the value of the Donor's Fund in his estate is reducing). For example, before he takes his first capital payment of £5,000 from the trust, his taxable estate will include the full capital value of the Donor's Fund of £80,289. If he receives and spends the £5,000 from the trust, his taxable estate will reduce to £75,289.

On his death, the entitlement to any residual Donor's Fund will pass under the terms of his will and in this respect John has left this to Jennifer. No inheritance tax arises on this due to the spouse exemption.

In view of the reduction of John's pension on his death, Jennifer may need to receive a higher level of benefits from the trust. If so, after John's death she could request payments of, say, £10,000 per annum from the investment bond. If this causes the trustees to exceed their annual 5% withdrawal allowances a chargeable event will occur. The first £1,000 of chargeable event gains will be taxed at 20% meaning no further liability arises on a UK bond. Chargeable event gains over and above this would, under current legislation, be assessed on the trustees at 40% (less a 20% income tax credit for internal fund taxation in the case of a UK investment bond). [*ITTOIA 2005, s 530*].

Assume Jennifer takes capital payments of £10,000 per annum for the next five years and then dies. At that time the residual Donor's Fund would be worth £67,121 (assuming 7% per annum growth net of charges). The value of the Gifted Fund would be £221,520.

Had Jennifer not died and the Donor's Fund became totally extinguished, then the trustees could have made cash available to her by periodically making an absolute appointment of benefits from the Gifted Fund of the desired amount to her. At that time:

•   Any income tax charge on the chargeable event gains arising will be taxed on the trustees at 40% with a 20% income tax credit on a UK investment bond to the extent that they exceed the trustees £1,000 standard rate tax band. [*ITTOIA 2005, s 530*].

•   Provided proper appointments of capital are made to Jennifer, these should be free of income tax in her hands.

As it happens, following Jennifer's death, the trustees decide to distribute the trust benefits to the two granddaughters who are then adult. They appoint benefits irrevocably and absolutely to the two granddaughters and assign segments in the investment bond to each of them. Whilst this could theoretically give rise to an exit charge, in practice no IHT arises because no IHT was paid on the trust fund at the last ten-year anniversary.

59.34   **Benefits of the arrangement.** John and Jennifer have reduced their combined taxable estates by £100,000 so saving IHT of £40,000 on current rates on the second death. The saving is, in reality, more because the £100,000 investment would have grown in value during their joint lifetimes.

John and Jennifer have enjoyed a tax free 'income' during their retirement. This increased after John's death. At any time during his life John (and, after his death, Jennifer) could have demanded full payment of the outstanding Donor's Fund had a need for capital arisen.

The growth in the value of the investment bond subject to the Gifted Fund part of the trust has been free of inheritance tax. Assuming growth of 7% per annum net of charges, a sum of £221,520 would be available free of inheritance tax for the benefit of the beneficiaries when Jennifer dies. The sum of £67,121 representing the residual value of the Donor's Fund would form part of her taxable estate.

Had Jennifer predeceased John with John subsequently dying at age 75, based on a growth rate of 7% per annum net of charges, the value of the Gifted fund, which is available for the beneficiaries, would be £157,941 which is very likely to be free of inheritance tax. This represents a total value for the investment bond of £246,800 less the value of £88,859 being the outstanding Donor's Fund.

As trustees of the trust (while alive) John and Jennifer, together with Albert, have kept control over who the beneficiaries of the trust fund are.

In setting the level of withdrawals at outset, John and Jennifer should give due consideration to the period of years over which they hope to draw 'income' from the Plan.

59.35   **CASE STUDY 11 — STANLEY AND SONIA WHITE**

Stanley and Sonia are both 68 years old and are both retired. Stanley's pension from his ex-employer's pension scheme together with income from his investments amounts to about £16,000 per annum. On the advice of his tax adviser, Stanley transferred a number of his investments to Sonia five years ago. The capital value of these investments, mainly invested in deposit accounts, is now about £140,000. These produce a gross annual income of about £7,000.

They have three children and four grandchildren. Their home is worth £300,000 and their villa in Spain about £125,000. They now spend about two months a year in Spain during January and February but have no intention of moving abroad permanently and so changing their domicile. They are aware of the high potential inheritance tax liability on their joint estates but they are not prepared to make outright gifts. They estimate that Stanley will live for at least another ten years. However, Sonia has had heart trouble of late and may well predecease Stanley. Apart from Stanley's gift to Sonia, they have made no previous gifts.

Stanley and Sonia therefore require an investment that can:

1.   reduce their potential inheritance tax liability;

2.   provide them with a tax efficient income;

3.   provide access to capital should the need arise; and

4.   provide them with flexibility should they live longer than expected.

59.36   **Solution.** Sonia can use some of her deposit capital to set up a loan plan to meet these objectives. She implements this plan by taking the following steps:

She establishes a discretionary trust under which Sonia, Stanley and Ralph (her younger brother) are trustees. Sonia is not a beneficiary under the trust. The trust is established with the specific purpose of receiving an interest-free loan from Sonia. The trust will become completely constituted when it holds trust property, i.e. the loan or an investment representing the loan – see below.

> (i) During the Trust Period the Trustees shall have power by deed or deeds revocable (whether by the persons making the deed or some other persons) during the Trust Period or irrevocable to appoint the Trust Fund and the income thereof for such one or more of the Beneficiaries in such one or more shares and for such interests and subject to such trust powers and provisions (including protective trusts discretionary trusts or powers operative or exercisable at the discretion of the Trustees or any other persons) as the Trustees shall in their absolute discretion think fit.

Under the trust Sonia names her three children as ultimate default beneficiaries. These people will benefit in the unlikely event of the trust fund not having been distributed after 80 years. Her children and grandchildren are among the discretionary beneficiaries under the trust. In other words, the trustees can appoint benefits to any of these persons in the future should they so wish. Her husband Stanley is also a discretionary beneficiary under the trust and so the trustees can appoint benefits to him at a later date. However, this is not recommended while Sonia is alive as she may indirectly benefit from amounts appointed to Stanley and the gift with reservation rules [*FA 1986, s 102*] could apply thus neutralising the inheritance tax advantages. Therefore appointments of capital to Stanley should only occur, if necessary, after Sonia's death. No gift with reservation can occur at that time.

Sonia then uses £80,000 of her deposits to make an interest-free loan repayable on demand to the trustees. The trustees use the loan to effect a life assurance investment bond, written as a number of identical segmented policies, on the lives of the children on a joint lives last survivor basis.

Sonia envisages that in the future she will demand loan repayments of £4,000 per annum from the trustees. These will be financed by the trustees making part surrenders from the investment bond bought with the loan.

59.37 Tax effects.

The £80,000 loan made to the trust is not:

- a transfer of value (because although it is interest-free, it is repayable on demand);

- a gift with reservation because there is no gift of 'property' [*IHTA 1984, s 272*] and no benefit to the lender.

Sonia's taxable estate has not reduced. The loan is still owed to her estate and will form part of her estate on death.

All growth in the value of the investment bond is outside of her taxable estate. For example, assuming no loan repayments are taken and the investment bond bought with the loan is worth £157,372 (assuming 7% per annum growth net of charges) after 10 years (assuming no periodic charge arises and this is likely—see below), £77,372 of this will be free of inheritance tax.

HMRC has confirmed in their guidance notes that the POAT rules will not apply to loan trusts because:

- the settlor is excluded from all benefit under the trust and

- the loan is not a settlement.

Therefore both of the required essential conditions for the POAT rules to apply (see earlier) are lacking from the two constituent parts of the arrangement.

Ongoing IHT implications for the trust itself

As this is a discretionary trust, this means that special IHT charging rules apply. Under these rules there may be IHT charges:

- on every ten-year anniversary of the trust—'the Periodic Charge'; or

- whenever property leaves the trust (e.g. when capital is advanced to a Beneficiary)— 'the Exit Charge'.

The periodic charge. Periodic charges at ten-yearly intervals may be applied to the value of the assets in the trust. It is important that under the Gift and Loan Trust the value of the trust assets will be determined *after* deducting the amount of the outstanding loan.

The rate of inheritance tax charged will be determined based on an assumed transfer by an assumed transferor. This will mean that it will, broadly, be necessary to take account of:

- the value of the property in the trust on the ten-year anniversary (the assumed transfer)

- the settlor's cumulative total of transfers immediately before he made the trust (the cumulative total of the assumed transferor) plus any sums on which exit charges were imposed in the ten years immediately preceding the date of the periodic charge.

The maximum liability will be 6% of the value of the trust property less the outstanding loan but frequently it will be much less or nil.

In cases where the settlor has not made any chargeable transfers in the seven years before he creates the trust (as in the case of Sonia), no payments (other than loan repayments) have been made out of the trust in the previous ten years and there has been no added property, there will be no liability provided the value of the trust less the outstanding loan does not exceed the nil-rate band applicable at the ten-year anniversary. Any excess over the then nil-rate band will suffer IHT at 6%.

It is therefore very unlikely that any IHT charge will arise on Sonia's Gift and Loan Trust.

It should be remembered that for the purpose of calculating the value of the trust fund at any time the value of the outstanding loan must be deducted from the trust fund in order to arrive at its value for IHT purposes.

The exit charge. Exit charges will be based on the value of property leaving the trust. No exit charge will arise on loan repayments (or loans granted by the trustees to a Beneficiary).

Exit charges within the first ten years will be nil if the value of the initial amount going into the trust after deducting the initial value of the loan and taking account of any added property is nil. If there is an initial value (which is highly unlikely) then it will be necessary to take into account the cumulative total of the settlor's chargeable transfers in the seven years prior to creating the trust. If the combined total of these, together with any added property, is below the nil-rate band when the trust is created, there will be no exit charge.

Under a loan trust it is highly unlikely that there would be any 'exits' other than 'inoffensive' loan repayments. However, if there were the amount of any exit charge occurring after the first ten years will depend on the rate of tax charged at the previous ten-year anniversary (if any) and the length of time (in quarters) that the property has been in the trust since the last periodic charge. In many cases with a loan trust there will have been no periodic charge (see above) so no exit charge would arise.

It is reiterated that no IHT charge will arise on property paid out of the trust if there was no IHT charge at the last ten-year anniversary.

Certain transactions, such as the value of the trust property on ten-year anniversaries and capital payments to the beneficiaries, may also have to be reported to HM Revenue & Customs on Forms IHT100c and 100d even if no actual tax liability arises.

59.38   **Further planning.** Stanley and Sonia require an immediate 'income' from their investment.

Sonia decides to request the trustees to repay £4,000 per annum as a part repayment of her loan. This is free of income tax in her hands—as it is a repayment of her loan it is treated as capital.

The trustees finance the loan repayments by making a 5% part surrender/withdrawal from the investment bond. This does not give rise to a chargeable event as it is within the 5% withdrawal entitlement. [*ITTOIA 2005, s 507*].

As loan repayments are made to Sonia and spent by her, her taxable estate will reduce (i.e. the outstanding £80,000 loan is reducing by £4,000 per annum).

Sonia dies when she is aged 73. She has received a total of £20,000 in loan repayments and therefore £60,000 of her loan is still outstanding. To ensure that her personal representatives do not demand repayment of the loan, she leaves the rights to the loan and repayments thereunder in her will to her husband Stanley. Therefore the £60,000 in respect of the outstanding loan that is included in her estate is covered by the spouse exemption and there is no inheritance tax liability. [*IHTA 1984, s 18*].

Stanley can continue to demand part repayments of the loan as Sonia had done in the past. The trustees continue to finance this by withdrawals from the investment bond. Now it will be Stanley's taxable estate that will reduce as he takes loan repayments and spends them.

Stanley decides to request increased loan repayments of £5,000 per annum. To finance such repayments the trustees need to make 6.25% part surrenders from the investment bond. They will, therefore, exceed the 20 year annual 5% withdrawal allowance and a chargeable event gain of £1,000 will arise each year. This will be taxed on the trustees. The first £1,000 of chargeable event gains will be taxed at 20% and so no further tax will arise in respect of UK bonds. The balance will be taxed at 40% which means for a UK investment bond, after a 20% lower rate tax credit for internal fund taxation, the liability will be 20%. [*ITTOIA 2005, s 530*].

When Stanley is aged 85, the loan will be completely repaid. The loan will then be completely removed from his taxable estate assuming he has spent the loan repayments. However, he may still require 'income'. This can be provided by the trustees appointing capital to him and taking part surrenders from the investment bond to finance these. The tax implications of this action are:

- for a UK investment bond chargeable event gains arising on the part encashments (that exceed the trustees £1,000 basic rate band) will be taxed on the trustees at 40% with a 20% tax credit for internal fund taxation (i.e. they will pay net tax at 20%). [*ITTOIA 2005, s 530*];

- provided proper irrevocable appointments of capital are made to Stanley, these would be free of income tax in his hands.

If Stanley died at age 85, assuming 7% pa growth net of charges, the bond would then be worth £111,454. The trustees decide to encash the investment bond and distribute the proceeds to Stanley's three children. They encash the investment bond and appoint benefits irrevocably and absolutely to the children. Ignoring the £1,000 standard rate band, this will give rise to an income tax charge at 20% on the trustees for a UK investment bond. [*ITTOIA 2005, s 530*]. Although a theoretical exit charge arises, as no IHT was paid at the last ten-year anniversary there is no IHT due on exit.

It may be that the trustees could, instead, make an absolute appointment of benefits to the children and assign the trust policies to them. No chargeable event will arise on such an assignment and chargeable event gains arising on the subsequent encashment of the policies will be taxed on the children. If they are not higher rate taxpayers after taking account of the top-sliced gain under the investment bond, no tax charge will then arise in the case of a UK investment bond. Such an assignment should not give rise to an exit charge for the reason previously given for the trustees encashing the bond and making a distribution.

59.39   **Benefits of the arrangement.** Stanley and Sonia have reduced their combined taxable estates by £80,000 (IHT saving £32,000 on current rates on second death). They have enjoyed a tax free 'income' during their retirement. This increased after Sonia's death.

Before the loan was completely repaid Sonia (and later Stanley) could have demanded full repayment of the outstanding loan if a need for capital arose.

The growth in value of the investment bond is likely to be free of inheritance tax as periodic charges and exit charges look unlikely. On Stanley's death at age 85, the investment bond would have been worth £111,454 based on the growth and withdrawal assumptions made above.

As trustees of the trust (whilst alive) Stanley and Sonia with Ralph have kept control over who the beneficiaries of the trust fund are.

In setting the level of withdrawals at outset, Sonia and Stanley should give due considera-tion to the period of years over which they hope to draw 'income' from the Plan.

Case studies 10, 11 and 13 have been provided by Technical Connection. For further information on this firm you can visit their website at http://www.techlink.co.uk.

59.40   **CASE STUDY 12 — SANDRA AND DON BLACK**

Don Black died in early 2004 after entering into an *Eversden* type arrangement prior to June 2003 passing the house and contents into trust under which his wife Sandra solely took an initial interest in possession for 6 months but continues to live in the house alone paying no rent. Sandra is capable of benefiting in the reversionary interest. See 6.2 ANTI-AVOIDANCE. The house at the time of the gift was valued at £500,000. The annual rental value is, say, 5% of the value of the property and chattels. The property increases in value each year by £10,000 and on Sandra's death is valued at £600,000. Sandra has been left, by her late husband, a painting after Holbein painted by a student of his school. She enjoys the painting but gifts the asset into a discretionary trust in which she is a potential beneficiary. The Trustees allow Sandra retention and enjoyment of the painting, but draw up a lease agreement regarding the 'chattel' as detailed below whereby she pays £700 per annum rent to reflect 100% of the current open market value. However, after a three-year rental review it turns out that the chattel is in fact an original and the annual rental value is £7,000 per annum. In February 2015 Sandra dies and her estate is worth £400,000 comprised of fixed interest Government securities which have given an overall interest rate each year of 4% i.e. £16,000 per annum.

59.41   **Compliance undertakings.** For avoidance of the pre-owned assets rules the donor will normally have to be wholly excluded from benefiting from the gifted property other than in the case of (A) below. Previously, however, certain schemes normally wholly excluded the donor from benefit in the gifted property and the dismantling of the scheme as detailed below is unlikely to be possible. However, see the note to the election at 59.42 below.

(A)   The income tax charge on pre-owned assets (occupying land, possession or use of chattels and benefiting from intangible assets) will not apply to the extent that the relevant property or other property deriving its value from the relevant property and being not *substantially* less than the relevant property is within the person's estate for IHT purposes. Where a person's estate includes property deriving its value from the relevant property which is substantially less that the value of the relevant property then the chargeable amounts under *FA 2004, Sch 15 paras 4, 7, 9* are to be reduced as is reasonable to take account of that property being included in the person's estate for IHT purposes. Therefore the relevant property is only treated as comprising in the person's estate to the extent that its value exceeds the amount of the excluded liability. [*FA 2004, Sch 15 para 11(1), (2)*].

(B)   The charging provisions do **not** apply to property within an 'exemption from charge' as follows:

- The asset, tangible or intangible, is still treated as part of the taxpayer's estate for IHT purposes under the gifts with reservation rules above (*FA 1986, Part V*). [*FA 2004, Sch 15 para 11(5)(a)*];

- The gift would fall within *FA 1986, s 102(5)(d)–(i)* as in 22.2 GIFTS WITH RESERVATION at (*a*)(iv)–(x). [*FA 2004, Sch 15 para 11(5)(b)*];

- Any enjoyment of the property for full consideration and this will include situations where the property was gifted to a family member(s) and the donor benefits from enjoyment of that property after a change in the donor's circumstances (*FA 1986, Sch 20 para 6(1)(b); FA 1986, s 102C(3)*). 'Full consideration' is not defined but see 22.2 (*C*), (*d*)(i)–(iv). [*FA 2004, Sch 15 para 11(5)(d)*];

- Where there is a sharing arrangement (no greater share than equates to the number of owners each paying their own share of household expenses) under *FA 1986, s 102B(4)* so that co-ownership and occupation of an undivided interest in the land the subject of a gift made on or after 9 March 1999 coming within *s 102B(4)* is exempt. [*FA 2004, Sch 15 para 11(5)(c)*].

[*FA 2004, s 84, Sch 15 para 11(5)(a)–(d)*].

(C)   In addition, the income tax charge on pre-owned assets will not apply for the purposes of the disposal/contribution conditions below at (G) and (H) to the extent that it comes within an 'excluded transaction' category or is disregarded as follows:

- The property (land and chattels only) originally owned by the taxpayer is now owned by their spouse or former spouse, either by gift or under the terms of a court order, or where the property is now held in trust and the spouse or former spouse has an interest in possession but not where the interest in possession has come to an end other than on the death of the spouse or former spouse. [*FA 2004, Sch 15 para 10(1)(b)(c), (3)*]. See 42 SETTLEMENTS–GENERAL;

- The property (land and chattels only) was disposed of by the taxpayer in an arm's length transaction with a person not connected with him—including a transaction such as might be expected between persons not connected with each other. This rather ambiguous insertion covers sales of property to connected persons for cash but it is not wholly clear as it presently stands. [*FA 2004, Sch 15 para 10(1)(a); Charge to Income Tax by Reference to Enjoyment of Property Previously Owned Regulations 2005, SI 2005/724, Reg 5*]. The matter has to a degree been clarified by a statement by the Paymaster General Dawn Primarolo MP on 8 March 2005 after the consultation period and the issue of a Technical Guidance Note on 17 March 2005. See http://www.hmrc.gov.uk/cto/pre-owned-assets.PDF. Certain equity release scheme cases will still be considered to be caught within *FA 2004, Sch 15* according to the statement. (Excluded from this anti-avoidance measure are equity release schemes provided by a commercial vendor of equity release schemes within *Reg 5(1)(a)*, see also **Case Study 13** below.) These schemes would, it appears, be sales of a part interest which are made otherwise than at arm's length as in the case where one member of a family needs cash with another member of the family able to provide the cash. However, *Reg 5(1)(b)(ii)* ensures that if a sale of a part interest is made in an arm's length transaction before 7 March 2005 to a connected person it will be exempt. If the sale is to a connected person on or after 7 March 2005 then there will be a charge. It is common for intra-family part disposals to arise from patterns of behaviour adopted for good family or business reasons and exemption may arise by reason of *Reg 5(1)(b)(I)*. An example given of this pattern of behaviour is where a child moves in with an aged parent and acquires an equitable interest in the shared property in consideration for care of the elderly parent or where younger members of the family acquire an equitable interest in a business from the partners who preceded them. It is also accepted that where asset owners have already sold a part interest in property within their family they are unlikely, given the law as it stood, to have chosen the scheme primarily for tax avoidance purposes. Therefore property sales, whether a part or whole disposal, completed at arm's length or otherwise not at arm's length, will be exempt from the regulations if the transaction was completed before 7 March 2005. This exemption will also apply to future disposals if those disposals are made for consideration other than money or readily convertible/realisable assets. For instance, where a daughter acquires an equitable interest in her father's property under an understanding that she, say, gives up work to care for her father, he will not incur the income tax charge or there property sharing and the division of expenses is 'broadly equal'. See http://www.hmrc.gov.uk/poa/poa_guidance4.htm#housesharing. [*ITEPA 2003, s 702; Charge to Income Tax by Reference to Enjoyment of Property Previously Owned Regulations 2005, SI 2005/724, Reg 5*]. See below and 13.8 CONNECTED PERSONS;

- The person disposes of property (land and chattels only) that falls within the disposition for family maintenance exemption within *IHTA 1984, s 11* or the disposal of the property is a transfer of value to an individual that is within the annual exemption under *s 19* or the small gifts exemption under *s 20*. [*FA 2004, Sch 15 para 10(1)(d)(e)*]. See 21.9 EXEMPT TRANSFERS;

- The chargeable person with an interest in a deceased's estate varies it by way of *IHTA 1984, s 17* (i.e. changes in the distribution of a deceased's estate) so that the disposition is not treated as a transfer for IHT purposes. [*FA 2004, Sch 15 para 16*]. See 14.5 DEEDS VARYING DISPOSITIONS ON DEATH.

- Where the taxpayer is neither UK-domiciled or deemed domicile (*IHTA 1984, s 267(1)* prior to a relevant disposal then *FA 2004, Sch 15* should not apply. Persons who are not resident in the UK cannot be chargeable to income tax under *FA 2004, Sch 15*. Persons who are UK-resident but non-domiciled are only liable in respect of property situated in the UK. This also means that where the spouse is non-domiciled the restriction for IHT purposes on gifts between spouses is not applicable. [*IHTA 1984, s 18(2)*]. See 17.3 DOMICILE.

- A person acting as guarantor in respect of any loan taken out by another person to acquire property is not to be regarded for these purposes as having funded the purchase. HMRC do not regard the contribution condition set out in *Sch 15, para 3(3)* as being met where a lender resides in property purchased by another with money loaned to him by the lender. HMRC's view is that since the outstanding debt will form part of the lender's estate on death for IHT purposes, it would not be reasonable to consider that the loan falls within the contribution condition. It is not therefore reasonably attributable to the consideration under *Sch 15, para 4(2)(c)*, even where the loan is interest free. It follows that the 'lender', in such an arrangement, would not be caught by a charge under *Sch 15*. See http://www.hmrc.gov.uk/poa/poa_guidance1.htm#thecontributioncondition.

[*FA 2004, Sch 15 para 17*].

- For the purposes of the contribution condition in *Sch 15, paras 3(3), 6(3)* the provision of consideration by a chargeable person for another's acquisition of any property is an excluded transaction if:

  (1)   the other person is a spouse or former spouse where provision of consideration has been ordered by the court. [*FA 2004, Sch 15 para 10(2)(a)*];

  (2)   the property acquired becomes settled property in which his spouse or former spouse is beneficially entitled to an interest in possession but not where the interest in possession has come to an end other than on the death of the spouse or former spouse. [*FA 2004, Sch 15 para 10(2)(b), (3)*];

  (3)   the provision of consideration is an outright gift of money (sterling or other currency) made at least seven years before the earliest date on which the chargeable person occupied the land under *paragraph 3(1)(a)* (occupation of land solely or together with other persons) or had possession or use of the chattel(s) under *paragraph 6(1)(a)* (possession or use of a chattel solely or together with other persons). [*FA 2004, Sch 15 para 10(2)(c)*];

  (4)   the provision of consideration by reason of *IHTA 1984, s 11* (dispositions for family maintenance). [*FA 2004, Sch 15 para 10(2)(d)*];

  (5)   the provision of consideration is an outright gift and is wholly exempt by reason of being within the annual exemption(s) or small gifts exemption. [*IHTA 1984, ss 19, 20; FA 2004, Sch 15 para 10(2)(e)*].

[*FA 2004, s 84, Sch 15 paras 3, 6, 10, 12, 16, 17*].

(D)   Where a person's estate is reduced by an excluded liability (see (A) above) then that property is not to be treated for these purposes as comprised in their estate except where the property exceeds the amount of the excluded liability. In this case any creation of a liability and any transaction increasing a person's estate or derived property resulting from that transaction were associated operations within *IHTA 1984, s 268*. This latter provision is introduced to counteract the home loan avoidance scheme. See 6.3 ANTI-AVOIDANCE. [*FA 2004, Sch 15 para 11(6), (7)*].

(E)   In determining whether the relevant property falls within *FA 2004, s 84, Sch 15 para 11(5)(b)–(d)* (see (B) above) where the contribution conditions of *Sch 15 paras 3(3), 6(3)* are met, then the exclusion of gifts of money within *FA 1986, Sch 20 para 2(2)(b)* is disregarded. This applies to outright gifts of cash but does not necessarily extend to gifts of chattels. SEE 22.3 GIFTS WITH RESERVATION. [*FA 2004, Sch 15 para 11(8)*].

(F)   In determining 'relevant property' above for these purposes it is property disposed of and the disposal/contribution condition (see (G) and (F) below) applies so that any time after 17 March 1986 the chargeable person has directly or indirectly provided any of the consideration given for the acquisition land or chattel or an interest in same. In the case of intangible property comprised in a settlement which is or represents property which the chargeable person settled after 17 March 1986 (or added to the settlement) then the income arising is treated as that of the settlor. [*FA 2004, Sch 15 para 11(9)*].

FA 2006, s 80 adds new subparagraphs to *FA 2004, Sch 15 para 11* to ensure that where relevant or derived property ceases to be comprised in a person's estate or the person has directly or indirectly provided consideration for the acquisition of relevant property then that property is not to be treated as being comprised in a person's estate and hence subject to an income tax charge. The new legislation basically seeks to deny the existing pre-owned assets exemption under the reverter to settlor rule where a taxpayer disposes of an asset but continues to enjoy it having been given an interest in possession in respect of the asset. See 6.4 ANTI-AVOIDANCE. Where an election is made under *FA 2004, Sch 15 para 21* in respect of the property then there will be a charge to IHT under the gifts with reservation rules under *FA 1986, s 102(3)(4)*. See Note (B) in example below. [*FA 2004, Sch 15 para 11(11)–(13); FA 2006, s 80*].

(G)   The *disposal condition* mentioned in (F) above will apply if the chargeable person, say X, at any time after 17 March 1986, owned relevant land or chattels or other property the disposal proceeds of which are directly or indirectly applied by another person, say Y, towards the acquisition of the relevant land and chattels, and then Y disposes of all or part of his/her interest in the relevant property i.e. land, chattels or other property. The disposal condition will also apply to the chargeable person's occupation or use of the property even if that property is not owned by them. For instance, if X sells the property and gifts the proceeds to Y so that he/she can use the proceeds to purchase the relevant property the *disposal condition* is satisfied unless it qualifies as an excluded transaction as in (C) above. Note that a disposal that creates a new interest in land or in a chattel out of an existing interest is taken to be a disposal of part of the existing interest.

(H)   The *contribution condition* mentioned in (F) above will apply if the person at any time after 17 March 1986 provides any of the consideration given by another person for the acquisition of an interest in the relevant land or chattel, or for the acquisition of any other property where the proceeds of disposal are or have been directly or indirectly applied by another person towards the acquisition of an interest in relevant land or a chattel. Similarly to the disposal condition above, if the provision of the consideration qualifies as an excluded transaction as in (C) above then this condition does not apply. For instance, the contribution condition applies not only when the contribution is directly applied to purchase the relevant land or chattel but where it is indirect too! If, say X, provides all or part of the consideration to Y so that he/she purchases property and then sells/disposes of the property using the proceeds to purchase the land/chattel used by X then the contribution condition will indirectly be satisfied, subject of course to the exclusions in (C) above.

(I)   With regard to intangible assets there is only one condition that has to be met in order for a charge to apply. [*FA 2004, Sch 15 para 8*]. The charge will apply where the chargeable person settles intangible property or adds intangible property to a settlement after 17 March 1986 on terms that result in any income arising from that settled property being treated as coming within *ICTA 1988, s 660A* (now *ITTOIA 2005, ss 622, 624, 625, 626, 627, Sch 2 para 132(1)(3)*) so that income arising to the settlement is treated as that of the settlor notwithstanding *s 660A(2)* (now *ITTOIA 2005, s 625(1)*). For these purposes intangible property means assets such as stocks or securities, insurance policies, bank and building society accounts, etc. Land and chattels do not come within the meaning of intangible assets.

CHATTEL LEASE

Continues:

4. Enjoyment and Housing

    4.1   The Trustees covenant with Sandra Black (provided Sandra Black pays the rent and perform the covenants) that Sandra Black shall peaceably hold and enjoy the Chattel during the term without any interruption by the Trustees or any person rightfully claiming under or in trust for any of them

    4.2   The Chattel shall be housed at ....[Name of property]... or at other locations from time to time agreed between Sandra Black and the Trustees

5. Rental

    5.1   The initial annual rental for the Chattel shall be £700 per annum (which is agreed by the Trustees and Sandra Black to reflect 100% of the current open market value of the Chattel)

    5.2   The rental shall be paid annually; the first year's rental is due on the signing of this agreement (and the Trustees acknowledge receipt of it); further annual rental payments shall be due on the anniversaries of this agreement. Such adjustment as is necessary on the termination of the agreement by the death of Sandra Black shall be made as is required; otherwise there shall be no adjustment

    5.3   The rental shall be reviewable by agreement at three-yearly intervals from the date of this Agreement to ensure that Sandra Black gives full consideration for the use and enjoyment of the Chattel. In default of agreement the reviewed rent shall be determined by a valuer appointed by the President for the time being of the Incorporated Society of Valuers and Auctioneers acting as expert and not an arbitrator; either party shall be at liberty to request the President to make such an appointment.

6. Insurance

Chattel lease agreement continues.

Notes to the Precedent Extract

(A)   The initial rent should be arrived at preferably by written negotiation between two competent valuers aware of the terms of the lease, the value and condition of the chattel, cost of insurance and security, etc.

(B)   In these circumstances the benefit of the use of the chattel avoids the gifts with reservation application as full consideration in money or money's worth is exchanged. [*FA 1986, Sch 20 para 6(1)(a), (3)*]. However, after a three year rental review it turns out that the chattel is in fact an original and the 'appropriate amount' is £7,000 per annum. A charge therefore is calculated under *FA 2004, Sch 15 para 7* in respect of the difference between the interest paid at the valuation date with regard to the chattel and the actual amount i.e. £6,300 for each year. See Tax Planning and Mitigation below.

(C)   'Enjoy' for these purposes means, in the case of land, occupation of that land and in the case of chattels, it is possession or use of the chattel such as paintings, furniture, vehicles, boats, jewellery, musical instruments, wines and collectible items. 'Occupation' would not apply if the property is let but if the property was used for storage or the individual has the sole means of access to the property and uses the property from time to time then this would constitute occupation. However, HMRC have set out examples which come within the *de minimis* occupation criteria in Revenue Interpretation 55. [*FA 2004, Sch 15 para 21(4)*]. See http://www.hmrc.gov.uk/leaflets/iht.htm.

$$\frac{DV}{V} \times N$$

where

DV   is the value at the valuation date of the interest in the chattel that was disposed of by the chargeable person or, where the disposal was a non-exempt sale (i.e. sale for cash which is not exempt under *Sch 15 para 10*), the appropriate portion of that value. Where the chargeable person owned and disposed of an interest in other property including a non-exempt sale, the proceeds of which are applied to acquire an interest in relevant land, then that 'appropriate portion' of the value of the relevant land at the valuation date (see (E) below) as is reasonably attributable to the property originally disposed of by the chargeable person will become the element of DV;

V   is the value of the chattel at the valuation date (see (E) below). In the case of rental value for land it is the rent that would be chargeable for the period if the property is let to the chargeable person at an annual rent equivalent to the annual value. The annual value is the rent that might be reasonably be expected to be obtained on a letting from year to year where the tenant undertakes to pay all rates, taxes and charges that are usually paid by a tenant with the landlord bearing the cost of repairs and insurance of the building and other expenses necessary for maintaining the property to command such a rent; and

N   is the amount of interest that would be payable for the taxable period if the interest were payable at the 'prescribed rate' on an amount equal to the value of the chattel at the valuation date. The prescribed rate is currently set at 6.25% and is related to the official rate of interest as defined in *ITEPA 2003, s 181*. [*FA 2004, Sch 15 para 7(2); Charge to Income Tax by Reference to Enjoyment of Property Previously Owned Regulations 2005, SI 2005/724, Reg 3*].

Any amount so calculated above is reduced by any payments which, in pursuance of legal obligation, are made by the chargeable person during the period to the owner of the chattel in respect of the possession or use of the chattel. [*FA 2004, Sch 15 para 7(1), (2)*].

(D)   In the case of intangible property the chargeable amount in relation to the relevant property is:

$$N - T$$

where

N   is the amount of the interest that would be payable for the taxable period if the interest were payable at the prescribed rate an amount equal to the value of the relevant property at the valuation date. The prescribed rate has the same meaning as within *ITEPA 2003, s 181* and may change yearly but is currently set at 5%. [*FA 2004, Sch 15 para 9(1); Charge to Income Tax by Reference to Enjoyment of Property Previously Owned Regulations 2005, SI 2005/724, Reg 3*];

T   is the amount of any income tax or capital gains tax payable by the chargeable person in respect of the taxable period by virtue of any of the provisions under *ICTA 1988, ss 547* (now *ITTOIA 2005, ss 461, 463–468, 507, 527,*

530–534, 664, 878, Sch 1 para 147, Sch 2 paras 98, 109(1)–(3), 112(1), 114(1)), 660A, 739 or *TCGA 1992, ss 77, 86* so far as the tax is attributable to the relevant property.

(E)   When valuing land or chattels it is not necessary to make a valuation each year (whereas for intangible property it is necessary). Under the regulations the valuation should be made once every five years. Initially, there will be a first valuation which is the date the land or chattel first comes within the charging provisions. For existing schemes already coming within the pre-owned assets charge this would be the valuation as at 6 April 2005. [*FA 2004, Sch 15 paras 4, 7; Charge to Income Tax by Reference to Enjoyment of Property Previously Owned Regulations 2005, SI 2005/724, Reg 4*]. Thereafter the valuation date will be the fifth anniversary of the 6 April in the year of assessment in which the provisions of *Sch 15* first applied to the chargeable person. This could in fact be a period of less than five years unless coincidentally the charge first arose on 6 April five years previously. Where there is an interruption in the person's use or occupation of the property and the five-year cycle is broken so that it is not chargeable then the year in which the occupation of the property is again resumed and is chargeable under the *Sch 15* provisions will be treated as the next five-year anniversary. For instance, X is chargeable under the provisions of *Sch 15* on 16 June 2005 for the first time. The first five-year anniversary will be 6 April 2009 for revaluation purposes and every five years thereafter i.e. 6 April 2014, etc. However, if on 4 April 2008 he leaves to go abroad for five years and returns on 26 April 2013 after being non-resident abroad and consequently not chargeable to income tax for that period then the five-year revaluation date will be the year in which he returns and the date when the provisions of *Sch 15* apply again. When valuing land in a case of a non-exempt sale (see above) for the purposes of ascertaining the appropriate rental value the formula

$$\frac{MV \text{ minus } P}{MV}$$

MV is the value of the interest in the land at the time of the sale

P is the amount paid.

59.42   **Tax planning and mitigation.** Had Sandra Black effected a deed of variation within two years of her husband's death to ensure that the chattel was the subject of a nil-rate band discretionary trust as if the deceased had wanted this then the result would be that the chattel would not have come within the charge. Where a surviving spouse becomes beneficially entitled to property it is possible to effect a discretionary trust under *IHTA 1984, s 142* (see below) but no consideration in any form should be received for the variation. It must be questioned whether the use of the chattel subsequently by the surviving spouse can be classed as extraneous consideration and thereby lose the effectiveness of the discretionary trust gift. Otherwise the use of the discretionary trust in this way can be effective in planning to avoid both the 'gift with reservation' under *FA 1986, Sch 20* and income tax charge under *FA 2004, Sch 15 paras 6, 7*.

Under *FA 2004, s 84, Sch 15 para 16* relating to 'Pre-owned assets' provides that under *IHTA 1984, s 17* where beneficiaries of a deceased's estate agree between themselves to vary the will or the intestacy provisions then any party to the variation shall not be taxed as a former owner by reason of having had an interest under the original will or intestacy provisions. As an election may be made within two years of the death under *IHTA 1984, ss 142, 147* and *Administration of Estates Act 1925, s 47A* this gives a period of grace with no charge arising in respect of rental value of the property or chattels in question where these are enjoyed by a 'relative' within *ITA 2007, s 993 formerly ICTA 1988, s 839* including uncle, aunt, nephew and niece. 'Settlement' , 'settlor' and 'trustee' have the same meaning in this context as they do for *IHTA 1984*. See 42.6 SETTLEMENTS —GENERAL. This applies from 6 April 2005 and consequently the two-year period of grace mentioned above would only fully apply from deaths on or after that date.

The income tax charge is to be applied in respect of any benefit received in chargeable circumstances arising in or after the tax year 2005–06 but the donor will not be chargeable if the scheme has been dismantled, or the donor decides to pay a full market rent. This anti-avoidance legislation institutes latent retrospective taxation and applies to existing arrangements that have been in place for many years as well as future arrangements. [FA 2004, Sch 15 paras 3, 6, 10]. See also 56 VALUATION. After further consultation was undertaken in respect of the method of ascertaining the values of the tangible and intangible assets subject to the income tax charge HMRC issued a Technical Guidance note in March 2005 as to the method of ascertaining values. See (D) and (E) above. However, no income tax charge will apply where the total appropriate/chargeable amount for any given tax year is no more than £5,001. See also Tolley's Income Tax 2007–08. [FA 2004, Sch 15 paras 4, 7, 9; Charge to Income Tax by Reference to Enjoyment of Property Previously Owned Regulations 2005, SI 2005/724, Regs 2–4].

In order to provide an escape route from incurring the income tax charge detailed above taxpayers who have existing schemes that come within the charge may elect for special treatment that allows them to avoid the charge to income tax by dismantling the original gift scheme. The election must be made on or before 'relevant filing date' which means by 31 January in the year of assessment that immediately follows the initial year. In certain circumstances a late election may be accepted by HMRC such as serious illness or loss of financial records by reason of fire, flood or theft of papers. See note (A) to the election below. The election is to take effect from the beginning of the year of assessment ('the initial year') for which it is to apply. This will then ensure that the asset is treated as part of the individual's taxable estate for IHT purposes while the individual continues to enjoy the property in accordance with the gifts with reservation rules as above. Under the gifts with reservation rules the property would be potentially eligible for IHT reliefs and exemptions e.g. BPR, APR etc. providing the necessary requirements for those reliefs and exemptions were met. However, it may still in certain circumstances be appropriate to suffer the income tax charge under existing schemes and avoid the IHT charge. See below.

	IHT payable £
IHT charge after gift of house	
June 2003	
Gift of house into trust	
FA 1986, s 102 disapplied by FA 1986, s 102(5)(a). Associated operations do not apply re *FA 1986, Sch 20 para 6(1)(c)*.	—
February 2015	
Death estate £400,000	
Tax £54,800 (i.e. £400,000 – 263,000* × 40%)	54,800
Total tax due as result of Sandra Black's death	£54,800
Income Tax charge from 6 April 2005	
Annual charge is £25,000 + £500 (compound) each year (10 yrs) × 22%	£61,050
Total tax charge	£115,850

IHT assuming no gift of house
February 2015
Death estate £1,000,000 (i.e. £400,000 + £600,000)
Tax at death rates (i.e. £1,000,000 – 263,000* × 40%)   £294,800
*Nil rate band assumed to be static but annual increases of £8,000 × 10 (£32,000)
yrs × 40% would reduce the IHT payable by

Total IHT due after indexing the Nil rate band   £262,800

Notes to the example

(A) The personal financial circumstances in this case are such that Sandra Black's investment portfolio enables her to have sufficient funds to pay the annual market rent for the property. However, in many cases this will not be the case and the above scenario would not be appropriate in circumstances where the individual would be unable to meet the rental demands. In these cases where an existing scheme is in operation consideration may have to be given to an election under *FA 2004, Sch 15 para 21(2)* whereby the chargeable person elects within *Sch 15 para 23* to have the relevant property i.e. the land and property in this case, as if it were treated as a 'gift with reservation' within *FA 1986, Part V* so that the property forms part of their estate if that person continues to enjoy it until their death or otherwise. [*FA 2004, Sch 15 para 23(5)*].

(B) Where a chargeable person elects under *FA 2004, Sch 15 para 21(2)(b)(i–iii)* in respect of land and chattels (IHT 500 below) the IHT exemption for settled property does not apply and the asset will be treated as part of that person's estate valued on the date of their death or, if the interest comes to an end on an earlier date, that particular date. Where a person makes an election and then dies before the date of Royal Assent to the *FA 2006* i.e. 19 July 2006 then any IHT due as a result will fall for payment 14 days after enactment. Similar rules apply to intangible property which is the object of a settlement where a chargeable person elects under *FA 2004, Sch 15 para 22(2)(b)(i–iii)* for a charge to IHT under the gifts with reservation rules under *FA 1986, s 102(3)(4)*. [*FA 2006, s 80(3)(4)*].

The form of election within (A) using the prescribed form IHT500 recommended by HM Revenue and Customs which, in the event of the individual's death, the personal representatives may sign is as follows: [See overleaf].

Notes to the election

(A) The legislation merely refers to an election being made in the 'prescribed manner'. [*FA 2004, Sch 15 para 23(2)*]. The form (i.e. IHT 500 above) has now been issued and therefore constitutes the prescribed manner and should, when completed, be sent to HMRC Inheritance Tax, Pre-Owned Assets Unit. The difficulty arising with such an election is that it does not revert the donor back to the position prior to the gift for IHT purposes because unless the donee(s) join in a revocation of the gift, which in many cases it is debatable whether this is possible, then the original gift cannot be undone, but see note (B) below. Clearly the election will result in the property being comprised in the original donor's estate but there will not be an automatic CGT uplift for the donee(s) on the subsequent death of the donor which may be many years later when the property has increased substantially in value. Any election should have been deferred until just prior to 31 January 2007 because if an election was made early and the donor dies prior to 31 January 2007 all potential IHT savings will have been lost with only a small saving by reason of the income tax charge. A late election may have been preferable because a subsequent revocation of the election is not possible after death and the delayed income tax charge, if applicable because it exceeds the *de minimis* amount, will in any case merely have accrued from 6 April 2005. Elections for existing schemes should have been made by 31 January 2007 in the normal course of

Inland Revenue
Capital Taxes

Election for Inheritance Tax to apply to asset previously owned

Fill in this form if you are chargeable to income tax on the benefit you receive from property you previously owned but want to elect for the property to be treated as part of your estate for inheritance tax purposes.

You should read the notes in form IHT501 as you fill in this form. Please provide information for all sections, inserting "not applicable" where appropriate.

About the person making the election

Title	Surname
	Other name(s)
	Date of birth / /
	Income Tax district and reference
	Unique Taxpayer Reference (UTR)
	National Insurance number
	Address

About the property subject to the election

The property is: an interest in land ✓

a chattel ☐

intangible property ☐

Description of the property

IHT 500 (Substitute)(LexisNexis Butterworths)

IR CT Approval ref: L4/05

59.42   Working Case Study

Who are the legal owners of the property?	
What is the nature and extent of your interest in the property?	
Name(s) of anyone else who receives a benefit from the property	
Details of disposal(s) or contribution(s)	
Is the property conditionally exempt from IHT or CGT on an earlier event?	Yes ☐ No ☐
If "yes", please provide details	

The election

I elect that the property specified above is to form part of my estate for inheritance tax purposes under the provisions of paragraphs 21 to 23, Schedule 15 to the Finance Act 2004.

Signature of person making the election	
Capacity	
Date	

This election applies from the year of Assessment beginning on 6 April

When you have completed this form send it to:

Pre-owned Assets Section
Inland Revenue Capital Taxes
PO Box 38
Castle Meadow Road
Nottingham
NG21BB

**Probate and inheritance tax
Helpline 0845 3020900**

Document Exchange: DX 701201 Nottingham 4.

events. However, *FA 2007* inserted an amendment to the 2004 legislation so that HMRC may allow a later filing date in particular cases that are deemed appropriate. [*FA 2004, Sch 15 para 23(3) as inserted by FA 2007, s 66*]. See http://www.hmrc.gov.uk/poa/late-election-guidance.htm. Otherwise, elections must be made on or before 'relevant filing date', which means by 31 January in the year of assessment that immediately follows the relevant year (see IHT500 above). There is also the question of whether the donee(s) can in any case revoke the gift under general law and if so whether this in turn would be tantamount to a gift being made by the donee(s) to the donor. For the notes concerning the preparation of IHT 500 see http://www.hmrc.gov.uk/poa/iht501.pdf.

However, one matter that has been clarified by HMRC is where an election, as detailed above, is made but the taxpayer dies within a few years of making the election and the deceased's estate faces the possibility of a double charge to IHT effectively on the same underlying asset. For instance, where one trust is created to buy a settlor's asset(s) in exchange for an IOU which is then gifted into a separate second trust to exclude it from the settlor's taxable estate. Where the donor dies within seven years the estate will be liable to IHT on the IOU but, in addition, where an election has been made under *FA 2004, Sch 15 para 23* the deceased's estate might also have been liable to IHT on the underlying asset. See Example 1 in 22.10 GIFTS WITH RESERVATION. The consultation document raised concerns about this potential for a double charge if electing under *FA 2004, Sch 15 paras 21–23* and regulations have been issued to ensure that such a double charge in these circumstances is avoided. However, where an IOU has formally been written off and the donor dies within seven years there may still have been the possibility of a double charge but this has been clarified as not being the case in the Paymaster General's statement dated 21 July 2005. See http://www.hmrc.gov.uk/poa/ms-pre-ownedassets.pdf. New regulations ensure that relief is given where the former owner of an asset of an asset disposes of it such that the provisions of *Sch 15* apply and gifts the proceeds into a trust but is given an IOU in exchange as detailed above. Whilst the regulations have effect from 4 January 2006 they apply in any case where an individual dies on or after 6 April 2005 and has dismantled the arrangement but died within seven years of the gift into the trust. [*FA 1986, s 104; Charge to Income Tax by Reference to Enjoyment of Property Previously Owned Regulations 2005, SI 2005/724, Reg 6; Inheritance Tax (Double Charges Relief) Regulations 2005, SI 2005/3441, Reg 3*]. An example of the effects of the double IHT charge is shown in the Technical Guidance Note at Point 4.8. See http://www.hmrc.gov.uk/cto/pre-owned-assets.PDF.

(B)   In a letter to HMRC Inheritance Tax in October 2006, STEP/CIOT raised the point that if an election is made in order to avoid an income tax charge from 6 April 2005 onwards if the property is back in the person's estate, then the effect of the election ceases to apply for IHT purposes and the spouse exemption and charity exemptions would in the normal course of events apply. If the election is made and the scheme is not then unravelled, the spouse exemption is not available. HMRC Inheritance Tax confirmed that:

'If evidence is produced that property, in respect of which an election under Schedule 15 legislation had been made, has been appointed back to the estate, we would ignore the existence of the election for the purposes of determining the IHT estate on death.'

59.43   CASE STUDY 13 —WILLIAM AND MARY PINK

William and Mary are both 73 years old and are both retired. William's pension from his ex-employer's pension scheme is £25,000 per annum. William has cash deposits of about £75,000 and stock market investments worth about £50,000. Mary has £37,500 in a building society account and PEPs, ISAs and National Savings Certificates worth £25,000.

59.44   Working Case Study

Following a recent inheritance from William's uncle they have £175,000 in a joint bank account awaiting more permanent investment. Inheritance tax has been paid on this legacy.

They have two children and three grandchildren. Their private residence is worth £400,000 and owned in joint names. Their Wills leave all the deceased's assets to the surviving spouse on the first death.

They are aware of the high potential inheritance tax liability on their joint estates but they are not prepared to make outright gifts because they need income from their investment capital. However, they are unlikely to need capital.

They would like to take action in such a way as to secure immediate inheritance tax savings and an income payment throughout their joint lifetimes and for the lifetime of the survivor.

Both William and Mary are in reasonably good health and expect to live for at least another ten years. They have made no previous gifts.

William and Mary's estates are as follows:

	William £	Mary £	Joint £
Private residence			400,000
Cash deposits	75,000	37,500	175,000
Stock market investments	50,000		
PEPs/ISAs and National Savings		25,000	
	125,000	62,500	575,000

They have executed Wills leaving all of their estate to the survivor on the first death.

This means that no inheritance tax (IHT) will arise on the first death but on the second death both estates will be aggregated giving rise to IHT of £185,000 (based on tax year 2007/08).

Clearly there is a substantial potential IHT problem.

59.44   **Financial requirements.** William and Mary wish to use their cash deposits to make an investment that can give them

- an immediate IHT saving

- tax efficient 'income'

- without necessarily having access to capital.

A loan-based trust (see **Case Study 11**) would not be appropriate because of their need for immediate IHT savings.

As they are both in reasonably good health, a discounted gift trust would meet all of their requirements. They have a requirement for income throughout both their lives and, as the bigger cash deposit is held in joint names, a joint settlor investment would be most appropriate.

59.45   **Discounted gift trust solution.**

1.   **The structure**

- William and Mary wish to use £100,000 of their joint cash deposit to invest in a discounted gift trust. They therefore execute a discounted gift trust deed under which they jointly pay £100,000 to the trustees. Both are therefore treated as settlors as to £50,000. Under the trust, two benefits are paid. A fixed capital sum will be paid to the settlor(s) each time they survive to a future date. This is known as the Settlor's Fund and provides the settlors with 'income'. Under the trust they request an 'income' of £5,000 per annum. This 'income' will be paid to them throughout their joint lifetimes and will continue to the survivor after the first death.

- The balance of the benefits (i.e. the balance of the trust fund after payments to the settlors) is held on discretionary trusts for the benefit of William and Mary's family. Default beneficiaries have to be named and this would normally be William and Mary's children failing whom, their estates. The default beneficiaries will only ultimately benefit if the trustees have failed to appoint benefits at the end of 80 years.

- Following the establishment of the trust, the trustees make an application for a single premium investment bond on the lives of the default beneficiaries under the trust (i.e. the children) on a joint lives last survivor basis for a premium of £100,000 and use the gift of £100,000 to pay the premium under the bond. The bond is then issued to the trustees.

- As the settlors are entitled to a capital payment of £5,000 each time they survive to an anniversary date of the trust, the trustees can normally arrange for this to be paid by requesting that the provider pay this directly into the settlors' bank account. As and when the settlors survive to the anniversary dates these payments will then be credited to their account.

2.   **The taxation effects**

- The retention by William and Mary of a regular flow of the right to cash payments each year will be a valuable asset in their estates. This means the loss to their estate for inheritance tax purposes when they establish the trust will be the cash invested less the value of retained rights.

- The present value of the right to future capital payments of £5,000 per annum on their survival to specified future dates will need to be determined. This will need to be actuarially valued based on their age, health and the levels of payments to which William and Mary will be entitled. It will also need to take account of each settlor's possible right to benefit from the full capital payment if they survive the first to die. HMRC have issued guidelines of this calculation. For illustration purposes, let's assume that in William's case the value of his retained rights is £20,000 and for Mary it is £25,000.

- Because William and Mary's retained rights are valued at £20,000 and £25,000 respectively and they each invest £50,000 in the trust, the differences of £30,000 and £25,000 are the gift elements for IHT purposes. This is called a 'discounted gift' because it is less than the amount they are each investing in the trust (which is the actual amount by which each estate reduces on death). The gift is a chargeable lifetime transfer. No IHT will arise if this does not cause the settlor to exceed his nil rate band taking account of chargeable lifetime transfers in the last seven years.

- On each death, no value will be attributable to the deceased's right to the stream of capital payments because this needs to be valued immediately before death.

- Should either William or Mary unfortunately die immediately after setting up the trust, it will mean that the full trust fund will be available for their beneficiaries, yet the deceased will only be treated as having made a gift of £30,000 or £25,000 as appropriate—hence the expression 'discounted gift'. (This is subject to underwriting at inception confirming that this is an accurate discounted gift value so that a return can then be made to HMRC on Forms IHT100, 100a and D34.)

- After William and Mary's survival for seven years, the discounted gift will fall out of account meaning that on the second death, the full value of the fund can be paid free of IHT.

- As the £5,000 'income' payable to William and Mary is a capital payment, it is tax free in their hands. As it is funded by a 5% annual withdrawal from the bond, no income tax arises on these part surrenders for 20 years (although they will need to be taken into account in calculating the chargeable event gain on final encashment).

- On final encashment of the bond, a chargeable event will occur and income tax may be payable. It may be possible to mitigate this by assignment of the bond to an adult beneficiary before encashment.

Ongoing IHT implications for the trust itself

As this is a discretionary trust, this means that special IHT charging rules apply. Under these rules there may be IHT charges

- on every ten-year anniversary of the trust—'the periodic charge'; or

- whenever property leaves the trust (e.g. when capital is advanced to a beneficiary)— 'the exit charge'.

The periodic charge. Periodic charges at ten-yearly intervals may be applied to the value of the assets in the trust (although special rules apply to determine the value of trust property for discounted gift trusts—see below). The rate of inheritance tax charged will be determined based on an assumed transfer by an assumed transferor. This will mean that (provided no other settlements are created on the same day – these are known as related settlements) it will, broadly, be necessary to take account of

- the value of the property in the trust on the ten-year anniversary (the assumed transfer);

- the settlor's cumulative total of transfers immediately before he made the trust (the cumulative total of the assumed transferor) plus any sums on which exit charges were imposed in the ten years immediately preceding the date of the periodic charge.

The maximum liability will be 6% of the value of the trust property (see below) but frequently it will be much less or nil.

In cases where the settlor has not made any chargeable transfers in the seven years before he creates the trust (as in the case of William and Mary), no payments have been made out of the trust in the previous ten years and there has been no added property, there will be no liability provided the value of the trust does not exceed the nil-rate band applicable at the ten-year anniversary. Any excess over the then nil-rate band will suffer IHT at 6%.

For the purposes of calculating the value of the trust fund for the periodic charge, HMRC has confirmed that the present value of the settlor's right to future cash payments at that time (i.e. at the ten-year anniversary) should be deducted from the value of the trust fund (i.e. the investment bond). This means that an amount in respect of the then value of the settlor's rights would need to be deducted from the value of the investment bond.

No IHT liability is therefore likely at the tenth anniversary of William and Mary's Discounted Gift Trust.

If all the trust fund is distributed before the tenth anniversary, no tax charge will arise (see next section). If assets remain in the trust after a distribution (or in the unlikely event of further assets being added to the trust), the trustees will need to seek specialist tax advice.

The exit charge. Exit charges will be based on the value of property leaving the trust.

HMRC has confirmed that no exit charge will arise on payments made to the settlor under a discretionary discounted gift trust because this property is already held absolutely on bare trust for him.

Exit charges within the first ten years will be nil if the value of the initial chargeable transfer going into the trust (i.e. the discounted gift) plus the cumulative total of the settlor's chargeable transfers in the seven years prior to creating the trust plus the value of any added property is below the nil-rate band when the trust is created (this assumes no related settlements were made). If an exit charge does arise, it will increase according to the number of quarters that have expired since the trust was created.

The amount of any exit charge occurring after the first ten years will depend on the rate of tax charged at the previous ten-year anniversary (if any) and the length of time (in quarters) that the property has been in the trust since the last periodic charge. If there is no periodic charge at the immediately preceding ten-year anniversary then there will be no exit charge in the next ten years.

Exit charges are therefore unlikely to arise when the trust assets are ultimately distributed to the beneficiary(ies).

Certain transactions, such as the value of the trust property on ten-year anniversaries and capital payments to the beneficiaries, may also have to be reported to HM Revenue & Customs on Forms IHT100c, 100d and D34 even if no actual tax liability arises.

If there are joint settlors for all IHT purposes, the trust is effectively treated as two separate trusts, each settled by one settlor, based on his/her discounted gift at outset.

59.46 **Tax planning and mitigation.** Assuming William dies eight years after establishing the trust he will have therefore have received £2,500 per annum under the trust on each annual anniversary of the trust.

At that time, assuming growth at a rate of 8% per annum net of charges, the value of the bond would be £131,910. No IHT arises because:

- Although William has now died because he survived his gift by seven years, it has fallen out of account for inheritance tax.

- No value is included in William's estate for his right to future capital payments.

Under the terms of the trust William's £2,500 capital entitlement will now continue to Mary provided she survives to the stated anniversary dates. This means that Mary now receives 'income' of £5,000 in total each time she survives to an appropriate anniversary date. The trustees fund this continuing entitlement by making 5% withdrawals from the bond.

Five years later (thirteen years after the trust was established) Mary dies. The bond, again assuming 8% per annum growth net of charges, is then worth £164,486. No IHT arises because:

- Mary has survived her initial gift by seven years

- No value is included in Mary's taxable estate for her right to future capital payments.

The trustees have a choice over how they distribute the Beneficiaries' Fund. Either:

- They can encash the investment bond and distribute cash to the beneficiaries. This will give rise to a chargeable event giving rise to a chargeable event gain of £129,486 (i.e. (£164,486 + £65,000) less £100,000). If they encash the bond in the same tax year as that in which Mary died, then one-half of the chargeable event gain would be assessed on the trustees and one-half on Mary. If they encash the bond in a tax year after that in which Mary's death occurred, the first £1,000 of chargeable event gains would be taxed at 20% which would mean no tax charge would arise on a UK bond. Gains in excess of this would be taxed at 40% which would give rise to a 20% tax charge on a UK bond.

- Alternatively, the trustees could make an absolute irrevocable appointment of benefits and assign the bond to the adult beneficiary concerned. No chargeable event will occur on the assignment. On a later encashment by that beneficiary, chargeable event gains will be taxed on that beneficiary which may produce a lower income tax charge. No exit charge would arise if there was no IHT charge at the last ten-year anniversary.

Or

- The trustees/beneficiaries could, of course, decide to keep the bond running.

The trust has conferred the following benefits:

- An immediate reduction in the IHT liability.

- A further reduction in the IHT liability after survival for seven years.

- A tax efficient 'income' stream in the form of regular capital payments.

- Flexibility via the trustees as to who ultimately benefits under the trust.

59.47   **CASE STUDY 14 — AMELIE AND CAROL**

Amelie and Carol have lived together in the village and conducted a same sex relationship for many years. They have decided with the introduction of the *Civil Partnership Act 2004* (CPA 2004), which received Royal Assent on 18 November 2004, to have their relationship legally recognised following a registration process (without the requirement for an exchange of vows) and will then acquire legal rights similar to heterosexual married couples. See 59.48 below for the formal procedure required. This will be after the Act is implemented towards the end of 2005 and civil partners have completed the registration process. Once the civil partners have their registration certificate they will be treated similarly to married couples with regard to both legal and taxation matters including IHT. [*FA 2005, s 103; The Tax and Civil Partnership Regulations 2005, SI 2005/3229*].

Amelie, who is a French domiciliary (see also **Case Study 7** above for the effects of French domicile), lives with Carol in the town in her detached property which is valued at £450,000 excluding the chattels and other effects in the property which are valued at £25,000. Amelie has a small property in Salisbury valued at £100,000 which she occupied many years ago but now rents out at an annual rental of £9,000 per annum. Her personal furniture and effects are in storage and are valued at £15,000. Neither has any life insurance in favour of the other and both work at Coleman's Pies Ltd and have specifically named each other as sole beneficiary of the company pension payment (amounting to four times their current salary of £24,000 each) should either die. See 59.49 below. Carol has savings in gilts amounting to £47,500.

59.48   **Compliance undertakings.** Amelie and Carol will apply for a registration certificate (see below) under the *Civil Partnership Act 2004, s 2* and once they have this they will be treated for the purposes of all taxes in the same way as a married couple. The *CPA 2004* creates a new legal status of civil partner in respect of their relationship and applies from 5 December 2005 when the *CPA 2004* came into force. One effect of this is that where one civil partner has been living in another's property and/or being supported then they can make application under *Inheritance (Provision for Family and Dependants) Act 1975* for reasonable financial provision. [*CPA 2004, Sch 4 paras 15–27*]. See paragraph 24.5 of the Chancery Guide at http://www.hmcourts-service.gov.uk/cms/publications.htm. For tax purposes civil partners will be treated the same way as married couples and tax charges and anti-avoidance rules apply in equal measures. For IHT purposes transfers between the two of them will be exempt from tax during lifetime and on death. The same treatment applies for CGT purposes so that in the situation where two properties are owned by them one will have to be treated as the main residence as with married couples. An election should be made within two years of the certificate being issued. [*TCGA 1992, s 222(5)(6)*]. Where only one property is owned, whether jointly or solely by one partner or both, then it will be treated as the main residence for principal private residence exemption purposes. Carol wishes Amelie to share the house as a joint tenant/tenant in common and there are both CGT and IHT implications of this action. See below. As with married couples, Amelie and Carol will be treated as 'connected persons' as will the close relatives of each other. In addition, if one partner settles property on trust such that the other partner can benefit from the settlement then the settlor is liable to CGT by reference to capital gains realised by the trustees. The anti-avoidance provisions relating to settlements will also apply so that if either partner transfers assets into trust so that the other benefits by receiving income that is taxed at their marginal rate, being less than the settlor's marginal rate, then the anti-avoidance rules will apply. [*ICTA 1988, s 660A* (now *ITTOIA 2005, ss 622, 624, 625, 626, 627, Sch 2 para 132(1)(3)*)].

Further anti-avoidance provisions apply so that the transfer of assets abroad by one party in favour of the other will be caught. [*ITA 2007, Ch 2 formerly ICTA 1988, ss 739–746*]. This prevents individuals avoiding income tax by the transfer of assets abroad so that the non-resident or non-UK domiciliary benefits in that income. Where this is so the income tax charge will apply to the civil partner making the transfer where by associated operations or otherwise the transfer is deemed to be avoidance. If, however, Amelie has income arising outside the UK that is not taxed under *ITA 2007, s 737* then by concession this will not be taxed on Carol.

Amelie and Carol may apply to the Registrar of Births, Deaths and Marriages in Salisbury to advise the Registrar of their 'Notice of Intent of Partnership'. Under the formal procedure rules they will both have to attend the Register Office with proof of identity e.g. passport and also a utility bill that shows their address and names printed on the bill. The earliest that they could have registered a formal partnership within *CPA 2004* was fifteen clear days after the Act coming into force on 5 December 2005 i.e. 21 December 2005, because their names had to be shown on the Registry Office notice board for that period. It will cost Amelie and Carol £30 each to give notice and an 'Authority of Intent' is then issued after fifteen clear days. Slightly different formalities will apply in varying parts of the UK. The fact that Amelie is French will not cause any delays in the registration as she is a national of an EU member i.e. France. Under *CPA 2004, ss 213, 214, Sch 20* there are provisions for an overseas relationship to be treated as a civil partnership provided it is either a 'specified relationship' or meets certain other conditions but in this particular case Amelie and Carol's relationship is likely to be legally recognised in any case. See *Wilkinson v Kitzineger and Another [2006] TLR 21* August 2006. If Amelie had registered a *Pacte Civile de Solidarité* in France under Law 99–944 with another partner then it may be worth effecting a dissolution of that partnership because as from 5 December 2005 only a formal dissolution would be valid in the UK under the new law. In other cases pertaining to a national of a non-EU member there may be a delay in the registration procedure whilst checks are made.

59.49   **Tax planning and mitigation.** Whilst the Act does not contain provisions regarding taxation further details with regard to the tax provisions of civil partnerships will be published in due course by way of regulation so that civil partnerships are treated the same way as married couples for tax purposes. [*FA 2005, s 103*]. Therefore once the certificate (or 'civil partnership document' under *CPA 2004, s 2(1)*) is received Amelie and Carol may wish to equalise their estates for the purposes of IHT. The transfer of part of Carol's property into Amelie's ownership will be exempt similarly to *IHTA 1984, s 18*. See also 60 TAX CASES regarding *Burden & Burden v United Kingdom*. A *joint tenancy* may be appropriate in order that on the death of either, their share automatically transfers to the survivor whereas a *tenancy in common* will result in the share becoming part of the deceased's estate so that it may be left to each party's other beneficiaries. Under the provisions of *CPA 2004, Sch 4 para 13* amendment is made to *Intestates' Estate Act 1952, s 5, Sch 2* to ensure that the surviving civil partner acquires the home shared with the deceased in priority to other family members of the deceased. As the house was originally Carol's this may be ideal if she is the survivor whereas a *tenancy in common* would result in the share becoming part of the Amelie's estate where Carol predeceases her so that it might be left to Amelie's beneficiaries in France although, under *Trusts of Land and Appointment* *of Trustees Act 1996, s 5, Sch 2*, there would no longer a duty to sell the property and the trustees can postpone the sale unless there is a reason to sell such as bankruptcy. Also, as Amelie has been contributing financially to the property and these funds may have been used to improve the property, Amelie could claim an increased share of that property as a result of her contributions under *CPA 2004, s 65*. This right may be excluded by express agreement and this is something Amelie and Carol will have to discuss with their solicitor when preparing their new wills. Any transfer by one civil partner to the other of a share in the property will be exempt from SDLT. Their wills will need to be redrafted to take into account the revocation of existing wills within *CPA 2004, Sch 4 para 2* and use made of the subsequent tax planning opportunities afforded by the new legislation. On equalising their estates Amelie's assets will be valued at £340,000 (previously £115,000) and Carol's estate £297,500 (previously £522,500) giving a saving in IHT using 2007 rates (see table at 41.1 2007.A1) of £73,000. Amelie may wish to transfer some of her income from property to Carol in recompense and this will be an exempt transfer under *IHTA 1984, s 18*.

As Amelie and Carol would each like the other to benefit from their estate on their death their wills can be drawn up to reflect this mutual desire. However, whilst each would wish the other to wholly benefit on their respective deaths, they would not wish the other's family to benefit in a case where *commorientes* was to apply because of, say, a disaster (see Example below) where both died together but in circumstances where it was not known which one of them died first. See also *CPA 2004, Sch 4 para 5* which states that the surviving civil partner takes priority. Under current rules of the *Law of Property Act 1925, s 184* it is provided that where two persons have died in circumstances where it is uncertain which of them survived the other, for all purposes affecting the title to property, the younger is deemed to have survived the elder. If there is medical evidence which states that one person survived the other, even if only for a few minutes, the section does not apply. The deaths need to have occurred by reason of a common disaster, see *Hickman v Peacey [1945] 2 All ER 215*. The *Law of Property Act 1925, s 184* may be overridden by the terms of either of the deceased's wills so that a clause inserted into the wills making provision for the disposition of the estates in the event of the deaths simultaneously will generally be effective.

Under the provisions in the *FA 2006, Sch 20* where the spouse or civil partner of the transferor has the first interest in possession, under a trust created during the transferor's lifetime after 21 March 2006, exemption from IHT will be available under *IHTA 1984, s 18*. One point that arises is that original trust deeds excluding any benefit for the settlor or the spouse may not have included any reference to civil partner. It is probable therefore that any newly drafted trust deeds should refer to civil partners and existing deeds be appropriately amended. See *Unmarried Settlor v IRC [2003] STC SCD 274 Sp C 345*. Where an interest in possession for a surviving spouse or civil partner is created by will or on intestacy there will be exemption under *IHTA 1984, s 18* for the property subject to the interest if the interest is an 'immediate post-death interest'. See 43.1 SETTLEMENTS WITH INTERESTS IN POSSESSION. This is one which can only come to an end in favour of absolute interests, or interests which vest absolutely at 18 for children of the testator or intestate, e.g. where residue is left to the surviving spouse or civil partner for life with remainder to the deceased's children in equal shares absolutely although in Amelie and Carol's particular circumstances this is not the case. An interest in possession for a surviving spouse or civil partner which is subject to an overriding power of appointment, or followed by a trust for children subject to attaining the age of 25, will not qualify for exemption from IHT under *IHTA 1984, s 18*.

In the case of married couples (and now civil partnerships) the *Law Reform (Succession) Act 1995, s 1* requires that a spouse must survive the other by 28 days (applying from 1 January 1996) before acquiring a beneficial interest.

> I appoint ....provided she survives me by 28 days.

For the purposes of establishing if there has been a transfer on death, where it cannot be known which of two or more persons died first they are assumed to have died at the same instant (i.e. the rule in the *Law of Property Act 1925, s 184* that the elder is deemed to have died first does not apply for these purposes). [*IHTA 1984, s 4(2)*]. In the case of married couples (and now civil partnerships) this may require a survivorship condition to be imposed in their respective wills but that the survivorship condition should not apply in the will of the elder in the situation where there are simultaneous deaths of Amelie and Carol. The survivor condition inserted into Carol's will, as the elder, would be worded along the lines of

> '... if Amelie [my civil partner] survives me by 30 days, or she is deemed to survive me under *section 184* under the *Law of Property Act 1925*, I give the residue of my estate to her absolutely.'

This would ensure that on the event of simultaneous deaths that Carol's estate would pass to Amelie and then out of her estate immediately to the default beneficiaries i.e. Carol's family. In cases where the above condition is not written into the will it may be possible to cover this simultaneous death situation by a deed of variation but Amelie's personal representatives may not of course agree to this and therefore the survivor condition in Carol's will would be preferable. However, if Carol did not particularly wish to benefit her family or omitted to include a survivor condition then the result may be as follows:

Example

If Amelie and Carol died in the same avalanche in a skiing accident, it being not known who died first, any property bequeathed by Carol, the elder of the two, passes to Amelie's estate (since Carol is deemed under the rule quoted above to have died first) and then to the beneficiaries under Amelie's will, but inheritance tax is chargeable only on the transfer of the property to Amelie's estate and not again on the transfer of it to the beneficiaries of Amelie's estate.

In the case of spouses/civil partners who die in *commorientes* circumstances then the situation is complicated further by the potential effect of the anomaly regarding inter-spouse exemption under *IHTA 1984, s 18* which one would assume will apply to civil partnership situations although this is not presently clear due to the lack of guidance; as there is an exempt transfer on the death under *section 18(1)* then the transfer to the younger spouse/partner is not a chargeable transfer. However, the younger of the spouses is deemed to have inherited the elder spouse's estate under the *Law of Property Act 1925, s 184* but for the purposes of IHT under *IHTA 1984, s 4(2)* eliminates mutual gifts between individuals in such circumstances and there is no transfer of value to the younger spouse on which inheritance tax can be charged. There is a view therefore that the elder's estate escapes inheritance tax completely and therefore a survivorship condition, which is normally desirable, is deliberately excluded in the event of the spouses dying simultaneously. This view though is not universally accepted (see British Tax Review 1995 p 390). See IHTM12197 for text and a useful example, which supports the view above.

As Amelie is domiciled in France and the *Law of Property Act 1925, s 184* does not apply in cases of uncertainty of persons dying domiciled outside England and Wales. Therefore in the case of Amelie's death evidence of the law of survivorship of the place of domicile i.e. France (see Rule 30(1)(b) below) would be required. Such evidence will not be necessary where the court of the place of domicile has entrusted someone with the administration of the estate (Rule 30(1)(a) below) so that the place of domicile i.e. France is satisfied on the point of survivorship before granting representation. The Non-Contentious Probate Rules 1987, Rule 30 provides:

59.49   Working Case Study

---

(1)   Subject to paragraph (3) below where the deceased died domiciled outside England and Wales a district judge or registrar may order that a grant, limited in such way as the district judge or registrar may direct, do issue to any of the following persons:

    (a)   to the person entrusted with the administration of the estate by the court having jurisdiction at the place where the deceased died domiciled; or

    (b)   where there is no person so entrusted, to the person beneficially entitled to the estate by the law of the place where the deceased died domiciled or, if there is more than one person so entitled, to such of them as the district judge or registrar may direct; or

    (c)   if in the opinion of the district judge or registrar the circumstances so require, to such person as the district judge or registrar may direct.

(2)   A grant may be made under paragraph (1)(a) or (b) above may be issued jointly with such person as the district judge or registrar may direct if the grant is required to be made to not less than two administrators.

(3)   Without any order under paragraph (1) above:

    (a)   probate of any will which is admissible to proof may be granted

        (i)   if the will is in English or Welsh language, to the executor named therein; or

        (ii)   if the will describes the duties of a named person in terms sufficient to constitute him executor according to the tenor of the will, to that person, and

    (b)   where the whole or substantially the whole of the estate in England and Wales consists of immovable property, a grant in respect of the whole estate may be made in accordance with the law which would have been applicable if the deceased died domiciled in England and Wales.

The current pension tax legislation is to be amended so that references to civil partners will be included. This will enable Carol and Amelie to ensure that any pension rights written in favour of the other on death will allowed so that each may benefit on the death of the other. However, in the case of the pension scheme at Coleman's Pies Ltd, the Letter of Wishes to the scheme administrators has already been completed to ensure that any proceeds are paid out at the discretion of the scheme trustees. This will ensure that any lump sum payable on death of four times salary i.e. £96,000 will not form part of either of their estates for the purposes of IHT:

For the guidance of the Management Committee, I nominate the person(s) named above to be the beneficiary/beneficiaries in the event of my death. I request the Management Committee to consider paying a pension and/or cash sum to the above person(s). I understand that my wishes cannot be binding on the Management Committee but that they will be considered when benefits become payable..............

Please read these notes carefully before completing the form.

On your death, certain benefits will be paid from the .... Pension Scheme.

So that these benefits can be paid free of inheritance tax, the Rules of the .... Pension Scheme give the Management Committee absolute discretion regarding the people to whom pensions and cash are paid.

In reaching its decision, however, the Management Committee will take account of your wishes and you can complete this nomination form with details of the person(s) you would like to receive a benefit on your death.

Where a life insurance policy is expressed to be for the benefit of the spouse, civil partner or children under the *Married Women's Property Act 1882*, a trust is created in their favour so that the person whose life is assured never has an interest in the policy and the proceeds will not be included in his estate on his death. [*Married Women's Property Act 1882, s 11 as amended by Civil Partnership Act 2004, s 70*]. Money payable under a policy in this particular category will not form part of the estate of the deceased but will apply to a policy on the civil partner's life whether this is for the benefit of their partner and/or either of their children.

This chapter includes summaries not only of IHT/CTT cases but also a number of other, mainly estate duty and anti-avoidance, where the principles established are relevant to IHT. Some of the legislation interpreted in the earlier cases has been amended, repealed or replaced. Nevertheless, the cumulative nature of IHT means that knowledge of the law in earlier years will continue to be necessary for some time to come. Where the CIR (or, in Scotland, the Lord Advocate) are a party, the case is listed under the name of the other party only. Judicial review cases are listed under the name of the applicant and the person who is the subject of the review but again excluding the CIR etc.

Legislative references marked with an asterisk (*) are to legislation which has replaced, or is substantially similar to, that involved in the case summarised.

A Beneficiary v CIR

Japanese citizen avoiding liability to taxation.

A woman (B) was born in the UK, of an English father and a Japanese mother. In 1991/92 B's maternal grandfather (G), who was a Japanese citizen, transferred a large sum of money to the UK for the purpose of benefiting B. On the advice of a solicitor, and in order to avoid liability to IHT, G subsequently (in June 1992) established a discretionary settlement in Jersey and transferred the money from the UK to this settlement. G informed the trustee of the settlement that he wished B to be the principal beneficiary (and did not want the money to be used to benefit B's mother). G died in Japan two years later. The Revenue issued a 1992/93 assessment charging tax on B under *Sec 740*. B appealed, contending that *Sec 740* did not apply, since 'the purpose of avoiding liability to taxation was not the purpose or one of the purposes for which the transfer or associated operations ... were effected'. The Special Commissioners accepted this contention and allowed B's appeal. Applying *dicta* of Lord Templeman in *New Zealand Commr of Inland Revenue v Challenge Corporation Ltd*, G's motives in transferring the money from the UK to Jersey were tax mitigation rather than tax avoidance. The Commissioners observed that, by virtue of *IHTA, s 157(1)*, if G had arranged for the funds to be left in the UK in the form of foreign currency, no IHT would have been payable. By virtue of *IHTA, s 6(1)*, property situated outside the UK was excluded property if the person beneficially entitled to it was domiciled outside the UK. The Commissioners held that there was no 'difference in principle between an action designed to take advantage of the provisions of *s 157* as against actions designed to take advantage of the provisions of *s 6*'. On the evidence, the Commissioners found that, although UK tax was 'a consideration of (G's) advisers ... the tax implications of siting the trust in Jersey were a matter of indifference to (G)'. *[1999] STC SCD 134 Sp C 190.*

AC Smith v HMRC (and related appeals)

IHTA 1984, s 263—annuity purchased in conjunction with life policy.

In October 1996 a married couple took out three life assurance policies coupled with three annuities, and executed three 'declarations of trust' in favour of their children. The wife died in 2000 and the husband died in February 2003. HMRC issued notices of determination that the vesting of the life assurance policies under the terms of the 'declarations of trust' was a transfer of value under *IHTA 1984, s 263*. The executors and the beneficiaries appealed, contending that the purchase of the annuities and the making of the life assurance policies should not be treated as 'associated operations' by virtue of Revenue Statement of Practice E4. The Special Commissioner rejected this contention and dismissed the appeals, observing that Statement of Practice E4 only applied where a policy 'was issued on full medical evidence', which was not the case here. The questionnaire, which had been issued by the life assurance company, 'would not give ... a complete picture of the assured's health at the time of underwriting'. *[2007] Sp C 605.*

Alexander v CIR

Valuation of leasehold flat.

In March 1983 A acquired a leasehold flat for £35,400 under the provisions of the *Housing Act 1980*. The market value of the lease was taken to be £60,000, and the lease contained a covenant requiring A to pay the landlords a percentage of the difference of £24,600 if she should dispose of the flat within five years. A died in 1984. However, her death did not constitute a disposal under the terms of the covenant. The Revenue issued a determination on the basis that the value of the lease for CTT purposes was £52,000 (after taking into account the potential obligation to make a payment to the landlords if the flat were sold before March 1988). A's executor appealed to the Lands Tribunal, which determined the open market value of the lease at A's death as £63,000, and held that it had no jurisdiction to allow any deduction in respect of the potential obligation to make a payment to the landlords, considering that this was not a question of land valuation. The Revenue appealed to the CA, which remitted the case to the Tribunal. The liability to make a repayment of the discount allowed on the purchase of the flat was an encumbrance on the property and therefore a question as to the value of land, to be decided by the Tribunal. Applying the principles in *CIR v Crossman*, the Tribunal was required to determine the amount which, on a hypothetical sale, a purchaser would be willing to pay to acquire the lease subject to the obligation which would fall on the hypothetical purchaser to make a repayment to the landlords in the event of a disposal, but on the basis that the hypothetical sale did not itself give rise to such a disposal. *CA 1991, 64 TC 59; [1991] STC 112; [1991] 26 EG 141.*

Alford v Department for the Environment, Food and Rural Affairs

Restoring derelict farmland to previous levels of agricultural production did not involve using the land for intensive agricultural purposes—Environmental Impact Assessment (Uncultivated Land and Semi-Natural Areas)(England)Regs 2001.

The defendant owned land at Vixen Tor Farm, Merrivale, Dartmoor and undertook projects that involved the application of farmyard manures and calcified seaweed to four fields that had been left in their natural state for many years. The boundary walls and fences had fallen into disrepair and livestock from common land had relatively unrestricted access to the farm. On 10 June 2004 the defendant faced four charges of carrying out projects on land she owned without obtaining a screening decision or the grant of consent by the Secretary of State for the Environment, Food and Rural Affairs contrary to *Environmental Impact Assessment (Uncultivated Land and Semi-Natural Areas)(England) Regs 2001, SI 2001/3966, s 19.* In the case stated the deputy district judge found that from 1966 to 2002 the tenant farmers appeared to have abandoned the farm. There was no evidence of cultivation and nothing had been applied to the fields in terms of fertilizer or additives and it was kept as grazing moorland. The land was kept in its natural state. The land was then taken in hand by the defendant and the manures and seaweed applied to make the grass palatable for the cattle. Also boundary walls and fences were repaired to make the fields stock proof resulting in the charge that the unauthorised increase in productivity, or the intensification of the use to which the land had been put fell foul of the environmental protection law such that under *Environmental Impact Assessment (Uncultivated Land and Semi-Natural Areas)(England) Regs 2001, SI 2001/3966, s 2(1)* the projects constituted a) the execution of construction works or other installations or schemes; or b) other interventions in the natural surroundings and landscape, involving the use of uncultivated land or semi-natural areas for intensive agricultural purposes.

The question for the High Court was what was meant by the phrase 'intensive agricultural purposes' in regulation 2(1)? The circumstances of this case were such that the projects were not capable of being described as an intervention for intensive agricultural purposes, and although EEC Council Directive (97/11/EC) (OJ 1997 No L73/5) had a wide scope and a broad purpose, the framers of the legislation did not intend it to catch a project that was concerned only to bring land back to a normal level of agricultural productivity. The project did not amount to an intervention in the natural surroundings and landscape involving the use of uncultivated land or semi-natural areas for intensive agricultural purposes. *[2005] TLR 30 May 2005.*

Anand v CIR

Beneficial ownership of bank accounts

An individual (J), who had been born in India, died in 1988 domiciled and resident in Iran, with substantial funds in a number of UK bank accounts. The Revenue issued a notice of determination charging IHT on the basis that J was the beneficial owner of these funds. His executors appealed, contending that much of the money belonged to a family partnership which had been established in Iran, and that the partnership had transferred the money to London because of the political situation in Iran. The Special Commissioner accepted the executors' evidence and allowed their appeal, holding that the funds were 'partnership funds in origin and remained such. Placing them in an account in the deceased's sole name did not make him the sole beneficial owner.' J had been a 'trustee or nominee' of the funds, which 'belonged beneficially to the deceased and his three sons in equal shares'. *[1997] STC SCD 58 Sp C 107* .

Anderson (Anderson's Executor) v CIR

Scotsman resident in England at time of death—whether English domicile acquired.

An individual (A) was born in Scotland in 1909. He lived in Scotland until 1974, when he sold his property in Scotland and moved to Cornwall. A few months after moving, he suffered a serious heart attack. He died in 1982, having lived in Cornwall for eight years and leaving his widow as his executrix. Following her subsequent death, the Revenue considered that A had acquired a domicile of choice in England. Her executor (who was A's son) appealed contending that A had retained his domicile of origin in Scotland. The Special Commissioner accepted this contention and allowed the appeal, observing that there was 'an inherent improbability in a 65-year old Scotsman, who lived in Scotland all his life, abandoning his roots and intending to acquire a domicile of choice in England'. There was 'nothing inconsistent with an elderly Scottish gentleman acquiring a residence in the south of England at his retirement without having any intention to acquire a domicile in England'. It was significant that A had no English will or English Solicitor and the scattering of his ashes near his former home in Scotland were inferences that he had not intended his final resting place to be Cornwall. *[1998] STC SCD 43 Sp C 147.*

Arkwright and Another (Williams' Personal Representatives) v CIR

Related property under IHTA 1984, s 161.

A married couple owned a freehold property as tenants in common. The husband (W) died in 2001. By his will, he gave his widow a life interest in his 50% share of the property, with the remainder to his daughters. In January 2002 his widow and the daughters executed a deed of variation so that W's interest in the property vested in his daughters. The Inland Revenue issued a notice of determination that IHT was due on £275,000 (being 50% of the agreed open market value of the property). W's daughters (as his personal representatives) appealed to the Special Commissioners, contending that W's interest should be valued at less than 50% of the vacant possession value, because his widow had the right to occupy the property and not have it sold without her consent. The Commissioner accepted this contention and allowed the appeal in principle, holding that the value of W's interest should be determined in accordance with *IHTA 1984, s 161(3)*, and making various observations concerning the effect of *s 161(3)*. The Inland Revenue appealed to the Ch D, contending that the Commissioner had exceeded her jurisdiction and that the case should be referred to the Lands Tribunal. The Ch D accepted this contention. Gloster J held that 'the Special Commissioner was clearly entitled to conclude that, because *section 161(4)* did not apply, the value of the deceased's interest in the property was not inevitably a mathematical one-half of the vacant possession value'. However, she had exceeded her authority in purporting to determine 'that, as matter of fact, the value of his interest was indeed less than a mathematical one-half of the vacant possession value. That was properly an issue that should have been referred to the Lands Tribunal for determination by it.' *Ch D [2004] STC 1323.*

Arnander, Lloyd & Villiers (McKenna's Executors) v HMRC

Farmhouse and adjoining buildings—whether qualified for agricultural property relief—not main dwelling from which the agricultural operations over the land were conducted and managed.

A married couple had owned a small country estate comprising a large house with six acres of gardens and some domestic outbuildings, and 187 acres of land, most of which was farmland. They both died in 2003. HMRC issued notices of determination charging IHT on the house (while accepting that 110 acres of land and a farm outbuilding qualified for agricultural property relief). The executors appealed, contending that the house was a farmhouse which also qualified for agricultural property relief, as did 11 more outbuildings on the estate. The Special Commissioner reviewed the evidence in detail and held that three of the outbuildings qualified for relief but that the main house and eight of the outbuildings did not. The Commissioner observed that the farming activities were carried on by contractors who were managed by a land agent in a nearby town. The house which the couple lived in was not 'the main dwelling from which the agricultural operations over the land were conducted and managed'. [2006] STC SCD 800 Sp C 565.

Aspden v Hildesley

Transfer of assets under Court Order on divorce.

The taxpayer and his wife had jointly owned certain property, not the private residence of either. They had been separated since 1970 and were divorced by decree nisi on 12 February 1976. The Court Order (by consent) provided, *inter alia*, for the taxpayer's half share of the property to be transferred to his wife, while she undertook to give an irrevocable order to her personal representatives that, should she die before 10 December 1984 and before her husband, a sum equal to half the equity in the property was to be paid to him out of her estate. The taxpayer was assessed on the footing that he had disposed of his share in the property on 12 February 1976, and that by virtue of *CGTA 1979, s 19(3)(a)** and *TCGA 1992, ss 18, 286** the consideration was to be taken as the market value. The Ch D upheld the assessment, reversing the decision of the Commissioners. On the facts, the taxpayer's interest in the property was transferred at the time of the decree nisi, the consent order being an unconditional contract for the transfer. As the decree was not then absolute, the parties were still married and *CGTA 1979, s 19(3)(a)** applied by virtue of *TCGA 1992, ss 18(2)*, 286(2)**. (Note. *CGTA 1979, s 19(3)* was repealed by *FA 1981* and replaced by what is now *TCGA 1992, s 17.) Ch D 1981, 55 TC 609; [1982] STC 206; [1982] 1 WLR 264; [1982] 2 All ER 53.*

A-G v Boden and Another

Valuation—partnership goodwill—whether transfer for full consideration.

A father in partnership with his two sons was not required to devote as much time to the business as his sons. On his death his share accrued equally to his sons, subject to their paying his estate the value of his share exclusive of any amount of goodwill. The obligations of the sons under the partnership deed were held to constitute full consideration for the deceased's share of the goodwill. *KB 1911, [1912] 1 KB 539; 105 LT 247.*

A-G v Farrell

Gifts with reservation—settlements.

A reservation of benefit arises where a settlor is included as a potential beneficiary under a discretionary trust. *[1931] 1 KB 81.*

A-G v Heywood

Gifts with reservation—settlements.

A reservation of benefit arises where a settlor is included as a potential beneficiary under a discretionary trust. *QB, [1887] 19 QBD 326.*

A-G v Ralli

Valuation—partnership reserves—whether transfer for full consideration.

The deceased was a partner in a partnership of bankers which held large reserves for the partnership business. The partnership deed provided that each partner's share in the reserves accrued on his death or retirement to the remaining partners. The court held that ED was not payable on the deceased's interest in the reserves. There was no gift but merely an ordinary commercial transaction for full consideration. *KB 1936, 15 ATC 523.*

A-G v Seccombe

Gifts with reservation—exclusion of donor from enjoyment.

The KB held that a donor may remain a guest in a house he has given away without tax being attracted provided that there was no agreement to this effect and it was a *bona fide* gift. *KB, [1911] 2 KB 688.* (Note. This proposition is, however, open to question following *Chick v Commrs of Stamp Duties of New South Wales PC, [1958] AC 435; [1958] 2 All ER 623; [1958] 3 WLR 93.*)

A-G v Worrall

Gifts with reservation—exclusion of donor from any benefit.

A collated annuity to the donor secured by personal covenant was held to be a benefit. *QB [1895], 1 QB 99; [1891–94] All ER 861.*

Baird's Executors v CIR

Valuation—renunciation of agricultural tenancy—valuation of interest transferred.

A father (B) and son were joint tenants of a farm in Scotland. In September 1977 the son was killed in a car accident. In December 1977 B renounced his tenancy in favour of his daughter-in-law and his grandson. This transfer was accepted by the landlord, and thereafter the land was farmed by the transferees in partnership with B until his death in 1985. The Revenue took the view that B had made a chargeable transfer of the tenancy, the value of which the District Valuer determined as £138,000 (being 25% of the agreed vacant possession value). B's executors appealed, contending that the tenancy had no value because it could not have been transferred without the landlord's consent, and that B's interest was in only a half share of the tenancy. The Lands Tribunal allowed the appeal in part, holding that the Revenue's valuation of the tenancy was correct, but that the chargeable transfer was of a half share in the tenancy, the half share previously held by B's son having passed to his widow rather than reverting to B. The Tribunal therefore determined that the amount of the chargeable transfer was £69,000. *Lands Tribunal 1990, SVC 188.*

Barclays Bank Trust Co Ltd v IRC

Business property relief regarding whether cash held by a company an excepted asset. IHTA 1984, s 112.

A married woman (W) died in 1990. Her estate included a 50% shareholding in a family company, which held cash of about £450,000 at her death. The Revenue issued a notice of determination, accepting in principle that the shares qualified for business property relief, but computed on the basis that the company only required cash of some £150,000 for the purposes of its business, and that the balance of £300,000 was an 'excepted asset', within *IHTA, s 112(2),* and did not qualify for relief. W's executor appealed, contending that the company had held the cash 'as a contingency measure' in case 'an appropriate business opportunity should arise', so that the cash was 'required ... for future use', within *IHTA, s 112(2)(b)*. The Special Commissioner rejected this contention and dismissed the appeal, holding on the evidence that the £300,000 was not 'required'. The Commissioner held that, for the purposes of *s 112*, 'required' did not include 'the possibility that the money might be required should an opportunity arise to make use of the money in two, three or seven years' time ...' The word "required" implies some imperative that the money will fall to be used upon a given project or for some palpable business purpose'. [*1998] STC SCD 125 Sp C 22*.

Barrett (Barrett's Personal Representatives) v HMRC

Lands Tribunal decision—15% discount for joint ownership

An individual (B) was joint owner of a semi-detached house built in the 1930s. He died in 2002. HMRC determined the value of his interest in the property as £144,500. His personal representative (who was the other joint-owner) appealed, contending that the house should be valued at £288,000, and that with a 15% discount for the joint ownership, the value of B's interest should be taken as £122,400. The Lands Tribunal reviewed the evidence in detail and held that the house should be valued at £315,000, so that with a 15% discount for joint ownership, the value of B's interest was £133,875. Lands Tribunal 23 November 2005 unreported.

Battle and Another v CIR

Valuation—value of unquoted shares—minority shareholding.

An ED avoidance case is of interest because the principles to be considered in establishing the discount on the asset value of a minority shareholding were discussed. The precise amount of the discount was not material to the outcome of the case but, on the facts, the stockbroker giving evidence for the Revenue suggested the discount should be in the region of 10 to 15% while the Capital Taxes Office [now HMRC Inheritance Tax] broadly concurred with a figure of 15%. Although the chief valuation witness for the taxpayers argued that other considerations should be taken into account in this particular case, he did, in general, accept the valuation principles indicated by the Revenue witnesses. *Ch D 1979, [1980] STC 86.*

Baylis v Gregory

Avoidance schemes—the Ramsay principle.

The managing director of a company (PGI) controlled the company through his own and trustee shareholdings. Another company, C, entered into negotiations to acquire PGI, and the taxpayer and his associates set up a Manx company to exchange their shares in PGI with shares in the Manx company. However, C ended the negotiations. Nevertheless the share exchange was proceeded with and completed in March 1974. No further steps were taken to sell PGI until May 1975 when a third company, H, became interested in it. Eventually, the Manx company sold the PGI shares to H. The Special Commissioners allowed the taxpayer's appeals and their decision was upheld by the Ch D, the CA, and the HL. The transactions were not a 'pre-ordained series of transactions'. *HL 1988, 62 TC 1; [1988] STC 476; [1988] 3 WLR 423; [1988] 3 All ER 495.*

Beckman v IRC

Relevant business property—IHTA, s 105(1).

A woman (H) and her daughter (B) had carried on business in partnership for many years until H retired in 1993. B then continued the business as sole proprietor. H died in 1997, having retained an interest in the business through her capital account. The Revenue issued a notice of determination charging IHT on the amounts owed by B to H at H's death. B appealed, contending that the amounts in question were 'relevant business property' within *IHTA, s 105(1)*. The Special Commissioner rejected this contention and dismissed the appeal. For the purposes of *IHTA, s 105*, H's interest in the business 'ceased when she retired from the partnership'. Following H's retirement from the business, her rights 'were simply those of a creditor of the business'. *[2000] STC SCD 59 Sp C 226*.

Begg-McBrearty v Stilwell (Trustee of the GE Coke Settlement)

Exercise of power of appointment in favour of grandchildren of settlor—whether grandchildren acquiring an interest in possession at age of 18 or 21.

In 1975 the trustees of a settlement made in 1959 exercised their power of appointment in favour of the settlor's three grandchildren, and thereafter held the trust fund contingently for the grandchildren contingently on their reaching the age of 21. The eldest grandchild became 21 in 1990, and thus became absolutely entitled to a one-third share of the settled property. The Revenue issued a 1990/91 assessment on one of the trustees, charging CGT on the deemed disposal to the grandchild in accordance with *TCGA 1992, s 71**. The trustee appealed, contending that the gain should be held over by virtue of an election made under *TCGA 1992, s 260(2)(d)**. The Ch D rejected this contention and upheld the assessment. The disposal could not be held over under *TCGA 1992, s 260(2)(d)** because the grandchild had become entitled to an interest in possession in her share of the settled property in 1987, when she reached the age of 18. Before the exercise of the power of appointment, the grandchild had had only a revocable interest in the trust property. Her relevant interest arose from the power of appointment. Since this had been exercised in 1975, it fell within the provisions of *Family Law Reform Act 1969* (which had reduced the age of majority to 18 with effect from 1 January 1970), even though the original settlement had been made before the date on which that act took effect. *Ch D 1996, TL 3473; [1996] STC 413; [1996] 1 WLR 951; [1996] 4 All ER 205*.

Benham's Will Trusts re (Lockhart v Harker & Others)

IHTA 1984, s 41—allocation of exemptions.

A testatrix bequeathed her residuary estate between some charitable beneficiaries and some non-charitable beneficiaries. The executor issued an originating summons seeking the opinion of the court as to whether the non-charitable beneficiaries should receive their shares subject to IHT (as the charitable beneficiaries contended) or whether their shares should be grossed up (as the non-charitable beneficiaries themselves contended). The Ch D upheld the contention of the non-charitable beneficiaries, holding that the plain intention of the executrix was that each beneficiary in the list should receive the same amount, that this was not inconsistent with the provisions of *IHTA 1984, s 41*, and accordingly that the non-charitable beneficiaries should receive grossed-up shares. *Ch D 1994, [1995] STC 210*.

Bennett & Others v CIR

Gifts to sons—whether exempt from IHT as 'normal expenditure of the transferor'—IHTA 1984, s 21.

Under a will, the shares in a family company were held on trust, with the income from the shares and the residuary estate being paid to the testator's widow for her life and thereafter to the testator's three sons. The trustees sold the shares in 1987, as a result of which the income of the trust was greatly increased. The testator's widow was 87 years of age and had a settled lifestyle. She authorised the trustees to distribute equally between her three sons such of the trust income for each accounting year as was surplus to her financial requirements. In February 1989 the trustees paid £9,300 to each of the sons, and on 5 February 1990 they paid £60,000 to each of the sons. The widow died suddenly on 20 February 1990. The Revenue issued determinations that the payments to the sons were chargeable to IHT. The sons appealed, contending that the gifts were exempt from IHT under *IHTA 1984, s 21(1)* as 'part of the normal expenditure of the transferor'. The QB accepted this contention and allowed the appeals. Lightman J held that ' "normal expenditure" connotes expenditure which at the time it took place accorded with the settled pattern of expenditure adopted by the transferor ... For an expenditure to be "normal" there is no fixed minimum period during which the expenditure shall have occurred. All that is necessary is that on the totality of evidence the pattern of actual or intended payments shall have been established and that the item in question conforms with that pattern ... The pattern need not be immutable; it must however be established that the pattern was intended to remain in place for more than a nominal period and indeed for a sufficient period (barring unforeseen circumstances) fairly to be regarded as a regular feature of the transferor's annual expenditure. Thus a "death bed" resolution to make periodic payments "for life" and a payment made in accordance with such a determination will not suffice ... The fact that the objective behind the expenditure is tax planning, e.g. to prevent an accumulation of income in the hands of the transferor liable to inheritance tax on his death, is no impediment.' On the evidence, the widow had adopted 'a pattern of expenditure in respect of the surplus, and the payments to the sons were made in accordance with this pattern'. *Ch D 1994, [1995] STC 54.*

Brown's Executors v CIR

IHTA 1984, s 105—Proceeds of sale of a nightclub held on deposit to be reinvested—allowed.

An individual (B), who owned a 99% shareholding in an unquoted UK company, died in 1986. The company had operated a nightclub, but had sold this in 1985. The proceeds of the sale were held on short-term deposit pending re-investment in similar premises, but no such premises had been acquired at the time of B's death. The executors claimed that B's shareholding qualified for business property relief. The Revenue rejected the claim on the basis that the company's business consisted 'wholly or mainly ... of making or holding investments'. The executors appealed, contending that until B's death, the company had been actively seeking alternative sites to open a new nightclub, and accordingly should not be treated as an investment-holding company. The Special Commissioner accepted the executors' evidence and allowed the appeal. *[1996] STC SCD 277 Sp C 83.*

Buccleuch (Duke of) & Another v CIR

Valuation—division of estate into units.

In an ED case the Revenue valued a substantial estate by dividing it into 532 'natural units' for valuation purposes. The trustees appealed, accepting that 46 of the units could be sold individually but contending that the remaining 486 could only be sold within a reasonable time if they were sold as a whole to an investor or speculator, and that the price payable by such a buyer would be some 20% less than the total valuation of the individual units. Their appeal was dismissed by the Land Tribunal, the CA and the HL. The HL held that the open market value was to be determined by reference to the aggregate of the proceeds of sale in a hypothetical market of each individual unit. The fact that it would have taken a long time to sell individual units separately, and that delay would have been caused by the need to avoid flooding the market, were held to be irrelevant. *HL 1966, [1967] 1 All ER 129; [1967] 1 AC 506.*

Bullock, CIR v

Domicile.

A Canadian married a woman of English parentage in 1946 and came to live in the UK. By 1966, he had given up any idea of returning to Canada during his wife's lifetime. He was held not to have acquired an English domicile of choice for the relevant years (1971–72 and 1972–73). *CA 1976, 51 TC 522; [1976] STC 409; [1976] 1 WLR 1178; [1976] 3 All ER 353.*

Burden & Burden v United Kingdom

IHTA 1984, s 18—whether any breach of European Convention on Human Rights.

Two elderly sisters lived together in a jointly-owned house on land which they had inherited from their parents. They lodged a complaint with the ECHR, contending that the provisions of *IHTA 1984, s 18* (as amended by the *Tax and Civil Partnership Regulations 2005*) were a breach of *Article 14* of the *European Convention on Human Rights*, because when one of them died, the survivor would be required to pay IHT on her sister's share of their home, whereas no IHT would have been charged if they had lived together as a registered lesbian civil partnership. The ECHR rejected their application, holding that 'the inheritance tax exemption for married and civil partnership couples ... pursues a legitimate aim, namely to promote stable, committed heterosexual and homosexual relationships by providing the survivor with a measure of financial security after the death of the spouse or partner'. The United Kingdom's decision 'to treat differently for tax purposes those who were married or who were parties to a civil partnership from other persons living together, even in a long-term settled relationship' was within the 'margin of appreciation' available to national authorities. *[2006] ECHR Case 13378/05* unreported.

Burkinyoung (Burkinyoung's Executor) v CIR

Business property relief—deeds of variation.

Martin & Horsfall v CIR was applied in a similar case where the deceased had let four flats on shorthold tenancies. The Commissioner held that the letting of the flats was a business which was 'wholly one of making or holding investments', so that the effect of *IHTA 1984, s 105(3)* was that business property relief was not due. *[1995] STC SCD 29 Sp C 3.*

Burmah Oil Co Ltd, CIR v

Avoidance schemes—the Ramsay principle.

A company (H), which was a member of a group, was dormant but owned stock with a market value substantially less than its acquisition cost. Its parent company (B) carried out a series of transactions including a capital reorganisation and the loan of £160 million to H via another company in the same group. At the end of these transactions, B held the stock previously held by H, which had been put into liquidation. B claimed that it had made a loss of £160 million on the disposal of its shareholding in H. The HL rejected the claim (reversing the decision of the CS). The whole and only purpose of the scheme had been the avoidance of tax. Applying *WT Ramsay Ltd*, the transactions had 'no commercial purpose apart from the avoidance of a liability to tax', and should be disregarded. *HL 1981, 54 TC 200; [1982] STC 30.*

Bushell v Faith

Company law—special voting rights attached to shares.

The share capital of a company comprised 300 shares of £1 each which were held as to 100 each by F and his two sisters. By Article 9 of the articles of association 'in the event of a resolution being proposed at any general meeting of the company for the removal from office of any director, any shares held by that director shall on a poll in respect of such resolution carry the right to three votes per share'. The HL upheld the effectiveness of the article. The weighting of votes on the particular resolution does not infringe *CA 1985, s 303*. [1970] AC 1099.*

Buswell v CIR

Domicile.

A South African who married an Englishwoman, and who in the relevant years lived in the UK, was held not to have acquired an English domicile of choice. (In so deciding, the CA reversed the decisions of the Special Commissioners and the Ch D.) *CA 1974, 49 TC 334; [1974] STC 266; [1974] 1 WLR 1631; [1974] 2 All ER 520.*

Cancer Research Campaign and others v Ernest Brown & Co

Duty to exercise reasonable care in advising a deceased's beneficiary of the possibility of executing a deed of variation – IHTA 1984, s 142.

N died on 11 December 1986 leaving a will dated 21 December 1985 giving his residuary estate to his sister who then died on 28 May 1988. Seven charities named as residuary beneficiaries under the testatrix's will dated 14 September 1987, brought an action for damages for negligence against the defendant firm of solicitors. The plaintiffs claimed that by reason of the solicitors' negligence they were unable to take advantage of a deed of variation under *IHTA 1984, s 142* at a cost to them of some £200,000 of unnecessarily paid IHT on N's estate because the statutory election period had expired on 10 December 1988. The plaintiffs contended that the solicitors were in breach of their duty of care during the testatrix's lifetime in failing to advise her of the possibility of executing a deed of variation of N's bequests. In addition, a breach of duty of their care had arisen, following the testatrix's death, in the administration of the estate in failing to notify them of their prospective legacies.

The court could not accept that there was a duty to advise an intended testator/testatrix about the tax avoidance schemes of another estate. The executor's duty was to collect the assets and he was under no obligation to inform the beneficiaries of the contents of the will as well as owing no duty to inform a legatee that there was a prospective legacy. The action was dismissed. *[1997] STC 1425.*

Challenge Corporation Ltd, New Zealand CIR v

Tax avoidance—distinction between avoidance and mitigation.

In a New Zealand case heard by the PC and relating to NZ legislation which has no counterpart in UK legislation, Lord Templeman discussed the distinction between 'tax avoidance' and 'tax mitigation'. Tax mitigation occurs where a taxpayer obtains a tax advantage by reducing his income or by incurring expenditure in circumstances in which the taxing statutes afford a reduction in tax liability. Tax avoidance takes place where a taxpayer seeks to avoid a liability to tax by entering into an arrangement without actually incurring the expenditure or loss which would permit the desired reduction in liability. *PC [1986] STC 548; [1987] 2 WLR 24; [1987] AC 155.*

Charkham v IRC

Valuation of a joint owners minority interest in undivided shares in property secured varying discounts of 15%, 20% and 22.5%-LPA 1925, s 30 and TLATA 1996, s 14.

A joint owner's interest in *investment* properties are routinely discounted by between 10%–15% but in this case the taxpayer's valuer chose to adopt an income approach in arguing that a minority owner could not obtain an order for sale. A multiple was calculated by the valuer derived from the investment market. In its considerations the Tribunal chose to exercise its discretion on the basis of the likelihood of a holder of the percentage obtaining an order for sale from the court. In this connection the holder as a purchaser would be aware of the uncertainty of a *LPA 1925, s 30* application and therefore discount the open market value. Also, there should be a single discount notwithstanding the difference in the IHT values of 24.04% to 6.04%. In applying this the Tribunal held for discounts of 15% on certain properties (Tottenham Court Road) and 20% and 22.5% on other properties (Alderney Street). *Charkham v IRC Lands Tribunal 1997.*

Chick v Commrs of Stamp Duties of New South Wales

Gifts with reservation—exclusion of donor from enjoyment.

See under *A-G v Seccombe* above. *PC, [1958] AC 435; [1958] 2 All ER 623; [1958] 3 WLR 93.*

Cholmondeley & Another v CIR

Protective trust—failure or determination.

By a deed of appointment dated 11 June 1979, the trustees of a settlement appointed seven farms to be held on protective trusts for M for life. By a deed of advancement dated the following day, three of the seven farms were advanced to M's eldest son, to be held in trust for him absolutely. The Revenue charged CTT on the basis that the deed of advancement ended M's protected life interest in the three farms. The trustees appealed, contending that the trust had been determined within *IHTA 1984, s 88(2)**, so that no CTT was chargeable. The Ch D dismissed the appeal, holding that *IHTA 1984, s 88(2)** only applied where there was a failure or determination of the protected life interest as such, rather than in relation to any particular assets. Since the protected life interest continued in relation to the other four farms, *IHTA 1984, s 88(2)** did not apply. Furthermore, the deed of appointment and the deed of advancement should be read together, so that the 'trust period' expired when the deed of advancement came into effect. *Ch D 1986, CTTL 29; [1986] STC 384.*

Civil Engineer v CIR

Taxpayer setting up trusts in Guernsey and Jersey—Guernsey trust was discretionary in form and the Jersey trust was established under Jersey law to pay income and capital for such charitable objects as trustees thought fit—Trustees of the Jersey trust resident outside the UK. Whether chargeable transfers for IHT purposes—Whether Jersey trust charitable under UK law—Whether Guernsey trust discretionary.

The taxpayer was born in England and he was English domicile. He worked in England as a consulting civil engineer in 1949. In 1960 he moved to Hong Kong and took up a permanent and pensionable post with the Hong Kong government. In 1967 he also became a partner in a London firm of consulting engineers. He and his wife were also shareholders of a Dutch company, HBV. He left Hong Kong in September 1989. Whilst in Hong Kong he rented accommodation but from 1960 to 1976 he owned property in the United Kingdom. Following changes in the Finance Act 1974 he closed his London office and ceased to own any property. His visits to the United Kingdom varied between zero and 36 days in a tax year between 1980 and 1988. He left Hong Kong in September 1989 severing his business and social connections with Hong Kong in November 1990. His P86 recorded that he had left for Jersey 31 January 1990 and returned to the UK permanently on 23 April 1990. On 22 March 1990 he created the S Foundation, a charity, under Jersey law (£75,000) and A Trust in Guernsey on 27 March 1990 (£375,000). All the Trustees were resident in Jersey and A Trust was discretionary naming only the Red Cross of Geneva as beneficiary but with the power to add other beneficiaries.

The Inland Revenue took the view that the transfers on 23 April 1990 were chargeable transfers and IHT was payable. The taxpayer appealed stating that he had acquired a domicile of choice of Hong Kong and that A Trust and S Foundation were not properly constituted or alternatively that A Trust was a life interest Trust and S Foundation a charity. Leaving Hong Kong with the intention of not returning revived the UK domicile of origin and therefore at the time of the transfers to the Trust and Foundation he was within the UK for IHT purposes. A Trust and S Foundation were valid trusts and A was a discretionary trust. S Foundation was not governed by the law of part of the UK and not subject to the jurisdiction of the UK courts. See *Camille and Henry Dreyfus Foundation Inc v CIR [1955] All ER 97.*

A letter of wishes signed by the taxpayer and his wife that was inconsistent with it being a interest in possession trust. The Trustees had wide discretionary powers and these included fixed monthly payments to the taxpayer and his wife. There was nothing to show that it was not a valid trust. The foundation is not subject to the jurisdiction of the UK courts and therefore not charitable for UK tax purposes. The appeal was dismissed. *[2002] STC SCD 72.*

Clark & Southern (Clark's Executors) v HMRC

Company's business consisted 'mainly of holding investments'.

A woman owned a number of shares in a company which owned more than 100 different properties from which it received rents, and also managed 141 dwellings owned by members of the family for which it charged 7.5% of the rent. The company had its own workforce for carrying out building work, maintenance and refurbishment of all properties. More than half the income was from the company's own properties. Her executors claimed business property relief. The Revenue rejected the claim on the basis that the shares were not 'relevant business property', because the company's business consisted mainly of 'making or holding investments', within *IHTA 1984, s 105(3)*. The executors appealed, contending that because the company carried out maintenance work on the properties itself, it should not be treated as falling within *s 105(3)*. The Special Commissioner rejected this contention and dismissed the executors' appeal, holding that 'the company's maintenance activity is not the separate provision of services; it is inherent in property ownership'. On the evidence, the company's business consisted 'mainly of holding investments'. *[2005] STC SCD 823 Sp C 502.*

Clay, CIR v

Valuation—definition of open market value.

Special circumstances existed which meant that one potential purchaser would have been prepared to give more for a house than what would otherwise have been the market price. Knowledge of local conditions and requirements, including the existence of such a purchaser, were held to be factors to be taken into account in establishing the open market value of the house. *CA 1914, [1914–15] All ER 882; [1914] 3 KB 466.*

Clore (deceased), Re (CIR v Stype Investments (Jersey) Ltd)

Jurisdiction—intermeddling—executor de son tort.

In May 1979 C, a wealthy man who had recently left the UK and was in poor health, transferred valuable land in England to S, a Jersey company, as his nominee. Two days later, S contracted to sell the land for more than £20 million. C died in July 1979. The sale was completed in September 1979, the sale proceeds being paid in Jersey. At the request of the Revenue, the QB granted injunctions ordering C's executors (none of whom were UK-resident) and S not to remove any of C's or S's assets from English jurisdiction. Meanwhile, the Family Division granted letters of administration of the estate to the Official Solicitor. The CA upheld the injunctions and the letters of administration, holding that the cause of action arose in England, so that the English courts had jurisdiction. S's acts in procuring payment outside England constituted an intermeddling with C's English estate within *IHTA 1984, ss 199(4), 200(4)* and rendered S liable to pay CTT in England as an executor *de son tort*. The letters of administration had been properly granted to the Official Solicitor. Templeman LJ commented that the conduct of S and the executors 'may have been the product of a criminal conspiracy to defraud the Revenue'. *CA 1982, CTTL 15; [1982] STC 625; [1982] 3 WLR 228; [1982] 3 All ER 419.*

Clore (deceased) (No 2), Re (Official Solicitor v Clore and Others)

Domicile.

Sir Charles Clore died in London on 26 July 1979, an immensely wealthy man. The Revenue claim to CTT on his free estate outside the UK, and on the assets of a Jersey settlement he had made on 20 February 1979, depended on whether, as considered by the Revenue, he was domiciled in England when he made the settlement and at his death. Towards the end of his life he spent part of each year abroad for tax reasons, and had been provisionally accepted by the Revenue as not resident or ordinarily resident in the UK since February 1977. He had taken steps to be associated with Monaco, as an acceptable 'tax haven', but there was no convincing evidence that he had formed a settled intention to reside permanently in Monaco. The Ch D held that, on the evidence, his father was domiciled in England when Sir Charles was born. His domicile of origin was therefore England and he had not abandoned this domicile at his death. *Ch D, [1984] STC 609.*

Clore (deceased) (No 3), Re (CIR v Stype Trustees (Jersey) Ltd and Others)

Delivery of accounts.

Foreign trustees contended that their admitted liability to pay CTT did not mean that they were liable to deliver accounts of the trust property under *IHTA 1984, s 216**. The Ch D rejected the trustees' argument that there was a territorial limitation to the section and held that their liability to pay tax meant that they were liable to comply with the administrative machinery of delivering accounts which normally precedes payment of tax. On a separate point, a former trustee was required to deliver an account giving details of settlement property 'to the best of his knowledge and belief'. 'Knowledge' was held to extend to the contents of documents in his possession, custody or power, but no further. He was not required to act as an information gatherer. *Ch D, [1985] STC 394; [1985] 1 WLR 1290; [1985] 2 All ER 819.*

Coates v Arndale Properties Ltd

Avoidance schemes—transfers within a group of companies.

Three companies, members of the same group, entered into transactions, not disputed to be genuine, but admittedly to secure expected favourable tax consequences. One company, SPI, had acquired and developed at a cost of £5,313,822 property the market value of which had fallen by March 1973 to £3,100,000. On 30 March 1973 it assigned the property to a property dealing company, A, for a consideration of £3,090,000. On the same day, A assigned the property for £3,100,000 to an investment company, APT. No cash passed, the matter being dealt with by book entries. A then purported to make an election under *TCGA 1992, s 161(3)**; the consequence would be that, by virtue of *TCGA 1992, s 171(1)**, the transfer from SPI to A would give rise to no loss or gain for CGT purposes, and in computing A's Case I profits it could treat the cost of the property as its market value plus the CGT loss which would have accrued under *TCGA 1992, s 161(1)** if the election had not been made. The Revenue assessed A under Case I on the footing that the election was invalid, contending that A had not acquired the property as trading stock within the meaning of *TCGA 1992, s 173(1)**. The HL upheld the assessment, holding that A never did decide to acquire, and never did acquire, the lease as trading stock. The transfer of the lease from SPI to A and from A to APT was procured with the object of obtaining group relief without in fact changing the lease from a capital asset to a trading asset. A lent its name to the transaction but it did not trade and never had any intention of trading with the lease. In these circumstances it was unnecessary to consider the principles enunciated in *CIR v Burmah Oil Co* and *Furniss v Dawson* or the dividend-stripping cases which had been considered in the courts below. *HL 1984, 59 TC 516; [1984] STC 637; [1984] 1 WLR 1328; [1985] 1 All ER 15.*

Cohen, CIR v

Domicile.

A taxpayer born in England, but who had spent a great deal of his life in Australia and who had in the relevant years had no permanent residence in the UK, was held to have retained his English domicile of origin. *KB 1937, 21 TC 301.*

Cook & Daw (Watkins' Executors) v CIR

Property division—Interest in possession.

A married woman (W) died in December 1999, having owned a house in Cardiff, which was divided into two flats. She had let the ground floor flat to tenants, and had lived in the first floor flat with her husband. By her will, she gave the house to trustees (her children by a previous marriage), but gave her husband the right to live in it 'and use it as his principal place of residence'. However, following her death, her husband stayed with his daughter for just over three weeks, before being admitted to hospital, where he died two months later. The Revenue issued a notice of determination to W's executors, ruling that her husband had not acquired an interest in possession in the house. They appealed. The Special Commissioner reviewed the evidence in detail and allowed the appeal in part, holding that the husband had acquired an interest in possession in the first floor flat but not in the ground-floor flat. *[2002] STC SCD 318 Sp C 319.*

Craven v White

Avoidance schemes—the Ramsay principle.

Three members of a family owned all the shares in a UK company (Q), which owned a number of shops. From 1973 they conducted negotiations with various other companies with a view to selling Q or merging it with a similar business. In July 1976, at a time when they were negotiating with two unconnected companies, they exchanged their shares for shares in an Isle of Man company (M). Nineteen days later M sold the shares in Q to one of the two companies with which negotiations had been in progress at the time of the share exchange. The sale proceeds were paid by M to the shareholders over a period of five years. The Revenue issued CGT assessments for 1976–77 on the basis that, applying the *Ramsay* principle, the disposal of the shares to M and their subsequent sale by M should be treated as a single composite transaction and that the transfer of the shares to M was a fiscal nullity. The Special Commissioners reduced the assessments, holding that the transfer could not be treated as a fiscal nullity but that the shareholders were assessable on the amounts they had received from M at the time of receipt. The Revenue's appeals against this decision were dismissed by the Ch D, the CA, and (by a 3–2 majority) the HL. In giving the leading judgment for the majority, Lord Oliver indicated the limitations of the principle adopted in *CIR v Ramsay*, as defined by Lord Brightman in *Furniss v Dawson*. The principle in question—that the Commissioners are not bound to consider individually each step in a composite transaction intended to be carried through as a whole—applied only where there was a 'pre-ordained series of transactions' or 'one single composite transaction' and where steps were inserted which had no commercial purpose apart from the avoidance of a liability to tax. Although the decision in *Furniss v Dawson* extended the *Ramsay* principle, by applying it to a linear transaction as opposed to a circular self-cancelling one, it did no more than apply that principle to different events. It did not lay down any proposition that a transaction entered into with the motive of minimising tax was to be ignored or struck down. In the *Ramsay* case, Lord Wilberforce had emphasised the continuing validity and application of the principle enunciated by Lord Tomlin in *Duke of Westminster v CIR* Lord Fraser had echoed this view, as had Lord Bridge in *Furniss v Dawson*. (The speech of Lord Roskill in that case, which implied the contrary, did not appear to represent the view of the majority.) The criteria by reference to which the *Ramsay* principle applied were not logically capable of expansion so as to apply to any similar case except one in which, when the intermediate transaction or transactions took place, the end result which in fact occurred was so certain of fulfilment that it was intellectually and practically possible to conclude that there had indeed taken place one single and indivisible process. For the principle to apply, the intermediate steps had to serve no purpose other than that of saving tax; all stages of the composite transaction had to be pre-ordained with a degree of certainty with the taxpayer having control over the end result at the time when the intermediate steps were taken; and there should be no interruption between the intermediate transaction and the disposal to the ultimate purchaser. In this case, however, the transactions that the Crown sought to reconstruct into a single direct disposal were not contemporaneous. Nor were they pre-ordained since, at the time of the share exchange, it was not certain what the ultimate destination of the property would be. Lord Jauncey considered that 'a step in a linear transaction which has no business purpose apart from the avoidance or deferment of tax liability will be treated as forming part of a pre-ordained series of transactions or of a composite transaction if it was taken at a time when negotiations or arrangements for the carrying through as a continuous process of a subsequent transaction which actually takes place had reached a stage when there was no real likelihood that such subsequent transaction would not take place and if thereafter such negotiations or arrangements were carried through to completion without genuine interruption'. Lord Oliver concurred with this definition. *HL 1988, 62 TC 1; [1988] STC 476; [1988] 3 WLR 423; [1988] 3 All ER 495.*

Crawford Settlement Trustees v HMRC

Assignation of interest in trust fund—whether IHTA 1984, s 71(3) applicable.

An individual (B) was born in 1969. He was due to become entitled to an interest in a trust fund, created under a 1954 settlement, on reaching the age of 21. In 1989, when he was 19 years old, he assigned the whole of his prospective interest to the trustees of a discretionary trust in which there was no interest in possession. The Revenue issued a notice of determination on the basis that the assignation of B's interest gave rise to a charge to IHT under *IHTA 1984, s 71(3)*. The trustees of the 1954 settlement appealed. The Special Commissioner allowed the appeal, holding that *IHTA 1984, s 71(3)* did not apply because 'immediately after the assignation, the trust comprised exactly the same property as immediately before the assignation; and viewing matters as at the date the assignation took effect, one or more persons "will" on or before attaining the age of 21 become beneficially entitled to an interest in possession in it. The conditions set forth in *section 71(1)* were met immediately after the assignation took effect in the same way they were met immediately before the assignation took effect. It cannot therefore be said that settled property ceased to be property to which *section 71* applied by virtue of the effect of the assignation. It follows that the assignation did not give rise to a charge to tax under *section 71(3)*.' *[2005] STC SCD 457 Sp C 473.*

Crossman and Others, CIR v

Valuation—value of unquoted shares subject to restrictions on transfers.

The open market value of unquoted shares had to be established for ED purposes. The articles of association imposed restrictions on transfer including a right of pre-emption in favour of existing shareholders. The value was not limited to that fixed by the pre-emption clause, but was estimated at the price obtainable in a hypothetical open market on the terms that the purchaser was registered as holder of the shares and held them subject to the same restrictions as his predecessor. *HL 1936, 15 ATC 94; [1936] 1 All ER 762; [1937] AC 26.*

Curnock (Curnock's Personal Representatives) v CIR

Cheque clearance after date of death but gift made before treated as part of deceased's estate.

A pensioner (P) had granted a power of attorney to his father (C). On 21 December 2001 C issued a cheque for £6,000 on behalf of P. On 22 December 2001 P died. The cheque was not cleared until 27 December. The Revenue issued a Notice of Determination on the basis that the £6,000 was part of P's estate. C (who was P's personal representative) appealed, contending that the £6,000 did not form part of P's estate, since he had disposed of the money on the day before he died. The Special Commissioner rejected this contention and dismissed C's appeal. Applying *dicta* of Pollock MR in *Re Swinburne, CA [1926] Ch 38*, a cheque was 'nothing more than an order to obtain a certain sum of money … and if the order is not acted upon in the lifetime of the person who gives it, it is worth nothing'. Accordingly, the £6,000 was part of P's estate when he died. *[2003] STC SCD 283 Sp C 365.*

Daffodil (Daffodil's Administrators) v CIR

Right under Administration of Estates Act 1925—whether 'property' within IHTA 1984, s 272.

A married couple owned a bungalow as tenants in common. In 1994 the husband died intestate. His widow was entitled to apply for a grant of letters of administration of his estate, but did not do so, and continued to live in the bungalow. She died in 2000, leaving the couple's son (D) as administrator of her estate. He was advised by his solicitor that, in order to sell the bungalow, he would need letters of administration of his father's estate, which he duly obtained. The Revenue issued a notice of administration on the basis that, when D's mother died, the bungalow which she occupied formed part of her estate. D appealed, contending that because his mother had not obtained letters of administration of her husband's estate, his estate (including his 50% share of the bungalow) did not form part of her estate. The Special Commissioner rejected this contention and dismissed D's appeal. Under *Administration of Estates Act 1925*, D's mother had had the right to require the whole of her husband's estate to be transferred to her. The effect of *IHTA 1984, s 272* was that this right formed part of her estate. *[2002] STC SCD 224 Sp C 311.*

Delamere's Settlement Trusts, Re (Kenny and Others v Cunningham-Reid and Others)

Interest in possession—effect of Trustee Act 1925, s 31.

An appointment in 1980 by trustees of a settlement which partly revoked the trusts of a 1971 appointment of income was expressed to have effect only if no interest in possession already subsisted in the relevant property for CTT purposes. The question before the CA was to what extent the *Trustee Act 1925, s 31* applied to the 1971 appointment. If it applied, a minor beneficiary's share of the accumulated income would fall back into the general capital of the trust in the event of his death before attaining 18 or marrying, and his interest in the accumulations would although vested, be defeasible. If *s 31(2)* did not apply, the accumulated income vested in the minor beneficiary as it accrued and was held by the trustees for him indefeasibly. The CA held that *s 31(2)* did not apply. The use of the word 'absolutely' and the fact that no time limit was placed on the duration of the income interests appointed, indicated the intention that the interests should not be defeasible in any circumstances during the subsistence of the 1971 appointment. *CA 1983, [1984] 1 WLR 813; [1984] 1 All ER 584.*

Dextra Accessories Ltd and others v MacDonald

Payments to employee benefit trust—whether FA 1989, s 43(11) applicable.

Six associated companies claimed deductions for payments which they made to an employee benefit trust. The Inland Revenue rejected the claims, considering that the payments were 'potential emoluments' within *FA 1989, s 43(11)* so that no deduction was allowable until the relevant employees were taxed on the fund as an emolument. The companies appealed, contending that the payments should not be treated as 'potential emoluments' within *s 43(11)*. The House of Lords unanimously rejected this contention and dismissed the companies' appeals. Lord Hoffmann held that 'in the ordinary use of language, the whole of the funds were potential emoluments. They could be used to pay emoluments.' He observed that this was 'the result of an arrangement into which the taxpayers have chosen to enter. Any untoward consequences can be avoided by segregating the funds held on trust to pay emoluments from funds held to benefit employees in other ways.' See also now *FA 2003, Sch 24*. This was intended to provide, with effect from 27 November 2002, that any contributions into an employee benefit trust will only attract corporation tax relief for the sponsoring company when payments subject to income tax and NICs have been made to the underlying employees. See Inland Revenue Budget Notice BN27, reproduced at SWTI 2003, pp 737–738. *HL [2005] UKHL 47.*

Dixon v CIR

Garden and orchard—whether 'agricultural property' for the purposes of Agricultural Property Relief under IHTA 1984, ss 115(2), 117(a).

A woman (B) died in 1998, owning 60% interest in a property consisting of a cottage, garden and orchard, with a total area of 0.6 acres. B had sometimes allowed a neighbouring farmer to graze sheep on the land, and had sometimes sold damsons from the orchard. The Inland Revenue issued a notice of determination charging IHT. B's executor appealed, contending that the property qualified for agricultural property relief. The Special Commissioner rejected this contention and dismissed the appeal, finding on the evidence that the property was not 'agricultural land or pasture' but was occupied as a private residence. *[2002] STC SCD 53 Sp C 297.*

Dreyfus (Camille & Henry) Foundation Inc v CIR

Charities—overseas trusts.

A foundation for the advancement of chemistry, etc. incorporated in the USA claimed exemption under *ICTA 1988, s 505(1)(c)** in respect of royalties. The claim was refused. The relief is limited to bodies and trusts subject to the jurisdiction of the courts of the UK. (The question of whether the foundation was established for charitable purposes was not considered.) *HL 1955, 36 TC 126; [1956] AC 39; [1955] 3 All ER 97.*

Dunstan v Young Austen Young Ltd

Avoidance schemes—whether issue of new shares not acquired at arm's length constituted a capital reorganisation.

The taxpayer company (Y) carried on business as a mechanical engineering contractor. In 1977 it acquired for £16,100 the 1,000 issued £1 shares of a company (J) in the same line of business. Shortly afterwards it joined a large group; one of the shares in J was registered in the name of a fellow-subsidiary (T), the remainder being registered in its own name. J was not trading profitably. By March 1979 it had incurred debts of £200,911 to other companies in the group, mainly to Y, and it was decided to sell it. An arm's length purchaser was found, and J issued a further 200,000 £1 shares on 12 June 1979. These were allotted to Y for £200,000 cash, which was promptly repaid to Y to clear its indebtedness. On 29 June an agreement was completed between Y, T and the purchaser for the sale of the 201,000 shares for £38,000. The appeal was against an assessment for the year to September 1979. The profits were agreed at nil and the substantive issue was whether Y had incurred a capital loss on its disposal of the shares in J and, if so, of what amount. It was common ground that Y acquired the additional 200,000 shares 'otherwise than by a bargain made at arm's length' and by virtue of *CGTA 1979, s 19(3)** the consideration for them should be taken to be their market value, which the Special Commissioner found to be nil 'or so near to it as to make no matter'. However, Y contended that the issue of the further 200,000 shares constituted a reorganisation of J's capital within *TCGA 1992, ss 126, 128**, with the consequence that the new shares would not be treated as a separate acquisition and that the £200,000 would be treated as having been given for the original 1,000 shares, making their cost £216,100 and the loss £178,100. This contention was upheld by the CA, reversing the decision of the Ch D and restoring that of the Special Commissioner. Properly construed, the phrase 'reorganisation of a company's share capital' in *TCGA 1992, s 126** included an increase in a company's share capital and the allotment of the new shares to its parent company for cash. (*Note. CGTA 1979, s 19(3)* was repealed by *FA 1981*. See now *TCGA 1992, s 128(2)* as regards reorganisations on or after 10 March 1981.) *CA 1988, 61 TC 448; [1989] STC 69.*

Edwards v Bairstow & Harrison

Appeals—distinction between fact and law.

Two individuals were assessed under Case I on the profits from the sale in five lots of cotton spinning plant purchased for resale. The General Commissioners allowed their appeals, holding that there was no trade or adventure in the nature of trade. The HL allowed the Revenue's appeal and restored the assessments, holding that the only reasonable conclusion on the evidence before the Commissioners was that there had been an adventure in the nature of trade. (A leading case establishing the principle that the courts will not disturb a Commissioners' conclusion on a question of fact if it was one to which they were entitled to come, notwithstanding that the court or another body of Commissioners might have reached a different conclusion on the same evidence. This was approved and restated by Lord Brightman in *Furniss v Dawson*, to the effect that 'an appellate court ... can and should interfere with an inference of fact drawn by the fact-finding tribunal which cannot be justified by the primary facts'. But 'if the primary facts justify alternative inferences of fact' the court should not 'substitute its own preferred inference for the inference drawn by the fact-finding tribunal'.) *HL 1955, 36 TC 207; [1956] AC 14; [1955] 3 All ER 48.*

Eilbeck v Rawling

Avoidance schemes—the Ramsay principle.

A taxpayer made a chargeable gain of £355,094 in 1974–75 as to which there was no dispute. Later in the same year he entered into a chain of transactions with the object of creating a commensurate allowable loss, at a cost to him of only £370 apart from the fees, etc. paid for the scheme, which was an 'off the peg' avoidance device obtained from a Jersey company. The central feature of the scheme involved his acquiring reversionary interests in two trust funds, one held by Jersey trustees and the other by Gibraltar trustees. Under a special power of appointment, the Gibraltar trustees advanced £315,000 to the Jersey trustees to be held on the trusts of the Jersey settlement. The taxpayer then sold both reversionary interests, making a gain on the sale of his interest under the Jersey settlement (claimed to be exempt under *TCGA 1992, s 76(1)**) and a matching loss of £312,470 on the sale of his interest under the Gibraltar settlement (claimed as an allowable loss). The CA refused the claim on the ground, *inter alia*, that the exercise of the power of appointment did not take the £315,000 outside the Gibraltar settlement; hence the sale of his reversionary interest in the £315,000 was a part sale of his interest under the Gibraltar settlement. The taxpayer appealed to the HL. The appeal was considered with *W T Ramsay Ltd*, and dismissed for the same general reason that, on the facts, the scheme was to be looked at as a composite transaction under which there was neither gain nor loss apart from the £370. Furthermore, the HL upheld the CA decision that the sale of the reversionary interest in the £315,000 was a sale of part of the taxpayer's reversionary interest in the Gibraltar settlement. (*Note.* The device would also now be caught by the value shifting provisions of *TCGA 1992, s 30*.) *HL 1981, 54 TC 101; [1981] STC 174; [1981] 2 WLR 449; [1981] 1 All ER 865.*

Essex & another (executors of Somerset deceased) v CIR

Relevant date for the purposes of FA 1986, s 102(5).

In 1988 a married woman (S) settled a 95% interest in a house on trust, to pay the income to her husband for life, and after his death to hold the capital and income on discretionary trusts for a class of beneficiaries that included herself and her children. S's husband died in 1992 and she died in 1998. The Inland Revenue issued a notice of determination on the basis that, at her death, the property held by the settlement fell to be treated as her property by reason of *FA 1986, s 102*. Her executors appealed, contending that the effect of *FA 1986, s 102(5)* was that no IHT was due, since the settlement had taken advantage of the exemption under *IHTA 1984, s 18* for transfers between spouses. The Special Commissioners accepted this contention and allowed the appeal, holding that the creation of the settlement involved a single gift to S's husband. This was an exempt transfer between spouses to which *s 102(5)* applied. For the purposes of *s 102(5)*, the relevant date was the date of the settlement, rather than the date of S's death. *[2002] STC SCD 39 Sp C 296.*

Eversden and Another, CIR v

Relevant date for the purposes of FA 1986, s 102(5).

In 1988 a married woman (S) settled a 95% interest in a house on trust, to pay the income to her husband for life, and after his death to hold the capital and income on discretionary trusts for a class of beneficiaries which included herself and her children. S's husband died in 1992 and she died in 1998. The Revenue issued a notice of determination on the basis that, at her death, the property held by the settlement fell to be treated as her property by virtue of *FA 1986, s 102*. Her executors appealed, contending that the effect of *FA 1986, s 102(5)* was that no IHT was due, since the settlement had taken advantage of the exemption under *IHTA 1984, s 18* for transfers between spouses. The Special Commissioner accepted this contention and allowed the appeal, holding that, for the purposes of *FA 1986, s 102(5)*, the relevant date was the date of the settlement, rather than the date of S's death. The Ch D and CA upheld this decision. Carnwath LJ held that 'the "disposal of the property by way of gift" was the transfer of the property in 1988'. This was accepted as an exempt transfer under *IHTA 1984, s 18*. It was, therefore, outside the scope of *FA 1986, s 102*. He also observed that the effect of *IHTA 1984, s 49* was that 'in the present case, the estate of the settlor's husband is taxed on the property, but that of the settlor is not. There is nothing in *section 102* to modify that ... If that is of concern to the Revenue, they must look for correction to Parliament, not to the Courts.' (*aka Essex & Essex (Somerset's Executors) v CIR*), *CA [2003] STC 822; [2003] EWCA Civ 668*. (*Note*. On 20 June 2003 the Government tabled an amendment to the 2003 Finance Bill (resulting in *FA 2003, s 185*) to amend *FA 1986, s 102* to reverse the effect of this decision. See the Inland Revenue Press Release issued on 20 June 2003.)

Farmer and another (Executors of Farmer deceased) v CIR

Relevant business property—deceased carrying on business of farming and letting some buildings and land on the farm—whether BPR excluded as consisting mainly of making or holding investments.

An individual (F), who owned a farm comprising 449 acres, died in 1997. Several of the properties at the farm were surplus to the requirements of the farm, and he had let these to tenants. The farm had an agreed probate value of £3,500,000. It was accepted that £2,250,000 of this related to the farmhouse, farm buildings and farmland, and qualified for 100% agricultural property relief. The balance of £1,250,000 related to the properties that had been let. F's executors claimed business property relief on the basis that there was a single business which qualified for relief (accepting that, by virtue of *IHTA 1984, s 114(1)*, the business property relief was restricted to the £1,250,000 which did not qualify for agricultural property relief). The Revenue rejected the claim and issued a notice of determination that the farm business consisted mainly of making or holding investments, within *IHTA 1984, s 105(3)*, and therefore was not 'relevant business property'. The executors appealed, accepting that the letting of property was 'making or holding investments' but contending that F's business had consisted mainly of farming. The Special Commissioner accepted this contention and allowed the appeal, holding on the evidence that 'the overall context of the business, the capital employed, the time spent by the employees and consultants, and the levels of turnover, all support the conclusion that the business consisted mainly of farming'. The fact that the lettings were more profitable than the rest of the business was not conclusive. See *[1999] STC SCD 321 Sp C 216*.

Faulkner (Adams' Trustee) v CIR

Licence to occupy property given to third party—whether interest in possession within IHTA 1984, s 49(1)—present right to present enjoyment of the property even though not occupied by the deceased.

In 1980 a widower (R), with no children, made a will allowing a friend (H) and his wife 'or the survivor of them for the time being still living' to live in his house 'and have the use of the furniture as long as he she or they so wish'. R died in 1981 and the couple duly moved into the house. H died in 1998 (having outlived his wife) and the house was sold later that year. The Revenue issued a notice of determination to R's surviving trustee, on the basis that H's right of occupation had been an interest in possession in settled property, within *IHTA 1984, s 49(1)*. The trustee appealed, contending firstly that R's will had given H a licence to use the house but had not conferred an interest in possession, and alternatively that if H had had an interest in possession, he should be deemed to have shared it with the three residuary beneficiaries under R's will. The Special Commissioner rejected these contentions and dismissed the appeal, holding that H had had a 'present right to the present enjoyment of the house'. This was an interest in possession in the whole of the house. *[2001] STC SCD 112 Sp C 278*.

Faye v CIR

Domicile.

An Australian woman, after 30 years in Australia, married a Frenchman, who acquired a domicile of choice in England. The marriage was dissolved and she remained in England and was held to be domiciled in the UK for the relevant years. *Ch D 1961, 40 TC 103*.

Fetherstonhaugh & Others v CIR

Business property relief—death of life tenant using settled property for business purposes.

In 1977 the life tenant of settled land, who had used that land in his farming and forestry business, died. The trustees claimed that the value of the settled land qualified for business property relief. The Revenue rejected the claim but the CA allowed the trustees' appeal. Although the land itself was not relevant business property, the life interest in the land was an asset used in the business. For CTT purposes the asset had to be valued as if the deceased was beneficially entitled to the land itself. 50% business property relief was therefore due. (*Note.* The relief would now be 100%—see *IHTA 1984, s 104* as amended by *F(No 2)A 1992, 13 Sch 1.*) *CA 1984, CTTL 21; [1984] STC 261; [1984] 3 WLR 212.*

Fielden v CIR

Domicile.

A taxpayer born in England, but who had spent part of his life in the USA and married a US citizen, was held to be domiciled in the UK in the relevant years. (He had obtained a domicile of choice in the USA at one time, but had since lost it.) *Ch D 1965, 42 TC 501.*

Fitzwilliam (Countess) & Others v CIR

Discretionary trust—mutual transfers of value—whether Ramsay principle applicable.

Trustees, appointed under a will, had discretion to appoint the residue among a class of beneficiaries during a period of 23 months from the testator's death. The main beneficiaries were the testator's widow (F), who was aged 81 and in poor health, and her daughter (H). There was a potentially heavy liability to CTT and the trustees undertook a number of transactions to mitigate the tax liability. On 20 December 1979, they declared that £4m should be held in trust as to both capital and income for F absolutely. On 9 January 1980 F made a gift to H of £2m net of CTT. On 14 January 1980 the trustees appointed £3.8m to be held on trust, subject to the income being paid to F until 15 February 1980 or her death, one half for H absolutely (the vested half) and the other half for a contingent interest. On 31 January 1980 F assigned to H, for £2m, her beneficial interest in the income of the contingent half. On 5 February 1980 H settled £1,000 on trust to pay the income to F until 15 March 1980 or her death, whichever was the earlier, and subject thereto in trust absolutely for herself. On 7 February 1980 H assigned to the trustees of her settlement her beneficial interest in the vested half of the trust established on 14 January 1980, to be accrued to the £1,000 as one fund. The Revenue served a notice of determination on the trustees, charging CTT on the basis that £4m and £3.8m had been appointed absolutely to F and H respectively. The trustees appealed, contending that the £4m was within what is now *IHTA 1984, s 144** and that the gift of £2m was exempt under *FA 1976, ss 86, 87.* The Ch D allowed the trustees' appeals and the HL upheld this decision (Lord Templeman dissenting). The Revenue's contention that the steps amounted to a single composite transaction within the *Ramsay* principle and that the original testator, rather than H, should be deemed to be the settlor of the settlement of the vested half made on 5 February were rejected. The steps taken in January and February 1980 could not be treated as a 'single and indivisible whole in which one or more of the steps was simply an element without independent effect'. The fact that they formed part of a 'pre-planned tax avoidance scheme' was not sufficient in itself 'to negative the application of an exemption from liability to tax which the series of transactions (was) intended to create', unless the series was 'capable of being construed in a manner inconsistent with the application of the exemption'. The series of transactions here could not be construed in such a way. *Craven v White* applied; *Furniss v Dawson* distinguished. With regard to the Revenue's alternative contention, the fact that the settled funds were historically derived from the original testator did not mean that he could reasonably be regarded as having provided property for the settlement made on 5 February 1980. *HL, [1993] STC 502; 1 WLR 1189; [1993] 3 All ER 184.*

Floor v Davis

Arrangements to reduce liability—interpretation of TCGA 1992, s 29(2)—exercise of control over shares.

It had been arranged that, subject to contract, the share capital of a company (IDM) would be sold (at a substantial profit to the shareholders) to another company (KDI). F and his two sons-in-law, who together controlled IDM, carried out a scheme under which the following transactions took place shortly after each other. They transferred their IDM shares to FNW, a company set up for the purpose, for preferred shares in FNW; FNW sold the IDM shares to KDI for cash; a Cayman Islands company, D, acquired a relatively insignificant holding of preferred shares in FNW; following a rights issue open to all preferred shareholders but accepted only by D, D became the sole ordinary shareholder in FNW; FNW went into liquidation and because of the differing rights attached to the two classes of shares, D, as the ordinary shareholder, became entitled to six-sevenths of the assets of FNW. The upshot was that the greater part of the proceeds of sale of the IDM shares reached D. The CA held (Eveleigh LJ dissenting), that F had disposed of his IDM shares to FNW (and not, as contended by the Revenue, to KDI) with the consequence that under *TCGA 1992, s 135** his FNW shares were treated as the IDM shares he originally held. However, the CA unanimously held that value had passed out of the FNW shares within the meaning of *TCGA 1992, s 29(2)** and F was assessable accordingly, on the grounds that (i) 'person' in *TCGA 1992, s 29(2)** includes the plural by virtue of *Interpretation Act 1889, s 1(1)(b)* and the definition of 'control' (see *TCGA 1992, s 288(1)**) and (ii) F and his sons-in-law had exercised their control, notwithstanding that two of them had not voted on the resolution to wind up FNW. The HL rejected F's appeal on this point. (The Revenue's contention that F had disposed of the shares to KDI was therefore not argued in the HL. See now as to this *Furniss v Dawson*, in which the dissenting judgment of Eveleigh LJ, who upheld the Revenue's contention that the shares had been disposed of to KDI, was approved.) (*Notes.* (1) The relevant transactions took place in 1969. See now for value-shifting transactions after 13 March 1989, *TCGA 1992, ss 30–34*. (2) The *Interpretation Act 1889* has since been repealed. See now *Interpretation Act 1978, s 6(c)*.) *HL 1979, 52 TC 609; [1979] STC 379; [1979] 2 WLR 830; [1979] 2 All ER 677.*

Fox (Lady), Gray (Executor of) v CIR

Valuation of related property.

Duke of Buccleuch was applied in a case where the freeholder of a large estate had, at the time of her death, held a 92.5% interest in a partnership which farmed the land. The Revenue issued a Notice of Determination claiming IHT on the combined value of the deceased's freehold reversion and her interest in the partnership. The CA upheld the Notice of Determination (reversing the decision of the Lands Tribunal). Hoffman LJ held that the hypothetical sale had to be supposed to have taken the course which would get the largest price provided that it did not entail 'undue expenditure of time and effort'. The freehold reversion and the partnership should be valued as one unit of property. *CA [1994] STC 360.*

Frankland v CIR

Distribution from property settled by will—whether IHTA 1984, s 144 applicable.

A married woman died on 26 September 1987, leaving property on discretionary trusts for the benefit of her husband and children. On 22 December 1987 the property was transferred to a trust, the income from which was to be paid to the deceased's husband for the duration of his life. The object of the transfer was to secure the benefit of the spouse exemption of *IHTA 1984, s 18(1)* in respect of the charge to tax otherwise payable in respect of the death. The Revenue issued a notice of determination on the basis that the spouse exemption did not apply since the transfer had not been made by the deceased. The trustee appealed, contending that the effect of *IHTA 1984, s 144* was that the husband's interest in possession should be treated as having arisen under the deceased's will. The Ch

D rejected this contention and dismissed the appeal, holding that *IHTA 1984, s 144* did not apply. The effect of *IHTA 1984, s 65(4)* was that, since the December transfer had taken place within three months of the death, that transfer itself was not an event giving rise to a charge to tax. *IHTA 1984, s 144* only applied where there was an event on which tax would otherwise be chargeable. The wording of *IHTA 1984, s 144* was unambiguous. Accordingly the transfer could not be treated as having been made by the deceased, and the spouse exemption did not apply. The Court of Appeal reaffirmed the decision. *CA [1997] STC 1450.*

Friends' Provident Life Office v British Railways Board

Lease—variation of lease.

A variation of a lease may, depending upon the facts, constitute a deemed surrender and re-grant. *[1996] 1 All ER 336.*

Fuller v Evans and Others

Accumulation and maintenance settlement—settlor divorced and beneficiaries were the children of the settlor—whether Trustees could exercise their discretion in the payment of school fees thereby relieving the settlor of financial responsibility for same.

A settlement that created an accumulation and maintenance trust for the benefit of the present and future children of the settlor. On the divorce between the settlor and his wife, a consent order was made which included provision for the settlor to make periodical payments to the mother of his children for general maintenance and for school fees inclusive of reasonable extras. The Clause 12 of the trust deed provided, inter alia, that no part of the capital or income of the trust fund be applied either directly or indirectly for the benefit of the settlor. The question raised was whether clause 12 precluded the trustees from exercising the power where the interests of the beneficiaries required its exercise if such exercise might incidentally benefit the settlor, and in particular might relieve the settlor from the actual or perceived need because of some legal or moral obligation, in this case an obligation arising under the consent order. Despite the breadth of the clause 12 Justice Lightman in the Chancery Division found it very difficult to read the settlement as paralysing the trustees in this situation. Clause 12 did little if anything more than vigorously reaffirm the duty of the trustees to have regard exclusively to the best interests of the beneficiaries and ignore those of the settlor. Therefore clause 12 did not preclude the trustees from exercising the power conferred upon them by reason of any incidental and unintended conferment of relief on the settlor.

Furniss v Dawson (and related appeals)

Avoidance schemes—the Ramsay principle.

The shareholders in two family companies wished to dispose of their shares, and found an unconnected company (W) willing to acquire the shares at an agreed price. Before disposing of the shares, they exchanged them for shares in a Manx company which in turn sold them to W. The Revenue issued assessments on the basis that the shares should be treated as having been disposed of directly to W, since the interposition of the Manx company had been designed solely to take advantage of the law then in force with regard to company reconstructions and amalgamations. The HL unanimously upheld the assessments (reversing the decision of the CA). Applying *WT Ramsay Ltd*, the transactions should be regarded as a single composite transaction. Lord Bridge of Harwich observed that 'the distinction between form and substance ... can usefully be drawn in determining the tax consequences of composite transactions'. Lord Brightman held that the *Ramsay* principle applied in cases where there was a 'pre-ordained series of transactions; or ... one single composite transaction' and steps were 'inserted which have no commercial (business) purpose apart from the avoidance of a liability to tax—not "no business effect"'. If these two ingredients exist, the inserted steps are to be disregarded for fiscal purposes. The court must look at the end result.' *Furniss v Dawson HL 1984, 55 TC 324; [1984] STC*

153; [1984] 2 WLR 226; [1984] 1 All ER 530. (Notes. (1) See also *TCGA 1992, s 137.* (2) Although the decision was unanimous, there was implicit disagreement as to the continuing validity of the Duke of Westminster principle. Lords Bridge and Scarman indicated that the principle still applied, but Lord Roskill specifically refrained from endorsing the Westminster decision. For subsequent developments, see the judgment of Lord Templeman in *Ensign Tankers (Leasing) Ltd v Stokes*, and that of Lord Keith in *Countess Fitzwilliam v CIR*.)

Furse (deceased), In re, Furse v CIR

Domicile.

A US citizen came to England as a boy in 1887. After completing his education in England he took up employment in America, where he married an American. In 1923, originally on medical advice, he came with his family to England, where his wife purchased a farm which remained the matrimonial home until he died in 1963, aged 80. From 1950 onwards he said that he would remain at the farm so long as he was able to do physical work there; he remained so able until his death. In an application by his executor for a declaration of his domicile for estate duty purposes, he was held to have acquired an English domicile of choice, distinguishing *CIR v Bullock. Ch D, [1980] STC 597; [1980] 3 All ER 838.*

Gartside v CIR

Meaning of interest in possession.

In an ED case which received much consideration in *Pearson and Others v CIR* the HL held that the objects of a discretionary trust, who were not entitled either individually or collectively to receive any part of the trust income in any year, did not have interests or interests in possession in the trust fund within the meaning of the relevant ED provisions. Per Lord Reid, an interest in possession must mean an interest which enables a person to claim now whatever may be the subject of his interest. *HL 1967, [1968] 2 WLR 277; [1968] 1 All ER 121; [1968] AC 553.*

George and Another, CIR v

Business Property Relief claim regarding caravans—provision of services not the holding of investments.

A widow (S) had owned 85% of the shares in a company which operated a residential caravan park, comprising 167 mobile homes, and a country club with a licensed bar. The Revenue issued a notice of determination on the basis that her shares in the company were not 'relevant business property', because the company's business consisted mainly of 'making or holding investments'. S's executors appealed. The Special Commissioner reviewed the evidence in detail and allowed the appeal, observing that the company had several full-time employees and was classed as a trading company for corporation tax purposes, and finding that '72% of the site fees goes in overheads (*sic*) ... most of which relate to the provision of upkeep of the common parts'. On the evidence, the Commissioner held that the company's business was 'the provision of services and not the business of holding investments'. The Ch D upheld the notice. Laddie J held that the business of receiving site fees from the owners of the mobile homes in return for the right to use the company's land, and the receipt of fees for the storage of caravans, constituted the exploitation of the proprietary rights in the land and amounted to the holding of an investment. Accordingly the shares in the company failed to qualify for business property relief. *[2002] STC SCD 358 Sp C 323; Ch D [2003] All ER (D) 376 (Feb); Ch D 2003, TL 3683; [2003] STC 468; [2003] EWHC 318.*

George & Loochin (Stedman's Executors) v CIR

The holding of property as an investment was only one component of the business, and did not prevent the company from qualifying for business property relief.

A woman (S) had owned 85% of the shares in a company which operated a residential caravan park, comprising 167 mobile homes, and a country club with a licensed bar. The

Revenue issued a notice of determination on the basis that her shares in the company were not 'relevant business property', because the company's business consisted mainly of 'making or holding investments'. S's executors appealed. The Special Commissioner reviewed the evidence in detail and allowed the appeal, observing that the company had several full-time employees and was classed as a trading company for corporation tax purposes, and finding that '72% of the site fees goes in overheads ... most of which relate to the provision of upkeep of the common parts'. On the evidence, the Commissioner held that the company's business was 'the provision of services and not the business of holding investments'. The Ch D reversed this decision but the CA restored it. Carnwath LJ held that, on the evidence, the holding of property as an investment was only one component of the business, and did not prevent the company from qualifying for business property relief. *CA [2003] EWCA Civ 1763; [2004] STC 147.*

Gladstone v Bower

Agricultural holding—agreement to let land for a fixed period.

A landlord let a farm to a tenant for a fixed term of 18 months. He gave no notice to quit but at the end of the term brought an action for possession of the farm. The tenant contended that the letting took effect as a tenancy from year to year and could only be terminated by notice to quit. The CA held that, since the letting for 18 months created an interest greater than a tenancy from year to year at common law which could be terminated at the end of the first year, the landlord was entitled to possession. *CA [1960] 3 All ER 353.*

Goodchild and Another v Goodchild

Husband and wife with wills drawn up under identical terms—whether mutually binding and failure to make reasonable provision for adult son. Inheritance (Provision for Family and Dependants) Act 1975.

A testator and his wife executed identical wills in favour of the survivor and then each in favour of their son. The wife died and the testator received all her estate. The testator then remarried and made a new will leaving all his estate to his new wife. The testator died and proceedings were brought against the inheriting wife by the testator's son seeking a declaration that the new wife held the testator's estate on trust for the son and to give effect to the provisions set out in the mutual wills and for reasonable financial provision to be made to the son. The mistaken belief held by the testator's first wife that the wills were mutually binding imposed a moral obligation on the testator which constituted special circumstances justifying the son's claim under the *Inheritance (Provision for Family and Dependants) Act 1975.* The sum of £185,000 was awarded to the son. An appeal against the decision was made and also a cross appeal by the son stating that the wills should have been deemed to be mutually binding. In the Court of Appeal the appeal and cross appeal were dismissed but comments by the Judges with regard to the case in matters of tax efficiency are relevant. See *Re Sainsbury's Settlement, Sainsbury v First C B Trustee Ltd [1967] 1 All ER 878, [1967] 1 WLR 476. [1996] 1 All ER 670, CA [1997] 3 All ER 63.*

Goulding and Another v James and Another

Variation of Trusts Act 1958, s 1. Application to vary contrary to testatrix's intentions—use in planning.

In 1994 the testatrix revoked her will made two years earlier and replaced it with a new will providing for the creation of a will trust under which the daughter J had a life interest in possession subject to the grandson, M, taking an absolute interest on his attaining the age of 40. J and M applied to the Court for a variation under the *Variation of Trusts Act 1958, s 1(1)(c)* so that the residuary estate would be held as to 45% for J absolutely, 45% for M absolutely and the remaining 10% held on the trusts of a grandchildren's trust fund. Since J and M were *sui juris* and legally entitled to do what they want and having also actuarially valued the contingent interest of the future children of M under the existing will at only 1.85% there was no reason for the beneficiaries not to exercise their proprietary rights to overbear and defeat the intention of the testatrix. Incidentally, the fund would also be taken offshore and, according to the proposed variation, be managed by professional trustees. The Court of Appeal allowed the appeal and consented to the variation. *CA [1997] 2 All ER 239.*

Grey (Earl) v A-G

Gifts with reservation—exclusion of the donor from any benefit.

A covenant by the donee to pay the donor's debts and funeral expenses is a benefit. *[1900] AC 124; [1900–1903] All ER 268.*

Grey and Another v CIR

Time of disposition—disposition of equitable interest in settled property.

In a stamp duty case, an oral direction that an equitable interest in property be held on the trusts of a settlement was held not to be a valid disposition as it was not in writing. *HL, [1959] 3 All ER 603; [1960] AC 1.*

Grimwood-Taylor & Mallender (Mallender's Executors) v CIR

IHTA 1984, s 103 (3)—business 'carried on otherwise than for gain'.

An individual (M) died in 1986, owning substantial shareholdings in two companies. Each of the companies had purchased property, which was occupied by shareholders. The Revenue issued notices of determination charging IHT on the value of shares in the companies. M's executors appealed, contending that the shares qualified for business property relief. The Special Commissioner rejected this contention and dismissed the appeal, holding that the effect of *IHTA, s 103(3)* was that the shares did not qualify for relief, because the companies had used their funds to purchase land for occupation by their shareholders, so that their businesses had been carried on 'otherwise than for gain'. *[2000] STC SCD 39 Sp C 223.*

Guild v CIR

Bequest for sporting purposes—whether within IHTA 1984, s 23.

A testator left the residue of his estate to the town council of North Berwick for use in connection with the North Berwick sports centre or for 'some purpose in connection with sport'. The Revenue issued a determination to capital transfer tax, against which the executor appealed, contending that the bequest was charitable under the *Recreational Charities Act 1958, s 1*, and was therefore exempt from CTT by virtue of what is now *IHTA 1984, s 23(1)*. The HL allowed the executor's appeal (reversing the decision of the CS). The facilities at the sports centre were provided with the object of improving the conditions of life of the community generally. The phrase 'some similar purpose in connection with sport' implied a bequest which would display the leading characteristics of the sports centre, which lay in the nature of the facilities provided there and the fact that they were available to the public at large. *Dicta* of Bridge LJ in *CIR v McMullen & Others* approved and applied; *dicta* of Walton J in the same case disapproved. *HL, [1992] STC 162; [1992] 2 WLR 397; [1992] 2 All ER 10.*

Gully v Dix; In re Dix, deceased

Inheritance (Provision for family and Dependants) Act 1975—whether temporary separation still within section 1 of the Act re living together in the same household definition.

A woman (W) living with her husband (H) had to leave the household due to H's continual drunkenness and antisocial behaviour which had caused her to leave the home she had shared with H over 27 years. After leaving the home in August 2001 H was found dead in the garden in October 2001. *Section 1* of the *Inheritance (Provision for Family and Dependants) Act 1975* required the claimant to be living in the same household and to be maintained by the deceased 'immediately' before the death of H. The issue was whether the claimant's leaving and living apart from the deceased during the last three months of his life had the consequence that W could not show their living in the same household during the whole of the period of two years ending immediately before the death, nor that, immediately before his death, she was being maintained by him. It was found that the claimant could still have been living with the deceased in the same household at the moment of his death even if they had been living separately at the moment in time. This would be substantiated if they were tied by their relationship, manifested by various elements, not simply living under the same roof; the public and private acknowledgement of the mutual society, protection and support that bound them together. Was there an acceptance or recognition that their relationship was in truth at an end? The claimant did not consider this to be the case. She still entertained the hope that, with the modification of the deceased's drinking, it would have been possible for her to return to H. Therefore a claim for financial provision by a woman who had lived with the deceased for 27 years succeeded despite her living elsewhere at the time of the deceased's death. *CA [2004] TLR 28 January 2004.*

Hall v Hall (Hall's Executors) v CIR

Making or holding investments—BPR

A widow (H) had owned a caravan park. The caravans were let from March to October each year. The park also contained 11 chalets which were let on 45 year leases. H's executors appealed against a notice of determination, contending that the park qualified for business property relief. The Special Commissioners rejected this contention and dismissed the appeal. On the evidence, almost 84% of H's income from the park consisted of rent and standing charges. It followed that H's business consisted 'mainly of making or holding investments' within *IHTA 1984, s 105(3). [1997] STC SCD 126 Sp C 114.*

Hardcastle & Hardcastle (Vernede's Executors) v CIR

Lloyd's Underwriter owing money on accounts open at date of death—whether 'liabilities incurred for the purpose of the business'—IHTA 1984, s 110(b).

A Lloyd's underwriter (V) died in 1994. It was accepted that his underwriting activities constituted a business, within *IHTA 1984, s 105(1)(a)*, qualifying for business property relief. The Revenue issued a determination charging IHT on the basis that, when computing the net value of V's business for the purposes of business property relief, the amounts owing on accounts open at the date of his death constituted 'liabilities incurred for the purposes of the business', and should be deducted from the value of the assets used in V's business. His executors appealed, contending that the amounts owing were not 'liabilities incurred for the purposes of the business', and should therefore be deducted from the value of his other estate. The Special Commissioner accepted this contention and allowed the appeal. Applying the principles in *Van den Berghs v Clark*, the insurance contracts in question were 'ordinary commercial contracts made in the course of carrying on the trade' and were not 'assets used in the business' for the purposes of *IHTA 1984, s 110*. Accordingly, the money owing on open accounts 'was not a liability incurred for the purposes within the meaning of *section 110(b)'. [2000] STC SCD 532 Sp C 259.*

Harding & Leigh v CIR

Appointment by Trustees in favour of testator's widow—whether IHTA 1984, s 143 applicable.

A married man died on 14 November 1993, leaving property on discretionary trust for the benefit of his wife and children. On 25 January 1994 the executors executed a deed of appointment, giving the deceased's widow a life interest in residue. The Revenue issued a notice of determination on the basis that the spouse exemption in *IHTA 1984, s 18* did not apply, since the appointment had not been made by the deceased, and that *IHTA 1984, s 144* did not apply for the reasons set out in *Frankland v CIR* . The executors appealed, contending that the appointment should be treated as a transfer made by the deceased by virtue of *IHTA 1984,s 143*. The Special Commissioner rejected this contention and dismissed the appeal, holding that *section 143* did not apply. Firstly, while 'in some contexts a legatee may include a trustee', the trustees here could not be treated as legatees for the purposes of *section 143*. Secondly, an appointment of property was not the same as a transfer of property. Thirdly, the Commissioner found that 'the evidence falls short of showing that the appointment was made in accordance with the deceased's wishes'. *[1997] STC SCD 321 Sp C 140.*

Hatton v CIR (and related appeals)

Two settlements executed on successive days—whether a preordained series of transactions—whether Ramsay principle applicable.

In August 1978 C, who was terminally ill, granted a power of attorney to her daughter (H) and her solicitor. The solicitor executed a settlement which provided that a fund was to be held on trust and that the income from the fund should be paid to C until midnight on the following day or until her death, whichever was the shorter period, and that subsequently the fund was to be held for the absolute benefit of H. On the following day a settlement was executed whereby H assigned her interest under the previous settlement to trustees to pay the income to C until midnight on the following day or until C's death, whichever occurred first, and subsequently to hold the fund for the absolute benefit of H. C died nine days later. The Revenue issued notices of determination on the basis that C had effected a chargeable transfer. H appealed, contending that what is now *IHTA 1984, s 53(3)** applied, and that no CTT was due since the property in question had reverted to her as settlor. The Special Commissioners upheld the notices of determination, holding that the creation of the two settlements was a 'preordained series of transactions' within the principle laid down in *W T Ramsay Ltd v CIR*. Accordingly C was to be treated as the settlor of both settlements and *IHTA 1984, s 53(3)** did not apply. The Ch D upheld the Commissioners' decision. The conditions laid down by Lord Oliver in *Craven v White* were satisfied. The transactions constituted a single composite transaction whereby C had created a settlement under which she was entitled to a beneficial interest in possession in the settled property at midnight two days after the creation of the settlement. As she was then living, tax was chargeable as if she had effected a chargeable transfer at that time. (Chadwick J commented that, even if the *Ramsay* principle had not applied, C would still fall to be treated as a joint settlor of the second settlement.) *Ch D, [1992] STC 140.*

HD Lyon's Personal Representatives v HMRC; Trustees of the Alloro Trust v HMRC

FA 1986, s 102(1)—settlor retaining powers of revocation over discretionary trust—whether a gift with reservation.

In 1999 a settlor (L) gave £2,700,000 to the trustees of a discretionary trust. Under the trust deed, L retained the power of revocation, and was also a potential beneficiary of the trust. During his lifetime, L received distributions totalling £15,965 from the trust. L died in 2004. Following his death, HMRC issued a notice of determination on the basis that his transfer of the £2,700,000 to the trust was a 'gift with reservation', within *FA 1986, s 102*. The trustees, and L's personal representatives, appealed. The Special Commissioner dismissed the appeals, holding that there had been a 'reservation of benefit', within *s 102(1)(b)*. Furthermore, the manner in which the trust had been operated meant that the 'possession and enjoyment of the property' had not been 'bona fide assumed by the donee at the beginning of the relevant period', within *s 102(1)(a)* [2007] Sp C 616.

Heirs of Van-Hilten Van der Heijden v Inspecteur van der Belastingdienst/Partculieren/Ondernemingen buitenland te Heerlen

Netherlands Law of Succession that levied inheritance tax on the estate of a person who resided in the Netherlands at the time of death—died within ten years of moving from the Netherlands. National had continued to reside in that member state.

The Netherlands Law of Succession that levied inheritance tax on the estate of a person who resided in the Netherlands at the time of death, and provided that a Netherlands national who died within ten years of ceasing to reside in the Netherlands was deemed to be resident in the country at the time of death. A double-taxation law provided that the estate of a person so deemed was amenable to relief from tax to allow for tax charged in another state. Mrs V, a Netherlands national who had lived in the Netherlands and subsequently in Belgium then Switzerland, died within ten years of moving from the Netherlands, leaving an estate with assets in the Netherlands.

The ECJ ruled that Article 73B of the EC Treaty (prohibition of restrictions on the movement of capital) did not preclude legislation of a member state by which the estate of a national of that member state who died within ten years of ceasing to reside in that member state was to be taxed as if that national had continued to reside in that member state, while enjoying relief in respect of inheritance taxes levied by other states.[2006] (Case: C-513/03); [2006] WTLR 919; STI 535.

Henderson & Henderson (Black's Trustees) v CIR

IHTA 1984, s 64—charge at ten-year anniversary of settlement without interest in possession.

The Revenue issued a notice of determination under *IHTA 1984, s 64*, on the ten-year anniversary of a settlement without interest in possession. Following the determination, the trustees of the settlement appealed, and provided more information concerning the value of the property comprised in the settlement, which the Revenue accepted. The Commissioner upheld the determination in principle and confirmed it in the amended amount. *[2000] STC SCD 572 Sp C 263.*

Higginson's Executors v CIR

IHTA 1984, s 115(2) re large hunting lodge in 134 acres not a farmhouse.

In 1954 H purchased an estate comprising 134 acres and including a large hunting lodge, built in the early nineteenth century. He farmed the estate until 1985, from when he let the farmland but continued to live in the lodge. He died in 2000, and the property was sold in 2001 for £1,150,000. The Inland Revenue accepted that the land and agricultural out-buildings qualified for agricultural property relief, but issued a ruling that the lodge was not 'of a character appropriate to the property' for the purposes of *IHTA 1984, s 115(2)*, and thus did not qualify for agricultural property relief. H's executors appealed. The Special Commissioner dismissed the appeal, holding that 'for the purposes of *section 115(2)* the unit must be an agricultural unit: that is to say that within the unit, the land must predominate … (and) any qualifying cottages, farm buildings or farmhouses must be ancillary to the land'. However, in view of the price paid for the property, it was clear that 'within this particular unit it is the house which predominates, and that what we have here is a house with farmland going with it (and not vice versa)'. Accordingly, the lodge was not a 'farmhouse' for the purposes of *s 115(2)*. *[2002] STC SCD 483 Sp C 337.*

Holland (Holland's Executor) v CIR

IHTA 1984, s 18—whether exemption for transfers between spouses applicable to transfers to common law wife.

An individual (H) separated from his wife in 1965 (and subsequently divorced). In 1968 he began living with another woman (K). They did not marry, but had two children together, and continued to live together until his death in 2000. H left his entire estate to K. The Inland Revenue issued a notice of determination charging IHT. K appealed, contending that she should be entitled to the inter-spouse exemption of *IHTA 1984, s 18*. The Special Commissioners rejected this contention and dismissed her appeal, holding that 'the word "spouse" in (*IHTA 1984, s 18*) means a person who is legally married and does not include a person who has lived with another as husband and wife'. *[2003] STC SCD 43 Sp C 350.* (*Note*. The Commissioners also held that this did not contravene the *Human Rights Act 1998*.)

Holmes & Another v McMullen & Others (re Ratcliffe (deceased))

IHTA 1984, s 41—allocation of exemption.

The decision in *Lockhart v Harker & Others (re Benham's Will Trusts)*, see above, was not followed (and was implicitly disapproved) in this subsequent case in which the testatrix had left half her estate to two relatives and the other half to be held on trust for four charities. The executors issued a summons seeking the court's declaration as to the correct method of administering the net residuary estate. The Chancery Division held that the half shares were to be calculated before the payment of inheritance tax due in respect of the relatives' shares (so that the net amount received by the relatives would be less than the net amount received by the charities). Blackburne J held that an equal division of disposable residue between the relatives and charities inevitably meant that the inheritance tax attributable to the relatives' share had to be borne by that share, since to subject the charities' share to any part of that burden was prohibited by *IHTA 1984, s 41(b)*. *[1999] STC SCD 262*.

Howarth's Executors v CIR

IHTA 1984, s 221—Notices of Determination.

A woman died in 1985. There were three executors. The Revenue issued Notices of Determination under *IHTA 1984, s 221* on each of the executors. They appealed. The Special Commissioner upheld the Notices and dismissed the appeals, observing that the fact that one of the executors had subsequently been made bankrupt, and that another was suffering from ill-health, did not provide any defence to the Notices. Applying *dicta* of Scott J in *CIR v Stannard*; 'the liability in respect of capital transfer tax for which a personal representative becomes liable … is necessarily an original liability which is in terms imposed on the personal representative'. *[1997] STC SCD 162 Sp C 119*.

HSBC Trusts Co (UK) Ltd (Farmbrough's Executor) v Twiddy

Valuation of a minority interest in property.

A woman (F) had held a 16.25% interest in two large buildings comprising 28 flats and 9 shops. The Lands Tribunal held that since this was a minority interest, it should be valued on an income basis, declining to follow the earlier decision in *Charkham v CIR, Lands Tribunal 1996, [2000] RVR 7*. The Tribunal assumed a net yield of 6.5% and therefore multiplied the net income of £170,000 by 15.38 to give a figure of £2,614,600 for the whole property and £425,000 (rounded to the nearest £1,000) for F's share. *Lands Tribunal 24 August 2006 unreported.*

Inglewood and Another v CIR

Accumulation and maintenance settlements—power of revocation.

By a 1964 appointment property was held on trust for the children of B who attained 21 or married under that age, subject to powers of revocation and reappointment and with interim powers of accumulation and maintenance. On 5 May 1975 B's eldest child became 21 and on 29 March 1976 the trustees released their power of revocation. The Revenue argued that a CTT charge arose on the former event under *FA 1975, 5 Sch 6(2)*, and on the latter under *FA 1975, 5 Sch 15(3)*. The trustees contended that the exemption for accumulation and maintenance settlements provided by *FA 1975, 5 Sch 15(1)(2)* applied so that no CTT was chargeable by reference to either event. The CA dismissed the trustees' appeal holding that the provisions of *para 15(1)(a)* were not satisfied by a trust subject to a power of revocation and reappointment under which the beneficiary's interest could be destroyed at the absolute discretion of the trustees and reappointed solely for the benefit of third parties at ages exceeding 25. The word 'will' in 'will … become entitled to' implied a degree of certainty inconsistent with such a power. *CA 1982, CTTL 16; [1983] STC 133; [1983] 1 WLR 366*. (*Note. FA 1975, 5 Sch 15* was replaced by *IHTA 1984, s 71** for events after 8 March 1982 or, in some instances, 31 March 1983 or 31 March 1984.)

Ingram and Another v CIR

Transfer of freehold interest in property to family trust—equitable leasehold interest retained by transferor—whether a gift with reservation.

In 1987 a widow transferred a property which she owned to her solicitor, who executed declarations that he held the property as her nominee. The solicitor executed two leases purporting to give the widow a rent-free leasehold interest on the estate for 20 years, and the land subject to the leases was transferred to a family trust. The widow continued to live at the property until her death in 1989. The Revenue treated the transfer as a gift with reservation, within *FA 1986, s 102,* and issued a notice of determination accordingly. The House of Lords allowed the executors' appeal. Lord Hoffman held that 'although (*s 102*) does not allow a donor to have his cake and eat it, there is nothing to stop him from carefully dividing up the cake, eating part and having the rest. If the benefits which the donor continues to enjoy are by virtue of property which was never comprised in the gift, he has not reserved any benefit out of the property of which he disposed.' For these purposes, 'property' was 'not something which has physical existence like a house but a specific interest in that property, a legal construct, which can co-exist with other interests in the same physical object. *Section 102* does not therefore prevent people from deriving benefit from the object in which they have given away an interest. It applies only when they derive the benefit from that interest.' The policy of *section 102* was to require people to 'define precisely the interests which they are giving away and the interests, if any, which they are retaining'. The interest, which the widow retained, was 'a proprietary interest, defined with the necessary precision'. The gift was 'a gift of the capital value in the land after deduction of her leasehold interest in the same way as a gift of the capital value of the fund after deduction of an annuity'. *Munro v Commrs of Stamp Duties of New South Wales,* and *dicta* of Lord Simonds in *St Aubyn v Attorney-General, HL 1951, [1952] AC 15; [1951] 2 All ER 473* applied. Furthermore, the leases were valid in law. Applying *Rye v Rye, HL [1962] AC 496; [1962] 1 All ER 146,* an owner of freehold property could not grant a lease to himself. However, a 'trustee in English law is not an agent for his beneficiary'. (The House of Lords declined to follow the Scottish stamp duty case of *Kildrummy (Jersey) Ltd v CIR, CS [1990] STC 657,* where the Court of Sessions held that the lease granted by a landowner to a nominee acting on his behalf was equivalent to the grant of a lease to himself.) *Dicta* of Goff J in *Nichols v CIR,* see below, disapproved. *HL [1999] STC 37; [1999] 1 All ER 297.*

Iveagh (Earl of) v Revenue Commissioners

Domicile—jurisdiction of Courts in relation to determination of domicile.

In an Irish case, the High Court reversed a decision by the Special Commissioners that the taxpayer had not given up his domicile of origin. The Supreme Court held that domicile is a question of fact and the Commissioners' decision, if one of fact, could not be reviewed by the Courts. However, in this case the Special Commissioners had approached the question as one of law and had misconstrued the law. The case was remitted to them to determine the question of domicile as one of fact. *SC(I) 1930, 1 ITC 316; [1930] IR 431.*

Jacques v HMRC

TMA 1970, s 31A—whether notice of appeal must specify grounds of appeal.

An accountant sent a notice of appeal against a penalty notice to the Special Commissioners, stating that 'due to the conduct of HMRC Officers we will not disclose the reasons for appeal'. HMRC applied for a ruling that the notice of appeal was invalid, as it had failed to state the grounds of appeal, as required by *TMA 1970, s 31A(5).* The Commissioner accepted this contention, holding that the purported notice of appeal was invalid. *[2006] STC SCD 40 Sp C 513.*

Jones & Another (Ball's Administrators) v CIR

Uncompleted contract for sale of land—whether relief under IHTA 1984, s 191 available.

A farmer (B) died on 26 June 1988. On 25 June 1991 his administrators entered into a contract to sell the farm for £300,150. However, the contract was not completed and the farm was eventually sold for £400,000 under another contract in 1992. The probate value of the farm was agreed at £447,000, but the administrators claimed relief under *IHTA 1984, s 191*, contending that for IHT purposes the farm should be valued at £300,150 (the price payable under the 1991 contract). The Revenue rejected the claim and the Ch D dismissed the administrators' appeal. An abortive contract was not a sale, and the farm had not been sold within three years of B's death. Accordingly IHTA 1984, s 191 was not applicable and the farm had to be valued at its probate value of £447,000. *Ch D 14 February 1997, [1997] STC 358.*

Judge & Judge (Walden's Personal Representatives) v HMRC

Testator's widow continuing to occupy property at trustees' discretion—whether testator's will conferred interest in possession.

A woman (W) was widowed in 2000. Her husband's will gave his house to trustees, with a declaration that they should allow W to occupy the house 'for such period or periods as they shall in their absolute discretion think fit'. W continued to occupy the house until her death in 2003. The Revenue issued a notice of determination on the basis that her husband's will had given her an interest in possession in the house. Her personal representatives appealed. The Special Commissioner allowed their appeal, holding that the effect of W's husband's will was that she 'had no right to occupy the property but the trustees were given a discretion (but not a duty) to allow her to occupy'. Accordingly W did not have an interest in possession in the property. *[2005] STC SCD 863 Sp C 506.*

Kempe and Roberts (personal representatives of Lyon, deceased) v CIR

Life policy designation—whether deceased beneficially entitled to sum assured by reason of having a general power to dispose as he thought fit under IHTA 1984, s 5(2).

A company insured the life of one of its employees (L). Under the policy, L was allowed to designate the beneficiaries who would benefit on his demise and he nominated his two sisters as the beneficiaries in the event of his death. L died in 2001. The Inland Revenue issued a notice of determination charging IHT on the basis that the death benefits payable under the policy formed part of L's estate. His sisters (who were his personal representatives) appealed contending that the policy was not part of the estate of the deceased as it was for the benefit of the next of kin and to treat it as part of the estate of the deceased was to defeat the primary purpose of the policy. The Special Commissioner dismissed their appeal, holding that 'the deceased had a general power under (*IHTA 1984, s 5(2)*) which enabled him to dispose of the sum assured under the policy as he thought fit. That means that he was beneficially entitled to the sum assured and so it formed part of his estate and accordingly is chargeable to tax.' *[2004] STC SCD 467 Sp C 424.*

Kwok Chi Leung Karl (Executor of Lamson Kwok) v Commissioner of Estate Duty

Situation of property—contract debt.

New York Life Insurance Co Ltd was followed in a Hong Kong case where the testator had, on the day before his death, transferred assets to a Liberian company for a non-negotiable promissory note. The Privy Council, reversing the decision of the Hong Kong Court of Appeal, held that the fact that the document recording the debt was located in Hong Kong did not alter the principle that the debt was located where the debtor, rather than the creditor, resided. There was no suggestion by the Hong Kong Commissioner at any state of the proceedings that the transactions carried out so close to the testator's death were a sham. The Privy Council therefore had to treat them as genuine arm's length transactions. Per Lord Oliver, 'it would be unwise to assume that the genuineness of similar transactions in the future will necessarily be beyond challenge'. *PC [1988] STC 728.*

Lake v Lake & Others

Rectification of deeds.

A testator died in November 1986, and a Deed of Variation was executed three months later by his widow and the trustees. However, the solicitors drew up the Deed incorrectly, resulting in an increased inheritance tax liability. A second Deed was subsequently executed to correct the error, but following the decision in *Russell & Another v CIR*, the liability was nevertheless determined in accordance with the original Deed. The widow sought an Order for the rectification of the original Deed in accordance with the intentions, which the Ch D granted. On the facts, there was no doubt that the original Deed did not carry out the intentions of the parties, and the fact that there was no issue before the court did not present an obstacle to rectification. *Ch D [1989] STC 865.*

Lawton, In re

Domicile—whether English domicile of origin abandoned.

In an estate duty case, a testator who had been born in 1871 with an English domicile, but who from about 1890 onwards had lived abroad, was held, on the facts, to have been domiciled in France on his death in 1955, notwithstanding a declaration in his will made in 1948 that he had not abandoned his English domicile of origin. *Ch D 1958, 37 ATC 216.*

Lee & Lee (Lee's Executors) v CIR

IHTA, s 179(1)—application of twelve-month time limit.

An individual died in November 2000. In February 2002 his executors discovered that he had some investments in a unit trust, which had declined in value. They claimed relief under *IHTA 1984, s 178*. The Revenue rejected the claim, as it had been made outside the twelve-month time limit of *IHTA 1984, s 179(1)*. The Special Commissioner dismissed the executors' appeal. *[2002] STC SCD 41 Sp C 349.*

Lloyds Private Banking Ltd v CIR

Life interest in matrimonial home given to husband, daughter absolutely entitled on death of her father—whether an interest in possession conferred by the wife on husband. IHTA 1984, s 43(2).

A married couple lived together as tenants in common. The wife died in 1989. By her will, she appointed a trustee and bequeathed her 50% share in the matrimonial home to the trustee, directing that her husband should be permitted to continue to live there until his death, and that her share should then pass to her daughter. The husband continued to live in the property until his death in 1993. The Revenue issued a notice of determination, charging IHT on the basis that the deemed transfer of value on the husband's death included the entire interest in the property, on the basis that his wife's will had given him an interest in possession in her 50% share of the property. The trustee appealed, contending that the will did not confer an interest in possession, and that the will had conferred no new rights on the husband, who was entitled to the use and enjoyment of the property as a co-owner. The Special Commissioner accepted this contention and allowed the appeal. On the wife's death, the husband had continued to enjoy the right to reside in the property and that right could only have been terminated by the husband's volition or by a court order under Law of Property Act 1925, s 30. The effect of the wife's will was that there had been an absolute gift of her 50% share in the property to her daughter, subject to a direction to the trustee to postpone sale. The case was taken on appeal to the Chancery Division and in a reserved judgment Lightman J allowed the appeal brought by originating summons by the Inland Revenue. Lightman J stated that the critical issue was whether clause 3 was dispositive or merely laid down administrative directions to the Trustee. Clause 3 was dispositive and conferred on Mr Evans a determinable life interest in the half share although it was dressed up as a set of administrative instructions. See also dicta of Wood VC in *Maddison v Chapman, 1859, 4 K & J 709*, and Farwell J in *Re Shuckburgh's Settlement, Ch D [1901] 2 Ch 794*, applied. *[1997] STC SCD 259 Sp C 133; [1998] STC 559.*

Lloyds TSB plc (Antrobus' Personal Representatives) v CIR

Farmhouse set in 132 acres was 'a farmhouse with a farm and definitely not a house with land'.

A deceased estate included a six-bedroomed house, part of which had been built in the sixteenth century, and a number of agricultural buildings, set in about 132 acres of agricultural land. The site had been used as a farm by the same family for more than 90 years. The Revenue issued a notice of determination that the house was not 'of a character appropriate to the property' for the purposes of *IHTA 1984, s 115(2)*, and thus did not qualify for agricultural property relief. The company which acted as the deceased's personal representative appealed. The Special Commissioner allowed the appeal, finding that the property 'was in a poor state of repair and maintenance. The result was that, even if the dwelling-house had at one time been a family home of some distinction, it had, both in appearance and in use, become a farmhouse on a working farm.' On the evidence, the house was 'a farmhouse with a farm and definitely not a house with land'. It was 'of a character appropriate to the property' for the purposes of *s 115(2)*. *[2002] STC SCD 468 Sp C 336.*

Lloyds TSB plc (Antrobus' Personal Representative) v Twiddy

Lands Tribunal decision—30% discount for farmhouse to reflect agricultural value.

HMRC issued a notice of determination that the farmhouse (see case report above) in question had a market value in excess of its value as agricultural property, so that IHT was payable on the amount by which the market value exceeded the agricultural value. The personal representatives appealed, contending that the agricultural value was the same as the market value. The Lands Tribunal reviewed the evidence in detail, rejected this contention and dismissed the appeal, holding that the open market value of the farmhouse should be discounted by 30% to arrive at its 'agricultural value'. *[2004] DET/47/2004.*

Lynall (deceased), In re

The amount or value of the consideration for an asset—value of unquoted shares while public flotation under consideration.

In an estate duty case the question at issue was the price which certain unquoted shares 'would fetch if sold in the open market at the time of the death of the deceased'. At the time of the death, the directors were considering public flotation and favourable confidential reports had been made to them for that purpose by a firm of accountants and a firm of stockbrokers. The HL held, *inter alia*, that although no general rule could be laid down as to the information a hypothetical purchaser in an open market may be deemed to have, the board could not be deemed to disclose confidential information. *HL 1971, 47 TC 375; [1972] AC 680; [1971] 3 All ER 904.* (*Note.* See now *TCGA 1992, s 273*, deriving from *FA 1973*. The substantive decision here is therefore no longer applicable, but the judgments include a useful review of estate duty cases dealing with the valuation of unquoted shares. See also *Battle v CIR* and *CIR v Crossman, Caton's Administrators v Couch* and *Clark (Clark's Executor) v CIR*.)

Macaulay & Another v Premium Life Assurance Co Ltd

Unsuccessful CTT avoidance scheme—action alleging negligence by promoters of scheme.

In 1984 an individual (M) undertook a scheme marketed by a life assurance company, which the company claimed would avoid liability to capital transfer tax (subsequently renamed inheritance tax). However, the scheme failed to take account of *IHTA, s 3(3)**, so that the whole of M's free estate became liable to IHT on her death (on 4 March 1991). On 3 March 1997 M's executors issued a writ against the life assurance company, alleging that it owed a duty of care to ensure that its brochure was accurate and pointed out any CTT risks inherent in the scheme. The company defended the action, contending that the writ had been issued outside the six-year time limit laid down by *Limitation Act 1980*. The Ch D rejected this contention and held that the writ had been issued within the six-year period. The cause of action had accrued when M died. Her executors were not suing in respect of a lost opportunity suffered by M in her lifetime; they were suing in respect of the IHT liability which arose on her death, and which did not exist until she died. Liability for IHT was payable by M's estate, and was not imposed on the deceased. M's executors were suing for a loss or damage which did not exist until M's death. *Ch D 29 April 1999 unreported.*

McDowall & Others (McDowall's Executors) v CIR (and related appeal)

Power of attorney—gifts out of deceased estate—whether valid.

In 1993 an elderly man (M) granted a deed conferring a power of attorney on his wife, and providing that if she predeceased him, the power should pass to his son-in-law. M's wife died in 1996. M's son-in-law used the power of attorney to make substantial gifts out of M's estate. M died in April 1998. His solicitors submitted an inventory to the Capital Taxes Office [now HMRC Inheritance Tax], accepting that gifts of £604,000 were chargeable transfers on which IHT was due, but treating gifts totalling £147,800 as exempt transfers. The Revenue issued notices of determination to M's executors, determining that these gifts were not allowable as deductions from M's estate in determining the IHT liability. The executors appealed. The Special Commissioners reviewed the evidence in detail and dismissed the appeals, holding that on a proper construction of the power of attorney, M's son-in-law had no authority to make the gifts. Applying *dicta* of Russell J in *Re Reckitt, CA [1928] 2 KB 244,* 'the primary object of a power of attorney is to enable the attorney to act in the management of his principal's affairs. An attorney cannot, in the absence of a clear power to do so, make presents to himself or to others of his principal's property.' The gifts which M's son-in-law had purported to make were *ultra vires*, and M's executors were entitled to recover them. Therefore the amounts in question formed part of M's estate at the time of his death, and were chargeable to IHT accordingly. *[2004] STC SCD 22 Sp C 382.*

MacNiven v Westmoreland Investments Ltd

Anti-avoidance—payments of money borrowed from the pension fund constituted payments of interest for the purposes of s 338—meaning of 'paid'.

A property-holding company (W) suffered financial difficulties and was loaned substantial sums of money by its major shareholder (a pension fund). Subsequently it obtained further interest-free loans from the same source and paid accrued interest on the earlier loans. It claimed that these payments should be treated as charges on income. The Revenue rejected the claim, considering firstly that W did not qualify as an investment company, secondly that the accrued interest had not been paid for the purposes of *s 338,* and alternatively that even if the interest were held to have been paid, the payment was not wholly and exclusively for the purpose of W's business. The Special Commissioners allowed W's appeal, holding that W was an investment company within *s 130* and that the payments of interest were genuine, had been made for the purpose of W's business, and were effective for the purpose of *s 338.* The HL upheld the Commissioners' decision. The payments of money borrowed from the pension fund constituted payments of interest for the purposes of *s 338,* and the Commissioners were entitled to find that they had been made wholly and exclusively for the purpose of W's business. Lord Nicholls observed that 'the source from which a debtor obtains the money he uses in paying his debt is immaterial for the purpose of *s 338*'. Lord Hoffmann observed that 'the only apparent reason for the insistence on payment of yearly interest is that payment gives rise to an obligation to deduct tax. In the present case, (W) complied with that obligation. The Crown's real complaint is that the scheme, as an exempt fund, was able to reclaim the tax. But this cannot be remedied by giving the word "paid" a different meaning in the case of a payment to an exempt lender. The word must mean the same, whatever the status of the lender.' Lord Hutton observed that 'the obligation undertaken by (W) to pay interest on the sums it had been lent by the scheme trustees was a genuine one which existed in the real world'. Furthermore, the anti-avoidance provisions of *s 787* did not apply. *HL 2001, TL 3631; [2001] STC 237; [2001] 2 WLR 377; [2001] 1 All ER 865.*

Macpherson & Another v CIR

Associated operations.

On 29 March 1977, trustees of a discretionary settlement entered into an agreement with D which meant, in effect that D would have custody of some valuable trust paintings for 14 years. Although the agreement was on commercial terms, it reduced the value of the trustees' interest in the paintings. On the following day, the trustees appointed a protected life interest in the paintings, subject to the agreement, to D's son. The Revenue charged CTT on the reduction in value, and the trustees appealed, contending that *IHTA 1984, s 10** applied since the transactions had not been intended to confer gratuitous benefit. The HL rejected this contention and upheld the charge to CTT. The agreement and appointment were associated operations, and together constituted a transaction intended to confer gratuitous benefit on D's son. *HL [1988] STC 362; [1988] 2 WLR 1261; [1988] 2 All ER 753.*

Magnavox Electronics Co Ltd (in liquidation) v Hall

Date of disposal.

In September 1978 a company (M) exchanged contracts for the sale of a factory to another company (J) for £1,400,000. Completion was arranged for February 1979, but for financial reasons J was unable to complete the purchase, and forfeited its deposit. Meanwhile, M had gone into voluntary liquidation in December 1978. The liquidator did not rescind the contract of sale, but arranged for M to acquire an 'off-the-shelf' company (S), to which it assigned its beneficial interest under the contract on 6 July 1979. Three days later certain variations in the contract were agreed, including a reduction of the purchase price to £1,150,000 and a new completion date of 9 October 1979. On the same day S exchanged contracts with a fourth company (B) for the sale of the factory on terms practically identical with those in the original contract as varied. B duly completed. The Revenue issued an assessment on the basis that the disposal had taken place after M had gone into liquidation. M appealed, contending that the disposal had taken place in September 1978 (so that trading losses of that accounting period could be set against the gain). The Special Commissioners dismissed M's appeal, and the Ch D and CA upheld their decision. The disposal to B was not under the 1978 contract, but under a new contract made in July 1979. Furthermore, the interposition of S was part of an artificial avoidance scheme which could be disregarded, applying *Furniss v Dawson*. *CA 1986, 59 TC 610; [1986] STC 561.*

Maitland's Trustees v Lord Advocate

Deed of appointment executed by trustees—whether accumulation and maintenance settlement established.

The trustees of a discretionary settlement executed a deed of appointment with the intention of establishing a discretionary and maintenance settlement. The appointment was declared to be conditional on the power of accumulation being valid under the *Trusts (Scotland) Act 1961*, and provided that if the accumulations were contrary to law, the appointment should be void. The Revenue refused to accept the deed as establishing an accumulation and maintenance settlement, considering that *IHTA 1984, s 71(1)(a)** was not satisfied. The CS allowed the trustees appeal. The word 'will' in *IHTA 1984, s 71(1)(a)* did not require absolute certainty. Both the Revenue and the trustees agreed that there was no illegality, and the fact that a third party might question this in future did not prevent *IHTA 1984, s 71(1)(a)* being satisfied. The deed was not *ultra vires*, and the fact that the trustees might not safely make any distribution to the primary beneficiaries until the doubt as to the law was resolved did not affect the position. *CS, [1982] SLT 483.*

Mallender & Others (Drury-Lowe's Executors) v CIR

IHTA 1984, s 110(b)—Lloyd's underwriter—commercial property charged to bank—whether 'assets used in the business'.

A Lloyd's underwriter (D) died in 1993. His underwriting business was supported by several bank guarantees. In consideration for the guarantees, D had indemnified the bank against all liabilities and had secured this liability by a charge over some commercial property which D owned. The Revenue issued notices of determination on the basis that the commercial property did not qualify for business property relief. D's executors appealed, contending that the effect of the charge over the commercial property was that it was within the definition of 'assets used in the business', within *IHTA 1984, s 110(b)*. The Ch D rejected this contention and upheld the notices (reversing the decision of the Special Commissioner). Jacob J held that an asset used as a security for a guarantee was not 'relevant business property' within *IHTA 1984, s 105(1)(a)*. The property was not itself used in the business, and did not qualify for relief. *STC SCD 574 Sp C 264; Ch D [2001] STC 514.*

Mark v Mark

Person habitually resident and having a domicile of choice in England and Wales even though presence in the United Kingdom was a criminal offence—residence/domicile a question of fact not necessarily lawful.

Section 5(2) of the *Domicile and Matrimonial Proceedings Act 1973* provides for the following: '(2) The Court shall have jurisdiction to entertain proceedings for divorce or judicial separation if (but only if) either of the parties to the marriage (a) is domiciled in England and Wales on the date when proceedings are begun; or (b) was habitually resident in England and Wales throughout the period of one year ending with that date'. In an appeal from a decision by the Court of Appeal the House of Lords decided that Mrs Mark, a party to divorce proceedings, who was habitually resident and having a domicile of choice in England and Wales was domiciled here even though her presence in the United Kingdom was a criminal offence. There was no reason why, in principle, a person whose presence here, although unlawful under the *Immigration Act 1971*, could not acquire a domicile of choice in England and Wales. Either a person had acquired a domicile of choice in England and Wales or they had not. If having done so, that person was not to be denied it because the court considered the case unmeritorious or tainted with moral or legal turpitude. If that person had not done so, they were not to be granted it because the court considered them to be virtuous. The matter lay with the facts of the case whether the person had the required intention at the relevant time. *HL [2005] UKHL 42.*

Martin & Horsfall (Moore's Executors) v CIR

Business property relief—relevant business property—IHTA 1984, s 105(3).

A widow owned a number of industrial units. On her death, the Revenue issued a notice of determination. Her executors appealed, contending that the industrial units qualified for business property relief. The Special Commissioner dismissed the appeal, holding that the effect of *IHTA, s 105(3)* was that the property was not 'relevant business property', since the widow's business consisted 'wholly or mainly … of making or holding investments'. The Commissioner noted that *s 105(3)* derived from *FA 1976*, and that, during the relevant Finance Bill Debates, the Chief Secretary of the Treasury had stated that the letting of land did not qualify for business property relief. *[1995] STC SCD 5 Sp C 2.*

Masterman-Lister v Jewell and another; Masterman-Lister v Brutton and Co

Practice and procedure—Parties—Capacity to litigate and compromise—Claimant suffering brain damage as result of road traffic accident—Claimant issuing proceedings arising out of accident—Claimant agreeing to settle claim—Claimant alleging he was a patient at time of settlement—Burden of proof—Test to be applied—RSC Ord 80, rr 1, 10—CPR Pt 21.

The claimant was born in 1963. In 1980, he was involved in a serious road traffic accident with a milk float driven by J, who was employed by the second defendant. As a result, the claimant suffered severe brain damage. The claimant instructed B and Co, who were the defendants to the second action, to issue a claim against J and HCD. In 1987, the claimant accepted an offer from HCD to compromise the action on the basis of £76,000 and costs. He returned to work some nine months after the accident, but was only able to perform menial tasks. He resigned in 1989, and had not worked since. He lived with his parents until 1992, when he purchased his own house. In 1993, he issued proceedings against the first defendant in relation to their conduct of that litigation. In 1997, the claimant was advised by a consultant in neuropsychiatric rehabilitation that he was, and had been since the accident, a patient within the meaning of *s 94(2)a* of the *Mental Health Act 1983*. The claimant sought to reopen the settlement of his personal injury action on the basis that it never received the approval of the court, as would have been required at the relevant time pursuant to RSC Ord 80 r 10b. RSC Ord 80 r 1c, which defined 'patient', was replaced by CPR 21.1(2)(b)d. The issue of whether the claimant was a patient within the 1983 Act was tried as a preliminary issue. The judge ruled that the court should only take over the individual's function of decision making when it was shown on the balance of probabilities that such person did not have the capacity sufficiently to understand, absorb and retain information, including advice, relevant to the matters in question sufficiently to enable him or her to make decisions based upon such information. He then considered the evidence and concluded that since 1983 at the latest, the claimant had been fully capable of managing and administering his property and affairs and therefore was not a 'patient' for the purposes of either the 1983 Act, RSC Ord 80 or CPR Pt 21. The claimant appealed. On appeal issues arose as to the burden of proof and the test for determining capacity to litigate and compromise.

The appeal would be dismissed.

(1) The burden of proof rested on those asserting incapacity. The fact that there was evidence that as a result of a head injury sustained in an accident it was agreed that the claimant was incapable of managing his property and affairs did not mean that he could rely on the presumption of continuance, although if there was clear evidence of incapacity for a considerable period then the burden of proof might be more easily discharged. There was no requirement that a judicial officer had to consider medical evidence or be satisfied as to incapacity before a person could be treated as a patient. However, following the implementation of the *Human Rights Act 1998* in order that a party was not deprived of his civil rights by being treated as a patient, the court should always, as a matter of practice, at the first convenient opportunity, investigate the question of capacity whenever there was any reason to suspect that it might be absent. That meant that, even where the issue did not seem to be contentious, a district judge who was responsible for case management would almost certainly require the assistance of a medical report before being able to be satisfied that incapacity existed.

(2) For the purposes of RSC Ord 80 and CPR Pt 21, the test to be applied was whether the party to legal proceedings was capable of understanding, with the assistance of such proper explanation from legal advisers and experts in other disciplines as the case might require, the issues on which his consent or decision was likely to be necessary in the course of those proceedings. If the party had capacity to understand that which he needed to understand in order to pursue or defend a claim, there was not reason why the law, whether substantive or procedural, should require the interposition of a next friend or a litigation friend. Moreover, a person should not be held unable to understand the information relevant to a decision if he could understand an explanation of that information in broad terms and simple language. Further, he should not be regarded as unable to make a rational decision merely because the decision which he did, in fact, make was a decision which would not be made by a person of ordinary prudence; *White v Fell* (12 November 1987, unreported, QBD) considered [2002] All ER (D) 297 (Dec); CA [2003] All ER (D) 59 (Jan).

Matthews v Martin & Others

Rectification of deed of family arrangement.

A widow agreed with her children that her late husband's estate should be distributed in a manner different from that laid down in the *Intestacy Rules*. The deed was executed within two years of the deceased's death as required by *IHTA 1984, s 182*, but it contained errors of which the parties only became aware after the expiry of the two-year period. The Ch D granted the widow's application for retrospective rectification of the deed. The deed was clearly defective and did not reflect the proper agreement of the parties. The fact that the sole purpose of seeking rectification was the obtaining of a fiscal advantage was not a bar to granting the relief sought. *Lake v Lake & Others* and *Seymour & Another v Seymour* applied. *Ch D 1990, [1991] BTC 8048.*

Mawson v Barclays Mercantile Business Finance Ltd (aka ABC Ltd v M)

General anti-avoidance—capital allowances.

A UK finance company (B) agreed to purchase a pipeline, which was accepted as plant and machinery, from the Irish Gas Board for £91,000,000 and to lease the pipeline back to the Board for 31 years. The Board in turn subleased the pipeline to a UK subsidiary company (G). Arrangements were agreed whereby the whole of the purchase price paid by B was deposited with a Jersey company (D), so that it was not available for immediate use by the Board, but was ultimately paid by D to B's holding company. B claimed capital allowances on the £91,000,000. The Revenue rejected the claim on the basis that the money was not expenditure incurred on the acquisition of plant or machinery, within *CAA 2001, s 11**. The CA allowed the company's appeal and the HL unanimously upheld this decision, observing that 'the object of granting the allowance is … to provide a tax equivalent to the normal accounting deduction from profits for the depreciation of machinery and plant used for the purposes of a trade. … When the trade is finance leasing, this means that the capital expenditure should have been incurred to acquire the machinery or plant for the purpose of leasing it in the course of the trade.' These requirements were 'in the case of a finance lease concerned entirely with the acts and purposes of the lessor'. On the evidence, the purchase and leaseback were part of B's 'ordinary trade of finance leasing'. What subsequently happened to the purchase price did 'not affect the reality of the expenditure by (B) and its acquisition of the pipeline for the purposes of its finance leasing trade'. *Mawson v Barclays Mercantile Business Finance Ltd (aka ABC Ltd v M), HL 2004, 76 TC 446; [2005] STC 1; [2004] UKHL 51; [2005] 1 All ER 97.* (*Note.* See now, however, *CAA 2001, ss 221–228,* largely deriving from *F(No 2) A 1997, s 46.*)

Melville and Others v CIR

IHTA, s 272—definition of 'property'.

In 1993 a settlor (M) made a discretionary settlement under terms which conferred on him a general power to direct the trustees to exercise a power of apportionment, and included the power to direct the trustees to transfer the whole of the trust fund to him absolutely. In 1999 the Revenue issued a notice of determination on the trustees. They appealed, contending that M's right to require them to revest all or part of the settled property on him was part of the 'rights and interests of any description' which, by virtue of *IHTA, s 272,* formed part of M's estate immediately after the settlement. The Ch D accepted this contention and allowed the appeal. Lightman J noted that the settlement had been intended 'to create a situation in which the settlor is able to make a substantial transfer of assets into a settlement which gives rise to a charge to inheritance tax in respect of the entire disposal, while at the same time ensuring that the amount of inheritance tax actually payable is negligible'. However, he held that not to treat the general power of appointment as 'property' within *s 272* would open the way 'to the artificial diminution of settlors' estates by the purchase of valuable consideration of enduring general powers of appointment under unconnected settlements'. A general power of appointment was 'something of very real value vested in the appointor'. *[2000] STC 628; Ch D [2000] All ER(D) 832; CA [2001] STC 1271.* The Court of Appeal upheld this decision. (*Note.* See now *FA 2002, s 119.* This is intended to ensure that, with effect from 17 April 2002, 'powers over trust property are to be disregarded for IHT purposes … except where doing so would create new scope for tax avoidance'.).

Miller & Others v CIR

Interest in possession—power to appropriate revenue to meet depreciation of capital value of assets—whether administrative or dispositive.

Property was held in trust to pay the whole of the free annual income to the wife for life but with the trustees having power, before striking the free income from any year, to appropriate such portion of the revenue as they thought proper to meet depreciation of the capital value of any asset or for any other reason they deemed advisable in their sole discretion. On the death of the wife, survived by her husband and children, the husband was entitled to one-third of the free income and the remainder was held for the maintenance and education of the children, also subject to the trustees' power to appropriate revenue to meet depreciation of assets etc. Following *Pearson and Others v CIR*, the CS held that, on the facts, the powers given to the trustees were administrative and not dispositive and that the wife had an interest in possession in the whole fund. On her death, therefore, a liability to CTT arose, subject to the exemption to the extent of the one-third interest passing to the husband, under the provisions of *CGTA 1984, ss 4(1), 5(1), 49(1)**. *CS 1986, [1987] STC 108.*

Millington v Secretary of State for the Environment

Wine making can be agriculture. Section 55, Town and Country Planning Act 1990.

Land was used for the creation of a new product from produce grown on that land, the land was still capable of being used for the purpose of agriculture and therefore was exempt from planning control. Mr Millington owned a site of nine hectares which included part of an old Roman city and this was turned over to vine growing, wine making and visits to the Roman site. The planning authority served Mr Millington with an enforcement notice relating to that part of the site on which a building stood which stored wine, wine making equipment and retail area. Mr Millington appealed to the Secretary of State who dismissed the appeal but granted planning permission for an existing building to provide facilities for the making of wine but selling the wine from the premises was disallowed. The Millingtons appealed and Judge Rich, QC, after due consideration remitted the case back to the Secretary of State. The Court of Appeal held that the making and selling of wine made from grapes grown on the land was capable of being an agricultural use. *[1999] TLR 29 June 1999.*

Moggs (Moggs' Executor) v CIR

Informal gift of 50% interest in property before the formal transfer—whether value of deceased's estate immediately before death included entirety of house with vacant possession.

In 1996 a woman (G), who was separated from her husband, moved into a house owned and occupied by her uncle (M). In August 2000 M, who had been diagnosed as having prostate cancer, formally transferred a 50% interest in the property to G. M died in April 2001. His executor appealed against a subsequent Notice of Determination, contending that M had made an informal gift of the 50% interest in the property before the formal transfer. The Special Commissioner rejected this contention and dismissed the executor's appeal. *[2005] STC SCD 394 Sp C 464.*

Montagu Trust Co (Jersey) Ltd and Others v CIR

Excluded property—trust fund invested in government securities—beneficiaries domiciled abroad.

The trust fund of a settlement made by K in 1970 was invested in a single holding of 1976 Treasury Loan Stock. This stock was exempt from taxation so long as it was in the beneficial ownership of persons neither domiciled nor ordinarily resident in the UK. K's daughter, W, made a similar settlement in 1976. The settlor, trustees and beneficiaries were all domiciled outside the UK but the trust was to be governed by English law. The trustees of the two settlements transferred the 1970 settlement trust fund to themselves as trustees of the 1976 settlement, to be held on trusts for the exclusive benefit of W's four children and their issue. On the following day the trustees executed a deed of appointment whereby each child became entitled to an interest in possession of one quarter of the trust fund. The Revenue raised assessments on the ground that the making of the appointment constituted a deemed capital distribution. The trustees' appeals were dismissed by the Ch D. There was a possibility that the fund might benefit people domiciled in the UK. On the facts, the trusts of the 1976 settlement were not exclusively for the benefit of W's four children, but might also benefit W's grandchildren. Accordingly there were resulting trusts to persons who might be resident in the UK and thus the trust fund was not excluded property. *Ch D, [1989] STC 477.*

Moodie v CIR & Sinnett

Tax avoidance schemes.

Under a tax avoidance scheme similar to that considered in *CIR v Plummer*, two taxpayers received sums from a registered charity in return for making five 'annual payments' to the charity. The taxpayers claimed to deduct the amounts of the payments in computing their income for tax purposes. The Revenue raised assessments on the basis that the payments were not deductible as 'annual payments', since the scheme should be treated as a fiscal nullity under the principles laid down in *W T Ramsay Ltd v CIR*. The HL upheld the assessments (reversing the decision of the CA and restoring that of the Special Commissioners). The taxpayers had not made annual payments within the meaning of *ICTA*, because the steps taken under the scheme were self-cancelling. The schemes had no object or effect other than the manufacture of claims that the taxpayers had reduced their income. The taxpayers had not reduced their actual income and had not been put to any capital expense other than the cost of the scheme. The decisions in *Plummer* and *Ramsay* were inconsistent. The decision in *Plummer* had been made on the assumption that payments had been made in implementation of each of the steps which constituted the scheme, and the fact that the scheme was self-cancelling had not been considered. In the subsequent case of *Ramsay*, however, the HL had held that schemes whereby an alleged loss was manufactured by a pre-arranged series of self-cancelling transactions were to be considered as a whole, and treated as fiscally ineffective. If this principle had been applied to the facts in *Plummer*, the decision in *Plummer* would have been different. Therefore the decision in *Ramsay* should be followed and the inconsistent decision in *Plummer* should be ignored. *HL 1993, 65 TC 610; [1993] STC 188; [1993] 1 WLR 266; [1993] 2 All ER 49.*

Moore and Osborne v CIR, In re Trafford's Settlements

Interest in possession—sole object of discretionary trust.

A settlor directed that income from certain trust funds was to be held upon protective trusts during his life, and that the trustees were to pay or apply the income to himself or to any wife or children he might have as they in their discretion saw fit. When he died in 1978 he was unmarried and childless, and the question arose as to whether or not he was beneficially entitled to an interest in possession in the trust funds immediately before his death. The Ch D upheld the trustees' contention that he was not so entitled. On the true construction of the relevant clause, the settlement had created an immediate discretionary trust rather than (as the Revenue argued) a protected life interest. The fact that the settlor was the sole existing object of the discretionary trust did not give him an interest in possession. The possibility, although remote, that another discretionary beneficiary might come into existence was sufficient to prevent him from having the necessary immediate entitlement to trust income as it arose. *Ch D 1984, CTTL 20; [1984] STC 236; [1984] 3 WLR 341; [1984] 1 All ER 1108.*

Moore's Executors v CIR

Domicile

A US citizen (M), born in Missouri, moved to the UK in 1991 and acquired a property in London. He lived in the UK until his death in 1997, although he continued to use a US passport. He left two wills, a US will leaving his US assets to two individual beneficiaries, and an English will, disposing of his non-US assets to a wide range of beneficiaries. The Inland Revenue issued a notice of determination that he had acquired a domicile of choice in England. The executors of his English will appealed. The Special Commissioners allowed the appeal, observing that M had remained a US citizen and taxpayer, and holding on the evidence that 'his living solely in London had been determined more by ill-health than by a desire to make England his permanent home'. *[2002] STC SCD 463 Sp C 335.*

Mrs Patch's Executors v HMRC

IHTA 1984, s 52(1)—effect of deed of partition.

A testator (P) left his widow a life interest in his residuary estate, with the remainder passing to his two children (by a previous marriage). In July 2000 the trustees executed a deed of partition under which the widow assigned two-thirds of the trust fund under P's estate to the reversioners, and received an absolute interest in the remainder. In December 2000 the widow died. HMRC issued a notice of determination on the basis that the deed of partition had resulted in a transfer of value under *IHTA 1984, s 52(1)*. The executors appealed, contending that the deed of partition should not be treated as giving rise to a transfer of value. The Special Commissioner rejected this contention and dismissed the appeal. *[2007] Sp C 600.*

Munro v Commrs of Stamp Duties of New South Wales

Gifts with reservation—exclusion of the donor from any benefit.

Arrangements between the donee and a third party to give the donor benefit is within the provisions but retention of rights under a contract made prior to the gift and quite separate from it is not. The gift of land already subject to a lease to the donor is not a gift with reservation as the lease is not part of the gift. *PC [1934] AC 61; [1933] All ER 185.*

Nadin v CIR

Irregular payments to close relatives—whether exempt from IHT as 'normal expenditure of the transferor'—IHTA 1984, s 21.

An elderly spinster (P) died in 1995. During the years before her death, she had made a number of irregular payments to close relatives. The Revenue issued a notice of determination charging IHT on the basis that the gifts made in the seven years before P's death were transfers of value. Her executor appealed, contending that the gifts were exempt from IHT under IHTA 1984, s 21 as 'part of the normal expenditure of the transferor'. The Special Commissioner rejected this contention and dismissed the appeal. On the evidence, the payments in question were abnormal expenditure rather than normal expenditure, and thus failed to qualify for exemption. Dicta of Lightman J in *Bennett & Others* applied. *[1997] STC SCD 107 Sp C 112.*

New South Wales Commrs of Stamp Duties v Permanent Trustee Co of New South Wales Ltd

Gifts with reservation—exclusion of donor from enjoyment.

The PC held that this condition is not fulfilled if at some later date after the gift the property or income therefrom is voluntarily applied by the donee to the donor, even if the latter is under an obligation to repay sums used by him. *PC [1956] AC 512; [1956] 2 All ER 512; [1956] 3 WLR 152.*

New South Wales Commrs of Stamp Duties v Perpetual Trustee Co Ltd

Gifts with reservation—settlements.

A settlement of shares in favour of an infant child with absolute gift provided he reached the age of 21 but with a resulting trust to the donor if the child failed to reach that age was not a gift with reservation as the property comprised in the gift was the equitable interest which the donor had created in the shares. *PC, [1943] AC 425; [1943] 1 All ER 525.*

New York Life Insurance Co Ltd v Public Trustee

Situation of property—simple contract debt.

A simple contract debt is situate in the country in which the debtor resides. If there is more than one country of residence the terms of the contract may serve to localise the debt. *CA 1924, 40 TLR 430; [1924] 2 Ch 101.*

Nichols v CIR

Gifts with reservation—exclusion of the donor from any benefit.

A gift of land subject to an agreement to a lease-back created at the same or a later time is the grant of the whole with something reserved out of it and not a gift of a partial interest leaving something in the hands of the grantor which he has not given away. *CA, [1975] STC 278; [1975] 2 All ER 120; [1975] 1 WLR 534.*

Ninth Marquess of Hertford and others (Executors of Eighth Marquess of Hertford deceased) v CIR

IHTA, s 110(b)—historic house used for business purposes and as private residence—whether 'assets used in the business'.

Part of a historic house was open to the public, while part was used as a private residence and not open to the public. The freeholder died in 1997. The Inland Revenue issued a notice of determination charging IHT on 22% of the value of the house, on the basis that only 78% of the house was open to the public and thus only 78% of the house qualified for business property relief. The freeholder's executors appealed, contending that the house was a single asset and that the effect of *IHTA 1984, s 110(b)* was that the whole of the house qualified for business property relief even though 22% of the house was not open to the public. The Special Commissioner accepted this contention and allowed the appeal, observing that *s 110* made no provision for apportionment, and holding that 'it is natural to consider a single building as a single asset where the unencumbered freehold is in single ownership'. The house was 'plainly important as a single structure and the whole building is a vital backdrop to the business carried on. The whole of the exterior is essential to the business.' *[2005] STC SCD 177 Sp C 44.*

Oakes v Commrs of Stamp Duties of New South Wales

Gifts with reservation—exclusion of the donor from any benefit.

Remuneration paid to the settlor as trustee, but not money spent on the maintenance and education of the donor's children, is a benefit. *PC [1954] AC 57; [1953] 2 All ER 1563; [1953] 3 WLR 1127.*

Oakley & Hutson (Jossaume's Personal Representatives) v CIR

Testator's will giving company right to occupy property—whether testator's widow had interest in possession.

A company director (J) died in 1993. Under his will, as modified by a deed of family arrangement, he gave his shares in the company to his son, and two freehold properties to trustees, with directions to pay the trust income to his widow for her lifetime and thereafter to his three children in equal shares. One of the freehold properties was occupied by the company, and J directed that the trustees of his will should not require the company to pay any rent. J's executors treated the property as having been transferred to his widow, and as qualifying for the exemption for transfers between spouses. J's widow died in 2000, and the Inland Revenue issued a notice of determination that IHT was chargeable on her interest in possession in the premises which were occupied by the company. Her personal representatives appealed, contending that the executors had made an error in treating the interest in the premises as having been transferred to J's widow, that J's will had conferred an interest in possession on the company, and that his widow did not have an interest in possession. The Special Commissioner accepted this contention and allowed the appeal, holding that J had intended that his will should 'protect the position of the company and ... preserve its use and occupancy' of the premises. The will gave the company a right to occupy the premises, and that right arose 'solely under the will'. The right in question was 'a present right to present enjoyment of property' and was an 'interest in possession' within *IHTA 1984, s 49(1).* (The Commissioner observed that the effect of this decision was that IHT 'will have become due in respect of the transfer of the yard at his death ...

(but) that a lower amount of inheritance tax will be payable than would have been the case'
if IHT had been charged on the death of J's widow.) *[2005] STC SCD 343 Sp C 460.*

O'Neill and others v IRC

*Deposit account in joint names of deceased and daughter—whether general power to dispose of
the whole account. IHTA 1984, s 5.*

An individual (O) died in 1992. In 1980 and 1984 he had opened deposit accounts in an Isle
of Man bank, in the joint names of O and his daughter. He had deposited substantial sums
in the accounts. The Revenue issued a notice of determination charging IHT on the basis
that the whole of the amounts in the deposit accounts formed part of O's estate. O's
daughter and executors appealed, contending that only 50% of the sums in the accounts
should be treated as part of O's estate. The Special Commissioner rejected this contention
and dismissed the appeals, holding on the evidence that O 'enjoyed the entire beneficial
interest in the accounts during his lifetime'. O's daughter had not known that the accounts
existed until after her father's death. The fact that O's daughter was never informed of the
accounts in her father's lifetime rebutted the presumption of advancement except to the
extent that it applied to the right of survivorship. While she had a beneficial right of
survivorship, she did not have 'a present beneficial interest in the accounts during her
father's lifetime'. Only O had been able to operate the accounts, and this *de facto* control of
the accounts was 'a clear pointer to the conclusion' that he had not made a lifetime gift of an
immediate interest in the accounts to his daughter. *[1998] STC SCD 110 Sp C 154.*

Ontario (Treasurer for) v Aberdein

Situation of property—registered shares.

In a Canadian case the PC held that registered shares which could be dealt with in two
countries were situate in the one in which in the ordinary course of affairs the shares would
be dealt with by the registered owner. *PC 1946, [1947] AC 24.*

Oughtred v CIR

Time of disposition—disposition of equitable interest in settled property.

An oral agreement was not effective to transfer an equitable reversionary interest. Such a
transfer could only be effected in writing. *HL, [1959] 3 All ER 623.*

Owen, Re, Owen v CIR

Time of disposition—time of gift by cheque.

More than three years before his death O gave a cheque to each of three relatives. However
the cheques were not presented for payment until within the three year period before O's
death. The gifts were held to have been made when the cheques cleared into each donee's
own account and were therefore liable to ED as being gifts made within three years of the
donor's death. *Ch D, [1949] 1 All ER 901.*

Pearson and Others v CIR

Meaning of interest in possession.

Subject to the trustees' overriding power of appointment, to their power to accumulate
income and to the possibility of partial defeasance on the birth of further children to the
settlor, property in a 1964 settlement was held upon trust in equal shares absolutely for the
three daughters of the settlor upon their attaining the age of 21. They were all 21 by the
end of February 1974. On 20 March 1976 the trustees appointed the income of £16,000 to
one of the daughters, F. The Revenue determined that F had become entitled to an interest
in possession in the £16,000 at a time when no such interest subsisted in that part of the
trust fund and that accordingly CTT became payable by virtue of *FA 1975, 5 Sch 6(2)*. By a
three to two majority, and reversing the unanimous decision of the CA in favour of the
trustees, the HL upheld the Revenue's determination. The trustees' power of accumula-

tion prevented the interests the daughters obtained upon reaching 21 from being interests in possession. For there to be an interest in possession there must be a present right to the present enjoyment of something and the power of accumulation prevented the daughters from having an immediate right to anything. A distinction was drawn by Viscount Dilhorne between trustees' administrative powers, such as those to pay duties, taxes etc., and their dispositive power to dispose of the net income of the trust fund. A mere administrative power will not prevent an interest from being in possession. *HL 1980, CTTL 5; [1980] STC 318; [1980] 2 All ER 479; [1980] 2 WLR 872.*

Pemsel v Special Commissioners

The meaning of 'charitable purposes'.

Lands were vested in trustees to apply the rents in maintaining (i) certain missionary establishments, (ii) a school for the children of ministers and missionaries, and (iii) certain other religious establishments. The trustees were held to be entitled to exemption under *ICTA 1988, s 505(1)(a)**. (This is the leading case on the meaning of 'charitable purposes' in *ICTA 1988, s 505*. The Revenue's argument, based on an 1888 decision of the Court of Session (*Baird's Trustees v Lord Advocate CS 1888, 25 SLR 533*), was that 'charity' should be given its popular meaning of the relief of poverty, and not the wider technical meaning evolved over the years in English courts; that technical meaning differed from the technical meaning under Scottish law, and in an Act applying to both countries it should have the same meaning. In a series of judgments containing a comprehensive review of the relevant law, the HL by a majority held that 'charity' should be given its technical meaning under English law and comprises (per Lord Macnaghten) 'four principal divisions; trusts for the relief of poverty, trusts for the advancement of education, trusts for the advancement of religion, and trusts beneficial to the community and not falling under any of the preceding heads. The trusts last referred to are not the less charitable ... because incidentally they benefit the rich as well as the poor.' These rules have been extensively applied in subsequent charity cases.) *HL 1891, 3 TC 53; [1891] AC 531.*

Pepper v Hart

Concessionary fees for sons of staff at public school—Parliamentary history of legislation.

Nine schoolmasters and the bursar of a public school had their sons educated at concessionary reduced fees of approximately one-fifth of the standard fees. The reduced fees covered the direct costs attributable to each boy, but did not include any indirect costs. The boys occupied surplus places at the school and their education there was at the discretion of the school, rather than an entitlement. The Revenue raised assessments on the basis that, in computing the cash equivalent of the benefits for the purpose of *ICTA 1988, s 156**, the overall running costs of the whole school should be apportioned pro rata to the concessionary places. The taxpayers appealed, contending that only the marginal costs should be assessed. The HL allowed the taxpayers' appeals against the assessments (reversing the decision of the CA and restoring that of the Special Commissioner). The wording of *ICTA 1988, s 156** was ambiguous. It derived from *FA 1976*, and, during the Parliamentary debates which preceded its enactment, the then Financial Secretary had clearly stated that the intention of the legislation was to assess such in-house benefits on the marginal cost to the employer, rather than on the average cost. Hansard could be used as an aid to interpretation where 'legislation is ambiguous or obscure, or leads to an absurdity; the material relied upon consists of one or more statements by a Minister or other promoter of the Bill together if necessary with such other Parliamentary material as is necessary to understand such statements and their effect; and the statements relied upon are clear'. In the light of these statements, the ambiguity should be resolved by construing the relevant legislation in such a way as to give effect to the intentions of Parliament. *HL 1992, 65 TC 421; [1992] STC 898; [1992] 3 WLR 1032; [1993] 1 All ER 42.*

Perry v CIR

IHTA 1984, s 200(1)—transfer on death—person liable.

A property dealer (K) had a joint bank account with a young woman (P), who lived in a property which K owned. K died in 1989, at which time there was more than £1,000,000 in the account. K's executors (a solicitor and an accountant) provided the Revenue with details of his estate, but made no reference to this bank account. In 1991 P replaced the accountant as K's personal representative. In 1995 the personal representatives (P and the solicitor) presented a bankruptcy petition, declaring that the estate was insolvent. The Revenue subsequently ascertained details of the bank account, and in 1997 they issued a notice of determination that P was liable to IHT in respect of half of the money in the account at K's death. The Special Commissioner upheld the determination and dismissed P's appeal, holding on the evidence that 'the joint account constituted a gift from (K) to the appellant of the balance for the time being in the account'. The effect of *IHTA 1984, s 200(1)(c)* was that P was liable to account for tax on the money in question. (The Commissioner also upheld a further notice of determination, holding that in 1984 K had given P 'an irrevocable licence to occupy rent-free ... for life' the property in which she lived.) *[2005] STC SCD 474 Sp C 474.*

Phillips and Others (Phillips' Executor) v HMRC

Business property relief—activities of a money-lender who lent money to family companies qualified for business property relief.

A widow held a majority shareholding in a company (P) which lent money to related family companies. Her executors claimed business property relief. The Revenue rejected the claim on the basis that the shares were not 'relevant business property', because P's business consisted mainly of 'making or holding investments', within *IHTA 1984, s 105(3)*. The Special Commissioner allowed the executors' appeal, finding that P was 'a banking arm for in-house transactions' and holding that 'few would regard the activities of a money-lender as investment'. On the evidence, P 'was in the business of making loans and not in the business of investing in loans ... the loans were not investments for their own sake but the provision of a finance facility to the other companies'. Accordingly, the shares in P qualified for business property relief. *[2006] STC SCD 639 Sp C 555.*

Phizackerley (Personal Representative of Dr PJR Phizackerley) v HMRC

FA 1986, s 103—treatment of certain debts.

A married woman died in 2000. Her will left an amount equal to the IHT nil rate band to a discretionary trust for her husband (P) and their children, and the residue to P. He agreed to pay £150,000 plus indexation to the discretionary trust in return for his wife's half-share in the matrimonial home. P died in 2002, and HMRC issued a notice of determination charging IHT on his estate. His personal representative appealed, contending that the £153,222 which P owed to the discretionary trust should be deducted from the value of his estate. The Special Commissioner rejected this contention and dismissed his appeal, holding that the effect of *FA 1986, s 103* was that the debt was not deductible. The Commissioner also held that *IHTA 1984, s 11* (providing that a 'disposition for maintenance' is not a 'transfer of value') did not apply to a situation 'when a husband puts a house in joint names of himself and his wife during their marriage'. *[2007] STC SCD 328 Sp C 591.*

Plummer v CIR

Domicile—whether foreign domicile of choice acquired.

A taxpayer aged 18 at the beginning of the relevant years, whose domicile of origin was English, claimed that she was domiciled in Guernsey for the purpose of a claim under *ICTA 1988, s 65(4)**. She was born in London of English parents. When she was aged 15, her mother and a sister went to take up residence in Guernsey with her grandmother. From then the taxpayer divided her residence between England and Guernsey, generally continuing her education and training in England (where she was reading for a degree at London University in the relevant years) and living with her father there during the week, and going with him to Guernsey for the week-end. She gave evidence before the Special Commissioners of her attachment to Guernsey and her intention to live and work there. The Commissioners held that she had not become an 'inhabitant' of Guernsey in the years of claim and therefore could not be said to have acquired a domicile of choice in Guernsey. Hoffmann J upheld their decision. A person who kept a residence in his domicile of origin could only acquire a domicile of choice in another country if the residence established there was his chief residence. On the facts the Commissioners were entitled to conclude that the taxpayer had not yet settled in Guernsey and therefore had not acquired a domicile of choice there. *Ch D 1987, 60 TC 452; [1987] STC 698; [1988] 1 WLR 292; [1988] 1 All ER 97.*

Portland, Duchess of, CIR v

Domicile—domicile acquired on marriage—effect of Matrimonial Proceedings Act 1973.

The taxpayer's domicile of origin was Canada. She acquired her husband's English domicile by dependence on her marriage. She lived in England with her husband but had a house in Canada which she visited annually and where she intended to live on her husband's retirement or death. The Ch D, reversing the decision of the Special Commissioners, held that by virtue of the *Matrimonial Proceedings Act 1973, s 1(2)* she retained her English domicile as a deemed domicile of choice, and her visits to Canada did not amount to an abandonment of that domicile. *Ch D 1981, 54 TC 648; [1982] STC 149; [1982] 2 WLR 367; [1982] 1 All ER 784.*

Postlethwaite's Executors v HMRC

Payment by close company to FURBS for controlling shareholder—whether IHTA 1984, s 10* applicable.

A motor racing engineer (P) incorporated a Jersey company (L) in 1990. In 1991 L agreed to provide P's services to an Italian company (G) for £600,000 pa, and also agreed to employ P at a salary of £75,000 pa. In 1993 L paid £700,000 to a funded unapproved retirement benefits scheme for P. P died in 1999, aged 55. Subsequently the Inland Revenue issued a notice of determination that the payment of £700,000 was a transfer of value within *IHTA 1984, s 94*. P's executors appealed, contending that the payment was a disposition not intended to confer gratuitous benefit, within *IHTA 1984, s 10*. The Special Commissioners reviewed the evidence in detail, accepted this contention and allowed the appeal. The Commissioners observed that the fees paid by G to L were 'in line with the cost of the services of comparable motor racing engineers'. By contrast, 'the basic salary paid by (L) to (P) was very low for a person of his standing'. The payment of £700,000 was not unreasonable or gratuitous, since 'if (P) had contributed at the maximum allowable level to an approved UK scheme until he was 60 and his salary of £75,000 had increased with inflation, the pension which he would have obtained was about the same as that which the £700,000 would secure'. Furthermore, 'the fact that on legal analysis the payment was for past consideration does not mean that it was made with the intention of conferring a gratuitous benefit'. *[2006] Sp C 571.*

Powell & Halfhide, executor of G E Pearce v CIR

IHTA 1984, s 105(3). Business of managing a caravan park—making or holding investments.

The deceased and her daughter ran a caravan park where 23 of the 33 caravans were privately owned. The deceased or her representative needed to be in attendance at the site at all times. The profits of the business were assessed to tax under Schedule D, Case I. On death the personal representatives claimed relief under *s 105(3)* and this was refused by the Inspector who argued that the 'making or holding investments' applied in this instance. The activities undertaken in the caravan park were either required under the terms of the lettings or the terms of the site licence which governed the lettings, or consisted of activities such as the social visits and organised medical visits, for which no charge was made, and so accordingly fell to be in the ambit of 'making and holding investments'. On the facts of the case it was determined that there was little difference in principle between, say, the owner of a portfolio of long leases receiving ground rents and the instant case where the main source of income was derived from pitch fees from long-term residents who owned their own caravans. The case has been withdrawn from application to be heard in the High Court by the taxpayers. *[1997] STC SCD 181 Sp C 120.*

Powell-Cotton v CIR

Interest in possession—life interest in settlement sold in consideration for shares in close company—subsequent transfer of shares by way of gift—whether a disposal of interest in possession in settled property.

In 1941 the taxpayer sold to a close company his life interest under a settlement for £25,000, to be paid by 25,000 £1 shares in the company. In 1964 he reacquired from the company his life interest in part of the settled property. His interest in the remainder of the settled property continued to be vested in the company. In 1982 the taxpayer transferred 2,999 of his shares to a charity by way of gift. Immediately before the transfer, he had held 8,993 of the 46,000 shares in the company. Accordingly, by virtue of what is now *IHTA 1984, s 101(1)* he fell to be treated as having been entitled to a part (8,993/46,000) of the interest in possession in the part of the settled property retained by the company. Following the transfer, he fell to be treated as being entitled to 5,994/46,000 of the interest in possession in question. The Revenue issued a notice of determination on the basis that he had made a transfer of value equal to (2,999/8,993 × 8993/46,000) of the settled property vested in the company. The taxpayer appealed, contending firstly that no part of the interest in possession had come to an end within *s 52(1)*, so that he had not made a disposal within *s 51(1)*, and alternatively that any transfer of value was exempt since it was attributable to property given to a charity within the meaning of what is now *IHTA 1984, s 23(1)*. The Ch D dismissed his appeal. The provisions of what is now *IHTA 1984, s 101(1)* required the interest in possession held by the close company to be treated as vested in the participators in that company. Accordingly, on the disposal of the shares, part of the taxpayer's interest in possession had come to an end within *IHTA 1984, s 52(1)*. The corollary of *IHTA 1984, s 101(1)* was that the company could not be treated as having an interest in possession in the settled property, since that would be inconsistent with the beneficial ownership attributed to the participator, and the company's right to the income of the retained part therefore had to be disregarded. Additionally, the effect of *IHTA 1984, s 56(3)* was that the deemed transfer of part of the settled property was not exempted by *IHTA 1984, s 23(1); Ch D, [1992] STC 625.*

Prosser (Jempson's Personal Representatives) v CIR

Interest charge under IHTA 1984, s 233(1)(b).

A personal representative failed to pay IHT of £8,000. The Revenue imposed an interest charge under *IHTA 1984, s 233(1)(b)*. The Special Commissioner upheld the charge to interest and dismissed the personal representative's appeal. *[2003] STC SCD 250 Sp C 362.*

R v Brentford Commissioners (ex p Chan & Others)

Application for judicial review.

A partnership had been under investigation for ten years, and negotiations with their accountant, a sole practitioner (G), were still in progress. At the request of the inspector, the clerk to the General Commissioners arranged a special meeting on 10 August 1983 to dispose of the matter. Notice of the meeting reached G's office on 18 July when he was on holiday. The inspector was also on holiday, returning on 8 August. G had a previous appointment on 10 August, and on 9 August he asked the inspector to agree to an adjournment, but the inspector refused. Accordingly the partners were represented at the meeting by W, an employee of G, who was qualified but who had had insufficient time to prepare his case. The Commissioners refused his request for an adjournment and determined the appeal against the partners. W expressed dissatisfaction and the Commissioners duly stated a case. The partners sought leave to apply for judicial review. The QB rejected the application, observing that *TMA 1970, s 56* gave the High Court the widest possible powers to remit the case to the Commissioners, and holding that the appeal, already under way, should proceed by way of Case Stated. *QB 1985, 57 TC 651; [1986] STC 65.*

R v CIR (ex p Goldberg)

Revenue information powers—legal professional privilege.

A barrister was served with a notice under *TMA 1970, s 20(3)*, requiring him to deliver or make available to the Revenue certain copies of documents in his possession which had been sent to him by a US attorney for legal advice. He refused to comply with the notice and the Revenue began penalty proceedings. His application for judicial review was granted, and a declaration made that the documents were subject to legal professional privilege and so excluded by *TMA 1970, s 20B(8)* from the application of *TMA 1970, s 20(3); QB, 1988, 61 TC 403; [1988] STC 524.* (Note. The decision was disapproved by the CA in *Dubai Bank Ltd v Galadari CA, [1989] 3 WLR 1044; [1989] 3 All ER 769.*)

R v CIR (ex p Kaye)

Application for judicial review by shareholders selling shares before publication of Statement of Practice.

In January 1989 a married couple sold shares to a German company. Four months later, the Inland Revenue published SP 5/89, stating that where, after 31 March 1982, a taxpayer acquired shares by a no gain/no loss transfer from someone who held them on that date, those shares would, together with any shares held by the taxpayer in the same company on 31 March 1982, be treated as a single holding acquired at market value on that date. The husband realised that, if his wife had transferred her shares to him before selling them, they could have been treated as a single holding, with a higher market value at 31 March 1982. He applied by way of judicial review for a declaration that the shares should be valued as if his wife had transferred them to him. The QB dismissed the application. There had not been an inter-spouse transfer of the shares, and the Revenue had a duty to demand the tax actually due. *QB 1992, 65 TC 82; [1992] STC 581.*

R v CIR (ex p Matrix Securities Ltd)

Application for judicial review—withdrawal of assurance given by Inspector—assurances based on inadequate disclosure of information by applicant.

A company sponsored a scheme which was designed to take advantage of the availability of industrial buildings allowances (at the rate of 100%) in designated enterprise zones. Under the scheme, 67.5% of the price payable by potential investors would be covered by loans from a merchant bank, so that the investors would make no net contribution. The loans themselves would be repaid under special 'exit arrangements', so that the investors would assume no significant risk. In July 1993 the company's solicitors submitted a letter giving some details of the scheme to an inspector of taxes, who agreed that the payments would qualify for industrial buildings allowances. Subsequently the Revenue received further information concerning the scheme, and in October 1993 the Revenue Financial Institutions Division wrote to the company informing it that the assurances made by the inspector had been wrongly given, and that it was not bound by them. The company applied for judicial review, seeking a declaration that the withdrawal was unfair and amounted to an abuse of power. The application was dismissed by the QB, the CA and the HL. The information submitted by the company had been 'inaccurate and misleading'. The Revenue were therefore entitled to withdraw the clearance. Lord Browne-Wilkinson and Lord Griffiths observed that the applicant had been aware that the Revenue required applications for clearance to be made to its Financial Institutions Division, so that a clearance by a local inspector was not to be treated as binding. *HL 1994, TL 3396; [1994] STC 272; [1994] 1 WLR 334; [1994] 1 All ER 769.*

R v CIR (ex p MFK Underwriting Agencies Ltd & Others)

Application for judicial review where taxpayers allegedly misled by informal statements by Revenue officers.

Between April 1986 and October 1988, there were more than 60 issues of index-linked bonds which were denominated in Canadian and US dollars. Various approaches were made to the Revenue, both by those considering issuing such bonds and by those considering them as an investment, to clarify whether the indexation uplift, reflected in the sale price or redemption values of the securities, would be taxed as capital or as income. In three cases inspectors informed the enquirers that they would be taxed as capital, and the Revenue proceeded accordingly. However, in several other cases the Revenue did not give an unequivocal reply until October 1988 when it issued a circular declaring that the indexation uplift was assessable as income. Five applicants (all Lloyd's underwriting syndicates or managing agents) sought judicial review of the Revenue's decision. The QB refused the applications. The Revenue could not be held to be bound by anything less than a clear, unambiguous and unqualified representation. In the five cases in question, the Revenue had neither promised nor indicated that it would follow a particular course and accordingly there had been no abuse of power. *QB 1989, 62 TC 607; [1989] STC 873; [1990] 1 All ER 91; [1990] 1 WLR 1545.*

R v CIR (ex p National Federation of Self-Employed and Small Businesses Ltd)

Tax amnesty—whether subject to judicial review.

In 1978, the Revenue offered an amnesty, on certain conditions, to casual workers in the newspaper industry who had been evading tax by using fictitious names. A federation of small businessmen, with a membership of 50,000, applied by way of judicial review for a declaration that the amnesty was unlawful and for a *mandamus* to the Revenue to collect the tax evaded. The HL, unanimously reversing the majority decision of the CA, held that the federation did not have a sufficient interest in the matter to support the application. The action taken by the Revenue had been 'genuinely in the care and management of the taxes, under the powers entrusted to them'. The HL opinions are a comprehensive and extensive discussion of the scope of judicial review in relation to a statutory body such as the CIR. *HL 1981, 55 TC 133; [1981] STC 260; [1981] 2 WLR 722; [1981] 2 All ER 93.*

R v CIR (ex p Rothschild (J) Holdings plc) (No 1) (and cross-appeal)

Application for discovery of Revenue documents in judicial review proceedings.

In a stamp duty case, a company sought discovery of documents relating to the Revenue practice in applying *FA 1973, 19 Sch 10* to share exchange transactions. Simon Brown J made an order limited to internal Revenue documents of a general nature, but excluding documents relating to individual and particular cases. Both sides appealed to the CA, the Revenue contending that the judge should not have made an order for discovery, and the company contending that the order should be varied to include, *inter alia*, copies of certain documents relating to successful applications under the relevant legislation. The CA dismissed both the appeal and the cross-appeal. *CA 1987, 61 TC 178; [1987] STC 163.*

R v CIR (ex p Taylor)

Application for order of discovery.

The taxpayer, a solicitor, was required by a notice under *TMA 1970, s 20*, to deliver certain documents to an inspector. He applied for an order of *certiorari* to quash the notice. He also applied to the QB for an order of discovery of a submission and report made to the Board of Inland Revenue by the inspector examining his affairs prior to the issue of the notice. His application for discovery was refused. The submission was subject to legal professional privilege, and he had not produced evidence suggesting that the decision to issue a notice was unreasonable. *CA 1988, 62 TC 562; [1988] STC 832; [1989] 1 All ER 906.*

R v HMIT (ex p Brumfield and Others)

Judicial review—interest paid by partnership on money lent by it to a partner.

A family partnership borrowed £120,558 from a bank at interest. It lent this amount to one of the partners interest-free. That partner used the loan to buy land in his name. The partnership claimed that the bank interest paid was deductible in computing its profits. The Revenue refused the claim. Twenty-six months later the partnership applied for judicial review. Peter Gibson J refused the application. SP 4/85, on which the partnership relied, did not apply in cases where a loan was made to a partnership and the money then made available to one of the partners. Furthermore, although it was strictly unnecessary to consider the point, the delay of 26 months in making the application was inexcusable. *QB 1988, 61 TC 589; [1989] STC 151.*

R v HMIT (ex p Fulford-Dobson)

Gift by wife to husband about to become non-resident—application of extra-statutory concession D2.

On 18 August 1980 the taxpayer entered into a contract of employment in Germany. He was required to begin work on 15 September and he left the UK for this purpose on 29 August 1980. From that date he became resident in Germany, having previously been resident and ordinarily resident in the UK. Acting on professional advice, and admittedly to take advantage of ESC D2, his wife by deed of gift transferred to him on 29 August a farm she had inherited in 1977 and had been considering selling in 1980. The farm was in fact sold by auction on 17 September. In due course the husband was assessed to CGT for 1980–81 on the substantial gain on the sale. It was common ground that apart from ESC D2 he was chargeable, but under the concession he would not be chargeable on gains accruing to him in the part of the year during which he was not resident in the UK. The Revenue refused to apply the concession, pointing out that, as is stated inside the front cover of the pamphlet IR1 listing the extra-statutory concessions in operation, a 'concession will not be given in any case where an attempt is made to use it for tax avoidance'. The taxpayer thereupon applied by way of judicial review for an order to quash the assessment. McNeill J refused the application, holding, after an extensive review of decisions in which the courts have considered the Revenue practice of making extra-statutory concessions, that they are lawful and within the proper exercise of managerial discretion. *QB 1987, 60 TC 168; [1987] STC 344; [1987] 3 WLR 277.*

R v HMIT (ex p Kissane and Another)

Whether ICTA 1988, s 776(8)* assessments made for the purposes authorised by statute.

The applicants were partners of a firm of solicitors and directors of a UK company (S), a subsidiary of a Jersey company (N). In 1981, N purchased land in the UK for £325,000 which it later sold to S for £1,125,000. S then resold the land to an independent purchaser for £1,150,000. The applicants were assessed under *ICTA 1988, s 776(8)**, on the basis that they had directly or indirectly provided an opportunity for another person to realise a gain. They applied for judicial review to quash the assessments, contending that there was no evidence that the tax assessed was due from them and that the inspector had acted improperly, having made the assessments for the purpose of making enquiries about other individuals of a kind not authorised by the statutory powers of enquiry. Nolan J, applying *R v Special Commissioners (ex p. Stipplechoice Ltd) (No 1)*, granted leave. It was arguable that there had been a misunderstanding by the Revenue in relation to material facts and that the inspector had acted irrationally. Moreover, although the points advanced could equally well be taken before the Special Commissioners, the applicants, if successful, would be prejudiced in that they would not be able to recover their costs in the appeal. *QB [1986] STC 152; [1986] 2 All ER 37.*

R v HMIT and Others (ex p Lansing Bagnall Ltd)

Whether 'may' in FA 1972, 16 Sch 3(1) mandatory or permissive.

A close company had made covenanted donations to charities in its four accounting periods to 30 April 1982. In 1984 the inspector served notices on the company for the annual payments to be apportioned among the participators, pursuant to *FA 1972, 16 Sch 3(1)*. The company applied, by way of judicial review, for the notices to be quashed, contending that 'may' in *16 Sch 3(1)* was permissive and that the inspector should have taken into account the company's representations in the matter. The QB granted the application and the CA upheld this decision. On the evidence, the inspector responsible for the issue of the notices had refused to consider the company's representations, regarding it as her duty to issue the notices. The wording of the legislation, however, conferred a general discretion to apportion the income of a close company and did not impose on the Revenue a duty to exercise the powers of apportionment. *CA 1986, 61 TC 112; [1986] STC 453. (Note. FA 1972, 16 Sch 3* was subsequently amended by *F(No 2)A 1987, s 61*. This case was subsequently distinguished in *Baylis v Roberts*.)

R v Hudson

Taxpayer prosecuted for fraud—whether indictable.

A taxpayer had submitted false accounts and a false certificate of disclosure and as a consequence was convicted on charges of making false statements to the prejudice of the Crown and the public revenue with intent to defraud, and was fined. He appealed on the ground that the offence charged was not one known to the law. The CCA held that he had been rightly convicted because the facts disclosed a fraud on the Crown and on the public which was indictable as a criminal offence. *CCA 1956, 36 TC 561; [1956] 2 QB 252; [1956] 1 All ER 814.*

R v Special Commissioners (ex p Emery)

Prerogative orders—jurisdiction of Divisional Courts.

A taxpayer applied to the QB for an order of *mandamus* to the Special Commissioners to amend a Stated Case. In the event, the applicant and the Revenue reached an agreement which made remission to the Commissioners unnecessary. However, Donaldson LJ observed that applications should normally be made to the Ch D as the specialised court in tax matters. The QB has residual jurisdiction over the supervision of such matters as the validity of, or errors in, the proceedings. *QB 1980, 53 TC 555; [1980] STC 549.*

R v Special Commissioners (ex p Esslemont)

Application for judicial review.

A taxpayer, whose appeal against a Schedule E assessment had been dismissed by the Special Commissioners, objected to their wording of the Case Stated, and applied for judicial review of their refusal to amend it in accordance with his wishes. His application was dismissed by the QB and the CA. *CA 1984 STI 312.*

R v Special Commissioners (ex p Morey)

Prerogative order sought to quash assessments.

On appeal, Special Commissioners confirmed certain out-of-time assessments made by the inspector with the leave of a General Commissioner. The taxpayer applied for an order of *certiorari* to quash the assessments. The order was refused. Per Widgery CJ, the Court will not normally interfere by way of prerogative order with the system of appeals under the Income Tax Acts. *CA 1972, 49 TC 71.*

R v Special Commissioner (ex p Stipplechoice Ltd) (No 1)

Leave given under TMA 1970, s 41—application for judicial review.

A Special Commissioner granted the Revenue leave to make an out of time assessment on a company, which thereupon applied for a judicial review of the decision. The CA allowed the application. There was no special provision for an appeal against the decision, and the company had an arguable case that the Commissioner had exercised her powers in so unreasonable a manner that it became open to review. (The facts are complex.) *CA, [1985] STC 248; [1985] 2 All ER 465.*

R v Special Commissioners (ex p Stipplechoice Ltd) (No 3)

Application for judicial review.

An order of *certiorari* was granted, quashing the determination of an appeal by a Special Commissioner, in a case where the accounting period of the assessment under appeal had been amended by the inspector by virtue of *ICTA 1988, s 12(8)** without adequate notice or information having been given to the taxpayer prior to the hearing of the appeal. The QB held that a taxpayer must know the nature of the assessment being made on him, and if the nature of the assessment changes, the taxpayer must know of the change and of the reasons why it is made before it can be confirmed on appeal. *QB 1988, 61 TC 391; [1989] STC 93.*

R v Tavistock Commissioners (ex p Worth and Another)

Judicial review—effect of delay in claim for judicial review.

In February 1982, General Commissioners determined appeals against assessments on a married couple who traded in partnership. In June 1982 the couple engaged a new accountant, and in March 1984 they applied for judicial review of the Commissioners' decision. The QB dismissed the application, holding that there was no good reason for extending the time limit laid down by *RSC Order 53, r 4(1); QB 1985, 59 TC 116; [1985] STC 564.*

R v Walton Commissioners (ex p Wilson)

Judicial review.

A 'higher-paid' employee had the use of a company car. The amounts of the resultant taxable benefits were taken into account in his codings for 1978–79 to 1980–81, by deduction from his allowances. He appealed, contending that only monetary payments could be dealt with under PAYE. The General Commissioners dismissed his appeal, whereupon he applied by way of judicial review for orders quashing the decision and ordering the inspector not to make the deductions in his coding. The application was refused. The relevant notices of coding were spent; the amount of any conceivable claim to interest by the taxpayer would be very small. This disposed of the matter, but in any event the notices of coding were correct. 'Income' in *ICTA 1988, s 203** and the PAYE regulations is wide enough to cover all emoluments within Schedule E including benefits in kind. *CA, [1983] STC 464.*

R v Williams and Another

Situation of property—registered shares.

Per Lord Maugham, shares are situate where they can be effectively dealt with as between the shareholder and the company so that the transferee will become legally entitled to all the rights of a member. *PC, [1942] 2 All ER 95; [1942] AC 541.*

Ramsay (W T) Ltd v CIR

Artificial avoidance scheme—whether a nullity for tax purposes.

A company, having made a substantial gain on the sale of a farm, carried out a number of share and loan transactions with the object of creating a large allowable loss at little cost to itself. The loss emerged as one of about £175,000 on shares it subscribed for in a company formed for the scheme, the success of which depended on its establishing that a loan to the same company, sold at a profit of about £173,000, was not a debt on a security within *TCGA 1992, s 251(1)**. The acceptance of the offer of the loan was given orally, but evidenced by a statutory declaration (*vide Statutory Declarations Act 1835*) by a director of the borrowing company. The CA held that the loan, being evidenced by the statutory declaration, which represented a marketable security, was a debt on a security. The scheme therefore failed. The company appealed to the HL, where the appeal was considered with that in *Eilbeck v Rawling* and in both cases the Revenue advanced the new argument that the scheme should be treated as a fiscal nullity producing neither loss nor gain (other than a loss of £370 in *Eilbeck v Rawling*). The HL accepted this approach. Lord Wilberforce held that although the *Duke of Westminster* principle prevented a court from looking behind a genuine document or transaction to some supposed underlying substance, it did not compel the court to view a document or transaction in blinkers, isolated from its context. A finding that a document or transaction is genuine does not preclude the Commissioners from considering whether, on the facts, what is in issue is a composite transaction or a number of independent transactions. The Commissioners are not 'bound to consider individually each separate step in a composite transaction intended to be carried through as a whole'. The question of whether what is in issue is a composite transaction or a number of independent transactions is a matter of law, reviewable by the courts. Such an approach does not introduce a new principle when dealing with legal avoidance, but applies existing legislation to new and sophisticated legal devices; 'while the techniques of tax avoidance progress, the courts are not obliged to stand still'. Turning to the facts here, it was clear that the scheme was for tax avoidance with no commercial justification, and that it was the intention to proceed through all its stages to completion once set in motion. It would therefore be wrong to consider one step in isolation. The true view was that, regarding the scheme as a whole, there was neither gain nor loss. The company's appeal was dismissed. Furthermore, although this ended the appeal, the CA had been correct in holding that the relevant debt was a 'debt on a security'. *HL 1981, 54 TC 101; [1981] STC 174; [1981] 2 WLR 449; [1981] 1 All ER 865.*

Re Applications to Vary the Undertakings of 'A' and 'B'

IHTA 1984, s 35A—variation of undertakings.

The Inland Revenue had agreed that the owners of certain valuable works of art should have the benefit of 'conditional exemption' from IHT in respect of those items, in return for the owners having entered into undertakings, within *IHTA 1984, s 31*, that there would be 'reasonable access to the public'. The owners required members of the public who wished to view the items to make appointments before doing so. Subsequently the Inland Revenue made applications, under *IHTA 1984, s 35A*, to vary the undertakings so as to give wider publicity to the existence of the items, and wider access to them. The Special Commissioner reviewed the evidence in detail and dismissed the Inland Revenue's applications, holding that 'the accumulated burdens placed on the particular owner' would 'so outweigh the benefit to the public as to make it neither just nor reasonable for me to direct that the proposals take effect'. There would be 'a serious intrusion into the family lives of the owners', and 'the increased risks of theft and damage to the owners' possessions' would go 'beyond what Parliament had in mind when empowering the inclusion of extended access requirements and publication requirements'.*[2005] STC SCD 103 Sp C 439.*

Reed v Nova Securities Ltd

Avoidance scheme—whether TCGA 1992, s 173(1) applicable.

Transactions resembling those in *Coates v Arndale Properties Ltd* were considered in another case a few months later. The taxpayer company (N) had traded in shares and securities since 1955. In March 1973 it was acquired by the well-known Littlewoods group. On 17 August 1973 Littlewoods sold to it shares owned by Littlewoods in, and debts owing to Littlewoods by, certain foreign companies. The sale price for the assets was £30,000, their market value, but their capital gains cost to Littlewoods was nearly £4m. When offering the assets to N, Littlewoods' Board said that about £55,000 would be received in part repayment of the debts and N had received a payment of £35,447 in 1979. They were not part of Littlewoods' trading stock. N purported to make an election under *TCGA*

*1992, s 161(3)** in respect of the assets acquired, and the issue in the appeal was whether they were trading stock, as defined in *ICTA 1988, s 100(2)** (see *TCGA 1992, s 288**). The General Commissioners found that they were and their decision was upheld by the Ch D and the CA. The HL unanimously upheld the decision as regards the debts but reversed it as regards the shares. The Commissioners had determined the appeal on the basis of an agreed statement of facts, without recourse to oral evidence, and no reasonable body of Commissioners could have concluded that the company had acquired the shares as trading stock; its acquisition of shares that had no value was without commercial justification. *HL 1985, 59 TC 516; [1985] STC 124; [1985] 1 WLR 193; [1985] 1 All ER 686.*

Reynaud & Others v CIR

Settlement of shares in company followed by purchase of shares by company—whether IHTA, s 268 applicable.

Four brothers were negotiating to sell their shares in a family company (C). Before the sale took place, they each transferred some of their shares to a discretionary trust. On the following day C purchased the shares from the trustees, and the remaining shares in C were sold to an unrelated purchaser (M). The Revenue issued notices of determination charging IHT on the transfer, on the basis that the settlement of the shares in C, and the subsequent purchase of those shares by C, were 'associated operations' (so that, by virtue of *IHTA 1984, s 268(3)*), business property relief was not available on the transfer of the shares). The brothers appealed, contending that C's purchase of the shares 'was not a relevant associated operation because it did not contribute anything to the transfer of value', so that the transfer of the shares to the trusts qualified for business property relief. The Special Commissioners accepted this contention and allowed the appeal, finding that 'when the discretionary trusts were made, there was a real possibility that the sale to (M) would not proceed' and that 'the discretionary trusts had more than just a tax purpose' since they also had the purpose of 'benefiting the families of the settlors and charity'. Although the transfer of shares to the trusts, and C's subsequent purchase of those shares, were 'associated operations' within *IHTA 1984, s 268*, an associated operation was relevant to a disposition 'only if it is part of the scheme contributing to the reduction of the estate'. The value of the brothers' estates 'were diminished as a result of the gift into settlement alone. The purchase of own shares contributed nothing to the diminution which had already occurred and was not therefore a relevant associated operation.' *[1999] STC SCD 185 Sp C 196.* (*Note.* The Commissioners also held that the principles in *WT Ramsay Ltd v CIR*, did not apply, finding that 'completion of the sale took place after a day of negotiations with the purchaser and there must have been a reasonable likelihood that the negotiations would fail. Accordingly ... the two transactions were not part of a single composite transaction for the purpose of the doctrine.' Furthermore, there was no 'inserted step which could be cut out in such a way so as to transform the gift of shares into a gift of cash'.)

Robertson v CIR

IHTA 1984, s 216(3A)—whether personal representatives made 'the fullest enquiries that are reasonably practicable'.

A woman (S) died in October 1999. She owned a house and its contents in Scotland, and a cottage in England. Her executors, one of whom was a solicitor, wished to sell the properties as soon as possible. In November the solicitor (R) submitted an inventory of S's estate to the Capital Taxes Office [now HMRC Inheritance Tax], showing the Scottish house at a value of £60,000; its contents at £5,000; and the English cottage at £50,000. Although R had instructed valuers to carry out valuations of the two properties, he had not received these valuations at the time of submitting the inventory. Later that month the contents of the Scottish house were valued at £24,845, and in December the house was sold for £82,000. In January 2000 the English cottage and its grounds were valued at £315,000. R submitted a corrective inventory to the Capital Taxes Office, and paid the additional IHT due. The CTO informed him that they considered that the executors had not made 'the fullest enquiries that are reasonably practicable', as required by *IHTA 1984, s 216(3A)*, and they proposed to charge a penalty of £9,000, under *IHTA, s 247*. The Special Commissioner reviewed the evidence and held that R was not liable to any penalty, since he had made the fullest enquiries that were reasonably practicable in the circumstances. On the evidence, R had made a thorough examination of S's home shortly after her death, had appreciated that a valuation of the contents would be required, and had instructed a valuation promptly. In the meantime, he had, in accordance with accepted practice, inserted estimated valuations in the inventory and had disclosed that they were estimates. He had followed what was acceptable practice in the legal profession, and had fulfilled his duties as an executor and as a solicitor. The Revenue were not justified in seeking to impose a penalty. *[2002] STC SCD 182 Sp C 309.*

Note. The Special Commissioner held that the Revenue were not justified in seeking to impose a penalty on a solicitor who had submitted an estimated valuation in his capacity as an executor. The solicitor subsequently applied for costs under *Special Commissioners (Jurisdiction and Procedure) Regulations 1994 (SI 1994 No 1811), Reg 21(1)*. The Commissioner awarded costs to the solicitor, holding on the evidence that the Revenue had acted 'wholly unreasonably in connection with the hearing'. *[2002] STC SCD 242 Sp C 313.*

Robertson v HMRC

Lump sum payments received from ex-husband.

A married couple divorced in 1987. The husband agreed to make monthly maintenance payments to the wife (M). In 2001 he also made a lump sum payment of £20,000, and in May 2002 he made a similar payment of £6,000. M died in October 2002. The Inland Revenue issued a Notice of Determination charging IHT on her estate. Her personal representative appealed, contending that the lump sum payments totalling £26,000, which M had received from her ex-husband, should be returned to him and should not be treated as part of her estate for IHT purposes. The Special Commissioner rejected this contention and dismissed the appeal. *[2005] STC SCD 723 Sp C 494.*

Rose v Director of Assets Recovery Agency

Trade of dealing in drugs—finding 'on the balance of probabilities' that R was not carrying on a trade.

The Director of the Assets Recovery Agency issued assessments on an individual (R), on the basis that he was carrying on a trade of dealing in drugs. R appealed, contending that he was not carrying on a trade of dealing in drugs. The Special Commissioner allowed his appeal, finding 'on the balance of probabilities' that R was not carrying on a trade. *[2006] STC SCD 472 Sp C 543.*

Rose, Re, Rose and Others v CIR

Time of disposition—registered shares.

A transfer under seal in the form appropriate to the company's regulations, together with delivery of the transfer and share certificate to the transferee, was held sufficient to constitute the transferee the beneficial owner of the shares at that time, although the transferee did not register the shares until a later date. So far as lay in his power the transferor had done all that he could to divest himself of his interest in the shares. *CA, [1952] 1 All ER 1217; [1952] Ch 499.*

Rowley, Holmes & Co v Barber

Employee and personal representative the same person-power as a PR to contract with himself as an individual.

G, a solicitor in practice, employed B for many years. G died and appointed B as his sole executor and trustee and bequeathed to B his practice. As B was unqualified he could not run the practice and sold the goodwill of the practice to R, a qualified solicitor, and was employed by R until R made B redundant. The firm contended that G's death had broken the continuity of the employment and that B was entitled to £292.50 but B contended that the redundancy payment should reflect continuous employment since 1954. It was held that the office of personal representative was capable of giving power to the PR to contract in his representative capacity with himself as in his individual capacity and therefore the redundancy payment should rightly apply to the longer period. Reference was made to Halsbury's Laws of England (9 Halsbury's Laws (4 Edition) para 204) concerning the power of an individual to contract with himself and this applies also to a trustee, executor, administrator or agent. *[1977] 1 All ER 801.*

Rosser v CIR

'Farmhouse' for the purpose of IHTA 1984, s 115(2).

P and his wife owned a farm with 41 acres of land. In 1989 they gave 39 acres to their daughter (R), who was carrying on a farming business with her husband seven miles away. P and his wife retained the farmhouse and two acres of land. Following the transfer, R and her husband farmed all 41 acres of land, including the two acres which P and his wife continued to own. P died in April 2001, and his wife died seven weeks later. The Revenue issued a notice of determination charging IHT on the farmhouse and a barn. (The Revenue accepted that the two acres of land were 'agricultural property' within *IHTA 1984, s 115(2).*) R appealed, contending that she was entitled to agricultural property relief. The Special Commissioner allowed the appeal in part, holding that by 2001 the house was not a 'farmhouse' for the purpose of *IHTA 1984, s 115(2)*, since its 'prime function' was 'as a retirement home'. However, the barn was 'a working farm building' and qualified for relief. *[2003] STC SCD 311 Sp C 368.*

Royal Trust Co v A-G for Alberta

Situation of property—specialty debt.

A specialty debt is situate where the bond or specialty is kept. *PC 1929, 46 TLR 25; [1930] AC 144.*

Russell & Another v CIR

Business property relief—deeds of variation.

A testator's residuary estate included a reserve fund at Lloyd's which qualified for business property relief. His executors entered into a Deed of Variation in 1983 and executed a further variation in 1985. The Revenue made a determination to the effect that business property relief was not available on the first variation. The Revenue also refused to accept that the second variation was within the scope of the relieving provisions in *FA 1978, s 68* (subsequently *IHTA 1984, s 142*). It was held that the second variation was not effective for capital transfer tax, as *FA 1978, s 68* did not apply to variations of dispositions previously varied under *FA 1978, s 68*. However, business property relief was held to be due in respect of the first variation because on the facts of the case the legacies in question could only be satisfied out of qualifying assets. (The rules on which the case was decided have been altered by *IHTA 1984, s 39A* with effect from 18 March 1986.) *Ch D, [1988] STC 195; [1988] 1 WLR 834; [1988] 2 All ER 405.*

Rye v Rye

Conveyance by persons to themselves.

Two brothers carried on a partnership business, the profits of which were divisible between them in unequal shares. They had purchased in equal shares the premises used for the business and in order to reconcile their inequality as partners with their equal ownership of the premises, they agreed orally to grant to the partnership a yearly tenancy of the premises. Following the death of one of the brothers, his son became one of the owners of the premises and, subsequently a partner in the business. When the partnership was subsequently dissolved, the son continued to occupy part of the premises for his own business use and the surviving brother brought an action claiming possession of the property as the surviving tenant under the yearly tenancy. The HL held that, on the fact, the inference that the partners purported to grant an annual tenancy to themselves was justified but such grant was ineffective for two reasons. First, a 'conveyance' only applies, unless the context of a particular enactment requires otherwise, to an instrument in writing as distinct from an oral disposition. Secondly, *Law of Property Act 1925, s 72(3)* does not enable an individual to grant a lease to himself, nor several persons to grant a lease to themselves. *HL [1962] AC 496; 1962 All ER 146.*

Rysaffe Trustee Co (CI) Ltd v CIR

Valuation of settled property which comprised five discretionary settlements comprising trust funds of £10 each by way of a cheque for £50 with property to be added at a later date—deferred shares in a private company of which the settlors were members and directors were subsequently transferred to the five settlements. Was each settlement for the purposes of the ten yearly tax charge to be taken as property comprised in one settlement—whether creation of five settlements and transfer of shares to trustee associated operations—whether five settlements comprised five dispositions of property resulting in one settlement. IHTA 1984, ss 43(2), 64, 268(1)(b) and 272.

A settlor executed five settlements within a period of 35 days, and transferred shares of equal value to each settlement. The Inland Revenue issued a notice of determination that the five holdings should be treated as a single settlement for the purposes of the charge to tax under *IHTA 1984, s 64*. The company which acted as the trustee of the settlements appealed. The Ch D allowed the appeal, holding that there were five separate settlements for the purposes of *s 64*. Park J held that 'it is up to the settlor who places property in trust to determine whether he wishes to create one trust or several trusts, or for that matter merely to add more property to a settlement which had already been created in the past'. Each settlement was created by a 'disposition' within *IHTA 1984, s 43*. The 'associated operations' provisions of *IHTA 1984, s 268* did not apply, since *s 268* was 'not an operative provision which of itself imposes inheritance tax liabilities. It is a definition of an expression (associated operations) which is used elsewhere. The definition only comes into effect in so far as the expression "associated operations" is used elsewhere, and then only if the expression in another provision is relevant to the way in which that other provision applies to the facts of the particular case.' The CA unanimously upheld this decision. Mummery LJ held that 'the inclusion of "associated operations" in the statutory description of "disposition" is not intended for cases, such as this, where there is no dispute that there was a "disposition" of property falling within *section 43(2)*. They are intended for cases where there is a dispute as to whether there was a relevant "disposition" at all.' In this case, the Revenue were 'not seeking to use the extended sense of "disposition" to determine what is to be taken as a settlement or what is the property comprised in a settlement. They are seeking to use it for the purpose of determining the different question of counting how many settlements there are in a given case. The provisions do not entitle the CIR, in the absence of clear language, to conduct the exercise of shrinking the number of settlements which satisfy the definition of a "settlement" in *s 43(2)*, or to aggregate the settled property comprised in each of the separate settlements, so as to treat, for inheritance tax purposes, property subject to discrete settlements as if it were comprised, along with other settled property, in a single settlement'. *CA [2003] EWCA Civ 356; CA [2003] STC 536.*

Scottish Provident Institution, CIR v

Taxation of financial instruments—qualifying contracts—FA 1994, s 147A.

In 1995 a bank (C) and a company (S) initiated a series of transactions, admittedly designed as a 'tax avoidance scheme', under which each party granted a call option to the other party. The scheme was designed to take advantage of the provisions of *FA 1994, ss 147A, 150A* and produce a deemed net loss of £20,000,000. The Revenue issued an assessment on the basis that the relevant transactions should be treated as a single composite transaction having no commercial purpose, and giving rise to no gain or loss. The HL unanimously upheld the assessment, observing that 'the purpose of the transaction was to create a tax loss, not a real loss or profit'. The Special Commissioners had found that 'there was an outside but commercially real possibility that circumstances might occur in which the two options would not be exercised so as to cancel each other out'. Nevertheless, this did not require the Commissioners to treat the options as separate transactions. The HL held that 'it would destroy the value of the *Ramsay* principle of construing provisions such as (*FA 1994, s 150A(1)*) as referring to the effect of composite transactions if their composite effect had to be disregarded simply because the parties had deliberately included a commercially irrelevant contingency, creating an acceptable risk that the scheme might not work as planned. We would be back in the world of artificial tax schemes, now equipped with anti-*Ramsay* devices. The composite effect of such a scheme should be considered as it was intended to operate and without regard to the possibility that, contrary to the intention and expectations of the parties, it might not work as planned.' The scheme was a 'single composite transaction' which 'created no entitlement to gilts', so that 'there was therefore no qualifying contract'. *HL 2004, 76 TC 538; [2005] STC 15; [2004] UKHL 52; [2005] 1 All ER 325.*

Shepherd v HMRC

Ordinary residence claim failed—not temporarily resident and therefore liable to UK income tax. ICTA 1988, s 334.

An airline pilot (S), who was born and domiciled in the UK, purchased a flat in Cyprus in October 1998. He claimed that he was not ordinarily resident in the UK for 1999/2000. The Revenue rejected the claim and S appealed. The Special Commissioner dismissed his appeal, finding that during 1999/2000 he had spent 80 days in the UK, 77 days in Cyprus, 180 days flying in the course of his employment, and 28 days holidaying elsewhere. While in the UK, he had stayed in the house which he shared with his wife. The Commissioner held that 'the absences of (S) after October 1998 were temporary absences from the United Kingdom as were his absences when flying in the course of his duties'. S's time in Cyprus was only 'occasional residence abroad', within *ICTA 1998, s 334(a)*. The Ch D upheld the Commissioner's decision. *Ch D [2006] All ER(D) 191; [2006] STC 1821.*

Shepherd v Lyntress Ltd; News International plc v Shepherd

Applicability of Ramsay principle where subsidiary company acquired with accumulated tax losses.

A major public company (N) had acquired shares in companies that had appreciated in value. It decided to acquire companies which had accumulated tax losses so that the gains on the holdings could be realised and the accrued losses could be set off against them. Accordingly, in 1979 N acquired the issued share capital of L, a company claiming to have £4m of accumulated tax losses available for set-off. In 1980 N sold part of its holding of appreciated assets to L, and a few days later L realised the gains by disposing of the assets on the Stock Exchange. The Revenue raised assessments on N on the basis that the *Ramsay* principle applied, and that the sale of the assets by N to L was to be ignored for fiscal purposes, so that the transactions would fall to be treated as disposals on the Stock Exchange by N, and on L on the basis that, again applying the *Ramsay* principle, the losses incurred within the company's former group were not available against gains accruing to a company outside that group. The Special Commissioners reduced the assessment on L, rejecting the Revenue's contention that the accumulated losses were not available for set-off. However, they upheld the assessment on N. Both sides appealed to the Ch D. Vinelott J allowed N's appeal and upheld the Commissioners' decision with regard to the assessment on L. On the facts, the Commissioners were clearly correct in rejecting the Revenue's contention that L's losses were not available for set-off. The real question in the case was whether the Commissioners were justified in concluding that the transfer and sale of the assets were part of a single composite transaction. Following *Craven v White*, this could not be held to be the case here, because no arrangements to sell the shares on the Stock Exchange had been made at the time when they were transferred from N to L. It was therefore impossible to conclude that the transfer of the shares to L, and their subsequent sale by L, was a single composite transaction within the *Ramsay* principle. L had an allowable loss at the time when its share capital was acquired by N. That loss remained an allowable loss after N had acquired L's share capital, and the gains which were realised when the transferred assets were sold on the Stock Exchange were gains realised by L at a time when it was a member of the same group of companies as N. *Ch D 1989, 62 TC 495; [1989] STC 617.*

Sillars and Another v CIR

The effect of IHTA 1984, s 5(2)was that the whole of a joint building society account formed part of the deceased's estate.

In 1995 a woman (S) transferred her building society account into the names of herself and her two daughters. On her death her personal representatives treated her as having owned only one-third of the balance in the account. The Revenue issued a notice of determination that IHT was due on the whole balance in the account. The personal representatives appealed. The Special Commissioner dismissed the appeal, holding on the evidence that S retained power over the account. She was able to dispose of the balance as she thought fit, and withdrawals were made for her benefit. The effect of *IHTA 1984, s 5(2)* was that the whole of the account formed part of her estate. *[2004] STC SCD 180 Sp C 401.*

Snapes v Aram and others

Windfall estate changes disinheritance position under Inheritance (Provision for Family and Dependants) Act 1975.

The father made his last will on 18 February 1980 and the estate comprised of a house and a plot of land. He made no financial provision for his daughter due to lack of funds. The land was used in the family business which was run by the sons and one daughter in the family. There was a specific provision in the deceased's will that if his wife predeceased him the remainder of the estate would be divided between the plaintiff, his other daughter and his seven grandchildren. In 1989 there was a change in the value of the land when Tesco bought the plot for £13 million. The widow died after the sale to Tesco and by her will she left the plaintiff a legacy of £1,000. The plaintiff did not make any application in respect of the mother's estate.

The main issues that arose on appeal were whether the father had made reasonable financial provision for the daughter and whether a subsequent windfall to the estate should change the original lack of financial provision to the daughter. From the will it was clear that the deceased was well disposed to the plaintiff and recognised that some provision ought, if resources permitted, to be made for her. That was a factor which it was to be taken into account under *section 3(1)(g)* and for the court to give such weight to. The judge was not obliged to find a special circumstance, such as moral obligation and was entitled to look at all the relevant matters under *section 3*. The Court of Appeal held that a subsequent windfall to the estate changed the position and an award was made to the plaintiff in respect of maintenance of £3,000 per annum. *TLR 8 May 1998.*

Soutter's Executry v CIR

IHTA 1984, s 142—whether deed of variation effective.

A woman (S) died in November 1999. The value of her estate was less than the IHT threshold. She owned a house, in which she lived with a friend (G). Under her will, she gave G the right to live in the house, rent-free. G died in November 2000. In an attempt to reduce the IHT due on G's death, S's executors and G's executors purported to execute a deed of variation of S's estate, under *IHTA 1984, s 142*, removing the provision whereby G could live in the house rent-free. The Revenue issued a notice of determination that the purported deed of variation was ineffective. S's executors appealed. The Special Commissioner dismissed the appeal, observing that 'the executors of a liferentrix have nothing they can vary'. G's executors 'had neither right, title or interest to any liferent'. They 'could not have continued to receive the liferent so they had nothing to give up or vary. The liferent was not and could not be assigned to them … a purported assignation of an expired liferent has no reality'. *[2002] STC SCD 385 Sp C 325.*

Spencer-Nairn v CIR

Sale of property at undervalue—whether any gratuitous benefit.

In 1976 a landowner sold a farm, several buildings on which were in need of repair and replacement, to a Jersey company for £101,350. His son was a major shareholder in the company, which was, therefore, connected with him for the purposes of both CGT and IHT. The Revenue took the view that the sale had been at undervalue, and the Lands Tribunal subsequently valued the property (for CGT purposes) at £199,000. The Revenue issued a determination on the basis that the disposition of the farm was within *IHTA 1984, s 3(1)**, and constituted a chargeable transfer of value. The landowner appealed, contending that he had not known that the purchasing company was connected with him for IHT purposes, and that he had had no intention of conferring a gratuitous benefit on the company. The Special Commissioner allowed his appeal and the CS upheld this decision. On the evidence, the tenant of the farm had not wished to purchase it and the farm was unlikely to have been of interest to institutional investors. Accordingly it was reasonable to conclude that the sale had not been intended to confer a gratuitous benefit on the Jersey company, and was a disposition which 'might be expected to be made in a transaction at arm's length'. The transaction was within *IHTA 1984, s 10(1)(b)** and there was no chargeable transfer of value. *CS 1990, [1991] STC 60.*

Standard Chartered Bank Ltd v CIR

Situation of property—registered shares.

Following *R v Williams and Treasurer for Ontario v Aberdein*, it was held that registered shares transferable in either England or South Africa were situate in South Africa because in the ordinary course of affairs that country was the one in which the deceased owner would have been likely to deal with those shares. *CIR Ch D, [1978] STC 272; [1978] 1 WLR 1160.*

Stannard, CIR v

Jurisdiction—personal liability of executor.

The Jersey resident executor of a testator who died resident and domiciled in England claimed that his Jersey residence made him immune from suit in England for unpaid CTT, and that he was liable for unpaid CTT only in a representative rather than in a personal capacity. The CA held, following *CIR v Stype Investments (Jersey) Ltd Re Clore (deceased)*, that the High Court has jurisdiction to deal with a claim for CTT arising on the death of a person resident and domiciled in England, and that the CTT liability arising on death could not be a liability of the deceased but was an original, personal liability of the personal representative. *Ch D 1984, CTTL 22; [1984] STC 245; [1984] 2 All ER 105; [1984] 1 WLR 1039.*

Starke & Another (Brown's Executors) v CIR

Agricultural property relief—definition of 'agricultural property'.

A deceased's estate included a 2.5 acre site containing a substantial six-bedroomed farmhouse and a number of outbuildings. The site was used as part of a moderately-sized farm. The Revenue issued a notice of determination under *IHTA 1984, s 221* that the transfer of the site was not a transfer of 'agricultural property' within *IHTA 1984, s 115(2)*, and thus did not qualify for agricultural property relief. The executors applied by way of an originating summons for leave to appeal and for a declaration that the determination was wrong. The Ch D dismissed the appeal and refused the declaration, holding that the site was not 'agricultural property', since it was not 'agricultural land or pasture'. The CA upheld this decision and dismissed the executor's appeal. *CA [1995] STC 689; [1995] 1 WLR 1439; [1996] 1 All ER 622.*

St Clair-Ford (Youlden's Executor) v Ryder

Joint owner of a retail shop—discount should be 15% rather than 10%. Lands Tribunal held that the discount should be 10%.

An individual (Y) was joint owner of a retail shop. He died in 2003. The Revenue determined the value of his interest in the shop as £175,000 (applying a 10% discount for joint ownership). Y's executor appealed, contending *inter alia* that the discount should be 15% rather than 10%. The Lands Tribunal rejected this contention and upheld the Revenue's determination, applying the decision in *Cust v CIR, KB 1917, 91 EG 11* and holding that the discount should be 10%. *Lands Tribunal 22 June 2006 unreported.*

St Dunstan's v Major

Variation of will by sole legatee—tax repaid to charity, IHT on estate reduced. Whether 'qualifying donation' within FA 1990, s 25.

The sole legatee under a will entered into a Deed of Variation, whereby £20,000 was bequeathed to a charity. The legatee claimed relief under *FA 1990, s 25* and signed a form R190(SD) certifying that he had paid £26,666 (i.e. £20,000 grossed-up at 25%) to the charity. The charity claimed a repayment of £6,666, which the Revenue made. Subsequently the Revenue formed the opinion that the donation of £20,000 did not satisfy the requirements of *FA 1990, s 25(2)(e)* and thus was not a 'qualifying donation', since the legatee had saved inheritance tax of £8,000, and had therefore received a benefit in consequence of making it, so that the charity should not have received any repayment. They issued an assessment to recover £6,666. The charity appealed, contending that the inheritance tax saving should not be treated as a benefit within *section 25(2)(e)*. The Special Commissioner rejected this contention and dismissed the appeal, holding that since the legatee was the 'sole or residuary beneficiary of the estate, he ultimately benefited from the inheritance tax saving'. Accordingly, the donation was not a qualifying donation within *FA 1990, s 25. [1997] STC SCD 212 Sp C 127.*

Steiner v CIR

Domicile—whether English domicile of choice acquired.

A Jew, born in Czechoslovakia, who acquired a domicile of origin in Germany but came to England in 1939 to escape Nazi persecution and obtained British naturalisation, was held to have acquired an English domicile of choice. *CA 1973, 49 TC 13; [1973] STC 547.*

Stenhouse's Trustees v Lord Advocate

Time of capital distribution—trustees in breach of trust.

On 8 April 1975, trustees of a discretionary trust appointed shares in the trust fund to the three daughters of the settlor. As the trustees only had power to make such an appointment to each daughter on her attaining the age of 22, and as the youngest was not yet 22, the trustees were in breach of trust. They therefore resolved that payment would not be made until all three had signed an indemnity. The question before the court was whether the three became entitled to interests in possession on 8 April 1975 (as opposed to the date the indemnities were signed or the date the youngest became 22). The CS held that the interests of the daughters were severable, and that the two who were already 22 became entitled to interests in possession on 8 April 1975. However, the youngest daughter did not, as it would have been *ultra vires* the trustees to confer an absolute entitlement on her on that date. *CS 1983, [1984] STC 195.*

Stoner and another (executors of Dickinson deceased) v CIR

Valuation—sale of land from deceased's estate—residuary estate to charity included freehold property which was sold by executors at prices exceeding probate values—executors made claim that sale prices values for IHT purposes—whether appropriate persons for IHTA 1984, ss 190, 191.

The deceased's will left the residue of her estate exceeding the nil rate band to charities. There was therefore no IHT payable. Freehold properties in the estate were valued at

£582,000. Some of these properties were sold and the CTO was informed of the amount £918,457. The executors were informed that confirmation by the CTO was not necessary as the since charity relief was applicable. In 1998 the executors made a formal claim under *IHTA 1984, s 191*. Reference in that section to 'appropriate person' making the claim was important to the executors as they wished the uplift in the values of the properties for CGT purposes. The IR issued a notice of determination in April 2001 that in relation to the deemed disposal for the purposes of *s 190(1)* there was no appropriate person to make the claim. The executors appealed contending that they were the appropriate person because they would have been liable for the tax if the residuary beneficiaries had not all been charities or if the value of the part estate not passing to the residuary beneficiaries had exceeded the nil rate band. The Special Commissioner noted the *s 191* was to grant relief where there was a fall in the value of the land after death. The section did not state that it should not apply to increases in values but did refer to 'appropriate person' who was defined as the person liable to IHT. Gifts to charities were exempt transfers and so no tax was chargeable. It followed that *s 190(1)* 'the person liable for inheritance tax' meant the person who either had paid the tax or had obligation to pay it. There was no person liable to pay IHT if there was no tax to pay. Therefore as there was no appropriate person under *s 191* the executors' appeal would be dismissed. *[2001] STC SCD 199 Sp C 288*.

Surveyor v CIR

IHTA 1984, s 6(1) re Hong Kong domicile of choice.

A surveyor had been born in England in 1958. He moved to Hong Kong in 1986, and married in 1990. In 1997 he and his wife received a 'right of permanent abode' in Hong Kong. In 1999 he established a discretionary trust in Jersey, for the benefit of his wife and children. He transferred £247,500 to the trustees. The Revenue issued a notice of determination that this was a chargeable transfer. He appealed, contending that he had lost his English domicile of origin and acquired a domicile of choice in Hong Kong (so that the money transferred to the trust was excluded property within *IHTA 1984, s 6(1)*). The Special Commissioner accepted this contention and allowed his appeal, finding that at the date of the transfer, he 'had the intention to reside permanently in Hong Kong'. *[2002] STC SCD 501 Sp C 339.*

Swales and Others v CIR

Interest in possession—effect of Trustee Act 1925, s 31.

In 1970 trustees appointed income from a trust fund to R absolutely, although the (complex) provisions of the trust prevented R's right to the income from vesting until one of her children became 21 in 1976 (the vesting date). The trustees disagreed with the Revenue as to whether an interest in possession was created in 1970 or in 1976. The interest in possession was held to have arisen in 1970. The 1970 appointment was a contingent appointment of income which was intended to carry the intermediate income of the fund before the vesting date, and *Trustee Act 1925, s 31(1)(ii)* applied so that R had a present right to that income as it arose and as such to an interest in possession in the trust fund. *Ch D 1984, CTTL 24; [1984] STC 413; [1984] 1 All ER 16.*

Thomas & Thomas v CIR

Protective trust—forfeiture before 12 April 1978.

In June 1976 a CTT avoidance scheme was used to take advantage of a loophole in the rules for protective trusts in *FA 1975, 5 Sch 18(2)* (subsequently *IHTA 1984, s 88(2)*). The Ch D rejected the Revenue's argument that a protective trust of income for the benefit of the settlor was not a trust 'to the like effect' as those in *Trustee Act 1925, s 33(1)*. *Ch D 1981, CTTL 8; [1981] STC 382.* (*Note.* The loophole was removed for forfeitures after 11 April 1978. *IHTA 1984, s 73** subsequently operated instead of *IHTA 1984, s 88(2)** where forfeiture was before 12 April 1978.)

Thomson (Thomson's Executor) v CIR

Determination under IHTA 1984, s 221 charging value on house bequeathed to daughter but non-evidence of transfer documents.

A widow died in 1971 and bequeathed her house to her daughter (J). J died in 2002. The Inland Revenue issued a Notice of Determination under *IHTA 1984, s 221*, charging IHT on the value of the house. J's executor appealed, contending that despite the terms of her mother's will, J should not be treated as having been the sole owner of the house, because she had never 'signed any document accepting the title to the house'. The Special Commissioner reviewed the evidence and dismissed the appeal, finding that J was the sole owner of the house, which accordingly formed part of her estate for IHT purposes. *[2004] Sp C 429.*

Thorogood v CIR

IHTA 1984, s 225—right of appeal to High Court.

An individual (T) had been the executor of his deceased son's estate, but was declared bankrupt. A solicitor was appointed as the trustee of the estate. The Inland Revenue issued a Notice of Determination in respect of certain shares. The solicitor appealed. T applied under *Special Commissioners (Jurisdiction and Procedure) Regulations 1994, SI 1994/1811)* to be joined as a party to the appeal. The Special Commissioner dismissed this application, and T appealed to the Chancery Division. The Chancery Division dismissed T's appeal. Laddie J held that *IHTA 1984, s 225* provided that only a 'party to an appeal' had the right of appeal against a Special Commissioner's decision. T was not a party to the appeal. (*Note.* The appellant appeared in person.) *[2005] All ER (D) 201; STC 897.*

Trustees Executors and Agency Co Ltd and Others v CIR

Situation of property—ships.

The artificial situs abroad of a ship registered abroad was displaced by the actual situs when within English territorial or national waters. *Ch D 1972, [1973] 1 All ER 563; [1973] Ch 254.*

Trustees of the Douglas Trust (for Mrs I Fairbairn) v HMRC

Whether 'inter vivos' trust conferred interest in possession.

In a Scottish case, an individual (D) transferred certain securities and investments to trustees in 1962. The income arising from the trust was treated for tax purposes as income of the settlor under *FA 1958, s 22* (now *ITTOIA 2005, ss 624–628*). D died in 1981 and then his wife died in 2002. HMRC issued a notice of determination on the basis that she had enjoyed an interest in possession in the settled property. The trustees appealed. The Special Commissioner dismissed the appeal, finding that D's widow had effectively enjoyed 'a power of veto: the whole of the free annual income of the trust fund had to be paid or applied to her or for her benefit from year to year unless or until she should concur with a consideration by the trustees that it was proper and expedient for a lesser amount to be so paid or applied'. Accordingly the trust deed had conferred an interest in possession. *[2007] STC SCD 338 Sp C 593.*

Two Settlors v CIR

Notices of Determination under IHTA 1984, s 221.

Two settlors transferred certain shares in the same company to two settlements. The Revenue issued purported Notices of Determination under *IHTA 1984, s 221* to the effect that there had been no loss to the transferors' estates. The settlors appealed, contending as a preliminary point that the Notices were premature and inappropriate, and that the Special Commissioner had no jurisdiction to decide whether there had been a transfer of a value, which was a matter to be decided in a future capital gains tax appeal. The Special Commissioner accepted this contention and held that the purported Notices of Determination were not within *IHTA 1984, s 221* and were not appropriate. The substantive issue of whether there had been any transfer of value 'will have to be determined in any subsequent capital gains tax appeal'. *[2004] STC SCD 45 Sp C 385.*

Von Ernst & Cie SA and Others v CIR

Discretionary settlement—whether capital distribution—whether excluded property— jurisdiction of High Court.

On 25 March 1976 the trustees of a discretionary settlement appointed property consisting of exempt government securities to the two children of the settlor. Neither was resident nor domiciled in the UK. On the failure of the trusts to the children the property would have been held on constructive discretionary trusts for two UK charities. The Board determined that the appointment was to be treated as giving rise to a capital distribution under *FA 1975, 5 Sch 6(2)*. The trustees appealed direct to the High Court, contending that para 6(2) did not apply because the property was excluded property as soon as there were interests in possession in it. After losing in the Ch D, the trustees adduced two new arguments before the CA. The CA held that (i) the question of whether settled property was excluded property for the purposes of *para 6(2)* depended on the state of affairs which existed immediately before the appointment; (ii) exemption from CTT depends on CTT legislation, not on *F(No 2)A 1931*; (iii) the exempt securities were excluded property before the appointment by virtue of *IHTA 1984, s 48(4)(b)** since the charities were not 'known persons' who might 'benefit' or become 'beneficially entitled' within the meaning of that provision. The appeal was therefore allowed. The Ch D had held that where a CTT appeal is taken direct to the High Court, the latter has the same power to quash etc. a determination of the Board as the Special Commissioners would have had if the appeal had gone first to them. (This was not contested in the CA.) *CA 1979, CTTL 6; [1980] STC 111; [1980] 1 WLR 468; [1980] 1 All ER 677.*

Walding & Others (Walding's Executors) v CIR

IHTA 1984, s 269(1)—whether deceased had control of company.

A woman held 45 of the 100 shares in a company at the time of her death. Of the remaining 55 shares, 24 were in the name of her four-year-old grandson. Her executors claimed that, since the grandson was not in a position to exercise the voting rights attached to his 24 shares, the deceased had had control of the company so that her shareholding qualified for business property relief. The Revenue rejected the claim and the Ch D dismissed the executors' appeal. *IHTA 1984, s 269(1)* dealt with the ambit of the powers of voting, not the capabilities of the shareholders in whose names the shares were registered. *Ch D 1995 [1996] STC 13.* (*Note.* See also *Hepworth v Smith Ch D 1981, 54 TC 396; [1981] STC 354*, a capital gains tax case, in which shares were taken into account for the purposes of *TCGA, s 163** although the relevant voting rights had never been exercised.)

Walker's Executors v CIR

Business property relief—casting vote gave control over the company IHTA 1984, s 269(1)—entitlement to BPR on land from which the company traded.

A married couple had formed a company to operate a road haulage business and petrol station. The husband died in 1983 and the wife died in 1996. At the time of her death, she was chairman of the company and held 50% of the shares in it, with a casting vote at general meetings. She also owned the land from which the company traded. The Revenue issued a determination charging IHT on the land. Her executors appealed, contending that she had control of the company by virtue of her casting vote, so that the land qualified for business property relief under *IHTA, s 105(1)(d)*. The Special Commissioner accepted this contention and allowed the appeal, holding that the casting vote had given her control of the company, within *IHTA 1984, s 269(1)*. *Dicta* of Rowlatt J in *CIR v BW Noble Ltd* applied. *[2001] STC SCD 86 Sp C 275.*

Wallach (deceased), In re

Domicile—husband's domicile retained on widowhood.

A widow had acquired her late husband's domicile on marriage. It was held, in an intestacy case, that she retained this until her death, not having changed it; her domicile of origin had not revived on her husband's death. *HC 1949, 28 ATC 486; [1950] 1 All ER 199.*

Walton (Walton's Executor) v CIR

Valuation of partnership interest in non-assignable agricultural tenancy.

The freehold of a farm was held by a father and his two sons as tenants in common in equal shares. The farm was let to a partnership comprising the father and one of the sons. In August 1984 the father died. It was agreed that the vacant possession premium (i.e. the difference between the open market value of the freehold interest in the farm with vacant possession and that when subject to the tenancy) was £200,000. The value of tenant-right and tenants' improvements, less dilapidations, was £40,000. The Revenue issued a notice of determination to CTT, valuing the tenancy at half the vacant possession premium with a 10% discount to reflect the part interest (i.e. at £90,000), plus the net value of tenant-right and tenants' improvements, thereby arriving at a value of £130,000. The father's half-share was, therefore, valued at £65,000. The executor appealed against the valuation, contending that it was excessive, since it assumed an immediate purchase by the freeholders, whereas in fact the freeholders would not have been interested in securing the surrender of the tenancy and did not have the financial resources for such a purchase. The Lands Tribunal accepted this evidence and allowed the appeal, holding on the evidence that the realisation of the vacant possession premium was 'so far from any market expectation as to make a valuation by reference to an apportionment of the vacant possession premium wholly inappropriate'. The property which was required to be valued in accordance with what is now *IHTA 1984, s 94* was an undivided beneficial interest in the joint tenancy as a partnership asset. The tenancy could only be sold and its value realised if the terms of the partnership agreement permitted it, which they did not. The sole value of the tenancy, as a partnership asset, rested upon the extent to which its terms enhanced the partnership profits by enabling the partners to exploit the partnership assets without paying a full market rent for the farm. The tribunal reviewed the evidence in detail and held that the value of the entire tenancy, on the basis of a valuation of profit rental and on the assumption that the landlords could not be regarded as a hypothetical purchaser, was approximately £12,600, so that the value of the deceased's share was £6,300. The Revenue appealed to the CA, which upheld the Tribunal decision as one of fact. The Tribunal had been entitled to conclude that the landlords were not to be regarded as a hypothetical purchaser, and it was for the tribunal to consider what premium (if any) any special purchaser would be prepared to pay. *CA 1995, [1996] STC 68.*

Ward and Others (Executors of Cook deceased) v IRC

Valuation of a deceased's interest in building society shares prior to conversion—whether deceased's interest in those shares to be valued at nil for IHT purposes.

The deceased, Cook, had a number of accounts with the Woolwich Building Society. The Society announced its proposed conversion into a public limited company subject to a number of conditions being met. In January 1997 the Woolwich sent out a copy of the transfer document. On 11 February at a special general meeting the members voted and the resolution to convert was carried. On 10 May 1997 Cook died. On 7 July 1997 the flotation took place. Under the transfer document the deceased was entitled to 450 free shares in Woolwich plc and an additional variable distribution. The first named executor was entitled to the shares as part of Cook's estate. The Revenue determined that on 10 May 1997 the anticipated benefit of the conversion enhanced the deceased's Woolwich holdings. The executors appealed saying that the deceased had merely a hope that she would receive the shares. Also, other arguments were advanced why the conversion might not have gone ahead. The Special Commissioners decided that the deceased held rights under the transfer document which transcended the mere hope that Cook would obtain shares in Woolwich plc. The rights conferred by the transfer document were part of Cook's property to which she was entitled and therefore held to be valued in calculating the extent of her estate and as such became part of her estate that Cook was deemed to have made immediately before her death. Therefore, the executors' valuation of nil would be rejected and the Revenue's valuation (see Table in 55.28) would be accepted. The executors' appeal was dismissed. *[1999] STC SCD 1 Sp C 175.*

Westminster (Duke of) v CIR

A taxpayer covenanted to make certain annual payments to a number of his domestic employees. The payments, having regard to the surrounding circumstances, were, in substance but not in form, remuneration. The HL held (Lord Atkin dissenting) that the payments were annual payments from which tax was deductible and were allowable deductions in arriving at the taxpayer's income for surtax. *HL 1935, 19 TC 490. (Notes.* (1) The covenants would now be 'caught'—see *ICTA 1988, ss 683, 684*.* The case remains of importance in relation to the meaning of 'annual payment' and in illustrating whether the courts will look at substance rather than form. (2) Lord Tomlin's judgment includes the celebrated dictum that 'every man is entitled if he can to order his affairs so that the tax attaching under the appropriate Acts is less than it otherwise would be'. This *dictum* has frequently been discussed in subsequent cases, particularly in the light of the *Ramsay* principle. It was applied by Lord Oliver in the 1988 case of *Craven v White.* However, in the 1992 case of *Ensign Tankers (Leasing) Ltd v Stokes,* Lord Templeman stated that 'subsequent events have shown that though this *dictum* is accurate as far as tax mitigation is concerned it does not apply to tax avoidance'. For the distinction between tax mitigation and tax avoidance, see *New Zealand Commissioner of Inland Revenue v Challenge Corporation.* In *Ensign Tankers,* Lord Templeman also specifically approved Lord Atkin's dissenting judgment in the *Duke of Westminster* case.)

Westminster's (4th Duke of) Executors v Ministry of Defence (aka Barty-King v Ministry of Defence)

Death on active service—cause of death.

The Duke of Westminster, who was wounded in action in 1944, died of cancer in 1967. The septicaemia caused by his war wound was noted on the death certificate as a significant condition contributing to the death 'but not related to the disease or condition causing it'. Exemption from estate duty was provided by *FA 1952, s 71* for the estate of any person who was certified by the Defence Council to have 'died from a wound inflicted … when … the deceased was a member of the armed forces of the Crown … on active service against an enemy'. The Defence Council turned down the executors' application for a certificate. The QB held that the executors were entitled to a declaration that they ought to have been granted a certificate. Although a wound had to be a cause of death, it did not have to be the direct or only cause. *QB 1978, CTTL 2; [1979] STC 218; [1979] 2 All ER 80. (Note.* The equivalent IHT exemption is provided by *IHTA 1984, s 154.*)

Weston (Weston's Executor) v CIR

Inheritance tax—exempt transfers and reliefs—business property—relevant business property—business of managing caravan park—whether business excluded from business property relief as consisting wholly or mainly of making or holding investments—IHTA 1984, s 105(3).

At the deceased's death in 1993 her estate included shares in a company. The business of the company, which was a single business, included the purchase and sale of caravans, the sale of caravans for commission on behalf of owners, and the grant of the right to pitch caravans on the caravan park run by the company for a consideration consisting of the pitch fees. The business also included the maintenance and administration of the park and the provision of facilities, and the supply for a consideration of electricity and bottled gas used by the pitch holders at the park. The park was situated near the M25 motorway, and was not a holiday park. It was entirely residential, and residents had to be over 50. It did not accommodate touring caravans or caravan rallies. The appearance of the park was that of a suburban residential development in miniature and the appearance of the caravans was that of small neat bungalows. The park had no shop or social club, but each caravan owner had the use of a brick built laundry and storeroom. The caravans were owned by their occupiers. Residents were obliged to purchase a caravan from the company or another resident, usually through the company, which took a commission on sales between residents. The number of sales of caravans was not large. The company's three employees spent a total of 111 hours per week on park maintenance and 37 hours per week on sales activities. The company's accounts, which were drawn up in accordance with normal accounting practice as laid down by the Companies Acts, showed that pitch fees exceeded in amount the sums realised by caravan sales in four out of the six years from 1989 to 1994. Also, the profits from pitch fees exceeded the profits from caravan sales in every year from 1988 to 1994, with the exception of 1989, and that from 1988 to 1994 there was a substantial excess of pitch fees, and bank interest produced by a considerable cash reserve, over caravan sales. Following the deceased's death the Revenue issued a determination, in relation to the deemed disposal for the purposes of inheritance tax on her death and her holding of shares in the company which formed part of her estate at her death, that that holding was not relevant business property for the purposes of relief from inheritance tax, on the ground that it was excluded from the category of relevant business property by *IHTA 1984, s 105(3)* because the business of the company consisted wholly or mainly in the making or holding of investments. The executor appealed.

The Commissioner concluded that, standing back and looking at the matter in the round in the light of relevant decisions of the Special Commissioners, the pitch fees were not ancillary to caravan sales; the caravan sales were ancillary to pitch fees at the park. The company operated a caravan park, and was not a dealer selling caravans. Accordingly, the business of the company consisted mainly in making or holding investments. The notice of determination would therefore be upheld. *[2000] STC SCD 30 Sp C 222.*

Subsequently W's executor appealed. The Special Commissioner dismissed the appeal, applying *Hall & Hall (Hall's Executors) v CIR*, and distinguishing *Furness v CIR*. The Ch D upheld this decision as one of fact. *[2000] STC 1064; Ch D [2000] All ER (D) 1870.*

Wheatley and another (Executors of Wheatley deceased) v CIR

Grazing of horses on pasture–whether meadow qualified for APR within provisions of IHTA 1984, s 117.

An individual (W) owned a meadow, which he let to a women who owned some horses. She used the meadow for grazing her horses, paying rent to W. W died in 1997 and the Revenue issued notices of determination charging inheritance tax. W's executors appealed, contending that the meadow qualified for agricultural property relief. The Special Commissioner rejected this contention and dismissed the appeal, holding that, although the meadow constituted 'pasture' within *IHTA 1984, s 115 (2)*, it was not 'occupied for the purposes of agriculture', as required by *IHTA 1984, s 117*. On the evidence, the horses which grazed the meadow 'were not connected with agriculture' but were used by their owner for 'leisure pursuits'. Horses were not 'livestock' and grazing by horses would only fall within the provisions of *section 117* if the horses were connected with agriculture, which was not the case here. *[1998] STC SCD 60 Sp C 149.*

Whittaker v CIR

IHT liabilities —IHTA 1984, s 162—foreign tax payable.

In a Scottish case where the facts are not fully set out in the decision, the Revenue issued a notice of determination in respect of a chargeable transfer of £334,771. The deceased's executor appealed, contending that the determination did not take account of a sum owed to the Italian tax authorities. The Special Commissioner dismissed the appeal, holding that the appellant had not shown that any further Italian tax was payable (and observing that, if any such tax were found to be due, double taxation relief would apply). *[2001] STC SCD 61 Sp C 272.* (*Note.* The appellant appeared in person.)

Wight and Moss v CIR

Valuation—joint property—value of half share.

Two women lived in a house which they owned as tenants in common in equal shares. When one of them died the value of her half share in the house had to be ascertained for CTT purposes. It was agreed that the other co-owner would be the most likely purchaser and that this was a relevant factor in the valuation. The Lands Tribunal held that the value was half vacant possession value less a discount to reflect the restricted demand for this type of interest. It was held that it was not likely that an outside purchaser would be able to obtain an order for sale under *Law of Property Act 1925, s 30* and, reflecting this, that the discount should be 15% rather than the 10% which had become customary following the earlier decision in *Cust v CIR (1917) 91 EG 11. Lands Tribunal, [1982] 264 EG 935.*

Williams (Williams' Personal Representative) v HMRC

'Broiler houses' used for intensive rearing of poultry—whether 'agricultural property' within IHTA 1984, s 115(2).

A farm occupied 7.41 acres of land. Part of the land was used for three 'broiler houses', which were used for the intensive rearing of poultry. In April 2000 the owner of the farm (W) let the broiler houses, and 2.59 acres of the land, to a company (S). W died in 2001. The Inland Revenue issued a ruling that the broiler houses, and the 2.59 acres of land which had been let to S, did not qualify as 'agricultural property' within *IHTA 1984, s 115(2).* W's personal representative appealed. The Special Commissioner reviewed the evidence in detail and allowed the appeal in part, holding that the effect of *s 115(2)* was that the broiler houses could only qualify for relief if they had been 'a subsidiary part of the purpose of an overall agricultural activity carried out on the land'. Since they had been let to a separate company, this was not the case. Accordingly, the broiler houses had not been 'ancillary' to the farm, within *s 115(2)*, and did not qualify for relief. However, on the evidence, the broiler houses only occupied 0.68 acres of land. The Commissioner held that the remaining 1.91 acres of land which had been let to S was within the definition of 'agricultural property' and did qualify for relief. *[2005] STC SCD 782 Sp C 500.*

Willett and another (Mrs Benson's Executors) v CIR

Valuation—value of freehold interest in tenanted agricultural property.

The owner of a freehold interest in tenanted agricultural land died in 1977. The Revenue valued the interest for CTT purposes at £45,000. The executors appealed, contending that the valuation should be £28,000. The Lands Tribunal reviewed the evidence in detail and held that the valuation should be £39,000. The Tribunal reaffirmed the principle that a valuation must assume property is suitably lotted if it would fetch a better price if sold in that way, applying *Earl of Ellesmere v CIR [1918] 2 KB 735.* Although the length of time the tenant would continue in occupation was a relevant factor in the executors' valuation, the Tribunal rejected a strict life expectancy approach in favour of the Revenue's method of using the number of years before his probable retirement at the age of 75. In one of the two methods of valuation used by the Revenue, the vacant possession value had been taken at £70,000, and an allowance of £25,000 had been deducted from this, being an estimate of the amount a prospective purchaser would consider appropriate to cover deferment and obtain possession. The Tribunal held that the estimate was too low in view of the fact that the purchaser would be taking a considerable risk as to whether the tenant would vacate for £25,000, and bearing in mind a purchaser's requirement for profit. The Revenue's alternative method was to divide the vacant possession value between the 'pure investment value' (taking the reversion in perpetuity) and the 'vacant possession element' and to add 40% of the latter to the former, 40% being assumed to be what the tenant would pay to obtain the freehold interest. The Land Tribunal upheld this method in principle but held that the addition should be 33% rather than 40%. *Lands Tribunal 1982, 264 EG 257.*

Winans and Another v A-G (No 2)

Situation of property—bearer securities.

Bearer securities transferable by delivery are situate in the UK if the certificate of title is in the UK. *HL 1909, [1910] AC 27.*

Wolff & Wolff v Wolff and Others

IHT avoidance scheme—whether transaction may be set aside. Scheme set aside by use of Civil Procedure Rules.

A married couple owned a freehold property. They sought advice from a solicitor with a view to avoiding inheritance tax. On the solicitor's advice, in 1997 they entered into a reversionary lease of the property in favour of their daughters, to begin in 2017. Subsequently they became aware that the effect of the lease was that they would have no right to remain in the property after 2017. They applied to the Ch D to set aside the reversionary lease under the *Civil Procedure Rules 1998, SI 1998/3132 Part 8.* The Ch D granted their application. Mann J observed that the relevant deed was 'manifestly defective as a piece of drafting' and that the solicitor 'did not fully understand the implications of what he had brought about'. On the evidence, the couple 'did not know that the effect of the lease was to deprive them of their right to occupy the property in 2017'. Applying *dicta* of Millett J in *Gibbon v Mitchell, Ch D [1990] 3 All ER 338,* 'wherever there is a voluntary transaction by which one party intends to confer a bounty on another, the deed will be set aside if the court is satisfied that the disponor did not intend the transaction to have the effect which it did'. *Ch D [2004] STC 1633.*

Woodhall (Woodhall's Personal Representatives) v CIR

IHTA 1984, s 50(5)—interest in part of property.

An individual (GW) died in 1957, leaving three children. Under his will, he left his house to his two sons as trustees, and directed that it should not be sold as long as any of his three children was living in it. One of his sons (EW) had already moved out when GW died, and his daughter moved out the following year. However, his other son (AW) continued to live in the house until he died in 1997. The Revenue issued a notice of determination on the basis that, when AW died, he had a beneficial interest in the whole of the house. His personal representative appealed, accepting that the house was settled property but contending firstly that AW was not beneficially entitled to an interest in possession, and alternatively that he only had such an interest in one half of the house, as his brother (EW) had a beneficial entitlement to the other half. (Their sister had died in 1971.) The Special Commissioner accepted this contention and allowed the appeal in part, holding that the effect of GW's will was that, in 1997, both AW and EW 'had the right to claim to occupy the house jointly with the other'. Accordingly, when AW died, he was beneficially entitled to an interest in possession in the house within the meaning of *IHTA 1984, s 49(1)*, but that his interest subsisted in only half of the house, within *IHTA 1984, s 50(5). [2000] STC SCD 558 Sp C 261.*

Young and Another v Phillips

Situs—location of letters of allotment.

Two brothers resident and ordinarily resident in the UK, but domiciled in South Africa, owned equally the ordinary shares of three associated UK companies, each with substantial sums to the credit of its profit and loss account. On professional advice, during 1978–79 they implemented a pre-arranged scheme with the aim of 'exporting' the shares outside the UK (and so taking them outside the scope of CTT) without incurring any CGT liability. In brief, each company created new preferred ordinary shares, ranking pari passu with the existing ordinary shares save for priority in a capital repayment on a winding up; capitalised the amounts credited to profit and loss; appropriated these amounts to the taxpayers and used them in paying up, in full, new preferred ordinary shares issued to them, in respect of which the company issued to them renounceable letters of allotment. Shortly afterwards two Channel Island companies, set up for the purpose, issued to the taxpayers shares at a premium of £1,364,216 and resolved to buy from them (by now directors of the Channel Island companies) their preferred ordinary shares in the UK companies for £1,364,216. The taxpayers then went to Sark with their letters of allotment and the scheme was completed by, *inter alia*, letters of renunciation in favour of the Channel Island companies. CGT assessments were made on the basis that there had been a disposal of assets situated in the UK. The Special Commissioners dismissed the taxpayers' appeals, and the Ch D upheld their decision. Nicholls J held that there had been a disposal of rights against the UK companies, and that these were situated in the UK irrespective of where the letters of allotment happened to be. Further, even had he held that there had been a disposal of assets outside the UK, *W T Ramsay Ltd* and *Furniss v Dawson*, would have applied, and he would have accepted an alternative Revenue contention that *TCGA 1992, s 29(2)** applied, the relieving provisions of *TCGA 1992, ss 127, 135** being curtailed by *TCGA 1992, s 137(1)** because one of the main purposes of the issuing of the shares in the UK companies was the avoidance of liability to tax. *Ch D 1984, 58 TC 232; [1984] STC 520.*

DECEMBER 1995. – VOLUME 1.1 CTO NEWSLETTER

COMPASS (COMPUTERISED ASSESSING).

The Capital Taxes Offices in Nottingham, Edinburgh and Belfast are all now linked up to a new computer system which we are calling COMPASS. This system will produce calculations of inheritance tax (IHT) automatically. The first ones are due to be generated in January 1996.

COMPASS can be used for calculations of IHT which arise on a death on or after March 1988. But as we have a rolling programme of training for our staff, you may still receive some of these calculations on the old coloured forms until the training is completed. (We hope this will be by March 1996).

The new forms The new calculation forms will retain the names "IHT 301" and "IHT 302". This identifier is shown in the bottom left-hand corner. The 302 is for tax on assets which qualify for the instalment option. You will get an IHT 302 if there is such property, even if you are not paying by instalments.

The form comes in two parts. You can keep Part 1, which shows the calculation. You send Part 2 with your payment for receipting. Instructions for "How to pay" are shown on Part 2.

Headings A word of explanation about the headings may not go amiss. The name of the deceased, date of death, CTO reference and your reference are all self-explanatory. But what about "*Title*" and "*Entry*"?

"*Title*" This relates to the title under which the property passes, for example if it is settled property', it might show "Will of Diane Veale" or "Peter Riley Settlement dated 15 May 1995". Often it will show "Free Estate" We use this term to cover all property passing under the Will (or by Intestacy) of the deceased and the joint property.

"*Entry*" This will identify the particular calculation you are looking at. For example, "A/NIOP-1/2". The first letter relates to the title. ("A" is the Free Estate.) "NIOP" ("non-instalment option property") is for the property which does not have the instalment option. "IOP" is for property which qualifies for the instalment option. "WIR" ("with interest relief") is for property which qualifies for interest free instalments. The first number identifies a group set up by the computer and the last number tells you which in a series of calculations this one is. So, in the example, it is the second calculation raised on the property passing under the Will of the deceased and on which tax can not be paid by instalments.

COMPASS CAN'T DO EVERYTHING!

There are some types of calculation which the system will not produce at first. These are for claims to tax which arose before 16 March 1988, claims on non-interest in possession trusts and lifetime transfers which give rise to an immediate claim to tax.

However, we are creating computer templates for these so that the calculations will be printed instead of hand-written. (You will be able to tell if the calculation was not produced by COMPASS because the form will be called "IHT 301 (or 302 or 307) Manual".)

The production of COMPASS calculations is tied to the entry of data from the original Inland Revenue Account (IRA) or Inventory. This means that if we have received it before the introduction of COMPASS, the calculation will not show full details of the amendments. But, please note that this is a temporary feature and our staff are instructed to give these details separately in a schedule or covering letter.

Cashiers You may have heard that there are plans to move IHT Cashiers from Worthing to Castle Meadow in Nottingham. This is true but we do not have a date yet. So, for now please *do not send money to Castle Meadow*. If the calculation-which we often call an "assessment"-is from our offices in Nottingham or London, please continue to send your payment to IHT Cashiers in Worthing. If the calculation is from our offices in Edinburgh or Belfast, please continue to send your payments to the Cashiers in those offices. The addresses for the CTOs in Edinburgh and Belfast are also on the back page [see 2.11 ACCOUNTS AND RETURNS]. Our Edinburgh Office deals with most estates where the grant has been taken out at Newcastle Probate Registry. So if you intend to apply to Newcastle for the grant, please send your pregrant payment to the Edinburgh Cashier (instead of Worthing).

Payments in advance You can still send money on account at any time, even if you have not received a calculation, and you can ask for a receipt.

When the CTO sends a calculation, it will show the advance payment as a deposit set off against the amount due. If the balance then due is £20 or less, the calculation will show "Calculation for information only". You will get a receipt for the amount actually paid, but do not send the balance. If later we have to make further changes to the liability, we may ask for the balance then. Similarly, if the amount on deposit is more than the amount due, but the excess is £10 or less, we will not automatically repay the excess. You are entitled to claim this, though, by writing to or telephoning the office that sent you the calculation. *Please remember that we can only make out repayments to the accountable persons unless we have their written authority to repay to someone else.*

Electronic transfers

You can pay IHT by this method. If you do you need to give the following details.

Office dealing with estate	Bank	Sort code	Account number
Nottingham or London	Bank of England	10-00-00	234 11007
Edinburgh	Royal Bank of Scotland	83-06-08	00 13 29 61
Belfast	Bank of Ireland	90-21-27	999 42208

You must also state the deceased's name and date of death. (If you don't it might take us a long time to trace the payment!) If you pay the tax due before the grant by electronic transfer, you still have to send the IRA to Cashiers for receipting before you can get the grant. (Section 109 of the Supreme Court Act 1981 provides that a grant cannot be issued until the Revenue account is receipted).

Pre-grant section The Pre-grant section of the CTO have asked us to mention a couple of problems that they are experiencing. The instructions currently state that solicitors should only refer to CTO Pre-grant when the case involves Foreign domicile, Settled land grants or payment of tax by National Savings. Otherwise Pre-grant exist to do the tax calculations for non-professional applicants.

It seems that a minority of solicitors think that they must send the accounts to the Pre-grant in all cases to check tax calculations, this is incorrect.

The arrangements for practitioners and referral to Pre-grant appear in greater detail in the leaflet IHT5 (practitioners notes), available from the CTO.

Formerly, reference had to be made to Pre-grant section when claiming conditional exemption for objects of national, scientific, historic or artistic interest or for land or buildings of outstanding interest. These exemptions will now be examined post-grant and so need not come to CTO before the issue of the grant.

MARCH 1996. – VOLUME 1.2 CTO NEWSLETTER

MANDATES.

We appreciate that since the 1992 Cheques Act, if a repayment cheque is made out to the personal representatives (PRs), they cannot simply endorse the back to make it payable to their agent. This has caused some irritation and delay to some of you-often just when you think you are finalising the estate. But we can only make out repayments to the accountable persons unless we have their written permission to repay to someone else. This has always been our policy, not least because the PRs are the accountable persons.

If you tell us about the changes to the estate on a corrective account, you can ask the PRs to sign the mandate at section 4. But many of you will have noticed that our staff have a more relaxed approach to amendments and often don't insist on a formal account. I suspect that you would not want this to change!

So how else can you and the PRs let us know you want us to make out the repayment to you? You can get supplies of Sect 66A from our Nottingham Stationery team. Then you can ask the PRs to sign it at whatever stage you think appropriate.

We are planning to include a mandate section on clearance certificate forms and the forms for claiming relief for loss on sales (Sect 5 and Cap 38 – Edinburgh have already included it on these two). Since all these forms need to be signed by the PRs anyway (and the claim forms usually result in repayment), we hope this will speed things up without causing extra work for you or us.

Of course, our staff need to check the validity of any mandate. There may be occasions when they believe it advisable to confirm it before repayment-for example, when the claim for a repayment comes out of the blue long after we thought the estate was finalised.

CLEARANCE CERTIFICATES: CAP 30.

We have received a variety of enquiries from practitioners about this aspect of dealing with an estate.

One question we are asked is whether we are prepared to keep on file an application for clearance, when the estate is not yet finalised. This occurs most frequently when there is a straight forward interest under a trust. The trust details are sorted out quickly, sometimes even before the grant to the free estate has been obtained. So, the application for clearance for the trust arrives in the CTO before we have had a chance to look at the estate.

Our instructions say:

> 'When you receive a Cap 30 and it is obvious both to ourselves and the parties that it cannot be issued for some time yet, it may be necessary to return the form to the parties for updating and resubmission at a later date.'

As you can see, we leave it to the discretion of the examiner and to their judgement of the circumstances of the case. They try to be helpful and sensible. This means that normal practice is to hold the application on file rather than bother the applicant by returning it.

But premature applications can cause problems and I would draw your attention to the first bullet note on the front of the form. (The latest print has our Castle Meadow address on it). This says, 'Do not send this form to us until you believe that it will not be necessary to change the amount of the tax or duty paid.'

It follows from this that an applicant should be sure that we have the final values at their title and should believe that we have the final values at other titles. This may involve correspondence with those responsible for the property at other titles.

If we keep the application on file, we put it in a prominent place so we cannot overlook it. So you do not need to remind us about it. As soon as all matters are finalised and we have collected all the tax, we will deal with the application.

DEEDS OF VARIATION.

Remember, you don't have to send in the original. You can send a certified copy for us to keep, instead if you wish.

SEPTEMBER 1996. – VOLUME 1.3 CTO NEWSLETTER

RELAXED RULES FOR EXCEPTED ESTATES.

The Revenue issued a Press Release on 6 June 1996 explaining the changes to the rules. The new rules apply if you seek a grant of representation after 30 June 1996 and the death was after 5 April 1996. There are three main changes.

Many practitioners and personal applicants have found it frustrating that they could not take out a grant under the excepted estate rules the estate was relatively small but the deceased had made straightforward gifts. To address this the changes introduce a new term — "specified transfers". These are chargeable transfers made in the seven years before the death of cash or quoted shares or securities whose total value is not more than £50,000. If the deceased made such transfers the estate may be excepted subject to the overall limit.

The overall limit has gone up from £145,000 to £180,000. But to see if this limit is exceeded you must add the value of any "specified transfers" to the gross estate.

The value limit for foreign assets has gone up from £15,000 to £30,000.

We expect these relaxations to the rules to bring around 7,500 estates in to the "excepted" category in the first year.

We have revised our leaflet IHT 12 in the light of these changes and the new leaflet is enclosed with this issue. The Scottish version, IHT 12(S) will be available soon from our Edinburgh office.

... and a common question about accounts for excepted states

We often get letters from practitioners who have taken out an excepted estate grant on behalf of the personal representatives. They ask us why we have written direct to the personal representatives, instead of to the solicitor, for an account on Form IHT 204. The answer is that the regulations require us to do so. [The personal representatives then have the option of whether to instruct their solicitor to deal with the account or not.]

LIST OF IHT FORMS (ENGLAND & WALES)

Form name	Description	Latest
Cap 29	Clearance application-person who paid IHT but is not ultimately liable for it	01/95
Cap 30	Clearance application by liable persons	08/95
Cap 38	Claim for loss on sale of interest in land	01/95
Cap A5C	Form of account for obtaining a special grant	10/95
Cap D3	Corrective account reporting amendments to the estate	02/94
IHT 26	Statement of domicile	01/93
IHT 37	Schedule of details of freehold/leasehold properties	01/93
IHT 40	Schedule of details of holdings of stocks and shares	01/93

IHT 44	Account for completion by personal applicants	09/95
IHT 100	Account of settled property in which deceased had an interest in possession and/or for a lifetime transfer	03/95
IHT 101	Account of a chargeable event in respect of a discretionary trust	10/93*
IHT 200	Inland Revenue Account (IRA) detailing the estate	01/93
IHT 201	IRA detailing the estate but deceased domiciled outside the UK	01/93
IHT 202	IRA detailing the estate but submitted by solicitor when below threshold	01/93
IHT 204	Account requested in excepted estates sample	09/95
IHT 205	Short account for completion by personal applicants for excepted estates	09/95
Sect 5	Claim for loss on sale of shares relief	11/94

* *IHT 101 is undergoing revision (for new addresses only) at the moment*

DECEMBER 1996. – VOLUME 1.4 CTO NEWSLETTER

TRUSTS AND FREE ESTATE.

Often, an account for a trust fund can be completed very soon after a person dies. Naturally, if you are the trustees, or acting for them, you would like clearance quickly. But, as you know, in most cases, we cannot give clearance until the Free Estate has also been finalised.

Our experience shows that in about 50% of cases where we receive the trust account first, the account for the Free Estate usually arrives within the next two months. This leaves half of the cases where we encounter further delay in getting the information we need. It may surprise you to learn that in some of these cases, the Free Estate representatives were either not aware they needed to get a grant; incorrectly took out an "Excepted Estate" grant or had not intended to get one because, for example, the Free Estate consisted entirely of joint property.

If you are dealing with a Trust Fund, you can help us to speed up the process by providing us with the names and addresses of the Legal Personal Representatives (LPRs) of the Free Estate (and their agents). If you do this when you send the trust account, and the Free Estate account is not delivered within a reasonable time, we will be able to chase up the information we need quickly.

It would also assist if you contact the LPRs or their agents to let them know that there is settled property comprised in the estate: they should not then obtain Probate without delivering an Inland Revenue Account (IRA). If you can give us an approximate value for the rest of the estate, this will often enable us to prepare a provisional calculation of tax soon after receipt of your account for the settled property.

NATIONAL HERITAGE DATABASE.

Where can you see a set of four 'Bacchanalia' tapestries?

You can find the answer on the Register of Conditionally Exempt Works of Art. This has been known in the CTO as 'Valerie', but we are looking for a new name, so let us know if you have any suggestions (preferably more decent than the aforementioned tapestries).

Some of you are already aware that we have been preparing to make the register available on the Internet. This is now ready. If you would like to know how you can view it or how to obtain a copy of the register, please ask for leaflet IR 156, 'Our heritage-your right to see tax exempt works of art'. This will be available soon from one of our branches or from the Tax Enquiry Centre.

Those of you who have access to the Internet can view the information at the following web site address:

http://www.cto.eds.co.uk/

DEEDS OF VARIATION.

Some of you send copies of Deeds of Variation to the Secretary to the Board of Inland Revenue at Somerset House. Guess what happens to them! Yes, they get sent to the CTO in Nottingham. So, please save yourself time and copying costs. We only need one copy to be sent to us direct.

CALCULATIONS OF IHT (COMPASS).

Our calculations of tax have an amendments section in the column headed "Summary of Estate". This shows increases or decreases to the taxable value of the Free Estate or trust to which the calculation relates.

Unfortunately our computer generated calculations also show amendments to other aggregable property in this section. For instance, an increase in the returned value of a will trust does affect the aggregate chargeable transfer upon which an estate's share of tax is based. But it does not alter the value of the Free Estate. The inclusion of amendments to aggregable property might suggest it does.

We are sorry for any confusion this might cause and are looking at ways to correct this anomaly. We can, however, assure you that actual calculations of tax are not adversely affected.

COMPUTER-GENERATED IHT ACCOUNTS.

You may recall our article in issue number two of the newsletter about substitute IHT forms. Several firms have since taken up the challenge of producing their own computer-generated substitute forms.

Although it is initially time-consuming to set up and obtain approval for substitute forms, some firms have reported considerable savings in time and resources when it actually comes to filling in the forms.

We have produced a new leaflet providing guidance for people who want to implement computer-generated IHT forms in their offices. Please ask the Customer Service team for a copy.

Even more firms have chosen to buy one of the approved packages sold under licence from the Inland Revenue. We have a list of these software companies that identifies which of our forms they can provide on disk. You can also get this list from Customer Service.

MARCH 1997. – VOLUME 2.1 CTO NEWSLETTER

ENFORCEMENT AND UNDERTAKINGS.

There are some cases where a Land Charge has been imposed in order to protect the interests of the Revenue. The property is subsequently agreed to be sold in order to pay the inheritance tax out of the sale proceeds.

Too often, we receive a telephone call or fax on the day of completion asking us to cancel the charge. As we require a professional undertaking that the tax will be paid in order to remove the charge, unavoidably delays occur. We now give the following advice in our letters.

"Should the property be sold so the inheritance tax can be paid out of the sale proceeds, we will require a professional undertaking that the tax will be paid before we cancel the charge. This should be given as soon as possible after a sale has been agreed but no later than the exchange of contracts if there is a reasonable time gap before completion. This will avoid any urgency later on."

DEEDS OF VARIATION (EXCEPTED ESTATES).

Copy of the grant Many deeds of variation sent to the CTO are for estates where the grant was obtained under the excepted estates' regulations. If you do send us one of these deeds, please attach a copy of the grant to the deed if possible.

If we receive a copy of the grant, we can process your deed much quicker. This saves us time to deal with other matters and you will consequently receive a quicker response.

EXCEPTED ESTATES AT NEWCASTLE.

Estates, which are not excepted estates, granted probate at the Newcastle District Probate Registry, or one of its sub-registries (Carlisle, Middlesborough or York), are usually dealt with by our Edinburgh office.

But if the grant was an *excepted estate* grant and you subsequently send us a deed of variation, please send the deed to Nottingham and not Edinburgh. Again, this will save you time as our Edinburgh office pass them on to Nottingham for processing anyway.

You should address all deeds of variation on English and Welsh excepted estates to Enquiries Section at Ferrers House in Nottingham.

INTEREST ON UNPAID TAX AND ON OVERPAYMENTS.

Interest on unpaid IHT is charged at an annual rate and the Capital Taxes Office calculates a daily rate from this using a 365 day year. It has been drawn to our attention that our system of calculation is not completely in line with that adopted elsewhere in the Revenue.

We have therefore amended our computerised assessing system and the interest factor tables we use. This change takes effect on 6 April 1997. Any interest accruing on or after that date is calculated as if every year is a leap year. This will give a small advantage to the taxpayer in three out of every four years.

The repayment supplement paid by the Revenue on overpayments of tax and interest will continue to be calculated using a 365 day year. Again, this will give the taxpayer a small advantage where the period includes 29 February.

JULY 1997. – VOLUME 2.2 CTO NEWSLETTER

ELECTRONIC TRANSFER OF IHT.

In the last issue of the newsletter we covered new procedures for payments of IHT and one of those procedures was payment by electronic transfer. This is sometimes used as a secure method of payment when large amounts are being paid.

If paying by BACS or CHAPS, you should use the Bank of England sort code 10-00-00. If you use the Bank Giro Credit method of payment the sort code is 10-53-92. In all cases the account number is 234 30 303.

However, there is one significant problem with electronic payment. You might imagine that using this method would speed up your application for probate, whereas the opposite is true. It takes a minimum of three working days for the paperwork to reach CTO from the Bank of England and just lately there have been some delays of more than three days. If speed is essential, please send us a cheque.

SOCIETY OF TRUST AND ESTATE PRACTITIONERS.

On the evening of 8 April 1997, the East Midlands Branch of the Society Of Trust & Estate Practitioners (S.T.E.P.) paid another visit to the CTO at Castle Meadow.

The visit was a success and included a lively question and answer session with the managers of the various inheritance tax divisions and our Customer Service and Compliance managers.

Many of the subjects covered will be of interest to Practitioners generally. We have picked out some of those questions and answers and listed them below for your information. We have concentrated on the subjects mentioned that were of a procedural rather than technical nature.

Q. Why can one never get a statement from the CTO of deposits lodged on account of tax?

A. This should never have really been a problem, as we were always willing to track the record of deposits for people, if they asked us to. The main difficulty was that following the application of sums from a deposit the balance was given a new deposit number. This will not happen under the new accounting system. We now issue a receipt for any money sent to us, therefore this perceived problem should no longer arise.

Q. To what extent is there information sharing between the CTO and other branches of the Inland Revenue? Do you routinely look at deceased's tax returns? Do other departments automatically look at the IR Account?

A. We do send extracts of estates to Inspector of Taxes to allow them to check their records and identify anything that should be in the estate. We also send extracts to FICO Scotland who deal with the taxation of any income arising during the period of administration in large estates.

Individual caseworkers do not routinely examine income tax returns, but rather use their discretion to call for tax files where they feel it necessary.

We never disclose information to departments outside the Inland Revenue.

Q. We recently declared an income tax repayment (ITR) in a corrective account. The supplementary IHT assessment was interest free and "ITR covers" was entered in the interest box. What is the logic behind this?

A. It has been part of our instructions for many years, that if the money is in the hands of the Revenue, we should not charge interest on it. Historically, income tax repayments rarely carried interest. Nowadays, repayment supplement is more likely to be due, particularly with the introduction of Self Assessment. We are therefore planning to review our instructions in this area.

Q. Life interest trusts — bank trust companies appear to charge 2% of the value of the fund as an allowance expense when determining the value at death of the life tenant. Is this a concession?

A. It is not a concession. We take the view that a deduction is justified for charges properly paid out of capital, normally in pursuit of a charging power in the trust document, where they were paid under a contractual obligation which normally existed from the time the trust was set up. Charges out of capital are only deductible if they have already fallen due before the material date. Charges properly paid out of income are not deductible.

CHARITY EXEMPTION.

To claim or not to claim? Charity (s 23 IHTA 1984) and Gifts for National Purpose (s 25) exemptions are two of the most frequently occurring inheritance tax exemptions. It is estimated that bequests through wills during 1996 amount to £1.6 billion.

The failure to claim s 23 and s 25 exemptions is a common reason for the repayment of tax by the Capital Taxes Office.

There are two ways in which you can help us to apply the correct exemptions to your cases. First, when drafting wills, please state the full name and address of the charitable body and include its UK Charity Registration Number (if it has one). Second, when you are filling in the account, please check the Will for possible exemptions and take them into consideration when calculating the tax due on delivery.

BELFAST AND EDINBURGH.

In the last issue we gave details of the new arrangements for payment of IHT in England and Wales.

Whilst we have always shown the addresses and telephone numbers for CTO Belfast and CTO Edinburgh on page 4 of this newsletter, we thought that a little more information might be useful.

We now show the telephone extensions for general enquiries in Edinburgh. In Belfast, general enquiries are currently dealt with on a rotational basis; you should simply dial the Belfast Office number and ask to speak to general enquiries.

For any payment of tax to these offices, you should address your correspondence to the Cashier and use the usual general address for the office.

You should make any electronic payments to the following accounts:

Bank of Ireland (for CTO Belfast
Sort code 90-21-27
Account number 99942208

Bank of Scotland (for CTO Edinburgh)
Sort code 83-06-08
Account number 00132961

You should always state the name and date of death of the person who has died to help us match up the payment.

DECEMBER 1997. – VOLUME 2.3 CTO NEWSLETTER

ALL EMPLOYEE TRUST AND PENSION SCHEMES.

Following a recent work reorganisation, all work on employee trusts (section 86 IHTA) and pension schemes (personal and occupational) has been transferred to our Edinburgh office.

Any enquiries and all future correspondence should be addressed in the first instance to Mrs Lesley Hoyle at the address shown on the back. Her extension is 102.

MEETING WITH TACT.

Three members of the Private Trust Committee of the Association of Corporate Trustees (TACT) paid a visit to Castle Meadow on 17 September 1997.

We arranged a meeting between them and three of our Divisional Managers in the IHT Group. This was a very amicable occasion and both sides felt that we gained a lot from our discussion.

Some of the questions and answers may be of general interest to our readers, so we have made a summary of these below.

Q. CTO has asked in the past for better referencing, particularly where a life tenant of a trust dies. Has this been successful?

A. It is less of a problem than it was. Although some agents are still not specific enough where several settlements exist with similar names. It does help us give a better service if correspondence shows our full reference and full names of the deceased or name of settlement.

More recently it has been our inundation with instruments of variation (IOV) on excepted estates that has caused us a lot of work for no discernible gain. We would like agents to clearly state that the IOV refers to an excepted estate and that no CTO reference exists.

Q. There was a well publicised case in the industry where personal liability for an IHT penalty was passed on to the clerk responsible for the negligence. Is this true?

A. Our policy is very clear on this. We only impose s 247 IHTA penalties against the legal personal representatives (LPR) and not against individuals within firms (unless of course the individual is acting as LPR in their own right). It is another issue entirely if firms chose to accept liability for their errors.

Q. Does CTO agree that discovered assets are best mentioned only at such time as a corrective account can be prepared rather than being declared to CTO straight away?

A. Yes, but only if the asset is relatively small in value. Generally, with items worth over £10,000 it is best to inform us as soon as possible.

Q. Apart from the mention in passing given to the gifts from normal expenditure out of income in some IHT leaflets, is there any other general guidance on how these are treated?

A. There is no rule of thumb. We basically judge each case on its merits. We do look very closely at the standard of living of the transferor. The test of 'normality' requires a pattern of giving to be established. That is why it is not always possible to say that, at the time it is made, a particular gift is or is not exempt as 'normal'.

Q. Is there any mileage in doing away with the requirement to pay IHT up front in order to get the grant.

A. From our point of view (and the Treasury's), the current system is desirable. The exchequer obtains a very large amount of money with relatively low collection costs and low risk of non-compliance. No change is contemplated.

Q. When different parts of the same corporate entity act as executor and as trustee to a settled fund, should not CTO treat them as separate entities and not assume that submission of a Cap 30 at one title indicates matters at the other title are settled?

A. We take the opposite view here. Many liable persons, whether or not professionally represented, do not apply for clearance. So, from our point of view, the absence of an application for clearance does not necessarily imply that amendments may be expected. In this light, we wonder whether the different sections of a corporate entity should check with each other before applying for clearance. In any case, it would be helpful to us if both forms are submitted together.

Q. Is there any possibility in relaxing the need to deliver accounts with full and accurate valuations where it is known that the spouse or charity exemption take the estate below the threshold?

A. As this would not save any work for CTO and would probably involve more work agreeing charity exemptions at the pre-grant stage, and possible delays getting the grant. We assume that the agents will need to provide a breakdown of individual assets anyway for their own purposes, so transferring data to the Account should not be too much extra work.

TAPER RELIEF.

One issue that can cause a degree of confusion for some agents and their clients is taper relief. The relief only applies to the tax payable on a gift in its own right. If the gift does not exceed the inheritance tax threshold, then no taper relief can be applied.

Leaflet IHT2 should help explain the rules to clients, while IHT 15 covers the subject in more detail.

Please write to us with any specific problems you may have. We will do our best to help.

MUTUAL SOCIETIES: TAKE-OVERS & MERGERS.

The qualifying members of a number of mutual societies have recently been receiving shares or cash on completion of a merger, take-over or conversion of the society business.

If a person died on or after the completion or vesting date, the shares or cash will form part of their estate. Additionally, we take the view that if a person died after the issue of a transfer document or prospectus but before the vesting date, the anticipated rights of the investor or borrower should be reflected in the open market value of that person's share in the society at the date of death.

The value of the qualifying member's share is determined by what is due or received at the anticipated market price. This is generally disclosed in the transfer document or prospectus. The value will attract an appropriate discount to reflect the uncertainty or delay in receiving the distributions due.

The Law Society has asked if they can publish guidance from the CTO. We have written to them with a copy of a table provided to our staff as an informal guide to the valuation of a qualifying member's share in a society when that person died before the vesting date.

You can obtain a copy of this table by writing to IHT HQ at Ferrers House, Nottingham.

MAY 1998. – VOLUME 2.4 CTO NEWSLETTER

BUDGET CHANGES.

This year's Finance Bill contains provisions to extend public access to tax exempt works of art, landed property, and property endowed by approved maintenance funds. We have already sent brief particulars of the proposals that were available on Budget Day to practitioners and owners of the works of art and other property affected. We sent some 700 letters on Budget Day itself and a further 200 the following day. As these letters explained, we shall need to review the cases where exemption has been allowed and maintenance funds approved, and we shall set about this task as soon as it becomes practicable to do so.

Please address any enquires about this to Mick Downs, Heritage Section or telephone Rona McKenzie on 0115 974 2490.

PROGRESSING CASES.

We are able to handle the vast majority of our cases quickly and efficiently due to regular contact with the professional firms representing the taxpayer-and this includes cases, which due to their magnitude or complexity take a number of years to settle. In a small number of cases, there are genuine reasons why the case may not progress quickly as either the taxpayer or we may like. There remains, however, a hard core of cases that do not move on as quickly as we would like and where there is no clear reason for the delay.

These cases take a disproportionate amount of our time to settle and take resources away from handling other cases. Long delay in respect of a few cases has an adverse impact across all other cases and may lead to frustration on the taxpayer's part when we are unable to give an apparently simple case the time to settle it quickly.

As a result, we have strengthened our procedures for reviewing *all* cases. We will be encouraging our staff to make more use of the telephone and if there are good reasons why a case is going to take some time to settle, please let us know.

If you are in regular contact with us, you are unlikely to notice any difference. But in cases where there is no good reason for the delay, we will be aiming to use our statutory powers to enforce payment or obtain information rather more quickly than we have done so in the past.

ESTIMATING VALUES.

Where the existence of an asset is known about at the time the Inland Revenue account is sent in, Section 216 IHTA 1984 makes it plain that the fullest enquiries that are reasonably practicable in the circumstances must be made to ascertain the exact value of an asset. However, if an exact value cannot be ascertained, a statement to that effect must be made and a provisional estimate of the value provided.

It is not sufficient to omit to mention an asset altogether in the absence of an exact value, on the basis that a corrective account will be submitted later. Our view is that, in these circumstances, the Inland Revenue account is *prima facie* incorrect and has been negligently delivered.

PENALTIES.

It appears, from feedback, that the published response to the question, "Are CTO taking a tough line on penalties?" (CTO Newsletter, September 1996) is open to misinterpretation. This note seeks to clarify the position.

Where there has been negligence in the incorrect completion of an Inland Revenue account, or in the provision of any other information or document, we would normally seek a penalty from the liable person(s). It is rare for a penalty to be sought from a practitioner *acting solely in the capacity of agent*. This is because the responsibility for the provision of the account, information or document remains with the liable person(s). However, in appropriate cases, penalties would be sought from practitioners under Section 247 (3) or (4) IHTA 1984.

If negligence is involved, a *practitioner acting as a legal personal representative*, renders herself/himself liable to a penalty in the same way as any other legal personal representative. The degree of negligence, from minor to extreme, is taken into account in arriving at the level of any penalty negotiated.

DEEDS OF VARIATION – RECENT GRANTS.

If you send a deed of variation to our Nottingham Enquiries Section where the grant was a recent one (say, within 2 months), please attach a photocopy of the grant itself.

This will help us to examine the deed more quickly as there is a delay of several weeks before we receive the details of the grants from elsewhere.

OPEN DAY, QUESTIONS AND ANSWERS

In the last issue of the newsletter we told you about our open day held in Nottingham on 30 October 1997. Here is a summary of some of the questions and answers from the open forum part of the day. If you would like further clarification of any point, please write to us and we will tell you what you need to know.

61 IHT Newsletter and Tax Bulletin extracts

Q. How does CTO choose which cases to take to litigation?

A. There is no set pattern. The Litigation Team receives cases as early as possible before irritation sets in on both sides. They will take a case to the Courts if it seems to have reached a state of readiness. The Lady Ingram case simply seemed nearer to readiness than 30–40 other similar cases.

Q. How does CTO decide which cases will go straight to the High Court?

A. We do not. If the taxpayer suggests it, we will normally agree if the issues are largely confined to matters of law. The High Court's an expensive way [of] finding facts.

Q. Does CTO have any comment on decisions made at the High Court by non-specialists ("gifted amateurs")?

A. Judges in the Chancery Division generally have a strong and highly professional background in taxation law. The Re Benham case was not, we understand, heard by such a judge but by one experienced in the Family Division.

Q. Are SVD prepared to value a shareholding that is not taxable for IHT purposes, but yet would still be useful to us for CGT and other purposes?

A. No. We are not resourced to investigate shareholdings if there is no tax payable. When a Probate Valuation is submitted, but we do not specifically agree it, the value has not been ascertained for CGT purposes.

Q. On what basis are CTO questioning deferred lease schemes?

A. We take the view that they are either gifts with reservation or open to challenge under s 163 as a contract made for no consideration which is disregarded at the next chargeable event, usually the death of the lessor.

Q. If there is an unusually long, and unavoidable, delay in agreeing values of property, is there any leeway in the charging of interest without putting money on deposit?

A. There is no scope for relaxing the period after which interest becomes chargeable. However, if the delays are substantial according to the Revenue Code of Practice, we will remit interest for the period of our delay.

Q. What level of "reasonable enquiries" do CTO expect agents to make into the history of lifetime transfers made by the deceased? Do you work to a checklist?

A. There is no checklist. We take the view that the solicitors and executors know best about the history of giving, particularly when they are close family members. We do appreciate that in certain cases the family will not be able to recall this information and we can only ask agents to make every effort in these cases. The level of enquiry must depend on the facts and knowledge of the deceased's financial affairs in his lifetime.

Q. What action would CTO take where the agents made reasonable enquiries and gifts subsequently came to light after clearance was given?

A. This has to depend on the facts. We will be as much concerned with what the legal personal representatives know or might have discovered as with what enquiries the agents made. Precisely how the gifts came to light and their nature will also be relevant. The extremes are on the one hand that we take no action and on the other hand that we ignore the certificate and pursue for additional tax and perhaps penalties.

Q. Do CTO have any advice on any action that can be taken by the executor where the executor has become liable for the IHT that should have been paid by the donee?

A. There is really nothing we can do directly. The problem lies with the executor to take legal action against the donee of the gift.

Q. Trusts of Land and Appointment of Trustees Act 1996 resulted in a change to s 237 (3) following the abolition of the doctrine of conversion. It is now possible to place a charge on joint property, what is the CTO's position on this?

A. We try to ensure that land charges are imposed responsibly so as not to penalise the other joint owner of the undivided share of land. If this change causes problems in practice the CTO would be interested to hear about them.

OCTOBER 1998 – VOLUME 3.1 CTO NEWSLETTER

ELECTRONIC TRANSFER OF IHT.

As mentioned previously in Volume 2.2 the payment of IHT by electronic transfer is slower than paying by cheque. It was considered necessary to remind people of the problem in paying by this method, because several of our customers have been experiencing delays recently when paying by electronic transfer. Please note that paying by cheque is still the quickest way of paying IHT, as when paying by electronic transfer it takes at least three working days for the paperwork to reach us from the Bank of England.

However, if you still wish to pay by this method if using BACS or CHAPs you should use the Bank of England sort code 10-00-00. If you use the Bank Giro Credit method of payment the sort code is 10-53-92. The account number to be used in all cases is 234 30 303.

STATIONERY REQUESTS.

Please note that, if after speaking to our Enquiries section, you need forms from our stationery department, but experience difficulty getting through, please try later, calling stationery direct on 0115 974 3040. Alternatively if you are not averse to speaking to a machine you can ring the Stationery's second line which is 0115 974 2982 where an answer machine is permanently switched on. Your request will be dealt with within the same time.

INVENTORIES.

We remind you that, unless you are dealing with a case where domicile is claimed, you do not need to send the inventory to us to calculate the tax due before the issue of Probate or Confirmation. You can complete the calculations yourself and send the Account/ Inventory direct to us with your payment. If no tax is payable you can lodge the Inventory direct with the Sheriff Clerk. You do not need to have the Inventory stamped by the CTO to show that no tax is payable.

Where you are claiming foreign domicile, you must send the papers to us to substantiate your claim before Probate or Confirmation is granted in any case where the estate in the UK exceeds £5,000.

If you are having difficulty with a calculation or require information about how to make payment we are, of course, willing to help you.

EXCEPTED ESTATES.

As you are probably aware from the press release of 10 June 1998 there have been changes in the thresholds for excepted estates. They are as follows:

For deaths after 5 April 1998

The limit for the gross estate is £200,000

The limit for lifetime transfers is £75,000

The limit for the gross value of foreign property is now £50,000

These changes will simplify the administration of some 5,000 smaller estates for Inheritance tax purposes. They were applied from 1 July 1998, to the estate of any person who died on or after 6 April 1998.

TELEPHONES.

The Edinburgh office installed a new direct dial telephone system on 6 March 1998. Communications issued from the office after that date show the direct number for the examiner dealing with the case or enquiry. The system also has a voice mail facility which will enable you to leave a message if the examiner is not available when you telephone. The numbers are on page 4. Customers of our Nottingham office certainly prefer direct dial, so we hope that you will be pleased about this change in Edinburgh.

KEY BUSINESS RESULTS.

We set out below our targets and results for 1997/1998, with the results from the previous year for comparison. These are published in our Annual Report, which will be in the House of Commons library from October. Or you can get a copy from us by contacting Carol Redmond.

We measure our performance by the length of time we take to settle cases, and how quickly we deal with correspondence. We also measure the quality of our work and the volumes of cases we handle.

Case settlement times	Result 1996/97	Target 1997/98	Result 1997/98
Inheritance Tax			
Death cases settled within 15 months	78%	73%	76%
Non taxpaying* death cases settled within 6 months	99%	95%	95%
Share Valuations			
Valuations settled within 12 months	71%	60%	73%
Average time taken to settle valuations	12 months	14 months	12 months

* 'Non-taxpaying' cases are those where the inheritance tax account showed no liability to tax but we need to review them to check, for example, that reliefs were properly due.

Dealing with correspondence	Result 96/97	Target 97/98	Result 97/98
Incoming correspondence dealt with within;			
28 days	83%	83%	81%
56 days	95%	95%	95%
Quality			
Death cases dealt with to a satisfactory or higher standard	96%	98%	97%
Share valuations dealt with to a satisfactory or higher standard	98%	98%	97%
Caseloads and outputs	Result 96/97	Forecast 97/98	Result 97/98

Inheritance Tax

Death cases received	18,705	15,800	18,587
Death cases settled	20,710	17,240	20,482
Death cases completed per head of staff	52	44	53

Share Valuations

Valuations received	24,592	25,300	20.329
Valuations settled	27,252	26,300	23,435
Valuations settled per head of staff	173	169	159

We forecast a reduction in new inheritance tax cases in 1997/98, in line with indexation of the threshold. But, prices of land, stocks and shares went up more than expected. So, in the event, we received and settled significantly more than we forecast. Because inheritance tax work accounts for most of our volume we missed our target of dealing with 83% of incoming post within 28 days.

On the other hand, we received far fewer new share valuations (20,329) than forecast. This is partly due to a timing difference resulting from the introduction of Self Assessment.

We settled 23,435 share valuations, which is also substantially below last year's total. However, we again settled considerably more valuations than we received, so we continue to eat into our work in progress.

We equalled or exceeded all our targets for how quickly we settle cases.

Yield and valuation adjustments The total yield from inheritance tax receipts was £1,684.3 million including £83.7 million arising as a direct result of our compliance action. Even though we settled fewer valuations than last year, our negotiations led to changes in values put forward by taxpayers of £3.5 billion.

SPECIAL EDITION – JUNE 1999 CTO NEWSLETTER

NEW LEAFLETS IR120 AND SVD1.

This Special Edition of our Newsletter launches the new versions of our leaflets IR120 – You and the Inland Revenue, Capital Taxes Office and SVD1 Shares Valuation Division: An Introduction. We hope you will find the leaflets useful.

One copy of each leaflet is enclosed with this newsletter. If you require further copies, you can get them by either faxing our Stationery section on 0115 974 3030 or phoning the Answer Machine on 0115 974 2982.

APOLOGIES FOR PREVIOUS ERROR.

As a lot of you are probably aware, the incorrect number was given as the fax number to order IHT30.

The number given 01115 974 2430 was in fact a phone number. The correct fax number is 0115 974 3030. We are sorry for any frustration this may have caused.

NOVEMBER 1999. – VOLUME 3.3 CTO NEWSLETTER

P26A AND COPY WILLS

The change in procedures in England & Wales involving the P26A is taking a little while to settle down so we hope the following reminders will be of use.

Deceased domiciled in the UK Deaths on or after 18 March 1986

- Taxable estates – send the Inland Revenue Account (IR A/c) and supporting papers, a copy of the Will, P26A and your payment to us altogether in one envelope. Provided all is in order, we will endorse form P26A and return it so you can apply for the grant. If you want us to send it back by DX, please put your DX address in the return address box.

- Non-tax estates — there is no need for us to endorse P26A in non-tax estates and you can send the P26A straight to the probate registry. Having worked out that there is no tax to pay, put "NIL" in box PS8 and sign the form. Send the IR A/c, supporting papers and a copy of the Will to us **at the same time** as you send form P26A with the other papers to the probate registry.

- Box PS3 is for the net value of settled property, but **only** if the deceased had and had exercised a general power of appointment over the settled property.

- One of the changes brought about by the P26A procedure is the need for a copy of the Will to be provided with the account. We receive many accounts without a copy of the Will. This prevents us from completing our initial processes so the benefit of the P26A procedure is lost. Please remember to provide a copy of the Will when you send the account to us.

- P26A does not apply to such deaths. Please use the correct form of account, CAP200 or the relevant Estate Duty form, both are available from our stationery section. If there is tax to pay, send the account and payment to us first — we will receipt and return the account. You can then send the account to the probate registry when you apply for the grant.

- P26A does not apply to this form. When you have completed the form, send it direct to the probate registry – there is no need for us to certify the account.

All estates

You must send the IR A/c and supporting papers, a copy of the Will and form P26A to us in all such estates, whether taxpaying or not, before you apply for the grant. At present, we assess the estate and, if appropriate, send you a calculation showing the tax that is due. Once the tax is paid, we endorse and return form P26A to you. We can speed up this process a little if you treat these estates in the same way as the estate of someone domiciled in the UK, "self-assess" the account and pay the tax. We will still need to consider the deceased's domicile and it will accordingly take more than the normal 2 or 3 working days to return form P26A to you. But this will enable us to endorse and return the P26A more quickly than under the present procedure.

PAYMENT OF TAX PRE-GRANT

The role of our pre-grant section is primarily to help unrepresented taxpayers with the calculation of the tax that must be paid before the grant. Pre-grant will also help practitioners out if the calculations are complex. But other than that, practitioners are required to work out how much tax must be paid before the grant and send a cheque when first delivering the account. And as mentioned above, we are extending this to include estates of those domiciled abroad.

If you do send a payment with the account, and all is in order, we should be able to get the P26A back to you within 2 or 3 working days. If you send the case in for us to assess, we will endeavour to reply within our published time limits, but it is unlikely to be as quick. If you include your reference somewhere on the form (the equivalent form with the new IHT 200 includes space for this) it will help you in tracing the papers when the form is returned.

NON-TAX ESTATES

As explained above we do not need to see the P26A in non-tax estates. Also we do not routinely acknowledge receipt of IR A/cs in estates where there is no tax to pay. We will write if we need to raise any matters with you. We also have a procedure to make sure that we have an IR A/c for every full grant that is issued. If we are unable to trace the IR A/c (this happens in a fraction over 1% of estates) we may write seeking your help in finding the IR A/c.

Other than in these circumstances we will not contact you where there is no tax to pay. If you wish to apply for clearance, you should do so in the normal way.

IHT 200

You may be aware that form IHT 200 is being redesigned. We have been piloting the account with a small number of solicitors and executor banks. We have also spoken to meetings of the Law Society's Probate Section, STEP, the Law Society of Scotland and at CLT conferences. The feedback we have received from these sources has been invaluable and we are close to settling on the final version of the account. We expect to launch the new IHT 200 in the first half of February next year. We will be sending an initial supply of all the forms and some copies of a practitioners guide to those who have applied for at least one full grant (i.e. not an excepted estate) during the last three to four months of 1999.

INSTRUMENTS OF VARIATION (IOVS)

We receive a large number of IOVs, many in estates where there is either no tax to pay or where the estate was an excepted estate. It takes a great deal of time to deal with these documents. The provisions of section 142 operate, in effect, as a relief against lifetime transfers, so it follows that if the transfer anticipated by the beneficiary is otherwise exempt *and* there is no inheritance tax to pay on the deceased's estate, then an IOV is not necessary. The obvious situation is where a beneficiary wants to pass on some of their inheritance to a charity. If there is no inheritance tax to pay on the estate, there is no advantage in delivering an election under S142 in connection with a gift to charity. If people only deliver an election where necessary, it would reduce the number that we receive and will help us to improve the service that we provide.

VALUATION OFFICE

We know that you are concerned with the time it can take in some cases before we give instructions to the Valuation Office and/or before the District Valuer makes a report. This is important as we always consult the Valuation Office when tax is, or might become, payable and the value of a freehold, or leasehold, property is required for IHT purposes.

Clearly, there will be some delay with two Offices involved but we are conscious of the importance of this aspect of our work and, together with the Valuation Office, we are doing all that we can to speed our processes and minimise the delay. We are currently engaged in a joint review of our respective internal procedures, with the aim of improving these, and reducing the collective time taken to complete the valuation process. This will include exploration of the opportunities for using current, and prospective, developments in the field of electronic communication to best advantage.

You should however know that in an increasing number of cases the District Valuer will consider the value returned and be able to accept it **without inspecting the property or making contact with you**. You may believe there is a delay when, in fact, the value offered has been considered.

We do not always keep you informed and we are looking at ways of improving on this. However, the fact that you have not been contacted about the value of a property need not hinder the administration. In cases where there is no tax to pay initially, you are entitled to assume that we have accepted the value unless, or until, we tell you otherwise. In taxpaying cases, we will contact you once the District Valuer has considered the value offered and reported back to us.

Either way, if you believe that the final figures in the estate have all been established, you can apply for a statutory clearance certificate. You can then give details of any adjustments (including a revised value for the property, on sale or otherwise, if you consider this appropriate). We may, by then, be in a position to deal with the clearance application (if we have heard from the District Valuer, where appropriate). Otherwise, we will let you know the current position.

EXCEPTED ESTATES — FIGURE GIVEN FOR THE NET VALUE OF THE ESTATE

We monitor estates where a grant of representation is taken out under the excepted estate regulations. We try to target our monitoring of estates on those where there may be issues that are worthy of further investigation. We do this by having regard to the value given for the net value of the estate. By doing so, and apart from a random sample of all excepted estates, we have been able to reduce the impact that our monitoring has on the lower value estates.

Following the introduction by the Probate Service of a flat rate fee for a grant of representation, practitioners need only record that the estate qualifies as an excepted estate. Unfortunately, that hampers our ability to target the monitoring of estates as we will not be able to identify the lower value estates. Consequently, it is likely that we will be asking the personal representatives of such estates to provide details of the assets etc. that make up the estate more often than we do now.

In a similar way, the Recovery from Estates section of the Benefits Agency examines the estates of all former Income support recipients to confirm that benefits have been correctly paid. Using the same monetary limit for both gross and net values will mean that they cannot identify estates where enquiries may not be needed. So they too will be writing to representatives unnecessarily.

Both we and the Benefits Agency can minimise this unnecessary correspondence if practitioners continue to indicate the net value (eg by using the bands that previously applied, particularly £100,000, £125,000 and £180,000). Although this may involve a little more work at the outset in arriving at a broad net value, it will save the personal representatives time and money later on and will help us to direct our resources in the most cost-efficient way.

INFORMATION NOTICES

We have been making a number of changes in the way we manage our casework to try to ensure that we only raise enquiries where we need to and to settle cases as quickly as possible when we do. But sometimes we find it difficult to progress cases because of delay by personal representatives in providing information.

When making enquiries into IHT accounts, we always seek any information we need informally in the first instance. We will of course continue to do so. However, the new powers introduced in the 1999 Finance Act (now s219A IHTA) give us the authority to issue a notice in writing requiring any person who has delivered or is liable to deliver an account to

• produce documents in their possession or power and

• furnish accounts or particulars

which are reasonably required to enquire into an account, determine whether, and the extent to which, it is incorrect and to make formal determinations.

Apart from continuing to seek information informally, we will also, when we do not receive replies, try and help personal representatives and agents to comply with our requests. We will telephone to find out the reasons for the delay and to agree a reasonable timetable for submission of the information we require. There may be a good reason why the information cannot be obtained right away or you may feel that our request is unreasonable. If so, tell us and if we still feel we need it we will explain why. However, when a person has not co-operated with our informal requests, or fails to produce information within a reasonable timescale, we will usually have no alternative but to issue a formal notice. There is a right of appeal against the notice to the Special Commissioners.

You may be aware from their recently published report that the House of Commons Public Accounts Committee have expressed concerns over delays in IHT casework. They naturally expect us to progress cases quickly and to use our new powers effectively to overcome external delays.

With the introduction of the new IHT 200, we are presently drafting a new Code of Practice for enquiries into the IHT account. This will set out the rights of personal representatives and how we will conduct enquiries. We will be consulting with professional advisors before this is published.

PENALTIES FOR NON-COMPLIANCE — FA 1999

Section 108 of Finance Act 1999 made changes to the penalty provisions in IHTA, including new penalties for failure to deliver accounts within the statutory time limits.

As you will know we have in the past sought penalties where appropriate. We will continue to do so where omissions from or understatements in accounts are discovered or disclosed, and we consider these understatements have arisen as a result of negligence (or fraud). We will also be seeking penalties, where appropriate, when accounts are sent in late.

We are revising our leaflet IHT 14 — The Personal Representatives' Responsibilities and this will set out what we expect from personal representatives when completing an account. But in broad terms we will consider a penalty for negligence where we feel the personal representative has not made sufficient enquiries or exercised sufficient care. We are also revising the leaflet IHT 13 which sets out why and how we seek penalties, including the policy for mitigation of the maximum penalties for disclosure, co-operation and gravity which mirrors that used for taxpayers generally. A copy of the proposed revised leaflet IHT 13 is attached and we would appreciate your comments on the draft. We will bear any such comments in mind when finalising the leaflet. We will also respond to the comments in a future edition of CTO Newsletter but we will not generally be able to respond to individual comments.

REMINDER

You can pay IHT out of a deceased's National Savings or holdings of certain Government securities. This helps to reduce the amount the personal representatives need to borrow to pay IHT before they get the grant or confirmation of the estate. For more details please see our leaflet IHT 11 or, if the estate is in Scotland, IHT 11(S).

AUGUST 2000. – CTO NEWSLETTER

OPEN DAYS

In last month's *Newsletter* we told you we are hoping to hold Open Days at our Nottingham and Edinburgh offices. Thank you to everybody who has replied. We have now finalised dates for these.

We have decided to run two events in Nottingham, on Wednesday 29 and Thursday 30 November, and two in Edinburgh, on Wednesday 24 and Thursday 25 January 2001.

We will be including items on, amongst other things, the new IHT 200, penalties and our relationship with the Valuation Office. We will also be including a session on technical issues, and plenty of time for questions from the floor. If there is anything you would particularly like to see on the timetable, please let us in the Customer Service Team know.

Also, if you would like to ask any questions in advance, please drop us a line and we will ensure they are answered on the day.

It is not too late to register your interest in attending. Let the Customer Service Team know if you would like to come along to any of the events. They will be issuing formal invitations in September to those who reply.

PENALTIES FOR NON-COMPLIANCE

Leaflet IHT 13. How and why we seek penalties We issued a draft of our proposed version of this leaflet with the November 1999 Newsletter. Thanks to those of you who commented on this.

Some of you thought the leaflet did not make it clear that we apply a percentage reduction to the fraud or negligence additions (£3,000 or £1,500) as well as to the additional tax maximum. We have rewritten the section concerned.

Following your suggestions we have also enclosed:

* examples of what we would and would not agree as reasonable excuse for late delivery of an account (Section 245 IHTA 1984)

* what we regard as unreasonable delay in notifying us of errors in accounts, information or documents (Section 248 IHTA 1984)

* what we regard as materially incorrect (Section 248 IHTA 1984)

We have altered the wording so that the leaflet is mainly addressed directly to people responsible for delivering an inheritance tax account.

A copy of the revised IHT 13 is enclosed with this Newsletter. We issue copies when we make penalty enquiries. One important reason for this is to make people aware that substantial reductions from the maximum penalty are available for disclosure and co-operation with our enquiries. You can also download copies from our website http://www.inlandrevenue.gov.uk/cto

Penalty enquiries We have not changed our policy on penalties, but you have noticed an increase in the number of enquiries (or perhaps received an enquiry for the first time) saying that we are considering whether a penalty may be due. We feel it is more open to explain this as soon as we start making our enquiries. Before, we used to refer to penalties only when replies to our initial enquiries led further.

We consider whether a penalty may be due whenever an asset is omitted from, or undervalued in, an inheritance tax account.

Sometimes it is plain from information we already have whether or not a penalty will arise. However, there are times when we need to make further enquiries of those responsible for delivering the account or their agents to enable us to decide.

It does not necessarily follow that we will seek a penalty in every case where we make an enquiry and issue an IHT 13 leaflet.

Penalty examples The following examples show two penalty situations and the likely penalty we would seek. You will probably find it helpful to refer to pages 6, 7 and 8 of the IHT 13 leaflet as you read through the examples.

Example 1

We discover that, within 2 years of death the deceased (a widow) made a gift of a house to her son. There was no mention of any gifts on the inheritance tax account delivered on 1 January 2000. The open market value of the house at the date of the gift was £100,000. The aggregation of this gift with the value of the estate declared results in an additional £40,000 tax. It is established that the personal representatives (unrelated to the deceased) had been negligent in delivering an incorrect account, because they had not checked whether any gifts had been made.

The maximum possible penalty is £1,500 + £40,000 = £41,500.

Consideration of reduction of the maximum penalty

Disclosure

The personal representatives were challenged about the non-inclusion of lifetime gifts. They initially maintained there had been no gifts, but after being presented with evidence of the gift of the house, they admitted that they had made no enquiries of the deceased's family nor of anyone else to find out whether there had been any gifts within the 7 years before death. **10% reduction allowed.**

Co-operation

The personal representatives were slow to reply to letters and initially refused to approach the deceased's family when asked to check with them whether there had been gifts. **25% reduction allowed.**

Gravity

It was accepted that there had been no fraudulent intent. However, the personal representatives had made no enquiries to find out whether there had been gifts and the additional tax was large. **20% reduction allowed.**

The total reductions amounted to 55% and so the penalty sought would be £41,500 × 45% = £18,675, rounded to the nearest £50, say, £18,650.

Example 2

A house is included in the inheritance tax account delivered on 5 October 1999 at a value of £124,000 at death. We refer the case to the District Valuer for advice, who challenges the value returned. The open market value of the property at death is later agreed to have been £200,000. An additional tax liability of £30,400 arises.

We asked how a figure of £124,000 was arrived at. It turns out to be the figure for which the property was insured. The deceased had estimated the value of the property when taking out insurance approximately 5 years before and his figure had been merely uprated by the insurance company each year since in line with a published index of rebuilding costs. The personal representatives had included the figure without checking whether the figure bore any relationship to the actual open market value at death. As the personal representatives had not taken proper care to ensure that the correct value for inheritance tax was included, they had negligently delivered an incorrect account.

The maximum possible penalty is £1,500 + £30,400 = £31,900.

Consideration of reduction of the maximum penalty

Disclosure

Amounts to full disclosure on challenge. **20% reduction allowed.**

Co-operation

Excellent throughout. All enquiries answered quickly, frankly and completely. **40% reduction allowed.**

Gravity

There was no evidence of fraud. The value had not simply been plucked out of the air, but there was no attempt to check whether the figure was a proper figure for inheritance tax purposes. The additional tax was large. **25% reduction allowed.**

The total reductions amount to 85% and so the penalty sought would be £31,900 × 15% = £4,785, rounded to the nearest £50, say, £4,800.

Notifying us about corrections The following question and answer appeared in the December 1997 edition of CTO Newsletter.

Q. Does CTO agree that discovered assets are best mentioned only at such time as a corrective account can be prepared rather than being declared straightaway?

A. Yes, but only if the asset is relatively small in value. Generally, with items worth over £10,000 it is best to inform us as soon as possible.

This matter has been reconsidered during the course of the recent consultations about our leaflet IHT 13 (see above). This was with particular reference to Section 248 IHTA 1984. That Section provides for penalties where any account, information or document is discovered to have been materially incorrect and the error is not remedied without unreasonable delay.

As explained in IHT 13, our view now is that any account, information or document is materially incorrect if the total tax arising from the correction, or corrections, amounts to £1,000 or more.

So where £1,000 or more of tax is at stake we want to know about errors (including newly discovered assets)

- in information or documents within 30 days of discovery at the latest

- in accounts within 6 months of discovery at the latest. This ties in with the time limit for delivering further accounts under Section 217 IHTA 1984.

In practice, this means that we expect to be told about changes, singly or in aggregate, amounting to £2,500 or more in value as soon as possible. Failure to tell us, within these time limits, about innocent errors resulting in tax of £1,000 or more may result in a penalty under Section 248 IHTA 1984.

Naturally we need to be told about smaller value changes in due course so that we can agree the final liability for inheritance tax.

We shall apply this limit to errors (including newly discovered assets) discovered on or after 1 September 2000.

Where errors in any account, information or documents arise as a result of negligence (or fraud), penalties under Section 247 IHTA 1984 can apply. We expect to be told immediately such errors are discovered,

IHT 200 IN SCOTLAND

The differences between the procedures in obtaining Confirmation and probate have meant that we needed to run a longer pilot of form IHT 200 in Scotland. We have received a lot of feedback about the new account and the new Inventory, form C1, and we have included many of the suggestions in the final versions. We are planning to launch the IHT 200 and new form C1 in Scotland on 25 September. We will continue to accept the existing forms A3, B3 and B4 for a short while but the new forms must be used for all applications made after 4 December.

We will be sending out a supply of the forms to over 400 different firms and organisations on 25 September. Please allow a couple of weeks for delivery, and if you have not received a supply in that time, call our orderline on 0845 234 1000. There are also electronic versions of both the forms and they will be available for download from the Internet at http://www.inlandrevenue.gov.uk/cto.

AMENDMENTS TO IHT 215

We have made a number of changes to the Practitioners Guide, form IHT 215, and we will be sending out the first set of amendments soon. If you do not receive enough copies for your firm/organisation, please let our Customer Service team know so we can update our mailing list. You will also be able to download the amendments from our website at the address above and if you are using our software to complete the forms on a PC, you will be able to download an updated copy of the whole Guide to replace the file used for the help feature.

When ordering, please remember the IHT 215 includes IHT 210, 213, 214 and all the notes to go with the supplementary D pages. So you don't need to order these as well.

EXEMPT ESTATES

We have for some time been conscious of the burden that delivering form IHT 200 places on the taxpayers where the deceased's Free Estate passes to a surviving spouse or charity. And a number of you have written to us about it. We need to be sure that the estate as a whole is complying with the law and we need enough information so that if (when) an Instrument of Variation is executed, we can accept that the document satisfies the requirements. But provided we can achieve this aim, we do not need a fully detailed account of an exempt estate. We are working on a solution to this with the Law Society and STEP and we hope to be able to put a formal procedure in place soon.

NATIONAL COAL BOARD (NCB) COMPENSATION CLAIMS

A simplified probate application procedure Practitioners acting for the estates of former miners may find that they need to make late Grant applications solely in order to pursue claims for compensation against the NCB. A simplified procedure for this has been agreed with the Court Service and is now in operation.

It has been introduced to reduce the administrative burden for Practitioners of completing a full Inland Revenue Account for estates of de minimis value most of the claims relate to pre-1981 deaths, to which the Excepted Estates regulations do not apply.

The vast majority of Applications are being handled by NCB-nominated firms of Solicitors but single-estate Applications are also within the terms of the scheme. If you are not one of the nominated firms and are asked about a potential claim, it is suggested that you speak to our contact point below before proceeding.

The relevant details required in respect of *each* estate are as follows:-

• The name of the Probate Registry you intend to use to obtain the Grant

• The name(s) of the of the intending administrator(s) or executor(s)

• The name of the deceased and

• The date of death

In addition we require the following declaration:-

I confirm that we require the Letters of Administration (or other) in the estate(s) of the former miners listed in order to pursue a claim under the Law Reform Act 1934 and/or the Fatal Accidents Act 1976. To the best of my knowledge, information and belief the value of the assets in the estate of each of the deceased at the date of death did not exceed the Nil rate band for Estate Duty or the tax threshold for Capital Transfer Tax or Inheritance Tax (as appropriate). This declaration needs to be signed, preferably by the intending administrator or executor.

A form P26A must also be completed in respect of each estate. This form is not strictly appropriate for deaths that occurred in CTT and ED eras and has been replaced generally now by the D18. However, it is to be retained and used for this particular exercise to help us to identify the NCB compensation claims more easily in our Initial Processing Section.

A form D18 will not be rejected if submitted but the whole process could be delayed if the nature of the requirement is not recognised when first received. Supplies of form P26A can be obtained from the CTO Nottingham.

The procedure applies only to non-taxpaying cases. Indeed, it is expected that the value of the estates will commonly be nil or at the most a negligible figure. The amount of the anticipated compensation should not be included in the value of the estate.

All completed lists of estates and P26As should be forwarded to our Nottingham office (*marked for the attention of IHT Support*) regardless of where the Grant is likely to be obtained. The P26As will then be endorsed as valid and returned to the sender to take to the Probate Registry.

We hope the simplified procedure will benefit all parties involved with the claims.

If there are any problems please contact Jon Bridger on 0115 974 2696.

ELECTRONIC FORMS

We have now produced an integrated version of form IHT 200 and it is available to download from our website now. This links all forms together and calculates the tax and interest payable on delivery for you. For taxpayers in Scotland, we are still working on a version that will provide some links between the IHT 200 and C1.

In addition to the account, we have produced a calculator that works out the chargeable estate in most cases where grossing-up is necessary. This too is available to download now, as are electronic versions of forms IHT 30 (clearance certificate), IHT 35 (relief for loss on sale of shares) and IHT 38 (relief for loss on sale of land). We hope to turn our attention to the other forms of account, IHT 100 and IHT 101, Cap D3 and the corrective Inventory (for Scotland) in due course.

DECEMBER 2000. – TAX BULLETIN

INHERITANCE TAX: ACCUMULATION & MAINTENANCE TRUSTS

Most practitioners will be familiar with the inheritance tax (IHT) provisions for 'Accumulation and Maintenance' trusts (AMTs). Among other things, these provide exemption from the periodic IHT charge on discretionary trusts either:

* so long as all beneficiaries are grandchildren of a common grandparent (or a surviving spouse of such a grandchild); or

* in other cases, for a maximum period of 25 years since the tests for AMTs were first satisfied.

No IHT charge has arisen yet under this second leg, because the 25 year period has not so far run out for any trust subject to it. But this category includes a significant class of trusts which were already in place when these rules for AMTs were finalised in 1976. So for all those which are still subject to this test, the grace period runs out on the same date 25 years on, at the close of 15 April 2001. Practitioners responsible for pre-75 AMTs may want to note that a charge potentially arises at this point. More generally, they will want to take note that IHT charges at the 25 year point will arise from then on for other trusts set up or modified since the mid-70s, at the particular anniversary dates appropriate to each trust.

IN MORE DETAIL

Trusts are liable to an IHT charge once they fail to qualify under Section 71 of the Inheritance Tax Act 1984 (IHTA) because they no longer meet the conditions for grandparent/grandchildren or a 25 year period has elapsed.

The 25 year period runs form the latest of:

* 15 April 1976;

* the date the settlement commenced; and

* the date of attainment of accumulation and maintenance status.

Settlements **not** affected are those set up by a common grandparent for grandchildren, whether or not with contingency provision for the widow or widower of any grandchild who dies before becoming entitled to the property.

For those settlements which **are** affected, IHT is calculated at a flat rate (Section 71(5)) which tapers over time on property which ceases to be held on AMTs or when the trustees make a disposition which reduces the value of the property. The tax charge for a 25 year period is 21% calculated as follows:

* 0.25% for each of the first 40 complete successive quarters in the relevant period;

* 0.20% for each of the next 40 complete successive quarters in the relevant period;

* 0.15% for each of the next 40 complete successive quarters in the relevant period.

Thereafter the normal rules for ten-yearly and proportionate charges for discretionary trusts apply to these settlements.

DECEMBER 2000. – IHT NEWSLETTER

EDITORIAL

Welcome to the latest edition of what is now our *IHT Newsletter*. Our first article explains the reasons for this change.

Our Nottingham Open Days took place on 28 and 29 November. Thank you to everybody who came along – we hope you found them valuable. We will include a feature about the Open Days, including the events in Edinburgh on 24 & 25 January 2001, in our next edition.

The next edition of the *Newsletter* will be March 2001.

In the meantime, we would like to wish you all a very merry Christmas and a happy New Year.

Customer Service Team

INLAND REVENUE (CAPITAL TAXES)

You may have heard about some organisational changes that are currently taking place in the Inland Revenue.

Capital Taxes Office has merged with parts of Capital and Savings which deal with Inheritance Tax and policy and technical advice on capital gains. The changes are part of a wider reorganisation of Capital and Savings, which is taking place between now and next April.

The new business, to be called Inland Revenue (Capital Taxes) – hence the change of name to our *Newsletter* – will be responsible for all aspects of inheritance tax as well as policy development, technical advice and clearance applications for capital gains. It will also deal with all Shares Valuation work.

Local tax offices will still be responsible for issuing returns, answering questions and dealing with the tax liabilities on capital gains.

There will be no immediate change for customers, who should continue to write to or telephone the people they normally deal with. However, we hope this reorganisation will help us improve our service in the long run by bringing together related areas of work and by bringing policy development closer to operational work.

The Business Director of Inland Revenue (Capital Taxes) is Jonathan Leigh Pemberton.

IHT200 & C1 – SCOTLAND

The new Inland Revenue Inheritance Tax Account, form IHT200, and the new Confirmation form C1 were introduced on 25 September 2000. These forms should be used for all applications from 4 December 2000 unless the estate is an excepted estate or the application is in respect of a death prior to 18 March 1986.

Capital Taxes in Edinburgh is running workshops to help practitioners become familiar with the layout, requirements and processing of the forms. There are vacancies at these workshops in our offices at Meldrum House on:

15 January 2001 – AM session only

18 January 2001 – AM session only

19 January 2001 – AM & PM sessions

29 January 2001 – AM & PM sessions

30 January 2001 – AM & PM sessions

It is intended that each workshop will last approximately 2 hours. There will be 24 places at each workshop and will be allocated on a first come first served basis.

If any member of your firm would like to attend, please telephone either Eleanor Dignan on 0131 777 4186 or Jane Thornton on 0131 777 4188 with the names of those wishing to attend.

THE NEW IHT200

The new IHT200 was launched in England, Wales and Northern Ireland in February and in Scotland in September. This new form should now be used in all Probate or Confirmation applications unless the estate or the application is in respect of a death prior to 18 March 1986.

The more detailed information required on the new form has enabled us to reduce the number of enquiries we raise. This is good news for probate practitioners as it will help us to deal with estates more quickly and with fewer exchanges of correspondence. It is also good news for us as it enables us to concentrate on reviewing the accounts and only raising enquiries where additional information is essential.

Working out the tax Solicitors should always calculate the tax due and send payment to the Capital Taxes with IHT 200. Form IHT(WS) should be used to calculate the tax. The guide '*How to fill in form IHT(WS)*' explains how to do this. If you have any difficulty calculating the tax, please phone our Helpline for advice. Our Helpline numbers can be found on the back of this Newsletter. Alternatively, the account is available on the Internet. If you complete the integrated account form on line it will calculate the tax and interest for you. Our web address is http://www.inlandrevenue.gov.uk/cto. If you do not calculate the tax before sending the IHT200 to us, we will have to calculate the tax and write to you asking for payment. This will delay the issue of the grant. And we have to devote resources to preparing calculations and asking for payment.

Even if no tax is payable, you should still complete the summary of the estate at section H of the IHT200. This will enable us to review the account more quickly.

Probate Summary D18 There is still some confusion about when the probate summary (supplementary page D18) should be sent to us and when it should be sent to the Probate Registry.

If Inheritance Tax is payable, or the deceased was not domiciled in the United Kingdom, the D18 must be sent to us with the IHT200 to certify the tax paid or, in foreign domicile cases only, that no tax is payable. If you do not enclose the D18, we will have to ask you to forward this. This will delay the issue of the grant.

If no Inheritance Tax is payable, and the deceased was domiciled in the United Kingdom, the D18 should be sent to the Probate Registry (with the other papers necessary to apply for a grant) at the same time as the IHT200 is sent to us. If you send the D18 to us, the Probate Registry will be unable to issue the grant until we forward it to them. This will delay the issue of the grant.

Other Supplementary Pages If the answer to any of the questions on page 2 of the account is 'Yes', you must attach the appropriate supplementary page except in the case of an exempt estate which satisfies the criteria for delivery of a reduced account. Unless the supplementary pages are attached, the account is incomplete and we are unable to certify the D18. If you do not enclose these supplementary pages we will have to ask you to forward them. This will delay the issue of the grant.

We have found that people do not always include the supplementary pages because they do not think that these provide any useful information. For example, an executor might answer 'Yes' to the question on page 2 of the account about pensions and then 'No' to all three questions on the supplementary page D6. As none of the boxes on the D6 have been completed, you might think it unnecessary to send us the D6. However we do still need the

D6 in these circumstances. Without it we do not know the answer to the three questions is 'No' and we will have to ask for the D6. This will delay the issue of the grant.

If a supplementary page has to be completed, it is necessary to answer all the questions fully. These are designed to elicit the basic information we need to review the account. If the questions are not fully answered, we will have to contact you in order to obtain the information we need. The aim of the new IHT200 is to avoid having to contact you for information as this delays the settlement of the estate.

PENALTIES AND URGENT GRANT CASES

Personal representatives have a statutory duty to deliver an account of all appropriate property and the value of that property (Section 216(1) IHTA 1984). Section 216(3) allows them to include an estimated value, if an exact value cannot be obtained, but only after the fullest enquiries reasonably practicable have been made.

We recognise that even this provision can pose practical difficulties if there is a proven need for obtaining a grant urgently.

We have always been prepared to discuss the need for urgent grants on a case by case basis and do all we can to assist.

Where we accept there is a genuine need for a quick grant we still expect the personal representatives to make such enquiries as they can in the time they have in order to include as considered an estimate as is possible.

But we will not seek penalties in these cases when the account contains estimated values, even if this is the best the personal representatives could do in the time available to them.

This does not mean that all values in such accounts need be estimates. If you do have the correct value for the asset that is the value that we expect you to include.

On a practicable level we suggest that if you believe you have an urgent need for a grant it would help us if you faxed us a letter outlining the circumstances. We will then telephone you to discuss and agree whether or not we accept the need for an urgent grant.

Fax number to use – 0115 974 3045.

ELECTRONIC FORMS C1 & C2

We have received a lot of feedback about difficulties in completing our electronic versions of forms C1 & C2 on screen. Consequently, we have produced an alternative version and we need some people to test it for us. If you are using our software for these forms and would like to test the alternative version, please contact Tony Key on 0115 974 2650.

PENALTIES AND THE NEW REDUCED ACCOUNT

The new form IHT19 outlines the conditions under which we will accept the delivery of a reduced account, IHT200.

Where a reduced account is delivered under this relaxed application of the statutory requirements, personal representatives are able to include their own estimate of value for an asset passing to an exempt beneficiary.

A reduced account may still be regarded as incorrect for the purposes of Section 247 IHTA 1984 if it contains incorrect or incomplete information, but we will not regard it as incorrect because of the inclusion of the personal representatives' own estimates allowed under this relaxation.

Where a corrective account is subsequently required because the estate is found not to meet the conditions for a reduced account (either as a result of an instrument of variation or otherwise) then that corrective account must include open market values. Including a value other than the open market value in the corrective account may give rise to a penalty.

INTEGRATED ACCOUNT

We discovered a minor 'bug' in our electronic integrated account. Anyone who has used this in the past should download a copy of the new version that we have now put on the website. http://www.inlandrevenue.gov.uk/cto.

OUR COMPLIANCE STRATEGY

We want to tell you a little about our strategy for handling our compliance work.

Our purpose in carrying out this work is to

- maximise compliance with the law as it relates to Inheritance Tax (IHT) and the valuation of assets referred to us for all fiscal purposes
- collect or enable the collection of tax properly payable at the right time and in an efficient manner.

The strategy in a nutshell is to

- encourage and improve voluntary compliance
- detect and challenge non-compliance.

The strategy sets out a number of ways in which we hope to achieve these goals.

For example, to help voluntary compliance, we aim to:

- help taxpayers and agents to help us
- minimise compliance costs
- convince our customers that we are fair and approachable.

Our strategy includes the following approaches to address non-compliance:

- risk assessment
- improved working methods
- effective and sustained action to establish and collect the correct liability
- a well trained workforce
- enhanced liaison with other parts of the department.

We recognise that setting out a strategy is like imagining permanent blue skies. So we make an annual analysis of where we are now and compare that with where we want to be. And we use that analysis to make a practical and achievable annual Compliance Plan to get us along the road to fully achieving our strategic aims.

This year (2000–2001) our Compliance Plan includes action to:

- encourage the greater use of the telephone and of meetings to advance the handling of taxpayers' affairs
- work towards electronic filing of accounts by taxpayers
- reviewing the operation of the new IHT200
- updating official instructions to ensure consistent practice
- learn from complaints made by taxpayers
- improving the way we select cases to take up for enquiry
- set and meet targets for quality and post turnarounds
- improve our debt management

- continue to reduce the number of old cases.

In future editions, we shall let you know more about the progress we have made.

OUR CUSTOMER SERVICE AIMS

Our overall aim is to provide taxpayers, whether they deal with us direct or through professional advisers and agents, with the high quality of service they require and to their need to comply with their obligations. This means not only that our staff must be trained to understand and apply the legislation accurately but also that we have procedures and processes in place that are easily understood and meet your needs.

We believe that we have improved the service we provide over recent years: this view is supported by what you have told us in previous customer surveys. However we know that there are many areas and ways where we must improve further. But we need your help with this, so we do need to know when we get things wrong. We take all complaints seriously and always critically examine our procedures and actions. Our Customer Service Team certainly welcome suggestions for improvement and always pass them on to the operational managers and staff.

Please do not be afraid to let us know when and where we do not provide the service you require. It also helps if we learn of our good work, when you believe that we have met your needs and have provided a high level of service.

We are now conducting a survey of practitioners. Some of you will receive a questionnaire shortly. Alternatively, you may have already received a request to comment on how we have dealt with you in connection with a specific estate as part of our programme of random customer surveys. We want to know what we do well, not so well or even badly from your and your clients' point of view. We do use our surveys to decide where we need to improve. If you receive a questionnaire, we hope you will spare the time to complete and return it.

We currently judge ourselves against a variety of targets and goals that cover both the customer service and compliance elements of our work. We review them annually and want to be sure that they are truly aimed at you and your clients' needs. You cannot judge this without knowing what they are and how in fact we are performing. Details of some of our performance indicators follow and we shall give details of others in our next *Newsletter*.

1. We aim to process and respond on the first delivery of 95% of Inland Revenue Accounts where inheritance tax is payable within 7 working days of receiving the account. This applies when payment of the tax accompanies the account (when we issue a receipt and the D18) **and** when we are asked to calculate the tax and request payment. We have struggled in Nottingham to meet our target with the latter situation but believe we are currently doing this.

2. We believe that we should start and finish our work in connection with each estate as quickly as possible. We have recently introduced two aims: to complete our processes and decide whether we have any enquiries (including the need to consult the Valuation Office) within 3 months in 95% of estates; to settle the final liability for tax, on the information we have, within 12 months in 90% of estates. We are on course to meet the second of these targets (and we are trying to let you know in all taxpaying estates when we have no further enquiries) but we have more work to do with the former. This year to date we are achieving 94% across our three locations. We are doing less well in Nottingham than in Belfast and Edinburgh.

3. We aim to take the appropriate action on receipt of 80% of post within 15 working days and of 97% within 40 working days. We look at all our post for this purpose (including letters that require no reply) and, on this basis, we are meeting our targets. We hope that you accept that some correspondence requires considerable analysis and thought and to expect a reply within 15 days is neither reasonable nor crucial. But you may believe that some types of correspondence should always be dealt with within 15 days, if not sooner.

4.   When correspondence is under way you should have the name and the extension of the member of our staff who can help you. We aim to answer 90% of calls within 15 seconds. We are (just) achieving this with calls to our Nottingham Helpline. We hope that our Helpline provides a valuable service but we must improve the speed of our response to these enquiries in Nottingham. As always, your views on this service are important – what service do you expect and are we providing it?

ICELANDIC WATER TRAWLERMEN SCHEME

In the August issue we outlined a simplified procedure for obtaining a Grant in cases involving compensation claims against the NCB. We have now agreed a similar, but not identical, process with the Probate Registry in cases where claims are being made under the Icelandic Water Trawlermen Scheme.

The majority of these cases appear to be being dealt with by Personal Applicants but if you find that you require further details of the simplified procedure please contact Liz Clark on 0115 974 2715 or Jon Bridger on 0115 974 2696.

APRIL 2001. – IHT NEWSLETTER

EDITORIAL

Welcome to the latest edition of our *IHT Newsletter.*

Helen Smith, the Customer Service Manager has now moved on within the Inland Revenue and David Wright has taken over the role of Customer Service & Complaints Manager.

Deborah Walsh will be Deputy Customer Service Manager and Julie Boole has joined the team from our Shares Valuation section.

The team would like to thank Helen Smith for all her help and guidance during her time at the Capital Taxes.

The next edition of the *Newsletter* will be August 2001.

OPEN DAYS

The Edinburgh Open days took place on 24 & 25 January 2001. We would like to thank all those who attended.

The feedback received from both the Edinburgh & Nottingham Open Days has been very useful for us.

Articles have recently been published in legal journals, which show the events in a positive light. Stephanie Lemmy of Halliwell Landau wrote in the Jan/Feb edition of *Trusts & Estate Tax Journal,* and David Wright, our Customer Service Manager, gave a response in the March edition. An article also appeared in issue *146 of Taxes – The Weekly Tax News* dated 8 December 2000.

Thank you once again to everyone who came along – we hope you found the events valuable.

EX-GRATIA PAYMENTS TO BRITISH POWS

On 24 January, a Press Release announced a new ESC whereby the ex-gratia payment of £10,000 made to Britons held prisoner by the Japanese during World War II was to be left out of account in determining the chargeable value of their estate on death. As this applies to the estate as a whole, the benefit needs to be given through an adjustment to tax, rather than to capital. It means if the deceased's Free Estate is exempt, because it passes to say, the

61   IHT Newsletter and Tax Bulletin extracts

surviving spouse, the benefit of the reduction can still be given to other chargeable components such as settled property or GWR [gifts with reservation].

In order to apply the reduction correctly, you should reduce the amount of tax charged on the estate by the lesser of

- 40% of the payment(s) received, or

- the actual tax charged before allowing the reduction.

You should include the figure for the reduction in box WS21 (normally reserved for QSR [quick succession relief]) on form IHT(WS), so that it is carried to box J6 on form IHT 200. In the rare event the QSR is also due, simply add the figures together.

BUDGET CHANGES

The Inheritance Tax threshold has been increased to £242,000. This applies to deaths and chargeable events on or after 6 April 2001.

HERITAGE EXEMPTIONS: FINANCE ACT 1998

a) **access to tax–exempt chattels by prior appointment only.** The Finance Act 1998 changed the rules for 'conditional exemption' of heritage assets, amongst other things by providing for the possibility of open access to chattels which are currently seen by prior appointment only. Practitioners acting for owners of such chattels will know that we have to consider in each case whether it is 'just and reasonable in all the circumstances' to propose such changes, and have asked owners to tell us about circumstances which they think are relevant. In reviewing the cases where we believe we now have enough material to come to a considered view, we have recently been able to tell more than 200 owners, covering nearly 4,000 chattels, that we do not presently propose any change to their existing 'by appointment' obligation. We will be continuing to process cases where we have the material to do so. And of course we will be happy to consider any change to their existing 'by appointment' obligation. We will be continuing to process cases where we have the material to do so. And of course we will be happy to consider any further responses from owners and advisers about their individual circumstances and the consequences which are considered to flow from them.

b) **claims for exemption: time limit.** The Finance Act 1998 also introduced a time limit within which to claim conditional exemption of heritage assets and exemption of funds to be held on approved maintenance fund trusts. The time limit is two years after the date of the death or transfer or other relevant event. The law gives the Inland Revenue discretion to allow a longer period, and we shall consider any application to make a late claim on its merits. But oversight on the part of a claimant or adviser, or post death variation of inheritance, will not normally by itself be an acceptable reason to allow a late claim. Neither will the failure of a claim for some other relief. For example there may be a primary claim for agricultural or business property relief, which we would normally expect to be settled within two years of the death or other event. If, however, practitioners believe that this claim may not be determined within the two year period, they might like to consider a secondary, protective, claim for heritage exemption, which might revive if the primary claim fails.

In order to constitute a claim for heritage exemption – and this applies equally to a protective claim along the lines just mentioned – the claimant should within two years of the date of death or transfer:

- provide a statement that exemption is being claimed, specifying the event to which the claim relates

- clearly identify each asset or group of assets covered by the claim

- provide a brief statement of why each asset is considered to qualify for exemption, including confirmation that proposals to provide public access will be made, and;

- confirm that there is no present intention to sell the asset(s).

DX POSTAL SERVICE

It has been brought to our attention that some solicitors firms in Scotland are no longer using Hays DX postal service. It is important that our records are updated so if you have withdrawn from this service, can you let us know by writing to Caroline Aikman in our Edinburgh office and confirm your Royal Mail address.

KEEPING YOU INFORMED OF PROGRESS

One of the benefits of the changes to form IHT200 is that we are now able to accept, without additional correspondence, the position as returned in a greater number of estates. But this means that we have no cause to contact you routinely in these estates and this may leave you wondering how things stand. To address this, we introduced a process last year – for every taxpaying estate and those non-tax estates where we do initiate correspondence – to write and confirm when we are satisfied with the information given.

But this process does not apply to most non-tax estates and the problems this brings were highlighted at our November Open days.

As the majority of non-tax estates remain that way we try to commit only the amount of resource essential to handling these estates. The commitment to issue a similar letter in all non-tax estates would be considerable. So to meet this we propose an extra module to the IHT200 which, when appropriate, can be completed by the taxpayer and delivered with the IHT200. We can then easily return the form using a window envelope when we have completed our examination of the IHT200.

The form will let you know that we are content with the information given about the estate and inform you of our reference should you need to write to us later. Although it does not have the standing of a statutory certificate of clearance we hope that, in most cases, this will suffice. We have written to the various Law Societies and to STEP to ask for their views about this suggestion. A copy of the draft form is on page 4 [see 35.9 PAYMENT OF TAX] of this Newsletter – if you would like to comment on the suggestion, please write to our Customer Service Team in Nottingham.

REDUCED ACCOUNT – LEAFLET IHT 19

Following feedback about the reduced account, we will be amending the IHT 19 in due course to reflect the points below. You may wish to note these on your own copy of the leaflet and apply the changes with immediate effect.

It was always our intention that the facility to deliver a reduced account should apply to any estate which is below the threshold due to spouse or charity relief. However, the word 'most' in the second box in the flowchart would exclude, for example, an estate of £300,000 where the nil-rate passes to chargeable beneficiaries. We will amend the IHT19 to replace the word 'most' with 'any'.

On page 2 of the IHT19, we say that only forms D1 – D6 must be completed. But this means that where there are foreign assets that pass to an exempt beneficiary, no details are provided on form IHT200 as it only contains the chargeable value – which may well be nil. So, in addition to forms D1 – D6, if the answer to question D15 is 'Yes', form D15 must also be filled in – although where the foreign assets pass to an exempt beneficiary, estimated values can be used in the same way.

END OF CASE SURVEYS

We mentioned in our last Newsletter that we were conducting random customer surveys. **Thank you to those people who have replied to the surveys already carried out.**

We piloted this in Nottingham with a short questionnaire issued with a clearance certificate asking how we handled that particular case. We asked for marks out of 5 for different aspects – where 5 meant 'totally satisfied' and 1 'totally dissatisfied'.

The % results for markings 4 or 5 (or 1 or 2) so far received are as follows:

- Speed of written responses 53% (14%)
- Keeping you informed of progress 55% (15%)
- Clarity of explanations 87% (4%)
- Courtesy of communications 89% (2%)
- Knowledge shown by staff 89% (4%)
- Accuracy of calculations 94% (4%)
- Overall rating of our service 82% (5%)

Overall the results are therefore generally encouraging but some of the marks, and comments made, show that there is room for improvement. The article on page 3 is one example of how we are trying to improve on how we keep you informed. We will keep you in touch with our plans on how we propose to address other areas in future *Newsletter*.

AUGUST 2001. – IHT NEWSLETTER

EDITORIAL

Welcome to the latest edition of our *IHT Newsletter*.

We have just heard that we have been awarded a Charter Mark for excellence in public service. We are very proud to have received this recognition of our hard work in improving the service we provide to our customers.

Of course, Charter Mark is not only about recognition. The application gave us a framework for assessing our own performance and with the expert feedback received, a tool kit for further improvement.

We will be letting you know more in future *Newsletters* about the feedback we have received and how we intend to use it. We also intend to issue a *Newsletter* shortly detailing the results of our latest customer survey.

KEEPING YOU INFORMED OF PROGRESS – FORM D19

In our April *Newsletter* we told you about our proposals to keep you in touch with what was happening in estates where there is no tax to pay. We invited your comments on a new module to the IHT 200. Overall, the responses were favourable and so we have implemented the proposal.

The D19 is a new module to form IHT200 which is to be used in estates where there is no tax to pay. If you do not want to know that we are content with details of an estate as given in the IHT200, you should fill in all the white boxes on the form D19 and send the form to us with the IHT200. Provided we are content that, on the basis of the information provided, there is no IHT to pay, we will stamp and return the form to you, taking the opportunity to tell you our reference number for the estate in case you need to contact us in the future.

If our mailing list shows that you hold a copy of the Practitioner's Guide, a supply of form D19 is enclosed with this *Newsletter*. It can be used straight away. D19s can also be obtained from our stationery orderline on 0845 2341000, or downloaded from our Internet website.

CHANGES TO IHT200

We have made some changes to two of the modules that support IHT200. Form D3 contains an extra question about gifts with reservation to reflect the FA 1999 changes to s 102 FA 1986. And form D14 contains an extra question about winding up and liquidation of a company. Answering this new question on the D14 will save Shares Valuation troubling you by having to raise the point after grant.

In Scotland, we have also made a small change to the Inventory, form C1, by separating the questions on page 4 about small and excepted estates.

You should use the new versions of the forms with effect from 13 August, although we will continue to accept the old forms for estates that are currently in progress.

AMENDMENTS TO THE PRACTITIONER'S GUIDE

If our mailing list shows that you hold a copy of the Practitioner's Guide, the second release of amendments to the Guide is enclosed with this *Newsletter*. This release reflects the feedback we have received and the changes to the D3 and D14. You can obtain amendments from our stationery orderline on 0845 2341000 – be sure to ask for the July 2001 amendments to form IHT215.

ON-LINE FORMS

We have included all the changes in the on-line forms available on our website and we have added the D19 into the integrated IHT200. If you use this software we recommend that you download updated copies from the Internet. We have provided details of the changes to those of you who produce substitute forms and to the commercial software providers. We expect that the new versions of the software will be available in due course.

IHT200 – SUPPLEMENTARY PAGES

Please could you remember to answer all the questions on the supplementary pages of the IHT200 that you have to complete.

We have had particular problems with people not answering all the questions on the D4 about joint property and the D9 about life insurance and annuities.

Please check that you have answered all these questions before sending us the account so that we do not have to raise the points in correspondence with you.

Thank you for your co-operation.

REPAYMENTS OF TAX

We have been told in our surveys and at our Open Days that we often take too long to make repayments of tax. We accept this. Clearly we have to exercise extra care and have extra checks before making repayments but we should complete our processes as quickly as we can and not delay repayments properly due.

We hope that you will have noticed improvements recently. The IHT200 provides the opportunity for the names of the payees to be provided at the outset. This has cut out one process as previously we only obtained this information when we knew that a repayment was necessary.

We have also increased the resources we devote to the security and other checks made at the final stage and so speeded up our turnaround times in our Nottingham office where the problem was so acute.

Finally, the payable orders themselves are now prepared and issued by the Accounts Office at Shipley rather than Worthing. This will provide a more consistently prompt level of service and reduce the time between the claim for a repayment being made and the payable order being issued.

IHT 35 (loss on sale of shares relief) We are looking at ways to reduce delays further. We currently make some 18,000 repayments annually and expect that with the recent overall drop in value of quoted stocks and shares we shall be making rather more than normal in the next few months. It would help us if you could bear the following in mind when you make claims for relief under section 179 of the IHTA 1984.

Note 3 on front of the form IHT35 explains that you may claim provisional relief within 12 months of the date of death (the claim will be reviewed later, as necessary) if the last sale was at least two months before the date of the latest signature on page 4 of the form. The relief will be provisional if the 12-month period has not expired **and** further sales by the appropriate person(s) (see Note 2 on IHT 35) are possible. But it will be final if you are able to confirm that any remaining qualifying investments are being transferred in specie to the beneficiaries, as no further sales by the appropriate persons are then possible.

Of course, if there are any further sales of qualifying investments by the appropriate person(s) within 12 months of the date of death, a further IHT 35 should be submitted with full details, whether those sales have resulted in a gain or loss compared to the value adopted for IHT purposes. Please do not wait for our review.

Finally, please remember that we do not give relief, provisionally or otherwise, if the IHT 35 is signed within 2 months of the last sale included in the claim. We will return the form if this 2-month period has not expired and this will result in delay.

INTEREST CHANGE

Interest on unpaid and overpaid IHT is payable at 4% from 6 May 2001.

BANK ACCOUNTS OF HOLOCAUST VICTIMS

ESC A100 published in April explained that compensation paid to the claimants under the 'Restore UK' initiative would be exempt from 'death duties'. In the nature of these cases, the present-day claimant will have acquired their interest in the account by succession on one or more deaths up to 60 years ago. And since the accounts are UK situs assets, these transfers were all, with hindsight, potentially chargeable to Estate Duty, CTT or IHT. The ESC makes clear that people interested in these accounts may pursue their claims and receive payment in full without worrying about these potential past liabilities.

If your clients succeed with a claim under this initiative, there is accordingly no need to send us details. However, although the payment is exempt from 'death duties' on the death of the account holder (or of the intervening owners in the chain of inheritance) to the extent that the cash proceeds form part of the estate of the successful claimant, they will be liable to IHT in the normal way.

SOFTWARE COMPATIBILITY

Adobe Acrobat 5 is now available. You should find our software will operate on Version 5 just as easily as with Adobe Acrobat 4.

BELFAST OPEN DAY

Some of you will already be aware that we will be holding an Open Day at the Europa Hotel in Belfast on Thursday, 4 October 2001. The programme will begin at 10 am and close no later than 4 pm.

We intend to explain the nature of our work and how we go about it. We will be including our latest thoughts on completing the IHT200, and on penalties. We will also cover a number of technical issues, such as pensions and insurance policies. There will be input from IR:Trusts and from the Valuation of Lands Agency, and time for questions from the floor.

If you would like to attend and have not already received or replied to a formal invitation, please write to Denise Donnelly or Tara Roy in our Belfast Office. Alternatively, you can call Denise on 028 9050 5337 or Tara on 020 9050 5335, or fax them on 028 9050 5305.

REMINDER

We as a department have a use for all the information you provide in the Inland Revenue Account (IHT200).

Of particular importance to us are the deceased's National Insurance number and their Income Tax District details on page one of the Account.

If this information is available to you, please enter it in the designated boxes on the front of the Account.

VALUATION OFFICE AGENCY (VOA) LINKS

At each of the last Open days (in Nottingham and Edinburgh) we explained the measures being taken to improve co-operation with the VOA. In brief:-

- A new Service Level Agreement, effective from May 2000, with tighter turnaround targets for completion of work

- More regular, and meaningful, interim reports on progress

- Clearer lines of internal communication and responsibility for handling of cases

- Better co-ordinated arrangements for keeping you informed of progress

Results for the Financial Year 2000/01 Generally, the new arrangements have been successful and have produced encouraging results.

- VOA outputs in the financial year 2000/01 were well up on the two preceding years (from 18,700 to 21,900 over the period)

- Unit cost per valuation is down over the same period (from £315 to £281)

- Overall throughput achieved in 2000/01 saw some 60% of the work completed within 2 months, 75% completed within 3 months and 90% completed within 6 months.

Current Developments Collectively, we are trying to do more to build on last year's achievements. Two particular developments are:-

- The VOA has restructured its business, with effect from 2 July

- Increased e-mail links – IR (CT) Caseworker to valuer – that are about to go live.

VOA Restructuring There is now a dedicated Business Stream within the VOA – the District Valuer Services (DVS) – which provides valuation services to IR (CT). VOA work previously handled by 24 Group Offices will now be dealt with by 9 geographically-based Units. All existing local Offices will remain open and there are now dedicated Agency resources and a single management chain, accountable for delivery of agreed annual targets.

Operational managers will no longer be faced with competing calls on their resources across the wide spectrum of VOA services. Within DVS, there should be greater flexibility to respond more quickly to both your and our needs.

In the immediate short term this change may cause some disruption while the new arrangements bed in and staff changes are completed. But we will do our best to keep this, and any knock-on delays in individual cases, to a minimum.

E-mail links Very shortly, we intend to extend the facility for direct e-mail links between the IR (CT) and the VOA to all staff engaged in the examination and valuation process. The initial commission from this Office will still be on paper for the moment because of the number and format of the attachments we need to forward to the VOA.

But thereafter the intention is for subsequent exchanges to be electronic as far as possible. Trials have shown this should lead to significant time savings. We are hoping that this step forward will have a knock on benefit on the future level of service that we can provide to you in terms of concluding the valuation aspect of the estate.

OCTOBER 2001. – IHT NEWSLETTER

EDITORIAL

Welcome to this special edition of our newsletter, which gives details of the results of the customer survey we conducted between November 2000 and January 2001. It has taken us a little longer than we had hoped to produce this report. But we wanted to analyse the results in detail and tell you in this *Newsletter* what we have done so far in response to them. We will continue to do this in future editions.

Also, on page 5 there is an article about annual monitoring of conditionally exempt land and buildings.

And on page 4 we tell you about our new Customer Information leaflet, which we are launching this month.

The *Newsletter* will return as usual in December.

Customer Services Team

CUSTOMER SURVEY

[This survey may be viewed on http://www.inlandrevenue.gov.uk/cto and is not reproduced here].

Customer information leaflet During October we will be launching a new leaflet with general information about our organisation and inheritance tax. Amongst other things, it will include contact names and addresses and details about our customer service targets and complaints procedures.

The leaflet will be issued to practitioners or unrepresented taxpayers in every estate where there is inheritance tax to pay.

HERITAGE

Annual monitoring of conditionally exempt land and buildings Conditional exemption from Capital Taxes can be claimed for, among other things:

- Outstanding land.

- Outstanding buildings and their amenity land (and any other chattels historically associated with these buildings).

In return for the exemption the owner of the property has to undertake to satisfy certain conditions concerned with the maintenance and preservation of the property, and to give the public reasonable access to it. And the owner is expected to provide a report every year to show whether he or she is complying with these conditions.

In the past, The Heritage Advisory Agencies, such as Countryside Agency and Historic Scotland, had the responsibility for requesting and obtaining these annual reports. They then passed the reports on to heritage Section in Capital Taxes. But, as from 1 April 2000, Heritage Section itself took over this responsibility and now deals with owners (or their agents). The Advisory Agencies are still involved – they see the reports and evaluate them.

We have been reviewing progress for 2000/01, the first full year that we have operated the new system. overall we have found the results encouraging.

The main features are:

- We have received most reports (about two thirds) within 2 months of asking for them.

- We had to return about 20% of reports because they did not contain all the information we wanted.

- Well over 90% of fully completed reports received have been accepted as satisfactory.

We would like to thank all those owners who returned their reports to us within a reasonable time. Their co-operation has been a big factor in producing the positive start to the new system.

Where we are not satisfied with reports – for example, where there are issues of inadequate advertising of the property, or quality of the estate management or public access arrangements – we have taken these matters up with the owners concerned. And in cases where, despite written and telephone reminders a report has still not been provided, we have reminded owners of the provisions of section 219 IHTA 1984 and issued Information Notices when necessary.

For 2000/01, we expect that owners (or their agents) will be more familiar with the new system and the amount of information we need. So we do not anticipate having to return many reports. And we are also looking to increase the proportion of reports we receive within two months. We would very much appreciate the continued co-operation of owners in helping us to achieve these objectives.

DECEMBER 2001. – INLAND REVENUE TAX BULLETIN ISSUE 56

MISCELLANEOUS

Inheritance Tax: Wartime Compensation Payments Extra-Statutory Concession F20 was revised and published on the IR website on 16 October. The text of the announcement is reproduced [in Chapter 23] but has been updated to reflect that claims by Jewish claimants will be handled by the Conference on Jewish Material Claims against Germany and those of non-Jewish claimants will be handled by International Organisation for Migration.

"Inheritance tax concession extended to include further wartime compensation payments

Extra-Statutory Concession F20 is revised from today, 16 October 2001, to cover payments being made from German public law foundation 'Remembrance, Responsibility and Future'. The foundation provides financial compensation of fixed amounts for claimants (or, where appropriate, the surviving spouse) who were slave or forced labourers or other victims of the Nationalist Socialist regime during the Second World War. Claims by UK claimants are being dealt with by the International Organisation for Migration (non-Jewish claimants) and those claimants entitled to this concession are being advised by them at the time of their successful claim. The extended concession aligns these payments with comparable ex-gratia amounts from the UK Government to British groups held prisoner by the Japanese during World War II.

Under present inheritance tax (IHT) rules, rights to such compensation, or subsequent proceeds, could form part of the claimant's estate for IHT purposes. Extra–Statutory Concession (F20) allows the amount of any compensation payment to be deducted from the claimant's IHT chargeable estate, whether payment is made to the claimant before their death or is made subsequently to their personal representatives. [See Chapter 23 of this publication].

DECEMBER 2001. – IHT NEWSLETTER

EDITORIAL

Welcome to the latest edition of our *IHT Newsletter*.

Firstly, a very big thank you to everybody who attended Capital Taxes' first ever open day in Belfast in October. We hope that you found it valuable. And we will use the *Newsletter* to tell you about similar events in future.

This edition includes an article by our colleagues from IR Trusts in Edinburgh, who deal with CGT and income tax aspects for most estates in administration valued at over £400,000. We realise that we share many of the same customers and will be including further articles in future *Newsletters*.

The next edition will be April 2002. In the meantime, we would like to wish you all a very merry Christmas and a happy New Year.

IHT 200 – SUPPLEMENTARY PAGES

Just a couple of changes and reminders about some of the supplementary pages to form IHT200.

Form D13 Questions 2a and 2b on this form reflect the alternative requirements of s. 117 IHTA, but the wording on the original version of the form did not accurately relay the statutory requirements. The latest version of this form corrects this.

Form D18 In England & Wales and Northern Ireland, please make sure you complete and send form D18 to us in all taxpaying estates and in all estates where you consider that the deceased was domiciled abroad.

Conversely, we do not need to authorise form D18 in non-tax estates where the deceased was domiciled in the UK. In such estates, you can complete the form and send it with your application for a grant at the same time as sending the IHT200 to us. Form D18 does not apply in Scotland.

Form D19 If there is no tax to pay on an estate and you would like us to confirm that we agree this is the case, please complete form D19 and send it to us with the IHT200. Where we agree that there is no tax to pay, we will stamp and return the form to you so keeping you informed about the progress of your estate.

With both forms D18 and D19, if you use the DX system and include that address in the return address box, we can get these forms back to you more quickly.

REDUCED ACCOUNT

In last December's issue of our *Newsletter*, we told you about the facility to deliver a reduced account where the chargeable value of the estate is below the threshold due to spouse or charity exemption. This facility should cut down the length of time it takes to apply for a grant and reduce costs in doing so. Our leaflet IHT19 sets out the full details and we recommend that you make use of this facility whenever it is appropriate.

INTEREST RATE CHANGE

Interest on unpaid and overpaid IHT is payable at 3% from 6 November 2001.

NATIONAL COAL BOARD / BRITISH COAL COMPENSATION CLAIMS

In our August 2000 *Newsletter*, we told you about the simplified procedure that had been agreed with the Court Service where a grant of representation was necessary to pursue a claim against British Coal. Although many claims will be in respect of coal miners who died some years ago, we have been asked what should be included in form IHT200 where a miner has died more recently.

Until Mr Justice Turner's decision on 23 January 1998, the likelihood of succeeding with a claim against British Coal was speculative and so where a miner died before that date, you should include the value of the right to make a claim at nil. Where a miner died on or after that date, you should include a discounted value, dependent on the likely success of the claim, the maximum amount payable under the head of claim and the delay before the money could be received. Where a miner dies having received their compensation, the money is fully liable to IHT in the normal way.

For CGT purposes, the capital element of any compensation payment will not be chargeable to CGT in view of S. 51(2) TCGA 1992. However, if the payment includes compensation of an income nature, for example recompense specifically for loss of earnings or accrued interest to account for delay in establishing the amount of compensation, that proportion is not capital in nature and would not be covered by S.51(2).

IR TRUSTS – EDINBURGH

IR Trusts – Edinburgh is part of the new Inland Revenue Trusts Business Stream created in April 2001. We deal with CGT and income tax aspects for all estates in administration valued at over £400,000 (excluding cases where there is a continuing trust, which are dealt with by the appropriate Trust Office).

Here are a few of the questions we are most frequently asked:

1)   **Can I make a voluntary payment?**

Yes, as long as:

- No form SA900 has been issued.

- The liability for the whole of the Administration Period is fully met by one payment.

- The total liability of the estate is less than £10,000.

- **The payment is accompanied by a simple calculation showing details of the charge.**

In all other cases we would expect you to complete a Trust & Estate Return.

2)   **What forms do we send out?**

- SA 900 (Trust & Estate Tax Return). This form is designed to let personal representatives self assess their liability.

- 922 (Statement of Residuary Income). Personal representatives use this to let us know how the residuary income has been calculated, and we use it to determine how much income the beneficiaries should be returning.

3) **When does the administration period end?**

The administration period ends when the residue has been ascertained and the personal representatives are able to either distribute the estate or hand it over to a body of trustees. In practice we may use the date to which final estate accounts are drawn up as the date of completion but this will depend on individual circumstances. We do not need either returns or forms 922 for the estate for any period after the administration has ended.

If you need additional help or guidance on these or any other subjects please either:

Contact our Administration Period helpline on 0131 777 4030, visit our website at http://home.inrev.gov.uk/inlandrevenue /trusts/index.htm or write to us direct at IR Trusts – Edinburgh, Meldrum House, 15 Drumsheugh Gardens, Edinburgh, EH3 7UB (or DX 542000).

SHARES VALUATION

Most practitioners will be familiar with Shares Valuation (SV) but its name can lead to a misunderstanding of its role.

People in SV, like our Inheritance Tax caseworkers, are part of IR Capital Taxes and (as Shares Valuation Division or SVD) were part of the old Capital Taxes Office.

What SV Does In spite of its name, SV does not deal with the valuation of quoted shares and securities, except in relation to shares in foreign companies. The majority of valuation requests reaching SV are actually for CGT or share option scheme purposes. In relation to IHT, its main role is to consider, in conjunction with technical group colleagues where the issue is contentious, whether Business Relief is available on unquoted shares and, if not, to value them. For death estates, if form D14 is fully completed, it may well be unnecessary for SV to write to you, as the information on the form and our internal check of Companies House records may well be sufficient for us to agree that Business Relief is due. For non-death transfers, we try to use internal resources to the maximum to determine whether Business Relief is due. However, for both death and non-death transfers, we may have to write to you to seek information which will enable us to determine whether the conditions for relief are satisfied.

Once we are satisfied that Business Relief is due, we will confirm the position for the IHT caseworker and, if we have written to you, also to yourself. If, once all the necessary information has been gathered, we consider that Business Relief is not due in full, we will write explaining our reasons. Where Business Relief is not due, for instance because the company is an investment company, we will need to consider and, if necessary, negotiate a value with you or any other agent appointed by the taxpayer.

If a valuation needs to be agreed, we aim to reach an agreement as soon as possible. However, share valuation is not an exact science and differences of opinion can sometimes result in lengthy negotiations. Once we have all the information we need to formulate an opinion of value, we will, if at all possible, put a reasoned valuation to you.

We aim to use all means to reach an agreement, whether a letter, a telephone call or a face-to-face meeting is most appropriate. If you think a meeting would help to resolve an issue with SV, please let us know.

What are SVs Targets? Shares Valuers have similar targets to their IHT colleagues for dealing with correspondence. We aim to reply substantively to 82% of correspondence within 15 working days and to 98% within 40 working days. We also aim to settle 83.5% of cases within twelve months and we carefully monitor old cases to ensure that they are settled as quickly as possible.

What does SV value apart from unquoted shares? SV have specialists who consider the value of foreign assets of any kind (quoted foreign shares and foreign immovable property are two examples), goodwill, intellectual property, copyrights, ships, bloodstock, livestock and underwriting interests. The IHT caseworker may call upon the expertise of these specialists as necessary.

SV's Customer Service Facilities If you have a general query regarding any of the activities undertaken by SV, you can telephone the SV Helpline on 0115 974 2222. The SV Foreign Helpline is 0115 974 2300 and the helpline in our Edinburgh Office is 0131 777 4180.

If you are dissatisfied with the service provided by Shares Valuation, please tell the SV valuer concerned in the first instance. If you remain dissatisfied or if you have a complaint or comment of wider significance, our SV Customer Service Manager, Bob Cartwright (telephone 0115 974 2374), would be pleased to hear from you.

S.142 IHTA — DEEDS OF VARIATION AND THE REAL WORLD

It is perhaps not immediately obvious that a variation must be implemented in the real world. S. 17(a) IHTA expressly provides that a variation or disclaimer to which s. 142(1) applies is not a transfer of value, so the instrument in writing must be more than an empty piece of paper. That provision and s.142, in previous incarnations, were in effect a form of relief from double charges under the CTT regime. It is a pre-requisite if the provisions are to have any impact that a 'real life' disposition or transfer took place, so that the transferor can decide whether or not to make an election in order to trigger the deeming provisions.

As Mr R T Oerton put it in Capital Tax Planning July 1992 'In the real world of property law, where questions about ownership and the transfer of ownership are decided, the deceased does not make the changes: the beneficiaries do. And the deceased cannot be deemed in the true world to bring about effects which the beneficiaries cannot, or do not, bring about in the real world'.

Let us take the situation in which, under the will of A, B has an interest in possession in settled property, and on its cesser the beneficial interest in possession passes to C. In other words A leaves a life interest in property to B, with remainder to C. Following B's death within two years of A, C makes a deed of variation – still within that two year period – which purports to vary the will of A by redirecting B's interest to C or to extinguish it totally. In the real world B's interest does not exist, there is nothing for the deed to bite upon, and so s.142 simply cannot apply. If the situation had been that it was possible for B's executors to disclaim his life interest as a matter of general law, then that should fall within the protection of s.142.

It has been found that some of these inoperative deeds have been accepted as effective variations. The inconsistency of treatment is regretted, and assurances that have been given in the past will be binding upon the Revenue.

CHANGES TO OUR FORMS

IHT100 & IHT101 We are reviewing forms IHT100 and IHT101. These forms are used mainly to account for lifetime transfers and charges relating to non-interest in possession settlements.

As with the redesigned IHT200, the aim of the redesign will be to enable taxpayers and practitioners to provide as much information as possible that might be relevant in determining the amount of tax payable.

We will be consulting practitioners about the new forms and piloting them during the Spring and Summer 2002 and we are seeking volunteers to participate in this pilot.

If anyone is interested in helping they should contact Ted Watts on 0115 974 2755.

CAP D3 & CAP D1 We are also working to amalgamate the Corrective Account (form Cap D3) and the Corrective Inventory (form Cap D1). All being well, we hope to be in a position to consult with professional bodies in early 2002.

APRIL 2002. – INLAND REVENUE TAX BULLETIN ISSUE 58

MISCELLANEOUS

Inheritance Tax Concession Extended to Include Further Wartime Compensation Payments The revised version of extra-statutory concession F20, published on the IR website on 13 March 2000 reflects the addition of further schemes anticipated in the text of the 16 October 2001 version. The common theme is that these payments are made in modest amounts and is compensation for personal hurt or injury rather than property loss. The text of the announcement is reproduced below.

Inheritance Tax: Wartime Compensation Payments Ministers have agreed to requests to extend extra-statutory concession F20 from today, 13 March 2002, to include further schemes which compensate original victims or their spouses for the personal hurt suffered at the hands of the National Socialist regime during World War II. Claims in respect of the German Public Law foundation "Remembrance, Responsibility and Future" and Holocaust Victim Assets Litigation (Swiss Bank Settlement) are being dealt with for non-Jewish claimants by the International Organisation for Migration, and for Jewish claimants by the Conference on Jewish Material Claims against Germany. Claimants entitled to the concession in respect of these claims are being advised by the relevant organisation at the time of their successful claim. The extended concession aligns these payments with comparable ex-gratia amounts from the UK Government to British groups held prisoner by the Japanese during World War II.

Under the present inheritance tax (IHT) rules, rights to such compensation, or the subsequent proceeds, could form part of the claimant's estate for IHT purposes. Extra-statutory concession (F20) allows the amount of any compensation payment to be deducted from the claimant's IHT chargeable estate, whether the payment is made to the claimant before their death or is made subsequently to their personal representatives.

The revised text of the concession is detailed below.

F20. Late Compensation for World War II Claims Schemes continue to be established in the UK and abroad which provide compensation for wrongs suffered during the World War II era. When this is received by the original victim or their surviving spouse, this almost inevitably comes late in life when their plans for the disposal of their wealth have already been made. Ministers have agreed that the cash value of these claims may be excluded from inheritance tax in the following cases where compensation is paid in modest round-sum, or otherwise cash-limited, amounts:

- single ex-gratia lump sums of £10,000 payable to each surviving member of the British groups-or their surviving spouse-interned or imprisoned by the Japanese during World War II as announced by the Government on 7 November 2000;

- financial compensation of fixed amounts payable from the German foundation "Remembrance, Responsibility and Future" or the Austrian Reconciliation Fund to claimants-or their surviving spouse-who were slave or forced labourers or other victims of the National Socialist regime during the World War II;

- financial compensation of $1,000 payable from the Holocaust Victim Assets Litigation (Swiss Bank Settlement) to each of the slave or forced labourers qualifying under the aforementioned German foundation scheme;

- financial compensation by way of fixed amounts to the victim or their surviving spouse from the Swiss Refugee Programme;

- financial compensation by way of fixed amounts to the victim or their surviving spouse from Stichting Maror-Gelden Overheid (Dutch Maror); and

- financial compensation by way of a one-time payment to the victim or their surviving spouse from the following:

  - monies allocated by the Federal German Government (the Hardship Fund);

  - the Austrian National Fund for Victims of Nazi Persecution;

  - the French Orphan Scheme.

Payments of this kind would normally increase the value of a deceased person's chargeable estate at death, either because a claim paid in their lifetime has increased their total assets, or because the right to a claim not yet paid is itself an asset of their estate.

By concession, where such a payment has been received at any time, either by the deceased or his or her personal representatives under the arrangements, the amount of the payment may be left out of account in determining the chargeable value of his or her estate for the purposes of inheritance tax on death. Similarly, where a person qualifies for more than one payment then each amount may be left out of account.

All enquiries about this extra-statutory concession in particular cases (quoting the full name and date of death of the deceased plus the Inland Revenue Capital Taxes reference number if known) should be directed to: Inland Revenue Capital Taxes – IHT Ferrers House PO Box 38
Castle Meadow Road Nottingham NG2 1BB

For members of the DX system: Inland Revenue Capital Taxes DX 701201 Nottingham.

APRIL/MAY 2002. – IHT NEWSLETTER

INTRODUCTION

Welcome to the latest edition of our IHT Newsletter. We are sorry that it has been slightly delayed, but we had to wait a liitle longer for the Budget this year. We think that you might find the article on page 2, about some proposals in this year's Finance Bill in connection with Instruments of Variation, particularly interesting.

Our new Assistant Director joined us in November. Anne King has taken over the job previously done by Trevor Plumb, who many of you will remember. Anne's responsibilities include all Customer Service and processing matters in connection with inheritance tax, including the IHT Helpline.

The next edition of the Newsletter will be August 2002.

INSTRUMENTS OF VARIATION (IOVS)

This year's Finance Bill contains some proposals that remove the need to deliver an election before an IoV can have effect for IHT/CGT purposes. Please note that this change only applies to IoVs executed after **1 August 2002**; the existing requirements of s 142(2) and s 62(7) continue to apply to all IoVs executed before that date.

At present, you need to send all IoVs to us where the parties to the Instrument elect that the provisions of s 142(1) and/or s 62(6) apply, irrespective of whether there are any immediate tax consequences. This places an unnecessary burden on taxpayers and is costly for us.

Under the proposals, the IoV will have effect for IHT and/or CGT purposes if it contains a statement of intent, made by the parties to the IoV, that the provisions of s 142(1) and/or s 62(6) should apply. Elections are abolished and you only need to send the IoV to us where it has an immediate effect – usually on the inheritance tax payable.

We will be revising our leaflets about IoVs to reflect this change and will be providing a checklist that you may wish to use to help make sure that an IoV meets the requirements of s 142 and/or s 62.

REVIEW OF FORMS IHT100 & IHT101

In December's *Newsletter* we announced that we are redesigning forms IHT100 and IHT101. These forms are used mainly to account for lifetime transfers and charges relating to non-interest in possession trusts.

We have now started to pilot new forms and to consult practitioners about them. This process will last until the autumn.

If any practitioners would like to take part in the pilot or find out more about the new forms, they should contact Ted Watts on 0115 974 2755.

SEPTEMBER 11TH: INHERITANCE TAX CONSEQUENCES

We have been asked about IHT treatment of estates of UK victims of September 11, particularly given the large compensation payments that are now being finalised.

There is no explicit IHT relief for civilian casualties of events like these; but the compensation payments themselves are not subject to IHT. The Victim's Compensation Fund of 2001 was established by US legislation as an alternative to any legal proceedings that the victims' estates could take under the law as it stood on September 11. Since the legislation was not passed until after September 11, claims under the compensation fund have no value at that date for IHT purposes.

The value of any "underlying" legal claims (i.e. under the law as it stood on September 11) is in principle chargeable to IHT. But our US advisors have told us that this value is in practice negligible. So, in effect substantial parts of victims' estates will not be subject to IHT. If any practitioner acting for the estate of a victim has not already been in touch with us, we would invite them to do so.

IHT200 UPDATE

Some of the main reasons for introducing the new IHT200 were to help taxpayers deliver a full and complete account at the outset, and to cut down unnecessary correspondence later. Most accounts are completed very well. However, we do sometimes find that not all of the questions on the supplementary pages to the account are being answered fully.

Module D1 – the will As well as replying to the questions, please could you also attach a copy of the will you are submitting to probate, unless the gross value of the estate is below the inheritance tax threshold and no instrument of variation is anticipated.

Module D2 – domicile outside the United Kingdom Please use box 6 on the reverse of the form to provide a rough guide to the deceased's worldwide estate. The value of this will obviously have a big impact on the extent to which we need to consider the question of domicile.

Module D3 – gifts and other transfers of value You do not need to list outright gifts between individuals which are covered by exemptions. But you do need to include payments by the deceased of insurance premiums on a policy for the benefit of another, which are usually made to the policy trustees or the insurance company. Please therefore give details of these payments on form D3, even if you are claiming exemption as normal expenditure out of income. If the deceased was paying monthly premiums you can give one figure for each year's worth of premiums. Please could you also provide copies of the policies and related documentation in all of these cases.

Module D4 – joint and nominated assets We need all of the information that is requested on this form before we can agree the extent of the deceased's interest in jointly owned assets. We have had particular problems with people not answering all the questions on D4. This is one way to make sure that we select your case for enquiry!

Module D6 – pensions Question 2 asks for details where a lump sum is payable under a pension scheme or a personal pension policy as a result of the deceased's death. If this was payable at the trustees' discretion, please could you provide a letter from the company, or a copy of the relevant part of the policy or scheme rules, to confirm this.

Module D9 – life assurance and annuities Section 2 asks for details where the deceased was entitled to benefit from a life insurance policy that does not pay out following their death. If you answer 'yes' to either question 2a or 2b, you should include the value of the deceased's interest in the policy as provided by the insurance company. Please could you also remember to provide a copy of the insurance policy.

Module D12 – land, buildings and interests in land Section 1 asks for details of the person the District Valuer should contact, and you often give the name and address of your own valuers. This is fine if you have already instructed your valuers to negotiate with the DV. In many instances, that is not the case – and the DV tells us that they can often sort out minor problems with you – so we recommend that you include your own details in this box.

Module D13 – agricultural relief We are still receiving vague descriptions of the agricultural activities carried out on farms. The answers 'general farming' or 'grazing' will ensure that the case is picked for enquiry, so please could you answer the character appropriate question on page 2 for each residential property on the farm individually.

Thank you for your co-operation on these points – it will help to increase the number of estates that we can accept on delivery.

INHERITANCE TAX – WARTIME COMPENSATION PAYMENTS

In drawing up the changes below we worked very closely with the organisations to ensure that people who benefit from this special concession are aware of it. Most of these further schemes are non-UK schemes and almost all claimants will not be liable to IHT. The original basis of the concession still applies, i.e. it covers modest payments for personal injury – property claims are not included – paid to elderly " first generation claimants". The effect of the concession is to give extra relief from IHT for the amount of the compensation payment for every eligible claimant, whether paid to them or their personal representatives. The text published on the IR website follows.

Ministers have agreed to requests to extend extra-statutory concession F20 from today, 13 March 2002, to include further schemes which compensate original victims or their spouses for the personal hurt suffered at the hands of the National Socialist regime during World War II. Claims in respect of the German Public Law foundation "Remembrance, Responsibility and Future" and Holocaust Victim Assets Litigation (Swiss Bank Settlement) are being dealt with for non-Jewish claimants by the International Organisation for Migration, and for Jewish claimants by the Conference on Jewish Material Claims against Germany. Claimants entitled to the concession in respect of these claims are being advised by the relevant organisation at the time of their successful claim. The extended concession aligns these payments with comparable ex-gratia amounts from the UK Government to British groups held prisoner by the Japanese during World War II.

Under the present inheritance tax (IHT) rules, rights to such compensation, or the subsequent proceeds, could form part of the claimant's estate for IHT purposes. Extra-statutory concession (F20) allows the amount of any compensation payment to be deducted from the claimant's IHT chargeable estate, whether the payment is made to the claimant before their death or is made subsequently to their personal representatives.

The revised text of the concession is detailed below.

F20. Late Compensation for World War II Claims Schemes continue to be established in the UK and abroad which provide compensation for wrongs suffered during the World War II era. When this is received by the original victim or their surviving spouse, this almost inevitably comes late in life when their plans for the disposal of their wealth have already been made. Ministers have agreed that the cash value of these claims may be excluded from inheritance tax in the following cases where compensation is paid in modest round-sum, or otherwise cash-limited, amounts:

- single ex-gratia lump sums of £10,000 payable to each surviving member of the British groups-or their surviving spouse-interned or imprisoned by the Japanese during World War II as announced by the Government on 7 November 2000;

- financial compensation of fixed amounts payable from the German foundation "Remembrance, Responsibility and Future" or the Austrian Reconciliation Fund to claimants-or their surviving spouse-who were slave or forced labourers or other victims of the National Socialist regime during the World War II;

- financial compensation of $1,000 payable from the Holocaust Victim Assets Litigation (Swiss Bank Settlement) to each of the slave or forced labourers qualifying under the aforementioned German foundation scheme;

- financial compensation by way of fixed amounts to the victim or their surviving spouse from the Swiss Refugee Programme;

- financial compensation by way of fixed amounts to the victim or their surviving spouse from Stichting Maror-Gelden Overheid (Dutch Maror); and

- financial compensation by way of a one-time payment to the victim or their surviving spouse from the following:

  - monies allocated by the Federal German Government (the Hardship Fund);

  - the Austrian National Fund for Victims of Nazi Persecution;

  - the French Orphan Scheme.

Payments of this kind would normally increase the value of a deceased person's chargeable estate at death, either because a claim paid in their lifetime has increased their total assets, or because the right to a claim not yet paid is itself an asset of their estate.

By concession, where such a payment has been received at any time, either by the deceased or his or her personal representatives under the arrangements, the amount of the payment may be left out of account in determining the chargeable value of his or her estate for the purposes of inheritance tax on death. Similarly, where a person qualifies for more than one payment then each amount may be left out of account.

All enquiries about this extra-statutory concession in particular cases (quoting the full name and date of death of the deceased plus the Inland Revenue Capital Taxes reference number if known) should be directed to Capital Taxes at Nottingham.

S.142 IHTA 84 – YOUR QUESTIONS ANSWERED

We have received some post in response to an article in our last Newsletter – "S.142A IHTA – Deeds of Variation and the Real World". We thought that it would be useful to reproduce some of the letters that we received and give our responses to them.

Q: With regards to your article "S.142A Deeds of Variation and the Real World", it would appear that in a situation where A dies leaving his estate outright to his widow B, who dies within two years leaving her estate to her children, your view is now that a Deed of variation redirecting the estate to the children would be ineffective. Is this correct?

A: The example you give in your letter is one where an absolute interest is given to the survivor. On the death of the survivor, the property inherited on the first death still exists in the survivor's estate and it is therefore possible, in the real world, for those inheriting on the second death to redirect the estate of the first to die. Contrast this with the example given in our Newsletter where, on the first death, the survivor is given a life interest in property. That interest is extinguished on the death of the survivor, so that when, in the real world, those inheriting on the second death come to consider a variation, there is nothing for the variation to bite on.

Q: We have recently received your Newsletter and note in particular your comments in S.142A IHTA 1984 – Deed of Variation and the real world. We do not understand your comments in the example you give re: the life interest. You say that B's life interest does not exist because "there is nothing for the deed to bite upon". Surely a) the interest exists until the variation b) it is a type of property which can be disposed of by B (or his Personal Representatives) at any time up to the Deed of Variation.

A: As the variation was made after the death of the life tenant there was then no life interest in existence. Whilst such an interest is capable of disposition by the life tenant, the fact that it ceases on his death means that it is not capable of being disposed of after that has occurred.

MAY 2002. – SPECIAL EDITION IHT NEWSLETTER

ESTIMATED VALUATIONS IN INHERITANCE TAX CASES

A recent decision of the Special Commissioner in Edinburgh on the application of Inheritance Tax Act 1984 sections 216(3A) and 247 has highlighted certain issues which will be of interest to those acting as personal representatives or their advisers.

The key facts of the case are as follows. Mrs Stanley died on 10 October 1999. Her will appointed Mr Robertson, a solicitor, as one of her executors. Mrs Stanley's estate included a house in Scotland ("Ingleside") and a cottage in England ("Jeffs"). Ingleside was left to the Church of Scotland who wished to have the property sold quickly so as to prevent it from deteriorating during the winter months. It was Mr Robertson's practice only to advertise property for sale once he had applied for Confirmation (the equivalent of Grant of Probate in English law). This practice ensures that the executors have full title to complete a sale of the property.

In late November 1999 Mr Robertson submitted an Inventory of Mrs Stanley's estate to the Capital Taxes Office ("CTO") and also to the appropriate Scottish authority to obtain Confirmation. The Inventory contained values of £50,623 for Jeffs and £5,000 for the contents of Ingleside. These values were clearly identified as estimates. Mr Robertson made these estimates himself and they were provisional on receiving expert advice. In early January 2000, Mr Robertson submitted revised (and substantially higher) valuations for this property to the CTO. These later valuations were made by suitable professional experts and were accepted by the Revenue for purposes of determining the Inheritance Tax due.

Section 216(3A) of the Inheritance Tax Act 1984 allows a personal representatives who, after making the fullest enquiries that are reasonably practicable in the circumstances, is unable to ascertain the exact value of any particular property to submit instead a provisional estimate of its value. at the same time the personal representative must give an undertaking to deliver a further account of the property as soon as its value is ascertained. The Special Commissioner accepted that in this case Mr Robertson acted appropriately in submitting estimated values in the original Inventory in order that the sale of Ingleside could proceed as quickly as possible.

The Special Commissioner also approved of other aspects of Mr Robertson's conduct of this matter. In particular the fact that he recognised that he did not have sufficient expertise to make final valuations of either Jeffs or the contents of Ingleside (which contained some valuable pieces). He therefore instructed appropriate professionals to carry out these valuations which were promptly forwarded to the CTO once they became available.

The Special Commissioner observed that the Revenue form that Mr Robertson had used when he submitted the initial Inventory (Cap A3) did not contain an express declaration to the effect that where estimates are supplied the personal representative undertakes to provide exact valuations as soon as practicable. Form Cap A3 has now been replaced by form IHT 200 which already incorporates a printed declaration along the lines of the one suggested by the Special Commissioner.

The Revenue is keen to provide assistance to personal representatives to enable them to fulfil their obligations without incurring penalties. In most circumstances we would expect the exact value of the property to be given when form IHT 200 is submitted and not merely an estimate. However we accept that if there is a proven need to obtain a grant urgently personal representatives may find themselves in a position where they think that they need to submit an estimated account of the value of a particular item of property. In such circumstances they should ensure that they have made the fullest enquiries that are reasonably practicable before doing so, and the estimate should be as accurate as possible. The Personal Representative should, for example, contact the professional who is going to value the property formally to ensure that the estimate is a reasonable one.

The Revenue is more than happy to discuss the circumstances of particular cases with personal representatives and their agents. If you would like further guidance from us, please let us have the details by fax on 0115 974 3045, or write to us at our Nottingham address.

Inland Revenue Capital Taxes Office, Ferrers House, PO Box 38, Castle Meadow Road, Nottingham NG2 1BB

DX 701201 Nottingham 4

AUGUST 2002. – IHT NEWSLETTER

INTRODUCTION

Welcome to the latest edition of the IHT Newsletter.

This Newsletter is larger than usual because it contains a lot of important information about changes to the excepted estates regulations. It also includes more information about the new requirements in connection with instruments of variation.

Please do take the time to read carefully through this Newsletter. If you have any questions at all, then please contact our Customer Service team at our Nottingham address.

DOWNLOADING FORMS FROM THE INTERNET

Many of our forms can be downloaded from the Internet-but hitherto you needed to have the full version of Adobe Acrobat on your computer to be able to save a copy of the completed forms on your hard disk. Some of you may have found the cost (£200+) prohibitive.

Adobe has now released Acrobat Approval, which is effectively Acrobat Reader with a save facility. This retails at less than £50, which you may find more affordable if you want to use and save our forms electronically.

EXCEPTED ESTATES

As part of our drive to keep down the costs of compliance, we have made some changes to the excepted estates regulations. As well as increasing the monetary limits, we have listened to feedback from the professions and have extended the scope of the regulations. For the first time now, estates where the deceased had a life interest in a small trust can qualify, as can those where a lifetime gift of the home has been made. And we have further extended the regulations to include the small UK estates of overseas investors. Altogether, we estimate that around 7,000 more estates will be excepted from delivering an account.

The regulations are contained in the Inheritance Tax (Delivery of Accounts) (Excepted Estates) Regulations 2002 (SI 2002 No. 1733). These come into effect on 1 August 2002 in respect of deaths occurring on or after 6 April 2002.

Our leaflet IHT12 (or IHT12 (S) for Scotland) contains more detail and some flowcharts to take you through the new conditions. You can get the leaflet from our stationery Orderline or the Revenue website. And we have reproduced the new conditions at the end of this article. But first, there are two important practical consequences that we need to highlight.

1. Previously an account was needed whenever the deceased died entitled to a life interest in settled property, so many trustees sent in their account as soon as they had been notified of the death-and well before the deceased's Free Estate has been quantified. Now, where an estate includes a small trust, the trustees may not need to deliver an account.

    So, we recommend that trustees should contact the personal representatives or their agents to find out whether or not the estate as a whole qualifies as an excepted estate, because if it does, there will be no need for any accounts to be delivered at all.

    But, if you are acting for the trustees of a small trust and you are certain that the estate as a whole will not qualify as an excepted estate, you are welcome to send in your account as soon as you wish. Please do make it clear in your covering letter that you know that the estate as a whole will not be an excepted estate.

Accounts from overseas investors

2. If you are acting for the executors of an overseas investor whose estate qualifies as an excepted estate, there is no longer any need to deliver an account. In England & Wales and Northern Ireland there will be no form D18 to be endorsed for domicile before you apply for a grant. You can apply for excepted estate grant in the same way as someone with a "UK" domicile, but as the deceased's domicile will be shown as overseas, please remember to use the £100,000 limit for the value of the gross estate and not £220,000.

The New Rules To qualify as an excepted estate, the conditions that must be met depend on the domicile of the deceased. In either case below, **all** the conditions must be fulfilled.

1. If the deceased died domiciled in the United Kingdom, the estate will qualify as an excepted estate where

    •   the gross value of the estate, including the deceased's share of any jointly owned assets (whether passing by survivorship or under the will) and any 'specified transfers' does not exceed £220,000, **and**

    •   if the estate includes assets held in trust, they are held in a single trust and their gross value does not exceed £100,000, **and**

    •   if the estate has foreign assets, their gross value does not exceed £75,000, **and**

    •   if there are any 'specified transfers', their gross value does not exceed £100,000, **and**

    •   the deceased had not made a gift with reservation of benefit.

    'Specified transfers' are chargeable transfers of

    •   cash, or

    •   quoted shares or securities or

    •   land and buildings (and contents given with them) transferred from one individual to another; but only where the donor did not retain any interest or benefit in the assets given away.

2. If the deceased died domiciled outside the United Kingdom, the estate will qualify as an excepted estate where

    •   the deceased's UK estate consists **only** of cash or quoted shares or securities passing under a Will or intestacy or by survivorship and the gross value does not exceed £100,000, **and**

    •   the deceased has never been domiciled in the United Kingdom, nor treated as domiciled in the United Kingdom.

    And finally, a reminder. When you are working out whether or not the overall limit of £220,000 is exceeded, please remember to add up the total of

    •   assets which pass under the deceased's Will or intestacy,

    •   the deceased's beneficial interest in any joint assets, including assets passing by survivorship, even if they are exempt,

    •   assets held in trust in which the deceased had an interest in possession,

    •   nominated assets, and

    •   specified transfers.

PRACTICE DIRECTION OF 22 MARCH 2002

The President of the Family Division issued a Practice Direction in March this year that changed the requirement regarding the net value of an excepted estate in England & Wales. With effect from 15 April 2002, the net value of an excepted estate must be rounded up to the next whole thousand, and expressed as "not exceeding £....". Feedback received by the Court Service suggests that this change has been taken to mean that an "accurate" valuation of land and buildings is now necessary, which increases costs and delay.

When personal representatives (prs) deliver a full Inland Revenue Account, we expect them to have made full and diligent enquiries so that their account includes, to the best of their knowledge and belief, all appropriate property and the value of that property, ascertained in accordance with s.160 IHTA. We do not insist on a professional valuation for land and buildings-or any other assets for that matter-it is up to the prs to judge whether or not they need to retain a professional valuer in order to satisfactorily fulfil their statutory obligations, bearing in mind the nature of the asset and the extent of their own expertise.

We expect prs to apply the same standard when they are establishing whether or not an estate meets the excepted estate criteria. That means considering the need for a valuer whenever the prs' preliminary estimate puts the overall gross estate nearer to the £220,000 limit. And we expect prs to make a realistic estimate rather than use a nominal value whatever the size of the gross estate. But if the gross value of the estate (as defined in the previous article) is clearly going to be well below the overall limit, it would be quite acceptable for prs to adopt their own realistic estimate as the value for any of the assets. All this assumes that there are no non-tax reasons why prs do not need to establish precise values.

JOINT PROPERTY – A REMINDER

We continue to see estates where joint property – particularly that passing by survivorship-is not included. Whilst a grant of representation is not needed to deal with survivorship property, the assets are still "appropriate property" under s.216(3) and must be included in **every** estate when working out the aggregate chargeable transfer. The executors run a very real risk of incurring a penalty if joint assets are omitted from their account of the estate.

One of the most common reasons for us to investigate a case where a grant has been taken out under the excepted estate procedures is because joint property has been excluded. We hope that the articles in this newsletter and this reminder have made it abundantly clear that you must **always** take the deceased's share of all jointly owned assets into account. This applies both when you are working out whether the estate qualifies as an excepted asset and when a full account is needed. And it applies whether the jointly owned assets pass by survivorship or not.

EXCEPTED SETTLEMENTS

We have received representations about the need for trustees of discretionary trusts to deliver an account in circumstances where the trust property has never been more than a nominal amount. In response to this, the Board has made regulations that will except such "pilot" trusts from delivering an account.

The regulations are contained in the Inheritance Tax (Delivery of Accounts) (Excepted Settlements) Regulations 2002 (SI 2002 No. 1732). These come into effect on 1 August 2002 in respect of chargeable events occurring on or after 6 April 2002.

To qualify as an excepted settlement, **all** the conditions below must be fulfilled

• the trust has been created by a gift of cash to UK resident trustees who have remained resident for the duration of the trust,

• no interest in possession exists in the trust property,

• the trust assets are held in cash throughout,

• no additions of capital are made,

• no other trusts were created by the settlor on same day, and

• the total value of the trust assets at the same time of the chargeable event is less than £1,000.

WARTIME COMPENSATION PAYMENTS

We published details about ESC F20 in our last Newsletter. We understand that payments are continuing to be made under the schemes covered by this concession. Remember, the full text is in Tax Bulletin 58 and on our website.

INSTRUMENTS OF VARIATION (IOVS)

Our April Newsletter told you about proposals contained in the Finance Bill 2002 that do away with the need to deliver an election before an IoV can take effect for IHT/CGT purposes. The proposals remain unchanged after consideration by Parliament and should be law by the time you receive this Newsletter. **This means that in most cases, you will no longer need to send IoVs to us.** Any IoVs executed on or after 1 August 2002 that are sent to us and which have no immediate tax consequences will be returned without comment.

We have rewritten our booklet about IoVs (IHT8) and you will be able to download a copy of it from the Revenue website from 1 August. Unfortunately, for reasons beyond our control, the paper version of the booklet will not be available immediately.

As we will no longer see the vast majority of IoVs, we have prepared a checklist to help you make sure that your document will meet our requirements, should your clients want the IoV to take effect for tax purposes. It is form IOV2 and the notes on the reverse of the form repeat the key points from IHT8. The form is available from our stationery Orderline and a version that can be filled in on screen using Adobe Acrobat software is available from the Revenue website.

If an IoV alters the amount of IHT that is payable by an estate, you **will** still need to send the IoV to us-and if it increases the tax, you must send it to us **within six months**. If you have used the checklist please send a copy of that too, as it will help us to review your IoV more quickly. In all other cases, the signatories should retain the IoV or a copy in case it is needed in the future.

Finally, if you have delivered a "reduced account" and included exempt assets at the prs' own estimate of their value, those values will need to be reviewed-and if necessary corrected if the assets are redirected so as to become chargeable. After 1 August 2002, you should deliver a corrective account updating the open market value of those assets **only** where tax is at stake and you need to deliver the IoV (as explained in the previous paragraph). Please bear in mind that if a variation increases the chargeable estate but still keeps it below the tax threshold, you do not need to send the IoV (or corrective account) to us. But when working out whether or not a proposed variation will affect the amount of IHT that is payable, you will need to remember that the values initially given in a reduced account may have been approximate.

FEEDBACK FOR PRACTITIONERS

Extending the rules for both excepted estates and the new rules for IoVs will reduce compliance costs for both the Revenue and the taxpayer-but only if we can maximise take-up. To help with this we will be changing the way we deal with accounts or IoVs that are sent to us unnecessarily. In the future, we will be returning accounts or IoVs, with an explanation why they are not required where

- the trustees deliver an account for a small trust, but it is not clear whether the estate as a whole might qualify as an excepted estate,

- a full IHT200 is delivered, but the estate nevertheless qualifies as an excepted estate, or

- we receive an IoV executed after 1 August 2002 which has no immediate IHT consequences.

We hope that this service will help you to streamline your work and reduce costs for all concerned.

Also, it is common to see a Will or IoV drafted so that "all such property, after taking into account gifts made in my lifetime and other property liable to IHT, up to the value of the IHT threshold shall pass to chargeable beneficiaries". The residue then passes to an exempt beneficiary, usually the spouse. Such a bequest is often referred to as a "nil rate band legacy".

If the Will or IoV has been written in this way, there can be no immediate IHT consequences unless there are lifetime gifts with a value over the threshold or other aggregable property exceeding the threshold. We will not enter into discussions about the availability of reliefs, exemptions or values where there are no immediate IHT consequences, including "nil rate band legacy" cases. Where an IoV is written in this way and there can be no immediate IHT consequences we will not need to see it.

CORRECTIVE ACCOUNT

Our December 2000 Newsletter told you that we were revising our Corrective Account-form Cap D3 and (in Scotland) forms Cap D1 and C4. We have amalgamated the three forms to give one Corrective Account, form C4, that can now be used throughout the UK. There is a continuation sheet, form C4(C), and a supplement, form C4 (S), that addresses the particular requirements of Confirmation and Recording in Scotland.

The new forms will come into use on 1 August and are available from our stationery Orderline. Versions that can be filled in on screen using Adobe Acrobat software can be downloaded from the Revenue website.

During our consultations about the new corrective account, practitioners expressed concerns about the need to file a formal corrective account where we presently accept notification of amendments by letter. We do not expect this practice to change. Where there are a small number of amendments, or the overall change in value is not significant, we are happy to accept notification by letter.

Where there are a number of changes or the change in value is significant, it is preferable to use a corrective account-and we reserve the right to call for a formal corrective account in any estate where we feel this is necessary. And, in Scotland, a corrective Inventory will always be required whenever an Eik to Confirmation is necessary.

GUARANTEED ANNUITIES

If the deceased was receiving payments under an annuity and died before the end of the guarantee period, the right to receive the remainder of the payments is an asset of the estate. You should include the value of that right in answer to question 1 on form D6. We have produced some software to help you work out the open market value of the right to receive these remaining payments. You can download this from the Revenue website.

OLD FORMS

We will not be accepting the old version of form IHT200, or (in Scotland) the old Inventories A3, B3 and B4 after 1 October 2002. Please make sure that you only use the new forms for deaths after 18 March 1986. For deaths before that date, the appropriate CTT or Estate Duty forms should still be used.

PLANNED SERVICE IMPROVEMENTS

We are aiming continuously to improve our service. We normally achieve our published service standards but I am very aware that some of our standards provide a service that is less speedy than all of us would wish. I appreciate, too, that on some occasions a number of you have not been kept as well informed as you would like about the progress of our enquiries.

This can best be illustrated by an example: initial research and risk assessment may take two or three months, and the case may then require consideration by the District Valuer. The Valuer, within the terms of his service agreement with us, may respond agreeing the valuation submitted within six weeks. Allow a further three weeks for us to deal with the valuation, and it can be seen that we have met our service standard, but a simple case may none the less take up to six months to finalise. As we do not write to you specifically at each stage of this process, you will not always know in the interim what stage we have reached.

We do not think that this level of service is good enough, so we are looking at all sorts of ways to substantially reduce the timescale for finalising a simple case where further enquiries do not arise. This will involve faster referrals to the Valuer or Shares Valuation where appropriate, and the introduction of robust processes to make sure cases do not stall whilst individuals are on holiday, training or struggling with conflicting demands on their time. Our aim is to submit most necessary valuations to the Valuer within 10 working days of receipt of an account, and the Valuation Service are piloting a plan to substantially reduce the time taken to respond to us in cases where they do not think further enquiries are warranted. More generally, we intend to make better, more consistent, use of electronic communication.

I hope you will notice improved turnaround times shortly. In the meantime you will notice that our new processes mean that a case will not necessarily be worked by the same person for its duration. To ensure that improvements are achieved across the board teams rather than individuals will own cases. This should not cause any difficulty; all correspondence will carry an extension number and the person taking the call will be qualified to deal with it unless some particular technical problem presents itself. Your co-operation in discussing the case with whoever takes the call will be greatly appreciated. But if you do experience any problem please just ask to speak to the manager who will deal with the difficulty straight away. You will also notice that successive letters on a case will not necessarily be written by the same person.

Your support in helping us to introduce the new system smoothly will be greatly appreciated. The transition is taking place at the moment. And I hope we will be seeing the improvements we are trying to achieve within a very short period of time.

DECEMBER 2002. – IHT NEWSLETTER

INTRODUCTION

Welcome to the latest edition of the IHT Newsletter. You will find that it is slightly shorter than previous editions, but we are enclosing some additional material with it.

If we know that you have copies of our Practitioners Guide to completing the IHT200, we are enclosing some new amendments to it-see article opposite.

Also, we are enclosing a survey, which we hope that you will complete in connection with your dealings with Capital Taxes in the last twelve months-Anne King's article on page 3 gives more details.

The next edition of the Newsletter will be April 2003. In the meantime, we would like to wish you all a merry Christmas and a happy new year.

IHT215 — THE PRACTITIONERS GUIDE

We have issued some amendments to this guide. These include the revisions to D4/D9 for joint life policies, (see page 3) expand on what we expect personal representatives to take into account when valuing realty, along with some other minor changes. If we know you have copies of the guide, you should find these amendments enclosed with this newsletter – they are otherwise available on our Orderline or the Revenue website. If you do not receive any amendments with this newsletter and would like to do so in the future, please let our Customer Service team know.

CLEARANCE FOR TRUSTEES IN EXCEPTED ESTATES

In the August edition of our Newsletter, we told you about the new regulations for excepted estates. One of the changes was to include estates with a small trust within the definition of an excepted estate. From the feedback we have received you would like to know how we intend to apply the automatic clearance contained in the regulations to trustees. Much will hinge on co-operation and good communication between personal representatives and trustees (or their agents). We envisage the following steps to the process.

1.   Agents for trustees and personal representatives agree that an estate qualifies as an excepted estate – personal representatives apply for a grant.

2.   Trustees will need to know when the grant of representation is issued, and whether or not we have issued a notice requiring an account from the personal representatives within the prescribed period.

3.   If no account has been requested within the prescribed period, regulation 6 will apply and discharge trustees from any claim for tax. We consider that the automatic clearance operates in the same way as formal clearance under s 239. In other words, once the prescribed period has expired, trustees are entitled to rely on that clearance should, for example, an additional asset in the Free Estate come to light which gives rise to a tax liability.

4.   Where trustees know that we have asked for an account, we suggest that they write to us and seek confirmation that we accept that the estate does qualify as an excepted estate. We cannot issue formal clearance to trustees as they have not delivered an account, but we will be able to provide the confirmation requested, if appropriate. Trustees should **only** write to us for this confirmation **where they know that we have requested an account from the personal representatives.**

5   If, having requested an account from the representatives, we establish that the estate is not an excepted estate we will have to consider whether an account is required from trustees. We may dispense with this requirement if, for example, the estate is not an excepted estate, but exemption from IHT means that the estate cannot exceed the threshold. Each case will be considered on its facts and we will be able to let trustees know what is required when we reply to their latter mentioned in 4 above. If an account is required and subsequently delivered, we will be able to provide formal clearance on application from trustees in the usual way.

What if the deceased had a life interest in assets worth less than £100,000, but no grant is needed? This could happen, where the deceased's own assets are very small, or are all owned jointly.

To be aware of this situation, trustees must have been in contact with the deceased's representatives to know that the latter are not going to apply for a grant. And trustees will need to have satisfied themselves that the estate would not meet the other excepted estate provisions, including the cash limits before they can take the decision not to deliver an IHT100. Having made that decision, what protection will trustees have should it turn out that the estate is not an excepted estate – or IHT is due?

Without an account we cannot grant a formal clearance, and the automatic clearance will not apply because there is no event to start the 35-day period. In these circumstance, provided trustees can produce evidence that they made adequate enquiries to satisfy themselves that the estate qualifies as an excepted estate and that no account is otherwise required, we will not hold them accountable or liable for any tax should the position change at a later date.

IHT200 AND FORM D9

Our current guidance tells you to include the deceased's interest under a "joint life and survivor" policy at question 2 on form D9. In the majority of estates, this has no impact in establishing the chargeable estate, but in rare combination of circumstances it can result in the chargeable estate being overstated. To eliminate risk, we have changed form D9 and the instructions. Although we still refer to this sort of policy on form D9, you should, with immediate effect, include details of such policies and the value of the deceased's share on form D4 (Joint Property) as property passing by survivorship. The new form D9 is available from our Orderline or the Revenue website.

SCOTTISH JOINT PROPERTY – A REMINDER

Further to the article on Joint Property in the August 2002 edition, we would like to draw your attention to the position in Scots Law where bank or building society accounts are held in joint names *and the survivor.*

Under Scots Law the "survivorship destination" does not by itself pass the ownership of the funds in the account to the survivorship. An account with a bank or building society is not a document of title as it is not a Deed of Trust in terms of the Bank Bonds and Trusts Act 1696. Rather it is a contract between the bank and the customer which regulates the conditions on which the account is to be operated and is for administrative convenience only. See for example: – *Cairns v Davidson 1913 S.C. 1054*

The result is therefore that the question of the ownership of the funds in the account falls to be determined according to the ordinary principles of ownership. The owner of the funds deposited in the account remains the owner unless and until some transfer of ownership has occurred.

So where a husband and wife open account, governed by Scots Law, in their joint names and the survivor, and the husband has provided the whole funds, then on his death survived by his wife: –

- Include the whole account on the supplementary page D2 of the IHT200.

- Enter the total in Box JP1 on the D4 and carry that figure forward to section F8 on page 3 of the IHT200.

- List any liabilities, enter the total in Box JP2 on D4 and carry that figure forward to the liabilities section on page 4 of the IHT200.

- Do not complete boxes JP3, 4 and 5 on the D4.

If under the terms of the Will/Intestacy the funds in the account do not pass wholly to the surviving spouse then Inheritance Tax will be payable as appropriate.

If under the terms of the Will/Intestacy the funds in the joint account pass to the spouse, then spouse exemption should be claimed on page 4 of the IHT200 under the head "Exemptions and Reliefs".

This applies to all bank/building society accounts governed by Scots Law so this is a point which English practitioners should also bear in mind when administering an estate.

SURVEY OF PROFESSIONAL CUSTOMERS 2002

In recent years we have asked our professional customers to complete a satisfaction survey at intervals of about every three years.

We are increasingly aware that customer perception of our services id the real measure of our performance, and so we have used the information from our customer surveys to set ourselves some challenging new performance targets.

Our aim is to achieve steady, year-on-year improvements in our customer satisfaction ratings, in the areas of speed of response, accuracy, availability and courtesy. We shall also be seeking guidance in making improvements to our services from the comments included in the surveys, and from whatever other information we receive from you and from personal applicants, who are our other main customer group.

Because these customer results are to be an important element of our business planning for the foreseeable future, we intend to survey one of our two major customer groups each year. We will also be issuing the surveys in time to enable us to process the results and monitor our performance by the end of our financial year.

Therefore, you will find a survey enclosed with this Newsletter. *Please could you take a few minutes to complete this and return it to the Customer Service team at our Nottingham address (see page 4).*

Because it is only two years since the last survey, I felt that I should explain the reasons why we are asking you to give up a little time to complete this more frequently than before. The decision in Capital Taxes to include targets like these was entirely our own, and does demonstrate our commitment to providing services that our customers want, not merely those that are convenient or traditional for us to provide.

APRIL 2003. – IHT NEWSLETTER

INHERITANCE TAX DIRECT PAYMENT SCHEME

Following discussions with the British Banker's Association and the Building Societies Association, we have agreed a process whereby personal representatives can draw on money held in the deceased's account(s) to pay the IHT that is due on delivery of form IHT200.

The scheme came into effect on Monday 31 March 2003. The process, which is set out in more detail in form D20(Notes), will work as follows

1.   Prior to submitting an IHT200, you should apply to us for an IR CT reference number. You should tell us the deceased's full name and any aliases, the date of death and date of birth. You can call our Helpline with this information – in which case please also tell us which Probate Registry or Sheriff Court you will be applying to – or you can fill in and send form D21 to the appropriate IR Capital Taxes office. We will either give you the reference number over the telephone or return the reply slip with a note of the reference number allocated.

2.   When you have worked out how much tax there is to pay, you should fill in form D20 and have it signed by the personal representatives who will be applying for a grant. The personal representatives will need to have identified themselves to the bank/ building society in much the same way as they do now when opening an executor's account.

3.   When you are ready to apply for a grant, send form D20 to the bank/building society and form IHT200 (etc) to us.

The bank/building society will transfer money to our account; once we are notified of the transfer and have confirmed the amount paid is correct, we will stamp and return form D18 (or in Scotland the Inventory, form C1) to you.

There are a number of points to note

- The scheme is voluntary on the part of the financial institutions, so you should check with the bank/building society whether they are part of the scheme.

- The scheme only applies to account's in the deceased's sole name. (The surviving owner(s) of a joint account can access those funds if they are to be used to pay the tax.)

- If the deceased had a number of accounts with a bank/building society-including loan and credit card accounts-only the net balance is likely to be available for transfer to pay the tax.

- Where the deceased has more than one account with the same bank/building society, you should arrange to have the necessary sums transferred to the account from which the transfer is to be made.

- Withdrawal of funds will be subject to normal banking rules, so if the account is a 'notice' account, there may be a loss on interest or a fee to pay.

- You will need to fill in a separate form D20 for each bank/building society from which the personal representatives wish to transfer money.

- The process from the start to the return of form D18/C1 will take longer than if you had paid the tax by cheque. But we hope the time and cost saved in arranging a loan will more than offset this.

To make use of this facility, you will need forms D20 and D21 (or licensed substitutes) and the instructions, D20 (Notes). Please make sure that you follow the instructions carefully.

From 7th April 2003 the new Helpline number will be 0845 30 20 900.

We will be centralising all our Helpline facilities in one location, with the advantage of a local call rate number. This will enable us to provide a speedier and more consistent service, at less cost to the customer.

You will find that some correspondence will carry this number. If you are phoning in response to a letter please use the number shown, this will help us provide the most efficient response.

New IHT100

A new form IHT100 will be introduced in April 2003. This form will replace the current forms IHT100 and IHT101.

The new form must be used to tell us about all events that give rise to inheritance tax, other than death, from the time it becomes available. These events, which are referred to as chargeable events, are

- Gifts and other transfers of value (including failed potentially exempt transfers).

- Ending of interests in possession in settled property.

- Proportionate charges on non-interest in possession (discretionary) trusts.

- Principal charges on the ten-year anniversary of a discretionary trust.

- Flat rate charges arising when assets cease to be held on special trusts such as temporary charitable trusts.

- Recapture charges arising on the ending of a conditional exemption on Heritage property.

The new IHT100 is the lead form in a set of forms consisting of

- IHT100 which is the main form for providing information about the assets in the transfer.

- Supplementary pages, D31 to D40. These are forms used to provide more detailed information about the assets in the IHT100.

- Event forms, IHT100a to IHT100f. These are to provide the further information about the chargeable event that we need to work out the tax. One of these must be filled in for each chargeable event.

- Worksheet, IHT100WS. This new facility can be used to work out the tax. Unlike the IHT200 there is no requirement to pay the tax on delivery of form IHT100, but this form gives you the option to work out the tax and make payment on delivery if you want to.

Explanatory notes "How to fill in form IHT100" (IHT110) and "How to fill in form IHT100WS" (IHT113) will accompany the forms.

If you want more information about the new IHT100 contact Edward Watts on 0115 974 2755.

All the new forms; D20, D21, IHT100 etc and associated guidance will be available on the Internet at http://www.inlandrevenue.gov.uk/. Please note that the IHT100 will be available from April 2003.

Copies of the new forms are available from our Orderline. The numbers are:

Telephone: 0845 234 1000

Fax: 0845 234 1010

E-mail: ir.purchasing@gtnet.gov.uk

MAY SPECIAL EDITION 2003. – IHT NEWSLETTER

INTRODUCTION

Welcome to this Special Edition of our IHT Newsletter.

David Wright, the Customer Service and Complaints Manager has now moved on. Mr Ashley Baldwin has now taken over the role.

The team would like to thank David for all his help and guidance during his time at Capital Taxes.

This Newsletter is slightly larger than usual and includes a lot of important articles containing, for example, information on the Budget, the new IHT100 form, Excepted Estates & Returns From Trustees. These are to name but a few, so we won't keep you any longer. Happy reading!

The next edition of the Newsletter will be August 2003.

BUDGET ANNOUNCEMENTS

The Inheritance Tax threshold has increased to £255,000 for deaths occurring on or after 6th April 2003.

In addition to the threshold change, there are two proposals affecting holdings in authorised unit trusts (AUTs) and open-ended investment companies (OEICs). These will apply to IHT occasions of charge on or after 16 October 2002 (the date when they were first announced). First, holdings in AUTs and OEICs will be excluded property if held by a non-UK domiciled individual or a trust made by a non-UK domiciled settlor. Second, holdings in OEICs will count as "qualifying investments" for the purposes of the relief for the loss on sale of shares.

EXCEPTED ESTATES & RETURNS FROM TRUSTEES

In our August and December Newsletters, we explained how we saw the extension of the excepted estate regulations might work where the estate contains a small trust. It is apparent from your feedback that our suggestions are not wholly practical. We have therefore decided that trustees should continue to submit form IHT100 and (IHT30 for clearance) in the following circumstances.

- Where trustees establish that we have issued a notice to the personal representatives to deliver an account under regulation 4, the automatic clearance given by regulation 6 will not apply. Trustees should not wait for us to contact them, but should deliver form IHT100/IHT30 as soon as possible. The personal representatives will be able to give the trustees the CT reference number.

- Where trustees establish that the personal representatives do not intend to take out a grant of representation (for whatever reason), they may deliver form IHT100/IHT30 in respect of the trust assets.

- Where trustees are uncertain whether or not an estate qualifies as an excepted estate, and they are unable to satisfy themselves from the information provided by the personal representatives, they may deliver form IHT100/IHT30 in respect of the trust assets.

With the second and third bullet above, please make sure that your covering letter explains what you are doing and why, or there is a very real risk that your account will be returned. If possible, please give us the name and address of the person to contact in connection with the Free Estate. We will make the necessary enquiries to establish whether the estate qualifies as an excepted estate and we will issue form IHT30 to trustees at the appropriate time.

This work may take a little while and we would be grateful if you did not remind the issue of form IHT30 too frequently.

So this means that the only time when trustees should not deliver form IHT100 is when a grant has been extracted as an excepted estate and no notice has been sent to the personal representatives. In these cases (which are likely to be the majority) the automatic clearance contained in the regulations will apply at the end of the specified period.

PAYING INHERITANCE TAX (IHT) BY A TRANSFER OF ASSETS

As many practitioners know, people liable to pay IHT (and interest) may meet some or all of their liability by transferring certain national heritage property to the Crown. The relevant statutory provision is section 230 Inheritance Tax Act 1984. We already provide guidance on this area in the Practitioners Guide that supports the IHT 200 and we will be clarifying some aspects of this guidance when the Guide is next revised. In the meantime, we hope practitioners will find the following statement of our practice helpful.

In our view, people may make a valid offer to transfer assets in lieu of tax only if they are at that time liable to pay IHT or interest. In other words, if people have already paid their IHT bill in full, we will not entertain a subsequent offer to transfer assets.

But we will entertain an offer to transfer assets where

- all the tax has been paid upfront in order to obtain the grant or confirmation, provided that at or around the time of payment we are notified of the possibility that an offer in lieu of tax will be made;

- we are holding money on account of a liability to pay tax or interest; as the money is held to the payer's order, the liability remains unpaid.

ANNUITY CALCULATOR

We have identified a minor problem with the annuity calculator which has now been corrected. In the very rare cases where the problem may arise, the value calculated is slightly lower than it should be.

If you have downloaded a copy of the calculator before 31st March 2003, please download the revised copy now.

THE NEW FORM IHT100

By the time you read this we expect to have introduced a new form IHT100. The new form must be used to tell us about all events that give rise to inheritance tax, other than death.

These events, referred to as chargeable events, are:

- Gifts and other transfers of value (including failed potentially exempt transfers).

- Ending of interests in possession in settled property.

- Proportionate charges on non-interest in possession (discretionary) trusts.

- Principal charges on the ten-year anniversary of a discretionary trust.

- Flat rate charges arising when assets cease to be held on special trusts such as temporary charitable trusts.

- Recapture charges arising on the ending of a conditional exemption on Heritage property or the disposal of timber or underwood.

The new form IHT100 replaces the earlier forms IHT100 and IHT101 which will be phased out over the next six months.

The form IHT100 is the lead form of a set of forms consisting of:

- IHT100
- Supplementary pages D31 to D40.
- Event forms IHT100a to IHT100f.
- Worksheet IHT100WS.

The form IHT100 follows the style of the form IHT200. In the IHT100 we ask for details about the assets on which inheritance tax arises or could arise. We also ask for details about the person who is chargeable and, where appropriate, the settlement involved.

The supplementary pages closely follow the supplementary pages that go with the IHT200 and perform the same role. They ask for more detailed information about certain assets included in the form IHT100 as well as exemptions that are being claimed.

In addition to the usual information about the chargeable person and the assets on which tax is chargeable we need other information to enable us to work out the tax that is due. This information differs depending on which chargeable event is being considered. To gather this information we have introduced separate forms, known as event forms. There are six of these. Each is tailored to ask for the additional information that relates to one of the six chargeable events the form IHT100 deals with. The appropriate event form must be returned with the form IHT100.

We have also introduced a worksheet, form IHT100WS. This is offered as a facility for those who wish to work out the tax themselves. Unlike the IHT200 there is no requirement to pay the tax on delivery of form IHT100, but this form gives you the option to work out the tax and make a payment on delivery if you want to.

The new forms will be available on the Internet at http://www.inlandrevenue.gov.uk/

Copies of the new forms may be obtained from our Orderline. The numbers are:

Telephone 0845 234 1000

Fax 0845 234 1010

E-mail ir.purchasing@gtnet.gov.uk

If you want more information about the new forms, please contact Edward Watts on 0115 974 2755.

CHARGES ON HERITAGE PROPERTY

As the article about the new form IHT100 explains, this is the appropriate form to tell us about the ending of an inheritance tax conditional exemption on Heritage property. It is the responsibility of the owner to deliver an account within 6 months from the end of the month in which the event giving rise to the tax charge occurs. In the future we will charge a penalty if we are not notified on time. Form Cap100 is appropriate for the ending of a capital transfer tax conditional exemption, but we will not generally insist on this being completed provided we are notified promptly of the event giving rise to the ending of the exemption and all necessary information is provided.

If the conditionally exempt item is sold, it will be clear that a charge to tax arises. But there are other circumstances where it **may** be possible to preserve the exemption if a replacement undertaking is given.

These circumstances include:

- A gift of the exempt item.

- The death of the person entitled to the item, if no new conditional exemption is being claimed.

- A change in the access arrangements.

However, if Heritage Section, Capital Taxes are not advised promptly of such a change in circumstances, the owner will be in breach of their undertaking giving rise to a claim for tax. A change in contact will not require a replacement undertaking. But failure to notify us promptly of a change is likely to be a breach of the undertaking to provide public access.

There is no prescribed form of account on which to notify us of the ending of an Estate Duty conditional exemption. However the owner is obliged to notify us promptly of any sale or other disposition of the exempt item giving all relevant details.

LATE ACCOUNTS & S.245 PENALTIES

From 1st April we are changing the process by which we deal with potential penalties on tax paying accounts sent to us outside the normal 12 month period allowed under s.216 Inheritance Tax Act 1984.

A standard letter will now automatically be issued, as part of our initial processing of the new account, which explains that the account is late and a penalty arises. At the bottom of the letter is a payment slip to accompany the payment of any penalty.

Attached to the letter will be a form that allows the personal representatives or their agent to provide an explanation if they believe a reasonable excuse exists so that the penalty does not have to be paid. An extract from our leaflet IHT 13, "Inheritance tax and penalties" will also be provided in every case. It contains examples of what we may agree as a reasonable excuse.

We know that sometimes explanations for the delay are provided with the account itself. We will do our best to identify those cases but accept that occasionally such explanations might be overlooked in the volume of papers accompanying the account and a standard letter might be inappropriately issued.

To help us minimise that risk it would greatly assist us if any explanations being offered at the outset for the account being late are included in the body of your accompanying letter and not contained in a note within the account itself.

SOFTWARE REMINDER

For those of you who download our forms and leaflets from the Internet, please remember to download new versions of the literature at least once a year.

This will help to ensure that you are using the most up to date versions, and will also allow for any changes to the tax rate and threshold, as well as amendments to the forms.

NATIONAL COAL BOARD (NCB) COMPENSATION CLAIMS

The simplified probate application procedure.

The August 2000 edition of the Newsletter introduced and outlined a simplified procedure for obtaining probate in cases where a grant was being sought in a non-taxpaying case solely as a means to pursue a claim for compensation against the National Coal Board.

Under this procedure applicants, instead of completing a full IHT account, were required to send a form P26A or D18 to Inland Revenue Capital Taxes together with a set declaration that the assets of the estate did not exceed the taxable limit or threshold at the date of death.

This procedure has been working well over the last couple of years and has cut down on the amount of work involved in the claims for all concerned.

Having reviewed the operation of the process we are pleased to announce that this procedure has been simplified still further.

It has been agreed with the Court Service that, with immediate effect, the completion of a form P26A or D18 will not be required. As a result, Inland Revenue Capital Taxes will no longer be part of the process. From now on, the intended legal personal representative(s) of an estate will need only to:

- Complete and sign the declaration.

- Send this, together with the Grant application, direct to the appropriate Probate Registry.

We hope this further simplification will mean less effort all round and will enable Grant applications to be dealt with more swiftly. If there are any problems with the new procedure please contact our Helpline on 0845 3020 900.

STATIONERY ORDERS

You are now able to order copies of our forms and leaflets from our Purchasing Team by email.

The email address is: ir.purchasing@gtnet.gov.uk

GILTS & FIXED INTEREST STOCKS:

Should gross or net interest be included as part of the estate? This article concerns the amount of accrued interest to be included in the estate on death in respect of gilts or other fixed interest stocks that are taxed under the Accrued Income Scheme (AIS). As explained below, we believe that interest on AIS securities quoted "cum- div" should be included net of basic rate tax. Similarly, where the securities are "ex-div" at the death, the allowance for interest accruing after the death should be net of tax.

Since 6 April 1996, a person's death has not been an occasion of charge under the AIS. As a result, valuations of holdings of AIS stocks prepared for IHT purposes have included gross interest and IHT has been charged accordingly. However, it has been suggested to us that this treatment may contain an element of double taxation. IHT is being charged on the gross interest accrued to the date of death. At the same time, when the next interest payment is made, the personal representatives are taxed on the whole payment, including the part accruing up to the death.

Since no part of the personal representatives' liability attaches to the deceased, no direct deduction is available on the death. Nevertheless, we now believe that including interest net of basic rate tax would be the correct approach.

This is based on the fact that, as with any property forming part of an estate on death, the stock has to be valued on the basis of a hypothetical sale in the open market. In such a sale, a seller of securities within AIS would be taxed on the interest apportioned up to the sale and the buyer would receive an appropriate credit against his or her tax.

We assume that these factors would have an appreciatory effect on the quoted price of an AIS security that is cum-div at the date of death. Since that is the value for IHT purposes, it is reasonable to make an allowance for the tax that would have been paid by the seller. Where, at the date of death, an AIS security is ex-div, we imagine that the quoted price would be depreciated by the fact that the tax on interest accruing from the date of the deemed transfer to the date the interest is paid would be borne by the buyer and not the seller. On this basis, we believe the allowance in the IHT calculation for interest accruing after the death should also be net of basic rate tax.

JOINT PROBATE & IHT HELPLINE

As well as changing the telephone number (see our April Edition) our new Helpline will now be operated in partnership with the Probate Service. This will provide a single point of contact for people wanting advice about probate procedures and inheritance tax and will be called the Probate and Inheritance Tax Helpline. However, if you need to call about a particular probate application you should, as at present, call the probate registry dealing with the case.

GUIDANCE ON PROPERTY VALUATIONS

The Royal Institute of Chartered Surveyors (RICS) published a new Guidance Note, GN 21, effective from 1st August of last year, which gives advice to members of RICS on the meaning of 'market value' for CGT and Inheritance Tax purposes.

The contents of GN 21 have also been approved by the Valuation Office Agency (VOA).

The Guidance Notes forms part of the RICS 'Appraisal and Valuation Manual' which is commonly referred to as 'The Red Book'.

This should help to resolve difficulties that have sometimes arisen in the past when surveyors have provided their clients with advice on Inheritance Tax or CGT valuations "in accordance with The Red Book" but on an incorrect basis.

In future we would recommend that if you require a valuation for CGT or Inheritance Tax purposes, you instruct the valuer to provide a valuation on the basis set out in GN 21 of the Red Book.

Further guidance on property valuations for CGT, IHT and other taxes, together with a full explanation of the 'market value' basis of valuation can be found in the VOAs CGT and IHT Manuals which can be viewed on their website http://www.voa.gov.uk/ under 'Publications'.

PAYMENT OF INHERITANCE TAX BY CHEQUE

We have been told by Cardiff Tax Office that cheques for Inheritance tax payments have been sent to them in error. If you intend to send a cheque, please remember that payments should be made to the Cashiers in Nottingham.

The cheque should be made payable to the 'Inland Revenue' and should include the name of the deceased, date of death or IRCT reference number if known.

AUGUST 2003. – IHT NEWSLETTER

EXCEPTED ESTATES

The overall limit for excepted estates has been increased to £240,000.

This change takes effect for all applications for a grant made on or after 1 August 2003 and applies to deaths occurring on or after 6 April 2003.

There are no other changes to the regulations.

Our leaflets IHT12 & IHT12(S) will be amended in due course.

IHT100

The new IHT100, introduced in April, should be used for all IHT non-death chargeable events.

The IHT100 is the core account, which should always be used. The appropriate event form (IHT100a to IHT100f) and supplementary pages, if any, should accompany it.

Some of you have been sending us event forms on their own. This will cause delay as we then have to ask you to fill in an IHT100.

DIRECT PAYMENT SCHEME

In our April Newsletter, we announced the introduction of this scheme. Banks and building societies have agreed to release monies directly to us, to pay inheritance tax due, prior to the Grant. So, it has become less necessary to have to arrange a loan to pay the tax.

We would like to make a few useful suggestions and comments, now that the scheme is up and running.

- The Scheme is there to supplement and not replace any prior arrangements that solicitors may have had with banks and building societies to release money. As far as we are concerned, those prior arrangements can continue and the Scheme only need be used if the institution will not release funds otherwise

- As part of the Scheme, people can either request a reference using the form D21 or they can telephone 0115 974 2540 (for a reference only). If you require information on the Scheme, you can call our Helpline 0845 30 20 900.

- We are finding that people are requesting a reference for purposes other than using the Scheme and, that there are some misunderstandings on how it operates. Whilst it is understandable that people would like a reference to quote in all correspondence, this can cause problems. When a reference is supplied, we create a file and computer record for that estate. The file then sits, awaiting that payment, with a specific team who deal with direct payments only.

We have had a number of cases where payments are intended to be made using National Savings. This is currently not within the Scheme although we are in discussion with National Savings to extend the Scheme to their products. You think that we are contacting

National Savings and we think you are arranging a transfer from the bank, so nothing happens! If you want to know how to make payments using National Savings, please call our Helpline.

We would please ask you only to get a reference if you intend to make a direct payment under the Scheme, otherwise by doing so, it may well delay the processing of your account.

- When payments are made, they need to be by CHAPS and not by cheque to the Bank of England, or the Royal Bank of Scotland. Details of the accounts are at TR5 on the form D20.

- Under the Scheme banks and building societies will not receive assessments from us and it is not their job to check or verify in any way that the tax is correct.

- Please send the D20 form to the bank or building society and not to us.

In general, the Scheme is working well and we hope the above pointers will help it run even more smoothly.

DECEMBER 2003. – IHT NEWSLETTER

IHT 100 – A REMINDER

The new form IHT100 is used to account for all events that give rise to an Inheritance Tax charge apart from the one that is deemed to occur immediately before death.

When we introduced the new form IHT100 last April, we said that we would accept returns on the old forms IHT100 and IHT101 for six months. That six-month period came to an end on 31 October 2003.

This is to remind you that from now on, only the new form IHT100 should be used to tell us about non-death events that give rise to an Inheritance Tax charge.

TO BE, OR NOT TO BE, THAT IS THE HYPOTHETICAL QUESTION?

Like all parts of the Inland Revenue, Capital Taxes gives advice under the Code of Practice 10 'Information and Advice'.

The Code says that we can give you general guidance on your tax affairs. We can also give information and guidance on our interpretation of tax law in five specified areas. The relevant ones for us are:

- *The interpretation of legislation passed in the last four Finance Acts;*

- *The application of double taxation agreements;*

- *Statements of practice and extra-statutory concessions;*

- *Other areas concerning matters of major public interest in an industry or in the financial sector.*

The Code goes on to say:

'However, we will not help with tax planning, or advise on transactions designed to avoid or reduce the tax charge, which might otherwise be expected to arise. And your query must arise from genuine uncertainty about the meaning of law'.

We are here to enable you to comply with the law. In order to do this we:

(1)   Publish a wide range of information, such as our leaflets and this Newsletter, which are available on the Inland Revenue website. We are expanding our available informa-

tion. For example, we have recently republished a greatly expanded leaflet IHT2 'Inheritance tax on lifetime gifts'. It is planned to publish the IHT Manual on the Revenue Internet by Spring 2004.

(2)   We provide general information and advice, through our Helpline 0845 30 20 900. We can help you complete an Account or advise on claiming an exemption/relief (after the chargeable event). We can also discuss in general terms how a relief or exemption operates. What we can do, is give specific rulings where no immediate charge to tax has arisen.

(3)   Where we have settled on any aspect of IHT law, we can give some indication of that view.

Our Helpline covers all Probate and Inheritance tax matters, but not Capital Gains Tax (CGT). General enquiries for CGT should be referred to the National Self-Assessment Helpline on 0845 9000 444. For specific CGT enquiries, please call the taxpayer's local tax office (numbers are available in the office directory, on the website under Inland Revenue/contact us).

Copies of the Code are also available on the Revenue website.

GILTS & FIXED STOCK INTEREST

We have been asked to clarify when the change to the inclusion of Gilts & Fixed Stock Interest took effect (see page 5 of the May 2003 Newsletter).

The benefit of the changed approach is available to any case received in IR Capital Taxes on or after 6 May 2003, the date on which the newsletter was published. If, in such a case, the gross interest has been taxed, a revised calculation of interest net of basic rate tax may be submitted.

GUIDANCE ON PROPERTY VALUATIONS

The Royal Institute of Chartered Surveyors (RICS) previously produced Guidance Note 21, which gives guidance on valuations for Inheritance Tax purposes. Please note that this has now been renumbered to Guidance Note 3.

Revised Forms IHT35 and IHT38

To help us reduce the number of occasions when we need to contact you, the claim forms for loss on sale relief have been redesigned. As you may be aware, the rules for claiming loss on sale of land say that the claim cannot be submitted within four months of the date the land was sold. For loss on sale of shares it is two months from the date the last shareholding was sold. If you have not sold the qualifying property, the relief will not be final until four years from the date of death for land and twelve months from the date of death for shares.

The claim forms IHT 35 and IHT 38 now include additional tick boxes, allowing you to tell us whether or not the relief you have claimed is final. If you tell us that the relief is final, we will be able to deal with your claim before the four and two month periods have elapsed. In addition, we will be able to issue clearance as soon as all other matters on the estate have been agreed.

The additional tick boxes are included on page 4 of the claim forms. Please can you make sure you tick the appropriate box on claims for loss on sale submitted to this office.

Application for Grant of Probate

There are two distinct processes to follow when applying for a grant of representation in England & Wales and Northern Ireland. Which process will apply depends on whether the estate qualifies as an excepted estate or not. Unfortunately, we are finding an increasing number of estates where the due process is not being followed.

There are a number of estates where an application for a grant is made as an excepted estate very soon after the deceased had died. Then during the administration, when it transpires that estate does not (and probably never did) qualify as an excepted estate, an IHT200 is submitted and the tax paid. Alternatively, where it is clear that the estate is not an excepted estate, form D18 is submitted to the probate registry showing that there is no tax to pay, but the IHT200 is not delivered to us. Then again, at a later point (convenient for the taxpayer) the account is delivered and the tax paid.

Neither is the correct or proper process and you can expect us to make more detailed enquiries into estates where we find this has happened. No matter what the circumstances, we expect the intending personal representatives to make the fullest enquiries reasonably practical to ascertain the content and composition of an estate before applying for a grant. Where an estate does not qualify as an excepted estate the personal representatives should fill in form IHT200 and deliver it to us – along with the tax due if appropriate – at the same time as they apply for a grant.

We do understand that there are circumstances where you need to obtain a grant quickly. If so, please get in touch by faxing us a letter on 0115 974 3045 headed 'Urgent Grant Request' and setting out the circumstances, rather than taking either route above. We will do what we can to help.

INTEREST RATE CHANGE

Interest on unpaid and overpaid IHT is payable at 3% from 6 December 2003.

NON-TAXPAYING ESTATES – D18 AND C1

Our legislation states that if there is no tax to pay **and** the deceased was domiciled in the UK, D18's and C1's for non-taxpaying cases can be sent to the Capital Taxes office first.

We have been receiving D18's and C1's on such cases for them to be stamped before they are forwarded to the Probate or Commissary Office.

Please note that we do not need to stamp these forms. In UK domicile non-taxpaying cases, please send them direct to the appropriate Probate or Commissary Office.

APRIL 2004. – IHT NEWSLETTER

INTRODUCTION

Welcome to this edition of the IHT Newsletter. Firstly we would like to say a big thank you to all of you who attended our recent series of Inheritance Tax Open Days and helped to make them a huge success.

Secondly, we report changes in the Customer Service team. Ashley Baldwin, the Customer Service and Complaints Manager has now moved on. Stuart Whitney has been appointed as the new Complaints Manager, taking on the responsibility for dealing with complaints within IR Capital Taxes. Should you wish to contact Stuart you can call him on 0115 974 2431 or email him at IRCTcustomerserviceteam@gtnet.gov.uk.

Deborah Walsh is the new Customer Relations Manager. She will be dealing with Customer Service work and you can contact her on 0115 974 2430 or by email as above.

We would like to thank Ashley for all his help and guidance during his time in the team.

Customer Service Team

NEW FORM D3A – FOR NORMAL OUT OF INCOME CLAIMS

Many of you will have been frustrated by the need to gather and collate all the necessary information to support claims for normal out of income exemption. Details of the gifts, the income, the tax on the income, and the expenditure all need to be set out in such a way that a regular pattern of gifts can be discerned.

It has been equally frustrating for us when those details are sent in spread over several separate schedules, so we decided to produce a new form to bring all the relevant details together. It is form D3, the form used to report details of lifetime gifts. A new question (1e) has been added to that form, and if the answer is 'yes', you are asked to go on to complete the new form D3a.

The form can be obtained either by ringing our Orderline on 0845 234 1000 or it can be downloaded from the Internet site www.inlandrevenue.gov.uk/cto/forms3.htm

FORTHCOMING CHANGES TO EXCEPTED ESTATES REGULATIONS

Background Capital Taxes, in line with the rest of the Inland Revenue and indeed with other government departments needs to continually review the burden of compliance that we place on the public. Under the current regime, over 30,000 people a year complete IHT accounts relating to estates which do not attract any liability to IHT. We have been looking critically to find ways of reducing the paperwork in cases where there is no likelihood of any tax liability, whilst carefully managing the risk to the Exchequer of extending the current regulations governing excepted estates.

New proposals Changes to the regulations will therefore be made over the course of the summer. Essentially the purpose of the changes will be to bring within the definition of excepted estates those estates with a gross value of less than £1 million, which are exempt from Inheritance Tax because of spouse or charity exemption. At the same time we intend to align the excepted estates limit with the IHT threshold.

The other principal feature of the change is to bring excepted estates within reach of the penalty regime. We hope this will deter the misuse of the excepted estates process to facilitate grant applications in cases where an IHT account is properly required at the time of the grant application.

At the time of going to press, consultation was underway with various professional representative bodies. Once consultation is complete, details of the process can be finalised. We will then notify you of any changes to the process for personal or professional applicants.

Next steps We are working closely with the Probate Service and will be looking critically at any duplication of information; it has to be right that the same information should not need to be sent in more than once for government purposes. They still have to make decisions about implementing some of the changes following the review of the probate services and the consultation that followed this. Both departments are determined to use every opportunity to streamline the process for the benefit of everyone involved in the administration of estates.

BUSINESS & AGRICULTURAL RELIEF

The valuation requirements for IHT are contained in s. 160 IHTA and the obligation in s. 216(1) for the personal representatives to deliver an account of all appropriate property and its value means that an open market value should be used. But how does this sit with the asset that qualifies, or is likely to qualify, for 100% business or agricultural relief?

The answer is that an open market value should still be used, but the personal representatives may feel that their own considered estimate of that value would be sufficient, rather than go to the expense of obtaining a full professional valuation – particularly as if we accept that 100% relief is due, the value of the asset returned for IHT will not be 'ascertained' within the meaning of s. 274 TCGA 1992.

Nominal or ill-considered values should not be used in any circumstances, not least because if it transpires that relief isn't due, a substantial uplift to the open market value may give rise to a penalty.

Both Shares Valuation and the District Valuer can often accept that the shares or land qualifies for 100% relief without getting in touch with you. It helps us to deal with these claims for relief if you fully complete forms D13 & D14 and send them with the IHT200.

BUDGET CHANGES

The inheritance tax threshold has been increased to £263,000.

This applies to deaths and chargeable transfers or events on or after 6 April 2004.

INSTRUMENTS OF VARIATION & STAMP DUTY

Prior to 1 December 2003 all instruments of variation were either liable to Stamp Duty, or certified exempt from Stamp Duty under Categories L or M in the schedule to the Stamp Duty (Exempt Instruments) Regulations 1987. From 1 December 2003, any instrument of variation effecting a land transaction only, does not require stamping, as such transactions fall within the new Stamp Duty Land Tax regime. Any instrument of variation that varies the devolution of land only, requires no certificate of exemption to be attached.

Other instruments of variation will not require stamping, or certification of exemption either, unless they vary the devolution of stock, shares or marketable securities. (Stamp Duty was abolished on all instruments, under Section 125 FA 2003, apart from those relating to these items.)

For Inheritance Tax purposes therefore, the Category M exemption certificate is only required to be attached where an instrument of variation alters the destination of stock, shares or marketable securities. A simple example of a variation requiring certification would be an estate comprising £1m of stocks and shares passing by will to the spouse, which is varied to give the nil rate band to chargeable beneficiaries.

AUGUST 2004. – IHT NEWSLETTER

INTRODUCTION

Welcome to this edition of the IHT Newsletter. We would like to say a very big thank you to those of you who took part in the recent focus groups. The feedback we have received has been very useful to us and we have included an article to tell you our thoughts on the results.

This edition also includes some important information about changes to the excepted estates regulations. Please do take time to read this article.

The next edition of the Newsletter will be in December. In the meantime, if any of your contact details change please remember to let our Customer service team know.

Please note our new email address

InheritanceTaxCustomerService@gtnet.gov.uk.

Happy reading!

Customer Service Team

EXTENDING THE EXCEPTED ESTATES REGULATIONS

New regulations are currently being prepared to extend the excepted estate regulations. This extension means that apart from very large estates, or estates that otherwise fail to qualify as an excepted estate, form IHT200 will only be needed where there is an IHT liability. This change will mean that a further 30,000 estates per year will be excused of having to deliver an IHT200. As this goes to press some loose ends are still being tied up, but these do not impact on the main thrust of the changes. The regulations are being extended in two ways. An estate will be able to qualify as an excepted estate where the gross value of the estate for IHT purposes, plus the chargeable value of any transfers in the 7 years prior to death, does not exceed

- the IHT threshold (subject to some limitation for applications between 6 April and 1 August each year), or

- £1,000,000 and the net chargeable estate after deduction of spouse and/or charity exemption only is less than the IHT threshold.

The circumstances in which spouse and charity exemption may be deducted to establish whether an estate qualifies will be restricted to the most straightforward (and therefore common) situations. It is important to recognise that because an exemption reduces the tax liability to nil, it does not mean that the exemption can automatically be taken into account in establishing whether the estate is an excepted estate. If the nature of the legacy concerned is outside the restrictions in the regulations, the exemption cannot be taken into account when establishing whether the estate is an excepted estate and the personal representatives (prs) will need to deliver an IHT200.

In Scotland, the spouse or charity exemption will be calculated by taking into account the possibility of claims to legal rights against the estate.

Extending the regulations in this way increases the risk of loss to the Exchequer. To help combat this, and to tackle those who exploit the present excepted estate regulations to their advantage, the process to apply for a grant as an excepted estate is to change.

With effect from the Autumn (probably 1st November), an application for a grant of representation in England & Wales and Northern Ireland will need to be accompanied by either

- an IHT205 (or IHT207 for those domiciled abroad) for excepted estates, or

- a D18 in all other cases.

In Scotland, a C5 or C5(OUK) will need to accompany the Inventory when it is delivered to the Sheriff Clerk, unless the estate is one where an IHT200 has been completed. Where Confirmation is applied for under the Small Estates Acts, a much simpler form C5 will apply.

The IHT205 is a short 4 page document that is currently completed by unrepresented taxpayers. This has been amended and improved so that it can accommodate all three categories of excepted estate. In Scotland, the C5 will compliment the detailed information already provided by the Inventory. Neither of these documents is asking for any more information over and above that which should be obtained and considered before applying under the existing regulations; nor will be required to apply under the extended regulations.

None of these documents is an "account" for IHT purposes. But the information therein which is supplied to the Probate Registry/Sheriff Court will be deemed to be information delivered to the Revenue. This means that where that information is provided fraudulently or negligently and a liability to tax arises as a result, the IHT penalty regime will apply. This will include penalties for the late delivery of an account that was due either at the outset or as a result of changes to the estate after the grant.

We understand that providing this information on a Revenue form where one is not currently needed may be seen as a retrograde step. We believe, however, that this is a necessary step if we are to successfully address a number of issues, namely to

- balance the need to minimise the number of estates that must deliver a full IHT200, whilst at the same time minimising the risk of loss of tax,

- provide an assurance that the prs have considered the whole estate that is relevant for IHT purposes, rather than just the estate devolving under the Will or by intestacy, (omitting to take account of gifts, joint or trust property remains the most common reason why an IHT200 is later found to be required-and in some cases, tax paid),

- remove the anxiety for prs created by the issue of the current IHT204 and IHT204(S) (this process will become obsolete),

- ensure the prs are aware-through signing a document containing the appropriate warnings-that they may be liable to penalties if they are negligent in applying for a grant through the excepted estate route,

- prevent those who currently exploit the existing process to their advantage from continuing to do so.

We do intend, however, to try to ensure that the information needed in estates that are well below the IHT threshold is kept to a minimum.

We will continue to police the operation of excepted estates. The Probate Registry/Sheriff Clerk will send the papers to us every week so that we can review estates without troubling the prs further. We will continue to take a random sample across the whole population and we will use other information sources to identify those estates nearer to the IHT threshold where we feel tax may be at risk.

The automatic discharge will continue to apply in that unless we write to the prs (or their agent) asking for more detailed information within the 35 day period (60 days in Scotland), the liable persons will be discharged from tax. The conditions that currently apply to this discharge will continue to apply.

Should the prs discover that an estate no longer qualifies as an excepted estate, they have six months from discovery to deliver a Corrective Account (form C4) containing details of the changes. The same applies should the beneficiaries of an estate execute an Instrument of Variation (IoV) which changes the devolution so that an estate no longer qualifies. A simple example here is where an estate containing relievable property of, say, £300,000 is left wholly to the spouse, but the relievable property is subsequently redirected to, say, the children. Although there may still be no tax to pay, the estate no longer qualifies as an excepted estate and a Corrective Account showing the reduction in spouse exemption (and deducting any appropriate new relief) should be delivered. To help us process such estates more quickly; a copy of the signed IHT205/C5 etc should be attached to the C4 along with a cheque for any tax and interest.

We are happy to adopt this less formal process that was suggested during our consultations, instead of insisting on a full IHT200 being delivered. If the change results from an IoV a copy of the Instrument will assist.

We are working with the commercial software suppliers to ensure that they have the new forms available in time and our own on-screen version will be available to download from the Internet. If you produce your own substitute forms, we will be letting you have a copy of the new forms shortly so you can develop your own form. The new paper forms will be available from our Orderline in due course.

Two final matters. Firstly, for estates where the gross value exceeds £1,000,000, but spouse and/or charity relief applies, the facility to deliver a reduced account will continue to apply.

Secondly, when the new regulations take effect, we will be changing the D18 process in England & Wales and Northern Ireland so that the Probate Registry will not issue a grant unless the D18 bears our authorisation. So in every case where you deliver an IHT200, you will need to send the D18 to us for authorisation first.

The equivalent procedure in Scotland will change in a similar way so that, on delivery to us, every IHT200 must be accompanied by the Inventory. We will stamp the form and return it to you to apply for Confirmation. Unless, therefore, the estate qualifies as an excepted estate, the Sheriff Clerk will not grant Confirmation if the Inventory is not authorised by us.

WHAT YOU THINK, WHAT WE THINK

We recently commissioned a market research company to organise a series of focus groups with professional firms who have regular contact with us in connection with inheritance tax and shares valuation. We asked the company carrying out the research to explore what aspects of our service are important to you and what you think is done well or less well.

We wanted to ascertain whether the move to teamworking within our service areas has caused any difficulties, to explore if our in depth enquiries are perceived to be carried out in a professional manner and to seek your views about how the process of applying for a grant and dealing with inheritance tax might be streamlined and improved. We also wanted feedback on the Probate and Inheritance Tax Helpline, our Orderline, this Newsletter and our Internet pages.

Among the many views expressed was some displeasure with the occasionally self-congratulatory tone of this Newsletter, and do not therefore intend to dwell upon the many appreciative comments that were made except to say thank you. We are very grateful to all of you who took part in the survey and any changes we introduce will be devised with your needs and preferences in mind.

Unavoidably this article is rather long so we have divided it into topics in the hope you will be able to quickly identify information relating to topics that may be of particular interest to you.

Penalties The view was expressed by some that we are taking a more "aggressive" approach to inheritance tax penalties. Certainly our compliance teams have taken an assertive stance on both fraud and negligence since more robust legislation came into effect in 1999. Perhaps worth mentioning is the fact that the legislation followed a report of the Public Accounts Committee who stated that they expected the department to give active consideration to penalty action wherever material understatements of tax liability arose through negligence or fraud. Our aim is to concentrate on cases where there has been serious negligence or fraud; so while penalties in individual cases may be higher we may seek to impose them on fewer occasions.

There may certainly be a perception that we are more eager to start the penalty process earlier. That may be because, as a result of changes brought about by the Human Rights Act, we are now required to inform you about the penalty process as soon as we consider a penalty *might* be an issue. We have standardised our initial letter making it clear at the outset, we hope that we are making enquiries only and not immediately launching into a penalty claim.

There is also confusion about using estimates in accounts. We clearly define in the IHT200 notes (IHT215) and our leaflet IHT14 what sort of enquiries we expect personal representatives to make before submitting an account. The legislation makes it clear that personal representatives must make "*the fullest enquiries that are reasonably practicable in the circumstances*" to establish the exact value of any particular property. If they have gone through that process and still cannot establish an exact value then, and only then, are they entitled to include a provisional estimate of the value of that property. The estimate provided should nonetheless be a realistic one (nominal values are not acceptable) and based on the best available information those enquiries produce. You should make it clear that the value of this particular asset is estimated and tell us the exact value as soon as it is known.

Solicitors do have an obligation to emphasise to their client the gravity of their responsibilities and that we will level a penalty where personal representatives have acted negligently or fraudulently in completing the account. Providing a value that is substantially less than the true open market value certainly might amount to negligence.

If you are unsure about whether those requirements have been met in any particular case you can write to our Compliance team to explain the position before submitting an account. They will do everything they can to advise you what they think reasonably needs to be done for the personal representatives to meet their statutory obligations.

We are also willing to make presentations clarifying our approach to penalties to professional gatherings, although we would normally expect an audience of at least 20 to make this worthwhile. If your organisation would like a presentation on a particular IHT topic, please let our Customer Service team know.

Submissions to the Valuation Office There are concerns about cases where significant delays are perceived to arise in cases submitted to the Valuation Office. Examples were quoted of cases where many months have passed before an appointment was made for the valuer to visit a property. All our records show that these are isolated examples and that the majority of cases are dealt with promptly, but this is clearly an area where we must continue to work. In our Nottingham office we have recently changed our initial processing of inheritance tax accounts and we are fortunate in that we now have a team of Valuation Office staff working alongside our Capital Taxes people. We expect this gradually to result in a faster turnaround of cases where the valuation provided is acceptable. In the majority of cases we aim to refer to the Valuation Office within a very few days of our receiving the account. We have a service level agreement with the Valuation Office and we regularly monitor and discuss performance. All of this however is of little help if one of your cases has somehow become lost or stuck in the system. Please let us know in any case where you are waiting for a valuation for more than 6 weeks and have had no contact from a valuer, or there appears to have been unreasonable delay at any stage of the process. We can and do expedite individual cases. In cases of particular urgency please do not hesitate to telephone or write and explain the exact nature of the difficulty that you are facing and we will do everything we can to bring these cases to the front of the queue.

The direct payment scheme The direct payment scheme has generally been received very favourably. There is however a lack of clarity about which banks and building societies are involved. Many banks and building societies will in any case simply advance money from the estate for payment of inheritance tax and in these cases there is of course no problem. Other banks and building societies may however prefer to use the formal process. One way or another most clearing banks and building societies will now advance funds from the estate, but again let us know if there are any particular difficulties and we will try and address these. We will, later in the year look at whether we can include other assets of the estate.

Non-taxpaying cases The survey indicated some concern about the amount of information required in cases where there is no inheritance tax liability. Forthcoming changes to the excepted estate regulations will mean that most non-taxpaying cases with the gross value of less than £1,000,000 will no longer need to complete IHT200s. The new regulations are expected to come into effect in October and an article on page 1 contains a detailed explanation of the new process. We believe that the new processes will meet many of the demands for a simplified process for non- taxpaying estates.

Scottish issues There were two particular issues raised in Scotland. The first concerned a perceived lack of expertise on the part of our Helpline staff about Scottish issues. We will consider what further training may be needed. There was also concern about the extent to which there was duplication between the Scottish Confirmation form C1 and the IHT200. We are working with the Court Service in Scotland, as in England, to simplify and streamline the entire process that needs to be followed and as part of this we will look at the forms in more detail. The format of the C1 is prescribed by statute and changes to it may prove difficult but we would like to move to a system where there is as little duplication as possible. On the other hand the IHT200 would run to very many pages if every asset had to be identified as in the C1. So there isn't an easy solution, but it is something we will work on.

Internet Increasingly we want to rely upon the Internet as a means of making information available to you. Any suggestions as to how we can encourage more people to use the Internet as a first port of call will be gratefully received. Updating paper versions of forms and leaflets is extremely difficult whereas the Internet is much more easily kept up to date, so using this form of communication is in all our interests.

IHT Newsletter Not all the participants in the meetings had seen the Newsletter or read it regularly. How can we best make sure that information that you want gets to the right people at the right time? Firstly please let us know if your contact details change. There may also be other publications that are widely read where it would be useful for us to include information. Your thoughts on this and any other means by which we might best communicate with you will be gratefully received. Please e-mail our Customer Service team with any suggestions you may have at InheritanceTaxCustomerService@gtnet.gov.uk.

INSTRUMENTS OF VARIATION

We have been asked to clarify paragraphs 2 & 3 of the article in the last issue on Instruments of Variation & Stamp Duty requirements. We can confirm that even when an instrument effects a variation in the destination of stocks and shares, *no* stamp duty certificate is required, except in the unusual case where the instrument is itself acting as a transfer form for the shares, rather than the far more common case where a separate stock transfer form is executed to effect the transfer. There is a Stamp Duty requirement for that form, but that is entirely separate from the document that is the Instrument of Variation.

HERITAGE – CONFIDENTIALITY & VALUATION

Practitioners and private individuals sometimes ask us for details of conditionally exempt assets, or to consider new claims for conditional exemption on death in advance of delivering accounts. This is unlikely to present any problems and we welcome such evidence of compliance. But we need to be aware of the rules concerning confidentiality.

We need to be quite sure before entering into correspondence that we do not provide information or details to which the recipient is not entitled. Before responding we need to identify the person who has enquired as either accountable (or prospectively accountable) or as acting for such persons.

If you or your firm need to contact us for reasons of this kind–indeed whenever someone else's confidentiality is in point–please be sure to enclose evidence that you are entitled to what you seek from us. Otherwise we should have to ask you for it with resulting delay and inconvenience to all concerned.

The "Business & Agricultural Relief" article on page 2 of the April 2004 edition of this newsletter covered valuation issues which also have general application for cases where conditional exemption claims are made under section 30 IHTA 1984.

The article refers to the use of a 'considered estimate' in cases where the personal representatives expect 100% AR or BR to apply. It must be borne in mind that this does assume the accountable persons are in a position to be able to arrive at a 'considered estimate', particularly in the case of potential conditionally exempt property. If that is not the case then seeking professional advice may still be the only way they can meet their obligations under s160 & s216 IHTA 1984

IHT direct payment scheme The scheme has been running for little over a year now. Despite the useful suggestions in our August 2003 Newsletter, we are aware of some dissatisfaction amongst our customers with the process. We welcome your feedback on the scheme. If you have any thoughts or concerns please let us know. You can telephone John Lovell on 0115 974 2853 or email us.

IHT PENALTY CHANGES

The Finance Bill contains a number of changes to the IHT penalty regime to align it more with Revenue penalties generally

Late delivery The penalty in s.245 for the late delivery of an account is changed to a fixed sum of £100 or £200 depending on whether the account is delivered more than 12 or 18 months after the date of death. This remains subject to the overriding rule that the penalty cannot exceed the tax. This change does not take effect until 6 months after Royal Assent.

A new penalty is introduced where the accountable person continues to fail to deliver their account. This applies where the account is delivered more than 24 months after the date of death, but only where an IHT liability arises. The maximum penalty is £3,000 and is subject to the defence of reasonable excuse. This change applies where the due date for the delivery of an account expires after Royal Assent-where the due date has expired before Royal Assent, the penalty does not apply until 12 months after Royal Assent.

Similarly, there is a new penalty of a maximum of £3,000 where a person continues to fail to comply with the provisions of s.218A and does not notify us within 18 months of the Instrument of Variation (IoV) being executed that it increases the IHT liability. This change applies where the due date for notification expires after Royal Assent-where the due date has expired before Royal Assent, the penalty does not apply until 12 months after Royal Assent. The reasonable excuse defence is extended to obligations under s.218A. for all IoV notification failures which arise after Royal assent.

Incorrect account, information or document The provision in s.247(1) whereby a sum of £1,500 or £3,000 is added to the culpable tax is removed, so that a penalty under this head can only now be charged where there is an IHT liability and is limited to the amount of tax concerned.

The differentiation between negligence and fraud in s.247 (3) is removed and replaced with a single penalty not exceeding £3,000.

These changes to s.247 above take effect for accounts, information and documents delivered after Royal Assent.

EXCEPTED ESTATES, DOUBLE DEATHS AND INSTRUMENTS OF VARIATION

We have been asked how (or whether) form IHT200 should completed where

- there are two deaths – usually husband and wife-within 2 years of each other,

- within 2 years of the first death, the beneficiaries of the second to die effect an Instrument of Variation (IoV) to redirect property from the first estate away from the second such that both estates, for IHT purposes, are below the excepted estate limit.

The answer is best given by way of an example, but the underlying principle is that the hypothesis created by the IoV only takes effect for IHT purposes. It does not alter the real world position of the second estate at the date the second person dies. So if, in the real world, the second estate did not qualify as an excepted estate, form IHT200 is required.

Let us consider the estate of a husband and wife. The husband owns assets worth £50,000 in his own right, the wife £60,000. Their home is owned jointly as beneficial joint tenants and has an open market value of £350,000. They each leave their whole estate to the other. The husband dies first. On his death, his IHT estate is valued at £225,000 (being £50,000 plus one half of the house), so the estate qualifies as an excepted estate and IHT200 is not required. The widow inherits the whole estate and becomes sole owner of the house by survivorship.

When the widow dies, her estate is worth £460,000. To make use of both nil-rate bands, the beneficiaries of her estate execute an IoV (before applying for probate) to redirect the husband's estate and his share of the joint property to themselves. The effect of the IoV is to reduce the widow's estate *for IHT purposes* to £235,000. But this does not alter the fact that, in reality, at the date of her death the widow's estate was valued at £460,000. Her estate is therefore outside the excepted estate regulations.

Form IHT200 should be completed by the widow's prs declaring the true gross value of the estate in sections F & G. Then to give effect to the IoV, the assets that are being redirected away from the estate should be deducted in the "Exemptions and reliefs" boxes. This way, the correct value for the gross and net estate is carried forward to form D18 and to the probate papers and the taxable value of the estate for IHT purposes is also correctly calculated.

Are your IHT forms gathering dust Our Orderline receives over 75 requests per day. Some of these are for over 100 copies of each form. It would be appreciated that when ordering stationery, you ask for supplies that you are likely to use within say the next 6 months. This will enable us to manage our stock more effectively, ensuring you have the most up to date versions.

DECEMBER 2004. – IHT NEWSLETTER

INTRODUCTION

Welcome to the latest edition of our Newsletter.

The Complaints Manager, Stuart Whitney has now moved on. Owen Jones has been appointed as the new Complaints Manager, taking on responsibility for dealing with complaints within IR Capital Taxes. Should you wish to contact Owen about a complaint or suggestions on how we can improve our service you can call him on **0115 974 2431** or email him at **InheritanceTaxCustomerService@gtnet.gov.uk.**

Deborah Walsh continues as the Customer Relations Manager. You can contact her on **0115 974 2430** or by email as above.

The next edition of the Newsletter will be in April 2005.

In the meantime, we would like to wish you all a very merry Christmas and a happy New Year.

Customer Service Team

HOUSEHOLD AND PERSONAL GOODS – IHT200 & IHT100

Forms D10 for the IHT200 and D35 for the IHT100 are designed for those submitting accounts to give details of any household and personal goods that form part of the estate or transfer. Form D4 is used where the goods are jointly owned. The guidance notes that accompany them explain the steps we expect accountable people to take to complete the forms accurately and completely.

When we receive completed accounts in IR Capital Taxes the two areas we look at for these assets are:

- Does the IHT account constitute a complete return of the household and personal goods owned by the deceased, transferor or trust? And

- Has the value of those goods been ascertained in accordance with the correct statutory principles?

The statutory principles are set out in section 160 of the Inheritance Tax Act 1984: the value of property for inheritance tax purposes is \u8220\'81the price which the property might reasonably be expected to fetch if sold in the open market\u8221\'81.

Areas that cause us particular difficulty include:

- Where it is unclear on what basis a valuation has been made. Valuations for insurance purposes or for "probate" may provide a starting point but do not necessarily represent the open market value. Some valuations do not show on what basis they have been made at all.

- Where the accountable person has made an estimated valuation themselves. We would welcome as full an explanation as possible of the basis on which the value has been arrived. This should include mention of what comparisons have been made.

- Where the goods have been described as having no value. We would expect a full explanation of the circumstances and the basis on which that conclusion has been reached.

- Where there was a vehicle but insufficient details are given. We may need to seek further information if the make, exact model and year of registration are not given. We would also like to know the registration number even if it is considered that there is no separate value for it.

- Where a valuer has provided a range of values and the accountable person has included values from the bottom of the range. Whilst the decision to do this rests with the accountable people, there is a general expectation that the most likely price goods would fetch on the open market would be nearer the middle of the range.

- Where goods are jointly owned and the questions on form D4 are not completely answered or answered at all. This is less an issue where the property is owned jointly by spouses but in other instances we need to know on what facts accountable people have established the joint ownership.

- Where circumstances indicate there has been a sale at an undervalue or a forced sale. We expect the value to be adjusted to represent the open market value or a reasoned explanation why the sale value should be taken as such.

- Where the estate includes property situate abroad–for example a holiday home–and there is no mention of household and personal goods there. It is possible that the contents are included in the valuation of the property but unless this is explicit we may seek clarification. It is also possible that the valuer may not have valued on the statutory basis.

In all of these circumstances there is an increased likelihood that we will want to open an enquiry and ask for further information or seek an explanation of the value offered. We may also want to ask what steps the accountable people have taken to ensure that all of the goods have been accounted for.

From January 2005 we will be paying particularly close attention to the values included for household and personal goods. In appropriate cases we will open an enquiry and ask you for further information to satisfy ourselves that all of the goods have been included and that they have been valued on the statutory basis.

We may ask:

- For evidence of the instructions given to valuers
- About the steps taken by accountable people to satisfy themselves that the valuation is on the statutory basis
- For photographs and further details of specific items
- To inspect and photograph items which have not been sold.

We will tell you that the estate is one that has been selected for enquiry in this way.

Where we consider that accountable people or their valuers have been negligent we will consider whether a penalty is appropriate.

IHT Customer Information The IHT Customer Information Leaflet has been withdrawn, as it was out of date. You may have already seen its replacement, our new IHT Customer Information sheet. This is being issued with official receipts on delivery of the Inland Revenue Account.

INHERITANCE TAX MANUAL

We have now completed the drafting of the first forty sections of the IHT Manual. This manual will replace the Capital Taxes\u8217\'81 Advanced Instruction Manual, General Examination Manual and Debt management Manual.

We expect to publish the manual on the Inland Revenue internet site during December 2004 but because of the volume of material it may not be possible to publish all of the sections from the outset. The table below shows the titles of the sections being published.

We aim to publish the remaining three sections during 2005. These will cover Heritage matters, Non interest in possession trusts and the text and notes for the Inheritance Tax double taxation conventions and agreements.

IHT Manual	
1	Office Structure
2	Communications
3	Files
4	What is IHT charged on
5	What happens when someone dies
6	Excepted estates
7	Initial processing
8	Account amendment work
9	Investigating accounts
10	Accounts and accountability
11	Exemptions
12	Succession
13	Domicile
14	Lifetime transfers
15	Joint/nominated property

16	Settled property
17	Pensions
18	Stocks and shares
19	Capital debts due to estate
20	Life policies
21	Household goods and personal effects
22	Interest in unadministered estates QSR
23	Land and buildings
24	Agricultural relief
25	Business relief and businesses
26	Calculating the estate
27	Foreign property
28	Liabilities
29	Enquiry procedures
30	Payment of tax and liability
31	Assessing
32	Reminding/progressing cases
33	Loss on sale of land relief
34	Loss on sale of shares relief
35	Changes to devolution of estate
36	Penalties
37	Notices of Determination
38	Debt Management
39	File Closure
40	Clearance certificates

HIDE & SEEK!

We have recently found an increasing number of cheques in amongst correspondence. When enclosing a cheque please place it on the top of any correspondence – this will help us and will also help you.

IHT 200 – STOCKS, SHARES & INVESTMENTS

We have noticed that where a stockbroker\u8217\'81s or other professional valuation has been produced for the personal representatives there is a tendency to just put in a global figure on the form D7.

In fact, the notes relating to the D7 ask that you break down the valuation or any other schedule into the four following groups:

1.   Quoted Stocks & shares

2.   UK government & municipal securities

3.   Unquoted stocks & investments

4.   Traded unquoted stocks & shares, e.g. AIM or OFFEX stocks.

It does help us to process your cases more quickly if you can break the holdings down into these groups. In particular, if groups 3 & 4, the unquoted stocks, shares & investments, are highlighted in this way, Shares Valuation can get involved at an earlier stage. We are also more likely to pick up on any missed claims for business relief–so it is not only for our benefit!

EXCEPTED ESTATE REGULATIONS

Please note the changes to the excepted estate regulations came into effect on 1st November 2004; our August 2004 Newsletter refers. If you have any questions please telephone the Probate and Inheritance Tax Helpline.

APRIL 2005. – TAX BULLETIN

RECOGNISED STOCK EXCHANGES

Please note this article replaces the article entitled Recognised Stock Exchanges Overseas in Tax Bulletin Issue 40.

The phrase "recognised stock exchange" occurs throughout the Taxes Acts and in various regulations.

The definition of a recognised stock exchange is at Section 841 ICTA 1988. It includes the London Stock Exchange and any such stock exchange outside the UK as is designated by an Order of the Board of the Inland Revenue.

The list of recognised stock exchanges in Tax Bulletin 40 is no longer up to date. The current list of recognised exchanges is available.

Please note that recognition under Section 841 ICTA is for income tax, corporation tax, capital gains tax and, to a limited extent, SDRT purposes only. Section 841 does not extend to Inheritance Tax, although, in practice, an exchange under section 841 will also be regarded as recognised for the purposes of Inheritance Tax. Recognition for these tax purposes does not imply recognition or approval for regulatory or other purposes.

APRIL 2005. – IHT NEWSLETTER

INTRODUCTION

Welcome to the April edition of our IHT Newsletter.

We are always happy to hear your comments and would ask that if you have any suggestions about how to improve it, or any new features that you would like to see, please email the Customer Service Team at InheritanceTaxCustomerService@gtnet.gov.uk or call us on **0115 974 2430**.

The Newsletter and many of our forms and leaflets are available on our website at www.inlandrevenue.gov.uk/cto. Also, many of you will be pleased to know that most of the chapters of the IHT Manual have now been published. We are sorry that it has been delayed.

On page 3 we have included details of the inheritance tax threshold changes following the recent budget.

61 IHT Newsletter and Tax Bulletin extracts

The next edition of the IHT Newsletter will be in August 2005.

Customer Service Team

EXCEPTED ESTATES

The changes to the excepted estate regulations appear to have been implemented quite smoothly. We are receiving fewer IHT200s in estates where there is no liability to tax, but there is still some way to go. If the estate you are dealing with qualifies as an excepted estate, please do use the IHT205 (or C5 in Scotland) rather than going to the trouble of completing an IHT200.

We are also finding that we do not have cause to raise enquiries into many of the IHT205s/C5s we select for sample. We hope this is evidence that the forms are doing their job and helping people to get things right, and to get them right first time.

When dealing with excepted estates, please keep focussed on the gross value of the estate. If the gross value of the estate does not exceed the appropriate IHT threshold, there is no need to deduct any exemption that may be due. After all, there can be no tax to pay, so whether the exemption is due or not is irrelevant.

This focus on the gross value of the estate is particularly important in low value estates where assets pass to the deceased's spouse. In determining if the estate is an excepted estate, spouse exemption can only be deducted if **both** the deceased and their spouse were

- born in the United Kingdom, and

- had their permanent home in the United Kingdom throughout their lives.

However, these conditions do not need to be considered if the gross estate does not exceed the excepted estate limit in any event. Low value estates can still qualify as an excepted estate by means of value alone.

We are grateful to those of you who have provided some feedback about the changes and we would like to draw your attention to some areas where problems have been identified.

The process

If your estate qualifies as an excepted estate, fill in form IHT205 and send it direct to the probate registry. We do not need to see the form first (or a copy of it) and there is no need to complete a D18 as well as the IHT205.

If the estate does not qualify as an excepted estate, fill in form IHT200. You must send this to us together with a D18 first for stamping. We cannot deal with a D18 on it's own.

Booklet IHT206

There are a couple of errors in the booklet that we will correct at the next reprint.

- On page 4 we say that in order to use form IHT205 the deceased must have been born in the UK as well as having their permanent home here and there being no tax to pay. There is no requirement that the deceased was born in the UK – all that is required is that they were domiciled in the UK at the date of death and there is no tax to pay.

- On page 22 we say that box 13.2 is for mortgages on property in the deceased's sole name. That box is to deduct any mortgages secured on property disclosed in section 11 of the form – and that can include a share in property owned as tenants-in-common. If there was a mortgage secured on a property owned as tenants-in-common, you should deduct the deceased's share of the debt in box 13.2.

Which IHT certificate to use in the Oath for Probate

Following the Senior District Judge's Direction of 27th October; there are now three alternative IHT certificates to use in the oath to apply for a grant. Please make sure that you use the correct one. They are detailed below.

1.   For an excepted estate where the gross value does not exceed the IHT threshold

"To the best of my/our knowledge, information and belief the gross estate passing under the grant does not exceed £............... and that the net estate does not exceed £............... and this is not a case in which an Inland Revenue Account is required to be delivered." (The net estate figure should be rounded to the nearest £'000.)

2.   For an excepted estate where the gross value exceeds the IHT threshold but does not exceed £1m and the chargeable estate after deducting spouse/charity exemption does not exceed the IHT threshold

"To the best of my/our knowledge, information and belief the gross estate passing under the grant amounts to £............... and that the net estate amounts to £............... and this is not a case in which an Inland Revenue Account is required to be delivered."

3.   For estates which are not excepted estates

"To the best of my/our knowledge, information and belief the gross estate passing under the grant amounts to £............... and that the net estate amounts to £..............."

Please use the first of the IHT certificates above for low value estates; but do not use this certificate for estates under £1m where there is still no tax to pay because of an exemption, where it is the second certificate that is appropriate.

INVENTORY FORM C1 & IHT200 – SCOTLAND

We would like to draw your attention to a couple of issues surrounding the completion of these forms.

- Despite the wording on page 4 of the form, there is no need to complete section 3 on page 4 when you are delivering form IHT200 with the Inventory – it is only necessary to complete these boxes when you are applying for Confirmation as an excepted estate. We will amend the form to make this clear at the next reprint.

- If, on a supplementary page to form IHT200, you refer back to the C1; can you please give the item number(s) on the C1 that you are referring to. And if you have attached a schedule to the C1, and refer back to that from the IHT200, it would help if you could attach a copy of the schedule to the relevant 'D' form.

IHT Direct Payment Scheme You can pay some or all of the IHT that is due on delivery of form IHT200 by using this scheme.

You must apply to us for a Capital Taxes reference number. To do this you can fill in form D21 and send it to us. Alternatively, you can telephone us on **0115 974 2540**.

PROBATE & INHERITANCE TAX HELPLINE

Scottish Issues Survey results last year highlighted a perceived lack of expertise on the part of our Helpline staff about Scottish issues. All our advisors have now received further training and we hope you will continue to use the Probate and Inheritance Tax Helpline for all Scottish issues.

PROSECUTION FOR IHT FRAUD

In the first case of its kind, the Revenue's Special Compliance Office in Edinburgh has successfully prosecuted a taxpayer for defrauding the Revenue of inheritance tax amounting to £163,000.

John Lamberton took over responsibility for his aunt's share portfolio previously managed by a bank and valued at £402,000. He sold the shares and opened a stockbroker's account for himself which received the proceeds. He set up a BVI company and used it and other offshore accounts to pass the money through. Lamberton moved to Spain where he purchased a house and set up an estate agency.

He failed to declare the investments in his aunt's SA return and, as executor, failed to show the investments on the IHT200 either as assets of the estate or as a gift to him. As one of two residuary beneficiaries, his actions also defrauded the other beneficiary of part of his entitlement.

Lamberton was found guilty of one count of embezzlement and two counts of fraud and was jailed for 7 years. The Crown Office is currently pursuing the confiscation of Lamberton's assets.

As well as being the first prosecution for IHT fraud, it is the first case where the perpetrator has been extradited back to Scotland for a tax-related offence and it is one of the longest sentences handed down for a Revenue case.

The case does illustrate that we take the delivery of a correct and complete account very seriously indeed and that we will pursue those who try to avoid making a full and complete return.

BUDGET CHANGES

The inheritance tax threshold has been increased to £275,000.

This applies to deaths and chargeable transfers or events on or after 6 April 2005.

For establishing whether an estate is excepted, £263,000 continues to apply to all applications made before 6 August 2005.

JUNE 2005. – SPECIAL TAX BULLETIN

INHERITANCE TAX

General The permanent HMRC guidance on this topic will be incorporated in the IHT manual.

As with CGT, PE [Payment Entitlement] is subject to the normal IHT rules. So the following references to "transfers" include the most common occasion when an IHT charge arises, i.e. the transfer that is deemed to take place on death, where the value transferred at that time for IHT purposes is equivalent to the value of the deceased's estate immediately before death.

Transfers before 1 January 2005 of a farming business, or an interest in a farming business, whose value reflects the expectation of future PE should be valued for IHT purposes with the benefit of that expectation. Transfers of PE on or after 1 January 2005 (whether before or after actual establishment) are liable to IHT as any other asset.

Agricultural Property Relief (APR) APR can apply to "agricultural property" only. This is defined in section 115(2) IHTA 1984 as agricultural land or pasture (including woodland and certain agricultural buildings). So PE itself, being an asset which is separate from land, cannot qualify for APR. (This will of course not affect the availability of APR for any other asset which does qualify as "agricultural property".)

APR applies to agricultural property which has been either occupied by the transferor for agricultural purposes for the two years immediately before the transfer, or owned by the transferor throughout the seven years immediately before the transfer and throughout that period has been occupied for agricultural purposes whether by the transferor or by another (section 117 IHTA).

Agricultural land which is taken out of production can still qualify for APR (including GAEC land) because section 117 IHTA does not require the land to be in production either continuously or at a specific time (though there must be an intention or expectation that the land will be back in production at some time in the future). So, for example, agricultural land set aside to rotational, or even permanent, fallow can still qualify as agricultural property within the definition of section 115(2) IHTA 1984 and as occupied for the purposes of agriculture within the meaning of section 117 IHTA.

Land used for grazing leisure horses does not satisfy the "occupied for the purposes of agriculture" test and so cannot qualify for APR.

Business Property relief (BPR) Land which formerly qualified for APR but which no longer does so (for example, because it ceases to be occupied for agricultural purposes) may nonetheless qualify for BPR if it is an asset of a trading business which satisfies the normal conditions of the relief.

BPR is available for transfers of "relevant business property" which the transferor has owned as such throughout the two years immediately before the transfer. "Relevant business property", which can qualify for BPR at 100 per cent, includes certain categories of business (or an interest in a business, for example a partnership interest) and some types of shares and securities. So in the normal case where the transferor is a farmer who has been farming for at least two years, PE (whether in expectancy pre-1/1/05, or on or after that date regardless of whether PE has actually been established) will qualify for 100 per cent BPR as an asset of the business, on the assumption, which will normally be the case, that the resulting payment will be used in the business or be required for future use in the business. PE will still qualify for BPR where the owner has put farmland out of production, for example into set-aside in order to receive SP, provided the farmer is still carrying on a business on a commercial basis, and provided the nature of the business remains essentially that of a trading concern rather than one that consists of dealing in land or making or holding investments.

As with any asset, the transfer of PE by someone who is not carrying on a trading business will not qualify for BPR. Similarly, the transfer of PE as an individual asset, rather than the business itself, or an interest in the business, will not qualify for BPR.

AUGUST 2005. – IHT NEWSLETTER

INTRODUCTION

Welcome to the latest edition of our IHT Newsletter.

On 18 April 2005 the Inland Revenue merged with HM Customs & Excise to form our new department HM Revenue & Customs (HMRC).

However, despite all of the changes we will continue to be responsible for Inheritance Tax and you can still contact our Probate and Inheritance Tax Helpline on 0845 30 20 900.

Alternatively, all our forms and guidance are available on our website. Please note our new address www.hmrc.gov.uk/cto.

Thank you to all of you that took part in our recent survey. We will be informing you on how we are planning to take your comments forward in the next edition of the Newsletter, which is due to be published in December 2005.

Customer Service Team

IHT DIRECT PAYMENT SCHEME (DPS)

Now that this scheme is fully established as a way of paying Inheritance Tax we are keen to ensure that it remains as easy to use as possible.

Our recent customer survey shows that an increasing number of our customers (over 66%) are now paying their tax directly from the deceased's bank or building society accounts. This is not necessarily through our scheme, as many banks and building societies operate independent schemes of their own, but it does demonstrate that this is becoming an easier way to pay. Awareness among our customers of this method of payment has also increased as well.

We have worked with the British Bankers' Association and The Building Societies Association to continue to improve in this area and have undertaken to let them know of difficulties that our customers come across with their members. We are pleased that these problems now seem to be few and far between.

If you have any comments regarding the scheme, please contact John Stratford on 0115 974 2853. We are always interested to hear views that may help us to improve the service we offer still further.

EXCEPTED ESTATES

We have been monitoring the extent to which personal representatives have been taking advantage of the changes to the excepted estates regulations introduced last year. Although we are receiving fewer IHT200s in estates where there is no liability to tax, significant proportions of the accounts we still receive are for estates that qualify as excepted estates. All that was needed in these estates was an IHT205 (or C5 in Scotland). Using these shorter forms will save your clients both time and money in dealing with the estate and saves us time in processing the form when it arrives. Please do use the right form(s).

There may be a mistaken belief that delivering an IHT200 for an excepted estate reduces the risk of a penalty should it transpire later that the estate did not qualify. This is not the case. The same consequences will flow whether it is an incorrect account (IHT200) that has been negligently delivered to the Board or incorrect information (IHT205/C5) that has been negligently produced to the probate service/sheriff clerk.

The Probate Service in England & Wales has asked us to draw to your attention a number of common errors in the information provided in excepted estates. They have recommended that before you send off your application for a grant that you should check that:

- The deceased's name is the same on both the IHT205 and the oath.

- The date of death is the same on both the IHT205 and the oath.

- The figures in the Probate Summary on the IHT205 match those that have been included in the oath.

- The appropriate IHT certificate is used (we explained which certificate to use in our April Newsletter).

- The IHT205 is signed by all the executors/administrators applying for the grant.

IHT PENALTIES

Just a reminder that all the provisions of s.245(4A) IHTA 1984 came into effect on 23 July 2005. This means that where an account is delivered more than two years after the end of the month in which the death/event occurred (without reasonable excuse) and there is tax to pay, those delivering the account may be liable to a penalty of up to £3,000. This penalty also applies where someone fails to comply with s.218A and notify us of an Instrument of Variation that increases the IHT payable on the death.

IHT206/IHT206A

The Probate and Inheritance Tax Helpline have received a number of calls from executors, where their solicitors forwarded them a copy of the IHT205 for completion but have forgotten to enclose a copy of the accompanying IHT206/IHT206A notes.

This obviously causes difficulties for the executors and generates unnecessary calls to the Helpline and no doubt the solicitors as well.

If you require additional copies of the notes, please contact our Stationery department by fax on 0845 234 1010 or by email at ir.purchasing@gtnet.gov.uk.

STAPLING & BINDING

A number of IHT200s and cheques have been received which have been stapled or bound together using corner or spine binding methods. Unfortunately, these are hampering the initial processing of the accounts, and can result in a delay in the IHT200 being examined, and cheques being overlooked. The binding and stapling must be removed prior to a file being created.

In view of this, could you please refrain from using these items when submitting correspondence to us.

IHT EXEMPTION FOR COMPENSATION PAID ON BANK ACCOUNTS OF HOLOCAUST VICTIMS

On 19 July the Paymaster General announced to Parliament a tax exemption for compensation for Holocaust victims, paid from foreign banks holding their war era accounts. The necessary legislation will be included in next year's Finance Bill.

Effect for Inheritance Tax

The exemption recognises that successful claimants for compensation will often trace their relationship to the original account holder through predecessors who are now dead. So the Finance Bill will include exemption from any additional inheritance tax (and the taxes it replaced) on their estates which might be thought to arise from the discovery of these accounts. The exemption will apply to any potential claimant who died before the respective award scheme was opened for claims.

Once a scheme is open for claims, normal IHT tax rules will apply to present-day recipients. So the proceeds of a successful claim or, where appropriate, the value of a claim or of the right to make a claim where an award has not yet been made, would form part of a deceased person's estate like any other asset.

If you believe that IHT has been paid in a situation where the payment may qualify for exemption, you should write to us at our Nottingham address (see over). Please quote the name and date of death of the deceased person. Alternatively, you can ring our Probate and Inheritance Tax Helpline on 0845 30 20 900. Further general information can be found at www.hmrc.gov.uk/individuals/holocaust.htm.

COVERING LETTERS

You may have already noticed that we no longer send out covering letters with routine calculations of inheritance tax.

In the majority of cases, you will already know about the reason for the tax calculation being issued because, for example; you have notified us of amendments or you have agreed a revised value with the District Valuer or Shares Valuation.

In view of this we have decided that covering letters will no longer be issued with straightforward calculations of tax. We will however make appropriate use of the notes box on the calculation to remind you of the reason for the calculation.

This will save us time and allow us to deal with cases more quickly.

LEAFLETS & IHT215

In accordance with Better Guidance procedures, the following Inheritance Tax leaflets and the IHT215 Practitioners Guide have been withdrawn from print.

IHT 2	Lifetime gifts
IHT 8	Alterations to inheritance after death
IHT 14	The personal rep's responsibilities
IHT 15	How to calculate the liability
IHT 16	Settled property
IHT 17	Businesses, farms and woodlands
IHT 18	Foreign aspects

These leaflets will continue to be available on the Internet at http://www.hmrc.gov.uk/cto.

DECEMBER 2005. – IHT NEWSLETTER

INTRODUCTION

Welcome to this edition of the IHT Newsletter.

During the Christmas and New Year period the office will be closed on 26 and 27 December and 2 January.

The next edition of the Newsletter will be April 2006. In the meantime, we would like to wish you all a very merry Christmas and a Happy New Year.

Customer Service Team

EXECUTOR'S OATH IN ENGLAND & WALES

Our Helpline receives a number of calls from solicitors seeking assistance about the wording of the Oath to be included in an application for a grant of representation. Our Helpline are not trained to deal with this sort of request; if you need to discuss the wording of the Oath to be used in particular circumstances, please contact your local Probate Registry or call the Solicitors line at the Principal Probate Registry on 0207 947 7431/7414.

CIVIL PARTNERSHIPS

The Civil Partnerships Act 2004 will come into force on 5 December 2005. Under the Act same-sex couples will be able to get legal recognition for their relationships by registering a civil partnership.

The parties to a civil partnership will be treated equally to married couples in a whole range of areas including Inheritance Tax. Very broadly, the rules on Inheritance Tax that at present apply to married couples will be extended to civil partners.

Inheritance Tax returns and explanatory notes will reflect the new legislation. From December the revised forms will be available on our website, www.hmrc.gov.uk/cto or they can be ordered by telephoning 0845 30 20 900.

We will continue to accept returns on the existing forms.

IHT205 & EXCEPTED ESTATES

Coverage in the National Press has suggested that the primary purpose of the IHT205 (C5 in Scotland) is to gather data about all estates so that assets can be traced through to the estates of surviving spouses (or civil partners). We would like to reassure you that this is not the case.

The primary aim of the IHT205/C5 is to take everyone through the filters that should be applied in deciding whether an estate qualifies as an excepted estate. If an estate success-fully passes the tests, recording the evidence in support of that conclusion provides reassurance for all concerned that an excepted estate grant has been applied for correctly.

We make use of that same information to monitor the operation of the excepted estate regulations and can do so without troubling the personal representatives any further. We only need to contact the personal representatives where we consider there is a risk to tax. Other than estates that are selected for review under our monitoring or subsequently become taxpaying, the information recorded on the IHT205/C5 is not indexed or entered on any IT systems.

We would also like to mention a couple of procedural points with excepted estates

- There is no need to report alterations to the information provided on the IHT205/C5 unless these give rise to a tax liability. Where a liability does arise, you should record the adjustments on a corrective account, form C4, and send it to us with a copy of the IHT205.

- If any property included in an excepted estate is sold, there is similarly no need to provide details of the sale unless this gives rise to a tax liability. The value you originally included in the IHT205/C5 is not "ascertained" for CGT purposes and, unless there is a liability, there is no need for us to agree whether the sale price should replace the value returned. You will need to deal with any CGT implications of the sale with the appropriate Inspector of Taxes.

- Unless you have delivered a corrective account, an application for clearance using form IHT30 is not appropriate for an excepted estate. The regulations contain an automatic clearance once the prescribed period has expired and that clearance holds good, even if there are alterations to the value of estate, as long as the estate continues to qualify as an excepted estate.

NHS CONTINUING CARE PAYMENTS

We have been asked how payments under the NHS Continuing Care Scheme should be treated for IHT. Our view is that the right to make a claim for reimbursement under this scheme is an asset of the estate and is liable to inheritance tax and interest. However that right must be valued in accordance with the provisions of s.160 and we consider that a discount is appropriate to reflect the uncertainty of success and likely delay in receiving the payment. The discounts, shown in the table below, reflect the impact on the scheme of the Coughlan case and subsequent reports by the Health Service Ombudsman.

Date of death	Discount
Prior to 17/7/99	100%
17/7/99 – 13/2/03	75%
14/2/03 – 16/12/04	40%
On or after 17/12/04	10%

Where a claim was underway at the date of death and an offer had been made by the Strategic Health Authority/Primary Care Trust you should include the offer, after the appropriate discount, as an asset in the IHT200. Please let us know the final figure when the payment is made. If the claim has not been quantified, or was not known about at death, you should report details of the amount eventually paid, again after the appropriate discount, as an amendment to the estate in due course.

It is important to take such a claim into account when establishing whether or not the estate qualifies as an excepted estate.

NEW PROCEDURE WHEN APPLYING FOR A GRANT AT THE NEWCASTLE PROBATE REGISTRY AND IN NORTHERN IRELAND

In order to make most efficient use of our resources, from 9 January 2006 our Nottingham office will be responsible for the initial handling of all estates where form IHT200 is completed and the grant is to be obtained in England, Wales and Northern Ireland.

So from that date, where previously you would have sent the IHT200, supporting papers and, if appropriate, payment to our Edinburgh (for Newcastle) or Belfast offices, please send the papers (and payment, if due) to our Nottingham office. Payments for such cases using the DPS should be made to the Bank of England.

Once we have completed our initial processing, the cases will be allocated to caseworkers across all three offices as now. For the avoidance of doubt, this change only applies to estates where form IHT200 is required; all applications for a grant in an excepted estate should continue to be sent to the appropriate Probate Registry.

IHT calculations issued by Belfast: with effect from the 31 January 2006 all payments made in respect of IHT calculations issued by Belfast should be sent to Nottingham Cashiers (electronic transfers should use the Bank of England 10-00-00 / 23430303). All other correspondence and adjustments to the estate should be notified to Belfast.

DECORATIONS FOR VALOUR OR GALLANT CONDUCT: EXTRA STATUTORY CONCESSION F19 (THE ESC)

Decorations which are awarded for valour or gallant conduct can command significant values and so increase the value of an estate or transfer for IHT purposes. Beneficiaries may therefore wish to keep them for personal or sentimental reasons, but be unable to afford to pay the tax on them.

Addressing this, Inland Revenue Press Release PR138/2000 announced on 21 August 2000 the following extra-statutory concession:

> "A decoration awarded for valour or gallant conduct is—by concession—to be treated for inheritance tax purposes as excluded property if it is shown **never** to have been transferred for consideration in money or money's worth."

The decoration (as distinct from a group of which it might form a part) must satisfy both conditions. It must have been awarded for valour or gallant conduct, although not necessarily in a military context, and never been sold. While it may be clear that a particular decoration was for gallantry (eg The Victoria Cross or The George Cross) some are not clear cut (e.g. The Order of the Bath or decorations awarded during the Napoleonic Wars) and others clearly do not qualify (e.g. campaign and general service medals).

The decoration need not have remained in the family of the original recipient. And it does not have to be a medal. Other decorations might include a piece of silverware or a presentation sword. The important thing is that it must demonstrably have been awarded for valour or gallant conduct.

You can invoke the ESC with a rider to the account. This should contain a description of the decoration, the circumstances in which it was awarded, and confirmation that, prior to the chargeable occasion, it had never been sold or transferred for consideration in money's worth. (But a sale during the administration of the estate in which the ESC is claimed would not prevent the ESC' applying.)

Please direct all enquiries about this concession to: Heritage Team, Capital Taxes, Ferrers House, PO Box 38, Castle Meadow Road, Nottingham NG2 1BB (or DX 701201 Nottingham 4) Telephone enquiries: 0115 974 2494.

For more information about extra-statutory concessions and a list of those currently in force please refer to: **http://www.hmrc.gov.uk/specialist/esc.pdf.**

INCOMPLETE ACCOUNTS

We are receiving a number of Inheritance Tax Accounts with missing schedules or incomplete answers/information on schedules where they are supplied. Often the missing information or schedules are required in order to consider the account and this will necessitate phoning or writing to you for the required information. This will unfortunately delay processing the account, and delay any referral to the District Valuer, which in turn will slow down the time taken to finalise matters.

We strive to make your dealings with this office run as smoothly and quickly as possible. Therefore, we would like to stress the importance of reading the explanatory notes prior to completion of the account IHT200 to ensure you have done everything in accordance with the guidance. Furthermore, can we ask that the account is checked thoroughly before it is submitted to ensure all required schedules are completed fully and any supporting information or documents are forwarded. We would like to remind you that all of our explanatory notes are available on our website and that our helpline is on hand should you require any assistance or advice.

STATIONERY ORDERS

There are several ways of obtaining forms and explanatory notes from Capital Taxes

• You can download them from our website www.hmrc.gov.uk/cto,

• requests can be emailed to hmrc.ihtorderline@gtnet.gov.uk or,

• faxed to 0845 234 1010.

Alternatively, you can telephone Capital Taxes to request the forms. From December 2005 if you wish to order our forms and explanatory notes by telephone, please use the Probate and Inheritance Tax Helpline number 0845 30 20 900. If you know which forms and notes you require press option one and you will be able to leave details of your request.

CUSTOMER GUIDE TO INHERITANCE TAX

We have started to publish a new Customer Guide to Inheritance Tax on the Internet. The new guide will be built up into a comprehensive guide between now and the end of 2005.

The guide will explain inheritance tax in a straightforward way. It is supported by a glossary of terms, which can be accessed from the text using the links provided. It also has links to the inheritance tax forms and the Inheritance Tax Manual. By structuring the guide in this way our customers will be able to choose the amount of information they need.

As well as information about inheritance tax the new guide will include information about personal representatives' responsibilities and how to pay inheritance tax. There will be links to the Court Service website where there is information about probate.

The new guide is being developed as part of our drive to improve the quality of our website. It will be easier to maintain. This means that we will be able to update it more quickly. It will be more flexible than the existing leaflets. As a result we will be able to tailor the content to meet our customers needs.

The Customer Guide to Inheritance Tax will in due course replace the existing range of inheritance tax leaflets that currently appear on our website. As it will only be published on the Internet we will continue to have a range of printed leaflets, but we expect that there will be fewer of them. We also expect that they will be supported by a number of fact sheets, each of which will deal with a single subject.

We welcome feedback from our customers. Any feedback on the Customer Guide to Inheritance Tax should be sent to: Edward.watts@hmrc.gsi.gov.uk.

IHT CUSTOMER SURVEY

Back in the spring we commissioned a survey of IHT customers, both professional and personal. The final report has just been published on the HMRC website. We are pleased to have this opportunity to thank those of you who took part, we need feedback if we are to improve our service but we are aware of the many calls on your time and we do appreciate your willingness to engage with us in the process.

We also want to share the main findings and our thoughts as to what we will do as a result.

The results reflect the views of over 500 professional customers who took part in the survey. Overall the results show a high level of satisfaction, with 96% of those surveyed describing themselves as satisfied or very satisfied with the service we provide.

We are particularly challenged by the need to provide accurate, up to date guidance at reasonable cost. We therefore asked specific questions about use of the internet. We are encouraged that most (90%) of you have adequate internet access, but we still have work to do to improve our online guidance so material is easy to find. Since the survey was held we have further developed the online guidance, and we would welcome any feedback about what more is needed.

Over 80% of those who responded prefer written guidance in the form of a separate booklet, rather than included in the body of a form. However, many non-professional customers fail to read the accompanying guidance when completing the IHT account. To reconcile differing needs here we will expand the guidance on straightforward issues included in the body of the form, but continue to provide further in depth information in the accompanying notes.

It is clear that we need to improve our calculations; 29% of professional customers do not find them easy to understand. We would welcome any specific ideas about making them more explicit, so if you have instances of specific difficulties or any other thoughts on the topic please do e-mail the Customer Service Team.

Similarly 25% of professionals did not find the direct payment scheme easy to use. We have made changes, not least by encouraging you to telephone for references rather than write, and hopefully this is seen as an improvement. If it isn't, please let us know.

Overall our aim is to reduce the burden on those involved in administering estates. We will continue to work closely with the Probate Service and eliminate as far as possible any duplication in the information applicants are asked to provide. Increasingly information will be provided online, although we are sensitive to the fact that not all personal applicants will have internet access or choose to use this channel of communication. Above all we will continue to ask you for your views, and involve you in devising efficient services that meet your needs in the 21ˢᵗ Century.

INTEREST RATE CHANGE

With effect from the 6 September 2005, interest on unpaid and overpaid tax is charged at 3%.

DIRECT PAYMENT SCHEME (DPS)

To obtain a Capital Taxes reference for use with this scheme, we would much prefer you to telephone our Helpline on 0845 30 20 900 and we will be able to give you a reference over the phone. If, however, you would prefer to apply for a reference by post, we have changed the D20 so that it doubles as the form to use to obtain the reference and to make application to the bank. The D21 has been made obsolete.

If you are applying for a reference by post, fill in the deceased's name and date of death on the front of the form and put your own return address and reference on the back. We will allocate the reference, record it on the D20 and send it back to you.

APRIL 2006. – IHT NEWSLETTER

INTRODUCTION

Welcome to the April 2006 edition of our IHT Newsletter. Our new Assistant Director joined us in March. Janet Blow has taken over the job previously done by Anne King. Janet's responsibilities include all initial processing matters and primary compliance for IHT, including the Probate & Inheritance Tax Helpline. The next edition of the Newsletter will be in August 2006.

Customer Service Team

DELIVERY OF A COMPLETE IHT200

The primary purpose behind the current version of form IHT200 is to help the taxpayer deliver a correct and complete account at the outset. This should keep contact after the grant to a minimum and hopefully keep costs down on both sides. When the form was introduced a little over 6 years ago, the "failure" rate – the number of accounts that were either not filled in properly or were missing "D" pages and attachments – was less than 2% (around 8 cases a week). At the last count, this had grown to around 10% (around 65 cases a week), which is a significant increase given the rise in workload over the same period.

To provide a high level of customer service, we have been releasing form D18 (or the Inventory in Scotland) before insisting that the omissions be corrected. Unfortunately, and with the higher number of "failures", chasing missing information after release of the D18/Inventory is creating a disproportionately large amount of unnecessary work.

We would sooner deploy the resource used in chasing missing information against our rising caseload so that we can continue to settle estates in as short a time as possible. You can help us to do so by making sure that the IHT200 is fully completed, that all the "D" pages you intend to send to us are included with the form and that any other information that we ask for in the guidance notes is supplied.

To help drive the "failure" rate down, we will be reverting to our previous practice of retaining the D18/Inventory until a complete account is delivered. To avoid any delay in the issue of the grant/Confirmation this would bring, please ensure that a full and complete IHT200 is delivered at the outset.

EXCEPTED ESTATES, DOUBLE DEATHS & INSTRUMENTS OF VARIATION (1)

Our Probate & Inheritance Tax Helpline have received a number of enquiries from solicitors about how, or whether, form IHT200 should be completed where

- there are two deaths – usually husband and wife – within 2 years of each other, and

- within 2 years of the first death, the beneficiaries of the second to die effect an Instrument of Variation (IoV) to redirect property from the first estate away from the second so that both estates, for IHT purposes, are below the excepted estate limit.

Our August 2004 Newsletter covered this issue in some detail but to recap ...

The underlying principle is that the hypothesis created by the IoV only takes effect for IHT purposes. It does not alter the real world position of the second estate at the date the second person dies. So if, in the real world, the second estate did not qualify as an excepted estate, form IHT200 is required.

Form IHT200 should be completed declaring the true gross values of the estate in sections F and G. Then to give effect to the IoV, the assets that are being redirected away from the estate should be deducted in the "Exemptions and reliefs" boxes. This way, the correct value for the gross and net estate is carried forward to form D18 and to the probate papers and the taxable value of the estate, for IHT purposes, is also correctly calculated.

INSTRUMENTS OF VARIATION (2)

May we remind you please that there is no need to send an IOV to us unless it has a "tax effect". There is no requirement to "register" an IOV and we will not pass any comment about the impact of an IOV, particularly in excepted estates, where it does not affect the IHT that is payable.

If you are unsure about whether an IOV meets the requirements of Section 142 IHTA 1984, a checklist on form IOV2, which will take you through all the issues that need to be considered, is available from our website at www.hmrc.gov.uk/cto.

IHT PENSION HELPLINE

The Capital Taxes Pension Helpline have changed their telephone number to **0131 777 4296**.

Please note that this number is for inheritance tax pension enquiries only.

PROSECUTION FOR IHT FRAUD

In our April 2005 Newsletter we told you about the first prosecution for IHT fraud. In the second such case, and the first in England, Shaun Gray was found guilty on each of 3 counts of false accounting and 2 of forgery in January 2006. He was sentenced to 3 years on each count, the terms to run concurrently.

Mr Gray delivered an incorrect Inheritance Tax Account in respect of the estate of Helen Guiterman, to whom he was distantly related, omitting some £500,000 of assets. The investigators also established that he had forged Helen Guiterman's Will, making himself the major beneficiary. Under a previous Will, Miss Guiterman had left her important collection of David Roberts' paintings to the National Art Collections Fund (NACF) and most of the residue of her estate to charity. As a result of the investigation, the Roberts collection has been recovered from Mr Gray and returned to the NACF.

Both these cases illustrate that we take the delivery of a correct and complete account very seriously indeed and that we will pursue those who try to avoid making a full and complete return.

BUSH HOUSE

The Stamp Office counter at Bush House has been closed with effect from 30th March 2006. This means that it is no longer possible to pay IHT over the counter and receive a receipted D18 in return.

We have considered whether we can continue with this service at alternative premises. But with the facility for local offices to bank payments being withdrawn, and in view of the very small fraction of payments that were made this way, we have concluded that there is no realistic prospect of providing an alternative.

IHT MANUAL – DISCRETIONARY TRUSTS

You may like to note that a new section, Section 42 Discretionary Trusts, will be added to the IHT Manual during April. This section will include guidance on the IHT charges, relevant property and trust powers, as well as a comprehensive subsection on Employee Benefit Trusts. If you find it useful, or not, please let us know. You can email us at InheritanceTaxCustomerService@gtnet.gov.uk.

HOUSEHOLD & PERSONAL GOODS

IHT200 & IHT100 In our December 2004 Newsletter we told you that from January 2005 we would be paying close attention to the values included for household and personal goods. We said that in appropriate cases we would open an enquiry to satisfy ourselves that all of the goods had been included and that they had been valued on the statutory basis.

In our December 2005 Newsletter we explained the difficulties caused by incomplete accounts with missing information and/or schedules. Investigating the household and personal goods in a number of estates has highlighted the difficulties with missing or incomplete information in this area. Some of the issues that cause us concern are.

- The question about household and personal goods on page 2 of the IHT200 has been answered "no" and form D10 has not been completed. When we make enquiries into these estates we invariably find that there were household and personal goods, although the personal representative(s) may have considered them valueless. In these circumstances the personal representative should answer "yes" to the question on page 2. Form D10 should be completed giving details of the household and personal goods and a full explanation of why they are considered to have no value.

- Form D10 is completed to show a nil value for the household and personal goods but no explanation of why is provided. As explained in the D10 (Notes) you should give details of the household and personal goods and a full explanation of why they are considered to have no value.

- Form D10 simply shows a value and no other information. As explained in the D10 (Notes) you should complete the form to give details of the household and personal goods and a full explanation of how the value was arrived at. If a professional valuation was obtained, a copy of this should be attached. If the value was an estimate by the personal representative(s), you should explain whether they have expertise in valuing such items and say how they estimated the value and whether they used any comparisons.

- A professional valuation has been obtained but the Valuer has not stated that the valuation is on an open market basis. If the valuation was made on an open market basis the Valuer should be asked to confirm this and the confirmation attached to the valuation.

- There is a car but this is not mentioned separately on form D10 and its value is included in a global figure for household and personal goods. If there is a car you should state the value placed on this and detail the make, exact model, year of registration and the registration number.

- The deceased owned a holiday home but no household goods are included for that property. Even if these are considered to have a nil value we still need to have details and a full explanation of the value.

- The household and personal goods in the house are included but we have found that items elsewhere are sometimes overlooked. When taking an inventory be sure to check the contents of sheds and garages, and for vehicles parked on the drive or even in the street. Items are sometimes stored with a bank, relative or friend for safekeeping, so this also needs to be considered.

If you provide full information about the household and personal goods we are more likely to be able to satisfy ourselves that they have been properly accounted for and to accept the values returned without the necessity of opening an enquiry.

In the long term we are planning to re-design the form D10 to make it easier for you to provide us with the information we need.

DIRECT PAYMENT SCHEME

We are finding that people are requesting a Capital Taxes reference number for purposes other than using the Direct Payment Scheme.

We would please ask you only to request a reference prior to submitting the Inheritance Tax Account if the estate is taxpaying and you intend on paying the tax through the scheme.

DEVELOPMENT VALUE

There appears to be some confusion over whether the potential of development (or hope) value needs to be accounted for where an estate contains land or buildings. The simple answer is, yes it does.

When completing an Inheritance Tax Account, we expect personal representatives to take all appropriate steps to provide (as close as possible) a value that the land or building may expect to achieve if sold on the open market (section 160 IHTA 1984). When considering this value the personal representatives must account for any feature that may make it attractive to a builder or developer, for example large gardens or access to land.

We expect all evidence available to be considered when completing the Inheritance Tax Account. Even if a professional valuation has been obtained, further information may come to light (for example marketing advice) which casts doubt on whether the original valuation still properly reflects the open market value as at the date of death.

If this is the case, we consider it reasonable to expect the personal representative to account for the new information when including the final valuation in the account or, if the account has been delivered, for this office to be notified as quickly as possible. Where it is evident that reasonable and adequate steps have not been taken to ascertain the open market value, based on all information that was available, penalties may be sought.

LOSS ON SALE OF LAND

We are receiving an increasing number of C4 corrective accounts where we are being asked to accept the lower sale price for property/land included in the estate. Please note a claim must be made on form **IHT38**. We cannot accept a claim on a C4 corrective account or by letter.

If a value has been agreed with the Valuation Office Agency (DV), we will consider if relief can be granted, and whether it should be provisional or final relief, on receipt of form IHT38.

If a value has still to be agreed with the DV you should contact the Valuer involved, making them aware of the sale. Alternatively, you can contact the Capital Taxes office dealing with the estate, and they will pass the information on to the DV.

You can download form IHT38 from our website www.hmrc.gov.uk/cto or you can email us at hmrc.ihtorderline@gtnet.gov.uk. You can also request the form from our Probate & Inheritance Tax Helpline on 0845 30 20 900 or by fax on 0845 234 1010.

EMPLOYEE BENEFIT TRUSTS

Trusts that satisfy the requirements of section 86 Inheritance Tax Act 1984 (IHTA) are excluded from the IHT regime for discretionary trusts.

In order to satisfy section 86, settled property must be held on trusts ensuring that it can be only applied for (broadly speaking) employees and their relatives and dependants. More particularly, under section 86(1)(b), among the class of eligible persons are those "... of a class defined by reference to a relationship to ..."(an employee).

We have been advised that "relationship" should be given a wide meaning for the purposes of section 86. In our view, the term embraces not only relatives, as defined for IHT purposes in section 270 IHTA (incorporating section 286 Taxation of Chargeable Gains Act 1992), but anyone who could be regarded as being "in a relationship" with an employee. Such a person might often be referred to as a "partner". Thus a trust that enabled settled property to be applied, among others, to the partners of employees would satisfy section 86, assuming of course that it met the other requirements of that section.

APPLYING FOR A GRANT IN NORTHERN IRELAND – A REMINDER

All IHT200's, D18's, supporting papers and, if appropriate, payments should now be sent to our **Nottingham** office. Sending these to our Belfast office may result in unnecessary delays, as they no longer have the facility to stamp D18's or to bank payments. This change only applies to estates where form IHT200 is required.

BUDGET 2006

As you will know by now, the Budget contained a number of changes to IHT. The operational consequences of these changes are as follows.

IHT Threshold

The threshold is increased to £285,000 for chargeable events occurring on or after 6th April 2006. Please remember that in establishing whether an estate qualifies as an excepted estate, the threshold remains at £275,000 where the deceased died on or after 6th April 2006 and an application for probate or confirmation is made before 6th August 2006.

Settled Property

Most transfers into trust are now immediately chargeable to IHT when made. The exception is where the trust is set up for a disabled person. You will need to report all such transfers to us on form IHT100. This means that the excepted transfer and termination regulations will have more purpose than previously and we will be reviewing the cash limits in those regulations. A&M trusts may now be subject to ten-year and exit charges.

Pensions

There are two aspects to changes to the IHT treatment of pensions. Firstly, where a scheme member dies under age 75, the Finance Bill contains legislation that will enable us to continue with our existing treatment in relation to a scheme member's dealings with their pension scheme. As now, our pension specialists in Edinburgh will continue to consider whether any such dealings give rise to a charge to IHT.

The second change provides for an IHT charge where assets remain in a fund that has provided a scheme member with an Alternatively Secured Pension (ASP). Where a scheme member dies on or after age 75 and the left-over ASP funds are used to pay benefits to a surviving spouse, civil partner or financial dependent, an IHT charge will arise when the survivor's entitlement ceases, usually on their own death. In other cases (unless the funds are left to charity), the charge will arise on the death of the scheme member. We will be revising form IHT100 and form D6 to cater for this latter situation and will produce a new form for scheme providers to notify us of the former.

Dormant Bank Accounts

The value of any right to claim compensation in respect of dormant bank accounts belonging to Holocaust victims before any formal compensation scheme is opened is now exempt from IHT. But payments received by a victim, or as the heir of one and included in their estate will be liable to IHT in the normal way – as will the value of any outstanding claim under an existing scheme – and should be included on form IHT200.

Pre-Budget Report

The proposals announced in the Pre-Budget Report about excluded property trusts and the measure to prevent revertor – to – settlor trusts circumventing the Pre-Owned Assets charge took effect from 5 December 2005.

CAPITAL TAXES – PROCESSES

We have recently run an event to review our processes with the aim of improving efficiency, customer service and streamlining our processes. This will involve our front end process from the point we receive an account up to the file reaching a caseworker. This is to let you know that we will be running a pilot from 24th April 2006. Therefore, when an account is sent to us it will either go through the usual route or to the pilot team. The pilot team will be a multi function team aiming to smooth workflow and reduce lead times. The pilot will run for at least three months after which we will evaluate the results.

INVENTORY FORM C1 – COMPLETION OF PAGE 4

We have noticed that the information contained on page 4 of the Inventory form C1 is not always fully completed.

Although this page is not part of the public record, it does play a vital part in helping us to quickly identify the different categories of the estate and to direct our resources to deal with the incoming work as best we can. Can we ask you please to make sure that page 4 of form C1 is fully completed in every case?

AUGUST 2006. – IHT NEWSLETTER

INTRODUCTION

Welcome to August's edition of the IHT Newsletter.

This Newsletter is slightly shorter than previous editions but it does, however, contain a lot of important information. For example, there is an article about changes to the excepted estate regulations. There is also information on the Finance Act 2006 and the implications that this has on Inheritance Tax.

Please do take the time to read carefully through this Newsletter. If you have any queries at all then please phone our Probate & Inheritance Tax Helpline on 0845 30 20 900. Any feedback on the articles contained in this Newsletter can be sent to the Customer Service team at our Nottingham address.

FOREIGN ASSETS – IHT200 & IHT100

When completing the IHT200, form D15 is used to give details of any foreign assets that form part of the estate. For a transfer where the IHT100 is appropriate, form D39 is used to give details of foreign assets. The guidance notes that accompany these forms explain the steps we expect people to take to complete them accurately and completely. Jointly owned foreign assets are included on the D15 or D39, and you should include answers to the joint property questions from the D4 on these forms.

When we receive completed accounts that include foreign property, the questions that we consider are:

- Does the IHT return constitute a complete return of the foreign assets owned by the deceased, transferor or trust? For example, if a house abroad is included in the account would there normally be household goods?

And

- Has the value of these assets been ascertained in accordance with the correct statutory principles? These are set out in section 160 of the Inheritance Tax Act 1984: the value for inheritance tax purposes is "the price which the property might reasonably be expected to fetch if sold in the open market". A foreign valuer used to a different tax system may not have valued on the statutory basis.

Where it is unclear if all the foreign assets have been included, or that they have been valued correctly, there is an increased likelihood that we will ask for further information or seek an explanation of the value offered.

For the remainder of 2006 we will be paying particularly close attention to foreign assets. In appropriate cases we will open an enquiry and ask you for further information to satisfy ourselves that all of the foreign assets have been included and that they have been valued on the statutory basis. We will tell you if the estate is one that has been selected for enquiry in this way. Where it appears that the accountable people have been negligent we will consider whether a penalty is appropriate.

FINANCE ACT 2006

The Finance Act 2006 has made some significant changes to IHT. There have been some changes to the original Budget proposals, but with Royal Assent, we now know the new shape of IHT.

IHT treatment of trusts

The most significant change concerns the treatment of property in trusts. Potentially Exempt Transfer treatment for most inter vivos transfers into trust has been withdrawn and unless the trust now qualifies as a disabled person's trust, the transfer into trust is immediately chargeable to IHT. This means that the transferor will need to complete and deliver form IHT100.

The concept that beneficial entitlement to an interest in possession means that the underlying trust assets are part of the estate is now restricted to

- an immediate post-death interest (defined in s.49A IHTA 1984),
- a disabled persons interest, (now defined in s.89B IHTA 1984) or
- a transitional serial interest (defined in s.49B to E IHTA 1984).

This means that, apart from the particular types of interest mentioned above and beneficial interests in possession that already existed on 22 March 2006, most trust assets will no longer be aggregated with a person's Free Estate. The corollary is, however, that those trusts which no longer form part of a person's estate will all be subject to the separate charging regime for trusts under Part III Chapter III IHTA 1984 with ten-yearly and exit charges applying.

This year's measures also affect the IHT treatment of accumulation and maintenance trusts (A&Ms). New trusts for minor children will secure complete freedom from the Part III Chapter III charging regime only if they arise under an intestacy or the Will of a deceased parent and they provide for an absolute entitlement at age 18. Alternatively they may secure partial relief from this regime by providing for absolute entitlement at age 25.

Pre-22 March 2006 A&Ms will become subject to Part III Chapter III by 6 April 2008 unless by then they provide for absolute entitlement at age 18 or 25 in order to secure complete or partial freedom from this regime.

Funds in alternatively secured pensions (ASPs)

New charges under s.151A-C IHTA 1984 will apply to funds in ASPs. In many cases, no charge will arise on the scheme member's death; but that charge will be recaptured when the dependent who inherited the fund dies. On the scheme member's death, the ASP fund is "appropriate property" and the deceased is treated as beneficially entitled to the assets. Consequently, it will be necessary for personal representatives to establish details of the fund and provide that information in form IHT200. However, it will be the scheme administrator who is accountable and liable for the funds' share of the tax.

Excluded property trusts

This change is an anti-avoidance measure that applies when a UK domiciled individual buys an interest in possession in an overseas trust. Where the interest has been acquired on or after 5 December 2005, the Finance Act ensures that the underlying property will not be excluded property for IHT purposes, even if it is situated outside the UK.

There is more information about these changes in our Customer Guide on the Internet and we will be making the necessary changes to our forms and guidance notes. The revisions to the Customer Guide have already been made and we hope the new forms will be available on the HMRC website before the end of August, that is before the due date for interest for someone who died on or after Budget day, whose estate is affected by these changes.

We would welcome feedback about the changes incorporated into the Customer Guide and the forms and guidance, particularly where you feel that an issue may need clarification or expansion. Please send your feedback to the Customer Service Team.

EXCEPTED ESTATES

The following changes to the excepted estate regulations take effect for deaths on or after 1st September 2006.

- the cash limit for specified transfers is increased to £150,000;
- the cash limit for settled property is increased to £150,000;
- the cash limit for foreign property is increased to £100,000; and

- the cash limit where the deceased was not domiciled in the UK is increased to £150,000.

Any estate where a charge arises on an alternatively secured pension fund under s.151A-C IHTA 1984 is **excluded** from qualifying as an excepted estate.

EXCEPTED ESTATES
The overall limit for an excepted estate is now £285,000 for deaths on or after 6 August 2006

EXCEPTED ESTATES WITH NO LIABILITY TO IHT

The changes made to the excepted estate regulations over the last couple of years should minimise the number of estates that need to deliver an IHT200 where there is no liability to IHT – yet last year we received around 18,000 returns from such estates. We have looked carefully at these returns and they breakdown into three distinct groups

- estates where the gross value exceeds the IHT threshold; but exemption, relief or liabilities keep the chargeable estate below the threshold,

- estates where the gross value is below the IHT threshold; but the estate is not within the conditions to qualify as an excepted estate; and

- estates which do qualify as excepted estates; but form IHT200 is delivered in any event.

While we balance the risk to the Exchequer, there is little we can do about the first group and we hope that the net effect of the changes from 1st September will cut back further the second group of estates.

But with regard to the third group (around 5,500 cases per year), can we urge you please to use the correct process to apply for a grant of probate/Confirmation as an excepted estate and use form IHT205 (or C5 in Scotland) rather than form IHT200. Doing so will mean you can get on with administering the estate without needing our sanction. With pressure on our resources, we have to prioritise our work and dealing with unnecessary IHT200s is the lowest of those priorities. So to avoid the risk of delay and to keep both your clients' costs and ours to a minimum, please do use the correct process where an estate qualifies as an excepted estate.

DEDUCTION OF RELIEF IN EXEMPT ESTATES

Where a deduction for, say, agricultural or business relief is made in an estate which is nevertheless not liable to tax because an exemption is available, we will not consider the validity of the deduction of the relief, or extent to which relief would otherwise be available. This is because with ever tightening resources, we cannot justify the costs of investigation to the taxpayer or Exchequer where there can be no tax consequences. If an application for clearance is made, we will issue a certificate, but that is no indication that we have considered or accepted any deduction for a relief against the estate. Should the availability of the relief affect the IHT payable on another estate; for example the subsequent death of a spouse/civil partner, we will consider the deduction for relief at that time and will not be bound by the fact that we have issued clearance in an estate where similar circumstances applied, but tax was not payable for other reasons.

IHT PAYMENTS – New process

Changes will take place later in the year that will affect our IHT banking facility at Meldrum House in Edinburgh.

61 IHT Newsletter and Tax Bulletin extracts

HM Revenue & Customs has taken the decision that **all** cheque handling should be through the Accounts Office at Shipley. Consequently, all local banking facilities are being withdrawn over a period of time (HMRC Working Together, February 2006). You may have seen from the December 2005 IHT Newsletter that the banking facilities have already been withdrawn from our Belfast office; and our banking facilities in Edinburgh will cease later this year. This will bring all IHT cheque handling to Nottingham, until such time as responsibility for all IHT payments is transferred to Shipley.

With the impending move to Shipley, we will need to begin using a bank-approved payslip that conforms to clearing bank standards. This change will initially apply to the payment of IHT calculations issued **after** Confirmation and Probate. We will enclose a payslip and pre-addressed envelope with every calculation; the cheque and payslip should be put in the envelope and sent to our Nottingham office.

We will then extend this use of a payslip to the initial payment required on delivery of the IHT200 & C1 in Edinburgh. This means that it will be necessary for an IHT reference to be allocated to every 'taxpaying' estate before the payment is made (so that we can quickly tie up the payment made to Nottingham with the papers delivered to Edinburgh and release the C1). We do not anticipate any problems in this regard, as staff in Edinburgh will have real time access to our accounting system; they will be able to see when the payment has been received.

The process to apply for an IHT reference number already exists where payment is to be made using the Direct Payment Scheme; we will simply extend this process to all estates where there is tax to pay.

Hopefully from October and only in Scotland you can telephone 0131 777 4236, 4179 & 4245 to request an IHT reference number. Alternatively, you may apply for a reference by post. We will re-introduce form D21 (Application for an Inheritance Tax reference). The D21 will, however, ask for one further piece of information; we need you to supply preferably the deceased's **National Insurance Number** or, if exceptionally this is not available, their **Income Tax reference**. This information is necessary so that we may confirm the identity of the deceased. If you telephone us for a reference, please ensure you have this additional information to hand.

When we receive your D21, or when you telephone us, we will create a record and allocate a reference number. We will send you a payslip [showing the reference] and a reply envelope. You should then send the completed IHT200 & C1 to our Edinburgh Office and your payment to Nottingham in the reply envelope. Please don't forget to include the IHT payslip with your payment.

We hope to begin using IHT payslips for all IHT calculations in September this year and for initial payments in Scotland in early October. We will contact solicitors in Scotland separately once a date has been decided. And we will keep you informed about when we will start to use payslips for the initial payment required on delivery of the IHT200 to Nottingham (England & Wales and Northern Ireland cases).

STAPLING & BINDING

A number of IHT200's and cheques have been received which have been stapled or bound together using corner or spine binding methods. These are hampering the initial processing of the accounts, and can result in a delay in the IHT200 being examined, and cheques being overlooked as the binding and stapling must be removed prior to a file being created.

If you prefer to secure all of the paperwork together please can you use a hole punch in the top left-hand corner and attach a treasury tag. This method is used to secure the IHT200 when it is placed in our files.

DECEMBER 2006. – IHT NEWSLETTER

INTRODUCTION

Welcome to December's edition of the IHT Newsletter.

Our new Assistant Director joined us in October. Linda Trippier has taken over as manager of the Inheritance Tax Compliance team, the job previously done by Mike Williams.

During the Christmas and New Year period the office will be closed on 25 and 26 December and 1 January. Our Edinburgh office will also be closed on 2 January.

The next edition of the Newsletter will be in April 2007. However, things are changing … you may wish to pay particular attention to the article on page 3. In the meantime, we would like to wish you all a Merry Christmas and a Happy New Year.

Please do take the time to read carefully through this Newsletter. If you have any queries at all then please phone our Probate & Inheritance Tax Helpline on 0845 30 20 900. Any feedback on the articles contained in this Newsletter can be sent to the Customer Service team at our Nottingham address.

D18 TURNAROUND

We are finding that we spend a lot of time responding to telephone enquiries about when the form D18 will be issued. Many of these enquiries arise within a short time of us receiving the IHT200. This is proving to be counterproductive in that time which could be spent processing accounts is being taken up responding to individual requests, thereby slowing down the processing of other accounts.

We aim to issue the majority of forms D18 within 7 working days of us receiving payment of the correct amount of tax and the supporting documentation.

Where we receive

- a complete account with all relevant supplementary pages and information provided;

- a correct calculation of the tax currently due; and

- payment of that amount

the D18 will normally be issued sooner than this. In future, our Helpline staff will ask when you sent your payment to us. If this is within 7 working days you will be asked to wait for the process to complete its normal course. We will follow up any delays in issuing the D18 beyond this time period. Please help us by not chasing us for forms D18 until 7 working days after you sent your payment to us.

JOINT ASSETS

In our April 2006 Newsletter we explained that we were receiving an increasing number of IHT200s that were not fully completed. We told you that we were responding to this by retaining the D18/Inventory until a complete account is delivered. The most common problem with the IHT200 is that full information on joint assets is not provided either because form D4 is not completed or because it is not completed fully. This article discusses some of the main issues.

- We receive a number of accounts where the question about joint property on page 2 of the IHT200 has been answered 'No', and no form D4 has been submitted, but where the form D12 indicates that the deceased owned a fractional share of a property. When we ask why a D4 was not completed we are often told that it is unnecessary because the property was owned as 'tenants in common' or, occasionally, because it was owned as 'joint tenants'. This is incorrect. If property is owned jointly, whether as 'tenants in common' or 'joint tenants', a completed form D4 is always required. If one is not submitted with the IHT200 we will ask for one before we will issue the D18/Confirmation. This will of course delay the issue of the grant/Confirmation. You can avoid this by ensuring a form D4 is always completed where there are fractional shares of property.

- We also find that where a form D4 is submitted with the IHT200, it is not always fully completed. Again, this means we have to ask for missing information before we can issue the D18/Confirmation, thereby delaying the issue of the grant/Confirmation. The D4 (Notes) provide guidance on what information is required and the issues that may arise. You may wish to use a separate D4 for each item of joint property, rather than trying to squeeze all the information about several items onto one form.

- We need to know who the other joint owner(s) are. It is helpful to us if you state their relationship to the deceased; this gives us a clearer picture of the joint ownership. It is particularly important to tell us when the joint ownership began. If it began many years ago we may not need the exact date; '20 years ago' or '1986' would suffice. But, if the joint ownership began within, or just outside, 7 years of the date of death we will need the exact date.

- It is also important to say how much each joint owner provided. In some cases the position will be quite clear, for example where a deceased and his sister inherited a house from their father, or where the deceased opened a joint bank account with his son and provided all the money in the account. In other cases, for example where both joint owners contributed but the contribution was unequal, it may be more complex. We also need to know how any income from joint assets was dealt with, as this may be indicative of the beneficial ownership. Whatever the circumstances, we need full details in order to consider exactly what claims for tax arise.

- Where the joint asset is a bank or building society account we need to know about withdrawals from the account. This is because any withdrawals by the joint owner(s) in excess of any funds provided by them will constitute gifts by the deceased.

- Finally we need to know whether the joint asset passes by survivorship or under the deceased's will or intestacy. This is particularly important where part of the estate devolves to an exempt beneficiary.

Providing full details of the joint property on delivery of the IHT200 will help avoid delay in the issue of the grant/Confirmation. It will also make it more likely that we can agree the extent of the claim without the need for additional enquiries. In the longer term we are planning to redesign the form D4 to make it easier for you to provide the information we require.

THE LATE CAPITAL TAXES

Capital Taxes no longer exists as an entity – so we will stop using the name. In future we will be known as HMRC Inheritance Tax. Over time all references to Capital Taxes, CT and CTO will be removed from our letters, forms and guidance. This change will not affect the work that we do and we will strive to provide you with the highest quality service possible.

OBTAINING AN IHT REFERENCE

Our April 2003 Newsletter introduced the Direct Payment Scheme (DPS), a process where personal representatives can draw on money held in the deceased's bank or building society account(s) to pay the IHT that is due on delivery of form IHT200. In order to use the scheme the personal representatives have to first obtain an Inheritance Tax reference either by telephone or using form D20. It is only necessary to apply for a reference in this way if you intend to use the DPS.

Since the scheme was introduced we have found that a number of people have applied for a reference when they do not actually need one, because the estate is an excepted estate and no IHT is payable. This causes unnecessary work for the personal representatives in applying for a reference that they do not need, and unnecessary work for us in creating a reference which is not needed and then following it up to find out why no IHT200 has been delivered.

Please do not apply for a reference if you are intending to apply for an excepted estate grant. If you do apply for a reference, and subsequently decide it is not required, because the estate is excepted, it would be helpful if you could let us know so that we can close our papers.

COMMUNICATING WITH OUR CUSTOMERS

IHT Newsletter – online

The IHT Newsletter is currently produced three times a year (in April, August and December). It is printed and distributed to approximately 7,000 practitioners and is published on the HMRC website at www.hmrc.gov.uk/cto/newsletter.htm.

We have recently reviewed our IHT Newsletter, considering whether we should only publish it on the HMRC website and stop providing a printed version.

However, the obvious benefit of a paper version is that it actually lands on your desk, so our main concern was how to let you know when a new edition of the newsletter had been released.

We have investigated a number of options for publicising this and have decided that the easiest way for us to let you know a newsletter has been issued is to email you.

But, we do have a problem with this. We do not currently have your email details recorded on our mailing database. So, if you wish to receive notification that the IHT Newsletter has been published please email us at InheritanceTaxCustomerService@gtnet.gov.uk.

Alternatively you can write to the Customer Service Team at our Nottingham office.

We hope to move to an online only version by August 2007.

IHT Presentations

From time to time we are asked by groups of customers – a local branch of the Society of Trust and Estate Practitioners for example – to give a presentation on an IHT-related topic. We have been reviewing our policy in this area, mainly with the objective of securing value for money from this activity, as we must do from all aspects of our business.

When considering requests to give presentations in future, we shall be taking into account factors such as the cost to us in delivering the presentation, the likely size of the audience and whether the chosen topic is one that would allow us to get across or reinforce messages about aspects of our business. Our new policy means that we will not be able to say "yes" to all requests for presentations. But we are still very keen to talk to groups of you face-to-face. With this in mind, we do intend to use the IHT Newsletter to give you information about those areas of the IHT business about which we would be happy to come to talk to you. We hope you will find this helpful.

APRIL 2007. – IHT NEWSLETTER

INTRODUCTION

Welcome to the April edition of the IHT Newsletter.

This edition includes important information regarding the Finance Bill 2007 and the implications on Inheritance Tax with regard to:

- IHT Nil Rate Band
- IHT Rules for Pensions: registered pension schemes
- ASP's
- Pre-Owned Assets

We are always happy to hear your comments and would ask that if you have any features that you would like to see, please email the Customer Service Team at: InheritanceTaxCustomerService@gtnet.gov.uk.

Please do take the time to read carefully through this Newsletter. If you have any queries at all then please phone our Probate & Inheritance Tax Helpline on 0845 30 20 900. Any feedback on the articles contained in this Newsletter can be sent to the Customer Service Team at our Nottingham address.

Customer Service Team

IMPORTANT PAYMENTS OF INHERITANCE TAX

We have explained in earlier Newsletters about the closure of Cashiers in our Belfast & Edinburgh offices. As a consequence of this, we are now closing our accounts with the Bank of Ireland and the Royal Bank of Scotland.

With effect from 27 March 2007 the only account to be used for paying Inheritance Tax is Bank of England account number 23430303. For all electronic payments the sort code is 10-00-00. If you are using a bank giro credit the sort code is 10-53-92.

If you are paying Inheritance Tax by cheque, please make sure you send them to Section K, PO Box 38, Ferrers House, Castle Meadow Road, Nottingham NG2 1BB or DX 701205, Nottingham 4. This includes payments made on delivery of the Inheritance Tax return, payment of calculations, or payments on account.

Any payments received in Belfast and Edinburgh cannot be processed in those offices and sending payments to these offices will only delay our handling of your case.

DIRECT PAYMENT SCHEME

The Direct Payment Scheme allows you to pay the initial payment of IHT, due on delivery of forms IHT200, using funds from the deceased's bank and building society accounts. However, the scheme is voluntary on the part of banks and building societies, so you should check with the branch holding the deceased's account(s) that they will accept your instructions before proceeding.

To use the scheme, you fill in both sides of form D20 and send it to the Inheritance Tax office where you will be delivering your account. We will allocate a reference for the deceased and return the D20 to you duly noted. Then, send the D20 to the bank or building society concerned at the same time as you send form IHT200 to us.

Once the funds are transferred to us and provided everything else is in order, we will authorise form D18 (or C1 in Scotland) and return it to you.

Please note you will need a separate D20 for each bank/building society and each account from which you wish to transfer funds.

JOINTLY OWNED ASSETS

We occasionally receive accounts from practitioners where joint assets passing by survivorship have been omitted. Joint assets form part of the deceased's estate for Inheritance Tax purposes even when they pass by survivorship to a spouse or civil partner. The requirements of HMRC IHT differ in this respect from those of the Probate Service or Sheriff Court.

In our December 2006 Newsletter we reminded you that joint assets should be included on form D4, as well as on any other relevant supplementary form such as D12, when form IHT200 is completed. We would like to emphasise that this includes any assets which pass to a spouse or civil partner and are exempt, even when these pass by survivorship, for example a house or (in England) bank accounts in joint names. (NB: an individual's beneficial interest in a Scottish bank account does not pass to the joint holder by survivorship.)

Assets which appear both on form D4 and another supplementary form, such as D12, will not be counted twice. If an IHT205 or a C5 is being completed the joint assets passing by survivorship, whether to the spouse, civil partner or otherwise, should be included in the appropriate box.

INHERITANCE TAX & TRUSTS OFFICES

The Inheritance Tax Office and Trusts Office are now run by the same senior manager and we are aiming to bring the work of the two offices closer together where it is sensible to do so. It occurs to us that a number of you who receive the IHT Newsletter may also have dealings with the Trusts Office and so we are considering whether or not to turn the IHT Newsletter into the IHT & Trusts Newsletter. Please let us know what you think – and if you have any issues around the Trusts business that you would like to see addressed in a joint Newsletter, please let us know what these are by contacting our Customer Service Team via email on: InheritanceTaxCustomerService@gtnet.gov.uk.

Or by writing to them at our Nottingham address detailed on the back page.

INTEREST RATES

Interest Period	Interest Rate
6.10.94 to 5.03.99	5%
6.03.99 to 5.02.00	4%
6.02.00 to 5.05.01	5%
6.05.01 to 5.11.01	4%
6.11.01 to 5.08.03	3%
6.08.03 to 5.12.03	2%
6.12.03 to 5.09.04	3%
6.09.04 to 5.09.05	4%
6.09.05 to 5.09.06	3%
6.09.06 to date	4%

FINANCE BILL 2007

The Finance Bill 2007 contains a small number of proposed changes for IHT. There is also a minor change to the tax rules for pre-owned assets. Although the charge (under Schedule 15 Finance Act 2004) is to income tax, its purpose is to counter avoidance of IHT, so the change may be of interest to IHT practitioners.

IHT nil-rate band

First, the IHT nil-rate band for 2010/11 has been set at £350,000. The nil-rate band for 2007/08 is £300,000 as announced in Finance Act 2005 (and Finance Act 2006 set 2008/09 at £312,000 and 2009/10 at £325,000).

IHT rules for pensions: registered pension schemes

Second, there are two changes that apply to pensions. For pension schemes, the proposal is to allow the exemption from IHT charges to operate within the same time frame as permitted by the rules of a registered pension scheme for payment of lump sum benefits following the death of a scheme member.

Under the tax rules operating before 6 April 2006, schemes were allowed a period of up to two years from the date of the member's death in which to pay out the death benefits. Our practice recognised this rule, so provided the benefits were paid out within the same timeframe, no IHT charges under the relevant property regime arose on the trust property. The pension rules for registered pension schemes are being amended so that the time allowed for payment will run from the date on which the scheme is notified or if earlier, the date the scheme could have reasonably been aware of the member's death.

This timing will be mirrored for IHT so that provided lump sums are paid within the time allowed by the pension scheme rules on or after 6 April 2006 the scheme funds will not attract charges under ss. 64 to 69 IHTA. Failure to meet the deadline will have the effect, as before, that the protection from the IHT charges will have ceased at the date of death of the scheme member.

Alternatively secured pensions (ASPs)

For ASPs, the changes mean that all charges arising under s.151A–C are now "top slice" charges. This ensures that the nil-rate band is used in priority against the remainder of the estate passing on death first and where a charge does arise on left-over ASP funds, that this can be settled without reference to the remainder of the estate. Additionally, in order to accommodate the interaction of IHT and the income tax resulting from unauthorised payment pension charges being introduced, where the ASP funds on death of the scheme member are transferred to other scheme members, the IHT charge will now take account of any such income tax that has already been paid before the IHT charge arises. Where the estate (excluding ASP funds) is not liable to IHT and IHT is due before the unauthorised payment pension charges, a new formula for calculating any IHT due on left-over ASP funds is introduced to take account of both the unused IHT nil-rate band and the unauthorised payment charges.

Finally, there are now specific provisions for dealing with left-over pension pots on the death of scheme members who were aged over 75 before they were traced by the scheme provider. Any left-over funds on death of such a scheme member are brought within the IHT framework, but the reporting requirements are altered so that scheme administrators have six months from the end of the month in which they discovered the scheme member's death to file their return.

Pre-owned assets

The third change proposed is to the Pre-Owned Assets legislation to allow us to accept a late election. The normal filing date for an election will continue to apply (i.e., 31st January in the tax year following the year of assessment concerned); and there is no change to the date to withdraw an election. This measure is aimed at people who may have been unaware that they were liable to the POA charge. Provided they elect into IHT as soon as practical after discovering they were liable to the POA charge, we will normally be able to accept a late election.

CLOSING CASES & CLEARANCE CERTIFICATES

When we are content that the IHT due on a case has been paid (or that no tax is due) we will normally write to you to confirm that position. In addition, the provisions of s.239 provide for the liable person(s) to apply for a formal clearance certificate and we receive a significant number of such applications each year.

From our perspective, the application for and issue of a clearance certificate does not add any value to the case – we have written to say that our enquiries are complete and, subject to any changes that you may need to notify later, that is the end of the matter. Handling a large number of applications for clearance diverts resource that could be used more productively in dealing with working cases.

We understand that the statutory nature of the certificate provides a level of assurance over and above that of a letter; but we would very much like to reduce the number of applications for clearance that we receive so we can use our limited resources more effectively.

We will therefore be changing the effect that our closure letter will have from 30th April 2007.

We will continue to write to you when our enquiries are complete and we are closing and putting away our files. The letter will provide the necessary confirmation that our enquiries are settled and that either

• no tax is due,

• all the tax has been paid, or

• all the tax has been paid except for any tax being deferred (e.g. on timber) or otherwise being paid later (by instalments).

The letter will be signed and stamped and we will treat that letter as having exactly the same effect as a formal certificate. So, for example, if we have sent such a closure letter both to the executors and to the trustees of a Will Trust and the former notify us of an increase in value of the Free Estate, we will regard the trustees as protected by that letter and we will not seek to collect any additional tax that is attributable to the trust.

This change will apply both to death and settlement cases, whether or not a liability arises. We will issue the letter in every case, so forms D19 & D42 will be withdrawn in due course. It will not apply to lifetime transfers, whether PETs or immediately chargeable transfers, given that a (further) liability may arise should the transferor die within 7 years of making the gift.

This change will bring benefits to us both; you will have confirmation we are content with the position sooner; there will be one less form for your clients to fill in and sign and we can deploy our resources more effectively.

But we need your help to bring this change about. So with effect from 30th April, we would urge you to rely on the assurance provided by our closure letter without the need to apply for a clearance certificate as well.

IHT NEWSLETTER ONLINE

Just to remind you that we are planning to move to an online only version of the IHT Newsletter by August 2007.

We want to let you know when a new edition of the newsletter has been released. The easiest way for us to do this is to email you.

If you haven't already done so, please let us know your email address. You can email us at InheritanceTaxCustomerService@gtnet.gov.uk.

Alternatively, you can write to the Customer Service Team at our Nottingham office.

INHERITANCE TAX NIL-RATE BAND

The Inheritance Tax nil-rate band has been increased to £300,000.

This applies to deaths and chargeable transfers or events on or after 6 April 2007.

For establishing whether an estate is excepted, £285,000 continues to apply to all applications made before 6 August 2007.

62   Finance Act 2007—Summary of IHT Provisions

(Royal Assent 19 July 2007)

s 4

The nil rate band becomes £350,000 for 2010–11. For the three years 2007–08, 2008–09 and 2009–10 the thresholds have been agreed as £300,000, £312,000 and £325,000 respectively. See also *FA 2006, s 155*. 1.7 INTRODUCTION AND BASIC PRINCIPLES and 41.1 RATES OF TAX.

s 66

In connection with the pre-owned assets income tax rules within *FA 2004, Sch 15*, elections for existing schemes should have been made by 31 January 2007 for 2005/06 in the normal course of events. However, *FA 2007, s 66* has inserted an amendment to the 2004 legislation so that HMRC may allow a later filing date in particular cases that are deemed appropriate. [*FA 2004, Sch 15 para 23(3) inserted by FA 2007, 66(1)*]. See 6.4 ANTI-AVOIDANCE and 59.42 WORKING CASE STUDY. Otherwise, elections must be made on or before 'relevant filing date', which means by 31 January in the year of assessment that immediately follows the relevant year (see HMRC Form IHT500) at 59.42 WORKING CASE STUDY.

s 69, Sch 19
paras 19, 20

Finance Act 2007, Sch 19 changes the inheritance tax rules to ensure that an income tax charge arising because of an unauthorised payment charge under *FA 2004, Part 4* is taken into account in calculating the tax liability. Also, alternatively secured pension (ASP) scheme liabilities arising under *IHTA 1984, s 151A* are 'top-sliced' from 6 April 2007 to ensure that the nil rate band, if available, is used against the non-ASP part of the estate in priority to the ASP. If there is part of the nil rate band remaining after setting it against the non-ASP estate of the scheme member then this may be available to set against ASP funds and any IHT liability is settled by the ASP scheme administrator. Where a scheme member dies with funds in a pension scheme that would have been an ASP had the scheme administrator been able to trace them before their reaching the age of 75 years, the date that the scheme administrator becomes aware of the scheme member's death will be the date for the purposes of *s 151A(a)(b)* in calculating the 'relevant amount' to be subject to tax. See 37.2 PENSION SCHEMES.

Sch 19 paras 19, 21, 22	ASP scheme liabilities arising under *IHTA 1984, s 151B* are 'top-sliced' from 6 April 2007 to ensure that the nil rate band, if available, is used against the non-ASP part of the estate of the original scheme member in priority to the ASP. Where a relevant dependant entitled to a pension fund inherited from a scheme member dies with funds in a pension scheme that would have been an ASP had the scheme administrator been able to trace the scheme member before their reaching the age of 75 years, the date that the scheme administrator becomes aware of the scheme member's death will be the date for the purposes of *s 151B(a)(b)* in calculating the amount to be subject to tax. New taxing rules in such circumstances follow those within *s 151A* allowing, on the cessation of the relevant dependant's pension, for unused nil rate band of the original scheme member to be grossed up under *s 151A(4C)* and set against the balance of the ASP funds remaining on the cessation of the dependant's pension. The nil rate band to be taken into account for these purposes is that applying at the time of the cessation of the relevant dependant's pension. If there has been a reduction in the tax rates since the scheme member's death then for these purposes the tax rate to be applied will be the most up-to-date in force at the time of the scheme member's death. See 37.2 PENSION SCHEMES.
Sch 19 paras 19, 23	Where a relevant dependant dies with another pension fund within *s 151C* any ASP arising under *IHTA 1984, s 151C* is 'top-sliced' from 6 April 2007 to ensure that the nil rate band, if available, is used against the non-ASP part of the estate of the original scheme member in priority to the ASP. Any income tax charge arising because of an unauthorised payment charge under *FA 2004, Part 4* is taken into account in calculating the tax liability. The income tax relieved within *s 151C(3)(a)* in this way is that which arose before IHT was charged in relation to any unauthorised member payments. Where there is an ASP and any unused nil rate band of the original scheme member has not been fully utilised against the non-ASP funds, the balance may be grossed up under *s 151C(3C)* and set against the balance of the ASP funds not previously assessed under *s 151A*. This 'previously untaxed dependant's alternatively secured pension fund amount' is that part of an individual's ASP that has not given rise to an unauthorised payment charge before IHT arose on the ASP. See 37.2 PENSION SCHEMES.
Sch 19 paras 19, 24, 25	Provision is made for situations where there is a left-over pension pot at the death of the scheme member who was over the age of 75 on death and which was traced after their death by the scheme administrator. In such cases, the left-over ASP funds are brought within IHT by *s 151A(6)* but the scheme administrator has twelve months from the end of the month in which he discovers the scheme member's death to file the return. See 2.6 ACCOUNTS AND RETURNS.
Sch 19 paras 19, 26	IHT due on ASP funds in such circumstances as above is payable within six months from the end of the month in which the administrator discovered the scheme member's death. See 35.1 PAYMENT OF TAX.

63   Table of Cases

Where the CIR (or, in Scotland, the Lord Advocate) are a party, the case is listed under the name of the other party only. Judicial review cases are listed under the name of the applicant and the person who is the subject of the review but again excluding the CIR etc. Note that most cases are summarised at Chapter 60.

63 Table of Cases

63 Table of Cases

64   Table of Statutes

Note: The legislation referred to in this book has been divided into three sections below, viz. Miscellaneous Legislation, the Taxes Acts and Statutory Instruments.

65 Statutory Instruments

Note: Statutory instruments relating to delivery of accounts will be found at 2.1–2.11 (and see 35.9), those relating to double taxation agreements will be found at 18.2, and those relating to interest on tax will be found at 27.1.

Others are as follows

66   Index

This index is referenced to chapter and paragraph number.

The entries in **bold capitals** are chapter headings in the text.